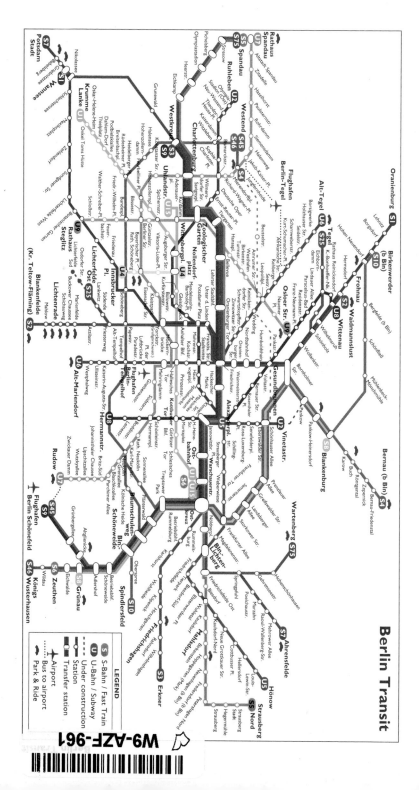

Berlin Transit

LEGEND

- **S** S-Bahn / Fast Train
- **U** U-Bahn / Subway
- ---- Under construction
- ○ Station
- ◎ Transfer station
- ✈ Airport
- → Bus to airport
- ⟶ Park & Ride

W9-AZF-961

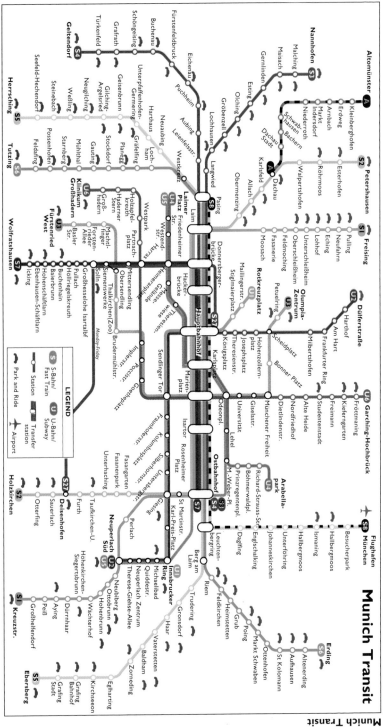

Munich Transit

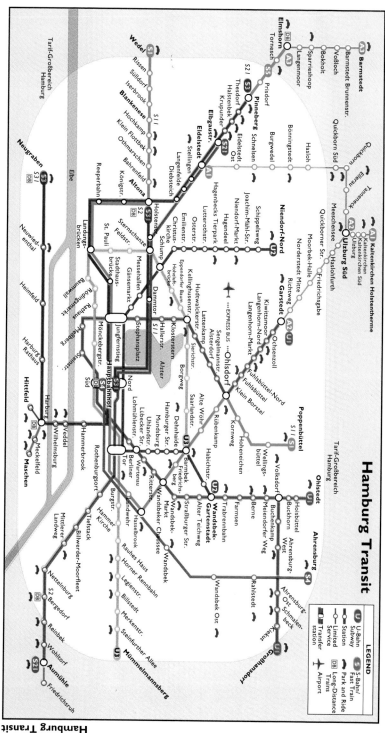

Hamburg Transit

Frankfurt Transit

 Let's Go writers travel on your budget.

"Guides that penetrate the veneer of the holiday brochures and mine the grit of real life."

—The Economist

"The writers seem to have experienced every rooster-packed bus and lunar-surfaced mattress about which they write."

—The New York Times

"All the dirt, dirt cheap."

—People

Great for independent travelers.

"The guides are aimed not only at young budget travelers but at the independent traveler; a sort of streetwise cookbook for traveling alone."

—The New York Times

"Flush with candor and irreverence, chock full of budget travel advice."

—The Des Moines Register

"An indispensible resource, *Let's Go*'s practical information can be used by every traveler."

—The Chattanooga Free Press

Let's Go is completely revised each year.

"Only *Let's Go* has the zeal to annually update every title on its list."

—The Boston Globe

"Unbeatable: good sightseeing advice; up-to-date info on restaurants, hotels, and inns; a commitment to money-saving travel; and a wry style that brightens nearly every page."

—The Washington Post

All the important information you need.

"*Let's Go* authors provide a comedic element while still providing concise information and thorough coverage of the country. Anything you need to know about budget traveling is detailed in this book."

—The Chicago Sun-Times

"Value-packed, unbeatable, accurate, and comprehensive."

—Los Angeles Times

Let's Go Publications

Let's Go: Alaska & the Pacific Northwest 2001
Let's Go: Australia 2001
Let's Go: Austria & Switzerland 2001
Let's Go: Boston 2001 **New Title!**
Let's Go: Britain & Ireland 2001
Let's Go: California 2001
Let's Go: Central America 2001
Let's Go: China 2001
Let's Go: Eastern Europe 2001
Let's Go: Europe 2001
Let's Go: France 2001
Let's Go: Germany 2001
Let's Go: Greece 2001
Let's Go: India & Nepal 2001
Let's Go: Ireland 2001
Let's Go: Israel 2001
Let's Go: Italy 2001
Let's Go: London 2001
Let's Go: Mexico 2001
Let's Go: Middle East 2001
Let's Go: New York City 2001
Let's Go: New Zealand 2001
Let's Go: Paris 2001
Let's Go: Peru, Bolivia & Ecuador 2001 **New Title!**
Let's Go: Rome 2001
Let's Go: San Francisco 2001 **New Title!**
Let's Go: South Africa 2001
Let's Go: Southeast Asia 2001
Let's Go: Spain & Portugal 2001
Let's Go: Turkey 2001
Let's Go: USA 2001
Let's Go: Washington, D.C. 2001
Let's Go: Western Europe 2001 **New Title!**

Let's Go *Map Guides*

Amsterdam	New Orleans
Berlin	New York City
Boston	Paris
Chicago	Prague
Florence	Rome
Hong Kong	San Francisco
London	Seattle
Los Angeles	Sydney
Madrid	Washington, D.C.

Coming Soon: *Dublin* and *Venice*

Let's Go

GERMANY
2001

Paul C. Dilley editor
Megan M. Anderson associate editor
Filip Wojciechowski map editor

researcher-writers
David A. Boyajian
Margaret Coe
Karoun Demirjian
Liz Glynn
Dan Koski-Karell
Aram Yang

St. Martin's Press ✖ New York

HELPING LET'S GO If you want to share your discoveries, suggestions, or corrections, please drop us a line. We read every piece of correspondence, whether a postcard, a 10-page email, or a coconut. Please note that mail received after May 2001 may be too late for the 2002 book, but will be kept for future editions. **Address mail to:**

> **Let's Go: Germany**
> **67 Mount Auburn Street**
> **Cambridge, MA 02138**
> **USA**

Visit Let's Go at **http://www.letsgo.com,** or send email to:

> **feedback@letsgo.com**
> **Subject: "Let's Go: Germany"**

In addition to the invaluable travel advice our readers share with us, many are kind enough to offer their services as researchers or editors. Unfortunately, our charter enables us to employ only currently enrolled Harvard students.

Maps by David Lindroth copyright © 2001, 2000, 1999, 1998, 1997, 1996, 1995, 1994, 1993, 1992, 1991, 1990, 1989, 1988 by St. Martin's Press.

Distributed outside the USA and Canada by Macmillan.

Let's Go: Germany Copyright © 2001 by Let's Go, Inc. All rights reserved. Printed in the United States of America. No part of this book may be used or reproduced in any manner whatsoever without written permission except in the case of brief quotations embodied in critical articles or reviews. Let's Go is available for purchase in bulk by institutions and authorized resellers. For information, address St. Martin's Press, 175 Fifth Avenue, New York, NY 10010, USA.

ISBN: 0-312-24676-5

First edition
10 9 8 7 6 5 4 3 2 1

Let's Go: Germany is written by Let's Go Publications, 67 Mount Auburn Street, Cambridge, MA 02138, USA.

Let's Go® and the thumb logo are trademarks of Let's Go, Inc.
Printed in the USA on recycled paper with biodegradable soy ink.

CONTENTS

MAPS

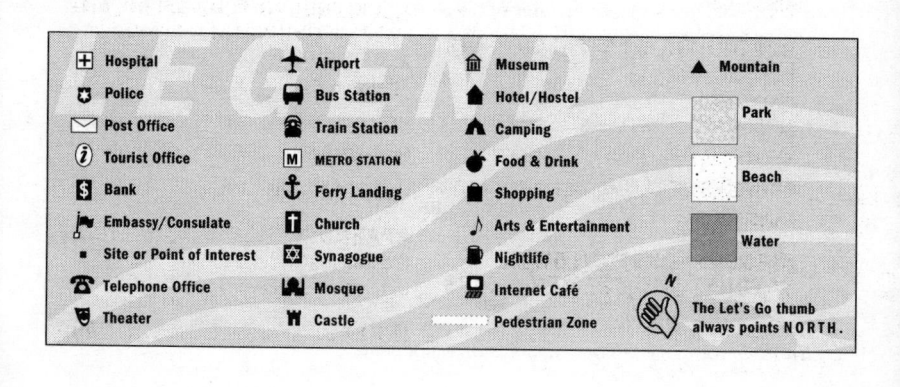

✚ Hospital	✈ Airport	🏛 Museum	▲ Mountain
🚓 Police	🚌 Bus Station	🏨 Hotel/Hostel	Park
✉ Post Office	🚆 Train Station	⛺ Camping	
ⓘ Tourist Office	Ⓜ METRO STATION	🍎 Food & Drink	Beach
🏦 Bank	⚓ Ferry Landing	🛍 Shopping	
⚑ Embassy/Consulate	✝ Church	♪ Arts & Entertainment	Water
■ Site or Point of Interest	✡ Synagogue	🍸 Nightlife	
☎ Telephone Office	☪ Mosque	💻 Internet Café	The Let's Go thumb always points NORTH.
🎭 Theater	♜ Castle	⋯⋯ Pedestrian Zone	

RESEARCHER-WRITERS

David A. Boyajian *Bavaria*

In the hands of the right person, libido can be a dynamic force, initiating the creative drive; luckily for us, David attacked his research job as tenaciously as he did the singles scene, covering mammoth portions of Bavaria, from the snow-covered Alps to the cow-pattied valleys. With Aram, he revolutionized the Munich coverage, coming up on the cleaning end of an epic night at the *Biergarten*. And so, after capping his tour de force with a conquest of the Bavarian Alps, he returned home where we crowned him "Bayerische Boyajian," king of Bavarian tourism.

Margaret Coe *Berlin, Sachsen, and Thüringen*

From the Sächsische Schweiz to the streets of Leipzig and Berlin, Maggie demonstrated a traveling savvy complemented by a gift for the poetic. She and Liz teamed up to deliver stunning coverage of Berlin, raving at its hottest clubs during the massive Love Parade by night and exploring its first-rate museums by day. Though the experience tainted Maggie's love of pink fur skirts, her passion for all other things German was clear in her lyrical writing and upbeat approach.

Karoun Demirjian *Niedersachsen, Nordrhein-Westfalia, and Rheinland-Pfalz*

This "Armenian Princess" navigated the Lorelei's favorite hunting grounds, scaled the tower of Köln's legendary Dom, dodged Bonn's lingering bureaucracy, and biked her way across the Lüneburg Heath. In between it all, she cheered up her editors with accounts of her wild escapades, unbalanced diet, and erstwhile romances. Karoun also found time to explore the wide and wonderful world of traditional German dress and may just bring the Dierndl back to fashion's forefront.

Liz Glynn *Berlin, Hessen, Niedersachsen, Sachsen and Sachsen-Anhalt*

Liz hopped successfully and artfully between Germany's biggest and smallest. From the tiny towns of the haunted Harz Mountains to the behemoth Berlin, Liz consistently researched with stamina and creativity and wrote with humor and precision. Never at a loss for adventures, she proved herself a resourceful and ingenious traveler and a dedicated researcher. Our hats are off to Liz for her wonderful work and invaluable contributions and insights.

Dan Koski-Karell *Brandenburg, Hamburg, Mecklenburg-Vorpommern, and Schleswig-Holstein*

Dan taught us all something about the open water in the summer of 2000. This land-lover scorned the land-locked Maschsee in Hannover for the World's Fair, but once he saw the harbors of Hamburg he fell in love. Partying there with students and sailors, the "Righteous *Rüder* of the North" hugged the sea in Lübeck and Kiel. Taking the coast of Rügen Island by bike, he then turned inland to finish his itinerary in the outskirts of Berlin, where the flowing rivers of the Spreewald symbolically led the first mate of Team Germany's heart back to the expansive waves.

Aram Yang *Bavaria, Baden-Württemberg, and Hessen*

Aram, backpacker extraordinaire, flew to Frankfurt and instantly took to the flashy culture of young, hip Germans. Rugged on the outside, but with avant-garde flair inside, this intrepid researcher infiltrated the world of the yuppie *Schicki-Micki*, adopting the alias Schicki-Aram. He gained information on Stuttgart, only letting down his guise temporarily to bare all in the mineral baths. Schicki-Aram left the cities to expose the Schwarzwald, but then returned to Munich, covering the hipper bars and pulling off a secret meeting with another researcher in a local *Biergarten*. After his finale on the German Wine Road, we raised a glass of *Riesling* for a toast to our capable correspondant.

ACKNOWLEDGMENTS

Team Germany thanks: Team Germany 2000, specifically former editor Max Hirsh for his advice on the book plan; Melissa Rudolph, production, and typesetting for their technical art; John Fiore and Mapland, specifically Filip Wojciechowski and his insider knowledge of Germany and Berlin; Anne Chisholm; Annette von Schmidt at the GNTO office in New York; Rose Schwartz at Deutsche Bahn; Ulrrcih Blaschke for his knowledge, insights, and tips about Nürnberg and Würzberg; all of our readers who sent us helpful suggestions over snail- and e-mail.

Paul thanks: Alice, for a sharp wit and helpful pen; Megan, for her format wizardry and dedicated work; my RWs, for their excellence, loyalty, teamwork, and resilience in adverse situations; 60 Banks, for budget living with style, successfully hosting FCD and BF, and especially Windom for the "road trip" and that hot-as-hell Alabama chili; my office pod for "bathroom" and a return to functionalist architecture; Ahura Mazda and the Avesta for establishing order, and theological French; the powerful kickball; Becky, for the cheerios; MW, MC, JD, JR and the usual suspects; as always, Sarah, Ryan and Danice; my crew from Kirkland House; Helmut Koester and ARNTS for important work and intellectual challenge; AnneMarie Luijendijk, the "punk-ass," with best wishes for her baby; Jason, for buying me lunch; and of course, *die Familie Dilley, für alles, was ihr mir gegeben habt.*

Megan Thanks: Paul for his leadership, creativity, hard work, ruthless cutting skills, and for reading all the funny parts out loud; Alice for keeping us and our copy lively; the RW's for the incredible amount of work they have put into this project and for letting us be a part of their experiences; the Axis pod and rubber ducky for making bathtime—and the summer—so much fun; and the phoenix, for being a perfect metaphor for each and every town in Germany. I'd also like to thank Robert, who never ceases to amaze me, and my famiy for their love, support, and laughter. Mom, Dad, Aaron, and Neil, I love you very much.

Editor
Paul C. Dilley
Associate Editor
Megan M. Anderson
Managing Editor
Alice Farmer
Map Editor
Filip Wojciechowski

Publishing Director
Kaya Stone
Editor-in-Chief
Kate McCarthy
Production Manager
Melissa Rudolph
Cartography Manager
John Fiore
Editorial Managers
Alice Farmer, Ankur Ghosh,
Aarup Kubal, Anup Kubal
Financial Manager
Bede Sheppard
Low-Season Manager
Melissa Gibson
Marketing & Publicity Managers
Olivia L. Cowley, Esti Iturralde
New Media Manager
Daryush Jonathan Dawid
Personnel Manager
Nicholas Grossman
Photo Editor
Dara Cho
Production Associates
Sanjay Mavinkurve, Nicholas
Murphy, Rosalinda Rosalez,
Matthew Daniels, Rachel Mason,
Daniel Visel
Some Design
Matthew Daniels
Office Coordinators
Sarah Jacoby, Chris Russell

Director of Advertising Sales
Cindy Rodriguez
Senior Advertising Associates
Adam Grant, Rebecca Rendell
Advertising Artwork Editor
Palmer Truelson

President
Andrew M. Murphy
General Manager
Robert B. Rombauer
Assistant General Manager
Anne E. Chisholm

ABOUT LET'S GO

FORTY-ONE YEARS OF WISDOM

As a new millennium arrives, *Let's Go: Europe*, now in its 41st edition and translated into seven languages, reigns as the world's bestselling international travel guide. For over four decades, travelers criss-crossing the Continent have relied on *Let's Go* for inside information on the hippest backstreet cafes, the most pristine secluded beaches, and the best routes from border to border. In the last 20 years, our rugged researchers have stretched the frontiers of backpacking and expanded our coverage into Asia, Africa, Australia, and the Americas. This year, we've introduced a new city guide series with titles to San Francisco and our hometown, Boston. Now, our seven city guides feature sharp photos, more maps, and an overall more user-friendly design. We've also returned to our roots with the inaugural edition of *Let's Go: Western Europe*.

It all started in 1960 when a handful of well-traveled students at Harvard University handed out a 20-page mimeographed pamphlet offering a collection of their tips on budget travel to passengers on student charter flights to Europe. The following year, in response to the instant popularity of the first volume, students traveling to Europe researched the first full-fledged edition of *Let's Go: Europe*, a pocket-sized book featuring honest, practical advice, witty writing, and a decidedly youthful slant on the world. Throughout the 60s and 70s, our guides reflected the times. In 1969 we taught travelers how to get from Paris to Prague on "no dollars a day" by singing in the street. In the 80s and 90s, we looked beyond Europe and North America and set off to all corners of the earth. Meanwhile, we focused in on the world's most exciting urban areas to produce in-depth, fold-out map guides. Our new guides bring the total number of titles to 51, each infused with the spirit of adventure and voice of opinion that travelers around the world have come to count on. But some things never change: our guides are still researched, written, and produced entirely by students who know first-hand how to see the world on the cheap.

HOW WE DO IT

Each guide is completely revised and thoroughly updated every year by a well-traveled set of nearly 300 students. Every spring, we recruit over 200 researchers and 90 editors to overhaul every book. After several months of training, researcher-writers hit the road for seven weeks of exploration, from Anchorage to Adelaide, Estonia to El Salvador, Iceland to Indonesia. Hired for their rare combination of budget travel sense, writing ability, stamina, and courage, these adventurous travelers know that train strikes, stolen luggage, food poisoning, and marriage proposals are all part of a day's work. Back at our offices, editors work from spring to fall, massaging copy written on Himalayan bus rides into witty, informative prose. A student staff of typesetters, cartographers, publicists, and managers keeps our lively team together. In September, the collected efforts of the summer are delivered to our printer, who turns them into books in record time, so that you have the most up-to-date information available for your vacation. Even as you read this, work on next year's editions is well underway.

WHY WE DO IT

We don't think of budget travel as the last recourse of the destitute; we believe that it's the only way to travel. Living cheaply and simply brings you closer to the people and places you've been saving up to visit. Our books will ease your anxieties and answer your questions about the basics—so you can get off the beaten track and explore. Once you learn the ropes, we encourage you to put *Let's Go* down now and then to strike out on your own. You know as well as we that the best discoveries are often those you make yourself. When you find something worth sharing, please drop us a line. We're Let's Go Publications, 67 Mount Auburn St., Cambridge, MA 02138, USA (email: feedback@letsgo.com). For more info, visit our website, www.letsgo.com.

HOW TO USE THIS BOOK

For many years, our publication has been jockeying to stay on top of Germany as it's grown, changed, and unified. Although *Let's Go: Germany 2001* is a budget travel guide, it still concentrates on quality; cheap and enjoyable often coincide on the road in Germany, and we strive to guide you to where they do. In 2001, we're hand-picking web addrees and the latest deep-house clubs, and giving you all the insider tips. You'll find restaurant write-ups, Internet access, car-pooling services, and all the gritty details you need to thrive and travel without a hitch.

Don't speak German? Don't worry, our guide has comprehensive introductions to all locations, sights, and establishments, and our **Appendix** outlines some easily learnable basics of the language for the intrepid. As you plan your odyssey, sift through regions, cities, towns and trails you're interested in by looking at their introductions and sights sections. Our innovated **Discover** section outlines broad themes and more specific tours that take you straight to Germany's best, from discos to fairy-tale castles. Before you lose yourself in either escape, read through our **Essentials** section, 40 pages of hard information on bank cards, railpasses, contact lenses, and how to call home. If the in-flight movie fails to captivate, we've included a rich **History and Culture** section, explaining Germany past and present.

The book is divided into 14 regional chapters, roughly by federal states, for quick reference. The capital city Berlin is at the beginning, and the rest of the country follows in clockwise geographical order. Each town includes an **Orientation and Practical Information** section that offers everything from tourist and post offices to train times and average prices. After that comes **Accomodations, Food, Sights and Entertainment,** in which establishments are listed in order from best to worst, except for HI hostels and Mensas, which are always first. Our absolute favorites are so denoted by the highest honor given out by the series, the *Let's Go* **thumbs-up** (🖑). The **phone code** for each region, city, or town appears opposite the name of that region, city, or town, and is denoted by the ☎ icon. **Phone numbers** in text are also preceded by the ☎ icon. **Grayboxes** at times provide wonderful cultural insight, at times simply crude humor. In any case, they're usually amusing, so enjoy. **Whiteboxes** provide important practical information, such as warnings (⚠), helpful hints, and further resources (📖) locally supplementing **Essentials.** The updated, specific **maps** of selected cities and regions should suffice for getting around; locations of accomodations, food, nightlife and sights are all marked.

Besides being better than all the guides from the "other century," *Let's Go: Germany 2001* includes significantly expanded and reorganzied coverage of Berlin, Germany's newly united city, newly restored capital, and international cultural mecca. Munich, that other city down south, has also been carefully updated and expanded. We've also included a new series of day hikes, where we guide you through some of Germany's most beautiful outdoor locales. Anyone in moderate shape can attempt them; to plan, see the sections on **Wilderness Safety** and **Equipment** sections in the **Essentials** chapter. It may be hard to put this book down. But remember that your guidebook should be a pleasure, not a habit. No matter how beautiful our cover is, leave it in your bag sometimes—it might not match your outfit. After all, it's your vacation. Go get 'em.

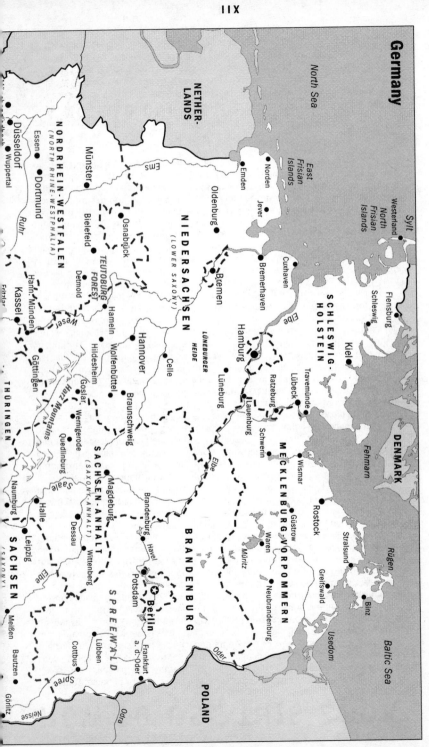

Germany

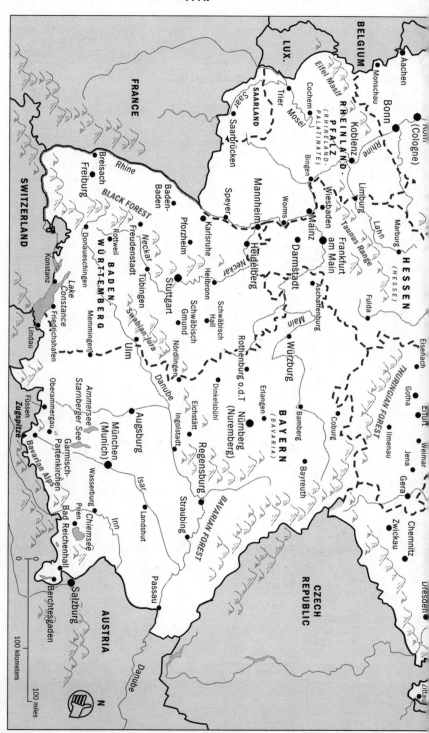

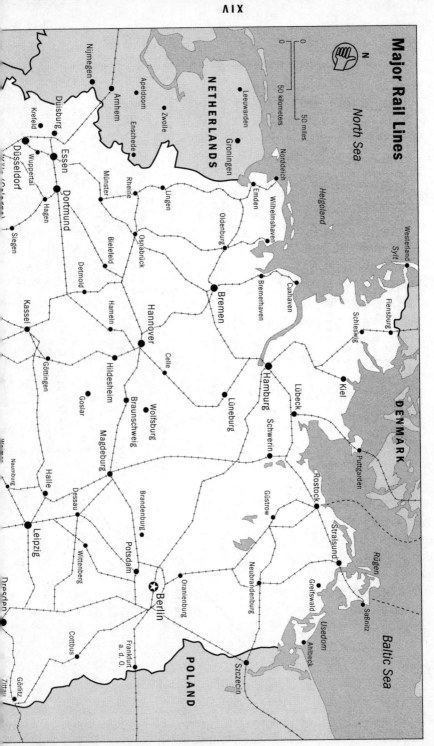

Major Rail Lines

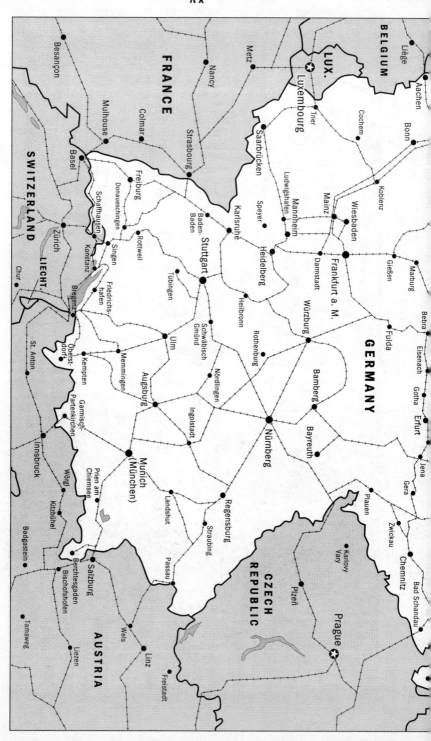

DISCOVER GERMANY

Germany attracts the rest of the world with an unparalleled combination of the old, even the ancient, and an avant-garde modernity. Whether mixing traditional mineral baths with the Daimler-Benz Museum in Stuttgart or the neoclassical majesty of the Brandenburger Gate with Potsdamer Platz's feverish building in Berlin, this exciting dichotomy grabs the traveler's attention. Germany—the country that produced and perfected the youth hostel and houses Europe's most advanced rail system—stands ready to whisk you from metropolises to medieval castles to snow-covered Alps, and back. Discover Germany in 2001.

FACTS AND FIGURES

The **total land area** of Germany is slightly smaller than that of Montana.

Germany has the world's **third largest economy,** behind the US and Japan, yet unemployment remains high in certain spots of the former East Germany. Social welfare benefits, including unemployment benefits, are comprehensive.

The German **national football team** has won an unprecedented 3 World Cups and 3 European Championships, but in the past two years has performed more poorly than ever before in its history. Germany will host the **World Cup** in 2006.

Germany's **total population** is approximately 82,087,361.

Over 20% of Germans describe themselves as **unaffiliated to a religion.**

Germany's **population growth rate** has slowed to .01%, with more deaths (10.76) than births (8.76) per 1,000 inhabitants. Only the positive migration rate, including **political refugees,** keeps the growth rate positive.

At 2.4% of the population, **Turks** form the largest ethnic minority.

Germany celebrates the **Tag der deutschen Einheit** (Day of German Unity) on October 3.

WHEN TO GO

Temperatures and airfares rise in July and August along with the number of tourists. The cloudy, temperate months of May, June, and September are the best time to go, as there are fewer tourists and the weather is pleasant. Be aware that most schools go on *Klassenreise* (extended field trips) in June, and that youth hostels may be inundated with schoolchildren. In winter months, some German hostels hibernate, and museum hours may be abbreviated. Winter sports gear up in November and continue through April; high season for skiing is mid-December to mid-January and February to March. For a temperature chart, see **Climate** (p. 587) For a chart detailing the holidays in Germany, see **Holidays,** p. 36.

THINGS TO DO

Among Germany's Alpine wonderlands and seaside resorts, medieval cities and cosmopolitan metropolises form one of the most prosperous regions in all of Europe. Each of the country's historically distinct cities and regions pulls Germany in its own direction: Munich, for example, revels in beer-drenched tradition, while Berlin steps to a cutting-edge beat, combining the achievements and spectres of the past with a gripping future as the political and cultural capital of Germany. For those who think blisters make the best souvenirs, there's hiking, biking, and skiing in the Bavarian Alps, the Black Forest, and the lesser-known yet worthy areas of the Harz Mountains and Swiss Saxony. The traveler in Germany could easily spend weeks in the medieval castles of Bavaria or in dynamic urban centers like Köln and Dresden, with their stunning cathedrals and clusters of half-timbered facades, never imagining the scenery that awaits a few hours away. Even a sprawling city like Hamburg offers picturesque sailing only a subway ride from a nightlife where everything—and we mean everything—is for sale.

For more specific regional attractions, see the **Highlights of the Region** section at the beginning of each chapter.

CHURCH HOPPING: ECCLESIASTICAL TOURS OF GERMANY

Germany has a rich ecclesiastical history, most clearly visible in its many churches. The country's Roman Catholic past is embodied in several magnificent cathedrals. No tour of Germany is complete without seeing the magnificent **Kölner Dom** (see p. 449), the largest High Gothic cathedral in the world. Köln itself is a city renowned for its many churches, including a collection of medieval examples in the Altstadt. Other important cathedrals include the tall and imposing **Münster** (see p. 372) in Freiburg, with the oldest bells in Germany; the **Frauenkirche** (see p. 254) in Munich and its two distinctive towers in the city skyline; the magnificent spires of the **Dom St. Peter** (see p. 301) in Regensburg; and the **Münster** (see p. 372) in Ulm, flaunting the largest spire in the world at 161m.

There are also many important protestant churches in Germany. Indeed, Lutherstadt Wittenberg is home to the **Schloßkirche** (see p. 193), upon which Martin Luther nailed his *95 Theses* in 1517, opening the floodgates of the Protestant Revolution. Important protestant churches are all over northern Germany: in Lübeck, the **Marienkirche** (see p. 549), destroyed during WWII but completely restored, sports the largest mechanical organ in the world, and Hamburg's **Große Michaelskirche** (see p. 538), the site of many concerts, has a famous baroque tower which is the city's distinctive symbol. The **Nikolaikirche** (see p. 186) in Leipzig is doubly famous as the church in which Bach composed his *St. John's Passion* and the rallying point for the demonstrations in early October of 1989, which hastened in the fall of the GDR and its communist regime.

PUMPING YOU UP: GERMANY AND THE OUTDOORS

There are many attractive locales for hiking in Germany, with options for both the intense and the initiate. The new **day hike** feature in Germany 2001 detail routes that are convenient for travelers who are focused on sight-seeing but who are also interested in taking time off from their routes to see the great outdoors. Despite its dense population, Germany has an extensive national park system, and beautiful, varied wilderness. The **Harz Mountains** (see p. 201) in Sachsen-Anhalt offer wooded pathways and the haunted history popularized by Goethe, a precursor to *Blair Witch* mystique. Further east in Sachsen are the national parks of the **Sächsische Schweiz** (see p. 168), a popular destination with exhilarating high, forested mountains and unique sandstone formations. For the more experienced (or even just fit) hikers, Germany offers the unmatched breathtaking beauty of the **Allgäu** (see p. 266) and the **Bavarian Alps** (see p. 269); many of their heights can be scaled with the aid of ski-lifts, albeit for a steep price. The rolling and verdant hills of the **Lüneburger Heath** (see p. 511) provide welcoming bike paths among the curiously comforting purple plants that cover the landscape. The islands in the north offer many opportunities for exploring the sandy white beaches and desolate terrain; The touristy **Sylt** (see p. 560) and slightly less crowded **Rügen Island** (see p. 576) in the east are both easily accesible from major cities like Hamburg and Rostock.

OLD GERMANY: HOW MEDIEVAL IS MEDIEVAL?

Many tourists travel to Germany to visit antiquated remains that dwarf the oldest sights of the modern age. In fact, virtually every city has an **Altstadt** where these sights are concentrated. But let the traveler beware: most of these sites have been restored heavily, especially after the heavy bombing suffered during World War II. Nonetheless, great care has been taken to reproduce damaged or destroyed buildings, and the sites often detail the nature and the extent of these repairs.

Quedlinburg (see p. 206), a meticulously preserved medieval town in Sachsen-Anhalt near the Harz Mountains, has been designated a cultural treasure by UNESCO and features a 13th-century fortress built on earlier remains. **Rothenburg ob der Tauber** (see p. 312) is another well-preserved medieval town, located on the Romantic Road in Bavaria. The town is famous for its well preserved medieval walls; although the Altstadt suffered from bombing during World War II, it was meticulously restored according to its 16th-century architectural basis.

▓ LET'S GO PICKS

BEST ACCOMMODATIONS: Reconciling human living space with tourism, Dessau's **Bauhaus** architectural school (see p. 194) offers single and double rooms. Berlin's **Circus** (see p. 100) is an all-star hostel for potential party-goers. The **Jugendlager Kaputzinerhötzl** (see p. 248) in Munich alleviates the city's tight housing with a merry tent of 400 fellow budget travelers.

BEST BIERGARTEN: Two establishments in Munich, undisputed king of the Biergarten, are in a dead-heat. The **Augustinerkeller** (see p. 260) serves the best brew in town, and is most beloved by native Müncheners, but the **Hirschgarten** (see p. 260), the largest Biergarten in Europe, brings an unbeatable charm with its park and carousel.

BEST BEACHES: Affluent German tourists frequent the ritzy island **Sylt** (see p. 560); if you want to avoid the crowds, run across to **Amrum** (see p. 562) at low tide, but watch out for the quicksand. The **Bodensee** (see p. 384), in the south, is a tropical respite from Germany's climate.

BEST PEEPSHOW: Bad Wimpfen's **Pig Museum** (see p. 345) features a peepshow with swine doing the nasty in three different positions, all in the name of scientific inquiry.

BEST PLACES TO DANCE: Berlin's **SO36** (see p. 139) draws a friendly, eclectic crowd; **U60311** (see p. 427) in Frankfurt offers house music mixed by high quality DJs to the young and beautiful. Try Munich's **Kunstpark Ost** (see p. 263) if its museums have numbed your attention span.

BEST RELICS OF THE GDR: Thrill to the concrete pomposity along **Straße der Nationen** (see p. 179) in Chemnitz, the city formerly known as Karl-Marx-Stadt. In Berlin, **Karl-Marx-Allee** (see p. 124) is prime for a parade of Western tourists.

BEST BATHTIMES: Backpackers will feel refreshingly out of their element after a bath and pink-towel nap in Baden-Baden's **Friedrichsbad** (see p. 367). Stuttgart's **Mineralbäder** (see p. 357) are rumored to have curative properties.

BEST UNDISCOVERED COUNTRY: Dessau (p. 190), home of Bauhaus, was the fount of modern design; **Wittenberg** (p. 190), home of Luther and his many monuments, is the source of Protestantism; both bide their time in a quiet corner of Sachsen-Anhalt. For secluded beauty in the mountains of Bavaria, be sure to visit the town of **Ramsau** (see p. 281): reports tell us it "kicks most excellent booty."

DISCOVER

SUGGESTED ITINERARIES

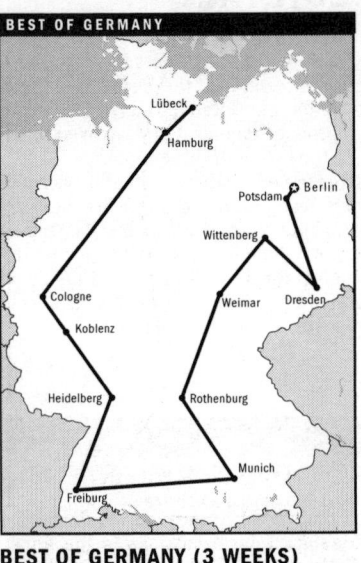

BEST OF GERMANY

BEST OF GERMANY (3 WEEKS)

Enter Germany at its center, **Berlin** (p. 85). The capital's enormous cultural and historical treasures, not to mention its chaotic nightlife, sprawl over an area eight times the size of Paris. Save time for a daytrip to the neoclassical splendors of nearby **Potsdam** (p. 146). If Berlin is too intense for you, **Dresden** (p. 156) won't help much. With its jumping nightlife and exquisite palaces and museums, the city is neatly counterpointed by a trip to **Lutherstadt Wittenberg** (p. 216); this is the small town where **Martin Luther** started the Reformation in 1517, and the city's center still seems absorbed in that event. Traveling to **Weimar** will further highlight the former GDR. The most thoroughly rebuilt city in Eastern Germany, Weimar rests solidly on the cultural heritage of Goethe, the Bauhaus architectural movement, and Germany's first liberal constitution. Continue your trip into Germany's past in **Rothenburg** (p. 312), a medieval city that deserves to be as kitschy as it wants to be. **Munich** (p. 238), takes bucolic merriment to a frothy head as the capital of Bavaria; the condition of its excellent museums and jovial beer halls both bear witness to its prosperity. Continuing south, the castles of **Neuschwanstein, Hohenschwangau,** and **Linderhof** make up the fairy-tale triumvirate of mad King Ludwig's **royal castles** (p. 273). Head west into Baden-Württemberg to live out your favorite Grimm's fairy tales in the **Black**

Forest (p. 376); from the winding alleys of **Freiburg** (p. 369) to the mountain-top lakes at **Titisee** and **Schluchsee** (p. 376), the region can't fail to impress. To the north, **Heidelberg** (p. 337) is home to Germany's oldest, most prestigious, and most scenic university, sitting below the brooding ruins of the city's castle. Next stop: **Koblenz** (p. 392), gateway to the Rhein and Mosel. Take a daytrip to the **Lorelei** cliffs of the **Rhein Valley** (p. 396) and embark on a side-trip to the wine-growing **Mosel Valley** (p. 402). Next, saunter northward to **Cologne** (p. 444), site of Germany's largest cathedral, the magnificent Gothic **Kölner Dom,** and home to a pounding nightlife. Much further north, reckless **Hamburg** (p. 531), Germany's largest city after Berlin, fuses the burliness of a port town with cosmopolitan flair, while the stolid townhouses of **Lübeck** (p. 546) recall an earlier age when the town was capital of the Hanseatic league.

VALLEY TOUR (1 WEEK)

The famous valleys of Rheinland-Pfalz and Baden-Württemberg are tightly grouped, suggesting an excellent bike or bus tour. Trains are often less convenient, but it is possible to travel to the area's major towns and then make daytrip excursions into the valleys. Start off in **Stuttgart** (p. 354) and spend a day walking the nearby fountains of the Schloßgarten or partying on Königstraße. Then move on to Germany's most popular Uni-town, **Heidelberg** (p. 337), taking time to look at the city's famed castle

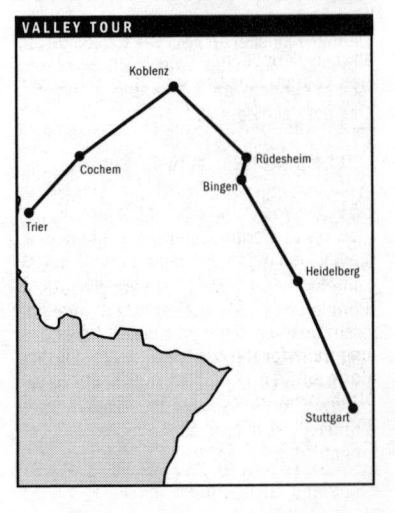

VALLEY TOUR

from the Philosophenweg trail across the Neckar. Heidelberg is a perfect base for day-trips down the **Neckar Valley** (p. 344), a miraculously untouristed stretch of the river that weaves between lookout castles and thickly forested hills. Take a train from Heidelberg to **Bingen** (p. 399), from where you can explore the legendary Lorelei cliffs of the **Rhein Valley** (**p. 396**). From Bingen, ferry across the Rhein to touristy **Rüdesheim** (p. 398), or stay aboard and trundle down the entire castle-lined gorge. Stop off for a visit to the famed wineries of **Bacharach** (p. 397), or continue on to the **Lorelei** cliffs (p. 396), a towering section of the river difficult to navigate and renowned for its mythical siren, who lured sailors onto the rocky crags that line the shore. Consider spending the night below the Lorelei in **St. Goar,** or move on to **Koblenz** (p. 392), where the Mosel and Rhein rivers converge at the **Deutsches Eck** peninsula, a memorial to the foundation of the Teutonic state. From Koblenz, the **Mosel Valley** (p. 402) is at your fingertips. Not as staggeringly steep as the cliffs of the Rhein, the valley is also less touristed, and its vineyards are too dense to bear commercial cheapening. Be sure to sample the fruity vines of **Cochem** (p. 402), or take a detour into the shaded valley where **Burg Eltz** (p. 404), one of the oldest intact medieval castles, keeps watch. At the end of the Mosel's most scenic stretch sits the ancient city of **Trier** (p. 405), fully equipped with vineyards, producing famous white wines, and Roman ruins, such as the **Porta Nigra,** heralding the city's great age and former glory as a capital of the Holy Roman Empire.

ROMANTIC ROAD (1 WEEK)

Officially dubbed the Romantic Road by German tourist officials in 1950, the route between Würzburg and Füssen has since become the most heavily touristed area in the country. **Würzburg** (p. 316) is home to the Residenz, one of the largest Baroque palaces in Germany. Continue to **Rothenburg** (p. 312); venturing behind its old ramparts is like stepping into the 16th century. **Dinkelsbühl** (p. 314), to the south, pulls the same medieval tricks. Everything is old in **Nördlingen** (p. 315), a town built in a 15-million-year-old crater whose bell tower has rung daily for the past 500 years. Further along on the Lech River, the abbey of **Ottobeuren** (p. 267) is the topographical and architectural climax of the Baroque style. Where the Lech tumbles down from the Alps, **Füssen** (p. 282) enchants with its castle and ancient fortifications, and is an

ROMANTIC ROAD AND ROYAL CASTLES

Würzburg
Rothenburg
Dinkelsbühl
Nördlingen
Ottobeuren
Füssen

ideal base for excursions to the **Royal Castles** (p. 273). Alpine getaways of mad King Ludwig, the castles are the product of eccentric Romantic imagination with money to burn. **Schloß Neuschwanstein** (p. 273), the castle upon which Walt Disney modeled the Magic Kingdom, towers above the Pöllat Gorge, recreating "the true style of German knights" with more success than any animated film could. While the nearby **Schloß Hohenschwangau** (p. 273) has perhaps a slightly more realistic medieval style, its personable interior is done in competing Biedermeier and Oriental styles. **Schloß Linderhof** (p. 274), placed deep in one of the Alps wildest valleys, comprises a Rococo palace with Renaissance gardens that are themselves enclosed by an English park. For tips on travel between the castles, see p. 275.

NIGHTLIFE (1 WEEK)

Germany's nightlife scene is one of the most varied and extensive in all of Europe. Any tour of the country should include at least a few nights at the Biergarten; but Germany isn't all beer and *Schnitzel,* as a trip to one of the country's too-hip-for-their-own-good dance clubs will prove. Begin your downfall in **Berlin** (p. 137), the epicenter of Teutonic debauchery and the undisputed capital of techno. Get your feet wet in one of the relaxed *Kneipen* along Oranienburger Str.; move on to Kreuzberg and Mitte's techno clubs or, if that's not your scene, to the cutting-edge hard-core raging in Prenzlauer Berg

DISCOVER

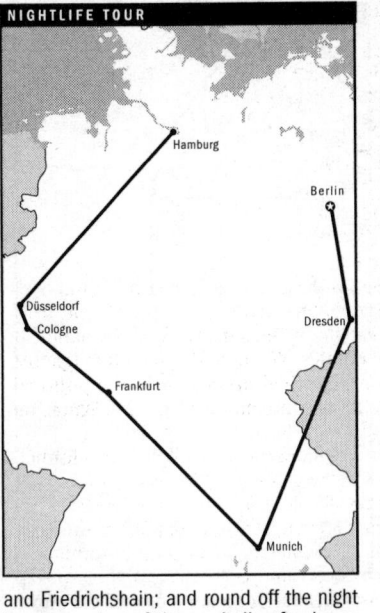

NIGHTLIFE TOUR

and Friedrichshain; and round off the night in any number of the capital's after-hours "chill-out" bars. Berlin also boasts the largest **gay and lesbian scene** in continental Europe (p. 143), with venues ranging from the super-chill to the super-cruisey. Take your pick. Once you've regained consciousness, hop on a train to **Dresden** (p. 164) for a taste of eastern Germany's rapidly evolving nightlife scene. If Berlin is the herald of all things illicit and avant-garde, then **Munich** (p. 259) is the guardian of Germany's most respected ritual, i.e. the mass consumption of beer. Despite its traditional appearance, the Bavarian metropolis still manages to foster impressive punk and gay scenes (p. 264). If money is what you want, head to the fashion-conscious economic capital, **Frankfurt** (p. 426), where only the super-rich and super-pretty will make it past the bouncer. Or high-tail it to **Cologne** (p. 453) and indulge in a few (dozen) rounds of *Kölsch*. If you have time, stop off in **Düsseldorf** (p. 473) and pay homage to what is reputed to be the longest bar counter in the world, with 500 pubs stretching across the Old Town. Last stop: **Hamburg** (p. 543), where everything—and we mean *everything*— is for sale. Indulge in the pleasures of the flesh along the Reeperbahn, Germany's most notorious legalized prostitution strip, or chill with the happy student crowd in the Sternschanze. Phew. All tired out? Oh, hell— go back to Berlin and start over.

NORTHERN GERMANY (1-2 WEEKS)

This tour surveys regions popular with vacationing Germans but generally overlooked by foreign tourists. Begin your exploration in **Hannover** (p. 484), the host of **EXPO 2000**, the first world exposition of the new millennium. From the Hauptbahnhof, head for the rolling purple plains of the **Lüneburger Heide** and its eponymous gateway, **Lüneburg** (p. 511). Charmingly well-preserved towns, such as the half-timbered **Celle,** await in this heath. Germany's largest port, **Hamburg** (p. 531) hosts a befuddling mix of students, strippers, and sailors. Next stop: **Sylt** (p. 560), whose majestic dunes and rideable surf make the island Germany's premier beach resort. Travelers with a bit more time should head for **Amrum** (p. 562), Sylt's less commercial sibling to the south, and the city **Schleswig** (p. 557), home to the remains of a Viking settlement and a superb collection of Expressionist paintings and Jugendstil design. Otherwise, high-tail it to **Lübeck** (p. 546). The city's legacy as a Hanseatic powerhouse funded one of the most beautiful Old Towns in Germany. After crossing the former East-West divide, head to **Rostock** (p. 569), the northeast's largest city and a hopping university town. Admire the Gothic spires of **Stralsund** (p. 569) on your way to **Rügen Island** (p. 576). Once the summer digs of Berlin's pre-war glitterati, the island boasts isolated beaches and the stunning chalk cliffs of **Jasmund national park** (p. 579). Back on the mainland, **Waren** (p. 567) is the gateway to the **Müritz,** Germany's largest freshwater lake. The surrounding national park hosts some of the best hiking and bird-watching opportunities in the country. If you've tired of the country, fear not—the urban hedonism of **Berlin** (p. 85) is less than two hours away.

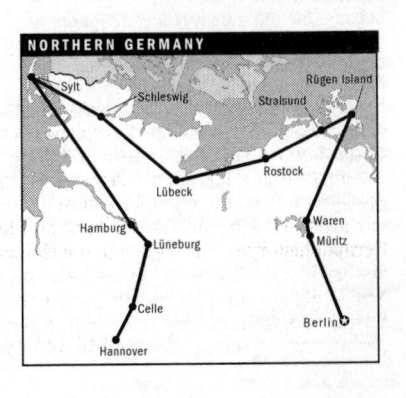

NORTHERN GERMANY

HISTORY AND CULTURE

More than a decade after the fall of the Berlin Wall, Germans are still working to fashion themselves an identity for the 21st century. After centuries of war, fragmentation, occupation, and division, Germany now finds itself a wealthy nation at the forefront of both European and global politics. Yet, bound by an often ignoble past, Germans are hesitant to draw upon historical precedent in the political sphere as a source of unity and pride: one finds contemporary cultural figures on **Deutschmarks** rather than earlier leaders.

Germany has long been a wellspring of revolutionaries and innovators—for better and for worse. One of the first heroes of German history, **Charlemagne** (Karl der Große) unified post-Roman Europe under relatively enlightened rule. **Martin Luther** went from small-town German monk to one of the most influential figures in Western history when he authored his **95 Theses,** spawning the Protestant Reformation. Communist pioneers **Karl Marx** and **Friedrich Engels** equipped the revolutionaries of 19th-century Europe with an ideology that precipitated the major conflicts of the second half of the 20th century. And one of the most horrifying figures in history, **Adolf Hitler,** forever tainted Germany's international reputation with his expansionist dreams of a greater Germany and genocidal race theories. This last image colors subsequent German history, as Germany has become inextricably linked to the horrors of the Holocaust and concentration camps. Today, Germans must grapple with the fact that the same country that produced Goethe, Kant, and Beethoven was also the breeding ground of Hitler, Goebbels, and Mengele.

To combat this incongruous legacy, Germans are now working to further integrate themselves into the economic and political institutions of the international future, while still coming to terms with the problems brought on by the remarkably quick reunification of the country eleven years ago. In the wake of Europe's most recent revolutions, Germany's pivotal role between East and West is even more important than it was during the Cold War. Germany is assuming an increasingly assertive role in the global community, and while a clear prospect of the country's future continues to be elusive, Germany enters the next millennium more unified and stable than ever before.

HISTORY

Entering into the fray surrounding German history can feel a little like wine tasting in the Moseltal: every historian will tout a different theory as the most salient. One of the longest-running historical debates is over the questionably teleological *Sonderweg*, the idea that German history has been on a particular—and divergent—path from the rest of Western history since its very origin. *Sonderweg* theory arose largely through historiographers' constant search for a version of German history that can explain the Holocaust. Even the starting point of German history is a debatable issue, as Germany first became a unified nation in 1871. Nominally speaking, "German" history began in 90 BC, when the Roman author Posidonius first applied the word to the peoples that migrated from Southern Scandinavia to central Europe around 1000 BC. That's where we pick up the story.

EARLY GERMAN HISTORY: 58BC–1517

AD 9
Chief Hermann
leads Germanic
tribes to victory
over the Romans
in the Teutoburg
forest

German history of the first millennium is more rightly considered prehistory, as the notion of a German nation didn't come to fruition until the 19th century. However, the clans of peoples in the region now known as Germany became a real political entity much earlier, when they were forced to defend themselves against the powerful **Roman Republic**. Despite many years of war with the "barbaric" German tribes, Rome expanded its borders to the Rhein by 58BC. Allied Germanic tribes, under the leadership of **Hermann,** earned themselves the nickname **"Teuton"** when they scored a great upset against the Romans in the Teutoburg Forest (see p. 476). The battle, which most likely took place near what is now Osnabrück, is lauded as the first assertion of truly Germanic culture. Five centuries of often antagonistic relations preceded a series of successive pillages of Rome by Germanic tribes. This led to the seizure of the city by the Ostrogoths and the end of the Roman Empire in 476AD. Still, Christianity continued to take root and German peoples appropriated many of the later Roman religious institutions.

800
Charlemagne
crowned emperor
of Holy Roman
Empire

While the southern German tribes were busy moving upon their well-heeled Roman neighbors, the **Franks** expanded their power into the Rhein Valley. Three centuries later, under the rule of **Charlemagne** (whom Germans know as Karl der Große), nearly all the Germanic kingdoms of Europe were united. Pope Leo III crowned Charlemagne **Emperor of Romans** on Christmas Day in the year 800, inviting comparisons between the emerging Europe and the former Roman Empire. Charlemagne initiated administrative reforms and cultural advancements; under his rule monasteries became centers of learning and commerce within Europe and with the Arab and Byzantine worlds was revived. This Dark Age "renaissance" soon came to an end, however, as invasions from outsiders, weak infrastructure, and disputes over succession after Charlemagne's death prompted the Treaty of Verdun in 843, which split the empire into three kingdoms. A leader of the Frankish kingdom, **Otto I,** pushed the Franks' borders east to the Oder River, earning himself the title of Holy Roman Emperor in 962. Over the next half millennium, the would-be German lands were further divided into a feudal society by destructive internal disputes. Still, in the 12th and 13th centuries, the kingdoms continued to expand in a fever of political competition. The **Hohenstaufen** family bears perhaps the closest resemblance to a dynasty during this period, with **Friedrich I (Barbarossa) and Friedrich II** as the most prominent rulers. Still, the grand aspirations of a succession of regional princes such as **Heinrich der Löwe** (Henry the Lion), maintained the decentralization of the emerging German nations.

843
Treaty of Verdun
splits the Empire
into three kingdoms, marking off
the territory that
would become
Germany

1356
The Golden Bull
splits authority
between archbishops and electors in
choosing the
emperor

Despite the continued existence of the Holy Roman Empire, quarrels between religious and political leadership arose repeatedly in the centuries preceding the signing of the **Golden Bull of 1356,** which declared that seven electors—three archbishops and four secular leaders—would approve the selection of each emperor. Large-scale bribing of these electors ensued, clearing the way for the ascent of the **House of Habs-**

burg, which occupied the throne for the next five centuries. Under Habsburg leadership, the German nation began to define itself more clearly; the **Hanseatic League** banded a number of North Sea merchant towns together in 1358, and outlying areas of the Holy Roman Empire, including Italy, slipped out of the Habsburgs' control entirely.

THE REFORMATION: 1517–1700

On All Saints' Day 1517, **Martin Luther,** a monk and professor of Biblical studies at the University of Wittenberg (p. 190), posted his **Ninety-Five Theses** on the door of the city's castle church. Luther took issue with the Roman Catholic Church for the extravagance of the papal court in Rome and for its practice of selling **indulgences**—gift certificates for the soul that promised to shorten the owner's stay in purgatory. He insisted that salvation came only through God's grace, not through paying fees to clergy. The dramatic repercussions of the **Protestant Reformation** could not have been anticipated even by the movement's founder. The greatest cultural contribution to the Reformation was Luther's **new translation of the Bible,** a document whose publication greatly helped crystallize the many German dialects into a standard, literary High German language.

The German electoral princes soon adopted Lutheranism, captivated by hopes of stemming the flow of money and power to Rome without the threat of getting held up in Purgatory. Armed conflicts soon erupted and quickly developed beyond purely religious conflicts. The serfs rebelled during the **Peasants' Wars** in 1524-1525, demanding their rights from the **Junker** class of noble landholders. The ensuing chaos exceeded the bounds of Luther's initial objectives, and he supported the princes' efforts to suppress the bands of peasants. But Lutheranism as a political movement continued to spread throughout Europe. The Habsburg Emperor **Karl V,** the most powerful leader since Charlemagne, initially declared his intention to uproot the subversive doctrine and destroy those who professed it. However, in the 1555 **Peace of Augsburg,** Karl granted individual princes the right to choose the religion practiced in their respective territories, an arrangement that led to a number of overnight conversions and further divided the empire.

Karl's successors were less than enamored of this agreement. When Archduke Ferdinand of Austria tried to impose Catholicism on Bohemia, the Protestant inhabitants rebelled, leading to the 1618 **Defenestration of Prague,** when an unsuspecting papal representative was hurled out of a window and had his fall broken by a pile of steamy horse dung. The **Thirty Years War** (1618-48) that ensued was a catastrophic setback in Germany's development. At least one-third of the population was killed in what became the longest and bloodiest conflict to embroil Europe. The **Peace of Westphalia,** which ended the war, served as the *de facto* constitution of the empire until its abolition in 1806; it granted 300 princes the right to elect the emperor. The Habsburg's imperial administration was dismantled, and although the Holy Roman Empire lingered for another 150 years, it was actually a dead institution. Germany's power was divided among the various regional monarchs.

1517
Martin Luther posts his 95 Theses, inaugurating the Protestant Reformation

1618-1648 Thirty Years War between Protestants and Catholics wipes out about a third of Germany's population. With the Peace of Westphalia, Germany becomes a land of overwhelming territories and a decentralized system of government

THE RISE OF BRANDENBURG-PRUSSIA: 1700–1862

1709
Friedrich the Great establishes Berlin as the capital of Prussia

1806
Napoleon creates the Confederation of the Rhine

1815
Congress of Vienna pushes Napoleon out and establishes the German Confederation

1848
Frankfurt National Assembly drafts Germany's first liberal constitution

The war indirectly benefited the leaders of **Brandenburg-Prussia.** Friedrich II—known as **Friedrich the Great**—consolidated the rising Prussian state. Friedrich is remembered in German history as an enlightened despot, the initiator of administrative and military reform as well as a patron of the arts. When Maria Theresa became empress of the Habsburg domains in 1740, Friedrich seized the opportunity and snatched the prosperous province of Silesia. By the end of the resulting **Seven Years War** in 1763, Prussia was recognized as one of Europe's great powers. **Friedrich II** and his nephew then joined forces with Russia and Austria and began to **partition Poland** in 1772 and to link Brandenburg to Prussia physically for the first time, piecing together a kingdom for the Habsburg's dynastic rivals, the **Hohenzollern.**

These skirmishes pale in comparison to the havoc wreaked upon Germany by post-revolutionary France. **Napoleon** conquered and disbanded what remained of the Holy Roman Empire and created a subservient **Confederation of the Rhine** in 1806. After incorporating hundreds of thousands of German soldiers, Napoleon's armies were bogged down in Russia, and a general rebellion known as the **Wars of Liberation** ejected Napoleon from German territory (see Jena, p. 223). The 1815 **Congress of Vienna** partially restored the pre-war German state system, creating the Austrian-led **German Confederation.** In 1834, Prussia sponsored the **Zollverein,** a customs union that linked most German territories in a free trade zone.

In 1848, revolution broke out again in France, and discontent spread rapidly to other parts of Europe. The German Confederation agreed to let an elected assembly decide its future. The **Frankfurt National Assembly** drafted a liberal constitution, and invited **Friedrich Wilhelm IV** of Prussia to serve as emperor. He spurned the offer, refusing to accept a cardboard Bürger King crown with limited powers of authority. The assembly disbanded, and the ensuing revolt in Frankfurt was crushed by the Prussian army (see p. 424). Subsequent economic growth heralded the coming of industrialism.

SECOND REICH: 1862–1914

1864-71
Bismarck's wars of unification assert Germany's strength throughout the continent

In 1862, Prussian King Wilhelm I appointed a talented aristocrat named **Otto von Bismarck** as chancellor. The originator and greatest practitioner of *Realpolitik* ("the ends justify the means"), Bismarck exploited a remarkably complex series of alliances and compromises that were frequently dissolved in favor of more violent tactics. Blood and iron, Bismarck proclaimed, were paramount to the creation of a strong and unified German nation. To demonstrate the consolidating effect of war, he fought Denmark in 1864 and seized control of Northern Schleswig. This led to conflict with Austria, which Prussia quashed in 1866 at Sadowa. Bismarck made it clear that Prussia would now dominate German affairs, voiding the current constitution and excluding Austria. In 1867, he disbanded the Confederation and replaced it with the Prussian-dominated

North German Confederation. Bismarck realized that France would never willingly acquiesce to a fully united Germany under Prussian domination, so he suckered France into a misguided declaration of the **Franco-Prussian** war in 1870 with a series of trivial diplomatic slights. The technologically superior Prussian army and its allies swept through France and trounced the French army, capturing Emperor Napoleon III. Parisians declared a republic and vowed to carry on the fight. Bismarck gleefully besieged Paris and had Wilhelm crowned **Kaiser of the German Reich** at the Palace of Versailles. With France disposed of, Bismarck founded the **German Empire** on his own terms in 1871. He presented German liberals with an offer they couldn't refuse: unification in exchange for an authoritarian monarchy. The so-called conservative empire garnered popular support by promoting an aggressive nationalism.

Germany underwent **industrialization** at breakneck speeds in the last decades of the 19th century. In less than 40 years, it developed the most advanced industrial base on the continent, yet retained a political system unaccommodating to the newer liberal ideals; Bismarck came to power in a political climate still controlled by the **Junker** class of noble, landed aristocracy. Many historians attribute Germany's problems in the early 20th century to this belated industrialization and despotism.

By the 1870s, reformist sentiment was gaining ground in Germany. Led by a burgeoning trade union movement and the **August Bebel**-founded **Social Democratic Party** (*Sozialdemokratische Partei Deutschlands*—SPD), working-class radicalism began to pose a serious threat to the established order, while the Catholic church threatened the authority of Prussia's secular institutions, affirming its ultimate loyalty to the Pope. To consolidate power, Bismarck engaged in a series of initiatives known as the **Kulturkampf** which alternatively revolved around reforms and repression. Bismarck pioneered social welfare programs such as unemployment insurance for the working class, but harshly repressed trade unions and the Social Democrats with the **Anti-Socialist Laws** of 1878. Appeasing potential radical factions with these welfare-like programs and alliances, Bismarck quelled revolt. Facing mounting problems with his own constitution and disputes with the new Kaiser Wilhelm II, Bismarck resigned in 1890.

Such rapid transitions produced tremendous social friction. The numbers of the proletariat exploded, while protectionist tariffs kept food prices high. Germany accelerated its foreign adventurism in part to shift the focus from unrest at home—a policy derisively known as **"Flucht nach vorn"** (escape forward). Bismarck's successors realized the need for a German navy able to compete with Britain in the race for overseas colonies, though Germany's sense of imperialism, like its industrialization, lagged far behind its European peers. Disputes over colonial issues left Germany diplomatically isolated in Europe, and tension between Germany and its neighbors rose. Germany boasted the most powerful army in the world at the turn of the century, prompting Britain, France, and Russia to unite as the **Triple Entente.** Meanwhile, democratic opposition began to pose a challenge within the regime itself. To the Kaiser and his supporting elite, it appeared that dramatic and militaristic action would be required for self-preservation.

1871
Wilhelm I crowned Kaiser of a unified Germany, heralding the Second Reich. After an initial lag, Germany pursues industrialization and colonization with a vengeance

1880s
Bismarck quells dissent through the Kulturkampf, but is eventually crushed under a political system of his own making

1907
Increasing international tension prompts Britain, France, and Russia to form the Triple Entente

WORLD WAR I: 1914–1918

1914
Europe erupts in war, with Germany and Austria-Hungary allied as the Central Powers

Trench and submarine warfare result in unprecedented casualties

1918
WWI concludes with the Treaty of Versailles, with Germany under conditions of heavy reparations

On the eve of WWI, Europe found itself in a complex web of alliances where a minor dispute could easily escalate into full-blown continental war. The first domino fell in 1914, when a Serbian nationalist assassinated the Habsburg heir to the Austrian throne, **Archduke Franz-Ferdinand,** in Sarajevo.

Austria quickly marched on Serbia in retaliation, and Russia came to the aid of its Slavic brethren. After Russia ignored Germany's ultimatum to rescind their advance, Germany entered the war on the side of Austria, forming the **Central Powers**, and in turn prompting France to mobilize. This provoked a rush of nationalist sentiment, receiving great popular support from the young generation of Germans. The German General Staff designed the **Schlieffen Plan** for war on two fronts: a lightning thrust through Belgium would deliver a knock-out blow to France, freeing German troops to turn eastward and defeat the Russian Czar before he could prepare his backward army. This plan, however, was not so easily executed. Germany declared war on France and demanded that Belgium allow its army to pass through its territory. Belgium refused. Britain, treaty-bound to defend Belgian neutrality, declared war on Germany. Germany quickly advanced through Belgium and northern France. All of Europe was suddenly swept into war.

After advancing within 50km of Paris, the German offensive was stalled at the **Battle of the Marne.** Four years of agonizing **trench warfare** ensued. The slaughter was staggering, magnified by new weapons such as machine-guns, tanks, planes, flame-throwers, and poison gas. Germany's policy of unrestricted submarine warfare against all ships entering European waters provoked the United States to enter the war on the side of France and Britain. A British naval blockade rapidly choked Germany. Coupling the blockade with the industrial capacity and fresh armies of the US, the Entente emerged victorious.

THE WEIMAR REPUBLIC: 1918–1933

1918
Weimar Republic founded in the midst of political chaos and cultural renaissance

In late 1918 the German army was on the brink of collapse, and riots broke out on the home front. On November 9, 1918, Social Democratic leader **Philipp Scheidemann** declared a republic in Berlin, with **Friedrich Ebert** as its first president. France insisted on a harsh peace in the **Treaty of Versailles,** which imposed staggering reparation payments, reduced the German army to 100,000 men, and ascribed the blame for the war to Germany. The new republican government had little choice but to accept the treaty, as the continuing Allied blockade cut off the country's decreasing supply of food. Even before a constitution was drawn up, the newborn republic was branded by the humiliating treaty. Because the Kaiser had promised a smashing victory right up to the end, Germans were psychologically unprepared for defeat. And the sudden transition to parliamentary democracy put Germany's political structure in a precarious state.

Building on this unsettled sentiment, the newly formed **Communist Party** (*Kommunistische Partei Deutschlands*—KPD), led by **Karl Liebknecht** and **Rosa Luxemburg,** launched a revolt in Berlin that found some support (see p. 89). The Republic crushed the revolution by appealing to bands of right-wing army veterans called **Freikorps,** who in turn launched their own coup d'état under **Wolfgang Kapp.** Workers, however, didn't share in the revolutionary fervor: they demonstrated support for the new republic through a general strike, organizing a force of 50,000-80,000 against the coup. The republic emerged bruised but intact. Its leaders drew up a constitution in **Weimar** (see p. 216). Chosen for its legacy as the birthplace of the German Enlightenment, Weimar now gave its name to a period of intense cultural activity between the world wars.

Outstanding war debts and the burden of reparations produced the hyperinflation of 1922-23. Germany was closer to collapse than it had been since 1871. The Republic achieved stability with help from the American **Dawes Plan,** which reduced the amount of war reparations, and an age of relative calm and remarkable artistic production ensued. However, the old, reactionary order still clung to power in many segments of society. When an Austrian corporal named **Adolf Hitler** was arrested for treason after the abortive 1923 **Beer Hall Putsch** uprising in Munich, he received the minimum sentence of five years—of which he served only 10 months. During his time in jail, Hitler wrote *Mein Kampf* and decided that his party, the **National Socialist German Workers Party** (*Nationalsozialistische deutsche Arbeiterspartei*—NSDAP), also known as the **Nazis,** would need to seize power by constitutional means. Two aspects of the Weimar constitution, intended to ensure a perfectly representative and functional democracy, expedited this process. Purely proportional representation encouraged a spectrum of political parties and discouraged stable governments, while the infamous **Article 48** (drafted by sociologist Max Weber) gave the chancellor power to rule by decree during crises, creating the potential for a dictatorial state.

The Nazi party expanded its efficient, faithful bureaucracy and nearly quadrupled its membership to 108,000 by 1929. Even so, it was still a fringe party in 1928, receiving only 2.6% of the vote. But when the Great Depression struck in 1929, 25% of the population was unemployed within months. Membership in the NSDAP exploded to more than a million by 1930—the **SA** *(Sturmabteilung)*, its paramilitary arm, grew as large as the German army. The Nazis campaigned on an anti-Semitic, xenophobic platform; Hitler failed in a presidential bid against the nearly senile war-hero Hindenburg in 1932, but parliamentary elections made the Nazis the largest party (winning 37% of the seats) in the *Reichstag*. After various political maneuvers, President Hindenburg reluctantly appointed Hitler chancellor of a coalition government on January 30, 1933.

THE THIRD REICH: 1933-1945

Although Hitler now held the most powerful government post, the Nazi party had difficulty obtaining a majority in the *Reichstag*. Within two months of taking control, Hitler convinced the ailing and aging Hindenburg to dissolve the *Reichstag* and hold new elections, allowing Hitler to invoke Article 48 and to rule by decree for seven weeks. During this reign of terror, he curtailed freedom of the press, authorized his special security arms (the Special State Police, known as the **Gestapo,** the **SA** Storm Troop-

1920
Communist Party uprising suppressed in Berlin

1922-23
Hitler stages unsuccessful Beer Hall Putsch; Germany suffers in conditions of hyperinflation

Late 1920s
Nazi party slowly gains power during a period of extreme political vulnerability

1933
Hitler consolidates power, declaring himself *Führer* of the Third Reich

1935
Racial Purity Laws enacted, depriving Jews of German citizenship and prohibiting intercourse between "Aryans" and Jews

1938
Jewish property destroyed during *Kristallnacht*

ers, and the **SS** Security Police) as auxiliary police, and brutalized opponents. Politically astute, he seized the opportunity of the mysterious Reichstag fire one week prior to the elections to declare a state of emergency and round up his opponents, many of whom were relocated to newly-built **concentration camps.** In the ensuing election on March 5, 1933 the Nazis gained 44% of the votes, once again falling short of a majority. Nonetheless, they arrested and browbeat enough opposing legislators to secure the passage of an **Enabling Act** of 1933 making Hitler the legal dictator of Germany. Characteristic humility led Hitler to place himself as the successor to the previous *Reichs:* the Holy Roman Empire (800-1806) and the German Empire (1871-1918).

Vilifying the Weimar government as soft and ineffectual, Hitler's platform played on German anxieties that had accumulated since 1918. Germany's failing economy encouraged a public largely receptive to ideas of anti-Semitism and German racial superiority. Aided by **Joseph Goebbels,** his propaganda chief, Hitler embarked upon a campaign of self-promotion to an insuperable degree; Nazi rallies were masterpieces of political demagoguery, and the Nazi emblem, the **swastika,** embellished everything from propaganda films to the fingernails of loyal teeny boppers. *Heil Hitler* and the right arm salute became a legally obliged greeting.

In 1934, after Hindenburg's death, Hitler appropriated the presidential powers for himself. The following year, the first of the anti-Semitic **Racial Purity Laws** deprived Jews of German citizenship. November 9, 1938 **Kristallnacht** (Night of Broken Glass), in retaliation for the assassination of a German diplomat in Paris by a young Jewish emigré, Nazis destroyed thousands of Jewish businesses, burned synagogues, killed nearly 100 Jews, and sent at least 20,000 to concentration camps.

Hitler directed his wrath not only at Jews, but also toward gypsies, communists, Social Democrats, gays, lesbians, artists, free-thinkers, and the disabled, as well as anyone who publicly demonstrated any sympathy toward these groups. The Third Reich's gained momentum as a massive program of industrialization restored full employment. This productivity, however, was hardly innocent: German business was mounting a war effort. Hitler abrogated the Versailles Treaty, freeing Germany from reparations payments and beginning rearmament. Next, he stared down the Western Allies and annexed Austria—the infamous **Anschluß** in 1938. He then demanded territorial concessions from Czechoslovakia, on the grounds that the Sudetenland served as a home to thousands of ethnic Germans. British Prime Minister Neville Chamberlain assured Hitler in the notorious 1938 **Munich Agreement** that Britain would not interfere with this hostile takeover. The Allies tolerated Germany's aggressive expansionism until war was all but inevitable.

WORLD WAR II: 1939–1945

On September 1, 1939, German tanks rolled across the eastern border into Poland. Britain and France, bound by treaty to defend Poland, declared war on Germany but did not attack. The Soviet Union likewise ignored the German invasion, having secretly divided up Eastern Europe with Germany under the **Molotov-Ribbentrop Pact.** In a month, Poland was crushed by Germany's new tactic of mechanized **Blitzkrieg** (literally, "lightening war"), and Hitler and Stalin carved it up accordingly. On April 9, 1940, Hitler overran Denmark and Norway. A month later, *Blitzkrieg* roared through Luxembourg and quickly overwhelmed Belgium, the Netherlands, and France. However, the Nazis failed to bomb London into submission in the aerial **Battle of Britain.** Preparations for a cross-channel invasion were shelved as Hitler turned his attentions to Russia. The German **invasion of the USSR** in June 1941 ended the Hitler-Stalin pact. Despite the Red Army's overwhelming manpower, the German invasion came close to success. At the peak of his conquests in late 1941, Hitler held an empire stretching from the Arctic Circle to the Sahara Desert, from the Pyrenees to the Urals.

The Soviets suffered extremely high casualties, but *Blitzkrieg* faltered in the Russian winter and Hitler sacrificed thousands of German soldiers in his adamant refusal to retreat. The bloody battle of **Stalingrad** was the critical turning point in the East. Hitler committed a fatal error in declaring war on the United States after his ally Japan bombed Pearl Harbor. His attempt to save Mussolini in North Africa led to the Nazi's first battlefield defeats, and soon Germany was retreating on all fronts. The Allied landings in Normandy on **D-Day** (June 6, 1944) preceded an arduous, bloody advance across Western Europe. The Third Reich's final offensive, the **Battle of the Bulge,** failed in December 1944. In March 1945, the Allies crossed the Rhein. The Red Army took Berlin in April 1945. With Russian troops overhead, Hitler killed himself in a bunker. The Third Reich, which Hitler had boasted would endure for 1000 years, lasted only 12.

1939
Axis and Allied powers meet in the second global clash of the century

Germany invades and occupies most of Europe with its lightning offensive

1945
WW II concludes with the Allied defeat of Germany

THE HOLOCAUST

By the outbreak of the War, the persecution of the Jews was virtually complete in scope. Jews, and Christians of Jewish heritage, were barred from serving in any public capacity and wore the Star of David patch as a reminder of their lost citizenship. In the years before 1939, **pogroms** became increasingly frequent, and Jews were herded into ghettos. Hitler's racial ideology, the central plank of the Nazi platform, was that the German *Volk* were meant to triumph or perish forever. He made no secret of his desire to exterminate all Jews, who, associated with internationalism, communism, pacifism, and democracy, representing the scourge of German nationalism.

Early in the war German **SS** troops invading eastward massacred entire towns of Jewish inhabitants. As the war progressed, institutions of mass execution were developed. The **"Final Solution to the Jewish problem,"** the Nazis' horrific designation for the genocide of European Jewry, called for expansion of the persecution, deprivation, and deportation to which Jews had been subjected since the first days of the Third Reich. The mass gassing of Jews in specially constructed **extermination camps** began in 1942. Seven full-fledged extermination camps, **Auschwitz, Buchenwald** (see p. 225), **Chelmno, Treblinka, Majdanek, Sobibor,** and **Belzec,** plus dozens of nominal "labor" camps such as **Bergen-Belsen** (see p. 514), **Dachau** (see p. 265), and **Sachsenhausen** (see p. 127) were operating before the war's end. Nearly six million Jews, two-thirds of Europe's Jewish population, mostly from Poland and the Soviet Union, were gassed, shot, starved, worked to death, or killed by exposure. Five million other victims—pris-

1942-45
"Final Solution," the attempted extermination of European Jewry, kills six million Jews in concentration and labor camps

oners of war, Slavs, gypsies, homosexuals, the mentally retarded, and political opponents—also died in Nazi camps. The atrocities of the Nazi years reach beyond the scope of tragedy into the realm of inconceivable horror.

OCCUPATION AND DIVISION: 1945-1949

1945
The Allies and Soviets convene at the Potsdam Conference to divide Germany into occupation zones

1945
Nürnberg war trials prosecute Nazis for war atrocities

1949
Soviet forces blockade Berlin. Soviet and Allied relations deteriorate, pulling the nation in both directions until the seams split. The Cold War, FRG, and GDR are born

Germans call their defeat at the end of WWII *Nullstunde*— "Zero Hour"—the moment at which everything began again. The economy was in shambles, most cities were bombed to ruins, more than five million German soldiers and civilians died in the war, and millions remained in POW camps. In July 1945, the United States, Great Britain, France, and the Soviet Union met at **Potsdam** to partition Germany into zones of occupation: the east under the Soviets, the west under the British and Americans, and Berlin under joint control. All German territory east of the Oder and Neisse rivers—a quarter of the nation's land—was confiscated and placed under Soviet and Polish administration, while the coal-rich Saarland was put under French control.

The three-pronged Allied program of **Occupation**—demilitarization, democratization, and de-Nazification (including the 1945 trials of the Nazi war criminals in Nürnberg)—proceeded apace, but growing animosity between the Soviets and the Western allies made joint control of Germany increasingly difficult, paving the way for total division in 1949. In 1947, the Western Allies merged their occupation zones into a single economic unit known as **Bizonia** (later Trizonia, after a French occupation zone was carved out of the British and American zones). The Western Allies began rebuilding their zone along the lines of a market economy with the aid of huge cash infusions from the American **Marshall Plan.** The Soviets, who suffered immeasurably more in the war than the US or Britain, had neither the desire nor the resources to help the East rebuild—they plundered it instead, as allowed by the Potsdam agreement. The Soviet Union carted away everything that wasn't fixed in concrete and a lot of things (such as factories and railroads) that were. The Western Allies ceased their contribution to the East in 1948 and then effectively severed the East's economy from the West's by introducing a new currency, the **Deutschmark.** The currency reform dispute was the proximate cause of the **Berlin Blockade** and the resultant **division of Germany** in 1949.

THE FEDERAL REPUBLIC OF GERMANY

The Federal Republic of Germany (*Bundesrepublik Deutschland*—FRG) was established as the provisional government of West Germany on May 24, 1949. The new government set up camp in the sleepy university town of **Bonn.** A **Basic Law,** drawn up under the direction of the Western Allies, safeguarded individual rights and established a system of Federal States with freely elected parliamentary assemblies. The tripartite government of the FRG (with emphasis on the legislative and judicial, rather than executive, branches) was also a clear case of Allied adoption. One of the most visionary paragraphs of the Basic

Law was the one that established a Right of Asylum, guaranteeing refuge to any person fleeing persecution. Ratification of the Basic Law, however, did not restore German sovereignty; the Allies retained the right to claim ultimate political authority over the country.

As the only party untainted by the Third Reich, the **Social Democratic Party** (*Sozialdemokratische Partei Deutschlands—*SPD) seemed poised to dominate postwar German politics. Another new party, the **Free Democratic Party** (*Freidemokratische Partei—*FDP), assembled bourgeois liberals and professionals along with several former Nazis. A third party, the **Christian Democratic Union** (*Christlich Demokratische Union—*CDU), managed to unite Germany's historically fragmented conservatives and centrists under a nondenominational platform. With **Konrad Adenauer** at the helm, the CDU won a small majority of *Bundestag* seats in the Federal Republic's first general election in mid-1949.

Adenauer, 73 years old when he assumed office, was perhaps the federal republic's greatest chancellor. He simultaneously pursued the integration of Germany into a unified Europe and the return of German national self-determination. He achieved both of these aims, first in 1951 with West Germany's entrance into the European Coal and Steel Community—the precursor of the modern European Union (EU)—and then in 1955 when the Western Allies recognized West German sovereignty. The idealistic Adenauer also helped to restore the self-esteem and purpose of his defeated people without rekindling nationalism. Rebuilding progressed rapidly: Germany achieved full employment by the late 1950s and soon began recruiting thousands of foreign **Gastarbeiter** (guest workers). The speedy economic recovery secured the dominance of the CDU. This *Wirtschaftswunder* (economic miracle), led by economist **Ludwig Erhard,** built it into the world's fourth-largest economy during the 1950s and 60s.

The SPD, whose fortunes seemed so promising in 1945, floundered for over 20 years. The party's Marxist rhetoric prevented it from expanding beyond a working-class base. In 1961, the SPD jettisoned Marx and found a dynamic young leader in **Willy Brandt.** Germany's first postwar recession in 1967 badly hurt the CDU and the 1969 *Bundestag* elections catapulted the SPD toward power. With Brandt as chancellor, the **Social-Liberal Coalition** of the SDP and FDP enacted a number of overdue reforms in education, governmental administration, social security, and industrial relations. Its most dramatic policy innovation, however, was in foreign relations. Brandt's **Ostpolitik** (Eastern Policy), actively sought improved relations with East Germany, the Soviet Union, and other Eastern Bloc nations. Brandt and his foreign minister **Walter Scheel** concluded several important treaties, including an agreement **normalizing relations** with the GDR, for which Brandt received the Nobel Peace Prize in 1971.

After Brandt resigned in the wake of a 1974 spy scandal, Social Democrat **Helmut Schmidt** became chancellor. Under Schmidt, West Germany racked up an economic record that was the envy of the industrialized world. Nevertheless, persistent structural problems in heavy industry contributed to **mounting unemployment** and dissatisfaction with the SPD in the late 1970s. In 1982, new partners FDP and CDU formed a government under **Helmut**

HISTORY & CULTURE

1949
Allied powers oversee the drafting of the Basic Law, promoting individual rights and a republican form of government

1949
Konrad Adenauer becomes the Federal Republic's first chancellor

1950s
FRG makes an overnight recovery from post-war ruins to economic power, necessitating the importation of thousands of foreign workers

1970s
Through a policy of *Ostpolitik,* the Federal Republic adopts a friendly neighbor attitude toward the GDR

1980s
The Greens, an environmentally-conscious political party, find a niche amidst an increasingly capitalist economy

Kohl. Kohl's government pursued a policy of welfare state cutbacks, tight monetary policy, and military cooperation with the US. At the same time, a new political force emerged in Germany: the **Green Party** *(die Grünen)*. By fighting for disarmament and environmentalism and rejecting traditional coalition politics, the Greens won a surprisingly large following. In 1984, **Richard von Weizsäcker** of the CDU was elected to the symbolic post of president. He urged Germans to shoulder fully their moral responsibility for the Third Reich—an implicit rebuke of politicians like Kohl who spoke of "the grace of late birth."

THE GERMAN DEMOCRATIC REPUBLIC

1949
Modeled upon Soviet Communism, the Socialist Unity Party forms a one-party dictatorship. A steady stream of GDR citizens leaks to the West

When Soviet troops occupied eastern Germany, a cadre of German Communists who had spent the war in exile came close on their heels. Even before the surrender was signed, these party functionaries began setting up an apparatus to run the Soviet occupation zone. The first party licensed to operate in the Soviet sector was the **German Communist Party** *(Kommunistische Partei Deutschlands)* under **Wilhelm Pieck** and **Walter Ulbricht,** but versions of the western parties were established shortly afterwards. At first, the German Communists pledged to establish a parliamentary democracy and a distinctively "German path to socialism." However, their dependence on Moscow quickly became apparent. Through some fancy political maneuvers the Social Democrats were forced to join the KPD in a common working-class anti-fascist front, the **Socialist Unity Party** *(Sozialistische Einheitspartei Deutschlands*—SED).

In Berlin, the SPD was permitted to operate freely, and the SED was soundly defeated at the ballot box. The Soviets responded by not holding any more open elections; future elections required voters to approve or reject a "unity list" of pre-selected candidates that ensured SED dominance. On October 7, 1949, a People's Congress selected by this method declared the establishment of the **German Democratic Republic** *(Deutsche Demokratische Republik*—GDR) under Pieck, with the national capital in Berlin. Although the first constitution of the GDR guaranteed civil liberties and paid lip service to parliamentary democracy, these were empty promises. Real power lay in the hands of the SED's *Politbüro* and the party's secretary. Economic, religious, and journalistic regimentation drove many GDR citizens to seek refuge in West Germany.

After Stalin's death, political conditions relaxed somewhat in the GDR, though the nationalization of industry proceeded without hesitation. Impossibly high work goals, made more unrealistic by an exodus of workers to the West, led to a **workers' revolt** across the GDR on June 17, 1953, which was ruthlessly crushed with the aid of Soviet tanks. In response to the FRG's normalization of relations with the Western powers, the GDR was recognized by the USSR in 1954 and became a member of the **Warsaw Pact** in 1955.

In 1961, when the tally of *Republikflüchtige* (illegal emigrants) from East to West Germany reached 3 million, the GDR decided to remedy the exodus of skilled young workers. Although borders to the West had already been sealed off, escape through Berlin remained a possibility. On the night of

August 12-13, the first rudimentary barriers of the **Berlin Wall** were laid. The regime called it an "anti-fascist protective wall," but Berliners knew which way the guns were pointed. Ulbricht to launched his hard-line **New Economic System** and established the GDR's **second constitution** in 1968. This document jettisoned most constitutional rights, already ignored in practice, and abandoned all pretense of parliamentary democracy.

1961
Berlin Wall erected at the height of the Cold War. Stasi secret police terrorize the GDR with a formidable network of 2 million agents

Ulbricht's iron grip on power was broken in 1971 when he ran afoul of his Soviet patrons. His replacement, **Erich Honecker,** returned East Germany to unquestioning subservience to the Soviet Union and eliminated the possibility of reform. Relations with the West improved remarkably during the era of Willy Brandt's **Ostpolitik,** and many Westerners were permitted to visit relatives in the GDR for the first time. Despite war's scars and the shortcomings of central planning, East Germans enjoyed the highest standard of living in the Eastern Bloc by the late 1970s, yet still lagged far behind their western neighbors. The secret police, the **Stasi,** maintained a network of agents to monitor every citizen; one in seven East Germans was a paid informant.

With the ascension of the *glasnost*-minded **Mikhail Gorbachev** to the leadership of the USSR in 1985, reform began to spread throughout the Eastern Bloc—except in the GDR, which ignored the liberalizing reforms. Nevertheless, discontent over the increasingly apparent economic disparities between East and West as well as the alarmingly high level of pollution in East German cities continued to pose a challenge to the SED's grip on power. *Die Wende* (the turning or the change, as the sudden toppling of the GDR is referred to in Germany), began in May 1989 when Hungary dismantled its barbed-wire border with Austria, giving some 55,000 East Germans an indirect route to the West. By October, Czechoslovakia tolerated a flood of GDR citizens into the West German embassy; thousands emigrated. On October 6, while on a state visit to celebrate the GDR's 40th birthday, Gorbachev announced that the USSR would not interfere in the GDR's domestic affairs. Dissident groups such as **Neues Forum** (New Forum) began to operate more freely, organizing massive **anti-government demonstrations** *(Demos)*, which started in Leipzig and spread to Dresden, Berlin, and other cities. East Germans demanded free elections, a free press, and freedom of travel. Faced with rising pressure, Honecker resigned. His successor, **Egon Krenz,** promised reforms. Meanwhile, tens of thousands of GDR citizens—largely young professionals—continued to flee via Czechoslovakia, which completely opened its border with West Germany. The entire GDR *Politbüro* resigned on November 8. A day later, a Central Committee spokesperson announced the **opening of all borders to the West,** including the Berlin Wall.

1980s
Mounting economic disparities between East and West lead to widespread political discontent

1989
East German regime collapses

REUNIFICATION AND ITS AFTERMATH: 1989–THE PRESENT

The opening of the Wall marked the **Wende,** the most symbolically significant turning point for Germans since the end of WWII. However, the it did not immediately herald the demise of the GDR or the Communist regime. Elected four days after the opening of the wall, East German Prime Minister **Hans Modrow** pledged to hold free elections. The constitution was re-written to

1989
Fall of the Berlin Wall

remove references to the SED's leading role, but the party remained in power and the *Stasi* continued to operate despite intense pressure. The SED renamed itself the **Party of Democratic Socialism (PDS),** whose initials, critics joked, really stood for *Pack deine Sachen* ("pack your bags"). The year 1990 began with another ecstatic celebration on top of the Berlin Wall, which belied the furious political struggle going on in both Germanies. In the East, opposition parties took shape and assumed positions in the existing government, while the West's political parties scrambled to assert their influence in preparation for March **elections.** The SPD was crippled by its expressed reluctance about the prospect of reunification. Buoyed by Kohl's success at getting Moscow to assent to unification, the CDU-backed **Alliance for Germany** emerged the winner. In the East, a broad coalition government of non-Communist parties authorized **economic and social union** with the Federal Republic. On the day of the *Währungsunion,* July 1, 1990, GDR citizens exchanged their worthless Ostmarks for mighty Deutschmarks. The signing of the **Four-Plus-Two Treaty** by the two Germanies and the four occupying powers on September 12, 1990, signaled the **end of a divided Germany.**

1990
The *Wende.* Germany reunifies. East Germany is absorbed into the FRG. The socialist net is pulled out, and a reunified but unprepared Federal Republic experiences its worst recession. Foreign workers bear the brunt of discrimination and resentment during economic hardship

Despite the designation *Wiedervereinigung* (reunification), East and West Germany did not unify on an equal basis to create a new nation-state. Rather, East Germany was absorbed into the institutions and structures of the Federal Republic, leading some to call the union *der Anschluß* (annexation). Under the Basic Law's paragraph 23, any territory had the power to accede, or simply declare themselves ready to be consumed by, the FRG. This was a fast route to nominal unity, and after a great deal of debate, it was the one Germany took. On **October 3, 1990,** the Allies forfeited their occupation rights, the GDR ceased to exist, and Germany became one united, sovereign nation for the first time in 45 years. Germans now distinguish between East and West with the labels **"new federal states"** and **"old federal states."**

Immediately following the events of 1989-90, nationalistic euphoria blurred the true state of matters for Germans on both sides of the wall. The collapse of East Germany's inefficient industries and institutions led to massive unemployment and the Federal Republic's worst-ever recession. Many westerners resented the inflation and taxes that were the cost of rebuilding the new federal states, while easterners had to give up the generous social benefits communism afforded them.

In the years following, economic frustrations led to the scapegoating of foreigners, especially asylum-seekers from Eastern Europe and the *Gastarbeiter,* many of whom had been living in Germany for decades. German law does not automatically grant citizenship to children born in Germany; parentage is considered the determining factor. This has become a more and more troubling point as the children of immigrants grow up in Germany, speak only German, know no other home, but are defined as aliens. The violent attacks on foreigners reached horrible proportions in 1992 and 1993, when wide-scale assaults were launched against immigrants in Mölln and Rostock, resulting in numerous deaths. Soon after, the liberal Asylum Law was repealed. Fortunately, violence has decreased significantly since the early 1990s.

After the dramatic fall of the Berlin Wall in 1989, Kohl and his CDU seemed insurmountable. Carrying their momentum into the first all-German elections, the CDU scored a stunning victory. After that, however, Kohl's popularity plummeted to the point where, during one visit, eastern voters pelted him with rotten vegetables, and his party failed to carry his own state in state elections. The CDU bounced back in 1994, only to be resoundingly ousted in 1998 by the left-wing parties.

Europe, or more specifically the new Germany's place in it, remains the big political question. The burden of the past makes everyone, including Germans themselves, nervous about Germany's participation in international military operations, highlighted most recently by the **Kosovo** crisis, in which Germany played a pivotal role in negotiating a peace accord. A persistent feeling among many Germans now is that they should stay out of foreign policy, acting instead as a large, benign economic machine at the heart of the European Union. But Germany is not Switzerland; such a neutral stance will not always be possible for the most populous and economically powerful nation in Europe. Yet most questions surrounding Germany's larger role in world affairs remained unanswered at the close of the 20th century.

1990s
Helmut Kohl and his political party, the CDU, ride the roller-coaster of public opinion

RECENTLY IN GERMANY

The fall 1998 elections unseated Kohl after 16 years as chancellor; in his place, **Gerhard Schröder** led the SPD to victory as the largest party in the Bundestag; to achieve a majority, however, Schröder formed a coalition with the Greens, and propelled longtime environmental politician **Joschka Fischer** to the post of secretary of state. This distinct leftward shift led to the reopening of a number of old debates. In January, Fischer announced the government's intention to **shut down all of Germany's remaining nuclear reactors.** The declaration caused much friction in Europe, as France and the UK demanded billions in reparations for the nuclear reprocessing contracts that were effectively canceled by the government's new energy policy. The progressive climate also spawned heated debate over Germany's contentious **citizenship laws,** which have been criticized as outdated given Germany's increasingly multicultural demographics. Measures to extend citizenship to non-Germans were strongly opposed by the CDU, who feared diminished returns at the ballot box in the wake of the enfranchisement of the several million Turks residing permanently in Germany. This year also marked the **fiftieth anniversary of the founding of the Federal Republic,** accompanied by appropriately well-tempered celebrations of the FRG's democratic institutions. Anxiety surrounded the Bundestag's move to Berlin, which restored the city's role as political capital of Germany for the first time in more than 50 years and inaugurated the much-anticipated **Berlin Republic.**

1998
Gerhard Schröder takes over the chancellorship following Kohl's 16-year tenure

1999
The national government moves back to Berlin after 55 years' absence

1999
Fiftieth anniversary of the founding of the German Republic.

GERMANY IN 2000

The campaign finance scandal that rocked the CDU received perhaps enormous international coverage. The CDU was unable to account for millions of *Deutschmarks* it received, some of which was transferred to the party by the CDU parlia-

2000
Helmut Kohl impli-
cated in CDU
finance scandal.
Reparations pay-
ments for forced
labor during WWII.
Continued negoti-
ations on nuclear
power. World's
Fair in Hannover.
Important meet-
ings with French
and Russian digni-
taries.

mentary group. Former Chancellor Helmut Kohl admitted to illegally accepting 2 million DM in campaign contributions, but refused to name the donors, citing the need to honor his word. No legal or civil action will be taken, but the controversy has weakened the CDU, which is striving to make a comeback under their secretary general, **Angela Merkel.** Meanwhile, Chancellor Gerhard Schröder and the SPD have labored to keep their coalition government with the Greens, despite differences over such issues as the maximum tenure of nuclear power plants, the size of army cuts, and the use of a solely private army.

In other news, public and private sources in Germany pledged 5 billion DM in **reparations payment for forced labor** during WWII. Although the German economy continued to grew, unemployment remained around 10%. Immigration was hotly debated, as radical right wing attacks on foreigners continued. Although Schröder and others advocated reducing immigration to stop the violence, a number of green cards were granted to foreigners highly trained in information technology, amid calls for supporting German education instead. German armed forces were present in the peace-keeping missions of the former Yugoslavia, and also helped flood relief in Africa.

It was a significant year for Germany's international relations. Hannover hosted the World's Fair, **Expo 2000.** Prominent visitors included President Clinton, who received the Charlemagne award, despite tense discussions of the possible American missile defense system's implications. In an address to students at Humboldt University in Berlin, **President Chirac** of France visited Germany and argued that the two countries should lead the EU towards more cooperative actions; he previously suggested giving Germany a permanent seat on the UN Security Council. Chancellor Schröder had long and productive meetings with the newly elected **President Putin** of Russia, in which the close relationship of the two countries was affirmed amidst business agreements and discussions of European missile defence initiatives; in a symbolic move of restoration, the two leaders side by side walked through the Brandenburg Gate.

FURTHER READING

Great overviews for those seeking a broader education in German history from its beginnings to the present include Mary Fulbrook's *Concise History of Germany* and Hagen Schulze's *Germany: A New History.* Gordon Craig's *Germany 1866-1945* provides a definitive history of those years. Detlev Peukert's *The Weimar Republic* is a thorough examination of the major trends of the interwar period, while Craig's *The Germans* offers an excellent general picture of modern German society. For an in-depth look at postwar German history, pick up Henry Ashby Turner's *The Two Germanies Since 1945* or Peter J. Katzenstein's *Policy and Politics in Western Germany.* Ralf Dahrendorf's *Society and Democracy in Germany* is a great treatment of "the German Question," while Fulbrook's *Anatomy of a Dictatorship: Inside the GDR, 1949-1989* offers a concise retrospective of the East German state.

CULTURE

Germany is the land of *Dichter und Denker*—poets and philosophers. The humanities in Germany have had an enormous influence on the development of artistic, literary, and musical trends in Europe and the world, to say nothing of the pivotal role German research has had in the natural sciences.

VISUAL ART

It was the late 8th- and 9th-century Frankish emperor **Charlemagne** who first marshaled Germanic drawing boards in a big way, commissioning Romanesque churches and illuminated manuscripts by the dozen. German painting during the late Gothic period was successful, albeit limited in theme to religious themes painted on wall panels. Little changed until Renaissance painters like **Matthias Grünewald** and **Hans Holbein the Younger** brought a strong sense of realism to the form. Their set also took up portraiture, as did the singularly prolific **Lucas Cranach,** who also brought historical and mythological themes to German art (see p. 221). The most exciting and enduring work of this time was done by **Albrecht Dürer,** master of the woodcut. His *Adam and Eve* still peppers advertisements today and his *Self-Portrait at 20,* one of the first self portraits in Europe, painted in 1500, resembles a humanist messiah.

Soon the **Protestant Reformation** ushered in a long period of turmoil. While **Baroque** and **Rococo** movements adopted from France and Italy made their architectural marks, the visual arts suffered from discontinuity and conflict brought on by the Thirty Years War. However, in the 19th century German critics encouraged **Romantic** painting (and rebuffed Neoclassicism) by advocating a return to traditional German masterworks—divinely inspired and individually interpreted. This idea easily bled into the expressive landscapes of **Philipp Otto Runge** and **Caspar David Friedrich.** Like much Romantic art, Friedrich's melancholy paintings of chalk cliffs (see Rügen, p. 579), and ancient ruins (see Eldena, p. 583) seem to be inspired by humanity's longing and loneliness in the face of nature.

In the 20th century, German art exploded. **German Expressionism** recalled the symbolist tendencies of Viennese **Jugendstil** (Art Nouveau) and French Fauvism (see Schleswig, p. 559). Its deliberately anti-realist aesthetics intensified colors and the representation of objects to project deeply personal emotions. **Die Brücke** (The Bridge) was the earliest Expressionist group, founded in Dresden in 1905. Its artists, especially the celebrated **Ernst Ludwig Kirchner,** used jarring outlines and deep color planes inspired by the primitivism of **Emil Nolde** to make paintings and sculptures loud and aggressively expressive. A 1911 exhibition in Munich entitled **Der Blaue Reiter** (The Blue Rider), led by Russian emigré **Wassily Kandinsky,** marked the rise of a second Expressionist school. Kandinsky's contribution was a series called *Improvisations.* Painted in 1910-11, they are considered the some of the first totally non-representational paintings in Western art. Other members include **Franz Marc,** of "Blue Horses" fame, and **Paul Klee,** whose primitive style has remained influential throughout the century.

World War I and its aftermath interrupted the flow of German art movements. Artists became increasingly bold and political in reaction to the rise of Fascism. **Max Beckmann** painted severely posed figures whose gestures and symbolism expressed a tortured view of man's condition. **Max Ernst** started a **Dadaist** group expressing artistic nihilism with collage and composition in Köln. The grotesque, satirical works of **Otto Dix** walked a tightrope between Expressionism and Dada before embracing the **Neue Sachlichkeit** (New Objectivity), a movement that sought to come to terms with the rapid modernization of the times through matter-of-fact representation. **Georg Grosz** and **John Heartfield** brought a sharp edge to *Neue Sachlichkeit* with almost violent collage and sketch satires of their increasingly fascist surroundings. The smaller German **Realist** movement devoted itself to bleak, critical works such as the social reform posters of **Käthe Kollwitz** (see Berlin, p. 131, and Moritzburg, p. 166). Sculptor **Ernst Barlach** infused realism with religious themes, inflaming Nazi censors (see Güstrow, p. 568).

The rise of Nazism drove most artists and their work into exile. Themes of *Blut und Boden* (Blood and Soil) dominated Nazi visual arts, depicting the mythical union of folkish blood and German soil through idealized images of workers, farmers, and soldiers of the "master race." In 1937, the Nazi's famous **Entartete Kunst** (Degenerate Art) exhibit placed pieces by Kandinsky, Kirchner, and other masters next to paintings by psychotics, sending a clear message to all artists in Germany.

After the war, German art made a quick recovery. In **East Germany,** state-supported **socialist realism** dominated the scene. Leipzig in particular became prominent for its paintings thematizing class struggle and socialist economic advances. While Realism reigned in the East, **abstraction** dominated West German art. As time went on, installations, "actions," and other art pieces that combined new technologies, especially video, edged out painting, although **Sigmar Polke** and a few other masters kept the medium alive. Polke was a member of the **Junge Wilde,** a group of late 1970s neo-expressionists that also included **Anselm Kiefer.** Kiefer commented on Nazism and the **Holocaust** with rare irony, first in symbolic photography and later on huge canvases. He also studied with **Josef Beuys** and his **constructivist sculpture** school at Düsseldorf (see p. 472). Along with Düsseldorf, Berlin and München stand as centers of contemporary art in Germany. The hottest (or at least the biggest) thing to see in contemporary German exhibitions is **documenta,** a summer-long exhibition of art from around the world that takes place every five years; the next event, documenta XI, will draw hordes to Kassel from June 8 through September 15, 2002.

ARCHITECTURE AND DESIGN

Long ago, German architecture and design began to pave the way for a thriving tourist industry. Churches and romantic castles around the country manifest stunning Romanesque, Gothic, and Baroque styles, all made possible by Germany's unique history and geography. The **Romanesque** period, spanning the years 1000 to 1300, arose from direct imitation of Roman ruins. Outstanding Romanesque cathedrals can be found along the Rhein at Speyer, Trier, Mainz, and Worms. Note that in German a cathedral is a **Dom** or **Münster.** Such cathedrals often feature a cloverleaf floor plan, numerous towers, and sometimes a mitre-like steeple.

The **Gothic** style, with its pointed rib vaulting, gradually replaced the Romanesque form between 1300 and 1500. Gothic cathedrals often take the form of a cross, facing east so that the morning sunrise will shine down onto the altar. Gothic cathedrals dominate the skylines of Regensburg and Magdeburg, and the cathedral at Köln is one of the most famous structures in Germany. Gothic style was also often employed in brick structures such as those at Lübeck, Stralsund, and Greifswald. Secular architecture at the end of the Middle Ages is best remembered through the **Fachwerk** (half-timbered) houses that still dominate the Altstädte of many German cities. The **Renaissance** influence can be found in south, in the Augsburg Rathaus (see p. 310) and the Heidelberg Schloß (see p. 340).

By 1550, Lutheran reforms put a damper on the unrestrained extravagance of cathedrals in the north, while the Counter-Reformation in the Catholic south spurred a splendid new **Baroque** style. The later 18th-century German Baroque sought to achieve an impression of fluidity and contrast, achieved through complex forms and sinuous contours. The **Zwinger** in Dresden (see p. 163) is a magnificent example. Baroque eventually reached a fanciful extreme with **Rococo,** as exemplified by **Schloß Sanssouci** at Potsdam (see p. 148). Versailles set a decadent precedent that influenced Bavarian castles, notably **Herrenchiemsee** (see p. 285) and the **Königsschlößer** (see p. 273).

Eventually this exuberance ran its course. The late 18th century saw an attempt to bring Greco-Roman prestige to Germany in the form of **Neoclassical** architecture. This was spurred on by contemporary archaeological digs at Pompeii and the pomp of **Karl Friedrich Schinkel** (see p. 129), state architect of Prussia. The **Branden-burger Tor** and the buildings along **Unter den Linden** in Berlin (see p. 114) were prod-ucts of this new, simpler period.

The **Maltidenhöhe** buildings at Darmstadt (see p. 430) are products of a much more modern movement, **Jugendstil,** which derived its name from the Munich mag-azine *Die Jugend.* This style, strongly influenced by *art nouveau*, spanned the decades before and after the turn of the century. In the 1920s and early 30s, a new philosophy emerged with **Walter Gropius,** who began his career with several sensa-tional buildings featuring clean forms, flat roofs, and broad windows, all made possible by new concrete-and-steel construction techniques. In 1919, Gropius founded the **Bauhaus** school in Weimar (see p. 220). A ground-breaking school of design, Bauhaus combined theoretical training in new principles of efficiency with exposure to the realities of mass production. "Form follows function" was its oft-quoted principle. The school moved to Dessau in 1925 (see p. 195) where Gropius designed its new facility, which quickly became a symbol of the modern style.

Hitler disapproved of the new buildings. He named a design school reject, **Albert Speer,** as his minister of architecture, and commissioned ponderous, neoclassical buildings appropriate to the "thousand-year Reich." Many were intended for public rallies, such as the **congress hall** and **stadium** at Nürnberg (see p. 325) and the **Olym-pic Stadium** at Berlin (see p. 122). After the war, Soviet architecture began to clut-ter East Germany, reaching a high-point with the 365m high **Fernsehturm** (TV tower) in Berlin (see p. 118). For the serious lover of Stalinist architecture, Karl-Marx-Allee is rich in **Plattenbauten,** the dispassionate pre-fab apartment buildings that can be found throughout East Germany (see p. 118). In all of Germany, recon-struction of war-torn Altstadt architecture fostered a revival of old forms.

LITERATURE

German literary history begins around 800, with the epic verse concerning the struggle between the heroic **Hildebrand** and his son. The next several centuries showed an intriguing mix of Christianity and the culture of the German tribes; for instance, the ninth-century **Heliand** interprets Christ as a prince, and his disciples as feudal vassals. As soon as chivalry took hold in Germany, a tradition of lyric poetry on the theme of unrequited love emerged, best represented by **Walter von der Vogel-weide.** This genre, called **Minnesang,** marked a high point in medieval literature. However, by the mid-13th century the chivalric ideal of love without satisfaction wore thin, and the **lyric ballad** became popular with a new, less elite public influ-enced by Renaissance Italy. Epic poetry in German continued, the most famous example being the 13th-century **Nibelungenlied,** by an anonymous author, concern-ing the struggles of the hero **Siegried.** Part of this text was used by **Wagner** when he composed **Der Ring des Nibelungen.** By the late 15th century, the best minds of Ger-many were thinking about the **Reformation,** and poetry took a more serious turn. **Martin Luther** produced his translation of the **Bible** in the 1530s, laying the founda-tion for a written form of modern German as well as the lumbering **protestant hymn.**

What Luther did for language, **Martin Opitz** did for poetics a century later, insist-ing that word accent and metrical stress coincide and that meter have regular stresses. Although sometimes constraining, these new linguistic rules allowed Ger-man literature to adopt foreign forms; during the chaos of the Thirty Years War many poets, such as **Andreas Gryphius,** found solace in an intense religious life that could be recorded in structured meter. The first significant German novel, **Hans J. C. von Grimmelshausen's** roguish epic *Simplicissimus,* was written in this period. Ultimately, however, the Reformation and the Thirty Years War fragmented Ger-many and stunted political development such that German literature had no equiv-alent to the French *grand siècle*. Often, Germany simply imitated France. **Gotthold Ephraim Lessing,** who admired Shakespeare, rebelled against this humiliating pos-turing by writing plays that broke with the French adherence to the Aristotelian unities of time, place, and motive with plays like *Nathan der Weise,* which is set in the Middle East and features a plot several days in length (see p. 510).

In the mid-18th century, a sentimental, unusually personalized poetry arose, and soon the literary giant **Johann Wolfgang von Goethe** was writing his early poetry (see p. 424). Goethe's lyrics possessed a revolutionary immediacy and drew on rediscovered folk songs and ballads. His novel *Die Leiden des jungen Werthers* (The Sorrows of Young Werther) eschewed formula and drew the attention of Europe to the budding **Sturm und Drang** (Storm and Stress) movement, which would greatly influence early Romantic literature. Goethe later turned to the *Bildungsroman* (novel of educational development) and themes of classicism and orientalism. His masterpieces are numerous; his retelling of the **Faust** legend is often considered the pinnacle of a German literature that had moved from the provincial to the center of Europe's attention by the time Goethe died in 1832. His friendship with **Friedrich Schiller** (see p. 361) was crucial to the molding of German literature, and their adopted base of Weimar (p. 219) and the surrounding region are full of literary history (see Thüringer Wald, p. 232).

In the early 19th century, **Romanticism** began to flower, with **Novalis** as its great poet. The movement continued to mature with the 1805 publication of *Des Knaben Wunderhorn*, an influential collection of popular folk tales, and the more celebrated collection by the **Brothers Grimm**, *Grimms' Fairy Tales*, followed in 1812. The **novella**, usually a story based on a reported event, served as a primary vehicle for new tales; **Heinrich von Kleist** (see Berlin, p. 126) and **Ludwig Tieck** were its chief practitioners. **E.T.A. Hoffmann** wrote ghost stories that were later analyzed by Freud (see Bamberg, p. 331). At the same time, **Johann Christian Friedrich Hölderlin** was writing a unique, myth-laden poetry until he succumbed to an insanity that had been haunting him for years and moved to a tower in Tübingen (see p. 364), where he lived out the rest of his life, composing quatrains on the four seasons.

The romantic attempt to transcend the limitations of practical life eventually turned to gritty, sometimes ironic resignation. A rush of realistic political literature exploded around the time of the revolutions of 1848. **Heinrich Heine** was the finest of the **Junges Deutschland** (Young Germany) movement and also one of the first German Jews to achieve literary prominence (see Düsseldorf, p. 471). From self-exile in France, he wrote telling satires as well as romantic poems like *Die Lorelei* (see p. 396), while **Georg Büchner** wrote several strikingly modern plays, *Woyzeck* among them, which was later prized by both Expressionists and Marxists. Another social dramatist, **Gerhart Hauptmann**, achieved great influence around the turn of the century, and **Theodor Fontane** wrote realist novels which commented on Prussian society.

Opposite this *fin-de-siècle* realism, the **Symbolist** movement of the early 20th century concentrated on fleeting, sonorous image-poems; the **George-Kreis** (George Circle), led by critic and poet **Stefan George,** combined passions for literature and stylishness. The spirituality of **Hermann Hesse** showed an Eastern flair; his 1922 quasi-Buddhist novel *Siddhartha* became a paperback sensation in the 1960s. **Thomas Mann** carried the modern novel to a high point with *Der Zauberberg* (The Magic Mountain) and *Doktor Faustus*, two allegorical recountings of Germany's fateful history (see Lübeck, p. 549). Also vital to the period were German-language writers living in Austria-Hungary, among them **Rainer Maria Rilke** and **Franz Kafka**.

In the years before WWI, Germany produced a violent strain of Expressionist poetry that partially mirrored developments in painting. This poetry was well suited to depict the horrors of war, although several of its finest practitioners were killed in battle. The **Weimar Era** was filled with surprisingly lively artistic production. Its most famous novel was **Erich Maria Remarque's** *Im Westen nichts Neues* (All Quiet on the Western Front), a blunt, uncompromising account of war's horrors which became embroiled in the political turmoil of the era. **Bertolt Brecht's** dramas and poems present humankind in all its grotesque absurdity (see Berlin, p. 120); his *Dreigroschenoper* (Three-Penny Opera) was set to music by **Kurt Weill** (see Dessau, p. 195). The years of the Third Reich were more about burning books than publishing them; the Nazi attitude toward literature was summed up by Goebbels: "Whenever I hear the word 'culture,' I reach for my gun."

GÜNTER GRASS: LITERARY SUPERSTAR

Considered Germany's most celebrated contemporary writer, Günter Grass was born in Danzig (now Gdańsk, Poland) in 1927. In the immediate postwar period, he quickly came to prominence in the literary group Gruppe 47. His brilliant "Danzig Trilogy" (*The Tin Drum, Cat and Mouse,* and *Dog Years*) looked at the Nazi experience from the periphery, treating WWII as it came to the townspeople of Danzig. While Grass' early novels scandalized the German public at their first printing, they are now part of most university curricula. Grass continues to write against the grain, especially through his political essays. Since 1989, he has consistently professed a strong, and increasingly isolated, criticism of German unification. In his 1990 *Two States—One Nation?* Grass argues that with Auschwitz, Germany lost for all time the right to reunify. His millennial *My Century* was published in December 1999. Grass was awarded the Nobel Prize for literature in 1999.

While the prolific literature of the Weimar period seemed to succeed WWI almost effortlessly, the second world war left Germany's artistic consciousness in shambles. Some thinkers, such as **Theodor Adorno** (see Philosophy, below), even questioned the propriety of writing certain types of literature after the **Holocaust** had so tragically called human consciousness into question. To nurse German literature back to health, several writers joined to form **Gruppe 47,** named after the year of its founding. The group included many who would become world-class writers: **Günter Grass** and (more peripherally) the poet **Paul Celan.** Much of the ensuing literature dealt with the problem of Germany's Nazi past; the novels of Grass and **Heinrich Böll** and the poetry of **Hans Magnus Enzensberger** turned a critical eye to post-war West Germany's repressive, overly organized tendencies.

The state of letters in the **GDR** was largely determined by the waxing and waning of government control. Many expatriate writers, particularly those with Marxist leanings from before the war (such as Brecht), returned to the East with great hopes. But the communist leadership was not interested in eliciting free artistic expression. The combination of personal danger, the burden of censorship, and simple disillusionment led many immensely talented writers to emigrate, including **Ernst Bloch, Uwe Johnson, Sarah Kirsch,** and **Heiner Kipphardt.** In the 70s and 80s, some East German writers were able to publish in the West, though not at home, and took that option as a middle ground. **Christa Wolf,** one of the most prominent German women writers, voluntarily remained in the GDR. Radical GDR playwright **Heiner Müller** shocked audiences with his disgusted protagonists and stripped-down scenarios of Beckett-esque plays such as *Hamletmaschine.* Since reunification, there has been a period of artistic anxiety and occasional malaise; in the former East, many authors are caught up in controversies over complicity with the *Stasi.* The new world of global capitalism has filled the shelves of German bookstores with translations of American best-sellers, pushing many works by German authors to the side. For happening German literature, look for **W. G. Sebald, Monika Maron, Peter Schneider,** or **Bernhard Schlink.**

PHILOSOPHY

Germany's philosophical and theological tradition—one of the most respected in the world—is often very difficult reading. In 1517, **Martin Luther** defied the Catholic church, arguing against papal infallibility by claiming that only scripture was holy and that the individual should have a direct relationship with God. **Gottfried Wilhelm Leibniz** thought of God as a metaphysical watchmaker who set the individual's body and soul in motion like two synchronized clocks. He also developed a **calculus** independent of Newton.

Immanuel Kant, the foremost thinker of the **German Enlightenment,** argued that ethics can be rationally deduced. While Kant sought to reconcile empiricism and rationalism, **Johann Gottlieb Fichte** spearheaded the new **German Idealist** movement from Jena. Idealism stressed the importance of a postulated spirit or *Geist* in interpreting experience. Also in Jena (see p. 223), **Georg W. F. Hegel** added a dialectical twist to idealism, proposing that world history as well as the development of the individual consciousness could be understood through discerning conflicts of thesis and antithesis that would lead to a new synthesis. The two thinkers were laid to rest side by side in a Berlin cemetery (see p. 120). Hegel's view of world history would, after some distortion, eventually provide a theoretical backing for German nationalism. Meanwhile, **Johann Gottfried Herder** pushed for romantic nationalism, asserting that the spirit of a nation could be found in its folklore and peasant traditions. **Karl Marx** turned Hegel's dialectic around, asserting that class conflict was the stage on which world history was made—and the rest is history.

Similarly controversial, **Friedrich Nietzsche,** influenced by pessimist *par excellence* **Arthur Schopenhauer,** scorned the mediocrity of the hypocritical Judaeo-Christian masses. He advanced the idea of the *Übermensch,* a super-man so wise and self-mastered that he could enjoy life even to the point of eternal repetition. Later, Nietzsche went insane after hugging a horse, and for ten years he lay in bed while his sister contorted his works into **anti-Semitic** ideologies.

Max Weber accurately announced that we are trapped in a bureaucratic iron cage and spoke out against the archaic, retarding effect of noble **Junker** society on German agriculture. **Edmund Husserl** inaugurated the philosophy of **phenomenology,** which occupied great German philosophers for decades. Phenomenology emphasizes the observation of pure consciousness stripped of metaphysical theories or scientific assumptions. **Martin Heidegger,** Husserl's successor at Freiburg and sometime Nazi, went his own way with *Being and Time*. This confusing, cumbersome book details the importance for man to understand what it means to question the meaning of life in a world where one-sided technical development has led to a crisis of **existential alienation.**

While Heidegger was comfortable with Hitler, the members of the **Frankfurt School,** progenitors of **Critical Theory** and erstwhile Marxists in the tradition of **Walter Benjamin,** fled to Columbia University in New York. **Theodor Adorno** and **Max Horkheimer** returned to Frankfurt after the war; their *Dialectic of Enlightenment* explores the merits of a civilizing process that seemingly culminates in fascism. The most celebrated post-war exponent of the school, **Jürgen Habermas,** has criticized German re-unification, citing the danger of joining two nations that have been forced to adopt two very different cultures.

FILM

The newborn medium of film exploded onto the German art scene in the **Weimar era** thanks to numerous brilliant directors. *Das Cabinet des Dr. Caligari* (The Cabinet of Dr. Caligari), an early horror film directed by **Robert Wiene,** plays out a melodrama of autonomy and control against brilliantly expressive sets of painted shadows and tilted walls. **Fritz Lang** produced a remarkable succession of films, including *M., Dr. Mabuse der Spieler,* and *Metropolis,* a dark and brutal vision of the techno-fascist city of the future. **Ernst Lubitsch** also produced silent classics, while **F.W. Murnau's** *Nosferatu* crystallized German pathologies of "the other" in his portrayal of the Dracula legend. Meanwhile, **Josef von Sternberg** extended the tradition into sound with his satiric and pathetic *Der blaue Engel* (The Blue Angel), based on Heinrich Mann's novel *Professor Unrath,* which starred the inimitable **Marlene Dietrich.** Relics of German film's heyday are on display at the former **UFA** studio grounds in Potsdam and Babelsberg (see p. 150).

Heeding Hitler's prediction that "without motor-cars, sound films, and wireless, (there can be) no victory for National Socialism," propaganda minister **Joseph Goebbels** became a masterful manipulator. Most **Nazi films** were political propaganda. *Der Ewige Jude* (The Eternal Jew) and *Jud Süss* (Jew Süss) glorified anti-Semitism. The frighteningly compelling propaganda films of **Leni Riefenstahl,** including *Triumph des Willens* (Triumph of the Will), which documented a Nürnberg Party Rally (see p. 325), and *Olympia*, an account of the 1936 Olympic Games (see p. 122), took the art of the documentary to new heights.

Film continued to be one of the most vigorous artistic media in the latter half of the 20th century. The late 60s and the 70s saw the greatest flood of cinematic excellence. The renaissance began in 1962 with the **Oberhausen Manifesto,** a declaration by independent filmmakers demanding artistic freedom and the right to create the new German feature film; within a few years, the government was granting subsidies to a constellation of young talents. Meanwhile, **Rainer Werner Fassbinder** made fatalistic films about individuals corrupted or defeated by society, including an epic television production of Alfred Döblin's mammoth novel *Berlin Alexanderplatz.* Fassbinder's film *Die Ehe der Maria Braun* (The Marriage of Maria Braun) and **Volker Schlöndorff's** *Die Blechtrommel* (The Tin Drum, based on Günther Grass's novel) brought the new German wave to a wider, international audience. **Margarethe von Trotta** focused mainly on women and politics, notably in her film *Die bleierne Zeit* (Marianne and Juliane). **Wolfgang Petersen** directed *Das Boot* (The Boat), one of the greatest war films ever made. **Werner Herzog's** works, including *Nosferatu*, drew inspiration from the silent films of the 20s in an attempt to recall German cinema's golden age. **Wim Wenders's** "road films," such as *Alice in den Städten* (Alice in the Cities) and the award-winning *Paris, Texas*, examine unconventional relationships and the freedom of life on the road. In 1984, **Edgar Reitz,** one of the Oberhausen signatories, created the 15-hour epic *Heimat* (Home). The film met with overwhelming acclaim for its questioning of national and regional identities. Dorris Dörrie is another current German filmmaker whose works explore race and gender, including films such as *Männer* and *Happy Birthday Turke.*

East German film was subject to more constraints than other artistic media due to the fact that all films had to be produced under the aegis of the state-run German Film Corporation (DEFA). Just after the war, directors in the Soviet Occupation Zone produced several internationally acclaimed films, among them **Wolfgang Staudte's** *Die Mörder sind unter uns* (The Murderers are Among Us), about a Nazi war criminal who evades detection and goes on to lead the good life, **Kurt Maetzig's** *Ehe im Schatten* (Marriage in the Shadows), and **Erich Engel's** *Affaire Blum* (The Blum Affair). **Slatan Dudow** produced the first of the DEFA's films, *Unser täglich Brot* (Our Daily Bread), a paean to the nationalization of industry, and went on to make one of the best East German films, *Stärker als die Nacht* (Stronger than the Night), which tells the story of a communist couple persecuted by the Nazis. After a brief post-Stalinist thaw, few East German films departed from the standard format of socialist heroism or love stories. **Egon Günther's** 1965 film *Lots Weib* (Lot's Wife), an explicitly feminist exploration of marital breakdown and divorce, was one notable exception. The next year saw three major films, Maetzig's *Das Kaninchen bin ich* (The Rabbit is Me), **Frank Vogel's** *Denk bloß nicht, ich heule* (Just Don't Think I'm Crying), and **Frank Beyer's** *Spur der Steine* (Track of Stones). Beyer later made the critically acclaimed *Jakob der Lügner* (Jacob the Liar), which was nominated for an Oscar. Another promising director, **Konrad Wolf,** produced such films as *Ich war neunzehn* (I was Nineteen), *Goya*, and *Sonnensucher* (Sun Seekers), the last of which was not permitted to be released until 14 years after its completion. The GDR also devoted a healthy portion of its filmmaking resources to **documentaries,** with **Winfried Junge, Volker Koepp,** and **Jürgen Böttcher** making significant contributions to the genre. A handful of these films managed to critique the prevailing political situation, although the majority of directors concocted unremarkable films glorifying the Soviet Union and the SED and denouncing the Federal Republic and the United States.

MUSIC

The earliest forms of music that appeared in German lands were religious, and compositions were originally written for the church. A tradition of secular music began in the 12th century with the **Minnesänger,** German troubadours whose technique of singing poetry passed gradually to the **Meistersänger** of the 14th and 15th centuries. After advancing through five ranks from apprentice to *Meister* (master), commoners organized themselves into guilds; their instrumental counterparts were the town-pipers, whose own guilds heralded the modern orchestra. **Polyphony,** the musical phenomenon in which more than one melodic and rhythmic line operates simultaneously within a piece, developed during this period. Luther's new **German translation of the Bible** in the 16th century ushered in a reformation of the musical world as well. The German *cantata* and *oratorio* (sacred and secular forms, respectively) gained popularity because they were finally composed in the language of the homeland. **Michael Praetorious** was a music theorist and composer whose settings of Lutheran chorales provide important examples of the first German hymns. At the turn of the century, **Dietrich Buxtehude** wailed on his organ, adding more settings to the German canon. Another musical form, the *passion*, came into being; the work thematized a saint's transcendence. **Johann Pachelbel** (best known for his Canon in D) worked in these new musical modes.

Johann Sebastian Bach was the phenomenal standout in a long line of musically successful Bachs. His organ works construct worlds whose meticulous symmetries and regularities reflect a careful, uplifting order. In mid-career he produced more secular works; the *Brandenburg Concerti* are famous for their imaginative exploration of the contrast between solo instruments and the chamber orchestra in the Baroque concerto. In 1723, Bach's appointment as cantor of Leipzig's largest church, the Thomaskirche (see p. 186), caused him to return to Lutheran religious music. During his appointment here, Bach composed over 200 cantatas, with the requisite one per week just to keep his job. Both his *St. Matthew* and *St. John Passions* were composed during this time, as were his famous Easter and Christmas Oratorios; they consist of arias and choruses based on Biblical texts. Bach and his contemporary **Georg Friedrich Händel** composed during the Baroque period of the 17th and 18th centuries, which was known for its extravagant decoration and popularized the theme-and-variation idiom. Händel is the man behind every ad campaign that uses the Hallelujah Chorus; his 1742 work **The Messiah** has made its way to more audiences than the composer could have imagined.

The 19th century was an era of German musical hegemony. **Ludwig van Beethoven's** symphonies and piano sonatas bridged Classicism and Romanticism (see p. 458). He pushed classical forms to their limits as he focused on rhythmic drives, extremes of musical elements, and intense emotional expressionism. His monumental *Ninth Symphony* and late string quartets were written in the 1820s after he was completely deaf. The ethereal work of **Felix Mendelssohn-Bartholdy** is well represented by his overture to *A Midsummer Night's Dream*. Immigrant **Franz Liszt** pushed piano music and the symphonic form into still further reaches of unorthodox harmony and arrangement (see p. 221). The second generation of Romantic composers included **Johannes Brahms,** who imbued Classical forms with rich Romantic emotion. **Richard Wagner** was perhaps the most influential German composer after Beethoven. He composed many of the world's best-known operas—*Tannhäuser, Die Meistersinger, Der Ring des Nibelungen*—in an attempt to revolutionize the form of opera; his vision of **Gesamtkunstwerk** (total work of art) unified music and text, poetry and philosophy. Through the reappearance of a *Leitmotiv*, a musical figure that would appear throughout an entire piece, Wagner would give signature sound to dramatic action. The composer's works were highly nationalistic in their celebration of Germanic legend, and were easily exploited by German-Aryan supremacists.

The unstable economy of the Weimar Republic and the anti-Romantic backlash encouraged smaller, cheaper musical forms such as jazz. A new movement of *Gebrauchsmusik* (utilitarian music) engendered music for amateur players and film scores. Austrian **Arnold Schönberg** and his disciples **Anton Webern** and **Alban Berg** mastered the possibilities of 12-tone composition (using a scale based on 12 notes) and explored the expressions of dissonance. In 1921, Berg's opera **Woyzeck** set author Georg Büchner's harrowing tale of insanity to a jarring score. **Paul Hindemith** headed a group of Neoclassicists influenced by the *Neue Sachlichkeit* and the emphasis on craftsmanship introduced by the *Bauhaus*. They embraced the older, variational forms (such as the sonata) most suited to the abstract aesthetic of the time. **Carl Orff,** Hitler's favorite composer, is most noted for his eclectic *Carmina Burana*, a resurrection of bawdy 13th-century lyrics with a bombastic score. Music hall works prior to WWII bred satiric operettas with songs of the political avant-garde. **Kurt Weill's** partnership with Bertolt Brecht produced such masterpieces of the genre as *Die Dreigroschenoper* (Three-Penny Opera). The immediate post-war period was not conducive to much musical experimentation, and schmaltzy *Schlager* tended to dominate. A number of exiled musicians (like the renowned chanteuse **Lotte Lenya**) returned to Germany after the war and briefly revitalized the otherwise unremarkable music scene.

The current state of German musical tastes is dismally transnational; Germans are more likely to listen to the Backstreet Boys or Britney Spears than their own countrymen. Nonetheless, German artists continue to make significant contributions to both the national and global music scene. Apart from **Nena Hagen's** apocalyptic 80s hit *99 Luftballons* and, more recently, **Rammstein's** frightening tune *Du hast*, Germany is best known internationally for having pioneered **techno,** an umbrella term for various kinds of electronic music. In addition to **hardcore** and **gabber,** whose hard-hitting beats (upwards of 200 bpm) inspire fury on the international dance floor, techno has also spawned genres more conducive to crossover; outgrowths such as **house** and **jungle,** developed mainly in the United States and England, juxtapose techno with more established genres like hip-hop and funk. More recently, **ambient** and **trance**—less bass-heavy, more serene forms of electronica—have become quite popular in Germany, with artists like Berlin-based **Mijk van Dijk** receiving international attention. Alec Empire of the popular band **Atari Teenage Riot** gives poignant social criticisms of Berlin and Germany, and his label **Digital Hardcore Recordings** experiments with vocal and electronic music. Techno's most pronounced manifestation is the annual **Love Parade** in Berlin (see p. 138), when DJs such as **Dr. Motte** (the parade's founder), **Da Hool,** and **Phil Fuldner** induce hundreds of thousands of Germans to drop ecstasy and get down.

Apart from techno, Germany enjoys a modest rock scene, with such notable acts as **Die Ärtzte** and **Die fantastischen Vier.** Further afield, **Blümchen** has gained infamy for her bizarre combination of cutesy girl rock and ear-splitting techno beats. Influenced by American musical trends, Germans have also begun to dabble in hip-hop and rap, ranging from the comically adolescent girl group **Tic Tac Toe** to the cannabis-inspired tracks of the Hamburg-based hip-hop act **Fünf Sterne Deluxe.** One of the most prolific homegrown labels is undoubtedly **3p,** which from its base in Frankfurt bills itself as the number one source of *deutsche Soulmusik*. Under its aegis, numerous hip-hop and rap stars, among them **Sabrina Setlur, Xavier Naidoo,** and **Illmatic,** have come to the forefront of the German charts.

MEDIA

British dailies, such as the *Times* and *Guardian*, are widely available at newsstands in most cities. The *International Herald Tribune* and the European edition of the *Wall Street Journal* are the most common US papers. American and British armed forces maintain English-language radio stations in Western Germany. German speakers can keep track of things with German language papers both in print and on the web. Stay in touch with world events with the informative, Hamburg-based weekly *Der Spiegel* (www.spiegel.de), one of the world's leading newsmagazines. *Die Zeit* (www.zeit.de) is a left-leaning weekly. The *Frankfurter Allgemeine Zeitung* (www.faz.de) is a stodgy, more conservative daily. Munich's *Süddeutsche Zeitung* (www.sueddeutsche.de) is one of the country's best newspapers, though the reactionary tabloid *Bild* (www.bild.de) is far more popular. Coming at you from Berlin are the liberal *Berliner Tagesspiegel* (www.tagesspiegel.de) and the leftist *Tageszeitung* (www.taz.de). For a different spin on the news, check out the PDS's neo-communist daily *Neues Deutschland*.

HISTORY & CULTURE

THE WOEFUL DECLINE OF THE ß The story of the ess-tset ("ß") begins hundreds of years ago with the Goths, who devised a letter that efficiently did the work of a cumbersome double S with only one stroke, freeing more time for pillage and plunder. As time passed, the letter gained fame and renown, figuring prominently in the works of Goethe and Schiller. Yet the ess-tset may soon be a fugitive in its own land. It is perhaps the most visible victim of a recent series of language and spelling reforms concocted by representatives of all the German-speaking states of Europe as "a systematic dismantling of anomalies." Other reforms standardize and Germanize the spelling of assimilated foreign words and other eclectically spelled words. Thus far, opposition in Germany has been vocal; in a recent referendum, voters in Schleswig-Holstein soundly rejected the proposed changes. If the ess-tset is exterminated as planned, there will be no way of knowing whether somebody is drinking within limits *(in Maßen)* or excessively *(in Massen)*—so why not opt for the latter?

German television has expanded in the last 15 years. In addition to the three government-run channels (ARD, ZDF, and a third regional channel), Germans can now receive more than 30 channels, including the popular private networks RTL, SAT1, and Pro7. English speakers have access to numerous US and British stations, including CNN, NBC, and BBC. For an entertaining peek at pop culture, watch German MTV and its homegrown counterpart VIVA, or tune into Germany's highest-grossing soap, *Gute Zeiten, Schlechte Zeiten* (Good Times, Bad Times).

FOOD AND DRINK

German food gets bad press. Maybe not as compelling as other European cuisines, *Deutsche Küche* has a "robust" charm. Meat-and-potato lovers especially will find the food in Germany hearty and satisfying. And if the local food is not to your taste, Germany's cities offer a wide variety of quality ethnic restaurants. Be careful when ordering from a German menu if you don't speak the language; ingredients such as *Aal* (eel), *Blutwurst* (blood sausage), and *Gehirn* (brains) are not uncommon, and may necessitate an acquired taste.

Vegetarians should not be afraid of entering this land of carnivores. Since the 1970s, vegetarianism has steadily gained popularity in Germany, with a recent rise due to the fear of mad cow disease. Approximately one-fifth of Germany's population now eats little or no meat. Vegetarian restaurants abound in most cities, and vegetarian and *Biokost* (health foods) supermarkets are much more prevalent than in the rest of Europe. As most vegetarian fare relies heavily on cheese, vegans may have a more difficult time finding non-dairy options. For more information, see **Dietary Concerns** (see p. 79).

The typical German **Frühstück** (breakfast) consists of coffee or tea with *Brötchen* (rolls), several kinds of bread, butter, marmalade, *Wurst* (cold sausage), *Schinken* (ham), *Eier* (eggs), and *Käse* (cheese). **Mittagessen** (lunch) is usually the main meal of the day, consisting of soup, broiled sausage or roasted meat, potatoes or dumplings, and a salad or *Gemüsebeilage* (vegetable side dish). **Abendessen** or **Abendbrot** (supper) is a re-enactment of breakfast, only beer replaces coffee and the selection of meat and cheese is wider. **Dessert** after meals is uncommon, but many older Germans indulge in a daily ritual of **Kaffee und Kuchen** (coffee and cakes), a snack analogous to English "tea-time," at 3 or 4pm.

Germany's bakeries produce an impressive range of quality **Brot** (bread). *Vollkornbrot* is whole-wheat (which has a completely different meaning in Germany) and *Roggenbrot* is rye bread. *Schwarzbrot* (black bread) is a dense, dark loaf that's slightly acidic. Go to a *Bäckerei* (bakery) and point to whatever looks good. Generally they sell you the whole loaf; for half, ask for *ein Halbes*. German bread does not contain preservatives and will go stale the day of its purchase.

Besides bread, the staples of the German diet are *Wurst* (sausage, in dozens of varieties; see p. 226), *Schweinefleisch* (pork), *Rindfleisch* (beef), *Kalbfleisch* (veal), *Lammfleisch* (lamb), *Huhn* (chicken), and *Kartoffeln* (potatoes). Sampling the various **local specialties** around Germany gives a taste of the diverse culinary tradition. In **Bavaria**, *Knödel* (potato and flour dumplings, sometimes filled with meat) are quite popular, as is *Weißwurst*, a sausage made with milk. Thüringen and northern Bavaria are famed for their succulent grilled *Bratwurst*, the classic, roasted sausage slathered in mustard and eaten with potatoes or bought from a street vendor and clasped in a roll. Southwestern Germany is known for its *Spätzle* (noodles), and *Maultaschen* (pasta pockets) are also popular in **Swabia.** German *Pfannkuchen* (pancakes) are quite heavy and come with a range of toppings. *Kaiserschmarren* is a chopped-up pancake with powdered sugar. **Hessians** do amazing things with potatoes, like smothering them in a delectable *grüne Soße* (green sauce). The North and Baltic seacoasts harvest an assortment of seafood delights, including *Krabben* (shrimp) and *Matjes* (herring).

When Turks began emigrating to West Germany in the early 1960s, the indigenous palate was revitalized by such now-ubiquitous delights as the *Döner Kebab*, thin slices of lamb mixed with cucumbers, onions, and red cabbage in a wedge of *Fladenbrot*, a round, flat, sesame-covered bread (see **What's a Döner?**, p. 112). Asking for a *Döner mit Soße* adds a deliciously piquant garlic sauce. Other well-known Turkish dishes include *Börek*, a flaky pastry filled with spinach, cheese, or meat; and *Lahmacun* (sometimes called *türkische Pizza*), a smaller, spicier version of Italy's staple fast food. Turkish restaurants and *Imbiße*, popular and cheap fast food stands offering various cuisines, also proffer delicious *Kefir* (flavored yogurt drinks) and *Baklava* for dessert.

Beer and wine (see below) are the meal-time **beverages.** *Saft* (juice), plain or mixed with mineral water, is an alternative. Germans do not guzzle glasses of water by the dozen as Americans do, although they will sip a (small) glass of carbonated mineral water. If you ask for *Wasser* in a restaurant, you get mineral water, which isn't free. For tap water, ask for *Leitungswasser* and expect funny looks.

With very few exceptions **restaurants** expect you to seat yourself. If there are no tables free, ask someone for permission to take a free seat (ask *Darf ich Platz nehmen?*, pronounced "DAHRF eesh PLAHTS nay-men"). In traditional restaurants, address waiters *Herr Ober*, and waitresses (but no one else) as *Fräulein* (pronounced "FROY-line"). In a less formal setting, just say *hallo*. At the table, Germans eat with the fork in the left hand and the knife in the right and keep their hands above or resting on the table. While eating, it is polite to keep the tines of your fork pointing down at all times. When you're finished, pay at the table. Ask the server *Zahlen, bitte* (TSAH-len, BIT-teh: "check, please"). Taxes *(Mehrwertsteuer)* and service are always included in the price, but it is customary to leave a little something extra, usually by rounding up the bill by a Mark or two.

Eating in restaurants at every meal will quickly drain your budget. One strategy is to stick to the daily fixed-price option, called the *Tagesmenü*. A cheaper option is to buy food in **grocery stores.** German university students eat in cafeterias called **Mensen.** Some *Mensen* (singular *Mensa*) require a student ID (or charge higher prices for non-students), while some are open only to local students, though travelers often evade this requirement by strolling in as if they belonged. In smaller towns, the best budget option is to stop by a *Bäckerei* (bakery) for bread and garnish it with sausage purchased from a butcher *(Fleischerei* or *Metzgerei)*.

BEER

Where does the German begin? Where does it end? May a German smoke? The majority says no... But a German may drink beer, indeed as a true son of Germania he should drink beer.
　—Heinrich Heine

Germans have brewed frothy and alcoholic malt beverages since the 8th century BC, and they've been consuming and exporting them in prodigious quantities ever since. The state of Bavaria alone contains about one-fifth of all the breweries in the world. The Germans drink more than 150 liters of beer per person every year, more than any other country. According to legend, the German king Gambrinus invented the modern beer recipe when he threw some hops into fermenting malt. During the Middle Ages, monastic orders refined the art of brewing, imbibing to stave off starvation during long fasts. It wasn't long before the monks' lucrative trade caught the eye of secular lords, who established the first *Hofbrauereien* (court breweries).

The variety of German beers boggles even the most sober mind. Most beer is **Vollbier,** containing about 4% alcohol. **Export** (5%) is also popular, and stout, tasty **Bockbier** (6.25%) is brewed in the spring. **Doppelbock** is an eye-popping concoction reserved for special occasions. Ordering *ein Helles* will get you a light-colored beer, while *Dunkles* can look like anything from Coca-Cola to molasses.

Although generalizations are difficult, the average German beer is maltier and more "bread-like" than Czech, Dutch, or American beers. (An affectionate German slang term for beer is *flüßiges Brot,* "liquid bread.") Among the exceptions is **Pils,** or Pilsner, which is most popular in the north. Its characteristic clarity and bitter taste come from the addition of extra hops (see **Ein Bitt, bitte,** p. 557). From the south, especially Bavaria, comes **Weißbier,** also known as **Weizenbier,** a smooth, refreshing brew. Despite the name, *Weißbier* is not white, but a rich brown. The term *Weizenbier* refers to a lighter wheat beer, while **Hefeweizen** is wheat beer with a layer of yeast in the bottom. **Flaschenbier** is bottled beer, while **Bier vom Faß** (or **Faßbier**) comes from the tap.

Sampling local brews numbers among the finest of Germany's pleasures. In Köln, one drinks smooth **Kölsch,** an extraordinarily refined, light-colored beer; a Düsseldorf specialty is **Altbier,** a darker top-fermented beer. Berliners are partial to **Berliner Weiße,** a lighter beer; ordering it *mit Schuß* adds a shot of raspberry or woodruff syrup. On hot summer days, lightweight drinkers and children prefer **Radler,** a mix containing half beer and half lemon-lime soda. **Diesel** is a mixture of *Bier* and cola that will get your engine started.

The variety of places to drink beer is almost as staggering as the variety of brews. The traditional **Biergarten** consists of outdoor tables under chestnut trees; sometimes food is served as well. The broad leaves of the trees originally kept beer barrels cool in the days before refrigeration, until—according to one legend—an enterprising brewer figured out that they could do the same thing for beer drinkers. The **Bierkeller** is a subterranean version of the *Biergarten,* where local breweries dispense their product. To order *ein Bier,* hold up your thumb, not your index finger. Raise your glass to a *Prost* (cheers) and drink (for more on beer halls in Munich, see **Beer, Beer, and more Beer,** p. 259). Another option for beer drinking is the **Gaststätte,** a simple, local restaurant. It's considered bad form to order only drinks at a *Gaststätte* during mealtimes, but at any other time, friends linger for hours over beers. Many *Gaststätten* have a *Stammtisch* (regulars' table), marked by a flag, where interlopers should not sit. The same group of friends may meet at the *Stammtisch* every week for decades to drink, play cards, and chill; keep in mind that your visa has an expiration date. **Kneipen** are bars where hard drinks are also served.

DAS REINHEITSGEBOT: GERMANY'S BEER PURITY LAW
One of the most despised characters in medieval Germany was the shoddy brewer who tried to cut costs by substituting lesser grains for the noble cereal at the heart of beer—barley. In 1516, Duke Wilhelm IV of Bavaria decreed that beer could contain only pure water, barley, and hops. As a result, German beer is world-famous, but it also contains no preservatives and will spoil relatively quickly. Wilhelm's Purity Law *(Reinheitsgebot)* has endured to this day, with minor alterations to permit the cultivation of Bavaria's trademark wheat-based beers. The law even applies to imports—none of the filler-laden products of the major American breweries can be imported into Germany. But with the arrival of the European Union, the law was challenged by other European countries, who saw it as an unfair trade barrier. Now the "impure" foreign beers are being admitted to the market, but to the joy of drinkers worldwide, German breweries have reaffirmed their commitment to the *Reinheitsgebot.*

WINE AND SPIRITS

Although overshadowed by Germany's more famous export beverage, German wines win over connoisseurs and casual drinkers alike. Virtually all German wines are white, though they vary widely in character. Generally, German wines are sweeter and taste fresher than French, Mediterranean, or Californian wines. Because Germany is the northernmost of the wine-producing countries, the quality of a vineyard's produce can vary considerably with the climate.

The cheapest wines are classified as *Tafelwein* (table wine), while the good stuff (which is still pretty affordable) is *Qualitätswein* (quality wine). The label *Qualitätswein bestimmter Anbaugebiete*, or *Q. b. A.*, designates quality wine from a specific cultivation region. *Qualitätswein mit Prädikat* (quality wine with distinction) denotes an even purer wine derived from a particular variety of grape. The *Prädikat* wines are further subdivided according to the ripeness of the grapes when harvested; from driest to sweetest, they are *Kabinett*, *Spätlese*, *Auslese*, *Beerenauslese*, *Trockenbeerenauslese*, and *Eiswein*. The grapes that produce the *Trockenbeerenauslese* are left on the vine well into winter until they have shriveled into raisins and begun to rot—no kidding.

The major concentrations of viticulture lie along the Rhein and Mosel valleys, along the Main River in Franconia, and in Baden. Of the dozens of varieties, the most famous are *Riesling*, *Müller-Thurgau*, *Sylvaner*, and *Traminer* (source of *Gewürztraminer*). In wine-producing towns, thirsty travelers can stop by a *Weinstube* to sample the local produce. In Hessen, the beverage of choice is *Äppelwoi* or *Äpfelwein* (apple wine), a hard cider similar in potency to beer. After a meal, many Germans aid their digestion by throwing back a shot of *Schnapps*, distilled from fruits. *Kirschwasser*, a cherry liqueur from the Schwarzwald, is the best known and probably the easiest to stomach, but adventurous sorts can experiment with the sublimely tasty *Black Haus*, a delectable, 100 proof, blackberry *Schnapps* also from the Schwarzwald, which will get you *Haused* in a most delightful fashion. Each year, unsuspecting tourists are seduced into buying little green bottles of *Jägermeister*, one of Germany's numerous (and barely palatable) herb liqueurs.

SOCIAL LIFE

An afternoon of relaxation in a park or cafe will teach you more about Germany than one spent in a museum. Many Germans know Americans and Britons only through contact with soldiers, who haven't always made the best impression. Anti-Americanism is a powerful sentiment among young Germans concerned by the American military's role as a global police force. If you are sensitive to this concern, you will find that most Germans have a passionate interest in the US. Despite anti-American sentiments, Germans are obsessed with Americana, and English words and American popular culture pervade German media and fashion.

Take the time to actually meet people. Although Germans may seem reserved or even unfriendly, they are not as stand-offish as they first appear. Europeans in general are sincerely interested in other lands and cultures, but have a very strong sense of their own cultural background; if you insult or belittle it, you'll only seem arrogant (and rude). Above all, don't automatically equate the American, Canadian, British, Australian, etc. way with "better."

Germans are incredibly frank and will not hesitate to register their disapproval. To the uninitiated this may come across as confrontational, but it stems more from an intense honesty than anything else. Many Germans consider effusive chumminess insincere and superficial, and Americans are often perceived as disingenuous for being overly friendly.The multiple rules surrounding German etiquette make Ann Landers look like a gas station attendant. However, it is important to note that many of these precepts do not apply to people under 30 and in larger urban areas. In general, Germans are much more formal than Americans and Australians, and incredibly big on punctuality. An invitation to a German home is a major courtesy;

you should bring something for the hostess. Among the older generations, be careful not to use the informal *du* (you) or a first name without being invited to do so. *Du* is appropriate when addressing fellow students and friends at a youth hostel, or when addressing children. In all other circumstances, use the formal *Sie* for "you," as in the question *Sprechen Sie Englisch?*

Only waitresses in traditional restaurants are addressed as *Fräulein*; address all other women as *Frau* (followed by a name). Always ask if someone speaks English before launching into a question. Better yet, try to learn a little German and don't be afraid to test your talents. The language is related to English, and you can learn the pronunciation system and some useful phrases in about 15 minutes (see Appendix, p. 588). In any case, learn at least two phrases: **bitte** (please and you're welcome; BIT-teh) and **danke** (thank you; DAHNK-eh).

Everything you've heard about the Germans' compulsive abidance of the law is true. The first time you see a German standing at an intersection in the pouring rain, with no cars in sight, waiting for the "walk" signal, you'll know what we mean. Jaywalking is only one of the petty offenses that will mark you as a foreigner (and subject you to fines); littering is another. Many tourists also do not realize that the bike lanes marked in red between the sidewalk and the road are not for pedestrian use. The younger generation takes matters much less seriously. The drinking age is 16 for beer and wine and 18 for hard liquor, although neither is strictly enforced; driving under the influence, however, is a severe offense.

HOLIDAYS

DATE	HOLIDAY	ENGLISH
January 6	Heilige Drei Könige	Epiphany
February 28	Aschermittwoch	Ash Wednesday
April 13	Karfreitag	Good Friday
April 15	Ostersonntag	Easter Sunday
April 16	Ostermontag	Easter Monday
May 1	Tag der Arbeit	Labor Day
May 24	Christi Himmelfahrt	Ascension Day
June 3	Pfingstsonntag	Whit Sunday (Pentecost)
June 4	Pfingstmontag	Whit Monday
June 14	Fronleichnam	Corpus Christi
August 15	Maria Himmelfahrt	Assumption Day
October 3	Tag der deutschen Einheit	Day of German Unity
November 1	Reformationtag	Reformation Day
November 1	Allerheiligen	All Saint's Day
December 25-26	Weihnachtstag	Christmas

ESSENTIALS

FACTS FOR THE TRAVELER

DOCUMENTS AND FORMALITIES

GERMAN CONSULAR SERVICES ABROAD

The German embassy or consulate in your home country can supply legal information concerning your trip, arrange for visas, and direct you to a wealth of other information about tourism, education, and employment in Germany.

Australia: Embassy: 119 Empire Circuit, Yarralumla, Canberra, ACT 2600 (☎(02) 6270 19 11; fax 62 70 19 51; email embgerma@dynamite.com.); Consulates: **Melbourne,** 480 Punt Rd., South Yarra, VIC, 3141 (☎(03) 98 64 68 88; fax 98 20 24 14); **Sydney,** 13 Trelawney St., Woollahra, NSW. 2025 (☎(02) 93 28 77 33; fax 93 27 96 49; email consugerma.sydney@bigpond.com).

Canada: Embassy: 1 Waverly St., **Ottawa,** ON K2P OT8 (☎(613) 232 1101; fax 594-9330; email 100566.2620@compuserve.com). Consulate: **Montréal,** 1250 René-Lévesque Ouest, Suite 4315, H5B 4W8 (☎(514) 931 2277; fax 931 7239).

Ireland: Embassy: 31 Trimleston Ave., Booterstown, Blackrock, Co. **Dublin** (☎(012) 69 30 11; fax 269 39 46).

New Zealand: Embassy: 90-92 Hobson St., Thorndon, **Wellington** (☎(04) 473 60 63; fax 473 60 69).

South Africa: Embassy: 180 Blackwood St., Arcadia, **Pretoria,** 0083 (☎(012) 427 89 00; fax 343 94 01). Consulate, **Cape Town,** 825 St. Martini Gardens, Queen Victoria St., 8001 (☎021 424 24 10; fax 24 94 03).

UK: Embassy: 23 Belgrave Sq., **London** SW1X 8PZ (☎(020) 78 24 13 00; fax 78 24 14 35). Consulate: **Edinburgh,** 16 Eglinton Crescent, EH12 5DG, Scotland (☎(0131) 337 23 23; fax 346 15 78).

US: Embassy: 4645 Reservoir Rd., **Washington, D.C.** 20007-1998 (☎(202) 298 4000; fax 298 4249; www.germany-info.org). Consulates: **New York,** 871 U.N. Plaza, New York, NY 10017 (☎(212) 610 9700; fax 610 9702); **Los Angeles,** 6222 Wilshire Blvd., Ste. 500, LA, California 90048 (☎(323) 930 2703; fax 930 2805); other consulates in **Atlanta, Boston, Chicago, Houston, Miami,** and **San Francisco**.

FOREIGN CONSULAR SERVICES IN GERMANY

For the latest information, call the **Auswärtiges Amt** (foreign office) in Berlin at (030) 20 18 60.

Australia: Embassy: **Berlin,** Friedrichstr. 200, 10117 (☎(030) 880 08 80; info@australian-embassy.de). Consulate: **Frankfurt:** Grunebrückweg 55-62, 60322 (☎(49 69) 90 55 81 00; fax 90 55 81 09).

> **ENTRANCE REQUIREMENTS**
> **Passport** (p. 38). Required for citizens of Australia, Canada, Ireland, New Zealand, South Africa, the UK, and the US
> **Visa** (p. 39). Required only for citizens of South Africa.
> **Work Permit** (p. 39). Required for all foreigners planning to work in Germany.
> **Driving Permit** (p. 73). Required for non-EU citizens planning to drive.

Canada: Embassy: **Berlin,** Friedrichstr. 95, 23rd fl., 10117 Berlin (☎(49 30) 20 31 20; fax 20 31 25 90; email brlin@dfait-maeci.gc.ca). Consulates: **Düsseldorf,** Benrataerstr. 8, 40213 (☎(49 211) 172 170; fax 359 165). **Hamburg,** ABC-Str. 45, 20354 (☎(49 40) 35 55 62 95; fax 35 55 62 94). **Munich,** Tal 29, 80331 (☎(49 89) 219 95 700; fax 21 99 57 57; email munic@dfait-maeci.gc.ca).

Ireland: Embassy: **Berlin,** Ernst-Reuter-Pl. 10, 10587 (☎(030) 34 80 08 22; fax 34 80 08 63). Consulates: **Hamburg,** Feldbrunnerstr. 43, 20148 (☎(040) 44 18 62 13). **Munich,** Mauerkircherstr. 1a, 81679 (☎(089) 98 57 23).

New Zealand: Embassy: **Berlin,** Friedrichstr. 60, 10117. **Consulate: Hamburg,** Zürich-Dom-Str. 19, 20095 (☎(040) 442 55 50).

South Africa: Embassy: **Berlin,** Friedrichstr. 60, 10117 (☎(030) 22 07 30; email konsular@suedafrika.org). Consulate: **Munich,** Sendlinger-Tor-Pl. 5, 80336 (☎(089) 231 16 30; fax 231163-63; email SAConsulate_Munich@compuserve.com).

UK: Embassy: **Berlin,** Unter den Linden 32-34, 10117 (☎(030) 20 18 40; fax. 20 18 41 58). Consulates, **Düsseldorf,** Yorckstr. 19, 40476 (☎(0211) 944 80; fax 48 63 59). **Frankfurt,** Bockenheimer Landstr. 42, 60323 (☎(069) 170 00 20; fax 72 95 53). **Hamburg,** Harvestehuder Weg 8a, 20148 (☎(040) 448 03 20; fax 410 72 59). **Munich,** Bükleinstr. 10, 80538 (☎(089) 21 10 90; fax 21 10 91 55). **Stuttgart,** Breite Str. 2, 70173 (☎(0711) 16 26 90; fax 162 69 30). **Leipzig,** Gohliser Str. 7, 04105 (☎(0341) 56 49 67 2; fax 56 49 67 3).

US: Embassy: **Berlin,** Neustädtische Kirchstr. 4-5, 10117 (☎(030) 832 92 33; fax 83 05 12 15). Consulates: **Düsseldorf,** Willi-Becker-Alee 10, 40227 (☎(0211) 788 89 27). **Frankfurt,** Siesmayerstr. 21, 60323 (☎(069) 753 50). **Hamburg,** Alsterufer 27/28, 20354 (☎(040) 41 17 10; fax 41 76 65). **Leipzig,** Wilhelm-Seyfferth-Str. 4, 04107 (☎(0341) 21 38 40). **Munich,** Königinstr. 5, 80539 (☎(089) 288 80).

PASSPORTS

REQUIREMENTS. Citizens of Australia, Canada, Ireland, New Zealand, South Africa, the UK, and the US need valid passports to enter Germany and to re-enter their own country. Returning home with an expired passport is illegal, and may result in a fine.

PHOTOCOPIES. Be sure to photocopy the page of your passport with your photo, passport number, and other identifying information, as well as any visas, travel insurance policies, plane tickets, or traveler's check serial numbers. Carry one set of copies in a safe place, separate from the originals, and leave another set at home. Consulates also recommend that you carry an expired passport or an official copy of your birth certificate in a part of your baggage separate from other documents.

LOST PASSPORTS. If you lose your passport, immediately notify the local police and the nearest embassy or consulate of your home government. To expedite its replacement, you will need to know all information previously recorded and show ID and proof of citizenship. In some cases, a replacement may take weeks to process, and it may be valid only for a limited time. In an emergency, ask for immediate temporary traveling papers that will permit you to re-enter your home country. Your passport is a public document belonging to your nation's government. You may have to surrender it to a foreign government official, but if you don't get it back in a reasonable amount of time, inform the nearest mission of your home country.

NEW PASSPORTS. File any new passport or renewal applications well in advance of your departure date. Most passport offices offer emergency passport services for an additional fee. Citizens living abroad who need a passport or renewal should contact the nearest consular service of their home country.

Australia: Info ☎ 13 12 32; email passports.australia@dfat.gov.au; www.dfat.gov.au/passports. Apply for a passport at a post office, passport office (in Adelaide, Brisbane, Canberra, Darwin, Hobart, Melbourne, Newcastle, Perth, or Sydney), or overseas diplomatic mission. Passports AUS$128 (32-page) or AUS$192 (64-page); valid for 10 years. Children AUS$64 (32-page) or AUS$96 (64-page); valid for 5 years.

Canada: Canadian Passport Office, Department of Foreign Affairs and International Trade, Ottawa, ON K1A OG3 (☎(613) 994 3500 or (800) 567 6868; www.dfait-maeci.gc.ca/passport). Applications available at passport offices, Canadian missions, and post offices. Passports CDN$60; valid for 5 years (non-renewable).

Ireland: Pick up an application at a *Garda* station or post office, or request one from a passport office. Then apply by mail to the Department of Foreign Affairs, Passport Office, Molesworth St., Dublin 2 (☎(01) 671 1633; fax 671 1092; www.irlgov.ie/iveagh), or the Passport Office, Irish Life Building, 1A South Mall, Cork (☎(021) 27 25 25). Passports IR£45; valid for 10 years. Under 18 or over 65 IR£10; valid for 3 years.

New Zealand: Send applications to the Passport Office, Department of International Affairs, P.O. Box 10526, Wellington, New Zealand (☎(0800) 22 50 50 or (4) 474 8100; fax (4) 474 8010; www.passports.govt.nz; email passports@dia.govt.nz). Standard processing time is 10 working days. Passports NZ$80; valid for 10 years. Children NZ$40; valid for 5 years. 3 day "urgent service" NZ$160; children NZ$120.

South Africa: Department of Home Affairs. Passports are issued only in Pretoria, but all applications must still be submitted or forwarded to the nearest South African consulate. Processing time is 3 months or more. Passports around SAR80; valid for 10 years. Under 16 around SAR60; valid for 5 years. For more information, check out http://usaembassy.southafrica.net/VisaForms/Passport/Passport2000.html.

United Kingdom: Info ☎(0870) 521 0410; www.open.gov.uk/ukpass/ukpass.htm. Get an application from a passport office, main post office, travel agent, or online (for UK residents only) at www.ukpa.gov.uk/forms/f_app_pack.htm. Then apply by mail to or in person at a passport office. Passports UK£28; valid for 10 years. Under 15 UK£14.80; valid for 5 years. The process takes about 4 weeks; faster service (by personal visit to the offices listed above) costs an additional £12.

United States: Info ☎(202) 647-0518; www.travel.state.gov/passport_services.html. Apply at any federal or state courthouse, authorized post office, or US Passport Agency (in most major cities); see the "US Government, State Department" section of the telephone book or a post office for addresses. Processing takes 3-4 weeks. New passports US$60; valid for 10 years. Under 15 US$40; valid for 5 years. Passports may be renewed by mail or in person for US$40. Add US$35 for 3-day expedited service.

> **ONE EUROPE** The idea of European unity has come a long way since 1958, when the European Economic Community (EEC) was created in order to promote solidarity and cooperation between its six founding states. Since then, the EEC has become the European Union (EU), with political, legal, and economic institutions spanning 15 member states: Austria, Belgium, Denmark, Finland, France, Germany, Greece, Ireland, Italy, Luxembourg, the Netherlands, Portugal, Spain, Sweden, and the UK.
>
> What does this have to do with the average non-EU tourist? Well, 1999 established **freedom of movement** across 14 European countries—the entire EU minus Denmark, Ireland, and the UK, but plus Iceland and Norway. This means that border controls between participating countries have been abolished, and visa policies harmonized. While you're still required to carry a passport (or government-issued ID card for EU citizens) when crossing an internal border, once you've been admitted into one country, you're free to travel to all participating states. Britain and Ireland have also formed a **common travel area,** abolishing passport controls between the UK and the Republic of Ireland, meaning that the only times you'll see a border guard within the EU are traveling between the British Isles and the Continent—and of course, in and out of Denmark.
>
> For more important consequences of the EU for travelers, see **The Euro** (see p. 43) and **European Customs** and **EU customs regulations** (see p. 41).

VISAS AND WORK PERMITS

VISAS. Citizens of **Australia, Canada, Ireland, New Zealand,** the **UK,** and the **US** need only a passport to stay in Germany for up to 90 days within six months. Those seeking an extended stay, employment, or student status should obtain a visa and a residence permit. Citizens of **South Africa** need a visa to enter Germany; contact the nearest German Consulate General (see p. 37). Be sure to double-check on entrance requirements at the nearest embassy or consulate for up-to-date info before departure. US citizens can also consult www.pueblo.gsa.gov/cic_text/travel/foreign/foreignentryreqs.html.

STUDY AND WORK PERMITS. Admission as a visitor does not include the right to work, which requires a work permit, and entering Germany to study requires a special visa. Student visas require proof of financial independence and admission to a German academic institution. These procedures can take up to three months. For more information, see **Alternatives to Tourism,** p. 80.

IDENTIFICATION

When you travel, always carry two or more forms of identification on your person, including at least one photo ID; a passport combined with a driver's license or birth certificate usually serves as adequate proof of identity and citizenship. Many establishments, especially banks, may require several IDs in order to cash traveler's checks. Never carry all your forms of ID together; split them up in case of theft or loss. It is useful to bring extra passport-size photos to affix to the various IDs or passes you may acquire along the way.

STUDENT, YOUTH, AND TEACHER IDENTIFICATION. The **International Student Identity Card (ISIC),** the most widely accepted form of student ID, provides discounts on sights, accommodations, food, and transport.The ISIC is preferable to an institution-specific card (such as a university ID) because it is more likely to be recognized (and honored) abroad. All cardholders have access to a 24-hour emergency helpline for medical, legal, and financial emergencies (in North America call (877) 370- SIC, elsewhere call US collect +1 (715) 345 0505), and US cardholders are also eligible for insurance benefits (see **Insurance,** p. 53). Many student travel agencies issue ISICs, including STA Travel in Australia and New Zealand; Travel CUTS in Canada; usit in the Republic of Ireland and Northern Ireland; SASTS in South Africa; Campus Travel and STA Travel in the UK; Council Travel (www.counciltravel.com/idcards/default.asp) and STA Travel in the US (see p. 65). The card is valid from September of one year to December of the following year and costs AUS$15, CDN$15, UK£5, or US$22. Applicants must be degree-seeking students of a secondary or post-secondary school and must be of at least 12 years of age. The **International Teacher Identity Card (ITIC)** offers the same insurance coverage as well as similar but limited discounts. The fee is AUS$13, UK£5, or US$22. For more info, contact the **International Student Travel Confederation (ISTC),** Herengracht 479, 1017 BS Amsterdam, Netherlands (☎+31 (20) 421 28 00; fax 421 28 10; email istcinfo@istc.org; www.istc.org). The International Student Travel Confederation issues a discount card to travelers who are 26 years old or under, but are not students. This one-year **International Youth Travel Card (IYTC;** formerly the **GO 25** Card) offers many of the same benefits as the ISIC. Most organizations that sell the ISIC also sell the IYTC (US$22).

CUSTOMS

ENTERING GERMANY
Don't mention the war!
—Basil Fawlty (John Cleese)

Upon entering Germany, you must declare certain items from abroad and pay a duty on the value of those articles that exceed the allowance established by Germany's customs service. Unless you plan to import a BMW or a barnyard beast, you will probably pass right through the customs barrier with minimal to-do. Germany prohibits or restricts the importation of firearms, explosives, ammunition, fireworks, controlled substances, many plants and animals, lottery tickets, and obscene literature or films. To prevent problems with transporting **prescription drugs,** make sure that the bottles are clearly marked, and carry a copy of your prescription to show customs officials.

Travelers may "import" gifts and commodities for personal use into Germany. For EU citizens, "personal use" is interpreted relatively freely. For non-EU citizens, however, regulations are as follows: travelers may import 200 cigarettes, 100 cigarillos, 50 cigars, or 250g of smoking tobacco; 1L of spirits stronger than 44 proof, 2L of weaker spirits, or 2 liters of wines or liqueur; 50g of perfume and 0.25L toilet water; 500g of coffee and 200g of extracts. The total value of personal use goods cannot exceed DM350. You must be 17 or over to import tobacco and alcohol products. There are no regulations on the import or export of currency.

> **EUROPEAN CUSTOMS** As well as freedom of movement of people within the EU (see p. 39), travelers can also take advantage of the freedom of movement of goods. This means that there are no customs controls at internal EU borders (i.e., you can take the blue customs channel at the airport), and travelers are free to transport whatever legal substances they like as long as it is for their own personal (non-commercial) use—up to 800 cigarettes, 10L of spirits, 90L of wine (60L of sparkling wine), and 110L of beer. You should also be aware that **duty-free** was abolished on June 30, 1999 for travel between EU member states; however, travelers between the EU and the rest of the world still get a duty-free allowance when passing through customs.

GOING HOME

Upon returning home, you must declare all articles acquired abroad and pay a duty on the value of articles that exceed the allowance established by your country's customs service. Goods and gifts purchased at duty-free shops abroad are not exempt from duty or sales tax at your point of return; you must declare these items as well. "Duty-free" merely means that you need not pay a tax in the country of purchase. For more specific information on customs requirements, contact the following information centers:

Australia: Australian Customs National Information Line (in Australia call (01) 30 03 63, from elsewhere call +61 (2) 6275 6666; www.customs.gov.au).

Canada: Canadian Customs, 2265 St. Laurent Blvd., Ottawa, ON K1G 4K3 (☎(800) 461-9999 (24hr.) or (613) 993-0534; www.revcan.ca).

Ireland: Customs Information Office, Irish Life Centre, Lower Abbey St., Dublin 1 (☎(01) 878 8811; fax 878 0836; taxes@revenue.iol.ie; www.revenue.ie/customs.htm).

New Zealand: New Zealand Customhouse, 17-21 Whitmore St., Box 2218, Wellington (☎(04) 473 6099; fax 473 7370; www.customs.govt.nz).

South Africa: Commissioner for Customs and Excise, Privat Bag X47, Pretoria 0001 (☎(012) 314 9911; fax 328 6478; www.gov.za).

United Kingdom: Her Majesty's Customs and Excise, Passenger Enquiry Team, Wayfarer House, Great South West Road, Feltham, Middlesex TW14 8NP (☎(020) 8910 3744; fax 8910 3933; www.hmce.gov.uk).

United States: US Customs Service, 1330 Pennsylvania Ave. NW, Washington, D.C. 20229 (☎(202) 354-1000; fax 354-1010; www.customs.gov).

MONEY

If you stay in hostels and prepare your own food, expect to spend anywhere from $25-50 per person per day when traveling in Germany. Hotels start at about $25 per night; a basic sit-down meal costs at least $6. Transportation and alcohol will increase these

ESSENTIALS

figures. If you plan to travel for more than a couple of days, you will need to keep handy a larger amount of cash than usual. Carrying money around, even in a money belt, is risky but necessary. Personal checks from home probably won't be accepted in Germany no matter how many forms of identification you have, and even traveler's checks may not be acceptable in some locations (see **Traveler's Checks,** p. 42). Members can cash personal checks at AmEx offices throughout Germany.

CURRENCY AND EXCHANGE

The **deutsche Mark** or **Deutschmark** (abbreviated DM) is the unit of currency in Germany. It is one of the most stable and respected currencies in the world; indeed, in most markets in Eastern Europe, "hard currency" means US dollars and Deutschmarks exclusively. One DM equals 100 Pfennig (Pf). Coins come in 1, 2, 5, 10, and 50Pf, and DM1, 2, and 5 amounts. Bills come in DM5, 10, 20, 50, 100, 200, 500, and 1000 denominations, though DM5 bills are now rare. Although some (especially Americans) may think of minted metal disks as inconsequential pieces of aluminum, remember that a DM5 coin can easily buy you a meal. To make sure you're not getting duped, only accept bills with an embedded silver strip.

The currency chart below is based on August 2000 exchange rates between the Deutschmark (DM) and US dollars (US$), Canadian dollars (CDN$), British pounds (UK£), Irish pounds (IR£), Australian dollars (AUS$), New Zealand dollars (NZ$), South African Rand (SAR), and European Union euros (EUR€). Check a large newspaper or the web (e.g. finance.yahoo.com or www.bloomberg.com) for the latest exchange rates.

US$1=DM2.18	DM1=US$0.46
CDN$1=DM1.47	DM1=CDN$0.68
UK£1=DM3.23	DM1=UK£0.31
IR£1=DM2.48	DM1=IR£0.40
AUS$1=DM1.27	DM1=AUS$0.79
NZ$1=DM0.97	DM1=NZ$1.04
SAR1=DM0.31	DM1=SAR3.20
EUR€1=DM1.96	DM1=EUR€0.51

As a general rule, it's cheaper to exchange money in Germany than at home. However, converting some money before you go will allow you to zip through the airport while others languish in exchange lines. It's a good idea to carry enough Deutschmarks to last for the first 24 to 72 hours of a trip to avoid getting stuck with no money after banking hours or on a holiday. Travelers from the US can get foreign currency from the comfort of home: **International Currency Express** (☎(888) 278 6628) delivers foreign currency or traveler's checks overnight (US$15) or 2nd-day (US$12) at competitive exchange rates.

Watch out for commission rates and check newspapers for the standard rate of exchange. Banks generally have the best rates. A good rule of thumb is only to go to banks or tourist offices and exchange kiosks that have at most a 5% margin between their buy and sell prices. Since you lose money with each transaction, convert in large sums. Also, using an ATM card or a credit card (see p. 45) will often get you the best possible rates. Store your money in a variety of forms; ideally, you will at any given time be carrying some cash, some traveler's checks, and an ATM and/or credit card.

TRAVELER'S CHECKS

All German banks cash traveler's checks, though the prevalence of ATMs (see below) may make that a more convenient option. Large department stores and businesses in Germany will accept the checks for purchasing products, but for smaller stores and rural areas, you will need to cash the checks into Deutschmarks first. Traveler's checks (**American Express** and **Visa** are the most recognized) are one

THE EURO Since 1999, the official currency of 11 members of the European Union—Austria, Belgium, Finland, France, Germany, Ireland, Italy, Luxembourg, the Netherlands, Portugal, and Spain—has been the **euro**. (As of January 2001, Greece will be admitted as well.) But you shouldn't throw out your Deutschmarks just yet; actual euro banknotes and coins won't be available until January 1, 2002. On June 1, 2002, the Deutschmark will be entirely withdrawn from circulation and the euro will become the only legal currency in Germany. *Let's Go* lists all prices in Deutschmarks, as these will still be most relevant in 2001. However, all German businesses must by law quote prices in both currencies.

While you might not be able to pay for a coffee and get your change in euros yet, the currency has some important—and positive—consequences for travelers hitting more than one euro-zone country. For one thing, money-changers across the euro-zone are obliged to exchange money at the official, fixed rate (see below), and at no commission (though they may still charge a small service fee). So now you can change your guilders into escudos and your escudos into lire without losing fistfuls of money on every transaction. Second, euro-denominated travelers cheques allow you to pay for goods and services across the euro-zone, again at the official rate and commission-free.

The exchange rate between euro-zone currencies was permanently fixed on January 1, 1999 at 1 EUR = 40.34 BEF (Belgian francs) = 1.96 DM (German marks) = 166.39 ESP (Spanish pesetas) = 6.56 FRF (French francs) = 0.79 IEP (Irish pounds) = 1936.27 ITL (Italian liras) = 40.34 LUF (Luxembourg francs) = 2.20 NLG (Dutch guilders) = 13.76 ATS (Austrian schillings) = 200.48 PTE (Portuguese escudos) = 5.95 FIM (Finnish markka). For more info, see www.europa.eu.int.

of the safest and least troublesome means of carrying funds. Several agencies and banks sell them for a small commission. Each agency provides refunds if your checks are lost or stolen, and many provide additional services, such as toll-free refund hotlines abroad for help to those whose checks have been stolen or lost, emergency message services, and stolen credit card assistance.

While traveling, keep check receipts and a record of which checks you've cashed separate from the checks themselves. Also leave a list of check numbers with someone at home. Never countersign checks until you're ready to cash them, and always bring your passport with you to cash them. If your checks are lost or stolen, immediately contact a refund center to be reimbursed; they may require a police report verifying the loss or theft. Ask about toll-free refund hotlines and the location of refund centers when purchasing checks, and always carry emergency cash.

American Express: Call (800) 251 902 in Australia; in New Zealand (0800) 441 068; in the UK (0800) 521 313; in the US and Canada (800) 221-7282. Elsewhere call US collect +1 (801) 964-6665; www.aexp.com. Traveler's checks are available in Deutschmarks at 1-4% commission at AmEx offices and banks, commission-free at AAA offices (see p. 42). *Cheques for Two* can be signed by either of 2 people traveling together. The booklet *Traveler's Companion* lists travel office addresses and stolen check hotlines abroad.

Citicorp: In the US and Canada call (800) 645-6556; in Europe, the Middle East, or Africa call the UK +44 (020) 7508 7007; elsewhere call US collect +1 (813) 623-1709. Traveler's checks available in 7 currencies at 1-2% commission. Call 24hr.

Thomas Cook MasterCard: In the US and Canada call (800) 223-7373; in the UK call (0800) 62 21 01; elsewhere call UK collect +44 (1733) 31 89 50. Checks available in 13 currencies at 2% commission. Thomas Cook offices cash checks commission-free.

Visa: In the US call (800) 227-6811; in the UK call (0800) 89 50 78; elsewhere call UK collect +44 (1733) 31 89 49. Call for the location of their nearest office.

ESSENTIALS

ESSENTIALS

CREDIT CARDS

Credit cards often accepted in Germany, although fewer restaurants take them than in the English-speaking world. Major credit cards—**MasterCard** and **Visa**—can be used to extract cash advances in Deutschmarks from associated banks and teller machines throughout Germany. **Eurocard,** which is affiliated with Master-Card, is preferred in Germany, and is more widely accepted than Visa. Credit card companies get the wholesale exchange rate, which is generally 5% better than the retail rate used by banks and other currency exchange establishments. **American Express** cards also work in some ATMs, as well as at AmEx offices and major airports. However, transaction fees for all credit card advances (up to US$10 per advance, plus 2-3% extra on foreign transactions after conversion) tend to make credit cards a more costly way of withdrawing cash than ATMs or traveler's checks. In an emergency, however, the transaction fee may prove worth the cost. Credit cards offer an array of other services as well, from insurance to emergency assistance. Check with your company to find out what is covered.

CREDIT CARD COMPANIES. Visa (US ☎ (800) 336 8472) and **MasterCard** (US ☎ (800) 307 7309) are issued in cooperation with banks and other organizations. **American Express** (US ☎ (800) 843 2273) has an annual fee of up to US$55. AmEx cardholders may cash personal checks at AmEx offices abroad, access an emergency medical and legal assistance hotline (24hr.; in North America call (800) 554-2639, elsewhere call US collect +1 (202) 554-2639), and enjoy American Express Travel Service benefits (including plane, hotel, and car rental reservation changes; baggage loss and flight insurance; mailgram and international cable services; and held mail). The **Discover Card** (in US call (800) 347-2683, elsewhere call US +1 (801) 902-3100) offers small cashback bonuses on most purchases, but it may not be readily accepted in Germany.

CASH (ATM) CARDS

24-hour ATMs (Automated Teller Machines) are widespread in Germany. Practically all German cities and towns provide cash machine services, and withdrawing funds directly in German currency (your bank statements will read in your home currency) is convenient. Depending on the system that your home bank uses, you can probably access your own personal bank account whenever you need money. ATMs get the same wholesale exchange rate as credit cards. Despite these perks, do some research before relying too heavily on automation. There is often a limit on the amount of money you can withdraw per day (usually about US$500, depending on the type of card and account), and computer networks sometimes fail. Inquire as to the amount your bank will charge for each transaction.

PLEASE, SIR, MAY I HAVE SOME MORE? To use a cash or credit card to withdraw money from a cash machine (ATM) in Europe, you must have a **four-digit Personal Identification Number (PIN).** If your PIN is longer than four digits, ask your bank whether can just use the first four, or whether you'll need a new one. **Credit cards** in North America don't usually come with PINs, so if you intend to hit up ATMs in Europe with a credit card to get cash advances, call your credit card company before leaving to request one.

People with alphabetic, rather than numerical, PINs may also be thrown off by the lack of letters on European cash machines. The following handy chart gives the corresponding numbers to use: 1=QZ; 2=ABC; 3=DEF; 4=GHI; 5=JKL; 6=MNO; 7=PRS; 8=TUV; and 9= WXY. Note that if you mistakenly punch the wrong code into the machine three times, it will swallow your card for good.

The two major international money networks are **Cirrus** (US ☎ 800 4 CIRRUS (424 7787)) and **PLUS** (US ☎ (800) 843 7587). To locate ATMs in Germany, use www.visa.com/pd/atm or www.mastercard.com/atm; both web pages will indicate which money network is used at a given machine.

Visa TravelMoney (in Germany call ☎ (0800) 810 99 10) is a system allowing you to access money from any Visa ATM. You deposit an amount before you travel (plus a small administrative fee) and withdraw up to that sum. The cards give you the safety of not having to carry too much cash, the same favorable exchange rate for withdrawals as a regular Visa, and are especially useful if you plan to be traveling through many countries. Check with your local bank to see if it issues Travel-Money cards. **Visa Road Cash** (☎ (877) 762 3227; www.roadcash.com) issues cards in the US with a minimum US$300 deposit.

GETTING MONEY FROM HOME

AMERICAN EXPRESS. Cardholders can withdraw cash from their checking accounts at any of AmEx's major offices and many representative offices (up to US$1000 every 21 days; no service charge, no interest). AmEx "Express Cash" withdrawals from any AmEx ATM in Germany are automatically debited from the cardholder's checking account or line of credit. Green card holders may withdraw up to US$1000 in any seven-day period (2% transaction fee; minimum US$2.50, maximum US$20). To enroll in Express Cash, cardmembers may call (800) 227-4669 in the US; elsewhere call the US collect +1 (336) 668-5041.

WESTERN UNION. Travelers from the US, Canada, and the UK can wire money abroad through Western Union's international money transfer services. In the US, call (800) 325 6000; in Canada, ☎ (800) 235-0000; in the UK, ☎ (0800) 833 833; in Germany, (0180) 522 5822. The rates for sending cash are generally US$10-11 cheaper than with a credit card, and the money is usually available at the place you're sending it to within an hour. To locate the nearest Western Union location, consult www.westernunion.com.

FEDERAL EXPRESS. Some people choose to send money abroad in cash via FedEx to avoid transmission fees and taxes. In the US and Canada, call ☎ (800) 463-3339; in the UK, ☎ (0800) 123 800; in Ireland, ☎ (800) 535 800; in Australia, ☎ 13 26 10; in New Zealand, ☎ (0800) 733 339; and in South Africa, ☎ (021) 551 7610. While FedEx is reliable, note that this method is illegal and somewhat risky.

US STATE DEPARTMENT (US CITIZENS ONLY). In dire emergencies only, the US State Department will forward money within hours to the nearest consular office, which will then disburse it according to instructions for a US$15 fee. Contact the Overseas Citizens Service, American Citizens Services, Consular Affairs, Room 4811, US Department of State, Washington, D.C. 20520 (☎ (202) 647-5225; nights, Sundays, and holidays 647-4000; http://travel.state.gov).

TIPPING AND BARGAINING

Germans generally round up DM1-2 when tipping. However, tipping is not practiced as liberally as it is elsewhere—most Germans only tip in restaurants and bars, or when they are the beneficiary of a service, such as a taxi ride. Note that tips in Germany are not left lying on the table, but handed directly to the server when you pay. If you don't want any change, say *Das stimmt so* (DAHS SHTIMT ZO). Germans rarely bargain except at flea markets.

TAXES

Most goods and services bought in Germany will automatically include a **Value Added Tax (VAT)** of 15%. In German, this is called the *Mehrwertsteuer* (MwSt). Non-EU citizens can usually get the VAT refunded for large purchases of goods (not services). At the point of purchase, ask for a Tax-Free Shopping Cheque, then have it stamped at customs upon leaving the country or at a customs authority. (You will have to present the goods, receipt, and cheque.) The goods you have purchased must remain unused until you leave the country.

SAFETY AND SECURITY

EMERGENCY TELEPHONE NUMBERS	Police: 110 Fire/Ambulance: 112 Medical emergency: 115

Germany is on par with the rest of Western Europe when it comes to safety. Violent crime is rare, with incidents largely confined to urban areas. German modes of conduct are on the reserved side, so crime is more likely to be encountered in the form of theft, rather than assault. After reunification, incidents of crime against foreigners in Eastern Germany were more frequent, largely as a result of economic depression (see **Reunification and its Aftermath,** p. 19). Former GDR citizens are now more accommodated to travelers' presence, but right-wing groups maintain an uncomfortable presence in disadvantaged areas.

! **Violent crime** is less common in Germany than in most countries, but it exists, especially in big cities like Frankfurt and Berlin—as well as economically depressed regions of the East, such as Rostock and its surrounding areas. Most of Germany's neo-Nazis and skinheads subscribe to the traditional skinhead uniform of flight jackets worn over white shortsleeve shirts and tight jeans rolled up high to reveal high-cut combat boots. Skinheads also tend to follow a shoelace code, with white supremacists and neo-Nazis wearing white laces, while anti-gay skinheads wear pink laces. Left-wing, anti-Nazi "S.H.A.R.P.s" (Skinheads Against Racial Prejudice) also exist; they favor red laces.

BLENDING IN. Tourists are particularly vulnerable to crime because they often carry large amounts of cash and are not as street savvy as locals. To avoid unwanted attention, try to blend in as much as possible—avoid clothing emblazoned with name brands and university logos. Western styles are the norm in Germany, though, despite the image of a *lederhosen*-clad native. The gawking cameratoter is a more obvious target than the low-profile traveler. Familiarize yourself with your surroundings before setting out; if you must check a map on the street, duck into a cafe or shop. If you are traveling alone, be sure that someone at home knows your itinerary, and **never admit that you're traveling alone.**

EXPLORING. Find out about unsafe areas from locals or from the manager of your hotel or hostel. You may want to carry a **whistle** to scare off attackers or attract attention; memorize the emergency number of the city or area (see above). Whenever possible, *Let's Go: Germany* warns of unsafe neighborhoods and areas, but there are good general tips to follow. When walking at night, stick to busy, well-lit streets and avoid dark alleyways. Do not attempt to cross through parks, parking lots, or other large, deserted areas. Buildings in disrepair, vacant lots, and unpopulated areas are all bad signs. The distribution of people can reveal a great deal about the relative safety of the area; look for children playing, women walking in the open, and other signs of an active community.

SELF DEFENSE. There is no sure-fire set of precautions that will protect you from all the situations you might encounter while traveling. A good self-defense course will give you concrete ways to react to different types of aggression. **Impact, Prepare, and Model Mugging** can refer you to local self-defense courses in the United States (☎(800) 345 5425) and Vancouver, Canada (☎(604) 878 3838). Workshops (2-3 hours) start at US$50 and full courses run US$350-500. Both women and men are welcome.

FINANCIAL SECURITY

PROTECTING YOUR VALUABLES. Don't keep all your valuables in one place. **Photocopies** of important documents allow you to recover them in case they are lost or filched. Label every piece of luggage both inside and out. **Don't put a wallet with money in your back pocket.** Never count your money in public and carry as little

> **TRAVEL ADVISORIES** The following government offices provide travel information and advisories by telephone, by fax, or via the web:
>
> **Australian Department of Foreign Affairs and Trade:** ☎(2) 6261 1111; www.dfat.gov.au.
>
> **Canadian Department of Foreign Affairs and International Trade (DFAIT):** In Canada call (800) 267-6788 in Canada, elsewhere call +1 (613) 944-6788; www.dfait-maeci.gc.ca. Call for their free booklet, *Bon Voyage...But.*
>
> **New Zealand Ministry of Foreign Affairs:** ☎(04) 494 8500; fax 494 8511; www.mft.govt.nz/trav.html.
>
> **United Kingdom Foreign and Commonwealth Office:** ☎(020) 7238 4503; fax 7238 4545; www.fco.gov.uk.
>
> **US Department of State:** ☎(202) 647-5225, auto faxback (202) 647-3000; http://travel.state.gov. For *A Safe Trip Abroad,* call (202) 512-1800.

as possible. If you carry a purse, buy a sturdy one with a secure clasp, and carry it crosswise on the side, away from the street with the clasp against you. Secure packs with small combination padlocks which slip through the two zippers. A **money belt** is the best way to carry cash, available at most camping supply stores. It consists of a nylon, zippered pouch with a belt that sits inside the waist of your pants or skirt and combines convenience and security. A **neck pouch** is equally safe, although far less accessible. Refrain from pulling out your neck pouch in public, especially in big cities like Hamburg and Berlin; if you must, be very discreet. Avoid keeping anything precious in a fanny-pack (even if it's worn on your stomach): your valuables will be highly visible and easy to steal. Keep some money separate from the rest to use in an emergency or in case of theft.

CON ARTISTS AND PICKPOCKETS. Among the more colorful aspects of large cities are **con artists.** Con artists and hustlers often work in groups, and children are among the most effective. They possess an innumerable range of ruses. Be aware of certain classics: sob stories that require money, rolls of bills "found" on the street, mustard spilled (or saliva spit) onto your shoulder distracting you for enough time to snatch your bag. One scam reported in Frankfurt involves targeting young men to buy companies of women champagne, only later revealing the exorbitant price of the alcohol. Hmmm. The moral of the story is be on your guard! The area around the main train station in large German cities should be traversed with caution. Be especially suspicious in unexpected situations. Do not respond (often the advances will be in English) or make eye contact, walk away quickly, and keep a solid grip on your belongings. Contact the police if a hustler is particularly insistent or aggressive.

In city crowds and especially on public transportation, **pickpockets** are amazingly deft at their craft. Also, be alert in public telephone booths. If you must say your calling card number, do so very quietly; if you punch it in, make sure no one can look over your shoulder.

ACCOMMODATIONS AND TRANSPORTATION. Never leave your belongings unattended; crime occurs in even the most demure-looking hostel or hotel. If you feel unsafe, look for places with either a curfew or night attendant. *Let's Go* lists locker availability in the hostels and train stations of larger cities, but you'll need your own **padlock.** Lockers are useful if you plan on sleeping outdoors or don't want to lug everything with you, but don't store valuables in them. Most hotels also provide lock boxes free or for a minimal fee.

Be particularly careful on **buses,** carry your backpack in front of you where you can see it, don't check baggage on trains, and don't trust anyone to "watch your bag for a second." Thieves thrive on **trains,** yes, even on the Deutsche Bahn; professionals wait for tourists to fall asleep and then carry off everything they can. When traveling in pairs, sleep in alternating shifts, and when alone, use good judgement in selecting a train compartment. Never stay in an empty one, and use a lock to secure your pack to the luggage rack. Keep important documents and other valuables on your person and try to sleep on top bunks with your luggage stored above you or in bed with you.

ALPS   ASPEN

AT&T Direct® Service

AT&T Direct Service access numbers are the easy way to call home from anywhere.

Global
connection
with the AT&T
Network

AT&T
direct
service

AT&T Direct® Service

The easy way to call
home from anywhere.

AT&T Access Numbers

Austria ●	0800-200-288	France	0800-99-00-11
Belarus ×	.........8♦800-101	Gambia ●	00111
Belgium ●	0-800-100-10	Germany	0800-2255-288
Bosnia ▲	00-800-0010	Ghana	0191
Bulgaria ▲	00-800-0010	Gibraltar	8800
Cyprus ●	080-900-10	Greece ●	00-800-1311
Czech Rep. ▲	00-42-000-101	Hungary ●	06-800-01111
Denmark	 8001-0010	Iceland ●	800-9001
Egypt ●(Cairo)‡	510-0200	Ireland ✓	1-800-550-000
Finland ●	0800-110-015	Israel	1-800-94-94-949

AT&T Direct® Service

The easy way to call
home from anywhere.

AT&T Access Numbers

Austria ●	0800-200-288	France	0800-99-00-11
Belarus ×	.........8♦800-101	Gambia ●	00111
Belgium ●	0-800-100-10	Germany	0800-2255-288
Bosnia ▲	00-800-0010	Ghana	0191
Bulgaria ▲	00-800-0010	Gibraltar	8800
Cyprus ●	080-900-10	Greece ●	00-800-1311
Czech Rep. ▲	00-42-000-101	Hungary ●	06-800-01111
Denmark	 8001-0010	Iceland ●	800-9001
Egypt ●(Cairo)‡	510-0200	Ireland ✓	1-800-550-000
Finland ●	0800-110-015	Israel	1-800-94-94-949

The best way to keep in touch when you're traveling overseas is with **AT&T Direct®** Service. It's the easy way to call your loved ones back home from just about anywhere in the world. Just cut out the wallet guide below and use it wherever your travels take you.

For a list of AT&T Access Numbers, tear out the attached wallet guide.

AT&T

Italy ● 172-1011	Russia (Moscow) ▶▲●755-5042
Luxembourg ✦ ..800-2-0111	(St. Petersbg.) ▶▲● ..325-5042
Macedonia ● ..99-800-4288	Slovakia ▲ ..00-42-100-101
Malta 0800-890-110	South Africa ..0800-99-0123
Monaco ● 800-90-288	Spain 900-99-00-11
Morocco 002-11-0011	Sweden 020-799-111
Netherlands ● ...0800-022-9111	Switzerland ● 0800-89-0011
Norway 800-190-11	Turkey ● 00-800-12277
Poland ▲● ..00-800-111-1111	Ukraine ▲ ....8✦100-11
Portugal ▲ 800-800-128	U.A. Emirates ● 800-121
Romania ●.....01-800-4288	U.K..............0800-89-0011

FOR EASY CALLING WORLDWIDE
1. Just dial the AT&T Access Number for the country you are calling from.
2. Dial the phone number you're calling.   *3.* Dial your card number.

For access numbers not listed ask any operator for **AT&T Direct®** Service.
In the U.S. call 1-800-331-1140 for a wallet guide listing all worldwide AT&T Access Numbers.
Visit our Web site at: **www.att.com/traveler**
Bold-faced countries permit country-to-country calling outside the U.S.
- ● Public phones require coin or card deposit to place call.
- ▲ May not be available from every phone/payphone.
- ✚ Public phones and select hotels.
- ✦ Await second dial tone.
- ▶ Additional charges apply when calling from outside the city.
- † Outside of Cairo, dial "02" first.
- ✘ Not available from public phones or all areas.
- ✔ Use U.K. access number in N. Ireland.

When placing an international call *from* the U.S., dial 1 800 CALL ATT.

EMEA   © 8/00 AT&T

Italy ● 172-1011	Russia (Moscow) ▶▲●755-5042
Luxembourg ✦ ..800-2-0111	(St. Petersbg.) ▶▲● ..325-5042
Macedonia ● ..99-800-4288	Slovakia ▲ ..00-42-100-101
Malta 0800-890-110	South Africa ..0800-99-0123
Monaco ● 800-90-288	Spain 900-99-00-11
Morocco 002-11-0011	Sweden 020-799-111
Netherlands ● ...0800-022-9111	Switzerland ● 0800-89-0011
Norway 800-190-11	Turkey ● 00-800-12277
Poland ▲● ..00-800-111-1111	Ukraine ▲ ....8✦100-11
Portugal ▲ 800-800-128	U.A. Emirates ● 800-121
Romania ●.....01-800-4288	U.K..............0800-89-0011

FOR EASY CALLING WORLDWIDE
1. Just dial the AT&T Access Number for the country you are calling from.
2. Dial the phone number you're calling.   *3.* Dial your card number.

For access numbers not listed ask any operator for **AT&T Direct®** Service.
In the U.S. call 1-800-331-1140 for a wallet guide listing all worldwide AT&T Access Numbers.
Visit our Web site at: **www.att.com/traveler**
Bold-faced countries permit country-to-country calling outside the U.S.
- ● Public phones require coin or card deposit to place call.
- ▲ May not be available from every phone/payphone.
- ✚ Public phones and select hotels.
- ✦ Await second dial tone.
- ▶ Additional charges apply when calling from outside the city.
- † Outside of Cairo, dial "02" first.
- ✘ Not available from public phones or all areas.
- ✔ Use U.K. access number in N. Ireland.

When placing an international call *from* the U.S., dial 1 800 CALL ATT.

EMEA   © 8/00 AT&T

If you travel by **car,** try not to leave valuable possessions—such as radios or luggage—in it while you are away. If your tape deck or radio is removable, hide it in the trunk or take it with you. Similarly, hide baggage in the trunk.

DRUGS AND ALCOHOL

A meek "I didn't know it was illegal" will not suffice. Remember that you are subject to the laws of the country in which you travel, not to those of your home country, and it is your responsibility to familiarize yourself with these laws before leaving. If you carry insulin, syringes, or any other **prescription drugs** while you travel, it is vital to have a copy of the prescriptions themselves and a note from a doctor, both readily accessible at country borders. **Avoid public drunkenness;** it can jeopardize your safety and earn the disdain of locals. The drinking age in Germany is 16 for beer and wine and 18 for spirits, although it is skimpily enforced. The maximum permissible blood alcohol level while driving in Germany is 0.08%.

Needless to say, **illegal drugs** are best avoided altogether; the average sentence for possession outside the US is about seven years. Buying or selling narcotics may lead to a prison sentence. In 1994, the German High Court ruled that while possession of marijuana or hashish was still illegal, possession of "small quantities for personal consumption" was not prosecutable. Each *Land* has interpreted the quantities involved in "personal consumption" differently, with possession of 3 to 30 grams *de facto* decriminalized at publication time. The more liberal areas, notably Berlin and Hamburg, tend toward the higher end of this spectrum, while the more conservative states of Bayern and in Eastern Germany afford less leniency. Those interested should find out what the latest law is, including what quantities of possession are acceptable in the various *Länder*, before filling a backpack with hash bricks.

The worst thing you can possibly do is carry drugs across an international border; not only could you end up in prison, you could be blessed with a "Drug Trafficker" stamp on your passport for the rest of your life. If arrested, call your country's consulate. Embassies may not be willing to help those arrested on drug charges. Refuse to carry anyone's excess luggage onto a plane; it's not chivalrous, we know, but you won't wind up in jail for possession of a controlled substance.

HEALTH

Germany has no exceptional health issues. No vaccinations are required for a visit, unless you're traveling from a region which is currently infected with something. Check with the German embassy or consulate and with your travel agent if you're coming from an area with health issues, such as Latin America, Africa, or Asia; an inoculation against yellow fever is the most likely requirement. Longer stays may require other certification (see **AIDS, HIV, and STDs,** p. 53).

HEALTH For minor health problems, bring a compact **first-aid kit,** including bandages, aspirin or other pain killer, antibiotic cream, a thermometer, a Swiss army knife with tweezers, moleskin, decongestant for colds, motion sickness remedy, medicine for diarrhea or stomach problems (Pepto Bismol or Immodium), sunscreen, insect repellent, burn ointment, and a syringe for emergency medical purposes (get a letter of explanation from your doctor). **Contact lens** wearers should bring an extra pair, a copy of the prescription, a pair of glasses, extra solution, and eyedrops. Those who use heat disinfection might consider switching to chemical cleansers for the duration of the trip.

Common sense is the simplest prescription for good health while you travel. Travelers complain most often about their feet and their gut, so take precautionary measures: drink lots of fluids to prevent dehydration and constipation, wear sturdy, broken-in shoes and clean socks, and use talcum powder to keep your feet dry. To minimize the effects of jet lag, "reset" your body's clock by adopting the time of your destination as soon as you board the plane.

Obtain a full supply of any necessary medication before the trip, since matching a prescription to a foreign equivalent is not always easy, safe, or possible. The website www.rxlist.com lists the names for common medications in several languages, and is a convenient reference list. To get a prescription filled in Germany you must go to an *Apotheke;* a *Drogerie* sells only toilet articles. Most German cities have a rotating all-night pharmacy schedule to ensure that services are available 24 hours a day. Refer to the **Practical Information** section of each particular city for the location of a convenient pharmacy. In dire straits, check the front door of the *Apotheke* nearest a city's train station for a schedule of rotating all-night pharmacies. Carry up-to-date, legible prescriptions or a statement from your doctor, especially if you use insulin, a syringe, or a narcotic. While traveling, keep all medication with you in your carry-on luggage.

BEFORE YOU GO

Preparation can help minimize the likelihood of contracting a disease and maximize the chances of receiving effective health care in the event of an emergency. In your **passport,** write the names of any people you wish to be contacted in case of a medical emergency, and also list any **allergies** or medical conditions of which you want doctors to be aware. Allergy sufferers might want to obtain a full supply of any necessary medication before the trip. Carry up-to-date, legible prescriptions or a statement from your doctor stating the medication's trade name, manufacturer, chemical name, and dosage.

While Germany has no vaccination requirements for foreigners entering the country from developed areas (see above), you should take a look at your immunization records before you go. Travelers over two years old should be sure that the following vaccines are up to date: MMR (for measles, mumps, and rubella); DTaP or Td (for diptheria, tetanus, and pertussis); OPV (for polio); HbCV (for haemophilus influenza B); and HBV (for hepatitis B). Check with a doctor for guidance through this maze of injections.

MEDICAL CONDITIONS

Those with medical conditions may want to obtain a **Medic Alert** identification tag (US$35 the first year, $15 annually thereafter), which identifies the condition and gives a 24-hour collect-call information number. Contact the Medic Alert Foundation, 2323 Colorado Ave., Turlock, CA 95382 (☎(800) 825 3785; www.medicalert.org). Diabetics can contact the **American Diabetes Association,** 1660 Duke St., Alexandria, VA 22314 (☎(800) 232 3472), to receive a copy of the article "Travel and Diabetes" and a diabetic ID card, which carries messages in 18 languages explaining the carrier's diabetic status. If you are **HIV** positive, contact the Bureau of Consular Affairs, #4811, Department of State, Washington, D.C. 20520 (☎(202) 647 1488; auto-fax 647 3000; travel.state.gov).

USEFUL ORGANIZATIONS

The US **Centers for Disease Control and Prevention (CDC)** (☎(888) 232 3299; www.cdc.gov) are an excellent source of information for travelers around the world and maintain an international fax information service for travelers. The US **State Department** (www.travel.state.gov) compiles Consular Information Sheets on health, entry requirements, and other issues for every country. For quick information on travel warnings, call the **Overseas Citizens' Services** (☎(202) 647 5225; after-hours 647 4000). To receive the same Consular Information Sheets by fax, dial (202) 647-3000 from a fax and follow the recorded instructions.

For detailed information and tips on travel health, including a country-by-country overview of diseases, check out the **International Travel Health Guide,** Stuart Rose, MD (Travel Medicine, $20). Information is also available at **Travel Medicine's** website (www.travmed.com).For general health information, contact the **American Red Cross.** The ARC publishes *First-Aid and Safety Handbook* (US$5) available by calling or writing to the American Red Cross, 285 Columbus Ave., Boston, MA 02116-5114. (☎(800) 564 1234. Open M-F 8:30am-4:30pm.)

MEDICAL ASSISTANCE ON THE ROAD

Germany has excellent medical care. Most doctors speak English, and the hospital system is largely public. Private practices are smaller clinics, and less common.

EU citizens in possession of an E11 form can get free first aid and emergency services. If you are concerned about being able to access medical support while traveling, contact one of these two services: **Global Emergency Medical Services (GEMS)** (☎(800) 860 1111; fax 770 475 0058; www.globalems.com) *MedPass* provides 24-hour international medical assistance and support coordinated through registered nurses who have online access to your medical information, your primary physician, and a worldwide network of screened, credentialed English-speaking doctors and hospitals. Subscribers also receive a personal medical record that contains vital information in case of emergencies, and GEMS will pay for medical evacuation if necessary. Prices start at about US$35 for a 30-day trip and run up to about $100 for annual services. The **International Association for Medical Assistance to Travelers (IAMAT)** has free membership and offers a directory of English-speaking doctors around the world who treat members for a set fee, as well as detailed charts on immunization requirements, climate, and sanitation. Chapters include: **US,** 417 Center St., Lewiston, NY 14092 (☎716-754-4883; fax 519-836-3412; email iamat@sentex.net; www.sentex.net/~iamat); **Canada,** 40 Regal Road, Guelph, ON N1K 1B5 (☎(519) 836 0102) or 1287 St. Clair Avenue West, Toronto, ON M6E 1B8 (☎(416) 652 0137; fax 519 836 3412); **New Zealand,** P.O. Box 5049, Christchurch 5 (fax (03) 352 4630; email iamat@chch.planet.org.nz).

Doctors may expect you to pay cash for immediate health services. If your regular **insurance** policy does not cover travel abroad, you may wish to purchase additional coverage. With the exception of Medicare/Medicaid, most health insurance plans cover members' medical emergencies during trips abroad; check with your insurance carrier. (See **Insurance,** p. 53).

ENVIRONMENTAL HAZARDS

Heat exhaustion, characterized by **dehydration** and salt deficiency, can lead to fatigue, headaches, and wooziness. Avoid heat exhaustion by drinking plenty of clear fluids and eating salty foods, like crackers. Always drink enough liquids to keep your urine clear. Alcoholic beverages are dehydrating, as are coffee, strong tea, and caffeinated sodas. Whether hiking in Swiss Saxony or lounging on the beach in the island of Sylt, wear a hat, sunglasses, and a lightweight longsleeve shirt in hot sun. If you're prone to **sunburn,** bring sunscreen with you and apply it liberally and often. If you are planning on spending time near the water or in the snow, you are at risk of getting burned, even through clouds. Protect your eyes with good sunglasses. If you get sunburned, drink more fluids than usual and apply calamine or an aloe-based lotion.

A rapid drop in body temperature is the clearest warning sign of **overexposure to cold.** Victims may also shiver, feel exhausted, have poor coordination or slurred speech, hallucinate, or suffer amnesia. Seek medical help, and *do not let hypothermia victims fall asleep*—their body temperature will continue to drop and they may die. To avoid hypothermia, keep dry, wear layers, and stay out of the wind. In wet weather, wool and synthetics such as pile retain heat. Most other fabric, especially cotton, will make you colder. When the temperature is below freezing, watch for **frostbite.** If a region of skin turns white, waxy, and cold, do not rub the area. Drink warm beverages, get dry, and slowly warm the area with dry fabric or steady body contact, until a doctor can be found.

Travelers to **high altitudes** must allow their bodies a couple of days to adjust to lower oxygen levels in the air before exerting themselves. Alcohol is more potent at high elevations. High altitudes mean that ultraviolet rays are stronger, and the risk of sunburn is therefore greater, even in cold weather.

PREVENTING DISEASE

INSECT-BORNE DISEASES

Many diseases are transmitted by insects—mainly mosquitoes, fleas, ticks, and lice. Be aware of insects in wet or forested areas, while hiking, and especially while camping. **Mosquitoes** are most active from dusk to dawn. Use insect repellents, such as DEET. Wear long pants and long sleeves, and buy a mosquito net. Wear shoes and socks, and tuck long pants into socks. Soak or spray your gear with permethrin, which is licensed in the US for use on clothing. Natural repellents can be useful supplements: taking vitamin B-12 pills regularly can eventually make you smelly to insects, as can garlic pills. Calamine lotion or topical cortisones may stop insect bites from itching, as can a bath with a half-cup of baking soda or oatmeal. **Ticks**—responsible for Lyme and other diseases—can be particularly dangerous in rural and forested regions. Pause periodically while walking to brush off ticks using a fine-toothed comb on your neck and scalp. Do not try to remove ticks by burning them or coating them with petroleum jelly.

Tick-borne encephalitis, a viral infection of the central nervous system, is transmitted during the summer by tick bites, and also by consumption of unpasteurized dairy products. The disease occurs most often in wooded areas. Symptoms can range from nothing to headaches and flu-like symptoms to swelling of the brain (encephalitis). A vaccine is available in Europe, but the immunization schedule is impractical for most tourists, and the risk of contracting the disease is relatively low, especially if you take precautions against tick bites.

Lyme disease, also carried by ticks, is a bacterial infection marked by a circular bull's-eye rash of 2in. or more that appears around the bite. Other symptoms include fever, headache, tiredness, and aches and pains. Antibiotics are effective if administered early. Left untreated, Lyme can cause problems in joints, the heart, and the nervous system. If you find a tick attached to your skin, grasp the tick's head parts with tweezers as close to your skin as possible and apply slow, steady traction. If you remove a tick within 24 hours, you greatly reduce your risk of infection.

FOOD- AND WATER-BORNE DISEASES

Prevention is the best cure: be sure that everything you eat is cooked properly and that the water you drink is clean. Germans' compulsive tendencies extend into the culinary realm, and most food is prepared under strictly-monitored sanitary conditions. Use your own judgment when it comes to *Imbiß* (fast food) fare—some establishments are cleaner than others. German tap water is generally safe to drink except in the most polluted areas of the former GDR, though most Germans prefer bottled mineral water.

Traveler's diarrhea results from drinking untreated water or eating uncooked foods. It can last three to seven days. Symptoms include nausea, bloating, urgency, and malaise. Eat quick-energy, non-sugary foods with protein and carbohydrates to keep your strength up. Over-the-counter remedies (such as Pepto Bismol or Immodium) may counteract the problems, but they can complicate serious infections. The most dangerous side effect of diarrhea is dehydration; the simplest and most effective anti-dehydration formula is 8 oz. of water with a ½ tsp. of sugar or honey and a pinch of salt. Soft drinks without caffeine or salted crackers are also good. Down several of these remedies a day, rest, and wait for the disease to run its course. If you develop a fever or your symptoms don't go away after four or five days, consult a doctor. If children develop traveler's diarrhea, consult a doctor immediately.

OTHER INFECTIOUS DISEASES

Rabies is transmitted through the saliva of infected animals. It is fatal if untreated. Avoid contact with animals, especially strays. If you are bitten, wash the wound thoroughly and seek immediate medical care. Once you begin to show symptoms (thirst and muscle spasms), the disease is in its terminal stage. If possible, try to locate the animal that bit you to determine whether it does indeed have rabies. A rabies vaccine is available but is only semi-effective. Three shots must be administered over one year.

Hepatitis B is a viral infection of the liver transmitted through the transfer of bodily fluids, by sharing needles, or by having unprotected sex. A person may not begin to show symptoms until many years after infection. The CDC recommends the Hepatitis B vaccination for health-care workers and sexually active travelers. Vaccination consists of a 3-shot series given over a period of time, and should begin 6 months before traveling.

Hepatitis C is like Hepatitis B, but the modes of transmission are different. Intravenous drug users, those with occupational exposure to blood, hemodialysis patients, or recipients of blood transfusions are at the highest risk, but the disease can also be spread through sexual contact and sharing of items like razors and toothbrushes, which may have traces of blood on them.

AIDS, HIV, AND STDS

For detailed information on **Acquired Immune Deficiency Syndrome (AIDS)** in Germany, call the **US Centers for Disease Control's** 24-hour hotline at (800) 342-2437, or contact the **Joint United Nations Programme on HIV/AIDS (UNAIDS),** 20 av. Appia 20, CH-1211 Geneva 27, Switzerland (☎+41 (22) 791 36 66, fax 791 41 87). Council's brochure, *Travel Safe: AIDS and International Travel,* is available at all Council Travel offices and on their website (www.ciee.org/lsp/safety/travelsafe.htm). Note that Germany can require the screening of incoming travelers for AIDS, primarily those planning extended visits for work or study and deny entrance to those who test HIV-positive. Contact the nearest consulate of for up-to-date information or see http://travel.state.gov/HIVtestingreqs.html.

The easiest mode of HIV transmission is through direct blood-to-blood contact with an HIV-positive person; *never* share intravenous drug, tattooing, or other needles. The most common mode of transmission is sexual intercourse. Health professionals recommend the use of latex condoms. Since it isn't always easy to buy condoms when traveling, take a supply with you before you depart for your trip.

Sexually transmitted diseases (STDs) such as gonorrhea, chlamydia, genital warts, syphilis, and herpes are easier to catch than HIV, and can be just as deadly. **Hepatitis B** and **C** are also serious sexually-transmitted diseases (see **Other Infectious Diseases,** above). Warning signs for STDs include: swelling, sores, bumps, or blisters on genitals, rectum, or mouth; pain during urination and bowel movements; itching around sex organs; swelling or redness in the throat, flu-like symptoms with fever, chills, and aches. If these symptoms develop, see a doctor immediately.

WOMEN'S HEALTH

Women traveling in unsanitary conditions are vulnerable to **urinary tract** and **bladder infections,** common and very uncomfortable bacterial diseases that cause a burning sensation and painful (sometimes frequent) urination. To try to avoid these infections, drink plenty of clean water and juice rich in vitamin C, and urinate frequently, especially after intercourse. Untreated, these infections can lead to kidney problems, sterility, and even death. If symptoms persist, see a doctor.

Women are also susceptible to **vaginal yeast infections,** a treatable but uncomfortable illness. Wearing loosely fitting trousers or a skirt and cotton underwear will help, as will over-the-counter remedies like Monostat or Gynelotrimin; an *Apotheke* can hook you up with the German equivalents such as Gyno-Canerteh and Canifug, which are stronger, in many cases, than their American counterparts. **Tampons, pads,** and reliable **contraceptive devices** are plentiful in Germany, but your preferred brand will rarely be available, and you may want to consider bringing supplies with you. Women on the pill should bring enough to allow for possible loss or extended stays. Bring a prescription, since forms of the pill vary.

Women considering an **abortion** abroad should contact the **International Planned Parenthood Federation (IPPF),** Regent's College, Inner Circle, Regent's Park, London NW1 4NS (☎(020) 7487 7900; fax 7487 7950; www.ippf.org), for more information.

INSURANCE

Travel insurance generally covers four basic areas: medical problems, property loss, trip cancellation/interruption, and emergency evacuation. Although your regular insurance policies may well extend to travel-related accidents, consider purchasing travel insurance if the cost of potential trip cancellation/interruption is greater than you can absorb. Prices for travel insurance purchased separately generally run about US$50 per week for full coverage, while trip cancellation/interruption insurance may be purchased separately at a rate of about US$5.50 per US$100 of coverage.

Medical insurance (especially university policies) often covers costs incurred abroad; check with your provider. **US Medicare does not cover foreign travel.** Canadians are protected by their home province's health insurance plan for up to 90 days after leaving the country; check with the provincial Ministry of Health or Health

Plan Headquarters for details. **Homeowners' insurance** (or your family's coverage) often covers theft during travel and loss of travel documents up to US$500.

ISIC and **ITIC** (see p. 40) provide basic insurance benefits, including US$100 per day of in-hospital sickness for up to 60 days, US$3000 of accident-related medical reimbursement, and US$25,000 for emergency medical transport. Cardholders have access to a toll-free 24-hour helpline for medical, legal, and financial emergencies overseas (US and Canada ☎ (877) 370-4742, elsewhere call US collect +1 (713) 342-4104). American Express (US ☎ (800) 528-4800) grants most cardholders automatic car rental insurance (collision and theft, but not liability) and ground travel accident coverage of US$100,000 on flight purchases made with the card.

Council and **STA** (see p. 65) offer a range of plans that can supplement your basic coverage. Other private insurance providers in the **US and Canada** include: **Access America** (☎ (800) 284-8300); **Berkely Group/Carefree Travel Insurance** (☎ (800) 323-3149; www.berkely.com); **Globalcare Travel Insurance** (☎ (800) 821-2488; www.globalcare-cocco.com); and **Travel Assistance International** (☎ (800) 821-2828; www.worldwide-assistance.com). Providers in the **UK** include **Campus Travel** (☎ (01865) 258 000) and **Columbus Travel Insurance** (☎ (020) 7375 0011). In **Australia,** try **CIC Insurance** (☎ 9202 8000).

PACKING

Though German climate is temperate, planning trips to the northernmost islands, ascending the Bavarian Alps or expecting the inevitable shower are cause for particular packing consideration. It's always a good idea to bring a rain jacket, a warm jacket or wool sweater, and sturdy shoes and thick socks. You may also want to add one dressy ensemble and a nicer pair of shoes for clubbing if you have the room. **Flip-flops** or waterproof sandals are crucial for grubby hostel showers. If you plan to visit any religious or cultural sites, remember that you'll need something besides tank tops and shorts to be respectful. If you are doing a lot of hiking, see **Camping and Hiking Equipment,** p. 58. **Pack light:** lay out only what you absolutely need, then take half the clothes and twice the money. The less you have, the less you have to lose (or store, or carry on your back). Any extra space will be useful for souvenirs or items you might pick up along the way.

LUGGAGE. If you plan to cover most of your itinerary by foot, a sturdy **frame backpack** is unbeatable (see p. 59). Organizations that sell packs through mail-order are listed on p. 58. Toting a **suitcase** or **trunk** is fine if you plan to live in one or two cities and explore from there, but a very bad idea if you're going to be moving around a lot. In addition to your main piece of luggage, a **daypack** (a small backpack or courier bag) is a must.

SLEEPSACKS. Some youth hostels require that you rent their sheets, but you can avoid linen charges by making the requisite sleepsack yourself: fold a full size sheet in half the long way, then sew it closed along the open long side and one of the short sides. Sleepsacks can also be bought at any Hostelling International outlet store. In some areas of Bavaria, the Thüringer Wald, and the Sächsiche Schweiz, hostels are at high altitudes; it can be useful to use a sleepsack in addition to the linen provided.

WASHING CLOTHES. *Let's Go: Germany* provides information on laundromats, called *Wäschereien*, in the **Practical Information** listings for larger cities, but it's cheaper to use a sink. Bring a bar or tube of detergent soap, a small rubber ball to stop up the sink, and a travel clothes line.

ELECTRIC CURRENT. In Germany, electricity is 220 volts AC, enough to fry any 110V North American appliance; sockets only accept a two-prong plug. Visit a hardware store for an adapter (which changes the shape of the plug). Americans and Canadians also need to pick up a converter (which changes the voltage). Don't make the mistake of using only an adapter unless appliance instructions explicitly state otherwise. New Zealanders, South Africans, and Australians only need to purchase an adapter.

TOILETRIES. Toothbrushes, towels, soap, talcum powder (to keep feet dry), deodorant, razors, tampons, and condoms are widely available, but it may be difficult or impossible to find your favorite brands. **Contact lenses,** on the other hand, may be expensive and difficult to find, so bring enough extra pairs and solution for your entire trip. Also bring your glasses and a copy of your prescription in case you need emergency replacements. If you use heat-disinfection, either switch temporarily to a chemical disinfection system (check first to make sure it's safe with your brand of lenses), or buy a converter to 220/240V.

FILM. Film in Germany is of excellent quality and available at photo shops and drug stores; the same businesses usually process and develop film. If you're not a serious photographer, you might want to consider bringing a **disposable camera** or two rather than an expensive permanent one. Despite disclaimers, airport security X-rays *can* fog film, so either buy a lead-lined pouch, sold at camera stores, or ask the security to hand inspect it. Always pack it in your carry-on luggage, since higher-intensity X-rays are used on checked luggage.

OTHER USEFUL ITEMS. No matter how you're traveling, it's a good idea to carry a first-aid kit including sunscreen, insect repellent, and vitamins (see Health, p. 49). For safety purposes, you should bring a **money belt** and small **padlock.** Basic **outdoors equipment** (plastic water bottle, compass, waterproof matches, pocketknife, sunglasses, sunscreen, hat) may also prove useful. **Quick repairs** of torn garments can be done on the road with a needle and thread; also consider bringing electrical tape for patching tears. **Other things** you're liable to forget: an umbrella; sealable **plastic bags** (for damp clothes, soap, food, shampoo, and other spillables); an **alarm clock;** safety pins; rubber bands; a flashlight; earplugs; garbage bags; and a small **calculator.**

FURTHER READING
The Packing Book, by Judith Gilford. Ten Speed Press ($9).

Backpacking One Step at a Time, Harvey Manning. Vintage ($15).

ACCOMMODATIONS

HOSTELS
In 1908, a German named Richard Schirmann, believing that life in industrial cities was harmful to the physical and moral development of Germany's young people, built the world's first **youth hostel** in Altena—a budget dormitory that would bring travel within the means of urban youth. Germany has been a leader in hosteling ever since, and Schirmann is something of a mythical figure. Some hostels are housed in stunning castles, others in run-down barracks far from the city center. Hostels are generally dorm-style accommodations, often in large single-sex rooms with bunk beds, although some hostels do offer private rooms for families and couples. Whatever the locale, a bed in a hostel will average around DM20-30. They sometimes have kitchens and utensils, bike or moped rentals, storage areas, email terminals, and laundry facilities. There can be **drawbacks:** some hostels close during certain daytime "lockout" hours, have a curfew, don't accept reservations, impose a maximum stay, or, less frequently, require that you do chores. There's often little privacy and you may run into more screaming pre-teen groups than you care to remember. Many hostels require sleepsacks (see **Packing,** p. 54). Sleeping bags are usually prohibited for sanitary reasons, but almost all hostels provide sheets and blankets for a fee, usually about DM5.

Hostelling in Germany is overseen by **Deutsches Jugendherbergswerk (DJH),** Bismarckstr. 8, D-32756 Detmold, Germany (☎ (0 52 31) 74 01-0; fax (0 52 31) 74 01-74, email service@djh.de). DJH has recently initiated a growing number of **Jugendgästehäuser,** youth guest-houses that are generally more expensive, have more facilities, and attract slightly older guests. DJH has absorbed hundreds of hostels in Eastern Germany with remarkable efficiency, though some still lack the truly sparkling facilities of their western counterparts. Undoubtedly a hosteler's paradise, Germany currently has about **600 hostels**—more than any other country.

DJH publishes *Jugendherbergen in Deutschland* (DM14.80), a guide to all federated German hostels. It can be purchased at German bookstores and major train station newsstands, by writing to DJH, or from the **DJH webpage** (www.djh.de), which also has pictures, prices, addresses, and phone numbers for almost every hostel in Germany. Contact information can also be found on most German cities' official webpages, listed under the tourist office in the **Practical Information** section of many cities in this guide. **Eurotrip** (www.eurotrip.com) has information on and reviews of budget hostels and several international hostel associations. Also check out the **Internet Guide to Hostelling** (www.hostels.com), which provides a directory of hostels in addition to hostelling and backpacking tips.

Joining the youth hostel association in your own country (listed below) automatically grants you membership privileges in **Hostelling International (HI),** a federation of national hosteling associations. HI hostels are scattered throughout Germany, and many accept reservations via the International Booking Network (Australia ☎(02) 9261 1111; Canada ☎(800) 663-5777; England and Wales ☎(16295) 814 18; Northern Ireland ☎(12323) 247 33; Republic of Ireland ☎(01) 830 1766; NZ ☎(09) 379 4224; Scotland ☎(541) 55 32 55; US ☎(800) 909 4776). The web page of HI's umbrella organization (www.iyhf.org), which lists the web addresses and phone numbers of all national associations, is a great place to begin research on hostelling in a specific region.

Most HI hostels also honor **guest memberships**—you'll get a blank card with space for six validation stamps. Each night you'll pay a nonmember supplement (one-sixth the membership fee) and earn one guest stamp; get six stamps, and you're a member. Most student travel agencies (see p. 65) sell HI cards, as do all of the national hosteling organizations listed below. All prices listed below are valid for **one-year memberships** unless otherwise noted.

Australian Youth Hostels Association (AYHA), 422 Kent St., Sydney NSW 2000 (☎(02) 9261 1111; fax 9261 1969; www.yha.org.au). AUS$49, under 18 AUS$14.50.

Hostelling International-Canada (HI-C), 400-205 Catherine St., Ottawa, ON K2P 1C3 (☎(800) 663-5777 or (613) 237-7884; fax 237-7868; email info@hostellingintl.ca; www.hostellingintl.ca). CDN$25, under 18 CDN$12.

An Óige (Irish Youth Hostel Association), 61 Mountjoy St., Dublin 7 (☎(1) 830 4555; fax 830 5808; email anoige@iol.ie; www.irelandyha.org). IR£10, under 18 IR£4.

Youth Hostels Association of New Zealand (YHANZ), P.O. Box 436, 173 Cashel St., Christchurch 1 (☎(03) 379 9970; fax 365 4476; email info@yha.org.nz; www.yha.org.nz). NZ$40, ages 15-17 NZ$12, under 15 free.

Hostels Association of South Africa, 3rd fl. 73 St. George's St. Mall, P.O. Box 4402, Cape Town 8000 (☎(021) 424 2511; fax 424 4119; email info@hisa.org.za; www.hisa.org.za). SAR50, under 18 SAR25, lifetime SAR250.

Scottish Youth Hostels Association (SYHA), 7 Glebe Crescent, Stirling FK8 2JA (☎(01786) 89 14 00; fax 89 13 33; www.syha.org.uk). UK£6, under 18 UK£2.50.

Youth Hostels Association (England and Wales) Ltd., Trevelyan House, 8 St. Stephen's Hill, St. Albans, Hertfordshire AL1 2DY, UK (☎(01727) 85 52 15; fax 84 41 26; www.yha.org.uk). UK£12, under 18 UK£6, families UK£24.

Hostelling International Northern Ireland (HINI), 22-32 Donegall Rd., Belfast BT12 5JN, Northern Ireland (☎(01232) 32 47 33; fax 43 96 99; email info@hini.org.uk; www.hini.org.uk). UK£7, under 18 UK£3.

Hostelling International-American Youth Hostels (HI-AYH), 733 15th St. NW, #840, Washington, D.C. 20005 (☎(202) 783-6161 ext. 136; fax 783-6171; email hiayhserv@hiayh.org; www.hiayh.org). US$25, under 18 free.

 NO OLD PEOPLE ALLOWED—SORRY POPS HI-affiliated hostels in **Bayern (Bavaria)** generally do not admit guests over age 26, although families with young children are usually allowed even if parents are over 26.

HOTELS AND PRIVATE ROOMS

The cheapest hotel-style accommodations are places with **Pension, Gasthof, Gäste-haus,** or **Hotel-Garni** in the name. Breakfast *(Frühstück)* is almost always included. Hotels are quite expensive in Germany: rock-bottom for singles is DM30, for doubles DM40-45; in large cities, expect to pay at least DM50 per night for a single and DM90 for a double. Germany's budget hotels might come as a rude shock to pampered North American travelers: a bathroom of your own is a rarity and costs extra when provided. Hot showers may also cost extra.

The best bet for a cheap bed is often a private room *(Privatzimmer)* in a home. Private rooms are much, much quieter than hostels, and will bring you in direct contact with the local population. Prices generally run DM20-50 per person, and usually include warm and personal service. Rooms are reserved through the local tourist office or through a private **Zimmervermittlung** (room-booking office), either for free or for a DM2-8 fee. This option works best if you have a rudimentary knowledge of German, since homeowners prefer to lay down a few household rules before handing over keys for the night. Travelers over 26 who would otherwise pay senior prices at youth hostels will find these rooms within budget range.

LONGER STAYS

Those planning to remain in Germany for an extended period of time should contact the local **Mitwohnzentrale,** an accommodation-finding office, in the city where they plan to stay. Throughout Germany, *Mitwohnzentralen* match apartments with apartment seekers; look under the **Practical Information** listings of individual cities. The stay can last anywhere from a few days to eternity, depending on the availability of apartments and the price you are willing to pay. Also check postings in universities, where student housing can offer lodging and utilities for DM200-300 per month.

Another option is a home exchange. These offer the traveler various types of homes (houses, apartments, condominiums, villas—even castles in some cases), plus the opportunity to live like a native and cut down dramatically on accommodation costs. Once you join or contact one of the exchange services listed below, it is up to you to decide with whom you would like to exchange homes. Most companies have pictures of member's homes and information about the owners. A great site listing many exchange companies can be found at www.aitec.edu.au/~bwechner/Documents/Travel/Lists/HomeExchangeClubs.html. Home rentals are much more expensive than exchanges, but can be cheaper than comparably-serviced hotels. Both home exchanges and rentals are ideal for families with children or travelers with special dietary needs; you often get a kitchen, maid service, TV, and telephones. For more information, contact the organizations listed below.

HomeExchange, P.O. Box 30085, Santa Barbara, CA 93130 (☎(805) 898 9660; admin@HomeExchange.com; www.homeexchange.com).

Intervac International Home Exchange, c/o Helge and Dieter Guenzler, Verdiweg 2, 70771 Leinfelden-Echterdingen, Germany (☎(0711) 754 60 69; fax (0711) 754 28 31; email intervacgue@t-online.de; www.intervac.com). Offers 11,000 home exchanges in 50 countries.

The Invented City: International Home Exchange, 41 Sutter St., Suite 1090, San Francisco, CA 94104 (☎(415) 252-1141; fax 252-1171; email info@invented-city.com; www.invented-city.com). For US$75, you get your offer listed in 1 catalog and unlimited access to the club's database containing thousands of homes for exchange.

CAMPING AND THE OUTDOORS

Germans love the outdoors, and their enthusiasm is evidenced by the 2,600 campsites that dot the outskirts of even major cities. Though the offerings in Germany are generally rather tame in comparison to those in Switzerland, Austria, or other more mountainous areas, the facilities for outdoor activities in Germany are among the best maintained in the world. Most are accessible by public transportation and include showers, bathrooms, and a restaurant or store. Often, however, campgrounds resemble battlegrounds, with weary travelers and screaming children vying for tiny grassy plots. Camping costs DM3-10 per person with an additional charge for tents and vehicles.

Blue signs with a black tent on a white background indicate official sites. **Deutscher Camping-Club (DCC),** Mandlstr. 28, 80802 München (☎(089) 380 14 20), and **Allgemeiner Deutscher Automobil-Club (ADAC)** (see **Getting Around: By Car,** p. 72) have specific information on campgrounds, and the National Tourist Office distributes a free map, *Camping in Germany*, with a list of campgrounds (see p. 83).

Hiking trails wind through the outskirts of every German city, and a national network of long-distance trails links the whole country together. The Black Forest and the Bavarian Alps are especially well-traversed, as are the Harz Mountains and Saxon Switzerland. Alpine clubs in Germany provide inexpensive, simple accommodations in splendid settings. The **German Alpine Association,** Von-Kahr-Str. 2-4, 80997 München (☎(089) 14 00 30; fax 140 03 11), maintains more than 14,000km of trails in the Alps and 252 huts open to all mountaineers. They also offer courses and guided expeditions.

USEFUL PUBLICATIONS AND WEB RESOURCES. For information about camping, hiking, and biking, contact the publishers listed below to receive a free catalogue. Campers should consider buying an International Camping Carnet. Similar to a hostel membership card, it's required at a few campgrounds and provides discounts at others. It is available in North America from the Family Campers and RVers Association and in the UK from The Caravan Club (below), and can usually be purchased at associated campsites.

Automobile Association, A.A. Publishing. Orders and enquiries to TBS Frating Distribution Centre, Colchester, Essex, CO7 7DW, UK (☎(01206) 25 56 78; www.theaa.co.uk).

The Caravan Club, East Grinstead House, East Grinstead, West Sussex, RH19 1UA, UK (☎(01342) 32 69 44; www.caravanclub.co.uk). For £27.50, members receive equipment discounts, a 700pp directory and handbook, and a monthly magazine.

Sierra Club Books, 85 Second St., 2nd fl., San Francisco, CA 94105, USA (☎(415) 977-5704; www.sierraclub.org/books). Publishes general resource books on hiking, camping, and women traveling in the outdoors.

The Mountaineers Books, 1001 SW Klickitat Way, #201, Seattle, WA 98134, USA (☎(800) 553-4453 or (206) 223-6303; www.mountaineersbooks.org). Over 400 titles on hiking, biking, mountaineering, natural history, and conservation.

WILDERNESS SAFETY

Stay warm, stay dry, and stay hydrated. The vast majority of life-threatening wilderness situations result from a breach of this simple dictum. On any hike, however brief, you should pack enough equipment to keep you alive should disaster befall. This includes raingear, hat and mittens, a first-aid kit, a reflector, a whistle, high energy food, and extra water. Dress in warm layers of **synthetic materials** designed for the outdoors, or **wool.** Pile fleece jackets and Gore-Tex raingear are excellent choices. Never rely on **cotton** for warmth. This "death cloth" will be absolutely useless should it get wet. Make sure to check all equipment for any defects before setting out, and see **Camping and Hiking Equipment,** below, for more information.

Check **weather forecasts** and pay attention to the skies when hiking—weather patterns can change suddenly. Don't hike when visibility is low. Whenever possible, hike with a companion, and let someone know when and where you are going hiking, either a friend, your hostel, a park ranger, or a local hiking organization. Do not attempt a hike beyond your ability—you may be endangering your life. Of particular concern in Austria and Switzerland is **glacier hiking.** Never hike over glaciers alone. Snow covered crevasses in glaciers have swallowed many an unsuspecting hiker. See **Health,** p. 49, for information about outdoor ailments such as heatstroke, hypothermia, giardia, rabies, and insects, as well as basic medical concerns and first-aid.

For more information, consult *How to Stay Alive in the Woods*, by Bradford Angier (Macmillan, US$8).

CAMPING AND HIKING EQUIPMENT

 ENVIRONMENTALLY RESPONSIBLE TOURISM The idea behind responsible tourism is to leave no trace of human presence behind. A campstove is the safer (and more efficient) way to cook than using vegetation, but if you must make a fire, keep it small and use only dead branches or brush rather than cutting vegetation. Make sure your campsite is at least 150 ft. (50m) from water supplies or bodies of water. If there are no toilet facilities, bury human waste (but not paper) at least four inches (10cm) deep and above the high-water line, and 150 ft. or more from any water supplies and campsites. Always pack your trash in a plastic bag and carry it with you until you reach the next trash receptacle. For more information on these issues, contact one of the organizations listed below.

Earthwatch, 680 Mt. Auburn St., Box 403, Watertown, MA 02272, USA (☎ (617) 776-0188; email info@earthwatch.org; www.earthwatch.org).

Ecotourism Society, P.O. Box 755, North Bennington, VT 05257, USA (☎ (802) 447-2121; email ecomail@ecotourism.org; www.ecotourism.org/tesinfo.html).

EcoTravel Center: www.ecotour.com.

National Audobon Society, Nature Odysseys, 700 Broadway, New York, NY 10003 (☎ (212) 979-3066; email travel@audobon.org; www.audobon.org).

Tourism Concern, Stapleton House, 277-281 Holloway Rd., London N7 8HN, UK (☎ (020) 7753 3330; www.gn.apc.org/tourismconcern).

Purchase equipment before you leave so that you'll know exactly what you have and how much it weighs. Spend some time examining catalogues and talking to knowledgeable salespeople. Camping equipment is generally more expensive in Australia, New Zealand, and the UK than in North America.

Sleeping Bag: Most good sleeping bags are rated by "season," or the lowest outdoor temperature at which they will keep you warm ("summer" means 30-40°F at night and "four-season" or "winter" often means below 0°F). Sleeping bags are made either of down (warmer and lighter, but more expensive, and miserable when wet) or of synthetic material (heavier, more durable, and warmer when wet). Prices vary, but might range from US$80-210 for a summer synthetic to US$250-300 for a good down winter bag. For **sleeping bag pads** you can choose from foam pads (US$10-20) or air mattresses (US$15-50). Both types cushion your back and neck and insulate you from the ground. Therm-A-Rest brand self-inflating sleeping pads are part foam and part air-mattress that partially inflate upon unrolling, US$45-80. Bring a **"stuff sack"** or plastic bag to store your sleeping bag and keep it dry.

Backpack: If you intend to do a lot of hiking, you should have a frame backpack. **Internal-frame packs** mold better to your back, keep a lower center of gravity, and can flex to allow you to hike difficult trails that require a lot of bending and maneuvering (external-frame packs are the skeletal ancestors of internal frame packs). Make sure your pack has a strong, padded hip belt, which transfers the weight from the shoulders to the legs. Any serious backpacking requires a pack of at least 3000 cubic inches (12,000cc). Sturdy backpacks cost anywhere from US$125-420. Before you buy any pack, try it on and imagine carrying it when full; insist on filling it with something heavy and walking around the store to get a sense of how it distributes weight before committing to buy it. A **waterproof backpack cover** will prove invaluable. Otherwise, plan to store all of your belongings in plastic bags inside your backpack.

Boots: Be sure to wear hiking boots with good **ankle support** regardless of the terrain you are hiking in. Your boots should fit snugly and comfortably over a pair of wool socks and a thin liner sock. Breaking in boots properly before setting out requires wearing them for several weeks; doing so will spare you from painful and debilitating blisters. If you're planning on doing any serious hiking your boots should be waterproof with Gore-Tex or a similar fabric. In addition, the fewer seams a boot has the more waterproof it will be–the best hiking boots are solid leather–flashy boots with different fabrics allow for many seams through which water can leak.

ESSENTIALS

Tent: The best tents are free-standing (with their own frames and suspension systems), set up quickly, and only require staking in high winds. Low-profile dome tents are the best all-around. Good 2-person tents start at US$90, 4-person at US$300. Seal the seams of your tent with waterproofer, and make sure it has a rain fly. Other tent accessories include a **battery-operated lantern,** a **plastic groundcloth,** and a **nylon tarp.**

Other Necessities: Raingear in two pieces, a top and pants, is far superior to a poncho. Three layer Gore-Tex is more waterproof and breathable than two layers, but the difference will be negligable for casual hikers. **Synthetic materials,** like polypropylene tops, socks, and long underwear, along with a pile jacket, will keep you warm even when wet. When camping in autumn, winter, or spring, bring along a **"space blanket,"** which helps you to retain your body heat and doubles as a groundcloth (US$5-15). Plastic **canteens** or water bottles keep water cooler than metal ones do, and are virtually shatter- and leak-proof. Large, collapsible **water sacks** will significantly improve your lot in primitive campgrounds and weigh practically nothing when empty. Bring **water-purification tablets** (iodine) for when you can't boil water, unless you are willing to shell out money for a portable water-purification system. Though most campgrounds provide campfire sites, you may want to bring a small metal grate or grill of your own. For those places that forbid fires or the gathering of firewood (virtually every organized campground in Germany), you'll need a **camp stove.** The classic Coleman stove starts at about US$40. Purchase a fuel bottle and fill it with propane to operate it. A **first aid kit, Swiss Army knife, insect repellent, calamine lotion,** and **waterproof matches** or a **lighter** are other essential camping items.

...AND WHERE TO BUY IT

The mail-order/online companies listed below offer lower prices than many retail stores, but a visit to a local camping or outdoors store will give you a good sense of the look and weight of certain items.

Campmor, P.O. Box 700, Upper Saddle River, NJ 07458 (US ☎(888) 226-7667; elsewhere call US +1 (201) 825-8300; www.campmor.com).

Discount Camping, 880 Main North Rd., Pooraka, South Australia 5095, Australia (☎(08) 826 23399; www.discountcamping.com.au).

Eastern Mountain Sports (EMS), 327 Jaffrey Rd., Peterborough, NH 03458, USA (☎(888) 463-6367 or (603) 924-7231; www.shopems.com)

L.L. Bean, Freeport, ME 04033 (US and Canada ☎(800) 441-5713; UK ☎(0800) 962 954; elsewhere, call US +1 (207) 552-6878; www.llbean.com).

Mountain Designs, P.O. Box 1472, Fortitude Valley, Queensland 4006, Australia (☎(07) 325 28894; www.mountaindesign.com.au).

Recreational Equipment, Inc. (REI), Sumner, WA 98352, USA (☎(800) 426-4840 or (253) 891-2500; www.rei.com).

YHA Adventure Shop, 14 Southampton St., London, WC2E 7HA, UK (☎(020) 783 68541). The main branch of one of Britain's largest outdoor equipment suppliers.

KEEPING IN TOUCH

MAIL

SENDING MAIL TO GERMANY

Mark envelopes "air mail" or "par avion" to avoid having letters sent by sea.

Australia: Allow 4-7 days for regular **airmail** to Germany. Postcards and letters up to 20g cost AUS$1; packages up to 50g AUS$1.50, up to 2kg AUS$46. **EMS** can get a letter to Germany in 3-5 days for AUS$32. www.auspost.com.au/pac.

Canada: Allow 4-7 days for regular **airmail** to Germany. Postcards and letters up to 20g cost CDN$0.95; packages up to 0.5kg CDN$10.45, up to 2kg CDN$39.20. www.canadapost.ca/CPC2/common/rates/ratesgen.html#international.

Ireland: Allow 3-4 days for regular airmail to Germany. Postcards and letters up to 25g cost IR£0.32. Add IR£2.30 for Swiftpost International. www.anpost.ie.

New Zealand: Allow 6-12 days for regular airmail to Germany. Postcards NZ$1.10. Letters up to 20g cost NZ$1.80-6; small parcels up to 0.5kg NZ$13.20, up to 2kg NZ$41.70. www.nzpost.co.nz/nzpost/inrates.

UK: Allow 3 days for airmail to Germany. Letters up to 20g cost UK£0.36; packages up to 0.5kg UK£2.67, up to 2kg UK£9.42. UK Swiftair delivers letters a day faster for UK£2.85 more. www.royalmail.co.uk/calculator.

US: Allow 4-7 days for regular **airmail** to Germany. Postcards/aerogrammes cost US55¢/60¢; letters under 1 oz. US$1. Packages under 1 lb. cost US$7.20; larger packages cost a variable amount (around US$15). **US Express Mail** takes 2-3 days and costs US$19/$23 (0.5/1 lb.). **US Global Priority Mail** delivers small/large flat-rate envelopes to Germany in 3-5 days for US$5/$9. http://ircalc.usps.gov.

Additionally, **Federal Express** (Australia ☎ 13 26 10; US and Canada ☎ (800) 247-4747; New Zealand ☎ (0800) 73 33 39; UK ☎ (0800) 12 38 00) handles express mail services from most of the above countries to Germany; for example, they can get a letter from New York to Germany in 2 days for US$25.50. Rates among non-US locations are prohibitively expensive (New York to Berlin, for example, costs upwards of $20 for overnight mail, depending on the weight). By **US Express Mail,** a letter from New York would arrive within four days and would cost US$1.

RECEIVING MAIL IN GERMANY
There are several ways to arrange pick-up of letters sent to you by friends and relatives while you are abroad.

General Delivery: Mail can be sent to Germany through **Poste Restante** (the international phrase for General Delivery; *Postlagernde Briefe*) to almost any city or town with a post office. Address *Poste Restante* letters to: Katie SCHULTZ, *Postlagernde Briefe*, D-20099 Hamburg, Germany. When picking up your mail, bring a form of photo ID, preferably a passport. There is generally no surcharge; if there is a charge, it generally does not exceed the cost of domestic postage. If the clerks insist that there is nothing for you, have them check under your first name as well. *Let's Go* lists post offices in the **Practical Information** section for each city and most towns.

American Express: AmEx's travel offices throughout the world offer a free **Client Letter Service** (mail held up to 30 days and forwarding upon request) for cardholders who contact them in advance. Address the letter in the same way shown above. Some offices will offer these services to non-cardholders (especially AmEx Travelers Cheque holders), but call ahead to make sure. *Let's Go* lists AmEx office locations for most large cities in **Practical Information** sections; for a complete, free list, call (800) 528-4800.

Surface mail is by far the cheapest and slowest way to send mail. It takes 1 to 3 months to cross the Atlantic and 2 to 4 to cross the Pacific—appropriate for sending large quantities of items you won't need to see for a while. When ordering books and materials from abroad, always include 1 or 2 **International Reply Coupons (IRCs)**—a way of providing the postage to cover delivery. IRCs should be available from your local post office and those abroad (US$1.05).

TELEPHONES
CALLING GERMANY FROM HOME
To call Germany direct from home, dial:
1. The **international access code** of your home country. **Access codes** include: Australia 0011, Ireland 00, New Zealand 00, South Africa 09, UK 00, US. 011.
2. 49 (Germany's country code).
3. The city code (see the city's **Practical Information** section) and local number. City codes are sometimes listed with a zero in front (e.g., 030), but after dialing the country code, drop initial zero (with an access code of 011 49, e.g., 011 49 30)

CALLING HOME FROM GERMANY

A calling card is probably your best and cheapest bet. Calls are billed either collect or to your account. **MCI WorldPhone** also provides access to MCI's Traveler's Assist, which gives legal and medical advice, exchange rate information, and translation services. Other phone companies provide similar services to travelers. To obtain a calling card from your national telecommunications service before you leave home, contact the appropriate company below.

USA: AT&T (☎(888) 288 4685); **Sprint** (☎(800) 877 4646); or **MCI** (☎(800) 444 4141).

Canada: Bell Canada **Canada Direct** (☎(800) 565 4708).

UK: British Telecom **BT Direct** (☎(800) 34 51 44).

Ireland: Telecom Éireann **Ireland Direct** (☎(0800) 250 250).

Australia: Telstra **Australia Direct** (☎13 22 00)

New Zealand: Telecom New Zealand (☎(0800) 000 000).

South Africa: Telkom South Africa (☎09 03).

To call home with a calling card, contact the Germany operator for your service provider by dialing:

AT&T: ☎(0800) 2255 288.

Sprint: ☎(0800) 8880 013.

MCI WorldPhone Direct: ☎(0800) 888 8000.

Canada Direct: ☎(0800) 888 0014.

BT Direct: ☎(0130) 80 0144.

Ireland Direct: ☎(0800) 180 0027.

Australia Direct: ☎(0130) 80 0061.

Telecom New Zealand Direct: ☎(0130) 80 0064.

Telkom South Africa Direct: ☎(0800) 180 0027.

Wherever possible, use a calling card for international phone calls, as the long-distance rates for national phone services are often exorbitant. German **Telefonkarten** (see below) can be used for direct international calls. Although incredibly convenient, in-room hotel calls invariably include an arbitrary and sky-high surcharge (as much as US$10).

If you do dial direct, you must first insert a *Telefonkarte*, then dial 00 (the international access code for Germany), and then dial the country code and number of your home. **Country codes** include: Australia 61; Ireland 353; New Zealand 64; South Africa 27; UK 44; US and Canada 1.

The expensive alternative to dialing direct or using a calling card is using an international operator to place a **collect call.** An English-speaking operator from your home nation can be reached by dialing the appropriate service provider listed above, and they will typically place a collect call even if you don't possess one of their phone cards.

CALLING WITHIN GERMANY

You can always be sure of finding a **public phone** *(Telefonzelle)* in a post office. Additionally, phones are located at all train and bus stations, on ICE trains, and on nearly every other street corner. Most public phones only accept telephone cards, though restaurants and bars sometimes have coin-operated phones. Telephones in transport hubs and near major attractions sometimes give you the option of paying by **credit card.** You can pick up a **Telefonkarte** (phone card) in post offices, at a *Kiosk* (newsstand), or at selected Deutsche Bahn counters in major train stations. The cards come in DM12, DM24, and DM50 denominations. If you purchase a card at a *Kiosk*, the salesperson will insert it in a machine to show you the balance.

To place **inter-city calls,** dial the **Vorwahl** (area code), including the first zero that appears in the code, followed by the **Rufnummer** (telephone number). There is no standard length for telephone numbers. The smaller the city, the more digits in the city code, while telephone numbers tend to have three to ten digits. The **national information number** is 11 833. For **international information,** call 118 34. **Phone rates** tend to be highest in the morning and afternoon, lower in the evening, and lowest after 9 p.m. and on Sundays and holidays. *Let's Go: Germany* lists **phone codes** at the end of each **Practical Information** section throughout the guide.

EMAIL AND INTERNET

While Germany lagged behind the US and UK for many years in the internet arena, more and more German citizens and companies are coming to rely on email and the web as a means of communication. Most German cities as well as a surprising number of smaller towns have at least one **internet cafe,** where patrons can check email, surf the web, and sip cappuccinos to the tune of DM3-7 per half hour. In addition, some German universities have banks of computers hooked up to the internet in their libraries, though ostensibly for student use. *Let's Go: Germany* lists internet access after post offices in the **Practical Information** section. For advice on traveling with the use of the internet, see the **World Wide Web,** p. 84.

Many web-based email providers offer **free email accounts;** check out Hotmail (www.hotmail.com), RocketMail (www.rocketmail.com), or Yahoo! Mail (www.yahoo.com) to subscribe. Most providers are funded by advertising and some may require subscribers to fill out a questionnaire. Almost every internet search engine has an affiliated free email service.

Travelers who have the luxury of a laptop with them can use a **modem** to call an internet service provider. Long-distance phone cards specifically intended for such calls can defray normally high phone charges. Check with your long-distance phone provider to see if they offer this option.

GETTING THERE

BY PLANE

When it comes to airfare, a little effort can save you a bundle. If your plans are flexible enough to deal with the restrictions, courier fares are the cheapest. Tickets bought from consolidators and standby seating are also good deals, but last-minute specials, airfare wars, and charter flights often beat these fares. The key is to hunt around, be flexible, and persistently ask about discounts. Students, seniors, and those under 26 should never pay full price for a ticket.

DETAILS AND TIPS

Timing: Airfares to Germany peak between June and September, and holidays are also expensive periods in which to travel. Midweek (M-Th morning) round-trip flights run US$40-50 cheaper than weekend flights. Return-date flexibility is usually not an option for the budget traveler; traveling with an "open return" ticket can be pricier than fixing a return date when buying the ticket and paying later to change it.

Route: Round-trip flights are by far the cheapest; "open-jaw" (arriving in and departing from different cities) and round-the-world, or RTW, flights are pricier but reasonable alternatives. Patching one-way flights together is the least economical way to travel. Flights between capital cities or regional hubs will offer the most competitive fares; Frankfurt will generally be the least expensive destination.

Boarding: Whenever flying internationally, pick up tickets for international flights well in advance of the departure date, and confirm by phone within 72 hours of departure. Most airlines require that passengers arrive at the airport at least 2 hours before departure. However, for scheduled flights departing from an EU country, you are entitled to full compensation if a flight is overbooked and you have a confirmed ticket (indicated by an 'ok' in the relevant box on the ticket), provided that you check in on time. One carry-on item (max 5kg) and 2 pieces of checked baggage (max 60kg) is the norm for non-courier flights; for flights within Europe, the checked baggage allowance is normally 20-30kg, regardless of the number of pieces. Consult the airline for weight allowances.

FLIGHT PLANNING ON THE INTERNET The Web is a great place to look for travel bargains—it's fast, it's convenient, and you can spend as long as you like exploring options without driving your travel agent insane.

Many airline sites offer special last-minute deals on the Web. Other sites do the legwork and compile the deals for you—try www.bestfares.com, www.one-travel.com, www.lowestfare.com, and www.travelzoo.com.

STA (www.sta-travel.com) and **Council** (www.counciltravel.com) provide quotes on student tickets, while **Expedia** (msn.expedia.com) and **Travelocity** (www.travelocity.com) offer full travel services. **Priceline** (www.priceline.com) allows you to specify a price, and obligates you to buy any ticket that meets or beats it; be prepared for antisocial hours and odd routes. **Skyauction** (www.skyauction.com) allows you to bid on both last-minute and advance-purchase tickets.

Just one last note—to protect yourself, make sure that the site uses a secure server before handing over any credit card details. Happy hunting!

Fares: Round-trip fares to Western Europe from the US range from US$400-600 (during the off season) to US$700-1000 (during the summer). Round-trip flights from the UK to Frankfurt are a comparative snip at UK£100-180.

BUDGET AND STUDENT TRAVEL AGENCIES

A knowledgeable agent specializing in flights to Germany can make your life easy and help you save, too, but agents may not spend the time to find you the lowest possible fare—they get paid on commission. Students and under-26ers holding **ISIC and IYTC cards** (see **Identification,** p. 40), respectively, qualify for big discounts from student travel agencies. Most flights from budget agencies are on major airlines, but in peak season some may sell seats on less reliable chartered aircraft.

usit world (www.usitworld.com). Over 50 **usit campus** branches in the UK (www.usitcampus.co.uk), including 52 Grosvenor Gardens, **London** SW1W 0AG (☎(0870) 240 1010); **Manchester** (☎(0161) 273 17 21); and **Edinburgh** (☎(0131) 668 33 03). Nearly 20 **usit now** offices in Ireland, including 19-21 Aston Quay, O'Connell Bridge, **Dublin** 2 (☎(01) 602 16 00; www.usitnow.ie), and **Belfast** (☎(02890) 32 71 11; www.usitnow.com). Offices also in Athens, Auckland, Brussels, Frankfurt, Johannesburg, Lisbon, Luxembourg, Madrid, Paris, Sofia, and Warsaw.

Council Travel (www.counciltravel.com). US offices include: Emory Village, 1561 N. Decatur Rd., **Atlanta,** GA 30307 (☎(404) 377 9997); 273 Newbury St., **Boston,** MA 02116 (☎(617) 266 1926); 1160 N. State St., **Chicago,** IL 60610 (☎(312) 951 0585); 931 Westwood Blvd., Westwood, **Los Angeles,** CA 90024 (☎(310) 208 3551); 254 Greene St., **New York,** NY 10003 (☎(212) 254 2525); 530 Bush St., **San Francisco,** CA 94108 (☎(415) 566 6222); 424 Broadway Ave E., **Seattle,** WA 98102 (☎(206) 329 4567); 3301 M St. NW, **Washington, D.C.** 20007 (☎(202) 337 6464). **For US cities not listed,** call (800) 2-COUNCIL (226 8624). In the UK, 28A Poland St. (Oxford Circus), **London,** W1V 3DB (☎(020) 74 37 77 67).

CTS Travel, 44 Goodge St., **London** W1 (☎(020) 76 36 00 31; fax 76 37 53 28; email ctsinfo@ctstravel.com.uk).

STA Travel, 6560 Scottsdale Rd. #F100, Scottsdale, AZ 85253 (☎(800) 777 0112; fax (602) 922 0793; www.sta-travel.com). A student and youth travel organization with over 150 offices worldwide. Ticket booking, travel insurance, railpasses, and more. US offices include: 297 Newbury St., **Boston,** MA 02115 (☎(617) 266-6014); 429 S. Dearborn St., **Chicago,** IL 60605 (☎(312) 786-9050); 7202 Melrose Ave., **Los Angeles,** CA 90046 (☎(323) 934-8722); 10 Downing St., **New York,** NY 10014 (☎(212) 627-3111); 2401 Pennsylvania Ave., Ste. G, **Washington, D.C.** 20037 (☎(202) 887-0912); 51 Grant Ave., **San Francisco,** CA 94108 (☎(415) 391-8407). In the UK, 11 Goodge St., **London** WIP 1FE (☎(020) 7436 7779 for North American travel). In New Zealand, 10 High St., **Auckland** (☎(09) 309 0458). In Australia, 366 Lygon St., **Melbourne** Vic 3053 (☎(03) 9349 4344).

Travel CUTS (Canadian Universities Travel Services Limited), 187 College St., **Toronto,** ON M5T 1P7 (☎(416) 979-2406; fax 979-8167; www.travelcuts.com). 40 offices across Canada. Also in the UK, 295-A Regent St., **London** W1R 7YA (☎(020) 7255 1944).

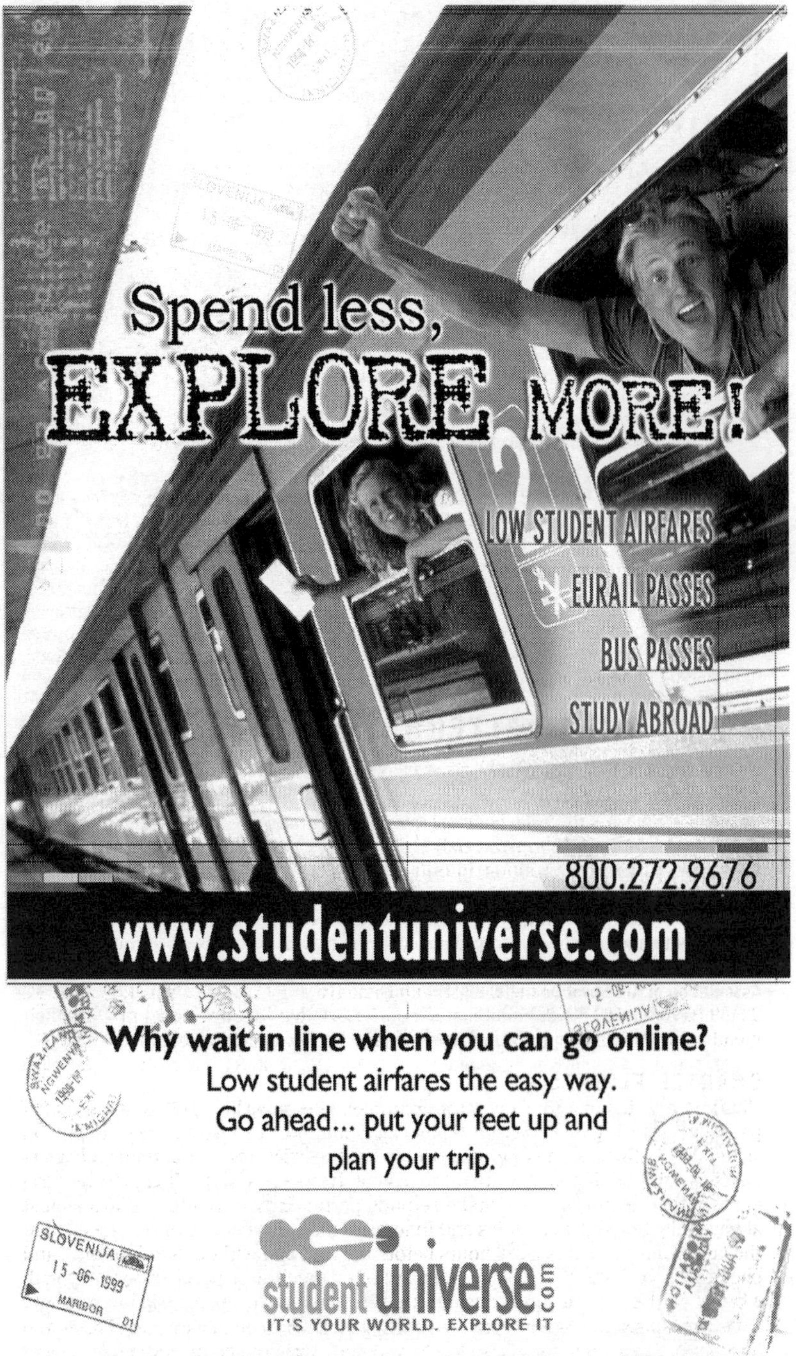

ESSENTIALS

Wasteels, Platform 2, Victoria Station, London SW1V 1JT (☎(020) 7834 7066; fax 7630 7628; www.wasteels.dk/uk). A huge chain in Europe, with 203 locations. Sells the Wasteels BIJ tickets, which are discounted (30-45% off regular fare), 2nd-class international point-to-point train tickets with unlimited stopovers for those under 26 (sold only in Europe).

COMMERCIAL AIRLINES

The commercial airlines' lowest regular offer is the **APEX** (Advance Purchase Excursion) fare, which provides confirmed reservations and allows "open-jaw" tickets. Generally, reservations must be made 7 to 21 days in advance, with 7- to 14-day minimum and up to 90-day maximum-stay limits, and hefty cancellation and change penalties (fees rise in summer). Book peak-season APEX fares early, since by May you will have a hard time getting the departure date you want.

Although APEX fares are probably not the cheapest possible fares, they will give you a sense of the average commercial price from which to measure other bargains. Specials advertised in newspapers may be cheaper but have more restrictions and fewer available seats. Popular carriers to Germany include:

Deutsche Lufthansa (☎(800) 645 3880 in the US and (800) 563 5954 in Canada; www.lufthansa.com), is Germany's premier airline and offers flights to the most cities, but fares tend to be high.

Icelandair (☎(800) 223 5500; www.centrum.is/icelandair), has last-minute offers and a standby fare from New York to Luxembourg. Reservations must be made within 3 days of departure.

KLM (☎(800) 374 7747; www.klm.com), is Dutch airline, with services throughout Europe and several North American cities.

LTU (☎(800) 888 0200; www.ltu.com), offers very reasonable rates to a number of German cities, including Frankfurt, Hamburg, and Düsseldorf. Service is only out of Miami, Orlando, Ft. Myers, and Los Angeles.

OTHER CHEAP ALTERNATIVES

AIR COURIER FLIGHTS

Couriers help transport cargo on international flights by guaranteeing delivery of the baggage claim slips from the company to a representative overseas. Generally, couriers must travel light (carry-ons only) and deal with complex restrictions on their flight. Most flights are round-trip only with short fixed-length stays (usually one week) and a limit of a single ticket per issue. Most of these flights also operate only out of the biggest cities, like New York. Generally, you must be over 21 (in some cases 18), have a valid passport, and procure your own visa, if necessary. Groups such as the **Air Courier Association** (☎(800) 282 1202; www.aircourier.org) and the **International Association of Air Travel Couriers,** 220 South Dixie Hwy., P.O. Box 1349, Lake Worth, FL 33460 (☎(561) 582 8320; email iaatc@courier.org; www.courier.org) provide their members with lists of opportunities and courier brokers worldwide for an annual fee.

CHARTER FLIGHTS

Charters are flights a tour operator contracts with an airline to fly extra loads of passengers during peak season. They can sometimes be cheaper than flights on scheduled airlines, some operate nonstop, and restrictions on minimum advance-purchase and minimum stay are more lenient. However, charter flights fly less frequently than major airlines, make refunds particularly difficult, and are almost always fully booked. Schedules and itineraries may also change or be cancelled at the last moment (as late as 48 hours before the trip, and without a full refund), and check-in, boarding, and baggage claim are often much slower. As always, pay with a credit card if you can, and consider traveler's insurance against trip interruption.

Discount clubs and **fare brokers** offer members' savings on last-minute charter and tour deals. Study their contracts closely; you don't want to end up with an unwanted overnight layover. **Travelers Advantage,** Stamford, CT (☎(800) 548 1116; www.travelersadvantage.com; specializes in European travel and tour packages ($US60 annual fee).

STANDBY FLIGHTS

To travel standby, you will need considerable flexibility in the dates and cities of your arrival and departure. Companies that specialize in standby flights don't sell tickets but rather the promise that you will get to your destination (or near your destination) within a certain window of time (anywhere from 1-5 days). You may only receive a refund if all available flights which depart within your date-range from the specified region are full, but future travel credit is always available.

Carefully read agreements with any company offering standby flights, as tricky fine print can leave you in the lurch. To check on a company's service record, call the Better Business Bureau of New York City (☎(212) 533 6200). It is difficult to receive refunds, and clients' vouchers will not be honored when an airline fails to receive payment in time.

Airhitch, 2641 Broadway, 3rd fl., New York, NY 10025 (☎(800) 326 2009 or (212) 864 2000; fax 864 5489; www.airhitch.org) and Los Angeles, CA (☎(310) 726 5000). In Europe, the flagship office is in Paris (☎01 47 00 16 30) and the other one is in Amsterdam (☎(020) 626 32 20). Flights to Europe cost US$159 each way when departing from the Northeast, $239 from the West Coast or Northwest, $209 from the Midwest, and $189 from the Southeast. Travel within the USA and Europe is also possible, with rates ranging $79-139.

TICKET CONSOLIDATORS

Ticket consolidators, or **"bucket shops,"** buy unsold tickets in bulk from commercial airlines and sell them at discounted rates. The best place to look is in the Sunday travel section of a major newspaper, where many bucket shops place tiny ads. Call quickly, as availability is typically extremely limited. Not all bucket shops are reliable establishments, so insist on a receipt that gives full details of restrictions, refunds, and tickets, and pay by credit card.

TRAVELING FROM THE US AND CANADA

Travel Avenue (☎(800) 333-3335; www.travelavenue.com) attempts to beat best-available published fares using several consolidators (for a fee). **NOW Voyager,** 74 Varick St., #307, New York, NY 10013 (☎(212) 431-1616; fax 219-1793; www.now-voyagertravel.com) arranges discounted flights, mostly from New York, to Barcelona, London, Madrid, Milan, Paris, and Rome. Other consolidators worth trying are **Interworld** (☎(305) 443-4929; fax 443-0351); **Pennsylvania Travel** (☎(800) 331-0947); **Rebel** (☎(800) 227-3235; email travel@rebeltours.com; www.rebeltours.com); **Cheap Tickets** (☎(800) 377-1000; www.cheaptickets.com); and **Travac** (☎(800) 872-8800; fax (212) 714-9063; www.travac.com). Yet more consolidators on the web include the **Internet Travel Network** (www.itn.com); **SurplusTravel.com** (www.surplustravel.com); **Travel Information Services** (www.tiss.com); **TravelHUB** (www.travelhub.com); and **The Travel Site** (www.thetravelsite.com). Keep in mind that these are just suggestions to get you started in your research; *Let's Go* does not endorse any of these agencies. As always, be cautious, and research companies before you hand over your credit card number.

TRAVELING FROM THE UK, AUSTRALIA, AND NEW ZEALAND

In London, the **Air Travel Advisory Bureau** (☎(020) 7636 5000; www.atab.co.uk) can provide names of reliable consolidators and discount flight specialists. From Australia and New Zealand, look for consolidator ads in the travel section of the *Sydney Morning Herald* and other papers.

FURTHER READING: BY PLANE

Air Courier Bargains, Kelly Monaghan. The Intrepid Traveler (US$15).

Courier Air Travel Handbook, Mark Field. Perpetual Press (US$10).

Consolidators FAQ (www.travel-library.com/air-travel/consolidators.html).

Consolidators: Air Travel's Bargain Basement, Kelly Monaghan. Intrepid Traveler (US$8).

The Worldwide Guide to Cheap Airfare, Michael McColl. Insider Publications (US$15).

Discount Airfares: The Insider's Guide, George Hobart. Priceless Publications (US$14).

The Official Airline Guide, an expensive tome available at many libraries, has flight schedules, fares, and reservation numbers.

Travelocity (www.travelocity.com). A searchable online database of published airfares. Online reservations.

Air Traveler's Handbook (www.cs.cmu.edu/afs/cs.cmu.edu/user/mkant/Public/Travel/airfare.html).

TravelHUB (www.travelhub.com). A directory of travel agents that includes a searchable database of fares from over 500 consolidators.

BY TRAIN

European trains retain the charm and romance their North American counterparts lost long ago. Nevertheless, bring food and a water bottle; the on-board cafe can be pricey, and train water undrinkable. Lock your compartment door and keep your valuables on your person.

Many train stations have different counters for domestic and international tickets, seat reservations, and information—check before lining up. Even with a railpass, reservations are often required on major lines, and are advisable during the busier holiday seasons; make them at least a few hours in advance at the train station (US$3-10). Use of many of Europe's high speed or quality trains (such as EuroCity and InterCity) requires a supplementary expenditure for those traveling with German railpasses.

For overnight travel, a tight, open bunk called a **couchette** is an affordable luxury, but watch your luggage. (About US$20; reserve at the station several days in advance.) Germany and the EU offer youth ticket discounts and youth railpasses. (See **Getting Around,** below.)

BY FERRY

Travel by boat is a bewitching alternative favored by Europeans but often over-looked by foreigners. Most European ferries are comfortable and well-equipped. Check in at least two hours early for a prime spot and allow plenty of time for late trains and getting to the port. Fares jump sharply in July and August. Ask for dis-counts; ISIC holders can often get student fares, and Eurail passholders get many reductions and free trips; check the brochure that comes with your railpass. You'll occasionally have to pay a small port tax (under US$10).

Ferries in the **North** and **Baltic Seas** are reliable and go everywhere. Ferries run from Hamburg, Kiel, Travemünde, Rostock, and Saßnitz to England, Scandinavia, Poland, the Baltic States, and Russia. Those content with deck passage rarely need to book ahead. If you really have travel time to spare, **Ford's Travel Guides,** 19448 Londelius St., Northridge, CA 91324 (☎818-701-7414; fax 701-7415) lists **freighter companies** that will take passengers worldwide. Ask for their *Freighter Travel Guide and Waterways of the World* (US$16, plus US$2.50 postage if mailed outside the US).

GETTING AROUND

BY TRAIN

Averaging 120km ☎ and connecting some 7,000 locations, the **Deutsche Bahn** network is Europe's best, and also one of its most expensive, although many discount oppor-tunities exist (see below). "In Germany, the trains run on time." It's a cliché, almost a joke, and not infallibly true. At the same time, it brings up an important truth about getting around in Germany—if the trains aren't perfect, they do go almost every-where a traveler would want to, with the exception of some very rural areas. In fact, the train system's obligation to run lines to inaccessible areas, even at a loss, is writ-ten into Germany's Basic Law. The German Rail webpage (www.bahn.de) is excel-lent; to check out times and prices go directly to http://bahn.hafas.de.

S-Bahn trains are commuter rail lines that run from a city's center to its suburbs; they are frequently integrated with the local subway or streetcar system. **RE** (Region-alExpress) and the slightly slower **RB** (RegionalBahn) trains include a number of rail networks between neighboring cities. **IR** (InterRegio) trains, covering larger net-works between cities, are speedy and comfortable. **D** trains are foreign trains that serve international routes. **EC** (EuroCity) and **IC** (InterCity) trains zoom along between major cities every hour 6am-10pm. Even the IC yields to the futuristic **ICE** (InterCityExpress) trains, which approach the luxury and kinetics of an airplane and run at speeds up to 280km per hour. You must purchase a **Zuschlag** (supplement) to ride an ICE, IC or EC train. (DM7 when bought in the station, DM9 on the train.)

Most German cities have a **main train station;** in German, **der Hauptbahnhof.** Unless otherwise noted, this is the location referred to when *Let's Go* gives directions "from the station." In train stations, yellow signs indicate departures *(Abfahrt)*, and white signs indicate arrivals *(Ankunft)*. The number under *Gleis* is the track number.

Second-class travel is pleasant, and compartments are excellent places to meet people of all ages and nationalities. Larger train stations have different counters for domestic tickets, international tickets, seat reservations, and information; check before lining up. On major lines, reservations are advisable even if you have a railpass; make them at least a few hours in advance at the train station.

Most European and German railpasses are best purchased before you leave home. Contact a domestic **budget travel agency** (see p. 65). Alternatively, contact Deutsche Bahn through their web page (www.bahn.de), or, once in Germany, by calling their toll-free hotline (☎(0180) 599 66 33).

GERMAN RAILPASSES

DEUTSCHE BAHN PASS. Designed for tourists, the German Railpass allows unlimited travel for four to 10 days within a four-week period. Non-Europeans can purchase German Railpasses in their home countries and—with a passport—in major German train stations. A second-class Railpass costs US$196 for 5 days of unlimited travel and $306 for 10. The **German Rail Youth Pass,** for tourists under 26, is US$156 for 5 days and $198 for 9. The second-class **Twin Pass,** for two adults traveling together, is US$294 for 5 days and $459 for 10.

BAHNCARD. A great option for those making frequent and extensive use of German trains for more than one month, the Bahncard is valid one year and entitles you to a 50% discount on all trains. Passes are available at major train stations and require a passport-sized photo. A **second-class** pass is DM260; a pass for those aged 17-22 or over 60, or any student under 27, is DM130; students under 17 pay DM65.

YOUTH, STUDENT, AND DISCOUNT FARES. Travelers under 26 can purchase **TwenTickets,** which knock 20-60% off fares over DM10; be sure to have an ID proving of your age. A **Schönes-Wochenende-Ticket** offers a fantastic deal for weekend trips. For a single price of DM35, up to five people receive unlimited travel on any of the slower trains (*not* ICE, IC, EC, D, or IR) from 12:01am Saturday until 2am on Monday. Single travelers often find larger groups who are amenable to sharing their ticket, either free or for a fraction of the purchase cost. The **Guten-Abend-Ticket** provides an excellent deal for long-distance night travel and entitles its holders to travel anywhere (*not* on InterCityNight or CityNightLines) in Germany between 7pm and 2am. Second-class tickets are DM59, with ICE surcharge DM69; first-class DM99, with ICE surcharge DM109; Friday and Sunday DM15 extra.

EUROPE-WIDE RAIL PASSES

There are two primary international European railpasses: the **Eurailpass** and the **Europass.** They are a good deal for travelers looking to cover a lot of ground in very little time. Ideally conceived, a railpass allows you to jump on any train in a given portion of Europe, go where you want whenever you want, and change your plans at will. In practice, it's not so simple. You still must stand in line to pay for supplements, seat reservations, and couchette reservations, as well as to have your pass validated when you first use it. More important, railpasses don't always pay off. For ballpark estimates, consult the **DER Travel** (www.dertravel.com) or the **RailEurope** railpass brochure (www.raileurope.com) for prices of **point-to-point** tickets. Add them up and compare with railpass prices. It may turn out that for a tour of Germany, Deutsche Bahn Passes, not Eurail nor Europass, are a better option.

Eurailpasses and Europasses can be purchased only by non-Europeans almost exclusively from non-European distributors. These passes must be sold at uniform prices determined by the EU, so no one travel agent is better than another as far as the price itself is concerned. However, some agents tack on a US$10 handling fee. Also, agents often offer different perks with purchase of a railpass, so shop around. Under both pass plans, children 4-11 pay half of adult prices.

EURAILPASS. Eurailpasses are valid in Austria, Belgium, Denmark, Finland, France, Germany, Greece, Hungary, the Republic of Ireland, Italy, Luxembourg, the Netherlands, Norway, Portugal, Spain, Sweden, and Switzerland. With your railpass you will receive a timetable for major routes and a map with details on possible ferry, steamer, bus, car rental, and hotels, and **Eurostar.**

  Eurail Saverpass: Unlimited 1st-class travel for those traveling in a group of 2-5. 15 days US$470; 21 days $610; 1 month $1072; 2 months $1072; 3 months $1324.

  Eurail Youthpass: Unlimited 2nd-class travel for those aged 12-25. 15 days US$388; 21 days $499; 1 month $623; 2 months $882; 3 months $1089.

  Youth Flexipasses: 2nd-class travel for those under 26. Days can be distributed over 2months: 10 days (US$458), 15 days (US$599). Children 4-11 pay half price, and children under 4 travel free.

EUROPASS. With a Europass you can travel in France, Germany, Italy, Spain, and Switzerland for five to 15 days within a window of two months. Second-class youth tickets begin at US$233 and increase incrementally by US$29 for each additional day of travel. With purchase of a first-class adult ticket, starting at US$348, you can buy an identical ticket for your traveling partner at a 40% discount. You can add associate countries for a fee; call for information. Be sure to plan your itineraries in advance before buying a Europass; you may be fined if you cut through a country you haven't purchased. Europasses are not appropriate if you like to take lots of side trips—you'll waste rail days.

PURCHASING A RAILPASS. You'll find it easiest to buy a Eurailpass before you arrive in Europe; virtually any travel agency handling Europe can sell them (p. 65), as does **Rail Europe,** 500 Mamaroneck Ave., Harrison, NY 10528 (in the US ☎ (800) 438-7245; fax (800) 432-1329; in Canada ☎ (800) 361-7245; fax (905) 602-4198; www.raileurope.com). If you're stuck in Europe and unable to find someone to sell you a Eurailpass, call an American railpass agent, who can send a pass by express mail. Eurailpasses are not refundable once validated, and you can get a replacement for a lost pass only if you have purchased insurance on it under the Pass Protection Plan (US$10).

INTERRAIL PASS. Travelers who have resided in Europe for more than six months and plan to travel through more than one country should consider InterRail Passes. For information and ticket sales in Europe, contact **Student Travel Center,** 24 Rupert St., 1st fl., London, W1V 7FN (☎ (020) 74 37 01 21, 74 37 63 70 or 74 37 81 01; fax 77 34 38 36; www.student-travel-centre.com). Tickets should be purchased in your country of residence and are available from travel agents and at larger train stations.

> **Under 26 InterRail Card:** 14 days or 1 month of unlimited travel within 1, 2, 3 or all of the 7 zones into which InterRail divides Europe. If you buy a ticket which includes your country of residence, you must pay 50% of the fare for travel within your country. UK£159-259.

> **Over 26 InterRail Card:** unlimited 2nd-class travel in 20 countries (Austria, Bulgaria, Croatia, Czech Republic, Denmark, Finland, Germany, Greece, Hungary, Republic of Ireland, Luxembourg, Netherlands, Norway, Poland, Romania, Slovakia, Slovenia, Sweden, Turkey, and Yugoslavia) for 15 days or 1 month. UK£215-275.

BY BUS

Germany does have a few regions that are inaccessible by train, and some bus lines fill the gaps. Bus service between cities and to outlying areas run from the local **Zentralomnibusbahnhof (ZOB),** which is usually close to the main train station. Buses are often slightly more expensive than the train for comparable distances. Railpasses are not valid on any buses other than a few run by Deutsche Bahn.

Europe's largest coach operator is **Eurolines,** 4 Cardiff Rd., Luton LU1 1PP (☎ (08705) 143 219; fax (01582) 400 694; in London, 52 Grosvenor Gardens, Victoria (☎ (01582) 404 511); email welcome@eurolines.uk.com). A **Eurolines Pass** offers unlimited 30-day (under 26 and over 60 UK£159; 26-60 UK£199) or 60-day (UK£199/ £249) travel between 30 major cities. Eurolines also offers **Euro Explorers,** seven travel loops through Europe with set fares and itineraries.

BY CAR

Cars offer speed, freedom, access to the countryside, and an escape from the town-to-town mentality of trains. Unfortunately, they also insulate you from the *esprit de corps* of rail traveling. Although a single traveler won't save by renting a car, four usually will. If you can't decide between train and car travel, you may benefit from a combination of the two; Rail Europe and other railpass vendors offer rail-and-drive packages for both individual countries and all of Europe.

German road conditions are generally excellent, with the exception of a few secondary roads in the former GDR that have yet to be renovated. Yes, there is no set speed limit on the **Autobahn,** or German highway; only a recommendation of 130km per hour (81mph) exists. Germans drive *fast.* Make a point to learn local driving signals and signs, and watch for signs indicating right-of-way (usually designated by a yellow triangle). The Autobahn is indicated by an intuitive "A" on signs; secondary highways, where the speed limit is usually 100km per hour, are accompanied by signs bearing a "B." Germans drive on the right side of the road, and it is illegal to pass on the right, even on superhighways. In cities and towns, speeds hover around 30-60kph (around 20-35mph).

Before setting off, know the laws of the countries in which you'll be driving. The **Association for Safe International Road Travel (ASIRT)** can provide more specific information about road conditions. Contact them at 5413 West Cedar Lane 103C, Bethesda, MD 20814 (☎(301) 983 5252; fax 983 3663; email asirt@erols.com; www.asirt.org). Germans use unleaded gas almost exclusively; prices run around DM7 per gallon, or about DM1.80 per liter.

MITFAHRZENTRALEN

Mitfahrzentralen pair up drivers and riders, who pay the agency a fee for the match and then negotiate the payment agreement with their driver.These agencies are indicated in the **Getting There and Getting Around** or **Practical Information** sections of cities throughout the guide. They provide a safe option for travel, as both the vehicle and driver must be registered with the office.

DRIVING PERMITS

Driver's licenses for most countries are valid in Germany for one year, after which a German license is required. Though it's not mandatory, it's strongly advised that you have an **International Driving Permit (IDP).** In case you're in a situation (e.g. an accident or being stranded in a smaller town where the police speak less English), the IDP is an excellent idea; information on the card is printed in ten languages, including German. The IDP, valid for one year, must be issued in your home country before you depart; AAA affiliates cannot issue IDPs valid in their own country. You must be 18 years old to receive the IDP. An application for an IDP usually needs to include one or two photos, a current local license, an additional form of ID, and a fee.

Australia: Contact the Royal Automobile Club (RAC) or the National Royal Motorist Association (NRMA) if in NSW or the ACT (☎(08) 9421 4298; www.rac.com.au/travel). Permits AUS$15.

Canada: Contact any Canadian Automobile Association (CAA) branch office in Canada, or write to CAA, 1145 Hunt Club Rd., Suite 200, K1V 0Y3 Canada. (☎(613) 247-0117; fax 247-0118;www.caa.ca/CAAInternet/travelservices/internationaldocumentation/idp-travel.htm). Permits CDN$10.

Ireland: Contact the nearest Automobile Association (AA) office or the Irish Automobile Association, 23 Suffolk St., Blackrock, Co. Dublin (☎(01) 677 9481). Permits IR£4.

New Zealand: Contact the Automobile Association (AA) or their main office at Auckland Central, 99 Albert St., Auckland (☎(09) 377 4660; fax 302 2037; www.nzaa.co.nz.). Permits NZ$8.

South Africa: Contact the Automobile Association of South Africa at P.O. Box 596, Johannesburg, 2000 (☎(011) 799 1000; fax 799 1010). Permits SAR28.50.

UK: Visit your local AA Shop, contact AA Headquarters (☎(0990) 448 866), or write to the Automobile Association, International Documents, Fanum House, Erskine, Renfrewshire PA8 6BW (☎(990) 500 600). Permits UK£4.

US: Visit any American Automobile Association (AAA) office or write to AAA Florida, Travel Related Services, 1000 AAA Drive (mail stop 100), Heathrow, FL 32746 (☎407-444-7000; fax 444-7380). Permits US$10.

CAR INSURANCE

Third-party insurance is mandatory to drive in Germany. Most gold and platinum credit cards cover standard insurance; otherwise check to make sure that your regular car insurance will carry over onto your rental car. If you rent, lease, or borrow a car, you will need a **green card,** or **International Insurance Certificate,** to prove that you have liability insurance. Obtain it through the car rental agency; most include coverage in their prices—although if your credit card provides insurance, you'll want to turn down the offer provided by the rental agency. If you lease a car, obtain a green card from the dealer. Verify whether your auto insurance applies abroad; even if it does, you will still need a green card to certify this to foreign officials. If you have a collision abroad, the accident will show up on your domestic records if you report it to your insurance company. Rental agencies may require you to purchase theft insurance in countries that they consider to have a high risk of auto theft. Ask your rental agency about Germany.

If you belong to the Australian or American AAA, the British AA, or the Canadian CAA, you are eligible for roadside assistance, discounts on some forms of car insurance, and other road services from the German motor club equivalent, **Allgemeiner Deutscher Automobil Club (ADAC),** Am Westpark 8, 81373 Munich (☎(089) 767 60). All cities have an ADAC branch.

RENTALS

You can **rent** a car from a US-based firm with European offices, from a European-based company with local representatives, or from a tour operator which will arrange a rental for you from a European company at its own rates. Multinationals offer greater flexibility, but tour operators often strike better deals. Expect to pay DM130-180 per week, plus 16% tax, for a teensy car. There is often an extra charge for drivers under 25. Reserve well before leaving for Germany and pay in advance if at all possible. It is always significantly less expensive to reserve a car from the US than doing so once in Germany. Always check if prices quoted include tax, unlimited mileage and collision insurance; some credit card companies cover this automatically. Ask about discounts and check the terms of insurance, particularly the size of the deductible. Non-Europeans should check with their national motoring organization (like AAA or CAA) for international coverage. Ask your airline about special fly-and-drive packages; you may get up to a week of free or discounted rental. Minimum age to rent in Germany is usually 21. At most agencies, all that's needed to rent a car is a US license and proof that you've had it for a year. Rent cars in Europe from these agencies:

Sixt, ☎(0180) 523 22 22; www.sixt.com.

Auto Europe, 39 Commercial St., P.O. Box 7006, Portland, ME 04101 (☎(888) 223 5555; fax 800-235-6321; www.autoeurope.com).

Avis, ☎(800) 331 1084 in US and Canada; in UK, (0990) 900 500; in Australia, (800) 225 533; www.avis.com.

Budget, ☎(800) 472 3325 in the US; in Canada, (800) 527 0700; in the UK, (0800) 181 181; in Australia, 13 2727; www.budgetrentacar.com.

Europe by Car, 1 Rockefeller Plaza, New York, NY 10020 (☎(800) 223 1516, (212) 581 3040; www.europebycar.com).

Europcar, 145 Avenue Malekoff, 75016 Paris (☎(800) 227 3876 in the US; (800) 227 7368 in Canada; 145 00 08 06 in France; www.europcar.com).

Hertz, ☎(800) 654 3001 in the US; in Canada, (800) 263 0600; in the UK, (0990) 996 699; in Australia, 13 30 39; www.hertz.com.

LEASING

For trips longer than 17 days, **leasing** can be cheaper than renting; it is often the only option for those under 21. The cheapest leases are agreements to buy the car and then sell it back to the manufacturer at a prearranged price. As far as you're concerned, though, it's a lease and doesn't entail enormous financial transactions. Leases generally include insurance coverage and are not taxed, though they may include a VAT. Expect to pay at least US$1200 for 60 days. Contact **Auto Europe** or **Europe by Car** (see above).

CAR SAFETY

If you are driving, make sure to learn local driving signals and signs (see **Getting Around: By Car,** p. 72). Wearing a seatbelt is the law in Germany, and children should sit in the rear seat; children under 40lbs. (17kg) should ride only in a specially-designed carseat, available for a small fee from most car rental agencies. Study route maps before you hit the road. If you plan on spending a lot of time on the road, you may want to bring spare parts. For long drives in desolate areas invest in a cellular phone and a roadside assistance program (see p. 73). Be sure to park your vehicle in a garage or well-traveled area. The legal cut-off for blood-alcohol levels is 0.08%. German police strictly enforce driving laws.

SPECIFIC CONCERNS

WOMEN TRAVELERS

Women exploring on their own inevitably face additional safety concerns, but it's easy to be adventurous without taking undue risks. German cities, especially, offers services—from women-only taxi services to **Frauenzentrum** (women's centers)—that cater to women's traveling needs; these resources are listed in the **Practical Information** section. Moreover, German standards of public behavior are fairly reserved, and harassment is less common than in other parts of Europe.

Still, German women inhabit a less central political and economic position, and the *Wende*, the change after reunification, is only slowly shifting this cultural reality. Many vestiges of a patriarchal government remain, both real and symbolic. For example, women have been able to serve in the Federal Republic's armed services since the induction of the **Basic Law** (see p. 16), which retains the possibility of female military service, but only in medical and musical capacity. It was not until 1999 that the Defense Ministry announced that women might soon be able to serve in guard duty capacity within the army, and a German woman appeared before the European Court of Justice to challenge the ban against combat duty; in 2000 the cabinet announced that women will be involved in all aspects of the military. However, in some respects German women have more life choices than anywhere else in the world; laws regarding work leave after birth are very liberal. For more information on feminist initiatives, visit the local *Frauenzentrum* and *Frauenbuchladen* (women's bookstore).

If you are concerned about safety, you might consider staying in hostels which offer single rooms that lock from the inside or in religious organizations that offer rooms for women only. Communal showers in some hostels are safer than others; check them before settling in. Stick to centrally located accommodations and avoid solitary late-night treks or subway rides. When traveling, always carry extra money for a phone call, bus, or taxi. **Hitchhiking** is never safe for lone women, or even for two women traveling together. Choose train compartments occupied by other women or couples; ask the conductor to put together a women-only compartment if he or she doesn't offer to do so first. Look as if you know where you're going and consider approaching older women or couples for directions if you're lost or feel uncomfortable.

Generally, the less you look like a tourist, the better off you'll be. Wearing a conspicuous **wedding band** may help prevent unwanted overtures. Some travelers report that carrying pictures of a "husband" or "children" is extremely useful to help document marriage status. Even a mention of a husband waiting back at the hotel may be enough in some places to discount your potentially vulnerable, unattached appearance. In cities, you may be harassed no matter how you're dressed. Your best answer to verbal harassment is no answer at all; feigned deafness, sitting motionless and staring straight ahead at nothing in particular will do a world of good that reacting usually doesn't achieve. The extremely persistent can sometimes be dissuaded by a firm, loud, and very public *Laß mich in Ruhe!* ("Leave me alone!"; LAHSS MEECH IN ROOH-eh). You can often rebuff a harasser by calling attention of passersby to his behavior. Don't hesitate to seek out a police officer or a passerby if you are being harassed.

Memorize the emergency numbers in Germany—**police: 110** and **ambulance: 112.** *Let's Go: Germany* lists other emergency numbers (including rape crisis lines) in the **Practical Information** listings of most cities. Carry a **whistle** or an airhorn on your keychain, and don't hesitate to use it in an emergency. An **IMPACT Model Mugging** self-defense course will not only prepare you for a potential attack, but will also raise your level of awareness of your surroundings as well as your confidence (see **Self Defense,** p. 47). Women also face some specific health concerns when traveling (see **Women's Health,** p. 53).

FURTHER READING

A Journey of One's Own: Uncommon Advice for the Independent Woman Traveler, Thalia Zepatos. Eighth Mountain Press (US$17).

Adventures in Good Company: The Complete Guide to Women's Tours and Outdoor Trips, Thalia Zepatos. Eighth Mountain Press (US$7).

Active Women Vacation Guide, Evelyn Kaye. Blue Panda Publications (US$18).

Travelers' Tales: Gutsy Women, Travel Tips and Wisdom for the Road, Marybeth Bond. Traveler's Tales (US$8).

A Foxy Old Woman's Guide to Traveling Alone, Jay Ben-Lesser. Crossing Press. (US$11).

TRAVELING ALONE

There are many benefits to traveling alone, among them greater independence and challenge. On the other hand, any solo traveler is a more vulnerable target of harassment and street theft. Lone travelers need to be well-organized and look confident at all times. If questioned, **never admit that you are traveling alone.** Maintain regular contact with someone at home who knows your itinerary.

A number of organizations supply information for solo travelers, and others find travel companions for those who don't want to go alone. A few are listed here:

Connecting: Solo Traveler Network, P.O. Box 29088, Delamont RPO, Vancouver, BC V6J 5C2, Canada (☎/fax (604) 737 7791; www.cstn.org). Bi-monthly newsletter features solo travel tips, single-friendly tips and travel companion ads. Advice and lodging exchanges facilitated between members. Membership US$25-35.

Travel Companion Exchange, P.O. Box 833, Amityville, NY 11701 (☎(631) 454 0880 or (800) 392 1256; www.whytravelalone.com). Publishes the pamphlet *Foiling Pickpockets & Bag Snatchers* (US$4) and *Travel Companions,* a bi-monthly newsletter for single travelers seeking a travel partner. Subscription US$48.

FURTHER READING
Traveling Solo, Eleanor Berman. Globe Pequot (US$17).

OLDER TRAVELERS

Senior citizens are eligible for a wide range of discounts on transportation, museums, movies, theaters, concerts, restaurants, and accommodations in Germany. If you don't see a reduced price listed, ask, and you may be delightfully surprised. Furthermore, Germany's excellent public transportation systems make most places easily accessible for older travelers. Agencies for senior group travel are growing in enrollment and popularity. These are only a few:

Elderhostel, 75 Federal St., Boston, MA 02110, USA (☎(617) 426-7788 or (877) 426-2166; email registration@elderhostel.org; www.elderhos☎org). Organizes 1- to 4-week "educational adventures" in Germany on varied subjects for those 55+.

The Mature Traveler, P.O. Box 50400, Reno, NV 89513, USA (☎(775) 786-7419, credit card orders (800) 460-6676). Deals, discounts, and travel packages for the 50+ traveler. Subscription$30.

FURTHER READING
No Problem! Worldwise Tips for Mature Adventurers, Janice Kenyon. Orca Book Publishers (US$16).

A Senior's Guide to Healthy Travel, Donald L. Sullivan. Career Press (US$15).

Unbelievably Good Deals and Great Adventures That You Absolutely Can't Get Unless You're Over 50, Joan Rattner Heilman. Contemporary Books (US$13).

BISEXUAL, GAY, AND LESBIAN TRAVELERS

Many bisexual, gay, and lesbian visitors to Germany are surprised to find a more acceptable environment than in their home country. While homophobic attitudes persist in rural areas as well as in ultraconservative Bavaria, Germans are generally more tolerant of homosexuality than Americans and Britons, though not quite as accepting as the Dutch. The German word for gay is *Schwul* (Sh-voohl), which refers exclusively to men; for lesbian, it's *Lesbe* (Lays-be). *Let's Go* provides information on local bisexual, gay, and lesbian culture in **Practical Information** listings and **Entertainment and Nightlife** sections of city descriptions. The epicenter of gay life in Germany, and possibly all of Europe, is Berlin (see p. 143). Other major centers include Hamburg (see p. 543), Frankfurt (see p. 426), Köln (see p. 460), and Munich (see p. 264). While tolerance is still very much a new concept in Eastern Germany, fairly prominent gay scenes have developed in Leipzig and, to a lesser extent, Dresden.

Women should look for *Frauencafés* and *Frauenkneipen*. It should be stressed that while such cafes are for women only, they are *not* for lesbians only. The local *Frauenbuchladen* (women's bookstore) is a good resource. There are dozens of regional and national gay and lesbian organizations; two of the largest are the **Bundesverband Homosexualität (BVH),** Greifswalder Str. 224, 10405 Berlin (☎(030) 441 24 98), and the **Schwulenverband Deutschland (SVD),** Friedrichstr. 165, 10117 Berlin (☎(030) 201 08 04). **Out and About** (www.planetout.com) offers a bi-weekly newsletter addressing travel concerns. Listed below are contact organizations, mail-order bookstores and publishers which offer materials addressing some specific concerns.

Gay's the Word, 66 Marchmont St., London WC1N 1AB (☎(020) 7278 7654; email sales@gaystheword.co.uk; www.gaystheword.co.uk). The largest gay and lesbian bookshop in the UK, with both fiction and non-fiction titles. Mail-order service available.

Giovanni's Room, 345 S. 12th St., Philadelphia, PA 19107, USA (☎(215) 923 2960; fax 923 0813; www.queerbooks.com). An international lesbian/feminist and gay bookstore with mail-order service (carries many of the publications listed below).

International Gay and Lesbian Travel Association, 4331 N. Federal Hwy., #304, Fort Lauderdale, FL 33308, USA (☎(954) 776 2626; fax 776-3303; www.iglta.com). An organization of over 1350 companies serving gay and lesbian travelers worldwide.

International Lesbian and Gay Association (ILGA), 81 rue Marché-au-Charbon, B-1000 Brussels, Belgium (☎/fax +32 (2) 502 24 71; www.ilga.org). Not a travel service; provides political information, such as homosexuality laws of individual countries.

FURTHER READING

Spartacus International Gay Guide. Bruno Gmunder Verlag. (US$33).

Damron's Accommodations, and *The Women's Traveller.* Damron Travel Guides (US$14-19). For more info, call US ☎(415) 255-0404 or (800) 462-6654 or check their website (www.damron.com).

Ferrari Guides' Gay Travel A to Z, Ferrari Guides' Men's Travel in Your Pocket, Ferrari Guides' Women's Travel in Your Pocket, and *Ferrari Guides' Inn Places.* Ferrari Guides (US$14-16). For more info, call (602) 863-2408 or (800) 962-2912 or try www.q-net.com.

The Gay Vacation Guide: The Best Trips and How to Plan Them, Mark Chesnut. Citadel Press (US$15).

TRAVELERS WITH DISABILITIES

Germany provides very competent services, information and accessibility to facilities for travelers with disabilities (**Behinderte** or **Schwerbehinderte**). Both national and regional tourist boards provide directories on the accessibility of various accommodations and transportation services. Germany's excellent public transportation systems make most places easily accessible for travelers with disabilities, and many public transport systems are wheelchair-accessible. The international wheelchair icon or a large letter "B" indicates access. Intersections in major cities have audible crossing signals for the blind.

Those with disabilities should inform airlines and hotels of their disabilities when making arrangements for travel; some time may be needed to prepare special accommodations. Call ahead to restaurants, hotels, parks, and other facilities to find out about the existence of ramps, the widths of doors, the dimensions of elevators, etc. All ICE, EC, and IC trains are equipped for **wheelchair accessibility,** and you can request free seat reservations. Rail is probably the most convenient form of travel for disabled travelers in Europe; for more information, contact Deutsche Bahn (see Getting Around: By Train, p. 70). **Guide dog owners** should be aware that Germany requires evidence of rabies vaccination from a licensed veterinarian at least 30 days but not more than 12 months before entering the country; a notarized German translation of this certificate is required. Hertz, Avis, and National car rental agencies have hand-controlled vehicles at some locations.

USEFUL ORGANIZATIONS

Mobility International USA (MIUSA), P.O. Box 10767, Eugene, OR 97440, USA (☎(541) 343-1284 voice and TDD; fax 343-6812; email info@miusa.org; www.miusa.org). Sells *A World of Options: A Guide to International Educational Exchange, Community Service, and Travel for Persons with Disabilities* (US$35).

Moss Rehab Hospital Travel Information Service (☎(215) 456-9600 or (800) CALL-MOSS; email netstaff@mossresourcenet.org; www.mossresourcenet.org). An information resource center on travel-related concerns for those with disabilities.

Society for the Advancement of Travel for the Handicapped (SATH), 347 Fifth Ave., #610, New York, NY 10016 (☎(212) 447-7284; www.sath.org). An advocacy group that publishes the quarterly travel magazine *OPEN WORLD* (free for members, US$13 for nonmembers). Also publishes a wide range of info sheets on disability travel facilitation and destinations. Annual membership US$45, students and seniors US$30.

TOUR AGENCIES

Directions Unlimited, 123 Green Ln., Bedford Hills, NY 10507, USA (☎(914) 241-1700 or (800) 533-5343; www.travel-cruises.com). Specializes in arranging individual and group vacations, tours, and cruises for the physically disabled.

FURTHER READING

Resource Directory for the Disabled, Richard Neil Shrout. Facts on file (US$45).

Wheelchair Through Europe, Annie Mackin. Graphic Language Press (US ☎(760) 944-9594; email niteowl@cts.com; US$13).

MINORITY TRAVELERS

Germany has a significant minority population composed mainly of about two million Turks. In addition, there are about a million residents from the former Yugoslavia. Eastern Germany also has about 100,000 Vietnamese residents. All the same, conspicuously non-German foreigners may stand out in less-traveled parts of both the East and West.

In certain economically depressed regions, tourists of color or members of certain religious groups may feel threatened by the small, but vocal neo-Nazi groups. While they represent only a fraction of the population, Neo-Nazi skinheads in the large cities of former East Germany, as well as in Western Germany, have been known to attack foreigners, especially non-whites. In these areas, common sense will serve you best. Keeping abreast of news of any such attack and then keeping away from the area in which it happened is perhaps the best (and only) real strategy for avoiding trouble.

RELIGIOUS TRAVELERS

The modern Basic Law states that "freedom of faith and conscience as well as freedom of religious or other belief shall be inviolable. The undisturbed practice of religion shall be guaranteed." Germany's legacy as a land of strong Catholic rule under the Holy Roman Empire was followed closely by a long tradition of Protestantism: it was here that Luther nailed his 95 Theses to the church door in Wittenberg, opening the floodgates of reform. Germany has developed as a Christian country (clergy are supported by the government), with the Protestant north slightly outnumbering the Roman Catholic south. Numerous significant monuments to Germany's Christian past stand throughout the country, and most cities of reasonable size have both Catholic and Protestant churches. The total Jewish population in Germany today is approximately 40-50,000 people. The largest Jewish congregations are in Berlin and Frankfurt, which together are home to more than 10,000 Jews; many cities in Germany do not have synagogues. An influx of foreign workers has brought with it a strong Islamic population; today, almost two million Muslims, mostly from Turkey, live in Germany, and mosques can be found in many cities. For information on worship and site-seeing opportunities, contact the following organizations:

Protestant: Kirchenamt der evangelischen Kirche in Deutschland, Herrenhäuser Str. 12, 30419 Hannover (☎(0511) 279 60; fax 279 67 07; email ekd@ekd.de).

Catholic: Katholisches Auslandssekretariat der Deutschen Bischofskonferenz Tourismus und Urlauberselsorge, Kaiser-Friedrich-Str. 9, 53113 Bonn (☎(0228) 91 14 30; fax 911 43 33).

Muslim: Islamische Gemeinschaft Berlin, Gesslerstr. 11, 10829 Berlin (☎/fax (030) 788 48 83; email mohammed.herzog@igdmb.de).

Jewish: Jewish community centers in each of the following cities: **Berlin,** Fasanenstr. 79-80 (☎(030) 880-280); **Bonn,** Tempelstr. 2 (☎/fax (0228) 21 35 60); **Frankfurt,** Westendstr. 43, 60325 (☎(069) 740 72 15; email yg.ssn@online.de); **Munich,** Reichenbachstr. 27, 80469 (☎(089) 202 40 00; fax (089) 201 46 04).

TRAVELERS WITH CHILDREN

Family vacations require that you plan ahead and often that you slow your pace. When deciding where to stay, remember the special needs of young children; if you pick a hostel or a small hotel, call ahead and make sure it's child-friendly. If you rent a car, make sure the rental company provides a car seat for younger children. Consider using a papoose-style device to carry a baby on walking trips. Be sure that your child carries some sort of ID in case of an emergency or if he or she gets lost, and arrange a reunion spot in case of separation when sight-seeing.

Restaurants often have children's menus and discounts. Virtually all museums and tourist attractions also have a children's rate. Children under two generally fly for 10% of the adult airfare on international flights, but this does not necessarily include a seat. International fares are usually discounted 25% for children from two to 11. Finding a private place for breast feeding is often a problem while traveling, so pack accordingly.

FURTHER READING

Backpacking with Babies and Small Children, Goldie Silverman. Wilderness Press (US$10).

Take Your Kids to Europe, Cynthia W. Harriman. Globe Pequot (US$17).

How to take Great Trips with Your Kids, Sanford and Jane Portnoy. Harvard Common Press (US $10).

Have Kid, Will Travel: 101 Survival Strategies for Vacationing With Babies and Young Children, Claire and Lucille Tristram. Andrews and McMeel (US$9).

Adventuring with Children: An Inspirational Guide to World Travel and the Outdoors, Nan Jeffrey. Avalon House Publishing ($15).

Trouble Free Travel with Children, Vicki Lansky. Book Peddlers (US$9).

DIETARY CONCERNS

Although Germany is unapologetically carnivorous, vegetarianism has become increasingly popular in the last ten years (see **Food and Drink,** p. 32). Mad Cow disease, growing health consciousness, and a blooming alternative scene have all contributed to a decline in meat consumption. Vegetarian restaurants have proliferated in larger cities, while health food shops, such as the well-known **Reformhaus,** provide a large selection of vegetarian and vegan products. *Let's Go: Germany* makes an effort to identify restaurants that offer vegetarian and vegan choices. Many of these establishments are ethnic restaurants; traditional German restaurants often offer no genuinely vegetarian dishes. For more information about vegetarian travel, contact:

European Vegetarian Union, Hildegund Scholvien, Friedhofstr. 12, 67693 Fischbach (☎(06305) 272; fax (06305) 52 56; email scholvien@folz.de).

Vegetarian Association of Germany, Blumenstr. 3, 30159 Hannover (☎(0511) 363 20 50; fax (0511) 363 20 07; email www.comlink.apc.org/vbd/).

North American Vegetarian Society, P.O. Box 72, Dolgeville, NY 13329 (☎518-568-7970; email navs@telenet.com; www.cyberveg.org/navs/). Publishes *Transformative Adventures*, a global guide to vacations and retreats (US$15).

Vegans International, c/o Heidrun Leisenheimer, Rosenheimer Landstr. 33a, 85521 Ottobrunn.

Kosher offerings in Germany are often discouragingly scarce. Travelers who keep kosher should contact synagogues in larger cities for information on kosher restaurants; your own synagogue or college Hillel should have access to lists of Jewish institutions across Germany. If you are strict in your observance, you may have to prepare your own food on the road.

The Jewish Travel Guide, lists synagogues, kosher restaurants, and Jewish institutions in over 100 countries, is available in Europe from Vallentine Mitchell Publishers, Newbury House 890-900, Eastern Ave., Newbury Park, Ilford, Essex IG2 7HH, UK (☎(020) 85 99 88 66; fax 85 99 09 84) and in the US ($16.95 + $4 S&H) from ISBS, 5804 NE Hassallo St., Portland, OR 97213 (☎(800) 944 6190).

FURTHER READING

The Vegetarian Traveler: Where to Stay if You're Vegetarian, Jed Civic. Larson Publishers (US$16).

Europe on 10 Salads a Day, Greg and Mary Jane Edwards. Mustang Publishing (US$10/UK£9).

ALTERNATIVES TO TOURISM

STUDY

Foreign study programs vary tremendously in expense, academic quality, living conditions, degree of contact with local students, and exposure to culture and language. Most American undergraduates enroll in programs sponsored by US universities, and many college offices give advice and information on **study abroad.** Ask for the names of recent participants in the programs and get in touch with them. Even basic language skills might be sufficient to allow direct enrollment in German universities, which—because they are publicly funded—are far cheaper than those in North America (and vastly cheaper than a study abroad program).

Studying in Germany requires a passport (see p. 38) and usually a student visa and resident permit (see **Visas and Work Permits,** p. 39). Sometimes a summer abroad program will not require a visa. An **International Student Identity Card (ISIC)** is highly recommended (see p. 40).

Deutscher Akademischer Austauschdienst (DAAD), 950 3rd Ave., 19th fl., New York, NY 10022 (☎(212) 758 3223; email daadny@daad.org; www.daad.org); in Germany, Kennedyallee 50, 53175 Bonn. Information on language instruction, exchanges, and the wealth of scholarships for study in Germany. The place to contact if you want to enroll in a German university; distributes applications and the valuable guide *Academic Study in the Federal Republic of Germany.*

Goethe-Institut, Helene-Weber-Allee 1, 80637 München (☎(089) 15 92 10; fax 15 92 14 50; mailing address Postfach 190419, 80604 München; email for adult students esb@goethe.de; for students under 26 esj@goethe.de; www.goethe.de), runs numerous German language programs in Germany and abroad; it also orchestrates high school exchange programs in Germany. For information on these programs and on their many cultural offerings, look on the web or contact your local branch (**Australia,** Canberra, Melbourne, Sydney; **Canada,** Montreal, Toronto, Vancouver; **Ireland,** Dublin; **New Zealand,** Wellington; **UK,** Glasgow, London, Manchester, York; **US,** New York, Washington, D.C., Boston, Atlanta, San Francisco, Los Angeles, Seattle) or write to the main office. 8-week intensive summer course DM2940, with room DM3740.

Council on International Educational Exchange (CIEE), 205 East 42nd St., New York, NY 10017 (☎(888) 268 6245 or (800) 407 8839; www.ciee.org/study) sponsors work, volunteer, academic, and internship programs in Germany.

Here's your ticket to freedom, baby!

NAME YOUR OWN PRICE!

**Wherever you want to go...
priceline.com can get you there for less.**

- Save up to 40% or more off the lowest published airfares every day!

- Major airlines serving virtually every corner of the globe.

- Special fares to Europe!

If you haven't already tried priceline.com, you're missing out on the best way to save. **Visit us online today at www.priceline.com.**

priceline.com℠
Name Your Own Price℠

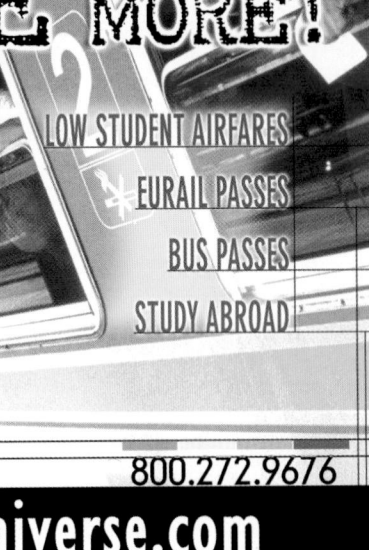

UNIVERSITIES

Most American undergraduates enroll in programs sponsored by US universities. Those relatively fluent in German may find it cheaper to enroll directly in a local university (though getting credit may be more difficult). Some schools that offer study abroad programs to foreigners are listed below.

Brown University: Brown-In-Germany, hosted by Humboldt University of Berlin. Fall (Sep. 18 - Feb. 19) and Spring (Mar. 10 - July 22) Terms. Complete curriculum, courses taught primarily in German. Open to sophomores, juniors and seniors of good academic standing, with at least 2.5 years of college coursework in German. Application with two letters of recommendation required. One Term: $12,312.

University of Kansas: Study Abroad in Bonn. Fall (Sep. 7 - Feb. 1) and Spring (Mar. 1 - Jun. 30). Complete curriculum, courses taught primarily in German. Open to juniros, seniors and graduate students of good academic standing, with at least 2 years of college coursework in German. Application with two letters of recommendation required. One Term: $4,310.

Wayne State University: Junior Year in Munich. Fall (Sep. 20 - Feb. 23) and Spring (Apr. 4 - Jul. 31). Complete curriculum, courses taught primarily in German. Opn to juniors, seniors and graduate students of good academic standing with at least 2 years of college coursework in German. Application with one letter of recommendation required. One term: $3,950.

FURTHER READING

Academic Year Abroad. Institute of International Education Books (US$45).

Vacation Study Abroad. Institute of International Education Books (US$40).

Peterson's Study Abroad Guide. Peterson's (US$30).

WORK

With **unemployment** in Western Germany still hovering over 10%, and rates even higher in the former GDR, Germany's days as a mecca for unskilled foreign workers are over. Millions of *Gastarbeiter* (guest workers) and former GDR citizens relocated in western Germany compete for positions, flooding an already tight bureaucracy and job market. Moreover, wading through the morass of German bureaucracy to obtain **work permits** can be disheartening, and the government takes documentation quite seriously, without which you will find the search impossible. However, if you are lucky enough to find work in Germany, take comfort in pay: wages are notably high, even among retail service industries.

There are often ways to make the search easier. Fluency in German will make employers much more likely to consider you. Friends in Germany can help expedite work permits or arrange work-for-accommodations swaps. EU citizens can work in Germany provided they have an EU residency permit *(EU-Aufenthaltserlaubnis)*; if your parents were born in an EU country, you may be able to claim dual citizenship or at least the right to a work permit. For US citizens and other non-Europeans, you will need to obtain a residency permit *(Aufenthaltserlaubnis)* and work permit *(Arbeitserlaubnis)*.

The German government maintains a slew of federally run employment offices, the *Bundesanstalt für Arbeit*, throughout the country. The *Bundesanstalt* tends to treat EU citizens with specific skills more favorably than those from other countries. The youth division is a bit more welcoming for foreign students ages 18-30 seeking summer employment; jobs frequently involve manual labor. Contact the central office before March, and be able to work for at least two months. With the proper certification and an offer in hand, you will be referred to a local employment office *(Arbeitsamt)* who will issue another work permit for your particular position. In recent years, private employment agencies have cropped up, although the unofficial monopoly is still in the federal arena.

The best tips on jobs for foreigners often come from other travelers, so be alert and inquisitive. Newspaper listings are another start. During the summer especially, the German tourist industry relies on students and illegal immigrants to blow the bellows at hotels, hostels, and resorts. Other fields such as fast food, agriculture, and nursing (for which you will need further health certification), and generally sectors involving skilled building labor, are friendlier to travelers. Ask around at pubs, cafes, restaurants, and hotels. Be sure to be aware of your rights as an employee; should a crafty employer try to refuse payment at the end of the season, it'll help if you have a written confirmation of your agreement. Consider work teaching English. Post a sign in markets or learning centers stating that you are a native speaker, and scan the classifieds of local newspapers.

If you are a full-time student at a US university, the simplest way to get a job in Germany is through work permit programs run by the **Council on International Educational Exchange (Council)** and its member organizations. For a US$225 application fee, Council can procure three- to six-month work permits and a handbook to help you find work and housing. No matter what your employment, make sure that you are covered by some type of health insurance (see p. 53).

AU PAIR

Accord Cultural Exchange, 750 La Playa, San Francisco, CA 94121 (☎(415) 386 6203; fax 386 0240; email leftbank@hotmail.com; www.cognitext.com/accord), offers au pair jobs to people aged 18-29 in Germany. Au pairs work 5-6 hours a day, 30 hours a week, plus 2 evenings of babysitting. Light housekeeping and childcare in exchange for room and board plus US$250-400 per month salary. Program fees US$750 for the summer, US$1200 for the academic year. US$40 application fee.

InterExchange, 161 Sixth Ave., New York, NY 10013 (☎(212) 924 0446; fax 924 0575; email interex@earthlink.net) provides information on international work and au pair positions in Germany.

Childcare International, Ltd., Trafalgar House, Grenville Place, London NW7 3SA (☎(020) 89 06 31 16; fax 89 06 34 61; email office@childint.demon.co.uk; www.childint.demon.co.uk) offers au pair positions in Germany. Provides information on local language schools. The organization prefers a long placement but does arrange summer work. UK£80 application fee.

TEACHING ENGLISH

International Schools Services, Educational Staffing Program, P.O. Box 5910, Princeton, NJ 08543 (☎(609) 452 0990; fax 452 2690; email edustaffing@iss.edu; www.iss.edu). Recruits teachers and administrators for American and English schools in Germany. All instruction in English. Applicants must have a bachelor's degree and two years of relevant experience. Nonrefundable US$100 application fee. Publishes *The ISS Directory of Overseas Schools* (US$35).

Office of Overseas Schools, A/OS Room 245, SA-29, Dept. of State, Washington, D.C., 20522-2902 (☎(703) 875-7800; fax 875-7979; email overseas.school@state.gov; state.gov/www/about_state/schools/). Maintains a list of schools abroad and agencies that arrange placement for Americans to teach abroad.

AGRICULTURE

Willing Workers on Organic Farms (WWOOF), c/o Miriam Wittmann, Postfach 210259, 01263 Dresden, Germany (email fairtours@gn.apc.org; www.phdcc.com/sites/wwoof). Membership ($10 or DM30) in WWOOF allows you to receive room and board at a variety of organic farms in Germany in exchange for chores.

FURTHER READING

Work Your Way Around the World: The Authoritative Guide for the Working Traveler, Susan Griffith. Peterson's (US$18). The Germany-specific information provides an incredibly thorough tour through the tangle of Germany's employment bureaucracy.

VOLUNTEERING

Volunteer jobs are readily available almost everywhere, and you may receive room and board in exchange for labor. You can sometimes avoid the high application fees charged by the organizations that arrange placement by contacting the individual workcamps directly.

Service Civil International Voluntary Service (SCI-VS), 814 NE 40th St., Seattle, WA 98105 (☎/fax (206) 545-6585; email sciivsusa@igc.apc.org). Arranges placement in workcamps in Europe for those over 18. Local organizations sponsor groups for physical and social work. Registration fees US$50-250, depending on the camp location.

Volunteers for Peace, 1034 Tiffany Rd., Belmont, VT 05730 (☎(802) 259-2759; fax 259-2922; email vfp@vfp.org; www.vfp.org). A nonprofit organization that arranges speedy placement in 2-3 week workcamps in Germany comprising 10-15 people. Projects include construction and restoration of low income housing and park maintenance. Most complete and up-to-date listings provided in the annual *International Workcamp Directory* (US$15). Registration fee US$195. Free newsletter.

FURTHER READING

International Jobs: Where They Are, How to Get Them, Eric Kocher and Nina Segal. Perseus Books (US$16).

How to Get a Job in Europe, Robert Sanborn. Surrey Books (US$22).

The Alternative Travel Directory, Clayton Hubbs. Transitions Abroad (US$20).

Work Abroad, Clayton Hubbs. Transitions Abroad (US$16).

International Directory of Voluntary Work, Victoria Pybus. Vacation Work Publications (US$16).

Teaching English Abroad, Susan Griffin. Vacation Work (US$17).

Overseas Summer Jobs 1999, Work Your Way Around the World, and *Directory of Jobs and Careers Abroad.* Peterson's (US$17-18 each).

OTHER RESOURCES

TOURIST OFFICES

For detailed information on any aspect of traveling in Germany, contact the **German National Tourist Office** in your home country or visit their website at www.germany-tourism.de, which includes suggested itineraries and links to over 50 major cities. The office will send you heaps of maps and brochures on Germany's 16 *Länder* and outdoor activities.

Canada: 175 Bloor Str. East, North Tower, Suite 604, Toronto, ON M4W 3R8 (☎(416) 968 1570; fax 416 968 1986; email germanto@idirect.com).

UK: P.O. Box 2695, London W1A 3NT (☎(020) 7317 0908; fax (020) 7495 6129; email German_National_Tourist_Office@compuserve.com).

US: 122 East 42nd St., Chanin Bldg., 52nd Floor, New York, NY 10168-0072 (☎(212) 661 7200; fax 661 7174; email gntony@aol.com).

USEFUL PUBLICATIONS

The publications we list here should be useful in preparing for your trip. If you're For books on Germany's culture and history, see **Further Reading,** p. 22. For information on German newspapers, see **Media,** p. 31.

A Traveller's Wine Guide to Germany, Kerry Brady Stewart. Traveller's Wine Guides, 1997. (US$17.95). Exactly what it says it is, by a well-known oenophile.

Atlantik-Brücke, Adenaueralle 131, 53113 Bonn. Devoted to promoting mutual understanding (hence "Atlantic Bridge"), it publishes *These Strange German Ways—a must for any American planning on living in Germany—as well as Meet United Germany, German Holidays and Folk Customs,* and *Speaking Out: Jewish Voices from United Germany.* Order the books from the Hamburg office (☎(040) 600 70 22).

Culture Shock! Germany, Richard Lord. Graphic Arts Publishing Co., 1996 (US$12.95). A readable low-down on living in Deutschland that isn't afraid to hold your hand.

Germany by Bike, Nadine Slavinski. Mountaineers Books, 1994 (US$14.95). Twenty tours throughout the *Länder,* with general information on getting your bike ready for the *Tour de...Deutschland.*

Wicked German, Howard Tomb. Workman, 1992 (US$4.95). A little guide to everything you really didn't need to know how to say in German.

TRAVEL BOOK PUBLISHERS

Hippocrene Books, 171 Madison Ave., New York, NY 10016 (☎(212) 685 4371; orders ☎(718) 454 2366; fax 454 1391; email contact@hippocrenebooks.com; www.netcom.com/~hippocre). Publishes travel reference books, travel guides, foreign language dictionaries, and language learning guides. Free catalog.

Hunter Publishing, 130 Campus Dr., Edison, NJ 08818-7816 (☎(800) 255 0343; email kimba@mediasoft.net; www.hunterpublishing.com). Has an extensive catalogue of travel books, guides, language learning tapes, and quality maps, and the *Charming Small Hotel Guide to Germany* (US$15).

Rand McNally, 150 S. Wacker Dr., Chicago, IL 60606 (☎(800) 234 0679 or (312) 332 2009; fax 443 9540; email storekeeper@randmcnally.com; www.randmcnally.com), publishes a number of comprehensive road atlases (each US$10).

THE WORLD WIDE WEB

Almost every aspect of budget travel (with the most notable exception, of course, being experience) is accessible via the web. Even if you don't have internet access at home, seeking it out at a public library or at work would be well worth it; within 10min. at the keyboard, you can make a reservation at a hostel in Germany, get advice on travel hotspots or experiences from other travelers who have just returned from Europe, or find out how much a train from Berlin to Dresden costs.

Listed here are some budget travel sites to start off your surfing; other relevant web sites are listed throughout the book. Because website turnover is high, use search engines (such as www.yahoo.com) to strike out on your own. But in doing so, keep in mind that most travel web sites simply exist to get your money.

LEARNING THE ART OF BUDGET TRAVEL

How to See the World: www.artoftravel.com. A compendium of great travel tips, from cheap flights to self defense to interacting with local culture.

Rec. Travel Library: www.travel-library.com. A fantastic set of links for general information and personal travelogues.

Shoestring Travel: www.stratpub.com. An e-zine focusing on budget travel.

INFORMATION ON GERMANY

CIA World Factbook: www.odci.gov/cia/publications/factbook/index.html. Tons of vital statistics on Germany's geography, government, economy, and people.

Foreign Language for Travelers: www.travlang.com. Provides free online translating dictionaries and lists of phrases in German.

MyTravelGuide: www.mytravelguide.com. Country overviews, with everything from history to transportation to live web cam coverage of Germany.

Geographia: www.geographia.com. Describes the highlights, culture, and people of Germany.

Atevo Travel: www.atevo.com/guides/destinations. Detailed introductions, travel tips, and suggested itineraries.

Columbus Travel Guides: http://www.travel-guides.com/navigate/world.asp. Helpful practical information.

LeisurePlanet: www.leisureplanet.com/TravelGuides. Good general background.

TravelPage: www.travelpage.com. Links to official tourist office sites throughout Germany.

PlanetRider: www.planetrider.com/Travel_Destinations.cfm. A subjective list of links to the "best" websites covering the culture and tourist attractions of Germany.

AND OUR PERSONAL FAVORITE...

Let's Go: www.letsgo.com. Our recently revamped website features photos and streaming video, info about our books, a travel forum buzzing with stories and tips, and links that will help you find everything you could ever want to know about Germany.

BERLIN

Now is the time to see Berlin. Projects are underway to transform it from the Allied-bombed and -occupied city of the post-WWII years into a sparklingly whole metropolis which will once again serve as Germany's capital, irreversibly changing the city's identity. Indeed, Berlin has always been dynamic; never in its history has it seemed a completed city, nor has it remained in any one pattern for a long period of time. Now city planners and architects envision a **"finished" Berlin,** claiming to know what it will look like and how it will function on a practical level after the construction is over four years from now. When the building is complete, the forests of yellow cranes collapsed and carted away, and the new glass Hauptbahnhof has finally become **Europe's transportation hub,** the character of the city will be greatly altered. The citizens of Berlin, though, are not a construction project that can be modeled or sketched. Their varying levels of approval for, discomfort with, or indifference to the astonishingly massive surface alterations planned for their city point to the lingering question of to what extent the arrival of the shiny new Berlin will change its social and cultural composition.

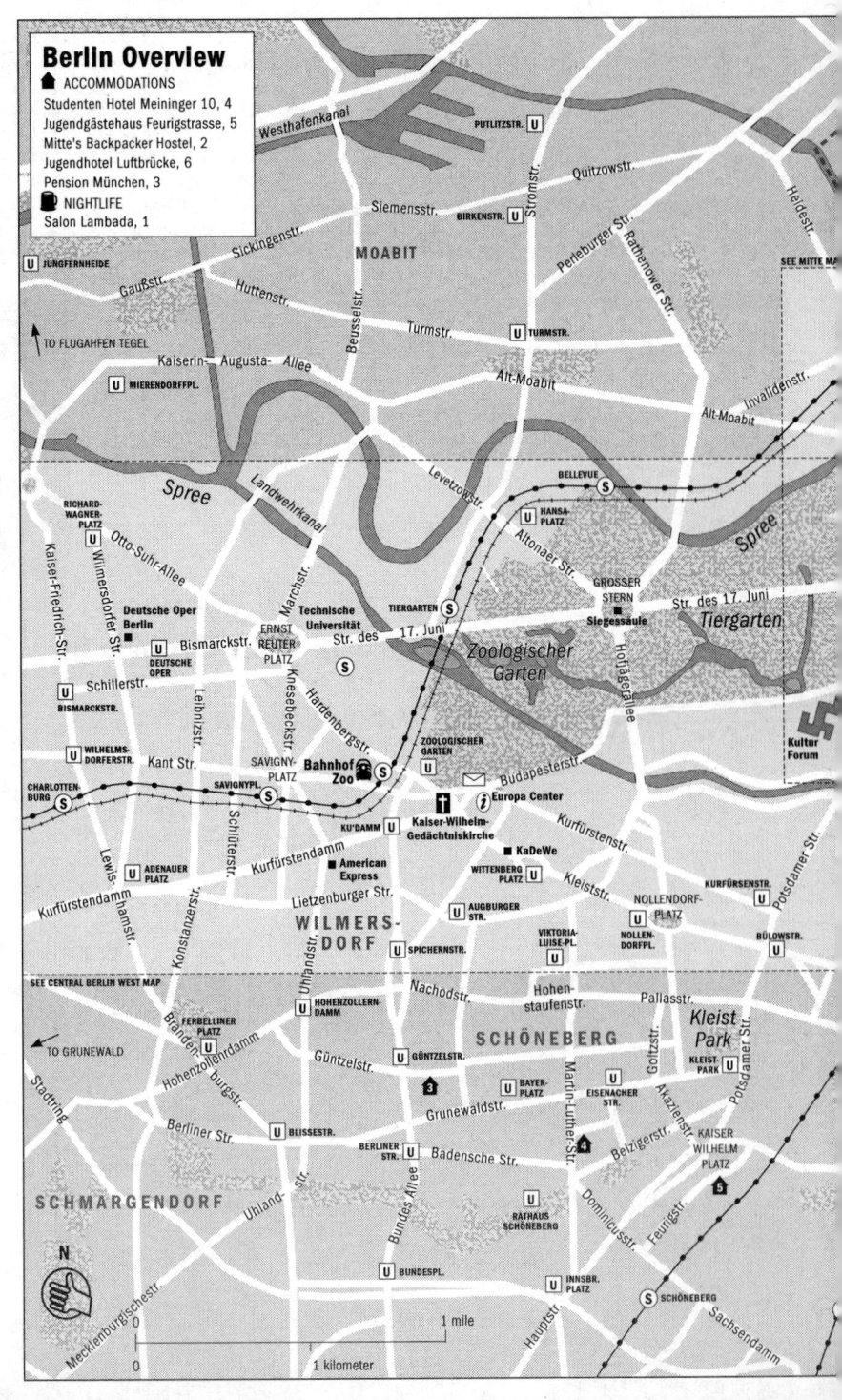

Berlin Overview

■ ACCOMMODATIONS
Studenten Hotel Meininger 10, 4
Jugendgästehaus Feurigstrasse, 5
Mitte's Backpacker Hostel, 2
Jugendhotel Luftbrücke, 6
Pension München, 3
■ NIGHTLIFE
Salon Lambada, 1

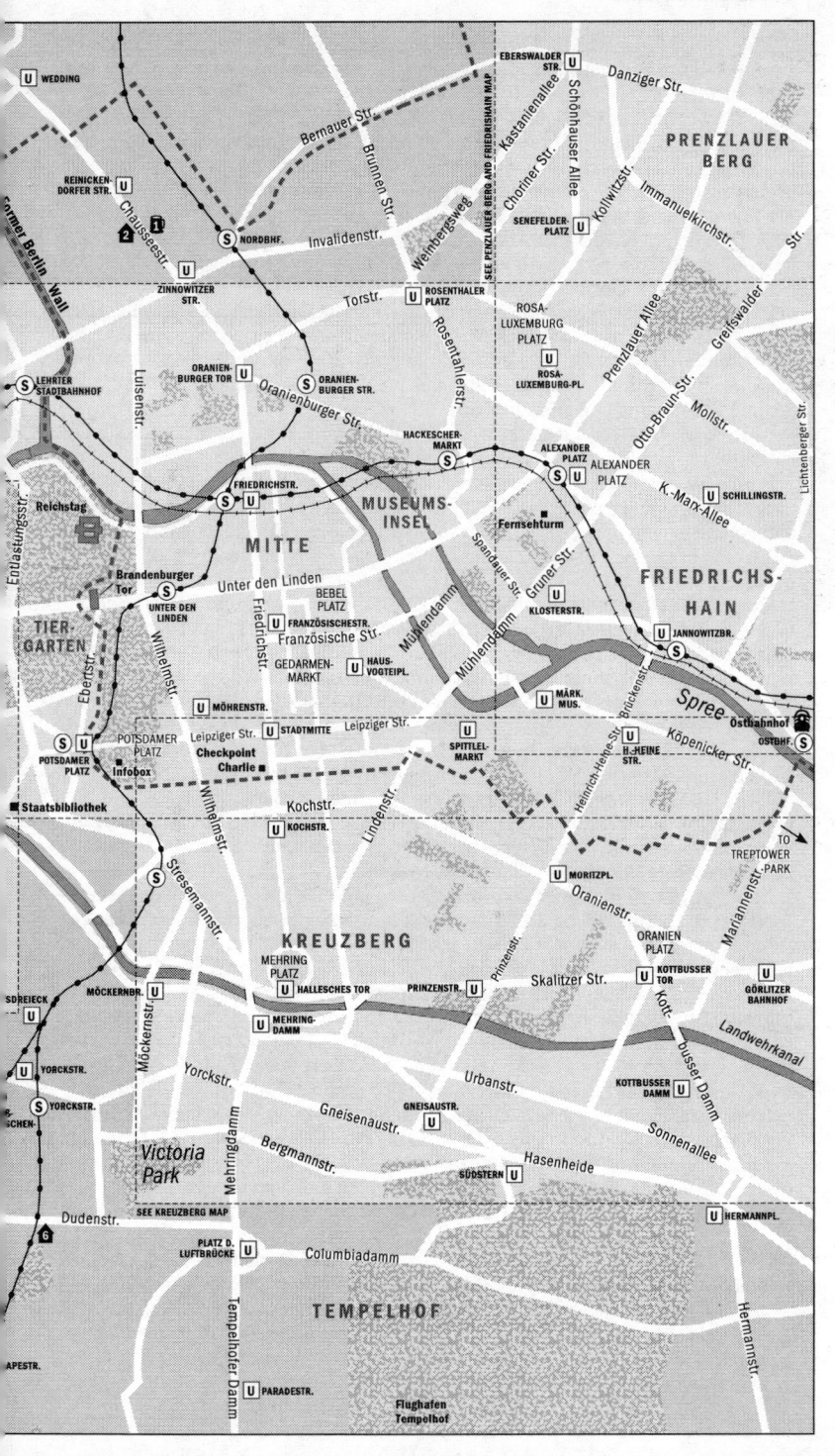

What has always made Berlin remarkable is its ability to flourish in times of adversity, but the established bureaucratic structure that Bonn's corps of civil servants has imported threatens to end this frenetic, Phoenix-like existence. Now that the government has almost completely moved back from Bonn, and Parliament once again meets in the glass-domed Reichstag, the population may soon settle into a more conservative stance befitting a capital city, and then very little will be left of the chaotic atmosphere which fed Berlin during the 20th century. Throughout the **debaucherous 1920s** of the Weimar Republic and again during the 40 years when the divided city personified the **Cold War,** Berlin's struggles forced its inhabitants to innovate. Raised in the shadow of global conflict, Berliners responded with a glorious storm of cultural activity and the sort of free-for-all nightlife you might expect from a population with its back against the wall. After the **collapse of the Berlin Wall** in 1989, the suddenly united city once more had the opportunity to reinvent itself. Communist governments fell across Eastern Europe, and Berlin found itself in a unique position, straddling the border of two distinct but no longer separate worlds. Almost overnight, it became a gateway— *the* gateway—between East and West. Yet at the same time, its two halves were sped along towards fusion, forming a complex, decentralized metropolis.

It remains unknown whether the **brilliantly colored, magnificently varied neighborhoods** that contain Berlin's true vitality will be affected by the presence of a united and complete city center, or whether they will maintain the individuality that has grown out of the lack of a true nexus over the past 50 years. In any case, the task of reconciling the twin cities is proving to be a difficult one. Plagued by a divisive **West-versus-East mentality** intensified by the rapidity of reunion, Berliners from both sides of the former divide are palpably less enthusiastic about sharing 'their' city a decade after the myopically euphoric reunification. High unemployment rates, skyrocketing rents, and Berlin's infamous reputation as an *ewige Baustelle*—perpetual construction site—have conspired against the Berliners' initial thrill of reestablishing their whole city as one of the world's most prominent cultural and political centers. Nonetheless, the city continues to gain momentum from its omnipresent and chaotic ambivalence toward the future. The threat of nuclear holocaust taught Berliners to live like there was no tomorrow, and this penchant for shortsighted excess continues to manifest itself in all aspects of the city's existence, from its ridiculously grandiose building endeavors to the **party-til-dawn atmosphere** that remains in its smoky nightclubs.

Now, as the former East and West Germany attempt to stitch themselves together, the result will be a new city for a new millennium, redefining Berlin as Germany's cultural center—or so the tourist brochures say. Yet at the heart of the city's current **problem of self-definition** is a hesitance to draw on a legacy to create an innovative, yet historically endowed, capital. For those who lived through the horrors of WWII, massive construction plans to turn Berlin into a center of intercontinental import are still overwhelmingly redolent of the fascist era; after all, the last man with plans for massive rebuilding was **Albert Speer,** Hitler's chief architect. Nearly as worrisome is the tendency to replicate other cities in order to achieve parallel fame. A few years ago, the influential news magazine *Der Spiegel* derided this peculiar propensity, warning that "Berlin should stop trying to imitate other metropolises such as London and Paris," for "the thirst for glory of a city is even more dangerous than the thirst for glory of an individual."

Questions of how to consider and remember the past continue to pose problems. Remnants of the Berlin Wall crumble daily on their own or are picked at by resourceful tourists, and nobody really knows whether to reinforce these physical reminders of the east-west divide for posterity, or to allow them to completely fall away as nature would have it. Hitler's bunker lies under an unmarked piece of grass, and Berliners avoid discussing the atrocities of the Third Reich whenever possible. As Weimar decadent **Karl Zuckmayer** wrote, "Berlin tasted of the future, and for that one happily accepted the dirt and the coldness as part of the bargain." The hope is that as the city is rebuilt, its history will not be dismantled.

HIGHLIGHTS OF BERLIN

Stroll the broad boulevards of **Str. des 17. Juni** and **Unter den Linden** to enjoy the green serenity of the massive **Tiergarten** as well as the imperial pomp of the **Siegessäule** (p. 119) and **Brandenburg Gate** (p. 115).

Among the building projects planned for Berlin, one of the most recently completed is Lord Norman Foster's design for the **Reichstag.** Take an elevator to the top and climb to the glass dome for a crane-ed view of the city's enormous construction sites.

Though little of the **Berlin Wall** remains, a visit to **Checkpoint Charlie** (p. 123) quickly recalls the days of the Cold War. To view the longest surviving stretch of the Wall, head to the **East Side Gallery** in Friedrichshain (p. 124).

To see the churned-up center of the world's largest construction site, head to **Potsdamer Platz** (p. 116), where multinational corporations are busily reworking the heart of pre-war Berlin.

Vast holdings of art and artifacts are on display at the museum complexes of **Dahlem, Museuminsel,** the **Kulturforum,** and **Schloß Charlottenburg** (p. 128).

Berlin's notorious **nightlife** (p. 137) centers on the districts of **Kreuzberg, Prenzlauer Berg,** and **Mitte,** with the beginnings of a scene sprouting up in **Friedrichshain.**

HISTORY

PRUSSIAN KINGDOM TO WORLD WAR I

Berlin took its time to attain international importance. The site of small Slavic settlements in marsh lands during the early Middle Ages, the city takes its name from the Slavonic word *birl,* or "swamp." The first mention of a neighboring settlement called **Cölln,** on an island in the **Spree River,** appears in 1237. The two towns united in 1307, and were closely connected with the nearby settlements of **Spandau** and **Köpenick.** Hohenzollern rule (as the **electors of Brandenburg**) came to the tumultuous region in 1411. After several centuries of building the capital to fit the power-hungry electors, Friedrich William (the Great Elector) bolstered the city by accepting Huguenot and Jewish refugees, and in 1701 Berlin became the capital of the Kingdom of Prussia. In the 18th century, Berlin flourished under the enlightened rule of **Friedrich II** (the Great), and in the following years such thinkers as **Gotthold Ephraim Lessing** and the **Humboldt brothers** made the growing city an intellectual center. Nonetheless, Berlin was little more than an ornate garrison town, as Friedrich's penchant for military pomp and circumstance (as well as young officers) turned the city into a series of grandiose parade grounds devoid of civilians. The city suffered a decline in the 19th century, during which time it was conquered by Napoleon in 1806 and beset by revolution in 1848. In 1871, Berlin became the capital of the German Empire established after Bismarck's wars (see p. 10). However, Imperial Berlin never became the center of the new nation in the same way that Paris was for France or London for Britain. Munich and Frankfurt remained cultural and commercial rivals, and many Germans felt little affection for the Prussian capital. It was not until the end of WWI and the establishment of the first German (Weimar) Republic that Berlin became the u ..disputed center of national life.

REVOLUTION AND WEIMAR CULTURE

WWI and the Allied blockade brought about near-starvation conditions in Berlin. A popular uprising led to the Kaiser's abdication and **Karl Liebknecht's** declaration of a socialist republic with Berlin as capital on November 9, 1918. Locally, the revolt—led by Liebknecht and **Rosa Luxemburg**—turned into a full-fledged workers' revolution that wrested control of the city for several days. The rival Social Democratic government, proclaimed by Philipp Scheidemann from the window of the Reichstag on the same day, enlisted the aid of right-wing mercenaries, the **Freikorps,** who brutally suppressed the rebellion and murdered Liebknecht and Luxemburg. The political and economic instability of the Weimar Republic hit the capital city hard until 1923, when chancellor Gustav Stresemann's economic plan and generous loans from the United States improved the situation. Meanwhile, Berlin had become one of the major cultural centers of Europe. Expressionist painting flourished, **Bertolt Brecht** developed revolutionary new theater techniques, and artists and writers from all over the world flocked to the city. The city's "Golden Twenties," however, ended abruptly with the 1929 economic collapse. With 10% of Germany's unemployed living in Berlin, the city erupted with bloody riots, radicalization, political chaos, and the ascent of the Nazis.

CAPITAL OF THE THIRD REICH

When Hitler took power on January 30, 1933, traditionally left-wing **"Red Berlin"** was not one of his strongholds. He consolidated his control over the city through economic improvements and totalitarian measures, and marshalled support for the savage anti-Semitic pogrom of November 9, 1938, known as **Kristallnacht.** Berlin was hit extremely hard during WWII; Allied bombing and the Battle of Berlin leveled one-fifth of the city, killing 80,000 citizens. With almost all healthy men dead or gone, it was Berlin's women, known as the **Trümmerfrauen** (rubble women), who picked up the broken pieces of the city, creating numerous artificial hills out of the tons of rubble strewn across the defeated capital. The pre-war population of 4.3 million sank to 2.8 million. Only 7,000 members of Berlin's once-thriving Jewish community of 160,000 survived the Holocaust.

After the war, the Allies took control of the city, dividing it into French, British, American, and Soviet sectors under a joint **Allied Command.** On June 16, 1948, the Soviets withdrew from the joint Command and demanded full control of Berlin. Ten days later, they began an 11-month blockade of most land and water routes into the Western sectors. The population would have starved were it not for a massive Allied airlift of supplies known as the **Luftbrücke** (air bridge). On May 12, 1949, the Soviets ceded control of West Berlin to the Western Allies.

A DIVIDED CITY

On October 5, 1949, the Soviet-controlled German Democratic Republic was formally established (see p. 18), with East Berlin as its capital. The city was thus officially divided. Dissatisfaction was great in East Berlin, and it manifested itself in the **workers' uprising** of June 17, 1953, when widespread popular demonstrations were crushed under Soviet tanks. One result of the repression was an increase in the number of **Republikflüchtige** ("Republic-deserters") who emigrated to West Berlin—200,000 in 1960 alone. On the morning of August 13, 1961, the East German government responded to this exodus with the almost instantaneous overnight construction of the **Berlin Wall,** which stopped virtually all interaction between the two halves of the city. The 165km Wall, or "anti-fascist protective barrier," as the East German government termed it, separated families and friends, sometimes even running through people's homes. In the early 1970s, a second wall was erected parallel to the first; the space in between them became known as the **Todesstreifen** ("death strip") as East German border guards were ordered to shoot any trespassers. The Western Allies responded to West Berlin's isolation by pouring millions into the city's reconstruction; to emphasize the glories of capitalism, the commercial center around Kurfürstendamm was created and nurtured to become *das Schaufenster des Westens* (the shop-window of the West).

West Berlin remained under joint French, British, and American control. Although there was an elected mayor, final say rested with the Allied commander-in-chief. The city was not officially a part of the Federal Republic of Germany but had "special status." Although Berlin adopted the resolutions of the Federal Parliament, the municipal Senate still had to approve them, and the Allies retained ultimate authority over the city right up until German reunification in 1990. One perk of this special status was the exemption of West Berliners from military conscription. Thousands of German artists, punks, homosexuals, and left-wing activists moved to Berlin to escape the draft and formed an unparalleled alternative scene. The West German government, determined to make a Cold War showcase of the city, subsidized its economic and cultural life, further enhancing its vitality.

THE WALL OPENS

On November 9, 1989—the 71st anniversary of the proclamation of the Weimar Republic, the 66th anniversary of Hitler's Beer Hall *Putsch,* and the 51st anniversary of *Kristallnacht*—a series of popular demonstrations throughout East Germany, riding on a decade of discontent and a year of rapid change in Eastern Europe, culminated in the opening of the Berlin Wall. The image of jubilant Berliners embracing beneath the Brandenburg Gate that night provided one of the most memorable images of the century. Berlin was officially reunited (free of Allied authority) along with the rest of Germany on October 3, 1990, to widespread celebration. Since then, the euphoria has evaporated. Eastern and Western Berliners have discovered many unexpected differences and obstacles to unity. Resignation to reconstruction has taken the place of the biting criticism and tasteless jokes that were standard immediately after reunification. Eastern Berlin remains politically volatile and economically disadvantaged, though the situation has improved somewhat in the past few years. The city is slowly knitting itself back together, but it will be years before residents on both sides of the divide consider themselves citizens of the same city. After a decade of planning, the *Bundestag* finally made the move from Bonn to Berlin in 1999, thus restoring Berlin to its pre-war status as the locus of German political power.

◪ GETTING THERE AND AWAY

> ☎ **PHONE CODE** Berlin's phone code is 030.

Berlin surveys the Prussian plains from the northeastern corner of Germany and is rapidly becoming the hub of the national rail network. About three hours southeast of Hamburg by train and eight hours north of Munich, Berlin has a web of rail and air connections to most other European capitals. The city is well-connected to Eastern European countries—Prague is five hours by rail, Warsaw six hours. Almost all European airlines, Western or Eastern, have frequent service to one of Berlin's three airports.

Flights: Berlin's airport authority has consolidated its telephone service. For information on all 3 airports, call ☎ (0180) 500 01 86. **Flughafen Tegel** is Western Berlin's main airport. Take express bus #X9 from Bahnhof Zoo, bus #109 from "Jakob-Kaiser-Pl." on U-Bahn #7, or bus #128 from "Kurt-Schumacher-Pl." on U-Bahn #6. **Flughafen Tempelhof,** Berlin's smallest airport, is used for intra-German travel and flights within Europe. U-Bahn #6 to "Pl. der Luftbrücke." **Flughafen Schönefeld,** southeast of Berlin, is used for intercontinental flights as well as travel to the former Soviet Union and developing countries. S-Bahn #45 or 9 to "Flughafen Berlin Schönefeld" or bus #171 from "Rudow" on U-Bahn #7.

Train Stations: While construction continues on the *Megabahnhof* of the future at Lehrter Stadtbahnhof, trains to and from Berlin are serviced by **Zoologischer Garten** (almost always called **Bahnhof Zoo**) in the West and **Ostbahnhof** (formerly the Hauptbahnhof) in the East. Most trains go to both stations, but some connections to cities in the former GDR only stop at Ostbahnhof, or stop there far more frequently. Many trains also connect to **Schönefeld** airport. A number of U-Bahn lines also make stops at **Oranienburg, Spandau,** and **Potsdam** before entering the city.

Rail Connections: One per hr. to: **Leipzig** (2hr., DM58); **Dresden** (2hr., DM59); **Rostock** (2¾hr., DM65); **Hamburg** (2½hr., DM81); **Frankfurt** (4hr., DM207); **Köln** (4¼hr., DM190); **Munich** (7½hr., DM249). **International connections: Stockholm** (15hr.); **Copenhagen** (7½hr.); **Amsterdam** (6½hr.); **Brussels** (7½hr.); **Paris** (9hr.); **Zurich** (9hr.); **Rome** (21hr.); **Vienna** (11½hr.); **Budapest** (12hr.); **Prague** (5hr.); **Kraków** (10½hr.); **Warsaw** (6hr.); and **Moscow** (27hr.). Times and prices change frequently—check your route at the computers located in the train stations.

Rail Information: Deutsche Bahn Information (☎ (0180) 599 66 33). Be prepared for a long wait and funky hold music. Also long lines at the *Reisezentrum* in **Bahnhof Zoo** (open daily 4:45am-11pm) and **Ostbahnhof.** Lines are separated according to whether you need information and reservations or just a quick ticket; be sure to wait in the right line. Both stations have recently installed computers, but there are sometimes lines for these, too—*arrive early.* All computers can be operated in English or German; if you're planning to purchase by computer, have your credit card ready because they don't take cash. For **recorded information** about departures and arrivals (in German) there are several lines depending on the direction of your destination: Hamburg, Rostock, Stralsund, Schwerin, and Scandinavia (☎01 15 31); Magdeburg, Frankfurt, Hannover, and Köln (☎01 15 32); Frankfurt (☎01 15 33); Leipzig, Nürnberg, and Munich (☎01 15 34); Dresden, Czech Republic, Slovakia, Austria, and Hungary (☎01 15 35); and Poland, Baltic States, and Ukraine (☎01 15 36). For information in **English,** check the helpful staff at **EurAide** (see **Tourist Offices,** p. 95).

Buses: ZOB, the central bus station (☎301 80 28), is by the *Funkturm* near Kaiserdamm. U-Bahn #2 to "Kaiserdamm" or S-Bahn #4, 45, or 46 to "Witzleben." Check *Zitty* and *Tip* for deals on long-distance buses, or call **Gulliver's** travel agency (☎78 10 21). Buses aren't so comfortable, but they are often much cheaper than trains. **Paris** (10hr., DM109 one-way); and **Vienna** (10½hr., DM79 one-way).

Mitfahrzentralen: City Netz, Joachimstaler Str. 17 (☎194 44; fax 882 44 20) has a computerized ride-share database. U-Bahn #9 or 15to "Kurfürstendamm." To **Hamburg** or **Hannover** DM12, **Frankfurt** DM17, **Munich** DM18. Open M-F 9am-8pm, Sa-Su 9am-7pm. **Branch office:** Südstern 2 (☎693 60 95), in Kreuzberg. U-Bahn #7 to "Südstern." Open M-F 10am-8pm, Sa-Su 10am-4pm. **Mitfahrzentrale Zoo** (☎31 03 31), on the U-Bahn #2 platform (Vinetastr. side) at "Bahnhof Zoo." Open M-F 9am-8pm, Sa-Su 10am-6pm. **Mitfahrzentrale Alex,** (☎241 58 20 or 241 58 21) in the "Alexanderpl." U-Bahn station between lines #2 and 8, specializes in Eastern Europe. Open M-W and F 10am-6pm, Th 10am-8pm, Sa-Su 11am-4pm. The **Mitfahrtelefon für Schwule and Lesben,** Yorckstr. 52 (☎194 20 or 216 60 21), matches gay and lesbian drivers and passengers. U-Bahn #7 to "Yorckstr." Open M-F 9am-8pm, Sa-Su 10am-4pm. Berlin has many small *Mitfahrzentralen;* check the magazines *Zitty, Tip,* or *030* for addresses and phone numbers.

Hitchhiking: *Let's Go* does not recommend hitchhiking as a safe mode of transportation. Remember that it is illegal to hitch at rest stops or anywhere along the highway. Those heading west and south (Hannover, Munich, Weimar, Leipzig) have been known to take S-Bahn #1 or 7 to "Wannsee," then bus #211 to the Autobahn entrance ramp. Those heading north (Hamburg, Rostock) report riding S-Bahn #25 to "Hennigsdorf," then walking 50m to the bridge on the right, or asking for the location of the *Trampenpl.* Both have crowds, but apparently someone gets picked up every few minutes.

⌐ GETTING AROUND

Public Transportation: The **BVG** *(Berliner Verkehrsbetriebe)* is one of the most efficient transportation systems in the world. While most reconstruction and expansion of the prewar transit grid has been completed, the BVG's mascot, **Max,** an inimitably affable cartoon mole, alerts travelers to disruptions in service. In most cases, the worst inconvenience is an extra 20min. wait.

Orientation and Basic Fares: It is impossible to tour Berlin on foot—fortunately, the extensive **bus, Straßenbahn** (streetcar), **U-Bahn** (subway), and **S-Bahn** (surface rail) systems of Berlin will get you to your destination safely and relatively quickly. Berlin is divided into 3 transit zones. **Zone A** encompasses downtown Berlin, including Tempelhof airport. Almost everything else falls into **Zone B,** while **Zone C** contains the outlying areas, including Potsdam and Oranienburg. An AB ticket is the best deal, as you can buy regional Bahn tickets for the outlying areas. A single ticket for the combined network (*Langstrecke* AB or BC, DM3.90; or *Ganzstrecke* ABC, DM4.20) is good for 2hr. after validation. Children under 6 accompanied by an adult travel free; children under 14 pay a reduced fare. **Within the validation period, the ticket may be used on any S-Bahn, U-Bahn, bus or streetcar.**

Special Passes: With the high cost of single tickets, it almost always makes sense to buy a transit pass. A **Tageskarte** (AB DM7.80, ABC DM8.50) is valid from the time of validation until 3am the next day. A **Gruppentageskarte** (AB DM20, ABC DM22.50) allows up to 5 people to travel together on the same ticket. The **WelcomeCard** (DM32) is valid on all lines for 72hr. The **7-Tage-Karte** (AB DM40, ABC DM48) is good for 7 days of travel.

For longer stays, an **Umweltkarte Standard** (AB DM99, ABC DM120) is valid for one calendar month. **Bikes** require an additional, reduced-fare ticket, and are permitted on the U-Bahn and S-Bahn but not on buses and streetcars.

Purchasing Tickets: Buy tickets from *Automaten* (machines), bus drivers, or ticket windows in the U- and S-Bahn stations. When using an *Automat,* make your selection before inserting money; note that the machines will not give more than DM20 change. Inspections have increased severely in the past two years, and the cost of cheating is steep (DM60). The "I didn't know I needed a ticket" excuse won't fly here—signs warn of the perils all over. *All tickets must be cancelled in the validation box marked "hier entwerfen" before boarding.*

Maps and Information: The **Liniennetz** map can be picked up for free at any tourist office or subway station. The BVG also issues an excellent **Atlas** of the entire city (DM13). For more information, visit the **BVG Pavillon** in the bus parking lot outside Bahnhof Zoo (☎25 62 25 62; open daily 6:30am-8:30pm) or the **BVG Kundenbüro** at "Turmstr." station on U-Bahn #9 (open M-F 6:30am-8:30pm, Sa 9am-3:30pm). One can also call the BVG's **information line** (☎194 49; open daily 6am-11pm) or check them on the **internet** (email auskunft@bvg.de; www.bvg.de).

Night Transport: U- and S-Bahn lines generally do not run from 1-4am, although most S-Bahn lines run once an hour during weekend nights. The **U9** and **U12** run all night Friday and Saturday. (The U12 line, which only runs F-Sa night, combines the "Ruhleben-Gleis-dreieck" leg of the U2 with the "Gleisdreieck-Warschauer Str." leg of the U1.) Most regular lines start their final runs by 12:15am. There is an extensive system of **night buses** centered on Bahnhof Zoo that run every 20-30min.; pick up the free *Nachtliniennetz* map at the BVG pavilion. Night bus numbers are preceded by the letter **N.**

Ferries: Stern und Kreis Schiffahrt, Puschkinallee 15 (☎536 36 00; fax 53 63 60 99), operates ferry services along the Spree Apr.-Oct. Ferries leave from locations throughout the city, including the Spreebogen, Friedrichstr., Museuminsel, the Dom, and the Nikolaiviertel. Five ferries run daily 10:30am-4:30pm; fares depend on distance traveled (DM3.50-22). Pleasure cruises available. *Berlin Kombi-Tageskarte* is valid on all regularly scheduled services. The tourist office and BVG Pavillon offer more information.

Taxis: ☎26 10 26, 21 02 02, or 690 22. Call at least 15min. in advance. Women may request a female driver. Trips within the city are priced at up to DM40.

Car Rental: The **Mietwagenservice,** counter 21 in Bahnhof Zoo's *Reisezentrum* (see above), represents *Avis, Hertz, Europacar* and *Sixt.* Open daily 4:45am-11pm. Most companies also have offices in the Tegel Airport.

Bike Rental: Hackescher Markt Fahrradstation, downstairs at the "Hackescher Markt" S-Bahn stop. Also try the red trailer off the **Lustgarten,** which rents bikes for DM5 per day. S-Bahn #3, 5, 7, 75, or 9 to "Hackescher Markt" for both locations. The government's **bikecity** program rents bikes for DM5 or 10 (depending on the bike) per day. The main rental station is at **Waldenserstr. 2-4,** U-Bahn #9 to "Turmstr." Call (☎39 73 91 45) for info during their open hours, M-Th 7:30am-4pm, F 7:30am-2:30pm. Other rental stations under the same program are at **Alexanderplatz,** near Hotel Forum (☎011 72 10 28 83), S-Bahn #3, 5, 7, 75, or 9 or U-Bahn #2, 5, or 8 to "Alexanderpl.," and Hardenbergpl. at Hertzallee (☎011 72 10 23 84), U-Bahn #2 or 12 or S-Bahn to "Zoologischer Garten." Both stations open daily 10am-6pm. Bikes are also available at several of the hostels—see p. 99.

SAFETY PRECAUTION! With thriving minority communities of all shapes and colors, Berlin is by far the most tolerant city in Germany. The media has sensationalized the new wave of Nazi extremism perhaps more than necessary; among major cities, Berlin in fact has the fewest hate crimes per capita. The majority of skinheads tend to target minority races and homosexuals. There are only an estimated 750 neo-Nazi skinheads in Berlin. However, there are still a few areas in which people of color as well as gays or lesbians should take precautions—the outlying areas in the eastern suburbs, particularly Bahnhof Lichtenberg, are best avoided late at night. If you see dark-colored combat boots with white laces, exercise caution, but do not panic.

✦ ORIENTATION

Berlin is an *immense* conglomeration of what were once two separate and unique cities: the former East, which contains the lion's share of Berlin's landmarks and historic sites, as well as an unfortunate number of pre-fab concrete socialist architectural experiments, and the former West, which functioned for decades as a small, isolated, Allied-occupied state and is still the commercial heart of united Berlin. The situation is rapidly changing, however, as businesses and embassies move their headquarters to Potsdamer Platz and Mitte.

The commercial district of Western Berlin lies at one end of the huge **Tiergarten** park and is centered around **Bahnhof Zoo** and **Kurfürstendamm** (Ku'damm for short). It is marked by the bombed-out **Kaiser-Wilhelm-Gedächtniskirche,** adjacent to the boxy tower of the **Europa-Center,** one of the few "skyscrapers" in Western Berlin. A star of streets radiates from Breitscheidpl.; toward the west run **Hardenbergstr., Kantstr.,** and the great commercial boulevard of modern Berlin, the renowned and reviled Kurfürstendamm. About a kilometer down Kantstr. lies **Savignyplatz,** one of many pleasant squares in **Charlottenburg,** home to cafes, restaurants, and *Pensionen.* Further afield, the regal splendor of **Schloß Charlottenburg** and its surrounding grounds hearken back to the city's imperial past. Southeast of the Ku'damm, **Schöneberg** is a pleasant residential neighborhood renowned for its cafe culture and as the traditional nexus of the city's gay and lesbian community. Further south, **Dahlem** houses Western Berlin's largest university and museum complex amidst opulent villas.

The grand, tree-lined **Str. des siebzehnten Juni** runs west-east through the Tiergarten to end at the triumphant **Brandenburg Gate,** which opens out onto **Pariser Platz,** a site of landmark public addresses. Heading south from the Brandenburg Gate and the nearby **Reichstag,** Ebertstraße runs haphazardly through the construction sites to **Potsdamer Platz.** Toward the east, the gate opens onto **Unter den Linden,** Berlin's most famous boulevard and the site of many historic buildings. The *Linden's* broad, tree-lined throughway empties into socialist-realist **Alexanderplatz,** the center of the East's growing commercial district and the home of Berlin's most visible landmark, the **Fernsehturm.** Southeast of Mitte lies **Kreuzberg,** a district home to an incongruous mix of radical leftists, Turks, punks, and homosexuals. Once confined to West Berlin's outer limits, Kreuzberg today finds itself bordering reunited Berlin's city center, a fact that is slowly pushing rents up and alternative types out as civil servants from Bonn descend on the area in a wave of gentrification.

Northeast of the city center, **Prenzlauer Berg,** a former working-class suburb-turned-squatter's paradise, rumbles with as-yet-unrestored pre-war structures and a sublime cafe culture. Southeast of Mitte, **Friedrichshain** is emerging as the latest center of Berlin's counterculture and nightlife, though the area suffers from its heavy concentration of pre-fabricated apartment complexes.

The **Spree River** snakes its way from west to east through the center of Berlin; it forms the northern border of the Tiergarten and splits just east of Unter den Linden to close off the **Museuminsel** (Museum Island). The windswept waters of the Wannsee, Tegeler See, and Heiligensee lap against the city's west side and are connected by narrow canals.

If you're planning to stay more than a few days in Berlin, the blue-and-yellow **Falk Plan** (available at most kiosks and bookstores) is an indispensable and convenient city map that includes a street index and unfolds like a book (DM11). Dozens of streets and subway stations in Eastern Berlin were named after Communist heroes and heroines. Many, but not all, have been renamed in a process only recently completed; be sure that your map is up-to-date.

✦ PRACTICAL INFORMATION

TOURIST OFFICES

Since privatization, tourist offices no longer provide the range of free services and information that they once did. However, they sell a useful **city map** (DM1) on which sights and transit stations are clearly marked. They book same-day **hotel** rooms for a DM5 fee—though room prices start at DM50 and rise to stratospheric heights. A free list of hotels and *Pensionen* is available, but most of the rooms aren't really budget options. Tourist offices also have free copies of the city magazines *030* and (for gays and lesbians) *Siegessäule* and *Sergej*, which have reasonably good entertainment listings. The monthly magazine *Berlin Programm* (DM2.80) lists museums, sights, some restaurants and hotels, and opera, theater, and classical music schedules. The city's main English-language magazine, *Berlin* (DM3.50), has good listings for classical music and opera but little else. Dig *deutsch?* You're better off buying *Tip* or *Zitty*, which have the most comprehensive listings for film, theater, concerts, clubs, and discos (DM4 each). For comprehensive information in English on the **internet,** check out www.berlin.de.

EurAide, in Bahnhof Zoo. Facing the Reisezentrum, go left and down the passage on your right. In English, French, and Spanish, heroic representatives dole out comprehensive travel information, make train reservations, find places to crash, and much, much more. The attendants will make **hotel reservations** for a DM7 fee and recommend hostels for free. Yes, they can get you to Prague. Arrive early—the office can get packed with twenty-somethings, and they don't accept phone calls. Open daily 8am-noon and 1-6pm.

Berlin Tourismus (☎25 00 25; fax 25 00 24 24) isn't the office you want to visit once you arrive, but it is nonetheless a useful resource for planning a trip; they'll send information and reserve **rooms.** Write to Berlin Tourismus Marketing GmbH, Am Karlsbad 11, 10785 Berlin. Other tourist offices do not give out phone numbers, so all telephone inquiries should be directed to this office.

Europa-Center, entrance on Budapester Str. From Bahnhof Zoo, walk along Budapester Str. past the Kaiser-Wilhelm-Gedächtniskirche; the office is on the right after about 2 blocks (5min.). The English-speaking staff will help with reservations and readily answer questions. A list of hostels, campgrounds, and budget-range *Pensionen* is available (DM1), as well as transit maps (free) and city maps (DM2). Open M-Sa 8:30am-8:30pm, Su 10am-6:30pm.

Brandenburger Tor, S-Bahn #1, 2, or 25 or bus #100 to "Unter den Linden." Facing the gates from Unter den Linden, on the left side. Reservations, general tourist info, and most of what the Europa Center office has, with shorter hours. Open daily 9:30am-6pm.

A.S. Airport-Service, at Tegel airport, behind the airport info desk, to the right of the escalator, second room on your left. They do baggage storage, hotel bookings, and general info. For the most specific questions, though, they'll send you to Europa-Center. Open daily 5am-10pm.

Infopoint Dresdner Bank, Unter den Linden 17. Open M, W, and F 8:30am-2pm, Tu and Th 8:30am-2pm and 3:30-6pm.

CITY TOURS

Berlin Walks (☎301 91 94; email berlinwalks@berlin.de; www.berlinwalks.com) offers a range of English-language walking tours, including tours of **Infamous Third Reich Sites,** of **Jewish Life in Berlin,** and **Discover Potsdam.** Their **Discover Berlin Walk** is one of the best ways to get acquainted with the city; the guides' competence and love for Berlin are remarkable. Tours last 3-7hr. and meet at 10am at the taxi stand in front of Bahnhof Zoo (Discover Potsdam meets at 9am); in summer, the Discover Berlin Walk also meets at 2:30pm. All tours DM18, under 26 years old, DM14. Tickets available at EurAide.

Insider Tour enjoys a reputation of providing a very thorough and intellectually stimulating historical narrative and hits all the major sights. Tours last 3½hr. and leave from the *McDonald's* by Bahnhof Zoo late Mar. to Nov. daily at 10am and 2:30pm (DM15).

Terry Brewer's Best of Berlin offers tours heavy on information with a personal touch. Guides Terry and Boris are particularly legendary for their vast knowledge and engaging personalities, making the long walk well worth it. Tours leave daily at 10am, 1:30 and 3pm from the Neue Synagoge on Oranienburger Str., near the intersection with Tucholskystr. The tour picks up guests at the **Circus, Odyssee** and **Clubhouse** hostels about a half-hour earlier (see Accommodations, p. 98). Take S-Bahn #1, 2, or 25 to "Oranienburger Str." DM15, under 14 free. Advertised as 5 hours, though some tours last as long as 8. No afternoon tour Nov.-Apr.

Bus tours are offered by various companies in English and German, leaving roughly hourly from the Ku'damm near the Europa-Center and Gedächtniskirche. Many bus tours also leave from Unter den Linden, near the Brandenburg gate. Most cost about DM33 for a full day of sightseeing.

BUDGET TRAVEL

STA, Goethestr. 73 (☎311 09 50), offers standard budget travel services. U-Bahn #2 to "Ernst-Reuter-Pl." Open M-W and F 10am-6pm, Th 10am-8pm. Also, Dorotheenstr. at the corner of Charlottenstr. U-Bahn #2 to "Hackescher Markt." Open M, Th, F 10am-6pm, Tu and W 10am-8pm.

Kilroy Travels, Hardenbergstr. 9 (☎31 000 40; fax 31 000 431; email berlin.sales@kilroytravels.de; www.kilroytravels.de), across from the Technische Universität, two blocks from Bahnhof Zoo. Kilroy specializes in student travel and will gladly find cheap flights or issue ISICs. For train tickets, though, you'll have to go to EurAide or the *ReiseZentrum*. **Branch offices** at: Takustr. 47 (in Dahlem; ☎831 10 25; fax 832 53 76; U-Bahn #1 to "Dahlem-Dorf"), Nollendorfpl. 7 (☎216 30 91; fax 215 92 21; U-Bahn #1, 2, 4, or 15to "Nollendorfpl."), Mariannenstr. 7 (in Kreuzberg; ☎614 68 22; fax 614 99 83; U-Bahn #1, 8 or 15 to "Kottbusser Tor"), Georgenstr. 3 (in Mitte; ☎203 90 30; S-Bahn #1, 2, 3, 5, 7, 25, or 75 or U-Bahn #6 to "Friedrichstr."). All open M-F 10am-6pm, Sa 11am-3pm. No credit cards accepted.

EMBASSIES AND CONSULATES

Berlin's construction plans include a new complex to house foreign dignitaries. While most embassies have moved to their new homes, the locations of the embassies and consulates remain in a state of flux. For the latest information, call the **Auswärtiges Amt Dienststelle Berlin** at ☎20 18 60 or visit their office on the Werderscher Markt. (U-Bahn #2 to "Hausvogteipl.")

Australian Embassy: Friedrichstr. 200 (☎880 08 80). U-Bahn #2 or 6 to "Stadtmitte." Also try Uhlandstr. 181-183 (☎880 08 80; fax 88 00 88 99). U-Bahn #15 to "Uhlandstr." Open M-F 9am-noon.

Canadian Embassy: Friedrichstr. 95 (☎20 31 20; fax 20 31 25 90)., on the 12th floor of the International Trade Center. S-Bahn #1, 2, 3, 5, 7, 9, 25 or 75 or U-Bahn #6 to "Friedrichstr." Open M-F 9am-noon, appointments at 2pm.

Irish Embassy: Friedrichstr. 200 (☎22 07 20). Open M-F 9:30am-noon, 2:30-4:45pm.

New Zealand Embassy: Friedrichstr. 60 (☎206 210; fax 20 62 11 14; email nzemb@t-online.de). Open M-F 9am-1pm, 2-5:30pm; closes F at 4:30pm.

South Africa: Embassy: Friedrichstr. 60, 10117 (☎ (030) 22 07 30; email konsular@suedafrika.org). **Consulate:** Douglasstr. 9 (☎82 50 11 or 825 27 11; fax 826 65 43). S-Bahn #7 to "Grunewald." Open M-F 9am-noon.

UK Embassy: Unter den Linden 32-34 (☎20 18 40; fax 20 18 41 58). S-Bahn #1, 2, 3, 5, 7, 9, 25 or 75 or U-Bahn #6 to "Friedrichstr." Open M-F 9am-4pm.

US Citizens Service: Clayallee 170 (☎832 92 33; fax 831 49 26). U-Bahn #1 to "Oskar-Helene-Heim." Open M-F 8:30am-noon. Telephone advice available M-F 2-4pm; after hours, call ☎83050 for emergency advice.

US Consulate: Neustädtische Kirchstr. 4-5 (☎238 51 74; fax 238 62 90). S-Bahn #1, 2, 3, 5, 7, 9, 25 or 75 or U-Bahn #6 to "Friedrichstr." Open 8:30am-5:30pm by appointment only.

LOCAL SERVICES

Currency Exchange: The best rates are usually found at offices that exclusively exchange currency and traveler's checks. The **Wechselstube** at Joachimstaler Str. 1-3 (☎882 10 86), near **Bahnhof Zoo,** has good rates and no commission. Open M-F 8am-8pm, Sa 9am-3pm. **Geldwechsel,** Joachimstaler Str. 7-9 (☎882 63 71), has decent rates and no commission. **ReiseBank,** at Bahnhof Zoo (☎881 71 17; open daily 7am-10pm) and Ostbahnhof (☎296 43 93; open M-F 7am-10pm, Sa 7am-6pm, Su 8am-4pm), is conveniently located in both major train stations, but has worse rates. **Berliner Bank** is in Tegel Airport. Open daily 8am-10pm. You can also change money at most **post offices,** which cash traveler's checks for DM6 per check. **Berliner Sparkasse** and **Deutsche Bank** have branches everywhere; their ATMs usually accept Visa and MC (as long as you know your PIN). Sparkasse changes cash for free, but charges a 1% commission on traveler's checks (with a DM7.50 minimum). **Citibank** has branches with **24hr. ATMs** at Kurfürstendamm 72, Wittenbergpl. 1, Wilmersdorfer Str. 133, and Karl-Marx-Allee 153. There's also a Citibank **ATM** at Tegel Airport.

American Express: Main Office, Bayreuther Str. 23 (☎21 49 83 63). U-Bahn #1, 2, or 15 to "Wittenbergpl." Holds mail and offers banking services. No commission for cashing AmEx traveler's checks. On F and Sa, expect out-the-door lines of travelers carrying *Let's Go*. Open M-F 9am-6pm, Sa 10am-1pm. **Branch office,** Friedrichstr. 172 (☎20 17 40 12). U-Bahn #6 to "Französische Str." Offers the same services. Open M-F 9am-5:30pm, Sa 10am-1pm.

Luggage Storage: In **Bahnhof Zoo.** Lockers DM2 per day, larger lockers DM4. 72hr. max. If all the lockers at Zoo are full, check your luggage at the center near the post office for DM4 per piece per day. Open daily 6am-11pm. Also at **Ostbahnhof** (lockers DM2 per day, larger DM4, 72hr. max.), **Bahnhof Lichtenberg,** and **Alexanderpl.** (lockers DM2 per day, 24hr. max.).

Lost Property: Zentrales Fundbüro, Pl. der Luftbrücke 8 (☎69 95). **BVG Fundbüro,** Fraunhofer Str. 33-36 (☎25 62 30 40). U-Bahn #2 to "Ernst-Reuter-Pl." For items lost on the bus, streetcar, or U-Bahn. Many, many umbrellas. Open M-Tu and Th 9am-3pm, W 9am-6pm, F 9am-2pm. **Fundbüro Berlin,** Mittelstr. 20 (☎29 72 96 12), at the Schönefeld airport train station. S-Bahn #9 or 45 to "Flughafen Berlin-Schönefeld."

Bookstores: Marga Schoeler Bücherstube, Knesebeckstr. 33 (☎881 11 12), at Mommsenstr., between Savignypl. and the Ku'damm. S-Bahn #3, 5, 7, 9, or 75 to "Savignypl." Large selection of books in English includes politics, history, poetry, literary criticism, and fiction. Lots of off-beat and contemporary reading material—perfect for the traveler tired of trashy romance novels sold on the one rack in the train station. Open M-W 9:30am-7pm, Th-F 9:30am-8pm, Sa 9:30am-4pm. The **British Bookshop,** Mauerstr. 83-84 (☎238 46 80), by Checkpoint Charlie. U-Bahn #6 to "Kochstr." An artfully stocked addition to Berlin's English book club, with well-chosen literature and history sections and English-language newspapers and mags. Open M-F 10am-7pm, Sa 10am-4pm. **Literaturhaus Berlin,** Fasanenstr. 23 (☎882 65 52), is in an old mansion complete with a garden and readings of German and international literature. U-Bahn #15 to "Uhlandstr." Their resident bookstore, **Kohlhaas & Co.** (☎882 50 44), has lots of German paperbacks, and excellent Judaica and Nazi history sections. Open M-F 10am-8pm, Sa 10am-4pm.

Libraries: Staatsbibliothek Preußischer Kulturbesitz, Potsdamer Str. 33 (☎26 61), and Unter den Linden 8 (☎210 50). 3.5 million books—one for every Berliner—but not all are stored on site. Lots of English-language newspapers. The Potsdamer Str. library was built for West Berlin in the 1960s, after the Iron Curtain went down on the original **"Staabi"** on Unter den Linden, next to the Humboldt-Universität (see p. 115). Now *Berliners* can choose between them—so can you. Both open M-F 9am-9pm, Sa 9am-5pm. Day-pass required for entry, DM1.

Cultural Centers: Amerika Haus, Hardenbergstr. 22-24 (☎31 50 55 70). Library includes English-language books, videos, and day-old editions of *The New York Times*. Occasionally hosts readings by visiting American authors. Offices open M-F 8:30am-5:30pm. Library open only by appointment, Tu and Th 2-8pm, W and F 2-5:30pm. **British Council,** Hardenbergstr. 20 (☎31 10 99 10), is next door, on the first floor of the Berliner Bank building. Open M-F 9am-12:30pm and 2-5pm. Library open M and W-F 2-6pm, Tu 2-7pm.

Language Instruction: Goethe-Institut, Schönhauser Str. 20 (☎25 90 63; fax 25 90 64 00), is the best known and the most expensive. Take S-Bahn #1 to "Feuerbachstr." All levels of German available. Office open M-Th 9am-5pm, F 9am-3pm. DM1690 for 4 weeks, DM3170 for 8 weeks; 25hr. of instruction per week. The magazines *Tip* and *Zitty* are filled with ads for other schools and private tutors—check the classifieds under "Unterricht" and shop around.

Laundromat: Wasch Centers at various locations: Leibnizstr. 72, in **Charlottenburg;** U-Bahn #7 to "Wilmersdorfer Str." Wexstr. 34, in **Schöneberg;** U-Bahn #9 to "Bundesplatz." Bergmannstr. 109, in **Kreuzberg;** U-Bahn #7 to "Gneisenaustr." Behmstr. 12, in **Mitte;** S-Bahn #1, 2, or 25 or U-Bahn #8 to "Gesundbrunnen." Jablonskistr. 21, in **Prenzlauer Berg;** U-Bahn #2 to "Eberswalder Str." Wash DM6 per 6kg, soap included. Dry DM2 for 30min. All open daily 6am-11pm. **Waschcenter Schnell und Sauber,** Uhlandstr. 61; U-Bahn #15 to "Uhlandstr." Torstr. 15, in **Mitte;** U-Bahn #8 to "Rosenthaler Pl." Oderberger Str. 1, in **Prenzlauer Berg;** U-Bahn #2 to "Eberswalder Str." Mehringdamm 32, in **Kreuzberg;** U-Bahn #6 to "Mehringdamm." Str. der Pariser Kommune 22, in **Friedrichshain;** S-Bahn #3, 5, 7, 9, or 75 to "Ostbahnhof." Wash DM6 per 6kg. Open daily 6am-11pm.

Emergency: Police, Pl. der Luftbrücke 6 (☎110). U-Bahn #6 to "Pl. der Luftbrücke." **Ambulance and Fire,** (☎112).

Crisis Lines: English spoken at most crisis lines. **American Hotline** (☎(0177) 814 15 10). Crisis and referral service. **Sexual Assault Hotline,** (☎251 28 28). Open Tu and Th 6-9pm, Su noon-2pm. **Schwules Überfall,** for victims of gay bashing, (☎216 33 36). Hotline and legal help. Open daily 6-9pm. **Schwulenberatung,** gay men's counseling, (☎194 46). **Lesbenberatung,** lesbian counseling, (☎215 20 00). **Drug Crisis,** (☎192 37). Open M-F 8:30am-10pm, Sa-Su 2-9:30pm. **Frauenkrisentelefon,** women's crisis line, (☎615 42 43). Open M and Th 10am-noon, Tu-W and F 7-9pm, Sa-Su 5-7pm. **Deutsche AIDS-Hilfe,** Dieffenbachstr. 33 (☎690 08 70). **Berliner Behindertenverband,** (☎545 87 99). Information and advice for the handicapped. Open M-F 8am-4pm.

Pharmacies: Europa-Apotheke, Tauentzienstr. 9-12 (☎261 41 42), near the Europa-Center and Bahnhof Zoo. Open M-F 9am-8pm, Sa 9am-4pm. **Münz-Apotheke,** Münzstr. 5 (☎241 10 83), just off Alexanderpl. Open M-F 8am-6:30pm, Sa 9am-1pm. Closed pharmacies post signs directing you to the nearest open one. For information about **late-night pharmacies,** call ☎011 89.

Medical Assistance: The American and British embassies have a list of English-speaking doctors. **Emergency Doctor** (☎31 00 31 or 192 42) and **Emergency Dentist** (☎89 00 43 33). Both available 24hr.

Post Offices: Budapester Str. 42, opposite the Europa-Center near Bahnhof Zoo. **Poste Restante** should be addressed: Postlagernd, Postamt in der Budapester Str. 42, 10787 Berlin. Open M-Sa 8am-midnight, Su 10am-midnight. Branch office at **Tegel Airport** (☎417 84 90). Open daily 6:30am-9pm. **Postamt Friedrichshain,** Str. der Pariser Kommune 8-10, 10243 Berlin, near Ostbahnhof. Open M-F 7am-9pm, Sa 8am-8pm. Neighborhood branches are everywhere (usually open M-F 9am-6pm, Sa 9am-noon); look for the little yellow POST signs.

Internet Access: Alpha, Dunckerstr. 72 (☎447 90 67), in Prenzlauer Berg. U-Bahn #2 to "Eberswalder Str." Open daily 3pm-midnight. DM12 per hr. **Cyberb@r,** Joachimstaler Str. 5-6, near Bahnhof Zoo. On the second floor of the **Karstadt** department store, Alexanderpl. DM5 per 30min. **Webtimes,** Chausseestr. 8 (☎280 49 890), in Mitte. U-Bahn #6 to "Oranienburger Tor." Speedy connections, quiet atmosphere. Open M-F 9am-midnight, Sa and Su 10am-midnight. DM7 per hr. **Com Line,** Innsbrückerstr. 56 (☎78 70 64 46, fax 78 70 64 48), in Schöneberg. Open M-Th noon-10pm, F & Sa noon-midnight, Su noon-8pm. DM 4 per 30 min. For the trendiest internet joint, see **Websites,** p. 111.

■ ACCOMMODATIONS

Although Berlin has become a favorite destination for tourists of all types, same-day accommodations aren't impossible to find thanks to the ever-growing hosteling and hotel industry. However, not making reservations will greatly limit your choice, and if you're cruising the hostel scene, it's likely you will have to take it day by day to know whether or not you have a bed, as some establishments are not sure if they have space until their reservations fail to show. For stays longer than a couple of days or on weekends, reservations are essential. For the **Love Parade** (see p. 138), the overly-eager begin making reservations at New Year's—if you want a choice of rooms, call at least two months early; for any bed at all you need at least two weeks. Note that some hostels increase prices by up to DM20 per night. Same-day space during this weekend is just about impossible to come by, and sleeping in the Tiergarten wouldn't be so bad if it weren't for all that urine.

For a DM5 fee, **tourist offices** will find you a room in a hostel, *Pension*, or hotel. Be prepared to pay at least DM70 for a single and DM100 for a double. There are also over 4000 **private rooms** available in the city; the overwhelming majority are controlled by the tourist offices. Expect to pay DM80 for singles, DM100 for doubles, plus a single-night surcharge of DM5. In that price range, there's a wide spectrum of locations, comfort levels, and amenities. Press for details, and be sure that they know your language abilities (if any). They often prefer to fill up the *Pensionen* first, so you may have to ask for private rooms. Although most accommodations are in western Berlin, the office does have some listings for private rooms in the eastern half of the city. The tourist offices also have the pamphlet *Accommodations, Youth Hostels, and Camping Places in Berlin*, which lists hostels and inexpensive guest houses and hotels in English and German (DM1).

For longer visits (more than 4 days), the various **Mitwohnzentralen** can arrange for you to housesit or sublet someone's apartment. Prices start at DM40 for a single, DM70 for a double, and DM80-100 for a two-person apartment. For longer stays, expect to pay DM500-800 per month for a studio. The fee decreases relative to the price the longer you stay. **Home Company Mitwohnzentrale,** Joachimstaler Str. 17, is the biggest, and the staff speaks English. (☎194 45. U-Bahn #9 or 15 to "Kurfürstendamm." Open M-F 9am-6pm, Sa 11am-2pm.) **Erste,** Sybelstr. 53, tends to be less chaotic. (☎324 30 31; fax 324 99 77. U-Bahn #7 to "Adenauerpl." Open M-F 9am-8pm, Sa 10am-6pm.) **Mitwohnzentralen** usually require you to pay up front unless you have—or can find a friend who has—a German bank account. Keep fees in mind—for short stays (less than a month) the standard commission is 20% of the final sum while for longer stays the rate is usually 25%, although the monthly prices are lower. Leases in Berlin start at any time—you don't need to wait for a new calendar month.

HOSTELS AND DORMITORY ACCOMMODATIONS

Hostels in Berlin fall into three categories: HI-affiliated, state-owned *Jugendherbergen* and *Jugendgästehäuser*, large, privately-owned hostels, and smaller, more off-beat private hostels. **HI hostels** can be a great, cheap sleep, but it's often very difficult to get a place, as they fill quickly with German school groups. Also note that state-run hostels often impose a **curfew,** putting a damper on late-night forays into Berlin's nightlife. Most HI hostels are for members only, though you can usually get a nonmember's stamp (DM6 extra) and spend the night. To purchase an **HI card,** head to Tempelhofer Ufer 32, where the staff issues membership cards (DM30) and reserves spots in the myriad hostels. (☎264 95 20. Open M, W, and F 10am-4pm, Tu and Th 1-6pm. U-Bahn #1, 15, or 2 to "Gleisdreieck.")

If you're looking for a more party-ready crew, shack up at one of the large, well-equipped **private hostels,** which have a mostly non-German clientele. These centers of youthful hipness are located near the train stations and major nightlife areas and have a guest turnover rate of about two days, so you'll never be bored—unless you tire of hearing more English spoken than German. These can vary depending on neighborhood or clientele attitude; read hostel descriptions carefully and pick the one that best suits your partying endurance. For more adventurous travelers, the **smaller independent hostels,** though often less central and with fewer amenities, are a better choice, offering a more relaxed atmosphere.

BERLIN HOSTELS Unless otherwise noted, hostel prices are *per person.*

MITTE

BERLIN

▨ **Circus,** Rosa-Luxemburg-Str. 39-41 (☎28 39 14 33; fax 28 39 14 84; email circus@mind.de). U-Bahn #2 to "Rosa-Luxemburg-Pl." Close to Alexanderpl., Circus makes a heroic effort at hostel hipness, offering cheap internet access and a disco ball in the lobby. Breakfast items and beverages available from the reception at menu prices. Laundry facilities, info on night-life, and a cafe/bar for guests only next door make Circus fully equipped with everything an English-speaking backpacker could ask for. Terry Brewer's walking tours (see p. 95) pick up Circus guests at 9:15 and 12:45. Spacious apartment with kitchen and private bath DM160. Sheets DM4. Bike rental DM12 per day. 24hr. reception. No curfew. Reservations in summer are a must and should be reconfirmed 1 day before arrival. Wheelchair accessible. 5-6 bed dorms DM25; singles DM45; doubles DM 40; triples DM35; quads DM40.

Clubhouse Hostel, Kalkscheunestr. 2 (☎28 09 79 79). S-Bahn #1, 2, or 25 to "Oranienburger Str." or U-Bahn #6 to "Oranienburger Tor." Enter the courtyard from Johannisstr. 2 or Kalkscheunestr. Great location in the center of the Oranienburger Str. club and bar scene, including a partnership with Club "Kalkscheune" downstairs (see p. 132). Breakfast buffet DM7, served 8-11am. Internet access DM1 per 5min. 24hr. reception and bar. No curfew. Call at least 2-3 days ahead. Wheelchair accessible. Terry Brewer's walking tours meet Clubhouse guests at 10:15am daily. 8-10 bed dorms DM25; 5-7 bed dorms DM30; singles DM50; doubles DM40.

Mitte's Backpacker Hostel, Chausseestr. 102 (☎262 51 40 or 28 39 09 65; fax 28 39 09 35; email backpacker@snafu.de; www.backpacker.de). U-Bahn #6 to "Zinnowitzer Str." Look for the giant orange sign on the wall outside. Ever striving to excel, the Backpacker has rooms with themes like "Garden of Eden" and "Under the Sea," but the fact that you may end up sleeping with a giant spider on your ceiling doesn't make up for the fact that most of your fellow hostel guests will be exhausted, city-a-day world travelers. The staff provides information on nightlife, travel, and sight-seeing. Sheets DM5. Laundry DM5 per load. Bikes DM10-12 per day. Internet access. Kitchen available for guest use; hostel guests also get a 10% discount at the restaurant downstairs. A thorough walking tour leaves the hostel daily at 9am and 2pm (6hr., DM10). No curfew. Reception 7am-9:30pm, plus a multi-purpose night-porter. Dorm beds DM25; 5-6 bed room DM27 to 29; doubles DM38; triples DM33; quads DM31.

Mitte

▲ **ACCOMMODATIONS**	🍅 **FOOD**	🏛 **MUSEUMS**	● **SIGHTS**
Circus, 6	Beth Café, 15	Alte Nationalgalerie, 28	Alte Bibliothek, 47
Clubhouse Hostel, 23	Cafe Edwin, 11	Altes Museum, 40	Bertolt-Brecht-Haus, 1
Mitte's Backpacker	Cafeteria Charlottenstr., 54	Bodemuseum, 26	Brandenburger Tor, 63
Hostel, 2	Mendelssohn, 14	Deutsche Guggenheim Berlin, 46	Deutsche Staatsbibliothek, 45
🍷 **NIGHTLIFE**	Mensa der Humboldt-U, 44	Deutscher Dom, 53	Deutsche Staatsoper, 48
b-flat, 7	Taba, 3	Deutsches Hist. Museum, 41	Ephraim-Palais, 33
Hackesche Höfe, 9	Trattoria Ossena, 20	Gemäldegalerie, 70	Fernsehturm, 30
Kalkscheune, 22	Village Voice, 4	Hamburger Bahnhof, 65	Französischer Dom, 51
Las Cucarachas, 16		Hanf Museum, 34	Führerbunker, 60
Mitte Bar, 18	✝ **CHURCHES**	Infobox, 58	Haus am Checkpoint Charlie, 55
Roter Salon, 5	Berliner Dom, 39	Kunstgewerbemuseum, 69	Hotel Adlon, 62
Silberstien, 12	Marienkirche, 29	Märkisches Museum, 36	Humboldt-Universität, 43
Sophienclub, 8	Nikolaikirche, 32	Musikinstrumentenmuseum, 67	Jüdische Knabenschule, 10
Tacheles, 19	St.-Hedwigs-Kathedrale, 49	Neue Nationalgalerie, 71	Knoblauchhaus, 35
Tränenpalast, 25		Pergamon-Museum, 27	Martin-Gropius-Bau, 57
Tresor/Globus, 59		Schinkelmuseum, 50	Neue Wache, 42
VEB-OZ, 17		Topographie des Terrors, 56	Neue Synagoge, 13
WMF, 24		Zeughaus, 41	Palast der Republik, 38
Zosch, 21			Reichstag, 64
♪ **ENTERTAINMENT**			Rotes Rathaus, 31
Konzerthaus, 52			Russian Embassy, 61
Philharmonie, 68			Sowjetisches Ehrenmal, 66
			Staatsrat, 37

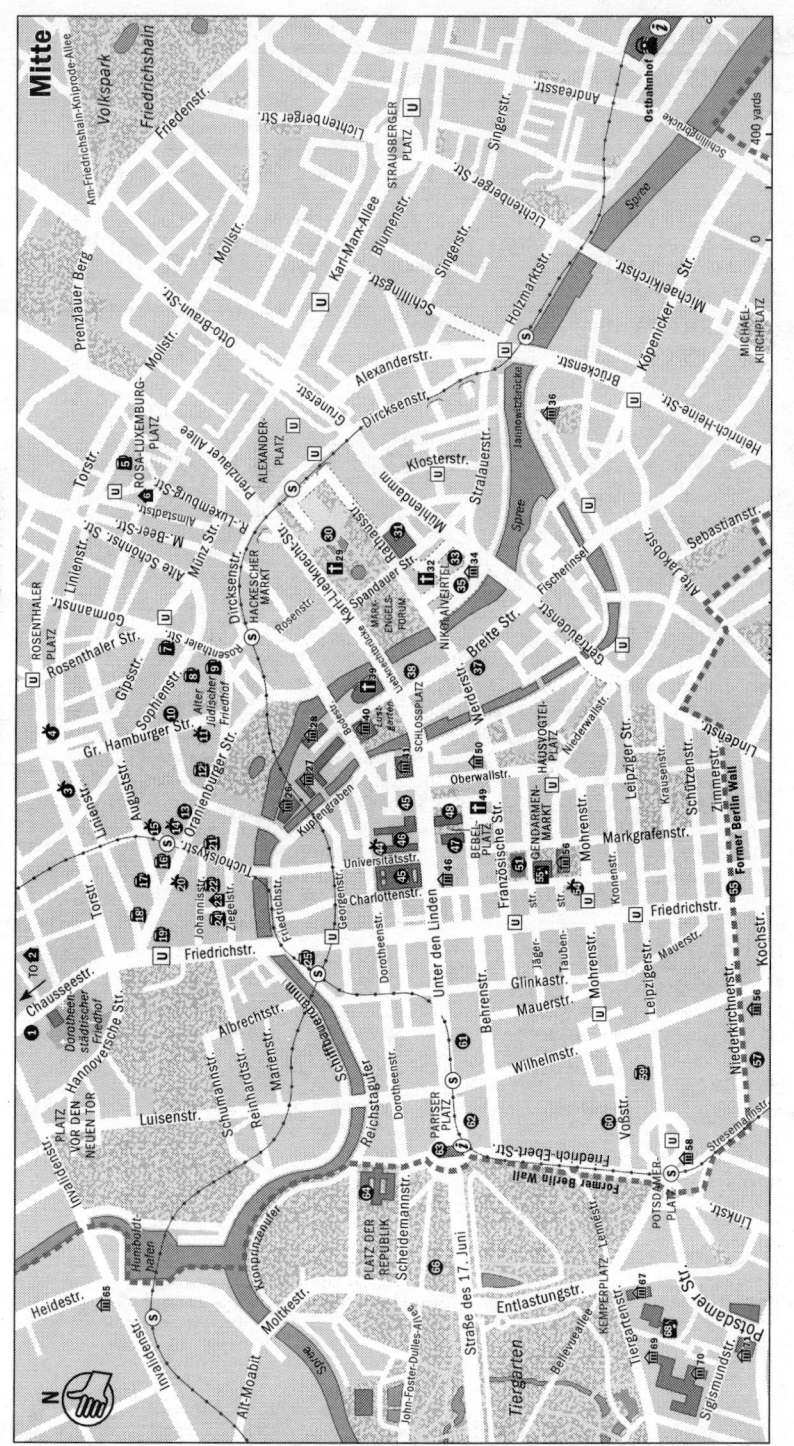

BAHNHOF ZOO

Jugendgästehaus am Zoo, Hardenbergstr. 9a (☎312 94 10; fax 401 52 83), opposite the Technical University *Mensa*. Bus #145 to "Steinpl.," or take the short walk from the back exit of Bahnhof Zoo straight down Hardenbergstr. Within spitting distance of Bahnhof Zoo. Bright rooms with enough space to go around. The wooden interior has seen a few too many years of backpack-bearing visitors, but the same-day convenience can't be beat. It's on the 5th floor; ride up in the elevator. Reception 9am-midnight. Check-in 10am. Check-out 9am. Lockout 10am-2pm. No curfew. No reservations accepted, but call in the morning to see if there's room. Grab a bite to eat at the adjacent **Café Hardenberg** (see p. 111). Small dorms (4-8 beds) DM35, over 26 DM40; Singles DM47, over 26 DM52; doubles DM85, over 26 DM95.

SCHÖNEBERG—TIERGARTEN

Jugendgästehaus (HI), Kluckstr. 3 (☎261 10 97 or 261 10 98; fax 265 03 83). From Bahnhof Zoo, take bus #129 (direction: "Hermannpl.") to "Gedenkstätte," or U-Bahn #1 to "Kurfürstenstr.," then walk up Potsdamer Str., go left on Pohlstr., and right on Kluckstr. The *Gästehaus* to end all *Gästehäuser* makes an effort to imitate its privately-owned competitors, offering an internet cafe, laundry facilities, and bike rentals in its enormous lobby, but it's just too damn big to shake off that HI feeling. Despite its staggering proportions, the dorm rooms are clean and contemporary. Breakfast and sheets included. Key deposit DM10. Lockers and laundry facilities available. Bike rental DM15 per day, students DM10. 24hr. reception. Curfew midnight; stragglers admitted every 30min. 12:30-6am. Lockout 9am-1pm. Reservations strongly recommended. 4-10 bed dorm rooms DM34, over 26 DM43.

Studentenhotel Meininger 10, Meininger Str. 10 (☎78 71 74 14; fax 78 71 74 12; email info@studentenhotel.de; www.studentenhostel.de). U-Bahn #4, bus #146 or N46 to "Rathaus Schöneberg." Walk toward the Rathaus on Freiherr-vom-Stein-Str., turn left onto Martin-Luther-Str. and then right on Meininger Str. The Studentenhotel reopened in January 2000 after being completely remodeled by an extremely enthusiastic and friendly group of university students. The results of their valiant efforts are not quite perfect, but their attitude carries over into the lively, friendly clientele. Breakfast included. 24hr. reception. DM10 deposit for locker keys. Free shuttle pick-up at Bahnhof Zoo for groups of 5 people or mores. 5% discount when you pull out your copy of *Let's Go*. Dorms DM25; singles DM66; doubles DM44; 3- to 6-bed rooms DM40.

Central Berlin West

🛏 ACCOMMODATIONS

Art Hotel Connection, 42
Charlottenburger Hof, 5
CVJM-Haus, 27
Frauenhotel Artemesia, 8
Hotel-Pension Cortina, 9
Jugendgästehaus (HI), 25
Jugendgästehaus am Zoo, 17
JugendKulturZentrum "Die Pumpe", 26
Hotel-Pension Hansablick, 19
Hotel Sachsenhof, 39
Pension Berolina, 6
Pension Knesebeck, 12

🍴 FOOD

Baharat Falafel, 31
Cafe Belmundo, 30
Cafe Hardenburg, 16
Cafe Sydney, 32
Cafe Voltaire, 7
Der Ägypter, 10
Filmbühne am Steinplatz, 15
Fish and Vegetables, 37
KaDeWe, 43
Mensa TU, 18
Schwarzes Café, 13
Sushi am Winterfeldtplatz, 36

🍷 NIGHTLIFE

A-Trane, 11
Cafe Berio, 33
Cafe Bilderbuch, 29
Connection, 41
Metropol, 34
Mister Hu, 28
Omnes, 40
Quasimodo, 14
Scheune, 38
Slumberland, 35

● SIGHTS

Aquarium, 44
Elefantentor, 45
Kaiser-Wilhelm-Gedächtiskirche, 46
Siegessäule, 20

🏛 MUSEUMS

Ägyptisches Museum, 2
Akademie der Künste, f
Bröhanmuseum, 4
Gemäldegalerie, 23
Kunstgewerbemuseum, 22
Neue Nationalgalerie, 24
Sammlung Berggruen, 3
Schloß Bellevue, 21
Schloß Charlottenburg, 1

BERLIN

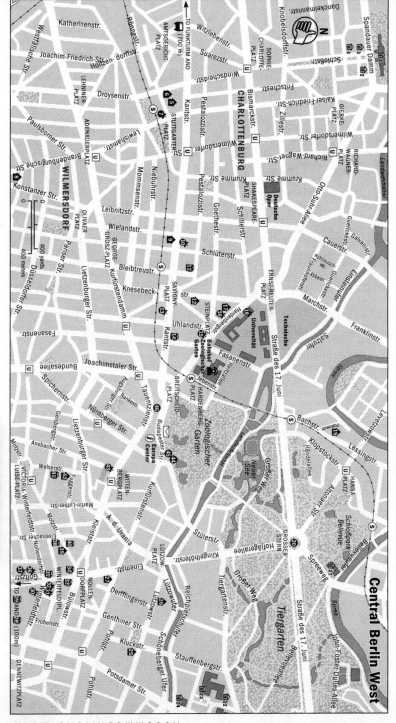

Central Berlin West

CVJM-Haus, Einemstr. 10 (☎264 91 00; fax 261 43 08). U-Bahn #1, 2, 4, or 15 to "Nollendorfpl." Young men: it's fun to stay at the German YMCA, despite the Christian institutional atmosphere. Palpably wholesome interior, all in tranquil blue. Popular with school groups. Conveniently located one block from Nollendorfpl.'s gay nightlife. Sheets DM3. Quiet time 10pm-7am and 1-3pm. Breakfast included. Reception 8-11am and 4-9pm. You can get a key for curfew-free revelry. Book ahead. DM40 per person for singles, doubles, and dormitory rooms.

Jugendgästehaus Feurigstraße, Feurigstr. 63 (☎781 52 11; fax 788 30 51). U-Bahn #7 to "Kleistpark," or bus #204 or 348 to "Kaiser-Wilhelm-Pl." Walk down Hauptstr., turn left onto Kollonenstr., and after a right onto Feurigstr., it will show up quickly on the left. An unadorned brown stucco building in a busy district relatively close to the Schöneberg bars. More popular with German school groups than with the traveling youth of America, you'll find respite from the English-speaking hostel scene here. Discount for groups of 10 or more. Breakfast included. Sheets DM5 if staying fewer than 3 nights, otherwise free. 24hr. reception, though staff is sometimes far from the desk; keep ringing. Call ahead. Dorms DM40 (DM27 after August); singles DM55; doubles DM50.

JugendKulturZentrum "Die Pumpe," Lutzowstr. 42 (☎26 48 48 30; fax 26 48 48 31). U-Bahn #1, 2, 4, or 15 to "Nollendorfpl." Take Einemstr. away from Nollendorfpl.; after a right onto Lützowstr., the "Pumpe" complex will appear two blocks later on the left (10 min). The cluster of buildings includes a restaurant/cafe ("Die Alte Pumpe"), day-care center, office, and dorm-style accommodations. The hostel caters to large groups, and tends to book them well in advance. Breakfast available only for groups of 10 or more, DM6. Door locked at 10pm, but you can get a key. DM30; DM31.50 with use of the kitchen. For groups of 10 or more DM25, DM26.50 with kitchen use.

KREUZBERG

Bax Pax, Skalitzer Str. 104 (☎69 51 83 22; fax 69 51 83 72; email info@baxpax.de; www.baxpax.de). U-Bahn #1 or 15 to "Görlitzer Bahnhof," right across the street. This brand-new addition to Berlin's private hosteling community offers dorm-style housing with fuzzy blue carpets, sparkling bathrooms, and an ultra-friendly staff. The atmosphere is very social, but what do you expect when the madness of Orangienstr. is just around the corner. Kitchen open 24 hours. Sheets DM5. Reception 7am-10pm. No curfew. DM25-30 per night.

Die Fabrik, Schlesische Str. 18 (☎611 71 16; fax 617 51 04; email info@diefabrik.com). U-Bahn #1 or 15 to "Schlesisches Tor" or night bus #N65 to "Taborstr." This consciously-cool converted factory, with spacious rooms, is within walking distance of Kreuzberg's nightlife. Breakfast in the cafe downstairs DM10. Bike rental DM20 per day. 24hr. reception. Reserve or call ahead. Curfew? Rage all night, little pumpkin. Surprisingly comfortable "sleep-in" deal puts you up in a 15-bed dorm for DM30; singles DM66; doubles DM47; triples DM40; quads DM36.

FRIEDRICHSHAIN

Frederik's Hostel, Str. der Pariser Kommune 35 (☎29 66 94 50 or 29 66 94 51; fax 29 66 94 52; email hostel@frederiks.de; www.frederiks.de). Take U-Bahn #5 to "Weberwiese" or S-Bahn #3, 5, 7, 9 or 75 to "Ostbahnhof." From the U-Bahn, exit on Karl-Marx-Allee and turn left on Str. der Pariser Kommune; the hostel will be on the right. From Ostbahnhof, walk to the farthest exit along the train tracks. Once downstairs, with your back to station, walk straight along Str. der Pariser Kommune; the hostel will be on the left side of the street (10min.). Laid-back hostel with a little bit of that alternative Friedrichshain spirit. Large kitchen and a cozy basement bar with just enough clutter to make it feel at home. Bright and cheery primary-colored bathrooms. Breakfast DM6. Sheets DM5. Kitchen facilities. Internet access. 24 hr. reception. 16-bed dorms DM23; 8-bed dorms DM26; singles DM59; doubles DM39; quads DM29.

Odyssee, Grünberger Str. 23 (☎29 00 00 81; www.hostel-berlin.de). U-Bahn #5 to "Frankfurter Tor" or S-Bahn #3, 5, 6, 7, 9, or 75 or U-Bahn #1 or 15 to "Warschauer Str." On the edge of the quickly growing Friedrichshain pub and club scene, this is one

BERLIN

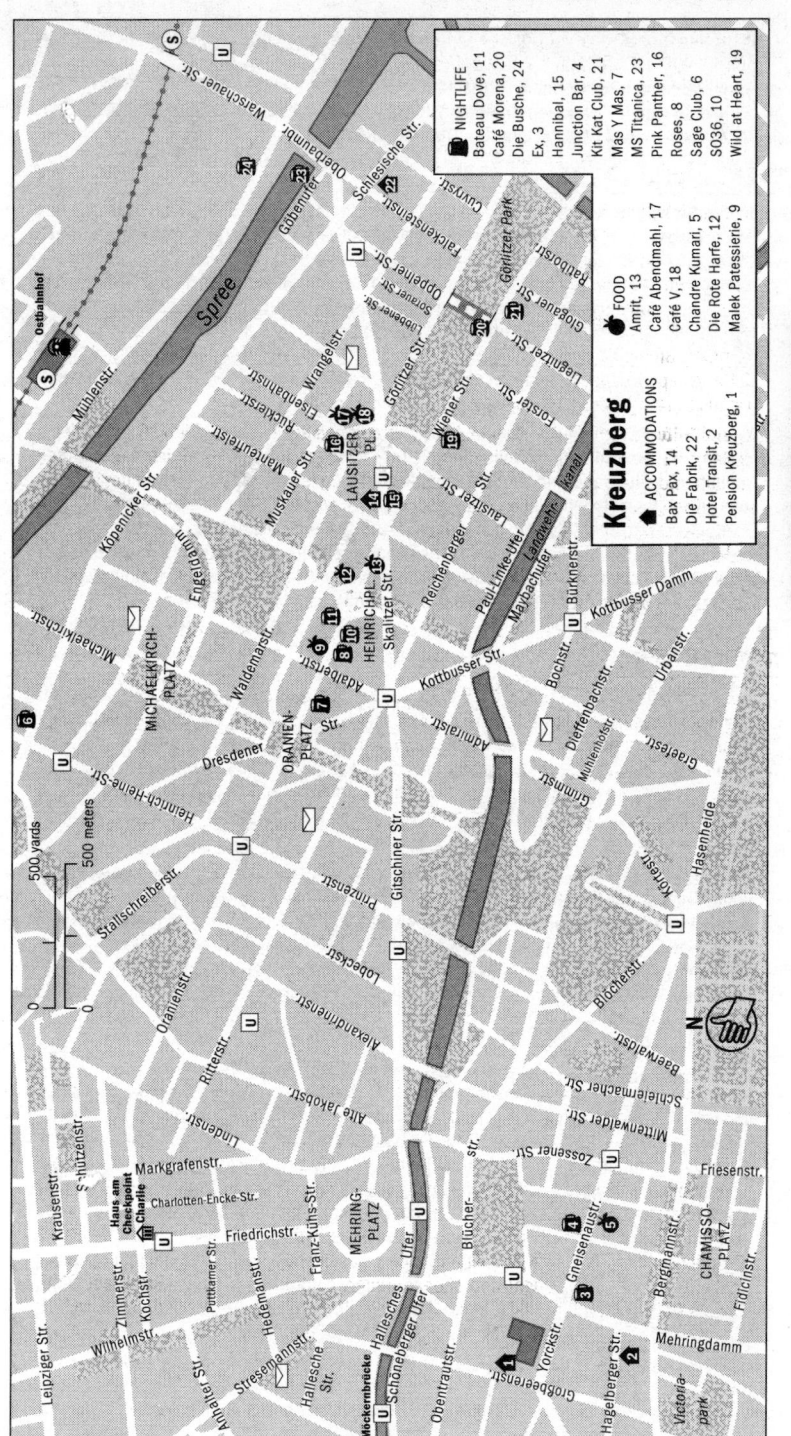

Kreuzberg

NIGHTLIFE
Bateau Dove, 11
Café Morena, 20
Die Busche, 24
Ex, 3
Hannibal, 15
Junction Bar, 4
Kit Kat Club, 21
Mas Y Mas, 7
MS Titanica, 23
Pink Panther, 16
Roses, 8
Sage Club, 6
SO36, 10
Wild at Heart, 19

FOOD
Amrit, 13
Café Abendmahl, 17
Café V, 18
Chandre Kumari, 5
Die Rote Harfe, 12
Malek Patessierie, 9

ACCOMMODATIONS
Bax Pax, 14
Die Fabrik, 22
Hotel Transit, 2
Pension Kreuzberg, 1

of the few hostels as cool as the surrounding neighborhood. Large, treehouse-style lounge with bar, colorfully painted bedrooms, and quite possibly the slickest bathrooms of all the hostels of Germany. Breakfast DM5. Internet access DM3 per 15min. Bar open until dawn. 24hr. reception. No curfew. Always reserve ahead. 8-bed dorms DM24; 6-bed dorms DM26; doubles DM36; quads DM32.

PRENZLAUER BERG

Lette'm Sleep Hostel, Lettestr. 7 (☎44 73 36 23; fax 44 73 36 25). U-Bahn #2 to "Eberswalder Str." The first hostel to open up in Prenzlauer Berg, a few blocks from Kollwitzpl. The hostel redefines the expressions "laid-back staff" and "relaxed atmosphere." Ideal place to crash for the hardcore club-goer. Kitchen facilities. Wheelchair access. Internet access DM1 per 5min. 3-6 bed dorms DM26-35.

TEGEL

Jugendherberge Ernst Reuter (HI), Hermsdorfer Damm 48-50 (☎404 16 10; fax 404 59 72). S-Bahn #25 to "Tegel" or U-Bahn #6 to "Alt-Tegel," then bus #125 or night bus #N25 (direction: "Frohnau/Invalidensiedlung") to "Jugendherberge." If you want a respite from the whirlwind touristers that flock to the city's hostels, Ernst Reuter presents a welcoming alternative with easy connections to the city center. The hostel will achieve complete hostel-chic with the addition of internet access, planned for the end of the 2000. Breakfast and sheets included. Lockers in the rooms. DM8 for laundry facilities, detergent included. 24 hour reception. Key deposit DM20. Reservations recommended, but a space or two is also usually available same-day if you call early in the morning. Closed Dec. 6-bed rooms DM28, over 26 and non-HI members DM35.

Backpacker's Paradise, Ziekowstr. 161 (☎433 86 40). S-Bahn #25 to "Tegel" or U-Bahn #6 to "Alt-Tegel," then bus #222 or night bus #N22 to "Titusweg." Next to the Jugendgästehaus Tegel. The signs in front of Tegel's proper hostel point you to the "International Camp for Young Backpackers," but you'll know where you've gotten yourself to as soon as you turn the corner and see the spray-painted logo. It's the next best thing to rolling a doobie in your VW van. Officially under 27 only, but rules are made for conformists, and they aren't into that sort of thing here. Breakfast buffet DM3. Free hot shower. Lockers DM1. Washing machines DM5. 24hr. reception. No reservations needed. Open late June-Aug. DM10 gets you a blanket and thermal pad under a tent; add DM3 for a summer-camp-like cot. Campfire every night.

Jugendgästehaus Tegel, Ziekowstr. 161 (☎433 30 46; fax 434 50 63; email JGH-Tegel@t-online.de). S-Bahn #25 to "Tegel" or U-Bahn #6 to "Alt-Tegel," then bus #222 or night bus #N22 (direction: "Alt-Lübars") to "Titusweg." On the north end of town by the Tegel parks. Old brick outside, new and bright inside. No English spoken, many school groups. Breakfast and sheets included. Reception 7:30am-11pm. No curfew, you get a house-key. Reservations are a must. 3-8 bed dorms DM37.50.

ELSEWHERE IN BERLIN

Jugendgästehaus am Wannsee (HI), Badeweg 1 (☎803 20 35; fax 803 59 08). S-Bahn #1 or 7 to "Nikolassee." From the main exit, cross the bridge and head left on Kronprinzessinweg; Badeweg will be on your right after 5min. 30min. from the center, but Wannsee has its own charm. From the DJH symbols on the cubes outside to the sanitary yellow brick inside, it's clear that this is no hip private hostel, but it's clean, organized, and friendly. 62 4-bed rooms. Toilets shared between 2 rooms, showers among 6. Breakfast and sheets included. Key deposit DM20. Large groups necessitate booking 2 weeks in advance from May to October. Members only. DM34, over 26 DM42.

Jugendgästehaus Nordufer, Nordufer 28 (☎45 19 91 12; fax 452 41 00). U-Bahn #9 to "Westhafen," left over the bridge and left onto Nordufer for about 15min. Away from the center, but on the pretty, blue Plötzensee. Some singles, but mostly quads. Swim in the adjacent pool for DM4, students DM3. Breakfast buffet and sheets included. Reception 7am-5pm; ring the bell at other times. No curfew. Dorm Beds DM37.50.

BERLIN

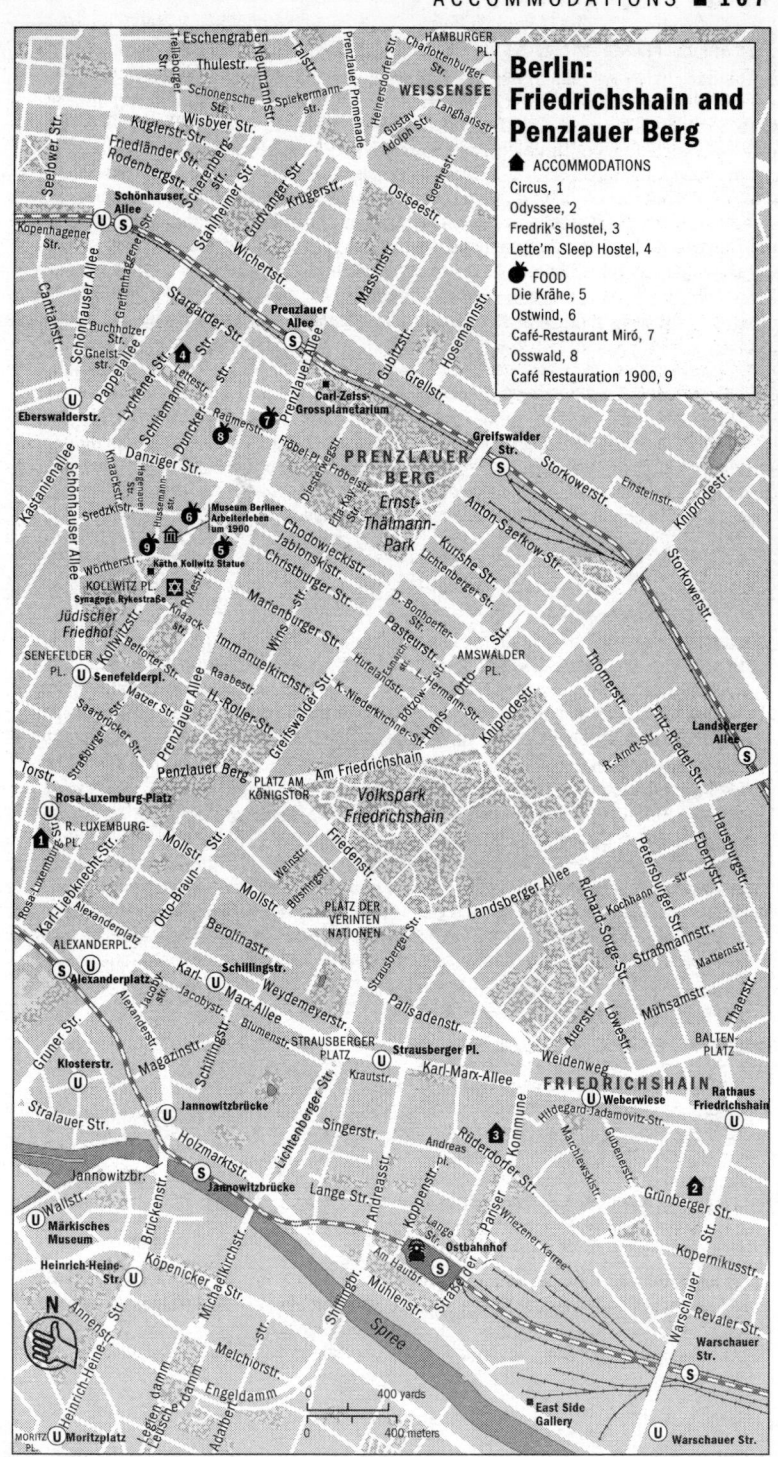

Berlin: Friedrichshain and Penzlauer Berg

🏠 **ACCOMMODATIONS**

Circus, 1
Odyssee, 2
Fredrik's Hostel, 3
Lette'm Sleep Hostel, 4

🍎 **FOOD**

Die Krähe, 5
Ostwind, 6
Café-Restaurant Miró, 7
Osswald, 8
Café Restauration 1900, 9

BERLIN

HOTELS AND PENSIONEN

Many small *Pensionen* and hotels are within the means of budget travelers, particularly since most establishments listed in *Let's Go* are amenable to *Mehrbettzimmer*, where extra beds are moved into a large double or triple. However, these benefits are really only for groups of three or more; hotels will not usually allow random individuals to crash together (lest an orgy spontaneously erupt). Most affordable hotels are in western Berlin; the hotels in Mitte are ridiculously expensive, and other areas in the east still lack the facilities to support many visitors. The best places to find cheap rooms is Charlottenburg, especially around Savignypl. and Wilmersdorfer Str.

TIERGARTEN

Hotel-Pension Hansablick, Flotowstr. 6 (☎390 48 00; fax 392 69 37; email reserv@hotel-hansablick.de; www.hotel-hansablick.de). S-Bahn #3, 5, 7, 9, or 75 to "Tiergarten." Somewhat pricey, but it's an absolute *Jugendstil* pearl, from the decorative ceilings to the marble entrance and lamps gracing the cobblestone streets in front. All rooms have bath, hair dryer, phone, and cable TV. Some have patios for watching ferries on the Spree. Few buildings like this survived WWII. Call, write, or fax ahead for reservations. In the low season (July-Aug. and mid-Nov. to Feb.), discount rates available upon request. 5% discount if you mention *Let's Go*. Safe available. 24hr. reception. Singles DM155, doubles DM185-225. Extra bed in the big doubles DM55.

CHARLOTTENBURG

Charlottenburger Hof, Stuttgarter Pl. 14 (☎32 90 70; fax 323 37 23). S-Bahn #3, 5, 7, 9, or 75 to "Charlottenburg" (across the street) or U-Bahn #7 to "Wilmersdorfer Str." The primary-colored, modern art-themed decor of this hotel is so chic that it could pass for a gallery, with Miró, Dalí, and Picasso lining the walls. Breakfast in the adjoining **Café Voltaire** DM7 (see p. 112). Laundry DM5. Sometimes has same-day space. All rooms include phones and TVs; the pricier doubles come with balconies and whirlpools. Singles DM80-120; doubles DM110-160; quads DM160-220.

Hotel-Pension Cortina, Kantstr. 140 (☎313 90 59; fax 312 73 96). S-Bahn #3, 5, 7, 9, or 75 to "Savignypl." High-ceilinged, bright rooms with a friendly staff and a great location right off the main S-Bahn line and within walking distance of Bahnhof Zoo. More expensive rooms have private showers. Breakfast included. 24hr. reception. Dorm-style accommodation DM35-60, depending on the time of year and the size of the group; singles DM60-90; doubles DM90-150.

Pension Berolina, Stuttgarter Pl. 17 (☎32 70 90 72; fax 32 70 90 73). S-Bahn #3, 5, 7, 9, or 75 to "Charlottenburg" or U-Bahn #7 to "Wilmersdorfer Str." Spartan rooms with linoleum floors, conveniently located near the S-Bahn station. Shared bathrooms. Breakfast DM8. Reservations recommended. Singles DM60; doubles DM80; triples DM90; quads DM100; quints DM110.

Pension Knesebeck, Knesebeckstr. 86 (☎312 72 55; fax 313 95 07). S-Bahn #3, 5, 7, 9, or 75 to "Savignypl." Just north of the park. Friendly, large *Alt-Berliner* rooms with faux Baroque stylings, couches, and sinks. Hearty buffet-style breakfast included. Laundry machines DM8. 24hr. reception. Phone reservations must be confirmed by fax or letter or with a credit card. Cheaper in winter. Singles DM75, with shower DM85; doubles DM110-120, with shower DM130-140; big *Mehrbettzimmer* DM50-60 per person.

SCHÖNEBERG-WILMERSDORF

Hotel-Pension München, Güntzelstr. 62 (☎857 91 20; fax 85 79 12 22; email hotel-pension.muenchen@arcormail.de). U-Bahn #9 to "Güntzelstr." Bright 3rd-floor *Pension* with balconies and art by contemporary Berlin artists. Clean, gracefully-decorated white-walled rooms with cable-TVs and phones. Breakfast DM10. Ask about *Mehrbettzimmer*. Checkout 11am. Written reservations are best as the hotel has many admirers. Singles DM66-70, with shower DM95-110; doubles DM80-90, with bath DM115-130.

Hotel Sachsenhof, Motzstr. 7 (☎216 20 74; fax 215 82 20). U-Bahn #1, 2, 4, or 15 to "Nollendorfpl." Small, well-furnished rooms with phone, TV, and leopard-print carpets. The hotel is in a lovely old house surrounded by Nollendorfpl.'s myriad cafes, and in the middle of its gay nightlife scene. Breakfast DM10. 24hr. reception. Call for reservations between 7am and 11pm. Singles DM57, with shower DM65; doubles DM99, with shower DM126; new double with shower DM 146, with full bath DM156; DM30 per extra bed.

Jugendhotel Luftbrücke, Kolonnenstr. 10-11 (☎78 70 21 30; fax 78 70 21 32; email jugendhotelberlin@t-online.de; www.Jugendhotel-Berlin.de). U-Bahn #7 to "Kleistpark." Walk down Hauptstr, turn left onto Kolonnenstr. After the bridge you'll see the sign in the window; the entrance is on Leberstr. (10 min.) In May 2001 a new building will open closer to the U-Bahn station. Similar to a hostel, this hotel doesn't call itself one because they do not put strangers together in dorm-style rooms. Clean, simple accomodations. Showers on the hallway. Breakfast included. Doors locked at night, but guests get a code for 24hr access. Reservations recommended. Singles DM50, doubles DM45, larger rooms (up to 10 beds) DM39. Off-season (Oct.-Jan.) DM32.50. The new building will offer rooms with private baths at DM65 for singles, DM55 for doubles.

Art Hotel Connection, Fuggerstr. 33 (☎217 70 28; fax 217 70 30; email info@arthotel-connection.de; www.arthotel-connection.de). U-Bahn #1, 2, or 15 to "Wittenbergpl.," on a side-street off Martin-Luther-Str. One of the most fabulous hotels in Berlin, the blue ceilings and antique elevator clue you in from the beginning that this is indeed an "art" hotel. For gay and lesbian guests only (though mostly men stay here), the rooms are nicely decorated and equipped with everything from phones and TVs to alarm clocks. For a really exciting getaway, ask for the "special room," fully equipped to guarantee that you have a little fun. Cheaper in winter. One two-room apartment with kitchen available. Breakfast included. Reservations required for weekends at least one month in advance. Singles DM110-150; doubles 150-210.

Frauenhotel Artemesia, Brandenburgische Str. 18 (☎873 89 05; fax 861 86 53; email frauenhotel-berlin@t-online.de). U-Bahn #7 to "Konstanzer Str." Pricey, but a rare bird—an immaculate, elegant hotel for women only, the first of its kind in Germany. Rooms celebrate famous women in Berlin's history, while an outdoor terrace provides a damn fine view of Berlin. The **Speiseraum** upstairs serves breakfast (M-F 7:30-10:30am, Sa-Su 8-11:30am) and evening drinks (5-10pm) to an all-female (straight and lesbian) crowd. Breakfast included. Children under 8 free. Reception 7am-10pm. Singles DM109, with shower DM148; doubles DM170, with bath DM198; extra beds DM40 per person. Discounted rates for stays of five nights or more in Jan., Feb., Aug., Nov., and Dec.: singles DM89-125; doubles DM145-165. Come on your birthday and stay the next three nights for free! Alternatively, try to get the "last-minute, same-day" specials, with singles from DM79 and doubles from DM129 (without breakfast).

KREUZBERG

Hotel Transit, Hagelberger Str. 53-54 (☎789 04 70; fax 78 90 47 77). U-Bahn #6 or 7 or night bus #N19 to "Mehringdamm." Big-screen MTV lounge with bar open 24hr. Rooms adorned with sleek, faux Bauhaus furnishings and showers. Breakfast included. 24hr. reception. If you anticipate a hangover, you can request breakfast at noon or later. Singles DM90; doubles DM105; triples DM140; quads DM180. Their "Sleep-In" deal allows you to share a *Mehrbettzimmer* for DM33.

Pension Kreuzberg, Großbeerenstr. 64 (☎251 13 62; fax 251 06 38). U-Bahn #6 or 7 or night bus #N19 to "Mehringdamm." Decently priced rooms, small but well decorated with things abstract in an old but grand building in a neighborhood that is purely Kreuzberg. Breakfast included. Reception 8am-10pm. Singles DM75; doubles DM98; *Mehrbettzimmer* DM44 per person.

CAMPING

Deutscher Camping-Club runs the following campgrounds in Berlin; both are adjacent to the imaginary line tracing the site of the Berlin Wall. Written reservations can be made by writing the Deutscher Camping-Club Berlin, Geisbergstr. 11, 10777 Berlin. Otherwise, call in advance. The DCC's central phone number is ☎218 60 71 or 218 60 72. Both sites charge DM9.70 per person, DM4.60 per child, DM7.20 per tent, and DM12.70 for trailers.

Dreilinden (☎805 12 01). S-Bahn #7 to "Griebnitzsee," then walk back between the station and lake. A city campsite, surrounded on 3 sides by the vestiges of the Berlin Wall. The remains of a stretch of the *Autobahn* which fell into disuse after 1949 can be seen through the trees. The site's bar is an old border checkpoint. Open Mar.-Oct.

Kladow, Krampnitzer Weg 111-117 (☎365 27 97). U-Bahn #7 to "Rathaus Spandau," then bus #135 (direction: "Alt-Kladow") to the end. Switch to bus #234 to "Krampnitzer Weg/Selbitzerstr.," then follow Krampnitzer Weg 200m. A store and restaurant complement the relaxed atmosphere by a swimmable lake. Open year-round.

◖ FOOD

Food in Berlin is a tasty surprise; its Turkish, Indian, Thai and Italian immigrants bring a wide variety of quality ethnic food to restaurants and stands throughout the city. Many offerings from German cuisine are quite tasty, but Berlin's most notable home-grown option is the sweet **Berliner Weiße mit Schuß,** a concoction of wheat beer with a shot of syrup. *Rot* (red) is the most popular variety, made with fruity *Himbeer* (raspberry) syrup; *grün* (green) is less palatable to the uninitiated, consisting of a lemony syrup with a piney aftertaste called *Waldmeister.*

Typical Berlin street food is Turkish, and almost every street has its own Turkish *Imbiß* or restaurant. The *Imbiß* stands are a lifeline for the late-night partier; most are open ridiculously late, some 24 hours. The *Döner Kebab*, a sandwich of lamb and salad, has cornered the fast-food market, with *Falafel* running a close second. Either makes a small meal for DM3-5. A second wave of immigration has brought quality Indian and Italian restaurants to Berlin.

While some *Kneipen* serve only drinks, the line between cafes and restaurants is extremely blurred. Both may offer meals of many sizes, and invariably have a lengthy drink menu. The leisurely breakfast is a gloriously civilized institution in Berlin cafes, often served well into the afternoon, sometimes 24 hours. Berliners read the paper and linger over their fruity, fatty breakfasts; join them and relax with *Milchkaffee*, a big delightful bowl of coffee with a giant mass of foamed milk.

Aldi, Plus, Edeka, and **Penny Markt** are the cheapest supermarket chains, followed by the pricier **Bolle, Kaiser's,** and **Reichelt.** Supermarkets are usually open Monday to Friday 9am-6pm and Saturday 9am-4pm, though some chains like Kaiser's are open until as late as 8pm on weekdays. At Bahnhof Zoo, **Ullrich am Zoo,** below the S-Bahn tracks, and **Nimm's Mit,** near the Reisezentrum, have longer hours (both open daily 6am-10pm). The best **open-air market** fires up Saturday mornings on Winterfeldtpl., though almost every neighborhood has one. For cheap vegetables and enormous wheels of *Fladenbrot*, check out the kaleidoscopic **Turkish market** in Kreuzberg, along Maybachufer on the Landwehrkanal, every Friday. Arrive early for the best produce. Take U-Bahn #8 to "Schönleinstr."

MITTE

Mensa der Humboldt-Universität, Unter den Linden 6, in the back of the university's main building. The cheapest *Mensa* in Berlin, conveniently located for sight-seeing in Eastern Berlin. Full meals DM2.50-4. Student ID required. Open M-F 11:30am-2:30pm.

Cafeteria Charlottenstraße, Charlottenstr. 55 (☎203 09 23 40). U-Bahn #6 to "Französische Str." or U-Bahn #2 or 6 to "Stadtmitte." Continuing construction may require you to enter from Taubenstr. At the **Hochschule für Musik,** near the Gendarmenmarkt. Meals DM2.55 for students, DM4.50 for others. Salads and grill items also available. Complete breakfast DM4.80. Open M-F 9am-3pm.

AROUND ORANIENBURGER STRASSE

Taba, Torstr. 164 (☎282 67 95). U-Bahn #8 to "Rosenthaler Pl." A lively, happening place with good Brazilian eats. Meals DM10-17, and excellent guacamole for DM8. Get your own Brazilian cigar for DM5. Live music F, Sa, and Su, disco every Saturday from midnight-4am. Open W-Su from 7pm.

Trattoria Ossena, Oranienburger Str. 65 (☎283 53 48). S-Bahn #1, 2, or 25 to "Oranien-burger Str." Surrounded on all sides by Oranienburger Str.'s myriad cafes, Ossena serves more substantial fare than the rest in the form of delicious Italian pastas and enormous pizzas. Most meals under DM20, many (especially pizzas) large enough to feed two. Try the *Pizza Treccose* (artichokes, ham, and mushrooms; DM14.80) or the *Lasagne con verdura* (vegetarian lasagna; DM14). Another location just opened at Rosenthalerstr. 42, S-Bahn #3, 5, 7, 9, or 15 to "Hackescher Markt." Open daily from 5pm.

Café Beth, Tucholskystr. 40 (☎281 31 35), just off Auguststr. S-Bahn #1, 2, or 25 to "Oranienburger Str." Kosher restaurant in the heart of the Scheunenviertel. Serves inexpensive Israeli specialties and a generous selection of kosher wines. Try the falafel (DM4.70) or a bagel with lox and cream cheese (DM4). Other dishes DM5-15. Open M-Th and Su 11am-10pm; F 11am-5pm, in winter 11am-3pm.

Mendelssohn, Oranienburger Str. 39 (☎281 78 59). S-Bahn #1, 2, or 25 to "Oranienburger Str." This swank locale serves Macedonian fare in a candlelit setting. Try the *Musaka* (DM12.80), a creamy layered dish of meat and potatoes, or the *Kifli* (DM5.50), a doughy pastry stuffed with goat cheese. Open M-F after 11am, Sa-Su after 9am. Kitchen opens at noon.

Café and Bistro Edwin, Große Hamburger Str. 15. A simple yet cheery yellow place, Edwin sells baguettes starting at DM5. Full meals DM10-15. Sitting outside puts you in the middle of a bustling but not overly crowded pedestrian street; inside you find marbled table-tops and green wall designs. Sundays from 7pm a *Caipirhina* goes for DM5.99; as the sign says, that's "Peanuts!" Sunday brunch buffet DM13.50. Open M 1pm-late, Tu-Sa 11am-late, Su 10am-late.

Village Voice, Ackerstr. 1a (☎282 45 50). U-Bahn #8 to "Rosenthaler Pl." Cafe-bar/ bookstore trying hard for NYC hipness. American literature and inexpensive Tex-Mex fare. Tacos DM9, nachos and chili each DM7.50. Cafe open M-F 11am-2am, Sa-Su noon-2am. Bookstore open M-F 11am-8pm, Sa noon-4pm.

AROUND BAHNHOF ZOO

Mensa TU, Hardenbergstr. 34 (☎311 22 53). Bus #145 to "Steinpl.," or walk 10min. from Bahnhof Zoo. The mightiest of Berlin's *Mensen* (behold its gigantic neon sign), serves decent food, including good vegetarian dishes. Meals DM4-5 for students, others DM6-7. Cafeteria downstairs has longer hours and slightly higher prices. *Mensa* open M-F 11:15am-2:30pm. Cafeteria open M-F 8am-7:45pm.

KaDeWe, Tauentzienstr. 21-24 (☎212 10). U-Bahn #1, 2, or 15 to "Wittenbergpl." Satiate every desire in the 6th-floor food emporium of this tremendous department store. Indulge in confectionery wonders, sample flavorful Italian *antipesto*, enjoy a glass of wine, or just get lost among the maze of counters. The best part? These classy indulgences are available at stunning prices. Open M-F 9:30am-8pm, Sa 9am-4pm.

Website, Joachimstaler Str. 41 (☎88 67 96 30; www.vrcafe.de). Berlin's trendiest cybercafe offers internet access to its *Milchkaffee*-drinking, cigarette-smoking, high-speed-downloading, cyberpunk patrons, and the homesick Americans sitting next to them. Set in a dark, digital-age lair complete with a glass floor that glows from the green bubbles underfoot. Pasta, salads, and omelettes under DM20. Breakfast (DM8-16) served all day. Snacks DM5-7. Open daily 10am-late.

Filmbühne am Steinplatz, Hardenbergstr. 12 (☎312 65 89). This cafe at one of Berlin's independent cinemas has an eclectic and extensive but generally inexpensive menu. The "Harry & Sally Breakfast" (DM28.50) serves two...or three or four. Sizable salads (from DM7), and a delicious variety of cakes which change daily. Open M-Sa 9am-3am, Su 9am-2am. Films are often subtitled rather than dubbed (DM11, Mondays DM8.50). Call ☎312 90 12 for film info.

Café Hardenberg, Hardenbergstr. 10 (☎312 33 30). Opposite the TU's *Mensa,* but with a lot more atmosphere. Offprint on the walls and a little bit of student-driven chatter make the cafe one of the most popular in the area. Order breakfast (DM5-12) day or night, and eggs and taters could arrive at your table in a sizzling skillet. Less dramatic, but equally good, are the salads and pasta dishes for DM5-13. Open M-F 9am-1am, Sa-Su 9am-2am.

CHARLOTTENBURG

Schwarzes Café, Kantstr. 148 (☎313 80 38; fax 215 29 54). S-Bahn #3, 5, 7, 9, or 75 to "Savignypl." In a district full of posh business-suit restaurants, this cafe caters to a pleasantly young crowd. The decor is a mix of brick, plaster, peeling red paint, and curious art (note the frogs' heads) but the most notable thing about the place is that it's *always* open, except for 8 hours from 3am-11am each Tuesday. Two floors of seating plus a patio out back point to its late-night popularity. Prices are a bit high (a milkshake is DM7), but breakfast is served around the clock; try the "Casablanca" (DM12.50): fruit salad, cheese, marmalade, and two croissants.

Der Ägypter, Kantstr. 26 (☎313 92 30). S-Bahn #3, 5, 7, 9, or 75 to "Savignypl." It's the one with King Tut's death mask blazing on the front. A little pricey (vegetarian entrees DM14-18), but where else can you get authentic Egyptian food in Berlin? Those who can't afford to eat here drool over the handicrafts on sale in the window before heading to the falafel (DM4) place next door. Open daily after 6pm.

Café Voltaire, Stuttgarter Pl. 14 (☎324 50 28). S-Bahn #3, 5, 7, 9 or 75 to "Charlottenburg," or U-Bahn #7 to "Wilmersdorfer Str." Cafe-bistro-gallery with a talkative crowd and Pollock imitations on the walls. Features an extensive menu of salads, omelettes, and baguettes along with great breakfasts (DM6-8; served 5am-3pm). Open daily 24hr.

SCHÖNEBERG

🍴 **Baharat Falafel,** Winterfeldtstr. 37. U-Bahn #1, 2, 4, or 15 to "Nollendorfpl." This ain't no greasy *Döner* stand - it's all about falafel. Five plump chick-pea balls in a fluffy pita, covered with veggies and heavenly sesame, mango, or chili sauce, for DM6-7. Falafel plates with tabouli, hummus, or other salad offerings are also available (from DM12). Wash it all down with fresh-squeezed *Gute-Laune Saft* (good mood juice). Open daily 11am-2am. Closed last week in July.

Bua Luang, Vorbergstr. 10a (☎781 83 81). U-Bahn #7 to "Kleistpark." Mild to spicy Thai food in a quiet residential section of Schöneberg. Feast on the hefty noodle dishes (DM10) or on the delectably spicy *Masaman* curried tofu (DM8). Order out or try to find a spot in the tiny cafe. Open daily 2pm-midnight.

Fish and Vegetables, Goltzstr. 32. U-Bahn #1, 2, 4, or 15 to "Nollendorfpl." In a fantastic tiled building alongside an Indian restaurant and a Spanish bar, Fish and Vegetables serves Thai food to a bustling lunch crowd as well as evening bar-hoppers. Order your meal by number and add a letter to specify type of meat; the generous portions of Pad Thai (DM9-11) come with ample peanut sauce, and the vegetables taste fresh and well cooked. Eat inside or out, but remember to clear your own plate.

Café Sidney, Winterfeldtstr. 40 (☎216 52 53). U-Bahn #1, 2, 4 or 15 to "Nollendorfplatz." With vaguely Australian interior decor and a second location in Ibiza, Spain, Sidney tries for worldly trendiness. It has mixed success, but breakfast from DM7 and baguettes with tomato and mozzarella for DM6.50 make it all work out in the end. A wide variety of drinks plus two pool tables in the back make it a good evening destination.

Sushi am Winterfeldtplatz, Goltzstr. 24 (☎215 49 30). U-Bahn #1, 2, 4, or 15 to "Nollendorfpl." Standing-room only Japanese cuisine in the heart of Schöneberg. Try the fresh sushi à la carte (DM3-8) or filling lunch platters (including miso soup) for DM15-19. Open M-Sa noon-midnight, Su 3pm-midnight. Delivery until 1hr. before closing.

WHAT'S A DÖNER? When this question was posed to Germany's *Döner* dealers, their response was utter bafflement. After all, everyone knows what a *Döner Kebab* is—chunks of spit-roasted lamb stuffed in a toasted Turkish *Fladenbrot* topped with vegetables and garlic sauce. Yet where does the name come from? Vendors in northern Germany unanimously insisted that it comes from Berlin and told us not to get any ideas about this being authentic Turkish food. But we learned that the German "Dön" comes from the Turkish word meaning "to turn," and that the meat is thus named a *Döner* because it revolves as it cooks. A *Döner* by any other name simply would not be the same.

Café Belmundo, Winterfeldtstr. 36 (☎215 20 70), opposite Baharat Falafel. U-Bahn #1, 2, 4 or 15 to "Nollendorfpl." Cheerful music and tasty baguettes, along with an inner courtyard patio for cozy outdoor seating. Nights are for the young, days for a slightly older clientele reading the newspaper. Sunday breakfast buffet (DM14) until 3:30pm. Salads and pasta DM5-10. Good selection of reasonably priced drinks. Open daily 9am-1am. Kitchen open 11am-11pm.

TeeTeaThé, Akazienstr. (☎217 662 40). U-Bahn #1, 2, 4, or 15 to "Nollendorfpl." A "Teesalon und cafe," this restaurant is notable not only for its wide variety of teas but also for its vegetarian entrees; it is one of few eateries in Berlin that offers veggie burgers (DM13.50). The cleverly named "Parisguettes" go for DM7-9. Breakfast served daily until 3pm. Daily specials served until 11pm. Open M-Sa 9am-midnight, Su 10am-midnight.

Café Asmarino, Grunewaldstr. 82. U-Bahn #7 to "Eisenacher Straße." Eritrean specialties in a small, clean restaurant. Meals DM11-20; try the *Taamot Rind* for DM11, or a vegetarian platter for two at DM25.

Pasodoble, Crellestr. 39 (☎784 52 44). U-Bahn #7 to "Kleistpark." An intimate *tapas* bar just off Schöneberg's busy Hauptstr., near Kaiser-Wilhelm-Pl. *Tapas* range from nachos to shrimp to calamari rings (DM6-9). Full meals (DM10-15), salads (DM4-7) and a wide selection of drinks round off the menu.

KREUZBERG

▨ **Amrit,** Oranienstr. 202-203 (☎612 55 50). U-Bahn #1 or 15 to "Görlitzer Bahnhof." Perhaps the best Indian food in Berlin, served under desert colored walls with just a touch of Kreuzberg flair. Fabulous vegetarian dishes like *Alu Saag* (DM12.50) as well as delectably spicy meat entrees; try the *Chicken Saag* (DM13.50). Menu in English and German. Open M-Th and Su noon-1am, F-Sa noon-2am.

Café V, Lausitzer Pl. 12 (☎612 45 05). U-Bahn #1 or 15 to "Görlitzer Bahnhof." Berlin's oldest vegetarian restaurant, with a dimly-lit yellow interior decorated with cool paintings. Some entrees are vegan-friendly, and fish entrees are also available. Try the *Auberginem-Tofu-Mosakka.* Open daily 10am-2am.

Chandre Kumari, Gneisenaustr. 4 (☎694 1203). U-Bahn #6 or 7 to "Mehringdamm." Sri-Lankan and Indian food are the specialties of this small cafe. Enjoy a variety of entrees (DM8-13) under the smiling moons and stars painted on the ceiling.

Melek Pastanesi, Oranienstr. 28 (☎694 89 48). U-Bahn #1, 8, or 15 to "Kottbusser Tor." Delicious Turkish pastries sold around the clock. Colorful cookies and other sweets for prices that are merely pocket change. A favorite stopping place for sugar-deprived late-night partygoers. 100g baklava DM1.40.

Café Abendmahl, Muskauer Str. 9 (☎612 51 70). U-Bahn #1 or 15 to "Görlitzer Bahnhof." While some of the *Ecce Homo* decorative motifs are a touch overbearing, the restaurant's delicious vegetarian and fish dishes are a favorite of gay and lesbian Berliners. Substantial salads DM9.50-16.50. Open daily after 6pm.

PRENZLAUER BERG/FRIEDRICHSHAIN

Sergena, Pappalallee 19 (☎44 05 41 67). This bright little cafe cooks up amazing food with slightly exotic flavors at great prices that are anything but the norm in this neighborhood. Substantial artichoke and cheese dish for DM10, and a range of salads (DM4-13). Open M-Th 3pm-1am, F-Su 2pm-1am.

Chop Bar, Pappalallee 29. Giraffe statues and wooden masks add an authentic feel to this African restaurant which exudes a friendly ambience warm as the desert sun. Entrees like the *Jaasa Djin* (DM16), as well as a substantial list of vegetarian options (DM14-16) are available. In the summer, 6-8pm, all entrees are only DM12. Open daily 6pm-midnight.

Ostwind, Husemannstr. 13 (☎441 59 51). U-Bahn #2 to "Senefelderpl." Chinese food that seeks to bridge the cultural divide between East and West. Prenzlauer hipsters indulge in the dim sum or *Shao-Lin Min* (noodles with tofu, lotus, broccoli, and carrots; DM13.90). Open M-Th 6pm-1am, F-Sa 10am-1am.

Die Krähe, Kollwitzstr. 84 (☎442 82 91), off Kollwitzpl. U-Bahn #2 to "Senefelderpl." White tablecloths combine with tasteful decor for a garden-like feel. Bright crowd orders from changing weekly menu; tasty breakfasts under DM10, crunchy salads DM12. The popular Sunday buffet lets you load up until you burst for DM13.50. Open M-Th 5:30pm-2am, F-Sa 5:30pm-3am, Su 10:30am-2am.

Sprelacarte, 18 Kollwitzpl. The pleasant cafe serves a variety of breakfast combos, like the *Käsefrühstück* (DM11), and daily dinner specials from DM9. But what makes this stand out from all the other cafes in Prenzlauer Berg? No one else has glowing fluorescent cows crawling up the side of a six-story building! Open daily 10am-1am.

Café-Restaurant Miró, Raumerstr. 29 (☎44 73 30 13). U-Bahn #2 to "Eberswalder Str." Generous portions of attractive and delectable Mediterranean cuisine. Breakfast DM7-11. Soups DM5, large appetizers DM8.50-15.50, salads DM7.50-16. Open 10am-late. Kitchen closes at midnight.

Osswald, Göhrener Str. 5 (☎442 74 50). U-Bahn #2 to "Eberswalder Str." A perfect place for breakfast, dinner, or a late-night drink, the restaurant/bar caters to locals and a few lucky tourists who read *Let's Go.* Excellent vantage point for people-watching, and simple but tasty dishes at great prices. Su breakfast buffet served until 5pm (DM12). Open daily 9am-4am.

Café Restauration 1900, Husemannstr. 1 (☎442 24 94), at Kollwitzpl. U-Bahn #2 to "Senefelderpl." Alternative interior with black and white drawings on a street decorated in Potemkin-village 19th-century style. Decent food at decent prices. Open M-Sa 11am-2am, Su 10am-2am. Kitchen open until midnight.

Situna, Kollwitzstr. 47 (☎44 04 30 11). U-Bahn #2 to "Senefelderpl." Tunisian and Sudanese cuisine cooked up to the sounds of tribal beats; a little corner of Africa curled up in Prenzlauer Berg. Staples like falafel (DM4) for the timid, or hearty plates of couscous (from DM7) for the daring. Open daily noon-10pm.

Yogi Snack, Simon-Dach Str. 11 (☎290 04 838). Inside an unassuming exterior hides a friendly, pink restaurant serving good, cheap Indian food. Sizeable entrees with salad and rice from DM8. Wash it down with a Yogi Tee (DM2). Open daily noon-midnight.

◪ SIGHTS

Berlin's sights are spread out over an area eight times the size of Paris. For a guide to the city's major neighborhoods, see **Orientation,** p. 94. Below, the sights are organized by *Bezirk* (district), beginning with Mitte and spiralling outward. Areas farther from the center are grouped together in **Outer Districts.** Many of central Berlin's major sights lie along the route of **bus #100,** which travels from Bahnhof Zoo to Prenzlauer Berg, passing the Siegessäule, Brandenburg Gate, Unter den Linden, the Berliner Dom, and Alexanderpl. along the way. To add an element of thrill to your sightseeing expedition, climb up to the second floor of the double-decker bus, and sit in the very first row: the view is unbeatable. Buying individual tickets every time you re-board the bus can get pricey; consider investing in a day pass (DM7.80) or a 7-day pass (DM40), as it's impossible to see everything on foot (see **Getting Around,** p. 92).

MITTE

Formerly the heart of Imperial Berlin, Mitte contains some of Berlin's most magnificent sights and museums. Much of the neighborhood languished in disuse and disrepair during GDR days, but now that the government is back in town, the district is once again living up to its name (*Mitte* means center), as embassies and national institutes pour back into the area's rapidly-renovating streets.

UNTER DEN LINDEN

The area between the Brandenburg Gate and Alexanderpl. is best reached by taking S-Bahn #1, 2, or 25 to "Unter den Linden" and heading east; alternatively, bus #100 runs the length of the boulevard every 4-6 minutes. The boulevard runs from the prominent Brandenburg Gate near the Reichstag through Pariser Pl. to the intersection with

Friedrichstr., where glitzy hotels named after other Communist capitals sprang up during the GDR and continue to mar reconstruction projects. Beyond Friedrichstr., impressive university buildings and museums join with two squares just south of the boulevard to form one of the largest collection of notable buildings in Berlin.

▓BRANDENBURGER TOR. For decades a barricaded gateway to nowhere, today the Brandenburg Gate is the most powerful emblem of reunited Germany and Berlin. Standing directly in the center of the city, it was within the no-man's land during the time of the wall. It opens east onto Unter den Linden and west onto the Tiergarten and Str. des 17. Juni. Built during the reign of Friedrich Wilhelm II as an image of peace to replace its crumbling medieval predecessor, the gate became a symbol—the symbol—of the Cold War East-West division (see p. 16). The images broadcast around the world of East and West Berliners dancing together atop the Wall were all filmed from the Brandenburg Gate, since this section of the wall was the only part with a flat top—everywhere else, the top was curved, preventing would-be escapees from getting a good grip.

PARISER PLATZ. The Brandenburger Tor opens eastward onto Unter den Linden, once one of Europe's best-known boulevards and the spine of old Berlin. Pariser Pl.'s garden serve as the entry way to this part of the city and from 1735 was ringed by impressive palaces. All but a few of the venerable buildings near the gate have been destroyed, including the *Stadtpalais*, which stood here from 1848 until its destruction in WWII. A massive reconstruction effort centered around the gate has already revived such pre-war staples as the **Hotel Adlon,** once the premier address for all visiting dignitaries and celebrities.

RUSSIAN EMBASSY. Rebuilding the edifices of the rich and famous wasn't a huge priority in the workers' state; one exception, however, is this imposing *Palais* on Unter den Linden 7. The building is massive, taking up nearly an entire block on the wide street. With the end of the Cold War, the *Palais* has reverted to being just another embassy, and the huge bust of Lenin that once graced its red star-shaped topiary was quietly removed in 1994.

DEUTSCHE STAATSBIBILIOTHEK. The stately library's shady, ivy-covered courtyard and cafe provide a pleasant respite from the surrounding landscape. *(Unter den Linden 8. ☎26 60. Library open M-F 9am-9pm, Sa 9am-5pm. DM1 for a day's admission. Cafe open M-F 9am-6pm, Sa 10am-4pm.)*

HUMBOLDT-UNIVERSITÄT. Just beyond the Deutsche Staatsbibliothek is the H-shaped main building of the Humboldt Universität, whose hallowed halls have been filled by the likes of Hegel, Einstein, the Brothers Grimm, Bismarck and Karl Marx. In the wake of the post-1989 internal ideological *Blitzkrieg*, in which "tainted" departments were radically revamped or simply shut down, international scholars have descended upon the university to take part in its dynamic renewal. Nevertheless, or perhaps consequently, Marx and Lenin's greatest hits are available for cheap from the book vendors outside. Near the university, the statue of **Friedrich the Great** atop his horse has been temporarily removed from the boulevard for restoration; according to official plan he should have been put back already, so the date of his return is uncertain. *(Unter den Linden 6. ☎209 30.)*

NEUE WACHE. The "New Guard-house" was designed by Prussian architect Karl Friedrich Schinkel in unrepentant Neoclassical style. During the GDR era, it was known as the "Monument to the Victims of Fascism and Militarism," and, ironically, was guarded by goose-stepping East German soldiers. After reunification, the building closed briefly but was reopened in 1993 as a war memorial. The remains of an unknown soldier and an unknown concentration camp victim are buried inside with earth from the Nazi concentration camps at Buchenwald and Mauthausen as well as from the battlefields of Stalingrad, El Alamein, and Normandy. A copy of Käthe Kollwitz's sculpture *Mutter mit totem Sohn* (mother with dead son) conveys the solemnity of the space and serves as an effective memorial to victims of war of all kinds. *(Unter den Linden 4. Open daily 10am-6pm.)*

BERLIN

BEBELPLATZ. On May 10, 1933 Nazi students burned nearly 20,000 books here by "subversive" authors such as Heinrich Heine and Sigmund Freud—both Jews. A plaque in the center of the square is engraved with Heine's eerily prescient 1820 quote: *Nur dort wo man Bücher verbrennt, verbrennt man am Ende auch Menschen.* ("Wherever books are burned, ultimately people are burned as well.") A few yards away, a glass-covered opening in the ground reveals a square room of silently empty shelves. The building with the curved facade is the **Alte Bibliothek.** Once the royal library, it is now home to the Humboldt's law faculty. On the other side of the square is the handsome **Deutsche Staatsoper,** fully rebuilt after the war from original sketches by Knobelsdorff, the same architect who designed Schloß Sanssouci in Potsdam (see p. 148). The distinctive blue dome at the end of the square belongs to the **St.-Hedwigs-Kathedrale.** Built in 1773 as the first Catholic church erected in Berlin after the Reformation, it was burnt to a crisp by American bombers in 1943. Designed after the Roman Pantheon, the church was rebuilt in the 1950s in high atheist style, such that the interior resembles a socialist nightclub more than a house of worship. Each Wednesday at 3pm, the massive organ plays for any passersby in the area to listen. *(Cathedral open M-F 10am-5pm, Sa 10am-4:30pm, Su 1-5pm. Free.)* Next to the cathedral, the **Bundeshauptstadt Berlin** shows an exhibit of the new buildings being constructed for the various governmental offices moving back into Berlin. It also tells the story of the controversial plan to rebuild Berlin's own *Schloß*, and has an enlightening interactive map of the city that points out all buildings planned or already built at the push of a button. *(Behrenstr. 39. ☎ 20 08 32 34. Open daily 9am-5:30pm. Free.)*

ZEUGHAUS. Once the Prussian army's hall of fame and military museum, the heavily ornamented building has calmed down a bit to become the Museum of German History (see Museums, p. 128). The exhibits will be housed in the Kronprinzenpalais across the street until 2002 while the Zeughaus undergoes renovations. Part of the renovation plan involves the addition of a second building designed by I.M. Pei. *(Unter den Linden 2. ☎ 20 30 40; fax 230 45 43.)*

GENDARMENMARKT

Berlin's most impressive ensemble of 19th-century buildings is a few blocks south of Unter den Linden on the **Gendarmenmarkt,** also known as the French Quarter, after it became the main settlement for Protestant Huguenots in the 18th century. Take U-Bahn #2 to "Französische Str." or U-Bahn #2 or 6 to "Stadtmitte." During the last week of June and the first week of July, the square transforms into an outdoor stage for open-air classical concerts; call ☎ 69 80 75 22 for details, or stop by one of the discount ticket offices for last-minute deals (see p. 132).

DEUTSCHER DOM. Gracing the southern end of the square, the Dom is not used as a church but instead houses **Fragen zur deutschen Geschichte,** a Bundestag-sponsored exhibition which traces German political history from despotism to fascism to democracy. *(Gendarmenmarkt 5. ☎ 22 73 21 41. Open Tu-Su 10am-7pm. Free.)*

FRANZÖSISCHER DOM. At the opposite end of the square from the Deutscher Dom. Built in the early 18th century by French Huguenots the Dom is now home to a restaurant and a small museum chronicling the Huguenot diaspora. The tower offers an interesting panorama of the surrounding construction sites. *(Gendarmenmarkt 5. ☎ 229 17 60. Museum open Tu-Sa noon-5pm. DM3, students DM2. Restaurant open daily noon-1am. Tower open daily 9am-7pm.)*

KONZERTHAUS AM GENDARMENMARKT. Located between the two churches. Designed by Karl Friedrich Schinkel in 1819 (see p. 24), the Konzerthaus was badly damaged in air attacks toward the end of WWII. It reopened in 1984 as the most elegant concert venue in Berlin and hosts a variety of performances from chamber music to concerts by international orchestras (see p. 133). *(Gendarmenmarkt 2. ☎ 203 09 21 01.)*

AROUND POTSDAMER PLATZ

■ **POTSDAMER PLATZ.** Caught in the death strip between the two walls during the Cold War, Potsdamer Pl. was the commercial and transport hub of pre-war Berlin. The square was built under Friedrich Wilhelm I in an approximation of Parisian boulevards with the primary purpose of moving troops quickly. After reunification, Potsdamer Pl. was chosen to become the new commercial center of united Berlin. The sight is now infamous as one of the world's largest construction sights of the 1990s, and the ending date has been pushed back to 2004. To find out more about the future of the square, visit the **Infobox,** the shiny red structure near the subway station (see **Museums,** p. 129). At the moment it appears in a moment of flux, the half-finished buildings, sand lots, and newly-constructed facades of glass and steel combining to create a landscape which is both a product and symbol of the cumbersome master plans that are attempting to hatch a new Berlin. *(No longer in the Wall's geographic limbo, Potsdamer Pl. is accessible by S-Bahn #1, 2, or 25 or U-Bahn #2 to "Potsdamer Pl.")*

FÜHRERBUNKER. Near Potsdamer Pl., unmarked and inconspicuous, lies the site of the bunker where Hitler married Eva Braun and then ended his life. In macabre irony, the actual bunker site is now a playground (behind the record store at Wilhelmstr. 92); tourists looking for it often mistakenly head for the visible bunker at the southern edge of Potsdamer Pl. Plans to restore the bunker were shelved amid fears that the site would become a shrine for the radical right.

LUSTGARTEN AND MUSEUMINSEL

After crossing the Schloßbrücke over the Spree, Unter den Linden passes by the **Museuminsel** (museum island), home to four major museums and the **Berliner Dom.** Take S-Bahn #3, 5, 7, 9, or 75 to "Hackescher Markt" and walk toward the Dom; alternatively, pick up bus #100 along Unter den Linden and get off at "Lustgarten." For information on the **Altes Museum, Pergamon, Bodemuseum,** and **Alte Nationalgalerie,** see **Museums,** p. 128.

ALTES MUSEUM. Across the Lustgarten from Unter den Linden. The museum was created by Schinkel, who envisioned Berlin as the "Athens on the Spree." The tubby granite bowl in front was supposed to adorn the main hall, but it didn't fit through the door. The immaculately green **Lustgarten** re-opened in 1999 after being redesigned to look as it did in the 19th century.

BERLINER DOM. Next door to the Altes Museum. The beautifully bulky, multiple-domed cathedral proves that Protestants can go overboard as much as Catholics. This is one of Berlin's most recognizable landmarks. Built during the reign of Kaiser Wilhelm II, the cathedral recently emerged from 20 years of restoration after being severely damaged by an air raid in 1944. The interior, with its distinctively Protestant icons (Calvin, Zwingli, and Luther), is quite ornate and striking. *(Open daily 9am-7:30pm. Admission to Dom DM5, students DM3. Comprehensive admission to the Dom, tower, and galleries DM8, students DM5. Free organ recitals W-F at 3pm. Frequent **concerts** in summer; buy tickets in the church or call ☎ 20 26 91 36 for more information.)* There's also the **Kaiserliches Treppenhaus** upstairs, with exhibits of period art and imperial booty. *(Open M-Sa 9am-8pm, Su noon-8pm. Free.)*

SCHLOßPLATZ. Across the street from the Lustgarten. Known as Marx-Engels-Platz during the days of the GDR, the square houses the glaring, amber-colored **Palast der Republik,** where the East German parliament met. In 1990, city authorities discovered that the building was full of asbestos and shut it down; a current reconstruction project aims to make it carcinogen-free. The problems associated with the building are further complicated by the fact that the entire square used to be the site of the **Berliner Schloß,** the Hohenzollern family palace. Remarkably, the palace survived the war, only to be demolished by GDR authorities in the 1950s in censure of its royal excess. The **Staatsrat,** currently the temporary office of the federal chancellor, resides on the site—look for the modern building with a slice of the palace facade embedded in the middle. The East German government preserved this section because **Karl Liebknecht** proclaimed a German socialist republic from its balcony. The newest plans for the site call for the Palast's demolition and the reconstruction of the Schloß's facade with a modern entertainment center behind it, but whether this will materialize is anybody's guess. Meanwhile, the Palast der Republik remains completely surrounded by construction walls.

MARX-ENGELS-FORUM. Across the Liebknecht-Brücke on the right-hand side of the street stands a memorial of steel tablets dedicated to the world-wide workers' struggle against fascism and imperialism. The giant, bulbous, cartoon-like statues of sitting Marx and standing Engels preside over the oft-graffittied exhibit. The park and the street behind it used to be collectively known as the Marx-Engels-Forum; the park has not been renamed, while the street is now called Rathausstr.

ALEXANDERPLATZ AND NIKOLAIVIERTEL

On the other side of Museuminsel, Unter den Linden becomes Karl-Liebknecht-Str., and leads into the monolithic **Alexanderpl.** Take S-Bahn #3, 5, 7, 9, or 75 or U-Bahn #2, 5, or 8 to "Alexanderpl."

ALEXANDERPLATZ. Formerly the frantic heart of Weimar Berlin, the plaza was transformed in East German times into an urban wasteland of fountains and pre-fab office buildings, including some concrete-block classics. In the 1970s, the grey drear was interrupted by enormous neon signs with declarations like "Medical Instruments of the GDR—Distributed in All the World!" in order to satisfy the people's need for bright lights. Today the signs have vanished, allowing chain stores like **Kaufhof** to pop up, and relying on the punks who spend their time in the plaza to fulfill the lust for color.

FERNSEHTURM. The TV tower, the tallest structure in Berlin at 365 meters, is a truly awkward piece of design intended to show off the new heights achieved through five-year plans; in fact, it looks more like something from the *Jetsons*. The project proved to be somewhat of a flop when it was discovered that the sun's reflection on the tower's amber-tinted windows creates a shadow that looks very much like a crucifix (known as the *Papsts Rache*—the Pope's revenge). The view from the top (the spherical node 203m up the spike) is magnificent. An elevator whisks tourists up and away. (☎ 242 33 33. Open daily Mar.-Oct. 9am-1am; Nov.-Feb. 10am-midnight. DM10, under 16 DM5.)

NIKOLAIVIERTEL. A carefully reconstructed Altstadt deriving its name from the Nikolaikirche, the Nikolaiviertel consists of a series of narrow, winding streets mostly occupied by cute little shops. Among the two dozen historic buildings is the **Knoblauchhaus,** home to a small museum documenting the life and times of architect Eduard Knoblauch. (Poststr. 23. Take the Rotes Rathaus exit from the Alexanderpl. station, walk straight through the pedestrian zone, cross Spandauerstr., and turn left on Poststr. ☎ 238 09 00. Open Tu-Su 10am-6pm. DM5, students DM2.50.) Nearby is the **Ephraim-Palais,** at the corner of Poststr. and Mühlendamm. The Nazis used this Rococo building as a sports museum; it now houses a collection of contemporary art from the era of Friedrich the Great. (Open Tu-Su 10am-6pm. DM3, students DM1.)

SCHEUNENVIERTEL AND ORANIENBURGER STRASSE

Northwest of Alexanderpl. lies the **Scheunenviertel,** once the center of Berlin's Orthodox Jewish community. Take S-Bahn #1, 2, or 25 to "Oranienburger Str." or U-Bahn #6 to "Oranienburger Tor." Prior to WWII, Berlin never had any ghettos. Jews lived throughout the city, though during the war they were deported to ghettos in Poland. Wealthier and more assimilated Jews tended to live in Western Berlin, while Orthodox Jews from Eastern Europe settled in the Scheunenviertel. Although evidence of Jewish life in Berlin dates back to the 13th century, the community was expelled in 1573 and not invited back for 100 years. Today the Scheunenviertel is better known for its teeming masses of outdoor cafes than for its historical significance as Berlin's Jewish center, but the past few years have seen the opening of several Judaica-oriented bookstores and kosher restaurants.

NEUE SYNAGOGE. This huge, "oriental-style" building was designed by Berlin architect Eduard Knoblauch. The synagogue, which seated 3,200, was used for worship until 1940, when the Nazis occupied it and used it for storage. Amazingly, the building survived *Kristallnacht*—the SS torched it, but a local police chief, realizing that the building was a historic monument, ordered the Nazis to extinguish the fire. The synagogue was destroyed by bombing, but its restoration, largely financed by international Jewish organizations, began in 1988. The temple's beautiful, gold-laced domes were rebuilt and opened to the public in 1995. Too big for Berlin's remaining Jewish community, the striking building is no longer used for services. The interior houses an exhibit chronicling the synagogue's history in addition to temporary exhibits on the history of Berlin's Jews. To enter, you must pass through a metal detector. *(Oranienburger Str. 30. ☎ 28 40 13 16. Open M-Th and Su 10am-6pm, F 10am-2pm. Museum DM5, students DM3. Entry to the dome DM3, students DM2.)*

ALTER JÜDISCHER FRIEDHOF. Destroyed by the Nazis, the site now contains only the restored gravestone of the Enlightenment philosopher and scholar Moses Mendelssohn; the rest is a quiet park. In front, a noticeable plaque marks the site of the **Jüdisches Altersheim,** the Jewish old-age home which after 1942 served as a holding place for Jews before their deportation to concentration camps. Across the street, between the two yellow cafes, plaques on the side of a bombed-out building memorialize its residents, listing their occupations and the years of their deaths. *(At the end of Große Hamburger Str., near the intersection with Oranienburgerstr.)*

JÜDISCHE KNABENSCHULE. Next to the cemetery, another plaque marks the location of Berlin's oldest **Jewish school,** where Moses Mendelssohn taught. The school's heavy metal guard-fences make the plaque on the side difficult to see, but it memorializes Mendelssohn, "the German Socrates," who translated the Hebrew Bible into German and supported interaction between Berlin's Jewish and non-Jewish communities. Corresponding with his humanist outlook, the school's enrollment was only half-Jewish. The building was reopened as a school in 1992; its student body is still half-and-half.

OTHER SIGHTS. Berlin's **first synagogue** opened in 1714 near the corner of Rochstr. and Rosenstr. Remarkably, this synagogue was not destroyed on *Kristallnacht* because of the presence of a post office that had been renting space in the building; however, it was later bombed during the war, never to be reconstructed. The former **Jewish welfare office** was located at Rosenstr. 2-4. In the adjacent park, a terra cotta memorial was erected in October 1995 on the 54th anniversary of the first deportation of Berlin's Jews. Now, the recently completed Alexander Plaza hotel and several radio stations occupy the spot, but a plaque on the wall details the significant protests against the deportation to Auschwitz that went on outside the building.

TIERGARTEN

In the center of Berlin, the lush **Tiergarten** is a relief from the neon lights of the Ku'damm to the west and the din and dust of construction work to the east. Stretching from Bahnhof Zoo to the Brandenburg Gate, the vast landscaped park was formerly used by Prussian monarchs as a hunting and parade ground. Today Berliners use the park to blow off steam, as the Tiergarten is filled with strolling families by day and cruising gay men at night. **Straße des 17. Juni** bisects the park from west to east, connecting Ernst-Reuter-Pl. to the Brandenburg Gate. The thoroughfare is the site of many demonstrations and parades; in early July, the Tiergarten becomes the sight of some serious original sin with the Love Parade.

SIEGESSÄULE. In the heart of the Tiergarten, the slender 70m victory column, topped by a gilded statue of winged Victoria, commemorates Prussia's humiliating defeat of France in 1870. In 1938, the Nazis moved the monument from its former spot in front of the Reichstag to increase its height and make it more impressive. Climb the monument's 285 steps to the top for a panorama of the city. Recently, Victoria has taken on a hipper pose once a year, donning flashing lights as she is surrounded by the millions coming to the climax point of the Love Parade. *(Großer Stern. Take bus #100, 187, to "Großer Stern." ☎391 29 61. Open Apr.-Nov. M 1-6pm, Tu-Su 9am-6pm. DM2, students DM1.)*

SOWJETISCHES EHRENMAL. At the eastern end of the Tiergarten stands the Soviet Memorial (yes, you're still in Western Berlin) guarded by a pair of red star-emblazoned tanks, the first two to enter Berlin in 1945. *(Bus #100 to "Pl. der Republik" and walk down Entlastungsstr. to Str. des 17. Juni.)*

⬛THE REICHSTAG

Just to the north of the Brandenburg Gate sits the imposing, stone-gray Reichstag building, former seat of the parliaments of the German Empire and the Weimar Republic, and current home of Germany's governing body, the Bundestag. In 1918 Philipp Scheidemann proclaimed a German republic from one of its balconies with the words "*es lebe die deutsche Republik*" ("long live the German Republic"). His move turned out to be wise, since two hours later Karl Liebknecht, in the Berliner Schloß a few kilometers away on Unter den Linden, announced a German Socialist Republic on the site that later supported the parliament of the GDR. Civil war followed in Berlin and much of the rest of Germany. The government fled to Weimar to draw up a new constitution, but over the course of the next decade the Reichstag became the fractured center of the economically troubled Republic (see p. 12). As the Republic declined, Nazi members showed up to sessions in uniform, and on February 28, 1933, a month after Hitler became Chancellor, fire mysteriously broke out in the building. The event provided a pretext for Hitler to declare a state of emergency, giving the Nazis broad powers to arrest and intimidate opponents before the upcoming elections. The infamous end result was the Enabling Act, which established Hitler as legal dictator and abolished democracy. A conceptual monument outside recalls the 96 members of the Reichstag executed by the Nazis. Inside the rooftop dome, a photography exhibit details the history of the government and the Reichstag.

In the summer of 1995, the Reichstag metamorphosed into an artsy parcel, when husband-and-wife team Christo and Jeanne-Claude wrapped the dignified building in 120,000 yards of shimmery metallic fabric. After the wrapping was torn down, the building was restored to its former glory and then some: a giant glass dome was constructed around an upside-down solar cone that powers the building. Most recently, the long-awaited move of Germany's parliament from Bonn to Berlin was executed in several stages throughout the summer and fall of 1999. The surrounding area, like much of Berlin, is littered with cranes and fencing as workers scramble to complete the nation's renewed center. But a little dust doesn't stop flocks of tourists from visiting; long lines await. However, the view from above, perhaps the best way to fully grasp the scope of the new city, is absolutely amazing and well worth the time it takes to obtain it. A walkway spirals up the inside of the dome, leading visitors around a panoramic view to the top of the cone. (☎ 226 29 933 or 227 27 453. Open daily 8am-midnight; last entrance at 10pm. Free.)

OTHER SIGHTS IN MITTE

BERTOLT-BRECHT-HAUS. If any single man personifies the maelstrom of political and aesthetic contradictions that is Berlin, it is **Bertolt Brecht,** who called the city home. "There is a reason to prefer Berlin to other cities," the playwright once declared, "because it is constantly changing. What is bad today can be improved tomorrow." Brecht lived and worked in the house near the intersection with Schlegelstr. from 1953 to 1956. If you understand German, take the guided tour, given in flamboyant Brechtian style. The **Brechtforum** on the second floor sponsors exhibits and lectures on artistic and metropolitan subjects; pick up a schedule. (Chausseestr. 125. U-Bahn #6 to "Zinnowitzer Str." ☎ 283 05 70 44. Entrance only with a tour. Tours every 30min. Tu-W and F 10-11:30am, Th 10-11:30am and 5-6:30pm and Sa 9:30am-1:30pm. Tours every hour Su 11am-6pm. DM4, students DM2.)

DOROTHEENSTÄDTISCHER FRIEDHOF. Attached to Brecht's house is the cemetery where he and his wife, Helene Weigel, are buried. Also at rest there are Karl Friedrich Schinkel, Heinrich Mann, and Hegel and Fichte, who lie side by side in the middle of the yard. A map near the entrance points out their locations. (Open May-Aug. daily 8am-8pm; Feb.-Apr. and Sept.-Nov. 8am-6pm; Dec.-Jan. 8am-4pm.)

CHARLOTTENBURG

The borough of Charlottenburg, one of the wealthiest areas in Berlin, includes the area between the Ku'damm and the Spree river. Like many of Berlin's neighborhoods, it was once a separate town.

KURFÜRSTENDAMM

Stretching several kilometers from Bahnhof Zoo, **Kurfürstendamm** (**Ku'damm** for short) is Berlin's biggest and fanciest shopping strip, lined with designer boutiques, department stores, and pricey hotels. For more on the Ku'damm's consumer delights, see **Shopping,** p. 136.

BAHNHOF ZOO. During the city's division, West Berlin centered around Bahnhof Zoo, the station which inspired U2's "Zoo TV" tour (the U-Bahn line with the same name as the band runs through the station. Clever.) The area surrounding the station is a spectacular wasteland of department stores and peepshows intermingled with souvenir shops and G-rated attractions.

ZOOLOGISCHER GARTEN. Across Bahnhof Zoo and through the corral of bus depots, the renowned Zoo is one of the best in the world, with many animals displayed in open-air habitats instead of cages. The diverse cast of creatures includes two pandas, and a variety of babies. The second entrance across from Europa-Center is the famous **Elefantentor,** Budapester Str. 34, a delightfully decorated pagoda of pachyderms. *(Open May-Sept. daily 9am-6:30pm; Oct.-Feb. 9am-5pm; Mar.-Apr. 9am-5:30pm. DM13, students DM11.)*

AQUARIUM. Next door to the Zoo is the excellent Aquarium, which houses broad collections of insects and reptiles as well as endless tanks of wide-eyed, rainbow-colored fish. Its pride and joy is the 450kg **Komodo dragon,** the world's largest reptile, a gift to Germany from Indonesia. Check out the psychedelic jellyfish tanks, filled with many translucent sea nettles. *(Budapester Str. 32. Open daily 9am-6pm. Aquarium DM12, students DM10. Combination ticket to the zoo and aquarium DM21, students DM17, children DM10.)*

KAISER-WILHELM-GEDÄCHTNISKIRCHE. Nicknamed "the rotten tooth" by Berliners, the shattered church, with jagged edges jutting out into an otherwise smooth skyline, stands in striking contrast to the surrounding fast-food chains and department stores as a quiet reminder of the destruction caused during WWII. Built in 1852 in a Romanesque-Byzantine style, the church has an equally striking interior, with colorful mosaics covering the ceiling, floors, and walls. The ruins house an exhibit showing what the church used to look like, as well as shocking photos of the entire city in ruins just after the war. While the post-war construction adjacent to the church looks rather dull in comparison, this enormous octagonal building has a silently beautiful interior which radiates a dim blue glow from the stained-glass blocks. In the summer, Berlin's many street performers and salesmen, foreigners, and young people often gather in front of the church to hang out, sell less-than-legal watches, and play bagpipes and sitars. *(☎218 50 23. Exhibit open M-Sa 10am-4pm. Church open daily 9am-7pm.)*

SCHLOß CHARLOTTENBURG

The broad Baroque palace commissioned by Friedrich I for his second wife, Sophie-Charlotte, drapes its yellow walls over a park on the northern edge of Charlottenburg. The sprawling complex provides ideal relief from the bustle of downtown, with lazy lawns and numerous buildings. The Schloß's many buildings include the **Neringbau** (or **Altes Schloß**), the palace proper, which contains many rooms filled with historic furnishings and gratuitous gilding; the **Schinkel-Pavilion,** a museum dedicated to Prussian architect Karl Friedrich Schinkel; **Belvedere,** a small building housing the royal family's porcelain collection; and the **Mausoleum,** the final resting spot for most of the family. The **Galerie der Romantik,** a state museum housing Berlin's first-rate collection of German Romantic paintings, is located in a side wing (see p. 128). Seek out the **Schloßgarten** behind the main buildings, an elysium of small lakes, footbridges, fountains, and carefully-planted rows of trees. *(☎32 09 11. Take bus #145 from Bahnhof Zoo to "Luisenpl./Schloß Charlottenburg" or U-Bahn #7 to "Richard-Wagner-Pl." and walk about 15min. down Otto-Suhr-Allee. Altes Schloß open Tu-F 9am-5pm, Sa-Su 10am-5pm; DM8, students DM4. Schinkel-Pavilion open Tu-Su 10am-5pm; DM3, students DM2. Belvedere open Apr.-Oct. Tu-Su 10am-5pm, Nov.-Mar. Tu-F noon-4pm and Sa-Su noon-5pm; DM3, students DM2. Mausoleum open Apr.-Oct. Tu-Su 10am-noon and 1-5pm; DM3, students DM2. Schloßgarten open Tu-Su 6am-9pm; free. Ticket to entire complex DM15, students DM10, under 14 free. Family card DM25.)*

BERLIN

OTHER SIGHTS IN CHARLOTTENBURG

OLYMPIA-STADION. At the western edge of Charlottenburg, the Olympic Stadium is one of the most prominent legacies of the Nazi architectural aesthetic. It was erected for the 1936 Olympic Games, in which Jesse Owens, an African-American, triumphed over the Nazis' racial theories by winning four gold medals. Hitler refused to congratulate Owens because of his skin color, but there's now a Jesse-Owens-Allee to the south of the stadium. Film buffs will recognize the complex from Leni Riefenstahl's infamous Nazi propaganda film *Olympia*. *(U-Bahn #2 to "Olympia-Stadion (Ost)" or S-Bahn #5 or 75 to "Olympiastadion." DM2. Open daily in summer 8am-8pm, in winter 8am-3pm.)*

FUNKTURM. Erected in 1926 to herald the radio age, the Funkturm is the Fernsehturm's marginally less impressive twin. Though not as touristed as its Alexanderpl. sibling, the tower offers a stunning view of the city atop its 200m-tall observation deck. Inside, the **Deutsches Rundfunkmuseum** chronicles the history of German broadcasting, including an exhibit dedicated to the world's first television transmission, made here in 1931. *(☎ 30 38 39 99. Take S-Bahn #45 or 46 to "Witzleben" or U-Bahn #2 to "Kaiserdamm." Panorama deck and museum open daily 10am-11pm. DM5.)*

GEDENKSTÄTTE PLÖTZENSEE. Housed in the terrifyingly well-preserved former execution chambers of the Third Reich, the memorial exhibits documents death sentences of "enemies of the people," including the officers who attempted to assassinate Hitler in 1944. More than 2,500 people were murdered within this small, stark red brick complex. Still visible are the hooks from which victims were hanged. The stone urn in front of the memorial contains soil from Nazi concentration camps. English literature is available. *(Hüttigpfad. Off the main road where the bus stops, down Emmy-Zehden-Weg on Hüttigpfad. ☎ 344 32 26. Take U-Bahn #9 to "Turmstr.," then bus #123 (direction: "Saatwinkler Damm") to "Gedenkstätte Plötzensee." Open daily Mar.-Oct. 9am-5pm, Nov.-Feb. 9am-4pm. Free.)*

SCHÖNEBERG AND WILMERSDORF

South of the Ku'damm, Schöneberg and Wilmersdorf are pleasant, middle-class residential districts noted for their shopping streets, lively cafes, and good restaurants. The birthplace of Marlene Dietrich and the former stomping grounds of Christopher Isherwood, Schöneberg is home to the more affluent segments of Berlin's gay and lesbian community (see **Gay and Lesbian Berlin,** p. 143).

RATHAUS SCHÖNEBERG. West Berlin's city government convened here until the Wall fell in 1989. On June 26, 1963, exactly 15 years after the beginning of the Berlin Airlift, 1.5 million Berliners swarmed the streets beneath the windowless tower to hear John F. Kennedy reassure them of the Allies' commitment to the city. Kennedy's speech ended with the now-famous words, "All free men, wherever they may live, are citizens of Berlin. And therefore, as a free man, I take pride in the words: *Ich bin ein Berliner.*" Of course, every German understood what Kennedy meant, but for the grammar buffs out there, the prez *did* say he's a jelly doughnut. Today, the fortress with the little Berlin bear on top is home to Schöneberg's municipal government as well as an exhibit on the life of former mayor and federal chancellor Willy Brandt. You can climb up to the top of the tower; just follow the signs that say "Zum Turm." *(John-F.-Kennedy-Pl. U-Bahn #4 to "Rathaus Schöneberg." ☎ 787 60. Rathaus open daily 9am-6pm. Exhibit open daily 9am-1pm. Tower open daily Mar. 15-Oct. 15 10am-5pm.)*

BAYERISCHER PLATZ. In 1993, a conceptual art exhibit was set up along the streets surrounding the square. If you look closely, you'll notice some of the street signs have black-and-white placards above them stating some of the Nazi edicts against Berlin's Jews. A map at the entrance to the park points out the locations of all of the signs, and a number of them can be seen on **Grunewaldstr.** *(U-Bahn #4 or 7 to "Bayerischer Pl.")*

FEHRBELLINER PLATZ. The Wilmersdorf square was erected by the Nazis as a vision of the fascist architectural future. These gruesomely regular, prison-like blocks were meant to be model apartment houses; try to imagine a city full of them. *(U-Bahn #1 or 7 to "Fehrbelliner Pl.")*

GRUNEWALD. In summer, clear your head in the Grunewald, a 745-acre birch forest. While there, visit the **Jagdschloß,** a restored royal hunting lodge housing a worthwhile collection of European paintings, including works by Rubens, van Dyck, and Cranach. Cranach's depiction of icy Judith with the head of Holofernes makes it worth the trip. The one-room hunting museum in the same building provides an interesting contrast, but if you're at all sensitive about animal cruelty be careful. The cabinets full of knives, guns, and spears are accompanied by racks on antlers, mounted wild boars, and everything from goblets to tea sets adorned with hunting scenes. *(Am Grunewaldsee 29. U-Bahn #1 or 7 to "Fehrbelliner Pl.," then bus #115 (direction: "Neuruppiner Str.") to "Pücklerstr." Walk west 15min. on Pücklerstr. until the castle. ☎813 35 97. Open Tu-Su 10am-5pm. DM4, students and seniors DM2.)*

KREUZBERG

If you find Kurfürstendamm's consumerism nauseating, Kreuzberg provides the perfect dose of counter-culture relief. Here lies the indisputable center of Berlin's alternative *Szene,* an eclectic population of diverse ethnic backgrounds, plenty of punks, lots of graffiti, a thriving gay and lesbian community and alternatives to everything. During President Reagan's 1985 visit to Berlin, authorities so feared protests from this quarter that they cordoned the whole Kreuzberg district off without warning—an utterly unconstitutional measure. Much of the area was occupied by *Hausbesetzer* (squatters) in the 1960s and 70s. A conservative city government decided to forcibly evict the illegal residents in the early 80s, provoking riots and throwing the city into total consternation.

■ **HAUS AM CHECKPOINT CHARLIE.** A strange, fascinating exhibition on the site of the famous border-crossing point with an uneasy mixture of blatant Western tourist kitsch and didactic Eastern earnestness, the Haus am Checkpoint Charlie is one of Berlin's most popular tourist attractions. The ground floor holds a pricey snack bar and a ticket desk completely buried under piles of highly marketable, Wall-related books, stickers, postcards and various knickknacks. Right by the door stands the car in which Johannes Ehret smuggled his girlfriend across the border in 1988. The upper floors are a giant collage of artwork, newspaper clippings, and photographs mixed in with all types of devices used to get over, under, or through the wall. Documentaries and dramas about the Wall are screened daily in the rooms upstairs. *(Friedrichstr. 44. U-Bahn #6 or bus #129 to "Kochstr." ☎251 10 31. Museum open daily 9am-10pm. DM8, students DM5. Films M-F at 5:30 and 7:30pm, Sa-Su at 4:30, 6, and 7pm.)*

JÜDISCHES MUSEUM BERLIN. Daniel Libeskind's winning design for this museum is truly eerie now that it has been realized: still empty, the museum is fascinating merely as an architectural experience. The building has no entrance except through the basement from the building next door. None of the walls are parallel, and the hallways take strange turns or lead to windows looking into voids frequently enough to make any visitor uncomfortable. The museum re-opens with exhibits in September 2001; until then only the basement floor will be open for visitors. Times and prices have not yet been set, so call for more info. *(Lindenstr. 9-14. U-Bahn #6 to "Kochstr." or "Hallesches Tor." ☎25 99 33.)*

AROUND MEHRINGDAMM. For a look at Kreuzberg's new, somewhat gentrified face, take the U-Bahn to "Mehringdamm" and wander around. The area around Chamissopl., bordered by Bergmannstr. and Fidicinstr., features an especially large number of old buildings and second-hand shops as well as excellent used music shops (see Shopping, p. 136). On the other side of Mehringdamm, the Viktoriapark contains Kreuzberg's namesake, a 66m hill featuring Berlin's only waterfall, albeit artificial. At night, many cafes and clubs line Gneisenaustraße, which heads west from the intersection with Mehringdamm. *(U-Bahn #6 or 7 to "Mehringdamm.")*

ORANIENSTRASSE. The colorful mix of cafes, bars, and stores hawking records and used clothing on Oranienstr. boast a more radical element; the May Day parades always start on Oranienpl., and the area was the site of frequent riots in the 1980s. The anarchists and left-wing radicals share the neighborhood with a mix of traditional Turkish families as well as a sizeable portion of Berlin's gay and lesbian population. This montage results in pure eye-candy for the alternatively-inclined: colorful plates of food from Indian to Turkish, outfits from spikes and leather to hemp and henna, all among graffiti colored walls. The scene at night is crazy; see **Nightlife,** p. 139. *(U-Bahn #1 or 15 to "Kottbusser Tor" or "Görlitzer Bahnhof.")*

EASTERN KREUZBERG. The **Landwehrkanal,** a channel bisecting Kreuzberg, is where Rosa Luxemburg's body was thrown after being murdered by the Freikorps in 1919 (see p. 12). The tree-dotted strip of the canal near Kottbusser Damm, **Paul-Linke-Ufer,** may be the most graceful street in Berlin, with its shady terraces and old facades. *(U-Bahn #8 to "Schönleinstr.")* The east end of Kreuzberg, near the site of the Wall and the **Schlesisches Tor,** is home to Turkish and Balkan neighborhoods, with a corresponding wealth of ethnic restaurants popular with radicals and students. At the end of Kreuzberg, the **Oberbaumbrücke** spanning the Spree was once a border crossing into East Berlin; it now serves as an entrance to Friedrichshain's nightlife scene. *(U-Bahn #1 or 15 to "Schlesisches Tor.")*

FRIEDRICHSHAIN AND LICHTENBERG

▨**EAST SIDE GALLERY.** The longest remaining portion of the Wall, the 1.3km stretch of cement and asbestos slabs also serves as one of the world's largest open-air art galleries. The murals are not the remnants of Cold War graffiti, but rather the efforts of an international group of artists who gathered here in 1989 to celebrate the end of the city's division. It was expected that the wall would be destroyed soon after, and the paintings lost, but in 1999, with the wall still standing, the same artists came together again to repaint their work, covering the scrawlings of later tourists. *(Along Mühlenstr. Take S-Bahn #3, 5, 6, 7, 9, or 75 or U-Bahn #1 or 15 to "Warschauer Str." and walk back toward the river. Open 24hr.)*

KARL-MARX-ALLEE. The cornerstone of the East German *Nationales Aufbauprogramm* (national construction program), Karl-Marx-Allee became the socialist realist showcase of the infant Communist government in the early 1950s, when it was known as Stalinallee. Billed as Germany's "first socialist road," the ludicrously broad avenue, widened in the 1960s to accommodate grandiose military parades, is flanked by scores of pre-fabricated gems, climaxing with the "people's palaces" at Strausberger Pl. *(U-Bahn #5 to "Strausberger Pl.")*

FORSCHUNGS- UND GEDENKSTÄTTE NORMANNENSTRASSE. In the suburb of Lichtenberg stands perhaps the most hated and feared building of the GDR regime—the headquarters of the East German secret police, the **Staatssicherheit** or **Stasi.** On January 15, 1990, a crowd of 100,000 Berliners stormed and vandalized the building to protest the continued existence of the police state. The building once contained six million individual dossiers on citizens of the GDR, a country of

WALKING MAN When you cross the streets in most of west Berlin, you see your standard green walking man telling you to go, and your standard red standing man telling you to stop. In east Berlin, you may notice a difference: the crossing-signal figures here are thicker, bolder, more attractive. The green walking man strides forward with his hat cocked back, and the red standing man throws both arms fully to the sides. The crossing-man of east Berlin, known as the *Ampel-Männchen,* or "little hanging man," was drawn by cartoonist Karl Peglau during the days of the GDR. His simple, cheerful design and easy visibility are supposed to appeal to children and the elderly, but apparently he is beloved by everyone. When the city was reunified and plans were made to standardize the symbols to the plain old boring western design, east *Berliners* protested. Now, the *Ampel-Männchen* is a favorite figure for *Berliners* and tourists alike, and has spawned his own line of merchandise. T-shirts, mouse pads, key-chains, and strings of lights featuring the little red and green men can all be purchased at most souvenir shops, and if you're willing to fork over DM4.50 you can even buy gummy reincarnations to munch on as you wait to cross the street.

only 16 million people. Since a 1991 law returned the records to their subjects, the "Horror-Files" have rocked Germany, exposing informants—and wrecking careers, marriages, and friendships—at all levels of society. Today the building maintains its oppressive drear, retaining the metal fencing on the stairs and an unmistakable general gloom. The exhibit displays the offices of Erich Mielke (the loathed Minister for State Security from 1957-1989), a large collection of tiny microphones and hidden cameras used for surveillance by the Stasi, and a GDR Stasi shrine full of Lenin busts and countless other kitchy relics which are nothing short of bizarre. The present-day museum, memorial, and research center contains fascinating artifacts, but the history and anecdotes are only written in German. Lichtenberg suffers from severe unemployment and so when visiting the memorial, be cautious among the remaining emblems of the GDR. *(Ruschestr. 103, Haus 1. U-Bahn #5 to "Magdalenenstr." From the station's Ruschestr. exit, walk up Ruschestr. and take a right on Normannenstr.; it's Haus #1 in the complex of office buildings.* ☎ *553 68 54. Open Tu-F 11am-6pm, Sa-Su 2-6pm. DM5, students DM3.75.)*

PRENZLAUER BERG

Northeast of Mitte lies Prenzlauer Berg, a former working-class district largely neglected by East Germany's reconstruction efforts. Many of the older buildings are crumbling at the edges, resulting in a charming state of age and graceful decay, slightly less charming for local residents with bad plumbing and no phones. However, recent years have brought the gentrification bird to Prenzlauer Berg, driving away those who fled to the neighborhood several years ago in search of cheaper rent, and replacing them with a more refined, chichi element. Unlike the loud, raucous scene in Kreuzberg and Mitte, Prenzlauer Berg is more refined and cerebral—which is not to say that it isn't lively. The streets here are studded with trendy but casual cafes and bars frequented by an ever-burgeoning crowd. To reach Kollwitzpl. and Husemannstr., take U-Bahn #2 to "Senefelderpl.," cross the street left and walk back through the park onto Kollwitzstr.

KOLLWITZPLATZ. The heart of Prenzlauer Berg's cafe scene, Kollwitzpl. offers a little triangle of greenery, centered around a statue of the square's namesake, visual artist **Käthe Kollwitz** (see p. 131). The monument has been painted a number of times in past years in acts of affectionate rather than angry vandalism, most notably with big pink polka-dots.

HUSEMANNSTRASSE. Just off Kollwitzpl., Husemannstr. is particularly representative of the new Prenzlauer Berg ambience. Lined with hip bars and cafes, it is also home to **Museum Berliner Arbeiterleben um 1900,** a meticulously accurate reproduction of a working-class family's apartment at the turn of the century. *(Husemannstr. 12.* ☎ *442 25 14. Open M-Th 10am-3pm. Free.)*

JÜDISCHER FRIEDHOF. Berlin's Jews found slightly remote Prenzlauer Berg ideal, slowly gravitating there during the 19th and early 20th centuries. The Jewish cemetery on Schönhauser Allee contains the graves of composer Giacomo Meyerbeer and painter Max Liebermann. *(Open M-Th 8am-4pm, F 8am-1pm. Men must cover their heads before entering the cemetery.)* Nearby stands the **Synagoge Rykestraße.** One of Berlin's loveliest synagogues, it was spared on *Kristallnacht* due to its inconspicuous location in a courtyard. *(Rykestr. 53.)*

CARL-ZEISS-GROSSPLANETARIUM. One of the last great feats of East Berlin's city planners, the planetarium opened in 1987 as the most modern facility of its kind in the GDR, and it remains one of the best in Germany. Operated by the vintage 1980s *Cosmorama* projector, the planetarium is an example of East German know-how at its best. *(Prenzlauer Allee 80.* ☎ *42 18 45 12. S-Bahn #4, 8, or 85 to "Prenzlauer Allee." DM8, students DM6.)*

OUTER DISTRICTS

The city districts listed below are accessible in about 20 minutes from the center of Berlin by public transportation and make good afternoon or daytrips. For excursions to Potsdam, see **Brandenburg** (p. 146).

WANNSEE

Most Berliners think of the town of Wannsee, on the lake of the same name, as the beach. Wannsee has long stretches of sand along the Havelufer-Promenade, and the roads behind the beaches are crowded with vacation villas. To reach the lake, take S-Bahn #1 or 7 to "Wannsee" or "Nikolassee" and walk 15 minutes to the beach. On summer weekends, a special bus shuttles bathers from the train station.

HAUS DER WANNSEE-KONFERENZ. The reputation of the charming village of Wannsee is tarnished by the memory of the notorious **Wannsee Conference** of January 20, 1942. Leading officials of the SS completed the details for the implementation of the "Final Solution" in the **Wannsee Villa,** formerly a Gestapo intelligence center. In January 1992, the 50th anniversary of the Nazi death-pact, the villa reopened as an excellent museum with permanent Holocaust exhibits and a documentary film series. The villa is discomfitingly lovely, and its grounds offer a dazzling view of the Wannsee. *(Am Großen Wannsee 56. Take bus #114 from the S-Bahn station to "Haus der Wannsee-Konferenz." ☎ 805 00 10. Open M-F 10am-6pm. Free.)*

KLEISTGRAB. Along the shores of the **Kleiner Wannsee,** the brilliant young author **Heinrich von Kleist** and his terminally ill companion committed suicide in 1811. A small grave marks the site of their demise. *(Bismarckstr. 3, below the Wannseebrücke.)*

PFAUENINSEL. Friedrich Wilhelm II built a *trompe l'oeil* "ruined" castle as a private pleasure house on the banks of Peacock Island. Here, he and his mistress could romp undisturbed for hours. A flock of the island's namesake fowl roams about the gardens surrounding the castle. *(Take bus #316 or A16 from the S-Bahn station to "Pfaueninsel" and hop on the ferry. Ferry operates May-Aug. 8am-8pm, Apr. and Sept. 9am-6pm, Mar. and Oct. 9am-5pm, Nov.-Feb. 10am-4pm. DM2, students and seniors DM1.)*

GLIENICKER BRÜCKE. At the southwestern corner of the district, the bridge crosses the Havel into Potsdam and what was once the GDR. Closed to traffic in Cold War days, it is famed as the spot where East and West once exchanged captured spies. The most famous such incident traded American U-2 pilot Gary Powers for Soviet spy Ivanovich Abel. To continue on the other side of the bridge, see p. 150. *(Bus #116 from the S-Bahn station (direction: "Glienicker Brücke (Potsdam)" to the end.)*

WANNSEE CRUISES. Two ferry companies run boats from the Wannsee waterfront just behind the park to the right of the S-Bahn station. **Stern und Kreis** (☎ 803 87 50) and **Reederverband** (☎ 434 89 80) both set sail once or twice an hour, though the ferries' leisurely clip means that they're meant more as pleasure cruises than as an efficient means of transport. *(Most cruises run DM10-12.)*

DAHLEM AND STEGLITZ

A southern suburb with small streets and shop windows, Dahlem is a quiet residential neighborhood home to affluent professionals as well as the sprawling **Freie Universität,** one of Berlin's three universities. The district also houses one of Berlin's most prestigious museum complexes (see p. 131). Next door to Dahlem, **Steglitz** is an unremarkable suburb noted for its busy shopping district *(U-Bahn #9 to "Schloßstr.")* as well as its exquisite botanical garden (see below).

BOTANISCHER GARTEN. One of the best botanical gardens in the world, the Botanischer Garten features traditional hot houses, but they're not afraid to experiment here: sprawling fields and naturalized patches of flowers and greens are allowed to go a little wild. Leafy treasures from around the world await—fragrant herbs, carefully arranged English flowers, and gnarled Japanese trees. The resulting scents are *dee*-vine. *(Königin-Luise-Str. 6. ☎ 83 00 61 27. S-Bahn #1 to "Botanischer Garten." Follow the signs from the S-Bahn station. Open May-July 9am-9pm, Apr. and Aug. 9am-8pm, Mar. and Oct. 9am-7pm, Nov.-Jan. 9am-4pm, Feb. 9am-5pm. Last admittance 30min. before closing. DM8, students DM4; Abendkarte, valid 2hr. before closing, DM4, students DM2.)*

TREPTOW

SOWJETISCHES EHRENMAL. This powerful Soviet War Memorial is a mammoth promenade built with marble taken from Hitler's Chancellery. The Soviets dedicated the site in 1948, honoring the millions of Red Army soldiers who fell in what Russians know as the "Great Patriotic War." Massive granite slabs along the walk are festooned with quotations from Stalin, leading up to colossal bronze figures in the socialist realist style, symbolically crushing Nazism underfoot. Even the trees bend their branches in sorrow with these powerful statues. It's quite moving, despite the pomp. Buried beneath the trees surrounding the monument are the bodies of 5,000 unknown Soviet soldiers who were killed during the Battle of Berlin in 1945. The memorial sits in the middle of **Treptower Park,** a spacious forest ideal for morbid picnics. Also in the park is the **Figurentheater,** Puschkinallee 15a, full of figures who perform *Märchen* (fairy tales) with wooden facial expressions. The neighborhood adjoining the park has many pleasant waterside cafes.

SPANDAU

Spandau is one of the oldest parts of Berlin and in many respects remains a separate city. Take U-Bahn #7 to "Altstadt Spandau." Many of the old buildings have been restored, though unfortunately they are now surrounded by car dealerships.

ZITADELLE. Encircled by waters once considered impregnable, the star-shaped enclosure was the anchor of Spandau in medieval days. During WWII, the Nazis used the fort as a chemical weapons lab, and in 1945 the Allies employed the *Zitadelle* as a prison to hold war criminals before the Nürnberg trials. Despite its grim name and past, the citadel is now a sort of wistful ghost town filled with old field-cannons, statues, a **medieval history museum,** and fields of grass on its ramparts. The thickly fortified **Juliusturm,** dating to circa 1200, is Spandau's unofficial symbol. (*Am Juliusturm. Take U-Bahn #7 to "Zitadelle."* ☎ *339 12 12. Open Tu-F 9am-5pm, Sa-Su 10am-5pm. DM4, students DM2.*)

OTHER SIGHTS. Spandauers defiantly constructed a somewhat unremarkable **Rathaus** from 1911 to 1913 (at a cost of DM3.5 million) in a futile effort to stave off absorption into Berlin. While this colossal brown structure once loomed over the area, today a busy street and the ever-present **Karstadt** are closing in. Take U-Bahn #7 to "Rathaus Spandau." **Spandau Prison** was demolished after its last inmate, Hitler's deputy Rudolf Hess, committed suicide in 1987 at age 93. Hess, a devoted party member from the beginning (he participated in the Beer Hall Putsch and took dictation for Hitler's *Mein Kampf*) was an unrepentant Nazi until his death.

ORANIENBURG AND SACHSENHAUSEN

To get to Sachsenhausen, take S-Bahn #1 (direction: "Oranienburg") to the end (40min.). The camp is a 20-min. walk from the station; follow the signs. (Str. der Nationen 22. ☎(03301) 80 37 15. Open Apr.-Sept. Tu-Su 8:30am-6pm; Oct.-Mar. Tu-Su 8:30am-4:30pm. Last entry 30min. before closing. Free.)

The small town of Oranienburg, just north of Berlin, was home to **KZ Sachsenhausen,** a Nazi concentration camp in which more than 100,000 Jews, communists, intellectuals, gypsies, and homosexuals were killed between 1936 and 1945. The **Gedenkstätte Sachsenhausen** was opened by the GDR in 1961. Parts of the camp have been preserved in their original forms, including sets of cramped barracks, the cell block where particularly "dangerous" prisoners were kept in solitary confinement and tortured daily, and a pathology department where Nazis performed medical experiments on inmates both dead and alive. Only the foundations of Station Z (where prisoners were methodically exterminated) remain, but the windswept grounds convey the horrors that were committed here. A GDR slant is still apparent; the main museum building features Socialist Realist stained-glass windows memorializing "German Anti-Fascist Martyrs." The museums, however, have been totally overhauled recently. The main one hosts special shows of Holocaust-related art or specific histories of imprisoned groups, as well as a fascinating permanent exhibit (in English and German) on the history of anti-Semitic practices throughout the world. The latest addition is a museum in the jail block detailing its uses and the punishments inflicted there, along with rotating exhibits on the individual prisoners.

🏛 MUSEUMS

Berlin is one of the world's great museum cities, with collections of art and artifacts encompassing all subjects and eras. The **Staatliche Museen Preußischer Kulturbesitz (SMPK)** runs the four major complexes—**Museum Insel, Kulturforum,
Charlottenburg,** and **Dahlem**—that form the hub of the city's museum culture. Since
these museums are government-run, their prices are standardized; a single admission costs DM4, students DM2. A *Tageskarte* (DM8, students DM4) is valid for all
SMPK museums on the day of purchase; the *Wochenkarte* (DM25, students
DM12.50) is valid for the whole week. The first Sunday of every month brings free
admission. Smaller museums deal with every subject imaginable, from sugar to
tarts. *Berlin Programm* lists museums and some galleries (DM2.80).

MUSEUMINSEL (MUSEUM ISLAND)

Museuminsel holds the treasure hoard of the former GDR in four separate museums, though one is currently closed for renovations. Modeled on ancient Athens,
the island's cultural temples are barely separated from the rest of Mitte by the
murky Spree. Many of the museums are undergoing extensive renovation, and
both the **Alte Nationalgalerie** and **Bodemuseum** remain closed until 2001 and 2004,
respectively. *(Take S-Bahn #3, 5, 7, 9 or 75 to "Hackescher Markt" or bus #100 to "Lustgarten." Unless otherwise noted, all Museuminsel museums are open Tuesday through Sunday 9am
to 6pm. All museums offer free audio tours in English.)*

▓ **PERGAMONMUSEUM.** One of the world's great ancient history museums, from
the days of the Empire when Western archaeology was king and Heinrich Schlie-
mann traversed the world, pillaging the debris of former civilizations and reassem-
bling it at home. Named for Pergamon, in present-day Turkey, the city from which
the enormous **Altar of Zeus** (180 BC) that fills its main exhibit hall was taken, the
museum features pieces of ancient Mediterranean and Near Eastern history as big
as they come. The big blue **Ishtar Gate** of Babylon (575 BC) and the Roman **Market
Gate of Miletus** are just several more of the pieces that astound; some are as old as
the 10th century BC. The museum houses extensive collections of Greek, Assyr-
ian, Islamic and Far Eastern art. *(Kupfergraben.* ☎ *203 55 00. Tours of Pergamon Altar
daily at 11am and 3pm. Tageskarte required for entry. Last entry 30min. before closing.)*

ALTE NATIONALGALERIE. Closed for renovations until 2001, the museum's collection of 19th-century German as well as French Impressionist painters is currently housed in the Altes Museum (see below).

ALTES MUSEUM. At the far end of the Lustgarten, the Altes Museum's galleries
are surprisingly untouristed. The lower level contains the *Antikensammlung*, a
permanent collection of ancient Greco-Roman decorative art, including a particularly fine slew of Greek vases and an interesting statue of a praying boy. Upstairs,
see the greatest hits of the Alte Nationalgalerie while their true home is renovated.
(Lustgarten. Tageskarte valid as long as the Alte Nationalgalerie collection remains there.)

AROUND MITTE

DEUTSCHE GUGGENHEIM BERLIN. Located in a newly renovated building
across the street from the Deutsche Staatsbibliothek (see p. 115). A joint venture
of the Deutsche Bank and the Guggenheim Foundation in New York, the museum
features changing exhibits of contemporary avant-garde art. The museum reopened in July 2000 with an exhibit called "Nach Alles" (After All), and shows new
exhibits every few months in its renovated space. *(Unter den Linden 13-15.* ☎ *20 20
93 13. Open daily 11am-8pm, Th and F until 10pm. DM8, students DM5; M free.)*

DEUTSCHES HISTORISCHES MUSEUM. Exhibits trace German history from the
Neanderthal period to the Nazis, while rotating exhibitions examine the last 50
years. Large quantities of GDR art in the "painting-of-a-happy-faced-worker" vein.
Until renovations of the Zeughaus are completed in 2002, the museum is housed in
the Kronprinzenpalais across the street. *(Unter den Linden 2, in the Zeughaus. S-Bahn
#3, 5, 7, 9, or 75 to "Hackescher Markt."* ☎ *20 30 40. Open Th-Tu 10am-6pm. Free.)*

SCHINKELMUSEUM. 19th-century French and German sculpture and an exhibit on the life and work of the famous Prussian architect Karl Friedrich Schinkel. The church housing the museum is almost more worthwhile than its exhibits. It was built in 1824-30 based on Schinkel's designs; destroyed in WWII, it was restored in 1987. *(Werderscher Markt, on the corner of Oberwallstr., south of Unter den Linden. ☎ 20 90 55 55. U-Bahn #2 to "Hausvogteipl." Open Tu-Su 10am-6pm. SMPK prices.)*

MÄRKISCHES MUSEUM. A beautiful building on the banks of the Spree housing a collection of early Berlin history and lots of applied art. Demonstration of automatophone Su at 3pm. *(Am Köllnischen Park 5, at the corner of Märkisches Ufer. U-Bahn #2 to "Märkisches Museum." ☎ 30 86 60. Open Tu-Su 10am-6pm. DM8, students DM4; W free.)*

HANFMUSEUM. Everything you wanted to know about marijuana is here in a small storefront space, including its medical and textile uses, and a history of the debate over the legality of non-medical usage. Mull over exhibits of hemp brownies, ice cream, oils, and cosmetics. Did you know that hemp can serve as a convenient insulation material? *(Mühlendamm 5. U-Bahn #2 to "Klosterstr." ☎ 24 72 02 33. Open Tu-F 10am-8pm, Sa-Su noon-8pm. DM5.)*

KULTURFORUM

The **Tiergarten-Kulturforum,** is a complex of museums at the eastern end of the Tiergarten, near the Staatsbibliothek and Potsdamer Pl. Right now its location is less than ideal; the area near Potsdamer Pl. is Europe's biggest construction site, and finding your way around is quite a task. *(On Matthäikirchpl. For all museums take S-Bahn #1, 2, or 25 or U-Bahn #2 to "Potsdamer Pl." and walk down Potsdamer Str.; the museums will be on your right. ☎ 20 90 55 55. All museums are open Tu-Su 10am-6pm, unless otherwise noted, and have SMPK prices.)*

■ **GEMÄLDEGALERIE.** One of Germany's most famous museums, and rightly so. It houses a stunning and enormous collection by Italian, German, Dutch, and Flemish masters, including works by Dürer, Rembrandt, Bruegel, Rubens, Vermeer, Raphael, Titian, and Botticelli. *(Open Th until 10 pm.)*

KUNSTBIBLIOTHEK/KUPFERSTICHKABINETT. A stellar collection of lithographs and drawings by Renaissance masters, including many Dürers, Goyas, and Botticelli's fantastic illustrations for the *Divine Comedy. (Tours Su at 3pm.)*

KUNSTGEWERBEMUSEUM. Including everything from spoons to plates to tables to chairs to tapestries to boxes, from the middle ages to art deco, the most interesting parts of the exhibit are the collections from the present-day. Never before have so many wacky chairs been together in the same room, and even an inflatable plastic one gets to be art for a while.

AROUND THE TIERGARTEN

NEUE NATIONALGALERIE. This sleek building, designed by Mies van der Rohe, houses interesting temporary exhibits upstairs in its huge windowed showroom, but the permanent collection downstairs is also worth a visit. Works by Warhol, Munch, Kirchner, Pechstein, Beckmann, and Ernst provide variety and provoke thought. *(Potsdamer Str. 50. Just past the Kulturforum. ☎ 266 26 62 or 266 26 56. SMPK prices for permanent collection; DM12, students DM6 for the whole museum. Open Tu-F 10am-6pm and Sa-Su 11am-6pm.)*

MUSIKINSTRUMENTEN-MUSEUM. Fittingly next door to the Philharmonic's bumpy yellow home, this is a truly fascinating museum of musical instruments. Housed in a bright (albeit small) space, the collection of instruments ranges from a glass harmonica and 12 foot alp horn to some really wacky violins. The computer lab downstairs allows visitors to choose music to listen to while testing their music trivia; a sound studio next door lets you try out some piano predecessors. *(Tiergartenstr. 1. S-Bahn #1, 2, or 25 or U-Bahn #2 to "Potsdamer Pl." ☎ 25 48 10. Open Tu-F 9am-5pm, Sa-Su 10am-5pm. DM4, students DM2. Tours Sa at 11am. DM3.)*

RAABGALERIE. A well-kept gallery with thoughtful exhibitions of famous and not-so-famous 20th-century artists. *(Potsdamer Str. 58. U-Bahn #2 to "Mendelssohn-Bartholdy-Park." ☎ 261 92 17. Open M-F 10am-7pm, Sa 10am-4pm.)*

BAUHAUS-ARCHIV MUSEUM FÜR GESTALTUNG. A building designed by Bauhaus founder Walter Gropius that houses an exhibit devoted to the school's development, along with a collection of paintings by Kandinsky and Klee. *(Klingelhöferstr. 14. Bus #100 or 187 to "Stülerstr." ☎ 254 00 20. Open M and W-Su 10am-5pm. DM5, students DM2.50; M free.)*

HAMBURGER BAHNHOF/MUSEUM FÜR GEGENWART. Berlin's foremost collection of contemporary art features some cheerfully amusing works by Warhol, and a few neat multimedia installations including Bill Viola's "He weeps for you," in which a magnified faucet drips slowly onto an amplified drum. Works by Beuys, Kiefer, and Twombley and Walter De Maria's "The 2000 Sculpture" fill the bright, airy spaces of this converted train station. *(Invalidenstr. 50-51. S-Bahn #3, 5, 7, 9, or 75 to "Lehrter Stadtbahnhof" or U-Bahn #6 to "Zinnowitzer Str." ☎ 397 83 11. Open Tu, W, F 10am-6pm, Th 10am-10pm, Sa-Su 11am-6pm. DM10, students DM5; first Su of the month free. Tours Sa-Su at 3pm.)*

AROUND POTSDAMER PLATZ

INFOBOX. Sponsored by Potsdamer Pl. investors, the Infobox brings everything you ever wanted to know about Europe's largest construction site just a click of the mouse away. The exhibits change regularly as building progresses, and address topics such as environmental concerns as well as the "mushroom concept," the overall idea behind the changes being made in the transportation systems. *(Leipziger Pl. 21. S-Bahn #1, 2, or 25 or U-Bahn #2 to "Potsdamer Pl." ☎ 226 62 40. Open daily 9am-7pm, Th 9am-9pm. Tours every hour on the hour 10am-4pm. Free.)*

MARTIN-GROPIUS-BAU. Walter Gropius' uncle Martin designed this neo-Renaissance wedding cake as a museum for and tribute to the industrial arts. The style is anything but Bauhaus slick—the ornate fixings are absolutely decadent. The building alone is worth the price of admission, and the temporary exhibits of modern art and history are top-notch. *(Niederkirchnerstr. 7. S-Bahn #1 or 2, or U-Bahn #2 to "Potsdamer Pl." ☎ 25 48 60. Open Tu-Su 10am-8pm. Admission varies.)*

TOPOGRAPHIE DES TERRORS. Built on top of the ruins of a Gestapo kitchen, the area used to be the site of the notorious Gestapo headquarters at Prinz-Albrecht-Str. (now Niederkirchnerstr.). The very comprehensive exhibit of photographs, documents, and German texts displayed amidst the crumbled buildings details the Nazi party's rise to power and the atrocities that occurred during the war. English guides are available, but you don't need to understand the captions to be moved by the photographs. A new exhibition building is under construction and scheduled to be completed at some point during 2001. *(Behind the Martin-Gropius-Bau, at the corner of Niederkirchnerstr. and Wilhelmstr. S-Bahn #1 or 2, or U-Bahn #2 to "Potsdamer Pl." ☎ 25 48 67 03. Open Tu-Su 10am-6pm. Free.)* The adjacent **Prinz-Albrecht-Gelände,** a deserted wasteland near the site of the Wall, contains the ruins of Gestapo buildings. *(Open 10am-dusk. Free.)*

SCHLOß CHARLOTTENBURG

The wide-flung wings and surrounding neighborhood of **Schloß Charlottenburg** (☎ 32 09 11) are home to a number of excellent museums. Take bus #145 from "Bahnhof Zoo" to "Luisenpl./Schloß Charlottenburg" or U-Bahn #7 to "Richard-Wagner-Pl." and walk about 15 min. down Otto-Suhr-Allee. For more on the Schloß and its grounds, see **Sights** p. 121.

■ **ÄGYPTISCHES MUSEUM.** This stern Neoclassical building contains a famous collection of ancient Egyptian art—animal mummies, elaborately-painted coffins, and original papyrus scrolls encrypted with hieroglyphics and the later Coptic language—dramatically lit for the full Indiana Jones effect. The most popular item on display is the stunning 3,300-year-old bust of **Queen Nefretiti** (1350 BC), thought by many to be the most beautiful representation of a woman in the world. *(Schloßstr. 70. Across Spandauer Damm from the palace. ☎ 20 90 55 55. Open Tu-Su 10am-6pm. DM8, students DM4.)*

■ **SAMMLUNG BERGGRUEN.** Five floors off a central spiralling staircase offer a substantial collection of Picasso's life's work, including numerous sketches, some of which were drawn when the artist was as young as 16. The bottom floor also exhibits works that influenced Picasso, including late French impressionist paintings and African masks; the top floor exhibits Paul Klee's paintings and Alberto Giacometti's sculptures. *(Schloßstr. 1. In an identical building across the street from the Egyptian museum.* ☎ *326 95 80. Open Tu-F 10am-6pm, Sa-Su 11am-6pm. DM8, students DM4.)*

GALERIE DER ROMANTIK. The museum holds the Prussian crown's dynamic collection of 19th-century art. The unquestioned show-stealers are the beautiful, bleak landscapes by Prussian artist Caspar David Friedrich, with looming skies and seas and tiny human figures placed precariously in their midst. *(In the palace's Neuer Flügel.* ☎ *20 90 55 55. Open Tu-F 10am-6pm, Sa-Su 11am-8pm. DM8, students DM4.)*

BRÖHANMUSEUM. Features two floors of *Jugendstil* and Art Deco furniture, housewares, and paintings in the sleekest of surroundings. Pieces date 1889–1939. *(Schloßstr. 1a. Next door to the Berggruen.* ☎ *321 40 29. Open Tu-Su 10am-6pm. DM8, students DM4.)*

DAHLEM

The **Staatliche Museen Preußischer Kulturbesitz Dahlem** complex looms near the Freie Universität. Several globe-spanning museums cram into one enormous building, plus another across the street; unfortunately, some are closed for renovations until 2001. Pick up a map at the entrance; the museums are laid out strangely. *(Take U-Bahn #1 to "Dahlem-Dorf" and follow the Museen signs. All have SMPK prices.)*

MUSEUM EUROPÄISCHER KULTUREN. A hop away from the main Dahlem complex, this museum is dedicated to artifacts of lower- and middle-class life from Germany and the rest of Europe from the past 400 years. The exhibit on post-war pop culture is charming—never thought you'd see *Garbage Pail Kids* in a museum, eh? *(Im Winkel 6-8.* ☎ *20 90 55 55. Open Tu-F 10am-6pm, Sa-Su 11am-6pm.)*

MUSEUM FÜR VÖLKERKUNDE. Fascinating collection of tools, artifacts, writings, musical instruments, weapons, and clothing from Africa, Polynesia, Central and South America, and Central and Southeast Asia. The Polynesian exhibit climaxes with a giant display of ornately decorated boats, many of which you can climb into. Play the baláfon (xylophone) in the African section. *(Lansstr. 8.* ☎ *20 90 55 55. Open Tu-F 10am-6pm, Sa-Su 11am-6pm. Free admission first Su of the month.)*

OTHER MUSEUMS

BRÜCKE MUSEUM. Tucked in a quiet residential neighborhood this museum exhibits the wildly colorful works by adherents of the Expressionist *Brücke* school, including work by Otto Dix. The adjacent Bernard Heihger Stiftung sculpture garden is also worth a peak. *(Bussardsteig 9. Take U-Bahn #1 or 7 to "Fehrbelliner Pl." then bus #115 (direction: "Neuruppiner Str.") to "Pücklerstr."* ☎ *831 20 29. Open W-M 11am-5pm. DM7, students DM3.)*

DEUTSCHES TECHNIKMUSEUM. The collection of this colossal museum includes aged trains, a history of film technology, and plenty of model ships. Where's the German touch? A historic brewery, circa 1910. A new aeronautical wing is under construction, slated for completion in 2001. Combined admission with a yard of antique locomotives down the street. English information available. *(Trebbiner Str. 9. U-Bahn #1, 2, or 15 to "Gleisdreieck" or U-Bahn #1, 7, or 15 to "Möckernbrücke."* ☎ *25 48 40. Open Tu-F 9am-5:30pm, Sa-Su 10am-6pm. DM5, students DM2; first Su of the month free.)*

KÄTHE-KOLLWITZ-MUSEUM. A marvelous collection of works by one of Germany's most prominent modern artists, Käthe Kollwitz, a member of the Berlin *Sezession*, whose radical social consciousness is often evident in her work. The museum also hosts changing contemporary exhibitions. *(Fasanenstr. 24. U-Bahn #15 to "Uhlandstr."* ☎ *882 52 10. Open M and W-Su 11am-6pm. DM8, students DM4.)*

ZUCKERMUSEUM. A cultural history of sugar explores its uses, such as sculpture, records, and alcohol. Yum. Why is all this important? *Ohne Zucker kein Alcohol,* "without sugar no alcohol." *(Amrumer Str. 32. U-Bahn #9 to "Amrumer Str."* ☎ *31 42 75 74. Open M-W 9am-5pm, Th 3-8pm, Su 11am-6pm. DM4, students DM2.)*

GALLERIES

Berlin has an extremely well-funded art scene, with many first-rate galleries. The work is as diverse as Berlin's cultural landscape, and includes everything from early Christian antiques in Charlottenburg to conceptual installations in Mitte. To get started, *Berliner Galerien* is a small pamphlet with maps of the Mitte and Charlottenburg galleries, available at most hotels. The best information, with complete show listings, is available in the comprehensive *ARTery Berlin* (DM3.50), which is written in English and German, or the *Berliner Kunst Kalender* (DM3): both include maps and can be picked up just about anywhere in the city.

The center of the gallery world lies in Mitte; pick up the Berlin Mitte pamphlet at one of the area galleries for listings and a map. Twice every year, in July and September, Mitte offers a *Galerienrundgang* tour of the galleries. Sophienstr., Gipsstr., Auguststr., Linienstr. and the surrounding areas fill with art; while some of these locations lack big glass windows onto the street, it only takes a quick peak at the name tags on the doors and a few steps back into the building to see some of the better galleries in the city. Charlottenburg also has a large selection of galleries, many of which tend to be more upscale—antique shops abound, but galleries like Haas and Fuchs offer more contemporary work as well. Kreuzberg hosts a handful of blissfully alternative spaces, and in recent years, a scene has developed in Prenzlauer Berg off of Danziger Str. Below are two of the larger institutions.

AKADEMIE DER KÜNSTE. This three-hundred-year-old institution has been the core of Berlin's art community for many years, promoting a variety of visual and communication media: film, literature, painting, photography, music architecture, performing arts, and more. The Akademie sponsors a variety of prizes and hosts exhibitions in its Hanseatenweg location. *(Hanseatenweg 10. S-Bahn #3, 5, 7, 9, or 75 to "Schloß Bellvue." ☎ 39 07 60; fax 39 07 61 75; email info@adk.de. Open daily 11am-7pm.)*

NEW BERLINER KUNSTVEREIN. This organization is putting art back into the hands of the public. Besides hosting a gallery space, it sponsors the weekly Treffpunkt NBK, a series of lectures, discussions with artists, performances and other related events. They also loan contemporary works to Berlin residents for a small fee through the **Artothek**, and have collected videos since 1972, amassing a large collection and a group called the **Video-Forum.** *(Chausseestr. 128/129. ☎ 280 70 20; fax 280 70 19; email nbk@nbk.org; www.nbk.org. Gallery open M-F noon-6pm, Sa-Su noon-4pm.)*

🔳 ENTERTAINMENT

Berlin has one of the most vibrant cultural scenes in the world: exhibitions, concerts, plays, and dance performances abound. Despite recent cutbacks, the city still has a generously subsidized art scene, and tickets are usually reasonable, especially with student discounts. Numerous festivals celebrating everything from Chinese film to West African music spice up the regular offerings.

Reservations can be made by calling the box office directly. Always ask about student discounts; most theaters and concert halls offer up to 50% off, but only if you buy at the *Abendkasse* (evening box office), which generally opens one hour before performance. Numerous other ticket outlets charge commissions and do not offer student discounts. There are also ticket counters in all **Karstadt** department stores (☎80 60 29 29; fax 80 60 29 22), and in the **KaDeWe** department store, Tauentzienstr. 21 (☎217 77 54), on Wittenbergpl. All offices charge a 15-18% commission. Remember that while most theaters do accept credit cards, most other ticket outlets don't. Most theaters and operas close from mid-July to late August.

Hektiket (☎230 99 30; fax 23 09 82 30), on Hardenbergstr. next to the gigantic **Zoo-Palast** cineplex. Sells last-minute tickets for half-price. Open M-F 9am-8pm, Sa 10am-8pm, Su 4-8pm.

Berliner Festspiele, Budapester Str. 48-50 (☎25 48 92 50; www.berliner festspiele.de). Tickets for a variety of shows, concerts, and events. Open M-F 10am-6pm, Su 10am-2pm.

Berlin Ticket, Potsdamer Str. 96 (☎23 08 82 30; fax 23 08 82 99). Reservations only by phone.

Theater & Konzertkasse City Center, Kurfürstendamm 16 (☎882 65 63; fax 882 65 67), at the corner of Joachimstaler Str.

Theaterkasse Centrum, Meineckestr. 25 (☎882 76 11; fax 881 33 32). Open M-F 10am-6:30pm, Sa 10am-2pm.

CONCERTS, OPERA, AND DANCE

Berlin reaches its musical zenith during the fabulous **Berliner Festwochen,** lasting almost the entire month of September and drawing the world's best orchestras and soloists. The **Berliner Jazztage** in November also brings in the crowds. For more information and tickets (which sell out months in advance), call or write to Berliner Festspiele (see above). In mid-July, the **Bachtage** offer an intense week of classical music, while every Saturday night in August, the **Sommer Festspiele** turns the Ku'damm into a multi-faceted concert hall with punk, steel-drum, and folk groups competing for attention.

Look for concert listings in the monthly pamphlets *Konzerte und Theater in Berlin und Brandenburg* (free) and *Berlin Programm* (DM2.80), as well as in the biweekly *Zitty* and *Tip.* The programs for many theaters and opera houses are also listed on huge posters in U-Bahn stations. Tickets for the *Philharmonie* and the *Oper* are often impossible to acquire through conventional channels without writing months in advance. Try standing out in front before performances with a small sign saying *Suche Karte* (seeking ticket)—invariably a few people will try to unload tickets at the last moment. Remember that concert halls and operas close for a few weeks during the summer months.

Berliner Philharmonisches Orchester, Matthäikirchstr. 1 (☎25 48 81 32; fax 25 48 81 35; email kartenbuero@philharmonic.sireco.de). Take S-Bahn #1, 2 or 25 or U-Bahn #2 to "Potsdamer Pl." and walk up Potsdamer Str. The big yellow asymmetrical building, designed by Scharoun in 1963, is as acoustically perfect within as it is unconventional without. The *Berliner Philharmoniker,* led for decades by the late Herbert von Karajan and under the baton of Claudio Abbado until late 2001, is one of the world's finest orchestras. It is well-nigh impossible to get a seat; check an hour before concert time or write at least 8 weeks in advance. The *Philharmonie* is closed from the end of June until the start of September. Tickets start at DM14 for standing room, DM26 for seats. Box office open M-F 3:30-6pm, Sa-Su 11am-2pm.

Konzerthaus (Schauspielhaus Gendarmenmarkt), Gendarmenmarkt 2 (☎203 09 21 01). U-Bahn #2 or 6 to "Stadtmitte." The opulent home of Berlin's symphony orchestra. Last-minute tickets are somewhat easier to come by. Box office open M-Sa noon-6pm, Su noon-4pm. The orchestra goes on vacation from mid-July to mid-Aug., but the *Deutsches Kammerorchester* continues to perform chamber music in the *Kleiner Saal.* Order tickets by writing to Deutsches Kammerorchester, Suarezstr. 15, 14057 Berlin; or call ☎325 42 29; or fax 32 60 86 10.

Komische Oper, Unter den Linden 14 (☎20 26 03 60; fax 20 26 02 60; email info@komische-oper-berlin.de; www.komische-oper-berlin.de). U-Bahn #6 to "Französische Str," or S-Bahn #1, 2, 25 to "Unter den Linden." Its reputation was built by the famous post-war director Felsenstein, but in recent years zany artistic director Harry Kupfer has revitalized the opera with clever stagings of the classics. Program ranges from Mozart to Gilbert and Sullivan. Tickets DM15-94. 50% student discounts almost always available 2hr. before performance. Box office open M-Sa 11am-7pm, Su 1pm until 1½hr. before performance.

Tanzfabrik, Möckernstr. 68 (☎786 58 61). U-Bahn #7 to "Yorckstr." Turn left on Yorckstr., then right onto Möckernstr. Modern dance performances and a center for dance workshops. Box office open M-Th 10am-noon and 5-8pm, F 10am-noon. Tickets DM15. Occasional weekend performances start at 8 or 8:30pm.

Deutsche Oper Berlin, Bismarckstr. 35 (☎341 02 49 for info, 343 84 01 for tickets; toll free ☎0 800 248 98 42; fax 345 84 55). U-Bahn #2 to "Deutsche Oper." Berlin's best and youngest opera, featuring newly commissioned works as well as all the German and Italian classics. Student discounts available 1 week or less before performance. Tickets DM15-140. Box office open M-Sa 11am until 1hr. before performance, Su 10am-2pm. Evening tickets available 1hr. before performance. For tickets, write to Deutsche Oper Berlin, Richard-Wagner-Str. 10, 10585 Berlin; or fax 343 84 55. For program information, write to Deutsche Oper Berlin, Bismarckstr. 35, 10627 Berlin. Closed July-Aug.

Deutsche Staatsoper, Unter den Linden 7 (☎20 35 45 55; fax 20 35 44 83; email contact@staatsoper-berlin.de; www.staatsoper-berlin.de). U-Bahn #6 to "Französische Str." eastern Berlin's leading opera company, with sets and costumes on a big, bold scale, led by Daniel Barenboim (also the conductor of the Chicago Symphony Orchestra). Ballet and classical music, too, although the orchestra fluctuates between good and mediocre. Tours daily at 11am. Tickets DM18-35. 50% student discount. Box office open M-F 10am-6pm, Sa-Su 2pm-6pm, and 1hr. before performance. Closed mid-July to mid-Aug.

THEATER

Theater listings are available in the monthly pamphlets *Kultur!news* and *Berlin Programm*, as well as in *Zitty* and *Tip*. They are also posted in most U-Bahn stations. In addition to the best German-language theater in the world, Berlin also has a lively English-language theater scene. Look for listings in *Zitty* or *Tip* that say *in englischer Sprache* (in English) next to them. There are a number of privately run companies called "off-theaters" that feature occasional English-language plays. As with concert halls, look out for summer closings (*Theaterferien* or *Sommerpause*); see the introduction to **Entertainment**, p. 132, for box office information. There is an international **theater festival** in May.

Deutsches Theater, Schumannstr. 13a (☎28 44 12 25). U-Bahn #6 or S-Bahn #1, 2, 3, 5, 7, 9, 25, or 75 to "Friedrichstr." or bus #147 to "Albrechtpl." Walk north on Friedrichstr., turn left on Reinhardtstr., and then right on Albrechtstr., which curves into Schumannstr. The word has spread to western Berlin: this is the best theater in the country. Max Reinhardt made it great 100 years ago, and it now has innovative productions of the classics and newer works. The repertoire runs from Büchner to Mamet to Ibsen. Box office open M-Sa 11am-6:30pm, Su 3-6:30pm. Tickets DM15-25. The **Kammerspiel des Deutschen Theaters** (☎28 44 12 26) has smaller, controversial productions. Tickets DM15-40, but 50% student discounts often available. Box office open M-Sa noon-6pm, Su 3-6pm.

Hebbel-Theater, Stresemannstr. 29 (☎25 90 04 27 or 25 90 04 36; email tickets@hebbel-theater.de). U-Bahn #1, 6, or 15 to "Hallesches Tor." The most avant of the avant-garde theaters in Berlin, drawing cutting-edge talent from all over the world. Order tickets by phone M-Su 4-7pm or show up 1hr. before performance.

Berliner Ensemble, Bertolt-Brecht-Pl. 1 (☎282 31 60 or 28 40 81 55). U-Bahn #6 or S-Bahn #1, 2, 3, 5, 7, 9, 25, or 75 to "Friedrichstr." The famous theater established by Brecht is undergoing a renaissance. Hip repertoire, including Heiner Müller and some young American playwrights, as well as Brecht's own plays. Also some premieres. Tickets DM12-40, 50% student discount available 1hr. before performance. Box office open M-Sa 11am-6pm, Su 3-6pm.

Maxim-Gorki-Theater, Am Festungsgraben 1 (☎20 22 10). U-Bahn #6 or S-Bahn #1, 2, 3, 5, 7, 9, 25, or 75 to "Friedrichstr.", or bus #100, 157, or 348 to "Deutsche Staatsoper." Excellent contemporary theater with wonderfully varied repertoire—everything from Schiller to Albee. Tickets DM5-25. Box office open M-Sa 1-6:30pm, Su 3-6:30pm., and 1hr. before performance.

Die Distel, Friedrichstr. 101 (☎204 47 04; fax 208 15 55). U-Bahn #6 or S-Bahn #1, 2, 3, 5, 7, 9, 25, or 75 to "Friedrichstr." During GDR days, this was a renowned cabaret for political satire—but reunification has taken the bite out of some of the jokes. Box office open M-F noon-6pm and 2hr. before performance.

Vagantenbühne, Kantstr. 12a (☎312 45 29). U-Bahn #2 or 9 or S-Bahn #3, 5, 7, 9, or 75 to "Zoologischer Garten." This off-beat hole-in-the-wall near the Ku'damm—the oldest private theater in Berlin—presents a healthy balance of contemporary German plays as well as such existentialist favorites as Sartre's *No Exit*. Tickets DM16-32, students DM12. Box office open M 10am-4pm, Tu-F 10am-7pm, Sa 2-7pm.

Friends of Italian Opera, Fidicinstr. 40 (☎691 12 11). U-Bahn #6 to "Pl. der Luftbrücke." The name is a joking reference to the mafia in *Some Like It Hot*, and belies its role as Berlin's leading English-language theater. The stage is home to the renowned Berliner Grundtheater company as well as a grab-bag of English-language performances with a penchant for the grotesque, ranging from Tennessee Williams to Katherine Anne Porter. Tickets DM15-20. Box office opens at 6:30pm. Most shows at 8pm.

FILM

Berlin is a movie-loving town; it hosts the international **Berlinale** film festival (Feb. 7-18, 2001), and on any night in Berlin you can choose from 100 different films, many in the original languages. *O.F.* next to a movie listing means original version (i.e., not dubbed); *O.m.U.* means original version with German subtitles. Check *Tip, Zitty,* or the ubiquitous *Kinoprogramm* posters plastered throughout the city. Numerous cineplexes offer the chance to see dubbed Hollywood blockbusters. **UCI Kinowelt Zoo-Palast,** Hardenbergstr. 29a (☎25 41 47 77), near Bahnhof Zoo, is one of the biggest and most popular, with more than a dozen screens. Mondays, Tuesdays, or Wednesdays are *Kinotage* at most movie theaters, with prices reduced a few DM. Bring a student ID for discounts.

Arsenal, in the Filmhaus at Potsdamer P. (☎86 95 51 00). U-Bahn #1, 2, or 15 to "Potsdamer Pl." Run by the *Freunde der deutschen Kinemathek,* the founders of the *Berlinale,* Arsenal showcases independent films as well as the occasional classic. Frequent appearances by guest directors make the theater a popular meeting place for Berlin's filmmakers.

Odeon, Hauptstr. 116 (☎78 70 40 19). U-Bahn #4 to "Rathaus Schöneberg." Odeon's venue is a mixture of mainstream American and British films with a pseudo-leftist slant. Reduced admission Tu and W. All films in English.

Filmkunsthaus Babylon, Rosa-Luxemburg-Str. 30 (☎242 50 76). U-Bahn #2 to "Rosa-Luxemburg-Pl." Shows classics and art films, often in their original languages. DM8, students DM7. Currently under renovation.

Babylon-Kino, Dresdener Str. 126 (☎61 60 96 93). U-Bahn #1, 8, or 15 to "Kottbusser Tor." The other branch of the Babylon plays offbeat comedies in English with German subtitles. Reduced admission Tu and W. Wheelchair accessible.

Freiluftkino: The summer brings a host of outdoor film screenings to Berlin. Two venues show films in English: **Freiluftkino Hasenheide** (☎62 70 58 85), at the Sputnik in Hasenheide park, screens anything from silent films to last year's blockbusters. U-Bahn #7 or 8 to "Hermannpl." **Freiluftkino Orangienpl.,** Mariannenpl. 2 (☎614 24 64), screens avant-garde contemporary films. U-Bahn #1, 8, or 15 to "Kottbusser Tor." DM10 for either theater. Reduced admission M and W.

Blow Up, Immanuelkirchstr. 14 (☎442 86 62). S-Bahn #4, 8, or 85 to "Greifswalder Str." Explosive and entertaining—see *Unzipped* followed by a fashion show, or catch them when they're showing the eternally cool Bogey flicks. The theater always screens something in English. DM9, Tu and W DM7.

◪ SWIMMING

Berlin is very concrete-intensive; during summer, the sidewalks are roasting. Though a fair amount of clothing comes off on the city's dance floors, the place to see the most skin and be cool in every way is in one of Berlin's *Freibäder and Sommerbäder.* Outdoor pools are generally open from May to August. In addition, Berlin is home to dozens of surprisingly clean lakes. In winter, the city's myriad indoor *Schwimmbäder* keep Berliners from frowning too hard by lulling them into a climate-controlled state of relaxation. A dip in a municipal pool costs DM6, students DM4. For more information, call the **Berliner Bäder-Betriebe's** service hotline at ☎(01803) 10 20 20. Other pools are in **Wilmersdorf,** Forckenbeckstr. 114, **Wannsee,** Wannseebadweg 25, and **Mügelsee,** Fürstenwalder Damm 838.

Sommerbad am Insulaner, Munsterdamm 80 (☎79 41 04 13). S-Bahn #2 or 25 to "Priesterweg." Beautiful outdoor pool beneath one of Berlin's towering *Trümmerberge,* hills made out of rubble left behind by WWII. Idyllic, except when someone toting a beer belly and speedo walks by.

Freibad Olympiastadion, Olympischer Pl. (☎30 06 34 40). S-Bahn #5 or 75 to "Olympiastadion" or U-Bahn #2 to "Olympia-Stadion (Ost)." Olympic-sized pool with a diving board the height of the Tower of Babel.

Schwimmhalle Fischerinsel, Fischerinsel 11 (☎201 39 85). U-Bahn #2 to "Spittelmarkt." Just a few blocks from Mitte's historic sights, the indoor pool complex features a sauna and bistro. Open M 6:30am-4pm, Tu and F 6:30am-10pm, W 9am-10pm, Th 6:30am-4pm, Su 10am-7pm. Wheelchair accessible.

🛍 SHOPPING

When Berlin was a lonely outpost in the Eastern Bloc consumer wilderness, Berliners had no choice but to buy native. Thanks to the captive market, the city accrued a mind-boggling array of things for sale: if a price tag can be put on it, you can buy it in Berlin. The high temple of the consumerist religion is the seven-story **KaDeWe department store** on Wittenbergpl. at Tauentzienstr. 21-24, the largest department store in mainland Europe. The name is a German abbreviation of "Department Store of the West" *(Kaufhaus des Westens);* for the tens of thousands of product-starved East Germans who flooded Berlin in the days following the opening of the Wall, KaDeWe *was* the West to individuals standing on the threshold of consumerism. The saccharine and pervasive materialism on display alternatively proves awe-inspiring and sickening. (☎212 10. Open M-F 9:30am-8pm, Sa 9am-4pm.) The food department, on the sixth floor, has to be seen to be believed (see **Food**, p. 110).

Two shopping districts have received a major face-lift in recent years. The **Kurfürstendamm**, near Bahnhof Zoo, has almost every kind of shop imaginable as well as a half-dozen monolithic department stores. The **Ku'damm Eck**, at the corner of Joachimstaler Str., and **Ku'damm Block**, near Uhlandstr., are the most notable areas. **Bleibtreustr.** has stores closer to the budget traveler's reach. **Friedrichstr.** is the commercial hub of Eastern Berlin. In particular, the **Friedrichstadtpassagen** are proof of just how much the area has changed in the past decade; flashy restaurants and clothing shops now stand where soldiers once guarded the entrance to the Soviet sector of the city. In addition, the new **Daimler-Benz** complex on **Potsdamer Pl.** has more than 100 new shops and many restaurants, cafes, and pubs.

Theodore Sturgeon astutely observed that "90% of everything is crap," and the **flea markets** that regularly occupy Berlin are no exception. Nevertheless, you can occasionally find the fantastic bargain that makes all the sorting and sifting worthwhile. The market on **Str. des 17. Juni** probably has the best selection of stuff, but the prices are higher than those at a lot of other markets. (U-Bahn #2 to "Ernst-Reuter-Pl." Sa-Su 10am-5pm.) **Winterfeldtpl.**, near Nollendorfpl., overflows with food, flowers, and people crooning Dylan tunes over their acoustic guitars (W and Sa mornings). The market on **Oranienburger Str.** by Tacheles offers works by starving artists and a variety of nonsensical Dada delights (Sa-Su 8am-3pm). Closer to Hackescher Markt, Oranienburger Str. is also home to a number of trendy shoe and clothing stores. The **Hallentrödelmarkt**, Nostitzstr. 6-7 in Kreuzberg, aims to help the homeless of Berlin. (U-Bahn #6 or 7 to "Mehringdamm." Tu 5-7pm, Th 11am-1pm, Sa 11am-3pm.) Other markets are located near **Ostbahnhof** in Friedrichshain (S-Bahn #3, 5, 7, 9, or 75 to "Ostbahnhof"; Sa 9am-3pm, Su 10am-5pm), and on **John-F.-Kennedy-Pl.** in Schöneberg. (U-Bahn #4 to "Rathaus Schöneberg." Sa-Su 8am-4pm.) There is a typical German *Fußgängerzone* (pedestrian zone) on **Wilmersdorfer Str.**, where bakeries, *Döner* joints, trendy clothing shops, and department stores abound (U-Bahn #7 to "Wilmersdorfer Str." or S-Bahn #3, 5, 7, 9, or 75 to "Charlottenburg"). For the latest in club gear, check out the trendy **Hennes & Mauritz** clothing chain (H&M for short), scattered throughout the city; convenient locations are **Kurfürstendamm 20**, near Bahnhof Zoo; **Friedrichstr. 79**, near Unter den Linden; and **Schönhauser Allee 78** in Prenzlauer Berg. If you're looking for that special something to wear to the **Love Parade** (see p. 138), **Waahnsinn Berlin** (☎282 08 29), at the corner of Hackescher Markt and Neue Promenade, should take care of your every pink furry desire.

Zweite Hand ("second-hand"; DM3.80), an aptly named newspaper appearing at newsstands on Tuesdays, Thursdays, and Saturdays, consists of ads for anything anyone wants to resell, from apartment shares and plane tickets to silk dresses and cats; it also has good deals on **bikes. Bergmannstr.**, in Kreuzberg, is a used clothes and cheap antique shop strip. Take U-Bahn #7 to "Gneisenaustr." **Made in Berlin**, Potsdamer Str. 106, generally has funky second-hand stuff, all quite cheap. Get your leather jacket here. (U-Bahn #1 or 15 to "Kurfürstenstr.") A larger selection of used clothes, albeit with less consistent quality, awaits at **Checkpoint**, Mehringdamm 59 (U-Bahn #6 or 7 to "Mehringdamm").

Berlin's enormous electronics store **Saturn**, Alexanderpl. 8, located right outside the train station has a respectable CD store in its basement level. Most CDs are DM25-30. (☎24 75 16. Open M-F 9am-8pm, Sa 9am-4pm. U-Bahn #2, 5, or 8 or S-Bahn #3, 5, 7, 9, or 75 to "Alexanderpl.") If you're looking for used CDs or LPs, snoop around the streets near the "Schlesisches Tor" U-Bahn stop (lines #1 and 15). A variety of used CDs and records are bought and sold at **Cover**, Turmstr. 52, but they're particularly into pop and top-40s music. (U-Bahn #9 to "Turmstr." ☎395 87 62. Open M-F 10am-8pm, Sa 10am-4pm.) To complete (or start) your trance, techno, house, and acid collection, head to **Flashpoint**, Bornholmer Str. 88. (☎44 65 09 59. S-Bahn #1, 2, 4, 8, 25 or 85 to "Bornholmer Str.")

◪ NIGHTLIFE

Berlin's nightlife is absolute madness, a teeming cauldron of debauchery that runs around the clock and threatens to inflict coronaries upon the faint of heart. Bars typically open around 6pm, and pack in around 10pm, just as the clubs are opening their doors. As the bar scenes wind down around 1am, the pace picks up and the smoke machines kick in at the clubs, which groove till dawn, when a variety of after parties and 24-hour cafes are waiting to keep up this seemingly perpetual motion. It's completely possible (if you can live without sleep) to party non-stop Friday night through Monday morning. From 1am to 4am, take advantage of the **night buses** and **U-Bahn #9** and **12**, which run all night on Fridays and Saturdays; normal transit service resumes after 4:30am. The best sources of information about bands and dance venues are the bi-weekly magazines *Tip* and the superior *Zitty* (both DM4), available at all newsstands, or the free *030*, distributed in several hostels, cafes and bars.

Western Berlin has a rather varied combination of scenes. **Savignypl.**, near Zoologischer Garten, offers refined, laid-back cafes in one of Berlin's oldest (and richest) neighborhoods. The Ku'damm is best avoided at night, unless you enjoy fraternizing with drunken businessmen, middle-aged tourists, and dirty old men who drool at the sight of strip shows. Gay life in Berlin centers around **Nollendorf Pl.**, where the crowds are usually mixed and establishments range from the friendly to the cruisey. **Gneisenaustr.**, on the western edge of Kreuzberg, offers a variety of ethnic restaurants and some good bars. The eastern Kreuzberg scene pushes up against the remains of the Wall, and anything else the Establishment dares put in its way. In the midst of a strong Turkish community lies a dizzying array of radically alternative clubs and bars centering around Oranienstr., and radiating outward several blocks, with more gay and lesbian establishments up around Muskauerstr. On the opposite bank of the Spree in **Friedrichshain**, several clubs have jumped off the capitalist bandwagon and headed East; check out the latest venues along Simon-Dach-Str. and Gabriel-Max-Str. (S-Bahn #3, 5, 6, 7, 9, or 75 or U-Bahn #1, 12, or 15 to "Warschauer Str.").

Berlin's best clubs are also located in eastern Berlin. While Kreuzberg tries to defend west Berlin's reputation as the dance capital of the world, competition is coming from all sides and there is no longer a clear winner. A few of the best clubs in the city are scattered around Mitte and Potsdamer Pl., but the eastern street-life centers around Orangienburgerstr. in Mitte (not to be confused with Kreuzberg's Oranienstr.) Trendy bars abound, and prices are relatively high. Further afield, Prenzlauer Berg, a neighborhood which once provided a fresh alternative to the more established scenes of Kreuzberg and Mitte, has now settled into its role as home for classy bars and cafes, centered around Kollwitzpl. Prices are on the rise, but the streets on the fringes, particularly the area around Danzigerstr., still hold onto a bit of the alternative spirit. Way out in Friedrichshain, a revolution is brewing in the punky, gothy tough-as-nails nightlife.

If at all possible, try to hit (or, if you're prone to bouts of claustrophobia, avoid) Berlin during the **Love Parade**, usually held in the second weekend of July (see **The Love Parade**, p. 138), when all of Berlin just says "yes" to everything. Rumors that the parade would move from Berlin to another city seem to have died down after 2000 hosted another successful romp through the Tiergarten. Now, the plan has changed to make Love a worldwide phenomenon. Vienna, Austria and Leeds, England each hosted a parade this year, so the spreading of the Love has already begun; it remains to be see how far this will go. It's also worth mentioning that Berlin has **de-criminalized marijuana possession** of up to eight grams. Smoking in public, however, has not been officially accepted, though it's becoming more common in some clubs. *Let's Go* does not recommend puffing clouds of hash smoke into the face of police officers.

BARS AND CLUBS

This is the section of *Let's Go: Germany* where we dance.

SAVIGNYPLATZ

Quasimodo, Kantstr. 12a (☎312 80 86; www.quasimodo.de). U-Bahn #2 or 12 or S-Bahn #3, 5, 7, 9, or 75 to "Zoologischer Garten." The wide variety of artists who come to play at this basement jazz venue attract a lively crowd; Tuesdays and Wednesdays are always a mere DM5, so students fill the club in the middle of the week. On weekends, cover depends on performance, ranging from free to DM40. Concert tickets available from 5pm or at Kant-Kasse ticket service (☎313 45 54; fax 312 64 40). No student discounts. Club open every Tu, W, F, Sa from 9pm; other days occasionally.

A-Trane, Bleibtreustr. 1 (☎313 25 50; fax 313 46 29; email a-trane@a-trane.de; www.a-trane.de). S-Bahn #3, 5, 7, 9, or 75 to "Savignypl." With a name partially inspired by John Coltrane, this club makes an effort to bring quality performers to its cozy setting. The small stage makes the vocal jazz groups and small combos that perform here very accessible to the audience. Hidden in a quiet corner of Charlottenburg, the venue is calmer and more staid than many, but the programmers work hard to bring performers from all segments of the jazz scene to their club. Cover DM10-20 (usually about DM15 on weekends); student discount usually DM5 with ID. Club open every day at 10pm; closes at 2am weekdays, later on weekends.

SCHÖNEBERG

Metropol, Nollendorfpl. 5 (☎217 36 80). U-Bahn #1, 2, 4, or 15 to "Nollendorfpl.," or night buses #N5, N19, N26, N48, N52, or N75. 650,000 watts of light! 35,800 watts of sound! Berlin's largest disco is decked out in extravagant ancient Egyptian motifs. Lately, the Metropol has taken to hosting the events of the former *Kit Kat Club*, taking on the combined name of **Kit Kat @ Metropol.** Lascivious? The word loses its meaning here. Erotic? This implies innuendo, a quality which has no place on this dance floor. Sex. SEXSEXSEX. People with varying degrees of clothing, some copulating, some just digging the cool trance music in the jaw-dropping fluorescent interior, leave their inhibitions outside. Go latex! Sexual-fantasy-outfit required on Fridays and Saturdays, and the

THE LOVE PARADE Every year during the second weekend in July, the Love Parade brings Berlin to its knees—its trains run late, its streets fill with litter, and its otherwise patriotic populace scrambles to the countryside in the wake of a wave of west German teenagers dying their hair, dropping ecstasy, and getting down *en masse.* What started in 1988 as a DJ's birthday party with only 150 people has mutated into an annual techno Woodstock, the world's only 1.5 million-man rave, and a massive corporate event dubbed *Die Größte Partei der Welt,* "the greatest party in the world." A huge "parade" takes place on Saturday afternoon, involving a snail-paced procession of tractor-trailers loaded with blasting speakers and topped by gyrating bodies that slowly works it from Ernst-Reuter-Pl. to the Brandenburg Gate. The city-wide party turns the Str. des 17. Juni into a riotous dance floor, and the Tiergarten into a garden of original—and sometimes quite creative—sin. To celebrate the licentious atmosphere, the BVG offers a "No-Limit-Ticket," useful for getting around from venue to venue during the weekend's **54 hours of nonstop partying** (DM10, condom included). Unless you have a fetish for tall people's hairy and sweaty armpits, the best way to see and enjoy the parade is to be up high (literally, of course)—the porta-potties are supreme watch towers. Club prices skyrocket for the event as the best DJs from Europe are imported for a frantic weekend of beat-thumping madness. It's an experience that you won't forget, unless you consume something that leaves you in a cloud of oblivion.

infamous **"Fuck Naked Sex Party,"** is now staged here Th and Su. The Metropol still manages to host concerts in between, though. Concert ticket prices vary; call ☎215 54 63 for information and prices. Open M-F 11am-3pm and 3:30-6pm. Cover F-Sa DM15.

■ **Slumberland,** Winterfeldtpl. U-Bahn #1, 2, 4, 12, or 15 to "Nollendorfpl." This cafe/bar must be seen to be believed. It boasts African motifs, complete with artwork, palm trees, and the crowning glory: sand for a floor! Head on in and listen to contemporary R&B as well as Bob Marley. The bar serves a wide variety of drinks including your favorite *Berliner Weisse* for DM5. It's less lively on weekdays than on weekends, but nevertheless the place is always a cheerful one. Open Su-F 5pm-4am, Sa 11am-4am.

Café Bilderbuch, Akazienstr. 28 (☎78 70 60 57). U-Bahn #7 to "Eisenacher Str." This sophisticated jazzy cafe teleports its clientele into a world of flappers and speakeasies. Chill on the plush sofas with the over-30 crowd while sipping a fruity *Berliner Weiße mit Schuß* (DM4.50), or tango the night away at one of the cafe's bi-weekly *Tanztees*. The tasty brunch baskets, served around the clock, culminate in the sumptuous Sunday buffet (DM15). Open M-Sa 9am-2am, Su 10am-2am.

Mister Hu, Goltzstr. 39 (☎217 21 11). U-Bahn #1, 2, 4 or 15 to "Nollendorfpl." This bar's mysterious name rhymes with the "Wozu?" written in red neon lights which provides the only light for the inner room. The silhouette of a slouching Mister Hu appears on the napkins as well on the men's bathroom door. The green bead lights and the rocky bar add to the mystique. Happy hour is 5-8pm, but if you come on Sunday all cocktails are just DM9.99, including ones with titles like "Bob get lost" (Maracuja, pineapple, Limette, and grenadine). Open daily from 5pm.

KREUZBERG

For a map of Kreuzberg's bars and clubs, see p. 105.

■ **SO36,** Oranienstr. 190 (☎61 40 13 06; www.SO36.de). U-Bahn #1, 12, or 15 to "Görlitzer Bahnhof" or night bus #N29 to "Heinrichpl." Berlin's only *truly* mixed club, with a clientele of hip heteros, gays, and lesbians grooving to a mish-mash of wild genres. Loud music, huge dance floor, and friendly people—just don't assume that what you see is what you get. Mondays are "electric ballroom," a trance party featuring Berlin's up-and-coming DJs and TV screens filled with anime. Th hip-hop, reggae, punk, or ska. Weekends run the gamut from techno to live concerts. For other nights, see **Gay and Lesbian Berlin,** p. 144. Open after 11pm. Cover varies.

Wild at Heart, Wiener Str. 20 (☎611 60 10; email info@wildatheartberlin.de; www.wildatheartberlin.de). This place is punk as f**k. Climb the stairs into this little cave of colored lights and red walls peppered with old show posters. Snarling guitars every night; if there's no live band, then a DJ or the jukebox will send your sinful soul straight to hell. It's all about the leather jackets and the tattoos, baby. Open daily from 10pm.

Café Morena, Wiener Str. 60 (☎611 47 16). U-Bahn #1, 8, 12, or 15 to "Görlitzer Bahnhof." The crowd may be a little on the loud side, but that's what happens when you have happy "hour" every day from 7-8pm and midnight-2am. A mix of trip-hop and trance flows over the stereo as freely as a rainbow of beverages. Try a *kokosshake* (DM6). Long drinks DM7, cocktails DM10. "American-style" bagel and burger platters DM14-15. Open M-Th and Su 9am-4am, F-Sa 9am-5am.

Ex, Mehringhof, Gneisenaustr. 2a (☎693 58 00). U-Bahn #6 or 7 to "Mehringdamm" or night bus #N4, N19, or N76. A bar, performance space, and club run by a leftist collective in a steel and concrete courtyard. Also a site for political meetings and (primarily) lesbian events, as well as an anarchist bookstore. They cook up an Indian storm bound to cause an intestinal revolution. Open Tu-F 3pm-late, Sa-Su until late.

Junction Bar, Gneisenaustr. 18 (☎772 76 77). U-Bahn #7 to "Gneisenaustr." or night bus #N4 or N19 to "Zossener Str." Funk, soul, jazz, and hip-hop on the weekends accompany American-style breakfast served until 2:30am. Shows at 7:30, 8:30, and 9:30pm weeknights, and DJ parties after 1am. Open daily after 6pm.

Sage Club, Brückenstr. 1. U-Bahn #8 to "Heinrich-Heine-Str." or night bus #N8. This club, practically on top of the train station, is a favorite of the cruising teen population and 20-somethings who wish they were that young. Th-Su from 11pm. Cover DM10-25.

Hannibal, corner of Wienerstr. and Skalitzerstr. U-Bahn #1, 12 or 15, or night bus N29 to "Görlitzer Bahnhof." Mornings (and afternoons until 3pm) are for breakfast and street-side tables. Evenings bring the action inside, where patrons share intense conversations under the shimmer of the disco ball. Open Su-Th 8am-4am, F-Sa 8am-5am.

The Pink Panther, corner of Waldemarstr. and Lausitzerpl. U-Bahn #1, 12, or 15 to "Schlesisches Tor." A little corner of Lausitzerpl. that is one of the coolest (in the Kreuzberg sense of the word) bars in the neighborhood. The music pumps while street-smart leather-wearing hipsters smoke cigarettes as they knock back bottles of beer. And yes, the interior is of course in pink. Open M-Th 3pm-2am, F-Sa 3pm-late.

Bateau Dove, Oranienstr. 10 (☎61 40 36 59). This friendly bistro-bar is a popular meeting place for locals to sit back and relax over coffee or beer before shakin' that thing across the street at SO36, making late night tables a sought-after commodity. Jazz music wafts through the room lit by paper lanterns.

Mas Y Mas, Oranienstr. 167. Wooden tables, an aging flowered couch, crystal chandeliers, and walls of scarlet and brick give this bar an old Victorian-house kind of coolness. Dimly lit, very chill; the perfect local to sip a cocktail over some deep conversation. All cocktails are 2 for 1 Wednesdays after 8pm. Open daily 4pm to late.

ORANIENBURGER STRASSE-MITTE

Tresor/Globus, Leipziger Str. 126a (☎229 06 11 or 612 33 64). U-Bahn #2 or S-Bahn #1, 2, or 25 or night bus #N5, N29 or N52 to "Potsdamer Pl." One of the most rocking techno venues in Berlin, packed from wall to wall with enthusiastic ravers. Upstairs the ceilings are higher, the music is slower; downstairs the more cramped space flickers and throbs in the strobe lights, and hard-working ravers sweat to hard-core techno. Tresor provides a good mid-week option, as it opens Wednesday when many other clubs stay closed. Open W and F-Sa 11pm-6am. Cover W DM5, F DM10, Sa DM15-20.

Tacheles, Oranienburger Str. 53-56 (☎282 61 85). U-Bahn #6 to "Oranienburger Tor" or S-Bahn #1, 2, or 25 to "Oranienburger Str." or night bus #N6 or N84. A playground for artists, punks, and curious tourists staying in the nearby hostels. Housed in a bombed-out department store and the adjacent courtyard, the primary decorative motif is hardcore graffiti and artwork made of scrap metal. Tacheles plays host to several art galleries, a *Biergarten*, **Cafe Zapata,** and vicious raves. The owners have staved off ambitious plans to convert the area into office buildings for several years. Open M-Su 24hr.

VEB-OZ, Auguststr. at the corner of Oranienburgerstr. S-Bahn #1, 2, or 25 to "Oranienburger Str." The name stands for *Verkehrs Behruhigte Ost Zone,* and the map of East Germany on the ceiling paired with Karl Marx on the wall and Bob Dylan over the speakers leave you with no doubt that this place has attitude. They neither post their hours nor have a menu, but when every other bar on Oranienburgerstr. has closed by 1am on a weekday, this place is still growling.

Café Silberstein, Oranienburger Str. 27 (☎281 28 01). S-Bahn #1, 2, or 25 to "Oranienburger Str." Three words say it all: sushi until midnight (and sometimes later). Plus, there are those funky red chairs, and a lively student crowd. Open daily after 10am; sushi served M-Th 4pm-midnight, F 4pm-2am, Sa noon-2am, Su noon-midnight.

WMF, Ziegelstr. 22. S-Bahn #1, 2, or 25 to "Oranienburger Str." or U-Bahn #6 to "Oranienburger Tor." It's like what would happen if you had a house-party and it went terribly wrong. Or maybe terribly right. The entrance leads into a courtyard complete with trailer toilets; inside several rooms with casual, unkempt couches and jumping beats. Drum 'n bass, house, and techno, depending on the night. Sundays feature GMF, a gay tea dance. Open W-Su after 11pm. Cover DM15-25.

B-Flat, Rosenthalerstr. 13. (☎283 31 23). U-Bahn #8 to "Rosenthalerpl." Acoustic music and jazz in a super relaxed atmosphere right near the happening strip of bars on Oranienburgerstr. Open daily from 8pm; happy hour 9-10pm, blue hour 1-2am. Cover varies from free to DM15; frequent student discounts of DM3-5. All cocktails DM9.

Hackesche Höfe, Rosenthaler Str. 40-41. S-Bahn #3, 5, 7, 9, or 75 to "Hackescher Markt." One of the few successful attempts at revitalizing northern Mitte, the Hackescher Höfe is a series of interconnected courtyards containing restaurants, cafes, clubs, galleries, shops, apartments, and a movie theater. The lively sound of *klezmer* bands vie with

BLUE HOUR. Just how nutty is Berlin's nightlife? *Let's Go* recommends that travelers find out for themselves, but one manifestation of the insanity is the discount drink policies pushed by many of the city's bars. Happy hour is just not enough—after all, one or two hours of drinking in the early evening is child's play. Recently, some establishments have decided to add another rush of alcohol to fuel more late night partying. While the early drinks hold onto the title "Happy Hour," the effects of the alcohol as the evening wears on make this a misnomer for the second round. So what to call it? "Blue Hour," of course. Glasses clink around midnight...

street performers, while the low-key **Oxymoron** club (☎28 39 18 85) offers daily jazz concerts to a 30-something crowd. Open M and W-Sa after 11pm, Tu after 8:30pm, Su after 10pm. Concerts DM15-20. The **Chamaeleon Variety Show** plays at one of the theatres here all week; call the box office (☎238 57 69) for ticket info.

Mitte, Oranienburgerstr. 46. U-Bahn #6 to "Oranienburger Tor." Painted in primary colors, Mitte gives a respite from the hip trend of painting bar interiors orange. A young crowd drinks cocktails (DM9-14) at hearty wooden tables while listening to anything from techno to the *Pulp Fiction* soundtrack. A small dance floor provides room for a casual disco Fridays and Saturdays from 11pm (DM3).

Sophienclub, Sophienstr. 6 (☎282 45 52). S-Bahn #3, 5, 7, 9, 75 to "Hackescher Markt." A cute little club notable because it focuses on its favorite genre, "Britpop." Soul, funk, and house also show up on Sophienclub's schedules. Open Tu, Th-Sa from 10pm. Cover DM10.

Roter Salon, Rosa-Luxemburg-Pl. (☎30 87 48 02). U-Bahn #2 to "Rosa-Luxemburg-Pl." The club is notable because it doesn't play any electronica...well, almost none. M drum 'n bass, Tu salsa, W tango, F-Sa vary, Su happy 60s tunes. Cover DM7-12.

Kalkscheune, Johannisstr. 2 (☎28 39 00 65). S-Bahn #1, 2, or 25 to "Oranienburger Str." or U-Bahn #6 to "Oranienburger Tor." Across from WMF, the two clubs occasionally host parties together. Kalkscheune plays anything from hip-hop to latin to house and techno, as well as hosting the occasional jazz group; call ahead to see what's on. Cover DM5-20, student discount of DM5 for performances. Usually open Sa-Tu.

Tränenpalast, Reichstagsufer 17 (☎2061 00 11; www.traenenpalast.de). U-Bahn #6 or S-Bahn to "Friedrichstr." Formerly the post at which east Berliners and visiting west Berliners were separated at the end of the allotted visiting period, the "Palace of Tears" now hosts everything from club nights to jazz festivals. Open nearly every day from 8pm, cover varies. For concerts, advance ticket purchase may be necessary, and can be done at any ticket vendor. Call ahead or check the web for details.

Salon Lambada, Chauseestr. 42a (☎22 35 75 75). S-Bahn #1, 2, or 25 to "Nordbahnhof." This self-styled *multi-funktionales Kulturhaus* located on the fifth floor (above ground) of a warehouse on the edge of Mitte offers a variety of shows, with a distinctly underground edge. Standards? Of course not. But if experimental is your thing, this is the place—just check club listings before trekking out.

Las Cucarachas, Oranienburgerstr. 38 (☎282 20 44). U-Bahn #6 to "Oranienburger Tor." A little pricey for dinner, budget travelers can still bask in the Mexican friendliness of this place while drinking an after-dinner Margarita (DM9-12). Open later than most bars on the strip, Las Cucarachas is lively, popular, and brightly lit. Nachos DM7. Open daily from noon.

Zosch, Tucholskystr. 30 (☎280 76 64). U-Bahn #6 to "Oranienburger Tor." A laid-back bar slightly removed from Oranienburgerstr.'s obvious scene, Zosch further removes itself from Berlin's nightlife trends by playing little techno. Open M-Sa from noon, Su from 10am.

PRENZLAUER BERG

KulturBrauerei, Knaackstr. 97 (☎44 05 67 56). U-Bahn #2 to "Eberswalder Str." Enormous party space located in a former East German brewery. This small village of *Kultur* houses numerous stages and dance floors, a pleasant cafe, a gallery, and a music theater. Because the venues include everything from hard-core *Ostrock* and disco to techno, reggae, and *Schlager,* it's best to call ahead. Well-known as a concert venue. Open Tu and Th-Su after 10pm. Cover DM3-5, more for special events.

Pfefferberg Club, Schönhauser Allee 176 (☎44 38 31 16). U-Bahn #2 to "Senefelderpl." or night bus #N58. A little bit of techno, but the main offering here is reggae and world music. Very chill garden in the summer, perfect to get back to the roots. Open Th-Sa after 11pm. Cover varies.

Cafe and Bar Houdini, Lychener Str. 35 (☎441 2560). U-Bahn #2 to "Eberswalder Str." A small bar a few streets away from of the slickness of Kollwitzpl., Houdini offers friendly ambiance with tasteful magic theme. A substantial drink menu is sure to play some tricks of its own—try a Merlin (DM9).

Icon, Cantianstr. 15 (☎44 33 27 62). U-Bahn #2 to "Eberswalder Str." Great space with psychedelic lights. Famed for its Friday reggae/hip-hop and Sa drum 'n bass parties. Open from 11pm, but things really get going around 1-2am. Cover DM10.

Duncker, Dunckerstr. 64 (☎445 95 09). U-Bahn #2 to "Eberswalder Str." A small, colorful club keeping up the spirit of Prenzlauer Berg. Music ranges from underground bands to techno DJs. Garden with grill in back. Cover DM5-10; Th usually free.

Knaack, Greifwalderstr. 224 (☎442 7061; fax 442 6140; email info@knaack-berlin.de; www.knaack-berlin.de). This club does billiards and beer, but that's not why it's important. The Knaack is one of the few clubs for indie rock in Berlin. Lots of touring bands, many of which are foreign. Tickets available on the billiard floor; cover varies. Check schedule for details.

FRIEDRICHSHAIN

Maria am Ostbahnhof, Str. der Pariser Kommune 8-10 (☎29 00 61 98). S-Bahn #3, 5, 7, 9, or 75 to "Ostbahnhof" Extremely popular. Concert nights bring clove smoke and hipsters that vary with the band. Disco nights crank up the bass and turn up the heat. Concerts W and Th, Disco F and Sa. Cover DM5-20. Open W-Sa 10pm-late.

Dackammer Bar (DK), Simon-Dach Str. 39. Bright, friendly, and super-popular with the Friedrichshain crowd, DK serves light entrees (from DM7.50), and plenty of drinks to go around. The music ranges from ska to rock; if you're lucky, someone brought an acoustic guitar to serenade the outdoor diners. Open Su-Th noon-11pm, F-Sa noon-midnight.

Paule's Metal Eck, Krossener Str. 15 (☎291 1624), corner of Simon-Dach Str. For all metal-heads out there, this is the real deal, not some tired old beer bar with *Metallica* in the jukebox, but a real metal bar. Solid German dishes like *Schnitzel & Brot* (DM7.50). Don't even think about cocktails, it's all about beer. Open noon until late.

Intimes, Boxhagener Str. 107 (☎29 66 64 57). U-Bahn #5 to "Frankfurter Tor." Greek joint that's also an evening spot. Meals run DM11-20, except on Wednesdays, when all dishes are only DM7. Open daily from 10am. Kitchen open M-Th and Su 10am-midnight, F-Sa 10am-1am.

Euphoria, Grünbergerstr. 60 (☎29 00 46 83), on the corner of Simon-Dach Str., This bright orange hot-spot serves what are perhaps the best mixed drinks in Berlin—5 pages worth! Revolutionaries can go for a Cuba Libre (DM10), and those craving a little action can sip Just Sex (DM12). Happy hour 4-6pm—all drinks half price. Light entrees and Sunday brunch also served. Open Su-Th 10am-midnight, F-Sa 10am-1am.

Zehn Vorne, Simon-Dach Str. 9. Zip up those leather pants, and pull up a seat inside Zehn Vorne, a tiny little corner of darkness in the middle of Simon-Dach Str.'s edgy bar scene. Admire the spray-painted planets on the walls or the flashing lights coming out from under the bar while sipping down a Caipirnha (DM8). Open daily from 3pm.

TREPTOW

⚄ Insel der Jugend, Alt-Treptow 6 (☎53 60 80 20). S-Bahn #4, 6, 8, or 9 to "Treptower Park," then bus #166, 167, or 265 or night bus #N65 to "Alt-Treptow." The name Insel der Jugend (island of youth) gives you that Pinocchio sort of feeling, and the guilty pleasures you find here will definitely lead to donkey ears. Located in the Spree River, Insel's 3 fiercely decorated floors of dancing have the feel of a fishbowl with fluorescent silver foil and netting all over the place; you'll have the memory of a goldfish if you linger too long on the side. Top 2 floors spin reggae, hip-hop, ska, and house (sometimes all at once), while the frantic techno scene in the basement claims the casualties of the upper floors. An outdoor patio overlooking the trees and river serves as a peaceful retreat for smokers. Open W after 7pm, Th after 9pm, F-Sa after 10pm. Cover Th-Sa DM5-15.

GAY AND LESBIAN BERLIN

Berlin is one of the most gay-friendly cities on the continent. During the Cold War, thousands of homosexuals flocked to Berlin to take part in its left-wing activist scene as well as to avoid West Germany's *Wehrpflicht* (mandatory military service). Even before the war, Berlin was known as a gay metropolis, particularly in the tumultuous 1920s. Traditionally, the social nexus of gay and lesbian life has centered around **Nollendorfpl.** and the surrounding **"Schwuler Kiez"** (gay neighborhood) of Schöneberg. Nollendorfpl. also offers the most gay-friendly accommodations (see p. 108). Christopher Isherwood lived at Nollendorfstr. 17 while writing his collection of stories *Goodbye to Berlin*, later adapted as the musical *Cabaret*. The city's reputation for tolerance was marred by the Nazi persecutions of the 1930s and 40s, when thousands of gay and lesbian Berliners were deported to concentration camps. A marble pink triangle plaque outside the Nollendorfpl. U-Bahn station honors their memory. With the fall of the Wall, Berlin's *Szene* was once again revitalized by the emergence of east Berlin's heretofore heavily oppressed homosexual community, and many of the new clubs that have opened up in the past few years are situated in the eastern half of the city. All of Nollendorfpl. is a gay-friendly environment, but the main streets, including Goltzstr., Akazienstr., and Winterfeldtstr., tend to contain mixed bars and cafes. Heading west down Motzstr. leads to the neighborhood's more traditionally solely gay areas.

The boisterous history of homosexuality comes out at the **Schwules Museum,** Mehringdamm 61. Take U-Bahn #6 or 7 to "Mehringdamm." (☎ 693 11 72. Open W and F-Su 2-6pm, Th 2-9pm. DM7, students DM4.) **Spinnboden-Lesbenarchiv,** Anklamer Str. 38, tends toward culturally hip lesbian offerings, with exhibits, films, and all kinds of information about current lesbian life. Take U-Bahn #8 to "Bernauer Str." (☎ 448 58 48. Open W and F 2-7pm.) **Lesbenberatung,** Kulmer Str. 20a, offers a library, movie screenings, and counseling on lesbian issues. Take U-Bahn #7 to "Kleistpark." (☎ 215 20 00. Open M-Tu, and Th 4-7pm, F 2-5pm.) The gay information center **Mann-o-Meter,** Motzstr. 5, off Nollendorfpl., gives out information on nightlife, political activism, and gay or gay-friendly living arrangements. (☎ 216 80 08. DM30-75 a night.) They also offer informal monthly tours for those new to the Berlin scene on the third Friday of every month at 9pm. Take U-Bahn #1, 2, 4, or 15 to "Nollendorfpl." (open M-F 5-10pm, Sa-Su 4-10pm).

For up-to-date events listings, pick up a copy of the amazingly comprehensive *Siegessäule* (free); less in-depth, but also useful, is *Sergej*, a free publication for men. **Prinz Eisenherz Buchladen,** Bleibtreustr. 52, stocks gay-themed books, many in English. They also sell the travel guide *Berlin von Hinten* (Berlin from Behind), which costs a hefty DM19.80 but has extensive information on gay life in English and German. (☎ 313 99 36. Bookstore open M-F 10am-7pm, Sa 10am-4pm.) **Lilith Frauenbuchladen,** Knesebeckstr. 86, is a women's bookstore with a focus on lesbian issues. (☎ 312 31 02. Open M-F 10am-6:30pm, Sa 10am-4pm.) **Marga Schoeller Bücherstube,** Knesebeckstr. 33 (☎ 881 11 22), offers women's issues books in English. All three bookstores can be reached by taking S-Bahn #3, 5, 7, 9, or 75 to "Savignypl." *Blattgold* (DM5 from women's bookstores and some natural food stores) has information and listings for women on a monthly basis. Most *Frauencafes* listed are not exclusively lesbian, but do offer an all-female setting.

The second half of June is the high point of the annual queer calendar of events, culminating in the ecstatic, champagne-soaked floats of the **Christopher Street Day (CSD)** parade, a six-hour long street party drawing more than 250,000 revelers. The weekend before CSD sees a smaller but no less jubilant **Lesbisch-schwules Stadtfest** (street fair) at Nollendorfpl. Exact dates had not been set for either event by press time; contact Mann-o-Meter for up-to-date information.

SCHÖNEBERG

Omnes, Motzstr. 8 (☎ 23 63 83 00). U-Bahn #1, 2, 4, or 15 to "Nollendorfpl." A mainly male gay bar, Omnes planned hours to accommodate revelers after a full night of partying and to provide a week-long breakfast venue. Dim black and red lighting behind the bar provides a chatty atmosphere. Weekly specials DM6-20, pasta DM7-10. Open M-F from 8am, Sa and Su from 5am.

Scheune, Motzstr. 25 (☎ 213 85 80). U-Bahn #1, 2, 4, or 15 to "Nollendorfpl." With fully covered windows and strong soundproofing, Scheune increases the mystique by requiring that you ring the bell to enter. Men only. Mostly techno. Open Su-Th 9pm-7am, F and Sa 9pm-9am. Cover varies.

Blue Boy Bar, Motzstr. U-Bahn #1, 2, 4, or 15 to "Nollendorfpl." A mixed-age crowd of gay men fills Blue Boy at its most popular times, between 8pm and midnight on weekends, but the bar remains open 24hrs. Its windows are painted over, but the interior is friendly and the music is of all types, tending toward "happy tunes" and oldies.

Café Berio, Maaßenstr. 7 (☎216 19 46). U-Bahn #1, 2, 4, or 15 to "Nollendorfpl." Bright, charming cafe caters to an easy-going crowd of gays and lesbians. Perfect for brunch or an early evening drink. Outdoor seating in summer. Open daily 8am-1am.

Anderes Ufer, Hauptstr. 157 (☎78 70 38 00). U-Bahn #7 to "Kleistpark." A quieter, more relaxed *Kneipe* away from the club scene. Occasional exhibits by local artists adorn the brightly painted interior. Open M-Th and Su 11am-1am, F-Sa 11am-2am.

Connection, Fuggerstr. 33 (☎218 14 32). U-Bahn #1, 2, or 15 to "Wittenbergpl." Sketchy, sketchy, sketchy. The name says it all. Find your soul mate (well, one-night stand) in the above-ground disco, then go downstairs to dimly-lit labyrinthine **Connection Garage.** You get the picture. Open M-Th 10pm-1am, F-Sa 10pm-6am, Su 2pm-2am. Cover DM12, including first drink. First weekend of the month mixed, otherwise men only.

ORANIENSTRASSE

Most bars and clubs on and around Oranienstr. lie between Lausitzer Pl. and Oranienpl. Take U-Bahn #1, 8, 12, or 15 to "Kottbusser Tor" or U-Bahn #1, 12, or 15 to "Görlitzer Bahnhof." After hours, night bus #N29 runs the length of the strip.

■ **S036,** while usually a mixed club (see p. 139), sponsors three predominantly homosexual events. The largest is **Hungrige Herzen** (Wednesdays after 10pm), a jam-packed gay and (somewhat) lesbian trance and drum 'n bass party. Delightful drag queens make the rounds with super-soakers to cool off the flaming crowd. **Café Fatal** (Sundays), has a more relaxed atmosphere, with ballroom dancing from 5pm followed by the obligatory *Schlagerkarusell* at 10pm. The second Saturday in the month brings **Gayhane,** a self-described "HomOrientaldancefloor" for a mixed crowd of Turks and Germans. The club also regularly invites famous gay and lesbian performers.

Flammende Herzen, Oranienstr. 170 (☎615 71 02). Pleasant cafe frequented by Kreuzberg's gay and lesbian community. People-watch outside or chill in the flaming orange interior among bizarre-looking faces. Drinks DM4-8. Open daily from 11am.

Rose's, Oranienstr. 187 (☎615 65 70). Voluptuous interior that's perpetually packed with people. The mixed gay and lesbian clientele kicks it amidst suspended fluffy red hearts and outrageously painted walls. Flashing lights and glitter. Lots of glitter. Margaritas DM8. Open daily 10pm-6am.

Schoko-Café, Mariannenstr. 6 (☎615 15 61). Lesbian central; a cafe with a cultural center upstairs, billiards, and dancing every second Saturday of the month (10pm). Very friendly, laid back; the perfect female gathering space. Open M-Th and Su 5pm-1am year-round, plus F-Sa from noon in the summer.

ELSEWHERE IN KREUZBERG AND FRIEDRICHSHAIN

Die Busche, Mühlenstr. 12. U-Bahn #1, 12, or 15 or S-Bahn #3, 5, 6, 7, 9, or 75 to "Warschauer Str." East Berlin's largest queer disco serves up an incongruous rotation of techno, top 40, and, yes, *Schlager.* Very cruisey. Open W and F-Su from 9:30pm. The party gets going around midnight. It *really* gets going around 3am. Cover DM6-10.

SchwuZ, Mehringdamm 61 (☎693 70 25). U-Bahn #6 or 7 to "Mehringdamm." Cafe *cum* club in southern Kreuzberg with a mostly male clientele. The relaxed *Kneipe* facade belies the intense dance floor scene inside. Th ballroom and tango from 8pm; F-Sa house, techno, and top 40 from 11pm. Cover DM5-15.

MS TitaniCa, on the MS Sanssouci boat off Göbenufer in the Spree River (☎611 12 55). U-Bahn #1 or 15 to "Schlesisches Tor." MS Sanssouci's gently swaying cafe transforms into a swinging lesbian party the first Friday of the month from 8:30pm.

PRENZLAUER BERG

Café Amsterdam, Gleimstr. 24 (☎231 67 96). S-Bahn #4, 8, or 85 or U-Bahn #2 to "Schönhauser Allee." To the beat of chill house music, Amsterdam's clientele downs cheap drinks, plays pool, or challenges one another to a game of backgammon or Monopoly. Drink specials: M shot of vodka DM1.50; Tu shot of tequila DM1.50. Open daily 4pm-6am.

BRANDENBURG

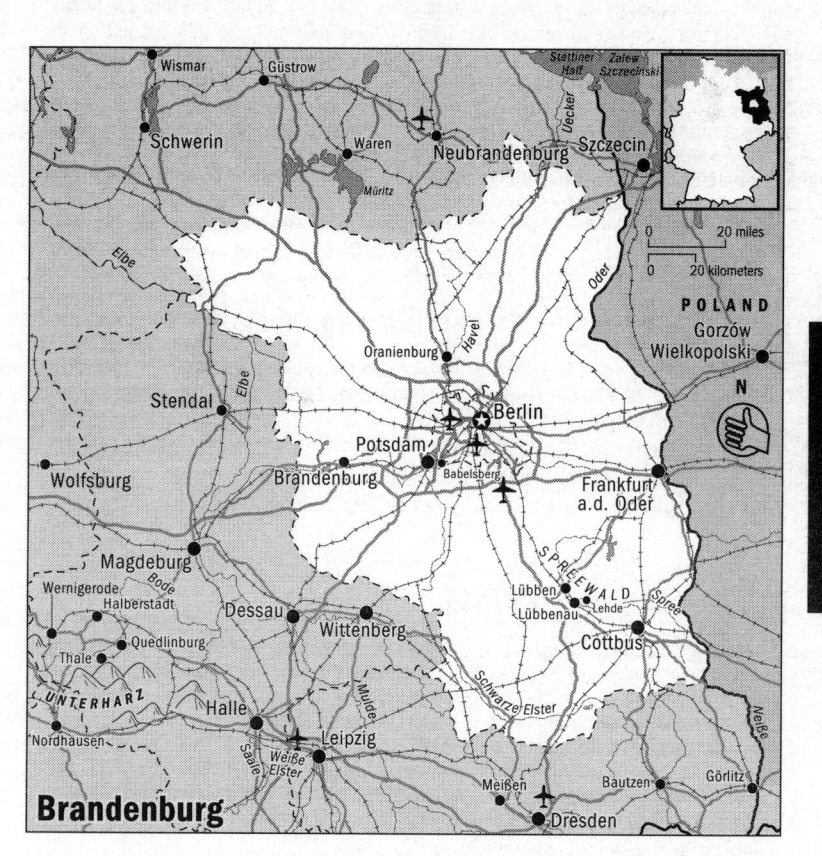

Surrounding Berlin on all sides, the *Land* of Brandenburg is often overshadowed by the sprawling metropolis within it. The infamous Hohenzollern family emerged from the province's forests to become the powerful rulers of Prussia, leaving their mark on the region by constructing more than 30 stunning palaces. Castles attract visitors to Brandenburg, but the pastoral lakes, forests, and canals that surround them are just as enticing. The entire region is an easy commute from Berlin, providing a peaceful break from the overloaded circuits of the non-stop metropolis.

HIGHLIGHTS OF BRANDENBURG

Potsdam (p. 146), with **Schloß Sanssouci** as its crowning glory, stands in regal contrast to the grit of nearby Berlin.

The winding canals of the swampy **Spreewald** (p. 152) make for a sort of rural Venice, with locals using the slow-moving rivers as streets. **Lübbenau** (p. 153) is an excellent base for exploring the woods and waterways.

POTSDAM ☎ 0331

Visitors disappointed by Berlin's distinctly unroyal demeanor can get their Kaiserly fix by taking the S-Bahn to nearby Potsdam, the glittering city of Friedrich II (the Great). While his father, Friedrich Wilhelm I ("the Soldier King"), wanted to turn Potsdam into a huge garrison of tall, tall men he had kidnapped to serve as his toy soldiers, the more eccentric Friedrich II beautified the city. In a second spurt of high heels, powder, and gilt, Potsdam served as Germany's "Little Hollywood" from 1921 until WWII, when the suburb of Babelsberg was one of the capitals of the nascent film industry. Although most of downtown Potsdam was destroyed in a 20-minute air raid in April 1945, the castle-studded Schloßpark Sanssouci still doubles the size of the city and stands as a monument to Friedrich II's (sometimes dubious) taste. As the site of the 1945 Potsdam Conference during which the Allies divvied up Germany, Potsdam's name became synonymous with Germany's defeat. After serving for 45 years as the home of Communist Party fat cats, the 1,000-year-old city recovered its traditional elitism and gained independence from Berlin in 1991 when Brandenburgers restored its status as the *Land's* capital.

▌ GETTING THERE AND GETTING AROUND

Trains: S-Bahn #7 runs from Potsdam-Stadt to **Berlin's** Bahnhof Zoo (30min., DM4.20). Hourly trains also run to **Magdeburg** (1½hr., DM32); **Dessau** (1½hr., DM30); and **Leipzig** (2hr., DM46).

Public Transportation: Potsdam lies in Zone C of Berlin's BVG transit network. For frequency and ticket prices, see **Getting Around**, p. 92.

Bike Rental: City Rad (☎ 61 90 52 or 270 27 29), 100m from the Potsdam-Stadt station on Bahnhofstr. Open May-Sept. M-F 9am-7pm, Sa-Su 9am-8pm. DM20 per day, DM35 for 2 days.

▌ PRACTICAL INFORMATION

Tourist Office: Friedrich-Ebert-Str. 5 (☎ 27 55 80; fax 275 58 99). Between the streetcar stops "Alter Markt" and "Platz der Einheit"; all streetcars from the Potsdam-Stadt station go to one of the two stops. To get there from the station, go across the Lange Brücke and make a right onto Friedrich-Ebert-Str. The office provides cheap city maps and books **rooms** for a DM5 fee. Rooms DM20-40 per person. Private bungalows DM35-50 per person. For accommodations information, call ☎ 275 58 16. Open Apr.-Oct. M-F 9am-6pm, Sa 10am-4pm, Su 10am-2pm; Nov.-Mar. M-F 10am-6pm, Sa-Su 10am-2pm. A **branch office,** in the train station, provides more expensive maps but also books rooms. Open M-F 10am-6pm, Sa 10am-2pm.

Tours: The tourist office offers 3hr. **bus tours** from the **Filmmuseum,** Schloßstr. 1. Tours leave Tu-Su at 11am. DM39 with admission to Sanssouci castle (students DM30), DM26 without. Alternatively, **Berlin Walks** (see p. 95) offers tours of Potsdam that leave from the taxi stand outside Berlin's Bahnhof Zoo W and Sa at 9am. DM26, students DM19. **City Rad** (see above) offers 3-4hr. **bike tours** Sa at 11:30am. DM15, not including bike rental.

Post Office: Platz der Einheit, 14476 Potsdam. Open M-F 9am-6pm, Sa 9am-noon.

▌ ACCOMMODATIONS AND CAMPING

Potsdam has no hostel—the closest is in **Wannsee** (see **Berlin,** p. 106), 10 minutes away by S-Bahn. The hostels in central Berlin are also a short S-Bahn ride away. Hotels are scarce, but the tourist office finds private rooms and offers a list of campgrounds in the Potsdam area. **Campingplatz Sanssouci-Gaisberg,** An der Pirschheide 41, is on the scenic banks of Templiner See. Take regional train #94 or 95 to "Bahnhof Pirschheide," and head down the lakeside road. (☎ 556 80. Open Apr.-Oct. DM10 per person, DM4 per child. Tents DM2.50-10. Bungalows DM45-70.)

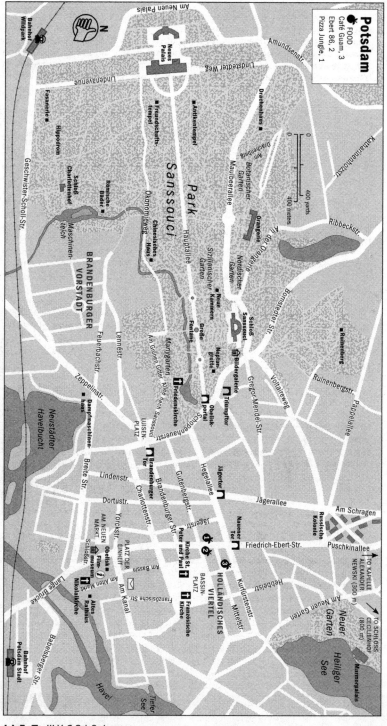

Potsdam

♣ FOOD
Café Guam, 3
Ebert 86, 2
Pizza Jungle, 1

FOOD

Bright, renovated **Brandenburger Str.,** the local pedestrian zone, encompasses most of the city's restaurants, fast-food stands, and grocery stores. The cafes near Brandenburger Tor are lovely but pricey. Similarly, the **Holländisches Viertel** (see **Sights,** below) is lined with chic little cafes where you can have a civilized afternoon glass of wine or coffee. The merchants at the **flea market** on Bassinplatz include a number of farmers with fresh produce and fake Levi's (open M-F 9am-6pm).

Pizza Jungle, Friedrich-Ebert-Str. 22 (☎270 12 87), around the corner from Mittelstr. Serves sandwiches (DM8), pizzas (DM7), and pasta (DM9). Open Tu-F 11am-8pm.

Ebert 86, Friedrich-Ebert-Str. 86 (☎270 63 22), serves *Döner,* falafel, and salads in a deli with Bauhaus-inspired stools. Most meals under DM5. Open daily 10am-1am.

Café Guam, Mittelstr. 38. Potsdam's hip crowd this cafe in the Holländiches Viertel for the small entrees (DM5-12) and plentiful drinks. Open M-F 4pm-2am, Sa-Su 2pm-1am.

SIGHTS

A good investment for sightseeing is a **day ticket,** valid and available at all castles in Potsdam (DM20, students DM15).

PARK SANSSOUCI. This kingdom of a backyard blends together two distinct parts. Half of the park is in the Baroque style—straight paths intersect at topiaries and statues of nude nymphs in geometrically pleasing patterns—and half is in the rambling, rolling style of English landscape gardens. The 600-acre park is Friedrich II's testament to the size of his treasury and the diversity of his aesthetic tastes. It doesn't all match, but it's exciting to wander through the wheat fields at the center of the park and then get lost among the rose trellises later on. For information on the park's myriad attractions, visit the **Info Center** at the windmill behind Schloß Sanssouci. (☎969 42 00. Open M-F 10am-5pm, Sa-Su 11am-4pm.)

SCHLOß SANSSOUCI. The park's main attraction, the Versailles-esque Schloß Sanssouci, sits atop a landscaped hill that defies all of nature's intentions. Built by Georg Wenzeslaus von Knobelsdorff in 1747, the yellow palace is small and airy, adorned with rich depictions of Bacchus and other Greek gods. **Tours** of the castle in German (strictly limited to 40 people) leave every 20 minutes, but the final tour (5pm) usually sells out by 2pm during the high season. Come early. If you want an English-language tour, go on the one led by the tourist office, but note that it includes only the main Schloß.

Inside, the style is cloud-like French Rococo (Friedrich was an unrepentant Francophile until his dying day)—all pinks and greens with startlingly gaudy gold trim. A high point is the steamy, tropical Voltairezimmer, decorated with colorful, carved reliefs of parrots and tropical fruit. Voltaire never stayed at the palace, this room was only built in his honor. The library reveals another of Friedrich's eccentricities: whenever he wanted to read a book, he had five copies printed, one for each of his palaces—*en français*, of course. By the way, the Ruinenberg (hill of ruins) the castle overlooks is fake. In a macabre reunification gesture, Friedrich's remains, spirited away in 1945 to a salt mine near Tübingen to save them from the Red Army, were brought back to the grounds in 1991. He's buried to the right of the Schloß in a plot of grass under six plain flagstones. (☎969 41 90. Streetcar #96 or 98 to "Schloß Sanssouci." Open Apr.-Oct. Tu-Su 9am-5pm; Nov.-Mar. Tu-Su 9am-4pm. DM10, students DM5, or free with a day ticket.)

NEUES PALAIS. At the opposite end of the park is the largest of the four castles, the 200-room Neues Palais, which was built by Friedrich to demonstrate Prussia's power and to house his guests. Inside is the 19th-century **Grottensaal,** a reception room whose walls glitter with seashells, and the **Schloßtheater,** which has occasional summer performances of plays, ballets, and concerts. (☎969 42 55. Open M-Th and Su Apr.-Oct. 9am-5pm; Nov.-Mar. 9am-4pm. DM6, students DM4. Tours DM2 extra.)

AROUND THE PARK. Next door to the Schloß Sanssouci lies the **Bildergalerie,** whose collection of Caravaggio, van Dyck, and Rubens (some of them copies—but still impressive) recently opened after extensive restoration with gorgeous results. (☎969 41 81. Open mid-May to mid-Oct. Tu-Su 10am-noon and 12:30-5pm; closed 4th W of each month. DM4, students DM2, or free with a day ticket.) On the other side of Schloß Sanssouci lie the **Neue Kammern,** which served as the guest house and recital hall for the dilettante king. (Open mid-May to mid-Oct. M-Th and Sa-Su 10am-5pm; Apr. to mid-May and mid-Oct. to early-Nov. Sa-Su only 10am-5pm. DM5 with a tour, DM4 without, students DM2.) The former ball and festival rooms are lavishly decorated; check out the Hohenzollern porcelain collection in a huge gold-trimmed closet room. Romantic **Schloß Charlottenhof,** whose park surroundings were a Christmas gift from Friedrich Wilhelm III to Friedrich Wilhelm IV, melts into landscaped gardens and grape arbors at the south of the park. Nearby lie the **Römische Bäder** (Roman baths). Overlooking the park from the north, the pseudo-Italian **Orangerieschloß** is famous for its 67 dubious Raphael imitations—they replace the originals swiped by Napoleon. (Open mid-May to mid-Oct. 10am-12:30pm and 1-5pm. Closed 4th Th of each month. DM6, students DM3.) The most "exotic" of the park's pavilions is the gold-plated **Chinesisches Teehaus,** complete with a rooftop Buddha toting a parasol. Inside, get a glimpse of the 18th-century *chinoiserie* porcelain or sip tea in the cafe (DM2). For some relative plainness, visit the **Friedenskirche** at the east entrance to the park. Friedrich Wilhelm IV and his wife Elizabeth are 'encrypted' below the glittering mosaics. (Free organ concerts W and Sa at 4pm.)

BRANDENBURGER TOR. A smaller, vanilla cousin of Berlin's Brandenburg Gate sits amid the traffic flowing through Luisenplatz. From here, Brandenburger Str. leads down to the 19th-century **Kirche St. Peter und Paul,** Bassinplatz, Potsdam's only Catholic church. (☎280 49 42. Open Tu-Su 1-5pm.)

HOLLÄNDISCHES VIERTEL. Friedrich's attempt to import Dutch craftsmen to beautify the city produced the Dutch Quarter around Friedrich-Ebert-Str. The neighborhood later fell into disrepair until 1990, when some entrepreneurs came on the scene and converted it into a row of shops and restaurants.

NIKOLAIKIRCHE. Toward the waterfront, the impressive dome of the Nikolaikirche rises above its neighbors. On closer inspection, the dome and the granite cube it sits on don't seem to match. The interior was renovated à la GDR with glass and sound-tiles that somehow lessen the aesthetic impact. (Am Alten Markt. ☎270 86 02. Open M 2-5pm, Tu-Sa 10am-5pm, Su 2-5pm. Vesper music Su at 5pm.)

NEUER GARTEN. Nuzzling the Heiliger See, Potsdam's second park contains several royal residences. The most worthwhile is **Schloß Cecilienhof,** built in the image of an English Tudor manor. Exhibits document the **Potsdam Treaty,** signed at the palace in 1945. It was supposed to be the "Berlin Treaty," but the capital was too bombed out to house the Allies' head honchos. Visitors can see the tacky rooms in which the Allied delegates stayed. (☎969 42 44. Open Tu-Su 9am-noon and 12:30-5pm. DM8 with a tour, DM6 without, students DM4.) The garden also contains the **Marmorpalais,** a stunning heap of marble, as well as various "ancient" monuments such as an Egyptian pyramid and Greek temple, which were actually used for food storage. (Marmorpalais open Apr.-Oct. Tu-Su 10am-5pm; Nov.-Mar. Sa-Su 10am-4pm. To get to the Neuer Garten, ride bus #694 to "Cecilienhof," or streetcar #92 to "Alleestr.")

RUSSISCHE KOLONIE. In the beginning of the 19th century, General Yorck brought 500 Russian soldiers to Prussia, and Friedrich Wilhelm III, a great fan of Russian culture and handsome soldiers, discovered that many of them had singing talent. Unfortunately, by the 1820s, only 12 of the original group were left—the rest died of homesickness. To mitigate the depressing atmosphere, Friedrich III built each soldier an ornate wooden house. The nearby onion-domed **Kapelle Alexander Newski,** designed by Karl Friedrich Schinkel, was also intended as compensation. (Streetcar #92 to "Puschkinalle" and follow the street north.)

OTHER SIGHTS. Potsdam has two other palace-parks. **Schloßpark Glienicke** contains a casino as well as its namesake, **Schloß Glienicke,** a less-than-stunning yellow-green affair built by Schinkel in 1828 for Prince Karl of Prussia. Berliner Str. leads through to the **Glienicker Brücke** (a.k.a. "The James Bond Bridge"), which used to be swallowed up by the death strip between the GDR and West Berlin. Until 1989, it was used for the exchange of spies, at which time it was known rather ironically as the "Bridge of Unity." *(Take streetcar #93 (direction: "Glienicker Brücke") to the end and walk back across the bridge.)* South of the station sit the **Einsteinturm** and **Meteorlogisches Obeservatorium**. Providing a breath of fresh air from palaces, the tower's design is as brilliant as the man himself. *(Cross the intersection south of the station to Brauhausberg, then a take a left onto Albert-Einstein-Str. Follow it into the woods.)*

🏛 MUSEUMS

FILMMUSEUM. Housed in an old Orangerie that once held Friedrich's stables, the film museum documents Potsdam's glory days as a film mecca with artifacts like Marlene Dietrich's costumes and a silent film archive. *(On the corner of Breite Str. and Schloßstr. ☎ 27 18 10. Open Tu-Su 10am-6pm. DM4, students DM2. Movies M-F from 2pm, Sa-Su from 3pm. DM8, students DM6.)*

FILMSTADT BABELSBERG. Back in the Golden Age of European cinema, the **UFA- Fabrik** in Babelsberg was *the* German studio, giving Marlene Dietrich, Hans Albers, and Leni Riefenstahl their first big breaks; in addition, Fritz Lang made *Metropolis* here. Tragically, apart from the films, few memorials of this era remain. The Disneylandish Filmstadt Babelsberg, built on the UFA lot, makes a feeble attempt to commemorate the greats of early German cinema, dishing out family fun of the worst sort in the form of video arcades and *historische Parades*. *(August-Bebel-Str. 26-52. Hop on S-Bahn #7 to "Babelsberg," then take bus #690 or 692 to "Filmpark." ☎ 34 56 72. Open Apr.-Nov. daily 10am-6pm. DM29, students DM26.)*

BRANDENBURG ☎ 03381

One-thousand-year-old Brandenburg has long been reluctant to wield its power; even when it was capital of the province to which it lends its name, it allowed Berlin civic freedom. When Albrecht the Bear built the town's cathedral in 1165, the surrounding city became the region's political epicenter. The city's industry took off during the 19th century, when the Brennabor bicycle factory and the Lehmann toy factory first began churning out their wares. Reconstruction of the decaying buildings is proceeding slowly, and the winding cobblestone streets are wistfully quiet. Anyone who is a fan of elegant roof tiling and strange, meandering canals can happily take up residence in this small town.

🚩 PRACTICAL INFORMATION. Two routes run to Brandenburg from **Berlin:** hop on trains heading toward **Magdeburg** and **Hannover** (DM11), or take S-Bahn #3 or 7 to "Potsdam-Stadt," then change to RB #33 (40min., DM7). The **tourist office,** Hauptstr. 51, is just off Neustädter Markt. From the train station, walk along Große Gartenstr., follow it right onto Jakobstr. past the **Soviet War Memorial** until it turns into Steinstr., and head left on Hauptstr. Or take streetcar #1, 2, or 9 from the station to "Neustädter Markt." The immensely helpful staff answers questions and books **rooms** for free. Private rooms run DM30 for singles, DM40 for doubles. The office also runs city **tours** and distributes free maps and brochures in English. (☎ 194 33; fax 22 37 43; email info@stadt-brandenburg.de; www.stadt-brandenburg.de. Open M-F 9am-6pm, Sa 9am-5pm.)

📷 ACCOMMODATIONS AND FOOD. The **Jugendherberge "Walter Husemann" (HI),** Havelstr. 7, sits right across from the Dom's Domlinden entrance. Bus B also stops near here; get off at "Domlinden" and walk one block toward the

Dom to Havelstr., which is on your right opposite the Dom. When the hostel is booked, they've been known to provide overflow housing in tents outside for DM12 per night. (☎/fax 52 10 40. Breakfast included. Reception 7-9am and 5-7pm. Curfew 10pm, but you can get a key. No English spoken. Members only. Closed Dec. 19-Jan. 4. Dorm beds DM20, over 26 DM25.) For cushier digs, head to **Pension Engel,** Große Gartenstr. 37, across the streetcar tracks from the train station. The *Pension* features basic, quiet rooms with phone and TV as well as a restaurant downstairs. (☎20 03 93; fax 20 03 94. Singles DM65, doubles DM110.) Or try **Pension Blaudruck,** Steinstr. 21. Call ahead because it's got so much character—and so few rooms. (☎22 57 34; fax 52 42 22. Singles DM45, doubles DM80.) **Campingplatz Malge** is in the middle of the woods 20 minutes away from the city center. Take Bus B from Neustädter Markt; ask the driver to let you off at the campground. (☎66 31 34. Showers included. Reception 9am-8pm. Open Apr.-Oct. DM6.50 per person. DM6-10 per tent. 2- and 4-person bungalows DM15-20.)

Inexpensive restaurants line the pedestrian area of **Hauptstr.,** which also features a **Spar supermarket,** Hauptstr. 35 (open M-F 8am-6pm, Sa 7-11am), and an open-air **farmers' market** (open daily 8am-6pm) behind the Katharinenkirche. For longer hours, head to **Nimm's mit,** in the train station behind the bike racks as you exit (open M-F 3am-11pm, Sa-Su 6am-10pm). Delicious, starchy meals await at the appetizingly named **Kartoffelkäfer** (potato beetle), Steinstr. 56 (☎22 41 18). It's a short walk from Neustädter Markt, or take bus #9 to "Steinstr./Kino." Substantial meals cost about DM10; *very* substantial meals run DM12-20. All meals revolve around the potato. **Pizzeria #31,** Steinstr. 31 (☎22 44 73), offers large and very large pizzas for under DM10. Wash down all that yummy dough with cheap beer. (DM2.70. Open M-Sa 11am-2:30pm and 5-10pm, F-Sa 11am-2:30pm and 5-11pm.)

🔯 **SIGHTS.** Brandenburg is surrounded by lush greenery and water. The **River Havel,** dotted with rowboats, flows gently by the **Dom St. Peter und Paul,** Burghof 11. This cathedral was begun in Romanesque style in 1165, completed in Gothic style, and is currently being refashioned in late-20th-century-construction-site style, with red bricks swaddled in green netting and hairy construction workers temporarily replacing the removed gargoyles. Before this modern overhaul, architect Friedrich Schinkel couldn't resist adding a few touches: the "Schinkel-Rosette" and the window over the entrance. The cathedral's many wings fold off from the center into darkness, ending in little rooms like the 13th-century-frescoed, crypt-like **Bunte Kapelle.** (☎20 03 25. Open M-Tu and Th-F 10am-5pm, W 10am-noon, Sa 10am-6pm, Su 11am-6pm.) The **Dommuseum** inside displays an array of vestments and local-history treasures. (Same hours as the Dom. DM5, students DM3.) To get to the Dom from Neustädter Markt, walk down Neustädtische Fischerstr. for 10min., or take bus A or B to "Domlinden." Back on Neustädter Markt, the **St. Katharinenkirche,** built at the end of the 14th century, is a beautiful example of *Backstein* (glazed brick) Gothic, now pockmarked by war damage (open daily 11am-6pm). Also near the Markt, the 14th-century **Steintorturm** on Steinstr. holds a town history museum and a steep stairway that knots its way to the parapet lookout like a small intestine. The summit offers an excellent vantage point for surveying Brandenburg and its many construction sites, but the stairs aren't much fun for anyone with an irrational fear of being digested by a tower-shaped monster. A monument outside the tower commemorates soldiers who died in WWII. (☎20 02 65. Tower open Tu-F 9am-5pm, Sa-Su 10am-5pm. DM4, students DM2, family pass DM8.) For 500 years, a 6m statue of the epic hero **Roland** has stood in front of the **Rathaus**—the GDR-era was just a ripple in time to this medieval symbol of free commerce. Several remaining towers from the 12th-century city walls add historic flavor to the Altstadt and the streets around **Neustädter Markt.** Incidentally, *Neustadt* (new town) is a relative term—it was founded in 1196.

SPREEWALD (SPREE FOREST)

The Spree River splits apart about 100km southeast of Berlin and branches out over the countryside in an intricate maze of streams, canals, meadows, and primeval forests stretching over 1000 square kilometers. This is the home of the legendary **Irrlichter,** German wood sprites who light the waterways for travelers who lose their way and lead those who refuse to pay to their deaths. Smart travelers now outwit the Irrlichter by warding them off with yellow-colored travel guides.

Folklore, tradition, and wildlife blossom in tiny villages and towns first settled in the Middle Ages. Hire a barge, rent a paddle boat, or take to the trails by foot or bicycle to see why locals insist that the Spreewald—not Amsterdam, Stockholm, or St. Petersburg—is the true "Venice of the North." Although the Spreewald lacks the urbanity of its Italian cousin, its canals are in constant use: farmers row to their fields and children paddle home from school. The fields and forests teem with owls, otters, and foxes, animals known to most Europeans only through textbooks or documentaries. In contrast to the streets of Berlin or the concrete monuments of other East German cities, the Spreewald is strikingly idyllic.

The Spreewald is now recognized as a *Biosphärreservat* (a biosphere nature reserve) by the UN. Some sections of the forest are closed to the public; other sections are closed during mating and breeding seasons, but not tourist season. Guided tours are offered by reservation, camping spots abound, bicycles can be rented everywhere, and excellent hiking trails and footpaths weave their way through the peaceful forest. Each local tourist office has information on these leisure activities. They won't let you forget, however, that the forest is protected by the government; tourists are urged to be environmentally responsible.

Lübben and **Lübbenau,** two tiny towns that open up into the labyrinths of canals that snake through the forest, are the most popular tourist destinations and lie within daytrip range of Berlin. The **Sorbs,** Germany's native Slavic minority, originally settled the Spreewald region and continue to influence its cultural identity (see **The Absorbing Sorbs,** p. 175).

LÜBBEN   ☎ 03546

With a web of canals and trails spreading out from the northern and southern ends of the city, scores of tourists crowd Lübben's tiny Altstadt with gondolas. Lübben also offers better access to wooded paths than neighboring towns, so pack your backpack, chomp on some juicy *Gurken* (cucumbers, the region's specialty), and get ready for an adventure.

🛉 PRACTICAL INFORMATION. Lübben is located along the Cottbus-Berlin rail line, making the city easily accessible by **train.** The tiny station is a gateway to **Berlin** (1hr., 1 per hr., DM19); **Cottbus** (30min., 1 per hr., DM17); and nearby **Lübbenau** (10min., every 30min., DM5.80). Rent **bikes** at the station for DM10 per day (open daily 7am-9pm) or at the tourist office. (DM1.50 per hr., DM10 per day. ID deposit required.) For a **taxi** call ☎48 12. The **tourist office** *(Spreewaldinformation),* Ernst-von-Houwald-Damm 15, spreads Spreewald love. From the station, head right on Bahnhofstr., then make a left on Luckauer Str., cross the two bridges, and you'll be on Ernst-von-Houwald-Damm. The office is on the right, in the large brick plaza. The staff finds **rooms** (DM30-60) for a DM5 fee (DM10 over the phone). They charge DM2.50 for a good **map,** but it's worth avoiding a mapless meander through town. During winter months and after hours, the office posts a list of private rooms just outside the entrance. (☎30 90; fax 25 43. Open daily 10am-6pm.) The **post office,** 15907 Lübben, awaits at Poststr. 4.

🖪🗗 ACCOMMODATIONS AND FOOD. The **Jugendherberge Lübben (HI),** Zum Wendenfürsten 8, is located in the middle of a wheat field on the outskirts of town. Although remote, the hostel itself is a dream, with cozy 4- to 10-bed rooms, nightly entertainment (watching cows stumble into electric fences), and a hip regular crowd of sharply dressed *Schulmädchen.* To get there, follow Bahnhofstr. to its end and turn left onto Luckauer Str. Turn right onto Burglehrstr. before the big crossing and right again onto Puschkinstr. Follow it until it splits, take the road on your left, and walk straight for approximately 3km. (☎/fax 30 46. Sheets DM6. Reception 9am-7pm. No curfew. DM21, over 26 DM26.) It takes a good 30 minutes to reach **Spreewald-Camping Lübben.** From the station, turn right on Bahnhofstr., left on Luckauer Str., right on Burglehrstr., and continue along the footpath to the campground. (☎70 53; fax 18 18 15. Reception 8am-noon and 3-8pm. Open mid-Mar. to Oct. DM9 per person; DM5-8 per tent. 4-person cabins DM40.) If you think your body deserves more than a bed in a dorm or tent, try **Pension Klauß,** Wiesenweg 8 (☎72 88). From the station, bear right and follow Bahnhofstr. until it ends. Turn left onto Luckauer Str., left again onto Lindenstr., and go straight. Count the bridges; after you have crossed four of them, look out for Wiesenweg, which should appear on your left just behind a gas station. (Breakfast included. Call ahead if you plan to arrive after 8pm. Dorm beds DM35 per person.)

While in Lübben, be sure to sample the Spreewald's particular pickled delicacies, famous throughout Germany. **Gurken Paule,** at the entrance of the tourist office plaza, is an outdoor stand offering the freshest of the Spreewald's unique *Gurken* assortment: *Salzdillgurken* (salty), *Senfgurken* (mustard), and *Gewürzgurken* (spicy). Expect to pay about DM0.30 per pickle, or DM5 for a jar (open daily 9am-6pm). For something warm, visit **Goldener Löwe,** Hauptstr. 14, which serves fish dishes and local specialties like the simple but mouth-watering *Quark mit Leinöl, Zwiebeln und Kartoffeln* (cottage cheese with onion and potatoes; DM9). The walls are decorated by paintings of Spreewald sprites and legendary beings, including the *Irrlichter.* (☎73 09. Open 11am-10pm.)

🏛🧗 SIGHTS AND HIKING. The Altstadt's architectural pride is the newly restored **Paul-Gerhardt-Kirche,** named for the most famous German hymn writer since Martin Luther (open May-Aug. W 10am-noon and 3-5pm). Gerhardt is buried inside. The entrance to Lübben's lush green park, **Der Hain,** is at the end of Breite Str. Most of Lübben's attractions lie outside the town in the surrounding forests—grab a bike, boat, or your own two feet and start exploring. The **Fährmannsverein Lübben/Spreewald,** Ernst-von-Houwald-Damm 15, offers boat trips exploring the Spreewald. (☎71 22. Open daily 9am-4pm. 1½-8hr., DM4-5 per hour). Trips depart from the Strandcafé Lübben after 9am; boats leave when full. Make a left out of the tourist office and the cafe will be on your left. The **Fährmannsverein "Flottes Rudel,"** Eisenbahnstr. 3 (☎82 69), offers boat and barge trips with picnics starting daily at 10am. Alternatively, rent a **kayak** at **Bootsverleih Gebauer** on Lindenstr. Turn right on the street before the tourist office. (☎71 94. You must be able to swim. Lifejackets provided for children. ID required. Open daily Apr.-Sept. 9am-7pm; Oct.-Mar. 10am-7pm. Boat rentals from DM8 per person per hour.)

LÜBBENAU ☎03542

Tiny Lübbenau is the most famous and perhaps the most idyllic of the Spreewald towns. For many tourists (and there are tons), the village serves as a springboard for trips into the kingdom of the *Irrlichter.* With several harbors and more gondolas than houses, the water trails are the main attraction. The landscape here is much denser than that around Lübben, and it is intricately interwoven with canals.

📋 PRACTICAL INFORMATION. Trains depart for **Berlin** (1½hr., 1 per hr., DM19.60); **Cottbus** (1hr., 1 per hr., DM17.60); and **Lübben** (10min., every 30min., DM5.80). For a **taxi** call 31 53. **Kowalski,** Poststr. 6, near the station, rents **bikes.** (☎28 35. Open M-Sa 9am-noon, 2-5pm; Su 9am-noon. DM10 per day.) Rent a kayak at the campsite (see below) or at **Manfred Franke,** Dammstr. 72. From the station, turn right down Bahnhofstr. and left at the next road. (☎27 22. Open Apr.-Oct. daily 8am-7pm. DM3-6 per hour.) The **tourist office,** Ehm-Welk-Str. 15, at the end of Poststr., has maps and finds **rooms** (DM25-45) for a DM5 fee. (☎36 68; fax 467 70. Open M-F 9am-7pm.)

ACCOMMODATIONS AND FOOD. Even though the closest hostel is in **Lübben** (10min. by train), finding a room isn't a problem in friendly Lübbenau. Check for *Zimmer frei* signs or ask for the *Gastgeberverzeichnis* brochure at the tourist office. **Pension Erlenhof,** Lindenstr. 5, is the cheapest *Pension* around. From the train station, it's a 25min. walk. Turn left onto Bahnhofstr. and go straight until Wiesengrund pops up on your right. Take a right and then a quick left onto Lindenstr. (☎460 73. Call ahead. Singles DM45, doubles DM70.) Directly on the road to Lehde, **Campingplatz "Am Schloßpark"** (☎/fax 466 54) offers 300 plots for tents with cooking and bathing facilities on site, as well as a store with soap, soup, pickles, and other necessities. (Bikes DM10 per day, boats DM28 per day. Reception 7am-noon and 2-9pm. DM7.50 per adult; DM3.50 per child. Tents DM5-8. Bungalows DM55 for up to 4 people. DM14 for trailer spots.)

For cheap food and pickles, beets, and beans by the barrel, check out the snack bars and stands along the **Grosser Hafe** (see below). Toward the campgrounds, **Café-Garten** (☎36 22), on the Lehde stream, is a self-service outdoor cafe with potato salad (DM2.50) and pike filet. (DM10.20. Open daily 9am-8pm.) In town, **Spreewald Idyll,** Spreestr. 13 (☎22 51), serves regional specialties like *Grützwurst* with potatoes (DM11.40), fish dishes (DM15-20), and salads (DM4-10).

SIGHTS AND HIKING. The Altstadt is a 10-minute trot from the station. Go straight on Poststr. until you come to the marketplace dominated by the Baroque **Nikolaikirche.** The carved stone pillar in front served as an 18th-century crossroads post marking the distance in *Stunden* (hours), an antique measurement equalling one hour's walk. *(Open M-F 2-4pm.)* The requisite **Schloß** is now a handsome (but terrifically expensive) hotel and restaurant. The lush castle grounds are open to the public and shelter the **Spreewaldmuseum,** which offers an overview of the Spreewald and its unique customs. *(Open Apr. to mid-Sept. Tu-Su 10am-6pm; mid.-Sept. to Oct. 10am-5pm. DM3, students DM2.)*

There are two main departure points for **gondola tours** of the forest: the **Großer Hafen** and the **Kleiner Hafen;** follow the signs from the town center or from the train station. The Großer Hafen offers a larger variety of tours, including two- and three-hour trips to Lehde. The boats, usually seating 20, take on customers starting at 9 or 10am and depart when full, continuing throughout the day. (2-9hr. DM8-17. No English tours, but they're hilarious if you speak German and can decipher the dialect.) From the Kleiner Hafen, at the end of Spreewaldstr., tours leave daily from 9am and last 1½ to 10 hours. *Genossenschaft der Kahnfährleute, Dammstr., is the biggest boat tour company. (☎22 25. Open Apr.-Oct. daily 9am-6pm. Round-trips to Lehde last three hours and cost DM10, children DM5; a 5hr. tour of the forest costs DM 23, children DM11.50.)*

It's only a hop and a paddle from Lübbenau to **Lehde,** a UNESCO-protected landmark and the most romantic village in the Spreewald, accessible by foot, bike, or boat. Walking, it's a 15-minute trek; follow the signs from the Großer Hafen. If you're partial to water, take a boat from the harbor. Check out the **Freilandmuseum,** where things remain as they were when entire Spreewalder families slept in the same room and newlyweds spent their honeymoons heaving in the hay. (Open Apr.-Oct. daily 10am-6pm. DM6, students and seniors DM4.) Just before the bridge to the museum, lies **Zum Fröhlichen Hecht,** Dorfstr. 1, a large cafe, restaurant, and *Biergarten.* Try *Kartoffeln mit Quark* (potatoes with sour curd cheese) in a special Spreewald sauce (DM10.50) or pickles with a side order of *Schmalz* (lard; DM1.70), another Spreewald "specialty." Say a prayer for your heart, and dig in. (☎27 82. Open daily 10am-5pm.)

BRANDENBURG

SACHSEN (SAXONY)

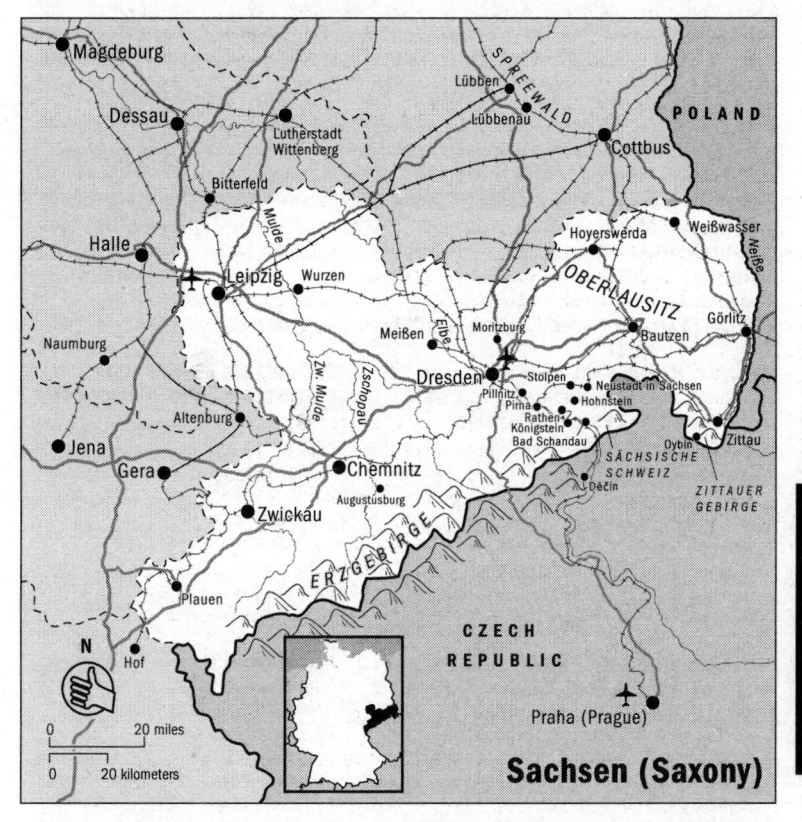

Sachsen (Saxony)

Sachsen is known primarily for **Dresden** and **Leipzig**, the largest cities in Eastern Germany after Berlin, but the entire region offers a fascinating historical and cultural diversity that reveals a great deal about life in the former East. The castles around Dresden attest to the bombastic history of Sachsen's decadent electors, while the socialist monuments of Chemnitz and the distinctive architecture of other major cities depict the former world of the GDR. On the eastern edge of Sachsen, the mountain ranges of the Sächsische Schweiz and the Zittauer Gebirge provide a respite from the aesthetic violence done by East Germany's city planners. Sachsen is also home to the Sorbs, Germany's only national minority, whose presence has infused a Slavic air to many of the region's eastern towns.

HIGHLIGHTS OF SACHSEN

Dresden (p. 156) is one of Germany's most compelling cities. Its sights, museums, and galleries will make you gasp, while its nightlife will leave you speechless—and sleepless.

Leipzig (p. 181) fostered East Germany's biggest anti-government demonstrations in 1989. A key trade city, it harbors an edgy *Uni*-culture and Europe's largest train station.

Climbing, hiking, and skiing abound in the **Sächsische Schweiz** (p. 168).

DRESDEN ☎ 0351

Dresden pulses with a historical intensity that is both vicious and sublime. The city was one of the cultural capitals of pre-war Germany and oversaw many key movements in European history, from the meetings of Goethe, Schiller, and Beethoven in Gottfried Körner's estate to the architectural revisionism of the 1920s. Sadly, no matter where you go, you will be unable to forget the Allied bombings of February 1945, which claimed over 50,000 lives and destroyed 75% of the city center. Warming up to the efforts of reunification, Dresden today engages visitors with spectacular ruins in the midst of world-class museums and partially reconstructed palaces and churches, featuring the exemplary Baroque designs of city architect Matthäus Daniel Pöppelmann. Reconstruction is scheduled for completion by 2006, the city's 800-year anniversary. However, the expectant energy driving present-day Dresden is not built solely on nostalgic appeals to the past; revitalization and reinvention go hand in hand. Dresden enters the new millennium as a young, dynamic metropolis propelled by a history of cultural turbulence.

▐▉ GETTING THERE AND GETTING AROUND

Flights: Dresden's **airport** (☎ 881 33 60, 881 33 62, or 881 33 70) is 9km from town. **Airport City Liners** buses leave both stations for the airport every hr. (DM8); call ☎ 251 82 43 for schedules and information.

Trains: From the **Dresden Hauptbahnhof** (☎ (0180) 599 66 33, or use the computerized schedule center in the main hall), travelers shoot off to **Leipzig** (1½hr., 34 per day, DM33); **Berlin** (2hr., 15 per day, DM52); **Munich** (8hr., 24 per day, DM148); **Frankfurt am Main** (6hr., 14 per day, DM136); **Budapest** (11hr., 4 per day, DM125); **Prague** (3hr., 12 per day, DM38); and **Warsaw** (8hr., 8 per day, DM55). Another station, **Bahnhof Dresden Neustadt,** sits across the Elbe and bears a striking resemblance to its mate; trains leave for **Bautzen** (1hr., 1 per hr., DM15); **Görlitz** (2hr., 1 per hr., DM29); **Zittau** (2½hr., 1 per hr., DM29); and other Eastern cities.

Ferries: The **Sächsische Dampfschiffahrt** (☎ 86 60 90, schedule information 866 09 40) grooves with a restaurant, band, and dancing. Ships travel up and down the Elbe from **Seußlitz** in the north to the Czech border town **Děčín** in the south. Ferries to **Pillnitz** (2hr., DM16) and **Meißen** (2hr., DM20). Day pass DM29.

Public Transportation: Dresden is sprawling—even if you only spend a few days here, familiarize yourself with the major bus and streetcar lines. **Punch your ticket as you board.** DM2.90; 4 or fewer stops DM1.80. Day pass DM8; weekly pass DM25, students DM19 (student ID required). Tickets and maps are available from friendly *Fahrkarten* dispensers at major stops and from the **Verkehrs-Info** stands outside the *Hauptbahnhof* or at Postpl. (both open M-F 7am-7pm, Sa-Su 8am-6pm), as well as at Albertpl. and Pirnaischer Pl. (open M-F 7am-7pm, Sa-Su 8am-4pm). Most major lines run every hour after midnight. Dresden's **S-Bahn** network reaches from **Meißen** (DM7.70) to Schöna by the Czech border (DM7.70). Buy tickets from *Automaten* in the *Hauptbahnhof* and validate them in the red contraptions; insert the ticket and press *hard.*

Taxis: ☎ 459 81 12 or 21 12 21.

Car Rental: Sixt-Budget, An der Frauenkirche 5 (☎ 864 29 72; fax 495 40 74), in the Hilton Hotel by the *Frauenkirche.* Open M-F 7am-8pm, Sa 8am-noon. **Europacar** (☎ (0180) 580 00) in the *Hauptbahnhof* near the Prager Str. exit. Open M-F 7am-9pm, Sa 8am-7pm, Su 9-11am. Offices also at *Bahnhof Neustadt,* to the left of the station and up the stairs. Open M-F 7:30am-6pm, Sa 8am-noon, Su 9-11am.

Bike Rental: ☎ 461 32 85. In the *Hauptbahnhof* near the luggage storage. DM10 per day. Open M-F and Su 6am-10pm, Sa 6am-9pm.

Mitfahrzentrale: Antonstr. 41 (☎ 194 40). From **Bahnhof Neustadt,** walk 400m along the tracks to the right of the station. DM0.10 per km plus finder's fee. **Berlin** DM21, **Frankfurt am Main** DM45, **Munich** DM43.50. Call 1-2 days in advance. Rides to west Germany are frequent. Open M-F 9am-7pm, Sa-Su 10am-2pm.

Hitchhiking: *Let's Go* does not recommend hitchhiking as a safe mode of transportation. Hitchers say they stand in front of the "Autobahn" signs at on-ramps; otherwise they are heavily fined or smacked by oncoming traffic. **To Berlin:** streetcar #3 or 13 to "Liststr.," then bus #81 to "Olter." To **Prague, Eisenach,** or **Frankfurt am Main:** bus #72 or 88 to "Luga," or bus #76, 85, or 87 to "Lockwitz."

ORIENTATION AND PRACTICAL INFORMATION

The capital of Sachsen, Dresden stands on the Elbe River 60km northwest of the Czech border and 200km south of Berlin. The city of half a million people is a major transportation hub between Eastern and Western Europe.

Dresden is bisected by the Elbe. The Altstadt lies on the same side as the Hauptbahnhof; Neustadt, to the north, escaped most of the bombing, paradoxically making it one of the oldest parts of the city. Many of Dresden's main tourist attractions are centered between the Altmarkt and the Elbe. From there it's a five-minute stroll to the banks of the Neustadt. Five immense bridges (Marienbrücke, Augustbrücke, Carolabrücke, Albertbrücke, and the "Blue Wonder" Loschwitzbrücke) connect the city's two halves. The area between the Altstadt and the Hauptbahnhof is packed with recent development, transforming the landscape into corporate shopping sprawl—this is the new Dresden. Across the river, the neighborhoods branching off of Königsbrücker pulse with vicious counter-culture vibrations and house Dresden's young, alternative *Szene*.

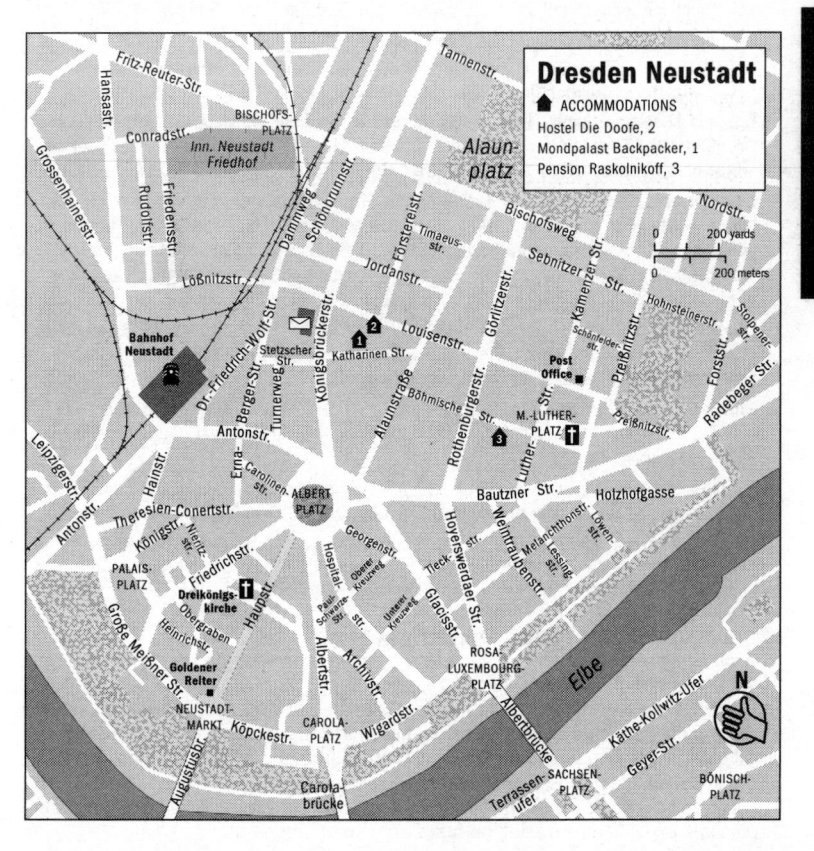

Dresden Neustadt

⌂ ACCOMMODATIONS
Hostel Die Doofe, 2
Mondpalast Backpacker, 1
Pension Raskolnikoff, 3

SAXONY

Tourist Office: Two locations: one on Prager Str., just across from the Hauptbahnhof, and another on Theaterpl. in the Schinkelwache, a small building in front of the Semper Oper. (☎49 19 20; fax 49 19 21 16. Both offices open M-F 10am-6pm, Sa-Su 10am-2pm.) The staff books rooms (DM6 fee per person) and hands out free maps. Consider buying a **Dresden Card,** which provides 48hr. of public transit and free or reduced entry at many museums (DM26). There are several special hotlines for general information (☎49 19 21 00), room reservations (☎49 19 22 22), city tours (☎49 19 22 30), and advance ticket purchases (☎49 19 22 33).

Currency Exchange: ReiseBank, in the main hall of the train station. Open M-F 7:30am-7:30pm, Sa 8am-noon and 12:30-4pm, Su 9am-1pm. 2.5-4.5% commission for currency exchange, depending on the amount; DM7.50 for traveler's checks. Other banks on Prager Str. After hours, the self-service exchange machine in the Hauptbahnhof will do, but the rates are poor.

American Express: Hoyerswerdaer Str. 20 (☎80 70 30), in Neustadt near Rosa-Luxemburg-Pl. Money sent, mail held, and other standard offerings. Open M-F 7:30am-6pm.

Luggage Storage and Lockers: At both train stations. Lockers DM2-4. 24hr. storage DM4 per piece. Open M-F 6am-10pm, Sa 6am-9pm.

Bookstore: Das Internationale Buch, Kreuzstr. 4 (☎495 41 90), directly behind the Kreuzkirche. English books on the 2nd floor. Open M-F 9:30am-7pm, Sa 9:30am-2pm.

Library: Haupt- und Musikbibliothek, Freiberger Str. 33-35 (☎864 82 33), in the World Trade Center. From the Hauptbahnhof, bear left and follow Ammonstr. up to Freiberger Str. A conveniently located library with tons of info, maps, and books about Dresden and Sachsen, plus a cool cafe. Open M-F 10am-7pm, Sa 10am-2pm.

Women's Center: Frauenzentrum "sowieso," Angelikastr. 1 (☎804 14 70). Open M 9am-1pm, Th 10am-7pm F 9am-1pm. Telephone advice W 3-5pm (general) and 7-10pm (lesbian issues). *Frauenkneipe* (women's bar) open Th-Sa from 7pm.

Gay and Lesbian Organizations: Gerede-Dresdner Lesben, Schwule und alle Anderen, Prießnitzstr. 18 (☎464 02 20; 24hr. hotline ☎802 22 70). From Albertpl., walk up Bautzner Str. and turn left onto Prießnitzstr. Open Tu 10am-noon and 3-5pm, Th 3-5pm.

Laundromat: Groove Station, Katharinenstr. 11-13. A laundromat and much, much more. Wash your clothes (DM5, dry DM3, cup of coffee included) and play a game of pool, have a few drinks, or brave the needles in the tattoo and piercing studio (most tattoos are going to take longer than your wash—maybe better to wait for the dryer). Open Su-F 11am-2am, Sa 10am-late. Öko-Express, on Königsbrücker Str., right next to Albertpl. DM3.50-5 per load. Open M-Sa 6am-11pm. Also at **Jugendherberge Rudi Arndt** (see Accommodations, p. 158) in the cellar. DM3-4 per load.

Emergency: Police, ☎110. Ambulance and Fire, ☎112.

Pharmacy: Apotheke Prager Straße, Prager Str. 3 (☎425 08). Open M-F 8:30am-7pm, Sa 8:30am-4pm. When closed, a sign on the door gives the nearest open pharmacies.

Post Office: The **Hauptpostamt,** Dresden 01099, Königsbrücker Str. 21/29 (☎819 13 70), is in Neustadt. Fax payphone available. Open M-F 8am-7pm, Sa 8am-1pm. Postamt 72, St. Petersburger Str. 26, is near the tourist office. Open M-F 8:30am-8pm, Sa 8:30am-noon.

Internet Access: Upd@te, Louisenstr. 30 (☎804 87 47). Close to **Die Boofe** (see Accommodations, p. 158). Speedy ISDN connections will make you bless modern technology. DM10 per hr. Open M-F noon-8pm, Sa noon-2pm.

ACCOMMODATIONS AND CAMPING

If there's one thing that attests to Dresden's status as a city on the rise, it's the state of its accommodations. New hotels and hostels are constantly being planned, built, and opened, but come the weekend, it's hard to get a spot in anything with a good location. In hotels, though, the reservation situation is just the opposite. The excess of available rooms means that you can often find same-day deals at some of the hotels on Prager Str. The tourist offices can also facilitate stays in private rooms and provide information on other accommodation options.

Jugendherberge Dresden Rudi Arndt (HI), Hübnerstr. 11 (☎471 06 67; fax 472 89 59). Streetcar #5 (direction: "Südvorstadt") or #3 (direction: "Plauen") to "Nürnberger Platz." Continue down Nürnberger Str., turn right onto Hübnerstr.; the hostel is at the first corner on the right. Or, from the Hauptbahnhof, walk down Fritz-Löffler-Str., bear right onto Münchener Str., turn right onto Eisenstuckstr. and walk up two blocks. Central location near the train station; friendly atmosphere makes up for the size of the rooms. Sheets DM5. HI members only. Check-in 3pm-1am. Curfew 1am. Reservations recommended. Dorm beds DM25, over 26 DM30.

Jugendgästehaus Dresden (HI), Maternistr. 22 (☎49 26 20; fax 492 62 99), formerly the Hotel-Kongress-Business-Center, is now an authentic glimpse into pre-fab hotel living. Go out the Prager Str. exit of the Hauptbahnhof and turn left, following the streetcar tracks along Ammonstr. to Freiberger Str. Turn right and take another quick right onto Maternistr. Newly renovated with more than 400 beds, the hostel attracts lots of school groups. Breakfast and sheets included. Check-in after 4pm, check-out 9:30am. No curfew. Wheelchair accessible. Rooms with washbasins DM38 per person; with private shower DM45. Single room DM15 extra.

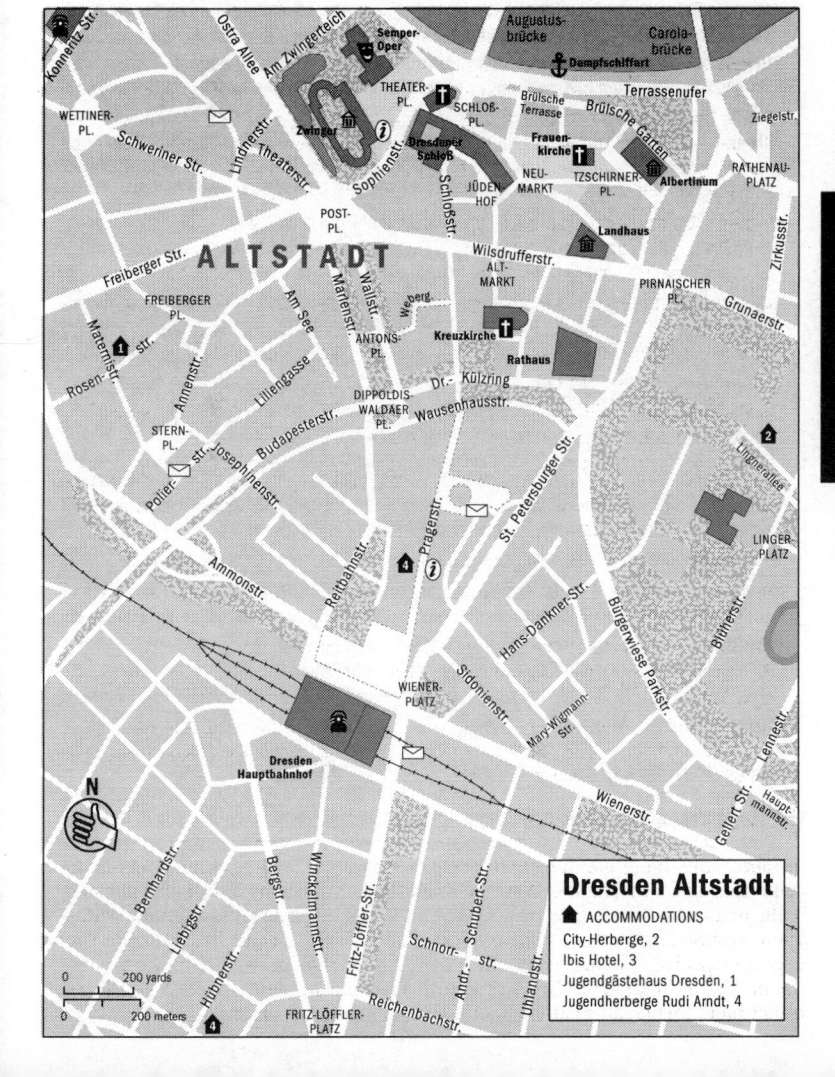

Dresden Altstadt

🏠 ACCOMMODATIONS

City-Herberge, 2
Ibis Hotel, 3
Jugendgästehaus Dresden, 1
Jugendherberge Rudi Arndt, 4

SAXONY

Mondpalast Backpacker, Katharinenstr. 11-13 (☎/fax 804 60 61), a 10min. walk from Bahnhof Neustadt, above **Groove Station** and **DownTown** (see p. 165). From Bahnhof Neustadt, walk down Antonstr. and turn left onto Königsbrücker Str. Cross the street and turn right on Katharinenstr.; the hostel is 100m ahead. A hostel created by backpackers for backpackers, located in the heart of the Neustadt scene. Themed room decor and a large kitchen, combined with the art gallery and cool facilities available at Groove Station, make this the hippest place in town. Breakfast DM8. Sheets DM5. 24hr. reception. Key deposit DM10. Internet access DM12 per hr. Call ahead. Credit cards accepted. 8-bed rooms DM25, 4-6 bed rooms DM27, doubles DM62.

Hostel Die Boofe, Louisenstr. 20 (☎801 33 61; fax 801 33 62). A renovated apartment building set back in a small courtyard, this hostel offers 54 beds in immaculate rooms in the middle of Neustadt. Cushy beds in cozy rooms that are more sleep-friendly than the caves after which the hostel was named. Bike rental DM10 per day. 24hr. reception. Reservations recommended. 2-5 bed rooms DM27. Sheets DM5, breakfast DM8. Doubles DM79, sheets and breakfast included.

City-Herberge, Lignerallee 3 (☎485 99 00; fax 485 99 01). From the Hauptbahnhof, walk up St. Petersburger Str., crossing over and using the right sidewalk. Turn right at Lignerallee. Central location with access to public transportation. The rooms are slick and well-decorated. While bathrooms are shared, they are private enough not to be an inconvenience. Breakfast included. Reservations recommended. May-June and Sept.-Oct. singles DM70, doubles DM100; all other times singles DM60, doubles DM80.

Ibis Hotel, Prager Str. (☎48 56 66 61). Three huge hotel skyscrapers on Prager Str., just across the street from the Hauptbahnhof, offer summer same-day specials that are a good bargain for people traveling in pairs. Simple but comfortable rooms, some with a beautiful skyscraper view at night. Suites include TV, phone, and shower or bath. 24hr. reception. Doubles May-June and Sept.-Oct. DM130, DM110 all other times. Apartments (DM145-175) are a good deal for families.

Pension Raskolnikoff, Böhmische Str. 34 (☎804 57 06), right above the restaurant and gallery. This tiny pension is squeezed into the same building as the restaurant and gallery; perfect for the authentic Neustadt experience. Double DM75, DM12 for every extra person. Call ahead.

Camping: Campingplatz Altfranken, Otto-Harzer-Str. 2 (☎410 24 00; fax 410 24 80). Thanks to the recent incorporation of Altfranken into greater Dresden, the campground is no longer outside the city, and is now conveniently located next to a bus stop. From the Hauptbahnhof, take streetcar #17 (direction: "Gorbitz") to "Tharandter Str.," then bus #90 all the way to "Altfranken." DM10 per tent. 24hr. reception.

⬛ FOOD

Unfortunately, the surge in Dresden tourism has yielded an increase in food prices, particularly in the Altstadt. The cheapest eats are at supermarkets or *Imbiß* stands along Prager Str. Most restaurants in the Altstadt cater almost exclusively to a tourist clientele; those in search of authenticity will probably prefer something outside of the center. The Neustadt area, between Albertpl. and Alaunpl., spawns a new bar every few weeks and clearly dominates Dresden's offerings of quirky, ethnic, and student-friendly restaurants. The free monthly *Spot*, available at the tourist office, details culinary options.

El Perro Borracho, Alaunstr. 70 (☎803 67 23). A tiny sparkle of sunny Spain in a friendly little patio. Try the tasty "mix & match" *tapas* and wash them down with *sangría*. All main courses DM12. Buffet breakfast before 4pm on weekends (DM10). Special deals for large groups. Open M-F 11:30am-1am, Sa-Su 10am-1am.

Blumenau, Louisenstr. 67 (☎802 65 02). One of the most popular restaurants in the Neustadt, this place offers a friendly environment perfect for *Milchkaffee* sipping in the mornings, and a nice spot for an evening drink. One of the cheapest restaurants in Dresden. Menu changes unpredictably but most dishes run DM6-10; Breakfast (DM5-11), served until 4pm. Open daily 10am-3am.

Raskolnikoff, Böhmische Str. 34 (☎804 57 06). A Dostoevskian haunt in a ramshackle pre-war brownstone. Savory Russian and Afghan fare (DM8-20), from goat cheese (DM6) to flaming kippers (DM14.50) to *Srasi* (potato pockets with mushrooms, DM12.50), served to a local crowd in a cozy dining room. Open daily 10am-2am.

Café Aha, Kreuzstr. 7 (☎492 33 79), across the street from the Kreuzkirche. A haven for environmentally-conscious idealism tucked in a neighborhood full of big corporate chains, the restaurant celebrates healthy food produced by ecologically sound means. Each interesting dish (DM8-20) promotes the idea of "fair trade"; the cafe changes its menu monthly to introduce foods from countries who can't compete in the world market. Downstairs is a shop with globally-friendly products of all types, and the loft holds changing political art exhibitions and occasional events. Open daily 10am-midnight.

Planwirtschaft, Louisenstr. 20 (☎801 31 87). Bright orange decor and solid German food served to locals and the hostelers who have wandered down from Die Boofe above. Try the pork chop with fried eggs and potatoes (DM14.50) or choose from a selection of fresh salads (DM7.50-13.50). English menu available. Open M-Th and Su 9am-1am, F-Sa 9am-3am.

☀ SIGHTS

ALTSTADT

From the banks of the Elbe, the **electors of Sachsen** once ruled nearly all of central Europe. Destroyed during WWII and partly rebuilt during Communist times, the *Altstadt* carries the city's legacy as one of the Continent's major cultural centers. Presently a gigantic restoration project, slated for completion in 2006, aims to re-establish Dresden as one of Germany's most beautiful cities. Most of Dresden's celebrated sights are located near **Theaterplatz.**

ZWINGER. The extravagant collection of Friedrich August I, a.k.a. August the Strong, Prince Elector of Saxony and King of Poland, is housed in this magnificent palace, designed by August's senior state architect, Matthäus Daniel Pöppelmann. Now championed as one of the most successful examples of Baroque design, the stately facade, with its extravagant modeling, attracts flocks of tourists every day to marvel at its wonders. The palace narrowly escaped destruction in the 1945 bombings, and while some of the statues lining the palace grounds are still charred, workers are busy sandblasting everything back to aesthetic perfection. The northern wing of the palace, a later addition, was designed by Gottfried Semper, revolutionary activist and master architect. The reconstruction of the Zwinger has become a symbol of the new Dresden, and today the palace is home to some of Dresden's finest museums (see **Museums,** p. 163).

SEMPER-OPER. Dresden's famed opera house reverberates with the same glorious luxury as the northern wing of the Zwinger palace. The painstaking restoration has returned the building to its original state, making it one of Dresden's major attractions. The interior is open for tours almost daily. *(Theaterplatz 2. ☎491 14 96; fax 491 14 58. Check the main entrance for tour times, usually midday. DM9, students DM6.)*

KREUZKIRCHE. This church on the *Altmarkt* was the site of the first Protestant celebration of communion in Dresden. After being leveled four times, in 1669 by fire, in 1760 with the Seven Years War, again in 1897 by fire, and finally in February 1945 with the Allied bombing, the interior remains in a damaged state, with rough plaster columns and half-headed cherubs, bearing a powerful reminder of the war's destruction. The tower offers a bird's eye view of downtown Dresden. *(An der Kreuzkirche 6. ☎439 39 20; fax 439 39 39. Open summer M-Tu and Th-F 10am-5:30pm, W and Sa 10am-4:30pm, Su noon-4:30pm; winter M-F 10am-4:30pm, Sa 10am-3:30pm, Su noon-4:30pm. Free. Tower closes 30min. before the church. DM2, children DM1.)* The church is also the home of the world-famous **Kreuzchor,** a boys' choir founded in the 13th century. *(Concerts Su 6pm. DM2.)*

DRESDENER SCHLOß. Standing across from the Zwinger, the residential palace of Sachsen's Electors and emperors was ruined in the Allied firebombing of February 13, 1945, but a good deal of its restoration is nearly complete—the few masses of crumbled brick that remain are quickly being rebuilt. Once the proud home of August the Strong, it features a display on the Renaissance and Baroque eras of the palace and the history of its reconstruction. The 100m tall **Hausmannsturm** hosts a small exhibition of photographs and texts (also available in English) discussing the details of the February 1945 bombings, and the top floor offers a 360° view of the city. *(Open Apr.-Oct. Tu-Su 10am-6pm. DM5, students and seniors DM3.)* The **Katholische Hofkirche** (Catholic royal church) used to be connected to the Schloß. *(Open M-Th 9am-5pm, F 1-5pm, Sa 10:30am-4pm, Su noon-4pm. Free.)* The **Fürstenzug** (Procession of Electors) along Augustusstr. is a mammoth (102m) mural made of 24,000 tiles of Meißen china depicting the rulers of Saxony from 1123 to 1904. If you've been mistaking Friedrich the Earnest for Friedrich the Pugnacious, you may want to stop in here for a history lesson. Where's August the Strong? In the middle, of course.

BRÜHLSCHE TERRASSE. Running along the river, the Brühlsche Terrasse offers a prime photo opportunity of the Elbe or the adjacent Katholische Hofkirche. Within its casements alchemist Johann Friedrich Böttger was imprisoned by August the Strong until he finally solved the secret recipe for porcelain in 1707. Böttger had originally promised to produce gold, but had to settle for dainty teacups and cow-shaped creamers instead. The same Meißen china (see p. 166) which comprises the *Fürstenzug* (above) was Böttger's invention, and made for a booming German trade in porcelain. Today the Terrasse offers a pathway lined with potted trees, perfect for a stroll down to the Albertinum from the Schloß.

FRAUENKIRCHE. Currently a hulking mass of scaffolding, ladders, and tarps crawling with construction workers, it is nearly impossible to see the original Frauenkirche, once Dresden's most famed silhouette until it collapsed after the bombings. For years the ruin remained a testament to the futility and horror of war. The most complex and expensive project of its kind in Germany, the reconstruction of the church began in 1994 and is scheduled for completion in 2006. The ruin was carefully taken apart and each stone examined and catalogued, so that the new structure will be built with both new and original parts. *(Neumarkt.* ☎ *498 11 31; fax 498 11 29. Tours available hourly; check the bulletin board outside for schedule changes and details.)*

NEUSTADT

On the other end of the magnificent **Augustusbrücke,** the city *Let's Go* of its history and enjoys the present. A few worthwhile sights float in a sea of socialist architectural oddities and the area's busy cultural life.

GOLDENER REITER. A gold-plated statue of August the Strong is located near the former Straße der Befreiung (Liberation Street, referring to when Soviet troops overran eastern Germany at the conclusion of WWII), now renamed Hauptstr. (Main Street) in a similar surge of nomenclatural genius. August's nickname was reputedly an homage to his remarkable (some might say unseemly) virility; legend has it he fathered 365 kids, though the official tally is 15. Today August sits in all his pompous glory atop an equally pretentious steed, rearing to gallop. Go August!

DREIKÖNIGSKIRCHE. Near Hauptstr., the Church of the Magi is one of the oldest structures in the city. Inside, check out the *Dresden Danse Macabre*, a 12.5m Renaissance monument, below the organ. *(Open M-Tu and Th-F 10am-6pm. Su noon-6pm. DM2.)* At the other end of Hauptstr., **Albertplatz** is surrounded by handsome 19th-century mansions, and marks the center of the Neustadt bar and restaurant scene.

ELSEWHERE IN DRESDEN

Dresden continues to surprise and impress farther away from the city center. Virtually untouched by the bombings, the outskirts of the city reverberate with spontaneity and local tradition. While the banks of the Elbe are perfect for a scenic stroll, the colorful architecture of the mansions and villas is also well worth a peek.

SCHLACHTHOFRINGE. The Schlachthofringe (Slaughterhouse Circle) is an original 1910 housing complex in a more dismal part of Dresden, commandeered during WWII as a camp for prisoners of war. Virtually forgotten by the tourist industry, the buildings have been left to waste away among a few less-than-thriving attempts at commerce. Novelist Kurt Vonnegut was imprisoned here during the bombing of Dresden, inspiring his masterpiece *Slaughterhouse Five*. Take bus #82 to "Ostragehege". On the way, you'll pass one of Dresden's architectural oddities, the former **Zigarettenfabrik** (cigarette factory). Keep an eye out for its brown, stained-glass dome and candy-striped pink and white facade. Built in 1907, it was modeled on a tobacco factory in Turkey, and now occasionally houses discos.

BLAUES WUNDER. A 19th-century suspension bridge connecting Blasewitz and Loschwitz, the Blaues Wunder ("Blue Wonder") was the only bridge the Nazis didn't destroy on the eve of the Soviet invasion at the end of WWII. A plaque remains as a memorial on this powder-blue steel darling. **Körnerplatz,** on the Loschwitz side, remains one of Dresden's prettiest squares, with its traditional German charm remaining unscathed by Dresden's tumultuous past century. Beyond Körnerplatz is the **Schwebebahn** (overhead railway). The vintage construction offers stunning views of Dresden and the Elbe. *(Take streetcar #1 (direction: "Tolkewitz") or #6 (direction: "Niedersedlitz"). DM4, DM6 return. Departs every 10min.)*

SCHILLERHÄUSCHEN. This tiny cottage was where Beethoven first heard Schiller's *Ode an die Freude*, which he later adapted for the finale of his Ninth Symphony. The house once belonged to Gottfried Körner, a well-to-do art patron who supported some of the greats during their stays in Sachsen. The Häuschen features a small museum of Schiller memorabilia. *(Schillerstr. 19. North of Körnerpl. in Loschwitz. ☎46 86 60. Open May-Oct. Sa-Su 1-5pm. DM1, students and seniors DM0.50.)*

🏛 MUSEUMS

After several years of renovations which are nearly complete, Dresden's museums are once again ready to compete with the rest of Europe. If you're going to visit the Albertinum, the Alte Meister collections, or the Zwinger museums, it may be worthwhile to invest in the **Tageskarte** (DM12, students and seniors DM7), which covers one-day admission to the Albertinum museums, the Schloß, most of the Zwinger and a number of other sights. The ticket covers so many sights that the ambitious museum-goers should probably get started right at 10 to see everything the ticket covers. Purchase it at any of the major museums. The **Dresden Card** (p. 158), also includes free or reduced entrance to many of the major museums.

ZWINGER COMPLEX

GEMÄLDEGALERIE ALTE MEISTER. From the Semper-Oper side, walk through the archway; the gallery entry is on the right. A world-class collection of paintings from 1400 to 1800. Cranach the Elder's luminous *Adam* and positively naughty *Eve* paintings (see p. 23), Rubens's *Leda and the Swan* and Raphael's *Die Sixtinische Madonna* are only a few of the masterpieces. *(Semper Wing. ☎491 46 19. Open Tu-Su 10am-6pm. DM7, students and seniors DM4. Tours F and Su at 4pm DM1.)*

RÜSTKAMMER. Fufllill your fantasies of chivalric valor with a collection of courtly toys that is nothing short of downright dangerous. Silver and gold plated suits, chain mail, ivory-inlaid guns and a stationary joust are just a few of the highlights. What appears to be a collection of midget armor is, in fact, that of the Wettin (Windsor) family's toddlers. *(Across from the Alte Meister in the Semper Wing. ☎491 46 19; fax 491 46 16. Open Tu-Su 10am-6pm. DM3, students and seniors DM2, covered by admission to the Gemäldegalerie Alte Meister.)*

PORZELLANSAMMLUNG. Entry across from the *Residenzschloß*. The "show-and-tell" centerpiece of Dresden, it traces Sachsen's porcelain industry through outlandishly delicate knick-knacks and makes you feel like a bull in a china shop. Unfortunately, the museum is closed for renovations and not scheduled to reopen until the summer of 2002. *(☎491 46 22. Open Su-W and F-Sa 10am-6pm. DM3, students and seniors DM2.)*

MATHEMATISCH-PHYSIKALISCHER SALON. Europe's oldest "science museum," this small room boasts a collection of historic scientific instruments—globes, clocks, atlases, etc. *(In the corner of the Zwinger courtyard closest to Postpl. ☎491 46 19; fax 491 46 16. Open Su-W and F-Sa 10am-6pm. DM3, students DM2.)*

ALBERTINUM

GEMÄLDEGALERIE DER NEUEN MEISTER. Out with the *alt*, in with the *neu!* A solid ensemble of tried-and-true German and French Impressionists, including many Renoirs and Degas', leads into a collection of Expressionists and *Neue Sachlichkeit* modernist works hard to match. Check out Otto Dix's renowned *War* triptych and other works by Germany's finest 20th-century artists (see p. 23). *(☎ 491 47 30. Open Su-W and F-Sa 10am-6pm. DM7, students and seniors DM4; includes admission to Grünes Gewölbe.)*

GRÜNES GEWÖLBE. If nothing else, the Grünes Gewölbe is proof that the House of Sachsen had a little too much money to burn. A miniature altar littered with hundreds of figures crafted in gold, silver, and porcelain is only one example of the absolute decadence; rows of priceless jewels are another. *(On the second floor of the Albertinum. Open Su-W and F-Sa 10am-6pm. Included in the admission to the Gemäldegalerie der Neuen Meister.)*

ELSEWHERE IN DRESDEN

STADTMUSEUM. Located in the 18th-century Landhaus, the museum tells the story of the city since its beginnings in the 13th century, with an entire exhibit devoted to a rather idyllic look at firefighting in the city. Early history just can't compete with the colorful collection of 20th century memorabilia, including the *Volksgasmask* (People's Gas Mask—then DM37). *(Wilsdruffer Str. 2, near Pirnaischer Pl. ☎ 49 86 60. Open May-Sept. M-Th, and Sa-Su 10am-6pm, W 10am-8pm; Oct.-Apr. daily except F 10am-6pm. DM4, students DM2.)*

VERKEHRSMUSEUM. Dresden's transport museum rolls through the history of German transportation, from carriages to bullet trains and BMWs. The silver AWF convertible is so slick it will make you cry. *(Augustusstr. 1, beside the Frauenkirche. ☎ 864 40. Open Tu-Su 10am-5pm. DM4, students and seniors DM2.)*

MUSEUM ZUR DRESDNER FRÜHROMANTIK. A small museum celebrating the German cultural accomplishments of the late 18th and early 19th centuries. A set-up of Caspar David Friedrich's studio, lots of furniture, letters, and other knickknacks following the lives of Muller, Kleist, and Wagner among others. Goethe? Of course, Goethe. *(Hauptstr. 13. ☎ 804 47 60. Open W-Su 10am-6pm. Last entry 5:30pm. DM3, students DM1.50.)*

KARL-MAY-MUSEUM. Dresden's Wild West. Karl May is a writer whose books about the 19th-century American West continue to charm generations of European children with Indians, buffaloes, and German cowboys who save the day. Includes a small exhibit devoted to the author. *(Karl-May-Str. 5. Take streetcar #4 (direction: "Weinböhle") to "Schildenstr." ☎ 837 30 10. Open Tu-Su 10am-4pm. DM8, children DM4.)*

DEUTSCHES HYGIENEMUSEUM. This ill-named museum long celebrated the health and cleanliness of GDR Germans. Now that the Party's over, the rather bizarre collection ranges from an examination of the culture surrounding hair, a fetus in a glass block, plenty of glass people with colorful innards, and an exhibit on AIDS that tries hard to shock. *(Lingnerpl. 1. ☎ 484 60. Open Tu and Th-F 9am-5pm, W 9am-8:30pm, Sa-Su 10am-5pm. DM5, students and seniors DM3.)*

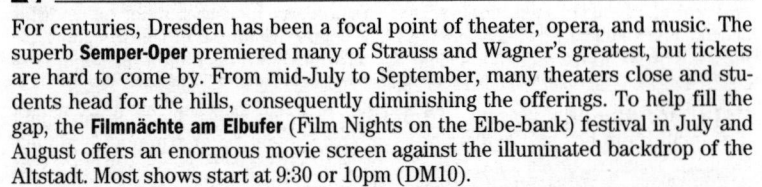 ENTERTAINMENT

For centuries, Dresden has been a focal point of theater, opera, and music. The superb **Semper-Oper** premiered many of Strauss and Wagner's greatest, but tickets are hard to come by. From mid-July to September, many theaters close and students head for the hills, consequently diminishing the offerings. To help fill the gap, the **Filmnächte am Elbufer** (Film Nights on the Elbe-bank) festival in July and August offers an enormous movie screen against the illuminated backdrop of the Altstadt. Most shows start at 9:30 or 10pm (DM10).

Sächsische Staatsoper (Semper-Oper), Theaterpl. 2 (☎491 17 30). See opera's finest in the most majestic of environs, newly restored. The box office unloads tickets for DM5-20 1hr. before performances, but you have to be lucky; otherwise, call ahead or go to the tourist office for tickets (DM12-140). Up to 50% student and senior discounts. Streetcar #4 or 8 to "Theaterpl." Box office at Schinkelwache open M-F 10am-6pm, Sa 10am-1pm, and 1hr. before performance.

Kulturpalast, Am Altmarkt (☎486 60). Home to the **Dresdner Philharmonie** (☎486 63 06) as well as other small music groups and dance ensembles. Box office at Schloßstr. 2. Main entrance open M-F 9am-6pm, Sa 10am-2pm.

Staatsoperette Dresden, Pirnaer Landstr. 131 (☎207 99 29). Musical theater from Lerner and Loewe to Sondheim. DM12-36. Discounted shows Tu and Th. Ticket office open M-F 10am-3pm. Sa 4-7pm, Su 1hr. before curtain.

Schauspielhaus, Ostraallee 47 (☎491 35 67; box office ☎491 35 55). Shows classics from Kleist to Shakespeare. Tickets DM25-40. Box office open M-F 10am-6:30pm, Sa 10am-2pm, and 1hr. before the show.

Schloßtheater, in the *Dresdener Schloß* (see p. 161; ☎491 35 55). This small ensemble performs German classics. Tickets are available through the *Schauspielhaus* (see above) and the tourist office.

projekttheater dresden, Louisenstr. 47 (☎804 30 41). Ultra hip, experimental theater with an international twist in the heart of the Neustadt. So cool they don't use capital letters. Tickets DM20, students DM15. Box office opens at 8pm, shows at 9pm.

Die Herkuleskeule, Sternpl. 1 (☎492 55 55). Cabaret with an angry political outlook revels in blasting US culture. Tickets M-Th and Su DM15-25, F-Sa DM20-30. Student discounts M-Th. Box office open M-F 1:30-6pm and 1hr. before performance.

Theater Junge Generation, Meißner Landstr. 4 (☎429 12 20). Shakespeare, opera, fairy tales, and more. Tickets DM12-18, 15-50% student discount. Tickets available M-Sa 10am-noon, extra hours W 2-6pm, F 2-7:30pm, and 1hr. before curtain.

Puppentheater der Stadt Dresden, in the Ufa-Palast on Prager Str. (☎496 53 70; fax 496 53 71). Children's performances during the day for young and old. DM6, children DM4, family ticket (up to five people) DM18. Occasional evening performance geared more toward adults DM12, students DM10. Box office open 30min. before shows on weekdays, 45min. before shows on weekends.

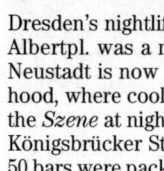 **NIGHTLIFE**

Dresden's nightlife scene is young and dynamic. Ten years ago, the area north of Albertpl. was a maze of gray streets lined with tired, crumbling buildings, but Neustadt is now the thudding heart of this fast-paced city. This lively neighborhood, where cool kids of every flavor come to shop during the day and partake in the *Szene* at night, comprises almost a full square kilometer, roughly bounded by Königsbrücker Str., Bischofsweg, Kamenzerstr., and Albertpl. At last count, over 50 bars were packed into this area; *Kneipen Surfer* provides a list and description of every one. Peruse the back of *SAX* (DM2.50 at the tourist office, or ask to see one at any bar) to see which concerts and dances are coming up. *Dresdner* is another free monthly available in many pubs with night-entertainment listings. Dresden is also a city that lives on posters, especially for the punkier shows.

Scheune, Alaunstr. 36-40 (☎804 55 32). From Albertpl., walk up Königsbrücker Str. and turn right onto Katharinenstr. Take a left on Alaunstr.; the club is on the other side of the street. The granddaddy of the Neustadt bar scene, in a former youth center. A culturally eclectic performance space with small-scale theater productions and obscure world music, in the same building as a popular cafe-bar. Check *SAX* for what's happening. Frequent concerts. Club opens at 8pm. Bar open M-F 11am-2am, Sa-Su 10am-2am. Cover varies.

DownTown, Katharinenstr. 11-13 (☎802 88 01), below the **Mondpalast** hostel (see Accommodations, p. 159). This place keeps the beat going, fast and furious, as Dresden's young and energetic scene grooves to the techno sounds. In the upstairs **Groove Station** (see **Laundromat,** p. 158), patrons numb themselves with drinks before getting tattooed and/or pierced or playing a game of pool just to chill out. F house and techno, Sa funk and occasional live music. Open 10pm-5am. Cover DM7, students DM5.

Mona Lisa (☎803 3151, Louisenstr., corner of Kamenzerstr). Streetcar #7 or 8 to "Louisenstr." Located in the heart of the Neustadt bar scene, Mona Lisa chills to techno beats every night of the week with live DJs. An atmosphere this chill is the perfect place to get a groove on without keeling over at the end. Happy hour 7pm-9pm, "Blue Hour" 11:30pm-1:30am. Open daily from 7pm.

AZ Conni, Rudolf-Leonhard-Str. 39 (☎804 58 58). From Albertpl., follow Königsbrücker Str. until the second set of traffic lights. Turn left, walk under the first railway bridge, and take a quick right. The club is up at top of the hill after the garden on the left. The first floor is a noisy bar, and the second is a dance floor or stage, depending on the night. Tu and Th are dance nights, but AZ is really know for its weekend concerts—one of the main venues for punk and hardcore in Dresden. Open daily 9pm until late. Cover varies.

Studentenklub Bärenzwinger, Brühlischer Garten 1 (☎495 14 09), not far from the Albertinum. Head toward the Carolabrücke, but make a sharp left down a little hill just before reaching the streetcar stop. A mainly student crowd gathers in this subterranean lair for what are quite possibly the cheapest drinks in Dresden, and a little disco action on the side. Sip a Caiprini for DM3, or take shots at a mere DM2.50. Over 18 only. Bring student ID for discounts. Tu, F, and Sa are usually dance. Open Tu-Th and Su 8pm-1am, F-Sa 9pm-3am for live shows and dancing. Cover DM8-12.

Queens, Görlitzer Str. 3 (☎803 16 50). A popular gay bar with plenty of sparkle to go around. Drinks, music, and occasional special entertainment. F 70s/80s night. Open daily after 8pm.

🄳 DAYTRIP FROM DRESDEN: MORITZBURG

Never one to be bashful about leaving his mark on the Saxon landscape, August the Strong tore down a little palace in 1723 and replaced it with 🄳**Schloß Moritzburg,** his titanic hunting lodge of ribaldry. The immense Schloß lounges arrogantly at the end of Schloßallee on an island in an artificial lake. Inside, lavish rooms and leering deer skulls commemorate the courtly hunting penchant, while the ornately embossed and painted leather wallpaper sets the standard for masculine, animal-killing prowess. A must-see is a portrait of one of Moritzburg's most "beautiful" oxen ever. To get to the Schloß from the **Schmalspurbahn** train station, join the pilgrimage out to the left and turn right on Schloßallee. (☎(035207) 873 18. Open Apr.-Oct. daily 9am-5pm; Nov.-Dec. and Feb.-Mar. Tu-Su 10am-5pm; Jan. open only Sa-Su 10am-5pm. DM7, students DM5.) Near the Schloß, the smaller **Fasanenschlößchen** was built by the great-grandson of August the Strong, Friedrich August III. Outside, sculptures of moose in tremendous pain remind you that this, too, is a hunting lodge. Unfortunately, the Fasanenschlößchen is closed indefinitely for repairs; ask the tourist office for information. From Schloß Moritzburg, follow Meißner Str. right until Große Fasanenstr.; the Fasanenschlößchen appears on the left. Farther down Große Fasanenstr., the structure peeking out of the forest is the **Leuchtturm** (lighthouse), which once served as a backdrop to the mock sea battles of the not-so-easily-amused princes. Moritzburg is also surrounded by extensive parks, a huge gaming reserve, and the **Sächsisches Langestüt** (Saxon Stud-Farm), where animals procreate as frequently as did August the Strong.

As the meeting place of *Brücke* artists from 1909 to 1911 (see p. 23), Moritzburg developed a rich art tradition. It continued to serve as a summer residence for many artists who came back to frolic in the waters. One of Germany's most-celebrated 20th-century artists, **Käthe Kollwitz** (see p. 23), resided in the region for a time: after Kollwitz's home in Berlin was bombed near the end of WWII, Prince Ernst Heinrich offered her a place of retreat here. Though Kollwitz passed away in 1945, only one year after her arrival, her house now holds the **Käthe-Kollwitz-Gedenkstätte,** Meißner Str. 7. The museum showcases her sculptures, woodcuts, and drawings, starkly and beautifully depicting the cruelty of war and poverty. Pictures and excerpts from letters and diaries help fill in the gaps about the artist. *(☎ (035207) 828 18. Open Apr.-Oct. Tu-Su 11am-5pm. DM3.50, students DM2.)*

The fastest way to Moritzburg from **Dresden** is by bus #326 (direction: "Radeburg") from Bahnhof-Neustadt to "Moritzburg, Schloß" (25min., DM5.20). The return trip runs from "Moritzburg, Markt" on Marktstr., parallel to Schloßallee. The most scenic route (but also the slowest, bumpiest, and noisiest) is the 110-year-old **Schmalspurbahn** (narrow-gauge railway) which leaves from Radebeul-Ost, accessible by S-Bahn to Meißen. (30min., 4 stops. S-Bahn and train DM7.40, students DM5.) Moritzburg's **tourist office,** Schloßallee 3b, provides information on guided tours of the Schloßpark, concerts in the Schloß, horse-and-carriage rentals, and books rooms (DM30-40 per person) for a DM2 fee. (☎ (035207) 854 10; fax 854 20. Open May-Oct. M-F 10am-5pm, Sa-Su noon-4pm; Nov.-Apr. M-F 10am-5pm.) Eating in Moritzburg cries out for one thing: a picnic. The classical gardens behind the castle provide the perfect backdrop, and they never close. If you forget your basket, try **Edeka,** Schloßallee 13 (open M-F 8am-6pm, Sa 8-11am), or **Zum Dreispitz,** Schloßallee 5, which offers *Sächsische* meat and mushroom dishes for DM10-20 (☎ (035207) 822 00; open daily 11am-midnight).

■ DAYTRIP FROM DRESDEN: PILLNITZ

August the Strong must have led a happy life. Among his many castles (almost as numerous as his mistresses), the magnificent gardens of **Schloß Pillnitz** (☎ 261 32 60) produce a singularly fantastic effect. The strongman inherited the nearly 300-year-old castle in 1694 and generously passed it on to Countess Cosel a few years later—who says *diamonds* are a girl's best friend? The Countess lived there from 1713 to 1715 until August decided to imprison her in the more poorly furnished Burg Stolpen and began the extensive remodeling that gave the complex its characteristic look. The turrets of the **Bergpalais** and **Wasserpalais** (modeled on Chinese architectural forms) swim in an amazing setting, surrounded on one side by the Elbe, and on the other by gardens in English, Chinese, and just plain decadent styles. The residences now house Dresden's **Kunstgewerbemuseum** (arts and crafts museum), some modern art displays, and lots of porcelain amidst the sumptuously sensual and suggestively salacious summer-like colors of the courtly rooms. Outside, brilliantly colored flowers heighten the mystical effect of the architecture. Concerts also take place in the garden during the summer; call for info. *(Museum open May-Oct. 9:30am-5:30pm. Bergpalais and Kunstgewerbemuseum closed M, Wasserpalais closed Tu. DM3, students and seniors DM2. Grounds open daily May-Oct. 10am-6pm, Nov.-Apr. 10am-4pm.)* To reach Pillnitz from **Dresden,** take streetcar #1 (direction: "Tolkewitz") or #6 (direction: "Niedersedlitz") to "Schillerpl.," then jump on bus #85 and continue to Pillnitz. Alternatively, **Weiße Flotte** can get you there by **boat.** (2hr. DM22, children DM15.) Head straight through the main garden to the "Alte Wache" **tourist office** for maps, information, and tours (open daily 10am-6pm).

MEIßEN   ☎ 03521
Just 30km from Dresden, Meißen sits on the banks of the Elbe as yet another testament to the frivolity of August the Strong. In 1710, the Saxon elector developed a severe case of *Porzellankrankheit* (the porcelain "bug") and turned the city's defunct castle into a porcelain-manufacturing base. Those visitors who would otherwise feel little affinity for the craft indulge in a couple of glasses of Meißen's fine wines and soon find themselves toasting the beauty of "white gold" (china, not cocaine). Meißen has a distinct aesthetic advantage over its comrade Dresden; its medieval nooks and crannies were barely scathed by WWII.

■ PRACTICAL INFORMATION. Meißen is an easily reached from **Dresden** by **train** (45min., DM7.70) or **scenic cruise** (round-trip DM25). The **tourist office,** Markt 3, is across the Markt from the church. Pick up maps or find a private room (DM25-55) for DM4. (☎ 419 40; fax 45 82 40. Open Apr.-Oct. M-F 10am-6:30pm, Sa-Su 10am-3pm; Nov.-Mar. M-F 10am-6pm, Sa 10am-3pm.) The **postal code** is 01662.

▓▓ ACCOMMODATIONS AND FOOD. The **Jugendherberge,** Wilsdrufferstr. 28, is a crap shoot—its 45 beds are often booked. Should they have space, they'll put you up in a crowded five-bed room. From the station, cross the Elbe footbridge and take Obergasse to the end where it meets Plosenweg. Turn left and continue uphill until you see the small **Edeka Markt;** the hostel is across the street. An infrequent bus (line C/C; direction: "Dr.-Donner-Str.") runs from the train station up the steep hill. (☎ 45 73 01. Breakfast included. Sheets DM5. Reception M-F 7am-noon and 4-8pm, Sa-Su 4-8pm. DM18.) A puffed, almost hollow pastry, the *Meißener Fummel,* owes its origin to August the Strong. One of his couriers was a spirited sort whose penchant for Meißen wine became known to the king. To keep tabs on his bacchanalian behavior, August ordered the Meißen bakers' guild to create an extremely fragile biscuit. The courier was to protect the *Fummel* from damage while delivering messages. That's how the story goes, anyway. Many Altstadt bakeries still sell this puffery. For less fluff, try *Zum Kellermeister,* Neugasse 10. Most Schnitzels run DM6-12. (☎ 45 40 88. Open M-F 11am-9pm.) The farmer's market is on the Markt (open Tu-F 8am-5pm). During the last weekend of September, Meißen frolics in merriment during its annual wine festival.

▓ SIGHTS. The narrow, romantic alleyways of the Altstadt climb up to the **Albrechtsburg,** a castle and cathedral overlooking the city. From the train station, walk straight onto Bahnhofstr. and follow the banks of the Elbe to the Elbbrücke. Cross the bridge, continue straight to the Markt and turn right onto Burgstr. At the end of Burgstr., on Schloßstr., you'll find the stairs that lead to the right up to Albrechtsburg. If the bridge is closed, use the railway bridge and walk along the river towards the Elbbrücke. Follow Elbstr., continue straight to the Markt, and follow the original directions from here on. Alternatively, board a bus at the Markt to save yourself the walk up the hill. The castle foundations were first built in 929 to protect the area's Sorb population (see **The Absorbing Sorbs,** p. 175). The interior was lavishly redecorated in the 15th century, and once again when porcelain profits started pouring in. The fantastically decorated rooms also house an extensive medieval sculpture collection. (☎ 47 07 10. Open Mar.-Oct. daily 10am-6pm; Nov.-Feb. 10am-5pm. Last entry 30min. before closing. DM6, students DM4.) Next door dwells the **Meißener Dom,** an early Gothic cathedral which ensures that its visitors get their money's worth with four priceless 13th-century statues by the Naumburg Master, a triptych by Cranach the Elder, and the metal grave coverings of the Wettins. (Open Apr.-Oct. daily 9am-6pm; Nov.-Mar. 10am-4pm. Last entry 30min. before closing. DM3.50, students DM2.50. Organ concerts May-Oct. daily at noon. DM4.)

Meißen's porcelain factory was once more tightly guarded than KGB headquarters for fear that competitors would discover its secret techniques. Across eastern Germany, museums still exhibit this precious product today. Porcelain was first discovered here in 1707, and today anyone can tour the **Staatliche Porzellan-Manufaktur** at Talstr. 9. The **Schauhalle** serves as a museum where visitors can peruse finished products (DM9, students DM7), but the real fun lies in the high-tech tour of the **Schauwerkstatt** (show workshop), which shows people working on different steps of the porcelain-manufacturing process. (☎ 46 82 07. Open daily 9am-6pm. DM5. English tapes available.) Meißen's Gothic **Rathaus** stands alongside the **Frauenkirche,** whose porcelain bells chatter every 15 minutes over the main market square. (Church open May-Oct. daily 10am-noon and 1-4pm.)

SÄCHSISCHE SCHWEIZ (SAXON SWITZERLAND)

The rest of Germany discovered the Sächsische Schweiz long ago, and it has since become one of the most popular national vacation destinations. In the summer, towns like Bad Schandau are full of strolling elderly couples or families with children, while the many hiking trails are never empty of Germans of all ages huffing

SAXONY

and puffing their way to another beautiful vantage point. However, apart from the occasional British biker, few other nations seem to have realized the convenience and richness of this veritably idyllic area. The region is "Swiss" because of the stunning landscape—striking sandstone cliffs emerge from dense vegetation, and the unique landforms allow each hike or summit to have its own particular character. The national park is divided into two regions, the *vorderer Teil* and the *hinterer Teil;* both are easily accessible from the south with Dresden's S-Bahn #1, which runs from inside Dresden's *Hauptbahnhof* all along the Elbe River. A regular ferry service, the **Sächsische Dampfschiffart,** also connects the towns along this section of the Elbe. The *Wanderwege* (footpaths) coil up the hills into the heart of the park, connecting all towns in the area in a spidery web. Visitors can obtain further information from the **Tourismusverband Sächsische Schweiz,** Am Bahnhof 6, 01814 Bad Schandau (☎/fax (035022) 49 50), or from the **Nationalpark-Verwaltung,** An der Elbe 4, 01814 Bad Schandau (☎ (035022) 900 60; fax 900 66). If you plan to explore more than one town in the region in a day, be sure to ask at a **Deutsche Bahn** information desk about the **Tageskarte** (DM8) and **Familientageskarte** (DM12), or buy one from any *Fahrausweis* machine. These day-passes allow unlimited travel on the S-Bahn, buses, and many of the ferries in the Sächsische Schweiz for a 24-hour period.

RATHEN AND WEHLEN ☎035024

Upstream from Dresden, just around the first bend in the Elbe, the magnificent sandstone begins. The first cliffs are called *Die Bastei* and were once the roaming grounds of—you guessed it—August the Strong, King of Poland and Elector of Saxony. Closest to Dresden lies **Wehlen,** and on the other end of the Bastei you'll find **Rathen.** To get to Wehlen, hop on S-Bahn #1; from the Bahnhof, take the ferry (DM1.30, children DM0.90). A tourist office in the Rathaus on the market finds rooms for free, and a list of accommodations is posted outside. (☎704 14, DM20-25. Open M-F 9am-6pm, Sa 9am-2pm.) Wehlen's best assets are its trails to Rathen. One of the paths climbs up onto the Bastei and was a favorite of August the Strong; look for the *Höllengrund an Steinern Tisch,* his mammoth dining table. The other path—shorter, easier, but much less impressive—is along the Elbe (45min.).

The Dresden S-Bahn stops in Rathen as well as Wehlen, but the hike to Rathen through the Bastei is a far more beautiful mode of transportation. Either way you choose to go, because of its location on the edge of the **Sächsische Schweiz National Park,** Rathen makes a good starting point for hikes of any length. Rathen also boasts the **Felsenbühne,** one of the most beautiful open-air theaters in Europe, with 2000 seats carved into a cliff and stone pillars looming over the stage. (Open 8am until 2hr. before rehearsal/event and 1hr. after rehearsal/event until 8pm.) To get there, walk into town from the ferry landing and take the first left; follow signs for "Felsenbühne." Tickets and schedules are available from the **Theaterkasse,** on the way to the theater. (☎77 70; fax 77 735. DM6-39.) A **tourist office,** upstairs in the *Gästeamt,* gives advice on hiking and finds rooms (DM25-35) for free. (☎/fax 704 22. Open M-F 9am-noon and 2-6pm, Sa 9am-2pm, closed Saturdays in winter.)

There are several options for accommodations. The most comfortable is the pricey **Gästehaus Burg Altrathen,** up the ramp near the ferry landing, in a castle perched above the Elbe. (☎700 37; fax 700 38. Singles DM40-45, doubles DM70-90, both with private shower.) For thriftier patrons, a **Bergsteigerzimmer** ("mountain climber's room") has a mattress for DM25. Alternatively, you can get the tourist office to find a private room, retreat across the river on a ferry to the S-Bahn station, or continue on two hours to **Hohnstein.**

HOHNSTEIN ☎035975

The small village of Hohnstein ("high stone" in old Saxon) sits atop a high, stony ridge, with grand forest vistas on all sides, and is linked to Rathen by two beautiful hikes through one of the national park's most stunning valleys. To get here from Rathen, follow the shorter (2hr.), more challenging path of the red stripe (the trail, not a Maoist paramilitary initiation), or the longer (3hr.) path of the green stripe.

SAXONY

On your way, be sure to stop at the **Hockstein,** an isolated outcropping providing a spectacular view of the valley below and of Hohnstein and its yellow church across the way. Heading left after coming down from the Hockstein will take you through the **Wolfsslucht,** a steep narrow passage between huge rocks. Watch your head at the bottom. Afterwards, you'll come to the valley of the Gauschgrotte, filled with beautiful green moss and rock formations. The **Museum der Geschichte des Burg Hohnstein,** housed in the **Naturfreundehaus** (see below), covers the history of the *Burg* with exhibits ranging from medieval armor and weapons to anti-fascist resistance in Dresden and the Sächsische Schweiz. The museum commemorates Konrad Hahnewald, the beloved father of Hohnstein's *Jugendherberge* (now the Naturfreundehaus) and later the first political refugee of the Hohnstein concentration camp. (☎ 809 87 or 812 02. Open daily Apr.-Oct. 9am-5pm. DM2, ages 6-16 DM1, under 6 and patrons of the Naturfreundehaus free.)

As an alternative to hiking, you can reach Hohnstein by taking the S-Bahn to "Pirna," and then bus #236 or 237 from the Bahnhof to Hohnstein "Eiche" or "Markt" (DM5.20). The tourist office, Rathausstr. 10, in the Rathaus, doles out information on the Burg and surrounding trails and finds rooms for free. (☎ 194 33; fax 868 10. Open M and W-F 9am-noon and 12:30-5pm, Tu 9am-noon and 12:30-6pm.) The town encircles the **Naturfreundehaus Burg Hohnstein,** Am Markt 1, a hostel in a fortress that includes a history and nature museum, lookout tower, cafe-restaurant, garden, and hostel. The hostel offers singles, quads, and titanic 6- to 18-bed rooms for the same price per person. (☎ 812 02; fax 812 03. Breakfast and sheets included. Reception open daily 7am-8pm. DM26-29, non-HI members DM33-37. DM1.20 tax per day. DM2 fee for stays under 3 days.)

🚶 DAYHIKE IN THE SACHSICHE SCHWEIZ
Estimated time: 7hrs.

Beginning from the Dresden S-Bahn stop in Wehlen, a solid day-hike from Wehlen to Rathen, and then up to Hohnstein and back, can be made in about 7 hours. On the way, you'll catch some of the highlights of this region of the national park, including **Die Bastei, Hockstein,** and the **Wolfsslucht.** For safety precautions to observe while hiking, and the necessary equipment, see p. 57.

Part 1: to the Bastei (1hr.). After you get off the S-Bahn in Wehlen, cross the Elbe by ferry, and look for the trail signs to Rathen. Two options exist; taking the longer trail marked **Wehlenerweg** starts you in a lush green valley on an easy, wide concrete path. When you reach the second bridge, turn right toward "Steinerner Tisch;" on your way to the **Bastei,** you'll pass this flat, table-like stone formation. The rest of the trip to the Bastei is mildly hilly and somewhat steep. You'll know you've arrived by the masses of people milling about at the hotel and restaurant placed just next to the cliffs. Stop for a bathroom break or just gawk at the extent of German commercialism, but once you're ready to move on take the stairs down next to the "Kaffeegarten" and head along the paths toward "Basteibrucke." Here you see the Bastei in all its splendor, with its startling outcroppings and several outlook points, the carefully built bridge among them, and the dizzying views of the valleys between the sand-stone monsters.

Part 2: the Felsenbühne (¾hr.). Once you've spent enough time marveling at the rock formations here, head on through and down the stairs at the other end. At the bottom, follow signs for the **Felsenbühne.** Follow the path past the box-office uphill until it takes you to the theatre. Sit in the audience and look at the cliffs that loom precariously above the stage before heading back out toward the main trails.

Part 3: to the Hockstein (1½hr.). Now the hike gets more serious. Following signs for "Hohnstein," you'll pass a dammed-off section of the river at which you can rent boats (DM5-8 for 30 min). After the boating area ends, hang a right toward **Hockstein.** The wide trail crosses a road, then passes a parking area, and then narrows. When you're close to the Hockstein, continue straight where the trail seems to go left and pass the first Hockstein "Lehrpfad." Cross the bridge and check out the vantage points. You can see the cheerful yellow Rathaus of Hohnstein across the way, and the gaping valley between.

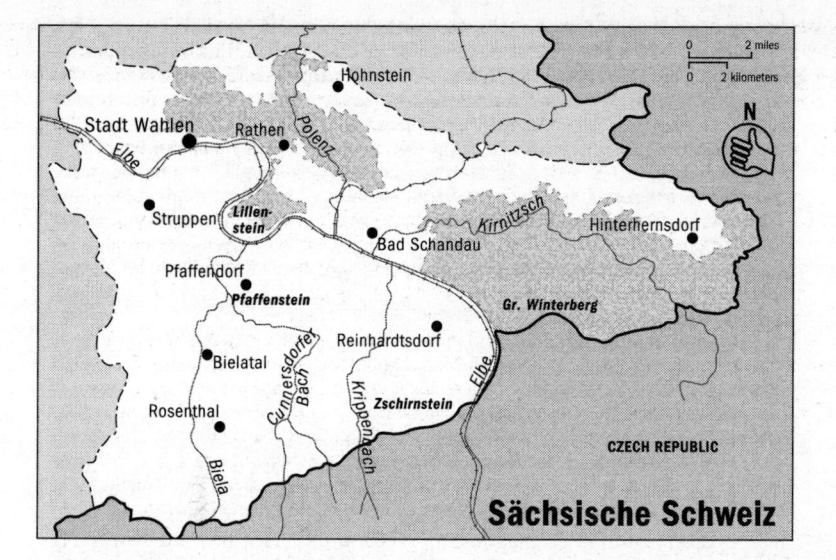

Sächsische Schweiz

Part 4: to **Wolfsslucht** (¼hr.) and **Hohnstein** (1hr.). On your way down, follow signs for the **Wolfsslucht.** When you reach it, watch your step. This narrow passage between two cold, hard rock overhangs is accessed by steep metal stairs; duck your head under the last overhang, and you've made it out. Turn left after you're through, look down at the cows grazing below you. This path will lead down to a road; be sure to turn right and follow the road until you reach a bridge; cross it (or wade if you prefer) and head up through the grottoes. These beautiful green areas are also some of the steepest parts of your climb. At the top of the steep rocky path, turn left toward **Hohnstein.**

Hohnstein is a lovely little town; if you've gotten a late start, divide up your hike and stay a night in its fortress-hostel. If not, check out the fortress' museum or stop at the cave-like Ratskeller for a drink. When you're ready to head back down to the Elbe, follow the trail back out, passing straight on by the end of the trail you came up through the grottoes. Follow signs back to Rathen, and soon you'll be back to the S-Bahn.

KÖNIGSTEIN   ☎ 035021

The next stop on the Dresden S-Bahn journey into the hills and dales of the Sächsische Schweiz is Königstein. Above the town looms the impressive fortress **Festung Königstein,** whose huge walls are built right into the same stone spires that made the Sächsische Schweiz famous. Replete with drawbridges and impenetrable stone walls, this castle belongs on the list of legendary royal abodes. An oft-exploited retreat for the kings of Sachsen, it was later converted into a feared state prison; **August Bebel** (see p. 10) was imprisoned here. During the Third Reich, it was used by the Nazis to stash stolen art. Between 1949 and 1955 it served as a juvenile correction center, and now the complex houses a variety of museums. From the city, it's a 40-minute struggle straight up from town, but the view is worth sweating for; follow the signs to the well-worn uphill path. (English pamphlets at the information office within the castle. Open daily Apr.-Sept. 9am-8pm; Oct. 9am-6pm; Nov.-Mar. 9am-5pm. DM7, students and seniors DM5.) The cheesy **Festungs Express** tours Königstein as it drags up tourists too tired to make the trek. Rides leave from Reißigerplatz, just to the right down Bahnhofstr. from the S-Bahn station. (Runs Apr.-Oct. 9am-6pm, every half hour. One-way DM4, children DM2; round-trip DM6, children DM3. Tickets available on board.) Paths also lead from

SAXONY

the town up to the challenging 415m **Lilienstein,** hiked by August the Strong in 1708. To get there, take the **ferry** (DM1.30) and the first right after getting off. Stay on this paved road until you see a sign for "Lilienstein" marked with a blue stripe. The steep 2km hike takes 1½ hours and gives striking views of the fortress opposite as well as a panorama of the fields and towns along the Elbe from Wehlen to Bad Schandau. The risk-takers of the world can be seen scaling the sheer rock-face, while the rest of us stick to the clearly marked steps and paths. The **tourist office,** Schreiberberg 2, two blocks uphill from the Festungs Express stop, books rooms (DM25-45), but in summer it's wise to call ahead. In addition to housing a post office, 01824 Königstein, the office has a list of available rooms, vacation houses, and *Pensionen;* prices are listed on a bulletin board outside when they're closed. (☎682 61; fax 688 87. Open Apr.-Oct. M-F 9am-noon and 2-6pm, Sa 9am-noon; Nov.-Mar. M-F 9am-noon and 3-5pm, Sa 9-10:30am.)

Königstein's Naturfreundehaus, Halbestadt 13, is an ideal place for families or groups to stay, but not necessarily for lone travelers; a surcharge of DM10 is added for single rooms. The rooms are clean and comfortable, the dining area is inviting, and out back an enormous chess board beckons you to play. To get there, take the ferry across the river and turn right. The hostel will appear on your right after about 10 minutes. (Breakfast included. Reception daily 6am-10pm. ☎9 94 80; fax 4 34 71. Price ranges from DM40.60 per person with just breakfast to DM70 with all meals and a single room.) The **campground** is on the banks of the Elbe about 10 minutes upstream from the station in the shadow of the fortress. It has washing facilities, a small supply shop, and a playground. (☎682 24. DM7.30 per person, DM6 per tent.) Fresh fruits and vegetables are sold at an open market on Tuesdays and Thursdays in the town's streets. Eat heartily among antlers and paintings of the Elbe at **Schräger's Gasthaus,** on Kirchgasse straight up Hainstr. from Reißigerplatz. (DM8-10. Vegetarian meals can be arranged.) If your thirst overcomes you after a day of hard hiking, check out **Bogart's,** just down the street from Reißigerplatz on Beilatalstr. Locals and vacationers alike meet here to watch *Fußball* and enjoy a beer in a tiny bar decorated with pictures of Humphrey Bogart and posters of Casablanca. The bartender (who, one could argue, looks a bit like Bogey himself) will also make any mixed drink you could ask for, including an *Erdbeer Daquiri* (DM8) from fresh strawberries, blended while you watch.

BAD SCHANDAU ☎034022

The biggest town in the Sächsische Schweiz, Bad Schandau takes advantage of its location between the two halves of the national park by offering plenty of hiking opportunities. Take the solar-powered *Kirnitzschtalbahn* train to the unimpressive **Lichtenhain waterfall,** a favorite starting point for three- and four-hour hikes on the **Schrammsteine.** (May-Oct. every 30min. DM6, DM8 round-trip.) Bad Schandau is also amply connected to the rest of Sachsen; the S-Bahn runs to **Dresden** (50min., every 30min., DM7.70), and trains go to **Bautzen** (2hr., every 2hr., DM16.20) and **Prague** (2hr., DM30.60). From the Bad Schandau train station, take the **ferry** (7:30am-9:30pm, every ½hr., DM1.30) and walk uphill to the Markt where you'll find the **tourist office,** Markt 12. The staff finds rooms (DM25-30), suggests hikes, and offers city tours and trips to the Czech Republic. (☎900 30. Open M-F 9am-6:30pm, Sa 9am-4pm.) To rent a bike, try **Rund Um's Fahrradverleih,** Poststr. 14. (☎428 83. Open M-F 9am-noon and 2-6pm, Sa 9am-noon. DM15 per day with ID.)

Bad Schandau is more of a family vacation spot than any other town in the area, and for this reason its hotels fill up quickly when the weather is good. The **Jugendherberge Bad Schandau (HI),** Dorfstr. 14, is a 30-minute walk along the Elbe down Rudolf-Sendig-Str. and then to the left up into the mountains along the difficult Wolfsgraben path. It is far from the center of town, the S-Bahn, and Dresden, but convenient to several trailheads and a good starting point for day-hikes. (☎424 8. DM24, HI members only.) The **Edeka supermarket** a few doors down at Dorfpl. 10 can provide you with food to last you through a day outdoors. In a town that closes down before 11pm, **Sigl's,** Kirnitzschtalstr. 17 (☎407 02), a bar-bistro, offers food and a wide selection of beers until 2am. The joint doubles as a hotel and is slightly cheaper than the hotels overlooking the river near the ferry dock. If you're interested in one of those, try **Hotel Elbterasse,** Markt 11 (☎ 485 60, fax 485 65).

OBERLAUSITZ (UPPER LUSATIA)

Forming Germany's border with two former Warsaw Pact neighbors, Oberlausitz works hard to overcome the negative image brought upon it by many years of economic stagnation prior to reunification. During GDR times, the Politburo *apparatchiks* let much of the region's magnificent medieval, Renaissance, and Baroque architecture decay, but as in much of Eastern Germany, Oberlausitz is currently undergoing extensive restoration in pursuit of its former shine. The area around Bautzen exemplifies the ongoing transformation of the region into an exciting destination for travelers.

BAUTZEN (BUDYŠIN)   ☎03591

Bautz'ner *Senf* (mustard): sausage in Germany just wouldn't be the same without it. But various mustard-covered offerings aren't the only reason to travel to Bautzen: with ancient towers on a hill high above the Spree River, a large population of Germany's sole national minority, the Sorbs, and a collection of crumbling Medieval, Baroque, and Art Nouveau architecture, Bautzen has proven itself a stalwart, millennium-old cultural capital. Despite the bilingual street signs, Bautzen's character is very German, and there's no shortage of *Wurst* to go with your *Senf.*

◪ PRACTICAL INFORMATION

Bautzen is a one-hour **train** ride from **Dresden** (1 per hr., DM14.80). The **tourist office,** Hauptmarkt 1, offers listings of accommodations and books **rooms** in hotels, *Pensionen,* and private homes (DM19-30). The staff also offers **city tours.** From the train station, walk straight through Rathenauplatz and bear left onto Bahnhofstr. Keep left on Postplatz and walk onto Karl-Marx-Str. Follow it straight, and Bahnhofstr. becomes Postplatz; keeping the **Post Office** on your right, cross through the Platz bearing slightly left onto Karl-Marx-Str. Walk until you see the Holiday Inn; before reaching it, cross the street near the artsy fountain. Up ahead is a tall white tower marking the beginning of Reichenstr. Follow Reichenstr. to the Hauptmarkt, the center of Bautzen's Altstadt. The tourist office is located to the right of the Rathaus, the big yellow building towering over the Markt. (☎ 420 16; fax 53 43 09. Open Apr.-Oct. M-F 10am-6pm, Sa-Su 10am-3pm; Nov.-Mar. M-F 10am-5pm, Sa-Su 10am-3pm. Tours W at 2pm, Sa and Su at 11am.)

◪◪ ACCOMMODATIONS AND FOOD

At the ancient defense-tower-turned-**Jugendherberge (HI),** Am Zwinger 1 (☎ 403 47), experience real Saxon hospitality (and great *Sächsische* accents) while sleeping in 2-, 3-, 4-, or 5-bed rooms. From the Hauptmarkt, go up Kornstr., and stick with it as it jogs right and turns into Schulerstr.; take a left after you go through the Schülertor, and the hostel will be on your right. (Breakfast included. Reception M-F 7am-8pm, Sa-Su 6-8pm. No lockout. Curfew 10pm, but you'll get a key. Reservations recommended. DM19, over 26 DM24.) If you don't dig the hostel scene, reserve a room at **Pension Stephan's,** Schloßstr. 1. From the Hauptmarkt, head uphill with the Rathaus on your right, past Dom St. Petri, and turn left. You'll see Stephan's in a light green building a block ahead on the left. This family-run *Pension* is centrally located and features immaculate rooms with private bath, telephones, and TV. (☎ 475 90; fax 475 91. Singles DM70, doubles DM110. Breakfast included, served until 10am. Doors lock at 10pm, but your room key works on the side entrance. Call ahead.) To find out more about Sorb culture, visit the **Sorbische Kulturinformation** office, Postpl. 2. The staff has information on cultural events and **homestays** with the local Sorb population. (☎ 421 05; fax 428 11. Open M-F 10am-6pm.) For a **taxi** call ☎ 422 22 or visit the taxi hut outside the Bahnhof (a cab ride from the Bahnhof to the Hauptmarkt costs DM6). The **AVIS** office at the train station rents cars. A self-service **laundromat** sits in a pink building on the corner of Lauenstr., just a few blocks downhill from the Hauptmarkt. The **post office,** 02625 Bautzen, is located on Postplatz (open M-F 8am-6pm, Sa 9am-noon).

The Hauptmarkt hosts a **market** three times a week (Tu, Th 8am-1pm, Sa 7-11am). ▓**Wjelbik,** Kornstr. 7 (☎420 60), serves tasty Sorbian specialities in a dimly lit, inviting interior complete with candles and real roses on every table. Try the *Sorbische Stulle,* a traditional pork sandwich (DM14), or relish a hefty veggie dish (DM16-17). *Sorbische Hochzeitsuppe* (wedding soup) is a mere DM 6. (☎420 60. DM16-17. Open daily 11am-3pm, 5-11pm.) If you think forks and knives are overrated, and all you like about monks, devils, and candles, try **Mönchshof,** Burglehn 1. Medieval cuisine (DM7-25) and a great atmosphere make the restaurant worth a visit. (☎49 01 41. Open M-Sa 11:30am-1am, Su 11:30am-11pm. Reservations recommended.) To experience the German approach to natural healing, visit **Zur Apotheke,** Schloßstr. 21. The restaurant prepares a wide range of meals rich in herbs (DM12-20), which, unlike most medicines, are very tasty. (☎48 00 35. Open daily from 11:30am-late.) With a decor heavy on gangsta motifs, **Al Capone's,** Schülerstr. 4, bangs out pizzas (DM9-12) and pastas. (DM9-14). (☎49 10 10. Open M 5pm-midnight, Tu-Su 11:30am-2pm and 5pm-midnight.)

◉ SIGHTS

REICHENTURM. The **Reichenturm** is the leaning tower of Bautzen. It was built in 1490, with a Baroque top added in 1715. It deviates exactly 1.44m from the perpendicular, and the view is marvelous. *(Up Kornmarktstr. on Reichenstr. Open daily Apr.-Oct. 10am-5pm. Last entrance at 4:30pm. DM2, students DM1.50, under 12 years DM1. Tours DM10.)* A block away, at the intersection of Wendischer Graben and Wendische Str., you'll find the **Wendischer Turm,** the tower attached to the **Alte Kaserne** (old barracks), an elegant building designed by Dresden master Gottfried Semper to accommodate unappreciative 19th-century troops, now serving as an office space.

HAUPTMARKT. This square contains the grand and yellow 13th-century **Rathaus,** with the **Fleischmarkt** behind it alongside the Gothic **Dom St. Petri.** *(Left from the Reichenturm and down Reichenstr. Open June-Sept. M-Sa 10am-4pm, Su 10am-1pm; May and Oct. M-Sa 10am-3pm, Su 10am-1pm; Nov.-Apr. M-F 11am-noon.)* First consecrated in 1221, the Dom has been Eastern Germany's only *Simultankirche* (simultaneously Catholic and Protestant church) since 1524. The division of the church, made official in a 1583 contract, was forcefully obvious due to the presence of a 4m-high fence in the middle that remained there until 1952.

DOMSTIFT. This ornate red-and-gold structure houses the Domschatz (cathedral treasury), a phenomenal collection of jewel-studded gowns, icons, and gold regalia. Ring the bell and ask to see the *Domschatzkammer.* *(Behind the cathedral. Open M-F 10am-noon and 1-4pm. Free.)*

NIKOLAITURM. Crossing under the gate of this tower, check out the face carved above the entrance. Locals claim that this is a likeness of a former mayor, who was bricked alive into the tower as retribution for opening the city to Hussite attackers in the 16th century. *(Follow An der Petrikirche downhill from the cathedral, on your right.)* Just through the gate and to the left is the **St. Nikolai Friedhof.** Since 1745 these ruins of the **Nikolaikirche,** destroyed in 1634 in the 30-Years-War, have been used as a gravesite; looking out through the gaping window-holes gives an excellent view of the Spree below. *(Open 8am-4pm in the winter, 7am-8pm May-July.)*

THE SORBISCHES MUSEUM. The museum exhibits detail the intriguing history and culture of the Sorbs. Displays include samples of their writing, life-sized costumes, the area's special Easter eggs, and those mysterious *Dudelsacks* (bagpipes), which look more like saxophones or psychedelic water-filtration devices than anything else. *(Ortenburg 3. On Schloßstr., through the Matthiasturm. ☎424 03. Open Apr.-Oct. daily 10am-5pm; Nov.-Mar. 10am-4pm. DM3, students and children DM2.)*

THE ABSORBING SORBS The Sorbs are a Slavic minority stemming from tribes who streamed into the Niederlausitz and Oberlausitz areas between the Spreewald and Lusatian mountains during the 6th and 7th centuries. Sorbian is similar to Czech and Polish and is divided into two basic dialects: Niedersorbisch (Low Sorbian); spoken in and around Cottbus, and Obersorbisch (High Sorbian); spoken in the Bautzen region. Since the crystallization of the Sorb nationalist movement in 1848, small Sorbian-speaking communities totalling about 75,000 members have maintained their regional identities. Under Hitler's *Reich,* Sorbian was ruthlessly suppressed in a program of liquidation initiated in 1937. After the war, a law was enacted to assure the protection and promotion of the Sorbs' culture and language, and a special bureau was created to guarantee Sorbians civil rights in the German constitution. The Sorbs enrich German culture with their ornamental Easter eggs, their *Osterreiten* (Easter rides) organized in various towns, and their traditional style of celebrating marriage and weddings. Dance and music abound during the festival of *Zapust,* which lasts from the end of January to the beginning of March. January 25 marks the *Vogelhochzeit* (birds' wedding), during which children in costume represent birds grateful for seeds left by their human friends in order to celebrate a marriage.

OUTER BAUTZEN. From the Nikolaiturm or the Sorbisches Museum, follow the scenic ◼**Osterweg** and ◼**Reymannweg** paths to the left around the city walls and along the Spree, taking in the views of the 1480 **Mühlbastei** (mill tower), the 1558 **Alte Wasserkunst** (old water tower), and the spire of the 1429 **Michaeliskirche.** On the other side of the fortress lies the brown-shingled **Hexenhäusrl** (witches' cottage). This small wooden structure, the oldest house in the area, was the only home to survive two devastating fires. The villagers later shunned the inhabitants as witches, though the fire was actually averted by a well inside the house.

GÖRLITZ ☎ 03581

The town of Görlitz lies right next to Germany's easternmost border; so close, in fact, that one can walk over a bridge in the southern part of town and find that the language and currency have suddenly changed to Polish. "Görlitzers," though, are determined not to let their distant town be overlooked. They are proud of its churches and towers, its magnificent Renaissance and Baroque buildings, and its position as a center of travel, history, and culture among the surrounding smaller, virtually unknown towns. They will quickly point out that their town is one of very few to have escaped WWII unscathed. The restoration projects begun here in the early 90s have helped to bring Görlitz out of Cold War decline, and as they near completion, the town looks increasingly splendorous.

◪ **PRACTICAL INFORMATION. Trains** chug to **Bautzen** (50min., 1 per hr., DM12); **Dresden** (2hr., 1 per hr., DM29); and **Zittau** (50min., 1 per hr., DM9.80). Travelers heading to Poland can catch connections to **Warsaw** (1 per day, DM27.40) and **Wrocław** (1 per day, DM16.80). The **tourist office,** Obermarkt 29, across from the Dreifaltigkeitskirche, sells maps and finds **rooms** (DM30-40) in private homes for free. (☎475 70; fax 47 57 27. Open M-F 10am-6:30pm, Sa 10am-4:30pm, Su 10am-1pm.) For a **taxi,** call ☎40 08 00. The **post office** is at Gasthofstr. 29, 92828 Görlitz (open daily 9am-noon and 2:30-8pm).

◪◌ **ACCOMMODATIONS AND FOOD.** Görlitz's **Jugendherberge (HI),** Goethestr. 17, is housed in an impressive building set sedately back from the street by a long driveway. Take the south exit *(Südausgang)* of the train station, bear left up the hill, turn right onto Zittauer Str., and continue until Goethestr. just past the **Tierpark.** Turn left, and the hostel is ahead on the right (15min.). Enter the gate up the stairs to reach the entrance on the right. The huge stained-glass windows are almost as brilliantly colorful as the comforters. Accordions and guitars are supplied for guests' use; you can also rent skis and grills. Rooms have two to eight beds; some family rooms are available. (☎/fax 40 65 10. Breakfast included. Sheets DM7 extra. Reception M-F 7am-9:30pm, Sa-Su 7-10am and 4-9:30pm. No lockout. Curfew 10pm, but you get a key. DM21, over 27 DM26.)

SAXONY

Two **Edeka supermarkets** make hunting for groceries easy: the one at Steinstr. 1 is in the Altstadt; enter from the Obermarkt (open M-F 8am-6:30pm, Sa 8am-noon). The second, Goethestr. 17, is a few doors down from the hostel (open M-F 8am-7pm, Sa 8am-1pm). Many cost-effective *Imbiß* options line Berliner Str., while the nooks and crannies of the Altstadt shelter numerous restaurants; see the beer glass key on the city map at the tourist office. **Destille,** Nikolaistr. 6, directly across from the Nikolaiturm and down the street from St. Peter's, serves *Soljanka* soup with bread (DM5) to the many locals who flock to its wooden tables, and a hefty farmer's omelette, served with potatoes and ham (DM 10). The option of sitting outside at the foot of the tower makes this a fine place to dine as the sun goes down. (☎40 53 02. Open daily 11:30am-11:30pm.) The immaculate seafood restaurant **Gastmahl des Meeres,** Struvestr. 2, whips up Alaskan fish for DM11.90. (☎40 62 29. Open M-Sa 11am-10pm, Su 11am-3pm.

🔲 **SIGHTS.** Berliner Straße, Görlitz's attractive pedestrian zone, intersects **Postplatz,** home to a central fountain surrounded by a motley collection of flowers; the darkly stained **Frauenkirche,** a late Gothic cathedral built in 1431; and the **post office,** a recent project of the restoration workers. The **Dicker Turm,** a squat gray tower with 5m-thick walls, stands tall and proud at **Marienplatz,** located right past the *Karstadt* department store.

Many of Görlitz's central sights are near the **Obermarkt,** which is reached by following Steinstr. Across the square to the right sits the faded yellow **Dreifaltigkeitskirche.** Originally a 13th-century Franciscan monastery, the church bears marks of frequent expansion. Walking past it down Brüderstr. leads to the **Rathaus,** by the **Untermarkt,** which bears several shiny clock faces, one of which ticks away under the constant gaze of the sculpted head above it. On the corner opposite the Rathaus is the **Ratsapotheke,** a Renaissance building from 1550 that still has an astrology and astronomy chart painted on its crumbling surface—the confluence of tweaked clocks is indicative of Görlitz's position on the 15-degree meridian, the center point of the Central European time zone. Don't miss the **Peterskirche,** near the Untermarkt. Its brightly adorned interior, speckled with gilded suns and clocks, is enough to impress even the most jaded tourists. Enter by the back side. (Open Tu-Sa 10:30am-4pm, Su and holidays 11:45am-4pm. Closed M.) Just down the street the view across the river shows a tower painted with an enormous head. Görlitz's **Städtische Kunstsammlung,** the city museum, displays collections pertinent to the Oberlausitz region. It is housed in the **Kaisertrutz** and the **Reichenbacher Turm,** located at the opposite end of the Obermarkt from the Dreifaltigkeitskirche.)

ZITTAUER GEBIRGE (ZITTAU MOUNTAINS)

The rocky cliffs of the Zittauer Gebirge rise in a sliver of Germany wedged between the Czech Republic and Poland. Once a favorite spot of medieval monks, these beehive-shaped mountains are the conquests of choice for skiers, hikers, and landscape lovers. The sublime surroundings were a fountain of inspiration for Romantic artists like Ludwig Richter. But matters have not always been so picture-perfect: in 1491, the region was the scene of the vicious **Bierkrieg** (beer war), when the citizens of Görlitz protested Zittau's success as a beer-brewing town by destroying barrels of the beverage. The horror! More recently, the workers and local forests of this region have been reeling from a nasty socialist hangover plaguing much of Eastern Germany; as inefficient factories are shut down, many residents remain unemployed.

ZITTAU   ☎ 03583

At the crossroads of three nations—Poland, the Czech Republic, and Germany—Zittau has served as a trading and cultural center for many years. Under the rule of the Bohemian kings, Zittau took on a dominant role in Oberlausitz; it later came to dominate the vital yarn and thread industries.

⚂ PRACTICAL INFORMATION. Trains roll in from **Dresden** (1½hr., every 2hr., DM29) and **Görlitz** (1hr., 1 every hr., DM9.80). The **tourist office**, Markt 1, on the first floor of the Rathaus near the left side entrance, provides city maps for free. (☎75 21 37; fax 75 21 61. Open M-F 8am-6pm, Sa 9am-1pm.) A pharmacy, Johannis Apotheke, Johannisstr. 2, has emergency services listed on the door. (☎51 21 64. Open M-F 8am-6pm, Sa 8am-noon.) **Deutsche Bank,** Bautzner Str. 20, is just down the street. (M-Th 8:30am-6pm, F 8:30am-1pm.) **Email** and other internet services can be found at the **Computer-Nutzer Laden,** Rosa-Luxembourg-Str. 34. To get there, turn left off Bahnhofstr. before Haberkorn Platz and continue around on Theaterring until Rosa-Luxembourg-Str. leads off to the left (open Tu-Th 3pm-midnight, F-Su 3pm-late). The **post office,** 02763 Zittau, is at Haberkornpl. 1 (open M-F 7:30am-7pm, Sa 8am-1pm). For a **taxi** dial ☎51 24 00.

⛶ ACCOMMODATIONS AND FOOD. There are no HI hostels in Zittau, but have no fear: the tourist office books rooms for free (DM25-45). Head up Johannisstr. from the tourist office for the old-fashioned beer-and-sauerkraut **Kloster Stüb'l,** Johannisstr. 4-6. Try the *Abernmaunke mit Brotwurscht und Sauerkroattch* (evening meal with sausage and sauerkraut; DM8.50) or pay more for a "medieval meal" you eat with your hands. (☎51 25 76. Open M-Th 11am-10pm, F-Sa 11am-midnight.) The **Savi Café and Bar** (☎70 82 97), on Bautzner Str. across from the Hotel Dreiländereck, serves salads and pasta as well as traditional dishes in a relaxed, modern atmosphere. If it's a bar you're looking for, varied options exist: **Filmsiß** in the Marktplatz, decorated with movie posters, is open until 1am F and Sa, while the **Felsenkeller,** Johannisstr. 10, serves *wurst,* beer, and mixed drinks until 2am every night except M. Zittau is, after all, a university town, so curiosities such as **House of Pain Tattoo and Record Store,** located across Bahnhofstr. from the Police, and **Titan Piercing,** Weberstr. 30 (just down the street from Johanneskirche), which also sells Dr. Marten's and all things British, can accommodate a tourist's need for excitement of any kind. Zittau is also a starting point for the 115km **Upper Lusatian Mountain Path;** ask at the tourist office for info on where to pick up the trail.

▣ SIGHTS. Most of the interesting sights lie in the **Altstadt.** The recently renovated exterior of the **Johanniskirche** shelters a dilapidated interior, which is currently being reconstructed (open M-F 10am-6pm, Sa-Su 10am-4pm). Climb up its *Aussichtsturm* to see the view (open Apr.-Oct. M-F 10am-6pm, Sa-Su 10am-4pm; Nov.-Mar. M-F 10am-4:30pm, Sa 10am-4pm). From the church, walk directly down Bautzner Str. to the grand **Marktplatz.** The Renaissance-style **Rathaus** was designed by Prussian architect Friedrich Schinkel in 1843 (see p. 24.). On Johannisstr., you'll find the late Gothic **Klosterkirche** and the adjoining **Stadtmuseum,** housed in a former 13th-century Franciscan monastery stocked with tourist-friendly medieval torture devices. (☎/fax 51 02 70. Open Tu-Su 10am-noon and 1-4pm. DM3, students DM2.) The recently-restored **Museum der Kirche zum heiligen Kreuz,** Frauenstr. 23, at the corner of Theaterring and Frauenstr., houses extremely rare 15th- and 16th-century tapestries on the life of Christ. (Open Tu-Su 10am-5pm. DM7, students and seniors DM4.)

OYBIN ☎035844

The neighboring spa town of Oybin is a love-child of beauty and kitsch that will make everyone smile. The surrounding scenery is sublime, with pine-forested hills punctuated by imposing mounds of twisted, eroded sandstone. At the top of the cliffs outside the town are the **ruins** of a high Gothic fortress and cloister built in the 14th century. In the summer, concerts and theater presentations are held in the halls of the cathedral. To get there, head up the stairs across from the tourist office. (Ruins DM5, under 16 DM2.) On your way up, stop inside the Bergkirche; its downward-sloping pews and colorful wall designs conjure up images of the Seven Dwarves deep in solemn prayer. After you've seen both church and cathedral, stay atop the mountain and wander over to the **camera obscura.** Ask for a demonstration of this unique telescopic tool from the little man inside the shed. There's good hiking and more stone on the other side of the village. Kitsch is king at **▨Märchenspiele,** a small *Biergarten* next to the train station which brings fairy tales to life with delightfully corny moving miniature dwarves and hikers. (Open M-Th and Sa-Su 10:30am-5:30pm. DM2, 5-6 DM1, under 5 free.)

To get to Oybin, hop on the Mr. Rogers-esque **Schmalspurbahn,** an adorable circa-1890 train just outside the Zittau train station (45min., 3-4 per day, DM5.40). To sleep over, stop by the **tourist office,** Hauptstr. 15, where they'll refer to you a list of accommodations ranging from DM20-125. They also have free hiking maps. (Open M-F 10am-5pm, Sa noon-4pm, Su 2-4pm; when closed, a list of accommodations is posted next to the door.) The **postal code** is 02797.

CHEMNITZ   ☎ 0371

In the midday sun, Chemnitz's industrial-looking metallic buildings gleam incessantly, blinding the eyes of a passerby strolling down the Str. der Nationens, the city's main boulevard. Even at the Theaterplatz, where an elegant new opera house and quality museums surround an open plaza crossed with yellow and grey stone patterns, shade is hard to find. Still, only a block farther down the street one finds the bust of Karl Marx staring off into the distance, casting a shadow on the skateboarding youths and the immense souveneir shop at his base. Chemnitz tries its best to move steadily into the future, and new building projects throughout the city demonstrate the significant amount of money and thought being spent on its revitalization. But the bust of Karl Marx, bringing gloom to the excessive shine and facing the wrong direction in an in-your-face place, gives a solemn reminder: the new image of excessive commercialism to which Chemnitz has committed itself is just not enough to accurately capture the history and culture of this city.

▌ PRACTICAL INFORMATION

Trains run to Chemnitz from **Leipzig** (1½ hrs.), **Dresden** (1½ hrs.), **Görlitz** (3 hrs.), and **Prague** (4 hrs.). Head straight down Georgstr. or Carolastr. from the Hauptbahnhof; after a block, you'll come to Straße der Nationen, the city's north-south axis. To your right, on the north end of the boulevard, lies a quiet neighborhood of old houses that centers on the Brühl, a serene pedestrian zone. The **tourist office,** Bahnhofstr. 6, is across from the train station. The staff finds private **rooms** (DM25-40) for a DM3 fee. (☎ 690 68; fax 690 68 30. Open M-F 9am-6pm, Sa 9am-1pm.) For a **taxi,** call ☎ 194 10. Down Carolastr., to the left along Straße der Nationen, looms the **post office,** 09009 Chemnitz (open M-F 8am-6pm, Sa 8am-2pm).

▌◖ ACCOMMODATIONS AND FOOD

A convenient overnight stay in Chemnitz is difficult to come by; in general the cheaper the establishment, the farther from the center of Chemnitz you must travel. The **Jugendherberge (HI),** Augustusburgerstr. 369 (☎ 71 331), is the cheapest option, though also far from where you want to be. Take Bahnhofstr. to Brückenstr., turn left and it immediately becomes Augustusburgerstr. The same buses that run to Augustusburg, T-244 and T-245, pass this way. A number of inexpensive pensions in the DM40 range do exist, but you may have to go to great lengths (and into less than desirable areas) to find them. Your best bets in this category are **Pension Art Nouveau,** Hainstr. 130 (☎ 402 50 71; fax 402 50 73. Singles from DM65 and doubles from DM90, breakfast included), and **Pension Renate Kästner,** Wildenbruchstr. 3. (☎/fax 85 51 16. Starts at DM40 for a single and DM80 for a double.) These two offer the best mix of proximity to the city's center and Bahnhof, and price. Farther out, but accessible by S-Bahn 5 to the "Altchemnitz Central" stop, the **Hotel Europark** complex offers pension singles for DM40, but the rooms in this massive corporate complex might be less than immaculate.

The **E Aktiv Markt,** just half a block further down Georgstr., is an Edeka of mammoth proportions, and can certainly fulfill your grocery desires (they even have water *without* carbonation!). In the early afternoon you'll always find a fruit market outside it or in front of the Rathaus. For a quick bite, swing by the market next to the **Rathaus,** which is always full of *Imbiße* during the day. For something more, stop by the

Brühl, or look along Str. der Nationen near the Rathaus. **Pizzeria Dolomiti,** just across the street from the un-missable **McDonald's,** shrinks from Marx's glare by placing its restaurant in the comfortable basement of its Str. der Nationens storefront. These Italians serve a "Studentenpizza" for DM6, and several varieties of pasta for DM10. Conveniently, the *Eiscafe* next door can give your meal a completely Italian theme.

◨ SIGHTS

Chemnitz builds up to its former socialist crescendo along ▧**Straße der Nationen;** every street corner boasts statues of frolicking children or happily scrubbed workers. But nothing outshines the **bust of Karl Marx,** an enormous concrete chunk that bears the likeness of the city's adopted philosopher; although Chemnitz was called Karl-Marx-Stadt for almost 40 years, Marx never lived here. A few blocks down Str. der Nationens lies the **Theaterplatz,** surrounded on three sides by large, serene buildings. Straight ahead, the 1992 **opera house** serves to demonstrate the kind of city Chemnitz would like to be. To the right is the **Petrikirche,** first opened in 1888 and since the early nineties painstakingly and gently refurbished. The city's museums, housed in the **König-Albert-Museumsbau,** include the **Städtische Kunstsammlungen Chemnitz** (municipal art collection) and the **Museum für Naturkunde Chemnitz** (natural history museum). The art museum features a nice sampling of 19th- and 20th-century German art, and a huge collection of paintings and woodcuts by local Expressionist Karl Schmidt-Rotluff. *(Open Tu-Su noon-7pm. DM4, students and seniors DM2.)* You'll find a peaceful park and the **Schloß complex** on Schloßberg 12. To reach the castle, dash to Str. der Nationen from the train station and turn right, take a left onto Bebelstr., which becomes Müllerstr., which leads to Schloßberg on the right. The castle that stood here was destroyed in the Thirty Years War; the **Schloßbergmuseum** occupies a reconstructed building that approximates the old structure. *(☎ 488 45 01. Open Tu-F 11am-5pm, Sa-Su 11am-6pm. DM4, students DM2.)* The goods reside upstairs in the **Stadtgeschichte** (city history) display, which documents the history of Chemnitz from its 12th-century foundation to the present. Particularly intriguing are the posters advertising Hitler's *Entartete Kunst* (Degenerate Art) exhibit, on display in Chemnitz at the outset of WWII, and the collections of Communist kitsch from the GDR days.

♫ ENTERTAINMENT

Chemnitz has developed quite an eclectic nightlife scene; search the free magazine *Blitz* for the latest nightlife information. Check out the **Chemnitz opera** or take in a play at the **Schauspielhaus.** Schedules and information for both are posted on Theaterplatz. (Opera tickets DM10-30, 50% student discount. Box office open M-F 10am-6pm, Sa 2-6pm.) If high culture is not for you, shake it at **Fuchsbau,** Carolastr. 8, where local cats head for disco, techno, and jazz. (☎ 67 17 17. Open W-Su, 9pm-2am.) The **Stadtkeller** on Str. der Nationen just before the Roter Turm has an industrial feel, and its dance scene is broadcast live on the radio two nights a week. The ultra-hip bar-cafe **Mox** sits just across the street from Fuchsbau at Carolastr. 5; from 8pm (6pm in the summer) until 3am, Mox and its cousin establishment **Bogart's,** at Hartmannstr. 7d (☎ 63 14 603), serve a variety of alcoholic and non-alcoholic beverages from smoothies and daquiris to beer and milkshakes (DM2-9), and some suspiciously American-sounding bar snacks, including "poppers" and "chicken wings." The **Beer Academy,** at the corner of the pedestrian zone at Rosenhofstr., with its curiously floral patterned plush bar stools, attracts a somewhat older crowd to its Rathaus-area locale. The newest addition to Chemnitz's commercial life is the shopping center called **Galerie Roter Turm,** which just opened in April 2000 across from the post office at Str. der Nationen and Rathausstr. Sleek and air-conditioned enough to be the newest Mall of America, the Roter Turm features three floors of shopping and, at the top of the escalator, a movie theater and gaming complex complete with air-hockey, slot machines, and internet access. (DM1 for 100 "points," or about 20 minutes.)

NEAR CHEMNITZ: AUGUSTUSBURG   ☎037291

A night at the lively castle in Augustusburg facilitates recovery from the exhaustion of post-industrialist, post-Marxist, monochromatic Chemnitz. The princely mountaintop hamlet can be reached by bus T-244 or T-245 (direction: "Schloßberg") from the Chemnitz *Busbahnhof*, down Georgstr. from the train station. (45min., operates 7am-7pm. DM5.80.) The bus stop is at the foot of the path leading to the castle. The Renaissance **hunting lodge** of the Saxon electors is perched 1500m above the town with a mesmerizing 360° panorama of the surrounding **Erzgebirge** mountains—look for the Czech Republic on the horizon. (Schloß open daily May-Oct. 9am-6pm; Nov.-Apr. 10am-5pm.) The obligatory guided tour of the royal playhouse leads through the **Brunnenhaus** (well house) and the intimate **Schloßkapelle** (church chapel), the only Renaissance chapel left in Sachsen. The altar is graced by a Lucas Cranach painting, portraying the dour Herzog August, his wife Anna, and their 14 pious children. (Tours every hour at 30min. past the hour. DM4, students DM2.50.) Also check out the Motorradmuseum (motorcycle museum), the Museum für Jagdtier- und Vogelkunde des Erzgebirges (hunting and game museum), and the Kutschenmuseum (carriage museum). A day pass for all museums costs DM10 (students DM6). Tickets for individual museums can also be purchased separately.

The real treat of a visit to Augustusburg is the ⬛**Jugendherberge (HI)**. Located inside the castle, the hostel has recently undergone restoration, and the bedrooms have all been refurbished; thus you are welcomed by immaculate wood floors, desks, chairs, and closets. Spotless washrooms down the hall leave you feeling squeaky clean. Rooms may have two beds on the floor or four bunked in pairs. Air-hockey and vending machines draw noisy schoolchildren eager to spend their change. Best of all, the castle grounds are yours to wander through as the sun is setting (☎202 56. Breakfast included. Reception 7am-8pm. Check-in after 3pm. Curfew 10pm but you get a key. DM26, students DM21.)

ZWICKAU   ☎0375

Zwickau is best known as the motor city of East Germany. For more than 35 years, the city's *Sachsenring-Auto-Union* produced the GDR's ubiquitous consumer car, the tiny *Trabant*. An ill-engineered, two-cylinder plastic jalopy, the *Trabi* was Communist industry's inferior answer to the West's *Volkswagen*, and, like cockroaches, the wheezing little cars persist. Officially, the city would prefer to play up its more genteel distinctions, such as its active artistic tradition, which launched composer Robert Schumann and a couple of members of the *Brücke* painting school to international renown and continues to show itself in the thriving theatrical community here. But it may be a losing battle; the tinny whine of a *Trabi* laboring uphill is never out of earshot.

🏫 **PRACTICAL INFORMATION.** Located in the middle of the busy Sachsen-Thüringfen rail network, Zwickau is easily reached by **train** as a daytrip from **Leipzig** (1½hr., 13 per day, DM22); **Dresden** (2hr., 26 per day, DM35); or **Altenburg** (40min., 17 per day, DM12). Its oldest attractions and most beautiful streets are confined to a circular region in the Altstadt, bounded by a bustling three-lane roundabout called **Dr.-Friedrichs-Ring.** For a **taxi** call ☎21 22 22. Zwickau's **tourist office,** Hauptstr. 6 (☎83 52 70; fax 29 37 15), lies in the center of the circle. From the **Hauptbahnhof,** head along the left fork, which becomes Bahnhofstr., until it ends at Humboldtstr. Follow the sidewalk around to the right, and then turn left on Schumannstr., then turn right onto Innere Plauensche Str., a pedestrian zone, which leads to the Marienkirche. After the church, a quick left brings you into the Markt; the office is right behind the *Burger King.* If you arrive at **Zwickau-Zentrum,** the new underground train station, just follow Schneebergerstr. into the Markt. The staff provides maps and books **rooms** (from DM35) for free. (Open M-F 9am-6:30pm, Sa 10am-4pm.) The main **post office,** Humboldtstr. 3, 08056 Zwickau, is just outside the Ring near the intersection with Humboldtstr. (Open M-F 9am-noon and 2-6pm, Sa 9-11am.)

❏ FOOD. The monthly *Stadtsreicher*, free at the tourist office, lists the major events in the area, ranging from shows to bars to food. The **Markt** hosts food stands (Th-F 8am-6pm). Other cheap dining options can be found along the Hauptmarkt and Innere Schneeberger Str. during the day, while the **SPAR supermarket,** across from the Schumannhaus, fills your grocery bags (open M-F 8am-6:30pm, Sa 8am-noon). Just outside the Ring lies **Dönerhaus,** Schumannstr. 10, an upscale *Imbiß* serving Turkish fare. (Meals DM4.50-8. ☎353 17 82. Open M-Sa 10am-11pm, Su noon-11pm.) Along Bahnhofstr., **Für Wenig Geld!** ("For Little Money") lives up to its name, offering half-chickens as well as more conventional meal items such as gyros for DM5. If you're looking for a more formal meal, the **Restaurant im Historischen Dünnebierhaus,** on Katharinenstr. just outside the market past the theatre, is surprisingly cheap for a building that doubles as a tourist attraction. (Meals DM7-12, vegetarian options DM5-8. Open M-Sa 5:30pm-late, Su 11:30am-2:30pm.) To imbibe some spirits and GDR nostalgia, head to **Roter Oktober,** at the corner of Leipziger Str. and Kolpingstr. Toast the hammer and sickle if you really feel like getting crazy (or beaten up). (Open M-Sa 7pm-1am.)

❏ SIGHTS. The dusky colored, virtually unmarked four-story **Robert-Schumann-Haus** stands at Hauptmarkt 5. The museum emphasizes Zwickau as Schumann's home city, and describes the musical community in which Robert Schumann met and married his wife, Clara Wieck, one of the most accomplished pianists of her day; Clara is memorialized as "the woman on the DM100 bill." The friendly staff will answer questions about any part of the exhibit, let you choose a Schumann CD to listen to while you examine the display, and proudly point out the plaques showing winners of Zwickau's Schumann prize. Musicians perform both Robert and Clara's works in the *Klavierhalle* monthly from September through April; contact the museum for dates. (☎21 52 69; fax 28 11 01. Open M-F 10am-5pm, Sa and Su 1-5pm. DM5, students and seniors DM3. Concerts DM15, students and seniors DM10.)

After visiting with Schumann, you can check out the **Marienkirche,** which sits near the market *(open daily 9am-6pm)* or rent paddleboats with disarmingly large swan heads on the **Schwanenteich,** along Humboldtstr and across the ring from the Markt *(rentals M-Sa 1-7pm, Su 10am-7pm, boats DM7/hr. or DM12 for solar-powered ones)*, but for a more interesting experience check out the **Automobilienmuseum.** Over a dozen *Trabant* models are on display, prompting wonder at the design's invulnerability to innovation over the years. The sight of the last *Trabi* ever produced (in 1991) in all of its pink splendor and emblazoned with the words *"Trabant:* Legend on Wheels" is enough to make even the most ardent Cold Warrior misty-eyed. *(Walter-Rathenau-Str. 51. Head north from Dr.-Friedrichs-Ring on Römerstr., which becomes Walther-Rathenau-Str., to the out-of-the-way building past the auto factory (20min.). ☎332 22 32. Open Tu-Th 9am-noon and 2-5pm, Sa-Su 10am-5pm. DM5, students and seniors DM3.50.)* The *Trabi* has a devoted following of worshippers, many of whom come to Zwickau every year in mid-June to participate in the *Trabantfahrertreffen*, and true aficionados can subscribe to the *Trabi* magazine.

LEIPZIG ☎0341

Leipzig's Innenstadt area is small and compact, bursting with sights and museums, cafes and university buildings, tourists, students, and everyday residents. From the university's pointed tower to the used clothing and record stores on Karl-Liebknecht-str. to the monuments to Bach and the quiet, staid church in which he worked, Leipzig has a varied and vibrant cultural history and an active cultural life in the present. The clean and easily-walkable Innenstadt area masks a city in which unemployment still poses something of a problem, but Leipzig's important role in historical change from the time of Napoleon to the demonstrations leading to the fall of the Berlin Wall tends to overshadow any problems currently faced by the city. The influence in world culture of former residents like Bach, as well as Nietzsche, Mendelssohn, Wagner, Leibniz, and Goethe, gives Leipzigers an attitude of cutting-edge hip-ness, making their social and cultural scene one full of innovation and confidence.

■ GETTING THERE AND GETTING AROUND

Flights: Flughafen Leipzig-Halle (information ☎224 11 56), in Schkeuditzgasse, about 20km from Leipzig. International service throughout Central Europe. An **airport city liner bus** leaves Goethestr. next to the tourist office every 30min. during the day, every hour at night. DM10, round-trip DM16.

Trains: Leipzig lies on the Berlin-Munich line, with regular InterCity service to Frankfurt. Trains zoom to **Halle** (20min., 2-3 per hr., DM9.40); **Dresden** (1½hr., 1 per hr., DM26); **Berlin** (2-3hr., 1 per hr., DM46); **Frankfurt** (5hr., every 2 hrs., DM90); and **Munich** (7hr., 1 per hr., DM113). Information counter on the platform near track 15, or ask at one of the counters in the huge and helpful *Reisezentrum* at the entrance of the station.

Public Transportation: Streetcars and buses cover the city; the hub is on Platz der Republik, in front of the Hauptbahnhof. Your best bet for tickets is either five 1hr. tickets for DM11, or a day card, valid all day after 10am, for DM6. After midnight, night buses (1 per hr.) provide transportation along the most trafficked routes. All night buses leave from the Hauptbahnhof. Tickets are available from the tourist office, vending machines, and drivers. For questions about public transit, call the hotline at 19 449.

Taxis: ☎48 84, 98 22 22, or 42 33.

Car Rental: Sixt-Budget and **Avis** both have counters at the Hauptbahnhof's *Reisezentrum*. Open M-F 7am-9pm, Sa-Su 8am-6pm. More offices are at the airport.

Mitfahrzentrale: Goethestr. 7-10 (☎194 40), just past the tourist office, organizes rideshares. Dresden DM16, Berlin DM22, Munich DM44, Prague DM29. Open daily 7am-10pm. Call ahead.

Hitchhiking: *Let's Go* does not recommend hitchhiking as a safe mode of transportation. Hitchers going to Dresden and Prague take streetcar #3, 6, or 8 (direction: "Sommerfeld") to "Paunsdorfer Allee," and turn left down Paunsdorfer Allee to the *Autobahn* interchange. To Berlin, take streetcar #16 (direction: "Messegelände") to "Essener Str.," switch to bus #86, get out at Sachsenpark, and walk to the *Autobahn*.

■ ORIENTATION AND PRACTICAL INFORMATION

Leipzig's **Innenstadt** is enclosed within a circular ring only about a kilometer in diameter; an enormous amount of what attracts a traveler to this city is within the ring, including the university, performance spaces, most of the museums, and an active nightlife. It's a 10-minute walk from the main train station on the north edge of the Innenstadt to **Augustusplatz,** the **Gewandhaus,** the university, and the main post office. The cavernous **Hauptbahnhof** is a sight in itself—its curved-beam roofs enclose Europe's largest train station and recall the grander days of rail travel. The station was recently renovated to include a three-story underground shopping center as crassly American as apple pie. (Most shops open M-Sa 9am-8pm.) Beyond this ring, to the south lies **Karl-Liebknecht-Straße,** where several cheap restaurants can be found, and to the northeast the areas called **Thekla** and **Schönefeld** house some cheaper accommodations, including the Jugendherberge.

Tourist Office: Leipzig Information, Richard-Wagner-Str. 1 (☎710 42 60; booking hotline 710 42 55; fax 710 42 71; email lipsia@aol.com). Walk across Willy-Brandt-Platz in front of the station and turn left at Richard-Wagner-Str. Among the gorgeous brochures, there's a useful free map of the center and suburbs with a street name index. They book **private rooms** and rooms in *Pensionen* for free and sell tickets.

Tours: The tourist office leads bus tours daily at 10:30am (in German. 2hr., DM20, students and seniors DM16) and 1:30pm (in German and English. 2½hr., DM28, seniors DM20, students DM16). Themed walking tours depart daily. Some guides are English-speaking (2hr., DM10-15). For more information and departure times, call 710 42 80.

Budget Travel: Campus Tours, on the corner of Universitätsstr. across from the Moritzbastei, sells discount airline tickets, issues ISICs, and serves other travel needs. STA-affiliated. Open M-F 9am-6pm, Sa 10am-1pm.

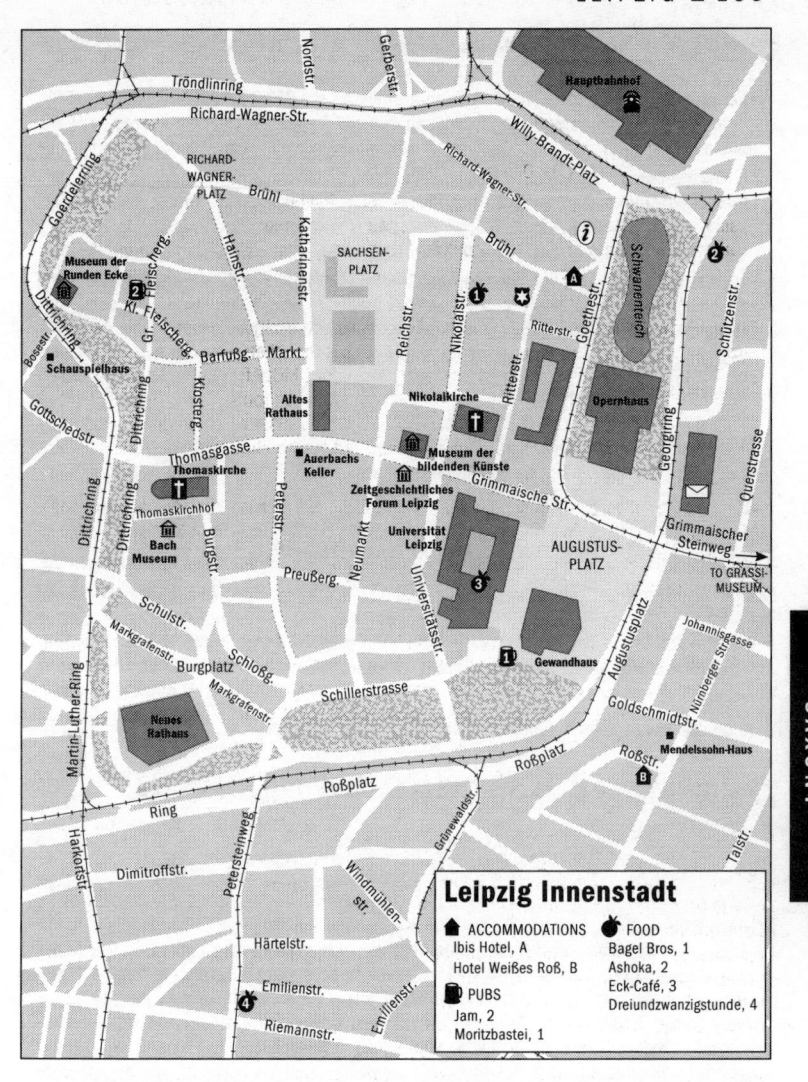

Leipzig Innenstadt

🏠 ACCOMMODATIONS
Ibis Hotel, A
Hotel Weißes Roß, B

🍎 FOOD
Bagel Bros, 1
Ashoka, 2
Eck-Café, 3
Dreiundzwanzigstunde, 4

🍺 PUBS
Jam, 2
Moritzbastei, 1

Consulate: US, Wilhelm-Seyferth-Str. 4 (☎21 38 40). Cross the Innenstadt ring behind the Neues Rathaus, and follow Tauchnitzstr. until Wilhelm-Seyferth comes up on the left. The entrance is on Wächstr., around the building to the right. Available in emergencies M-F 8am-7pm. No visas are issued, but US citizens may apply for passports M-F 2-5pm.

Currency Exchange: Dresdner Bank, Goethestr. 3-5, just off Augustuspl. Open M-Th 9am-6:30pm, F 9am-4pm. Several **ATMs.**

Library: British Council, Katharinenstr. 1-3 (☎140 64 10), near the Markt, stocks a reading room with English books a-plenty. Open M and W-F 1-6pm, Tu 1-8pm. Or check out the **Amerika-Haus Bibliothek** (☎213 84 25), in the US consulate (see **Consulate,** above). Open Tu 4-7pm, W-F 2-5pm.

Gay and Lesbian Resources: AIDS-Hilfe, Ossietzkystr. 18 (☎232 31 26; counseling hotline 194 11). Take streetcar #31 (direction: "Schonefeld") to "Ossietzkystr." The complex features a popular cafe (Open Tu and Th 3-9pm). Also offers the updated **Queer**

Stadtplan, a map of gay and lesbian nightlife. Office open M-Th 10am-6pm and F 10am-1pm. Counseling M, W 1-6pm and Tu, Th 1-9pm.

Mitwohnzentrale: ☎ 194 30, in the same office as the **Mitfahrzentrale** (see p. 156). Arranges long-term accommodation. Open 7am-10pm.

Women's Resources: Frauenkultur, Windscheidstr. 51 (**☎** 213 300 30; email hallo@frauenkultur.leipzig.w4w.net; www.frauenkultur.leipzig.w4w.net), is a center for art, meetings, and relaxation. Office open M-F 8am-2pm. Women's cafe W-F 6pm-midnight.

Laundromat: Maga Pon, Gottschedstr. 11 (**☎** 960 79 22), takes the cake as the jazziest laundromat in Sachsen—it doubles as a hep-cat bar and restaurant, so come in your coolest clothes (unless you want to wash them). Wash DM6, dry DM1 per 20 min. Open daily 9am-late. For a less intimidating (but also less edible) laundry experience, the **Prinz SB Waschsalon** at 76 Karl-Liebknecht-str. offers the same prices.

Emergency: Police, ☎ 110. **Fire** and **Ambulance, ☎** 112.

Pharmacies: Löwen-Apotheke, Grimmaische Str. 19 (**☎** 960 50 27). Open M-F 8am-8pm, Sa 8am-4pm. Posts a list of open pharmacies.

Internet Access: see **Café le bit,** p. 185.

Post Office: Hauptpostamt 1, 04109 Leipzig (**☎** 212 25 88), across from Augustuspl. on Grimmaische Str. Open M-F 8am-8pm, Sa 9am-4pm.

▎ ACCOMMODATIONS AND CAMPING

Budget accommodations in Leipzig are hard to come by, but not impossible. Finding something cheap generally means traveling at least 15 minutes by streetcar to a hostel or cheap hotel, but in a city with such punctual public transportation this rarely poses much of a problem. Private rooms, which can be booked for free at the tourist office, also serve as an alternative.

Jugendherberge Leipzig Centrum (HI), Volksgartenstr. 24 (**☎** 245 70 11; fax 245 70 12). Although "Centrum" would imply otherwise, the hostel is a 15min. streetcar ride from the city. Take streetcar #17, 27, or 31 (direction: "Thekla" or "Schönefeld") to "Löbauer Str." Walk past the supermarket along Löbauer Str. and take a right onto Volksgartenstr. Rooms with 2-6 comfortable beds fill the six floors of a functional, and somehow cheerful, high-rise. Bathrooms on the hallways. Breakfast included. Sheets DM6. Reception 2:30-11pm. Curfew 1am, ask at the desk or call in to make later arrangements. DM25, over 26 DM30.

▨ Hotel Weißes Roß, Roßstr. 20 (**☎** 960 59 51). Take the streetcar to "Augustuspl.," and walk down Augustspl. until it becomes Roßplatz and curves to the right. Go through the portal just to the left of center of the large, curving apartment building; the hotel is 100m straight ahead. Simple accommodations, but you get a set of house keys and the place very quickly begins to feel like your own. The attached restaurant serves a boisterous crowd of locals, and if you're lucky, you'll hear the proprietor singing and playing the guitar for them just before closing time. Breakfast included. Reception M-F 2-8pm. Reservations strongly recommended. Singles DM55 or 60 (depending on size), with private shower DM70. Doubles DM95, with private shower DM110. Breakfast included. Reception M-F 2-8pm. Reservations strongly recommended.

Pension Christin, Kochstr. 4 (**☎**/fax 2 32 93 66.) Take streetcar #11 or 28 (direction: "Markkleeberg," "Ost" or "West") and get off at Arndtstr.; facing away from the Innenstadt, Kochstr. curves off immediately to the right. Ring the bell for "Schmidt" if the door is locked. This pension offers clean rooms, sparkling shared bathrooms, and a green-upholstered common area with TV. Breakfast included. Reservations recommended. Singles DM 55, doubles DM 80.

Kosmos Hotel, Gottschedstr. 1 (**☎** 233 44 20). From the Hauptbahnhof, take a right along Tröndlingring; follow the ring around as it becomes Goerdelerring, then head straight on as it becomes K.-Kollwitz-str. and Kosmos will show up at the corner (10 min). Alternatively, take the streetcar to "Thomaskirche;" the building sits just across the ring from the Innenstadt. This hotel opened in fall 1999 and is part of a larger com-

SAXONY

plex including nightclub, theater, and restaurant. Singles and doubles with themes like "Jungle," or "France," come relatively cheaply for the area, but don't expect a quiet night's sleep; Gottschedstr. rocks until the wee hours. Breakfast about DM5 extra. Singles from DM50, doubles from DM70, all with private bathrooms.

ETAP Hotel Leipzig, Föpplstr. 7 (☎245 84 01). Take streetcar #17, 37, or 57 (direction: "Schönefeld" or "Thekla") to "Löbauer Str.," then bus #70, 84, or 90 (direction: "Mockau-West") to "Stöhrer/Braunstr." (30min.). Walk one more block away from Braunstr. and turn right onto Föpplstr. Remotely located in an industrial wasteland, but in a pinch it is reachable by public transportation and damn cheap for a hotel. Rooms are equipped with private showers and TV. This place is fully integrated into the modern technological world, so you can both check-in and unlock your door electronically. Breakfast DM8.90. Reception 6:30-10am and 5-8pm. Singles and doubles are both DM55—a great bargain for two. Breakfast DM8.90. Reception 6:30-10am and 5-8pm.

Hotel Ibis, Brühl 69 (☎218 60; fax 218 62 22). From the Hauptbahnhof, cross the street and head a block down Goethestr. Take a right onto the Brühl. If you run out of budget options, the Ibis is a 2min. walk from the train station, and in summer offers a per-room special price of DM89.90. Rooms normally DM125. Breakfast DM15. 24hr. reception.

Hostel Sleepy Lion, Käthe-Kollwitz-Str. 3 (☎993 94 80). Streetcar #1 or 31 (direction "Lausen") or #2 (direction "S-Bahnhof Plagwitz") to "Gottschedstr." Leipzig's newest hostel has been a long time coming; it fills a need for centrally located backpacker-friendly budget accommodations in the city. Brand new in August 2000, the hostel has 50 beds. All rooms with TV. Internet access. Breakfast DM5. Sheets DM4. 24hr. reception. 6-8 bed dorms DM27; singles DM45; doubles DM70; quads DM116.

Camping: Campingplatz Am Auensee, Gustav-Esche-Str. 5 (☎465 16 00), in the nearby suburb of Wahren. From the station, take streetcar #11 or 28 (direction: "Wahren") to "Rathaus Wahren." Turn left at the Rathaus, and follow the twisting main road for 10min. Reception M-Sa 6am-9:30pm, Su 6am-8:30pm. DM8 per person, DM5 per car, DM12 for caravans. Small tent-huts function as 2-bed bungalows. Small hut DM30, large hut with shower DM60.

FOOD

Budget meals are not as hard to find in Leipzig as budget rooms, but it's still no cakewalk. The Innenstadt is well supplied with Imbiß stands, bistros, and restaurants for consumption on the go. A **Kaiser's** supermarket pops up on the Brühl, near Sachsenplatz. (Open M-F 7am-8pm, Sa 7am-4pm.) There's a **market** on Sachsenplatz on Tuesdays and Fridays. You'll also find a daily **market** just south of the Innenstadt near Bayerischer Platz. For those with a flexible budget looking to find Leipzig's hottest coffee houses, Karl-Liebknecht-str., Gottschedstr., and Barfußgäßchen are full of chic cafes that double as bars; most of them also feature a sunday brunch from 11am-2pm that fits in the DM11-15 price range.

Avocado, Karl-Liebknecht-str. 79 (☎3 01 15 75), at the corner of Arndtstr. This vegetarian restaurant and bar serves many dishes made from its namesake veggie (and some not) in a friendly, clean, green atmosphere. Vegan options also available. Filling sandwiches such as the "Käse," made with mozzarella, tomatoes, and the restaurant's namesake Gemüse cost DM4-8. Pasta DM9-14. Sunday brunch buffet DM17.50. Open M-Th noon-1am, F and Sa noon-2am, Su 11am-2pm.

Eck-Café, in the university complex just off Grimmaische Str., across from the Mensa. Rub elbows with Leipzig University students as they meet for intellectual conversation over beer, coffee, and many cigarettes. Soup DM3-4, Wurst DM3-6. Open Oct.-Feb. and Apr.-Aug. M-Th 9am-9pm, F 9:30am-4pm.

Ashoka, Georgiring 8-9 (☎961 48 19), Facing the Hauptbahnhof, head to your right. Respectably good Indian food comes as a surprise in Germany, and the lunch buffet (M-F noon-3pm, DM 14.90) is a good deal. Dinner DM13-25. Open M-F noon-3pm and 5pm-11pm, Sa-Su noon-11pm.

Café le bit, Kohlgartenstr. 2 (☎998 20 2000; www.le-bit.de), right off Friedrich-List-Pl. Heading toward the train station on Georgiring, turn right on Schützenstr., which becomes Rosa-Luxemburg-Str. and leads straight there (10min. from the station). The bilingual staff is accustomed to dealing with visiting emailers as well as the crowd of local surfers. First 30min. free; DM2 each additional 15min. The bar menu includes great crepes (DM3-8.50). Open M-F 8:30am-3am, Sa 10am-late, Su 10am-1am.

Dreiundzwanzigstunden, corner of Emilienstr. and Petersteinweg. A 5min. walk from the Innenstadt; head down Petersteinweg from Roßpl. This self-service restaurant heaps on the German food at great prices, and throughout all 23 hours it remains surprisingly clean. *Schnitzel* (DM5.50-7.50), breakfasts (DM7). Open daily 6am-5am.

 SIGHTS

INNENSTADT. Leipzig's historic city center suffered from both WWII bombings and from the poorly planned architectural creations of the post-war era. The heart of the city beats on at the Marktplatz, a colorful, cobblestoned square guarded by the slanted 16th-century **Altes Rathaus,** with its elegant **clock tower** showing four bright-blue faces. Inside, a grand festival hall runs above the **Stadtgeschichtliches Museum Leipzig**, which offers a straightforward look at Leipzig's history. An attached exhibit hall shows temporary displays on contemporary history. *(☎96 51 30. Open Tu 2-8pm, W-Su 10am-6pm. DM5, students DM2.50.)*

AUERBACHS KELLER. Leipzig's most famous restaurant, inside the Mädlerpassage, it was in this 16th-century tavern that Mephistopheles tricked some drunkards in Goethe's *Faust*, before disappearing in a puff of smoke. The entrees don't quite make the budget range (DM25-30), but it's still worth taking a peek. *(Grimmaische Str. 2-4. From the Markt, head away from the Rathaus, and you'll see the Keller ahead. ☎21 61 00. Open daily 11:30am-midnight.)*

THOMASKIRCHE. A little farther down the street from the *Keller* stands the church in which Bach spent the last 27 years of his career. Though sparsely decorated, the church pays simple and fitting homage to Bach, and the grave to which his body was moved in 1949 lies beneath the floor in front of the altar. Performances of the **Thomanerchor,** one of Europe's most prestigious boys' choirs, take place Friday at 6pm, Saturday at 3pm and Sunday during services. *(Church open daily in summer 9am-6pm, in winter 9am-5pm.)*

NIKOLAIKIRCHE. The 800-year-old Nikolaikirche witnessed the birth of Bach's St. John Passion as well as the GDR's peaceful revolution. The sandstone exterior hides a truly exceptional interior. The late 18th-century redesign features green columns carved like palm fronds, 30 paintings of scenes from the New Testament, and alabaster reliefs. In 1989, the church became the gathering point for what would become a truly revolutionary political engagement. What began as regular Monday meetings at the Nikolaikirche turned into massive weekly demonstrations (Montagdemos), which eventually led to the fall of the GDR (see p. 19). *(On Nikolaistr., just a bit past the Thomaskirche in the direction of the university. Church open M-Sa 10am-6pm, Su after services. Free.)*

UNIVERSITÄT LEIPZIG. The former Karl-Marx-Universität lies on Universitätsstr. Its "sharp tooth" tower, a steel and concrete behemoth, was reportedly designed to resemble a partially open book standing upright. The tower is currently coated with scaffolding as builders work to strengthen its design and fill it with university facilities, offices, and a cafe in the top floors.

MENDELSSOHN-HAUS. This was the residence of composer Felix Mendelssohn-Bartholdy, during the years he lived in Leipzig and headed up a revival of interest in Bach. It was through Mendelssohn's urging that the monument outside the Thomaskirche was erected in 1843. *(Goldschmidtstr. 12. Take Augustuspl. away from the Opernhaus toward Roßpl., then turn left down Goldschmidtstr. ☎123 02 94. Open M-Sa 10am-6pm. The Mendelssohn-Saal hosts frequent concerts.)*

VÖLKERSCHLACHTDENKMAL. Outside the city ring, the memorial remembers the 400,000 soldiers engaged in the 1813 Battle of Nations—a struggle that turned the tide against Napoleon and determined many of Europe's current national boundaries. The monument, overlooking a large pool, is a massive pile of sculpted brown rock, with 500 climbable steps to the top. *(Streetcar #15 or 21 from the Hauptbahnhof (direction: "Meusdorf") to "Völkerschlachtdenkmal" (20min.). ☎878 04 71. Open daily Apr.-Oct. 10am-6pm; Nov.-Mar. 10am-4pm. To climb to the top DM6, students DM 3.)*

LEIPZIGER MESSEGELÄNDE. Finished in 1996, the trade grounds consist of five mammoth halls all clustered around an arched main building that resembles the Biosphere. The building hosts trade fairs nearly non-stop throughout the year, but the futuristic buildings themselves are more worth seeing than the yuppies networking inside. Ask the tourist office for more information. *(S-bahn #16 or 21 to "Messegelände." 45 min.)*

🏛 MUSEUMS

Leipzig's museums rely upon the compelling cultural endowments of the city's past to fill its hallowed halls. From remembering the days of Bach to documenting the struggle against the Communist regime, the museums acknowledge Leipzig's unique position on Germany's cultural landscape.

MUSEUM DER BILDENDEN KÜNSTE LEIPZIG. Since WWII, Leipzig's fine arts museum was housed in the pre-war supreme court building—until the court recently decided to reoccupy it, leaving the museum homeless. Until the new building on Sachsenplatz is completed in 2002, the museum is making do with the third floor of an old trade hall. Although presentation is a bit jumbled, the core of the collection is still on display, including some works by Rubens, paintings dating back to the late Middle Ages, and an excellent collection of 19th-century German paintings. *(Grimmaische Str. 1-7, just behind the Altes Rathaus. ☎21 69 90. Open Tu and Th-Su 10am-6pm, W 1-9:30pm. DM5, students and seniors DM2.50.)*

MUSEUM DER "RUNDEN ECKE". One of the more thought-provoking museums in the new *Bundesländer*. Housed in the regional headquarters of the East German Ministry for State Security, or *Stasi*, the museum presents a stunningly blunt exhibit on the history, doctrine, and tools of the secret police. Displays also chronicle the triumph of the resistance that overthrew the Communist regime. On the night of December 4, 1989, the people of Leipzig took over the *Stasi* building; inside, they found some 50,000 letters seized over the last 40 years and entire floors devoted to documentation of the actions of suspected resistors. Even more disturbing, perhaps, are the mountains of paper-pulp which were found outside, indicating that much of what went on inside the building will never be known. *(Dittrichring 24. ☎961 24 43. Open W-Su 2-6pm. Free.)*

JOHANN-SEBASTIAN-BACH-MUSEUM. The Thomaskirche and the **Bach Denkmal** across the street serve as fitting monuments to Bach's important work in Leipzig, but the Bach Museum's small exhibits emphasizing Bach's role as teacher and choir director also provide important background on his life and work in Leipzig, where he wrote his Mass in B minor and both St. John and St. Matthew Passions. The **Sommersaal** hosts concerts Wednesday at 3pm. *(Thomaskirchhof 16. ☎96 44 10. Open daily 10am-5pm. DM4, students and seniors DM2.50. Tours daily at 11am and 3pm; price depends on the size of the group. Concerts DM20, students and seniors DM15.)*

ZEITGESCHICHTLICHES FORUM LEIPZIG. Leipzig's newest museum provides a slick, multi-media look at the years after WWII until the present. The exhibit emphasizes the events of June 17, 1953 and the building of the Berlin Wall, as well as Leipzig's role in the events leading to its fall in 1989. The third floor holds changing temporary exhibits. *(Grimmaischestr. 6. ☎22 200; www.hdg.de. Open Tu-F 9am-6pm, Sa and Su 10am-6pm. Free. Exhibit descriptions available in English.)*

GRASSIMUSEUM. The museum is home to three smaller museums. The largest of the three, the **Museum für Völkerkunde** (anthropology museum), has a huge collection of life-size exhibits demonstrating the dress and customs of peoples from every continent except Europe. *(Open Tu-F 10am-5:30pm, Sa-Su 10am-5pm.)* The university's **Musikinstrumenten Museum** exhibits instruments from "krumhorns" and "shawms" to early pianos and mechanical instruments. Most are too fragile to use, but visitors can choose from among audio samples and try some out in the "sound laboratory." *(Open Tu-Sa 10am-5pm, Su 10am-1pm.)* Enter the courtyard to find the **Museum des Kunsthandwerk** (arts and crafts museum). The permanent collection contains 60,000 objects from the medieval age to the present, including a solid showing of Meissen's famous porcelain. *(All 3 museums located at Johannispl. 5-11. ☎21 42. Walk past the university and down Grimmaischer Steinweg. Open Tu and Th-Su 10am-6pm, W noon-8pm. Each museum DM5, students DM2. Combination ticket to all three museums DM9, students DM6.)*

🎵 ENTERTAINMENT

The patrons that frequent the super-cool, slightly artsy cafes scattered around Leipzig also support a throbbing theater and music scene. Be forewarned: most theaters, musical and otherwise, take a *Sommerpause* in July and August, during which there are no performances. The musical offerings are top-notch, particularly at the **Gewandhaus-Orchester**, a major international orchestra since 1843. Some concerts are free, but usually only when a guest orchestra is playing; otherwise buy tickets (DM7-60; 20% student discount) at the *Gewandhaus* box office, Augustuspl. 8 (☎1270 280; 12 70 480 for concert schedules; fax 1270 222), next to the university. (Open M 1-6pm, Tu-F 10am-6pm, Sa 10am-2pm.) Leipzig's **Opera** (☎126 10; 12 61 261 for tickets; fax 12 61 300), receives wide acclaim and gives Dresden's *Semper* company a run for its money. Tickets run DM18-60, with a 30% student discount, except for premieres. Head to the ticket counter at Augustuspl. 12 for more information. (Reservations by phone daily 8am-8pm. Counter open M-F 10am-8pm, Sa 10am-4pm, and 1½hr. before performances.)

The opera house is also an entry point to Leipzig's diverse **theater** scene. It hosts the experimental **Kellertheater** (☎126 12 61; fax 126 13 00) in its basement. Renowned for its theater, Leipzig has unleashed a wave of experimental plays in the wake of the latest revolution. The **Schauspielhaus**, Bosestr. 1 (☎126 80), just off Dittrichring, produces the classics, including offerings from Euripides, Heiner, Müller, and Brecht. (Box office open M-F 10am-6pm, Sa 10am-1pm and 1½hr. before performance. Tickets DM10-30. Student discount 30-50%.) The cabaret scene is centered in the understated **academixer**, Kupgergasse 6 (☎960 48 48), run by the Leipzig student body. (Open M-F 10am-6pm, Sa 10am-1pm.) Also check out the more brash **Gohglmohsch**, Markt 9 (☎961 51 11), and the **Leipziger Pfeffermühle**, Thomas Kirchhof 16 (☎960 32 53). Leipzig offers documentaries and short films at its annual late October **film festival** (call 980 39 21 for information, or ask at the tourist office). **Kino im Grassi,** Täubchenweg 2d (☎960 48 38) and **naTo,** Karl-Liebknecht-Str. 46 (☎391 55 39), show indie films, usually subtitled.

🌙 NIGHTLIFE

Free magazines *Fritz* and *Blitz* fill you in on nightlife, but the superior *Kreuzer* (sold at newsstands, DM2.50) puts these to shame. **Barfußgäßchen,** a street just off the Markt, serves as the see-and-be-seen bar venue for everyone from students to *schicki-Mickis* (Yuppies). In the summer, bar-goers spill out onto the streets into parasol-covered outdoor seating. **Café Baum,** the oldest in the city, **Markt Neun, Zigarre, Steel, and Varadero,** all fill up by 10pm, and though some crowds will dwindle by midnight, the most popular bars will stay packed until 3am on a good night. Just across Dittrichring on **Gottschedstraße** and **Bosessstraße** a similar scene takes place in bars such as **Neue Szene, Hemingway,** and **Diebels Faßkeller,** but with a slightly younger crowd and the music turned up a notch.

Karl-Liebknecht-Straße is just as Szene-ic without being quite as claustrophobic as Barfußgäschen. Take streetcar #11 (direction: "Markkleeburg-Ost") to "Arndtstr." At night, the cafes all double as bars, pouring drinks for Irish lovers (**Killiwilly** at #44), tough art-house film types (**naTo** at #46, see **Entertainment,** above), caffeine addicts (**KAHWE** at the corner of Arndtstr. and Karl-Liebknecht-Str.), and everyone else (**Weißes Rössel** right next door). Revelry of the get-down-and-boogie type is more difficult to find, and tends to serve a younger crowd, but clubbing does exist in Leipzig, and it gets most rocking between midnight and 3 am.

Moritzbastei, Universitätsstr. 9 (☎ 702 59 13; tickets ☎ 70 25 90; www.moritzbastei.de), next to the university tower. Leipzig university students spent eight years excavating this series of medieval tunnels so they could get their groove on. A chill atmosphere presides over the multiple bars and dance floors, enhanced by frequent concerts. **Café Barbakan** (open M-Sa after 10am), an **open-air movie theater** (screenings June-Aug. M-Tu and Th-Sa at 10pm, weather permitting), and the outdoor terrace and *Biergarten* (open in nice weather M-F 11:30am-midnight, Sa-Su 2pm-midnight) provide respite from the wild music scene. Things kick off after 9pm, with a salacious scene for the jam-packed Wednesday night "Papperlapop" disco. Cover DM4-7 for discos, slightly more for concerts. Some concerts require prior ticket purchase; office open M 2-6pm, Tu-F noon-2pm. Bring student ID for discount.

Distillery (☎ 963 82 11), at the corner of Kurt-Eisner-Str. and Loßinger Str. Streetcar #5 or 16 (direction: "Lößing") to the "K.-Eisner-Str./A.-Hoffman-Str." stop. Distillery is to the left at the dead end on Kurt-Eisner-Str. F special parties, Sa two floors of pulsing house and techno. Things usually get going after 11pm. Cover DM10-15.

Jam, Große Fleischergasse 12 (☎ 961 74 32). About as commercial as discos can get, but with one saving grace: the building was the former *Stasi* headquarters. One room features techno, the other is more top-40 oriented; both have full bars. Fridays feature a *Flirtparty*, while Saturdays are just too crazy to have a theme. Every second Sunday hosts a gay and lesbian party. Cover DM6-12, including a few drinks.

RosaLinde, Lindenauer Markt 21 (☎ 484 15 11). Streetcar #17 or 57 (direction: "Böhlitz-Ehrenberg") to "Lindenauer Markt." Described by some as the center of the gay and lesbian scene, it resides in the elegant brown building in Lindenauer Markt that is also home to the "Theater von Jungen Welt." The bar is open daily after 8pm (except on Thursdays), and hosts a disco every Saturday and the second Friday of each month.

SAXONY

SACHSEN-ANHALT

Sachsen-Anhalt's endless, mesmerizing grass plains offer one of the more tranquil landscapes in Eastern Germany. The fact that the region suffers from the highest unemployment rate in Germany doesn't seem to slow down the rapid process of reconstruction and modernization currently underway. Sachsen-Anhalt contains a number of worthwhile destinations including Wittenberg, the city of Martin Luther and cradle of the Protestant Reformation, Magdeburg, home to a splendid Gothic cathedral where the first Holy Roman Emperor is buried, and the witch-haunted Harz Mountains, a popular hiking region. The grand cathedrals filling the skyline attest to the region's former importance, while the many construction sites mushrooming across the *Land* point toward its future.

HIGHLIGHTS OF SACHSEN-ANHALT

Martin Luther, the instigator of the Reformation, posted his *95 Theses* on a church in **Wittenberg** (p. 190). The city still celebrates its native superstar and has recently been blessed with **a Hundertwasser**-designed high school.

The original **Bauhaus** demonstrates principles of the merger of form and function, imbuing the city of **Dessau** (p. 193) with design-school hipness.

The castle-spotted **Harz mountains** (p. 201) offer tons of outdoor fun. Walk in Goethe's footsteps to the top of the **Brocken** (p. 203) or visit the half-timbered towns of **Quedlinburg** (see p. 206) and **Wernigerode** (see p. 204).

WITTENBERG
☎ 03491

Wittenberg does its best to keep the memory of Martin Luther alive; in 1938, the town even went so far as to rename itself **Lutherstadt Wittenberg.** Luther claimed that the town was the source and fount of his life's work: he preached, taught, married (a scandal to the Catholic clergy), raised children, and led the Protestant Reformation in this picturesque town. The city's fondest memories are of Luther nailing the *95 Thesen* (95 Theses) to the Schloßkirche in 1517 and of his scandalous (and exceptionally contrived) wedding, the mildly debaucherous move Luther made as one final snub to Rome, a "made-for-TV" event that the town re-enacts every June. The infamous "Luther Year," 1996, witnessed the 450th anniversary of Martin Luther's death—an unparalleled tourist extravaganza. If you missed it, don't worry; Martin's remains remain. Although he died in Eisleben in 1546, his body was buried directly beneath the Schloßkirche's pulpit.

Luther managed to hang onto his celebrity status in the officially atheistic GDR; he was, after all, a harsh critic of Catholic wealth, inciting early bourgeois revolutions. He also had a presence in the civil sphere, and for many East Germans the image of Luther risking his life to nail up his *95 Thesen* became an emblem of courageous resistance. A successor of Luther at the Schloßkirche pulpit, Pastor Friedrich Schorlemmer, was a key player in the 1989 revolution against the GDR. Since that time, religious pilgrims have returned in full force to Luther's city. The slow shuffle of Scandinavian church groups has pushed up *Schnitzel* prices while giving a fresh gleam to the architectural remnants.

▧ ORIENTATION AND PRACTICAL INFORMATION

Trains: leave for **Berlin** (1½hr., every 2hr., DM39); **Dessau** (30min., 2 every 3 hrs., DM10); **Magdeburg** (1½hr., every 2 hrs., DM22); and **Leipzig** (1hr., every 2hr., DM16). The Hauptbahnhof is the departure point for most regional trains. To get to the main pedestrian zone from the station, go straight out of the main building, or left from the bus stop, walk down the street and follow the curve right. Cross the street and walk straight until the **Lutherhalle** appears on your left, and follow Collegien Str.

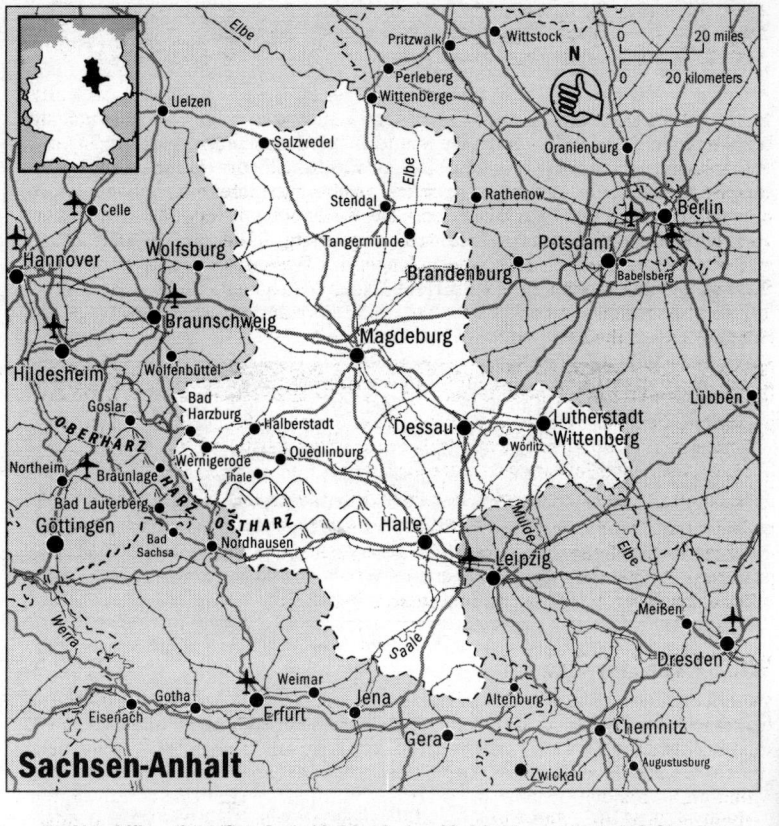

Sachsen-Anhalt

Tourist Office: Schloßpl. 2 (☎ 49 86 10; fax 49 86 11; email wb_info@t-online.de; www.wittenberg.de), at the other end of pedestrian zone, provides maps and books **rooms** (DM25-75) for a DM3 fee. Open M-F 9:30am-5:30pm, Sa 10am-3pm, Su 11am-4pm. **Tours** leave daily at 2pm from the Schloßkirche (DM10). English and other foreign language tours available at additional cost; arrangements are made in advance. The **regional tourist office,** Mittelstr. 33 (☎ 40 26 10; fax 40 58 57), across from the Lutherhalle, has information about cultural events and an eager welcome. A wealth of information about biking and hiking in the region is also available. Open Apr.-Oct. daily 9:30am-5:30pm; Nov.-Mar. M-F 9:30am-5:30pm.

Bikes: M&B Fahrradladen, Coswiger Str. 21 (☎ 40 28 49), rents for DM8 per day.

Pharmacy: on Marktpl., where painter Lucas Cranach pushed drugs to support an art habit, posts a schedule of all-night pharmacies (open M-F 8am-6:30pm, Sa 9am-noon).

Banks: Sparkasse, Markt 20, has several **ATMs** (open M-F 8:30am-6pm, Sa 9am-1pm).

Post Office, 06866 Wittenberg, is near the Lutherhalle on the corner of Friedrichstr. and Fleischerstr. (open M-F 8am-6:30pm, Sa 9am-noon).

▐ ACCOMMODATIONS

The **Jugendherberge (HI),** located in the castle, has bright rooms with just a touch of that Reformation severity. Cross the street from the tourist office and walk straight into the castle's enclosure, then trek up the spiraling stairs to the right. All rooms sport snazzy new bunk beds and closets as part of a renovation campaign that has also left the bathrooms immaculate. There are a few doubles and quads and a number of spacious 10- to 18-bed rooms. (☎/fax 40 32 55. Breakfast included. Sheets DM6. Reception 5-10pm. Lockout 10pm, but keys are available for a DM10 deposit. Reservations recommended, though the hostel sometimes offers floor space for a reduced rate if it's full. Dorm beds DM21, over 26 DM26.) While not centrally located, **Gästehaus Wolter,** Rheinsdorfer Weg 77, sings sweet lullabies with its truly homey ambience, complete with playground, family dog, sunny rooms with TV, and spotless bathrooms. Ride bus #302, 314, or 315 to "Elbedruckerei," walk in the direction of the bus, take the first right, and veer right on Rheinsdorfer Weg. If this sounds confusing, call Frau Wolter and she will happily pick you up from town. (☎41 25 78. Breakfast included. 24hr. reception. Singles DM35; doubles DM70-90.

FOOD AND ENTERTAINMENT

A number of delectable delights at low cost lie along the Collegienstr.-Schloßstr. strip, and a **City-Kauf supermarket** waits across from Coswiger Str. 15, about 20m from the tourist office (open M-F 7am-6:30pm, Sa 8am-12:30pm). **Bosphorus,** Collegienstr. 64, cooks up all the Turkish delights you could ever want. Tasty salads from DM4, spicy Döner combo plates, and much more. (☎41 15 90. Open M-Sa 9am-10pm Su 11am-10pm.) Get Guinness on tap at the **Irish Harp Pub,** Collegienstr. 71, where live English and Irish music rumbles on Saturdays. (☎41 01 50. Open daily 3pm-3am. Cover DM7.) Members of Wittenberg's artsy theater crowd occasionally burst into song or soliloquy at **Vis à Vis,** Sternstr. 14, a cozy alternative establishment with an almost entirely vegetarian menu (main courses DM10). The staff puts up musical productions, and local bands rock the house on weekends. (☎40 67 65. Open M-Th and Su 3pm-1am, F-Sa 3pm-2am.) Theater buffs get their fix at the **Mitteldeutsches Landestheater,** which puts on a variety of contemporary plays; buy tickets at Collegienstr. 74. (☎40 20 85 or 40 20 86. Box office open M-F 10am-12:30pm and 1-5:30pm.)

SIGHTS

Wittenberg's sights provide unending adulation of the eminently historical Luther. Plan your sight-seeing around **Collegienstr.;** the street is less than 1.5km long and encompasses all the major sights. The **Lutherhalle,** to which Martin moved in 1508, houses a museum chronicling the history of the Reformation through letters, texts, and art. Some highlights include the main lecture hall, complete with the original podium, where Luther first spoke about many of his ideas, and the musty "Luther Room" where his philosophy evolved during after-dinner discussions. Luther's ground-breaking translation of the Bible, considered a model of the German language, an original **Gutenberg Bible,** and many angry responses to the feisty minister's theses are also on display. An obnoxious tourist's graffiti has also been preserved: Russian Czar Peter the Great scribbled his name above the door when he stopped by in 1702. (Collegienstr. 54. ☎40 26 71. Open daily 9am-6pm. DM7, students DM4.) Turn right from the Lutherhaus and stroll down to Lutherstr. to the elm tree under which Luther defiantly burned a papal bull (a decree of excommunication, not a Catholic beast).

At the end of Mittelstr. on the Marktpl. lies the **Stadtkirche St. Marien,** known for its dazzling altar painted by pharmacist and hometown art genius **Lucas Cranach the Elder** (see p. 23) Stand on the altar where Luther preached, and be sure to take a glance at the massive organ lurking over the balcony. (Open May-Oct. M-Sa 9am-5pm, Su 11am-5pm; Nov.-Apr. M-Sa 10am-4pm, Su 11am-4pm.) Cranach lived in Wittenberg for most of his life. His home, **Cranachhof,** has a courtyard which is used as a lively open-air performance space; inside, the **Galerie im Cranach-Haus** hosts some interesting modern art exhibitions. (Markt 4. Opening times and admission fees vary, but the gallery is usually open Tu-Sa 10am-6pm, Su 1-6pm.) Wittenberg's elegant white **Rathaus** dominates the Markt with its stately facade. Matching statues of Luther and Reformation hero Philip Melanchthon share the square with the **Jungfernröhrwasser,** a 16th-century well whose refreshing waters flow through original wooden pipes.

The **Schloßkirche,** crowned by a sumptuous Baroque cupola, holds a copy of the complaints that Luther nailed to its doors. The sharp metal peaks of the altar and imposing pews make it an architectural sight worth reckoning with. At the front of the church, the man who fought to translate the scriptures into the common man's tongue is interred, ironically, under a Latin plaque. Also featured are the graves of Wittenberg's other important dead folks: Prince Electors Friedrich the Wise and Johann the Steadfast, and Reformation hero Philip Melanchthon. In the 1840s, it was arranged that 15 people would check that old Luther was really buried here. The crypt was opened in secret for fear that failure to find Luther would discredit the church. Happily, they found the remains— or so they said. The **tower** affords a sumptuous view of the surrounding countryside. *(Down Schloßstr. Church open May-Oct. M 2-5pm, Tu-Sa 10am-5pm, Su 11:30am-3:30pm; Nov.-Apr. M 2-4pm, Tu-Sa 10am-4pm, Su 11:30am-4pm. Free. Tower open daily noon-5pm. DM2, students DM1.)*

Recently, Wittenberg gained a new and unusual tourist attraction. A group of students at the local high school thought it would be fun to have the architect **Friedensreich Hundertwasser,** famous for his radical ideas, redesign their boring, pre-fab school building in his characteristically eccentric style. Apparently Hundertwasser thought it was a good idea as well, because Wittenberg now has what is perhaps the funkiest-looking high school in all of Germany. Follow Sternstr. out of the city center and turn right onto Schillerstr; the **Hundertwasser-Schule** is on the left. Shouldn't every building have trees growing from its roof?

DESSAU ☎ 0340

The **Bauhaus** school is perhaps the most significant architectural movement of the 20th century, and it was in Dessau, from 1925 to 1932, that its ideals and practices found a home. *Bauhaus* masters **Walter Gropius, Hannes Meyer, László Moholy-Nagy,** and their students struggled with aesthetic representations of modernity and attempted to reconcile human living space with 20th-century industrialization and urbanism. The resulting aesthetic was minimalist, yet powerful in its simplicity, and at the time very radical. Hannes Meyer described their results perfectly when he said, "Building is *not* an aesthetic process." What he meant, and as Mies van der Rohe said, is that form follows function, where functionality consists not merely of pragmatic requirements, but also of the body and soul's needs. In short, the *Bauhaus* sought a unity of the human, the material, and the aesthetic. Though Dessau was not transformed in these short years, the masters did leave behind a number of stunning buildings before fleeing into exile after the conservative post-Weimar government declared their style *"undeutsch"*. Unfortunately, Dessau *was* totally made over by WWII bombings; eighty-four percent of the city was leveled. Many *Bauhaus* buildings were obliterated, while others survived with considerable damage. However, Dessau has had more success in its post-war reconstruction than other former GDR cities. Though it has its share of run-down, faceless apartment blocks, many of Dessau's residential areas are lush and attractive, and its commercial areas are sleek and modern.

The history of Dessau stretches back into antiquity. Founded as a medieval fortress in 1341, Dessau became one of the first German Renaissance settlements. With the backing of Princess Henrietta Katharina von Oranien, Dessau flourished as a thriving center of cultural and economic importance. Dessau's famed Prince Leopold invented the method of marching in step, and introduced it into his regiment, thus creating a model for the Prussian army and stereotypes about German militarism. Dessau prides itself on a unique civic culture and its two major historical offspring. **Moses Mendelssohn,** one of the greatest German-Jewish philosophers and a fervent proponent of religious tolerance in the 19th century, lived in Dessau, as did the greatly admired modern composer **Kurt Weill,** whose critical theater encouraged artistic resistance against Nazism.

▮ PRACTICAL INFORMATION

Trains depart for **Berlin** (2hr., 1 per hr., DM33); **Leipzig** (1hr., every 2hr., DM15); and **Wittenberg** (35min., every 2hr., DM10). Rent **bikes** at **Fahrradverleih am Wörlitzer Bahnhof,** Unruhstr. 10. (☎221 32 34. Open M-F 9am-6pm. DM15 per day.) The **tourist office,** Zerbster Str. 2c, finds **private rooms** (from DM30) for a DM5 fee and books hotel rooms for free. Call or fax ☎220 30 03 for reservations. Take streetcar #1 or 2 from the train station's main exit to "Hauptpost." The office sits behind the building with the huge *Rathaus-Center* signs. Walk toward the center and veer left on Ratsgasse. Take the first right; the office is on your left. The staff also sells the **Dessau Card** (DM15), a three-day ticket that allows up to one adult and one child unlimited access to all buses and streetcars in Dessau, as well as entry to most sights and museums. (☎204 14 42; fax 204 11 42; email tourismus-marketing@dessau.de; www.dessau.de. Open Apr.-Oct. M-F 9am-7pm, Sa 9am-1pm; Nov.-Mar. M-F 9am-6pm, Sa 10am-1pm.) **Tours** depart from the tourist office; English tours are available for groups if arranged in advance. (Apr.-Oct. Sa at 10am. DM10, children DM1.50.) The **Cyberb@r** on the top floor of the *Karstadt* in the Rathaus-Passage mall provides **internet access.** (Open M-F 9:30am-8pm, Sa 9:30am-4pm. DM5 for 30min.)The **post office,** 06844 Dessau, is at the corner of Friedrichstr. and Kavalierstr (open M-F 8am-7pm, Sa 8am-noon).

▮▮ ACCOMMODATIONS AND FOOD

The **Jugendherberge (HI),** Waldkaterweg 11, is a 25-minute walk from the train station through suburban Dessau. Exit from the smaller *Westausgang* of the station through the underground tunnel, make a left onto Rathenaustr., and follow it to the end; at the intersection, zig-zag across and follow Kühnauer Str. for 10 minutes until you cross Kiefernweg. About 50m farther, a small path on the right with red and white poles leads to the hostel's woody entrance. The rooms are small and spartan, and the bathroom facilities are minimal. (☎61 94 52. Breakfast included. Sheets DM6. Reception M-F 8am-4pm and 7:30-9:30pm, Sa-Su 6-9pm. Check-out 9am. DM22, over 26 DM27.)Dessau offers a unique opportunity to spend a night in the famous ▮**Bauhaus** school building (☎650 83 18). Aesthetically pleasing singles (DM30) or doubles (DM50). Reservations are recommended; call ahead and ask for Frau Oede. Otherwise, knock on the door of room 318. For directions from the station, see Sights, below.

Affordable restaurants are difficult to come by in Dessau. The gleaming expanse of the newly built *Rathaus-Center* satisfies every craving for mall life, and the bakeries, produce stands, and **Tip supermarket** inside provide an easy end to the harrowing search for cheap eats (open M-F 8am-8pm, Sa 8am-4pm). The stunningly hip ▮**Klub im Bauhaus,** in the *Bauhaus* school basement, is the ideal spot to indulge in angsty pretense over a light meal. Ponder imminent revolution over the *Anarchistenfrühstück* (anarchist's breakfast)—a pot of coffee, some bread, and a *Karo* cigarette (DM4). For something less revolutionary, the spaghetti with pesto, cheese, or tomatoes (DM8) is enough savory food to fill the proletariat stomach. The silver and black *Bauhaus* furniture completes the sensory experience. (☎650 84 44. Open M-F 8am-midnight, Sa 10am-midnight, Su 10am-6pm.) The **Ratskeller,** Zerbster Str. 4, across the street from the *Rathaus-Center,* serves up *Milchreis* (DM10.80), a Dessau original that is best described as rice pudding with cinnamon, sugar, and *Bratwurst.* They've also got a tasty veggie and potato dish for DM14. (☎221 52 83. Open daily 11:30am-midnight.) **Kiez Café,** Bertolt-Brecht-Str. 29a, just off Kurt-Weill-Str., is where the young, offbeat, and artsy congregate for a bit of *alternativ kultur.* The cafe is a one-stop-shop for all your cultural needs, with a photo lab/dark room, theater, art studios, a cinema (DM7, students DM5), and **internet access** for DM6 an hour. (☎21 20 32 or 21 20 37. Cafe open M-Th and Su 8pm-1am, F-Sa 8pm-2am.)

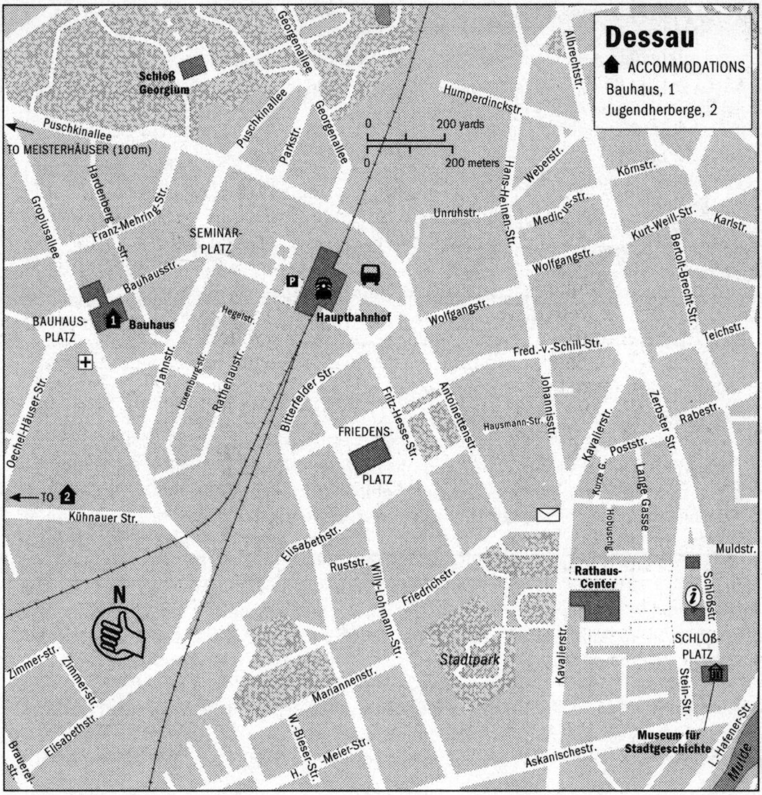
Dessau
ACCOMMODATIONS
Bauhaus, 1
Jugendherberge, 2
Schloß Georgium
Puschkinallee
TO MEISTERHÄUSER (100m)
Georgenallee
Puschkinallee
Parkstr.
Humperdinckstr.
0
200 yards
200 meters
Albrechtstr.
Hans-Heinen-Str.
Weberstr.
Körnstr.
Gropiusallee
Hardenberg-str.
Franz-Mehring-Str.
SEMINAR-PLATZ
Unruhstr.
Medicus-str.
Kurt-Weill-Str.
Karlstr.
Bertolt-Brecht-Str.
Bauhausstr.
Wolfgangstr.
Hauptbahnhof
BAUHAUS-PLATZ
Bauhaus
Hegelstr.
Wolfgangstr.
Teichstr.
Fred.-v.-Schill-Str.
Jahnstr.
Luxemburg-str.
Rathenaustr.
Bitterfelder Str.
Fritz-Hesse-Str.
Antoinettenstr.
Johannisstr.
Oechel-Häuser-Str.
FRIEDENS-PLATZ
Hausmann-Str.
Kavalierstr.
Zerbster Str.
Rabestr.
Poststr.
Kurze G.
Lange Gasse
TO 2
Kühnauer Str.
Hobusch
Muldstr.
Elisabethstr.
Ruststr.
Rathaus-Center
Schloßstr.
Friedrichstr.
N
SCHLOß-PLATZ
Stadtpark
Kavalierstr.
Willy-Lohmann-Str.
Zimmer-str.
Zimmer-str.
Mariannenstr.
Stein-Str.
Elisabethstr.
W.-Bieser-Str.
H.-Meier-Str.
Museum für Stadtgeschichte
Askanischestr.
L.-Hafener-Str.
Brauerei-str.
Mulde

SIGHTS

The Bauhaus began in Weimar in 1919, but the conservative local oligarchy pressured it to leave. The school packed up and brought its theory of constructive and artistic unity to Dessau in 1925; in 1932 the school fled yet again to the more brash Berlin before being exiled from the country in 1933 by the Nazis. Despite the necessity of remaining itinerant to avoid total dissolution, the *Bauhaus* masters inspired an architectural renaissance that attained its aesthetic zenith with the sleek skyscrapers of America's metropoli. After the war, as Dessau rebuilt, city planners translated the shapely *Bauhaus* legacy into building-block-shaped monotony. Today the **Bauhaus** houses a research institute and exhibition space for international architecture. The school currently decorates its sparsely linear walls with the works of legendary alumni Gropius, Klee, Kandinsky, and Brandt. To get there from the station, turn left and go up the steps, then head left over the railroad tracks. Veer left at the first street onto Kleiststr., then right onto Bauhausstr. Or take bus E or K to "Bauhaus." The building is open for self-guided tours and there are rotating exhibits on *Bauhaus* themes in the hallways and various spaces in the complex. *(Gropiusallee 38. ☎650 82 51; fax 650 82 26; email besuch@bauhaus-dessau.de; www.bauhaus-dessau.de. Building open 24hr. Free. 1-hour guided tours M-F 11am and 3pm; Sa and Sun. 11am and 2pm. Exhibition open Tu-Su 10am-5pm. DM5, students DM3.)*

The **Kurt-Weill-Zentrum** is located in the former house of designer and painter Lyonel Feininger. The center has been restored to its original splendor, thus providing lucid insight into the school's musings. Occasional concerts honor the wacky Weill. *(Ebertallee 63. ☎/fax 61 95 95. Open Tu-F 10am-5pm, Sa-Su noon-5pm. DM5, students DM3.)*

If you'd prefer an auditory impression of crazy Kurt, try to catch the annual Kurt Weil Festival in late February. The Zentrum is the first in the row of the three famous Bauhaus *Meisterhäuser;* Georg Muche and Oskar Schlemmer each resided in house number two, and the third served as home to Kandinsky and Klee. The **Kandinsky Klee Haus** has been renovated to accentuate its design, with sparse furnishings and an eye-popping paint-job. *(Meisterhäuser open Tu-Sun. 10am-5pm; DM8, students DM5. Combination ticket to the Bauhaus exhibition and the Meisterhäuser DM12, students DM8.)*

Several more spectacular Bauhaus buildings are scattered around town. To find them, pick up a copy of *Bauhaus Architecture in Dessau* (DM1) at the tourist office, available in English and German. Carl Fieger's **Kornhaus,** a 15-minute walk to the end of Elballee off Ebertallee, was designed as the ultimate party house, with a beer hall, cafe, dance floor, and two terraces. Today, the white tablecloths of a waterfront restaurant create a somewhat more refined atmosphere. To get a peek at the **Laubenganghäuser** on Peterholzstr., hop on streetcar #1 (direction: "Dessau-Süd") and hop off at "Damaschkestr." These were designed, in the true Bauhaus spirit, to be efficient, attractive housing tenements. Take a left onto Mittelring and behold an entire residential neighborhood in Bauhaus style. The **Moses-Mendelssohn-Zentrum** includes a museum about the philosopher's life and work as well as an exhibit on Jewish life in Dessau. *(Mittelring 38. ☎ 850 11 99. Open M-F 10am-5pm, Sa-Su noon-5pm. DM3, children DM2.)*

Dessau also has its share of ornate, old-school architecture. From the Bauhaus, make a right on Gropiusallee to reach **Schloß Georgium,** home to the **Anhaltische Gemäldegalerie.** The 17th-century country estate displays a range of lesser-known Old Masters' paintings from the 16th to the 19th century. The surrounding formal gardens are equally impressive. *(Puschkinallee 100. ☎ 61 38 74. Open Tu-Su 10am-5pm. DM5, students DM3. Gardens open 24hr.)* **Schloß Mosigkau** was built in 1752 for Princess Anna Wilhelmine. Furnished in opulent Baroque style, the castle displays works by such masters as Rubens and van Dyck. *(Knobelsdorffallee 3. Take bus D or L (direction: "Kochstedt") to "Schloß Mosigkau." ☎ 52 11 39. Open May-Sept. Tu-Su 10am-6pm; Apr. and Oct. Tu-Su 10am-5pm; Nov.-Mar. Tu-F 10am-4pm, Sa-Su 11am-4pm. DM5, students DM3.50.)* If you really like Dessau, visit the **Museum für Stadtgeschichte**. The museum has off-beat exhibits on Dessau's history and contemporary political and cultural concerns. *(Schloßplatz 3a, in the Johannbau. ☎ 220 96 12. Open Tu-Su, 10am-5pm. DM4, students DM2.)*

HALLE ☎ 0345

Halle an der Saale, the town saved by Katrin's drumming in the climactic scene of Brecht's *Mother Courage,* emerged from WWII relatively unscathed. The Altstadt offers some historic beauty, though the city seems held down by its dull physical landscape. Three months after the war came to a close, occupying Americans swapped Halle for a bit of Berlin under the terms of the Yalta agreement, and in the post-war decades, it served as Sachsen-Anhalt's political and industrial capital. Today Halle tries to draw attention to its cultural merits, calling itself the "Händel-Stadt" and promoting its city choir, orchestra, opera, theater scene, and museums. Continued unemployment plagues Halle, but the city's historical significance and university community energy often lend a distinct friendliness.

⁊ ORIENTATION AND PRACTICAL INFORMATION

Halle is divided into several districts; most significant are the GDR-style **Neustadt** and the historical **Altstadt,** separated by the scenic Saale River. Come nightfall, Neustadt is not secure, as political extremists (both right and left) reportedly roam this area. The train station and the major streetcar terminals are located in the Altstadt, and the city's energy is mostly concentrated there. Halle is a 40 minute train ride from **Leipzig** (1 per hr., DM10.40) or **Naumburg** (1 per hr., DM12.60.) Although most of Halle is walkable, streetcars efficiently cover the town (single ticket DM2.40, DM3 if bought on-board, day pass DM7). The system is easy to use, and all stops are clearly marked, though be wary of possible route changes while tracks are being replaced. The main street is Große Ulrichstr.; moving away from the **Marktplatz,** it becomes Geiststr., then Bernburger Str.

The **tourist office** is in the Roter Turm, on Marktplatz. From the main station, leave from the E.-Kamieth-Str. exit and head right to the buses, streetcars, and pedestrian tunnel to town. Follow the pedestrian tunnel and take a left on the pedestrian street Leipziger Str. past the Leipziger Turm to Marktplatz (15min.), or take streetcar #4 (direction: "Heide/Hubertusplatz") or #7 (direction: "Kröllwitz") four stops to "Markt." The office hands out city maps, sells tickets, offers a number of pamphlets on cultural events, and finds **rooms** (DM35-50) for free. (☎202 33 40; reservations ☎202 83 71; fax 50 27 98. Open M-F 10am-6pm, Sa 10am-2pm; May-Sept. also Su 10am-2pm.) **Tours** leave from Marktplatz. (M-Sa at 2pm. DM8.50, students and seniors DM5.) You can **exchange money** at several banks near Marktplatz, including **Deutsche Bank,** which has a 24-hr. **ATM** (open M, Tu, and Th 9am-6pm, W and F 9am-3pm). The **Weiberwirtschaft women's agency,** Robert-Franz-Ring 22, complements meetings and lectures with a hotline and cafe. (☎202 43 31. Office and help-line open M-F 10am-4pm; cafe Tu and F 4pm-midnight.) For advice on all things queer, contact **BBZ "Lebensart,"** Schmeerstr. 22 (☎202 33 85). The **post office,** 06108 Halle, is at the corner of Hansering and Große Steinstr., five minutes from the Marktplatz (open M-F 8am-6pm, Sa 9am-noon).

ACCOMMODATIONS AND FOOD

Hotels and *Pensionen* are generally far above the budgetary means of simple traveling folk, but the tourist office lists **private rooms.** Halle's **Jugendherberge (HI),** August-Bebel-Str. 48a (☎/fax 202 47 16), rests in a newly restored mansion north of the market. To get there, it's either a five-minute walk straight down August-Bebel-Str. from the Opernhaus on Universitätsring or a ride on streetcar #7 (direction: "Kröllwitz") to "Puschkinstr.," two stops from the Markt. Follow Geiststr. one block, turn right onto Puschkinstr., and take a right onto August-Bebel-Str. at the *Hong Kong* restaurant. Walk two blocks down; the hostel is on your left. The clean, elegant hostel is fantastically convenient to the city-center in a pleasant student neighborhood. Most rooms have six beds, though some doubles are available. Ask for room #7—it has a balcony. (Breakfast included; dinner DM7. Sheets DM6. Reception 5-11pm, but someone is usually there during the day. Curfew 11pm, but you can get a key. Call ahead. Breakfast included; dinner DM7. Sheets DM6. Dorm beds DM23, over 26 DM28.)

Affordable sit-down restaurants are difficult to find in Halle, but coffeehouses, ice cream parlors, and cafes line Leipziger Str. and Marktpl. Between Marktpl. and Moritzburg, cafes cater to a lively student crowd. The Marktpl. hosts an outdoor **market** daily until 6:30pm, and you'll find an **EDEKA** on Leipziger Str., approximately one block from the train station (open M-F 6:30am-8pm, Sa 8am-4pm). **Café Nöö,** Große Klausstr. 11, at the end of the street facing Domstr., is far töö cööl to say nöö töö. Occupying the ground floor of a building filled with social change and environmental groups, the cafe has hardly a sign marking its existence, and its dim, laid-back interior hosts patrons who know they don't need external approval of their hip-ness. Nöö serves affordable breakfast (DM4.90-6.50, with coffee DM9) and salads for DM6.40-7.20. (☎20 21 65 1. Open M-Th 8am-1am, F 8am-2am, Su 4:30am-8:30am and 10am-2am.) At **Café & Bar Unikum,** Universitätsring 23, there's serious hipster *Uni*-action going on amidst smoke and modern art. Cheap salads (DM4.50-6.30), sandwiches (DM3.30-3.90), and daily specials. (DM4.50-10) comprise the menu. (☎202 13 03. Open M-Th 8am-1am, F 8am-2am, Sa 4pm-2am, Su 6am-1am.) Local flavor suffers an identity crisis at **Zur Apotheke,** Mühlberg 4a, off Mühlgasse between the Dom and Moritzburg fortress, with Thüringer eats served in Sachsen-Anhalt. (DM6-13. Open M-Th 9am-1am, F-Sa 9am-2am, Su 9am-1am.)

SIGHTS

Central Halle revolves around the **Marktplatz,** which bustles with traffic, vegetable stands, and three-card monte con artists. At its center stands the **Roter Turm,** a 400-year-old bell tower. A number of popular myths surround the origin of the tower's name; some credit the copper roof, while others say the architect was a Commie. The most gruesome version relates that after it was built (1418-1506), the blood of the people being executed on the adjoining gallows splattered onto the tower, lending it a grisly tinge. Across from the tower lies the **Marktkirche unsere lieben Frauen,** whose altar is adorned with a triptych painted by Lucas Cranach's disciples. The organ on which Händel began his musical studies swings above the altar; the stops were silent for over 100 years until recent renovations. *(Open M-Tu, Th-F 10am-noon and 3-6pm, W 3-6pm, Sa 10am-noon and 3-5pm. Free 30min. organ concerts Tu and Th at 4pm.)* Just to the right of the church is the red 16th-century **Marktschlößchen,** an unassuming, rather small castle overlooking the Marktplatz. The **Galerie Marktschlößchen,** features works of lesser-known contemporary European artists. *(Markt 13. ☎202 91 41. Open M-F 10am-7pm, Sa-Su 10am-6pm. Free.)* The second floor houses the **Musikinstrumentensammlung des Händel-Hauses,** with an impressive collection of keyboard instruments, as well as three majestic music boxes, on display. *(Open W-Su 1:30-5:30pm. DM2, students DM1, Th free.)*

An 1859 centennial memorial to composer Georg Friedrich Händel decorates the Marktplatz, but the most important Händel shrine is his familial home. The outstanding **Händelhaus,** is a short walk from the market down Kleine Klausstr. *(Große Nikolaistr. 5. ☎50 09 00. Open M-W and F-Su 9:30am-5:30pm, Th 9:30am-9pm. DM4, students and seniors DM2, Th free.)* The museum chronicles Händel's life from his birth in Halle in 1685 to his death in London in 1759, where he lived for the last 50 years of his life. The exhibits demonstrate his facility with languages, as he set texts in German, Italian, and English. The museum also holds many historic instruments, as well as an exhibit on the history of Halle's proud musical tradition. If you call ahead, you can also get a cassette tour which covers the composer's career. From Händel's home, the **Dom** is a five-minute walk down Nikolaistr. *(Open M-Sa 2:30-4pm.)* This ancient complex, begun in 1250, remains a significant repository of religious relics. Today the church's most treasured offerings, renovations permitting, are 17 life-size figures by Peter Schroh from the 16th century. Witness the annual **Händel-Festspiele** (June 8-17, 2001), a celebration of Baroque music and one of its greatest masters. Tickets are available from the tourist office.

To reach the white-washed **Moritzburg fortress,** go around the far side of the Dom and head downhill, then turn right on Schloßburgstr. and walk up the hill. The **Staatliche Galerie Moritzburg** occupies most of the 15th-century giant. The largest art museum in Sachsen-Anhalt has three galleries; the largest and most interesting is directly up and to the left after the main entrance. It focuses mostly on 19th- and 20th-century German painters. Halle's once extensive Expressionist collection—including works by Max Beckmann, Paul Klee, and Oskar Kokoschka—offended Hitler, who drew heavily from this museum to furnish the infamous exhibit of *Entartete Kunst* (degenerate art) that toured Nazi Germany. Although much of the collection was either burned or sold off by the Nazis, the salvaged works remain an impressive monument to artistic freedom. Lyonel Feininger, Bauhaus headmaster and Expressionist painter, lived part-time in the tower at the entrance from 1929 to 1931 while completing his series of paintings of Halle; two still remain in the museum. The fortress is a fantastic place for an art gallery; the sloping and curving walls do a wonderful job of accentuating the excellent works inside. *(☎281 20 10. Open Tu 11am-8:30pm, W-Su 10am-6pm; last entry 30min. before closing. DM5, students DM3, Tu free.)*

🎵🎭 ENTERTAINMENT AND NIGHTLIFE

Halle's swiftly growing theater scene produces the classics as well as contemporary German plays. Pick up a free copy of the city magazines *Fritz* and *Blitz* at the tourist office or in cafes and bars to find out what's going on.

Halle hosts a number of organ concerts in the **Konzerthalle Ulrichkirche,** Kleine Brauhausstr. 26. *(☎221 30 26. Box office open M 10am-1pm and 3-6pm, Tu and Th 3-6pm, F 10am-1pm. Tickets DM12-38, students DM8-29.)* Tickets for the **Philharmonisches Staatsorchester Halle** can also be found at the Konzerthalle, and student tickets are only DM10. *(Box office open M-F 10am-1pm, W, Tu, Th 3-6pm. ☎221-30 00. Tickets regularly DM14-32.)* Completed in 1990, the **Neues Theater,** Große Ulrichstr. 50 *(☎205 02 22),* features a wide palate of works—everything from

Schiller, Shakespeare, Molière, and Brecht to Halle's own homegrown playwrights. (☎205 02 22. Box office open M-Sa 10am-8:30pm and 1hr. before performance. DM10-25, students DM7-15. No performances mid-July to Sept.) Halle's satirical theater, **Die Kiebitzensteiner,** in the Moritzburg fortress' south tower, is tucked beneath the fortress and serves as a contemporary forum for criticism, holding spicy and engaging performances. **Kiebitzkeller,** the restaurant downstairs, offers snacks and spirits for nightly performances. (☎202 39 81. Theater open Tu-Sa from 7pm. Ticket office open Tu-Sa 5-8pm and 1hr. before shows. Restaurant opens at 6pm on evenings of performances.) **Kleines Thalia Theater,** on Thaliapassage off Geiststr., premieres avant-garde theater productions and kiddie shows. (☎20 40 50. Box office open Tu and F 10am-noon and 1-4pm, W 10am-noon, Th 10am-noon and 1-6pm, and 1hr. before performances. DM12, children and students DM7.) **Turm,** in the northeast tower of the Moritzburg fortress, hosts the city's *Studentenklub* for Halle's literary set. The music is a mishmash of disco, punk, funk, blues, techno, and rock performed by local bands. A *Biergarten* and grill are outside. (☎202 37 37. Open daily 6-10pm.) Foreign students with ID (18 and over) are welcome. (Open Su, Tu, and sometimes Th from 8:30pm. Disco W and F-Sa from 10pm.) If Turm isn't your scene and Unikum is crowded for a football match, check out **das haus,** along Studentenring at Scharrenstr. 10 (☎202 20 45). The wood-and-metal decorating motif and funky chairs will make your beers and crêpes (DM6) go down easy. **Pierrot,** Großer Sandberg 10, just off Leipziger Str., is a popular gay and lesbian bar and disco. Wednesday hosts a singles party, while Thursday features house and techno. (☎290 32 31. Open M-Th and Su 6pm-late. F-Sa disco after 8pm. Sa cover DM5.)

NAUMBURG ☎03445

Naumburg's colorful Marktplatz buildings, lovely detailed cathedral, and cheerful, artsy atmosphere make it a special place to visit. The architectural restoration so prevalent in much of eastern Germany in recent years has been highly successful here, where building sites are far less common and historical buildings shine with clean, colorful facades.

🛈 **PRACTICAL INFORMATION.** Naumburg is an excellent sidelight during a visit to **Leipzig** (30min. by express train; those travelling on the cheap should take the 1½hr. local train via Großkorbetha, DM14.80); **Halle** (45min., 1 per hr., DM12); **Weimar** (45min., 31 per day, DM12); or **Erfurt** (30min., 31 per day, DM16.20). There are two competing **tourist offices** in Naumburg. One is on the market square at Markt 6. (☎20 16 14; fax 26 60 47. Open M-F 9am-6pm, Sa 9am-1pm.) The other is near the entrance to the Dom at Steinweg 15. (☎/fax 20 25 14. Open daily 10am-5pm.) Both are stocked with brochures and books on Naumburg and the surrounding region, and the office on the Markt arranges **private rooms** (from DM32) for free. To reach the Altstadt, head down Markgrafenweg from the train station, bearing right until you reach the end of the street. To the left is a winding cobble-stoned path that leads uphill to the town proper. At the top of the path a sign points to the Dom; follow it until the cathedral's huge towers poke above the rooftops to guide you.

📷🛏 **ACCOMMODATIONS AND FOOD.** To reach Naumburg's **Jugendgästehaus,** Am Tennispl. 9 (☎/fax 70 34 22), from the Marktplatz, follow Wenzelsstr. out of the old walled city to Bürgergartenstr., which appears slightly to the right at the end of Wenzelsstr., then go straight until you see signs for the hostel (30min.). Still undergoing renovations, Naumburg's hostel is nothing out of the ordinary, but many of its clean 2- to 6-bed rooms have attached bathrooms. (Breakfast included. Sheets DM6. Reception 5-10pm. Dorms DM24 per person, over 26 DM29; doubles DM27, over 26 DM32.) The hostel is a long hike out of town; for cheap accommodations in the city, call ahead to the tourist office for a private room. For a chic cup of coffee or light meal, try **Engelgasse 3** (☎20 07 70). To get there, face the Rathaus from the Markt and walk all the way around the building. A cafe, used book store, and art gallery, it has the retro, feel-good, funky style of renowned Leipzig illustrator Thomas Müller, further enhanced by omnipresent samples of the artist's work. Almost all of the ingredients on the menu come from small area farms; a *Brötchen* with *Bratwurst* or goat's milk gouda will run DM4.90-DM5.90. (Open M-W 11am-7pm, Th-F 11am-11pm, Sa 11am-4pm. Daily lunch specials served noon-2:30pm.) Cheap kebabs and other *Imbiß* fare are not hard to find on the way from the station or on streets off the Markt, and at **Cafe Kanzlei** on the Markt (☎20 06 10) you can get *Wurst* with *Brot* for DM4.50. **Kanzlei** and the **Ratskeller** across the way are both open until 1am daily, and their summer outdoor seating provides a lovely place to observe colorful Naumburg as the evening light fades.

🕘 SIGHTS. The **Naumburger Dom** has a captivating interior full of detail, from the procession of animals up the railing to the east choir and its original pews, to the depictions of the life of Christ along the top of the west choir screen and the twelve surprisingly realistic statues inside the west choir. Perhaps the best known of these statues, and certainly the most interesting, is Uta, who stands with her husband Eckehard on the right side. Uta is considered to be one of the best examples of realism between classical times and the Renaissance. Too humble to carve his name in the cathedral's stone, the artist is remembered today simply as the *Naumburger Meister*. The helpful staff at the front desk provides English pamphlets on request; English tours are also available. *(Open Apr.-Sept. M-Sa 9am-6pm, Su noon-6pm; Nov.-Feb. M-Sa 9am-4pm, Su noon-4pm; Mar. and Oct. M-Sa 9am-5pm, Su noon-5pm. DM6, students and seniors DM4. DM10 fee to take photos or use video cameras inside.)*

The rest of Naumburg has recovered amazingly well from its 45 years as a backwater Red Army post. A jaunt past the Dom on Steinweg leads to Naumburg's lively Marktplatz, which hosts a **market** on Mondays, Wednesdays, and Saturdays. Just off the market square is the **Wenzelskirche,** the Dom's runner-up. The renovation of the organ inside, to be completed in December 2000, should draw a larger portion of the musical community to the church's concerts. *(Open May-Sept. daily 10am-6pm; Mar.-Apr. and Oct. daily 10am-5pm; Nov.-Feb. M-Sa 9am-4pm, Su 10am-4pm. Tours Th at 2pm and Sa at 10am. Free. Organ concerts May-Oct. W and Sa-Su at noon. DM2.)* Lest you think Naumburg functions solely as a bastion of religious relics, Nietzsche, Fichte, and the world-famous founder of Egyptology, Richard Pelsius, all lived in Naumburg for parts of their illustrious lives. The **Nietzsche-Haus** has a well-presented display on Nietzsche's life, plus a second floor full of esoteric temporary exhibits. The philosopher lived in Naumburg from 1850 to 1858, and then returned in 1890 to live with his mother for seven years as his sanity degenerated. The samples of his handwriting on display demonstrate his degeneration during these years. *(Weingarten 18, off Jakobstr. ☎ 20 16 38. Open Tu-F 2-5pm, Sa-Su 10am-4pm. DM3, students DM1.50.)* The **Stadtmuseum "Hohe Lilie,"** contains exhibits detailing the history of the town, including a display on the region's *Bier* and a room dedicated to the town's patron saint, St. Wenzel. *(Grochlitzer Str. 49. ☎ 70 35 03. Open Tu-Su 10am-5pm. DM4, children under 14 free.)*

A pilgrimage to the Thomaskirche in Leipzig brings you right to the feet of J.S. Bach, where he lies under the floor of the upper level of the church. Bach wasn't always buried there, and his body did a good bit of moving around after his death, until finding final rest here in his own church in 1949. He was originally buried under the nearby Johanniskirche, but nobody knew exactly where; during the Bach-Renaissance of the 19th century, people began clamoring for a definite location of the body, so a professor of anatomy named Wilhelm His was called onto the scene and identified the body within reasonable certainty in 1849. It was then placed in a solid coffin and buried in the church's graveyard. The church was destroyed by a bombing on December 4, 1943, so on the 200th anniversary of his death, July 28, 1949, the city removed Bach from the ruins of the graveyard and brought him into the Thomaskirche. They didn't quite have his new coffin ready yet, so they watched over the body day and night until August 13, when they finally reclosed the coffin. A year later, on July 28, 1950, they finally lowered Bach into the floor, where he has been ever since.

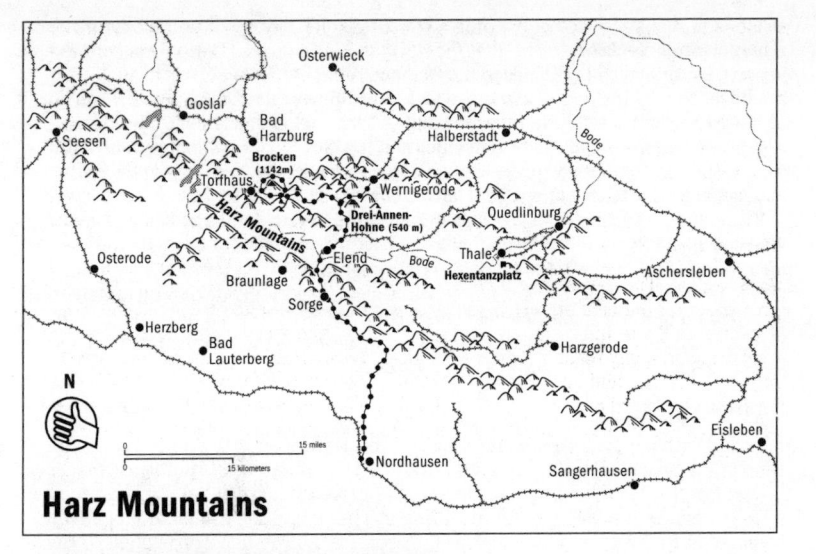

Harz Mountains

HARZ MOUNTAINS

Heinrich Heine wrote that even Mephistopheles stopped and trembled when he approached the Harz, the devil's dearest mountains. It's easy to see why Heine—as well as Goethe, Bismarck, and a host of others—fell in love with these mist-shrouded woodlands. Germany's 45-year division allowed the Harz Mountains to flourish in an artificial time warp. Since the region straddled the Iron Curtain, both East and West declared much of it off-limits, sparing it from development.

■ ORIENTATION. Now that the armed border guards have gone, visitors have taken their places and multiplied like mosquitoes; hikers and spa-fiends alike rush to these rugged hills in the heart of the restored nation. The range stretches from the northwestern **Oberharz** to the wind-sheltered valleys of the south and **Wernigerode** in the east. Throughout the Harz, historic villages compete with the lush, natural beauty of the mountains and valleys. In summer, the foliage offers great biking and hiking, while the first snow signals the beginning of the skiing, skating, and tobogganing season. The **Ostharz**, untouched by the deforming winds of capitalism, is endowed with gorgeous scenery and half-abandoned castles.

▣ GETTING AROUND. The **Harzquerbahn** and **Brockenbahn,** antique, narrow-gauge railways, steam from Nordhausen to **Wernigerode,** pass through the unfortunately named towns of **Sorge** and **Elend** (Sorrow and Misery), reach a 540m peak on Drei Annen Hohne, and chug along to Brocken, the Harz's highest peak (1142m). Trains run regularly in summer from 8:30am to 8:30pm. Schedules are available at most tourist offices, on the web at www.hsb-wr.de, and in the free monthly pamphlet *Brocken Tips.*

The easiest way to travel between the Ostharz and Oberharz is by **bus** between **Bad Harzburg,** the region's transportation hub, and **Wernigerode.** A **train** from Wernigerode to Bad Harzburg connects through Halberstadt and Vienenburg (1¾hr., 1 per hr., DM19.20). From Bad Harzburg, regular buses continue to Torfhaus and Braunlage. A more strenuous and interesting way involves a little jaunt through the woods. Torfhaus, Braunlage, Schierke, Elend, and Drei Annen Hohne all lie within a day's hike of one another.

▤ PRACTICAL INFORMATION. The **regional tourist office** in Goslar (p. 495) and the **regional bus station** in Wernigerode offer a wealth of information for navigating the region. Be sure to find times in advance; schedules vary greatly between seasons and some buses only come a few times per day. Pick up a copy of the *Fahrplan der Verkehrs- und Tarifgemeinschaft Ostharz* (DM3) for a comprehensive list of bus and rail lines in the Ostharz. A similar *Fahrplan* is available for the buses in the *Goslar Landkreis*, which runs all over the *Oberharz*. Always be prepared for bad weather here, especially sudden and violent rainstorms. Travelers should call the **Braunlage Wetterstation** at ☎ (05520) 13 20 for summertime (Apr.-Oct.) weather conditions (open 5:30am-11pm). During the winter months (Nov.-Mar.), call **Schneetelefon** at ☎ (05321) 340 40 or 200 24.

If possible, dive into the Harz and join in the immense regional celebration of **Walpurgisnacht** (April 30). The hedonistic festivities, immortalized by Goethe, center around legendary **witches** who sweep through the sky on broomsticks to land on the peak of **Brocken.** The legendary witches dance with the devil until midnight, at which point the May King cleans house. *Brocken Tips* lists events and activities in Wernigerode, Goslar, and Quedlinburg. For more on cultural happenings and hiking tips, pick up a free copy of *Harz-Blick* at any Harz tourist office.

BAD HARZBURG ☎ 05322

Perched in a prime locale at the edge of the Harz, just a few miles from the renowned Brocken peak, Bad Harzburg is a vital jumping-off point for hikers bound for glory in the mountains. Its integral place in the regional transportation network makes it a gateway for exploring the Harz, and the availability of cheap rooms makes it a great place to crash. In contrast to the hardcore hikers of the neighboring peaks, the majority of Bad Harzburg's tourist population is young only at heart, and frequents the spa scene to relieve aching bones.

⊡ PRACTICAL INFORMATION. Trains head to **Hannover** (2 per day, DM27); **Braunschweig** (every 2 hrs., DM 9.70); **Hildesheim** (every 2 hrs., DM17); and **Goslar** (every 2 hrs., DM4). Buses connect Bad Harzburg to **Torfhaus, Wernigerode,** and **Braunlage.** The **tourist office,** Herzog-Wilhelm Str. 86 (☎ 753 30; fax 753 29; email info@bad-harzburg.de; www.bad-harzburg.de), is located in the *Kurzentrum.* From the train station, walk straight down Herzog-Wilhelm Str. (15min.). The office has an automatic room reservation board with pictures, but the information is also available on paper. Free maps, and lots of information about everything one could ever want in Bad Harzburg are available. There is also a smaller office located in the train station. For a taxi, call ☎ 26 26.

⌐ ACCOMMODATIONS. Hotels and *Pensionen* are in endless supply in Bad Harzburg. There's one on almost every corner. The tourist office has a long list of private rooms, guest-houses, pensionen and hotels—finding a room under DM40 is *"kein Problem"* (no problem)—guest house start at DM20. For those in search of a vigorous crowd, the **Jugendherberge** is a bit of a hike from the train station (50min), but close to the trails of the National Park. (☎ 45 82; fax 18 67. Breakfast included. DM 25, over 26 DM 26; non-members DM29.) Try **Haus Königsmark** for pastoral bliss and a maternal manager; it's a 20-min. walk from the station. From the train station, turn right and follow Dr. Heinrich Jasper Str., then turn left on Am Schloß-park. (☎ 502 06. Breakfast included. Singles and doubles from DM30 per person.)

▣ SIGHTS. Travelers who have been hitting churches and castles by the dozens need to tone it down and ditch the running shoes in Bad Harzbug. This little town is all about relaxation, whether that involves hiking through wooded trails or soaking in sauna steam. The **Harzburger Sole-Therme,** Herzog-Wilhelm Str. 86, offers all kinds of aquatic cures—hot and cold baths (2 hr. DM13), saunas (DM20), and a variety of massage therapy. The bathers and steamers tend to be on the older side, but the occasional twenty-something does wander through. *(☎ 75 360. Open M-F 8am-9pm, Sa-Su 8am-7pm; Saunarium Men only 8am-1pm W, Women only 8am-9pm Th.)* For the more active set, **Nationalpark Harz,** located right of the *Sole-Therme,* offers pristine hills and loads of trails. *(☎ 918 90, fax 918 919, www.nationalpark-harz.de.)* The **Haus der Natur** on the edge of the park has hiking information, pictures and dried

samples of indigenous fauna and flora, and stuffed animals, including several adorable rodents and a gargantuan beast called the *Schwarzwild*. (☎ *17 74. Open daily
except Tuesday, 11am-5pm. Free.)* To see the sights of the *Nationalpark* without the
walk, the *Burgberg-Seilbahn* offers a short (very short) gondola-like lift up one of
the hills. (☎ *75 3 71. Up DM4; down DM 3; round-trip DM 6.)*

TORFHAUS   ☎ 05320

Torfhaus, a tiny cluster of buildings dropped on the highway between Bad
Harzburg and Braunlage, is barely large enough to be called a town. But this seem-
ing speck of a city is perhaps the most favored jumping-off point for hiking in the
Harz; it is home to the path to **Brocken**, the tallest peak in the Harz at 1142m. Since
Goethe's first ascent in 1777, pilgrims have tramped the **Goetheweg**, the 16km
round-trip trail to the summit. Though much of the path is littered in parts, it is still
lovely and historically interesting, occasionally following the old patrol road along
the Iron Curtain. To get to the *Goetheweg*, walk away from the bus stop (toward
Braunlage) and turn left at the yellow *Altenau—8km* sign. The Brocken peak
(2½hr. from Torfhaus) is now a full-fledged tourist trap. The **Brockenmuseum**,
inside the electronic warfare post of the former East German state security service, houses an information counter where you can buy hiking maps. (Open daily
in summer 9:30am-5pm. DM3, students DM2.) From the top of the Brocken, trails
head to the Ostharz, leading to Schierke and Drei Annen Hohne. The
Schmalspurbahn, a train that transports less nimble tourists to and from the
Brocken to Wernigerode, runs regularly, takes a long time, and costs a lot. (1hr.
One-way DM26, round-trip DM42.) The **Nationalparkhaus Torfhaus**, Torfhaus 21,
sells maps of Brocken's trails. (☎/fax 263. DM7.80. Open daily 9am-5pm.)

Torfhaus lies at the midpoint of **bus** #63 and 422 connecting Bad Harzburg and
Braunlage. **Ski-Verleih**, near the bus stop, rents cross-country skis for DM20 per
day. (☎203. Open daily 8am-5pm when snow adorns the ground.) Walking away
from Bad Harzburg, turn right at the *Altenau-8km* sign for the **Jugendherberge (HI)**,
Torfhaus 3. (☎242; fax 254. Members only. Ski rentals from DM10 per day. Reception 12:15-1pm, 4:30-5pm, and 6:15-7pm. Curfew 10pm. DM23, over 26 DM28.) The
postal code is 38667.

BRAUNLAGE   ☎ 05520

The ideal stop for hikers working the trails around Brocken, Braunlage provides a
needed rest from other excessively cute Harz villages. The town amply compensates for its lack of architectural panache with kilometers of excellent trails and
the luxury of spas at backpacker prices. Packed with spa connoisseurs in summer
and skiers in winter, Braunlage is also a likely bus stop for those traveling from the
Oberharz to the Ostharz.

🛈 PRACTICAL INFORMATION. Buses cruise in from **Bad Harzburg** (40min., DM7)
and **Torfhaus** (20min., DM4) to Braunlage. Disembark at the "Von-Langen-Str." stop
in the center of town. To get to the **tourist office**, Elbingeröder Str. 17, backtrack on
Herzog-Wilhelm-Str. and turn right onto Elbingeröder Str. You'll think you're entering a spaceship, but it's actually an enormous interactive electronic board that
indicates which hotels and pensions are full (red lights) and which have vacancies
(green lights). A brochure with a hotel list (on paper) is also available for luddites.
Maps and hiking trail information are also available. (☎ 194 33; fax 930 720; email
info@braunlage.de; www.braunlage.de. Open M-F 8am-12:30pm and 1:30-6pm, Sa
9:30am-noon.) The **Post-Apotheke**, Marktstr. 5, is the local **pharmacy**. (☎930 20. Open
M-F 8am-1pm and 3-6pm, Sa 8am-1pm.) The **post office**, 38700 Braunlage, is at
Marktstr. 16 (open M-F 9am-noon and 2:30-5:30pm, Sa 9am-noon).

📷 ACCOMMODATIONS AND FOOD. The view through the wall of windows
in the dining room of Braunlage's **Jugendherberge (HI)**, Von-Langen-Str. 28, provides reason enough to crash in its ideal location. The hostel often fills with school
groups, so call ahead. From the bus stop, follow Von-Langen-Str. uphill for 15

minutes. (☎22 38; fax 15 69. Breakfast included. Sheets DM5.70. Reception 1-10pm. DM22; over 26 DM27.) Braunlage has so many *Pensionen* (from DM30) and vacation homes (from DM25) you won't believe your eyes. Check out the electronic board at the tourist office or roam the streets. Pick up **groceries** at **Penny Markt,** Marktstr. 22 (open M-F 8am-8pm, Sa 8am-4pm), and fresh produce next door at **Fruchthaus Möller,** Marktstr. 21 (open M-F 9am-1pm and 3-6pm, Sa 9am-1pm). **Rhodos,** Elbingeröder Str. 3, whips up Greek specialties (DM10-20) and pizzas (DM8.50-13.50) in the company of pasty-skinned statues. (☎22 23. Open daily 11:30am-3pm and 5pm-midnight.)

🅰🈴 HIKING AND ENTERTAINMENT. The **Wurmbergseilbahn** chairlift is an exhilarating way to approach the hiking paths around Braunlage. Take the lift to the top (17min.) to access the hiking trail to Brocken (3hr.) Alternatively, disembark at the *Mittelstation* to reach the **Schierke** (2½hr.). The lift departs from the mountain base at the huge parking lot behind the ice rink. From the tourist office, turn left, then take the first right to its end. (☎725. Open May-Oct. 9am-5:20pm. One-way to the top DM8, round-trip DM13. To Mittelstation DM5, round-trip DM8.) When winter hits, cower inside the **enclosed lift** on your way up the slopes. (Open Dec.-Jan. daily 8:40am-4:40pm; Feb.-Apr. 9am-5:10pm. Day pass for open-air cabins and ski lifts DM32, for enclosed cabins and lifts DM35.) Rent **skis** at **Horst Bähr,** Harzburger Str. 23 (☎627) for DM20 per day, or try **Café Zur Seilbahn** at the chair lift station. (☎600. Open daily 9am-5pm. DM25 per day.) An **ice rink** on Harzburger Str. fulfills the need for winter sports year-round. (☎21 91. Open Tu and Th-F 10am-noon and 2-4pm; W and Sa 10am-noon, 2-4pm, and 8-10pm; Su 10am-noon, 1:30-3:30pm, and 4-6pm. DM5.50, with *Kurkarte* DM5. Skate rental DM4.50.) The **Kurmittelhaus,** Ramsenweg 2 (☎22 41), and the adjacent **Hallen- und Freizeitbad** (☎27 88) soak, steam, massage, and mud-pack the weary into clean, relaxed, well-adjusted personalities. (Kurmittelhaus open M-F 7:30am-noon and 2-5pm. Baths open M-W and F 9am-12:30pm and 2-6:30pm, Th 9am-12:30pm and 2-8:30pm, Sa 9am-6:30pm, Su 9am-5pm; Tu women only. Sauna DM15; pool DM9.)

WERNIGERODE ☎03943

Wernigerode was one of Goethe's secret spots in the hills, but with its central location between the Western and Eastern Harz, this secret was too hard to keep. Though the 20th century has plastered the town with many gray, block-shaped buildings, Wernigerode's *Altstadt* seems untouched by the passage of time, and the multitude of travelers who traipse through the Harz every year have taken notice. The half-timbered town is crowned by one of the most magnificent castles in the region. Riders of the **Querbahn** visit the town en route to Brocken, while others come to enjoy the wide pedestrian areas lined with well-preserved architectural treats and plenty of shopping options. Wernigerode is the natural crossing point from Western to Eastern Harz, making it the region's most touristed town.

🛈 PRACTICAL INFORMATION. To reach Wernigerode from **Magdeburg,** change **trains** at **Halberstadt** (30min., 1 per hr., DM7.60); trains also run directly from **Halle** (2hr., every 2hr., DM31), and a **bus** travels from **Bad Harzburg.** The town has two **train stations. Wernigerode-Westentor** is the next-to-last stop on the *Harzquerbahn* and close to the city center—head up Mittelstr., and then right on Bahnhofstr. to arrive at the Markt. The antique steamer also stops at the main **Bahnhof Wernigerode,** next to the regional **bus terminal.** To get to the Marktpl. and the tourist office from the train station, cross the street, walk right and then hang a left on Albert-Bartels-Str., which leads to the tourist office and the pedestrian zone.

The **tourist office,** Nicolaipl. 1, will be on your right around the corner from the *Rathaus.* The staff books **rooms** (from DM35) in private homes or hotels. The office also sells a small town guide (DM3) with an excellent pull-out map. (☎63 30 35; fax 63 20 40; www.harztourist.de. Open May-Oct. M-F 9am-7pm, Sa 10am-4pm, Su 10am-3pm; Oct.-Apr. M-F 9am-6pm, Sa-Su 9am-3pm.) **Tours** depart from the tourist office. (Tu at 10:30am, W-Th at 2pm, Sa at 10:30am and 2pm, Su at 2pm.

SAXONY-ANHALT

DM5.) There is a **Deutsche Bank** near the tourist office, at the corner of Kohlmarkt and Breite Str. (open M and W 8:30am-1pm and 2-6pm, T and Th 8am-1pm, F 8am-1pm). **Exchange currency** at the **post office,** Marktstr. 14, 38855 Wernigerode (open M-F 8am-6pm, Sa 8am-noon). There is a **pharmacy,** Rathaus-Apotheke, on Nikolaipl. (open M-F 8am-6:30pm, Sa 9am-1pm).

▐▐┇ ACCOMMODATIONS AND FOOD. To reach Wernigerode's **Jugendgäste-haus,** Friedrichstr. 53, from the "Westerntor" station, go right on Unter den Zindeln and turn right on Friedrichstr. (25min.). From the station, take bus #1, 4, or 5 to "Kirchstr." The hostel is on the corner of Friedrichstr. and Kirchstr. Rooms have been refurbished and sport modern facilities. The friendly staff serves a fresh breakfast buffet. (☎ 63 20 61. Breakfast included. Sheets DM6. Reception noon-9pm. DM21, over 26 DM27.) **Spar,** on Breite Str. near the *Rathaus*, takes care of all your **grocery** needs (open M-W and F 8:30am-6pm, Th 8:30am-7pm, Sa 8am-1pm). There's also a **farmer's market** in the pedestrian zone (Tu and Th 10am-5pm). **Euro-grill,** Westernstr. 6 (☎ 60 55 65), just off the *Markt*, serves salads (DM3-6) and lighter fare with a little twist. Better yet, they only charge DM4 for a *Döner;* on Saturday, it's a mere DM3.50. **Café Casa Nova,** Breite Str. 89, serves delicious pizzas for DM4-12. (☎ 63 30 60. Breakfast DM5-7. Open daily 11am-8pm.)

▩ SIGHTS. Wernigerode's **Schloß,** on its looming perch in the wooded mountains above town, is a plush and pompous monument to the Second Reich. Though the place was maintained by the GDR as a museum of feudalism, its guiding spirit was much more recent. Graf Otto, one of Bismarck's flunkies, hosted Kaiser Wilhelm I here for wildly extravagant hunting expeditions. The perfectly preserved **Königszimmer** guest suite, where the *Kaiser* stayed, oozes masculine luxury down to the deep green and gold brocaded wallpaper in the bedroom. The other regal rooms include a chapel, a Schreibzimmer that must have wiped out a small forest in its construction, and the jaw-dropping **Festsaal,** featuring a sky-high inlaid wooden ceiling, panoramic murals of glorious Teutonic dukes, and a teetering crystal chandelier. (☎ 55 30 30. Open May-Oct. daily 10am-6pm; Nov.-Apr. Tu-F 10am-4pm, Sa-Su 10am-6pm. Last entry 30min before closing. DM8, students DM7; DM1 additional for a tour.) The flower-trimmed terrace sports a vista of the **Brocken,** the Harz's tallest and supposedly most haunted mountain. The Schloß can be reached via the chugging **Bimmelbahn,** which leaves from the intersection of Teichdamm and Klintgasse behind the Rathaus. (☎ 60 40 00. May-Oct. daily every 20min. 9:30am-5:30pm; Nov.-Apr. every 45min. 10:30am-5:50pm. One-way DM3, under 10 DM2.) The more dignified take the gravel *Christiantalweg* path or the white brick road marked "Burgberg" and ascend the wooded park to the castle on foot (30min. from town center).

In the center of town, the renovated **Rathaus** looms over the marketplace with strikingly sharp slopes and petite wooden figures of saints, virgins, miners, and other Wernigerode notables decorating the facade of the 500-year-old building. Walk around the *Altstadt* for a nearly lethal dose of half-timbered architecture. The **Krummelsche Haus,** Breite Str. 72, is covered with ornate wood carvings to the point of suffocation. The **Älteste Haus,** Hinterstr. 48, is the oldest house in the city, having survived fires, bombs, and various acts of God since its construction in the early 15th century. The **Kleinste Haus,** Kochstr. 43, is 3m wide and the door is only 1.7m high. (Open daily 10am-4pm. DM1.) The **Normalste Haus,** Witzestr. 13, has no distinguishing traits.

HALBERSTADT
☎ 03941

Founded by Charlemagne in the 9th century as the seat of an episcopal see, this medieval town was destroyed in WWII, but partially restored by the GDR authorities. It remains a handsome city in the Harz worthy of attention.

▐ PRACTICAL INFORMATION. Halberstadt sits in the northeast region of the Harz. **Trains** travel between Halberstadt and **Magdeburg** (DM 15.40), and **Thale** (DM 7.80). Regular **buses** also travel to many of the nearby Harz towns. A system of **streetcars** runs through the city; the #1 and #2 run from the Hauptbahnhof into the

SAXONY-ANHALT

center (45-minute ticket DM1.50). The **tourist office,** Hinter dem Rathaus 6 (☎551 815; fax 551 089; email Halberstadt.Info@t-online.de; www.halberstadt.de), is right off the main pedestrian way. Free maps and room reservations await. The **post office** is located on Unter den Zwicken (☎66 00; open M-F 8am-6pm; Sa 8am-noon).

📷 **ACCOMMODATIONS AND FOOD.** Halberstadt doesn't cater to the budget traveler; just about everything in sight is 'business class.' The city lacks a youth hostel, and all of the cheaper pensionen are located prohibitively far away from the center of town. **Altstadtpension Ratsmühle,** Hoher Weg 1-2, is probably your best bet—from the tourist office, go right out the door, then right on the main street, and follow Hoher Weg down into a pedestrian zone; it's on your right. Inside this half-timbered facade, plush, renovated rooms come complete with large bathrooms, TVs, and telephones. (☎573 799. Breakfast included. Singles DM59, Doubles DM99.) Dining options are also a bit scarce. **Asia Bistro Mekong,** Fischmarkt Str., does budget Chinese dishes from DM3 with the compulsory dragon decor. (☎610 424. Open daily 9am-9pm.)

📷 **SIGHTS.** Most of Halberstadt's sights are centered around the **Domplatz,** across from the *Rathaus.* Ongoing renovations aim to bring this area up to speed with the other Harz towns; however, it is still very much a work in progress. The **Domplatz** centers around the **Dom St. Stephanus,** an impressive but well-worn structure dating back to the 800s. It is currently undergoing an intensive restoration process to restore some of its original splendor. The **Domschatz** claims the largest German collection of art from the Middle Ages held by a church. *(Dom and Domschatz open M-F 10am-5pm, Sat. 10am-4:30pm, Sun. 11am-4:30pm. DM2.50, children free.)* The Dom is flanked by a strip of museums; working back from the far end, the **Stadtisches Museum,** displays the city history, beginning with prehistoric clay pots and traveling through time past a gorgeous Victorian frock from the 1870s, a collection of early motorcycles, and even an early *die Grüne (*Green Party) leaflet from 1989. WWII buffs will be fascinated by horrific photographs of the city's devastation during the 1945 bombing. *(Domplatz 36. ☎55 14 71. Open Tu-F 9am-4pm, Sa-Su 10am-6pm.)* Sharing the same front yard, the **Museum Heineanum** offers a foray into nature with exhibitions directed at a young audience. *(Domplatz 37. ☎55 14 60. Open Tu-F 9am-5pm, Sa-Su 10am-5pm.)* Further down the walkway, the **Gleimhaus** traces the life of the Gleim family's role in classic German literature. Books, letters, and original furniture provide insight into the work, and the room full of oil-painting portraits looks like the *Guess Who?* game for German literature. *(Domplatz 31. ☎687 10; fax 687 40. Open M-F 9am-5pm, Sa-Su 10am-4pm.)* The *Gleimhaus,* along with the *Stadtisches Museum* and the *Museum Heinanum,* are covered by a combination ticket available for DM5, children DM2.50. Across the street from the *Dom* complex, the tower of the 13th-century **Martinikirche,** offers a sweeping view of the surrounding landscapes. *(☎445 360. Open May-Oct. daily 10am-5pm; Nov.-Apr. daily 11am-6pm. Tower DM1.)*

QUEDLINBURG ☎03946

Quedlinburg is a sightseer's paradise. Its narrow, winding streets are dripping with historically alluring eye-candy in the form of pastel-painted half-timbered houses, towering churches, and a castle on the hill to top it off. Today, much of the city appears much as it might have in 919 when Heinrich I waited in the market square for the news that he'd been chosen as emperor. The preservation efforts are part of massive restoration which took place after 1994, when UNESCO named Quedlinburg one of the world's most important cultural treasures. A walk through the intricately decorated market square is proof enough that they were right.

📷 **PRACTICAL INFORMATION. Trains** arrive every hour from **Thale** (10min., DM3) and **Magdeburg** (1½hr., DM20). There are also regular **buses** that depart from the train station to most Harz towns. Rent **bikes** at the **Fahrradverleih** at the station. (☎51 51 18. DM15 per day, mountain bikes DM20.) Quedlinburg's **tourist office,**

Markt 2, books **rooms** (from DM25) for free, sells museum tickets, and offers an invaluable map. (☎90 56 24 or 90 56 25; fax 90 56 29; email QTM@t-online.de; www.quedlinburg.de. Open May-Sept. M-F 9am-7pm, Sa 10am-4pm; Mar.-Apr., Oct., and Dec. M-F 9am-6pm, Sa 10am-3pm; Nov. and Jan.-Feb. M-F 9am-5pm.) **Tours** leave from the tourist office (Apr.-Oct. daily 10am and 2pm; Nov.-Mar. daily 10am). **Exchange money** or use the **ATM** in the **Deutsche Bank,** Am Markt 3 (open M, Tu, Thurs. 8:30am-12:30pm, 1:30pm-6pm, Wed. 8:30am-12:30pm, F 1:30pm-3pm; ATM 24 hours). The **post office,** 06484 Quedlinburg, stands at the intersection of Bahnhofstr. and Turnstr. (open M-F 8am-6pm, Sa 8:30am-noon).

░░ ACCOMMODATIONS AND FOOD. Quedlinburg's **Jugendherberge,** Neuendorf 28, is located in the heart of town, just a few streets away from the Markt. Two- and 4-bed rooms are hidden inside its half-timbered facade. (☎28 81; fax 916 53. Breakfast included. Sheets DM6. Dorm beds DM 24, over 26 DM 29.) Private rooms are also readily available at a prices suitable for a backpacking budget. Look for *Zimmer Frei* signs, inquire at the tourist office, or try **Gästehaus Biehl,** Blankenburger Str. 39. Head up Marktstr. from the *Markt* and turn left onto Marschlingerhof, which becomes Blankenburger Str. Set in a flowery residential neighborhood, this guesthouse offers rooms with TV, stereos, and baths in hall. (☎/fax 70 35 38. Breakfast included. Call ahead. Singles DM35, doubles DM60.)

Culinary delights await on every corner in town. On the way to the castle, grab a local brew at the **Brauhaus Lüdde,** Blasistr. 14. The interior is a high-ceilinged, circular brewing hall with a bar, filled with shiny copper brewing kettles. Try the light *Pilsner* (DM3.90) or the nutty *Lüdde-Alt* (DM3.30). Tasty snacks and meals run DM12. (☎70 52 06. Open M-Th 11am-midnight, F-Sa 11am-1am, Su 11am-10pm.) **Ollie's Bistro,** halfway down *Steinbrücke,* offers exquisite pastries and warm drinks at one counter and light pasta and sandwiches (DM4-9) at another. **Pasta Mia,** Steinbrücke 23, faces the **Marktplatz** and serves pizzas (DM8-14) and pastas (DM 9-15) to customers ranging from starry-eyed couples to cigarette-smoking teens. (☎21 22. Open M-Sa 11am-10pm.) Twice a week, local farmers sell their harvest on the Marktplatz (W 7am-5pm, Sa 7am-noon).

▨ SIGHTS. Overlooking the Markt stands the vine-covered seventeenth-century **Rathaus.** A remarkably resilient stone statue of **Roland** guards the grey giant after nearly four centuries underground. The statue was smashed and buried as punishment for the people after a failed insurrection in the mid-14th century. Tucked behind the Rathaus, the **Benediktikirche** graces the Markt with its 13th-century base. The altar's delicate angels and rich oil paintings are positively stunning. *(open M-F 11am-12:30noon, 1:30pm-3:30pm.)* On a street crowded with seemingly innocent half-timbered houses, the **Schreckensturm,** at the end of Neuendorf, served as Quedlinburg's 14th-century S&M torture palace.

The winding roads of **Schloßberg** insulate the **Schloß** complex with a narrow ring of recently-restored half-timbered cottages packed snugly together. Heinrich I died within the original walls of this old Saxon stronghold in 936. The current 13th-century structure has been a favorite residence-in-exile for the ruling family's widows and inconvenient relatives. The castle complex consists of three parts: the museum, the garden, and the church. The **Schloßmuseum** depicts city history from the Paleolithic era until the present, complete with the sarcophagus of Köigim Mathilde, circa 968 AD, and a *Kürassier* soldier uniform with huge black boots that will put any modern-day goth to shame. Several rooms are done-up in 18th-century style, including the **Wartesaal** and the **Thronsaal,** which is best described as raspberries and cream with gold on top. *(☎27 30. Open daily Tu-Su 10am-5pm; DM5, students DM3.)* Bordered by the castle, **Stiftskirche St. Servatius** houses the **Domsmuseum,** which is indeed more of a tourist-attraction than a bastion of religious sanctity. The first sight of the altar is breathtaking, until it is interrupted by the noise of foot traffic. Tourists traipse across the steps of the altar to view the gilded relics inside the Sükammer, and then around the crucifix to the once-solemn depths of the crypt. *(☎709 900. Open May-Oct., Tu-Sa 10am-5:30pm, Sun. noon-5:30pm;*

Nov.-Apr. Tu-Sa 10am-4pm, Sun. noon-4pm.) Loiter in the gardens around the *Schloß* with some chubby cherubs—the view includes almost every red roof in the city. *(Grounds open May-Oct. 6am-10pm; Nov.-Apr. 6am-8pm.)*

Underneath the castle, the **Lyonel-Feininger-Galerie** is tucked away in a smart, modern white house. Inside is an *Angst*-heavy collection of Feininger's bleak landscapes and portraits intersected by characteristic fracture lines, as well as temporary exhibits featuring works by contemporary artists. *(Finkenherd 5a. ☎ 22 38, fax 23 84. Open Apr.-Oct., Tu-Su 10am-6pm, Nov.-Mar., Tu-Su 10am-5pm. DM6, Students DM3.)* Next door, the **Klopstockhaus** is restored in memory of the classic German writer Friedrich Gottlieb Klopstock. Even if you aren't familiar with him, the furnishings are impressive. *(Schloßberg 12. ☎ 26 10. Open Tu-Sun. 10am-5pm. DM5, Students DM3.)* **Wipertikirche,** a squat, mostly rebuilt Romanesque church a short walk from the Schloß, stands guard over the 1,000-year-old crypt, resting on the site of Heinrich I's court. *(A short walk from the Schloß. ☎ 77 30 12. Open daily 11am-5pm.)*

THALE ☎ 03947

Above the dramatic front of Thale's flowing rivers, jagged cliffs, and splendid mountainside scenery lurks a region of legends, witches, and demons. Like most towns in the Harz, Thale boasts that Goethe fancied its **Bodetal** valley. The peaks on either side of the valley are the sites around which the region's rich folklore centers—lucky for us that Germany's witches just happened to do their thing in the middle of lush mountain forests and spectacular views.

■◪ **ORIENTATION AND PRACTICAL INFORMATION. Trains** leave for Thale from **Quedlinburg** (10min., 2 per hr., DM3). **Buses** depart to many Harz towns from the bus station next to the train station. Across the street from the train station, the **tourist office,** Rathausstr. 1, books **rooms** (DM25-40) for free. (☎ 25 97 or 22 77; fax 22 77; email info@Thale.de; www.Thale.de. Open May-Oct. M-F 9am-6pm, Sa-Su 9am-3pm; Nov.-Apr. M-F 9am-5pm.) A **Sparkasse** on Bahnhofstr. **exchanges money.** The **Hubertus-Apotheke,** Poststr. 15, is to the left as you exit the train station (open M-F 8am-6pm, Sa 8am-noon). The **post office,** Poststr. 1, 06502 Thale, lies across from the pharmacy (open M-F 9am-6pm, Sa 9am-noon).

▛▟ **ACCOMMODATIONS AND FOOD.** Thale's **Jugendherberge (HI),** Bodetal-Waldkater, deserves a lofty laud; its cavernous two- to six-bed rooms look out into the mountains and the running river below. The hostel may or may not be haunted; check with the tourist office for more details. Follow the directions to the cable car station, but instead of taking a right over the bridges, keep walking along the river on Hubertusstr. (☎ 28 81; fax 916 53. Breakfast included. Sheets DM6. Dinner DM7. Reception 3-6pm and 8-10pm. Dorm beds DM22, over 26 DM 27.) The hostel's cafeteria has lunch and dinner specials (DM7-9). Otherwise, the many food stands on Hexentanzplatz can fill your need for cheap eats. Straight ahead of the Sparkasse, Karl-Marx-Str. provides shops, restaurants, and amusements. The **Wolf und Sohn supermarket** (open M-F 7:30am-1pm and 2:30-6pm, Sa 7:30-11am) and the **J. Goethe bakery** fill the gaps. Thale goes crazy every year on April 30 for **Walpurgisnacht,** but only go if you dare commit to an orgy of sin.

▣ **SIGHTS.** Legend dates Thale's cultic history back to prehistoric times, when a sorceress named **Watelinde** led pagan rituals that forced incorrigible youths down a path of destruction in the fast-lane lifestyle of witchery. This heritage is celebrated in the **Hexentanzplatz,** a gathering of rocks and statues of demonic and ghoulish creatures adorned with parasitic animals. A witch bending over a rock in a provocative pose will distort every image of witches you might have picked up from Halloween decorations. Walk down the hill from the Hexentanzplatz and to the wildly entertaining **Walpurgishalle,** a museum commemorating the Harz's history of witchcraft. Displays range from the comical (plastic witches dancing on a a clay mountain), to the terrifying (an old black mask believed to be used in the original ceremonies). *(Open daily 9am-5pm. DM2, students DM1.)* Next to the museum is the impressive **Harzer Bergtheater Thale,** a huge, outdoor amphitheater, with performances vacillating between the sublime (anything from operas to Goethe's *Faust*) and the infernal (live performances by German *Schlager* stars). Shows run sporadically May-Sept. *(☎ 23 24. Tickets DM15-32; 30% discount for students.)* Ascend to the *Hexentanzplatz* either by following the adventure-filled **Winde** that begins by the hostel (30min.)—on foggy days its teeming life and poor visibility are reminiscent of Yoda's cave in the Dagobah system—or by means of the **Kabinenbahn,** a cable car that crosses the *Bodetal* to *Hexentanzplatz*. The ride offers spectacular views of the valley and adds an element of adventure to the trip by dramatically stopping every so often for no apparent reason, except perhaps to make you realize why, after the *Goethezeit* was well over, the valley was dubbed the "Grand Canyon of Germany." The **Roßtrappe,** a rocky peak across the valley from the Hexentanzplatz, can be reached by hiking up *Präsidentenweg* and then up Esselsteig; the trail starts a bit up-river from the chair lift station in the valley. Or take the **Sessellift.** *(☎ 25 00. Lift open in summer daily 9:30am-6pm; in winter Sa-Su 10am-5:30pm. Round-trip in the Kabinenbahn DM8, children DM6. Round-trip in the Sessellift DM6, children DM4. Combination ticket for both DM12, children DM8.)* Both cable cars depart from a station in the valley. From the tourist office, walk diagonally through the park, turn right onto Hubertusstr. and cross the bridges on the right.

🚶 DAY HIKE: THE HAUNTED HILLS.
Estimated distance: 25km; estimated time: 6-7 hours.

The witch-kitsch of the Harz Mountains may seem a bit ridiculous at times—perhaps the best way to get past the tourist tales for a real feel for this eerie area is a hike through the Haunted Hills. The journey begins with a sweep of the sights surrounding the **Hexentanzplatz,** then takes off into the whispering forest to the **Treseburg** overlook. From there the path descends to enter the **Bodetal** National Park and a winding trail by the river. Despite his sinister smirk, the devil at the **Teufelsbrücke** is a welcome landmark on the homestretch, a zig-zagging climb up the hill for a glimpse of the Roßtrappe or the view from the Bülshöhe cliff. For safety precautions to observe while hiking, and the necessary equipment, see p. 57.

Part 1: Pick up the invaluable **Stadt- und Wanderplan** from the tourist office across from the train station (DM5.70). Then, head left down Bahnhofstr. past the bus station and over the bridge. A left on **Goetheweg** leads to the **Kabinbahn** (see above), a magenta-colored gondola that will rocket you up to the first peak in style. Hop off your chariot at the top and hang a left down to the **Harzer Bergtheater,** where you can try to sneak a peek at an outdoor stage that's a production in and of itself. Another left will bring you to **Walpurgishalle** (see above), where you can get the lowdown on witch lore.

Part 2: After getting the skinny on those sinful sisters, return to the Kabinbahn and continue to the **Hexentanzplatz** (see above), their stomping grounds and sacrifice site of days long past, in a clearing atop the mountain. Take the first trail straight as you walk up the right edge of the Hexentanzplatz. The path runs about 8km to **Treseburg;** markers will come in three forms—be on the lookout for red circles, short stone pillars (follow the arrow to Treseburg, even if the 's' looks like a 'f'), and white rectangular signs (take the arrow to Treseburg with the red circle or continue in the direction opposite the arrow to Hexentanzplatz with the same mark). Soon the caged birds of the **Tierpark** will be singing on your left. Further up the trail lies a peculiar teepee-esque structure crafted of mud, overgrown by weeds, and supported, oddly enough, with a layer of chain-link fence. At first glance it could pass as the site of a demonic brewery, but it's only a resting-spot for tired travelers—enter if you dare. About ten minutes later, the trail will bounce off the road, but continue on a wider path to the right. The wooden ladders to nowhere propped against the fence look suspiciously like props from a movie about a witch named Blair; keep that video camera handy for noises in the brush. Up the path, **Pfeilsdenkmal,** a majestic bronze deer perched on a pedestal, awaits.

Part 3: Nearly an hour after leaving the Hexentanzplatz, a confusing three-way path awaits (not an orgy, it's on the trail, silly). Follow the markers mentioned above down the middle route despite its sketchy appearance. Finally, the **Treseburg** appears, delivering a full-blown, 180° view of the misty peaks clothed in an evergreen blanket. It's the view you've been trying to get all day peaking through the trees. A steep zig-zag descends to the bottom; on the way down, catch a glimpse of the water rushing below. The trail commences at the backside of a tiny cottage, and a bridge on the right leads to the road. On the road right around the corner bathrooms, cheap food, and other luxuries of civilization await. Instead of taking the large bridge across the river, swing a right and cross through the brown gates into the **Bodetal Nature Reserve.** The graphic representation of prohibitions is quite extensive (no smoking, swimming, eating mushrooms, etc. etc.), so be good! Follow the trail on its 10km dance with the river. The terrain can get a bit rocky—sometimes it's best to watch the trail ahead rather than admire the view. Boards along the route draw attention to the hidden treasures of the park's fauna and flora; however, the trail's greatest draw is the view of the **Bode** river. It's a long haul, but a sharp curve perched high above the river with a clearing and a bench around the corner are signs that the journey is nearly complete.

Part 4: Ten minutes later, one of Satan's little helpers smirks menacingly over **Teufelsbrücke.** The homestretch begins with the most difficult climb yet; a zig-zag ascent on a steep path up to the **Roßtrappe.** On the way up, the gravel-covered hills, tiny saplings, and their twisted parents make for a bizarre landscape that fits all too well with the area's legends. At the top, the right path leads to the Roßtrappe, where legend has it that beautiful Brunhilde, while fleeing the mad Bodo on a giant horse, sprang across the gorge and left a hoof-print in the rock. Bodo sprang after her, but came up a little short and fell into the river which today bears his name. Returning home, follow the signs to Thale. More souvenirs, restaurants, and even a hotel are patiently waiting. The exhausted or adventurous might consider taking the **Sessellift** (see above) down. For those who want to go *zu Fuß*, the beginning of the ascent is hidden off the landing on the right side of the hotel. At first the path is a bit overgrown, but it quickly widens. On the way down, the **Bülowshöhe** provides a lonesome-yet-excitingly-steep peak from which to view the valley. And if you thought you were sooo over the witch stuff, wait until you see the dark cave at the bottom of the trail! From here, a right turn will lead you towards the youth hostel, and a left in the direction of the tourist office and train station.

MAGDEBURG ☎ 0391

Magdeburg has three claims to fame: it has a spectacular cathedral, it is the birthplace of 18th-century composer Georg Phillipp Telemann, and it was devastated in both the Thirty Years War and WWII. On May 10, 1631, one of the most gruesome battles of the Thirty Years War decimated the city after Protestant town leaders refused to cut a deal with Catholic troops. As a major industrial center, it was later a prime Allied target in WWII. After the war, Magdeburg was rebuilt GDR-style—blessed with enviably broad boulevards and parks but cursed by concrete, cookie-cutter apartment blocks. In the months before reunification, Magdeburg had the good luck to triumph over Halle, becoming the new capital of Sachsen-Anhalt. In the same spirit as Berlin, Magdeburg has undertaken a vast construction project, turning the middle of the city into a giant sandbox, where dump trucks and bobcats frolic. However, progress is slow. The renovations are not yet nearing completion and frequently jeopardize the accessibility of many of the major attractions. However, Magdeburg is beginning to blossom, with the vibrance of the university and the increasing appearance of a fast-paced commercial center.

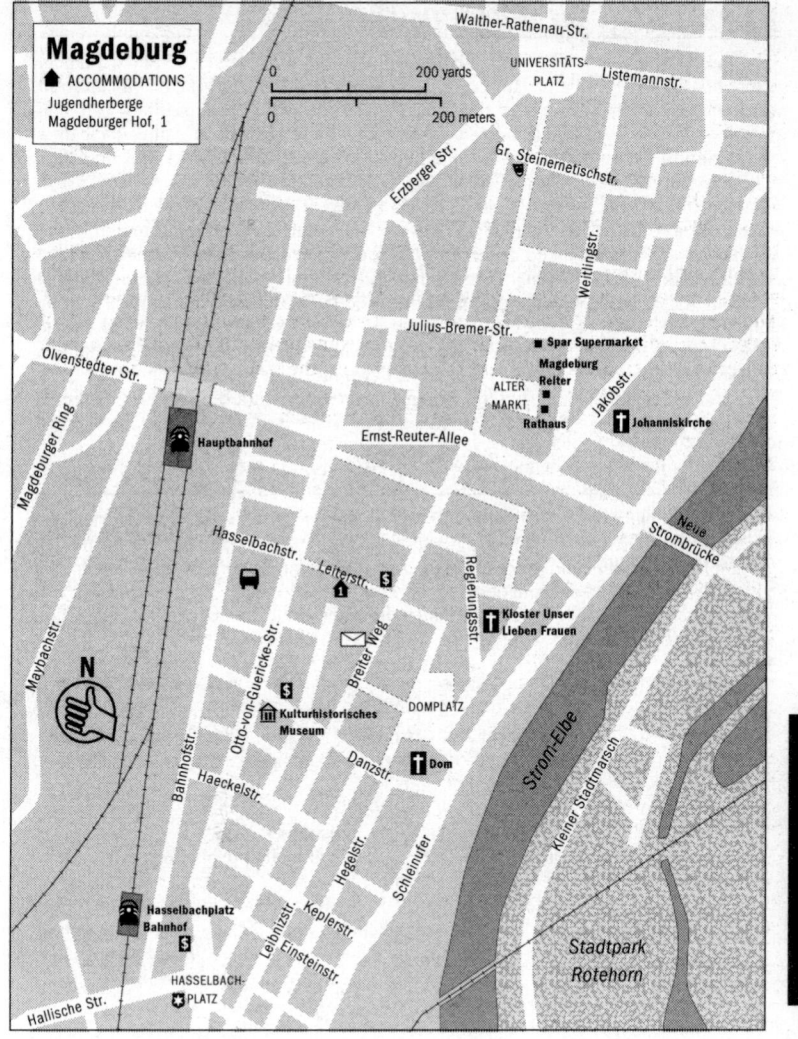

Magdeburg

⌂ ACCOMMODATIONS

Jugendherberge
Magdeburger Hof, 1

GETTING THERE

Trains connect Magdeburg with **Berlin** (1½hr., 1 per hr., DM40) and **Hannover** (1½hr., 2 per hr., DM37). Magdeburg is conveniently configured for pedestrians. Accesible from the train station via the perpendicular Ernst-Reuter-Allee, **Breiter Weg** cuts through the center of the city and serves as the main pedestrian route. Most of the museums and sights are located within a block or two of Breiter Weg, mainly between Ernst Reuter Allee and Haeckelstr. **Streetcars** shuttle between the major attractions. (Single ticket DM2.40; day pass DM5; for up to two adults and three kids, DM7; for up to five adults, DM9.)

🛈 PRACTICAL INFORMATION

The **tourist office** (☎ 194 33; fax 540 49 10; email mi@magdeburg.de; www.magde-burg.de) is a casualty of the construction chaos, having lost its permanent address while renovations in the Markt are underway; spray-painted red TIM logos on the sidewalk will guide you safely to their current location. Pick up a free copy of *Dates* magazine for a schedule of cultural activities and nightlife. The Zimmervermittlung (☎ 540 49 04), in the same office, finds rooms (DM25-75). The Kartenvorverkauf (☎ 540 49 02) sells tickets to shows, concerts, and other cultural events in town (office open M-F 10am-6pm, Sa 10am-1pm; the *Zimmervermittlung* and *Kartenvorverkauf* have the same hours, minus a lunch break from 1-1:45pm). Tours leave daily from the office at 11am (DM5). A 24-hour ATM squats outside the main doors of the **Karstadt** department store on Breiter Weg. For a taxi, call ☎ 73 73 73 or 56 56 56. **Courage,** Porsestr. 14 (☎/fax 404 80 89), is the local center for women's resources. **Internet access** is available in **Cyberb@r** (see Food, below) and **Orbit Cybercafé** (see Entertainment, p. 213). The **post office,** 39104 Magdeburg, sits in a late Gothic hulk on Breiter Weg (open M-F 7am-6pm).

🏠🍴 ACCOMMODATIONS AND FOOD

The ⚑**Jugendherberge Magdeburger Hof (HI),** Leiterstr. 10, hides a slick interior that could pass as a trendy cafe inside a rather unsightly, decaying brick structure. All rooms have showers and toilets, and the furniture is simple but tasteful. The hostel is a mere two minutes from the station and even closer to the main sights and museums. Follow the streetcar tracks to the right from the train station until you pass the bus station and walk up the stairs under the cement covering; the hostel is 30m down on the right. (☎ 532 10 10; fax 532 10 20. Breakfast and sheets included. Members only. Reception 2-10pm. Dorm beds DM34, over 26 DM39. Supplement for a single DM10, for a double DM5 per person.) Camp at **Campingplatz Am Barleber See.** Take streetcar #10 (direction: "Barleber See") to the end, continue down the main street and cross below the highway bridge. (☎ 50 32 44. Open May-Sept. Reception 7am-9pm. Tent DM5.)

Many inexpensive restaurants crowd the streets around the intersection of **Breiter Weg** and **Einsteinstr.** in **Hasselbachplatz.** This was the only downtown area to survive the bombing. Back up Breiter Weg, the **Alter Markt** proffers a bounty of cheap food like half-roasted chickens and fresh berries (open M-F 8am-5pm, Sa 7am-noon). The **Karstadt Restaurant-Café,** Breiter Weg 128, across from the market, offers **groceries** and a complete self-service cafeteria on the second floor (open M-F 9am-8pm, Sa 9am-4pm). Next door, the **Cyberb@r** brings the **internet** to Magdeburg. (Same hours as the restaurant. DM4 per 30min.) **Ratskeller,** in the *Alter Markt,* is a historical set-up in the basement of the Baroque Rathaus. Play your cards right and this can be the best food deal in Magdeburg: while *à la carte* will leave your pockets bare, the restaurant offers two special deals. Each weekday features a different *Stammesse* (lunch special) from 11am to 3pm, including an entree, starch, and dessert for a delightful DM8-10. Get there by 1pm if you can. The other sweet deal occurs daily: from 5 to 7pm, all items on the menu are available at *Ratsherrenpreise,* i.e. half the normal price plus DM2. (☎ 568 23 23. Open M-Sa 11am-11pm, Su 11am-9pm.) Further up Breiter Weg, **Rialto,** Breiter Weg 19a, serves Italian food in a popular outdoor setting under massive umbrellas. (☎ 543 34 72. Open daily 10am-midnight). **Mausefalle,** Breiter Weg 224, at the north end of Hasselbachplatz, attracts a young crowd, particularly students. Metal trees bearing lit-up leaves, a little bit of chrome, and a couple vintage posters add character to this already hopping hang-out. During the day, solid spaghetti dishes run DM10-14, salads DM12-15. (☎ 543 01 35. Open M-F 8:30am-3am, Sa-Su 11am-3am.) A **Spar supermarket** stands north of the intersection of Breiter Weg and Julius-Brenner-Str. (open M-F 7:30am-7pm, Sa 7:30am-2pm).

SIGHTS

Magdeburg's few dazzling sights seem strangely out-of-place among the drab neutral facades which cover the city. The main landmark and city symbol is the sprawling **Magdeburger Dom**, adjacent to the square on Breite Str. In fact, the *Dom* was famed as the largest cathedral in the nation until reunification forced it to yield that honor to Köln. But there's nothing second-rate about the spectacle of the wide courtyard quadrangle with the cathedral's twin dark towers spearing the skies above. At the front lies an inconspicuous tomb, the 973 grave site of Otto I, the second Holy Roman Emperor (after Charlemagne). Local ghost stories credit the Kaiser's spectral guardianship with preservation of the Dom during the destruction of 1631 (Catholic raiders) and 1945 (B-17 bombers). Ernst Barlach's famous wooden memorial to the victims of WWI, originally designed for the spot it now occupies, was removed by the Nazis, fortuitously spending the war years stored safely in Berlin's *Nationalgalerie. (☎541 04 36. Open in summer M-Sa 10am-6pm, Su 11:30am-6pm; in winter M-Sa 10am-4pm, Su 11:30am-4pm. Free. Tours M-Sa 10am and 2pm, Su 11:30am and 2pm. DM6, students DM3.)*

The ancient **Kloster unser lieben Frauen** lies near the Dom between many faceless apartments. This 11th-century nunnery now houses an art exhibition space, a concert hall, and a cafe. However, this shift in purpose has not compromised the monastic atmosphere—the grounds around the cloister still shimmer in sheltered tranquility. Wander among the statues of the garden or sit and cogitate on the benches or the remains of stone walls. *(Regierungsstr. 4/6. ☎56 50 20. Exhibition hall open Tu-Su 10am-5pm. DM4, students and seniors DM2. Cafe open Tu-Su 10am-6pm.)* Heading away from the *Dom* and crossing Breiter Weg on Danzstr., the **Kulturhistorisches Museum** will pop up on your left. As the building houses both a history and natural science museum, visitors can view everything from a potato bug model 15 times the bug's actual size to an exhibit on the city's history from the Stone Age (don't miss the mammoth hairs) to the demonstrations that led to the *Wende* in 1989. *(Otto-von-Guerike-Str. 68-73. Open Tu-Su 10am-5pm. DM4, students DM2.)* The **Johanniskirche** once stood as a memorial to the 1945 bombing, in which it was nearly destroyed. Recently, the church has been artfully rebuilt to its state of pre-war glory, and now holds a variety of temporary exhibitions. *(Almost on the Elbe behind the Alter Markt. ☎53 65 00. Open Tu.-Sun. 10am-5pm. Entrance DM1; exhibitions DM4.)* Across from the Johanniskirche rises the clock tower of the elegantly proportioned 17th-century **Rathaus.** On the Marktplatz in front of the Rathaus is a replica of the **Magdeburger Reiter** (built in 1240), the oldest free-standing equestrian figure in northern Europe. The original rides into the sunset at the Kulturhistorisches Museum.

🎵🍺 ENTERTAINMENT AND NIGHTLIFE

Magdeburg's cultural scene is packed. The magazine *Dates* and the pamphlet *Stadtpass* provide extensive information about what's going on in theaters, cinemas, and concert halls. *Uni Dates* gives information on the local club and bar scene, along with other essentials for the youthful wander. The **Theater Magdeburg,** Universitätspl. 9, is located at the corner of Breiter Weg and Erzberger Str. Its **Großes Haus** hosts big-name operas, ballets, and plays, while the **Podiumbühne** is somewhat more experimental. (☎540 64 44 and 540 65 55. Box office open Tu-F 10am-7:30pm, Sa 10am-2pm, and 1hr. before performance. Closed mid-July to early Sept.) The **Freie Kammerspiele,** Otto-von-Guericke-Str. 64, puts on modern interpretations of the classics. (☎598 82 26. Tickets available M-Th 4-6pm, F 2-6pm, and 1hr. before performances. Closed mid-July until early Sept.)

For bars, restaurants, and people-watching, there are three superior areas in Magdeburg: **Hasselbachplatz** (see **Food,** p. 212); **Sudenburg,** along Halberstädter Str. and its cross streets (S-Bahn #1 or 10 or bus #53 or 54 to "Eiskellerplatz" or

SAXONY-ANHALT

"Ambrosiusplatz"); and **Diesdorfstr.** (S-Bahn #1 or 6 to "Westring" or "Arndtstr."). Though far from the city center, Kurt Schmidt Str. and Schönebecker Str. offer a number of clubs as well.

As well prepared for emergencies as its namesake predecessor, the **Feuerwache** (fire station), Halberstädter Str. 140, answers calls for theater, art exhibits, and concerts while serving as a winter cafe and a casual summer beer garden. (☎60 28 09. Open daily 7pm-midnight.) From Halberstädter Str., take a right on Heidestr., where **Orbit Cybercafé,** Heidestr. 9, beams you up to a land with funky decorations, drinks of all sorts, occasional live DJs, and **internet access.** (☎620 98 35. Internet access DM5 per hr. Open M-F 6pm-1am, Sa-Su 6pm-2am.) The clientele at **Layla,** Lessingstr. 66, gulps down pints of Guinness in a chill setting. (☎731 70 28. Open M-Th 11am-1am, F 11am-2am, Sa 10am-2am, Su 10am-1am.)

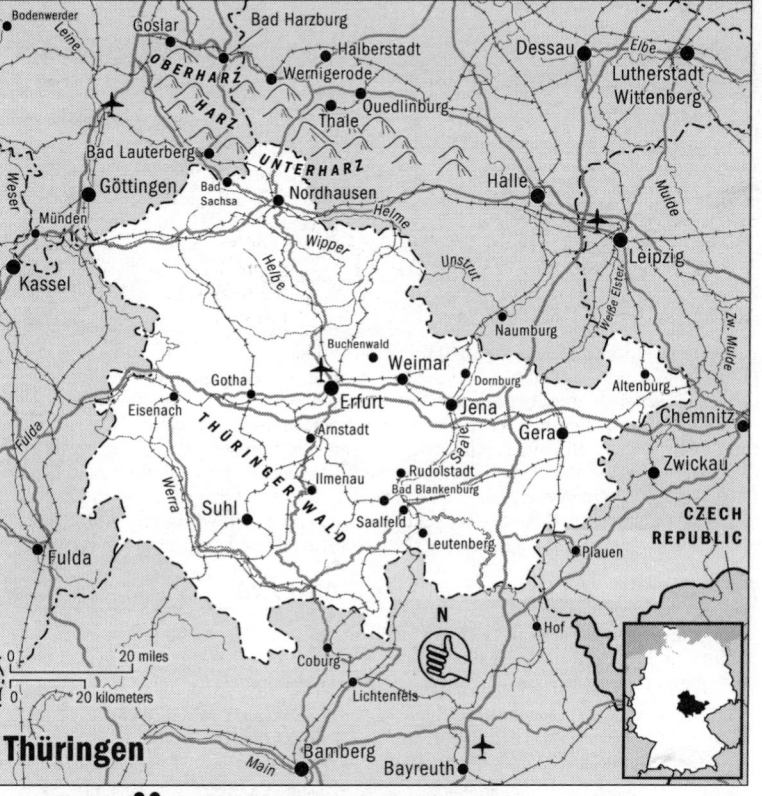

THÜRINGEN

The "Green Heart of Germany" offers tourists measure upon measure of goodness, from the hiking trails of the lush, hilly Thüringer Wald to the cultural significance of cities such as Weimar, Jena, and Eisenach, to the breathtaking views of Erfurt's cathedrals and Eisenach's stunning fortress, the solid **Wartburg**. The southern hills and highlands are cut by the historic **Rennsteig Trail,** and echo with the legacy of such important figures as Luther, Goethe, Schiller, and Wagner. One of the country's smaller *Länder*, Thuringen's cities are strung together by a convenient east-west rail line, easily accessed with the "Hopper Ticket," which provides same day round-trip travel within 50km for a mere DM8. The cities of Thüringen band together to further their cultural significance, too; magazines *Takt* and *Fritz* cover the entire region, and audiences for events like "Kulturarena Jena" come from all over the cozy area.

HIGHLIGHTS OF THÜRINGEN

To see the cities that generated the masterful work of Goethe, Schiller, Hegel, and Novalis, head to **Weimar (p. 216)** and the university town of **Jena (p. 223)**.

Erfurt, (p. 227) Thüringen's capital, boasts a busy and beautiful Innenstadt, an impressive cathedral, and the best nightlife in the region.

Eisenach's (p. 233) **Wartburg Fortress** once sheltered Luther, and now it overlooks the city where the birthplace of **J.S. Bach** still inspires musical extravaganzas.

The **Thüringer Wald** (p. 231) provides ample and beautiful hiking trails, from the 6hr. **Goethewanderweg** to the five-day **Rennsteig**.

WEIMAR
☎ 03643

Weimar's main claim to fame is its role in Germany's intellectual history; it was once home to such cultural giants as Goethe, Schiller, and Johann Gottfried von Herder, grandfather of the Romantics. Little Weimar was declared Europe's cultural capital in 1999, and so in the months leading up to the big celebration the entire city was cleaned up. Now its smooth, manicured surface still gleams, and it is one of the most completely renovated cities in east Germany. Weimar's cultural significance does not begin and end with Goethe. The *Bauhaus* architectural movement began here, and students at the Bauhaus Universität continue to be a source of energy and quirky culture within the seemingly perfect city. As the capital of Germany's ultimately unsuccessful attempt at a democratic republic after WWI, Weimar's political significance is also undeniable.

Weimar's cultural offerings attract tourists of all kinds, and the city thrives on this industry; it is more difficult to find the real intellectual substance behind the museums and *Häuser* carefully prepared for visiting guests. This intellectual substance shows itself most clearly in Weimar's **Neues Museum** and in its university student culture; visiting these in combination with the smoothly presented living quarters of Germany's great writers gives a fuller sense of Weimar's offerings. While the hype from the 1999 extravaganza has died down, the effects persist: revamped sites prevail, while budget stores and restaurants remain scarce. But with four solid hostels and a few cheap places to eat, visiting this beautiful city on a budget is still possible.

◖ GETTING THERE AND GETTING AROUND

Weimar is near the center of Germany, well-situated on the Dresden-Frankfurt and Berlin-Frankfurt rail lines. Its intelligently designed bus system runs through two nerve centers: the train station and the central Goetheplatz.

Trains: DB trains head to **Erfurt** (15min., 4 per hr., DM7.60); **Jena** (20min., 2 per hr., DM9.80); **Eisenach** (1hr., 3 per hr., DM19.40); **Leipzig** (1½hr., every 2 hrs., DM24.40); **Dresden** (3hr., 1 per hr., DM65); and **Frankfurt** (3hr., 1 per hr., DM78).

Public Transportation: Weimar operates an extensive **bus network,** with most buses running until midnight. Single tickets cost DM2.50 and can be bought on board, but better deals are to be had in advance: DM12 for 8 tickets, or a *Tageskarte*. A DM5 *Tageskarte* is good from the time of purchase until 6am the next day, and a DM6 *Tageskarte* is good for exactly 24 hours after validation. All tickets including your *Tageskarte* must be validated in the red machines upon boarding the bus. Both tourist offices sell bus tickets, but the main ticket office is located on Goethepl. Many newsstands also sell tickets; look for the green and yellow "H" signs.

Taxis: ☎ 90 36 00 or 90 39 00.

◖◖ ORIENTATION AND PRACTICAL INFORMATION

Weimar's center is located to the west of the Ilm River and south of the trainstation. A series of open squares strung together by side-streets make up the city's center and contain most of its sights and museums. From the train station, Carl-August-Allee stretches downhill to Karl-Liebknecht-Str. which leads into **Goetheplatz**(15 min). From there, **Theaterplatz** is down Wielandstr. to the left, and from Theaterplatz to the **Marktplatz** is just a short walk down Schillerstr.

Weimar offers two **discount cards:** the **WeimarCard** (DM25, students DM20) and the **Sammelkarte** (DM25, students DM15, children DM10). The WeimarCard is valid for 72 hours of local transportation, entry to many of Weimar's museums, and discounts on city tours. The Sammelkarte yields entry into 9 different museums. Both cards can be purchased at either of the tourist offices or at the **Stiftung Weimar Klassik**, Frauentorstr. 4 (☎ 54 50 or 54 51 02).

Tourist Office: The seriously modern and efficient **Weimar Information**, Marktstr. 10 (☎ 240 00; fax 24 00 40), is within view of the city's *Rathaus*. The office hands out free maps and books **rooms** for a DM5 fee. **Walking tours** leave the office daily at 11am and 2pm (DM12, students DM8; tours in English available upon advance request for

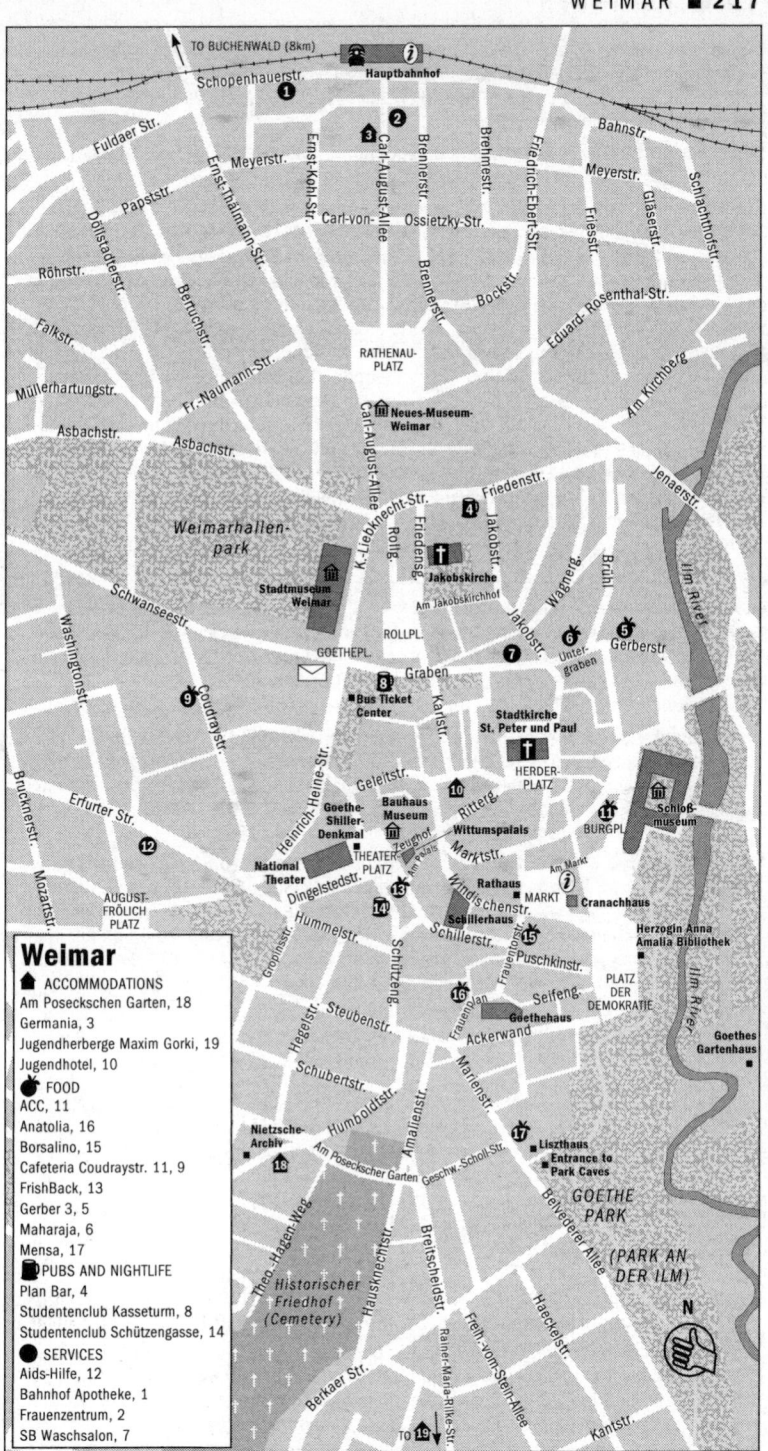

TO BUCHENWALD (8km)

Schopenhauerstr.

Hauptbahnhof

Fuldaer Str.

Meyerstr.

Papststr.

Ernst-Thälmann-Str.

Ernst-Kohl-Str.

Carl-August-Allee

Brennerstr.

Brehmestr.

Carl-von- Ossietzky-Str.

Friedrich-Ebert-Str.

Glaserstr.

Meyerstr.

Bahnstr.

Schlachthofstr.

Röhrstr.

Döllstädterstr.

Beruchstr.

Fr.-Naumann-Str.

Bockstr.

Eduard-Rosenthal-Str.

Falkstr.

Müllerhartungstr.

Asbachstr.

Asbachstr.

Am Kirchberg

Jenaerstr.

RATHENAU-PLATZ

Neues-Museum-Weimar

Weimarhallen-park

Schwanseestr.

K.-Liebknecht-Str.

Friedenstr.

Rollg.

Friedenstr.

Jakobstr.

Jakobstr.

Wagnerg.

Brühl

Ilm River

Jakobskirche

Stadtmuseum Weimar

Am Jakobskirchhof

Gerberstr.

ROLLPL.

GOETHEPL.

Graben

Unter-graben

Washingtonstr.

Coudraystr.

Erfurter Str.

Bruckerstr.

Mozartstr.

Bus Ticket Center

Karlstr.

Stadtkirche St. Peter und Paul

HERDER-PLATZ

Schloß-museum

BURGPL.

Heinrich-Heine-Str.

Geleitstr.

Goethe-Schiller-Denkmal

Bauhaus Museum

Ritterg.

Wittumspalais

Am Palais

Zeughof

Marktstr.

Am Markt

Cranachhaus

Herzogin Anna Amalia Bibliothek

AUGUST-FRÖLICH PLATZ

National Theater

Dingelstedtstr.

THEATER-PLATZ

Windischenstr.

Rathaus

MARKT

Schillerhaus

Schillerstr.

Puschkinstr.

PLATZ DER DEMOKRATIE

Hummelstr.

Gropiusstr.

Schützeng.

Hegelstr.

Steubenstr.

Frauenplan

Frauentorstr.

Seifeng.

Ackerwand

Goethehaus

Schubertstr.

Nietzsche-Archiv

Humboldtstr.

Am Poseckscher Garten

Geschw.-Scholl-Str.

Liszthaus Entrance to Park Caves

GOETHE PARK

Goethes Gartenhaus

Theo.-Hagen-Weg

Haussknstr.

Amalienstr.

Marienstr.

Breitscheidstr.

Freih.-vom-Stein-Allee

Belvederer Allee

(PARK AN DER ILM)

Historischer Friedhof (Cemetery)

Berkaer Str.

Rainer-Maria-Rilke-Str.

Kantstr.

TO 19

N

Weimar

ACCOMMODATIONS
Am Poseckschen Garten, 18
Germania, 3
Jugendherberge Maxim Gorki, 19
Jugendhotel, 10

FOOD
ACC, 11
Anatolia, 16
Borsalino, 15
Cafeteria Coudraystr. 11, 9
FrishBack, 13
Gerber 3, 5
Maharaja, 6
Mensa, 17

PUBS AND NIGHTLIFE
Plan Bar, 4
Studentenclub Kasseturm, 8
Studentenclub Schützengasse, 14

SERVICES
Aids-Hilfe, 12
Bahnhof Apotheke, 1
Frauenzentrum, 2
SB Waschsalon, 7

THURINGIA

groups of 5 or more), or go it alone with a walking-tour brochure available in various languages (DM1.50). Open Apr.-Oct. M-F 9:30am-7pm, Sa 9:30am-5pm, Su 9:30am-4pm; Nov.-Mar. M-F 10am-6pm, Sa and Su 10am-2pm. A branch office in the train station offers the same services from 10am to 8pm daily.

Currency Exchange: Four banks are spread out on Schillerstr. and Frauentorstr., but beware—none are open between F at 4pm and M at 8:30am.

Laundry: SB-Waschsalon, on Graben a few blocks down from Goethepl. Wash DM6 per load. Dry DM1 for 15min. Iron DM1 per 10min. Open M-Sa 8am-10pm; last wash at 8:30pm.

Pharmacy: Bahnhof-Apotheke, Carl-August-Allee 14 (☎543 20), near the train station. Evening hours as well as a *Notdienst* (emergency) buzzer and a list of which pharmacies are available on which nights. Open M-F 7:15am-7pm, Sa 9am-noon.

Women's Resources: Frauenzentrum, Schopenhauerstr. 21 (☎87 11 82), often hosts a **Frauencafé** from 2-6pm, and serves a "women's breakfast" once a month at 10am. Call for dates. Office open daily 2-6pm, usually longer, depending on what's planned.

Emergency: Police, ☎110. **Fire and Ambulance,** ☎112.

Post Office: Mail postcards of Goethe and Schiller from the **Hauptpostamt,** Goethepl. 7-8, 99423 Weimar (☎23 13 63). Construction on the post office began in May 2000, so for the time being you'll have to line up at the temporary headquarters around the back. Open M-F 8am-6:30pm, Sa 9am-1pm.

▌ ACCOMMODATIONS

Miraculously, Weimar's youth hostels and youth "hotel" are all clean, hospitable, budget-friendly places, so for student travelers Weimar is in ideal place to visit. For those who prefer to avoid hostels, private rooms and *Pensionen* are available through the tourist office (see above). These range widely in price and many swank hotels do exist in Weimar, but a single room for DM50-60 in a good location can still be found.

Jugendherberge Germania (HI), Carl-August-Allee 13 (☎85 04 90; fax 85 04 91). Within spitting distance of the train station, this hostel has convenience written all over it. Walk straight downhill 2min.; it will be on the right. One- to six- bed rooms in a lovely old house with a fresh coat of pastel-green paint. Sheets DM7. Lockout 10am-2pm. 24hr. reception. **HI members only.** Dorm beds DM25, over 26 DM30.

Jugendgästehaus Maxim Gorki (HI), Zum Wilden Graben 12 (☎85 07 50; fax 85 07 45). Take bus #8 from the station (direction: "Merketal") to "Wilder Graben." A converted villa in a tranquil Weimar suburb, Maxim Gorki often fills with jolly school groups, so call ahead. Careful: buses stop running in this direction early (around 8pm), and the walk back from downtown is poorly lit. Breakfast included. Sheets DM7. 24hr. reception. No curfew. Dorm beds DM25, over 26 DM30.

Jugendherberge Am Poseckschen Garten (HI), Humboldtstr. 17 (☎85 07 92), is situated near the city center, although fairly distant from the train station. Take bus #8 from the station (direction: "Merketal") to "Am Poseckschen Garten." Make a right onto Am Poseckschen Garten, then a left onto Humboldtstr.; the hostel is immediately on your left. A big turn-of-the-century brownstone with 8- to 10-bed rooms. The hostel tends to fill with young school groups due to its proximity to cultural attractions, so come early. Breakfast included. Lunch and dinner DM8 each. Sheets DM7. Reception 7am-8:30pm. Lockout 10am-2pm. Curfew 10pm. DM25, over 26 DM30.

▨ Jugendhotel Hababusch, Geleitstr. 4 (☎85 07 37; fax 40 26 15; email yh@uni-weimar.de; www.uni-weimar.de/yh). From Goethepl., follow Geleitstr.; after it takes a sharp right, you'll come to a statue on your left. The entrance to the Hababusch is hard to see; it's tucked in the ivied corner behind the statue.Word has gotten out that the Hababusch is *the* place for young travelers to stay in Weimar. Smack in the middle of the sights, the Hababusch is run by the architecture students who live upstairs, and it shows: check out the upside-down sink turned into overhead lighting in the bathroom. The laid-back atmosphere makes you feel like you've joined a friendly international commune, and the guests tend to sit around the large table to talk and share meals. No breakfast, but access to a full kitchen. DM20 key deposit. 24hr. reception. DM15 for a shared bedroom, doubles DM20 per person.

◑ FOOD

Unfortunately, of the bounteous establishments named for Goethe or adorned with his shadow in this city, few of them are budget restaurants. For a nice dinner, look in the area around Theaterpl., but if it's cheap eats you want you'll have to look a bit harder. Try the daily **produce market** at the Marktplatz (open M-F 8am-5pm, Sa 8am-noon), or the **Rewe grocery store,** in the basement of the *Handelhaus zu Weimar* on Theaterpl. (open M-F 7am-8pm, Sa 7am-4pm). There is also another **Rewe** at the intersection of Frauenplan and Steubenstr. (open M-F 7am-8pm, Sa 8am-2pm), and a smaller one just down the hill from the train station on Carl-August-Allee (open M-F 8am-6pm, Sa 8am-11am).

Mensa: Bauhaus-Universität, Marienstr. 13/15, just across the footpath in front of the *Bauhaus* building. Also accessible from Park an der Ilm. Flee the omnipresent Goethe and Schiller in this sanctuary of modernism, and fraternize with the German students in smoky ambience. Downstairs you can get coffee and pay cheap-ish prices in the cafeteria. Upstairs, in the **Mensa,** grab the grub for DM3-5. Cafeteria open M-Th 7:30am-7pm, F 7:30am-5pm, Sa 11am-2pm, mid-July to mid-Oct. M-F 7:30am-3pm; *Mensa* open 11am-2pm. The University has a **second Cafeteria** at Coudraystr. 11, which sells meals to students for DM3-5 and to others for DM5-8. Open M-F 7:30am-3pm. At all three a student ID is required for student prices.

Gerber III, Gerberstr. 3 (see **Entertainment and Nightlife** p. 221). This ultra-funky bar-like joint almost always has a pot of something cooking on a back burner (DM2-3). No bibs, mashed peas, or tiny plastic-coated spoons. Stop by weekdays noon-1:30pm and daily in the evenings to see what's on.

ACC, Burgpl. 1-2 (☎85 11 61; fax 85 12 63). This combination cafe and gallery is popular with students and sells relatively cheap food (meals DM8-13). Eat outside with a shaded view of the *Schloß* and then pop inside for a look at the artwork on display. Open daily 11am-1am.

Maharaja, Untergraben 9 (☎51 12 85). The first Indian restaurant in Weimar does a good job of keeping the food tasty and the prices down. A menu complete with mango lassis offers entrees for DM9-14. Open M-Sa 11am-2pm and 5-11pm, Su noon-11pm.

◉ SIGHTS

Weimar's main claim to fame is the number of famous people who lived, worked, wrote, thought, or visited here; each one has a Haus which tourists can visit for DM5-10. It is probably best to take only a moderate dose of house tours while in the city, and instead visit in some of the other, more interesting museum offerings such as the **Neues Museum** and the **Bauhaus Museum.**

■ **NEUES MUSEUM WEIMAR.** The opening of the new collection in February 2000 meant the introduction of a unique place to see modern art in Weimar. The collection is small, but varied enough to hold your interest. Downstairs, some 20th century Italian art mixes with Sol LeWitt and an installation by Pipilotti Rist involving giant red armchairs and a TV. Upstairs, a serious exhibit of art from the DDR is offset by Norbert W. Hinterberger's comical set of faucets supposedly taken from great thinkers' sinks; Nietzsche's faucets are marked with *gut* (good) and *böse* (evil) instead of hot and cold. *(Weimarplatz 4. At Rathenauplatz. ☎546 163; fax 546 101. Open Tu-Su 10am-6pm. DM6, students and children DM3.)*

GOETHEHAUS. While countless German towns leap at any excuse to build memorial *Goethehäuser* (proclaiming Goethe slept here, Goethe went to school here, Goethe once asked for directions here), Weimar features the real thing. The **Goethehaus** and **Goethe-Nationalmuseum** show off the immaculately preserved private chambers where the poet entertained, wrote, studied, and ultimately died after spending 50 years in Weimar. The famous *"Salve"* greeting emblazoned on tote bags in souvenir shops across Weimar can actually been seen here in the floor, beckoning entrance to Goethe's yellow salon. It's jammed to a bursting point with busts, paintings, and sculptures from Goethe's 50,000-piece art collection. To get the most out of the largely unlabeled exhibits, pick up the handy English guide "Goethe's House on the Frauenplan at Weimar" (DM3) at the desk. *(Frauenplan 1. Open mid-Mar. to mid-Oct. Tu-Su 9am-7pm; mid-Oct. to mid-Mar. Tu-Su 9am-4pm. Expect a wait of up to two hours during summer afternoons. DM8, students and seniors DM5, children DM2.50.)*

BAUHAUS-MUSEUM. This slick testament to the elegance of Modernism features historical artifacts about, and works produced by, the *Bauhaus* school of design and architecture (see p. 24). The exhibits detail the history of the school, pointing out Walter Gropius' April 1919 change of curriculum that would lead the school to fame; artists such as Feininger, Klee, and Kandinsky are listed as students and later as teaching masters. Weavings, sculptures, prints, furniture, books, toys, and other nifty objects bear testimony to the breadth of the school's philosophy and undertakings. *(Am Palais. Across from the Deutsches Nationaltheater. ☎ 54 60. Open Apr.-Oct. Tu-Su 10am-6pm; Nov.-Mar. Tu-Su 10am-4:30pm. DM5, students and seniors DM3.)*

NIETZSCHE-ARCHIV. Nietzsche spent the last three wacky years (1897-1900) of his life in this house; he was pretty far gone by the end, as is painfully evident from the cross-eyed glares emanating from the myriad pictures and busts. The archive was founded by Nietzsche's sister, Elisabeth, a woman whose misunderstandings set the stage for the Nazis' cynical distortion of her brother's philosophy—she gave Hitler a tour of the house in 1932. *(Humboldtstr. 36. Open mid-Mar. to mid-Oct. Tu-Su 1-6pm; mid-Oct. to mid-Mar. 1-4pm. DM4, students and seniors DM3.)*

PARK AN DER ILM. Flanking the river, the park was landscaped by Goethe. Of particular note are the fake ruins built by the Weimar shooting club and the *Kubus,* a huge black cube that is used as a theater and as a movie screen, complete with hammer and sickle. Perched on the park's far slopes is Goethe's **Gartenhaus,** the poet's first Weimar home and later his retreat from the city. Indicative of Weimar's commitment to Goethe-tourism, two replicas of the **Gartenhaus** have been built to satisfy tourists who are merely interested in the house's architecture. *(Gartenhaus on Corona-Schöfer-Str. Open mid-Mar. to mid-Oct. M and W-Su 9am-7pm; mid-Oct. to mid-Mar. M and W-Su 9am-4pm. DM5, students and seniors DM2.50.)* Also accessible from the Park is the **Herzogin Anna Amalia Bibliothek,** notable of course because Goethe used to visit, but also because of its impressive Rococo reading room. *(Platz der Demokratie 1. Reading room open Tu-Su 11am-12:30am, but tickets can only be bought at 10:30am daily.)*

HISTORISCHER FRIEDHOF. South of the town center, Goethe and Schiller lie in rest together at the cemetery, in the basement of the **Fürstengruft** next to a dozen or so Prussian princes. Goethe arranged to be sealed in an airtight steel case. Schiller, who died in an epidemic, was originally buried in a mass grave, but Goethe later combed through the remains until he identified Schiller and had him interred in a tomb. Skeptics argued for a long time that Goethe was mistaken, so a couple of "Schillers" were placed side by side. In the 1960s, a team of Russian scientists determined that Goethe was right after all. *(Cemetery open Mar.-Sept. 8am-9pm; Oct.-Feb. 8am-6pm. Tomb open daily mid-Mar. to mid-Oct. M and W-Su 9am-7pm; mid-Oct. to mid-Mar. M and W-Su 9am-4pm. DM4, students and seniors DM3.)*

DEUTSCHES NATIONALTHEATER. On Hummelstr., one block away from Schiller's erstwhile home, Schiller and Goethe are reconciled in bronze before the **Deutsches Nationaltheater,** which first breathed life into their stage works. The theater is the epicenter of Weimar's cultural and political spheres—in addition to operating as a first-run venue for their plays, it was also the locale from which the Weimar Constitution emerged in 1919. *(Am Palais. ☎ 75 53 34; fax 75 53 21.)*

SCHILLERS WOHNHAUS. Sitting a neighborly distance from Goethe's pad, this was Schiller's home during the last three years of his life after he resigned from his academic chair at Jena. Showcasing the backgrounds to *The Maid of Orleans* and *William Tell,* both written here, the house offers original drafts and early editions of plays and a detailed biographical chronicle of its owner's life. A room full of medallions and coins with Schiller's head imprinted on them is another of the interesting exhibits here. *(Schillerstr. 12. Open mid-Mar. to mid-Oct. M and W-Su 9am-7pm; mid-Oct. to mid-Mar. M and W-Su 9am-4pm. DM5, students DM3.)*

SCHLOßMUSEUM. The first floor is a major-league Lucas Cranach fest; the second floor is a minor-league collection of 19th- and 20th-century German works, including a sampling of the "Weimarer Malerschule" of the second half of the 19th century. The museum also features a ballroom with fancy chandeliers and real red carpets rolled down the stairs. *(Burgpl. 4. To the left of the Marktplatz. Open Apr.-Oct. Tu-Su 10am-6pm; Nov.-Mar. Tu-Su 10am-4:30pm. DM6, students and seniors DM3.)*

WITTUMSPALAIS. Here Goethe, Schiller, and Herder sat at the round table of their patron, Duchess Anna Amalia. Under the same roof, the **Wielandmuseum** documents the life and works of the extraordinary duchess. *(Am Palais 3. Open mid-Mar. to mid-Oct. daily 9am-7pm, mid-Oct. to mid-Mar. daily 9am-4pm. DM6, students DM4.)*

FRANZ-LISZT-HAUS. The composer spent his last years here. The instruments and furnishings are supposedly original, but given Liszt's torrid love life, the single bed seems improbable. *(Marienstr. 17. Open mid-Mar. to mid-Oct. Tu-Su 9am-1pm and 2-7pm; mid-Oct. to mid-Mar. Tu-Su 10am-1pm and 2-4pm. DM4, students and seniors DM3.)*

LUCAS-CRANACH-HAUS. The prolific 16th-century painter spent his last days behind this colorful Renaissance facade. Closed to the public except for an art gallery of fairly hip modern paintings, photos, and sculptures by still-to-be-discovered talents. *(On the Marktplatz. Gallery open Th and F noon-8pm, Sa 11am-3pm.)*

OTHER SIGHTS. The cobblestoned **Marktplatz,** straight down Frauentorstr., spreads out beneath the neo-Gothic **Rathaus,** which is closed to the public. Like every other German city, Weimar of course has a **Stadtmuseum;** Weimar's unique history at the center of German politics after WWI makes its city museum far more fascinating than many others. *(Karl-Liebknecht-Str. 5-9. ☎/fax 903 868. Open Apr.-Oct. Tu-Su 10am-6pm, Nov.-Mar. Tu-Su 10am-5pm. DM4, students DM2, children DM1.)* Cranach rests in the churchyard of the **Jakobskirche,** Am Jakobskirchhof 9. *(Open M-F 11am-3pm, Sa 10am-noon.)* The **Stadtkirche St. Peter und Paul** features Cranach's last triptych altarpiece. *(Down Jakobstr. Open M-Sa 10am-noon and 2-4pm, Su after services until noon and 2-3pm. Free.)* The church is also called the **Herderkirche,** in honor of philosopher and linguist Johann Gottfried von Herder, who preached here regularly in the 1780s. The church's interior is at odds with its solemn exterior: dazzlingly colorful coats of arms painted on all the balconies give the hall a festive air.

♫ 🎭 ENTERTAINMENT AND NIGHTLIFE

The obvious first place to go in Weimar is the **Deutsches Nationaltheater,** Am Palais. The theatre that got Goethe and Schiller started still presents *Faust* regularly, along with Mozart and Verdi operas and classics from folks like Shakespeare. (☎755 334. Box office open M 2-6pm, Tu-Sa 10am-6pm, Su 10am-6pm, and one hour before performances. Tickets for musical theatre events DM29-55, for plays DM19-45, for *Faust* DM10 extra per ticket. 30% student discount. "Theaterferien" during the month of August.) The rest of Weimar's nightlife is left to a small collection of student clubs. The student culture here is driven by quirky architecture students from the *Bauhaus,* so it definitely has its own character, but the scene is small and not as vigorous as the *Uni*-culture of nearby Jena. When something cool does happen, the *Bauhaus-Universität's Mensa* has posters and bulletin boards directing you to what's going down (see **Food,** p. 219).

Studentenclub Kasserturm in an old medieval tower on Goethepl. opposite the main post office. With a disco up top and a groovy beer cellar below, this is the oldest student club in Germany and a good place to chill. Open M-Sa 8pm-late. Disco W and F, live bands Sa. Cover varies.

Studentenclub Schützengasse, on Schützengasse, has a beer garden outside. Open M, W-Th 7:30pm-late, Tu and F-Sa 9pm-late. Disco Tu, F, and Sa. Cover DM3-6, admittance only for those 18 and older.

Gerber III, Gerberstr. 3, is a former squatters' house that now shelters all things leftist; a club, cafe, climbing wall, movie theater, and bicycle repair shop are all under the roof.

Part of the building also sometimes functions as a crazy disco. Stop by and pick up the detailed *Gerberei* pamphlet for details on what's happening.

AIDS-Hilfe (☎ 85 35 35), Erfurter Str. 17, holds a popular gay cafe Tu-Sa from 8pm. They also host a gay "safe sex" party on the last F of every month.

█ DAYTRIP FROM WEIMAR: BUCHENWALD

Two hundred fifty thousand Jews, Gypsies, homosexuals, communists, and political prisoners were imprisoned and murdered by the Nazis at the labor camp of Buchenwald during WWII. Now a memorial to those who suffered there, the compound comprises a vast expanse of gravel with the former location of the prison blocks marked by the number they were assigned during the war. Around the perimeter remain the more permanent buildings of the camp, such as the SS officers' quarters and the crematorium. The stark ugliness of the site and the horror of its history are in wrenching contrast to the beauty of the natural surroundings: the view from the compound of the surrounding countryside is breathtaking.

For the most part, Buchenwald served to detain and murder political enemies of Nazism and prisoners of war. Its first prisoners were German political prisoners, but from 1937 onward huge numbers of deported prisoners from Poland, Denmark, Belgium, Norway, and other countries made the camp swell to be the largest still in existence in 1945. A plaque near the former commandant's horse stable matter-of-factly states that an estimated 8,000 Soviet prisoners were executed by firing squad in the little space before the war's end. Many Jews were sent here, but after 1942, most were deported to Auschwitz. As the Red Army drew closer to Polish camps, more prisoners were carted out of Auschwitz and back to Buchenwald; as liberation drew nearer the camp became more and more crowded. The exhibits describe it as "a place for dying." The testaments given by the US soldiers who liberated the camp on April 11, 1945 express their disbelief at the magnitude of suffering experienced here. Soviet authorities used the site from 1945 to 1950 as an internment camp in which more than 28,000 Germans, mostly Nazi war criminals and opponents of the Communist regime, were held; 10,000 died of hunger and disease. An exhibit detailing the Soviet abuses opened in 1997. In the woods behind the museum rests a cemetery with the graves of both the victims and perpetrators of the Soviet abuses.

The **Nationale Mahnmal und Gedenkstätte Buchenwald** (☎ (03643) 43 00) has two principal sights: the **KZ-Lager** and the **Glockenturm**. The former refers to the remnants of the camp, while the latter is a solemn monument overlooking Weimar and the surrounding countryside. The museum in the large storehouse building at the KZ-Lager documents both the history of Buchenwald (1937-1945) and the general history of Nazism, including German anti-Semitism. The exhibits stand in stark gray metal boxes lined up in even rows, re-emphasizing the dim horrors they attempt to explain. Just outside the museum lies a powerful symbol: the charred stump of the **Goethe-Eiche** (Goethe oak), left standing in the middle of the camp to commemorate Buchenwald's former role as a get-away for Germany's greatest cultural figure. The memorial stones recently embedded in the ground around block #22 read, in English, German, and Hebrew: "So that the generation to come might know, the children, yet to be born, that they too may rise and declare to their children." The camp **archives** are open to anyone searching for records of family and friends between 1937 and 1945. Call ahead to schedule an appointment with the curator (☎ (03643) 43 01 54).

A 10-minute walk away, on the other side of the hilltop from the KZ-Lager, are the GDR-designed **Mahnmal** (memorial) and **Glockenturm** (bell tower). A path leads through the woods, emerging at a two-way fork in the road. Head right, walking past the parking lot and bus stop. Keep going as the street curves left. A recently added exhibit explains the history of debate over what kind of monument to build. The exhibit begins with the GDR-Soviet attempts to make it a monument to the defeat of National-Socialism by resistance fighters and the rise of a "better" Germany, and ends with the post-reunification reassessment of just how the crimes committed at Buchenwald should be memorialized and presented to the visiting public. The actual memorial consists of a series of carved blocks depicting stylized scenes of violence and oppression. Left from these blocks looms the somber bell tower with no marking other than an immense "MCMXLV" carved on each side. Behind the tower unfolds a commanding view of the surrounding countryside, overseen by the slightly awkward **Plastikgruppe,** a sculpture of ragged, stern-jawed socialist prisoners claiming their freedom.

The best way to reach the camp is by bus #6 from Weimar's train station or from Goethepl. Check the schedule carefully; some #6 busses go to "Ettersburg" rather than "Gedenkstätte Buchenwald." (M-F 1 per hr., Sa-Su every 2hr.). There is an information center near the bus stop at Buchenwald. (Exhibits and information booth open Tu-Su May-Sept. 9:45am-5:15pm; Oct.-Apr. 8:45am-4:15pm; outdoor camp area open daily until sundown.) Buses to Weimar stop at the *KZ-Lager* parking lot and at the road by the *Glockenturm.*

JENA   ☎ 03641

Once home to the country's premier university, Jena still triggers intellectual fire-works in the German historical consciousness. Under the stewardship of literary greats Schlegel, Novalis, Tieck, and Hölderlin, Jena first transplanted the Roman-tic movement to German soil. It was here that philosophers Fichte and Schelling argued for a new conception of intellectual and political freedom, and here, in 1806, that a then-unknown junior philosophy professor named Georg Wilhelm Friedrich Hegel wrote the epoch-making *Phenomenology of Spirit.* Today, the university bears the name of Friedrich Schiller, who, in 1789, graced its halls with his lectures on the ideals of the French Revolution. Even though the construction around the university tower creates an eyesore of a city center, Jena can't shake that exciting feeling of cutting-edge intellectual innovation. Nestled in a valley in hilly Thüringen, the town feels almost untouched by the outside world.

⚡ ORIENTATION AND PRACTICAL INFORMATION

Jena lies in the Saale Valley, 25km east of Weimar by **train** (30min., 3 per hr., DM7.80). Trains between **Dresden** and **Erfurt** stop at **Bahnhof Jena-West,** while trains on the Berlin-Munich line and on the Saale line between **Saalfeld** and **Naumburg** stop at the more distant **Jena Saalbahnhof,** 15 minutes north of the center. A third station, **Bahnhof Jena-Paradies,** brings trains from the Saalbahnhof closer to the city; most trains going there also make a stop at Jena-Paradies. Most of the city is connected by a bus and streetcar system that uses the "Zentrum" stop on Löbdergraben as its hub. (Single ride DM2; *Tageskarte* DM5). From Saalbahnhof, turn left down Saal-bahnhofstr. and take a right on Saalstr. to get to the center of town, or take bus #15. From Bahnhof Jena-West, head toward Westbahnhofstr. until it becomes Schiller-str. Turn left up Schillerstr. to the towering university building. From Jena-Paradies, take Kahlaischestr. to Neugasse, which leads to Holzmarkt and Löbdergraben. **Jena Tourist-Information,** Johannisstr. 23, on Eichpl., hands out free maps, leads city **tours,** and **books rooms** (DM30-45) for a DM6 fee. (☎ 194 33; fax 58 63 22; www.jena.de. Open M-F 9am-6pm, Sa 9am-2pm. Tours W,Su at 10am.) Rent **bikes** at **Kirscht Fahr-rad,** Löbdergraben 8, near the "Zentrum" bus stop. (☎44 15 39. Open M-F 9am-7pm, Sa 9am-4pm. DM15 per day.) For a **taxi** call ☎55 66 or 44 37 37. The **Goethe-Apotheke** is conveniently located on Weigelstr., just north of Eichpl.; a sign lists emergency **pharmacy** information. (☎45 45 45. Open M-F 8am-8pm, Sa 8am-4pm.) The **post office,** 07743 Jena, is at Engelpl. 8 (open M-F 9am-6:30pm, Sa 8am-1pm).

🏠🍽 ACCOMMODATIONS AND FOOD

Jena's budget accommodations aren't nearly as robust as its alternative culture. The **IB-Jugendgästehaus,** Am Herrenberge 3, is the cheapest bet. Take bus #10 or 13 (direction: "Burgau") to "Zeiss-Werk." Go right on Mühlenstr. up the hill until it turns into Am Herrenberge. Removed from the city-center but not hard to get to, the IB provides you with clean rooms and clean showers. (☎68 72 30. Breakfast included. Sheets DM7. Reception M-F 24hr., Sa 5-8pm, Su after 6pm. Dorm beds DM26; doubles DM31; singles DM45.)

The **market** on the Markt provides fresh produce (open Tu and Th-F 10am-6:30pm). A well-stocked **tegut** supermarket in the basement of the Goethe-Galerie off Schillerstr. provides more basics (open M-F 8am-8pm, Sa 8am-1pm). Jena's **Mensa** recently moved to its sparkling new digs in the University courtyard at Ernst-Abbe-Platz, across Leutragraben from the defuct tower. (Full meals DM2.50-5. Open M-F 8am-3pm.) A combination *Imbiß*, cafe, and restaurant, **Baboo's Internationale Spezialitäten,** Johannispl. 12, offers everything from *Döner Kebabs* (DM5) to tasty chicken curry (DM13), and you can have it to go, eat it at the table outside, or sit inside for a full-service meal. (☎42 66 66; fax 42 66 67. Open daily from 10am.) **Pizza und Pasta Lo-Studente,** Johannisstr. 18, serves the kind of crowd its name suggests, providing outdoor seating with a thought-provoking view of the less-than-attractive university tower. The cheap pizzas provide a filling meal. Pizza from DM7.50, pasta from DM6.50. (☎82 83 84. Open daily from 10am.) A crunchy clientele frequents **Café Immergrün**, Jenergasse 6, just off Fürstengraben. The fresh and friendly cafe is an unofficial environmental center. Vegetable and meat dishes with rice or baguette run DM3-8. (☎44 73 13. Open M-Sa 11am-1am, Su 3pm-late.)

👁 SIGHTS

The **Romantikerhaus,** Unterm Markt 12a, just off the old market square, once bubbled with the raw creative energy of the Romantic period. Owned by philosopher and fiery democrat Johann Fichte, it later hosted the poetry and philosophy parties of the Romantics. These days the museum inside is a bizarre mix of biographical info about the early Romantics and amusingly heavy-handed representations of their innovations. A room commemorates the meeting of Novalis, Schelling, and the Schlegels there in 1799; recordings of readings of their words allow you to hear them all talking at once. (☎44 32 63. Open Tu-Su 10am-1pm and 2-5pm. DM7, students and seniors DM3.) A few blocks to the southwest sits **Schillers Gartenhaus,** Schiller's swank summer home on Schillergäßchen, just off (you guessed it!) Schillerstr. Another museum where the furniture, including a standing desk, looks like it *could* have been used by Schiller—who knows? A helpful brochure in English brings some history to these recently renovated rooms and delightful sculpture garden. (☎93 11 88. Open May-Oct. Tu-Su 11am-3pm; Sept.-Apr. Tu-Sa 11am-3pm. DM2, students and seniors DM1.) The absolutely gigantic **University tower** is impossible to miss in Jena's landscape; hopefully the ongoing construction will bring some cheerfulness to the giant cylindrical monolith. Nearby, the **Goethe-Galerie,** an enclosed shopping mall off Leutragraben *(open daily 9am-midnight),* leads from Schillerstr. to Carl-Zeiß-Pl., where the city's one big name not affiliated with the university has his headquarters. Since the mid-19th century, Carl Zeiß' factory has produced microscopes and precision optics, and was the leader of the GDR's optics industry. The **Optisches Museum,** *Carl-Zeiß-Pl. 12,* presents this history as well as some more interesting exhibits on microscopes, telescopes, and magic lanterns. (Open Tu-F 10am-5pm, Sa 1-4:30pm, Su 9:30am-1pm.)

The **Stadtkirche St. Michael** presides proudly over **Luther's tombstone.** He's not resting here, though the stone was intended for him; the folks at the Stadtkirche claim it was held up in shipping during a war, while back at the grave site in Wittenberg, tour guides mutter something under their breath about 17th-century plundering. The 16th-century church is unusually frightening and weather-beaten outside, but the interior is graceful and light. (Off Eichpl. Open M-F 10am-5pm, Sa 10am-3pm.) Nearby stand the **Botanischer Garten** and the row of statues of the university's distinguished faculty—notice that teachers and students of **Marx** are given particularly large statues. (Up Weigelstr. and left down Fürstengraben. Open mid-Sept. to mid-May 9am-5pm; mid-May to mid-Sep. 9am-6pm.) But there's one glaring exception—Marx's intellectual godfather and Jena's most notorious professor, Hegel, has no bust at all. In fact, the only mention of him in the entire city is a plaque on the back of the Romantikerhaus. The **Zeiss-Planetarium,** Am Planetarium 5. the world's oldest, offers a rollicking good time for stargazers. (☎88 54 88. Open Tu-Sa 10am-4pm.)

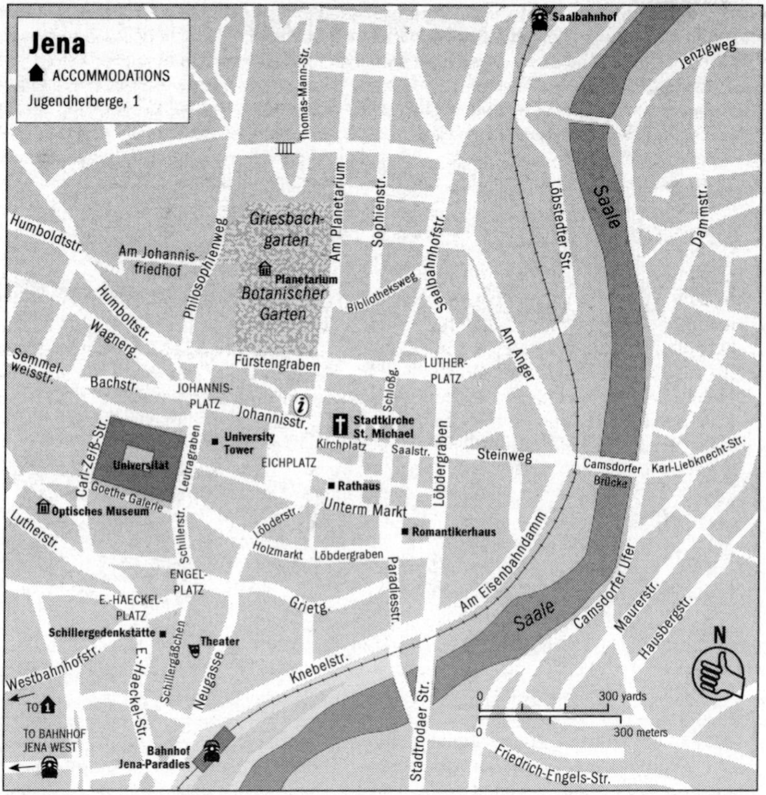

Jena

ACCOMMODATIONS
Jugendherberge, 1

(Map of Jena showing streets including Thomas-Mann-Str., Am Planetarium, Sophienstr., Saalbahnhofstr., Löbstedter Str., Saale, Jenzigweg, Dammstr., Humboldtstr., Am Johannis-friedhof, Philosophenweg, Griesbach-garten, Botanischer Garten, Planetarium, Bibliotheksweg, Am Anger, Fürstengraben, LUTHER-PLATZ, Schlofg., Semmel-weisstr., Bachstr., JOHANNIS-PLATZ, Johannisstr., University Tower, EICHPLATZ, Stadtkirche St. Michael, Kirchplatz, Saalstr., Steinweg, Camsdorfer Brücke, Karl-Liebknecht-Str., Universität, Goethe Galerie, Optisches Museum, Lutherstr., Rathaus, Unter Markt, Holzmarkt, Löbdergraben, Romantikerhaus, Paradiesstr., Am Eisenbahndamm, Camsdorfer Ufer, Maurerstr., Hausbergstr., ENGEL-PLATZ, E.-HAECKEL-PLATZ, Grietg., Schillergedenkstätte, Theater, Westbahnhofstr., E.-Haeckel-Str., Schillerstr., Neugasse, Knebelstr., Stadtrodaer Str., Friedrich-Engels-Str., Bahnhof Jena-Paradies, TO BAHNHOF JENA WEST, Saalbahnhof, 300 yards, 300 meters, N)

🎵🎭 ENTERTAINMENT AND NIGHTLIFE

Extending from Johannisstr., **Wagnergasse** is shaping up as Jena's funkiest area, filled with bars and restaurants. The university energy has clearly been funneled in this direction, and numerous trendy cafes and clothing stores line the street. At the end of the strip lies the **Studentenhaus Wagner**, Wagnergasse 26, the source of the funk, as it were. The university-sponsored hang-out and cafe doubles as a performance space for plays, readings, live music, and movie screenings. (☎93 06 80 or 93 06 81. Open M-F 11am-1am, Sa-Su 7:30pm-1am. Cafe open M-Sa from 6pm, Su from 7:30pm.) **Kassablanca**, Felsenkellerstr. 13a, sponsors a mind-boggling array of discos, concerts, and political discussions. The club hosts everything from freestyle to house. (☎282 60. Usually open W and F-Sa after 10pm. Cover DM5-8.) Kassablanca is also one of several annual sponsors of **Kulturarena Jena,** a month-long cultural festival featuring nightly performances. The area in front of Jena's theater at Engelpl. is transformed into an open-air performance space. Everything from Mozart opera to jazz to emphatic indie-rock is performed here from early July to mid-August. Buy the tickets at the tourist office, or join the crowds who line the sidewalks just outside and listen to the concerts for free (DM20-35, students DM15-30).

📷 DAY TRIP FROM JENA: DORNBURG

To reach Dornburg from Jena, hop on one of the hourly trains headed toward Naumburg from either Jena Saalbahnhof or Bahnhof Jena-Paradies.The castles are a 15-minute climb up a very steep hill. From the train station, head toward the castles and turn right on Am Born; the stairs are up the hill on the left. When you reach the main road, turn right and continue upward.

THURINGIA

TO WURST OR NOT TO WURST Wurst is believed to be
the very foundation of German national identity. "To *wurst* or not to *wurst*," pondered
an anonymous 11th-century German poet. Shakespeare later failed to convey the existential dilemma obvious to connoisseurs of all things German when he paraphrased
the credo in *Hamlet*. Arrogant English-speaking folks continue to believe that *Wurst* can
be translated literally as "German sausage" and often indulge in what may seem a
cheap and simple meal, oblivious to the true nature of the *Wurst*.

The only comprehensive categorization of different kinds of *Wurst* is said to have
been included in the lost pages of Aristotles' *Politics*. While no one is sure how many
types are currently available, four main varieties of *Wurst* can be distinguished:

Thüringer Bratwurst: The direct ancestor of the American "hot dog" comes cupped in a
flaky Brötchen, doused in mustard. Also known as a *Roster* or *Thüringer Brat*, this zesty
sausage puts the sickly pink American frank to shame. It's said to be a natural aphrodi-
siac, not to mention a possible cure for impotence.

Rheinländer Wurst: The *Rheinländer* is of religious significance to obscure tribal groups
inhabiting Western Germany. Legend has it that on special occasions Rheinlanders grab
a naked, greasy *Wurst* in their bare hands, alternately biting the meaty mass and a roll.

Bavarian Weißwurst: In the Middle Ages the *Weißwurst* was an essential element of a
popular medical practice. Known for its cleansing properties, it guarantees a stomach-
buckling experience, and was regarded as a perfect treatment for all sorts of digestive
disorders. Now that universal aesthetic and moral standards are finally imposing themselves on the German *Volk*, a medically indifferent and safer version prevails.

Frankfurter: This *Wurst* is produced following a secret recipe in a gruesome and morally
dubious process which involves stuffing the front legs of a pig into sheep intestines.
Though not chemically addictive, each *Frankfurter* comes with a legally mandated warning against frequent consumption, as prolonged use has been known to induce mental
instability and increased perspiration.

One of the more majestic summer estates in Thüringen lies 10 minutes north of
Jena. The **Dornburger Schlößer** are three royal palaces, running the gamut from
medieval to Baroque, perched along a white chalk cliff. First in line is the **Altes
Schloß,** the oldest and homeliest castle, built in 937 when the Kaisers still visited
Dornburg. The first German parliament met here; later, the building was used as a
prison by both the Nazi and Communist regimes. The interior is closed to the public. The summer residences of the Grand Duke of Sachsen-Weimar-Eisenach, the
Renaissanceschloß and the **Rokokoschloß** preside majestically and frivolously
(respectively) over the magnificent rose gardens where Goethe practiced his horticultural skills while writing letters to his lover, Charlotte von Stein. He was, of
course, ambidextrous. Inside the whitewashed, 16th-century Renaissance castle,
the plain royal belongings are spiced up with stories about Goethe's frequent visits
to the palaces. (DM2, students and seniors DM1.) One look inside the lush chambers of this 1740 Rococo pleasure palace will reveal why Goethe chose its ornate,
luxurious, and window-filled rooms for 19 of his 20 visits to Dornburg. Visitors
partake in the pleasure of gliding along the slick main hall in slippers provided to
protect its plum-tree wood. The gilded decorations and porcelain collection fall
somewhere between priceless treasures and gaudy kitsch. Unfortunately only the
Renaissance Schloß is currently open to visitors; the other two are closed until
June 2002 while being restored. (☎(03647) 222 91. Castles open W-Su Mar.-Oct.
9am-6pm; Nov.-Feb. 10am-4pm; castle grounds open daily 8am-dusk.)

Dornburg's abundance of roses, is celebrated during the last weekend in June
with the **Rosenfest,** marking the anniversary of King Karl August's lavish birthday
parties held here a century ago. The townspeople elect a rose queen on Saturday
who then leads a procession around the town on Sunday, distributing roses to
spectators. Locals don their party hats again during the last week in August to celebrate **Goethe's birthday.** The **post office** on the Markt also sells **groceries** (open M-F
8am-1pm and 3-5pm, Sa 8-10am).

ERFURT ☎0361

The capital of Thüringen, Erfurt has been renovated far more thoroughly and ingeniously than many towns and cities of the GDR. Its Altstadt area contains street after street of fascinating building facades. Sometimes referred to as "Thüringisches Rom" (Thurigian Rome), this capital city has a definite appeal. Though not a cultural powerhouse like Dresden or Weimar, Erfurt has a dynamic political history: Napoleon based his field camp here for more than a year, Konrad Adenauer lived here before WWII, and, more recently, West German Chancellor Willy Brandt met here in 1970 with East German leader Willi Stoph, commencing *Ostpolitik*, the difficult process of East-West reconciliation (see p. 19).

■ ORIENTATION AND PRACTICAL INFORMATION

Erfurt lies in the heart of Thüringen, only 15 minutes from Weimar, and is fittingly referred to as the gateway to the Thüringer Wald. The train station stands south of the city center. Head straight down Bahnhofstr. to reach the **Anger**—the main drag—and then the Altstadt, which is bisected by the **Gera River.** Across the river down Schlößerstr. lies the **Fischmarkt,** dominated by the **Rathaus.** From the square, Marktstr. leads left to the **Domhügel,** home to Erfurt's cathedral.

Trains: Trains chug to **Weimar** (15min., 4 per hr., DM7.60); **Leipzig** (2hr., 13 per day, DM32); **Dresden** (3hr., every 2hr., DM64); **Berlin** (3½hr., every 2hr., DM81); and **Frankfurt** (2½hr., 1 per hr., DM72).

Public Transportation: Buses and **streetcars** run through the pedestrian zones. DM2.50 per trip. Five trips DM8. *Tageskarte* DM5. Children and dogs 50% discount. Most buses and streetcars now have on-board ticket machines. Validate your ticket on board. Night streetcars (numbered with an "N" prefix) cover most stops on the daytime routes, running every 15 minutes or every half-hour all night long.

Taxis: ☎511 11 or, for those with bad memories, ☎555 55 or ☎66 66 66.

Bike Rental: Velo-Sport, Juri-Gagarin-Ring 72a (☎/fax 56 23 540). From the train station, take a right on Bahnhofstr. and walk left on Juri-Gagarin-Ring for about 3min. From DM15 per day. Open Apr.-Sept. M-F 10am-7pm, Sa 9am-4pm; Oct.-Mar. M-F 10am-7pm, Sa 9am-2pm.

Tourist Office: Erfurt Tourismus Gesellschaft, Benediktspl. 1 (☎664 00; fax 664 02 90), down the street to the left of the Rathaus. Pick up a copy of the monthly *Erfurter Magazin* with a worthy map in the center, and, for nightlife, *Takt* or *Fritz*. Maps of the Thüringer Wald are also available. The staff reserves tickets and books **rooms** (DM25-50) for a DM5 per person fee. Open M-F 10am-7pm, Sa-Su 10am-4pm. Two-hour **tours** of the city in German depart from the office Sa and Su at 1pm (DM6, students DM3).

Currency Exchange: ReiseBank, in the train station. Money transfers, phonecards, and cash advances on credit cards. Nice hours, but somewhat stiff rates. Open M 8am-1pm and 1:30-4pm, Tu-F 8am-7:30pm, Sa 9am-1pm and 1:30-4pm. Close to the train station, and with better rates and a **24hr. ATM,** is **DeutscheBank,** on the corner of Bahnhofstr. and Juri-Gagarin-Ring. Open M, W, and F 9am-4pm, Tu and Th 9am-6pm.

Laundry: SB Waschsalon, across the street and to the left as you exit the train station. Open daily 8am-11pm. DM6 per load.

Pharmacy: Apollo-Apotheke, Juri-Gagarin-Ring 94 (☎24 11 66), has a wide selection; all-night pharmacy listings are posted in the window. From the train station, go right on Bahnhofstr. to Juri-Gagarin-Ring. Take a left; the pharmacy should be just ahead. Open M-F 7:30am-7pm, Sa 8am-1pm.

Gay and Lesbian Resources: At the **AIDS-Hilfe,** Windhorststr. 43a (☎346 22 97). Streetcar #3 or 6 to "Robert-Koch-Str.," then continue on another block. On the edge of the city park near the train station the rainbow flag flies over a house filled with a library, archive, and cafe. Counseling Tu-W 10am-3pm and Th noon-5pm. **Café SwiB** open W, F, Su 7pm-midnight. Pick up *Buschlunk*, Thüringen's ultra-thorough, ultra-helpful monthly gay and lesbian magazine.

Women's Resources: Brennessel Frauenzentrum, Meister-Eckehart-Str. 5 (☎565 65 10; fax 565 65 11), in the center of the city, offers information and counseling, overnight stays, a cafe, sauna, and programs for lesbians. Open M-F 9am-5pm; events usually 8pm-midnight.

Internet access: On the second floor of the **Buch Habel** bookstore, Anger 7, across from the post office. Open M-F and Su 9am-8pm, Sa 9am-4pm. DM3 per half hour.

Emergency: Police, ☎110. **Fire and Ambulance,** ☎112.

Post Office: 99084 Erfurt. The main post office, the focal point of the Anger, occupies an ornate beast of a building probably larger than some of the punier European countries. Open M-F 8am-7pm, Sa 9am-1pm.

▌ ACCOMMODATIONS

Erfurt's one youth hostel is far from the center but easily accessed by public transportation and in a pleasant neighborhood. Other varieties of budget accommodations are hard to come by; try the tourist office's room-finding service.

Jugendherberge Erfurt (HI), Hochheimer Str. 12 (☎562 67 05; fax 562 67 06). From the station, take streetcar #5 (direction: "Steigerstr.") to "Steigerstr." Backtrack a little, and turn left onto Hochheimer Str.; the hostel is on the left corner at the first intersection. Institutional, but each 6-bed room has its own bathroom with shower. Breakfast included. Lunch and dinner DM8 each. Sheets DM7. Reception 6-9am and 3-10pm; tell the desk ahead of time if you plan on coming back any later than 10pm. Wheelchair accessible. Dorm beds DM25, over 27 DM30.

Pension am Park, Löberwallgraben 22 (☎/fax 345 33 44), at the near end of the park behind the train station. From the station, exit to the left and take an immediate left under the bridge on Bahnhofstr. Turn right onto Schillerstr., which leads to Löberwallgraben. After two blocks it will appear on the left. A lovely, quiet location. Breakfast included. Singles DM65, doubles DM100.

◖ FOOD

Cheap food in Erfurt is hard to come by, though the region's specialty, *Thüringer Bratwurst*, is sold at stands all over the city (DM2-3). For **groceries,** try the **Rewe supermarket,** to your right as you walk out of the train station (open M-W 6am-7pm, Th-F 6am-8pm, Sa 7am-1pm). There is also a **market** for fresh fruits and vegetables on Dompl. (open M-Sa 7am-2pm).

Ristorante Don Camillo, Michaelisstr. 29 (☎260 11 45), has delicious, moderately priced Italian food in a setting worthy of a higher price bracket. Pizzas DM8.50 and pastas from DM10. Open daily 11:30am-3pm and 5:30pm-1am.

Fellini, Am Fischmarkt 3 (☎642 13 75), is right in the middle of the action on the Fischmarkt, with outside seating and a view of the Rathaus. The friendly staff serves pastas like Tortelinni Aurora (DM12) and Gnocchi Pesto (DM11). The pasta portions are small, but the pizzas (from DM10) are filling. Open daily 10am-midnight.

Anger Maier, Schlösserstr. 8 (☎566 10 58), at the edge of Angerpl. heading toward the Fischmarkt, has a reasonably priced weekly menu (DM10-13), a *Biergarten*, and surprisingly sumptuous bagels. Sandwich with lox, DM5.90; with margarine, DM2.40. Open daily 10am-1am.

Kurdischer Döner Kebab, Meienbergstr. 21. This stand is noteworthy for its clean, sit-down facilities and fresh, quality ingredients. *Döner* DM5, pizza from DM6. Open M-F 9am-1am, Sa 10am-midnight.

◉ SIGHTS

■**KRÄMERBRÜCKE.** The quietly babbling **Gera** flows down Marktstr. and provides the *raison d'être* for one of Erfurt's most interesting architectural attractions. Completely covered by small shops, the medieval bridge dates back to the 12th century. In the 1400s, the bridge was part of a great trade route running from

THURINGIA

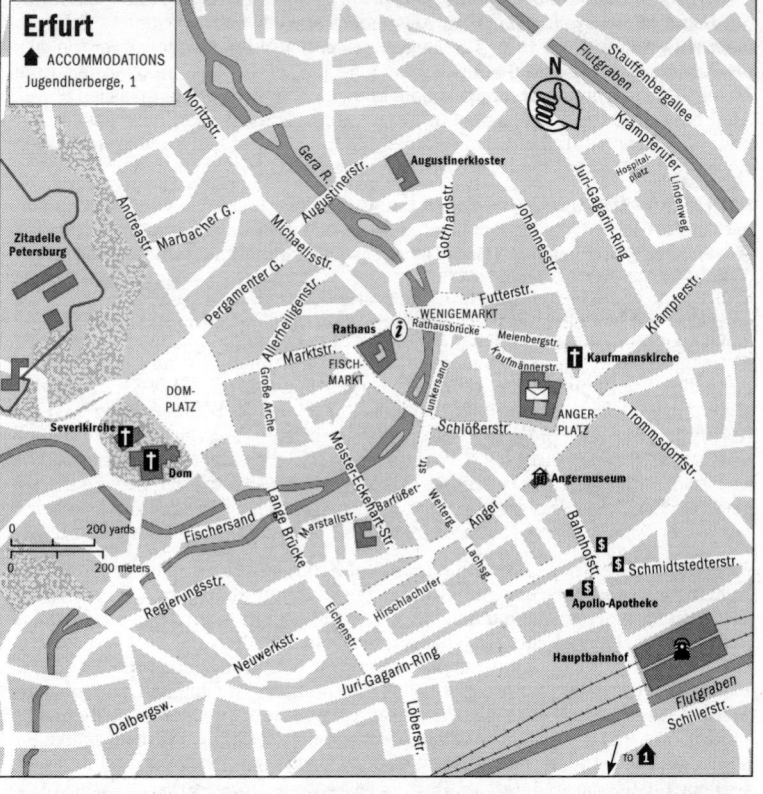

Erfurt

▲ ACCOMMODATIONS
Jugendherberge, 1

Kiev to Paris. Even more fascinating is the view from underneath—take one of the paths leading off the bridge to get a glance up from the water's edge. At the far end of the bridge from the tourist office, the **tower** of the **Aegidienkirche** is open for those interested in climbing some really rickety stairs for a nice view of Erfurt's red-roofed houses. *(Tower open sporadically M-Sa, but always Su noon-6pm. DM2.)*

MARIENDOM. The mammoth cathedral completely dominates the view from the marketplace at its perch on the **Domhügel**, impressing even the most ardent heathen. Today the church is a Gothic extravaganza, though its Romanesque foundation dates back to 1154. Inside, the most impressive part of the cathedral is the 15th-century **Hochchor** in the eastern wing; the **altar** is fully 17m high, embellished with miniature oil paintings, intricate carvings, and a painting by Lucas Cranach. The 15 **stained glass windows** are about halfway through a massive cleaning that will make them brighter than they've been in centuries. *(Domplatz. Open May-Oct. M-F 9-11:30am and 12:30-5pm, Sa 9-11:30am and 12:30-4:30pm, Su 2-4pm; Nov.-Apr. M-F 10-11:30am and 12:30-4pm, Su 2-4pm. Free.)*

SEVERIKIRCHE. The muted sandstone interior of this church proves less impressive than its turrets would lead one to believe. However, the enormous Baroque organ appendages scream with flying golden angels, flames, and fake pastel marble. *(Next to Mariendom. Open May-Oct. M-F 9-11:30am and 12:30-5pm, Sa 9-11:30am and 12:30-4:30pm, Su 2-4pm; Nov.-Apr. M-F 10-11:30am and 12:30-4pm, Su 2-4pm. Free.)*

ANGER. Erfurt's wide pedestrian promenade, the Anger, is one of the most attractive shopping areas in Eastern Germany. The architecture lining the street—most of it 19th-century Neoclassical or *Jugendstil*—is for the most part fascinating,

THURINGIA

though some GDR-era behemoths mar the cityscape. Across from the post office lies **House #6,** where Russian Czar Alexander I stayed when he came to Erfurt to meet with Napoleon in 1808. The **Angermuseum,** housed in a yellow mansion, is a pleasantly quiet museum that displays a collection of medieval religious art from around Erfurt. The medieval art is bold and colorful, with bright splashes of red. After pausing at the room painted by Expressionist Erich Heckel, head upstairs for pleasant 19th-century landscapes, mostly of the surrounding countryside. *(Anger 18.* ☎ *562 33 11. Open Tu-Su 10am-6pm. DM3, students DM1.50)*

KAUFMANNSKIRCHE. At the end of the Anger sits the church where Bach's parents tied the knot. Outside, feet planted firmly on a pedestal decorated with scenes from his days here, a squat **Martin Luther** casts an indifferent stare over the street. *(Open M-Sa 9am-7pm, Su 11am-5pm.)*

AUGUSTINERKLOSTER. Martin Luther spent 10 years as a Catholic priest and Augustine monk in this cloister. A Protestant college now occupies the site. Its **library** has one of Germany's most priceless collections, including a number of early bibles with personal notations by Luther himself. During WWII, the books were moved to make room for a bomb shelter. When US bombers destroyed the library in February 1945, 267 people lost their lives, but the books remained unscathed. *(From the tourist office, cross the Krämerbrücke, turn left on Gotthardstr., and cut left through Kirchengasse. Hourly tours Apr.-Oct. Tu-Sa 10am-noon and 2-4pm, Su once after services; Nov.-Mar. Tu-Sa 10am, noon, and 2pm. The cloister usually won't lead a tour if fewer than 6 people show up, so you may get bumped back an hour or more. DM5.50, students DM4.)*

RATHAUS. The stony neo-Gothic facade of Erfurt's Rathaus rests in sharp contrast to the decorations of its interior; running along the staircases and hallways of the main entrance to the building are beautifully colorful portrayals of mythical narratives, including Faust, Tannhauser, the Count of Gleichen, and even some of Luther's escapades. Multi-lingual plaques narrate each frame, and bring us periodically back to reality, pointing out that the Countess of Gleichen's supposedly pleased reaction to her husband's return from battle with a second wife has no basis in fact. The portrayals of Luther show a young, sprightly reformer, unlike the solid man portrayed in most statues; it seems that 95 theses can add a lot of bulk to a person. *(Fischmarkt 1. Open M, W, Th 7:30am-4pm, Tu 7:30am-6pm, F 7:30am-2pm, Sa and Su 10am-5pm. Free.)*

STAATSKANZLEI. Communists ruled the city from this massive building. Here, in a small salon on the second floor, Napoleon had breakfast with Goethe in 1808. Goethe later wrote that Napoleon spent the entire time chastising him for his gloomy tragedies—which the French emperor seemed to know inside and out—while Goethe listened passively. Both understood themselves to be immortals. Goethe also realized, however, that Napoleon's immortality was backed by an army. The building is not open to the public, but the exterior still merits a gawking. *(Bear right at the end of the Anger and follow Regierungstr. to have a look.)*

OTHER SIGHTS. From the Domplatz, Marktstr. leads down to the **Fischmarkt,** bordered by restored guild houses with wildly decorated facades. The exterior of Erfurt's **Stadtmuseum** at Johannisstr. 169, with its scowling lions' heads and blue-and-white squares, is far more intriguing than what it holds inside; apart from a few severed hands and some Bronze-Age skeletons, the museum is a fairly dry account of Erfurt's history.

♪ 🎭 ENTERTAINMENT AND NIGHTLIFE

Erfurt's 220,000 inhabitants manage a fairly indulgent nightlife. While the opera house is closed, a victim of stringent German safety regulations, the **Theater Erfurt** puts on regular shows at the nearby **Schauspielhaus,** with performances ranging from Mozart and Verdi operas to ballet and youth theatre. The **ticket office,** Dalbersweg 2, is in the green house just down the street from the opera house. (☎223 31 55. Office open Apr.-Aug. Tu-F 10am-1pm and 2-5:30pm, Sa 10am-1pm, Su 10am-noon, and 1hr. before performance; Sept.-Mar. closed Su. Ask about student discounts. Tickets can also be purchased at the tourist office.) Just off Domplatz, the **Theater Waidspeicher** charms all with a marionette and puppet theater, and cabaret crops up on weekends. (☎598 29 24. Box office at Dompl. 18. Open Tu-F 10am-2pm and 3-5:30pm. Puppet shows DM10-15, cabaret DM17-21.)

The area near Domplatz and the Krämerbrücke between **Michaelisstr.**, **Marbacher Gasse**, and **Allerheiligenstr.** glows at night with cafes, candlelit restaurants, and bars. **Johannisstr.** also has its share. The **Double b,** Marbacher Gasse 10, near Dompl., functions as a hybrid Irish pub, German beer garden, and Amsterdam cafe; all the cool cats in Erfurt show up there to chill in the fiercely hip vibe. (☎211 51 22. Open M-F 8am-midnight, Sa-Su 9am-1am.) **Silberschales,** Kürschnerg. 4, off Rathausbrücke near the Fischmarkt, has reasonably priced drinks and a delightful back deck with seating right over the shallow Gera, and (open daily until 1am, later on weekends). **Miss Marple,** Michaelisstr. 42, features photos of the Agatha Christie's humorous private eye on the walls and ceilings, and an entrance that looks just like a London phone booth. Daily specials, like a Tequila Sunrise for DM5 on Mondays, make repeated visits worthwhile. *Berliner Weiße* of both varieties is to be had for DM3.50. (☎520 33 99. Open daily from 6pm.) The **Studentenclub Engelsburg,** Allerheiligenstr. 20-21, just off Marktstr., is down with the disco and moderate punk scene, especially at the musical grotto within. Live bands from Erfurt and the surrounding area groove in the party room. (☎24 47 70. Open July-Sept. W and Sa 9pm-1am, Su 10pm-midnight; Oct.-June W-Sa 9pm-1am. Cover DM8, students DM4.) The club also contains **Café Duckdich,** a grooving student meeting place. (Open Tu-Th 8pm-2am, F and Sa 8pm-3am.) Erfurt also feeds a very healthy electronic music scene. Much of it is underground, but to find out what's up, stop by **Pure** on Meienbergstr., a record store that has fliers for every concert going on between Eisenach and Leipzig. (☎643 09 55. Open M-F 11am-8pm, Sa 11am-2pm.) Wanna dance? Erfurt makes it easy for you, offering a special bus to its two largest discos, **MAD** and **FUN. Bus #33** runs F-Su from the Anger to the discos and back, for DM2.50, the same price as a regular ride. Plan carefully, though, as the bus makes the full trip only every two hours.

THÜRINGER WALD (THURINGIAN FOREST)

"The area is magnificent, quite magnificent…I am basking in God's world," wrote Goethe in a letter from the Thüringer Wald more than 200 years ago. Goethe's exuberant exclamation is still accurate; the time-worn mountains make for perfect skiing during winter and excellent hiking, camping, and walking in summer. The greenness of the country is mind-boggling; any church-tower providing a view of Thüringen shows miles and miles of deep green mountains. Cradled within these mighty hills, the region's towns and villages have cultivated and inspired many German composers, philosophers, and poets; Goethe and Schiller wrote some of their most brilliant poetry on these slopes.

Snaking through the forest, the **Rennsteig** has been a renowned hiking trail for centuries. While history books date the trail to 1330, locals claim that it was first trodden by prehistoric hunter-gatherers. During the years of East-West division, much of the trail was closed because of its potential as an escape route. Now hikers wander the length of the 168km, 5-day trek from Hörschel near Eisenach south into Bavaria. The **tourist office** in Erfurt (p. 227) sells guides and maps for an extended jaunt. If you're thinking about taking on the Rennsteig, reserve trail-side huts well in advance. Write or call **Gästeinformation Brotterode**, Bad-Vibeler-Platz 4, 98599 Brotterode (☎(036840) 33 33), for more information.

THURINGIA

NEAR ERFURT: ILMENAU AND THE GOETHE TRAIL

Surrounded by the spectacular beauty of the Thüringer Wald, Ilmenau is a pleasant, friendly, and well-kept town, proud of its native ingenue, Johann Wolfgang von Goethe. The residents will proudly point out that Goethe visited their town a whole 28 times. The author first worked in Ilmenau as a government minister responsible for mining under the Duke of Weimar; later, he came back to the area as a poet in search of inspiration. Today the town capitalizes on Goethe and his fame to draw visitors, vaunting the sights he frequented about town in addition to the stunning 18.5km ■**Goethewanderweg** (Goethe Trail), marked by the author's over-flourished "G" monogram. Ilmenau also makes a good starting point for a hike along the 168km-long ■**Rennsteig**; take bus #300 (direction: "Suhl") to "Rennsteigkreuzung" (DM3.30). Cutting across a good swath of southern Thüringen, the Rennsteig links gorgeous scenery and traditional villages that lie scattered along the path.

Ilmenau can be reached by **bus** or **train** from **Erfurt** (1hr., 1 per hr., DM15). Pick up a map and ask for more information about the Goethewanderweg or Rennsteig at the **tourist office**, Lindenstr. 12. From the station, walk down Bahnhofstr. to Wetzlarer Pl. and follow the pedestrian zone until it becomes Lindenstr. (15min.). The staff provides hiking maps and books **rooms** (DM20-45) for a DM2 per-person fee. (☎(03677) 20 23 58 or 621 32; fax 20 25 02; email Stadtinfo@ilmenau.de; www.ilmenau.de. Open M-F 9am-6pm, Sa 9am-noon.) The **post office**, 98693 Ilmenau, Lindenstr. 1, is along the pedestrian zone before the tourist office (open M-F 8am-6pm, Sa 9am-noon).

Jugendherberge Ilmenau, Am Stollen 49 (☎(03677) 88 46 81; fax 88 46 82), offers a shower and bathroom for each four-bed room. From the station, take a left at August-Bebel-Str., crossing the tracks and veering right on the path along the tracks. After the sharp right curve, cross the bridge on your left, and continue on the trail until it merges with Am Stollen (15 min.). Though a bit far from the center among drab apartment buildings, the hostel is friendly and hospitable, and well situated as a jumping-off place for hikers. (Breakfast included. Reception 10am-10pm. Key deposit DM20. DM25, over 26 DM30.) Head to the **farmer's market** on the Markt for fresh produce (Tu and F 8am-6pm). For more substantial goods to sustain you through a day-hike, try the **Rewe** in the basement of the City *Kaufhaus* along F.-Hoffmann-Str. in the pedestrian zone (open M-W and F 9am-7pm, Th 9am-7:30pm, Sa 9am-4pm). **Die Arche,** Str. des Friedens 28, is a cafe featuring international cuisine as well as a shop for African and Indian trinkets. The walls on the bottom floor are covered with teas and herbs, while the top floor gives out on a colorful garden. Immerse yourself in the cloud of exotic scents, and enjoy a pot of tea—there are 170 options. (☎(03677) 89 41 11. Cup DM2.50, pot DM5. Open M-F 10am-6pm, Sa 9am-2pm, Su 1-6pm.) **Zur Post,** Mühltor 6, on Wetzlarer Pl., offers regional specialties at excellent prices (DM9-14). Try the *Thüringer Rostbrätel*, a pork roast with fried potatoes, for DM10. (☎(03677) 67 10 27. Open M-F 8:30am-midnight, Sa-Su 11am-midnight. Kitchen closes 11pm.)

▲ DAY HIKE: THE GOETHE WANDERWEG
Estimated time: 6-7 hrs.; Estimated distance: 18.5 km

Follow Goethe's very footsteps through his beloved hills of Thüringen along the **Goethewanderweg.** The hike begins in Ilmenau, at the top of the hill past the market, outside the town's **Goethe-Gedenkstätte,** a museum devoted to the author and his works. *(Am Markt 1. ☎20 26 67 or 60 01 06. Open May-Oct. daily 9am-noon and 1-4:30pm; Nov.-Apr. 10am-noon and 1-4pm. DM2, students and seniors DM1.)* The trail is well-marked by a large "G" monogram, while it meanders through green hills, runs above open pastures, passes ponds and crosses streams. For safety precautions to observe while hiking, and the necessary equipment, see p. 57.

Part 1: Goethe-associated landmarks appear throughout the trail; after lmenau's museum, the first is the grave of **Corona Schröter,** the first actress to portray Goethe's renowned Iphigenia. *(Following the signs out of the graveyard, continue along Erfurterstr. to Neue Marienstr. and head into the hills.)* Tall pines crowd both sides of the trail as it leads through magnificent greenery to the **Schwalbenstein,** an impressive outcropping upon which Goethe wrote Act IV of *Iphigenia*. The view into the valley is wonder-

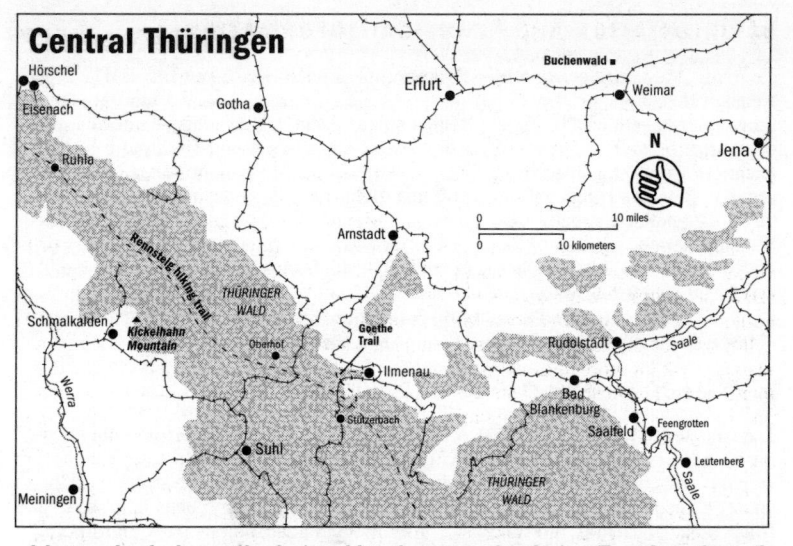

Central Thüringen

ful; on a cloudy day, puffs of mist add to the sense of seclusion. From here the trail gets steeper; follow it uphill and then keep with it as it turns back down toward the town of **Manebach;** be sure to stare back at the cows grazing on the sloped meadow. **Part 2:** From Manebach, the "G" signs point back up into the green. About 10km into the trail, the forlorn and tiny **Goethehäuschen** rests on the **Kickelhahn,** where the poetry the author scratched on the walls in his youth is on display. Farther along (11km) lies the **Jagdhaus Gabelbach,** the hunting house of Duke Karl August that Goethe frequented in the summer. The lodge features a display of the author's scientific experiments as well as some of his drawings. (☎ 20 26 26. Open W-Su Mar.-Oct. 9am-5pm; Sept.-Feb. 10am-4pm. DM4, students DM3.) The terrain evens out and the going gets easy for a while; deep in the forest, the trail passes a pond, then crosses **Finsteres Loch** and turns uphill once more. After Auerhahn, cross the road and head directly downhill; the signs will pick up after a few meters and will point toward the last three landmarks. **Part 3:** Goethe's meandering footsteps brought the end of the trail to **Stützerbach,** a tiny little valley town where the local glass-works magnate often hosted the poet. The house is now the **Goethehaus,** but, as a nod to the patron, there are demonstrations of traditional glass-blowing. (Open W-Su Mar.-Oct. 9am-5pm, Nov.-Feb. 10am-4pm. DM4, students DM3.) Unless you're prepared to hike the 6 hours back to Ilmenau, you'll need to catch a bus back from **Stützerbach.** Don't head for the defunct train station; go into town, turn right onto Bahnhofstr., and then cut to your left through the parking lot in front of the tourist office. Next take a right; this street soon becomes Unterstr., and leads over a bridge and right up to the bus stop called "Ilmenau, Erholung" on Schleusingerstr. (Buses run about every hr. until just before 9pm. DM2.50 to Ilmenau station.)

EISENACH   ☎ 03691

Birthplace of Johann Sebastian Bach and home-in-exile of Martin Luther, Eisenach boasts impressive humanist credentials. Adolf Hitler is said to have called the idyllic Wartburg "the most German of German castles," fighting a pitched (and unsuccessful) battle with the local church to replace its tower's cross with a swastika. The castle has done good things for Eisenach; the tourism it has always generated has kept the town well-off and pleasantly welcoming. Eisenach's automobile industry has marked the castle's rich contributions to the city, naming luxury cars after the Wartburg since 1899. Eisenach basks pleasantly beneath the sturdy shadow of the castle-on-a-hill, quietly reaping the benefits of being home to one of Germany's most treasured national symbols.

THURINGIA

⚡ ORIENTATION AND PRACTICAL INFORMATION

Frequent **train** connections link Eisenach to **Erfurt** (1hr., 3 per hr., DM14.80); **Weimar** (1hr., 3 per hr., DM19.50); **Kassel** (1½hr., 1 per hr., DM27); and **Göttingen** (2hr., 1 per hr., DM35). Eisenach's **tourist office**, Markt 2, has plenty of information on Wartburg, sells maps (DM2), offers daily city **tours** (2pm, DM5), and books **rooms** (DM30-40) for free. From the train station, walk on Bahnhofstr. through the arched tunnel, and angle left until you turn right onto the pedestrian Karlstr. (☎67 02 60. Open M 10am-6pm, Tu-F 9am-6pm, Sa and Su 10am-2pm.) Rent a **bike** at **Schmidt Fahrrad,** Johannispl. 12 (☎21 49 24; open M-F 10am-6pm, Sa 10am-1pm), or go for a ride on Eisenach's **buses** (2 trips DM2.40; 6 trips DM7.20). For a **taxi,** call ☎22 02 20. The **Ost-Apotheke,** Bahnhofstr. 29, has a list of night **pharmacies.** (☎20 32 42. Open M-F 8am-6pm, Sa 8am-noon.) Send your Wartburg postcard from the **post office,** 99817 Eisenach, on the Markt (open M-F 8am-6pm, Sa 8am-noon).

▓◌ ACCOMMODATIONS AND FOOD

Jugendherberge Arthur Becker (HI), Mariental 24, fills a comfortable old villa fairly far from the center, a bit beyond the Schloß. From the train station, take Bahnhofstr. to Wartburger Allee, which runs into Mariental. Walk down the street until the hostel comes up on your right, past the pond (35min.); alternatively, take bus #3 (direction: "Mariental") to "Lilienstr." About 100m past the bus stop, signs point the way up the sloping drive to the right. The hostel was completely renovated for 2000, and the squeaky-clean floors and brightly-painted orange walls attest. Putting glass doors on the showers in the co-ed bathrooms, though, wasn't a stroke of genius. (☎74 32 59; fax 74 32 60. Breakfast included. Sheets DM7. Reception 4-9pm. Curfew 10pm, but you can get a key. Dorm beds DM25, over 26 DM30.) Eisenach also offers an excellent, very central *Pension:* **Gasthof Storchenturm,** Georgenstr. 43, fills a secluded courtyard next to a park with a restaurant, *Biergarten*, and several clean and quiet rooms, all with showers (☎21 52 50; fax 21 50 82. Breakfast DM7.50. Restaurant open 7am-1am. Singles DM45; doubles DM70.) The nearest **camping** is at **Am Altenberger See,** offering showers, a sauna, and a view of the lake in the hamlet of Eckartshausen. From the Eisenach station, take the **bus** to "Bad Liebenstein" and tell the driver your destination. (☎21 56 37. 14 departures daily M-F; 7:43am, 1:43pm, and 5:23pm on weekends.) About 10km from town, the campground offers 13 cabins. (Reception 8am-1pm and 3-10pm. DM7 per person. Tent DM5. Car DM2.)

For **groceries** head to the **Edeka** on Johannispl. (open M-F 7am-7pm, Sa 7am-2pm). There's also a **Nimm's mit** supermarket in Eisenach's train station (open M-F 5:30am-8pm, Sa-Su 8am-8pm). Near the train station, **Café Moritz,** Bahnhofstr. 7, raises your daily caloric intake with Thüringer specialities (around DM8), served outside if the weather permits. (☎74 65 75. Open May-Oct. M-F 8am-9pm, Sa-Su 10am-9pm; Nov.-Apr. M-F 8am-7pm, Sa-Su 10am-7pm.) Just down the hill from Bach's house, **Café Brühem,** Treboniusstr. 8, serves soups (DM3-5), milkshakes (DM4.50) and a wide variety of cakes and coffees in a cheerful, casual locale (open M-F 9am-6pm, Sa 1pm-6pm).

◉ SIGHTS

▓ WARTBURG FORTRESS

(The foot of the hill can be reached by a stroll down Wartburgerallee from the train station. Tour buses run hourly 9am-5pm between the train station and the castle. One-way DM1.50, round-trip DM2.50. There are a number of well-cleared footpaths up the incline—hiking downhill is a blast. If you weigh 60kg (132 lbs.) or less, you can opt for a donkey ride for the last stretch; DM5. ☎770 73. Open Mar.-Oct. daily 8:30am-5pm; Nov.-Feb. daily 9am-3:30pm. DM11, students and children DM6, seniors and the disabled DM8. Museum and Luther study separately DM6 and DM5 respectively. Entrance to the castle only with a tour; tours (in German) leave every 10 minutes from "Eingang I.")

THURINGIA

Karl-Marx-Str.

Mühlgraben

Goethestr.

Thüringer
Landestheater

Jakobstr.

Uferstr.

Clemensstr.

TO AUTOMOBILBAU-
MUSEUM

Clemdastr.

Sommerstr.

JAKOBSPLAN

Sophienstr.

Alexanderstr.

Querstr.

Schillerstr.

Schillerstr.

Hauptbahnhof

Bahnhofstraße

TO

Georgenstr.

Wydenbrugkstr.

Nikolaikirche
KARLS-
PLATZ   Nikolaitor

Schloß

MARKT   Rathaus

Predigerkirche

Karlstr.

PREDIGER-
PLATZ

Pfarrberg

Markstr.

Goldschmiedenstr.

Georgenkirche

Dr.-Moritz-

STADTPARK

Mitzenheim-Str.

Lutherhaus   LUTHER-
PLATZ

Schmelzerstr.

Stadtbibliothek
JOHANNIS-
PLATZ

Domstr.

Lutherstr.

Frauenplan

Grimmelg.

J.-S.-Bach Str.

Bachhaus

Am Ofenstein

N

Barfüßerstr.

Wartburgallee

Hedwigstr.

Augustastr.

Marienstr.

Wandelhalle

Haintal

Reuter-Wagner-
Museum

Reuterweg

Gedenkstätte
"Goldener Löwe"

Kurstr.

Kartaus-
garten

200 yards

200 meters

Helltal   Hainteich

Wartburgallee

Mariental

TO WARTBURG
FORTRESS   TO

Prinzenteich

Waisenstr.

Ernst-Böckel-Str.

Prellerstr.

Eisenach

▲ ACCOMMODATIONS
Jugendherberge Artur Becke, 2
Pension Storehenturm, 1

THURINGIA

The castle high above Eisenach's half-timbered houses lords over the northwestern slope of the rolling Thüringer Wald. Wartburg has attracted visitors of all kinds for centuries. In 1521, it sheltered Martin Luther after his excommunication. To thwart the search, Luther grew a beard and spent his 10-month stay disguised as a noble named Junker Jörg. The Romanesque Wartburg is notable for the peaceful character of its history. Aside from sheltering Luther, it was a haven for the 12th-century *Minnesänger*, the originators of German choral music. The mural that inspired Wagner's *Tannhäuser*, a depiction of a 12th-century battle of musicians, adorns a wall in one of the castle's restored chambers. The castle's **Festsaal** preserves the memory of the 1817 meeting of 500 representatives of university fraternities who formed Germany's first bourgeois opposition (ruthlessly crushed two years later); a copy of the flag they toasted still hangs in the room. The first floor of the tower is a dungeon dating from darker days.

Much of the castle's interior is not authentically medieval; 19th-century additions from stricken Romantics are responsible for the impressive decorative interiors of many of the rooms; still, the Wartburg is worth a visit, and joining the parade of satisfied tourists who are led through its rooms can only bring happiness to your day. From the walls of Wartburg's courtyard or from the top of the climbable south tower, the view is spectacular—if you look opposite Eisenach, you see the Thüringer Wald and all the way across the former East-West border to Hessen. Get there early enough and you may not have to wait; any later than 10:30am and you may be sitting around for more than an hour. To kill the time, hike around the rich woods and grounds for free.

BACHHAUS. Where Johann Sebastian stormed into the world in 1685, the Bachhaus has recreated the family's living quarters. Downstairs are period instruments such as a clavichord, a spinet, and a beautifully preserved "house organ" from 1750, about the size of a telephone booth, with a little stool for the player. Roughly every 40 minutes, one of the museum's guides gives a presentation on Bach's life in German and English, supplementing the historical facts with humorous tidbits and beautiful musical interludes. *(Frauenplan 21. Turn off Wartburgallee down Grimmelgasse to reach the house. ☎ 793 40; fax 79 34 24. Open Apr.-Sept. M noon-5:45pm, Tu-Su 9am-5:45pm.; Oct.-Mar. M 1-4:45pm, Tu-Su 9am-4:45pm. DM5, students DM4.)*

OTHER SIGHTS. The **Reuter-Wagner-Museum,** below the fortress, is housed in the villa of writer Fritz Reuter, and commemorates his life as well as that of his friend, composer Richard Wagner. *(Reuterweg 2. Below the fortress. ☎ 74 32 93. Open Tu-Su 10am-5pm. DM4, students and seniors DM2.)* Town life centers on the pastel **Markt,** bounded by the tilting dollhouse of a **Rathaus** and the 800-year-old **Georgenkirche,** where Luther preached a few times and Bach was baptized. *(Open M-Sa 10am-12:30pm and 2-5pm, Su after services.)* Just up the street from the Markt sits the latticed **Lutherhaus,** young Martin's home in his school days. *(Lutherpl. 8. ☎ 298 30. Open Apr.-Oct. daily 9am-5pm; Nov.-Mar. daily 10am-5pm. DM5, seniors and the disabled DM4, students DM2.)* The one-room **Automobilbaumuseum,** where shiny vehicles are on glorious display, proudly celebrates 100 years of automobile-manufacture in Eisenach. *(Rennbahn 6-8. Leave from the station's "Ausgang Nord," and veer left; after an eight-minute walk, the museum is on the right. ☎ 772 12. Open Tu-Su 10am-5pm. DM4, students, seniors, and children DM2.)*

BAYERN
(BAVARIA)

Bayern is the Germany of Teutonic myth, Wagnerian opera, and fairy tales. From the tiny villages of the Wald, to the Baroque cities along the Danube, to Mad King Ludwig's castles perched high in the Alps, the region beckons to more tourists than any other part of the country. Indeed, when most foreigners conjure up images of Germany, they are imagining Bavaria, land of beer gardens, smoked sausage, and *Lederhosen*. This is in part a relic of Germany's 45-year division, which shifted Western perceptions southward and prevented iconoclastic Berlin from acting as a counterweight to more strait-laced Bavarian cities. Though mostly rural, Catholic, and conservative, the largest of Germany's federal states nurtures flourishing commerce and industry, including such renowned companies as the *Bayerische Motorwerke* (BMW).

However, these popular images of Bavaria present a somewhat inaccurate image of the whole of Germany, as the region's independent residents have always been Bavarians first and Germans second. It took wars with France and Austria to pull Bayern into Bismarck's orbit, and it remained its own kingdom until 1918. Local authorities still insist upon using the *Land*'s proper name: *Freistaat Bayern* (Free State of Bavaria). In a plebiscite, Bayern was the only state to refuse to ratify the Federal Republic's Basic Law, and the ruling CDU still abides by a long-standing agreement not to compete in Bavarian elections (instead, a related party, the Christian Social Union, represents the center-right). The insistent preservation of its unique tradition and history, amply demonstrated by the impenetrable dialect spoken in the region, animates stereotypes about German culture.

 REMINDER. HI-affiliated hostels in Bayern generally do not admit guests over age 26, although families and groups of adults with young children are usually allowed even if adults are over 26.

HIGHLIGHTS OF BAYERN

Brimming with beers, swathed with lush green parks, loaded with museums, and blessed with Germany's best-oiled tourist industry, **Munich** deserves its great reputation among travelers. Make reservations early for **Oktoberfest** (Sept. 22-Oct. 7, 2001), or try out one of the city's dozens of outdoor **beer gardens** (p. 259).

Like all great visionaries, King Ludwig II was a nut. His **Königsschlösser**, or royal castles (see p. 273), enormously extravagant retreats in the Bavarian Alps, now perch in the mountains near Füssen.

The South of Bayern borders the spectacular Alps. For high-altitude fun, head to either the **Bavarian Alps** (see p. 269) or the **Allgäu Alps** (see p. 269).

Haunted by its many associations with Germany's Nazi past, **Nürnberg** (see p. 320) is captivating and solemn, with many Nazi-era ruins still visible.

The **Romantische Str.** (see p. 311) snakes through western Bavaria, linking **Würzburg** to **Füssen** by way of well-touristed towns.

MÜNCHEN (MUNICH)   ☎089

The capital and cultural center of Bayern, Munich is a sprawling, relatively liberal metropolis in the midst of conservative southern Germany. The cities of Munich and Berlin are emblematic of the poles of German character. Munich, exuding a traditional air of merriment, stands in sharp contrast to Berlin, which thrives on its sense of fragmented avant-garde and is characterized by dizzying reconstruction.

Munich unabashedly displays West German postwar economic glory. World-class museums, handsome parks and architecture, a rambunctious arts scene, and an urbane population collide to create a city of astonishing vitality. Even in the depths of winter, citizens meet in outdoor beer gardens to discuss art, politics, and (of course) *Fußball*. An ebullient mixture of sophistication and earthy Bavarian *Gemütlichkeit* keeps the city awake at (almost) all hours. *Müncheners* party zealously during *Fasching* (Jan. 7-Feb. 27, 2001), Germany's equivalent of Mardi Gras, and during the legendary Oktoberfest (Sept. 22-Oct.7, 2001).

HISTORY

Although Munich revels in its cushy Southern German location, the city was actually founded by a Northerner, Heinrich the Lion, in 1158. Named after the city's early monk residents *(Mönche)*, Munich came under the rule of one of Europe's most stalwart dynasties, the **Wittelsbachs,** who controlled the city in strict Catholic piety from 1180 until the 18th century, when Napoleon's romp through Europe turned the city into a Napoleonic kingdom and ushered in the Bavarian Golden Age. At this time, "enlightened" absolutists rationalized state administration, promoted commerce, and patronized the arts. Ludwig I and Maximilian I contributed immensely to the expansion and evolution of the city, while its most famous king, **Ludwig II,** began his flight toward head-in-the-clouds extravagance. In 1871, after Bismarck's successful wars solidified Prussian dominance of Germany, Ludwig presided over the absorption of Bayern into the greater *Reich;* the process was facilitated by Bismarck's generous funding of Ludwig's loony architectural projects. Munich rose to become a cultural powerhouse, rivalling hated Berlin (a city that *Müncheners* regarded as a glorified garrison town), with artists flocking to its burgeoning scene.

The Golden Age came to an abrupt end with Germany's defeat in WWI. Weimar Munich was an incubator for reactionary and anti-Semitic movements: **Adolf Hitler** found the city such fertile recruiting ground for the new National Socialist German Workers Party (Nazis) that he later called it "the capital of our movement." In 1923, Hitler attempted to overthrow the municipal government and lead a march on Berlin to topple the Weimar Republic. His **Beer Hall Putsch** was quickly squashed and its leaders arrested, but evidence of his eventual success still haunts the city: Neville Chamberlain's attempted appeasement of Hitler over the Sudetenland is remembered as the **Munich Agreement,** and the Nazis' first concentration camp was constructed just outside the city at **Dachau.**

Despite Munich's fortuitous location deep inside the German air defenses, Allied bombings were devastating. By 1944, less than 3% of the city center remained intact; since then, much of it has been rebuilt in the original style. When Munich hosted the **1972 Olympics,** the city went to great lengths to revolutionize itself, pedestrianizing large portions of the city center, extending the subway system, and bringing the city's resources to their current, modernized state.

Though Munich's history appears to speak otherwise, the city was and is now an indulgent, celebratory place. Today's riotous upheavals are of a much less threatening variety. Consider a recent protest, 20,000 citizens strong, over—what else?—beer. The issue at hand in this "Bavarian beer garden revolution" was the **Waldwirtschaft beer garden,** which can accommodate 2,000 customers but has only 100 parking places. Numerous neighborhood complaints had finally led to a draconian court decision mandating a 9:30pm closing time for the beer garden. After *Müncheners* marched on Marienpl. in good revolutionary spirit a few years back, the court reversed its decision and they won back a half hour—enough time to chug at least one more *Maß*.

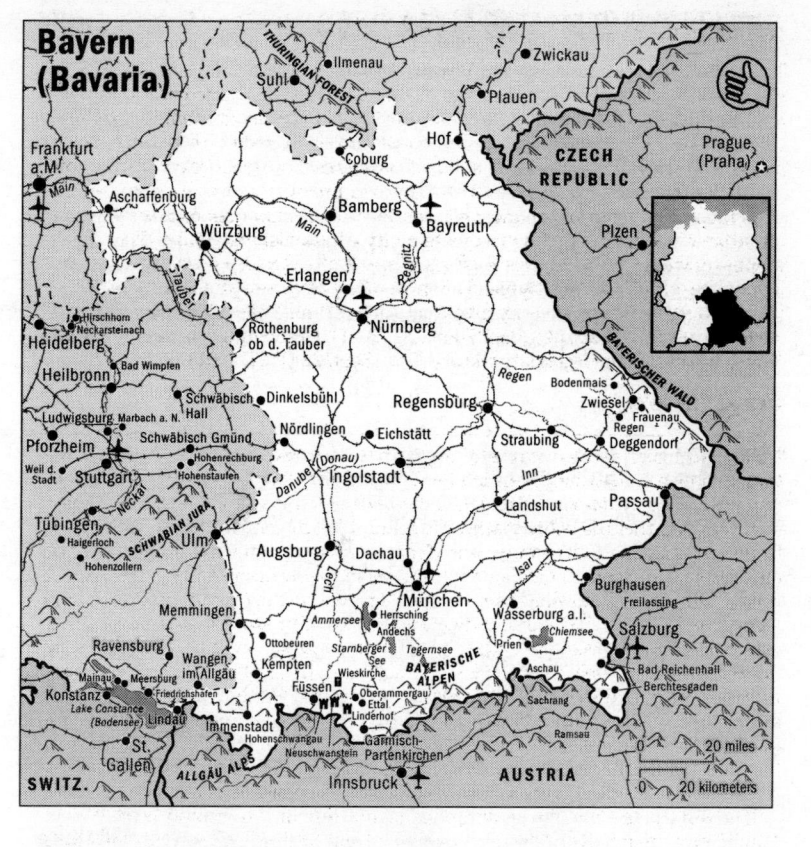

Bayern (Bavaria)

✈ GETTING THERE AND AWAY

Flights: Flughafen München (☎97 52 13 13). S-Bahn #8 runs to the airport and from the Hauptbahnhof every 20min. DM15.20 or 8 stripes on the *Streifenkarte*. Alternatively, a **Lufthansa shuttle bus** runs between the Hauptbahnhof and the airport (45min.), with a pickup at the "Nordfriedhof" U-Bahn stop in Schwabing. Buses leave from Arnulfstr., on the northern side of the train station every 20min. 6:50am-7:50pm. Buses return from Terminal A *(Zentralbereich)* and Terminal D every 20min. 7:55am-8:55pm. One-way DM16, round-trip DM26.

Trains: Munich's **Hauptbahnhof** (☎22 33 12 56) is the transportation hub of Southern Germany, with connections to **Füssen** (3hr., 1 per hr., DM36, youth DM29); **Frankfurt** (3½hr., 3 per hr., DM147, youth DM118); **Köln** (6hr., 2 per hr., DM173, youth DM138); **Hamburg** (6hr., 2 per hr., DM268, youth DM214); **Berlin** (7½hr., 2 per hr., DM277, youth DM222); **Innsbruck** (2hr., 1 per hr., DM48, youth DM37); **Salzburg** (1¾hr., 1 per hr., DM41, youth DM30); **Zürich** (5hr., every 2 hr., DM110, youth DM85); **Vienna** (5hr., 1 per hr., DM106, youth DM82); **Prague** (8½hr., 6 per day, DM113, youth DM85); **Amsterdam** (9hr., 1 per hr., DM248, youth DM198); and **Paris** (10hr., DM194, youth DM156). For schedules, fare information, and reservations, call ☎(0180) 599 66 33. Open 6am-10:30pm. **EurAide** (see **Tourist Offices,** p. 241), in the station, provides free train information in English. **Reisezentrum** information counters open daily 6am-11:30pm. Reservation desk open 7am-9pm.

Mitfahrzentrale: McShare Treffpunkt Zentrale, Klenzestr. 57b or Lämmerstr. 4 (☎ 194 40). Walk out the "Arnulfstr." exit of the train station and cross the street, then walk left of the Hypo-Vereins bank down Pfefferstr., and take a left down Hirtenstr. and a right on Lämmerstr. Matches McDrivers and McRiders. **Heidelberg** DM34, **Frankfurt** DM41, **Berlin** DM54. Open daily 8am-8pm. At the same location, **Frauer⌐mitfahrzentrale,** Klenzestr. 57b, arranges ride shares for women only. Open M-F 8am-8pm. **Känguruh,** Amalienstr. 87 (☎ 194 44), is in the Amalienpassage near the university. Open M-F 9am-6:30pm, Sa 9am-3pm, Su 10am-7pm.

Hitchhiking: *Let's Go* does not recommend hitchhiking as a safe mode of transportation. Those looking to share rides scan the bulletin boards in the **Mensa,** Leopoldstr. 13. Otherwise, hitchers try *Autobahn* on-ramps; *those who stand behind the blue sign with the white auto may be fined.* Hitchers going to Salzburg take U-Bahn #1 or 2 to "Karl-Preis-pl." For Stuttgart, take streetcar #17 to "Amalienburgstr." or S-Bahn #2 to "Obermenzing," then bus #73 or 75 to "Blutenburg." To Nürnberg and Berlin, take U-Bahn #6 to "Studentenstadt" and walk 500m to the Frankfurter Ring. To the Bodensee and Switzerland, take U-Bahn #4 or 5 to "Heimeranpl.," then bus #33 to "Siegenburger Str."

▐ GETTING AROUND

Public Transportation: MVV, Munich's public transport system, runs Su-Th 5am-12:30am, F-Sa 5am-2am. Eurail, InterRail, and German railpasses are valid on the S-Bahn but *not* on the U-Bahn, streetcars, or buses. Buy tickets at the blue *MVV-Fahrausweise* vending machines and **validate them** in the boxes marked with an "E" *before entering the platform.* Payment is made on an honor system, but disguised agents check for tickets sporadically; if you jump the fare or don't validate correctly, you risk a DM60 fine. **Transit maps** and **maps of wheelchair accessible stations** can be picked up in the tourist office or EurAide and at MVV counters near the subway entrance in the train station.

Prices: Single ride tickets DM3.80 (valid for 3hr.). **Kurzstrecke** (short trip) tickets cost DM1.90 and can be used for 2 stops on the U-Bahn or S-Bahn, or for 4 stops on a streetcar or bus. A *Streifenkarte* (11-strip ticket) costs DM16 and can be used by more than 1 person. Cancel 2 strips per person for a normal ride, or 1 strip per person for a *Kurzstrecke.* Beyond the city center, cancel 2 strips per additional zone. A **Single-Tageskarte** (single-day ticket) is valid for one day of unlimited travel until 6am the next day (DM9). A **Partner-Tageskarte** (DM14) can be used by 2 adults, 4 children under 18, and a dog. The **3-Day Pass** (DM22) is also a great deal. The best public transportation deal is the **München Welcome Card,** available at the tourist office and in many hotels, which is valid for 3 days of public transportation for DM29; a group ticket for up to 5 people runs DM42. The card includes a 50% discount on many of Munich's museums and on Radius bike rental (see below). Passes can be purchased at the MVV office behind tracks 31 and 32 in the Hauptbahnhof. Children under 15 pay reduced fares, and children under 4 ride free. For bikes you need a special ticket.

Taxis: Taxi-Zentrale (☎ 216 11 or 194 10) has large stands in front of the train station and every 5-10 blocks in the central city. Women can request a female driver.

Car Rental: Swing, Schellingstr. 139 (☎ 523 20 05), rents from DM45 per day. **Avis** (☎ 550 12 12), **Europcar/National** (☎ 550 13 41), **Hertz** (☎ 550 22 56), and **Sixt Budget** (☎ 550 24 47) have offices upstairs in the Hauptbahnhof. Prices start at DM130. **Flach's Leihwagen,** Landsberger Str. 289 (☎ 56 60 56), rents cars for DM60-112 per day. Open M-F 8am-8pm, Sa 9am-noon.

Bike Rental: Radius Bikes (☎ 59 61 13), at the far end of the Hauptbahnhof, behind the lockers opposite tracks 30-36. DM5 per hr., DM25 per day, DM75 per week. Mountain bikes 20% more. Deposit DM100, passport, or credit card. Students and Eurailpass holders receive a 10% discount. Open May to mid-Oct. daily 10am-6pm. **Aktiv-Rad,** Hans-Sachs-Str. 7 (☎ 26 65 06), rents for DM18 per day. U-Bahn #1 or 2 to "Fraunhofer Str." Open M-F 9am-1pm and 2-6:30pm, Sa 9am-1pm.

⚜ ORIENTATION

Munich rests on the banks of the Isar in the middle of south-central Bayern. Mad King Ludwig's castles and the Bavarian Alps are only a short trip through Munich's industrial outskirts.

A map of Munich's center looks like a skewed circle quartered by one horizontal and one vertical line. The circle is the main traffic **Ring**, which changes its name again and again as it bounds the city center. Within it lie the lion's share of Munich's sights. The east-west and north-south thoroughfares cross at Munich's epicenter, the **Marienplatz** (home to the **Neues Rathaus**), and meet the traffic rings at **Karlsplatz** (called **Stachus** by locals) in the west, **Isartorplatz** in the east, **Odeonsplatz** in the north, and **Sendlinger Tor** in the south. The **Hauptbahnhof** is just beyond Karlspl. outside the Ring in the west. In the east beyond the Isartor, the **Isar** flows by the city center, south to north. To get to Marienpl. from the station, go straight on Bayerstr. to the yellow buildings of Karlsplatz. Continue straight through Karlstor to Neuhauser Str., which becomes Kaufingerstr. before it reaches Marienpl. (15-20min.). Or take S-Bahn #1-8 (two stops from the Hauptbahnhof, direction "Ostbahnhof") to "Marienplatz."

To the north, at Odeonspl., the giant **Residenz** palace sprawls over a hefty piece of downtown land; **LudwigStr.** stretches north from there toward the university district. **LeopoldStr.,** the continuation of Ludwigstr., reaches farther toward **Schwabing.** This district, also known as "Schwabylon," is student country; it lies to the west of the maddeningly mobbed Leopoldstr. **Türkenstr., Amalienstr., Schellingstr.,** and **Barerstr.** meander through the funk. To the east of Schwabing sprawls the **Englischer Garten;** to the west is the **Olympiazentrum,** the complex constructed for the 1972 games, surrounded by the verdant **Olympiapark.** Farther west sits the posh **Nymphenburg,** built around the eponymous **Schloß Nymphenburg.** Southwest of Marienpl., **Sendlinger Str.** leads past shops to the Sendlinger Tor. From there, Lindwurmstr. proceeds to Goethepl., from which Mozartstr. leads to **Theresienwiese,** the site of Oktoberfest.

Several publications help visitors navigate Munich. The most comprehensive one (in English) is the monthly *Munich Found* (DM4); available at newsstands and bookshops; it provides a list of services, events, and museums. The tourist office distributes the encyclopedic *Monatsprogramm* (DM3), with a list of city events in chronological order. The bi-weekly *in München* (free) gives a more intensive insider's look at the Munich *Szene*, providing detailed movie, theater, and concert schedules. *Prinz* (DM5) is the hip and hefty monthly with endless tips on shopping, art, music, film, concerts, and food. EurAide's free publication, *Inside Track*, provides updated information in English on train connections as well as basic tips on getting started in Munich; it's available at EurAide (see below) or at the *Reisezentrum* in the main hall of the station.

🗗 PRACTICAL INFORMATION

TOURIST OFFICES

▓ **EurAide in English** (☎59 38 89; fax 550 39 65; email euraide@compuserve.com; www.euraide.de), along track 11 (room 3) of the Hauptbahnhof, near the Bayerstr. exit. Delve into the intricacies of Munich with one sound byte from EurAide's Alan R. Wissenberg, savior of frazzled English-speaking tourists. A nearly omniscient American, he points you in the right direction and **books rooms** for a DM7 fee. Also sells train tickets and offers the "Two Castle Tour," an outing to the Königsschlösser (see **Tours,** below). Open June-Oktoberfest daily 7:45am-noon and 1-6pm; Oct.-Apr. M-F 8am-noon and 1-4pm, Sa 8am-noon; May daily 7:45am-noon and 1-4:30pm.

Main Office: Fremdenverkehrsamt (☎23 33 02 57 or 233 03 00; fax 23 33 02 33; email Munich_Tourist_Office@compuserve.com; www.munich-tourist.de), located on the front (east) side of the train station, next to ABR Travel on Bahnhofpl. Although friendly and helpful, this office is usually inundated with tourists, and the staff rarely answers the phone. They do speak English, but for more in-depth questions, EurAide (see above) will probably better suit your needs. The tourist office **books rooms** for free with a 10-15% deposit and sells excellent English city maps (DM0.50). You can also purchase the **München Welcome Card** here, which offers free public transportation and reduced prices for 35 different sights and services (single-day ticket DM12, 3-day ticket DM29). The English/German young people's guide München Infopool (DM1) lists beer gardens and gives tips on cycling, sightseeing, and navigating the confusing public transportation system. Call for **recorded information** in English on museums and galleries (☎23 91 62) or sights and castles (☎23 91 72). Open M-Sa 9am-10pm, Su 10am-6pm. A large **branch office** roosts just inside the entrance to the Neues Rathaus on Marienpl. (☎23 33 02 72 or 23 33 02 73), offering free brochures and city maps (DM0.50). A counter on the opposite side of the room sells tickets for concerts and performances. Open M-F 10am-8pm, Sa 10am-4pm.

TOURS

April Munich Walks (☎(0177) 227 59 01;, fax 030 301 9194; email info@munich-walks.com; www.munichwalks.com). Native English speakers give guided historical walking tours of the city with 2 different slants: the comprehensive introductory tour of the Altstadt hits all the major sights (May-Nov. daily 10:15am, also M-Sa May-Aug. 2:15pm; Apr. daily 10:30am), while a more specialized tour visits haunting Nazi sites (May-Aug. M, Th, Sa 10:15am; Apr. Sa 2:30pm; Sept.-Nov. M, Sa 2:15pm). The 2½hr. tours cost DM18, under 26 DM14, under 14 free with an adult. Both tours leave from outside the EurAide office in the train station; simply show up there to participate.

Mike's Bike Tours (☎255 439 88; fax 651 4275; email Mike@bavaria.com; www.mikesbiketours.com). Ponder the "Eunuch of Munich," "hunt" lions, have lunch at a Biergarten in the Englischer Garten, and see the sights of the city by bike under the direction of entertaining and informative English-speaking tour guides. Tours leave from the Altes Rathaus by the Spielzeugmuseum. The 4hr., 6.5km city tour includes a lunch break and runs mid-Apr. to mid-Sept. daily 11:30am and 3pm; more frequently June thru mid-Aug. and at 12:30pm Mar. thru mid-Apr. and mid-Sept thru Oct. DM36. The 6hr., 16km. tour includes 2 beer garden breaks. (June-mid Aug. daily 12:30pm. DM46.) All prices include bike rental and rain gear.

The Bike and Walk Company (☎589 589 33; www.bikeandwalkcompany.de). This team of real Müncheners offers English biking or walking tours from a local's perspective, providing information on the history, culture, and nightlife of the city. City bike tours leave Apr. thru mid-Oct. at 11:30am, and also at 3:30pm mid-May thru mid-Sept. (3.5 hr, DM31; under 26 DM27). City walk tours leave Apr. thru mid-Oct. at 10:45am, and also at 4:45pm May-Aug. (2.5 hr. DM15, children under 14 free with parent.) A Third Reich walking tour is offered May thru mid-Oct. M, Th, Sa at 2:30pm. Both tours depart from the Neues Rathaus under the glockenspiel; no reservations necessary.

Spurwechsel Bike Tours (☎692 46 99; www.spurwechsel-muenchen.de). Entertaining German-speaking tour guides lead a 15km cycling spree around the Altstadt, Schwabing, and Englischer Garten, with a pause at the Chinesischer Turm beer garden for a pretzel and Weißbier feast. 2hr. DM24. Tours meet M, W, F, Su, and holidays at 11:15am at the Marienpl. fountain.

Panorama Tours, Arnulfstr. 8 (☎54 90 75 60 for day excursions, ☎55 02 89 95 for city excursions). Offers staid bilingual **bus** tours that leave from the train station's main entrance on Bahnhofspl. 1hr. tour in an open-air double-decker, May-Oct. daily 10, 11, noon, 1, 2, 2:30, 3, and 4pm. DM19, children DM10. A 2.5hr. tour leaves daily at 10am and 2:30pm; the 10am tour goes to the Residenz or the Olympic Park, while the 2:30pm tour visits the Peterskirche, the Olympic Park, or the Nymphenburg Palace. DM33, children DM17. Hotel pick-up available. 10% off day excursions with Eurailpass. Open M-F 7:30am-6pm, Sa 7:30am-noon, Su 7:30-10am.

Castles and other Bavarian sites: For those who want to enter the magical realm of Mad King Ludwig II (see p. 273), three options await: **Panorama Tours** offers a 10½hr. bus excursion (in English) to Schloß Neuschwanstein and Schloß Linderhof leaving Apr.-Oct. daily 8:30am; Nov.-Mar. Tu, Th, and Sa-Su 8:30am. DM78; with Eurailpass, InterRail, or German Railpass DM68; with ISIC DM59; Schloß admission not included. Book in advance. **Bus Bavaria** (www.busbavaria.com), a subsidiary of **Mike's Bike Tours**, offers guided day trips (in English) by bus and bike to Schloß Neuschwanstein, Berchtesgaden, and Dachau (mid-May to mid-Aug., DM80, DM80, and DM59, respectively). **EurAide** leads an English-speaking half-bus, half-train Schloß-schlepp that includes Neuschwanstein, Schloß Linderhof, and the Rococo Wieskirche. Meet June-July Wednesday at 7:30am by track 11 in front of EurAide. DM70; with Eurailpass, InterRail, or flexipass DM55. Admission to castles not included, but EurAide will get you a DM1 discount. Or drop by EurAide for train and public bus schedules to see the castles on your own (see **Hypertravel to the Castles,** p. 275).

CONSULATES

Canada: Tal 29 (☎219 95 70). S-Bahn to "Isartor." Open M-Th 9am-noon and 2-5pm, F 9am-noon and 2-3:30pm.

Ireland: Mauerkircherstr. 1a (☎98 57 23). Streetcar #20 or bus #54 or 87. Open M-F 9am-noon.

South Africa: Sendlinger-Tor-Pl. 5 (☎231 16 30). U-Bahn #1, 2, 3 or 6 to "Sendlinger Tor." Open M-F 9am-noon.

UK: Bürkleinstr. 10 (☎21 10 90), 4th floor. U-Bahn #4 or 5 to "Lehel." Open M-F 8:30am-noon and 1-5pm (F to 3:30pm).

US: Königinstr. 5 (☎288 80). Open M-F 8-11am. For a recording on visa information any time of day or night, call (0190) 27 07 89 (DM1.21 per min.); to speak to an official, call (0190) 88 22 11 M-F 7am-8pm (DM3.63 per min.).

LOCAL SERVICES

Budget Travel: Council Travel, Adalbertstr. 32 (☎38 83 89 70), near the university, sells ISICs for DM18. Open M-F 10am-1pm and 2-6:30pm, Sa 10am-3pm. **DER Reise-büro** (☎55 14 02 00; www.der.de) is in the main hall of the train station and sells train tickets and railpasses. Open M-F 9:30am-6pm and Sa 10am-1pm.

Currency Exchange: ReiseBank (☎551 08 37). 2 locations: one in front of the main entrance to the train station on Bahnhofpl. (open daily 6am-11pm); and the other around the corner from EurAide at track 11 (open M-Sa 7:30am-7:15pm, Su 9:30am-12:30pm and 1-4:45pm). Those with *Inside Track,* available at EurAide, get a 10-15% discount on commission if exchanging US$50 or more or cashing in US traveler's checks. Western Union services also available.

American Express: Promenadepl. 6 (☎29 09 00; 24hr. hotline (0130) 85 31 00), in the Hotel Bayerischer Hof. Holds mail and cashes traveler's checks. Open M-F 9am-5:30pm, Sa 9:30am-12:30pm. **Branch** office at Kaufingerstr. 24 (☎22 80 13 87), by the Frauenkirche. Open M-F 9am-6pm, Sa 10am-2pm.

Luggage Storage: At the **train station** (☎13 08 50 47) and **airport** (☎97 52 13 75). Staffed storage room *(Gepäckaufbewahrung)* in the main hall of the train station. Open M-F 6:30am-11pm, Sa-Su 7:30am-10pm. DM4 per piece per calendar day. Lockers in main hall and opposite tracks # 16, 24, and 28-36. DM2-4 per 24hr.

BAVARIA

Lost and Found: Fundbüro, Ötztaler Str. 17 (☎23 34 59 00). U-Bahn #6 to "Partnachpl." Open M-Th 8am-noon, Tu also 2-6:30pm, Fr. 7am-noon. For items lost on the S-Bahn, contact **Fundstelle im Ostbahnhof** (☎12 88 44 09). Open M-F 8am-5:30pm, Sa 8am-11:45pm or **Deutsche Bahn Fundbüro,** Landsberger Str. 472 (☎13 08 58 59). S-Bahn to "Pasing." Open M and W-F 8am-noon, Tu 8am-noon and 12:30-3pm.

Mitwohnzentrale: An der Uni (☎286 60 66; email mwz@mwz-munich.de; www.mwz-munich.de), at 6 Adalbertstr. (U-Bahn #6 to "Universität") has apartments available for 1 month or more. Open M-F 10am-6pm. **City Mitwohnzentrale,** Klenzerstr. 57b (☎194 40), lists apartments and houses throughout Germany. **Studentenwerk** offers extremely inexpensive housing for students (email stuwohn@studentenwerk.mhn.de; www.studentenwerk.mhn.de).

Bookstores: Anglia English Bookshop, Schellingstr. 3 (☎28 36 42), offers reams of English-language books in a gloriously chaotic atmosphere. U-Bahn #3 or 6 to "Universität." Open M-F 9am-6:30pm, Sa 10am-2pm. **Words' Worth,** Schellingstr. 21a (☎280 91 41), carries obscure novels in English as well as a full range of classic literature. Open M-Tu and F 9am-6:30pm, W-Th 9am-8pm, Sa 10am-2pm.

Libraries: Many of Munich's city libraries have a hefty English section. **Bayerische Staatsbibliothek,** Ludwigstr. 16 (☎28 63 80), the largest university library in all German-speaking countries, has 6.5 million books and a seemingly endless supply of magazines and newspapers. Open M-F 9am-7:30pm, Sa 9am-4:30pm. **Universitätsbibliothek der Universität,** Geschwister-Scholl-pl. 1 (☎21 80 24 28). Open Dec.-July M-Th 9am-8pm, F 9am-4pm; Aug.-Nov. M-Th 9am-7pm, F 9am-noon. **The Bookshelf,** Blumenstr. 36 (☎61 62 27), is an English lending library. U-Bahn #1 or 2 to "Sendlinger Tor." Open M, W, F 3-5pm, Sa 11am-1pm.

Cultural Centers: Amerika Haus, Karolinenpl. 3 (☎552 53 70; www.amerikahaus.de), is the cultural extension of the consulate. U-Bahn #2 to "Königspl." Cultural resources and advice for Americans wishing to teach, a library for reading and research, and language courses for Germans wishing to learn English. Internet DM5, DM2.50 for students. Open M-F 9am-noon, 2pm-5pm. The **British Council,** Rumfordstr. 7, offers the same resources, a video lending library, and free internet.

Gay and Lesbian Resources: Gay services information (☎260 30 56). **Lesbian information** and the **LeTra Lesbentraum** (Angertorstr. 3, ☎725 42 72). Telephone times M, W 2:30-5pm; Tu 10:30am-1pm; Th 7-9pm. See also **Gay and Lesbian Munich,** p. 264.

Women's Resources: Kofra Kommunikationszentrum für Frauen, Baaderstr. 30 (☎201 04 50). Job advice, magazines, lesbian politics, and books. Open M-F 4-10pm. **Frauentreffpunkt Neuperlach,** Oskar-Maria-Graf-Ring 20-22 (☎670 64 63; fax 67 92 09 71). An environmentally-conscious women's cafe and shop. Open Tu and Th-F 10am-1pm, W 10am-1pm and 3-6pm. **Lillemor's Frauenbuchladen,** Arcisstr. 57 (☎272 12 05), is a bookstore and center for women's events. U-Bahn #2 to "Max-Joseph-pl." Open M-F 10am-6:30pm, Sa 10am-2pm. **Fraueninfothek,** Johannispl. 12 (☎48 48 90). Open M 10am-1pm, Tu 10am-1pm and 2-5pm, Th 2-5pm.

Disabled Resources: Info Center für Behinderte, Schellingstr. 31 (☎21 17 0; fax 21 17 258; email info@vdk.de; www.vdk.bayern.com), has a list of Munich's resources for disabled persons. Open M-Th 9am-noon and 12:30-6pm, F 9am-5pm, Sa 9am-noon.

Ticket Agencies: To order almost all **tickets by phone** call **München Ticket** (☎54 81 81 81; fax. 54 81 81 54; www.muenchenticket.de). Advance tickets are available at the **München ticket** offices in the **Kaufhof** department store (☎260 32 49; fax 260 33 92) on **Marienpl.,** 3rd floor, or at **Karlspl.,** ground floor (☎512 53 36; fax 55 85 65). Marienpl. location open M-F 10am-8pm, Karlspl. M-F 11am-8pm. Both open Sa 9am-4pm. **Hertie** department stores at the Hauptbahnhof and at Marienpl. offer the same services. 9am-6:30pm, Sa 9am-2pm.

Laundromat: City SB-Waschcenter, Paul-Heyse-Str. 21, near the train station. Right on Bayerstr., then left on Paul-Heyse-Str. for 1½ blocks. Wash DM6, soap included. Dry DM1 per 10min. Open daily 7am-11pm. **Münz Waschsalon,** Amalienstr. 61, near the university. Wash DM6.20, soap DM1, dry DM1 per 10min. Open M-F 8am-6:30pm, Sa

8am-1pm. **Waschcenter,** Landshüter Allee 77. U-Bahn #1 to "Rotkreuzpl." Wash DM6. Dry DM1 per 15min. Open 24hr. Bring change for laundromats.

Swimming Pools: Pool season is May to mid-Sept. Choose from 16 local dives. **Müllerisches Volksbad,** Rosenheimer Str. 1 (☎23 61 34 29), has Art Nouveau indoor pools and steam baths for DM10. S-Bahn to "Isartor." Open M 10am-5pm, Tu and Th 8am-7:30pm, W 6:45am-7:30pm, F 8am-8:45pm, Sa 8am-5:30pm, Su 9am-6pm. The outdoor, heated **Dantebad,** Dantestr. 6 (☎15 28 74), in Neuhausen, is excellent and much less crowded—hardly hellish. Streetcar #20 or 21 to "Baldurstr." Open daily 8am-7:30pm. DM5. **Westbad,** Weinburger Str. 17 (☎88 54 41), offers indoor and outdoor pools, a sauna, tanning booths, water slides, and a large green lawn (DM15). From Karlspl., streetcar #19 to "Am Knie/Westbad." **Nordbad,** Schleißheimer Str. 142 (☎23 61 79 41), has similar offerings, including a whirlpool, for DM5. U-Bahn #2 to "Hohen-zollernpl." Open 7:30am-11pm daily.

EMERGENCY AND COMMUNICATIONS

Emergency: Police, ☎110. **Ambulance** and **Fire,** ☎112. **Emergency medical service,** ☎59 44 75.

Rape Crisis Line: Frauennotruf München, Güllstr. 3 (☎76 37 37).

AIDS Hotline: ☎520 73 87 or 520 74 12 (M-Th 8am-3pm, F 8am-noon); or 194 11 (M-Sa 7-10pm).

Pharmacy: Bahnhof-Apotheke, Bahnhofpl. 2 (☎59 41 19 or 59 81 19), on the corner outside the train station. Open M-F 8am-6:30pm, Sa 8am-2pm. 24hr. service rotates among the city's pharmacies—call ☎59 44 75 for recorded information (German only).

Medical Assistance: Klinikum Rechts der Isar, across the river on Ismaninger Str. U-Bahn #4 or 5 to "Max-Weber-pl." STD/AIDS tests are free and anonymous at the **Gesundheitshaus,** Dachauer Str. 90 (☎520 71). Open M-Th 8-11am and 1-2pm, F 8-11am. UK and US consulates carry lists of English-speaking doctors.

Post Office: Bahnhofpl., 80335 Munich (☎59 90 87 16). Walk out of the main train station exit and it's the large yellow building directly across the street. Open M-F 7am-8pm, Sa 8am-4pm, Su 9am-3pm. **Postamt 31** (☎552 26 20), up the escalator in the train station, sells stamps and phone cards and mails letters, but doesn't mail packages or exchange money. Open M-F 7am-8pm, Sa 8am-4pm, Su 9am-3pm.

Internet Access: Times Square Internet cafe, Bayerstr. 10a, located on the south side of the train station. The cafe offers beer (DM4.50-5.50), salads (DM7-16), and other specials (DM10-20). 15min. Internet access DM4.50. See also **Internet-cafe,** p. 253.

■ ACCOMMODATIONS AND CAMPING

Munich's accommodations usually fall into one of three categories: seedy, expensive, or booked solid. During times like Oktoberfest, only the last category exists. In summer, the best strategy is to start calling before noon or to book a few weeks in advance. Most singles (without private bath) run DM55-85, doubles DM80-120. If you're planning an extended stay in Munich, call the *Mitwohnzentrale* (p. 244) or try bargaining with a *Pension* owner. Remember, **Bavarian HI hostels do not accept guests over age 26.** The enforcement of this rule varies. At most of Munich's hostels you can check in all day, but try to start your search well before 5pm.

Don't even think of sleeping in any public area, including the Hauptbahnhof; police patrol frequently all night long. A few options for the roomless do exist: the Augsburg youth hostel (see p. 309) is 30 to 45 minutes away by train (until 11:20pm, 2-3 per hr., DM17), but be mindful of the 1am curfew. Alternatively, throw your luggage into a locker, party until 5am, and return to re-evaluate the hotel lists afterward.

BAVARIA

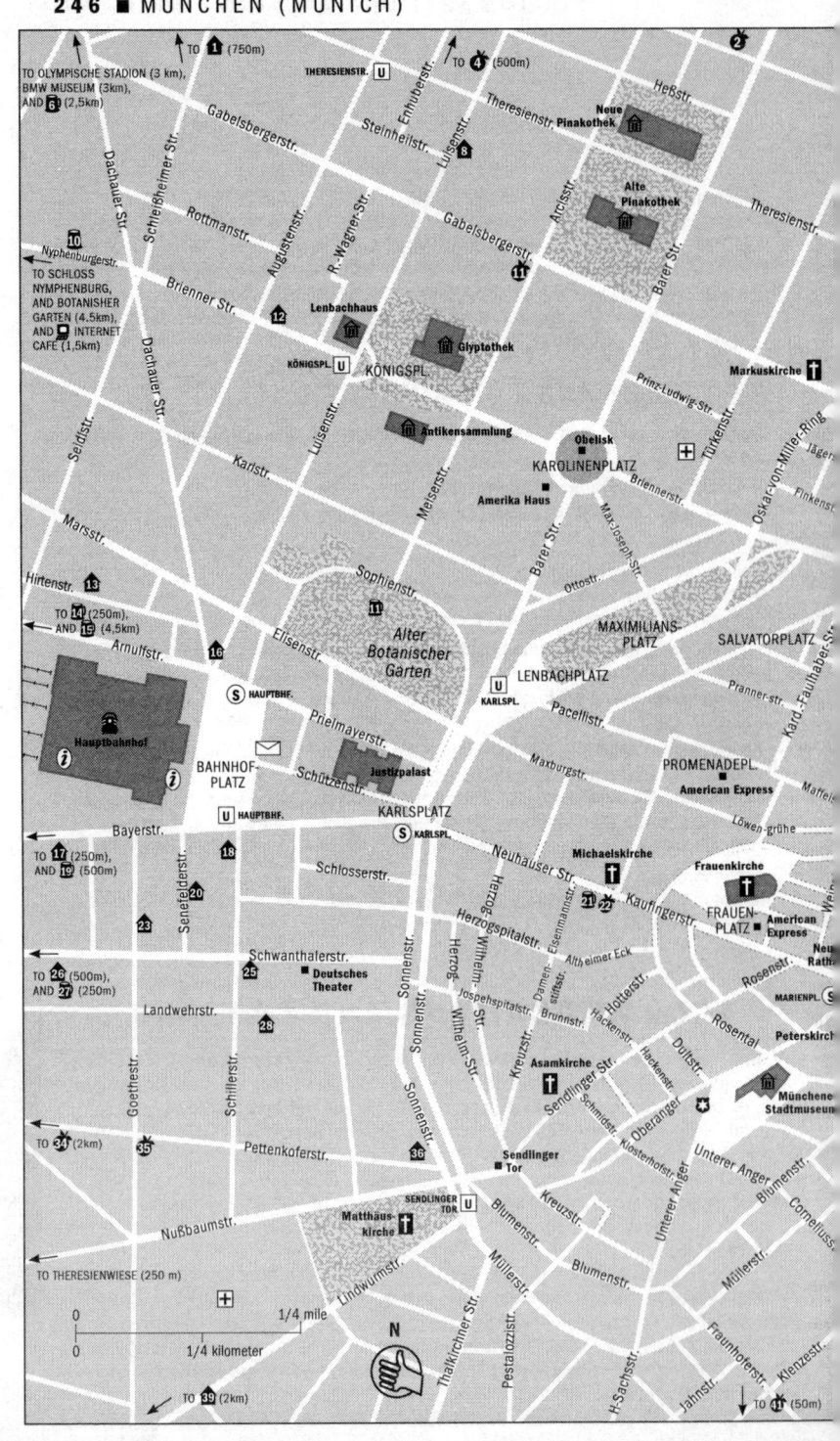

TO 1 (750m)
TO 4 (500m)
THERESIENSTR. U
Theresienstr.
Heßstr.
Neue Pinakothek
TO OLYMPISCHE STADION (3 km), BMW MUSEUM (3km), AND 6 (2,5km)
Gabelsbergerstr.
Steinheilstr.
Erzmu..str.
Lüisenstr.
8
Arcisstr.
Alte Pinakothek
Theresienstr.
Dachauer Str.
Schleißheimer Str.
Rottmanstr.
Augustenstr.
R. Wagner-Str.
Gabelsbergerstr.
Barer Str.
11
Nyphenburgerstr.
10
TO SCHLOSS NYMPHENBURG, AND BOTANISHER GARTEN (4,5km), AND INTERNET CAFE (1,5km)
Brienner Str.
12
Lenbachhaus
Glyptothek
Prinz-Ludwig-Str.
Markuskirche
Dachauer Str.
Luisenstr.
KÖNIGSPL. U KÖNIGSPL.
Antikensammlung
Obelisk
Türkenstr.
Oskar-von-Miller-Ring
Jäger..
Karlstr.
Meiserstr.
KAROLINENPLATZ
Brienner str.
Amerika Haus
Barer Str.
Max-Joseph-Str.
Ottostr.
Finkenst..
Marsstr.
Seidlstr.
Sophienstr.
MAXIMILIANS PLATZ
SALVATORPLATZ
Hirtenstr. 13
TO 14 (250m), AND 15 (4,5km)
Elisenstr.
Arnulfstr.
16
Alter Botanischer Garten
LENBACHPLATZ
U KARLSPL.
Pranner-str.
Kard.-Faulhaber-Str.
S HAUPTBHF.
Pfelmayerstr.
Pacellistr.
Hauptbahnhof
i i
BAHNHOF-PLATZ
Schützenstr.
Justizpalast
Maxburgstr.
PROMENADEPL.
American Express
Maffei..
U HAUPTBHF.
Bayerstr.
KARLSPLATZ
S KARLSPL.
Neuhauser Str.
Löwen-grühe
TO 17 (250m), AND 19 (500m)
18
Schlosserstr.
Herzogspitalstr.
Herzogstr.
Eisenmannstr.
Michaelskirche
21 22
Kaufingerstr.
Frauenkirche
FRAUEN-PLATZ American Express
Neu.. Rath..
Senefelderstr.
20
23
Schwanthalerstr.
25
Deutsches Theater
Herzog-Wilhelm-Str.
Damen-stiftstr.
Altheimer Eck
Josephspitalstr.
Brunnstr.
Hackenstr.
Rosenstr.
MARIENPL. S
Rosental
Peterskirch..
TO 26 (500m), AND 27 (250m)
Landwehrstr.
28
Sonnenstr.
Kreuzstr.
Asamkirche
Sendlinger Str.
Hackenstr.
Dultstr.
Oberanger
Münchener Stadtmuseum
Goethestr.
Schillerstr.
TO 34 (2km) 35
Pettenkoferstr.
36
Schmidstr.
Klosterhofstr..
Unterer Anger
Blumenstr.
Cornelius..
Sendlinger Tor
Nußbaumstr.
Matthäus-Kirche
SENDLINGER TOR U
Blumenstr.
Kreuzstr.
Müllerstr.
Unterer Anger
Müllerstr..
TO THERESIENWIESE (250 m)
Lindwurmstr.
Thalkirchner Str.
Pestalozzistr.
Blumenstr.
Fraunhoferstr.
Klenzest..
0   1/4 mile
0   1/4 kilometer
N
TO 39 (2km)
H-Sachsstr.
Jahnstr.
TO 41 (50m)

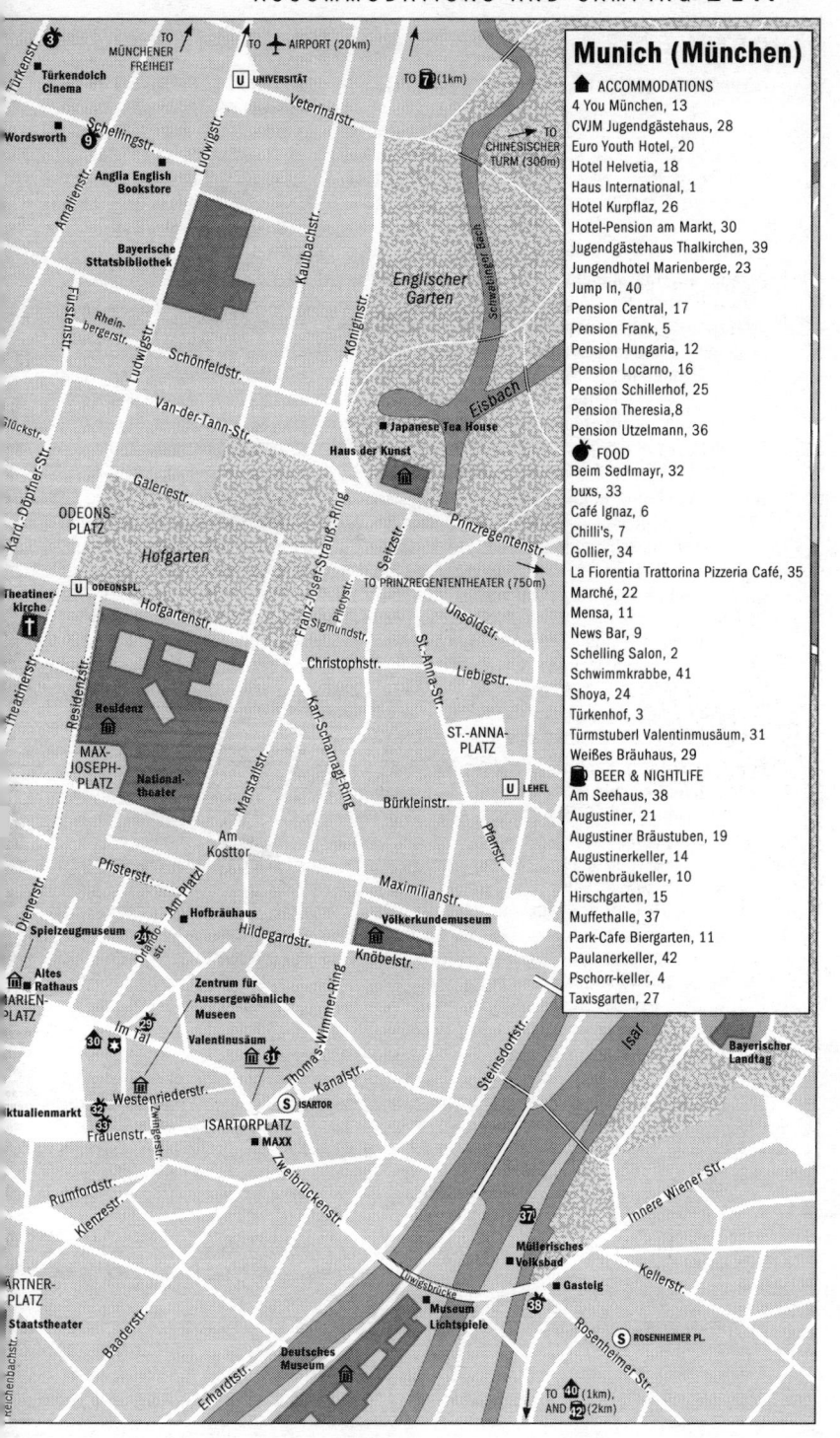

Munich (München)

▲ ACCOMMODATIONS
4 You München, 13
CVJM Jugendgästehaus, 28
Euro Youth Hotel, 20
Hotel Helvetia, 18
Haus International, 1
Hotel Kurpflaz, 26
Hotel-Pension am Markt, 30
Jugendgästehaus Thalkirchen, 39
Jungendhotel Marienberge, 23
Jump In, 40
Pension Central, 17
Pension Frank, 5
Pension Hungaria, 12
Pension Locarno, 16
Pension Schillerhof, 25
Pension Theresia, 8
Pension Utzelmann, 36

🍎 FOOD
Beim Sedlmayr, 32
buxs, 33
Café Ignaz, 6
Chilli's, 7
Gollier, 34
La Fiorentia Trattorina Pizzeria Café, 35
Marché, 22
Mensa, 11
News Bar, 9
Schelling Salon, 2
Schwimmkrabbe, 41
Shoya, 24
Türkenhof, 3
Türmstuberl Valentinmusäum, 31
Weißes Bräuhaus, 29

🍺 BEER & NIGHTLIFE
Am Seehaus, 38
Augustiner, 21
Augustiner Bräustuben, 19
Augustinerkeller, 14
Cöwenbräukeller, 10
Hirschgarten, 15
Muffethalle, 37
Park-Cafe Biergarten, 11
Paulanerkeller, 42
Pschorr-keller, 4
Taxisgarten, 27

HOSTELS

Jugendherberge Pullach Burg Schwaneck (HI), Burgweg 4-6 (☎ 793 06 43; fax 793 79 22), in a castle 12km outside the city center. S-Bahn #7 (direction: "Wolfratshausen") to "Pullach" (20min.). Exit the station from the side toward Munich and walk in the direction of the huge soccer field down Margarethenstr. and follow the signs (8min.). Clean rooms with green furniture are quiet and well-kept. Soccer games in the castle courtyard. Breakfast and sheets included. Dinner DM8. Reception 4-11pm. Curfew 11:30pm. Try to make reservations 7:30-10am. Singles DM37.50; doubles DM35.50; quads DM26; 6- to 8-bed rooms DM23. All prices per person.

Jugendherberge München (HI), Wendl-Dietrich-Str. 20. (☎ 13 11 56; fax 167 87 45; email jhmuenchen@djh-bayern.de). U-Bahn #1 (direction "Westfriedhof") to "Rot-kreuzpl." Go down Wendl-Dietrich-Str; to the left of the *Schwestern Schule* building; the entrance is ahead on the right. The most "central" of the HI hostels (3km from the city center). Safes in the reception area—*use them.* Breakfast and sheets included. Bike rental DM24. Mandatory DM20 key deposit. Check-in starts at 11am, but the lines form before 9am. 24hr. reception. No curfew. Reservations only accepted a week in advance; if you get one, arrive by 6pm or call ahead. Big dorm (37 beds) for men only DM25; 4- to 6-bed coed rooms DM30.

Jugendgästehaus Thalkirchen (HI), Miesingstr. 4 (☎ 723 65 50 or 723 65 60; fax 724 25 67; email BineMunich@aol.com). U-Bahn #1 or 2 to "Sendlinger Tor," then U-Bahn #3 (direction: "Fürstenrieder West") to "Thalkirchen." Take the Thalkirchner pl. exit and follow Schäftlarnstr. toward Innsbruck and bear right around the curve, then follow Frauenbergstr. and head left on Münchner Str.; follow the street as it curves left. Although distant, the Jugendgästehaus can be reached by a 15min subway ride from the city center. Rooms are comfortable and newly-renovated (some even have their own showers). TV room, billiards, and a washer/dryer (wash and dry DM5 each). Sheets and breakfast included. Bike rental DM24 per day, DM96 per week. Reception 7am-1am. Check-in 2pm-6pm (call first if later than 6pm). Curfew 1am. Call weeks in advance. Singles DM42.50; 2- to 15-bed rooms DM37.50.

■ **Euro Youth Hotel,** Senefelderstr. 5 (☎ 59 90 88 11; fax 59 90 88 77; email info@euro-youth-hotel.de; www.euro-youth-hotel.de). From the Bahnhofspl. exit of the Hauptbahn-nhof, make a right on Bayerstr. and a left on Senefelderstr.; the hotel will be on the left. Offers an outlandishly friendly and well-informed English-speaking staff loaded with bro-chures. Sleek bar open daily 8pm-2am (Maß DM3.50); happy hour 8-9pm (mixed drinks DM6.50). All-you-can-eat breakfast buffet DM7.90. Wash and dry DM6. 24hr. reception. No curfew or lockout. Doubles DM42, with private shower, telephone & breakfast DM60; triples and quads DM36; dorm beds DM29. All prices per person. Also inquire about their new location on the S-bahn 6 line, with close to 1000 beds and shuttle service to and from the airport, scheduled to open in Apr. 2001.

■ **Jugendlager Kapuzinerhölzl** ("The Tent"), In den Kirschen 30 (☎ 141 43 00; fax 17 50 90; email see-you@the-tent.de; www.the-tent.de). Streetcar #17 from the Hauptbahn-nhof (direction "Amalienburgstr.") to "Botanischer Garten" (15min.). Go straight on Franz-Schrank-Str. and left at In den Kirschen; The Tent is on the right. Night streetcars run at least once an hour all night. Spontaneous merrymaking around a bonfire at night; random films in English. Sleep with 250 fellow "campers" under a big circus tent on a wooden floor. DM15 gets you a foam pad, multiple wool blankets (you can use your sleeping bag also), bathrooms, a shower (not necessarily warm), a rudimentary break-fast, and enthusiastic management. Actual "beds" DM19. Camping available for DM8 per campsite plus DM8 per person. Laundry DM4. Lockers provided. Internet access DM2 for 15min. Bike rental DM12 per day. Free city tours (W 9am). Kitchen facilities available. Passport required as deposit. 24hr. reception. Reservations only for groups over 15, but rarely full. Open mid-June to Aug.

JCVJM Jugendgästehaus, Landwehrstr. 13 (☎ 552 14 10; fax 550 42 82; email info@cvjm-muenchen.org; www.cvjm-muenchen.org). Take the Bayerstr. exit from the train station, head straight down Goethestr. or Schillerstr., and take the 2nd left onto Landwehrstr.; it's on the right. Central location with modern rooms and showers in the hall. Nifty 70s-decorated restaurant offers pizza (DM7.80), soups, and salads Tu-Th 6:30-10:30pm, F 6:30-midnight. Co-ed rooms for married couples only. Breakfast included. Reception 8am-12:30am. Curfew 12:30am-7am. Reservations by mail, phone, fax, or email must arrive before 4pm and can be made up to a year in advance. Hostel closed during Easter and Dec. 20-Jan. 7. Reduced rates between Dec and Feb., increased rates during the Oktoberfest. Over 26 16% surcharge. Singles DM53; doubles DM90; triples DM126.

Jump In, Hochstr. 51 (☎48 95 34 37; www.jump-in.net), a new, small, private establishment founded by a brother and sister team tired of impersonal hostels. S-Bahn #1-8 to "Rosenheimer pl.," then take the Gasteig exit to the left and walk left on Hochstr. for 10min. Or take streetcar #27 or bus #51 to "Ostfriedhof." A little disorganized, but supremely amicable and delightfully informal. Easily accessible location, but rather spartan. Sinks in every room, showers and toilet off the hallway. Bed sheets DM5. Wash DM5. Reception 10am-noon and 5-10pm. No curfew. Mattresses on the floor DM29; real beds DM35; doubles DM39.

Haus International, Elisabethstr. 87 (☎12 00 60; fax 12 00 62 51). U-Bahn #2 (direction: "Feldmoching") to "Hohenzollernpl.," then streetcar #12 (direction: "Romanpl.") or bus #33 (direction: "Aidenbachstr.") to "Barbarastr." It's the 5-story beige building behind the BP gas station. Pleasantly clean dorms overlook a busy street. Cafeteria-style lunch and dinner available (DM12-14). Free indoor pool, small beer garden, TV room, and groovy disco with bar. 24hr. reception. Reservations recommended in summer. Singles DM55, with bath DM85; doubles DM49, with shower DM69; triples DM48; quads DM45; quints DM42.

4 you münchen, Hirtenstr. 18 (☎552 16 60; fax 55 21 66 66; email info@the4you.de; www.the4you.de), 200m from the Hauptbahnhof. Exit at Arnulfstr., go left, quickly turn right onto Pfefferstr., then hang a left onto Hirtenstr. Ecological youth hostel with restaurant and bar, hang-out areas, a playroom, and wheelchair-accessible everything. Breakfast buffet DM8. Sheets DM5. Key deposit DM20. Singles DM56; doubles DM40; 4-, 6- or 8-bed dorms DM32; 12-bed dorms DM26. Over 27 15% surcharge. In their **adjoining hotel,** breakfast is included. Reception 24hr. Reserve well in advance. singles with bath run DM79; doubles with bath DM129, extra bed DM49.

Jugendhotel Marienberge, Goethestr. 9 (☎55 58 05; fax 55 02 82 60; email invia.muenchen.marienherberge@t-online.de), less than a block from the train station. Take the "Bayerstr." exit and walk down Goethestr. Open only to women under 26. Staffed by merry nuns, the rooms in this hostel are spacious, cheery, and spotless. Breakfast included. Kitchen, laundry, and television facilities. Wash DM2, dry DM2. Reception 8am-midnight. Curfew midnight, before you turn into a pumpkin. Singles DM40; doubles DM35; triples DM35; 6-bed dorms DM30.

CAMPING

Munich's campgrounds are open from mid-Mar. to late October.

Campingpl. Thalkirchen, Zentralländstr. 49 (☎723 17 07; fax 724 31 77). U-Bahn #1 or 2 to "Sendlinger Tor," then #3 to "Thalkirchen," and change to bus #57 (20min.). From the bus stop, cross the busy street on the left and take a right onto the footpath next to the road. The entrance is down the tree-lined path on the left. Well-run, crowded grounds with jogging and bike paths. TV lounge, groceries, and a restaurant (meals DM3-8). Wash DM7, dry DM0.50 per 6min. Curfew 11pm. DM8.40 per person, DM2.50 per child under 14. DM5.50-7 charged per tent. Car DM8.50. Showers DM2.

Campingpl. Obermenzing, Lochhausener Str. 59 (☎811 22 35; fax 814 48 07). S-Bahn #3, 4, 5, 6, or 8 to "Pasing" then exit toward track 8 and take bus #76 to "Lochhausener Str." Head up Lochhausener Str. from the bus stop; it's on the left after about 10min. On the noisy *Autobahn,* but friendly and well kept. Reception 7:30am-noon and 3-8pm. DM7.80 per person, DM4 per child under 14. Tent DM7.50. Car DM6. Oktoberfest surcharge DM2.50. Showers DM2.

HOTELS AND PENSIONEN

While Munich—reputedly a city of 80,000 guest beds—has a surplus of dirt-cheap (and often dirty) accommodations, it is often a better idea to crash in a hostel. A clean room in a safe area costs at least DM55-65 for a single and DM80-100 for a double. **Always call ahead.** Call a few months in advance for Oktoberfest rooms, as some hotels are booked for the entire two weeks by early summer.

NEAR THE HAUPTBAHNHOF

■ **Hotel Helvetia,** Schillerstr. 6 (☎590 68 50; fax 59 06 85 70; email hotel-helvetia@t-online.de), at the corner of Bahnhofspl., next to the Vereinsbank, to the right as you exit the station. The friendliest hotel in all of Munich. Beautiful, newly-renovated rooms with oriental rugs, most with phones; free internet access 24-7. Breakfast included. Singles DM55-65; doubles DM72-95, with shower DM99-115; triples DM105-126. Also caters to backpackers with new **hostel-like dorms.** Breakfast DM7. Sheets DM4. Laundry service DM9.90. 24hr. reception. 6-bed rooms DM26 per person; 10-bed DM22. Rates rise 10-15% during Oktoberfest.

Hotel Kurpfalz, Schwanthaler Str. 121 (☎540 98 60; fax 54 09 88 11; email hotel-kurpfalz@munich-online.de; www.munich-hotels.com). Exit on Bayerstr. from the station, turn right and walk 5-6 blocks down Bayerstr., veer left onto Holzapfelstr., and make a right onto Schwanthaler Str. (10min.). Or streetcar #18 or 19 to "Holzapfelstr." (3 stops) and walk from there. The hotel's Sevdas brothers will win you over with their smiley proficiency in Americana. Satellite TVs, phones, and hardwood furniture in all rooms. All rooms have private bath. Breakfast buffet included. Free email access; internet surfing DM5 for 30min. 24hr. reception. Singles from DM89; doubles from DM109; triples (doubles with cots) DM165.

Pension Locarno, Bahnhofspl. 5 (☎55 51 64; fax 59 50 45; www.deutschland-hotel.de/muc/locarno.htm). From the train station's main entrance walk left across Bahnhofspl. and look for the building with the *Pension* sign. Plain, newly furnished and carpeted rooms, all with TV and phone. Helpful owners. Reception Su-M 7:30am-midnight, Tu-Sa 7:30am-5am. Mention "Let's Go" to get these rates: singles DM55-75, doubles DM85, triples DM125, quads DM140. DM5 less without breakfast.

Pension Schillerhof, Schillerstr. 21 (☎59 42 70; fax 550 18 35; email hotel-schillerhof@az-online.net; www.hotel-schillerhof.de). Exit onto Bahnhofpl. from the train station, turn right, and walk 2 blocks down Schillerstr. Tidy rooms with TV. Breakfast included. Reception 6am-10pm. Reservations can be made on-line. Singles DM60-80; doubles DM90-120. Extra bed DM20. Oktoberfest surcharge DM25-40 per person.

Hotel-Pension Utzelmann, Pettenkoferstr. 6 (☎59 48 89; fax 59 62 28). From the train station walk 4 blocks down Schillerstr. and go left on Pettenkofer; it's at the end on the left (10min.). Nostalgic, elegant rooms with upholstered furniture and oriental rugs. Breakfast included. Reception 7am-10pm. Singles DM55, with shower DM95, with bath DM130; doubles DM98, with shower DM115, with bath DM150; triples DM140, with shower DM160, with bath DM180; quads DM170, with shower DM190.

Pension Hungaria, Briennerstr. 42 (☎52 15 58). From the train station, go left onto Dachauer Str., right on Augustenstr., and across and to the right on Briennerstr.; it's the 2nd building to your left (10min.). Or U-Bahn #1 to "Stiglmaierpl."; take the Briennerstr./Volkstheater exit, and it's on the next corner at Augustenstr. Oriental rugs, comfortable furnishings, and a small travel library adorn this cozy pension. Breakfast included. Showers DM3. 24hr. reception 2 floors up. Singles DM60-65; doubles DM85-90; triples DM110; quads DM130. Oktoberfest surcharge DM10 per room.

Pension Central, Bayerstr. 55 (☎543 98 46; fax 543 98 47; email pension.central@t-online.de). Hang a right out of the Bayerstr. exit of the train station and walk 5 minutes up Bayerstr. The pension is on the left. Although the exterior may not please the eyes, you can't judge a book by its cover. Inside, the rooms are classy and spacious. 24hr. reception. Singles DM65, with bath DM75; doubles DM95, with bath DM110-120; triples DM120; quads DM160-180; quints DM200-220.

BAVARIA

SCHWABING/UNIVERSITY/CITY CENTER

Pension Frank, Schellingstr. 24 (☎28 14 51; fax 280 09 10; email pension.frank@gmx.net; www.pension-frank.de). U-Bahn #3 or 6 to "Universität." Take the Schellingstr. exit, then the first right onto Schellingstr.; it's 2 blocks down on the right. Curious combination of backpackers, student groups, and wannabe fashion models. Fabulous location for cafe and bookstore aficionados. Hearty breakfast included. Reception 7:30am-10pm. Check-out at 11. Single beds in shared rooms almost always available. Singles DM55-65; doubles DM95; 3- to 6-bed rooms DM40 per person.

Pension am Kaiserpl., Kaiserpl. 12 (☎34 91 90). Located a few blocks from nightlife central—a good location if you doubt your own sense of direction after a couple of beers. U-Bahn #3 or 6 to "Münchener Freiheit." Take the escalator to Herzogstr., then left; it's 3 blocks to Viktoriastr. Take a left at Viktoriastr.; it's at the end of the street on the right (10min.). Helpful owner offers elegantly decorated, high-ceilinged rooms. Breakfast included. Reception 7am-9pm. Singles DM59; doubles DM89, with shower DM99-105; each additional person DM40; 6-bed rooms DM240.

Pension Geiger, Steinheilstr. 1 (☎52 15 56; fax 52 31 54 71). U-Bahn #2 to "Theresienstr." Take the Augustenstr. S.O. exit, and walk straight down Theresienstr. towards Kopierladen München. Take a right on Enhuberstr. and a left on Steinheilstr.; enter through the double doors on the right (5min.). Family-run *Pension* located in a quiet neighborhood and decorated in soft, bright colors with comfortable sofas. Hall showers DM2. Reception (2 floors up) 8am-9pm. Arrive by 6pm or call. Closed Dec. 24-Jan. 31. Singles DM55, with shower DM80; doubles DM98, with shower DM108.

Pension Theresia, Luisenstr. 51 (☎52 12 50; fax 542 06 33). U-Bahn #2 to "Theresienstr." and take the Augustenstr. S.O. exit, head straight down Theresienstr., and take the second right onto Luisenstr.; the entrance is in the passageway left of the Dahlke store. Cheery red carpets and an elegant dining room complement the well-maintained, relatively spacious rooms. Breakfast included. Reception (2nd floor) 7am-10pm. Reservations by phone or fax. Singles DM52-68; doubles DM89-99, with shower DM95-145; triples and quads available, DM30 per extra person.

Hotel-Pension am Markt, Heiliggeiststr. 6 (☎22 50 14; fax 22 40 17), smack dab in the city center. S-Bahn #1-8 to "Marienpl.," then walk past the Altes Rathaus and turn right down the little alley behind the green Heiliggeist church. Aging photographs recall celebrities that once graced the hotel's small but spotless rooms—recognize anyone? Breakfast included. Singles DM62-64, with shower DM110; doubles DM110-116, with shower DM150-160; triples DM165, with shower DM205.

🗷 FOOD

The vibrant **Viktualienmarkt,** two minutes south of Marienpl., is Munich's gastronomic center, offering both basic and exotic foods and ingredients. It's fun to browse, but don't plan to do any budget grocery shopping here (open M-F 10am-8pm, Sa 8am-4pm). Located on every corner, the ubiquitous **beer gardens** (see **Beer, Beer, and More Beer,** p. 259) serve savory snacks along with booze. However, since the time of King Ludwig I, skinflints have been permitted to bring their own food to many of the gardens. To make sure that your fixings are welcome, ask a server or check for tables without tablecloths, as bare tables usually indicate self-service (*Selbstbedienung*). To stick your fangs into an authentic Bavarian lunch, grab a Brez'n (pretzel) and spread it with Leberwurst or cheese (DM5-6). **Weißwürste** (white veal sausages) are another native bargain, served in a pot of hot water with sweet mustard and a soft pretzel on the side. Don't eat the skin of the sausage; instead, slice it open and devour the tender meat. **Leberkäs,** also a Münchener lunch, is a slice of a pinkish, meatloaf-like compound of ground beef and bacon which, despite its name and dubious appearance, contains neither liver nor cheese. **Leberknödel** are liver dumplings, usually served in soup or with Kraut; **Kartoffelknödel** (potato dumplings) and **Semmelknödel** (made from white bread, egg, and parsley) are eaten along with a hearty chunk of German meat. Those not interested in chowing down on all things meaty can head to Munich's scrumptious and healthy vegetarian cafes.

BAVARIA

The large **A&P Tengelmann** in the Karlspl. subway station is convenient for **grocery** needs. From the Hauptbahnhof, walk east on Bayerstr., make a right onto Sonnenstr. and enter the U-Bahn after Schloßerstr. (open M-F 8:30am-8pm, Sa 8am-4pm). Another **A&P Tengelmann** with the same hours is located at Rotkreuzpl. (Nymphenburger Str. 170; take U-Bahn #1 to "Rotkreuzpl."). *Munich Found* (DM4) lists a few restaurants, while *Prinz* (DM5) offers a fairly complete listing of restaurants, cafes, and bars. Fruit and vegetable **markets** are held throughout the city, with many on Bayerstr. just a few blocks from the train station.

NEAR THE UNIVERSITY

The university district off **LudwigStr.** is Munich's best source of filling meals in a lively, unpretentiously hip atmosphere. Many reasonably-priced restaurants and cafes cluster on **Schellingstr., Amalienstr.,** and **Türkenstr.** Ride U-Bahn #3 or 6 to "Universität." **Plus supermarket,** Schellingstr. 38, provides **groceries** (open M-F 8:30am-7pm, Sa 8am-3pm).

Mensa, Arcisstr. 17, to the left of the Pinakothek just below Gabelsbergstr. on Arcisstr. U-Bahn #2 or #8 to "Königspl." In the cafeteria on the ground floor, snacks, sandwiches, and small warm entrees can be had for orgasmically low prices (DM1-3.50). The actual Mensa upstairs serves large portions of cheap food (DM3-5.50) and offers at least one vegetarian dish; to eat there, however, you need to procure a "Legic-Karte" in the library (DM10 deposit plus DM10 worth of buying power). Student ID required for both Mensa and the cafeteria. Open M-Th 7:45am-5:30pm, F 7:45am-4pm; during vacations open M-F 8am-4pm.

News Bar, Amalienstr. 55 (☎28 17 87), at the corner of Schellingstr. Trendy cafe teeming with younguns; serves large portions at reasonable prices. Breakfast menu (DM4.70-15.50); freshly pressed juice DM7.90. For lunch or dinner, choose from a wide assortment of salads (DM8.50-17.50), sandwiches (DM8.50-13.50), or pasta (DM12.90-17.90). Crepes DM12-14. Open daily 7:30am-2am.

Türkenhof, Türkenstr. 78 (☎280 02 35), offers a wide selection of global cuisine, including everything from Middle Eastern to Mexican to Thai. Immensely popular with the low-key student population. Smoky and buzzing from noon 'til night. Variable daily menu with numerous veggie options. Entrees DM10.80-15.80. Open M-Th and Su 11am-1am, F-Sa 11am-2am.

Schelling Salon, Schellingstr. 54 (☎272 07 88). Bavarian *Knödel* and billiard balls. Founded in 1872, this pool joint has racked the balls of Lenin, Rilke, and Hitler. Breakfast DM5.50-9.50, Wurst DM6-7. A free **billiard museum** displays a 200-year-old Polish noble's table and the history of pool back to the Pharaohs. Restaurant open Th-M 6:30am-1am; museum open at night, Sa-Su.

Gaststätte Engelsburg, Türkenstr. 51, at the corner of Schellingstr. This restaurant offers a healthy mix of traditional Bavarian dishes and faster food, and a crowd that is more town than gown. The daily "Menü" options usually include a soup and warm entree for about DM10. The take-out window serves currywurst with fries (DM5.90) and gyros (DM4.90), among others. Pizzas DM8.50-13.50. Open daily 10am-1am.

IN THE CENTER

Munich's touristy interior suffers from an overabundance of high-priced eateries, but there are some good options for the budget traveler. For **groceries**, try **HL Markt**, Tal 13 (open M-F 8:30am-8pm, Sa 8am-4pm).

Marché, Neuhauser Str., between Karlspl. and Marienpl. (☎260 60 61). The top floor of this monstrous eatery offers cafeteria-style food displays (try the fried goat cheese with salad for DM5.90), a make-your-own-pizza bar (DM8.50), and a Mövenpick ice cream stand. Downstairs, customers are given food cards before entering the area, which is decorated as a mini-Munich and filled with buffet and food stations where chefs prepare every food imaginable. Great vegetarian selections. You'll get a stamp for each item you take; pay on the way out. And, by the way, don't lose that card! If you do, you'll either throw down DM100 or spend the day washing dishes. Top floor open 11am-10pm, bottom floor open 8am-11pm.

Weißes Bräuhaus, Tal 7 (☎29 98 75), across from the *McDonald's* at the end of Marienpl. This traditional Bavarian restaurant, which made Marcellino's *Top Ten Restaurants in Munich* in 1997 and 1999, is brimming with affordable and delectable dishes.

Choose from the 40-50 options on the daily menu (DM8.90-25) as a portrait of Crazy Ludwig stares down at you. Open daily 7:30am-midnight.

Beim Sedlmayr, Westenriederstr. 14 (☎22 62 19), off the Viktualienmarkt. Anyone craving Weißwurst (DM7) will love this slice of Bavaria. Specials DM7-27. Beer DM5.70 for 0.5L. Open daily 9am-10pm. Kitchen open M-F 11am-9pm, Sa 8am-4pm.

La Fiorentia Trattorina Pizzeria cafe, Goethestr. 41 (☎53 41 85), a few blocks from the train station, specializes in generating exquisite, mouth-watering fragrances. Salivating cappuccino and pizza-lovers from the nearby medical university transform the cafe into an Italian culinary festival on weekday afternoons. Calzones DM11-12.80, pizza DM7-14. Open M-F 11:30am-11:30pm, Sa 3-11pm.

Chilli's, Rosenheimerstr. 10 (S-Bahn #1-8 to Isartor, exit "Deutsches Museum"). Tiny restaurant with tiny prices. Get a bowl of their homemade chilli for DM5.99, or sink your teeth into the 12-piece chicken wing platter (the most expensive item on the menu) for DM9.14. Vegetarians can enjoy the veggie burrito (DM4.79), and there is a breakfast menu for all you early birds. Open M-Sa 10am-10pm, Su noon-10pm.

Shoya, Orlandostr. 5 (☎29 27 72), across from the Hofbräuhaus. The most reasonable Japanese restaurant in town. Fill up on rice dishes (DM13-17), teriyaki (DM8-16), sushi (DM5-42), and meat and veggie dishes (DM7-16) as you listen to traditional Japanese music. Open daily 10:30am-midnight.

Turmstüberl im Valentin-Musäum, Tal 50, (☎29 37 62), in the Valentin-Musäum in the Isartorturm. S-Bahn #1-8 or Streetcar #18 or 20 to "Isartor." This curious nook at the top of the city's western tower serves up thick mugs of hot milk with honey (DM4.50) and savory Apfelstrudel with vanilla ice cream (DM7) in a comical and characteristically Valentin atmosphere. Must pay entrance fee for museum to get in. Open M-Tu and F-Sa 11am-5:30pm, Su 10am-5:30pm.

ELSEWHERE IN MUNICH

Internet-cafe, Nymphenburger Str. 145 (☎129 11 20), on the corner of Landshuter Allee. U-Bahn #1 to "Rotkreuzpl." With the addition of 12 terminals, this is an average Italian joint turned hopping, electronic haven—a Neuromancer's paradise. Unlimited free Internet access as long as you order pasta (DM5.30-7.50) or pizza (DM5.50-8.50); otherwise, the cost is DM5 for 30 min. Open daily 11am-4am. **Another location,** Altheimer Eck 12 (☎260 78 15), sits in the city center between Marienpl. and Karlspl. in the pedestrian zone Arcade-Passage. Same offerings. Open daily 11am-1am.

Schwimmkrabbe, Ickstattstr. 13 (☎201 00 80). U-Bahn #1 or 2 to "Fraunhoferstr.," then walk 1 block down Baaderstr. and turn right on Ickstattstr. Locals flock to this family-run Turkish restaurant. Try the delicious Etli Pide (lamb and veggies wrapped in a foot-long bread with salad; DM16). Filling appetizers DM6-14. Hearty dishes DM15-29. Belly-dancing darlings on F and Sa nights. Open daily 5pm-1am. Reserve on weekends.

VEGETARIAN RESTAURANTS

Gollier, Gollierstr. 83 (☎50 16 73). U-Bahn #4 or 5 or S-Bahn #7 or 27 to "Heimeranpl.", then walk 2 blocks north on Garmischer Str. and turn left on Gollierstr. Serves delicious homemade pizzas, casseroles, and crepes (DM6-19). Food to go from DM3.50. Lunch buffet DM13.50. Offers many summer specials such as reduced lunch buffet prices and early-bird dinner deals. Open M-F noon-3pm and 5pm-midnight, Sa 5pm-midnight, Su 10am-midnight.

café Ignaz, Georgenstr. 67 (☎271 60 93). U-Bahn #2 to "Josephspl.", then take Adelheidstr. one block north and make a right on Georgenstr. Earth-friendly cafe with a nutritious, inexpensive menu. Yogurt with fresh fruit DM6.50. Dinners (pasta, quiche, and stir-fry dishes) DM10-16.50. Crepes DM7-12.50. English menu available. Lunch buffet M-F noon-2pm DM13.50, brunch buffet Sa-Su 9am-1pm, DM13. Open M-F 8am-10pm, Sa-Su 9am-10pm.

buxs, Frauenstr. 9 (☎29 19 550), on the southern edge of the Viktualienmarkt on the corner of Westenriederstr. This up-scale cafe not only provides tasty, artful pastas, salads, soups, and bread, but it also has its own line of cookbooks. Self-serve everything, with a weight-based charge at the end. Be careful; an average plate of this high-quality food can easily cost DM20. Open M-F 11am-8:30pm, Sa 11am-3:30pm.

BAVARIA

🔦 SIGHTS

MARIENPLATZ. Numerous sacred stone edifices prickle the area around Marienpl., a major S-Bahn and U-Bahn junction as well as the social nexus of the city. An ornate 17th-century monument to the Virgin Mary, the **Mariensäule** was built to commemorate the fact that the amazing and powerful Swedes did not destroy the city during the Thirty Years War. At the neo-Gothic **Neues Rathaus,** the Glockenspiel chimes with a display of jousting knights and dancing coopers. According to legend, the barrel-makers coaxed townspeople out of their homes, singing and dancing, to prove that the Great Plague had passed. *(Daily 11am, noon, and 5pm.)* At bedtime *(9pm),* a mechanical watchman marches out and the Guardian Angel escorts the *Münchner Kindl* (Munich Child, the town's symbol) to bed. Don't miss the rooster perched above the knights; he crows three times after the bells stop tolling. *(Tower open M-F 9am-7pm, Sa, Su 10am-7pm. DM3, under 18 DM1.50, under 6 free.)* On the face of the **Altes Rathaus** tower, to the right of the Neues Rathaus, are all of Munich's coats of arms since its inception as a city—with one noble gap. When the tower was rebuilt after its destruction in WWII, the local government refused to include the swastika-bearing coat of arms from the Nazi era.

FRAUENPLATZ. Munich's Catholic past has left many marks on the city's architecture. From the Marienpl., walk one block towards the Hauptbahnhof on Kaufingerstr. to find the onion-domed towers of the 15th-century Frauenkirche—one (well, maybe two) of Munich's most notable landmarks. Inside, see the final resting place of Kaiser Ludwig der Bayer and take advantage of a free German language tour at 2pm. *(Towers open Apr.-Oct. M-Sa 10am-5pm. DM4, students DM2, under 6 free.)*

ASAMKIRCHE. A Rococo masterpiece, the Asamkirche is named after its creators, the Asam brothers, who promised God that they would build a church if they survived the wreckage of their ship. Rocks at the bottom of the facade represent rapids, the church's literal and metaphorical foundation. Inside, red and gray marble columns spiral heavenward among gold and silver adornments. Two priests give a tour of the church Sat at noon from June-Sept (DM5). *(Sendlinger Str. 32; four blocks down Sendlinger Str. from the Marienpl.)*

PETERSKIRCHE. The 11th-century Peterskirche, the city's oldest parish church, represents Munich's ecclesiastical past; its golden interior was Baroquified in the 18th century. More than 300 steps scale the tower, christened *Alter Peter* by locals; a spectacular view of Munich and (on a very clear day) the Alps awaits at the top. *(Rindermarkt and Peterspl., across Marienpl. from the Neues Rathaus. Open M-Sa 9am-5pm, Su 10am-7pm. DM2.50, students DM1.50, children DM0.50.)*

MICHAELSKIRCHE. Ludwig II of Bayern (of crazy castle fame) rests peacefully with 40-odd other Wittelsbachs entombed in the crypt of the 16th-century Jesuit Michaelskirche. The construction of the church, designed to emphasize the city's loyalty to Catholicism during the Reformation, almost bankrupted the state treasury. Father Rupert Mayer, one of the few German clerics who spoke out against Hitler, preached here. *(☎ 231 70 60. Crypt open M-F 9:30am-4:30pm, Sa 9:30am-2:30pm. DM2, students and children under 16 DM1.)*

RESIDENZ. Down the pedestrian zone from Odeonspl., the richly decorated rooms of the Residenz (Palace), built from the 14th to 19th centuries, form the material vestiges of the Wittelsbach dynasty. The grounds now house several museums. The beautifully landscaped **Hofgarten** behind the Residenz shelters the lovely temple of Diana. The **Schatzkammer** (treasury) contains jeweled baubles, crowns, swords, china, ivory work, and other trinkets from the 10th century on. *(Open daily from Apr. to mid. Oct. 9am-6pm, Th. 9am-8pm; in winter 10am-4pm. Last admission 1 hour before closing time. DM8; students with ID, seniors, and group members DM6; children under 15 free with adult.)* The **Residenzmuseum** comprises the former Wittelsbach apartments and State Rooms, a collection of European porcelain, and a 17th-century court chapel. German tours of the Residenzmuseum meet just outside the

BAVARIA

museum entrance. The walls of the **Ahnengalerie,** hung with 120 "family portraits," trace the royal lineage in an unusual manner. Charlemagne would be surprised to find himself accountable for the genesis of the Wittelsbach family. *(Max-Joseph-pl. 3.* ☎ *29 06 71. Take U-Bahn #3-6 to "Odeonspl." Open same hours as Schatzkammer. DM8; students and children DM6. Residenzmuseum tours Su, W 11am; Tu, Sa 2pm. DM8, Su DM10. Combination ticket to Schatzkammer and Residenzmuseum DM14; students and seniors DM11.)*

ENGLISCHER GARTEN. Extending from the city center to the studentenheim is the vast Englischer Garten, one of Europe's oldest landscaped public parks. On sunny days, all of Munich turns out to bike, fly kites, play badminton, ride horseback, swim in the Eisbach, or sunbathe. A couple beer gardens are on garden grounds, as is a Japanese tea house, Chinese pagoda, and Greek temple. Nude sunbathing areas are designated FKK on signs and park maps. Consider yourself warned (or clued in). Müncheners with aquatic daring-do surf--yes, that kind of surf--the white-water rapids of the Eisbach, which flows artificially through the park. The stone bridge on Prinzregentenstr., close to the Staatsgalerie Moderner Kunst, is an excellent vantage point for witnessing these marine stunts.

SCHLOß NYMPHENBURG. After 10 years of trying for an heir, Ludwig I celebrated the birth of his son Maximilian in 1662 by erecting an elaborate summer playground. Schloß Nymphenburg, in the northwest of town, is a handsome architectural symptom of Ludwig's dogged desire to copy King Louis XIV of France. Set in a winsome park, the Baroque palace hides a number of treasures, including a two-story granite marble hall seasoned with stucco and frescoes. Check out King Ludwig's "Gallery of Beauties"—whenever a woman caught his fancy, he would have her portrait painted (a scandalous hobby, considering that many of the women were commoners; as well as an ironic one, given that Ludwig grappled with an affection for men throughout his life). Do not confuse the "Gallery of Beauties" with the "Gallery of Horses" housed in the **Marstallmuseum** (carriage museum). Ludwig was a man of many fetishes. A few lakes and four manors also inhabit the palace grounds: **Amalienburg**, **Badenburg**, **Pagodenburg**, and **Magdalen hermitage**. *(Streetcar #17 (direction: "Amalienburgstr.") to "Schloß Nymphenburg." All attractions open Apr. to mid-Oct. daily 9am-6pm, Th. 9am-8pm; late-Oct. to Mar. 10am-4pm daily. DM6, students DM4. Museum open Tu-Su 9am-noon and 1-5pm. Badenburg, Pagodenburg, and Magdalen hermitage closed in winter. Schloß or Marstall museum DM7, students DM5. Each burg DM5, students DM4. Entire complex DM15; students DM12; children under 15 free with adult. Grounds open until 9:30pm. Free.)*

BOTANISCHER GARTEN. Next door to Schloß Nymphenburg, the greenhouses of the immense Botanischer Garten shelter rare and wonderful growths from around the world. Check out the Indian and Bolivian water lily room, the eight-foot tall, 100-year-old cycadee, and the prickly cactus alcove. *(Streetcar #17 (direction: "Amalienburgstr.") to "Botanischer Garten." ☎ 17 86 13 10. Open daily 9am-8pm. Open 9-11:45am and 1-7:30pm. DM4, students DM2, under 15 DM0.50.)*

NAZI-RELATED SIGHTS. Mixed with Munich's Baroque elegance are visible traces of Germany's Nazi past. Buildings erected by Hitler and his cronies that survived the bombings of 1945 stand as grim reminders of Munich's role as the ideological "Hauptstadt der Bewegung" (capital of the movement). The **Haus der Kunst,** built to enshrine Nazi principles of art, serves as a modern art museum; swastika patterns have been left on its porch as reminders of its origins (see **Museums,** below). The gloomy limestone building now housing the **Hauptschule für Musik und Theater** was built under Hitler's auspices and functioned as the *Führerbau*, his Munich headquarters. From its balcony, he viewed the city's military parades; it was also here that Chamberlain signed away the Sudetenland in 1938. At the **Königspl.**, one block away from the Führerbau between the Antikensammlung and the Glyptothek Museums, thousands of books were burned on the night of May 10, 1933.

OLYMPIC SPIRIT. An indoor sports and amusement park and Munich's newest nostalgic and interactive addition to its 1972 Olympic park, Olympic Spirit beckons sports buffs to check out its high-tech simulators that show various sports from the athlete's perspective, computer sports quizzes, booths to try out everything from bobsledding to basketball, videos of classic Olympic performances, and Sports cafe, which broadcasts live sports events daily from 10am-12:30am. *(Streetcar #21 (direction: "Westfriedhof") to "Olympic Spirit."* ☎ *30 63 86 26. Park open Tu-Su 10am-7pm. DM24, under 13 DM18.)*

🏛 MUSEUMS

Munich is a supreme museum city, and many of the city's offerings would require days for exhaustive perusal. The *Münchner Volksschule* offers tours of many city museums for DM8. A day pass for entry to all of Munich's museums is sold at the tourist office and at many larger museums (DM30).

MUSEUMSINSEL

DEUTSCHES MUSEUM. One of the world's largest and best museums of science and technology. Fascinating exhibits of original models include the first telephone and the work bench upon which Otto Hahn split his first atom. Don't miss the mining exhibit, which winds through a labyrinth of recreated subterranean tunnels. A walk through the museum's 46 departments covers over 17km; grab an English guidebook (DM6). The planetarium (DM3) and electrical show will warm any physicist's heart. *(Museuminsel 1. S-Bahn #1-8 to "Isartor.", or street car #18 to "Deutsches Museum".* ☎ *217 91; www.deutsches-museum.de. Open daily 9am-5pm. DM12, students DM5, children under 6 free.)*

KÖNIGSPLATZ

ALTE PINAKOTHEK. Contains Munich's most precious art. Commissioned in 1826 by King Ludwig I, the last of the passionate Wittelsbach art collectors, this world-renowned hall houses works by Titian, da Vinci, Raphael, Dürer, Rembrandt, Rubens, and other European painters of the 14th through the 18th centuries. *(Barerstr. 27. U-Bahn #2 to "Königspl."* ☎ *23 80 52 16, www.stmukwk.bayern.de/kunst/museen. Open Tu-Su 10am-5pm and Th until 8pm. DM7, students DM4; a combination ticket for the Alte and the Neue Pinakotheken can be purchased for DM12, students DM6.)*

NEUE PINAKOTHEK. Sleek space for paintings and sculptures of the 18th to 20th centuries: Van Gogh, Klimt, Cézanne, Manet, and more. *(Barerstr. 29.* ☎ *23 80 51 95, www.stmukwk.bayern.de/kunst/museen. Next to and with the same prices as the Alte Pinakothek. Open W-M 10am-5pm and Th until 8pm.)*

GLYPTOTHEK. Assembled by Ludwig I in 1825 in pursuit of his Greek dream to turn Munich into a "cultural work of such sheer perfection as only few Germans have experienced." Features 2,400-year-old pediment figures from the Temple of Aphaea as well as Etruscan and Roman sculptures. *(Königspl. 3. Around the corner from the Lenbachhaus. U-Bahn #2 to "Königspl."* ☎ *28 61 00. Open Tu-Su 10am-5pm and Th until 8pm. DM6, students DM3.50; free tour Thursdays at 6pm. A combination ticket for the Glyptothek and the Antikensammlung is available for DM10, students DM5.)*

ANTIKENSAMMLUNG. Flaunts a first-rate flock of vases and the other half of Munich's finest collection of ancient art, featuring Ancient Greek and Etruscan pottery and jewelry. *(Königspl. 1. Across Königspl. from Glyptothek. U-Bahn #2 to "Königspl."* ☎ *59 83 59. Open Tu-Su 10am-5pm and W until 8pm. DM6, students DM3.50; free tour Wednesdays at 6pm. Closed for renovations until Apr. 2001.)*

LENBACHHAUS. Munich cityscapes (useful if it's raining), along with works by Kandinsky, Klee, and the Blaue Reiter school. *(Luisenstr. 33.* ☎ *23 33 20 02; www.lenbachhaus.de. U-Bahn #2 to "Königspl." Open Tu-Su 10am-6pm. DM8, students DM4.)*

ELSEWHERE IN MUNICH

BMW-MUSEUM. The ultimate driving museum features a fetching display of past, present, and future products of Bavaria's second-favorite export. The English brochure, *Horizons in Time*, guides you through the spiral path to the top of the museum. Sit in a simulator of the car of the future, with on-board computer, as you listen to Rod Steward and Kool 'n' the Gang on the headphones. *(Petuelring 130. U-Bahn #3 to "Olympiazentrum."* ☎ *38 22 33 07. Open daily 9am-5pm. Last entry 4pm. DM5.50, students DM4.)*

ZAM: ZENTRUM FÜR AUSSERGEWÖHNLICHE MUSEEN. Munich's Center for Unusual Museums, a brilliant place that brazenly corrals under one roof such treasures as the Padlock Museum, the Museum of Easter Rabbits, and the Chamberpot Museum. Fan of Empress Elizabeth of Austria? Sass on over to the Sisi Museum, sweetie. *(Westenriederstr. 41. S-Bahn #1-8 to "Isartor" or streetcar #17 or 18. ☎ 290 41 21. Open daily 10am-6pm. DM8, students and children DM5.)*

MÜNCHENER STADTMUSEUM. A collection of exhibitions presenting interesting aspects of Munich's city life and history: film, fashion, musical instruments, weapons, puppetry, posters, and more. **Classic films** (DM8) roll every evening starting at 6pm. Foreign films shown in the original language with German subtitles; call ☎ 23 32 55 86 for a program. *(St.-Jakobs-pl. 1. U-Bahn #3 or 6 or S-Bahn #1-8 to "Marienplatz." ☎ 23 32 23 70; www.stadtmuseum-online.de. Open Tu-Su 10am-6pm. Museum DM5, students, seniors, and children DM2.50, under 6 free; DM3 extra for admission to special exhibitions.)*

STAATSGALERIE MODERNER KUNST. In the **Haus der Kunst** at the southern tip of the Englischer Garten, this sterling gallery celebrates the vitality of 20th-century art, from the colorful palettes of the Expressionists to the spare canvases of the Minimalists. Showcases Beckmann, Kandinsky, Klee, Picasso, and Dalí. Constructed by the Nazis as the Museum of German Art, it opened with the famous Entartete Kunst (degenerate art) exhibit that included works of the Expressionists and Dadaists. Excellent visiting exhibits DM4-6 extra. The collection will soon be relocated to the new Pinakotheck der Moderne Kunst, which is expected to reach completion in 2001. *(Prinzregentenstr. 1. U-Bahn #4 or 5 to "Lehel," then streetcar #17. ☎ 21 12 71 37. Open Tu-Su 10am-10pm. DM6, students DM3.50.)*

SPIELZEUGMUSEUM. Two centuries of toys—compare the "futuristic" WWI figurines to the evolution of the schicki-micki Barbie and her rather stiff date Ken. *(Marienplatz 15. In the Altes Rathaus. ☎ 29 40 01. Open daily 10am-5:30pm. DM5, children under 15 DM1, families DM10.)*

VALENTIN-MUSÄUM. Decidedly esoteric peek at the comical life of Karl Valentin, the German counterpart of Charlie Chaplin, and his partner Liesl Karlstadt. Curiosities include sham skeletons encased in the stone wall and a nail in the wall upon which Valentin hung up his first career as a carpenter. *(Isartorturm (Tal 50). S-Bahn #1-8 to "Isartor." ☎ 22 32 66. Open M-Tu and F-Sa 11:01am-5:29pm, Su 10:01am-5:29pm. 299Pfennig, students 149Pfennig.)*

🎷 ENTERTAINMENT

THEATER AND OPERA

Munich's cultural cachet rivals the world's best. Its natives are great fun lovers and hedonists, yet they reserve a place for folksy kitsch, cultivating a supreme and diverse *Szene* with something for everyone. Sixty theaters of various sizes are scattered throughout the city. Styles range from dramatic classics at the **Residenztheater** and **Volkstheater** to comic opera at the **Staatstheater am Gärtnerpl.** to experimental works at the **Theater im Marstall** in Nymphenburg. Standing tickets run around DM10. Munich's **opera festival** (in July) is held in the Bayerische Staatsoper (below) and is accompanied by a concert series in the Nymphenburg and Schleißheim palaces. The *Monatsprogramm* (DM2.50) lists schedules for all of Munich's stages, museums, and festivals.

Munich shows its more bohemian face with scores of small fringe theaters, cabaret stages, art cinemas, and artsy pubs in **Schwabing. LeopoldStr.,** the main avenue leading up from the university, can be magical on a warm summer night in its own gaudy way—milling youthful crowds, art students hawking their work, and terrace-cafes create an exciting swarm. At the turn of the century this area was a distinguished center of European cultural and intellectual life, housing luminaries such as Brecht, Mann, Klee, Georgi, Kandinsky, Spengler, and Trotsky.

■ **Bayerische Staatsoper,** Max-Joseph-pl. 2 (tickets ☎21 85 19 30; recorded information ☎21 85 19 19). U-Bahn #3-6 to "Odeonspl." or streetcar #19 to "Nationaltheater." Standing-room and reduced-rate student tickets (DM7-20) to the numerous operas and ballets are sold at Maximilianstr. 11 (☎26 46 20), behind the opera house, or 1hr. before performance at the side entrance on Maximilianstr. Box office open M-F 10am-6pm, Sa 10am-1pm. No performances Aug. to mid-Sept.

Gasteig Kulturzentrum, Rosenheimer Str. 5 (☎48 09 80). S-Bahn #1-8 to "Rosenheimer pl." or streetcar #18 to "Am Gasteig." The most modern concert hall in Germany, the Kulturzentrum hosts musical performances ranging from classical to non-Western in its 3 concert halls and visual arts center. The hall rests on the former site of the Bürgerbräukeller, where Adolf Hitler launched his abortive Beer Hall Putsch. Features the **Munich Philharmonic** and a wide range of events, readings, and ballet. Box office in the Glashalle (☎54 89 89) open M-F 10am-6pm, Sa 10am-2pm, and 1hr. before performances.

Staatstheater, Gärtnerpl. 3 (☎21 85 90 60). U-Bahn #1 or 2 to "Fraunhoferstr." and follow Reichenbachstr. to Gärtnerpl.; or bus #52 or 56 to "Gärtnerpl." Stages comic opera and musicals. Tickets available 4 weeks before each performance at the Staatstheater box office (☎20 24 11). Standing room tickets start at DM19. Open M-F 10am-6pm, Sa 10am-1pm, and 1hr. before performance.

Drehleier, Rosenheimer Str. 123 (☎48 27 42). S-Bahn #1-8 or bus #51 to "Rosenheimer pl." A mixture of theater, cabaret, and performance art romps across this offbeat stage. One of the best cabaret scenes in Munich. Kitchen serves inexpensive salads and noodle dishes (DM6-15) until 10pm. Reservations required. Open Tu-Sa 6:30pm-1am. Performances Tu-Sa 10:30pm. Tickets DM20-30.

Münchner Kammerspiele, Maximilianstr. 26 (tickets ☎233 37 00; recorded information ☎23 72 13 26). Streetcar #19 to "Maxmonument." Exceptional modern theater and classics grace its two stages. The **Schauspielhaus,** Maximilianstr. 26, shows Goethe and Shakespeare (tickets DM11-59). The **Werkraum,** Hildegardstr. 1, features avant-garde and critical leftist pieces. Standing room tickets DM1.50. Tickets available 1 week in advance. Box office open M-F 10am-6pm, Sa 10am-1pm. Renovations are anticipated for 2001-2003.

Prinzregententheater, Prinzregentenpl. 12 (tickets ☎21 85 28 99, recorded information ☎21 85 29 59). U-Bahn #4 to "Prinzregentenpl.", or bus #53 or 54 to "Prinzregentenpl.". Classic and modern opera, ballet, and plays, as well as lectures on these works, grace the many halls of this turn-of-the-century venue. Ticket prices vary from DM8 to as much as DM225, but most concerts and performances have significant student discounts. Box office open M-F 10am-6pm, Sa 10am-2pm.

FILM

English films are often dubbed; search for the initials "OF" (original language) or "OmU" (subtitled) on the poster before buying your popcorn. Munich's **film festival** generally runs for a week in late June or early July. For schedules and information, contact **Internationale Filmwoche,** Kaiserstr. 93, 80799 Munich (☎381 90 40). *In München* (free) lists movie screenings.

Cinema, Nymphenburger Str. 31 (☎55 52 55; www.cinema-muenchen.com), U-bahn #1 to Stiglmaierpl. and then walk 2 blocks west on Nymphenburger Str. This air-conditioned theater plays English language films almost exclusively, many of which are current and American. Tickets can be purchased up to a week in advance; admission DM9.50, students DM8.90; matinees weekdays before 5pm DM7.50.

MAXX, Isartorpl. 9 (☎24 63 62 99; www.cinemaxx.de), S-Bahn #1-8 to "Isartor" (follow exit signs for "Deutsches Museum") or streetcar #17 or 18 to "Isartorpl.". This self-proclaimed Film Palace on the Isartor plays a mix of current German and American films. Tickets can be reserved in advance for free online or for a charge of DM1 per ticket over the telephone. Admission M-Tu DM10, W-Th DM13.50 (matinees DM11.50), F-Su DM16.50 (matinees DM13); no student discount, but children under 12 DM9.

Museum Lichtspiele, Lilienstr. 2 (☎48 24 03), by the Ludwigsbrücke and the Deutsches Museum. S-Bahn #1-6 or streetcar #18 to "Isartor." Holds the world's record—24 years and counting—for most consecutive daily screenings of the *Rocky Horror Picture Show* (4pm). English-language films daily. Admission DM12.50; students and seniors DM10.50. Monday is Movieday, with reduced admission (DM8.50).

Türkendolch, Türkenstr. 74 (☎271 88 44), in the middle of the student district, has mini-film festivals dedicated to particular directors and themes. Admission M-Tu DM8.50, W-F DM12 (DM 9.90 matinee), Sa-Su DM12.

◪ NIGHTLIFE

Munich's nightlife is a curious collision of Bavarian *Gemütlichkeit* and trendy cliquishness. Representatives of the latter trait are often referred to as *Schicki-Mickis,* loosely defined as club-going German yuppies—expensively dressed, coiffed and sprayed, beautiful, shapely specimens of both sexes. With a healthy mix of students and other less pretentious locals, the streets bustle with raucous beer halls, loud discos, and exclusive cafes every night of the week. The locals tend to tackle their nightlife as an epic voyage. The odyssey begins at one of Munich's beer gardens or beer halls (see **Beer, Beer, and More Beer,** below), which generally close before midnight and are most crowded in the early evening. The alcohol keeps flowing at cafes and bars, which, except for Friday and Saturday nights, shut off their taps at 1am. Then the discos and dance clubs, sedate before midnight, suddenly spark and throb relentlessly until 4am. The trendy bars, cafes, cabarets, and discos plugged into **Leopoldstr.** in **Schwabing** attract tourists from all over Europe (see **Entertainment,** p. 257). For easy access, dig the jaded hipster-wear out of your pack, or at least leave the baseball hat and T-shirt at home. A few more tips: no tennis shoes, no shorts, and no sandals (no, not even Birkenstocks—or haven't you noticed yet that you're the only person in Germany wearing them?). On weekends, appearance is especially important.

The **Muffathalle,** Zellstr. 4 (☎45 87 50 10; www.muffathalle.de), in Haidhausen, is a former power plant that generates hip student energy with techno, hip-hop, jazz, and dance performances. Take S-Bahn #1-8 to "Rosenheimerpl." and walk toward the river on Rosenheimerstr. for two blocks, or streetcar #18 to "Deutsches Museum." (Open M-Sa 6pm-4am, Su 4pm-1am. Cover starts at DM10 and varies depending on events.) Munich's alternative concert scene goes on at **Feierwerk,** Hansastr. 39-41 (☎769 36 00), which has seven stages and huge tents. Take S-Bahn #7 or U-Bahn #4 or 5 to "Heimeranpl.," then walk left down Hansastr. (10min.). In summer, there's lots of independent music, comedy, beer gardens, *Imbiße,* blues, and rock. Beer gardens open at 6pm; doors usually open at 8:30pm and concerts begin at 9pm. **Münchener Freiheit** is the most famous (and most touristy) bar and cafe district. The southwestern section of Schwabing, directly behind the university on Amalienstr. and Türkenstr is more low-key. (see **Food,** p. 251).

Scads of culture and nightlife guides are available to help you sort out Munich's scene. Pick up *Munich Found, in München,* or *Prinz* (the hippest) at any newsstand to find out what's up. Big-name pop artists often perform at the **Olympihalle,** while the **Olympia-Stadion** on the northern edge of town hosts mega-concerts. Check listings for dates and ticket information or call ☎30 67 24 24.

BEER, BEER, AND MORE BEER

The six great Munich labels are *Augustiner, Hacker-Pschorr, Hofbräu, Löwenbräu, Paulaner,* and *Spaten-Franziskaner,* yet most restaurants and *Gaststätte* will pick a side by only serving one brewery's beer. There are four main types of beer served in Munich: **Helles** and **Dunkles,** standard but delicious light and dark beers; **Weißbier,** a cloudy blond beer made from wheat instead of barley; and **Radler** (literally "cyclist's brew"), which is half beer and half lemon soda. Munich's beer typically has an alcohol content of 3.5%, though in *Starkbierzeit* (which runs two weeks, beginning with Lent), Müncheners traditionally drink *Salvator,* a strong, dark beer that is 5.5% alcohol. *Prost!* In May, art folk clean their palates with *Marbock,* a blond Bockbier. *Frühschoppen* is a morning beer-and-sausage

---

BEER GARDEN HISTORY 101 The official coat-of-arms of Munich depicts a monk holding a Bible in his right hand. Unofficially, the monk's left hand firmly clenches a large, frothy beer, raising it high and, with a twinkle in the eye, saying *"Prost."* Sacrilege? Not at all. In 1328, the Augustiner monks introduced *Bier* to unsuspecting Müncheners, who have since continued the trend. Bayern proudly holds the title as the largest producer *and* consumer of beer in Germany—in a mighty big way. Local breweries produce 123 million gallons of "liquid bread" per annum; 150,000 seats in Munich beer gardens beckon the thirsty; and every year, the average local imbibes more than 220 liters of the amber dew, more than twice the average drunk in the rest of Germany (though the figure does include the mighty Oktoberfest, during which locals and visitors together swig five million liters). The tradition of beer gardens in Bavaria is said to have begun with King Ludwig I, who allowed brewers to sell beer, but not food, in an outdoor restaurant setting. All citizens could afford to indulge in this yummy beverage by bringing their own meals to the gardens. Many of Munich's beer gardens today are shaded by large-leafed chestnut trees, planted before the invention of refrigeration to keep the ground above the storage cellars cool. Proudly honoring the *Reinheitsgebot* (Beer Purity Law; see p. 34) of 1516, Bavarians reaffirm their exalted and earned reputation as the ultimate, tried-and-true beer connoisseurs.

---

ritual. *"Ein Bier, bitte"* will get you a liter, known as a *Maß* (DM8-11). If you want a half-*Maß* (DM4-6), you must specify it, but many establishments will only serve *Weißbier* in 0.5L sizes. Though some beer gardens offer non-meaty dishes, vegetarians may wish to eat elsewhere before hitting a beer garden for a post-meal swig. For an online guide to Munich's beer gardens, visit www.biergarten.com.

The longest beer festival in the world, Munich's **Oktoberfest** runs the last two weeks in September (Sept. 22-Oct. 7, 2001). The site of this uncontrolled revelry is the **Theresienwiese,** or *"Wies'n"* (shortened perhaps after one *Maß* too many). Ride U-Bahn #4 or 5 to "Theresienwiese." The festivities began in 1810 when Prince Ludwig married Princess Therese von Sachsen-Hildburghausen; ironically, no alcohol was served at the original reception. But it was so much fun that Müncheners have repeated the revelry every year. Oktoberfest kicks off with speeches, a parade of horse-drawn beer wagons, and the tapping of the ceremonial first *Faß* (barrel). The touristy *Hofbräu* tent is the rowdiest; fights often break out. Arrive early (by 4:30pm) to get a table—you must be seated to be served at Oktoberfest.

WITHIN MUNICH

🍺 **Augustinerkeller,** Arnulfstr. 52 (☎59 43 93), at Zirkus-Krone-Str. S-Bahn #1-8 to "Hackerbrücke." Founded in 1824, *Augustiner* is viewed by most *Müncheners* as the finest beer garden in town. Lush grounds and dim lighting beneath 100-year-old chestnut trees and tasty, enormous *Brez'n* (pretzels; DM5.50) support their assertion. The real attraction is the delicious, sharp *Augustiner* beer (*Maß* DM10.50), which entices locals, smart tourists, and students. Food DM4-28. Open daily 10am-1am; hot food until 10pm. Beer garden open daily 10:30am-midnight or 1am, depending on weather.

🍺 **Hirschgarten,** Hirschgarten 1 (☎17 25 91). U-Bahn #1 to "Rotkreuzpl.," then streetcar #12 to "Romanpl." Walk south to the end of Guntherstr. and enter the Hirschgarten—literally, "deer garden." The largest beer garden in Europe (seating 9000 people) is boisterous and pleasant, but somewhat remote near Schloß Nymphenburg. Families head here for the grassy park and carousel, and to see the deer which are still kept on the premises. Entrees DM7.60-25.90. For dessert, their *Münchener Apfelstrudel* with vanilla ice cream and Sahne (DM 8.60) is a worthwhile splurge. *Maß* DM9.30. Open daily 9am-midnight, kitchen open until 10pm. Restaurant closed Mondays Nov.-Feb.

Hofbräuhaus, Am platzl 9 (☎22 16 76), 2 blocks from Marienpl. In 1589, Bavarian Duke Wilhelm the Pious earned his epithet by founding the Münchener Hofbräuhaus for the worship of Germany's most revered beverages. Although the Hofbräuhaus was originally reserved for royalty and invited guests, a 19th century proclamation lowered the price of its beer below normal city prices to "offer the Military and working classes a healthy and good tasting drink". Since then, tourism has steadily inflated the cost. 15,000-30,000L of beer are sold per day, mostly to uninitiated souls who have pilgrimaged far and wide for a taste of Hofbräuhaus ambrosia. Yet, there remain many Stammtische (reserved tables) for locals, and a good number of *Müncheners* keep their personal steins in the beer hall's safe. Beer garden out back under chestnut trees. To avoid tourists, go in the early afternoon. *Maß* DM11.40. *Weißwürste* with pretzel DM7.90. Open daily 9am-midnight with live *Blasmusik* every day.

Am Seehaus, Kleinhesselohe 3 (☎381 61 30). U-Bahn #6 to "Dietlindenstr.," then bus #44 direction "Giesing" to "Osterwaldstr." Directly on the Kleinhesseloher See in the Englischer Garten. Beloved by locals for the lack of tourists. Observe the courtship rituals of several species of duck while enjoying a *Maß* (DM11) or small *Brez'n* (DM1.60). Open M-F 11am-midnight, Sa-Su 10am-midnight. Beer garden closes at 11pm.

Taxisgarten, Taxisstr. 12 (☎15 68 27). U-Bahn #1 to "Rotkreuzpl.," then bus #83 or 177 to "Klugstr.", then walk one block east on Tizianstr. This beer garden is a gem—its small size (1500 chairs) has kept it a favorite of locals and students. Almost always full. One of few places that serves a green variety of the normally orange Bavarian specialty *Obazer* (a mix of cheeses, DM3.80). Jumbo *Brez'n* DM5.50. *Maß* DM10.20, *Weißbier* DM5.50. Open daily 11am-11pm.

Paulanerkeller, Hochstr. 77 (☎459 91 30). U-Bahn #2 or 7 to "Silberhornstr.," then bus #15 or 25, direction "Max-Weber-Pl.", to "Ostfriedhof." Walk west down St. Bonifatius Str. over the bridge and to the right. It's big, old, and well-known among locals for its year-round sale of the strong, dark beer called *Salvator*. Remotely located on Nockherberg hill with a thirtysomething crowd. *Maß Salvator* DM11.80, *Maß* original *Münchner Helles* DM9.90. *Brez'n and Knödel* DM11.80. Open daily 10am-11pm.

Chinesischer Turm, (☎38 38 73 19), in the Englischer Garten next to the pagoda. U-Bahn #3 or 6 to "Giselastr." or bus #54 from Südbahnhof to "Chinesischer Turm." A fair-weather tourist favorite next to a very pricey restaurant; lots of kids. *Maß* DM11. Pretzels DM5.50. Open daily in balmy weather 10am-11pm.

Löwenbräukeller, Nymphenburger Str. 2 (☎52 60 21). U-Bahn #1 or 7 to "Stiglmaierpl." Castle-like entrance, festive and loud beer hall, pleasant garden. Come here to taste the real *Löwenbräu* if you dare. The bitter and somewhat dilute taste has a loyal core of local followers, despite general disapproval—it's considered by some to be the Budweiser of Munich beers. The *Speisenzeytung* (menu) is written in Bavarian dialect with German translations (traditional entrees DM8.90-28.90). 0.5L beer DM4.40. Kitchen open 11am-midnight. Open daily 8am-1am.

Pschorr-Keller, Theresienhöhe 7 (☎50 10 88). U-Bahn #4 or 5 to "Theresienwiese." An outpost of the *Hacker-Pschorr* brewery along with the Hackerkeller down the street; right next to the Oktoberfest grounds. Good stuff. Come here for an interesting, fruity brew, to be enjoyed mostly in the company of locals. *Maß* DM11.20. Meals DM10-20; weißwurst DM3.60 per piece. Open daily 11am-11pm.

Augustiner Bräustuben, Landsberger Str. 19 (☎50 70 47). S-Bahn #1-8 to "Hackerbrücke." Relatively new beer hall in the *Augustiner* brewery's former horse stalls. DM4.40 for 0.5L. For the hungry horse, try the *Bräustüberl* (duck, two types of pork, Kraut, and two types of dumplings; DM16.50). Other delicious heaps of Bavarian food come at excellent prices (DM7.50-18.80, daily specials DM7.50-11.50). *Maß* DM9. Especially popular in winter. Open daily 10am-midnight. Kitchen open 11am-11pm.

Augustiner, Neuhauser Str. 27 (☎23 18 32 57). Across from the Michaelskirche. Smaller manifestation of the Keller of the same name. Beer hall and sidewalk tables on the pedestrian zone between the station and Marienpl. The restaurant on the right offers the same selection of food, but at higher prices than the beer hall. Bavarian meals DM7.40-27.80. Beer hall *Maß* DM11.20. Ice cream desserts DM3.70-9.50. Beer hall and restaurant open daily 9am-midnight. Kitchen open until 11pm.

BEER GARDEN HISTORY 102: THE ROAD LESS TRAVELED

A well-kept secret guarded by locals in-the-know is Munich's close proximity to the Weihenstephan brewery, the oldest brewery in the world and, some would argue, home to the world's finest brew. In the year 1020, Benedictine monks built a monastery in the tiny town of Freising, 30km north of Munich. Twenty years later, under the direction of Arnold the Right, these crafty men of the cloth said, "Let there be beer"; hence, the world's oldest brewery was born. Since then, Weihenstephaner beer has nourished more than just the people of Freising; its quality was so high that the Hofbräuhaus served it for a time next to its own beer. In 1931, the good brothers at Weihenstephan built a small beer hall and garden at the brewery, and pilgrimages from Munich for a taste of these divine brews can be made with relatively little effort. To get there, take S-Bahn #1 to Freising, then walk down Vöttingerstr. out of the town proper; the brewery will be on your left at the top of the hill.

JUST OUTSIDE MUNICH

Waldwirtschaft Großhesselohe, Georg-Kalb-Str. 3 (☎79 50 88). S-Bahn #7 to "Großhesselohe Isartalbahnhof." From the train station, follow Kastanian Allee and turn right on Georg-Kolb-Str; bear left at the three-way and follow the sign (15min.). Relaxed beer garden with live music daily from noon (no cover). Classic and international jazz Sundays at noon. On a sunny day, schedule a Frühschoppen session for 11am or so. *Maß* DM11. Open daily 11am-11pm.

Forschungsbräuerei, Unterhachinger Str. 76 (☎670 11 69). From the train station, turn left on Schneckestr., right on Sebastian-Bauer-Str., left on Fasengartenstr., and left on Unterhachingerstr. (10min.). Pleasant, comfortable tables under arching trees. In-house brewery provides fresh beer using an experimentally taste-tested recipe; the name means "research brewery." *Maß* DM10.80. Open Tu-Sa 11am-11pm, Su 10am-10pm.

BARS

Many of the city's charming cafes (see **Food,** p. 251) double as hip nightly haunts. A few stalwarts only open the doors for drink after 5pm, and by 1am many squeeze revelers out into more late-night joints. Also see **Beer, Beer, and More Beer,** p. 259.

Reitschule, Königstr. 34 (☎33 34 02). U-Bahn #3 or 6 to "Giselastr." Above a club, with windows overlooking a horseback-riding school. Marble tables and a sleek bar. Also a cafe with a beer garden out back. Rumor has it this is where Boris Becker met his wife. *Weißbier* DM6. Breakfast served all day. Open daily 9am-1am.

Master's Home, Frauenstr. 11 (☎21 69 09). U-Bahn #3 or 6 or S-Bahn #1-8 to "Marienplatz." A tremendous stuffed peacock greets visitors as they descend the gold painted staircase to the subterranean bar and *faux* private home. Lounge in the elegant living room with books and velvet furniture, relax in the bedroom, or chill in the tub with a beer in hand. Gourmet Italian and *Schicki-Mickis* in the restaurant (meals DM15-30), with a more relaxed crowd in the bar. Mixed drinks DM11.50, other drinks similarly highbrow in price. Weekdays comfortable, weekends mobbed. Open daily 6:30pm-3am.

Scalar Lounge, Seitzstr. 12 (☎21 57 96 36.) U-Bahn to "Odeonspl." Small and hidden, you'll find the heaviest drinkers in München here—fish. Aquariums dot the walls of this tiny bar. Beer DM6.50. Drinks DM6-15. Open Tu-Su 9am-3pm.

Lux, Reichenbachstr. 37 (☎20 23 83 93). U-Bahn to "Frauenhofer." Large pastel asterisks decorate the walls of this popular hang-out. Sit at the bar or at one of the black lacquer tables. Drinks DM8-20. Open M-Th 6pm-1am, F-Sa 8pm-2am.

Günther Murphy's, Nikolaistr. 9a (☎39 89 11). U-Bahn #3 or 6 to "Giselastr." Cozy up in the "snuggle-box" with a Guinness (DM5-7.50). Irish cheer accompanies each serving of scrumptious British and American food (DM9-30). Sells cigars; DM2.50 for regular or DM4.90 for "Lewinsky" size. Open M-F 5pm-1am, Sa 2pm-2am, Su noon-1am.

Rincon Restaurant-Bar, Rumfordstr. 34 (☎21 93 93 40). U-Bahn to "Frauenhofer." Candles throughout the restaurant give Rincon a subtle glow—bright enough to check out people, and dark enough to make them look uncommonly good. Offers two stories of candlelight madness—check out the armchairs on the balcony. Restaurant is expensive, but a surefire way to impress your date. Open M-F 11am-1am, Sa-Su 10am-1pm.

Treznjewski, Theresienstr. 72 (☎22 23 49). U-Bahn #2 to "Theresienstr." Handsome bar with dark wood and stylish frescoes. Good cocktails and chatty crowds until way late. Entrees DM15-30. Beer DM5. Open daily 8pm-3am.

Tabacco, Hartmannstr. 8 (☎22 72 16). U-Bahn to "Marienpl." Have dessert (DM8.50), drink (DM8-20), and enjoy this bar blissfully overlooked by all the tourists passing by. Open M-S 5pm-3am.

MUSIC BARS

Nachtcafe, Maximilianspl. 5 (☎59 59 00). U-Bahn #4 or 5 or S-Bahn #1-8 to "Karlsplatz." Live jazz, funk, soul, and blues until the wee hours. The chic and the wannabes rub shoulders in this modern jet-black bar. Very *schicki-micki*. Things don't get rolling until midnight. Breakfast served after 2am. No cover, but outrageous prices and a bouncer—easy-going weekdays, very picky on weekends when you'll have to look the part. On warm summer evenings the porch cafe is packed with elegant Müncheners drinking cocktails by moonlight. Beer DM8 (0.3L).

Shamrock, Trautenwolfstr. 6 (☎33 10 81). U-Bahn #3 or 6 to "Giselastr." Live music runs the gamut from blues and soul to Irish fiddling to rock in this cozy Irish pub. Irish soccer highlights on Sundays. Guinness DM7.50. Pizza DM10-13. Open M-Th, Su 5pm-1am, F 5pm-3am, Sa 2pm-3am.

Zur Unterfahrt Club 2, Kirchenstr. 96 (☎48 95 06 36). S-Bahn #1-8 or U-Bahn #5 to "Ostbahnhof." Corner of Kirchenstr. and Orleanstr. Alternative rock and jazz nights; 2-3 live performances per week. Open daily 7pm-1am. Cover for shows DM10 and up.

DANCE CLUBS

🏠**Kunstpark Ost,** Grafinger Str. 6 (☎49 00 29 28; www.kunstpark.de). U-Bahn #5 or S-Bahn #1-8 to "Ostbahnhof;" follow signs for the "Kunstpark Ost" exit, turn right onto Friedenstr. and then left onto Grafinger Str; the Park is half a block down on the right. The newest and biggest addition to the Munich nightlife scene, this huge complex with 40 different venues swarms with young people hitting clubs, concerts, and bars—but most of all, dancing the night away. Try the psychedelic-trance **Natraj Temple** (☎49 00 18 95; open F-Sa), the alternative cocktail and disco joint **K41** (☎49 04 21 60, www.k41.de; open every night), the very chill cigars and drinks mecca **Cohibar** (☎49 00 33 12; open W-Sa), or the risque South American rock bar **Titty Twister** (☎49 04 21 10; open W-Sa), among many other venues and patios. Hours, cover, and themes vary—call the info and advance ticket number (above) or get ahold of the monthly magazine *Kunstpark* for details on specific club nights and specials.

Backstage, Helmholtzstr. 18 (☎18 33 30). S-Bahn #1-8 to "Donnersberger Brücke." Wide range of music, but mostly "little Seattle," hip-hop, and techno. Mixed crowd, with lots of nose rings and green hair. Huge outdoor beer garden. Open W-Th 9pm-3am, F 10pm-5am, Sa 9pm-5am. No cover.

Nachtwerk and Club, Landesberger Str. 185 (☎578 38 00). Streetcar #18 or 19 or bus #83 to "Lautensackstr." The older, larger **Nachtwerk** spins mainstream dance tunes for sweaty mainstream crowds in a packed warehouse. Saturday is the beloved "Best of the 50s to the 90s" night. Its little sister **Club** offers a 2-level dance floor, just as tight and swinging as its next-door neighbor. Mixtures of rock, trip-hop, house, acid jazz, and rare grooves. Be aware that Sunday night is a rehashing of German oldies. Beer DM4.50 at both places. Open daily 10pm-4am. Cover DM10 for both.

Reactor, Domagkstr. 33 (☎324 44 23), in the Alabamahalle. U-Bahn #6 to "Alte Heide." Situated along with three other discos on a former military base in Schwabing. Techno, house, and German oldies. Open F-Sa 9pm-4am. Try **Millennium Club** for techno highlights (Th-Su 9pm-6am; cover DM10-15), **Alabama** for German oldies (F-Sa 9pm-4am; drinks free until 1am), or **Schwabinger Ballhouse** for international jams (F-Sa 10pm-4am. Cover DM15, all drinks DM1).

Opera, Helmholtzstr. 12 (☎129 79 69). S-Bahn #1-8 to "Donnersberger Brücke." A wacky warehouse disco offering some of the cheapest drinks in town (DM1-3). Offers a mix of hip-hop, techno, and that oh-so-special Friday-night "drink-dance-and-kiss" party. Open W-Sa 10pm-4am. Cover DM7.

Pulverturm, Schleißheimer Str. 393 (☎351 99 99). U-Bahn #2 to "Harthof"; it's 15min. from the stop. A bit far out (geographically and otherwise), this dance club with beer garden lacks the pretension of Munich's other venues. Beer DM5.50. Anything from psychedelic to grunge; F is indie rock and Su kicks back with reggae. Open daily 10pm-4am. Cover DM10.

GAY AND LESBIAN MUNICH

Although Bayern has the reputation of being intolerant of homosexuality, Munich sustains a respectably vibrant gay nightlife. The center of Munich's homosexual scene lies within the **"Golden Triangle,"** stretching from the area south of the Sendlinger Tor through the Viktualienmarkt/Gärtnerpl. area to the Isartor. Bars, cafes, and clubs of all atmospheres abound. Pick up the free, extensive booklet *Rosa Seiten* at **Max&Milian Bookstore,** Ickstattstr. 2 (☎260 33 20; open M-F 10:30am-2pm and 3:30-8pm, Sa 11am-4pm), or at any other gay locale, for extensive listings of gay nightlife hotspots and services. The **Schwules Kommunikations- und Kulturzentrum** offers an array of telephone services for gay men. Some English is spoken, depending on the staff. (General information ☎260 30 56; violence hotline ☎192 28; counseling ☎194 46. Open Su-Th 7-11pm, F-Sa 7pm-midnight.) For lesbian information, call **Lesbentelefon.** (☎725 42 72. Open M,W 2:30-5pm, Tu 10:30am-1pm, and Th 7-9pm.) **Sapphovision,** a lesbian film center at the **Frauenzentrum Treibhaus,** Güllstr. 3 (☎77 40 41), shows films every second Friday of the month. **Lillemor's Frauenbuchladen,** Barerstr. 70 (☎271 12 05; www.divas.de), the oldest women's book store in Germany, provides information for lesbians is the homepage of the bi-weekly Divas Frauenfest and an excellent introduction to Munich's lesbian nightlife.

■ **Bei Carla,** Buttermelcherstr. 9 (☎22 79 01). S-Bahn #1-8 to "Isartor," then walk 1 block south on Rumfordstr., turn left on Klenzestr., then another left onto Buttermelcherstr. This charming and friendly lesbian cafe and bar is one of Munich's best-kept secrets. Many women, mostly in their 20s and 30s, flock here for pleasant conversation, a few cocktails, and a round or two of darts. Open M-Sa 4pm-1am, Su 6pm-1am.

Sappho, Corneliusstr. 16 (☎202 12 96). U-Bahn #1, 2, 7, or 8 to Fraunhoferstr., then walk north on Reichenbachstr. to Gärtnerpl. and turn right. This pleasant lesbian cafe transforms into a swinging disco on F and Sa nights; groove to chart hits and oldies under the gigantic gold disco ball. Open Su-Th 7pm-1am; F, Sa 7pm-3am.

Inge's Karotte, Baaderstr. 13 (☎201 06 69). S-Bahn #1-8 to "Isartor", then walk south on Baaderstr. for 2 blocks. The oldest lesbian bar in Munich, Inge's Karotte also attracts an older crowd (mostly women in their 30s and 40s). The tiny, dimly-lit bar provides an intimate environment. Open M-F 4pm-1am, Sa 6pm-1am.

Fortuna Musikbar, Maximiliansplatz. 5, (☎55 40 70; www.fortuna-muenchen.de). U-Bahn #4 or 5 or S-Bahn #1-8 to "Karlspl.," then walk northeast along the Ring until you hit Maximiliansplatz. A hip and popular disco for lesbians. The place on F evenings for salsa. Open Th-Sa 10:30pm-6am. Cover DM10.

Soul City, Maximilianspl. 5 (☎59 52 72; www.soul-city.de), at the intersection with Max-Joseph-Str. Purportedly the biggest gay disco in Bayern; music ranges from 70s disco to Latin to techno. Straights always welcome. Beer DM7.50 (0.3L). Open W-Sa, 10pm-late. Cover DM10-25.

Morizz, Klenzestr. 43 (☎201 67 76). U-Bahn #1 or 2 to "Fraunhofer Str." Reminiscent of certain Casablanca scenes, this relaxed cafe and bar is frequented by gay men. Settle into the low red sofa chairs and enjoy a cocktail (DM12-16). European and Thai dishes available until 12:30am; Thai curry DM19, pasta and other entrees DM18-26. Open Su-Th 7pm-2am, F-Sa 7pm-3am.

New York, Sonnenstr. 25 (☎59 10 56; www.newyork-munich.de). U-Bahn #1-3 or 6 to "Sendlinger Tor." Fashionable gay men dance the night away. Laser show F-Su 11:30pm. Open daily 11pm-4am. Cover F-Su DM10 (includes drinks).

cafe Nil, Hans-Sach-Str. 2 (☎26 55 45). U-Bahn #1 or 2 to "Fraunhofer Str." Take a right out of the U-Bahn down Klenzestr., a right on Ickstattstr., and a right on Hans-Sach-Str. Sleek cafe that's a day- and nighttime meeting place for gay men, mostly in their 30s. Mobbed on weekends. Beer DM5 (0.4L), pasta DM13.50. Open daily 3pm-3am.

✺ FESTIVALS: OKTOBERFEST

Every fall, hordes of tourists make an unholy pilgrimage to Munich, Edenic city of alcohol, when it is in full bloom. From the middle of September until early October, it's all about consuming beer, and the numbers for this festival have become truly mindboggling: six million participants chug five million liters of beer, but only on a full stomach of 200,000 *Würste*. The Oktoberfest was inaugurated on October 12, 1810, to celebrate the wedding of crown prince Ludwig (later king Ludwig I of Bavaria) and Princess Theresa. Representatives from all over Bavaria met outside the gates of the city, celebrating on fields they named the *Theresenwiese* in honor of the bride; the party was so successful they decided to have it again the following year. The Oktoberfest of old was marked by horse races, but this tradition has since been abandoned. However, the agricultural shows inaugurated in 1811 are still held every three years, and standard fair fare, including carousels and touristy kitch remain to amuse beer-guzzling participants.

The Oktoberfest begins with the "Grand Entry of the Oktoberfest Landlords and Breweries," which ends around noon with the drinking of the ceremonial first keg, to the cry of *O'zapft is!*, or "it's tapped." Other special events include international folklore presentations, a costume and rifleman's parade, and an open-air Oktoberfest music concert. Each of Munich's breweries set up tents in the Theresienwiese. You must have a seat to be served alcohol, and it's usually best to call in advance and reserve one. The drinking hours are relatively short (no all night Love-Parade-style partying on the fairgrounds), ranging from 9am to 10:30pm, depending on the day; the fairground attractions and sideshows are open slightly later. For all those who share a love of alcohol with their kin, there are family days with reduced prices.

🏃 DAYTRIP FROM MUNICH: DACHAU

From Munich, take S-Bahn #2 (direction: "Petershausen") to "Dachau" (20min., DM7.60, or 4 stripes on the Streifenkarte), then bus #724 (direction: "Kraütgarten") or 726 (direction: "Kopernikusstr.") from in front of the station to "KZ-Gedenkstätte" (10min., DM1.90 or one stripe on the Streifenkarte). Informative but lengthy two-hour tours of the camp in English leave from the museum. July daily 12:30pm, Aug.-June Sa-Su, and holidays at 12:30pm. DM5 donation requested. Call ☎(08131) 17 41 for more information.

"Once they burn books, they will end up burning people," wrote German poet Heinrich Heine in 1820. His warning is posted at the Dachau concentration camp, next to a photograph of a Nazi book-burning. The walls, gates, gas chamber, and crematorium have been restored since 1962 in a chillingly sparse memorial to the victims of Dachau, the first German concentration camp and the model for the network of 3,000 work and concentration camps erected in Nazi-occupied Europe. Once tightly-packed barracks are now, for the most part, only foundations. However, survivors ensured that at least two barracks would be reconstructed to teach future generations about the 206,000 prisoners who were interned here from 1933 to 1945. Residents of the city of Dachau—it is important to remember that there *is* a town here, which lives in the shadow of the camp every day—watch visitors with uncertainty, and even insecurity. While the concentration camp is treated as a tourist attraction by many, it is first and foremost a memorial.

BAVARIA

The wrought-iron gate at the **Jourhaus,** formerly the only entrance to the camp, reads *Arbeit Macht Frei* (Work Sets One Free); it was the first sight as prisoners entered the camp. There is also a Jewish memorial, a Protestant commemorative chapel, and the Catholic **Todesangst Christi-Kapelle** (Christ in Agony Church) on the grounds. (For more on the issues surrounding concentration camps, see **The Holocaust,** p. 15.) The museum, located in the former administrative buildings, examines pre-1930s anti-Semitism, the rise of Nazism, the establishment of the concentration camp system, and the lives of prisoners through photographs, documents, and artifacts. The thick guide (DM25, available in English) translates the propaganda posters, SS files, documents, and letters. Most exhibits are accompanied by short captions in English. Also on display are texts of the letters from prisoners to their families as well as internal SS memos. A short film (22min.) is screened in English at noon, 2 and 3:30pm. A new display in the **Bunker,** the concentration camp's prison and torture chamber, chronicles the lives and experiences of the camp's special prisoners and the barbarism of SS guards. The camp is open Tu-Su 9am-5pm.

Dachau's tiny **tourist office,** Konrad-Adenauer-Str. 1, has information on the city and sells maps for DM1. From the train station, follow Langhammerstr. to Münchnerstr., make a right and keep going straight when Münchnerstr. becomes Karlsberg. (☎(08131) 845 66; fax 845 29. Open M-F 9am-6pm, Sa 9am-noon.) A 16th-century castle and a parish church built in the year 920 top the Altstadt. Tours in German of the castle and the church leave from the front of the modern **Rathaus,** across the street from the tourist office. (Tours May-Oct. Sa-Su 3pm. DM6, children and students DM3. Castle open Tu-Su 10am-5:45pm. DM3, children DM1.5.)

ALLGÄU

Stretching from the balmy shores of the Bodensee (Lake Constance) to the snow-capped peaks along the Austrian border, the Allgäu region boasts inimitably charming villages, while the surrounding alpine landscape offers some of the most beautiful hiking trails in the world. Largely ignored by international tourists, the Allgäu region provides Germans with an exquisite haven for skiing and hiking

ACROSS THE WAVES. For coverage of Lindau and the Bodensee, see Baden-Württemberg, p. 389

MEMMINGEN   ☎ 08331

At the foothills of the Allgäu Alps, Memmingen is not a town of blinding glory, but the 13th-century fortifications of this former free imperial city and its colorful Rococo buildings can easily charm a visitor into a two-hour stroll. The smells of specialties from both Schwaben and Bayern fill the air, and locals indulging in these culinary pleasures sit munching and sipping on crowded pedestrian streets.

The white **Rathaus** in the Marktpl. sports a 16th-century facade, spruced up in 1765 with some Rococo additions. Off Marktpl. on Zangmeisterstr., the Gothic **St. Martinskirche,** built in the 15th century, swims in frescoes. Walking straight down Kramerstr. through the pedestrian zone and taking a left onto Lindentorstr., you'll chance upon Gerberpl. and the **Siebendächerhaus,** a half-timbered house with seven roofs designed for tanners to dry their skins, now home to an **Apotheke.**

Memmingen can be reached by **train** from **Ulm** (30min., 2 per hr., DM15); **Oberstdorf** (1½hr., 1 per hr., DM20); and **Munich** (1½hr., 1 per every 2 hrs., DM31). To get to the Altstadt, walk down Maximilianstr. from the station and take a right onto pedestrian Kramerstr. to **Marktplatz.** Or from the **ZOB** (bus terminal) near the train station take bus #4 or 6 to "Weinmarkt." (Every 30min., DM1.80.) The **tourist office,** Marktpl. 3, near the Rathaus, finds **rooms** and sells maps of nearby biking trails for DM9.80-14.80. (☎85 01 72; fax 85 01 78; email info@memmingen.de; www.memmingen.de. Open M-F 8am-5pm, Sa 9:30am-12:30pm.) Rent bikes from **Matthäus**

Fickler, Lindauerstr. 14, for DM10 per day (☎22 58; fax 481 22. Open M,F 9am-6pm; Tu-Th 9am-12:30pm, 2pm-6pm, Sa 9am-1pm.) The **post office,** Lindentorstr. 22, 87700 Memmingen, is near the station (open M-F 8am-6pm, Sa 9am-noon).

Memmingen's **Jugendherberge (HI),** Kempter Str. 42, pleases rowdy schoolgroups and ping-pong fans. Take Kramerstr. to Lindentorstr. and cross onto Kempter Str.; the hostel is near **Kempter Tor,** the southern gate of the city. (☎/fax 49 40 87. Breakfast included. Open Mar.-Nov. Dorm beds DM18.) Near the train station, **Gasthaus Lindenbad,** Lindenbadstr. 18, offers decent rooms. (☎32 78; fax 49 56 50. Breakfast included. Singles DM35, doubles DM70.) The historic **Roter Ochsen,** Kramerstr. 37, serves beer and food at reasonable prices in the lively pedestrian zone. (☎36 40. Open daily 11am-1am.) For cheaper *Imbiß* fare near the Marktpl., **George,** Ulmerstr. 3, has a K-E-B-A-P waterfall. (Falafel DM4, pizza DM8 and up. Open daily 9am-12:30am.) From June 6-June 16, 2001, Memmingen residents will dress in historic costumes and drink any tourist under the table during the annual **Stadtfest.**

OTTOBEUREN   ☎08332

The prime attraction of the Allgäu, Ottobeuren is renowned for its towering basilica and ▨**Benedictine Abbey,** considered the architectural height of the German Baroque. Since its foundation in 764, Ottobeuren's Benedictine abbey has metamorphosed many times. It finally settled into an 18th-century Baroque style modeled by a number of talented German and Italian artists. Marble swirls of light pink and yellow surround pudgy cherubs smiling upwards at the gold-rimmed domes. In this immense, detailed, and overwhelming bazaar of Catholic glory, a small, easily missed 12th-century statue of Christ on the first altar is the most venerated piece of art; its bent head and body position gave rise to the current layout of the abbey. Look around the main alter and see the Four Corners of relics of martyrs and saints. *(Church always open. Free.)* **Organ concerts** add song to the paradise *(Feb.-Nov. Sa at 4pm)*. The 25 monks who still roam the abbey's halls are proud to live in the most open and accessible monastery north of the Alps. Visitors are allowed to see the grandiose **library,** the impressive **Emperor's Hall,** adorned with statues of the Kaisers, and a **museum** of old church artifacts. *(Open Apr.-Oct. daily 10am-noon and 2-5pm; Nov.-Mar. M-F 10am-noon and 2-4pm, Sa-Su 10am-noon and 2-5pm. DM4, students DM2.)*

Ottobeuren does not have a functioning train station, but the town can be reached by **bus** from the Memmingen bus station, adjacent to the train station. Schedules are available at both towns' tourist offices. (Bus. #955 to "Ottobeuren," bus platform #3. 20min.; weekdays 1 per hr., Sa-Su every 2hr. DM4.30.) Get off at "Marktpl."; the church is just ahead. Rent **bikes** at **Anne's Bike Shop,** Rettenbacher Str. 8. (☎12 34. Open M-F 3-7pm and Sa 9am-1pm. DM8 per day, usually a minimum of 3 days.) To bike to Memmingen, follow Memminger Str. from the right side of the church until you see signs for the bike trail (50min). The **tourist office,** Marktpl. 14, finds **rooms** (from DM25) and hands out a phenomenal town brochure. (☎92 19 50; fax 92 19 92; email touristikamt@ottobeuren.de; www.ottobeuren.de. Open M-F 9am-12pm, M-Th 2pm-5pm. F 2pm-4pm.) The **postal code** is 87724.

Ottobeuren's **Jugendherberge (HI),** Kaltenbrunnweg 11 (☎368; fax 72 19), was founded in 1952 by a doctor who wanted an oasis of hostelling in the then-unsettled fields. Guests are required to remove their street shoes inside to preserve cleanliness. Facing the church, walk down Sebastian-Kneipp-Str. for 15min. and turn left onto Beethovenstr.; the hostel is on the second street down Kaltenbrunnweg. **Primrose cafe,** Luitpoldstr. 6, serves cheap eats (DM5-12) on a shady lane by Ottobeuren's puny brook. (☎93 73 90. Open daily 11am-1am.) Across from the tourist office, **Karin's bistro** serves ample regional specialties from DM7.50-DM24.

IMMENSTADT AND BÜHL AM ALPSEE   ☎08323

The small, misleadingly named town of **Immenstadt** and the even smaller hamlet of **Bühl am Alpsee** huddle deep in the gorgeous mountains of the Allgäu south of Kempten, a world away from the resorts to the south. Streams flowing down from the Alps feed two lakes, the **Großer Alpsee** and the **Kleiner Alpsee,** whose cool, clear waters are unimaginably refreshing after a hike into the surrounding hills.

The Kleiner Alpsee, a 30-minute walk from the center of Immenstadt, offers an extensive park where families play volleyball, take a dip, and sunbathe. Check out the swimming action at **Freibad Kleiner Alpsee**, Am Kleinen Alpsee, on the other side of the lake. From the train station, turn left on Bahnhofstr. and then take a right after the rotary onto Badeweg and continue straight for about 15min. (☎87 20. Open daily 9am-7pm, in case of bad weather 9:30am-1pm. DM5.) The Großer Alpsee has *Größer* wet and wild opportunities, but certain stretches are off-limits to swimmers. Take the bus (direction "Oberstaufen") to "Bühl." **Boat and windsurfboard rental** on the Großer Alpsee is also available; choose from paddle-boats, rowboats, sailboats, and catamarans. (From DM25 per hr., depending on boat.) Immenstadt is also close to two immense skiing and tobogganing areas: **Alpsee Skizirkus** (☎(08325) 252) and **Mittag Ski-Rodel Center** (☎61 49). The season runs roughly from December to Mar. Day passes cost DM26 in each area, while weeklong passes are DM130. Chairlifts and cable cars run summer-long for dedicated wanderers. (DM8 to the half-way point, DM14 to the top.) Hiking trails are innumerable here; one stunning trek leads to the lofty **Otmarkirche**; head down Grüntenstr. east of the Nikolaikirche. Continue behind the school and turn left down Weidachweg, following the *Sportzentrum* signs. The trail extends past the Auwaldsee and the **Iller** river, named after victims who drowned there in 1284.

Immenstadt can be reached by **train** from **Memmingen** (45min., 1 per hr., DM15) and **Füssen** (2hr., 1 per hr., DM28). The friendly **tourist office,** Marienpl. 3, books **rooms** (DM18-32) and doles out hiking maps (DM6.80-9.90). Rooms in neighboring Bühl are generally cheaper, starting at DM24. (☎91 41 76; fax 91 41 95; email immenstadt@allgaeu.org. Open mid-July to Sept. M-F 9am-6pm and Sa 10am-noon; Oct. to mid-July M-F 9am-1pm and 2-5:30pm.) From the station, follow Alleestr. and turn right on Rothesstr. **Goldener Adler** offers convenient rooms with average cleanliness (DM35-60. Breakfast included.) Refuel with a *Wurst* (DM4) or salad (DM5) at **Marianne's Steigbach Imbiß,** Landwehrpl. 2, a hut at the edge of the square. (☎516 66. Open daily noon-7pm.) A plentiful **market** of fruits, meats, and more pops up Saturday mornings on **Marienplatz.**

Next door to Immenstadt, tiny **Bühl** is accessible by bus (5min., 1 per hr., DM2) and by the exquisite but painful **Hornweg** trail, which begins at the cemetery trailhead. From Immenstadt, it's a 90-minute walk along the *very steep* mountainside; or amble down the pleasant **Badeweg** path (30-40min.). Bühl's **tourist office,** Seestr. 5, has many of the same maps and brochures as its Immenstadt sibling. (☎91 41 78; fax 89 96. Open June-Oct. M-F 8:30am-noon and 2-5pm, Sa 10am-noon; Nov.-May M-F 8:30am-noon and 2-5pm. Maps from DM9.90.) Camp on the Großer Alpsee at **Bucher's Camping,** Seestr. 25. (☎77 26. DM9 per person. DM7.50-9.50 per tent. DM2.50 per car. DM1.50 *Kurtaxe* per person. Open Easter to early-Oct.)

OBERSTDORF   ☎08322

Oberstdorf is heaven for hard-core hikers. Surrounded by the snow-layered Allgäu Alps, this mecca of outdoorsiness combines solitary forest paths with a refreshing sense of nature-oriented tourism. The town's large pedestrian zone deceives with its plethora of sporting goods stores, but beyond the commercial streets, narrow dirt trails taper enticingly toward alpine lakes and desolate hillsides. Foreign tourists are few and far between, as Oberstdorf remains a health resort populated by Germans seeking to enjoy their native landscape.

Three **Bergbahnen** (cable cars) whisk hikers to the heady heights of the Alps. The closest one delivers acrophiliacs to the top of **Nebelhorn,** at 2,224m the highest accessible mountain in the Allgäu Alps. (☎96 00 96 or 960 00. Operates mid-May to Oct. daily 8:30am-4:50pm). The **Fellhornbahn** climbs 2,037m for an equally thrilling view. Unfortunately, the prices are as eye-popping as the panoramas. (☎30 35. Mid-May to Oct. daily 8:20am-4:50pm. DM43 to the top of Nebelhorn; DM16 to the lowest station.) Not quite as ambitious, the **Söllereckbahn** (☎57 57) carries hikers up 1358m to several mountainous hiking paths (DM14). On the mountain, gravel trails wind among flowery meadows and patches of snow. Come winter, the Bergbahnen transport skiers and snowboarders ready to hit the slopes (winter prices from DM44 for half a day). To reach the Nebelhornbahn station, walk down Nebelhornstr. from Hauptstr. To reach the Fellhornbahn, ride the "Fellhorn" bus from the train station. Söllereck is accessible by bus #1.

For swimming fun against a mountain backdrop, splash around in the **Moorbad** (☎48 63). From the Marktpl., turn onto Oststr. and walk to the end. Follow the sign to the trail that leads to the Moorbad. One prime hiking route leads to the **Breitachklamm,** a vertical chasm in a rock face carved out by a frothy river. It's most easily approachable from Kornau, a sub-village of Oberstdorf. From the train station, take the bus (direction: "Klein Walsertal") to "Reute." (Every 20min. DM2.) Walk up the hill and hang a right after house #22. The road becomes a hiking trail over the Breitach river (45min. to the Klamm).

Trains link Oberstdorf to Immenstadt (30min., 2 per hr., DM8). Rent a **bike** at **Zweirad Center,** Hauptstr. 7, for DM15 per day, mountain bikes DM25. (☎44 67. Open M-F 9am-noon and 2:30-6pm, Sa 9am-noon.) The Oberstdorf **tourist office,** across from the train station at Bahnhofpl. 3, doles out loads of brochures on hiking possibilities and accommodations. (☎70 00; fax 70 02 36; email info@oberstdorf.de; www.oberstdorf.de. Open M-F 8:30am-noon and 2-6pm, Sa 9am-noon, 2-6pm. Hiking maps DM4.90-DM9.80.) A **branch office** at Marktpl. 7 is open 8:30am-6pm, Sa 9:30am-12pm.) The **post office,** 87561 Oberstdorf, is across from the train station (open M-F 8:30am-12:30pm, 1:30am-6pm).

Close to Oberstdorf, **Kornau** is home to the excellent **Jugendherberge Oberstdorf (HI),** Kornau Haus 8, in a gorgeous setting overlooking the Alps. Its spacious facilities include laundry and a rudimentary bar. Take the bus from Oberstdorf to "Reute," continue in the direction of the bus, and take the first right. Be forewarned: the last bus leaves town by 9pm. Stragglers suffer a DM15 taxi ride or an hour-long climb uphill in the dark. (☎22 25; fax 804 46. Breakfast included. Cross-country ski rental DM7 per day. Reception 8am-noon, 5-8pm, and 9:30-10pm. Open Jan.-Oct. Dorm beds DM26.) For a homey chalet in the center of the village near the station, try **Gästehaus Alois Zobel,** Obere Bahnhofstr. 2 (☎963 20). Restaurants close early and are high-priced; check out the self-serve **cafe Felixar** at Nebelhornstr. 48 (chicken, pizzas, and more DM4-13) or try the **grocery stores** near Hauptstr.

BAYERISCHE ALPEN (BAVARIAN ALPS)

Visible on a clear day from the spires of Munich are a series of snow-covered peaks and forested slopes spanning from southeast Germany across Austria and into Italy. It was in this rugged and magical terrain that Ludwig II of Bavaria, the certifiably batty "Fairy Tale King," chose to build his theatrical palaces. Mountain villages, glacial lakes, icy waterfalls, and world-class ski resorts lend color to the jagged gray cliffs and thickly-forested valleys. The rhythmic beat of cowbells ceases only at dusk, and, after a few days, the smell of cow dung no longer seems pungent and foul, but pleasant and therapeutic (well, almost). This is the region where people authentically wear *Lederhosen*, and everyone seems to be going to or coming back from a hike. Rail lines are sparse; buses cover the gaps. For regional travel information, contact **Fremdenverkehrsverband Oberbayern,** Bodenseestr. 113, in Munich. (☎(089) 829 21 80. Open M-Th 9am-4pm, F 9am-12:30pm.)

FÜSSEN   ☎08362

A brightly painted toenail at the tip of the Alpine foothills, Füssen has captivated visitors ever since the time of Mad King Ludwig. The town's plethora of scenic hiking trails, access to fabulous alpine ski resorts, and proximity to Ludwig's famed **Königsschlösser** (p. 273) lures legions here every month of the year. Under Henry VII, Füssen found itself a reluctant player in the game of European intrigue and politics. To help finance his Italian campaign, Henry put up the town as collateral

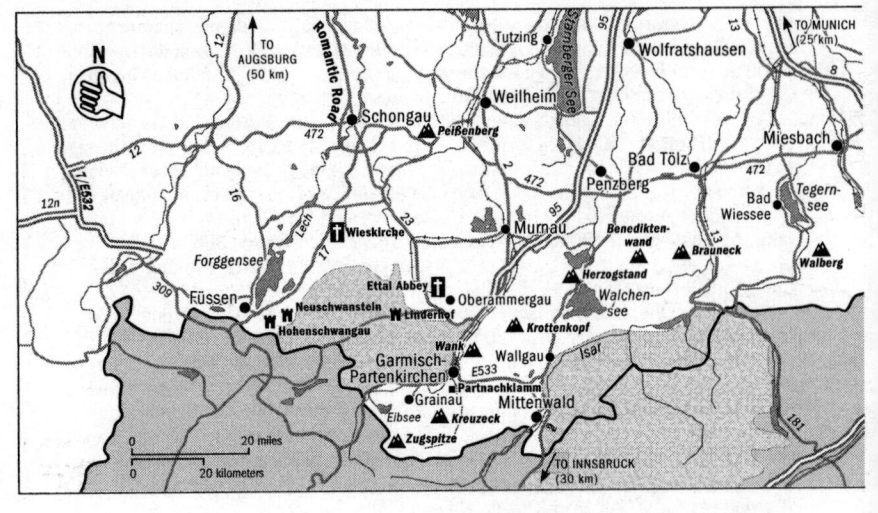

against a loan of 400 silver Marks from the prince-bishop of Augsburg. Henry died indebted, so the town was forfeited to the prince-bishop from 1313 until the great German Secularization of 1802. The Altstadt's lively pedestrian zone winds between ancient cemeteries, beneath Romanesque archways, and directly into the imposing castle walls. The landscape invites tourists to wander among pastures, bike the Roman road, or take a refreshing dip in a mountain lake.

7 PRACTICAL INFORMATION. Trains run to **Munich** (2hr., 1 per hr., DM36) and **Augsburg** (2hr., every 2 hrs., DM28). Füssen can also be reached by **bus** (#1084) from **Oberammergau** (1½hr., 5 per day, DM12.50). Along the Füssen-Schwangau county line, 80km of cycling paths make the town a haven for cyclists. Rent **bikes** at **Preisschranke,** to the left of the train station as you exit. (DM15 per day. ☎ (08368) 342. Open M-F 9am-6pm, Sa 9am-2pm.) The **tourist office** is on Kaiser-Maximilian-Pl. 1. From the station, walk the length of Bahnhofstr., then head straight on Luitpoldstr. to the big yellow building. The staff finds **rooms** for free, gives German language **city tours** Saturdays at 9:30am, and organizes whole- and half-day **guided hikes** of the area. (☎ 938 50; fax 93 85 20; email tourismus@fuessen.de; www.fuessen.de. Tours and hikes free with the *Kurkarte.* Office open Apr.-Sept. M-F 8:30am-6:30pm, Sa 9am-12:30pm, Su 10am-noon; Oct.-Mar. M-F 9am-5pm, Sa 10am-noon.) The **Bahnhof-Apotheke,** Bahnhofstr. 8, has a bell for night **pharmacy** service. (☎918 10. Open M-F 8:30am-1pm and 2-6:30pm, Sa 8:30am-12:30pm.) An **internet cafe** can be found in the Jugendhaus, Von Freyburgstr. 2½. (☎92 10 44. Open Tu-Th 4-8:30pm, F-Sa 3-9pm, and Su 3-7pm.) The **post office,** 87629 Füssen, is at the corner of Bahnhofstr. and Rupprechtstr., to the left of the train station as you exit (open M-F 8:30am-5:30pm, Sa 8:30am-noon).

🏛 SIGHTS. Reminders of the prince-bishop's medieval reign linger in Füssen's architectural wonders. The inner walls of the **Hohes Schloß** courtyard scream royalty with their arresting fifteenth-century *trompe l'oeil* windows and towers. The **Staatsgalerie** resides inside the castle walls, in the dens of late-medieval bishops and knights. The museum shelters a collection of regional late Gothic and Renaissance art. (☎90 31 64. Open Apr.-Oct. Tu-Su 11am-4pm; Nov.-Mar. Tu-Su 2-4pm. DM5, students and seniors DM4, children under 14 free; free tours W at 2:30pm.) Just below the castle rests the Baroque **Mangkirche** and its abbey, dating from the 8th century. An ancient fresco discovered during renovations in 1950 lights up the church's 10th-century subterranean crypt. Also in the abbey is the gaudy 18th-century Baroque library. (☎48 44. Tours July-Sept. Tu and Th 4pm, Sa 10:30am; May-June and Oct. Tu 4pm and

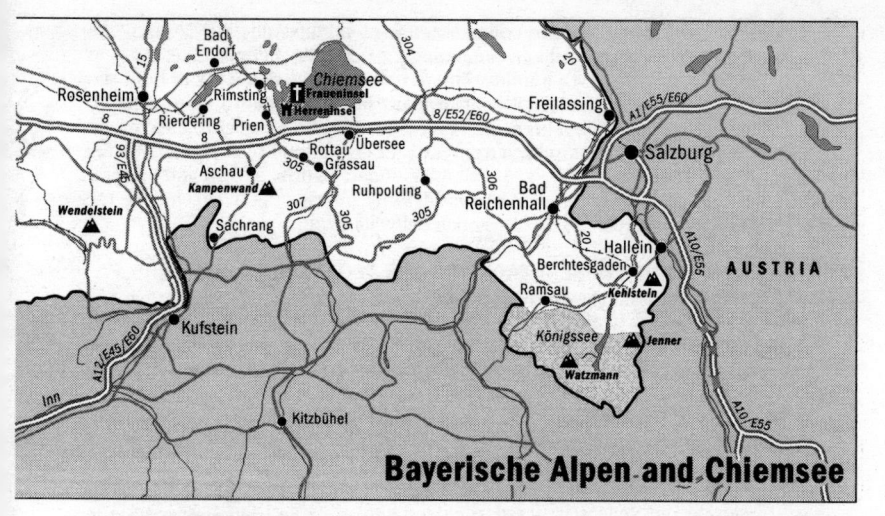

Bayerische Alpen and Chiemsee

Sa 10:30am; Jan.-Apr. Sa 10:30am.) The **Stadtmuseum** in the monastery details the history, art, and culture of the Füssen region in four distinct departments. One room devoted solely to the history of lutes and violins explores Füssen's role as home of Europe's oldest lutemakers guild (est. 1562). Inside the **Annenkapelle,** 20 macabre skeleton-decked panels depict everyone from the Pope and Emperor to the smallest child engaged in the *Totentanz* (death dance), a public frenzy of despair that overtook Europe during the plague. The purpose of the painting is best summarized by an inscription on one of the panels: *Sagt ja, Sagt nein, Getanzt Müß Seyn* (say yes or say no, all must dance). (☎ 90 31 45. Open Apr.-Oct. Tu-Su 11am-4pm, Nov.-Mar. Tu-Su 2-4pm. Adults DM5, children and students DM4.) The **▓Kombikarte** allows admission to both the Stadtmuseum and the Staatsgalerie for DM6.

▌ ACCOMMODATIONS AND FOOD. Füssen's **Jugendherberge (HI),** Mariahilfer Str. 5, is blessed by a lovely location and friendly staff. Turn right from the station and follow the railroad tracks (10min.). It's often packed, so make a reservation at least one day in advance. (☎ 77 54; fax 27 70. Sheets DM5.50. Basement lockers, DM1 deposit. Meals DM7.50-9. Reception 7-9am, 5-7pm, and 8-10pm. Curfew 11:30pm, but you can get the access code. Closed Nov. DM21 plus DM1.50 *kurtaxe.*) For a colorful, friendly room with breakfast, try **Pension Haslach,** Mariahilfer Str. 1b. (☎ 24 26. Singles DM35, doubles DM70.) Keep your eyes open for *Zimmer frei* signs in private homes.

Plus, on the corner of Bahnhofstr. and Luitpoldstr., is the cheapest **grocery** store around (open M-F 8:30am-6:30pm, Sa 8am-2pm). Many reasonably priced bakeries, meat shops, and *Imbiß* stands line the pedestrian zone on **Reichenstr.** For an excellent Greek sit-down meal, try **Poseidon,** Ottostr. 1½. Enjoy their lunch menu dishes (all under DM10) inside, on the patio, or in the beer garden. (☎ 384 57. Open daily noon-2pm, 5:30pm-midnight.) **Pizza Blitz,** Luitpoldstr. 14, offers gargantuan pizzas and calzones (DM6-13), making it a favorite local hangout. (☎ 383 54. Open M-Th 11am-11pm, F-Sa 11am-midnight, Su noon-11pm.)

▌ DAYTRIP FROM FÜSSEN: WIESKIRCHE. Any trek from Füssen or Oberammergau to the Ammergau Alps should include a brief stop at the **Wieskirche** (Church in the Meadows), a splendid Rococo pilgrimage church. Torrents of light bathe the church in astonishing brightness, and the effect is particularly riveting in the morning and evening when the sun shines directly through the arched windows. One of the earliest optical illusions created, the ceiling is actually completely flat, rising directly from the cornice for only 3m before flattening out entirely. The painter and sculptor collaborated to blend the gold-gilded ornaments into the frescoed walls and ceiling, eliminating the boundary between the two- and three-dimensional worlds. Dominikus Zimmermann, the architect who built the church from 1746-1754, could not bear to leave his most beautiful and accomplished masterpiece, and until his death he lived in a tiny house next to the church. The best way to get to Wieskirche is from the Füssen station. Bus #9715 leaves for the church daily at 12:25, 1:05, 3:25, and 4:35pm and returns at 3:15 and 3:50pm. 1hr. One-way DM7.80; save on the round-trip by purchasing a Tageskarte for DM10. Wieskirche (☎ (08861) 81 73) is open daily 8am-7pm.

⚠ DAY HIKE FROM FÜSSEN: TACKLING THE TEGELBERG
Estimated distance: 23km; estimated time: 7½ hours
There's no better way to admire Crazy King Ludwig's castles, take in the beauty of the Alps, and work off that beer gut than to plan a day hike in the Füssen-Schwangau region. An excellent, detailed topographical map of the area's numerous trails, **Zumstein Wanderkarte Füssen,** is available at the Füssen tourist office (DM8) and should be purchased and studied before the trip. **Aktiv Flugsport & Freizeit,** Bullachbergweg 34a, Schwangau (☎ (08362) 98 34 50), supplies hiking and climbing gear.

What follows is a blow-by-blow account of a hike through the mountains which ranges in altitude from 800m to 1880m, and gives stunning, unique views of Castles **Neuschwanstein** and **Hohenschwangau,** the deep blue waters of the **Alpsee,** and the dramatic **Pöllat Gorge.** The trailhead for this trek is the Hohenschwangau bus stop, which can be reached from Füssen by the Königschlösser bus (#9713; DM2.50). The trek is divided into three parts, which provides the option of bailing out (or bailing in) as you wish. This hike—especially the first portion—should only be attempted in good weather during the summer months, and by persons who are in good physical condition. The time estimates provided assume a constant, steady pace. For safety precautions to observe while hiking, and the necessary equipment, see p. 57.
Part 1: UP *(estimated time: 2½ hours)* From the bus stop and information center, walk east across Alpseestr. and through the parking lot to **Trail 32.** When the path forks, take a left up the wood stairs and merge into the paved road. Turn right onto **Trail 36** (direction: "Marienbrücke"). Cross the famous Marienbrücke over the Pöllat Gorge, and admire Neuschwanstein in all its beauty. Don't forget to say goodbye to the tourists as you head for the other end of the bridge. From here, your climb of Tegelberg begins in earnest. You'll be following **Trail 76a,** delineated by the blue trail markers on trees and rocks. Since the sometimes faint trail has many switchbacks, it's a good idea to turn around every 100m to look for trail markers and to make sure you didn't miss a turn. The first of many great views of Neuschwanstein, Hohenschwangau, and Alpsee opens up. For the next 45 minutes, you will occasionally encounter points when you must climb on all-fours, until you reach the **Holzerei,** and a couple of sketchy dudes with chain saws in the middle of the woods. Don't worry—they're after the wood, not you. In all likelihood, they will have moved on by the time this book is published, but the muddy slick caused by the lumbering may still make the trail extremely hard to navigate at this point. By now, you've hit the tree line, and are looking out on all of Southern Germany as you work your way to the summit. **Tegelbahnhaus. Bail-out Point #1:** the Tegelbergbahn can take you back down for DM15, and bus #9713 brings you back to the castles and to Füssen. Follow the sign for "Branderschrofen Gipfel", the very top of the mountain; you'll be looking for the red trail markers. The last 100m of this trail require all-fours scaling. Congratulations, you just climbed over 1km to the summit (1880m). You have a panoramic view of Germany to the north and the Austrian Alps to the southwest. To the west, you'll notice two towns separated by a forested hill—Füssen on the right, and Vils (Austria) on the left. The **Zugspitze,** Germany's highest mountain (2964m), looms in the distance to the south- southeast.
Part 2: DOWN *(estimated time: 2¾ hours)* After spending half an hour at the top resting and admiring the view, you're ready to move on. Descend back down to the Tegel Berghaus. Make a left onto **Naturpfad Ahornreitweg,** delineated by orange

trailmarkers. As you wind your way down, take a look back at the sparse pine trees and cold grey rock of the Tegelberg. Turn right at the sign to "Bleckenau" via the "Reitweg" trail. Soon Mount Hoher Straußberg (1933m), its streams glistening in the sunlight, stares you straight in the face. A couple paces more and you come across the Jagdhütte, a hut which provides a good opportunity for a short break. As you start to descend into the Pöllat Gorge, Mt. Säuling (2038m), the monster mountain of the region, towers above you. After another couple hundred meters, turn right at the dead end onto **Trail 75a**, the paved path heading back toward Neuschwanstein. This road takes you along the Pöllat river, as it speeds down from its Alpine source towards the castles. The Marienbrücke and Neuschwanstein are visible from a unique vantage point. **Bail-out Point #2:** If you're too tired for the victory lap around the Alpsee, **trails 36** and **32** bring you back to the bus stop, where you started.

Part 3: AROUND (THE ALPSEE) *(estimated time: 2¼ hours)* Make a sharp left up **Trail 39** and keep following those signs as you change trails from **Wasserleitungsweg** to **Oberer Winterzug Weg.** The first of many views of the bright yellow Schloß Hohenschwangau, with the deep blue Alpsee in the foreground, opens up. At the intersection where a small statue of Mary peers down from a tree, turn right onto **Trail 41** towards "Istraelitfelsen." Keep following signs for Trail 41. The Istraelit-felsen, a large granite outcropping, appears in the woods. Turn right on **Trail 43** towards the Alpsee. Now at the shore of the Alpsee, turn left onto **Trail 20** towards "Marienmonument," built by Ludwig in memory of his mother, and follow it as it hugs the shore. From here, follow **Trail 45** to Hohenschwangau. Turn right on Trail 45a to Pindarplatz, a rock outcropping over the Alpsee which provides splendid views of Neuschwanstein. Then take **Trail 45** to Fürstenstr., turn right, and follow to Hohenschwangau. Make your way back to the bus stop and take a load off!

KÖNIGSSCHLÖSSER (ROYAL CASTLES)

After Queen Marie bore Maximilian II two healthy sons, there was no reason to expect the fall of the Bavarian royal family—but it was soon to come. Otto, the younger son, developed schizophrenia as a young adult, leaving his brother Ludwig II to carry on the family name. In 1864, he assumed the throne at the tender age of 18, a shockingly handsome lad who was extremely naive about politics. A zany visionary and fervent Wagner fan, Ludwig used his cash to craft his dreams into reality, creating fantastic castles that soar into the Alpine skies, hoping to realize his fantasyland in an ugly and evil world. In 1886, a band of upstart nobles and bureaucrats deposed Ludwig in a coup d'état and imprisoned him in Schloß Berg on the Starnberger See. Three days later, the King and a loyal advisor were discovered dead in the lake under mysterious circumstances. Some hypothesize that it was a failed escape attempt, even though Ludwig was a first-class swimmer. Today, the captivating enigma of Ludwig's life, death, and self-fashioned dream-world lingers for the tourist.

▨ HOHENSCHWANGAU & NEUSCHWANSTEIN

Both castles open Apr.-Sept. 9am-6pm, Oct.-Mar. 10am-4pm. Required tours included in entrance fee. Tickets for both castles may be purchased at the Ticket-Service Center, Alpseestr. 12 (☎(08362) 93 08 30; fax 930 83 20; email info@ticket-center-hohenschwangau.de; www.ticket-center-hohenschwangau.de), about 100m south of the Hohenschwangau bus stop. Your tour's number and departure time are printed on the ticket. From Apr.-Sept., English tours of each castle are offered about every 20min. while German tours depart every 10min.; German and English tours depart every 30min. Oct.-Mar. Tours last 35min. Arrive early in the morning to avoid long lines at the Ticket-Service Center, and to be placed in a tour group that departs as soon as possible. Tickets may be reserved in advance with a credit card for a DM3 per person fee. Each castle DM14; students and children DM12; combination tickets DM26 and DM22, respectively. Tegelbergbahn cable car ☎983 60. Open daily 8:30am-5pm; in winter 8:45am-4:30pm. One-way DM16.50, students DM15.50, children DM8.50; round-trip DM28, students DM26, children DM14.

BAVARIA

Ludwig II grew up in **Schloß Hohenschwangau,** the bright yellow neo-Gothic castle rebuilt by his father. It was no doubt here that he acquired his taste for the romantic German mythologies of the Middle Ages. Atop a humble hill and forest, this authentic palace has rooms that actually appear to have been lived in. After Maximilian II died, Ludwig ordered the servants to paint a dreamy night sky upon the royal bedroom ceiling. The vast constellation of stars would shine brightly down upon the sleeping Ludwig when lit with oil lamps from above. The castle also houses Wagner's piano and a loaf of bread from the 1830s.

Ludwig's desperate building spree across Bavaria peaked with the construction of glitzy **Schloß Neuschwanstein,** built from 1869 to 1886, now Germany's most cliché tourist attraction and the inspiration for Disneyland's Cinderella Castle. The first sketches of the Schloß were reportedly drawn by a set designer, not an architect, which explains a lot. The young Ludwig II lived a mere 173 days within the extravagant edifice, in which 63 rooms remained unfinished. The completed chambers include a Byzantine throne-room, a small artificial grotto, and an immense *Sängersaal*—an acoustic masterpiece, built expressly for Wagnerian opera performances. A wood carving of a familiar but unidentifiable city skyline tops the king's bed; it depicts most of the famous towers of the world.

Consider spending the rest of the day hiking around the spectacular environs. For the fairy godmother of all views, hike up to the **Marienbrücke,** spanning the **Pöllat gorge** behind Schloß Neuschwanstein (10min.). Those with stout hearts and legs can continue uphill from here for a knockout view of the castle and nearby lake (1hr.). In the opposite direction, descend the mountain from Schloß Hohenschwangau to the lily pad-topped **Schwansee** (trail #49). Follow the Schwansee-Bundweg path (#13) through fields of wild flowers to a swan-infested beach area and a secluded swimming hole. Sane people and insane hang-gliders ride the **Tegelbergbahn** cable car for a glimpse of—or a dive into—the same panorama.

From Füssen, hop on bus #9713 marked "Königsschlösser," which departs from the train station (2 per hr., DM2.50). It will dump you at the base of a number of surrounding hills in front of the **information booth. (☎**81 98 40. Open daily 9am-6pm.) The Ticket-Service Center is a short walk uphill on Alpseestr. Separate paths lead up to both Hohenschwangau and Neuschwanstein. A less touristed path to Hohenschwangau is path #17, which starts from the left side of the information booth and meanders through the moss-covered forest (10min.). To Neuschwanstein, take path #32, from Car Park D; it's the shortest but also steepest trail to the top (25min.). Alternatively, clip-clop your way to the top in a horse-drawn carriage (uphill DM8, downhill DM4) from Car Park D or Hotel Müller. Consider trekking path #33 from Neuschwanstein back to the base of the hill (20min.; open only in summer). Virtually untouristed, this route winds its way down through the dramatic **Pöllat gorge.** Private **buses** run from Hotel Lisl to **Bleckenau,** a beautiful vantage point 650 steep meters uphill from Neuschwanstein (DM3.50 uphill, DM2 downhill, DM5 round trip). A **Tagesticket** (DM13) entitles castle-hoppers to unlimited regional bus use (including the ride to Linderhof); buy it from the bus driver.

▨ SCHLOß LINDERHOF

☎(08822) 920 30, fax 92 03 11. Open Apr.-Sept. daily 9am-6pm; Oct.-Mar. 10am-4pm. Apr.-Sept. obligatory castle tour DM11, students and seniors DM9; Oct.-Mar. DM8, students and seniors DM6; accompanied children under 18 free. Park is free and open to the public, Apr.-Sept. only.

Halfway between Garmisch-Partenkirchen and Oberammergau lies the exquisite **Schloß Linderhof,** Ludwig II's compact hunting palace, surrounded by a meticulously manicured park. Ludwig paid homage to the French Bourbon kings, in particular Louis XIV (the Sun King), just as he did with his Herrenchiemsee palace (see p. 285). Although it lacks Neuschwanstein's pristine exterior, the decadent palace is bathed in gold. The royal bedchamber, the largest room in the castle, is unbelievably lush, with gold leaf and a colossal crystal chandelier that weighs half a ton. Dark blue velvet (the king's favorite color) encases the king-size bed; though he topped 195cm (6' 5"), Ludwig had no trouble fitting in between the hand-carved head and foot boards.

Across the ceiling stretches the affirmation *Nec pluribus impar*, which roughly translates as "I am the MacDaddy of the DaddyMacs." The two malachite tables were gifts from Russian Czarina Marie Alexandrovna, who tried to match Ludwig (a bachelor to his death) with one of her daughters. Ludwig just kept the tables.

More impressive than the palace itself is the magnificent **park** surrounding it. The sheer force of water cascading down steps behind the palace powers the fountain in front. Once an hour, the dam is opened and water shoots higher than the top of the palace. Paths originating at the swan lake at the park entrance weave through the ornately landscaped grounds. To the right of the palace and up the slope is an enormous, artificial **grotto;** red and blue floodlights illuminate a "subterranean" lake and floating shell-boat. Farther along, brilliant red and blue stained-glass windows richly illuminate the **Maurischer Kiosk,** an elaborate, mosque-inspired building, and the only sight on the grounds not built expressly for Ludwig. He saw it at the 1867 World Exposition in Paris and liked it so much that he brought it home. Within these walls, Ludwig would smoke his water pipe and implore his servants to dress up in period costumes and read him tales from *1,001 Nights.* Following the path down the hill to the left (20min.) is the newly reconstructed **Hunding-Hütte,** another of Ludwig's flights of fancy, modeled after a scene in Wagner's *Die Walküre* from *Der Ring des Nibelungen.* Bearskin-covered log benches surround an artificial tree.

Bus #9622 runs between Oberammergau and the park (9:50am-6:15pm). The last bus leaves Linderhof at 6:40pm (20min., 1 per hr., DM9.20 round-trip). Hikers and cyclists can follow the well-kept gravel path along the river to Linderhof (10km). From the Oberammergau tourist office head left on Eugen-Papst-Str.; when the road forks at the bridge, select the gravel bike path straight ahead and follow the signs to Linderhof. Oberammergau is connected by **bus** to **Garmisch-Partenkirchen** (#1084 and 9606, 40min., 1 per hr., DM5.40), and **Füssen** (#1084, 1½hr., 8 per day, DM12.50). **Trains** run from **Munich** to Oberammergau, switching at Murnau (1¾hr., 1 per hr., DM25.60).

HYPERTRAVEL TO THE CASTLES

Seeing all three of the royal castles during a daytrip from Munich requires some fancy footwork and luck with connections (and can only be done M-F). Take the 6:50am train from Munich to Buchloe, and transfer here onto the 7:46am to Füssen. Arriving in Füssen at 8:57am, hop on bus #9713 at 9:15am to the Königsschlösser. Arriving at 9:23am, you'll have almost 4 hours to fight through the lines at Hohenschwangau and Neuschwanstein before you catch bus #1084 at 1:13pm to Oberammergau (changing in Steingaden), and from Oberammergau, bus #9622 at 3:05pm to Schloß Linderhof. Until 5:35pm, you can indulge in the surrounding opulence, but then it'll be time to mount bus #9622 back to "Oberammergau Post/Bahnhof." At 6pm you'll get to the Oberammergau train station with plenty of time to catch the 6:08pm train to Murnau, where you'll change trains at 6:47pm and hopefully grab a Löwenbräu at 7:55pm back in Munich. Double check your schedule with a timetable before departing. A simpler and more advisable option, particularly if you don't have a railpass, is to sign on with EurAide for a charter bus ride to Neuschwanstein, Linderhof, and Wieskirche (see p. 241).

OBERAMMERGAU AND ETTAL ABBEY   ☎ 08822

Situated in a wide valley surrounded by mountains, meadows, and forests, the tiny Alpine town of Oberammergau is home to the world-famous **Passion Play.** After the town was spared from a plague that swept through Europe in 1633, the inhabitants promised to re-enact the Crucifixion and Resurrection of Christ every 10 years. The cast is composed of about 1,000 locals who begin rehearsing far in advance, often growing long hair and beards. The plays last all day, with a short break for pretzels, Wurst, and beer around noon. As luck would have it, last year was a performance year—you'll have to wait until summer 2010 to see it. Start saving now, though; the cheapest seats in the house go for DM110. While the plays are not being performed, the most exciting things to do in Oberammergau are hike along scenic alpine ridges, visit nearby Ettal Abbey and Schloß Linderhof, admire the craftsmanship of the town's many wood carvers, and watch the beards grow.

🛈 PRACTICAL INFORMATION. The **tourist office** is located at Eugen-Papst-Str. 9a. Turn left from the station and right at the town center onto Eugen-Papst-Str. The staff offers maps and books **rooms** (DM25-40) for free. (☎923 10; fax 923 31 90; tourist-info@oberammergau.de; www.oberammergau.de. Open M-F 8:30am-6pm, Sa 8:30am-noon.) If the tourist office is closed, head to the information board with accommodations listings and a free hotel phone directly in front of the office. The **post office**, 87488 Oberammergau, is across the street from the train station. (☎920 70. Open M-F 8:30am-5:30pm, Sa 8:30am-2:30pm.)

🍴 ACCOMMODATIONS AND FOOD. Oberammergau's **Jugendherberge (HI)**, Malensteinweg 10, hunches over the gently flowing Ammer River seven minutes upstream from the train station. Head left up Bahnhofstr. for 100m and take a right on the gravel path just before the bridge; follow the path, keeping the river on your left—the hostel is ahead on the right. The four- to six-bed rooms are simple and spotless. (☎41 14; fax 16 95. Sheets DM5.50. Reception 7-11:30am and 4-10pm. Curfew 10pm. Closed Nov. 12-Dec. 25. DM21 plus DM2.50 *Kurtaxe*.) Oberammergau's pricey restaurants and lack of *Imbiße* may necessitate **grocery shopping;** stock up at **A&P Tengelmann**, Bahnhofstr. 9 (open M-F 8am-8pm, Sa 8am-4pm).

🔲 SIGHTS. In Oberammergau, a visit to the 18th-century Rococo **St. Peter & Paul Church,** Pfarrpl. 1, is well worth the trip. The church's unique marble columns, its intricate stucco work, and moving ceiling fresco depicting the martyrdom of Peter and Paul, create a truly other-worldly effect. From the tourist office, walk north on Eugen-Papst-Str., turn right on Verlegergasse, and make another right onto Dorf-str. *(open from dawn to dusk).* On your way, stop to admire the famous Lüftlmalerei (house fresco) on **Pilatushaus** (Verlegergasse); painted in 1784 by Franz Zwink, it illustrates Christ's condemnation by Pilate.

   In 1330, Ludwig I of Bavaria—not to be confused with the crazy Ludwig of Neuschwanstein fame (see p. 273)—founded the enormous **Abbey** in the tiny village of **Ettal,** 4km south of Oberammergau (a 45min. hike). Since then, the abbey has conducted a brisk business in house-fermented beer and spirits. The **Klosterladen,** to the right as you face the church, sells divine six-packs of Kloster-brewed beer (DM14.50); there are numerous other "licensed" Kloster Ettal pushers in the vicinity. Beautifully stuccoed and ornamented with gold and precious stones, this double-domed Baroque sanctuary assumed its present shape after 18th-century renovations. English guides to the history and architecture of the abbey cost DM4. *(www.kloster-ettal.de. Open daily Apr.-Sept. 7:45am-7:45pm, Oct.-Mar. 7:45am-noon.)*

   Buses #1084 and 9606 to Ettal from Oberammergau leave hourly from the train station (round-trip DM5.60). To **hike** to the abbey from the Oberammergau tourist office, swing a left onto Eugen-Papst-Str. and shimmy down the sidewalk until the road forks at the bridge. Follow the gravel bike path with signs to Ettal straight ahead. The Ettal **tourist office,** Ammergauer Str. 8, lists **rooms** (DM25-70) and a map of hiking trails. (☎35 34; fax 63 99. Open M-F 8am-noon.)

GARMISCH-PARTENKIRCHEN   ☎08821

Once upon a time, the 1,100-year-old hamlets of Garmisch and Partenkirchen were beautiful unassuming Bavarian villages whose location at the foot of the Zugspitze—Germany's tallest peak—ensured their tranquil isolation. Once the 19th-century nature movement discovered the mountains, however, the two towns quickly became renowned throughout Germany for their spectacular alpine ski slopes and magnificent hiking and rock-climbing routes. Hitler persuaded the Garmisch and Partenkirchen mayors to unite the two villages in 1935 in anticipation of the 1936 Winter Olympic Games. To this day, however, the towns remain geographically distinct—Garmisch in the west and Partenkirchen in the east—and their inhabitants assert their individuality. Both sides of town staunchly maintain that they speak different dialects, and their cows don't socialize in public.

⁊ PRACTICAL INFORMATION. Garmisch-Partenkirchen can be reached by **train** from **Munich** (1½hr., 1 per hr., DM27), or **Innsbruck** (1½hr., 1 per hr., DM20.20), and by **bus** #1084 from **Füssen** (2hr., 6-7 per day, DM13 with **Tagesticket**). **Public transportation** within the city costs DM2, but it's free with a *Kurkarte* (see below). Rent **bikes** at **Sport Total**, Marienpl. 18 (☎14 25; open M-F 9am-noon and 2-5pm; DM30 per day), or **Pro Shop Stefan Leiner**, Rathauspl. 11. (☎795 28 or 548 44. Open M-F 9am-6pm, Sa 9am-1pm. From DM18 per day.) The **tourist office**, Richard-Strauss-Pl. 2, distributes free maps and books **rooms** (DM35-55) for free. From the station, turn left on Bahnhofstr. and after 200m turn left again onto Von-Brug-Str.; the office faces the fountain on the square. (☎18 07 00; fax 18 07 55; email tourist-info@garmisch-partenkirchen.de; www.garmisch-partenkirchen.de. Open M-Sa 8am-6pm, Su 10am-noon.) For **snow** and **weather reports** for the Zugspitze or Alpspitze, call ☎79 79 79; for the Wank area, call ☎75 33 33. **Bahnhof-Apotheke,** Bahnhofstr. 36, to the right as you face the station, has a list in its window of opening times and addresses of all other **pharmacies.** (☎24 50. Open M-F 8:30am-noon and 2-6pm, Sa 8:30am-noon.) The **post office,** 82467 Garmisch-Partenkirchen, is across the street from the station (open M-F 8am-6pm, Sa 8am-12:30pm).

⁊⁊ ACCOMMODATIONS AND FOOD. Reasonably priced rooms exist in Garmisch-Partenkirchen, but you'll have to do a bit of detective work to find one. Drop by the tourist office or request a list of private rooms and call from the free hotel phone. Most locales require a three-night minimum stay. Note that a **Kurtaxe** (DM3.50) is levied on all overnight guests over the age of 16. The compensation for paying is a green **Kurkarte** entitling visitors to transport on the bus system and admission to various sights. Awake to the tolling of bells at the pleasant **Jugendherberge (HI),** Jochstr. 10. Cross the street from the train station, walk 25m to your left, and hop on bus #3 (direction: "Burgrain") or 4 or 5 (direction: "Farchant") to "Burgrain." Walk straight down Am Lahner Wiesgraben and turn right after two blocks onto Jochstr to get to the hostel's clean, somewhat institutional 6- to 10-bed rooms. (☎29 80; fax 585 36. Ages 18-26 only. Sheets DM5.50. Reception 7-9am and 5pm-midnight. Lockout 9am-3:30pm. Curfew 11:30pm. Open Jan. to mid-Nov. Dorm beds DM21.) The **Naturfreundehaus,** Schalmeiweg 21, is an independent hostel on the edge of the forest at the east end of Partenkirchen. From the station, walk straight on Bahnhofstr. as it becomes Ludwigstr., follow the rightward bend in Ludwigstr., and turn left on Sonnenbergstr. Continue straight as this first becomes Prof.-Michael-Sachs-Str. and then Schalmeiweg (25min.). Sleep in immaculate attic lofts with up to 16 other scruffy yet smiling backpackers. (☎43 22. Breakfast DM8. Quiet after 10pm, but no curfew. Call ahead. Dorm beds DM15.) **Campingpl. Zugspitze,** Griesener Str. 4, is on highway B24 at the base of the Zugspitze; take the bus from the station to "Schmölzabzweigung." (☎31 80. DM9.50 per person, under 15 DM5.50. DM5 per tent.)

Aldi, at the corner of Enzianstr. and Bahnhofstr., stocks the cheapest **groceries** in town (open M-F 8:30am-6pm, Sa 8am-2pm). **HL Markt,** at the intersection of Bahnhofstr. and Von-Brug-Str., has slightly better hours (open M-F 8am-8pm, Sa 7:30am-4pm). Garmisch's restaurants cater to a range of tastes and tax brackets. The best value in town is probably the friendly Italian **La Baita**, Zugspitzstr. 16, 100m from Marienpl. The restaurant offers delightful pasta dishes (DM8-16), omelettes (DM9), and pizzas (DM8-14. ☎787 77. Open M-Tu and Th-Su 11:30am-2:30pm and 5:30-11:30pm.) In the heart of Partenkirchen, grab a giant *Schnitzel* (DM9-11) at **Gasthof Fraudorfer**, Ludwigstr. 24, where Bavarian dishes are supplemented with traditional folk dances and songs after 7pm. (☎21 76. Open M and Th-Su 7am-1am, W 5pm-1am.)

⁊⁊ SIGHTS AND HIKING. The mountains are the main attraction in town—marvelous views in the summer, and snowy Alpine antics in the winter. There are three ways to conquer the **Zugspitze**, the highest peak in Germany, though they should only be attempted in fair weather. **Option 1:** Take the cog railway from the

Zugspitzbahnhof (50m behind the Garmisch main station) via Grainau to Hotel Schneefernerhaus, then a cable car, the **Gipfelseilbahn,** to the outlook, the Zugspitzplatt. (Departs hourly 7:39am-2:39pm. 1¼hr. Round-trip DM79, children 16-17 DM55, children 5-15 DM47, under 5 free.) Continue with the **Gletscherbahn** cable car. **Option 2:** Get off the railway at Eibsee and take the **Eibseeseilbahn,** one of the steepest cable car runs in the world, all the way to the top. (Departs hourly 8am-4:15pm. 80min. Same prices as option 1.) A **combination ticket** including the train from Munich or Augsburg and the Zugspitze tour costs DM90, students 16-17 DM65, children 4-15 DM51, under 4 free. **Option 3:** Hike it—the cheapest way to scale the 2,964m monster is to climb for about 10hrs., usually as part of a two-day trip. *Do not attempt this ascent unless you are an experienced climber.* Get a good map from the tourist office and check the weather before heading out.

For other Alpine views at lower prices, take the **Alpspitzbahn** to Osterfelderkopf peak (2050m, 9min., round-trip DM38), the **Kreuzeck** cable car to Kreuzeck (1650m, 8min., round-trip DM28), or the **Wankbahn** (1780m, 18min., round-trip DM29). Most trips depart hourly (May-June 8:30am-5pm, July-Sept. 8am-5pm, Oct.-Nov. 8:30am-4:30pm). A worthwhile daytrip includes biking to the **Eibsee,** 10km from Garmisch. The calm, crystal waters of a mountain lake against the soaring, snow-capped monumentality of the Zugspitze will remind you of a movie backdrop. To avoid the fairly steep uphill grade of the last 300m, take the Eibsee bus from Garmisch (round-trip DM5, half-off for German Bahncard holders). One of the most popular trails leads to the dramatic, 100m-deep **Partnachklamm** gorge (DM3). Hikers walk up to the gorge from behind the Olympic ski stadium (35min.) and then meander for another half hour in the narrow tunnels dug in the rocks, extremely close to the foaming water. **WN Alpin,** Zugspitzstr. 51 (☎503 40; www.wn-alpin.de; open M-F 9am-12:30pm & 2-6pm, Sa 9am-12:30pm), and **Conrad Outdoors,** Rathauspl. 2 (☎563 61; open M-F 8:30am-6pm, Sa 8:30am-1pm), specialize in mountaineering gear and rent **hiking and climbing equipment.** For information about hiking trails and rock climbing, contact the **German Alpine Association** in Munich (☎(089) 29 49 40).

BERCHTESGADEN ☎08652

Nestled in the southeastern corner of the Bavarian Alps, Berchtesgaden wins the affection of many world travelers for the natural beauty of its surroundings. Once part of the Archbishopric of Salzburg, the region was usurped by Bavaria in 1809 for its salt deposits and now comprises one of Germany's largest and most scenic national parks. The alpine peaks of Hoher Göll, Watzman, and Hochkalter, the Königsee and Hintersee's shimmering waters, and the Zauberwald's pristine forests encircle this charming town. Yet, Berchtesgaden is equally well-known for a sinister and often-visited attraction: Hitler's **Kehlsteinhaus**—a mountaintop retreat christened "Eagle's Nest" by the American troops who occupied it after WWII. Even the most beautiful splendors of the natural world cannot whitewash Berchtesgaden's ominous connection to this aspect of German history.

▛ GETTING THERE AND GETTING AROUND

Trains: run hourly to **Munich** (2½hr., change at Freilassing, DM48); **Salzburg** (1hr., change at Freilassing, DM12.20); and **Bad Reichenhall** (30min., DM6).

Buses: provide **public transportation** within Berchtesgaden (DM1.50); they also head to Bad Reichenhall (DM6.40), Königssee (DM5.40), and Salzburg (DM7.10).

Bikes: can be rented at **Full Stall Beierl,** Maximilianstr. 16 (☎94 84 50). From the Bahnhof, follow the signs marked "Zum Markt".

Cars: can be rented at **AVIS,** BP fuel station, Königsseer Str. 47 (☎691 07, ☎610 93 99 after hours). Open M-F 8:30am-noon. DM215 for a weekend rental including insurance and city tax.

⚡ ORIENTATION AND PRACTICAL INFORMATION

Crouched in the southeastern corner of Germany, Berchtesgaden is a lone German outpost among Austrian mountains.

Tourist office, Königsseer Str. 2 (☎96 71 50; fax 96 74 00; email info@berchtes-gadener-land.com; www.berchtesgadener-land.com), is opposite the train station in an off-white building with blue shutters. The office's **Wanderpass** brochure (DM5) includes tips on walking trails in the Berchtesgaden National Park; it comes with the **Kurkarte,** a tourist card given to tourists who pay the obligatory DM3 **Kurtaxe.** Open M-F 8am-6pm, Sa 9am-5pm, Su 9am-3pm. Call ☎96 70 for a recording of **hotel information.** Most establishments also accept Austrian schillings.

Post office, Bahnhofspl. 4, 83471 Berchtesgaden, is adjacent to the train station. Open M-F 8:30am-noon and 2-5:30pm, Sa 8:30am-noon.

🍴 ACCOMMODATIONS AND FOOD

The secret to finding inexpensive accommodations in Berchtesgaden is not to stay in Berchtesgaden; most private rooms and *Pensionen* run DM100-150 per night. Many less expensive establishments can be found in the neighboring town of Ramsau (inquire at the Berchtesgaden tourist office), which is reached by bus #9546 from Berchtesgaden every half hour (20 min trip, DM3.80).

Jugendherberge (HI), Gebirgsjägerstr. 52 (☎943 70; fax 94 37 37), is a 30-minute walk uphill from the station. Turn right from the station and follow Ramsauer Str. on the left for 15 minutes, then take the first right on Gmündbrücke, and follow the signs up the steep gravel path on the left. Or take bus #9539 (direction: "Strub Kaserne") to "Jugendherberge." All-you-can-eat breakfast included. Sheets DM5.50. Reception 8am-noon and 5-7pm, but you can check in until 10pm. Curfew midnight. Closed Nov.-Dec. 26. 10-bed dorm DM20, plus DM3 *Kurtaxe.*

Haus Achental, Ramsauerstr. 4 (☎45 49; fax 632 70), is a relatively inexpensive Gäste-haus right near the center of town. From the train station, take a right and walk five minutes down Ramsauer Str. Breakfast included. From DM65.

Campingplatz Allweglehen (☎23 96; fax 635 03; www.berchtesgaden.de/allweglehen) at Untersalzberg, is more than an hour's walk downstream from the station. DM11 with tent, children 6-16 years DM6.50.

Berchtesgaden is rife with restaurants for wealthy tourists. Pick up a *Wurst* from a vendor or score some groceries at the **Edeka Markt,** Königsseer Str. 22. Turn right when leaving the tourist center. (Open M-F 7:30am-6pm, Sa 7:30am-noon.)

Express-Grill Hendl, Maximilianstr. 8, is perhaps the least expensive meal in town. Traditional Bavarian dishes as well as hamburgers and cheeseburgers with fries are served up daily. From the train station, follow the signs marked "Zum Markt" and bear right on Maximillianstr. to munch on bratwurst with sauerkraut (DM5.60), or *bayerische Schweinhaxe* (DM 9.90). Open 11am-8pm.

Hotel Schwabenwirt, Königsseer Str. 1 (☎20 22), across the street from the tourist office, is slightly more expensive but relaxing. It features a sunny beer garden and English menus. Try a noodle dish (DM11.90-16.80), or the vegetarian lasagna with salad (DM14.80). Open 10am-10pm.

👁 SIGHTS AND HIKING

KEHLSTEINHAUS. The **Kehlsteinhaus,** called the **Eagle's Nest** by invading American soldiers, was built for the *Führer*'s 50th birthday as a refuge for entertainment. While Hitler only visited the mountaintop retreat 14 times, tourists bombard it constantly. The stone resort house is now a **restaurant** with no museum in sight (☎29 69; meals DM11-20). In fact, the best reason for visiting the Kehlsteinhaus is on

B A V A R I A

the way to the spectacular view from the 1834m mountain peak. The 6.5km road is something of an engineering marvel, hewn into solid rock by an army of 3000 men excused from conscription for health reasons. On the way back down, check out the 20+ buildings Hitler built for his officers and foreign dignitaries. They include an architectural studio, an experimental farm, a VIP hotel, and housing for SS officers *(Take bus #9538, direction: "Obersalzberg, Kehlstein" from the covered platform to the right of the train station to "Obersalzberg, Hintereck." June-Oct. roughly every 45min.; off-season much less regularly, check with the tourist office for schedules. Round-trip DM5.90. At Hintereck, catch bus #9549 to "Kehlstein Parkpl., Eagle's Nest." Every 30min. 9:30am-4pm. Open daily May-Oct. except on days of heavy snow. DM22, with Kurkarte DM19; children DM13, DM12. Alternately, you can buy the full round-trip ticket from the Bahnhof in Berchtesgaden for DM27.90.)* At Kehlstein, reserve your spot on a return bus (we mean it) at the booth when you get off. Reserving a place on a bus leaving one hour after the time of your Kehlstein arrival will give you enough time to explore the mountaintop if you don't plan to stop for lunch at the summit. *(Buses return to Hintereck and Berchtesgaden every 30min., last one at 5:05pm.)* From the parking lot, go through the tunnel and take the elevator to the Kehlsteinhaus. The elevator's golden mirrors are original, installed to quell Hitler's claustrophobia. Pack a jacket for the cool weather on the peak.

BERCHTESGADEN TOURS. A short, non-obligatory English-language tour of the **Kehlsteinhaus** departs daily at 10:30 and 11:40am. *(35min. DM7, children free. Meet at the tunnel entrance to the elevator.)* To catch the 10:30 tour, take the 9:00am bus from *Berchtesgaden* to Kehlstein; for the 11:40 tour, hop the 10:40am bus. A 4-hour English-language tour can be reserved one day in advance from Berchtesgaden Mini Bus Tours in the tourist office. *(☎649 71 or 621 72. DM55, under 13 DM27.50, under 6 free. Meet at the tourist office seven days a week at 1:30pm.)* The Bavarian hills are alive with the sound of minibuses; the same company also operates *Sound of Music* tours. Join English-speaking tour guides on a walk through the old city of Salzburg, Austria and a bus tour of the locations used in the film *The Sound of Music*. On the return to Berchtesgaden, sit back, relax, and listen to the "real-life" tale of the von Trapp family. *(4hr. DM50, children under 13 DM25, children under 6 free. Tours leave M-Sa 8:30am from the Berchtesgaden tourist office. Reservations required.)*

BERCHTESGADEN SCHLOß. The Berchtesgaden **Schloß** was a monastic priory until Bavarian rulers took over the area and appropriated the property. It now houses a collection of art and weaponry. Bear right from the station, through the overhang labeled *"Zum Markt,"* and go up the covered staircase. Cross over the train tracks on the footbridge behind the station and follow the *"Zum Markt"* signs to Maximilianstr. Bear right onto Maximilianstr., and veer right again at the cylindrical parking garage, veer left by Gasthof Triembacher and then veer no more—follow the signs around the corner to the Schloß. *(☎20 85. Open Easter-Sept. Su-F 10am-1pm, and 2-5pm; Oct. M-F 10am-noon and 2-4pm, Nov.-Easter M-F at 11am and 2pm. DM7, with Kurkarte DM6, students DM3.50, under 16 DM3.)*

KÖNIGSSEE. Wedged into extraordinary Alpine cliffs, the Königssee calmly mirrors the landscape on its blue-green surface. The walk from Berchtesgaden winds through fields and over brooks, and provides a breathtaking view of the Alps. From the train station, cross the street, turn right, and take a quick left over the bridge. Walk past the green-roofed building and take a left onto the gravel path near the stone wall. *(Follow the "Königssee" signs for a 5.5 km walk. Alternatively, take bus #9541 from the bus station near the train station, DM7.20 round trip, or the touristy Alpenexpress train, which departs from the Alpenexpress sign across the street from the train station and over the bridge. Every hour from 10am-4:55pm. DM8, under 16 DM6. By foot, bus, or train, you'll end up in the Königssee parking lot. Walk straight down Seestr. and look to your left for the Nationalpark Informationsstelle, which provides hiking information.)* At the end of Seestr. is the Königssee dock and the **Bayerische Seen Schiffahrt** counter, which offers cruises to other points along the Königssee. *(☎96 360; www.seenschifffahrt.de. Boats operate 8am-5:30pm. Roundtrips from DM19, under 14 DM9.50. 10% discount before 9am.)* The best lake view is from the **Malerwinkel** (painter's outlook), to the left of the lake, while the best aerial view is from the 1170m peak serviced by the Jenner cable car. (☎958 10. Take bus #9541, direction: "Königssee," from the train station to the end of the line. Open in summer 8am-5:30pm; in winter 9am-4:30pm. DM34, with Kurkarte DM33.)

SALZBERGWERKE. In the Salzbergwerke (salt mines) near town, visitors dress up in old miner's outfits, toboggan down snaking passages in the dark, and raft on a salt lake in mines that have been operating since 1517. The tour lasts an hour, but allow two hours for purchasing tickets, dressing up, and touring. (☎600 20. From the station, take bus #9548 to "Salzbergwerke." 1-2 per hr, 8:30am-7:40pm, DM1.50. Or, make the 30-minute trek across Königsseer Str. from the tourist office, through the parking lot and onto the gravel trail that runs along the river and eventually becomes a sidewalk. Open May to mid-Oct. daily 9am-5pm; mid-Oct. to Apr. M-Sa 12:30-3:30pm. DM21, children under 11 DM11.) To go moonlight rafting, call the Berchtesgaden Outdoor Club (☎50 01).

NEAR BERCHTESGADEN: RAMSAU ☎08657

Hiding among the alps 20km southwest of Berchtesgaden, the tiny village of Ramsau is a heaven-on-earth for hikers, white-water kayakers, cyclists, skiers, and all appreciators of Mother Nature's beauty. Dominated by the magnificent, snow-capped Waltzmann and Hochkalter mountains, Ramsau provides an ideal starting point for walks and mountain hikes in the **Berchtesgaden National Park.** In the winter, knicker-clad tourists take advantage of cross-country ski trails, sled runs, and ice skating on the Hintersee. The 16th-century **Pfarrkirche** (parish church), Im Tal 82 (☎988 60), rises magnificently from the Ramsauer Ache stream a couple sheep pastures down the road from the tourist office. To clear your sinuses, follow the white gravel-lined path across the road from the church and bear left at cafe Waldquelle to the **Kleingradierwerk Ramsau,** a small "outdoor brine inhalatorium" constructed out of hundreds of branches of mountain briar bushes. Even if your pains don't subside, a soothing 15 minutes of cool tranquility will dispel your hiking aches. Past the inhalatorium along a pebbly path is the **Kneipp-Gesundheitsanlage,** a mountain stream wading pool built by a local doctor to improve circulation. The ice-cold water can prep feet for a day in the sun or cool them after a day spent hiking long trails. (Always open. Free.)

From Ramsau, a vast network of well-marked hiking trails radiates throughout the surrounding Alpine landscape. One short but excellent hike leads from the center of town, following the Ramsauer Ache, through the **Zauberwald,** or "Magic Forest," to the sparkling green **Hintersee.** Hitch up your *Lederhosen* and follow Im Tal from the tourist office past the Pfarrkirche, taking a left on Fendtenweg by cafe Brotzeitstation. Cross the narrow foot bridge and, keeping the river on your right, follow the white-gravel trail to the Zauberwald and then on to the Hintersee. Weary legs make the return trip back to Ramsau by bus #9546 from Hintersee's bus station. (10min.; 1-2 per hr. DM3.25.)

Ramsau can be reached by bus, bike, or foot from Berchtesgaden. **Bus** #9546 runs hourly from the Berchtesgaden bus station, to the right of the train station. (15min. DM3.80 one-way, DM6.50 round-trip.) Rent **mountain bikes** at **Sport Brandner,** Im Tal 64. (☎790. Open M-F 9am-noon and 2-6pm, Sa 9am-noon. DM25 per day.) The friendly staff at the Ramsau **tourist office,** Im Tal 2, will shower you with trail maps and hiking information, and books rooms for them. (☎98 89 20; fax 772; www.ramsau-nationalparkgemeinde.de. Open Oct-June M-F 8am-noon and 1:15-5pm, Sa 9am-noon; July-Sept M-Sa 8am-5pm., Su 9am-noon and 2-5pm.) **Exchange money** and traveler's checks at **Raiffeisenbank,** Im Tal 89. (☎390. Open M-Tu and Th-F 8:30am-noon and 2-4:30pm, W 8:30am-noon and 2-3:30pm. 24hr. **ATM.**) The **post office,** Im Tal 87, 83486 Ramsau, is across from Gasthof Oberwirt. (☎275. Open M-F 8am-12:30pm and 2:30-6:30pm, Sa 8am-12:30pm.)

Although there is no youth hostel, Ramsau sports a wide selection of fairly inexpensive *Pensionen* and *Gästehäuser* (DM20-40, breakfast usually included). **Gästehaus Marxen,** Hinterseer Str. 22, is a quiet, friendly cottage up the hill from the "Marxenbrücke" bus stop. (☎213. DM21-26, including all taxes and breakfast.) **Campingpl. Simonhof,** Am Taubensee 19, basks in a beautiful location on the Lattenbach river five minutes from the "Taubensee" bus stop. (☎284. DM8.50, cars DM9, children 3-16 DM4.50.) The colorful **cafe Waldquelle,** Riesenbichl 25, offers seating on an outdoor patio with great opportunities for people-watching, or indoors among many of the local (stuffed) fauna of Bavaria. Slurp down home-made buttermilk or fill up on bratwurst with sauerkraut and potatoes while you listen to classic Bavarian folk music on the radio. (☎291. Open M-W and F-Su 11:30am-9pm. Most meals DM7-14.) At **Gasthof Oberwirt,** Im Tal 86, enjoy hot apple strudel and other local specialties as you gaze at Mt. Hochkalter. (☎225. Open 11am-8pm, DM8-23.) Buy **groceries** at the **Edeka,** Im Tal 60 (open M-F 7:30am-noon and 2:30-6pm, Sa 7:30am-noon). The **Bäckerei-Konditorei,** Im Tal 3, sells fresh bread and pastries, some of which are sold for half-price after 5pm. (☎12 51. Open M-F 6:30-noon and 2-6pm, Sa 6:30-noon.)

BAD REICHENHALL   ☎08651

In Bad Reichenhall, it is considered vital to sit in front of a salt water fountain daily, cover oneself in mud, and then inhale oxygen from an intimidating appara-tus. But even if you haven't come for the facials and cucumber eyepatches, the city's breathtaking views of the Austrian Alps and its "White Gold" (salt deposits) are just as pleasurable.

▊ PRACTICAL INFORMATION. Trains run to and from **Munich** (with a change in Freilassing, 2½hr., 1 per hr., DM43) and **Salzburg** (20min., 1 per hr., DM7.60). Both trains and **buses** are connected with Berchtesgaden (45min., 1 per hr., DM5.80). Rent a **bike** at **Sport Müller,** Spitalgasse 3. A half-day rental is DM12, and a full day runs DM15, children 20% off. (☎37 76; fax 69 511; email sport-mueller@t-online.de. Open M-F 9am-6:30pm, Sa 9am-1:30pm.) The **tourist office,** Wittelsbacherstr. 15, is to the right on the same road as the station, across from the Sparkasse bank. The staff provide maps and hiking tips. (☎606 303; fax 606 311; email info@bad-reichenhall.de; www.bad-reichenhall.de. Open M-F 8am-5:30pm, Sa 9am-noon.) **Club Aktiv,** Frühlingstr. 61, offers **rafting** and **canyoning** tours, and mountain biking and paragliding opportunities (☎672 38; www.rafting-fun.com; starting at DM60). The **post office,** Bahnhofstr. 35, 83435 Bad Reichenhall, is to the right as you exit the station (open M-F 8am-5:30pm, Sa 8am-noon).

▊▊ ACCOMMODATIONS AND FOOD. There is no youth hostel in Bad Reichen-hall and unfortunately most hotels are expensive. A small but very pleasant hotel is **Gästehaus Villa Fischer,** Adolf-Schmidt-Str. 4, which is among the least expensive accommodations in Bad Reichenhall proper, a short walk from the Kurgarten. (☎57 64. DM36-39. English and French spoken.) Still less expensive options can be found in the neighboring town of Bayerisch Gmain; inquire at the Bad Reichenhall tourist office for more information. Endless cafes and shops line the pedestrian zones of Salzburger Str. and Ludwigstr.; delectable Mozartkugeln (marzipan and chocolate balls) should be procured at the famous **Cafe Reber,** 10 Ludwigstr (M-Sa 9am-6pm, Su 10am-6pm; 2 pieces for DM2.40). At **Gasthof Bürgerbräu,** Am Rathauspl., traditionally dressed waiters and waitresses serve local beer direct from the in-house brewery (0.5L from DM4.10). Bavarian dishes run DM9.90-18.20, and vegetarian options can be had for DM7.90-16.90. (☎60 89. Open daily 9am-11:30pm.) **Restaurant Fuchsbau,** Inns-brucker Str. 19, serves pizza (DM9-14) and Bavarian meals for DM12.90-22.50. (☎58 59. Open Tu-Su 7pm-3am.) The cheapest meal in town, however, can probably be had at **Nordsee Restaurant** Ludwigstr. 16, a fast-food seafood mecca which offers sand-wiches from DM3-5, salads from DM3-8, and snack boxes from DM3-7. (☎55 14. Open 9am-8pm.) For basics, head to the **grocery** store **HL Markt,** Bahnhofstr. 20, to the right of the station (open M-F 7:30am-8pm, Sa 7:30am-4pm).

▊ SIGHTS. The **Salzmuseum,** Alte Saline, is peppered with exhibits on the his-tory and process of salt-making in the area. The obligatory tour in German winds through the damp underground passageways where brine (salt water) is pumped out of the mountain. (☎70 02 146. Tours May-Oct. daily 10, 11:30am, 2, and 4pm; Nov.-Apr.

T, Th 2 and 4pm. DM8.50, with Kurkarte DM7; children 6-16 DM4.50.) At the museum's **Glashütte,** visitors experience the beauty of glass-blowing and buying *(☎697 38; open M-F 9:30am-6pm, Sa 9am-1pm; free).* The reasonably priced **Glasofenwirtshaus,** on the second floor of the Glashütte, hosts a musical *Weißwurstfrühschoppen* (a Bavarian practice of getting plastered in the morning) every Saturday from 9am to 1pm with live music. *(Restaurant open M-F 9:30am-6pm, Sa 9am-1pm.)* The **Städtisches Heimatmuseum,** offers exhibits on the earliest settlements in the Saalach valley and the history of the town. *(Getreidegasse 4. ☎668 21. Open May-Oct. Tu-F 2-6pm and the first Sunday of the month from 10am-noon. DM 1.50, children DM 0.50, DM1 with Kurkarte.)*

The center of the town's spa circuit is the palatial **Kurgarten.** From the train station, turn right and walk down Bahnhofstr. Take a left onto Kurstr. and continue until you reach the Kurgarten on the left. *(Open Apr.-Oct. daily 7am-10pm; Nov.-Mar. 7am-6pm. Free.)* The **Altes Kurhaus** in the garden offers a therapeutic blue theater, a music pavilion, and a life-size chess set. At the Trinksole (salt spring fountain), buy a cup (DM0.20) to drink from the hot or cold salt springs. *(Open M-Sa 8am-12:30pm and 3-5pm, Su 10am-12:30pm.)* The 170m **Gradierwerk** out front is a bizarre wall known as an "open air inhalatorium." Built in 1912, it's covered with 250,000 *Dornbündel* (bundles of branches, briars, and thorns) through which salt-water mist trickles from Apr. to October. For best results, sit down-wind and inhale for 30 minutes daily. The **Predigtstuhlbahn,** the oldest twin-cable car in the world (1928), climbs 1614m of skiers' paradise to a beautiful lookout point and an expensive restaurant, situated in Südtirolerpl. across the Saalach River. *(☎21 27; fax 43 84. 1 trip per half-hour 9am-5pm. Round-trip DM24 if purchased at the tourist office, DM27 if purchased at the cable car; with Kurkarte DM26, students DM20, under 16 DM12, under 6 free.)* The **St. Zeno Minister,** Salzburger Str. 30, at the end of Zenostr., dates from the 12th century, and is the largest Romanesque Bascilica in Altbayern *(☎48 89).*

CHIEMSEE

For almost 2000 years, artists, architects, and musicians have chosen the Chiemsee region as the setting for their masterpieces. With its picturesque islands, meadows, pastures, forests, marshland, and dramatic crescent of mountains, the region first lured the 9th-century builders of the **Fraueninsel cloisters.** Later, the eccentric King Ludwig II arrived to build **Königsschloß Herrenchiemsee,** his third and last fairy-tale castle, on the **Herreninsel.** The poet Maximilian Haushofer lived and died in **Prien,** and 11-year-old Mozart composed a mass in **Seeon** while on holiday. Most modern visitors to "The Bavarian Ocean" are artists of leisure; the area has been overrun by resorts and prices have risen. But don't expect to find many foreigners—Chiemsee is where the German *nouveaux riches* vacation. Prien, the largest lake town, offers easy access to the ski areas of the **Kampenwand,** the surrounding curtain of mountains, and to the resort paradises **Aschau** and **Sachrang.** For information on white-water **rafting** in the Chiemsee area, call *Sport Lukas* ☎ (08649) 243. Throughout the summer several **Trachtenfeste,** traditional festivals featuring parades, folklore, and pilgrimages, take place in different towns at the end of July and in mid-August; entrance fees run DM5-7.

PRIEN AM CHIEMSEE ☎08051

Without question, Prien's best qualities are its idyllic Chiemsee coast and its highly frequented train station, which facilitates the use of the town as a base for sights elsewhere on the lake.

◪ **GETTING THERE.** Located on the northwestern corner of the Chiemsee, Prien has **train** connections to **Munich** (1hr., 1 per hr., DM36) and **Salzburg,** Austria (40min., 1 per hr., DM 34.) Call ☎28 74 for train information. Rent **bikes** at **Radsport Reischenböck,** Bahnhofpl. 6 (☎46 31; www.reischenboeck.de), 100m to your left after exiting the train station (DM14 for one day, open M-F 8am-noon and 2-6pm, Sa 8am-noon), or hook up a set of **inline skates** from **Intersport Erhard,** Bernauer Str.

16 (☎903 616). Walk right out of the station, left onto Seestr., and left at the next intersection to Bernauer Str. (☎903 616. From DM25 per day, knee and wrist pads included.) To paddle the Chiemsee, rent a **boat** from **Bootsverleih Stöffl**, at the red and white umbrella stand at the end of the path to the Chiemsee. Turn left before the ferries. (☎20 00 or 16 16. From DM 8 per boat per hr.; open daily Apr.-Oct.)

🔁 PRACTICAL INFORMATION. The train station is a few blocks from the city center and a 20-minute walk north of the lake. To reach the Altstadt, turn right as you exit the station and then turn left on Seestr., which becomes Alte Rathausstr. The large, modern **tourist office**, Alte Rathausstr. 11, five minutes away on the left, is full of free maps and brochures, and books **private rooms** for free. (☎690 50 or 69 05 55; fax 69 05 40; e-mail info@prien.chiemsee.de; www.prien.chiemsee.de. Starting from DM26-33, breakfast included. Office open M-F 8:30am-6pm, Sa 9am-noon.) Check out the **ticket booth** outside the train station for all your entertainment needs. (Open M-F 6:40am-7pm, Sa 8am-6pm, and Sun 8am-12:30pm and 1:20pm-6pm.) Putt around at **Minigolf Prien**, Seestr. 100 (Open 10am-10pm. DM 4.30, students DM4, children under 14 DM3), or dance the night away on the 3hr. **Chiemsee Tanzschiff river cruises,** leaving every F at 7:30pm from the Prien dock (☎60 90; DM30). Phone ☎10 37 to find out which **pharmacy** is open on each night.

🔃 ACCOMMODATIONS AND FOOD.
The cheapest bed in town is at the **Jugendherberge (HI),** Carl-Braun-Str. 66, a 15min. walk from the station and 10min. from the lake. From the station, go right on Seestr. and under the train overpass. After two blocks, take a left on Staudenstr., which curves right and turns into Carl-Braun-Str. (☎687 70; fax 68 77 15. Showers, lockers, and breakfast included. Sheets DM5.50. Reception 8-9am, 5-7pm, and 9:30-10pm. Lockout 9am-1pm. Curfew 10pm. Open early Feb.-Nov. 6-bed rooms DM25.) An inexpensive hotel is **Pension Dellner,** Am Berg 11. From the train station, bear right onto Seestr. and walk about 5min. Take another right on Jensenstr., walk for another 2min. and take a left onto Am Berg. (☎48 30; fax 469 17. Breakfast included. Open May-Oct. DM36; doubles DM72.) **Campingpl. Hofbauer,** Bernauer Str. 110, is a 30min. stroll from the center of town. From the station, turn left at Seestr., left again at the next intersection, and follow Bernauer Str. out of town past the gas station and McDonald's. (☎41 36; fax 626 57. Open Apr.-Oct. Reception 7:30-11:00am, 2-10pm. DM10.50 per person, children 14 and under DM5.50, DM10 per tent and car. Showers included.)

Gather **groceries** from **HL Markt,** Seestr. 11 (open M-F 8am-8pm, Sa 8am-4pm). Most of the restaurants in Prien cater to the vacationing bourgeoisie. Try **Scherer Restaurant,** Alte Rathausstr. 1, on the corner of Alte Rathausstr. and Bernauer Str. The self-serve restaurant cooks up hearty meals and filling salads. (☎45 91. DM9.50-23.50, daily specials DM6.90-8. Open M-F 9am-9pm, Sa 9am-3pm.) For a delicious Italian meal, descend into the green candlelight ambience of **La Piazza,** Seestr. 7 (☎56 52; open Tu-Su 11:00am-2:30pm, 5-11:30pm). The lively waitstaff serves savory pasta dishes (DM 11-13) and large, thin-crust pizzas (DM 9.80). Of course, the cheapest meal in town is found 15 minutes from the Marktpl. at the friendly **McDonalds,** Bernauer Str. 66, with familiar extra value meals (DM7.99).

📷 SIGHTS. To soothe that sore back, wade in the cold water of Prien's *Kneipp* water cure and then jump into a 90°F (32°C) **thermal bath.** The canary yellow **Mariä Himmelfahrt Church** rises heavenward from the Marktpl.; from the train station, take a right onto Hochriesstr., a left onto Seestr., and walk straight for two minutes toward the steeple. The red-and-blue marble interior of the church boasts beautiful 18th century chandeliers, paintings, statues, and ceiling frescos. On the square behind the church rests the **Heimatmuseum,** a testament to the distinctive Bavarian culture of the 17th century. With over 20 rooms, it houses enough clocks, fishing rods, guns, coins, and stuffed local fowl to fulfill any estate buyer's dreams. (*☎69 05 42; open Apr.-Oct. Tu-F 10am-noon and 3-5pm, Sa 10am-noon, Nov.-Mar. 10am-noon and 3-5pm Tu & F only; DM3, students and children DM2.)*

HERRENINSEL AND FRAUENINSEL

Ferries float across the waters of the Chiemsee from Prien to the **Herreninsel** (Gentlemen's Island), the **Fraueninsel** (Ladies' Island), and towns on the other side of the lake. (Roughly hourly departures from the Prien dock, 6:40am-7:30pm. Round-trip to Herreninsel DM10, under 15 DM5; to Fraueninsel or to both islands DM12.50, under 15 DM6.) Both islands are now co-ed, although this wasn't always the case—a monastery on Herreninsel once complemented the still-extant nunnery on Fraueninsel in religious chastity and isolation. Supposedly, mischievous members of the cloth (of both sexes) met up on **Krautinsel** (Herb Island) and practiced the eyebrow-raising act of gardening; nowadays, the island remains uninhabited and unferried. For more information on passage to the islands, call Chiemsee-Schiffahrt (☎ 60 90). To get to the dock, hang a right from the Prien train station's main entrance and follow Seestr. for about 20 minutes. Alternatively, a slow 19th-century green steam train, the **Chiemseebahn,** takes visitors from the train station to the dock roughly hourly; to get there, follow the *Chiemseebahn* sign. (Departs 9:40am-6:15pm. One-way DM3.50, round-trip DM6; children under 15 DM 1.50, DM3. Total package, including train shuttle and ship passage, DM 16.5.) The train station **information booth,** though central, has very limited hours (open July to mid-Sept. M-F 12:45-5:45pm).

SCHLOß HERRENCHIEMSEE. "Never can as unsuitable a location have been chosen for something as tasteless as this unfortunate copy of the palace at Versailles," Bavarian poet Ludwig Thomas pouted. Although some join Thomas in scowling at the Königsschloß's extravagance, year after year thousands of tourists faithfully flock to the Herreninsel to stroll the halls of this excessively furnished palace. To get to the palace from the ferry landing, either walk along the paved footpath (20min.) or take one of the horse-drawn carriages that run every 15 minutes. *(DM4, children under 15 DM2.50.)* The architecture of **Königsschloß Herrenchiemsee** is fabulously overwrought as only King Ludwig II could manage. *(☎ 68 870; fax 68 87 99; email info@herren-chiemsee.de; www.herren-chiemsee.de. Open Apr.-Sept. daily 9am-6pm; Oct.-Mar. 10am-4pm. Admission and obligatory tour DM11, seniors, students, and disabled persons DM9, under 16 free with adult. German tours every 10min.; English tours 10:30 and 11:30am, 1, 2, 3, and 4pm.)* Ludwig bankrupted Bayern while building the palace, resulting in an odd juxtaposition of starkly barren rooms and the 20 overadorned chambers which were completed. The entire U-shaped palace is a shameless attempt to be larger, better, and more extravagant than Versailles. Ludwig II was so obsessed with the "Sun King" that he commissioned exact replicas of Versailles originals to grace the walls of his palace. There's even a **Hall of Mirrors,** only Ludwig's is longer than Louis's. It took 25 people half an hour to light the more than 500 candles in this room when Ludwig decided to tour his palace. Candle-lit concerts are hosted here throughout the summer. For a more supernatural glow, check out the purple nightlight Ludwig had installed in his bedroom to mitigate his fear of the dark. None of Ludwig's other castles so well reflect his obsessive qualities or his relentless insistence on creating an alternate reality. A **museum** documenting Ludwig's life lies just inside the castle entrance. *(Open Apr.-Sept. 9am-5pm; Oct.-Mar. 10am-4pm. DM4, students DM3.)* In the summers, evening concerts take place at the castle; call the Prien tourist office for more information. For other Herrenchiemsee **tourist information,** call ☎ (08051) 30 69.

FRAUENINSEL. Despite its proximity to Ludwig's material world, the Fraueninsel is no material girl. In fact, it's quite the opposite: a small realm of hard-working nuns and fishermen that shuns the most material of all possessions—the automobile; only footpaths wind through this subdued village. From the dock, a marked path curls toward the **island cloister,** passing its medicinal herb garden. The nuns make their own marzipan, beeswax candles, and five kinds of liqueurs, for sale in the convent shop. (0.2L *Klosterlikör* DM8.50.) The abbey dates back to at least 866. St. Irmengard, the great-granddaughter of Charlemagne and earliest known abbess of the cloister, is memorialized in a **chapel** behind the main altar. Her sarcophagus was exhumed in the 17th century, and in 1928 her remains were encased in glass within the altar. They're not much to look at—that's what 1,000 years will do to you. More interesting are the countless messages written to Irmengard on the opposite wall in thanks for deliverance after prayer. The **Torhalle** (gate) is the oldest surviving part of the cloister; various artifacts, including the 8th-century Merovingian **Cross of Bischofhofen,** are displayed in the **Michaelskapelle** above the gate (DM2). The Torhalle also plays host to art exhibits which change yearly. *(☎(08054) 72 56. Open June-Sept, DM8.)* The entire island can be circumnavigated on foot in 45 minutes. There are quite a few *Gaststätte* scattered all over the island, but prices are high because owners know they have hungry tourists trapped. Bring some food or be prepared to splurge. If you are stranded and starving, try the food store next to the post office on the right sight of the island when you step off the ferry. For **tourist information,** call ☎(08054) 92 16.

ELSEWHERE NEAR THE CHIEMSEE

While Prien is considered the "metropolis of the Bavarian sea," countless other idyllic towns melt into the landscape, offering resort luxuries, nature hikes, and historical attractions. **Übersee,** a playground for bikers, sailors, and windsurfers, lies on the Chiemsee just past Prien on the Munich-Salzburg train line. Contact their **tourist office** (☎(08642) 295; fax 62 14; email info@uebersee.com; www.uebersee.com). Just northwest of the Chiemsee lies **Bad Endorf,** famed for its thermal baths and popular with older Germans; call the Kurverwaltung for more information (☎(08053) 30 08 22; fax 30 08 30; email info@bad-endorf.de; www.bad-endorf.de). Bad Endorf also has a **hostel (HI)** located 3km from the train station on Rankhamer Weg 11. Take a left onto Bahnhofstr. when you leave the train station and walk until you hit Traunsteiner Str.; go right and walk to Hauptstr., take a left and walk to Lederer Bergstr.; the Jugendherberge sign will be down on your left. The hostel is quiet, cheery, and cheap. (☎(08053) 509; fax 32 92. DM16.50, sheets DM5.50. Closed in Dec.) Little villages curl up at the foothills of the mountains. The tourist offices for **Grassau Verkehrsamt** (☎(08641) 23 40; fax 40 08 41; e-mail verkehrsamt@grassau-info.de; www.grassau-info.de), **Rimsting Verkehrsamt** (☎(08051) 68 76 21; fax 68 76 30; www.rimsting.de), and **Riedering Verkehrsamt** (☎(08036) 34 48; fax 37 58) can supply more information. **Rottau,** just south of the Chiemsee, nestles in a mountain ridge; contact its **Verkehrsamt** (☎(08641) 27 73; fax 14 19; email verkehrsverein-rottau@t-online.de; www.rottau.de).

    Aschau, a beautiful mountain town southwest of the Chiemsee, offers everything from horseback riding to mountain gondola rides, as well as solaria, tobogganing, skiing, and sailing. Head first to the **tourist office,** Kampenwandstr. 38. From the train station, take a left on Bahnhofstr., which turns into Kampenwandstr. (☎(08052) 90 49 37; fax 90 49 45; email info@aschau.de; www.aschau.de. Open May to mid-Oct. M-F 8am-noon and 2-6pm, Sa 9am-noon, Su 10am-noon; mid-Oct. to Apr. M-F 8am-noon and 1:30-5pm.) The office is located in the middle of a small pond in front of the Kurpark, where weekly summer concerts are held. Ten minutes further down Kampenwandstr. sits **Schloß Hohenaschau,** built atop Burg Hohenaschau as the erstwhile outlook and protection point for the Prien Valley in the 12th century. *(Required tours given May-Sept. Tu-Fr at 9:30, 10:30, and 11:30am; Apr. and October Th at 9:30, 10:30, and 11:30am.)* **Accommodations** can be found down the street from the tourist office at **Gästehaus Kirchlechner,** Kampenwandstr. 30. (☎(08052) 761. DM27-30 33 per person. Three night minimum.) Most restaurants in Aschau are expensive, but **Penny Markt,** Kampenwandstr. 22, offers a medium-size selection of your basic four food groups (open M-F 8:30am-7pm, Sa 8am-4pm). Aschau is easily reached by train from the Munich-Salzburg route via Prien, and buses link Aschau to Munich.

    To reach the tiny town of **Sachrang,** an exquisite Alpine village on the Austrian border, take bus #9502 from the stop in front of Aschau's train station. For more information on excellent skiing, mountain climbing, and walking tours, stop by the tourist office, **Sachrang Verkehrsamt,** Dorfstr. 20. (☎(08057) 378; fax 10 51, email info@sachrang.de, www.sachrang.de. Open M-Tu and Th-F 8am-noon and 2-5pm, W 8am-noon, Sa 9am-noon.)

BURGHAUSEN
☎ 08677

The proverbial castle-on-the-hill overshadows everything else in tiny Burghausen, a hamlet separated from Austria by the Salzach River. The town lies in the Ice Age sediment deposited from the Salzach glacier, which carved a deep valley into the surrounding cliff. In medieval times, the town was protected by the longest fortress in Europe, which continues to loom broodingly over the Altstadt.

▼ PRACTICAL INFORMATION. Burghausen is most easily reached by **train** from **Munich** (2hr., 1 per hr. via Mühldorf from 5:10am until 9pm), and **buses** run from Mühldorf, the transportation hub of eastern Bayern. Stepping off the train, you'll find yourself smack in the middle of suburbia. Don't panic. One hundred meters to your left at the end of the parking lot is a city map. Follow Marktlerstr. (directly in front of you) to the right; it's a 30 minute hike to the Stadtpl. Or take Bus #1 on Marktlerstr. around the corner from the train station. It's four stops to "Stadtpl." (Every 30min. 6:35am-7:35pm; fewer on weekends. DM1.70.) For a **taxi**, call ☎ 22 23. The **tourist office,** Stadtpl. 112-114, is located in the peppermint green **Rathaus** at the far end of the Stadtpl. (☎ 24 35; fax 88 71 55; email tourismundkultur@burghausen.de; www.burghausen.de. Open M-W and F 8am-noon and 1:30-5pm, Th 8am-noon and 1:30-6pm, Sa 10am-1pm.) To explore the Burghausen area by **boat,** join **Plättenfahrten** on a 1½ hour tour down the Salzach River on an ancient open-air salt gondola. Tours leave from the dock at Tittmoning, 18km south of Burghausen, and land at the Salzach boat launching dock in Burghausen. (☎ 24 35. Tours leave every Sunday from June to mid-Sept. DM12, children and disabled persons DM6.) The **post office,** In den Grüben 162, 84489 Burghausen, is one block down from the Rathaus.

▐▐▓ ACCOMMODATIONS AND FOOD. The **Jugendherberge Burghausen (HI),** Kapuzinergasse 235, is a schlep from the train station but close to the cafe-heavy In den Grüben. To avoid the 45 minute walk, take city bus #1 from the train station through Stadtpl. to "Hl.-Geist-Spital." Walk straight and turn left onto Kapuzinergasse (15min.). Or from Stadtpl., continue through the arch at the far side of the square onto In den Grüben. At the end, cross the intersection to the left of the church onto Spitalgasse and turn right onto Kapuzinergasse. The hostel offers immaculate, spacious four-bed dorms with private showers and an impressive view of the castle, and the staff speaks fluent English. (☎ 41 87; fax 91 13 18. DM24, sheets and breakfast included. Reception 8-9am, 11:45am-1pm, 5-7pm, and 9:30-10pm; closed Dec; no curfew.) Many cheap **private rooms,** starting from as little as DM10-20, including breakfast, can be found through the tourist office. If you're after Bavarian dishes, try **Hotel Post,** Stadtpl. 39. After 450 years, it knows its *Würstchen.* (☎ 96 50; www.hotelpost.de. Most meals DM13.80-19.80, beer DM4.) For A-plus "I" cuisine, try **Taj Mahal,** In den Grüben 166, which serves a unique mix of Indian and Italian dishes. Vegetarian options DM13.50-17, pizzas DM8-11.50, and pasta DM7.50-11.50 abound (open Tu-Sa 11:30am-2pm and 6-11:30pm, Su 11:30am-11pm). Buy **groceries** at **Edeka** on In den Grüben, across from the post office (open M-F 8am-1pm and 2-7pm, Sa 7am-2pm).

▧ SIGHTS. The 1034m **Burg,** the longest medieval fortress in Europe, was considered impregnable—and indeed, it was only breached once. In 1742, the Habsburg Empire, eager to extend its borders into Bayern, fell upon the border town of Burghausen. Cowed by the Austrian show of arms and lacking outside reinforcements, Burghausen opened its gates without a fight. Days later, on October 16, 1742, Burghausen's moment of glory came: the brash 26-year-old *Hofkaminkehrermeister* (Master Chimney Sweep) Karl Franz Cura recruited 40 grenadiers for the seemingly impossible task of breaking through the castle walls. In one fell swoop, Cura brilliantly freed the castle and the city. Burghausen remains a distinguished fortress town akin to Heidelberg and Rothenburg in its medieval glory, only much less trafficked.

These days, the **castle ramparts** can be walked without violent reprisals, and the Burg's friendly **Information Center** (Burg 9) can keep you abreast of the concerts, historical festivals, and art exhibits that now take place there. The Town of Burghausen's **historical museum** is housed in the upper halls of the Burg. (☎651 98. *Open May-Sept. daily 9am-6pm; mid-Mar. to Apr. and Oct.-Nov. 10am-4:30pm. DM2.50, children DM1.*) In addition, the **Staatliche Sammlung** contains collections of daily wares of the medieval inhabitants of the Burg. (☎46 59. *Open Apr.-Sept., F-W 9am-6pm, Th 9am-8pm; Oct.-Mar. 10am-4pm. DM5, children free.*) For the price of lugging your picnic basket up the steep footpath, the castle offers a grassy park area with a ravishing view of the town's red-tiled roofs and colorful gables. The footpath starts behind the **St. Jakobskirche,** a 12th century church across from the Rathaus. The castle's eerie **Folterturm** (torture chamber) was used until 1918. (*Open Apr. to early May 10am-5pm, May-Oct. 9am-6pm. DM3, children DM1.*) A peek out one of the upper story windows affords a view of the grassy banks of the Wöhrsee far below, a popular swimming hole in the hot summer months. The **Hexenturm** across the way held accused witches until 1751. Below the castle, the rows of pastel facades lining the **Stadtpl.** shimmer with such soft medieval splendor that you may suspect Burghausen to be a doll house city. At the far end of the Stadtpl. looms the magnificent Baroque **Studienkirche St. Joseph,** a 1630 Jesuit convent.

Across the Stadtpl. from the Studienkirche lies the late-night hotspot of Burghausen, **In den Grüben.** Most of its cafes, restaurants, and dance clubs don't open until 7 or 8pm, and stay open past midnight. Every year in the late spring, In den Grüben plays host to B'Jazz Burghausen, an annual jazz festival which has hosted musicians of international fame, such as Dizzy Gillespie. Check out www.b-jazz.com or call ☎14 11 for more information on this year's festival.

PASSAU   ☎0851

Baroque arches cast long shadows across the cobblestone alleyways of Passau, a 2000-year-old city situated at the confluence of the Danube, the Inn, and the Ilz Rivers. The heavily fortified medieval castle, musty Gothic Rathaus, and row of bishops' palaces bear witness to the fact that this *Dreiflüssestadt* (three-river city) was once a center both of secular and religious power. In 739, the Church awarded Passau the seat of a diocese. Centuries later the *Stephansdom*, originally a Gothic structure and rebuilt as a pink-columned Baroque cathedral after a destructive fire, inspired the construction of an offspring cathedral by the same name in Vienna. In the 13th century, enterprising local merchants monopolized the European salt trade—a very profitable achievement, given that Europeans then consumed six times more salt than they do today. Today *Eiscafes* and monasteries, shoe stores and art galleries line the streets of this ancient city.

▐ GETTING THERE AND GETTING AROUND

Trains: Hauptbahnhof located west of downtown on Bahnhofstr. (☎(0180) 599 66 33). Trains to **Regensburg** (1-2hr., every hr., DM32); **Nürnberg** (2hr., every 2hr., DM60); **Munich** (2hr., every hr., DM52); **Frankfurt** (4½hr., every 2hr., DM74-131); and **Vienna** (3½hr., 1-2 per hr.). The service point **information counter** at the train station has officials who will answer questions and provide information about train transportation. Open M-Sa 6:45am-9pm, Su 8am-7:30pm. The **ticket counter** is open M-Sa 5:50am-7:25pm, Su 8am-8:25pm. Dump your bags in **lockers** for DM2-4.

Buses: Service from the train station to various other cities in eastern Bavaria provided by **Regionalbus Ostbayern** (☎75 63 70). **SWP Passau** busses make a number of stops within the city and in neighboring towns; single ticket DM2, 4 rides DM5, 8 rides DM9. For schedules call ☎56 02 72 or check out www.swp-passau.de. The **City-Bus** runs from the station to the Rathaus (M-F 6:30am-10:10pm, Sa 7:30am-4:15pm; every 10-30min.; DM0.50).

Ferries: Donau Schiffahrt (☎92 92 92; www.donauschiffahrt.com) steamers chug along the Danube to **Linz,** Austria, May to Oct. daily at 9am, and also at 1:10pm June-Sept. (5hr.). To daytrip it, take the morning steamer to Linz and return to Passau by bus or train in the afternoon (one way ship DM38, round-trip ship plus bus or train DM48; children under 15 50% off). Or stay overnight in Linz and return with the steamer the next day at 2:15pm (arrives in Passau at 8:40pm). The **"Three Rivers" tour** of the city runs daily Mar. to Oct. (every 30 min from 10am-5pm, 45min. trip; DM11, under 15 DM5.50). For an elegant evening of live music and dancing, take an **evening river cruise** among a coupled clientele on the Tanzfahrten ab Passau steamer (4¾hr.; May-Oct. every Saturday at 7pm; DM28). All ships depart from the docks along the Fritz-Schäffer-Promenade by the Rathaus.

Bike Rental: From ÖBB at the Hauptbahnhof (☎530 43 97; open M-F 5:50am-6:45pm, Sa 5:30am-6:45pm, Su 8am-6:40pm). Prices depend on whether you came to Passau by train. The stunning **Donau Radweg** (bike path) begins in Donaueschingen and continues through Passau into Austria; ask at the tourist office for more information and for cycling maps of the area.

▲⚡ ORIENTATION AND PRACTICAL INFORMATION

To reach the city center from the train station, follow Bahnhofstr. to the right until you reach **Ludwigsplatz.** Bear left downhill across Ludwigspl. to Ludwigstr., the beginning of the pedestrian zone, which becomes Rindermarkt, Steinweg, and finally Große Messergasse. Continuing straight onto Schustergasse when the street ends, you will soon reach the **Altstadt;** hang a left on Schrottgasse and you'll stumble upon the **Rathausplatz.** From there, a glance upwards yields a picturesque view of the Danube and the steep hill, beyond which lies the **Veste Oberhaus** fortress. Heading farther east on the tip of the peninsula leads to the point where the three rivers converge.

Tourist Office: Tourist Information, Rathauspl. 3 (☎95 59 80; fax 351 07; email tourist-info@passau.de; www.passau.de), on the banks of the Danube next to the Rathaus (see directions above). Free brochures, schedules, and tour information as well as cycling maps and guides. The staff books rooms for a DM5 fee and provides information on cheaper hotels and *Pensionen* in the surrounding area (DM35-60). *WasWannWo,* a free monthly guide, chronicles everything going down in Passau. Office open Easter to mid-Oct. M-F 8:30am-6pm, Sa-Su 9:30am-3pm; the rest of the year M-Th 8:30am-5pm, F 8:30am-4pm. A smaller **branch,** across from the train station at Bahnhofstr. 36 (☎95 59 80; fax 572 98), has free maps and brochures stocked outside in case you get into town after hours. Open Easter to mid-Oct. M-F 9am-5pm, Sa-Su 9am-1pm; the rest of the year M-Th 9am-5pm, F 9am-4pm, Sa-Su 9am-1pm.

Tours: German-language walking tours of the city (1hr.) meet at the **Königsdenkmal** (monument) in front of the church at Dompl. Apr.-Oct. M-F 10:30am and 2:30pm, Sa-Su 2:30pm. DM4.50, children DM2. City tours in English may be arranged through the tourist office.

Budget Travel: ITO Reisebüro, Bahnhofstr. 28 (☎540 48), across the street from the train station in the Donau Passage. Open M-F 8am-6pm, Sa 9am-1pm.

Currency Exchange: Take a right out of the train station down Bahnhofstr. until Ludwigspl. to reach **Volksbank-Raiffeisenbank,** Ludwigspl. 1, which cashes traveler's checks for a DM2 fee per check. Open M-W and F 8:30am-12:30pm and 1:15-4:15pm, Th 1:15-5pm.

Laundromat: Rent-Wash, Neuburger Str. 19. From Ludwigspl., walk up Dr.-Hans-Kapfinger-Str., turn right onto Neuburger Str. and then bear left. Open daily 7am-midnight. Wash DM5; dry DM3.

Emergency: Police, Nibelungenstr. 17, ☎110. **Fire** and **Ambulance,** ☎112.

Hospital: Klinikum Passau, Bischof-Pilgrim-Str. 1, ☎530 00.

Pharmacy: 24hr. service rotates among the city's pharmacies; check the listings in the notices section of the daily newspapers (*Tagespresse* or *Passauer Neue Presse*) or in the window of the **Bahnhof Apotheke,** Bahnhofstr. 17 (☎150 301), to the right of the station. Open M-F 8am-6pm, Sa 9am-2pm.

Post Office: 94032 Passau, at Bahnhofstr. 27 (☎959 54 43), to the right of the train station as you exit. Open M-F 8am-6pm, Sa 8:30am-12:30pm.

BAVARIA

▮ ACCOMMODATIONS AND CAMPING

Most *Pensionen* in downtown Passau start at DM60, while vacation houses in the surrounding area (2-6 beds) run DM30-75. The only youth hostel in town is usually swarming with German schoolchildren, especially during June and July.

Jugendherberge (HI), Veste Oberhaus 125 (☎413 51; fax 437 09), is perched high above the Danube in the sentinel guards' living quarters above the main gate to the medieval castle. A 35-45min. walk from the train station and a 20-30min. uphill trek from the Rathaus. Cross the suspension bridge downstream from the Rathaus, then **ignore the misplaced sign** pointing up the steps straight ahead. Instead turn right and proceed through the lefthand tunnel. (Skeptics who follow the signs will get there, too— they'll just go through an extra 20min. of steep hell for their disbelief.) On your left will be a steep (but more direct) cobblestone driveway leading up to the hostel; when the path forks, take a left, walk through the yellow house, then turn right for the hostel. Or you can hop on the **shuttle** *(Pendelbus)* from Rathauspl. bound for the museum adjacent to the hostel (Easter to mid.-Oct. every 30min. M-F 10:30am-5pm, Sa-Su 11:30am-6pm; DM3, round-trip DM4). The hostel has a fantastic location and is beautiful and clean, but the 8-bed rooms feel very cramped. Breakfast included. Sheets DM5.50. Reception 7-11:30am and 4-11:30pm. New arrivals after 4pm only. Curfew 11:30pm. Reservations recommended. Dorm beds DM22.

▨ Rotel Inn, Hauptbahnhof/Donauufer (☎951 60; fax 951 61 00). From the train station, walk straight ahead down the steps, down Haissengasse, and through the tunnel to this outlandish hotel right on the river. Built in 1993 in the shape of a sleeping man to protest Europe's decade-long economic slumber, this self-proclaimed "Hotel of the Future" packs travelers into tight rooms bedecked with primary-color plastics. Inside, passionate graffiti depicts a monstrous Japanese auto industry trampling America and squashing Europe. Claustrophobes beware; each room has only three feet of walking space before your shins smash against the 4-by-8 foot wall-to-wall bed. Radios in every room. Breakfast DM8. 24hr. reception. Singles DM35; doubles DM50.

Pension Rößner, Bräugasse 19 (☎93 13 50; fax 931 35 55; e-mail roessner@passau.baynet.de; www.passau.baynet.de). From the Rathaus, walk downstream along the Danube. Directly on the Danube, these homey rooms are among the cheapest in the Altstadt. Call upstairs if there's no one at the reception. All rooms come with bath, radio, and telephone. Breakfast included. Price per person DM40-60.

Gasthof-Pension "Zur Brücke," Landrichterstr. 13 (☎434 75), on the Ilz river, 45min. from the Rathaus; cross the Luitpoldbrücke bridge and continue right along the curve, through the left-hand tunnel. Follow Halser Str. to the right of the yellow house, which eventually turns into Grafenleite, along the Ilz river for about 20min., then turn right on Pfarrer-Einberger-Weg and left on Pustetweg; take a right over the bridge and a quick right onto Landrichterstr. Even better, take bus #4 to "Hals." Quiet, sunny rooms are bargains for the idyllic location. Breakfast buffet included. Singles DM35; doubles with bath DM35 per person.

Camping: Zeltpl. Ilzstadt, Halser Str. 34 (☎414 57). Downhill from the youth hostel at a beautiful location on the riverbank. Walk down Halser Str. (see above) all the way to the riverbank; keep right when Halser Str. becomes Grafenleite. Or take buses #1, 2, 3, or 4 from "Exerzierpl." to "Ilzbrücke." Open May-Oct. No camping vehicles. Tent and hot showers included. Reception 5-10pm. DM10, under 18 DM8, under 6 free.

◖ FOOD

The student district centers on **InnStr.** near the university. From Ludwigspl., head down Nikolastr. and turn right on Innstr., which runs parallel to the Inn River; the street is lined with good, cheap places to eat. **Edeka,** on Ludwigstr. at Grabengasse (open M-F 8am-8pm, Sa 7:30am-4pm), and **SuperSpar,** Residenzpl. 13 (open M-F 7:30am-6pm, Sa 7:30am-12:30pm), provide supermarket eats.

▨ **Café Kowalski,** Oberer Sand 1 (☎350 96). From Ludwigspl., walk down Nikolastr. toward the Inn river; take a left on Gottfried-Schäffer-Str. and walk almost two blocks until you see the terrace on the left side of the street. Home of the largest schnitzel in Passau. Chic décor, a groovy bar, and a terrace with outdoor seating overlooking the Inn. Hordes of college students chill with ice cream specialties (DM4.80-10.80), funky drinks (DM4.50-6.90), fresh salads (DM12.80-14.80), and pasta (DM13.80-14.80). Daily lunch specials DM8.50; reduced menu prices during happy hours. Every Thursday there's a grill party on the terrace, and the house rocks to the vibes of live DJ's until 3am on the weekends. Open Su-Th 10am-11pm, F-Sa 10am-3am.

Café Duft, Theresienstr. 22. Folksy indoor and outdoor cafe boasting a garden in back, with little lighted trees and an aquatic theme. Lip-smackin' fruit-topped yogurt (DM4.20) and breakfast combos (DM8.50-19.50). Soups hearty enough to be meals (DM5.20-5.50). Vegetarian options include hors d'oeuvres and Mexican entrees. Open daily 9am-1am. Kitchen open until 11pm.

Innsteg Café Kneipe, Innstr. 13 (☎512 57), one block from Nikolastr. The black-painted interior is inviting to Mozart devotees and body-pierced revolutionaries alike. Very popular with students. Nurse a beer (Maß DM8.50) on the balcony over the riverbank. Daily menu DM4-23.50. Salads DM3.50-16.90. Open daily 10am-1am.

Café Venezia, Kastnergasse 2 (☎27 44), one block from the Dompl. on the Danube. Italian cuisine with a view of the river. Spaghetti, tortellini, and rigatoni dishes DM10.90-14.90; Italian ice cream specialties DM2-16.90.

Wirtshaus Bayerischer Löwe, Dr.-Hans-Kapfinger-Str. 3 (☎958 01 11). Authentic—or at least that's what the waves of tourists believe. For big German food and appetites, try their daily lunch specialty (DM9.90). Beer DM4.20-5.40. Open daily 9am-1am.

👁 SIGHTS

STEPHANSDOM. Passau's beautiful Baroque architecture reaches its zenith at this sublime cathedral. *(Open M-Sa 7:30-10:45am and 12:30-6pm. Free.)* Hundreds of cherubs are sprawled across the ceiling and the **world's largest church organ** stands above the choir. Its 17,774 pipes and multiple keyboards can accommodate five organists at once. *(Organ concerts May-Oct. M-Sa at noon. DM4, students, seniors, and children DM2. Th at 7:30pm. DM10, students, seniors, and children DM5. No concerts on holidays.)*

VESTE OBERHAUS. Over the Luitpoldbrücke bridge, across the river and up the footpath is the former palace of the bishopric. *(Open early Apr.-Oct. M-F, 9am-5pm, Sa-Su 10am-6pm; Nov.-Mar. Tu-Su 9am-5pm.)* Once a place of refuge for the bishop and a prison for various enemies of the cloth, the stronghold now contains the **Cultural History Museum,** whose 54 rooms of art and artifacts span the last 2000 years. In addition, special exhibits rotate through the museum on a yearly basis; the presentation in 2001 is on the relationship between the nations of Bavaria and Hungary. The same bus that goes to the hostel (see above) also stops in front of the Veste Oberhaus. *(☎49 33 50; DM7, students DM4. Every 30min. from the Rathauspl.; last bus leaves Oberhaus at 5:15pm.)*

ALTSTADT. Behind the cathedral is the **Residenzpl.,** lined with former patrician dwellings, as well as the **Residenz,** erstwhile home of Passau's bishops. The **Domschatz** (cathedral treasury) within the Residenz houses an extravagant collection of gold and tapestries. *(Enter through the back of the Stephansdom. Open Easter-Oct. M-Sa 10am-4pm. DM2, students and children DM1.)* Tours of the cathedral (in German) are given daily. *(May-Oct. M-F at 12:30pm, meet in front of the side aisle; Jan.-Apr. and Nov.-Dec. M-F at noon, meet underneath the main organ. DM2.)* Nearby stands the Baroque church of **St. Michael,** built and gilded by the Jesuits. *(Open Feb. and Apr.-Oct. Tu-Su 9am-5pm; Nov.-Jan. and Mar. 10am-4pm. DM3, students DM1.50.)* The less opulent, 13th-century Gothic **Rathaus** was appropriated from a wealthy merchant in 1298 to house the city government. *(Open Apr.-Oct. and Christmas-time 10am-4pm. DM2, students DM1.)* The **Prunksaal** (Great Hall) is a masterpiece showcasing rich wooden paneling and dark

BAVARIA

marble. In the heart of the Altstadt, bright, arched skylights shelter the **Museum Moderner Kunst,** Bräugasse 17 *(☎383 87 90. Open Tu-Su 10am-6pm, Th until 8pm. DM10, students and children DM6.)* The renowned **Passauer Glasmuseum**, next to the Rathaus in the Wilder Mann Hotel, houses 30,000 pieces of glass documenting the last 300 years of glass-making. *(☎350 71. Open daily in the summer 10am-4pm, in winter 1-4pm. DM5, students DM3, children under 13 free with parent.)*

ENTERTAINMENT AND NIGHTLIFE

After long days of work or study, Passau's large population of students and young professionals comes out to party at the city's many bars and clubs. Most of the action takes place on InnStr. by the university or across the footbridge in Innstadt. The best way to keep abreast of the nightlife scene is to get ahold of the magazine *Pasta*, a monthly publication with information on films, live concerts, happy hours, and various lascivious activities in Passau.

Bluenotes, Lederergasse 50 (☎343 77). Cross the Fünferisteg footbridge, make a left on Am Severinstor, and hang another left onto Lederergasse to find one of Passau's newest, jazziest bars. Enjoy your beer or cocktail to the tinkling of the baby grand (live jazz and blues music every Sunday night), or outside in the biergarten. Happy hour is all night on Wednesdays (cocktails DM8); bar open every night 6pm-1am.

Colors, Mariahilfstr. 8 (☎322 20), right across the Innbrücke in Innstadt, past the Kirchenpl. Gulp down a Helles (DM3.80-4.50) as you throw darts, shoot pool, or just plain relax in the biergarten. Tuesday night—all night—is happy "hour," when cocktails go for DM7 and DJs spin everything from reggae to easy listening. Hamburgers, cheeseburgers, and hotdogs always DM3.50. Open every night, 7pm-1am.

Camera, Frauengasse (☎343 20), around the corner from the McDonald's on Ludwigspl. The city center's grooviest dance lair, its stark black exterior foreshadows an underground pit of student angst and inebriation. Beer DM4.50-5.50. Open daily 10pm-3am, weekends and holidays until 4 am. Live music every Tuesday during spring, early summer, and fall; otherwise, get down to house oldies and chart music.

The Frizz, Dr.-Hans-Kapfinger-Str. 3 (☎958 01 11), directly below the Wirtshaus Bayerischer Löwe. Somehow, the fast cats at the Frizz have received special dispensation to stay open later than all the other bars in town. Mellow out with beer (DM4.50), long drinks (DM7.50), and cocktails (DM12) as you take in the yellow marble interior and the techno. Open W, Th 9pm-3am; F, Sa 9pm-4am.

Espresso, Lederergasse 3 (☎304 38), two blocks toward Kirchenpl. from Bluenotes (see above). The place to go for **Altbier,** a dark beer famous in northern Germany. Monday night is happy "hour." Open daily 8pm-1am in the winter, F-M in the summer.

LANDSHUT ☎0871

Residents of Landshut are quick to point out that the House of Wittelsbach did not always call Munich or any of the Königsschlößer home. Landshut served as the main seat of government for Maximillian and Ludwig's ancestors until 1255, and even after that it remained the capital of Lower Bayern. Less than an hour away from Munich by train, the city straddles the swiftly-moving Isar. Red-roofed houses, flower gardens, and pedestrian walkways frame the wide river, which is a popular stomping ground for cyclists, dog walkers, and landscape artists. The city frolics with style during the **Landshuter Hochzeit,** a three-week medieval orgy with authentic (read: excessive) feasting, jousting, dancing, and period plays. First celebrated in 1475 and resurrected in 1903, the festival, re-enacting the magnificent *Hochzeit* (wedding) that Duke Ludwig arranged for his son Georg and his bride Hedwig, takes place every four years. Modern-day knights and ladies will put on their best boots and wedding dresses for four consecutive weekends in 2001 starting June 30; information and tickets are available from the tourist office.

⊏ GETTING THERE AND GETTING AROUND

Landshut is best reached by **train** from **Munich** (45min., 2-3 per hr., DM20.20); **Regensburg** (45min., 2 per hr., DM17); or **Passau** (1½hr., 1 per hr., DM32). From the station, it's a 25-minute walk into town. Walk straight on Luitpoldstr. for about 10 minutes; follow the curve left and cross the bridge. Go through the town gates to your left, then continue straight ahead on Theaterstr.; turn left on Altstadtstr. and the Rathaus will be ahead on the right. Or use **public transportation;** all buses that stop at the station run to the center of town (one-way DM2; day card DM2.70). Purchase tickets from the bus driver.

⁊ ORIENTATION AND PRACTICAL INFORMATION

The **tourist office** (Verkehrsverein), Altstadtstr. 315, in the Rathaus, has primitive maps of the Altstadt for free and better ones of the entire city for DM2. There's no room-finding service, but they will provide a catalogue of available rooms; prices plummet beyond the magical "20-minute radius" from the city center. The tourist office also organizes city walking tours (DM5; May-Oct. W and Sa at 3pm, Nov.-Apr. Sa at 2pm). Pick up the *Monatsprogramm*, a pamphlet listing all concerts, art shows, dances, and films showing in any given month. For the latest on the nightlife scene in the Straubing/Landshut/Regensburg area, pick up a copy of *Bagpipes*. (☎92 20 50; fax 892 75; email verkehrsverein@landshut.de. Open M-F 9am-noon and 1:30-5pm, Sa 9am-noon.) **St. Michaels Apotheke,** Luitpoldstr. 58, lists on-call **pharmacies** (☎643 13; open M-Tu 8:30am-6:30pm, Th 8:30am-7pm, W and F 8:30am-6pm, Sa 8:30am-12:30pm, closed daily from 1-2pm). The **post office**, 84028 Landshut, is just to the left of the station as you exit (open M-F 8am-6pm, Sa 8am-noon).

⸙ ACCOMMODATIONS AND FOOD

The **Jugendherberge (HI)** is at Richard-Schirrmann-Weg 6. From the tourist office, walk to the left up Altstadtstr. and turn left onto Alte Bergstr. at the "Burg Trausnitz" sign. Pass the stairs leading to the Burg, and a few steps farther on your right follow Richard-Schirrmann-Weg to the end. The elegant modern villa sits on quiet, green grounds overlooking the town and provides comfortable but simple four-, six-, and eight-bed dorm rooms with private showers. (☎234 49; fax 27 49 47; email stadt.landshut.jh@landshut.org. Breakfast DM6. Sheets DM5.50. Reception M-F 9am-noon and 5-10pm, Sa-Su 9am-noon and 5-8pm. Closed Dec. 23-Jan. 7. Dorms DM15, DM18.50 with shower and toilet; doubles DM43.) One of the more affordable places in town is the **Weinstube Heigl,** Herrngasse 385, in the city center. Walk right from the Rathaus and take the fourth right onto Herrngasse. The rooms are freshly painted, and the staff is polite and cheery. (☎891 32; fax 27 31 04. Singles DM59, with bath DM69; doubles DM94, with bath DM104.) Halfway between the train station and the Altstadt, **Hotel Park cafe,** Papierstr. 36, offers friendly reception and the bare necessities of a room fifteen minutes from the station. Walk straight on Luitpoldstr., take a left on Rennweg, and a right onto Nikolastr. which becomes Papierstr. (☎693 39; fax 63 03 07. Breakfast included. Singles DM50-98, doubles DM96-140.) **Campingpl. Landshut-Mitterwöhr,** Breslauer Str. 122 (☎533 66), is located just outside of town along the banks of the Isar. From the Rathaus, walk right down Altstadtstr. and straight ahead over Heiliger-Geist-Brücke, then follow the sidewalk and gravel path directly to the right of the bridge along the river for about 20 minutes. At the second bridge, Adenauerbrücke, take the stairs up to the street and walk left down Adenauerstr.; turn right onto Breslauer Str. at the camping sign and the site is on your left. Minigolf, table tennis, and laundry are available. Showers and warm water included. Open Apr.-Sept. (DM10 per site; DM5 per tent; DM8 per person, children under 13 DM5, dogs DM2.)

HL Markt, Dreifaltigkeitspl. 177 at the southern end of Altstadtstr., provides **groceries** (open M-F 8am-8pm, Sa 7:30am-4pm). **Café Cappuccino,** Altstadtstr. 337, right down the street from the Rathaus, has tasty daily specials (DM12.20), salads (DM7-14), pasta (DM8.50-13.90), a breakfast menu (DM6.90-18.90), and, of course, cappuccino for DM4. (☎270 92. Open M-Th 9am-midnight, F-Sa 9am-1am, Su 2-11pm.) For an excellent Greek meal, head to ◼**Restaurant Pallas,** Altstadtstr. 191. Their delicious daily lunch specials are in the DM10 range. Try the house's specialty, gyros with onions, pilaf, and french fries for DM9.90. Vegetarian options DM11.80-15.90, lamb dishes DM15.90-17.90, pizzas DM9.50-15.50. (☎233 33. Open daily 11:30am-3pm, 5-9:30pm.) **Weißes Bräuhaus Krenkl,** Altsdatstr. 107, across the street and to the right of the Rathaus, has been serving up authentic Bavarian meals since 1457. Oma Krenkl and the gang cook up many meat dishes (DM12.50-21.50) and a lunch buffet. (DM10.50 for a big plate. ☎248 01. Open daily 9am-midnight.) A fruit and vegetable market appears Monday through Thursday and Saturday mornings in front of the Rathaus (7am-noon), and F on Am alten Viehmarkt.

◼ ♫ SIGHTS AND ENTERTAINMENT

The Landshut **Altstadt** features rows of gabled Gothic and Baroque houses filled with glitzy shops and restaurants. The proud, greenish-beige **Rathaus** stands at the center bearing Renaissance and neo-Gothic architectural facades. Fantastic murals inside the Prunksaal (main hall) upstairs depict Georg and Hedwig's wedding. (☎88 12 15. Open M-F 2-3pm. Free.) Across from the Rathaus stands the **Stadtresidenz,** the first Italian Renaissance-style palace to be built in Germany (1533-37), and the only one north of the Alps. Its gleaming white classical facade conceals a spacious courtyard with arcades of distinct Italian influence. The **museum** upstairs offers a glimpse of gloriously decadent palace rooms from the 16th to the 18th century, and also houses a regional collection of art with works from the 16th and 17th centuries. (☎92 41 10. 45min. tours every one or two hours, Apr.-Sept. daily 9am-6pm, last tour at 5pm; Oct.-Mar. daily 9am-noon and 1-4pm, last tour 3pm. DM4, students DM3, children under 15 free.)

Bricks zig-zag up the 130m spire of **St. Martin's Kirche,** the world's highest church tower of its kind. Inside, check out the hewn stone altar (1424), the 8m long crucifix crafted by Michael Erhart in 1495, and a late-Gothic **Madonna and Child** elaborately carved by Hans Leinberger in 1518 (open Apr.-Sept. daily 7:30am-6:30pm; Oct.-Mar. 7:30am-5pm). Farther up Altstadtstr., a sign points to **Burg Trausnitz.** To the left and up the crooked brick stairway (5-10min.) sits the hefty brick and red-tiled fortress built in 1204. The hard, seemingly impenetrable exterior conceals a soft yellow courtyard with tiers of delicate arches. The castle was the luxurious abode of the Wittelsbacher princes of Bavaria-Landshut until 1503. The amusing *Narrentreppe* (fool's staircase) inside displays frescoed scenes from famous Italian folk plays, the *Commedia dell'Arte*. The castle interior can only be seen with a German-language tour, but you can borrow an English translation or call ahead to arrange an English tour. (☎92 41 10. Tours same times as *Stadtresidenz Museum*. DM5, students and seniors DM4, children free if accompanied by parent.) A free shuttle runs from the Burg parking lot to the Altstadt (Sa-Su 1:20-6:50pm, every 30min). The new **Skulpturenmuseum im Hofberg** exhibits the modern sculptures and charcoal sketches of Fritz Koenig (1942-1997). (☎890 21. From the *Rathaus*, walk left on Altstadtstr., turn left on Kirchgasse, which then becomes Bindergasse and leads to the Museum. Open Tu-Su 10:30am-1pm and 2-5pm. DM6, students and school children DM4, kids under 10 free.)

STRAUBING

"They govern in Landshut, they pray in Passau, but you can really live in Straubing," said painter Carl Spitzweg of this historic town on the Danube, perched on the fringe of the Bayerischer Wald. And live they do. Each summer, Straubing lets down its hair for the 10-day **Gäubodenvolksfest** (Aug. 10-20, 2001). The festival, called the "Fifth Season" by locals, started as an agricultural fair in 1812 under King Maximillian. It has since evolved into a massive beer-guzzling phenomenon second in size only to **Oktoberfest.** Seven enormous beer tents welcome over a million revelers, who, after imbibing a few liters of the local brews, spend their week's earnings on a bevy of amusement park rides. Accompanying the *Volksfest* is the **Ostbayernschau** (East Bavaria Show), a regional trade and industry exhibition (i.e. more beer; Aug. 11-19, 2001). Both are held in the Fest area "Am Hagen," 5 minutes north of the Markt. When they aren't festing, Straubing's residents and visitors enjoy the city's beautiful churches, striking architecture, colorful houses, and cobbled pedestrian zone, as well as its zoo, water park, museums, and mother nature herself. For information about hiking into the Bavarian Forest from Straubing, call the Bayerischer Waldverein (☎412 39).

▐ GETTING THERE AND GETTING AROUND

Straubing is easily reached by train from **Regensburg** (30min., 1-2 per hr., DM12.60); **Passau** (1 hr., 7 per day, DM20.20); **Landshut** (1 hr., 1-2 per hr., DM15.40); and **Munich** (2 per hr., DM37). The information counter is at the **train station.** (☎(01805) 99 66 33. Open M 5:30am-6:15pm, Tu-F 6am-6:15pm, Sa 7:30am-12:30pm, Su 9:45am-6:30pm). **Stadtwerke Straubing** runs four bus lines through the city (single trip DM2.20, day card DM5); maps and schedules can be found at the tourist office. Rent **bikes** at **Bund Naturschutz,** Ludwigspl. 14, first floor. (☎25 12. DM10 with a DM50 deposit. Open M-F 8am-5pm, Sa 9am-1pm.)

▐ ORIENTATION AND PRACTICAL INFORMATION

The Altstadt lies northwest of the train station, five minutes away on foot. Cross the street in front of the station, and look left for the Fußweg-Zentrum sign that points you across a crosswalk and through a small park, at the end of which is another identical sign; follow it right down Bahnhofstr., through the pedestrian zone and the clock tower passage.

The **tourist office,** Theresienpl. 20, is to the left outside the clock tower tunnel. The office has free maps and extensive brochures on Straubing and neighboring towns, and helps you find **private rooms** (around DM30) for free. (☎94 43 07; fax 94 41 03; email tourismus@straubing.de; www.straubing.de. Open M-W and F 9am-5pm, Th 9am-6pm; Sa 9am-noon.) A public rest room is in the small tunnel just to the left of the tourist office. The staff gives German tours of the Altstadt. (1½hr. mid-May thru mid-Oct. W and Sa at 2pm. DM5, students and seniors DM3, under 6 free. Tours leave from the tourist office. English tours for groups by appointment.) The city's **pharmacies** rotate 24-hour service; check the listing on the wall to the left of the window of the **Agnes-Bernauer-Apotheke,** Bahnhofstr. 16. (☎806 75. Open M-F 8am-6:30pm, Sa 8:30am-1pm.) The **post office,** Landshuter Str. 21, serves all your mail-type needs. Walk left out of the train station and take a left on Landshuter Str. (open M-F 8am-6pm, Sa 8am-noon).

▐░ ACCOMMODATIONS AND FOOD

The **Jugendherberge (HI),** Friedhofstr. 12, is 15 minutes from the train station. Turn right from the front entrance of the station and follow the curve of Bahnhofspl. left. Turn immediately right onto Schildhauerstr. as it turns into Äußere-Passauer-Str., by the "Passau" sign. Cross the stream and turn left onto Friedhofstr.; the hostel is on your right. This very inexpensive hostel features creaking hardwood floors, comfortable leather sofas in the hallways, table-tennis, billiards, and an affectionate house dog. Informality and cleanliness reign supreme. One double is available if you're lucky, but most rooms are 4-, 6-, or 8-beds. (☎804 36; fax 120 94. Breakfast included. Sheets DM5.50. Reception 7-9am and 5-10pm. New arrivals after 5pm only. Lockout 9am-5pm. 10pm curfew, but keys available with DM10 deposit. Showers between 6-8am and 5-10pm. Open Apr.-Oct. DM17.50). Most hotels and *Pensionen* in Straubing begin at DM60; one small and tidy exception is

BAVARIA

Weißes Rößl, Landshuter Str. 65. Walk left out of the train station and left again down Landshuter Str. for 10 min.; the building is on your left. (☎ 325 81. Breakfast DM5. Showers off the hallway. Singles DM30; doubles DM60.) The other inexpensive pension in town, **Hotel Schedlbauer,** Landshuter Str. 78, is right across the street from the Weißes Rößl. Very clean rooms with clock radios. (☎ 338 38; fax 4640. Breakfast included. Showers off the hallway. Singles DM38; doubles DM65.) A **Campingpl.** is located at Wundermühlweg 9. From the tourist office, walk east down Ludwigspl., turn left on Stadtgrabenstr. which then becomes Chamer Str., and the site will be on your left. (☎ 897 94. Open May-Oct. 15. DM15-40.)

The supermarket era has not yet come to Straubing, a town peppered with fruit and vegetable stands, bakeries, and meat shops. Often the best (and most reasonably priced) meals can be found in the adjoining Imbiß of a Metzgerei. **Metzgerei Königsbauer,** Ludwigspl. 6, near the Stadtturm, serves a hefty lunch at its Stehcafe (standing cafe). Entrees are available for take-out, including Wienerschnitzel, Wurst, Knödel, and every other German meat specialty for DM4-8. (☎ 214 61. Open M-F 7:30am-6pm, Sa 7:30am-3pm.) **Schmankerl Passage,** Bahnhofstr. 2, half-way between the train station and the center of the Altstadt, combines a bakery, meat shop, and fruit stand with cafe-like tables for eating (most items under DM4; open M-Sa 7:30am-6pm). The restaurant in the **Hotel Bischershof,** Frauenhoferstr. 16, left out of the tourist office and another left down the third alleyway, serves salads (DM3.20-11.50), grill specialties (DM13.50-25), and, like everyplace in Straubing, super cheap beer (DM4-4.90). There's a Biergarten out back. (☎ 129 92. Open M-Sa 11am-2:30pm and 5:30pm-1am, Su 11am-1am.). Fresh fruits and vegetables are sold at the **market** on Ludwigspl. (open M-Th and Sa 7am-1pm, F 7am-6pm). A **farmer's market** is held Saturdays on Theresienpl.

👁🎵 SIGHTS AND ENTERTAINMENT

The five-turreted Gothic **Stadtturm** (fire- and watchtower) in the middle of the market square is the city's symbol. Dating from 1316, the teal-green structure with an inset gold figure of Mary splits the Marktplatz. (1hr. tours in German mid-Mar. thru mid-Oct. Th at 2pm; Sa-Su at 10:30am. Th and Sa tours leave from the tourist office; Su tours leave from the entrance to the watchtower. DM5, students DM3, under 6 free.) The **Basilika St. Peter,** a Romanesque basilica built during the 1180s, is surrounded by a fortified medieval graveyard with wrought-iron crosses, gravestones from as far back as the 13th century, and three Gothic chapels: the All Souls Chapel with frescos of the Totentanz (Dance of Death), the Agnes Bernauer Chapel which houses a red marble epitaph devoted to her memory, and the Gothic Chapel of Our Lady. From the Stadtturm, walk east on Ludwigspl., turn left onto Stadtgraben Str., and turn right just before the bridge onto Donaugasse; St. Peters is a 10min. walk. Inquire at the tourist office about tours of the complex. Tall, slender white columns and graceful sculptures of saints clothed in gold give the **Basilika St. Jakob,** Pfarrpl. 1a, a divine elegance. Two-story stained glass windows illustrating the Annunciation and the lives of the disciples shed color on the Rococo pulpit. The **Gäubodenmuseum,** Frauenhoferstr. 9, houses exhibits from the early Bronze Age, as well as a collection of regional art and folklore. (☎ 818 11. Open Tu-Su 10am-4pm. DM4, students DM3.) From the Gäubodenmuseum, walk two short blocks east on Hofstattstr. to the late-Gothic **Karmelitenkirche,** Albrechtsgasse 21. Angels and disciples peer down from the lavish gold altar and stolid white columns into the church's stunning Baroque interior.

One block down on Burggasse, the stunning **Ursulinenkirche** rests behind an off-putting white stucco facade. Built from 1736 to 1741 by the renowned Asam brothers as their last joint endeavor, the interior exhibits the overflowing opulence of the Rococo. Peach marble columns snake up to the ceiling, lavishly covered in flashy gold and fantastic frescoes. Down Fürstenstr. on the banks of the Danube, parts of the **Herzogsschloß** date from 1356. Most of the palace interior is closed to the public, its innards clogged with the cholesterol blockage of bureaucracy. A few renovated floors house a new **state museum,** with a rather bland exhibition of images of worship from the 17th to the 20th century. (☎ 211 14. Open Apr.-Sept. Tu-Su 10am-4pm. DM4, students DM3.)

Perhaps the hippest spot in Straubing for nocturnal prowlings is the ⚑**Roxy** on Apr.gasse, replete with an ample bar, plenty of seating, a dance floor packed with a good mix of teens to thirty-somethings, and *Fußball*. The DJ's collection includes over 1000 albums, many of which are LPs, and he spins the best collection of classic rock this side of the Atlantic. From the *Stadtturm*, walk one block west on Theresienpl. and turn left on Apr.gasse. (☎121 57. Open W, F 10pm-3am, Sa 10pm-4am. Cover DM5.) **Max**, Hebbelstr. 14, hidden in the Gäubodenpark shopping complex, is the place to trot to techno, trance, rap, and house. (☎34 31. Open W and F-Sa 10pm-3am. Beer DM4.50. Cover DM10.) From the train station, head left toward the post office. Follow the road to the left as it curves under the train overpass; the Gläuboden Park mall is ahead. **Peaches**, Steinergasse 14, just south of the *Stadtturm*, is a mellow cocktail bar that offers half-off on all cocktails and long drinks on Tuesday nights. (☎105 92. Open Su-Th 7pm-1am, F-Sa 7pm-2am. Cover for Tu DM4.)

Straubing's enormous swimming pool complex, **AQUA-therm**, Wittelsbacherhöhe 50-52, hosts an 80m waterslide, several massage parlors, an indoor pool, a steam sauna, and a warm salt-water pool. Follow the tunnel to the left of the Bahnhof down Landshuter Str. and turn right onto Dr.-Otto-Höchtl-Str., which becomes Wittelsbacherhöhe; it's on the right. Or take bus #2 from Ludwigspl. to "Aquatherm." (☎86 41 78 or 86 41 79. Open June-Aug. 10 daily 8am-9pm; Aug. 11-Sept. 14 M-F 8am-8pm, Sa-Su 8am-7pm. DM5, after 5:30pm DM3; students, seniors, and under 16 DM2; under 6 free.) **Bowl** yourself over at **Keglerhalle am Sportzentrum Peterswöhrd**, 20 minutes from the center of town. Take a right out of the tourist office down Ludwigspl. and then turn left on Stadtgraben; walk for five minutes. Take a right onto Donaugasse, then a quick left onto Uferstr., and after about ten minutes take a left onto Am Peterswöhrd.; the alley is on your right. (☎802 48. Open daily 10am-midnight.) Straubing is home to the only **Zoo** in eastern Bavaria, with more than 1400 closely-quartered animals and a large aquarium. From the tourist office walk right down Theresienpl. and follow the road as it becomes Regensburger Str.; continue for 20 minutes. Walk through the parking lot and follow the *Fußweg zum Tiergarten* sign. (☎212 77. Open Mar.-Sept. 8:30am-7pm; Oct.-Feb. 9am-dark. DM8, students and children 6-18 DM5, children under 6 DM3.)

REGENSBURG ☎0941

When Goethe visited Regensburg for the first time, he wrote to his friend Charlotte von Stein, "Regensburg is beautifully situated; the area couldn't help but attract a city." Indeed, almost two millennia ago in AD 179, Roman Emperor Marcus Aurelius laid the foundations of this city by building Fortress **Castra Regina** at the confluence of the Regen and the Danube. Although Roman structures still stand in Regensburg, the city's greatness did not crumble with Rome; it later became the first capital of Bayern, then the seat of the Perpetual Imperial Diet (see **Worms**, p. 363), and the site of the first German parliament.

⌐ GETTING THERE AND GETTING AROUND

Trains: To **Munich** (1½hr., 1 per hr., DM38); **Nürnberg** (1-1½hr., 1-2 per hr., DM27); and **Passau** (1-1½hr., 1 per hr., DM32). Ticket office open M-F 6am-7:30pm, Sa 6am-6:30pm, Su 7:30am-8:45pm.

Ferries: Regensburger Personenschifffahrt (☎553 59; www.schifffahrtklinger.de), on Thunerdorfstr. next to the Steinerne Brücke. The main ship of the fleet goes to Walhalla Apr.-Oct. daily at 10:30am and 2pm. 45min. One-way DM11, children DM5, families DM26. Round-trip DM16, children DM7, families DM38.

Public Transportation: Routes, schedules, and fares for Regensburg's **bus** system are available at the *Presse & Buch* store in the train station, or at the tourist office (DM1). The transport hub is "Bustreff Albertstr.," 1 block straight and to the right from the station. Single ride within the Altstadt DM1, within the inner-most zone DM2.80; day ticket for zones 1 and 2 DM6. Buses run until about midnight.

Taxi: ☎194 10, ☎570 00, or ☎520 52.

Bike Rental: Bike Haus, Bahnhofstr. 18 (☎599 81 94; www.bikeprojekt.de), in the west wing of the train station, rents bikes and also provides maps and route suggestions. Open daily 9am-7pm. DM15-17 per day, children DM10.

◪ 🔢 ORIENTATION AND PRACTICAL INFORMATION

The Altstadt sprawls over a square-shaped cobblestoned mecca; the Danube is to the north, the train station and Bahnhofstr. to the south, Kumpfmühlerstr. to the west, and Martin-Luther-Str. to the east. Maximilianstr. leads from the station into the heart of the city. The university lies behind the station in the opposite direction from the Danube.

Tourist Office: Rathauspl. (☎507 44 10; fax 507 44 19; email tourismus@info.regensburg.de; www.regensburg.de), in the Altes Rathaus. From the station, walk down Maximilianstr. to Grasgasse and take a left. Follow the street as it turns into Obermünsterstr., turn right at the end to Obere Bachgasse and follow it 5 blocks down Untere Bachgasse onto Rathauspl. The office, to the left across the square, provides free maps and books **rooms** for a DM1.50 fee. Open M-F 8:30am-6pm, Sa 9am-4pm, Su 9:30am-2:30pm. From Apr.-Oct. also open Su until 4pm.

Tours: 1½hr. English-language tours of the city depart from the tourist office May-Sept. W and Sa at 1:30pm. DM10, students DM5.

Lost and Found: At the Neues Rathaus (☎507 21 05).

Bookstore: Booox, Goldene-Bären-Str. 12 (☎56 70 14) near the Steinerne Brücke; entrance on Brückstr. Cluttered bookstore has tons of discount boooox along with a 2nd-floor shelf of cheap classics (DM7). Ooopen M-F 9am-8pm, Sa 9am-4pm. The **university bookstore** (☎56 97 50) is on the main plaza of the university (see **Mensa**, p. 300), and has 3 shelves of English novels. Open M-F 8:30am-6pm.

Emergency: ☎110. **Police:** Minoritenweg (☎192 22). **Fire** and **Ambulance,** ☎112.

Crisis Hotline: In case of rape or other trauma, contact **Caritas** (☎78 20).

Pharmacy: Maximilian-Apotheke, Maximilianstr. 29, 2 blocks from the train station, posts 24hr. emergency information to the left of the door. Open M-F 8:30am-6:30pm, Sa 8:30am-1pm.

Hospital: Evangelisches Krankenhaus, Emmeramspl. 10 (☎504 00), near the Thurn und Taxis Schloß, is the most centrally located.

Post Office: on Bahnhofstr., 93047 Regensburg, next door to the train station. Open M-F 6:30am-6:30pm, Sa 7am-12:30pm.

Internet: Internet cafe, Am Römling 9 (☎599 97 02). Walk down Goldene-Bären-Str. away from the Steinerne Brücke and turn left on Am Römling. DM5 per 30min. Open Tu-Su 7pm-1am.

▗ ACCOMMODATIONS AND CAMPING

Most of Regensburg's "cheap" lodgings are centrally located and fill up quickly in summer. For location, reserve, reserve, reserve. If the hotels and *Pensionen* are full, the tourist office might find a room in a private home (a coveted few in the DM30-50 range; most DM60-90). Otherwise, try the hotels in outlying parts of town—all are linked to the center by reliable bus service.

Jugendherberge (HI), Wöhrdstr. 60 (☎574 02; fax 524 11), on an island in the Danube. From the station, walk down Maximilianstr. to the end. Turn right at the Apotheke onto Pfluggasse and immediately left at the Optik sign onto tiny Erhardigasse. At the end, take the steps down and walk left over the Eiserne Brücke, then veer right onto Wöhrdstr. on the other side. The hostel is on the right (25min.). Or take bus #3, 8, or 9 from the station to "Eisstadion." The hostel is a few steps beyond the bus stop on the right. Carpeted, crayola-colored rooms. Breakfast and sheets included. Dinner DM9. Key deposit DM20. Reception 6am-1am. Check-in until 1am. No curfew. Reservations encouraged. Partial wheelchair access. Dorm beds DM28.

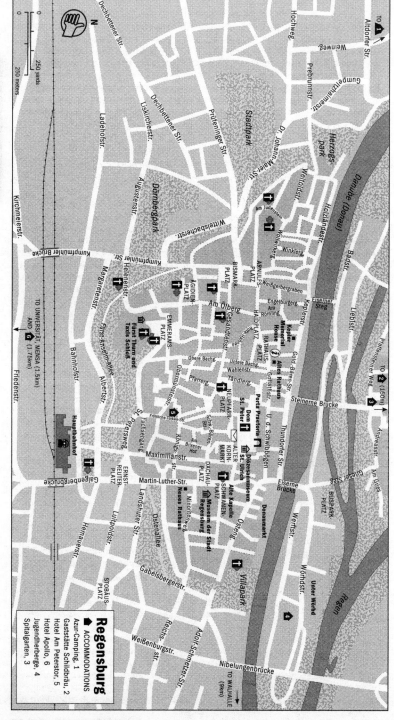

Regensburg

◆ ACCOMMODATIONS
Azur-Camping, 1
Gaststätte Schildbräu, 2
Hotel Am Peterstor, 5
Hotel Apollo, 6
Jugendherberge, 4
Spitalgarten, 3

Spitalgarten, St.-Katharinen-Pl. 1 (☎ 847 74; fax 890 31 68; email spitalgarten@t-online.de), inside a 13th-century hospital. Cross the Steinerne Brücke and make a left into St.-Katherinen-Pl. at the "zum Spitalgarten Fremdenzimmer" sign. Pass through another gate and go past the left side of the church. Or take bus #12 from the station to "Stadtamhof." Head into the pink Biergarten and inquire about the *Pension* with the staff behind the counter. Breakfast included. Reception until midnight. Call, fax, or write well ahead. Singles DM40; doubles DM80.

Gaststätte Schildbräu, Stadtamhof 24 (☎ 857 24), is over the Steinerne Brücke; follow the street for 5min. and it's on the right. Or take bus #12 from the station to "Stadtamhof." Clean and orderly rooms, with baths and geraniums spilling from every window. Breakfast included. Reception 7:30am-midnight. Call ahead. Singles DM65; doubles DM110; triples DM150; quads DM190.

Apollo Hotel, Neuprüll 17 (☎ 910 50; fax 91 05 70; email apollo-hotel-regensburg@t-online.de; www.hotelapollo.de). From the station, take bus #6 (direction: "Klinikum") to "Neuprüll" (15min., DM2.80). Proximity to the university and the giant breakfast buffet make it worth the trip. Rooms have cable TV, radio, and phone, and guests have access to a pool and sauna. Breakfast included. Reception M-Sa 6:30am-11pm. Singles with shower DM70; doubles with shower DM110.

Hotel Am Peterstor, Fröhliche-Türken-Str. 12 (☎ 545 45; fax 545 42), 5min. from the station. Head down Maximilianstr. and take the 2nd left onto St.-Peters-Weg, which becomes Fröhliche-Türken-Str. around the corner. Rooms are neat and simple, with bath and TV. Institutional, but fun anyway. Breakfast DM10. Reception 7-11am and 4-10:30pm. Singles DM75; doubles DM95.

Camping: Azur-Camping, Am Weinweg 40 (☎ 27 00 25; fax 29 94 32; email info@azur-camping.de; www.azur-camping.de). From station, bus #11 (direction: "Westbad") to "Westheim." Prices lower mid-Jan. to Mar. and Sept. to mid-Dec. Reception 8am-1pm and 3-11pm. DM10.50 per person. Tent DM7.50. Car DM6.

🍴 FOOD

The 17th-century English dramatist and diplomat Sir George Etherege commented that Regensburg's "noble, serene air makes us hungry as hawks"—a laudable attempt to blame his swelling belly on the atmosphere rather than the heavy Bavarian fare and beer. A tantalizing number of cafes, bars, and beer gardens await to tempt the Imperial Diet. A plethora of **supermarkets** in the city, however, will mend the proverbial holes in your pockets. **GM Markt,** Untere Bachgasse 2, on the way to the tourist office from the train station, is a good starting point for the makings of a lazy picnic. (☎ 51 36. Open M-F 8am-8pm, Sa 8am-4pm.) To stock up on fruit, vegetables, and other basics, head to the **Rettichmarkt** on Dompl. (open Mar.-Oct. M-Sa 7am-6pm, Su 10:30am-6pm). Otherwise, join the rest of Regensburg at a beer garden for a meal of *Würstchen*, pretzels, and of course, beer.

Mensa, on Albertus-Magnus-Str., in the park on the university campus. Take bus #6 (direction: "Klinikum") or #11 (direction: "Burgweinting") to "Universität Mensa" (DM2.80), or turn right from the station and take the bridge over the tracks onto Galgenbergstr. Follow this street for about 20min. and take a right on Albertus-Magnus-Str. The stairs on the left lead up to the Mensa. The cheapest meal in Regensburg, with a lively student crowd. Meals DM3-6. Open M-Th 11:15am-1:45pm and 5-7pm, F 11:15am-1:45pm and 5-6:30pm. From Nov.-Feb. and May-July also open on Sa from 11:15am-1pm.

▨ Bistro Rosarium, Hoppestr. 3a (☎ 268 85). The gorgeous solarium and outdoor patio/beer garden are set before the 7-hectare Dörnbergpark. Surprisingly cheap for this location: lunch menu with drink is DM13, breakfasts start at DM7. Open M-Sa 11am-1am, Su 10am-1am.

Hinterhaus, Rote-Hahnen-Gasse 2 (☎ 546 61), off Haidpl. down from Rathauspl. Crooked tables under dimly lit archways and white stucco walls decorated with post-modern art. A relatively young crowd mellows out to blues and jazz CDs. Excellent vegetarian dishes and salads DM5-14; meat dishes such as the "Italian lamb with potatoes and salad" DM8.80-14.80. Open daily 6pm-1am.

BEER GARDENS

 Historische Wurstküche, Thundorfer Str. (☎590 98), next to the Steinerne Brücke with a view of the river. A fun place to relax, sip a beer, and watch the ships drift by. Recently having celebrated its 850th birthday, the Wurstküche is the oldest operating fast food joint in Europe. Twelfth-century workers who built the bridge broke for lunch here, so put down your shovel and join the tradition yourself. Six small, delicious Würste from the smoky kitchen come with sauerkraut and bread (DM8.70; 0.5L beer DM4.80). Open daily 8am-7pm (Sundays Nov.-Mar. 8am-3pm).

Goldene Ente, Badstr. 32 (☎854 55). Under magnificent chestnut trees on the banks of the Danube just across the Eiserner Steg footbridge, upstream from the Steinerne Brücke. The oldest inn in Regensburg; during the summer the beer garden is packed with well-pilsnered students. Steaks, *Würstchen,* and *Schnitzel* grilled at student-friendly prices (DM9-14). Open M-Sa noon-11pm, Su 10am-11pm.

Kneitinger Keller, Galgenbergstr. 18 (☎766 80), to the right from the station and over the tracks (10min.). Regensburg's largest beer garden, with 1,200 seats. Devoted locals, thirsty tourists, and intelligentsia-in-training alike follow their noses: the smell of beer has pervaded the entire area since the brewery was established in 1530. *Maß* DM7.80, six *Würstchen* with bread DM8.70; *Wiener Schnitzel* with roasted potatoes and salad DM15.50. Open daily 9am-midnight.

🔍 SIGHTS

DOM ST. PETER. The Dompl. provides a stable foundation for the soaring high-Gothic Dom St. Peter and the **Diözesanmuseum St. Ulrich** adjacent to the church. Begun in 1276, the cathedral was finished in 1486, not counting the delicately carved 159m twin spires, which King Ludwig II added in characteristically grandiose style between 1859 and 1869. The richly-colored stained glass windows, many from the 13th and 14th centuries, dazzle. Inside the cathedral is the **Domschatz,** a priceless collection of gold and jewels purchased by the Regensburg bishops back in the days of indulgences and economic exploitation by the clergy. Underneath the Dom is the final resting place of many of Regensburg's bishops and recently-unearthed Roman ruins. *(Cathedral ☎597 10 02. Open Apr.-Oct. daily 6:30am-6pm; Nov.-Mar. 6:30am-5pm; free. Two-hour German language tours May-Oct. M-Sa 10, 11am, and 2pm, Su noon and 2pm; Nov.-Apr. M-Sa 11am, Su noon. DM5, students and children DM3. Call ahead for English tours for groups only. Diözesanmuseum St. Ulrich ☎516 88. Open Apr.-Nov. Tu-Su 10am-5pm. DM2, students DM1.50, families DM7. Domschatzmuseum ☎576 45. Open Apr.-Nov. Tu-Sa 10am-5pm, Su noon-5pm; Dec.-Mar. F-Sa 10am-4pm, Su noon-4pm. DM2, students DM1.50, families DM7. Wheelchair access to the Dom is on the cathedral's northern side, via the Eselturm.)*

ALTES RATHAUS. A few blocks away from the cathedral, the yellow Gothic town hall served as capital of the Holy Roman Empire until 1803. Four long iron rods are fastened on its side; these were the official measurement standards by which the merchants traded in the Middle Ages. The impotent Imperial Parliament, the first of many similar bodies in German history, lives on in the Reichstagsmuseum housed in the Rathaus. The differing heights of the chairs reflect the political hierarchy of the legislators. *(Tours in German Apr.-Oct. every 30min. M-Sa 9:30am-noon and 2-4pm, Su 10am-noon and 2-4pm; Nov.-Mar. tours hourly. English tours May-Sept. M-Sa at 3:15pm. DM5, students and seniors DM2.50.)*

KEPLERGEDÄCHTNISHAUS. The iconoclastic astronomer and physicist Johannes Kepler died here of meningitis in 1630. Period furniture, portraits, and facsimiles of Kepler's work are on display. Up the street at Keplerstr. 2 is **Keplers Wohnhaus,** a colorful house where he hung his hat and spent time away from his gold-nosed patron and taskmaster, Tycho Brahe. It now houses a tanning salon. *(Keplerstr. 5. ☎507 34 42. Open Tu-Su 10am-noon and 2-4pm, Su Nov.-Mar. 10am-noon only. 45min. tours at 10 and 11am, 2 and 3pm. Admission DM4, students DM2.)*

PORTA PRAETORIA. A Roman gateway, the Porta Praetoria and ruins from its accompanying wall sketch a hazy outline of the city's original fortifications. They have been incorporated into a house located on Unter den Schwibbögen between the Dom and the Danube. One of the earliest documents of Regensburg's past is found on the front wall of the house—a flat foundation stone from the Roman fort of Castra Regina, inscribed in AD 179.

WALHALLA. Down the river from Regensburg is Walhalla, an imitation Greek temple poised dramatically on the steep northern bank of the Danube. Ludwig I built the monument between 1830 and 1842 to honor Germans past and present whom he admired. Modeled after the Parthenon in Athens and named after the legendary resting place of Norse heroes, Walhalla stares imposingly down on the river as the boat from Regensburg approaches the dock (see p. 297). Ludwig called Walhalla "the child of my love." The climb up the steep steps (248 in all) to the monument is tough going, but the view of the river and the opposite bank is stunning. In summer, the hallowed steps provide a lively evening hangout for students who venture here by bike and car; probably not what poor Ludwig envisioned. *(Take bus #5 from the train station to "Donaustauf Walhallastr." (DM3.80), then continue walking on Wörtherstr. to the gravel path leading up the hill. ☎ 96 16 80. Open Apr.-Sept. daily 9am-5:45pm; Oct. daily 9am-4:45pm; Nov.-Mar. 10-11:45am and 1-3:45pm. DM3, students DM2.)*

FÜRST THURN UND TAXIS SCHLOß. Across from the station sits the Fürst Thurn und Taxis Schloß. Originally a Benedictine cloister from the 11th century, the 500-room compound has been the residence of the Prince of Thurn and Taxis since 1812; the new owners made the formerly Gothic buildings Baroque upon acquisition. The family earned its title from Kaiser Leopold I in 1695 in recognition of the booming postal business they had built. In recent times, with the nationalization of the post and the decline of nobility as a reliable profession, the royal family has fallen on hard times. In 1991, when the prince died, the princess had to sell the family jewels to pay the DM44million inheritance taxes. Luckily, the state bought the jewels and added them to the carriage museum in the castle to make the Thurn und Taxis Museum. Four hundred seventy five rooms of the private palace are still off-limits to the public, but the 25 other rooms are part of a tour leaving the main entrance. *(☎ 504 81 33. Open M-F 11am-5pm, Sa-Su 10am-5pm. DM8, students DM6. Tours Apr.-Oct. daily at 11am, 2, 3, and 4pm. Sa-Su additional tour at 10am; Nov.-Mar. Sa-Su at 10 and 11am, 2 and 3pm.)*

🎵🏛 ENTERTAINMENT AND NIGHTLIFE

Many of the cafes and beer gardens listed above double as local nighttime haunts, and good bars raise inebriation to Walhallian heights. Ask at the tourist office for a free copy of *Logo* or *Stadtzeitung*—two monthly publications that list the liveliest events and addresses of the hippest bars and cafes in Regensburg.

Alte Mälzerei, Galgenbergstr. 20 (☎ 730 33 or for tickets 757 49). Regensburg's self-proclaimed "Art and Culture Factory" is in an old malt processing plant that hosts a bar with pop, jazz, funk, reggae and blues. Beer DM4.20-4.90. Open daily 6pm-1am.

Wunderbar, Keplerstr. 11 (☎ 531 30). Young late-nighters pack into one of the only bars open after 1am, located just a few staggers from the Steinerne Brücke. Elaborately crafted cocktails DM10.50-13.50. The history of cocktail mixing appears for your edification on the menu. Open M-Th and Su 10pm-3am, F-Sa 9pm-3am.

Filmbühne, Hinter der Grieb 8 (☎ 579 26). Look for the staircase leading down within a green gate. Regensburg's funkiest scene attracts a diverse and bizarre crowd. Film posters, strange art, and disco balls are scattered everywhere. Open daily 9pm-1am.

Südhaus, Untere Bachgasse 8 (☎ 519 33). One of Regensburg's best discos. Tu "ultimate" alternative night; Th gay night. Beer DM5.50. Open Tu, Th 11pm-3am, F-Sa 11pm-4am. Cover Tu, Th DM5; F-Sa DM6.

BAYERISCHER WALD (BAVARIAN FOREST)

A coddled national treasure, the Bayerischer Wald is the largest range of wooded mountains in central Europe. Six thousand square kilometers of peaks (60 of which are over 1000m high) and countless rivers and creeks stretch from the Danube to the Austrian and Czech borders to form a vast hook that lures hikers, campers, and cross-country skiers throughout the year. The **Naturpark Bayerischer Wald,** the first national park in Germany, strictly prohibits any activities that might alter the forest ecosystem—this includes camping and building fires outside designated campgrounds. Clearly marked trails lace 8000 hectares (20,000 acres) of forest. You can trek it alone or sign up for free guided hiking tours, botanical tours, natural history tours, or tours of virgin woodlands. For information and schedules, or to book a tour (which you must do at least a day in advance), contact the **Hans-Eisenmann-Haus,** Böhmstr. 35, 94556 Neuschönau. (☎(08558) 961 50. Open daily Jan.-Oct. 9am-5pm.) For general information about the Bayerischer Wald, contact the **Nationalparkverwaltung Bayerischer Wald,** Freyunger Str. 2, 94481 Grafenau (☎(08552) 960 00; fax 46 90). Pick up a copy of the forest newspaper *Informationsblatt Nationalpark Bayerischer Wald* for the latest news about the forest, or the free *encyclopedia* of the Bayerischer Wald, which is filled to the brim with phone numbers, maps, and listings. Both are available at tourist offices in the area.

The Bayerischer Wald is much more than just a verdant paradise; palaces, churches, and castle ruins are tucked away in tiny villages throughout the region. **Burgruine Hals,** an extensive castle ruin high on a woody cliff north of Passau, dates from the 12th century. The 18th-century **Wiesenfelden** gardens surround the ruins. For information contact the **tourist office,** Schulstr. 3, 93497 Wiesenfelden. (☎(09966) 94 00 17.) **Frauenzell's** 15th-century Benedictine church is lavishly *barockisiert* and *funkisiert* (Baroquified and funkified), and parts of the **Annunciation Church** in **Cham** date from the 12th century.

The region is famous for its crafts, particularly **glass-blowing.** The glass produced here is prized (and dropped) throughout the world, particularly the dark green *Waldglas* (forest glass). Every little forest village seems to have its own *Glashütte.* For more information, contact the **Bergglashütte Weinfurtner,** Zellertalstr. 13 (☎(09945) 94 110; www.weinfurtner.de) in Arnbruck, or the **Freiherr von Poschinger Kristallglasfabrik,** Moosauhütte (☎(09926) 940 10), in Frauenau.

The remoteness of the towns attracts few English-speaking visitors, but the park maintains a heavy flow of Germans seeking healthy, peaceful vacations. Use the towns below as springboards for exploring the nooks and crannies of this region. An impressive 14 **HI youth hostels** dot the forest; Regensburg's tourist office (see p. 298) has a helpful brochure as well as current addresses.

ZWIESEL   ☎09922

The abundance of train connections running through Zwiesel makes it an excellent hub for scouting the heart of the Bayerischer Wald. A skier's paradise in the winter, in summer the focus flips to its 800-year history of glass-making, the modern-day incarnation of which is the production of postmodern wine glasses.

🛈 **PRACTICAL INFORMATION. Trains** run hourly from **Plattling** off the Nürnberg-Passau line (1hr., every hour, DM15.40). There is an information counter at the train station (open M-F 6:15-11:50am and 12:40-15:45pm, Sa 7:35am-12:45pm). The **tourist office,** Stadtpl. 27, in the **Rathaus,** provides maps and information on hiking and biking tours, and finds private rooms (DM25-90) for free. From the station, turn right and walk downhill on Dr.-Schott-Str. After a few blocks, veer left onto Innenriederstr. and cross the bridge, then take a gentle left onto Stadtpl.; the Rathaus is on the left. (☎84 05 23; fax 56 55; email zwiesel.tourist@t-online.de; www.zwiesel.de. Open M-F 8:30am-5:30pm, Sa 10am-noon; Nov.-Dec. M-F 8:30am-

5:30pm.) Four **city buses** make 11 trips through the town on weekdays and 4 on Saturdays; one trip DM2.20, DM14 for a 10-ride card. The **post office** is located at Dr.-Schott-Str. 55, 94227 Zwiesel (open M-F 8:30am-noon and 2-5:15pm, Sa 8:30-11:30am). There is a large wheelchair-accessible public telephone booth directly in front of the post office.

▟▙ ACCOMMODATIONS AND FOOD. The **Jugendherberge (HI),** Hindenburgstr. 26, is a 30-minute walk from the station. Follow the directions to Stadtpl., continue past the *Rathaus*, and turn right onto Frauenauer Str. Continue straight for 10 minutes and turn left on Hindenburgstr. (one block after the "AOK" sign); the hostel is just over the hill. Or take bus #1 from the station to "Jugendherberge" (DM2.20; 1 per hr.). This clean hostel is the choicest accommodation in the Bayerischer Wald. *Klein aber fein* (tiny but shiny), repeats the proud hostel mother. (☎10 61; fax 601 91. Breakfast included. Sheets DM5.50. Reception daily 5-7pm. Curfew 10pm, but they'll give you a key. DM20. Spacious doubles available.) For a small, inexpensive pension, try **Gästehaus Mühl,** Badstr. 5. From the train station walk left down Bahnhofstr. to the first intersection; take a left down Rabensteiner Str. and walk through the tunnel. Take the first left onto Badstr.; the house is on the left (10 min.). The inn features a common room with television and a balcony filled with flowers. (☎18 21. Breakfast included. DM25-28 per person.) Another inexpensive pension is **Haus Elfriede,** Anton-Pech-Str. 4. From the train station, follow directions to the Jugendherberge. Then, turn left up Böhmerwaldstr. and make a right onto Anton-Pech-Str. Enjoy cheap living amid retro furniture in this small and clean pension. (☎30 17. Breakfast included. Singles DM22; doubles DM29.) **Campingpl. TröpplKeller,** Langdorderstr. 56, is located on the Schwarzer Regen river, 2km from the center of town. From the train station, turn right and walk downhill on Dr.-Schott-Str. After a few blocks, turn right onto Schlachthofstr., then take another right onto Langdorfer Str. and walk about 800m to TröpplKeller on the left. (☎17 09 or 603 91. Campsite open year-round. DM8.50 plus DM1.50 *Kurtaxe.*)

The **Eiscafe-Pizzeria Rialto,** Stadtpl. 28 (☎47 03), has outdoor seating on a busy street. Feed the hungry beast with pizza (DM8-12.50), pasta (DM8-12), or an ice cream confection (DM6-11). For traditional Bavarian meals, try **Gasthaus zum Kirchenwirt,** Bergstr. 1 (☎25 70), which serves up specialties such as *Schweinbraten* with *Knödel* and *Sauerkraut* (DM8-12) and offers daily lunch specials for DM9.80-15.90 (open daily 11am-1am). The hotel-restaurant **Deutscher Rhein,** Stadtpl. 42 (☎841 00), prides itself in its *Niederbayerische* specialties (DM9.40-15.70). Saddle up to a bowl of goulash with potatoes for DM5.60, or try their fish and meat dishes (DM14-25). **Lidl,** up the street from the tourist office at the intersection of Stadtpl. and Oberzwieselaner Str., is a convenient and extremely cheap supermarket (open M-F 8:30am-7pm, Sa 8am-2pm).

◉ SIGHTS. Just north of town lies the **Glas Park Theresienthal,** a village of glassblowing houses with a museum that demonstrates to awed spectators how delicately these fancies are created *(park open M-F 9:30am-6pm, Sa 9:30am-4pm, Su from June-Oct. 11am-4pm).* Eleven buses per day shuttle to the Glas Park from the Stadtpl. *(M-F beginning at 7:55am; last return at 6:07pm. DM2.20.)* The **Waldmuseum,** Stadtpl. 29, behind the *Rathaus*, tells the tinkly tale of glass-making in the region, exhibits items from everyday life in the Bayerischer Wald, and educates about the forest itself. *(☎608 88; www.glasstrasse.com/waldmuseum. Open May 15-Oct. 15 M-F 9am-5pm, Sa-Su 10am-noon and 2-4pm; Oct. 16-May 14 M-F 10am-noon and 2-5pm, Sa-Su 10am-noon; closed in Nov. DM4, with Kurkarte DM3, disabled persons and students DM1.)* The **Spielzeugmuseum,** 20 meters behind the *Waldmuseum*, contains a large model train set, teddy bears galore, and toys of all kinds, spanning two centuries. *(☎55 26. Open daily June-Aug. 9am-5pm, Sept.-May 10am-5pm, closed Nov. to mid-Dec; DM4, children 14-17 DM3, children 2-13 DM2.)* For easy hiking near Zwiesel, head out of the Rathaus down Stadtpl. Follow the street to the edge of the city and look for green Fußwanderweg signs on your left.

⁂ DAYTRIP FROM ZWIESEL: REGEN

A nine-minute train trip from **Zwiesel** (1 per hr., DM3), Regen offers a well-designed **Landwirtschaftsmuseum,** Schulgasse 2. Displays of photos, tools, and a film present the history and development of the area from 18th-century Feudalism through the industrial revolution. (☎ (09921) 57 10 or 72 05. Open daily 10am-5pm. DM4, students and children DM2.) Just outside the town, the ruins of **Burg Weißenstein,** an 11th-century castle which now houses a historical/geological/archaeological museum as well as a glass factory, beckons visitors (open daily May-Sept. 9:30am-5pm). The **tourist office** is located next to the Rathaus on Schulgasse 2. Head left out of the train station and take a left at the first stoplight on Bahnhofstr. At the next stoplight take a right over Ludwigsbrücke onto the Stadtpl. Walk diagonally across the pl. and up the steps to the right of the Rathaus. The English-speaking staff boggles the mind with brochures. (☎ (09921) 29 29; fax 604 33; email tourist-information-regen@t-online.de; www.regen.de. Open M-F 8am-5pm, Sa-Su and holidays 10am-5pm.) Regen also offers a calming **Kurgarten** with bizarre modern sculpture and fountains—turn into the park from Bahnhofstr., before the Ludwigsbrücke. The **Restaurant am Rathaus,** Stadtpl. 3, directly downstairs and to the right of the tourist office, serves savory Bavarian cuisine (DM8-20) and offers a complete vegetarian menu (DM8-14), beer (DM4.50-5.50), and ice cream creations (DM5-8.50) in a large, relaxed space decorated with trophies and an assortment of liquor bottles. In case you haven't picked up on the differences between standard German and the Bavarian dialect, they've spelled it out for you in chart form on the napkins. (☎ 22 20. Open Th-Tu 10am-1am.)

EICHSTÄTT ☎ 08421

Sheltered in the valley of the Altmühl River, Eichstätt doesn't make it onto many tourist itineraries. But unlike many well-preserved Bavarian towns, Eichstätt's buildings are actively in use today, serving as more than props put up for a stream of visitors. The town's university and position at the heart of the **Altmühltal Nature Preserve** make it both an environmental and intellectual center.

⁊ ORIENTATION AND PRACTICAL INFORMATION

Trains run to Eichstätt-Bahnhof from **Ingolstadt** (25min., 2 per hr., DM8) and **Nürnberg** (1¼hr., 1 per hr., DM25.60). From Eichstätt-Bahnhof, another train takes you the last 5km to the **Eichstätt-Stadt** station (9min., 3 per hr., DM2.40). Information and ticket counter open M-F 7:30am-noon, 1-6pm; Sa 9am-2:10pm.) Rent **bikes** at **Fahrradgarage,** Herzoggasse 3, in the alley that leads from Marktpl. to the footbridge. (☎ 21 10 or 899 87. Open daily 9-11:30am and 2:30-7pm. DM13 per day.) **Heinz Glas,** Industriestr. 18, rents **canoes** for trips down the Altmühl River. (☎ 30 55. M-F DM20 per day, Sa-Su DM25; under 16 20% off.) The **tourist office,** Kardinal-Preysing-Pl. 14, has free maps and books rooms (DM25-30) for free. From the Bahnhof, walk right and follow the information sign across the Spitalbrücke. Turn right on Residenzpl. and follow the bend left to Leonrodpl., then bear right until you reach Kardinal-Preysing-Pl. on the left; the tourist office is up the street on the right. (☎ 988 00; fax 98 80 30; e-mail tourismus@eichstaett.de; www.eichstaett.de. Open Apr.-Oct. M-Sa 9am-6pm, Su 1-4pm; Nov.-Mar. M-Th 9am-noon and 2-4pm, F 9am-noon.) German language **tours** of the town leave from the tourist office. (1½hr. Apr.-Oct. Sa 1:30pm, also W at 1:30pm from July-Aug. DM5. Call ahead to arrange an English tour.) **Informationszentrum Naturpark Altmühltal,** Notre Dame 1, cloistered in a former monastery connected to the tourist office, also provides tourist information on trails and paths in the nature reserve. (☎ 987 60. Open May-Sept. M-Sa 9am-6pm, Su 10am-6pm; Oct.-Apr. M-F 8am-noon, 2-4pm) Exchange money at **Hypo-Vereinsbank,** Marktpl. 18. (open M-Tu and Th 8:30am-noon and 2-4:30pm, W 8:30am-noon, F 8:30am-3pm). A convenient **pharmacy** is **Dom-Apotheke,** Dompl. 16. (☎ 15 20. Open M-F 8am-6pm, Sa 8am-noon.) The **post office,** 85072 Eichstätt, is at Dompl. 7 (open M-F 8:30am-5:30pm, Sa 9am-noon).

▐▗◙ ACCOMMODATIONS AND FOOD

Eichstätt's **Jugendherberge (HI)**, Reichenaustr. 15, is modern and comfortable. Follow directions to Willibaldsburg (see **Sights**, below), but turn right halfway up Burgstr. onto Reichenaustr. at the Jugendherberge sign. (☎980 40; fax 98 04 15. Breakfast included. Sheets DM5.50. Reception 8-9am and 5-7pm. Lockout 10am-5pm. Curfew 10pm, but they'll give you a key if you're over 18. Closed Dec.-Jan. 6-bed dorms DM25.) A small *Pension* down the street from the Jugendherberge is **Haus Kirschner**, Elias-Holl-Str. 27. (☎54 42; fax 90 22 22. Doubles with TV and internet connections DM30 per person per night.) Other plentiful, inexpensive guest houses and *Pensionen* can be found through the tourist office.

Netto Marken-Discount, Buchtal 28, offers cheap **groceries** (open M-F 8am-6:30pm, Sa 8am-1pm). **Schneller's Backstube**, Marktpl. 20a, provides inexpensive fresh bread and delicious pastries (open M-F 7am-6pm, Sa 7:30am-1pm). To get to the university **Mensa**, Universitätsallee 2, walk toward the end of Ostenstr. and hang a right on Universitätsallee; look for the big "Mensa" sign on the right. Buy a card (DM20, 8 of which is a card deposit) from the machine on the first floor to eat in the actual Mensa. (☎93 14 60. ID required. Open during the semester M-F 11:30am-2pm; in summer 11:30am-1:30pm; closed Aug. to mid-Sept.) A relaxed **cafeteria** on the first floor, where you can pay with cash, has an outdoor garden (open M-Th 8:15am-7pm, F 8:15am-3pm; in summer M-F 8:15am-3pm). In town, **Zum Ammonit**, Luitpoldstr. 19, is a student hangout with beer (DM4.20 for 0.5L) and other snacks for DM7-15. (☎29 29. Open M-F 9:30am-1am, Sa-Su 9:30am-2am.) **L'Incontro**, Luitpoldstr. 21, is a deluxe coffee bar. (☎56 90. Same hours as Ammonit.) **La Grotta**, in back of Marktpl. 13, offers affordable pizzas (DM8-13.50) and pasta (DM8.50-12.50), as well as a nice terrace. (☎72 80 or 15 07. Open daily 11:30am-2pm and 5:30pm-1am. Kitchen open until 11pm.) For an excellent Greek meal, try **Restaurant Poseidon**, off the north-west corner of the Marktpl. at Westenstr. 17. The lunch menu contains 25 offerings in the DM10 range. (☎26 40. Open daily 11am-3pm and 5pm-12:30am.)

▐◉ SIGHTS

The **Willibaldsburg**, conspicuously watches over the town from its high perch across the river. To reach the castle from the station, take a right onto Freiwasserstr., then turn right again. At the main intersection, turn right onto Weißenburgerstr., then turn left on Burgstr. The 14th-century castle now houses the **Juramuseum**, filled with fossils from the Jurassic period found in the Altmühltal Valley, once covered by a vast prehistoric sea. See the fossil of the earliest bird ever to catch a worm, the Archaeopteryx, who lived over 150 million years ago. Dinosaur movies (no Spielberg) are screened daily at 10:15am and 2:30pm. The **Museum für Ur- und Frühgeschichte,** also in the Willibaldsburg, picks up the story at the debut of Homo Sapiens and continues through the era of Roman colonization. *(Burgstr. 19. Both museums open Apr.-Sept. Tu-Su 9am-6pm; Oct.-Mar. Tu-Su 10am-4pm. Juramuseum ☎29 56 or 47 30; DM6, students DM4, children under 15 free. Museum für Ur- und Frühgeschichte ☎894 50; DM10.)* Also on the Burg is the revived **Bastionsgarten,** once the *Hortus Eystettensis* of Prince Johann Konrad von Gemmingen (1561-1612). Abandoned after the Thirty Years War, this garden now blooms year round.

Across the river, Eichstätt proper is built around the extravagant **Residenzplatz,** surrounded by Rococo Episcopal palaces. The west wing has a particularly magnificent portal, and the interior is just as richly decorated. Free German-language tours of the **Residenz** begin here if there are at least five people. *(☎702 20. Easter-Oct. M-Th at 11am and 3pm, F at 11am, Sa-Su every 45 min. 10-11:30am and 2-3:30pm.)* In a corner of Residenzpl., in the middle of a fountain, stands the **Mariensäule,** an elaborate column depicting the Virgin Mary. Behind the Residenz is the 14th-century **Hoher Dom,** an eclectic product of the Romanesque, Gothic, and Baroque eras. *(Open M-Th 9:45am-1pm and 2:30-4pm, F 9:45am-3:30pm, Sa 9:45am-3pm, Su 12:30-5pm.)* The east apse features richly colored stained glass, and the north aisle shelters the intricate 15th-century stone **Pappenheim Altar.** On the other side of the altar is the entrance to the **Mortuarium,** resting place of Eichstätt's bishops, in which the Gothic **Schöne Säule** rises to meet the vault. Also in the cathedral complex, the **Diözesanmuseum** examines the 1,200-year history of the diocese with statues, folk art, and paintings. *(Residenzpl. 7. ☎507 42. Open Apr.-Oct. W-F 10:30am-5pm, Sa-Su 10am-5pm. DM2.50, under 18 free.)* Two blocks farther on Leonrodpl. is the Baroque **Schutzengelkirche,** built during the Thirty Years War, containing richly carved wooden pews and a striking golden sunburst above the high altar. Five-hundred sixty-seven sculpted angels fly about the church's interior. Start counting.

For a taste of the corporal world, head on over to the **Altmühltaler Schnapsmuseum.** There, exhibits and a video on the art of schnapps brewing (as well as a tasting bench) will tempt you to buy their delicious potent potables *(Weißenburgerstr. 5-6. ☎971 30. Open M-F 9am-noon and 2-6pm; Sa 9am-noon. Free.)*

INGOLSTADT ☎0841

The site of the first Bavarian university from 1472 to 1800, the old Danube city of Ingolstadt is now best known as the home of Audi. The name of this luxury car company was originally *Horch*, the last name of auto innovator and entrepreneur August Horch, and German for "eavesdrop." After WWII it was changed to the Latin *Audi* (listen) to help exports in an international market resistant to German-sounding products. It would take much more than a name change, however, to shake the traditional look of this old town. The Stadtmitte remains a tightly packed collection of old-school architecture, enclosed by lush greenery with no evidence of heavy industry in sight, and frequented by university students.

▐ GETTING THERE AND GETTING AROUND

Trains roll from Ingolstadt to **Munich** (1hr., 2 per hr., DM23.40); **Augsburg** (1hr., 1 per hr., DM17); and **Regensburg** (1¼hr., 1 per hr., DM20.20). **Bus** routes center around the **Omnibusbahnhof,** in the middle of the city (single ride DM2.70). The **Mitfahrzentrale,** Lebzeltergasse 5, arranges ride shares. (☎ 194 40. Open M-F 2-6pm.) For a **taxi** call ☎877 88. **Radverleih Fahrradinsel,** Münchener Str. 45, rents **bikes** for DM19 per day. (☎730 27. Open Tu-F 9am-12:30pm and 1:30-7pm, Sa 9am-4pm.)

▐ ORIENTATION AND PRACTICAL INFORMATION

Ingolstadt's **tourist office,** Rathauspl. 2, in the Altes Rathaus, hands out maps and helps find (relatively expensive) hotel **rooms.** To reach the tourist office and the Altstadt from the distant train station, take bus #10, 11, 15, 16, or 44 to "Rathausplatz." Or follow Bahnhofstr. to Münchener Str. and head straight over the bridge down Donaustr. to Rathauspl. (☎305 10 98; fax 305 10 99; email touristinformation@ingolstadt.de; www.ingolstadt.de. Open M-F 8am-5pm, Sa 9am-noon.) Free **tours** in German leave from the office Saturdays Apr.-Oct. at 2pm. **Exchange money** at **Volksbank,** Theresienstr. 32 (open M-W 8am-4:30pm, Th 8am-5:30pm, F 8am-2pm). **Franziskus-Apotheke,** Rathauspl. 13, posts late-night **pharmacy** information. (☎330 53. Open M-F 8am-6:30pm, Sa 8am-1pm.) The **post office,** 85024 Ingolstadt, is directly in front of the train station (open M-F 7:30am-6pm, Sa 8am-noon).

▐ ACCOMMODATIONS AND FOOD

Ingolstadt's superb **Jugendherberge (HI),** Friedhofstr. 4, is in a renovated section of the old town fortifications. From the tourist office, take Moritzstr. north and turn left on Theresienstr. to the Kreuztor. Walk through the gate and cross Auf der Schanz; the hostel is on the right (10min.). Large echoing rooms with private sinks, cavernous hallways, and a great location—hosteling rarely gets this good. (☎341 77; fax 91 01 78. Sheets included. Reception 8am-11:30pm; inquire in the kitchen if no one's at the front desk. Curfew 11:30pm. Dorm beds DM23.) **Pension Lipp** is at Feldkirchener Str. 16. Walk east down Schloßländestr. along the Danube, take a left up Frühlingstr., and then a right on Feldkirchener. This pleasant, small

BAVARIA

pension is struggling to survive amidst the rapidly expanding (and expensive) hotel industry, so give Oma a ring and keep her in business. (☎587 36. Singles DM40, with bath DM45; doubles DM75, with shower DM85.) The most inexpensive hotel in town is **Gästehaus Bauer,** Hölzlstr. 2, half-way between the station and the Altstadt. To make the 15min. walk from the train station, take Bahnhofstr. to Münchener Str., make a right at the Fiat dealership and proceed to Hölzlstr. (☎670 86; fax 661 94. Breakfast included. All rooms with TV and phone. Singles from DM65; doubles from DM85.) Campers head to **Campingpl. am Auwaldsee,** known as the "Blue Lagoon,"off the E45/Autobahn A9, a five minute drive from the town center. (☎961 16 16. Open year-round. DM7.10 per person. Tent DM5.10. Car DM9.90.)

Edeka, Ludwigstr. 27 in the basement of Galeria Kaufhof, sells **groceries** (open M-F 9am-8pm, Sa 9am-4pm). The **Kreuztor** might be the symbol of the Altstadt, but it's also the epicenter of all that's hip and new in town. Local nightlife centers around **Kreuzstr.,** which turns into **Theresienstr.** toward the center of town. **Sigi's cafe und Bistro,** Kreuzstr. 6, a few doors down from the Tor, is a small and chic cafe with nice outdoor seating. *Wurst,* sandwiches, and salads are all under DM11. (☎329 52. Open M-Sa 9:30am-2am, Su 2pm-2am.) **Restaurant Mykonos,** Ludwigstr. 9, dishes up Greek delights in a mini-Athens. Omelettes (DM7.20) and Mediterranean specialities (DM9-13) grace the affordable lunch menu; a free shot of *ouzo* accompanies your check (open daily 11am-3pm and 5pm-1am). The **Weissbräuhaus zum Herrnbräu,** Dollstr. 3, serves up traditional Bavarian fare for DM10-20 and was voted best Bavarian restaurant in Ingolstadt in 1998. (☎328 90. Open daily 9am-1am.)

Neue Welt, Griesbadgasse 7, off Kreuzstr., is home to the local art and music crowd with its own stage. Cabarets and alternative and R&B concerts premiere M, Tu, and F. Try the chili (DM8.50), a *Tsatsiki* (DM6), or vegetarian rigatoni with "special sauce." (DM9. Beer DM4.50. ☎324 70. Open daily 7pm-2am.) **Goldener Stern,** Griesbadgasse 2, is in a light yellow house nearby. Self-proclaimed student-friendly prices are a joy, and an amicable staff and peaceful *Biergarten* sweeten the deal. Beer starts at DM4; chocolatey and fruity crepes run DM5-7. (☎354 19. 18+. Open daily 7pm-1am.)

👁 SIGHTS

The old city wall is magnificently represented by the turreted **Kreuztor** (built from 1054-1070), topped by dainty stone ornamentations. Just beyond the gate outside the city wall is the **Stadtmuseum,** which explores the archaeological and cultural history of the area. *(Auf der Schanz 45. ☎305 18 85. Open Tu-Sa 9am-5pm, Su 10am-5pm. DM4, students and seniors DM2.)* Two blocks east of the Kreuztor stands the late Gothic **Liebfrauenmünster,** full of ornate altars and immense columns. A few blocks south on tantalizingly named Anatomiestr., the **Deutsches Medizinhistorisches Museum** features an 18th-century "do-it-yourself" enema stool complete with a hand-operated water pump and padded seat with protruding 3-inch-long pipe. This breathes new life into the term "self-service pump." The "skeleton room" displays skinned human corpses with dried-up muscles still attached and an eerie collection of shrivelled guts and limbs. The staff will lend you a thick English guidebook to interpret the German-only exhibits. *(Anatomiestr. 18-20. ☎305 18 60. Open Tu-Su 10am-noon and 2-5pm. DM4, students and seniors DM2.)* At the corner of Jesuitenstr. and Neubaustr. is the **Maria-de-Victoria-Kirche.** This once sparse chapel for students of the nearby Catholic school was rococo-ed with a vengeance in 1732, and an awe-inspiring frescoco by Cosmos Damion Asam depicting Mary as queen of Heaven now adorns the ceiling. *(Open Mar.-Nov. Tu-Su 9am-noon and 1-5pm; Dec.-Feb. Tu-Su 10am-noon and 1-4pm. DM2.50, students and children DM1.50, children under 12 free.)*

Across town on Paradepl. is the 15th-century **Neues Schloß,** Paradepl. 4, a red-tiled castle that houses a band of pierced-and-tattooed *Szene* kids and the less fascinating **Bayerisches Armeemuseum,** an exhibit of military artifacts collected by King Ludwig "if-I-weren't-crazy-I'd-be-dangerous" II. *(☎93 770. Open Tu-Su 8:45am-4:30pm. DM5.50, students DM2.)* The brand-new **Museum für Konkrete Kunst** is off Donaustr. near the Konrad-Adenauer-Brücke. The neon lights and funkadelic designs of the concrete art exhibits will make your head spin. *(Tränktorstr. 6-8. ☎305 18 75. Open Tu and Th-Su 10am-6pm, W 10am-2pm and 5-9pm. DM4, students DM2, children under 10 free. Tours every 2nd W of the month at 6:30pm, DM4.)* Have a burning fetish for automobiles? Call **Audi** for information on factory tours *(☎89 12 41).*

AUGSBURG   ☎0821

Founded by Caesar Augustus in 15 BC, Augsburg was the financial center of the Holy Roman Empire and a major commercial city by the end of the 15th century. The town owed its success and prestige mainly to the Fuggers, an Augsburg family that virtually monopolized the banking industry; Jakob Fugger "the Rich" was personal financier to the Hapsburg Emperors. Augsburg didn't fare well in WWII, however, and very little besides major monuments were reconstructed. Today its castles are scattered among modern office buildings, and industry is the main engine of Augsburg's economy.

⊓ ORIENTATION AND PRACTICAL INFORMATION

Augsburg is connected by **train** to **Munich** (45min., 4-5 per hr., DM17-30); **Nürnberg** (2hr., 2 per hr., DM45); **Würzburg** (2hr., 1 per hr., DM76); **Stuttgart** (1¾hr., 2 per hr., DM66), and **Zürich** (5hr., 2 per hr.). The ubiquitous **Europabus** line, canvassing the Romantische Str. route (see p. 311), stops at the Augsburg train station (northbound arrival 10:20am; southbound arrival 5:30pm). Augsburg's **public transportation** hub is at Königspl., two blocks east of the train station down Bahnhofstr.; for information on bus and streetcar routes, head to the **VGA Info Center** there (☎324 58 88; open M-F 7am-6pm, Sa 9am-1pm). The **tourist office,** Bahnhofstr. 7, off Königspl., about 300m from the station down Bahnhofstr., sells excellent maps and books **rooms** (DM40-60) for a DM3 fee. (☎50 20 70; fax 502 07 45; email stadtfuehrungen@regio-augsburg.de; www.regio-augsburg.de. Open M-F 9am-6pm.) A **branch** office on Rathauspl. has longer hours. From the station, walk to the end of Bahnhofstr. and take a left at Königspl. onto Annastr. Take the third right and Rathauspl. will be on the left; the branch office is on the right. (☎502 07 24. Open Apr.-Sept. M-F 9am-6pm, Sa 10am-4pm, Su 10am-1pm; Oct.-Mar. M-F 9am-6pm, Sa 10am-1pm.) Walking **tours** leave from the Rathaus (daily 2pm; DM12, students and children DM9), as do one-hour bus tours (Th-Su 10:30am; DM14, students DM10). For a **pharmacy,** head to **Stern-Apotheke**, Maximilianstr. 27 on Moritzpl., behind the fountain. (☎308 38. Open M-F 8:30am-6:30pm, Sa 8:30am-1pm.) **Sparkasse,** Halderstr. 3, two blocks east of the station, **exchanges cash** (3% fee, 2.55 €minimum; no fee to exchange American dollars) and **cashes traveler's checks.** (0.5% fee, DM7 minimum. Open M & Th 8:30am-6pm, Tu-W 8:30am-4pm, F 8:30am-3pm.) Augsburg's **post office,** Halderstr. 29, 86150 Augsburg, is on the right as you exit the station (open M-F 7am-8pm, Sa 8am-2pm, and Su 10am-noon).

⌐⌐ ACCOMMODATIONS AND FOOD

Augsburg's **Jugendherberge (HI),** Beim Pfaffenkeller 3, has an inner courtyard that allows for a sense of seclusion, in rooms which feel like converted second-grade classrooms. From the station walk up Prinzregentenstr. as it curves to the right through town. Turn left at Karolinenstr. and then right at the cathedral on Innere Pfaffengasse. Bear left as it becomes Beim Pfaffenkeller. (☎339 09; fax 15 11 49. Breakfast included. Sheets DM5.50. Key deposit DM20 or an ID. Reception 7-9am and 5-10pm. Curfew 1am. Closed Jan. Call ahead. Dorm beds DM21, adults over 27 accompanying youth DM25.) The cheapest privacy you'll find in a central location is at **Jakoberhof,** Jakoberstr. 39-41, 20min. from the station. Follow Prinzregentenstr. until it intersects with Mittlerer Graben, then fork right on Pilgerhausstr. (☎51 00 30; fax 15 08 44; email jakoberhof@t-online.de; www.mon.de/scw/jakoberhof. Breakfast included. Singles DM50, with shower DM75; doubles DM75, with bath DM105.) **Gasthof Lenzhalde,** Thelottstr. 2, is a 25-min. walk from the station. Bear right on Halderstr., take a sharp right onto Hermannstr., and cross the Gögginger Brücke. Take the first right onto Rosenaustr. and follow it for several blocks; when it curves right at the traffic light, the Gasthof is straight ahead. Very simple, tidy rooms overlook a park and train tracks. (☎52 07 45; fax 52 87 61. Singles DM42, with shower DM50; doubles DM78; triples DM110.) Pitch your tent at **Campingpl. Augusta,** ABA Augsburg-Ost, Am Autobahnsee. Take bus #23 (direction: "Firnhaberau") to "Hammerschmiede" and follow the signs; the camp is about 500m away. (☎70 75 75; fax 70 58 83. DM8 per person. Tent DM6. Car DM6.)

An outdoor **fruit and vegetable market** takes place on the Stadtmarkt, two blocks west of Rathauspl. (M-F 7am-7pm and Sa 7am-3pm). Stock up on **groceries** at **Penny Markt,** Maximilianstr. 71, a few blocks south of the Rathaus (open M-F 8am-8pm, Sa 8am-4pm). Myriad food stands line Maximilianstr. in the summer, but some of the *Imbiß* fare is surprisingly pricey. At **König von Flandern,** Karolinenstr. 12, Augsburg's first Gasthof-brewery, the pleasing, rustic smell of yeast and fermenting barley wafts up to visitors. Large portions of soup (DM5-6), salad (DM5-10), and meat (DM5.50-18.90) will satisfy ravenous Bavarian food fiends. (☎15 80 50. Open M-Sa 11am-1am, Su 5pm-1am.) A **Lech-Bäck** bakery and **Fleischwaren** meat shop team up at Karolinenstr. 16 to offer cheap eats. (Everything under DM5. Open M-F 7:30am-6pm, Sa 7:30am-1:30pm.)

SIGHTS

Jakob Fugger "The Rich", Augsburg's very own Daddy Warbucks, founded the **Fuggerei** quarter in 1519 as the first welfare housing project in the world. Perhaps dreading the day he would discover just how difficult it is for a camel to pass through the eye of a needle, Fugger established the Fuggerei "for the salvation of his soul and as an everlasting example to his fellow citizens and all posterity." Still in use almost 500 years later, the narrow cobblestone streets and 67 gabled houses are a haven for the elderly, who earn their keep by praying for the departed souls of the Fuggers and pay only DM1.72 (the equivalent of a "Rhein Guilder") rent annually. Sure beats hosteling, but budget travelers need not apply. The **Fuggereimuseum,** Mittlergasse 13 within the Fuggerei, is in one of the only flats whose original construction survived WWII, and is arranged to portray the typical decoration of the homes 500 years ago, as well as the financial predilections of its owners. *(To reach the Fuggerei from the Rathaus, walk behind the Perlachturm tower on Perlachberg, which becomes Barfüsserstr. and finally Jakoberstr., and turn right under the archway. The gates close at 10pm. Open Mar.-Dec. daily 9am-6pm. DM1, students and seniors DM0.50.)* Fugger lived and tended to his business in the **Fugger Haus,** Maximilianstr. 36-38, where a dispute between Martin Luther and Cardinal Cajetan in October of 1518 ensured church schism. Luther stayed with Prior Frosch in the **St. Anna Kirche** and convinced him to pioneer the Reformation in Augsburg from this church. *(On Annastr. near Königspl. Open Tu-Su 10am-12:30pm and 3-6pm).*

A jaunt down Maximilianstr. leads to the huge Renaissance **Rathaus,** which encloses the **Goldener Saal** on its third floor. The wide rectangular room, richly ornamented with golden cherubs and bright ceiling frescos, recalls the importance of commerce in Augsburg's past. *(☎324 91 80. Open daily 10am-6pm. DM3, children under 15 DM1.)* Down Hoher Weg to the left sits the **Hoher Dom,** the regional bishop's seat. Built in the 9th century, the cathedral was renovated in the 14th century in Gothic style and badly damaged in WWII. The chancel and high altar exemplify the Bauhaus-inspired design prevalent in German churches after the war. *(Open M-Sa 6am-5pm. German-language tours available M-Sa 10:15am-4pm.)* Another cultural treasure destroyed during WWII and later rebuilt is the **Synagoge.** Turn right from the station on Halderstr.; the synagogue is on the left. Set back from the street by a gated courtyard, the reconstructed early 20th-century synagogue includes an enormous Byzantine dome. Inside, the **Jewish Cultural Museum** displays valuable ritual objects from Judaism. *(☎51 36 58. Open Tu-F 9am-4pm and Su 10am-5pm. DM4, students and children DM2.)*

Bertolt Brecht's birthplace was renovated in 1998, on the 100th anniversary of his birth. The museum does a good job of chronicling the life of one of the most influential 20th-century playwrights and poets through photographs, letters, and poetry. From the station head up Prinzregentenstr. to tiny Schmiedgasse on the right. (Open W-Su 10am-4pm. DM2.50, students and children DM1.50.)

ROMANTISCHE STRAßE (ROMANTIC ROAD)

Groomed fields of sunflowers and wheat checker the landscape between Würzburg and Füssen. Circular cities, ornate castles, and dense forests seem laid out with the *Kitsch*-hungry traveler in mind. The region's beauty wasn't lost on the German tourism industry, which baptized it the **Romantische Straße** in 1950; the area has subsequently become the most heavily touristed region in Germany.

▛ GETTING AROUND. Deutsche Bahn's Europabus transports throngs of American and Japanese tourists daily from Frankfurt to Munich and back. Though this is the most popular way to travel the Romantische Str., it is also one of the least flexible—there is only one bus in each direction per day. On the **Frankfurt-Munich route,** southbound buses leave Frankfurt daily at 8am, while northbound buses depart from Munich daily at 9am. Stops include Würzburg

(southbound arrival 9:45am, departure 10am; northbound arrival 6:30pm, departure 6:45pm), Rothenburg (12:45pm, 2:30pm; 2:50pm, 4:15pm), Dinkelsbühl (3:25pm, 4:15pm; 12:45pm, 2pm), Nördlingen (4:55pm, 4:57pm; 11:55am, 12:15pm), Augsburg (6:20pm, 6:35pm; 10:20am, 10:35am), and Munich (7:50pm; 9am). On the **Dinkelsbühl-Füssen route,** southbound buses leave Dinkelsbühl at 4:15pm, and northbound buses leave Füssen at 8am. Stops on this line include **Augsburg** (southbound arrival 5:30pm, departure 6pm; northbound arrival 10:40am, departure 10:50am), **Wieskirche** (northbound only, arrival 8:35am, departure 8:55am), and **Hohenschwangau and Neuschwanstein** (7:55pm; 8:07am). Check schedules with a tourist office before heading to the bus. The Europabus is relatively expensive. (Frankfurt to Rothenburg DM63, to Dinkelsbühl DM76, to Munich DM121, Dinkelsbühl to Hohenschwangau or Füssen DM61; Students and under 26 10% off, under 12 and over 60 50% off, under 4 free. Eurail and German Railpass holders get a 75% discount, but BahnCard holders receive no discount.)

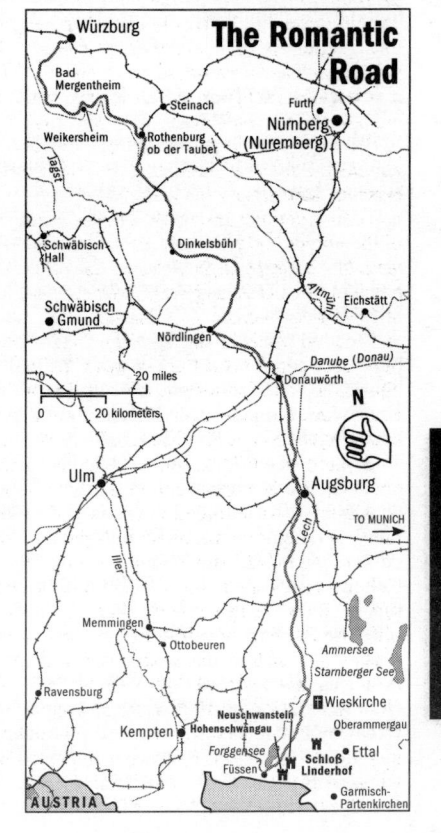

The Romantic Road

BAVARIA

A more economical way to see the Romantische Str. for those without the railpass discount is (paradoxically) to use the faster and much more frequent **trains,** which run to every town except Dinkelsbühl. Those traveling the Romantische Str. by **car** may have to park in lots outside the old city walls of some towns, but will have easy access to many suburban budget hotels, *Privatzimmer*, and campgrounds that lie outside the reach of bus or train. The Romantische Str. is an excellent opportunity for a leisurely **bike** journey, with campgrounds located 10 to 20km apart. Tourist offices offer excellent cycling maps and information on campgrounds along the road. For information or reservations, call **Deutsche Touring** in Frankfurt, Am Römerhof 17 (☎ (069) 79 03 50; fax 790 32 19; email service@deutsche-touring.com; www.deutsche-touring.com). For general information, contact the **Romantische Str. Arbeitsgemeinschaft,** Marktpl., 91550 Dinkelsbühl (☎ (09851) 902 71; fax 902 79 902 81; email romantischestrasse@t-online.de; www.romantischestrasse.de).

ROTHENBURG OB DER TAUBER ☎ 09861

Rothenburg ob der Tauber is *the* Romantic Roadstop, touched by everyone—and we mean *everyone*. While Rothenburg is busy enjoying the same commercialized fate as its favorite December holiday, don't knock all the touristic pomp; this small town is your best chance to see a nearly intact medieval walled city in Bayern. At the end of the 19th century, locals set up strict preservation laws in order to preserve their 16th-century town; unfortunately, Allied bombs destroyed 40% of Rothenburg in WWII. Afterwards, Rothenburg's legions of former tourists banded together to rebuild and restore the Altstadt, which is a gorgeous reminder of Bayern's architectural past.

◼ ORIENTATION AND PRACTICAL INFORMA.ION

Hourly **trains** run from **Würzburg** (40min, 1 per hr., DM15.40) and **München** (3hr., 1 per hr., DM60) to **Steinach,** where you can transfer for a quick trip to Rothenburg (15min., 1 per hr., DM3.30). **Buses** also serve the route, sometimes in place of the train in the evening. The **Europabus** leaves from the Busbahnhof, right next to the train station. For a **taxi** call ☎ 20 00 or 72 27. Rent **bikes** from **Herrmann Hat's,** Galgengasse 33 (☎ 61 11; open daily 8am-7pm; half-day DM10, full day DM15-18), or at **Rad und Tat,** Bensenstr. 17 (☎ 879 84; open M-Sa 9am-6pm, Su 9am-2pm; DM5 per hr. or DM20 per day).

Rothenburg's **tourist office,** Marktpl. 2, supplies maps in English and books **rooms** (DM35-60) for free or for a DM5 fee during the summer and Christmas. Walk left from the station, bear right on Ansbacher Str., and follow it straight to the Marktpl. (15min.); the office is on your right, across the square in the pink building with the clock on the upper stories. (☎ 404 92; fax 868 07; email info@rothenburg.de; www.rothenburg.de. Open May-Oct. M-F 9am-12:30pm and 1-6pm, Sa-Su 10am-3pm; Nov.-Apr. M-F 9am-12:30pm and 1-5pm, Sa 10am-1pm.) **Tours** in German depart daily from the steps of the Rathaus (90min.; Apr.-Oct. and Dec. at 11am and 2pm; DM5), while tours in English meet daily at the Rathaus at 2pm (DM6). The ◼**"night watchman"** leads a special tour with his candle-lit lantern and iron spear that is more entertaining than educating; meet at the Rathaus. (In English at 8pm; DM6. In German at 9:30pm; DM5.)

Wäscherei Then is a **laundromat** located at Johannitergasse 9. (☎ 27 75. Wash DM6.50, including soap. Dry DM3.50. Open M-F 8am-6pm, Sa-Su 8am-2pm.) **Löwen-Apotheke,** Marktpl. 3, has all your **pharmacy** phixins and a night bell for emergencies. (☎ 93 51 90. Open M-F 8am-6pm, Sa 8:30am-12:30pm.) **Internet access** is at **Planet Internet,** Paradeisgasse 5, to the right off Rödergasse. (☎ 93 44 15. Open Su-Th noon-midnight, F-Sa noon-1am; DM6 for 30min., DM9 for 1hr.) The **post office,** Bahnhofstr. 15, 91541 Rothenburg, is across from the station and to the right in the Zentro shopping complex (open M-F 9am-5:30pm, Sa 9am-noon).

ACCOMMODATIONS

An incredible number of **private rooms** (DM20-45) not registered with the tourist office are available; look for *Zimmer frei* signs. Just knock on doors bearing the signs to inquire. Despite their abundance, don't expect same-day availability in the summer or around Christmas. **Jugendherberge Rossmühle (HI),** Mühlacker 1, is in a former horse-powered mill that shelters modern two-to-six-bed rooms and a Calvin-Klein-ad-ready staff. Amenities include ping-pong and pool tables, a TV room where you can borrow movies, free storage lockers (DM5 deposit required), and washers and dryers (DM3.50 for each)—this is what all hostels should be like. Follow the directions to the tourist office, take a left down Obere Schmiedgasse, and go straight for about 10min. until you see the small, white Jugendherberge sign to the righ. (☎941 60; fax 94 16 20; email jhrothen@aol.com. Sheets and breakfast included. Dinner DM8.50, lunch and dinner DM15. Reception 7am-midnight. Check-in until 10pm. Curfew midnight, but they'll give you an access code. DM28) Rothenburg has an unbelievable number of *Pensionen* for a town its size, but most of them are expensive. For an exception, check out ⬛**Pension Raidel,** Wenggasse 3, on the way to the hostel. Head down Obere Schmiedgasse and make a left on Wenggasse. Bright rooms and featherbeds, each one built and decorated by the owner, make this the most charming of the affordable *Pensionen* in the Altstadt. (☎31 15; fax 93 52 55; email gaestehaus-raidel@t-online.de; www.romanticroad.com/raidel. Breakfast included. Call ahead. Singles DM35, with private bath DM69; doubles DM69, with private bath DM89.) **Pension Then,** Johannitergasse 8a, has a friendly staff. From the station, turn left, then right on Ansbacher Str. and right on Johannitergasse. (☎51 77; fax 860 14. Singles DM40, doubles DM80-86. Apartment with kitchen DM25 per person with a 3-day min. stay.)

FOOD

With a cozy Christmas theme year-round, it's not surprising that Rothenburg is famous for its heart-stopping *Schneeballen* (snowballs), large balls of sweet dough fried and then covered with powdered sugar. Today, non-traditional versions are dipped in various colors of chocolate, and have sweet centers of marzipan or amaretto. **Dillers,** Hofbronner Gasse 16 and Hafengasse 4, offers these doughy concoctions at industrially produced rates. (DM2.50-5.50. ☎866 23. Open Su-F 10am-6pm, Sa 10am-4pm.) For fast food, try Rödergasse, off Marktpl., where *Döners* and hamburgers run DM5. **Roter Hahn,** Obere Schmiedgasse 21, is the former home of the renowned wine-chugging Mayor Nusch whose tolerance for large doses of alcohol saved the town from destruction (see below). The ancient, traditional Bavarian restaurant caters to meat-lovers, but less atherosclerotic meals such as baked shrimp on salad (DM13.95) can be found. Most meals on the lunch menu cost less than DM14. (☎97 40. Open daily 11:30am-10pm.) **Pizzeria Roma,** Galgengasse 19, serves large portions of pasta (DM8-11), pizzas (DM9-12), and fresh salads (DM4.50-10) in a dark interior with a small plastic fountain. (☎45 40. Open daily 11:30am-midnight.) **Fränkisches Haus,** Galgengasse 13, offers regional specialties such as *Fränkischer Bratwurst* or *Mainländer Schnitzel* for DM10-17. (☎34 39. Open M-Tu and Th-F 8am-6pm, Sa 8:30am-6pm, Su 9am-6pm; closed W.) Pick up fresh goods from vendors on the **Marktpl.** (Sa 7am-noon), or stop by **Kupsch** on Rödergasse, inside the city wall as you enter town, for **groceries** (open M-F 8am-7pm, Sa 8am-2pm).

SIGHTS

On the Marktpl. stands the Renaissance **Rathaus;** its 60m tower affords a nice view of the town. *(Open daily 8am-6pm. Free. Tower open Apr.-Oct. daily 9:30am-12:30pm and 1-5pm; Nov.-Mar. M-F 9:30am-12:30pm, Sa-Su noon-3pm. DM2, children DM1.)* In 1631, the conquering Catholic general Johann Tilly offered to spare the town from destruction if any local could chug a wine keg containing almost a gallon of wine. Mayor Georg Nusch successfully met the challenge, then passed out for several days. His saving **Meistertrunk** is reenacted with great fanfare each year. The town clock acts out a slooow motion version of the episode over the Marktplatz *(hourly 11am-3pm and 8-10pm).* Inside the courtyard behind the Rathaus are the **Historien-Gewölbe,** which articulate Rothenburg's history during the Thirty Years War. *(☎867 51. Open May-Sept. daily 9am-6pm; Oct. to mid-Nov. and mid-Mar. to Apr. daily 9am-5pm. DM3, students DM2.)* Three gloomy stone cells lurk in the dungeon, where Mayor Heinrich Toppler and his son were once imprisoned by King Ruprecht.

The **Jakobskirche,** Klostergasse 15, is famed for its **Altar of the Holy Blood** by Tilman Riemenschneider, a 5,500-pipe organ, and its 14th-century stained glass windows. *(☎70 06 20. Open Apr.-Oct. M-Sa 9am-5:30pm, Su 10:30am-5:30pm; Dec. daily 10am-5pm; Nov. and Jan.-Mar. daily 10am-noon and 2-4pm. DM2.50, students DM1. Free German language tours at 11am and 2pm Apr.-Oct.)* The **Reichsstadtmuseum,** Klosterhof 5, housed in a restored 13th-century Dominican convent, displays implements used by medieval nuns and 13th-century Judaica. *(☎93 90 43. Open Apr.-Oct. daily 10am-5pm; Nov.-Mar. 1-4pm. DM5, students DM3.)* The town's **Medieval Crime Museum,** Burggasse 3-5, is definitely worth the entrance fee for anyone who can stomach the thought of iron-maiden justice. Take a picture of yourself in the stocks outside before heading into the dim, creepy basement housing the torture exhibits. Rooms upstairs continue the fun, with exhibits on "eye for an eye" jurisprudence and the special punishments once reserved for bad musicians, dishonest bakers, and frivolous gossips. All exhibits explained in English. *(☎53 59. Open Apr.-Oct. daily 9:30am-6pm; Nov. and Jan.-Mar. 2-4pm; Dec. 10am-4pm. DM5, students DM4, children DM3.)*

Kitsch holds brazen sway at Käthe Wohlfahrt's **Christkindlmarkt** (Christ Child Market), Herrngasse 2, and the more extensive **Weihnachtsdorf** (Christmas Village), Herrngasse 1. *(☎40 90; www.wohlfahrt.de. Open M-F 9am-6:30pm, Sa 9am-4pm; mid-May to Dec. also Su 11am-6pm.)*

DINKELSBÜHL
☎09851

Forty-five kilometers south of Rothenburg, the historic town of Dinkelsbühl boasts a bevy of medieval half-timbered houses, a climbable 16th-century church tower, and a navigable town wall with gateways, towers, and moats. Sound familiar? It is, though locals claim their town's superiority lies in Dinkelsbühl's authenticity; the Altstadt corrals the largest number of original, unrestored structures on the Romantische Str. (repainting, of course, doesn't count).

⊏ GETTING THERE. When traveling by **bus** to and from Dinkelsbühl, plan ahead. Regional buses go to **Rothenburg** (9 per day, 1-3 per day on weekends; transfer buses at Dombühl or Feuchtwangen; DM11.40), and to **Nördlingen** (7 per day, 4-5 per day on weekends). Schedules are available at the tourist office and are posted at the town's main stop, "Bahnhof". If you plan poorly, you might get stuck with the crowded and expensive Europabus, which takes tourists along the Romantische Str. (see p. 311).

⋒ PRACTICAL INFORMATION. The **tourist office,** on the Marktpl., finds rooms (around DM70 for doubles) for a DM3 fee. The office also **rents bikes** (DM7 per day). From the "Bahnhof" bus stop, turn right on Luitpoldstr. and then left through the Wörnitz Tor into the Altstadt. Walk to the Marktpl.; the tourist office is in the rust-colored building with a bell tower on your right. *(☎902 40; fax 902 79; email touristik.service@dinkelsbuehl.de; www.dinkelsbuehl.de. Open Apr.-Oct. M-F 9am-noon and 2-6pm, Sa 10am-1pm and 2-6pm, Su 10am-1pm; Nov.-Mar. M-F 9am-noon and 2-5pm, Sa 10am-1pm.)* German language **tours** of the Altstadt meet in front of St. Georgskirche daily at 2:30, 8:30, and 9:30pm (the last with the **"night watchman"**; DM3.50, students DM2.50). The **St. Pauls pharmacy** at Nördlinger Str. 7, has a night bell for help at all hours. *(☎34 35. Open M-F 8am-12:30pm and 2-6pm, Sa 8am-noon.)* The post office, 91550 Dinkelsbühl, is located next to the "Bahnhof" bus stop on Luitpoldstr. (open M-F 9am-5pm, Sa 9am-noon).

⛰️📷 ACCOMMODATIONS AND FOOD. Built in 1508 as a grain store, the **Jugendherberge (HI)**, Koppengasse 10, is a huge, half-timbered fortress with wide wooden hallways garlanded with dried flowers. From the tourist office, head west down Segringer Str., and take a right on Bauhofstr. after passing the Rathaus. At the first bus stop, swing left on Koppengasse; it's the large stucco building on the right. (☎95 09; fax 48 74. Breakfast included. Sheets DM5.50. Reception 5-7pm. Curfew 11pm. Open Mar.-Oct. 2- to 8-bed rooms DM20-24.) **Gasthof Zur Sonne**, Weinmarkt 11, has airy rooms with pastel color schemes. (☎576 70; fax 75 48; www.mfro.de/sonne. Breakfast included. Singles DM45; doubles DM74-100; triples DM99-150.) Camp north on Dürrwanger Str. at **DCC Campingpark Romantische Str.** (☎78 17; fax 78 48. DM7.50 per person. DM16.50 per tent and car.)

Buy **groceries** at **Feinkost Müller**, Marktpl. 1 (open M-F 8am-6pm, Sa 8am-4pm). Budget food is hard to find in touristy Dinkelsbühl. Head to **Ali Baba Imbiß**, Nördlinger Str. 8, for *Döner* and salads. (DM3.90-10. ☎55 36 15. Open daily 10am-midnight.) **cafe Rossini**, Nördlinger Str. 17, serves reasonably priced Italian cuisine like pasta (DM8.50-14), pizza (DM6.50-14), salads (DM6-14.50), beer (DM4), and elaborate ice cream concoctions (DM6.90-15. ☎73 70. Open daily 9am-midnight.)

🏛️🎭 SIGHTS AND ENTERTAINMENT. The late-Gothic **St. Georgskirche**, which dominates the Weinmarkt at the center of town, sports a Romanesque tower and striking fan vaulting. Its perfect balance and proportion and its mighty sandstone pillars leave a powerful impression on visitors. A tale for tourists explains why the houses along Nördlinger Str. are oddly shaped—medieval superstition held that homes with right angles housed demons.

The **Parkring** around the Altstadt separates the old and new parts of town, with a system of moats and dykes glorified by armies of ducks and willow trees. New to the old town is the spiffy **3-Dimensional Museum**, housed in the Nördlinger Tor of the town wall. The only such museum in the world, it encompasses all the different ways since the Middle Ages that people have represented thick stuff in thin ways. (☎63 36. *Open Apr.-Oct. daily 10am-6pm; Nov.-Mar. Sa-Su 11am-4pm. DM10, with tourist office coupon DM9, children under 14 DM7.*) The **Historisches Museum**, Dr.-Martin-Luther-Str. 6b, presents exhibits on the history of Dinkelsbühl and its role in the Thirty Years War, and displays paintings of the town over the centuries. (☎32 93. *Open Tu-Su 10am-4pm; DM3, children under 15 DM1.*)

Every summer the Dinkelsbühlers faithfully celebrate the salvation of their besieged town during the Thirty Years War with the **Kinderzeche Festival** (July 13-22, 2001). The town tots' tears and the sweet voice of Kinderlore, the beautiful daughter of the town watchman, reputedly persuaded the invading colonel of Swedish King Gustavus Adolphus II to spare Dinkelsbühl. A recreation of the event accompanies parades, fireworks, dances, and, of course, crying kids—a strangely satisfying experience for hosteling travelers (tickets DM4-16).

NÖRDLINGEN IM RIES   ☎09081

The placid town of Nördlingen was created in the chaos and heat of a meteorite impact some 15 million years ago. Well, not exactly, but the plain it was built on during the Middle Ages was once a crater, created when the meteorite crashed, and then a prehistoric lake, before the sands of time caused it to fill up with mud. The wall surrounding this perfectly circular town was built entirely from "Rieser Moonstones"—stones which formed as a result of the collision. Nördlingen is the only town in Germany where the original walls are complete and can be navigated in their entirety.

📋 PRACTICAL INFORMATION. Nördlingen can be reached by hourly **trains** from **Augsburg** (1¼ hr., 1 per hr., change at Donauwörth, DM20); **Nürnberg** (2hr., one every other hr., change at Donauwörth, DM35); and **Ulm** (2hr., 1 per hr., change at Aalen, DM30). Buses also run from **Dinkelsbühl** to Nördlingen (45min., 8 per day, DM7.50). The **Europabus** (see p. 311) stops daily at Nördlingen's Rathaus (southbound 4:55pm, northbound 12:15pm). The **tourist office**, Marktpl. 2, distributes maps and finds rooms for free. (☎43 80 or 841 16; fax 841 13; email verkehr-

BAVARIA

samt@noerdlingen.de; www.noerdlingen.de. Open Easter-Oct. M-Th 9am-6pm, F 9am-4:30pm, Sa 9:30am-1pm; Nov.-Easter M-Th 9am-5pm, F 9am-3:30pm.) One-hour **tours** in German meet daily at the tourist office at 2pm (DM4; children under 13 free). **Einhorn-Apotheke,** Polizeigasse 7, has a list of 24-hour pharmacies posted in the window and a night bell. (☎296 20. Open M-F 8am-6pm, Sa 9am-noon.) An **Internet cafe** lies in the Stadtbücherei on the Marktplatz (open Tu, Sa 10am-1pm, W, F 10am-1pm and 2pm-6pm, Th 2-6:30pm). The **post office,** 86720 Nördlingen, is to the right of the train station as you exit (open M-F 8:30am-5pm, Sa 9am-noon).

⌂ ACCOMMODATIONS AND FOOD. Nördlingen's **Jugendherberge,** Kaiser-wiese 1, a small hostel with tidy rooms, is just outside the city walls on the north side of town. From Marktpl., follow Baldinger Str. out of the city walls; the hostel is on your right in the parking lot one cross street beyond the walls. (☎27 18 16. Reception 4:30-6pm. Curfew 10pm. Open Mar.-Oct. DM18.) **Gasthof Walfisch,** Hall-gasse 15, is located in the center of town near Marktpl. Head left onto Windgasse and take a right on Hallgasse. Relish the cavernous hallways and somber rooms. (☎31 07. Singles DM30, with bath DM60; doubles DM70, with bath DM110.) **Drei Mohren Gasthof,** Reimlinger Str. 18, is just inside the town wall. From Marktpl., fol-low Schäfflesmarkt to Reimlinger Str; the hotel is on the right. (☎31 13; fax 287 59; email drei.mohren@nordschwaben.de. DM35 per person.)

Nördlingen has many small restaurants and street cafes folded into its narrow alleyways, but the majority are expensive. For **groceries,** head to **Norma,** Rüben-markt 6, behind St. Georg (open M-F 8am-6:30pm, Sa 8am-1pm). **Cafe Radlos,** Löps-ingerstr. 8, serves up everything from traditional Bavarian *Wurst* to Greek, Italian, and Asian specialties. Most dishes are under DM14. (☎50 40. Open daily 11am-mid-night.) The sprightly **Ciao Ciao Pizza Ristorante,** Luckengasse 15, serves pizza (DM10-12) and pasta dishes. (DM11-14. Open Tu-Sa 6pm-midnight, Su 5-10pm.)

◉ SIGHTS. Nördlingen's **St. Georg Dom** boasts a 90m Gothic bell tower nick-named "Daniel," from whose lofty height the town watchman has presided over the people below every evening for the last 500 years. Those who climb up the 350 steps to the keeper's chambers at the top are rewarded with a hawk's eye view of the town and countryside below. Elegant Gothic columns arch over the wide hall of St. Georg, dwarfing the people in the pews below. *(Tower ☎27 18 13. Open daily Apr.-Oct. 9am-8pm; Nov.-Mar. 9am-5:30pm. DM3, under 17 DM2. Dom open M-F 9:30am-12:30pm and 2-5pm, Sa 9:30am-5pm, Su 11am-5pm. Free organ concerts Sa June-Aug. at noon.)* Explore the history of the medieval town wall in Nördlingen's **Stadtmauermu-seum,** inside Löpsinger Tor. *(☎91 80, open Apr.-Oct. daily 10am-4:30pm. DM2, under 17 DM1.)* The history and culture of the region—from the first farming settlements of 6000BC, to masterworks of Renaissance painters such as Lucas Cranach and Peter Paul Reubens, to the present day—can be digested at Nördlingen's **Stadtmuseum,** Vordere Gerbergasse 1. *(☎273 82 30. Open Tu-Su Mar.-Oct. 1:30-4:30pm. DM5, students DM2.50.)* Space cadets can trek over to the **Rieskrater Museum,** Eugene-Shoemaker-Pl. 1, for the low-down on the Ries meteorite which struck the earth here millions of years ago. *(☎273 82 20. Open Tu-Su May-Oct. 10am-4:30pm, Nov.-Apr. 10am-noon and 1:30-4:30pm. DM5, students DM2.50).* To take in all of these sights, purchase the **Museums Card** (DM10) at the tourist office.

WÜRZBURG ☎0931

Würzburg's two great monuments, the Baroque Residenz, one of Germany's most ostentatious palaces, and the 13th-century Marienburg, stare at one another across two hills bisected by the Main River while tourists pass in and out of their ornate gates. As if this weren't enough splendor for one town to handle, Würzburg is also the unofficial capital of the Franconian Wine Region, with vineyards lining the town's outskirts. Although the city had its origins as a religious center, Würzburg is now known as a university town. It was here in 1895 that Wilhelm Conrad Röntgen discovered X-rays and their medical applications, for which he was awarded the first Nobel Prize six years later. Today, more than 20,000 students attend the renowned Julius-Maximilians-Universität, which boasts six Nobel Prize winners among its faculty. Cyclists, streetcars, and skateboarders battle it out on the wide car-free pedestrian zone, paved with pigeon feathers and lined with cafes and Gothic cathedrals. War-time bombings destroyed much of the town's 18th-century magnificence—all that remained intact in 1945 was the spire of the Marienkapelle—but its older giants remain unchanged, making Würzburg a scenic portal for Germany's great tourist trail, the Romantische Str.

▐ GETTING THERE AND GETTING AROUND

Trains: Depart to **Rothenburg** (1hr., 1 per hr., DM17); **Nürnberg** (1½hr., 2 per hr., DM28); **Frankfurt** (2hr., 2 per hr., DM38); and **Munich** (2½hr., 1 per hr., DM76).

Buses: Europabus traces the Romantic Road to Rothenburg (DM29) and Munich (DM89) daily at 10am, departing from bus platform #13 to the right of the station. The return bus to Frankfurt stops at Würzburg daily at 6:30pm. Students receive a 10% discount, seniors 50%, Eurail and German Rail Pass holders 75%. Reservations can be made 3 days in advance through the **Deutsche Touring Büro,** Am Römerhof 17, Frankfurt (☎(069) 79 03 50; fax 790 32 19; e-mail service@deutsche-touring.com; www.deutsche-touring.com).

Public Transportation: Info ☎36 13 52. **Streetcars** are the fastest and most convenient way around, but large sections are not covered. The **bus** network is comprehensive, though most routes do not run nights and weekends. Ask for **night bus** schedules at WSB kiosk in front of station. Single fare within the city DM2.30, 24hr. ticket DM7.

Bike Rental: Fahrrad Station, Bahnhofpl. 4 (☎574 45), to the left of the station as you exit. DM17-20 per day, DM14-16 if you've traveled to Würzburg by train. Open Apr.-Oct. Tu-F 9:30am-6:30pm, Sa 9:30am-1:30pm, Su 10am-1pm; Nov.-Mar. Tu and Sa 9:30am-1:30pm, W-F 9:30am-6:30pm.

Mitfahrzentrale: ☎194 48 or 140 85, in the kiosk to the left of the train station exit. Organizes ride shares, including gas costs, to **Frankfurt** (DM18), **Stuttgart** (DM19), **Munich** (DM31), **Berlin** (DM47), and other cities. Open M-W 10am-4pm, Th-F 10am-6pm, Sa 10am-1pm, Su 11am-1pm.

▐ ORIENTATION AND PRACTICAL INFORMATION

To get to the city's center at the **Markt,** follow Kaiserstr. straight from the station for 2 blocks, then take a right on Juliuspromenade, and hang a left on **Schönbornstr.,** the main pedestrian and streetcar road; the Markt is a few blocks down and to the right. Streetcars #1, 3, and 5 also run from the station to the Markt. The Main separates the rest of the city from the steep hills on which the fortress stands.

Tourist Office: The **principal office** (☎37 23 98) is located in **Haus zum Falken,** an ornamental yellow building on the Marktpl. They provide a packet with a free map and a hotel list, and also help find **rooms** on arrival for free. Open M-F 10am-6pm, Sa 10am-2pm; Apr.-Oct. also Su 10am-2pm. The **business office** (☎37 23 35; fax 37 36 52; email tourismus@wuerzburg.de; www.wuerzburg.de), which provides brochures and will help find **rooms via written request** in advance of your arrival, is located in the Palais am Kongresszentrum near the Friedensbrücke, where Röntgenring intersects the Main. Open M-Th 8:30am-5pm, F 8:30am-1pm.

Tours: 2hr. English-language tours depart from the Haus zum Falken office and include entrance to the Residenz. Apr.-Oct. daily at 11am. DM15, students DM12. A German-language tour without the Residenz departs mid-Apr. to Oct. daily at 10:30am. DM9, students DM7. For wholesome nocturnal adventures, join the **"night watchman"** (replete with lantern and spear) on his rounds of the Altstadt. May-Dec. M-Sa 9pm; DM5, children free. Free 1½hr. **Rathaus tours** in German every Saturday May-Oct. at 10am. 2hr. **bus tours** in German depart from the bus station. Mid-Apr. to Oct. M-Sa 2pm, Su 10:30am. DM15, students DM12.

Bookstore: Buchladen Neuer Weg, Sanderstr. 23-25 (☎35 59 10). Has a small but adequate selection of English-language novels. Open M-F 9am-8pm, Sa 9am-4pm.

Pharmacy: Engel-Apotheke, Marktpl. 36 (☎32 13 40), lists night pharmacies on the door. Open M-F 8:30am-6pm, Sa 8:30am-1pm.

Emergency: Police, ☎110. **Fire,** ☎112. **Medical Aid,** ☎192 22.

Internet cafe: H@ckm@c2, Sanderstr. 5 (☎528 45). 30 min. DM4; 1 hour DM6. Open M-F 9am-1am, Sa 10am-1am, Su 11am-1am.

Post Office: Bahnhofpl. 2, 97070 Würzburg, to the right of the train station as you exit. Open M-F 7am-7pm, Sa 8am-1pm.

◤ ACCOMMODATIONS AND CAMPING

The one drawback to this otherwise excellent city is the lack of budget accommodations. Finding single rooms for less than DM45 is harder (much harder) than finding Waldo. Würzburg's least expensive beds are in the commercial zone around the station, near **Kaiserstr.** and **Bahnhofstr.**

▓ **Jugendgästehaus (HI),** Burkarderstr. 44 (☎425 90; fax 41 68 62), across the river from downtown. Streetcar #3 (direction: "Heidingsfeld") or 5 (direction: "Heuchelhof-Rotten-bauer") to "Löwenbrücke," then backtrack. Go down the stairs with the Jugendher-berge/Kapelle sign, turn right, walk past 2 streets and a Sparkasse on the left, go through the tunnel, and it's on the left. Enormous villa with views of the fortress and river. Breakfast and sheets included. Reception 24 hours. Check-in 5-10pm. Curfew 1am. DM33.

Gasthof Goldener Hahn, Marktgasse 7 (☎519 41; fax 519 61), in a little golden build-ing with green-checkered stained glass windows directly off the Markt. Clean rooms with phone and TV. Singles DM50, with bath DM85; doubles with bath DM150.

Pension Spehnkuch, Röntgenring 7 (☎547 52; fax 547 60), to the right of the station down Röntgenring. Renovated rooms are very white and clean; some even have a bal-cony. Breakfast included. Singles DM50; doubles DM96, with private shower DM140.

Camping Kanu-Club, Mergentheimer Str. 13b (☎725 36). Streetcar #3 (direction: "Heidingsfeld") or #5 (direction "Heuchelhof-Rottenbauer") to "Judenbühlweg." Go left as you exit the streetcar, take the first left, and follow the "C" signs to the building with an enormous canoe in front. Only 18 idyllic, riverside spots—call ahead. Reception noon-10pm.Open Apr.-Oct. DM4 per person. Tents DM3-6.

◖ FOOD

To sample some of the Würzburg region's distinctive wines, try **Haus des Franken-weins,** Kranenkai 1 (☎39 01 10; www.weinland-franken.de). The city's sweeter answer to Munich's Oktoberfest, the lively **Kiliani-Volksfest** is the largest Volksfest in Lower Franconia (held annually in the summer; July 7-23, 2001). There is a farmer's **market** on the Markt (Tu 6am-6pm, W 6am-2pm, F 6am-6pm, Sa 6am-2pm). For inexpensive **groceries,** hit **Kupsch,** Kaiserstr. 5 near Barbarossapl. (open M-F 8am-8pm, Sa 8am-4pm).

University Mensa, in the large, grey Studentenhaus on Am Exerzierpl., through the doors to your left. Assembly-line eating. Würzburg University ID technically required for dis-counts, but even without one, it's cheap. Buy meal tickets at the machines outside the dining room. Meals DM2.25-4.50. Open mid-Oct. to mid-July M-F 11am-1:30pm, Sa 11:30am-1:30pm; dinner M-Th 5:30-7:30pm; Feb.-Mar. same hours but closed Sa. Closed mid-July to mid-October.

▓ **Meyers cafe & Piano Bar,** Bronnbacher Gasse 43 (☎173 00). One of the classiest, jazz-iest, and most supremely mellow joints in town, Meyers offers a wide selection of baguettes (DM4.60-7.20), salads (DM7.50-13.90), tasty beers (DM5), and cigars in their secluded outdoor patio and indoor bar. Live piano music Th-Sa 9pm-1am in the summer, daily 8pm-1am in the winter. Open daily 10am-1pm.

BAVARIAN BOOZE: MORE THAN JUST

BEER Frankenland (Franconia), today northern Bavaria, was blessed with a temperate climate, rolling hills, and lime-rich soil—a coincidence which has meant the production of that other-worldly ambrosia known as wine since at least 7000BC. Würzburg is located in the center of Frankenland's wine-producing region. Most of the region's wines are white wines, and, in addition to the well-known **Riesling**, three interesting grapes are characteristic to Frankenland. The **Silvaner** produces an excellent wine with neutral bouquet and mild acidity that accompanies most any meal well. The early-ripening **Müller-Thurgau** grape makes a more nutty, flowery wine which goes well with fish and pasta. The **Bacchus** produces a full-bodied, fruity wine, ideal for pork and red meat dishes. For an excellent, dry wine, look for the labels "Qualitätswein mit Prädikat" and "trocken", or you may find out that the overly-sweet stereotype of German wines is true. All *Frankenweine* are bottled in the traditional pear-shaped *Bocksbeutel*.

 Le Clochard, Neubaustr. 20 (☎ 129 07). Crepes (DM5.90-8.90), sandwiches (DM6.90-11.90), and vegetarian dishes like *Jogurt-Kartoffeln* (potatoes topped with yogurt, cucumbers, and tomatoes; DM11.90) jive with the dark wood interior and plastic furniture outside. Come by in the late afternoon to gawk at the throng of caffeinated citizens enjoying "Happy Coffee-Crepe-Hour" (buy the crepe and get the coffee free; daily 3-5pm). Open daily 10am-1am.

Uni cafe, Neubaustr. 2 (☎ 156 72), on the corner of Sanderstr. Relaxed student atmosphere and outdoor sidewalk seating with a great view of the Marienburg. Lunch specials DM7-11, breakfast DM3.50-9.50. Open M-Sa 8am-1am, Su 9am-1am.

cafehaus Brückenbäck, Zellerstr. 2, by the Alte Mainbrücke (☎41 45 45). From the hostel, turn left on Saalgasse and walk 2 blocks to the bridge. Breezy atmosphere along the Main enhanced by a light natural menu of salads (DM7-16), teas of the world (DM5.80-6.20), alcoholic ice cream specialties (DM8.20-8.80), and cigars (DM1.20-13.50). Open M-F 8am-1am, Sa-Su 8:30am-1am.

Kult, Landwehrstr. 10 (☎528 45), right off Sanderstr. toward the Ludwigsbrücke, keeps a low profile as a hip *Kneipe* for local customers. Salad and main dish DM8-10, spaghetti DM6.50, apfelstrudel with vanilla ice cream DM3.50. Mellow but crowded at night. Open daily 9am-1am.

■ SIGHTS

FESTUNG MARIENBERG. The striking symbol of the city has been keeping vigil over the Main since the 12th century. The footpath to the fortress starts a short distance from the **Alte Mainbrücke,** which is more than 500 years old and lined with statues of saints. Within the fortress stand the 11th-century **Marienkirche** (replete with relic shrines containing the bones of early Christian martyrs), the 40m high **Bergfried** watchtower under which lies the **Hole of Fear** (dungeon), the ship-shape **Fürstengarten** (built to resemble a ship), and the 102m deep **Brunnentempel** which supplied the castle with water. Artifacts from the lives of the prince-bishops, a display on the destruction of Würzburg at the end of WWII, and *objets d'art* cluster in the **Fürstenbaumuseum.** Outside the walls of the main fortress is the castle arsenal, which now houses the **Mainfränkisches Museum.** The long hallways of the Baroque arsenal are lined primarily with religious statues featuring the work of Tilman Riemenschneider, the Master of Würzburg. A genius of Gothic styling, Riemenschneider sided with the peasants in their 16th-century revolts. When the insurrection was suppressed, the sculptor's fingers were broken as punishment, and he never worked again. *(Take bus #9 from the train station to "Festung". Tours depart from the main courtyard Tu-F 11am, 2pm, and 3pm, Sa-Su hourly 10am-4pm; DM4, seniors, students DM3. Fürstenbaumuseum ☎ 438 38. Open Apr. to mid-Oct. Tu-Su 9am-6pm; mid-Oct. to Mar. Tu-Su 10am-4pm; last entry 30min. before closing. DM5, students DM4. Mainfränkisches Museum ☎ 430 16. Open Tu-Su 10am-6pm; Nov.-Mar. closes 4pm. DM5, students DM2.50, children under 14 free; pass to both museums DM8.)*

RESIDENZ. The Residenz was the base camp for Würzburg's prince-bishops during the Enlightenment. Towering over the sweeping Residenzpl., the palace's vibrant ceiling fresco by Johannes Zick in the first-floor garden room (which appears on the DM50 bill) was originally so bright it has never needed to be restored; in fact, his use of extravagant colors got him fired. The Italian painter Giovanni Tiepolo was hired to finish the job in a more sedate style. His ceiling fresco in the grand staircase is the largest in the world, and certainly among the most ostentatious. Crane your head and see if you can find an overweight officer in dress uniform. Too easy? See if you can spot the dead alligator, then. Also in the Residenz, the university's **Martin-von-Wagner-Museum** proudly displays a collection of Greek vases and fleshy Baroque paintings. The **Residenzhofkirche** is astounding—the gilded moldings and pink marble make this little church the apex of Baroque fantasy. Behind the complex is the **Hofgarten,** with cone-shaped evergreens and a vast maze of bushes perfect for a thrilling game of hide-and-seek. *(Residenzpl. ☎35 51 70. From the station, walk down Kaiserstr. and Theaterstr. Open daily Apr. to mid-Oct. 9am-6pm (Th until 8pm); mid-Oct.-Mar. daily 10am-4pm. Last entry 30min. before closing. DM8, students and seniors DM6. Martin von Wagner Museum's painting gallery open Tu-Sa 9:30am-12:30pm. Greek collection open 2-5pm. The two galleries alternate being open Su 9:30am-12:30pm. Both free. Church open daily Apr. to mid-Oct. 9am-6pm; mid-Oct. to Mar. daily 10am-4pm. Free. Gardens open dawn-dusk. Free.)*

DOM ST. KILIAN. The 950-year-old cathedral was rebuilt in the mid-1960s after being obliterated in 1945, though it is debatable whether the reconstruction improved its overall appearance. Tilman Riemenschneider was responsible for the Gothic highlights of this large Romanesque cathedral. *(Kilianspl. ☎321 18 30. Open daily 8am-7pm; free. Non-obligatory 1hr. tours Apr.-Oct. M-Sa at 12:20pm, Su at 12:30pm; DM4, students DM2. Organ concerts M-Sa at noon.)*

NÜRNBERG (NUREMBERG)   ☎0911

From the 14th until the 16th century, Nürnberg was a free city, answering to no one lower than the emperor. The city's days in the sun came to an end, however, as trade-routes shifted westward following the discovery of the Americas, and the Thirty Years War destroyed large parts of the city. Nürnberg took on a central role in German politics again in the 20th century, playing host to the massive Nazi Party rallies held between 1933 and 1938, and lending its name to the 1935 Racial Purity Laws. As Hitler's power grew, money started rolling in with the Nazis' armament industry. Accordingly, the Allies took aim, and 90% of the city was reduced to rubble in 1945. Because of Nürnberg's close ties to Nazi power, the Allies chose this city as the site for the war crimes tribunals. Today, the townspeople of Nürnberg are working to forge a new image for their home as the "Stadt der Menschenrechte" (City of Human Rights), and since the early 90's they have sought to recognize compassion among world leaders through the establishment of the Nürnberg Human Rights Prize. Nürnberg jives with a steady German beat. Known for its toy fair and Christmas market, its sausages and gingerbread, and its association with former resident Albrecht Dürer as much as its ties to Nazism, the city persists in both the historical and contemporary consciousness of the German landscape.

▐ GETTING THERE AND GETTING AROUND

Flights: Flughafenstr. 100 (☎937 00, 937 12 00 for flight information), 7km north of Nürnberg. U-Bahn #2 connects the airport to the city (DM3.30).

Trains: Trains chug to **Würzburg** (1hr., 2 per hr., DM35); **Regensburg** (1hr., every 2 hrs., DM30); **Munich** (2½hr., 1 per hr., DM64); **Frankfurt** (3hr., 1 per hr., DM76); **Stuttgart** (2¾hr., 6 per day, DM54); **Berlin** (6hr., every 2hr., DM142); and **Prague** (5hr., 2 per day, DM72.40). Computers outside the Reisezentrum help decipher schedules and sell tickets for travel within Germany.

Public Transportation: Choose from U-Bahn, streetcars, buses, regional trains (R-Bahn), and S-Bahn. Single-ride within the city DM3.30. *Kurzstrecke* (short distance) DM2.50. 10-stripe *Streifenkarte* DM13.60. Day or weekend card DM6.60. The **VAG Verkehrszentrum** (☎283 48 95), downstairs at the west end of the train station's basement (take the "Königstorpassage" escalator) offers free public transportation maps and deals for tourists. Open M-F 7am-8pm, Sa 9am-2pm.

Taxi: ☎194 10.

Bike Rental: Ride on a Rainbow, Adam-Kraft-Str. 55 (☎39 73 37), outside the northwest corner of the Altstadt. Take Johannisstr. to Frauenholzstr. and turn right; then make a quick right onto Adam-Kraft-Str. DM10 per day with DM100 deposit. Mountain bikes DM18 per day with DM300 deposit. Open M-F 10am-7pm, Sa 10am-3pm.

Mitfahrzentrale: Strauchstr. 1 (☎194 44). Streetcar #4 to "Dutzendteich." Open M-F 9am-6pm, Sa 10am-1pm.

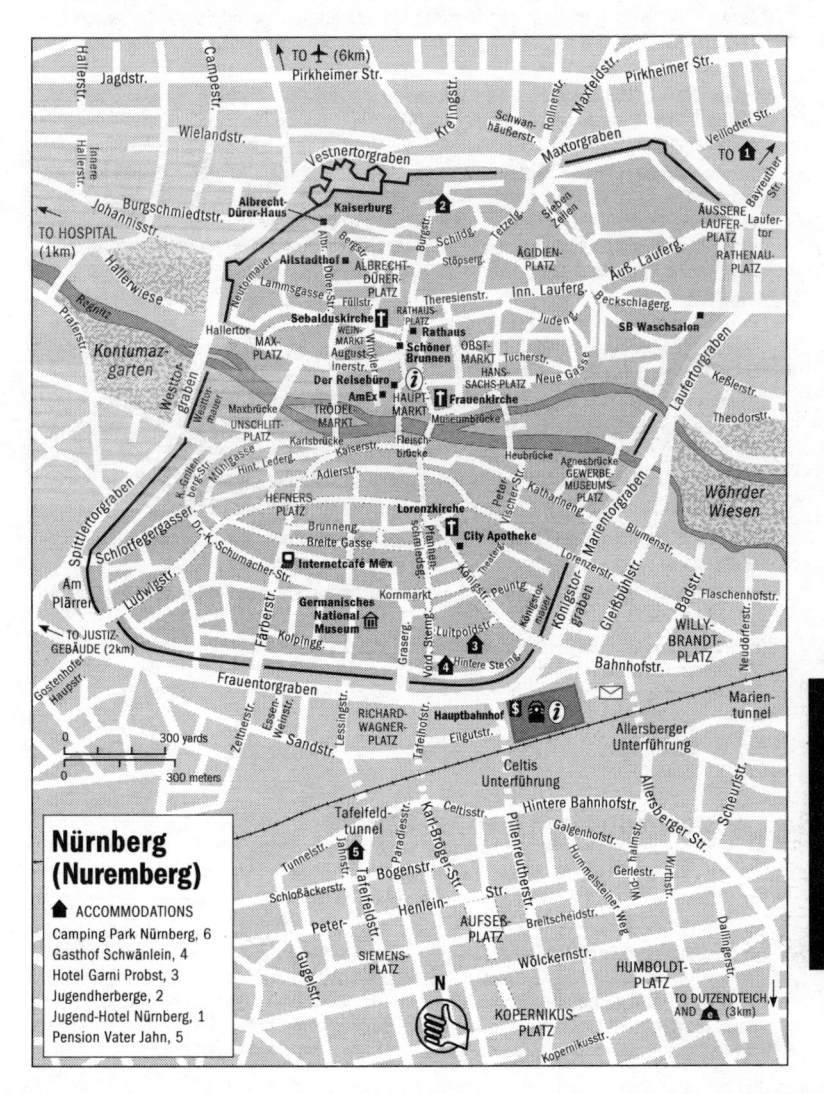

Nürnberg (Nuremberg)

▲ ACCOMMODATIONS
Camping Park Nürnberg, 6
Gasthof Schwänlein, 4
Hotel Garni Probst, 3
Jugendherberge, 2
Jugend-Hotel Nürnberg, 1
Pension Vater Jahn, 5

⊞ 🛈 ORIENTATION AND PRACTICAL INFORMATION

Nürnberg's thriving central district lies within the old city wall. From the train station, the main shopping area is across Frauentorgraben down **Königstr.**, which leads through the city walls. **Lorenzerpl.** and the **Hauptmarkt** lie just beyond this shopping district in the Altstadt's pedestrian zone. The **Burg** perches on a hill, overlooking the town from the northernmost part of the Altstadt.

Tourist Offices: Verkehrsverein (☎ 233 61 31; fax 233 61 66; email tourismus@nuernberg.btl.de; www.nuernberg.de), is in the train station near the main service desk. The staff offers free maps and a schedule of events and books **rooms** (DM45-65) for free. Open M-Sa 9am-7pm. A **branch office** (☎ 233 61 35) is on the Hauptmarkt near the golden fountain. Open May-Sept. M-Sa 9am-6pm, Su 10am-1pm and 2-4pm; Oct.-Apr. M-Sa 9am-6pm.

Tours: 2½hr. English tours depart from the Hauptmarkt tourist office May-Oct. daily at 1pm. DM12 (DM15 including Burg admission), children under 14 free if accompanied by an adult.

Budget Travel: DER Reisebüro, Hauptmarkt 29 (☎ 201 00), on the northwest corner of the Hauptmarkt, deciphers timetables and gives out information for a DM5 fee. Open M-F 9:30am-6pm, Sa 10am-1pm.

Currency Exchange: The **AmEx** office (below) is the cheapest option for those with or without The Card. Or head to the **Reisebank,** Bahnhofpl. 9 (☎ 22 67 78). Facing the train station's central service desk walk left out the side door to the small beige trailer. 4.5% commission on changing currency into DM. Open M-Sa 7:15am-7:45pm, Su 9:15am-12:30pm and 1:30-5:15pm.

American Express: Tuchgasse 10, on the corner of Winklerstr. (☎ 23 23 97), in the Hauptmarkt. Great rates. Nonmembers pay a 1% or DM2.50 fee to cash traveler's checks; everyone pays a DM4 commission on currency exchange. Open M-F 9am-6pm, Sa 9:30am-12:30pm. Cashier closed noon-2pm.

Laundromat: SB Waschsalon, Spitzenbergstr. 16, near the University Mensa. Wash off the beer stains for DM7 (soap included); dry DM1 for 12min. Make sure you bring coins—there's no bill changer. Open daily 6am-11pm.

Emergency: Police, Jakobspl. 5 (☎ 110). **Fire,** ☎ 112. **Ambulance,** ☎ 192 22.

Rape Crisis: (☎ 28 44 00). Counseling M 10am-noon, Tu 7-8pm, Th 4-6pm.

Pharmacy: City-Apotheke, Königstr. 31 (☎ 22 45 51). Open M-F 8:30am-6:30pm, Sa 9am-4pm.

Hospital: Städtisches Klinikum Nord, Flurstr. 17 (☎ 39 80). **Medical Assistance,** ☎ 53 37 71.

Internet Access: Internetcafe M@x, Färberstr. 11 (☎ 23 23 84), at the corner of Frauengasse. Head up to the 4th floor of the complex; the cafe is at the far end of the neon-lit hallway. Before 3pm 1hr. DM5; after 3pm 30min. DM5, 1hr. DM9. Open M-Sa noon-1am, Su 4pm-midnight.

Post Office: Bahnhofstr. 2, 90402 Nürnberg. Open M-F 8am-7pm, Sa 9am-2pm, Su 10am-1pm.

▐ ACCOMMODATIONS AND CAMPING

You don't have to trek outside the Altstadt walls to hang your hat in an inexpensive *Pension,* but it's best to call ahead in summer.

Jugendgästehaus (HI), Burg 2 (☎ 230 93 60; fax 23 09 36 11). From the station, cross Frauentorgraben, turn right, and walk along the outside of the city walls until you reach Königstor. Follow Königstr. through Lorenzerpl. over the bridge to the Hauptmarkt (10min.). Head in the direction of the golden fountain on the far left and bear right on Burgstr., then huff and puff up to the castle at the top of the hill in the direction of the sign pointing to Burgerstr. (about 20min.). Once a stable and grain storage for the imperial castle, the hostel's Romanesque arches, dizzying panorama over the city, and friendly desk staff (prone to playing with the loudspeakers) make for good hosteling fun. Dorms (4- to 6-bed rooms) DM30; singles DM60; doubles DM72. Reception 7am-1am. Curfew 1am. Reservations strongly recommended.

Gasthof Schwänlein, Hintere Sterngasse 11 (☎22 51 62; fax 241 90 08). From the station, take the underground passage to Königstr. and take an immediate left on Frauentormauerstr. Follow the town wall, then bear right onto Hintere Sterngasse; the hotel is about 200m down on the left. The quiet hallways of the Pension are soothing, although rooms are slightly cramped. Breakfast included. Reservations by fax or mail only. Singles DM40, with shower DM50, with bath DM60; doubles DM75, with shower DM80, with bath DM90.

Hotel Garni Probst, Luitpoldstr. 9 (☎20 34 33; fax 205 93 36). From the station, follow the underground passage to Königstor past Burger King; turn left on Luitpoldstr. The block is seedy, the location central. The jolly family establishment is 3 floors up, with tiny, oddly shaped rooms. Singles DM40, with shower DM78, with bath DM90; doubles DM88, with shower or bath DM110-130. Plentiful breakfast included.

Jugend-Hotel Nürnberg, Rathsbergstr. 300 (☎521 60 92; fax 521 69 54). From the station, take U-Bahn #2 (direction: "Flughafen") to "Ziegelstein", then bus #21 (direction: "Buchenbühl") to "Zum Felsenkeller." Rustic and cheerful, but far from the action. Nice surrounding grounds complement the dorm rooms, all with bath. Breakfast DM8.50. Reception 8am-10pm. Call ahead. Singles DM39.50; doubles DM59; triples DM75 (tip: many "singles" have 2 beds).

Pension "Vater Jahn", Jahnstr. 13 (☎44 45 07; fax 431 52 36). From the west exit of the station, head down Eilgutstr., then turn left on Tafelhofstr. through the underpass, turn right on Bogenstr. and right again onto Jahnstr. (10 min.). Gleaming rooms, some with TVs. Breakfast included. Singles DM45, with bath DM65; doubles DM75, with shower DM85, with bath DM95.

Camping: Campingpark Nürnberg, Hans-Kalb-Str. 56 (☎98 12 717; fax 98 12 718), southwest of the soccer stadium in Volkspark Dutzendteich. S-Bahn #2 (direction: "Freucht/Altdorf") to "Frankenstadion." Reception 2-10pm. Open year-round, except Nov. Call ahead. DM8.75 per person. Tent DM5-10. Parking DM12.50.

◖ FOOD

Nürnberg is famous for its cuisine: *Rostbratwurst* (rough but delectable grilled sausage), boiled *Sauere Zipfel*, and *Lebkuchen*, a candied variant of gingerbread, traditionally devoured at Christmas. For a food, film, and beer extravaganza, bust a move to **Cine Città** (see **Entertainment and Nightlife,** p. 326). **Edeka,** Hauptmarkt 12 near the Frauenkirche, has cheap **groceries** (open M-F 8:30am-7pm, Sa 8am-3pm).

Bratwursthäusle, Rathauspl. 1 (☎22 76 95), next to the Sebalduskirche, is the most famous and crowded *Bratwurst* joint in Nürnberg. The cooks of this rustic log cabin fire up 6 *Rostbratwürste* with *Sauerkraut* or potato salad for DM9.80; other Bavarian specialties DM4.50-12. Beer DM5.20. Don't have time to savor the sausage? Take home a *Vacupak* (10 bratwurst, DM8). Open M-Sa 10am-10:30pm (kitchen until 9:30pm).

Bratwurst Röslein, Rathauspl. 6 (☎21 48 60), the self-proclaimed largest *Brautwurst* house in the world, is a carnivorous paradise in an enormous beer hall. Liver dumpling soup (DM4.50), roast pork shoulder with dumplings and beer sauce, and all other meals run DM11.64. Open daily 10am-midnight. Kitchen closes at 11pm.

Enchilada, Obstmarkt 10 (☎244 84 98), behind the Frauenkirche. A popular Mexican restaurant and bar with a variety of vegetarian options. Nachos (DM10), Mexico salad (DM15), veggie quesadillas (DM17), and crazy cocktails (DM13-17). Happy hour every day 5-8pm (all cocktails half-price). Open daily 11am-1am.

Café Mohr, Färberstr. 3 (☎24 31 39), at the intersection with Karolinenstr. With an Art Deco atmosphere overlooking a lively square, the cafe is a fun meeting place. Crepes (DM5-9), salads (DM7-12), pineapple shakes (DM5), and cappuccino (DM4.20). Open M-Th 9am-midnight, F-Sa 9am-1am, Su 2pm-midnight.

👁 SIGHTS

Allied bombing left little of old Nürnberg for posterity. The churches, castle, and buildings were all reconstructed after the war; most churches display post-war photos and empty pedestals where exterior statues were lost in the bombing. From the station, the closest part of the Altstadt is a walled-in area filled with cottages and shops; this is the **Handwerkerhof,** a tourist trap masquerading as a historic attraction. The real sights lie farther up **KönigStr.,** in the northwest corner of the Altstadt at the foot of the castle, around the Hauptmarkt.

KAISERBURG. Atop the hill, Nürnberg's symbol offers the best vantage point of the city. Originally erected in a much smaller form in the 11th century, Germany's next emperor, Friedrich Barbarossa, expanded the Burg significantly. A war to defend the castle from the Hohenzollerns precipitated its near-total destruction in the 1300s, and the Gothic Kaiserburg extant today is largely a result of the 15th and 16th centuries. The spartan chambers housed every Holy Roman Emperor after Konrad III—it was law that every German Kaiser spend at least his first day in office here. Since the castle had no heating, however, the Kaisers usually spent their nights in the warm patrician homes of the Altstadt. Massive stone walls 13m tall and 7m thick surround the castle and the manicured gardens. Inside lurk the Romanesque chapel and the imperial living quarters. The 45-minute tour in German covers all parts and epochs of the Kaiserburg; the English-language tour (see p. 322) offered by the tourist office also covers the castle. (☎ 22 57 26. Burg open daily Apr.-Sept. 9am-6pm; Oct.-Mar. 10am-4pm. Garden open daily in summer, 8am-8pm. By tour only, every 30min.; last tour Apr.-Sept. 4:30pm; Oct.-Mar. 3:30pm. DM10, students and seniors DM8, children under 18 free with parent.)

AROUND THE ALTSTADT AND CASTLE

LORENZKIRCHE. Completely destroyed in WWII, the beautiful 13th-century Gothic structure has been restored and once again displays perfectly preserved works covering every surface. Of particular interest is the 20m high **tabernacle,** and its delicate stone tendrils curling up into the roof vaulting. The large wooden carving hanging in front of the altar is Veit Stoß's 1517 masterpiece *Engelsgruß* (Annunciation). (On Lorenzpl. ☎ 20 92 87. Open M-Sa 9am-5pm, Su 1-4pm. Free German language tours meet at the entrance in summer M-F 11am and 2pm; in winter M-F 2pm; call ahead for English tours.)

HAUPTMARKTPLATZ. The **Schöner Brunnen** (Beautiful Fountain) resembles nothing so much as the steeple of a Gothic church. Check out the 40 imaginatively carved figures, with Moses and the prophets up top. Hidden within the gate surrounding the fountain is an iron ring without seams (how it got there is a mystery); spinning it supposedly brings good luck.

The main attraction of the small 14th-century **Frauenkirche** is its ornate facade, practically the only part of the church that survived WWII intact. Crowds gather at noon to ogle at the **Männleinlaufen,** the mechanical clock in the center of the facade, where seven Electors pay homage to the seated figure of Kaiser Karl IV. Karl, who ordered the razing of a synagogue to make way for the church, commissioned its construction in 1350 (before he was elected Kaiser) to cement his political power. (☎ 20 65 60. Open M-Sa 9am-6pm, Su 12:30-6pm. Free summer tours M 12:10pm and W 6pm.)

SEBALDUSKIRCHE. The city's oldest parish church (constructed from 1230-1379) and home of Nürnberg's Protestant congregation since 1525, the late-Gothic Sebalduskirche stands across from the Rathaus. Once a year on the feast day of St. Sebaldus, the saint's remains are taken from their resting spot in the bronze tomb in front of the altar for a parade around town. (☎ 22 45 72. Open daily Mar.-May and Sept.-Dec. 9:30am-6pm; June-Aug. 9:30am-8pm; Jan.-Feb. 9:30am-4pm.)

RATHAUS. Begun in 1340 but built mostly in early Baroque style sprinkled with a little Renaissance Classicism, Nürnberg's Rathaus held the largest council chamber in central Europe before its destruction by fire in 1945. Beneath the oldest part of the building hide the spooky *Lochgefängnisse* (dungeons), where juicy medieval torture instruments are displayed. *(☎ 231 26 90. Open Tu-Su 10am-4:30pm. Obligatory tour every 30min.; English translation available. DM4, students and children under 15 DM2.)*

FELSENGÄNGE. This web of passageways and cellars below the Altstadt dates back more than 600 years. Bring a jacket; it's cold enough to store large barrels of beer. *(Bergstr. 19, in the Altstadthof. ☎ 22 70 66. 1hr. tours descend daily from Albrecht-Dürer-Pl. at 11am, 1, 3, and 5pm. DM7, students DM5, children under 11 free.)*

RUINS OF THE THIRD REICH

DUTZENDTEICH. The ruins of the site of the Nazi Party Congress rallies of 1934 and 1935 possess a deserted disquiet to remind visitors of a terrifying moment in German history. The rallies drew more than a half-million citizens annually. The park now holds the remains of Hitler's planned Nazi compound, which he proudly declared "the largest building site in the world". The predominant building style represents the apogee of Nazi architecture—massive and harsh, mixing modernist straight lines with Neoclassical pretension, constructed with the intent to make the individual feel small and powerless without the masses and the State. An exemplar of this architecture is the unfinished **Kongresshalle** at the north end of the Volkspark, begun in 1935 as a Party headquarters but abandoned for lack of money in 1938; the optical illusion created by the outer archways causes people standing under them to appear much smaller than they actually are. Leading from the Kongresshalle clear across the Volkspark, the 2km-long **Große Str.** was designed not only as a marching grounds for Nazi troops, but also as a symbolic link between Hitler and the Kaisers of German history, providing a clear view of Nazi headquarters at one end and the Kaiserburg at the other; Hitler planned to demolish parts of the Altstadt that obstructed the view.

The **Zeppelinwiese,** a field across the Großer Dutzendteich lake from the Kongresshalle, contains the **Tribüne,** the massive marble platform from which Hitler addressed more than 100,000 enthralled spectators. The very faint remains of a swastika stained into the marble are visible on the central promontory despite attempts to efface it. Poles spaced intermittently along the desolate field once held enormous banners, made infamous by Leni Riefenstahl's film **Triumph des Willens** (Triumph of the Will), which immortalized the 1935 Party rally in one of the most terrifying, enduring depictions of the Fascist aesthetic. The overwhelming emotional power of Nazi events—injecting elements of Wagnerian theater and Catholic ritual into Fascist grandiosity—can be seen in the exhibit **Faszination und Gewalt** (Fascination and Terror), accompanied by an excellent brochure; it's located inside the **Golden Hall,** at the rear of the Tribüne. The exhibits cover the rise of the Third Reich, Nürnberg's role in the growth of National Socialism, and the war crimes trials of 1946. The government has brainstormed uses for the abandoned structures; right now the wide steps of the Tribüne are used by skateboarders who pull their most daring stunts off the podium, while the Kongresshalle is used for storage. *(Take S-Bahn #2 (direction: "Freucht/Altdorf") to "Dutzendteich," then take the middle of the three exits, head down the stairs and turn left. 200m down the highway is Strandcafe Wanner; turn left just after it and follow the paved path. ☎ 981 37 23. Golden Hall open mid-May to Oct. Tu-Su 10am-6pm. DM5, students DM4, including informational booklet.)*

JUSTIZGEBÄUDE. On the other side of town, Nazi leaders faced Allied military judges during the infamous **Nürnberg war crimes trials** held in room 600 of the Justizgebäude. Soon after the trials, in October 1946, 10 men were hanged for their crimes against humanity. The building still serves as a courthouse, though it contains a small display on the trials. *(Fürtherstr. 110. Take U-Bahn #1 direction "Stadthalle" to "Bärenschanze" and continue farther on Furtherstr., walking away from the Altstadt. Tours Sa-Su at 1, 2, 3, and 4 pm. DM4.)*

BAVARIA

🏛 MUSEUMS

GERMANISCHES NATIONALMUSEUM. This gleaming, modern building chronicles Germanic art and culture from pre-history to the present, with huge displays of medieval sculpture and a reconstructed cloister. Highlights include a few of Rembrandt's self-portrait etchings and paintings by Cranach, including a portrait of Martin Luther. Outside the museum's main entrance, the **Str. der Menschenrechte** (Avenue of Human Rights) contains 30 white pillars, each engraved with a basic human right in many different languages. *(Kartäusergasse 1. From the Königstr. exit of the tunnel from the station turn left through the archway onto Frauentormauer and right on Kartäusergasse. ☎133 10. Open Tu and Th-Su 10am-5pm, W 10am-9pm. DM6, students and seniors DM3, free admission W from 6-9pm.)*

JÜDISCHES MUSEUM FRANKEN. This museum chronicles the history and culture of Jews in Franconia, as well as the present and future life of the community. Housed in Fürth, once the largest urban Jewish community in southern Germany, the displays showcase everything from medieval religious manuscripts to aspects of everyday life. *(Königstr. 89, Fürth. Take U-bahn #1 (direction: "Stadthalle") to "Rathaus." ☎77 05 77. Open Su-M and W-F 10am-5pm, Tu 10am-8pm. Tours Tu at 6:30pm and Su at 11am; DM3. Regular entrance DM6, students and seniors DM3.)*

ALBRECHT-DÜRER-HAUS. The residence of Nürnberg's favorite son and his long-suffering wife from 1509-1528, the house contains period furniture along with a very few of Dürer's etchings and copies of his paintings (most originals are on display in Vienna, Munich, and Berlin), as well as an exhibit of less-than-masterful Dürer-derived works by modern artists. Guides dressed as Agnes Dürer offer English tours through the house on Saturdays at 11am. *(Albrecht-Dürer-Str. 39. Uphill from the Sebalduskirche entrance. ☎231 25 68. Open Mar.-Oct. Tu-W and F-Su 10am-5pm, Th 10am-8pm; Nov.-Feb. Tu-F 1-5pm and Sa-Su 10am-5pm. DM8, students DM4; tours DM4.)*

ALTSTADTHOF. The *Hof* houses a small historic brewery. No free samples, but tempting 0.2L bottles of house brew cost a mere DM2.50. *(Bergstr. 19. ☎22 43 27. Tours of the Felsengänge end here.)*

🎵🎭 ENTERTAINMENT AND NIGHTLIFE

Nürnberg's nightspots run the gamut from ultra-traditional to hyper-modern. The Altstadt is packed with bars and clubs, the best of which reside in the west, near the river. Pick up the monthly *Plärrer* (DM5) at newsstands; the region's best entertainment magazine for the twenty-something crowd, it lists musical and cultural events and addresses of bars, discos, and cafes. The *Monatsmagazin* (DM2) lists all concerts, stage productions, and special museum exhibitions in Nürnberg, and can be found at the tourist office. The free guide *Doppelpunkt* is doled out at many bars and discos and can also be found online (www.doppelpunkt.de).

Cine Città, Gewerbemuseumspl. 3, packs seven cafes, twelve cinemas, an I-Max theater, and a disco into its multimedia megaplex. The multi-cultural, constantly morphing restaurants offer affordable meals. (☎20 66 60; www.cinecitta.de. Open M-Th and Su until 3am, F-Sa until 4am.) Although most movies are dubbed into German, the weekly *Filmtips* (www.filmtips.de) provides a schedule of films in their original language. **Roxy,** Julius-Loßman-Str. 16 (☎480 10 64 for program announcement, 488 40 for ticket reservation), shows more current English-language flicks, from trashy horror movies to love-sick romances. **Nicolaus-Copernicus-Planetarium,** Am Plärrer 41, projects the heavens onto a cement dome. (☎929 65 53 or 26 54 67 for program announcement; www.planetarium-nuernberg.de. Shows W 4 and 7:30pm, Th 7:30pm, and 1st and 3rd weekends of the month Sa-Su 4pm. Call for schedules. DM8, students DM5.)

BARS

Frizz!, Weißgerbergasse 37 (☎205 99 85), entrance on Maxpl. This hip bar sweats to the oldies as well as 80s rock and pop, and serves up cheap cocktails (DM6.50-10) and a few different varieties of *Lammsbräu* wheat beers (*Maß* DM9.90). Monday is singles' night, you sly fox. Open M-W 8pm-1am, Th 8pm-2am, F-Sa 8pm-4am.

cafe Ruhestörung, Tetzelgasse 21 (☎22 19 21). From the Rathaus, head right on Theresienstr., then left on Tetzelgasse. Mellow and dimly-lit, this place is quite a scene—people-watch with a vengeance. Outdoor seating with satanic red lighting. Serves breakfast (DM5.50-17.50), sandwiches, salads (DM5.50-12.50), and warm meals (DM8.50-13.50). Beer on tap DM5.50; double-shots of malt whiskey, aged 12 years DM11. Open M-W 7:30am-1am, Th-F 7:30am-2am, Sa 9am-2am, Su 9am-1am.

cafe Treibhaus, Karl-Grillenberger-Str. 28 (☎22 30 41), in the west part of the Altstadt, south of Westtor. Metal tables and dim lighting draw a well-heeled, older crowd trying to keep it real. Killer cocktails with snacks (DM3.50-12.50), salads (DM8-12.50), pastas (DM8-12.50), and breakfast (DM5-16.50). Their *Milchkaffee* (DM3.60) gives "foam" a new meaning—be initiated. Open M-W 8am-1am, Th-F 8am-2am, Sa 9am-2am, Su 9:30am-1am. Kitchen open until 10:30pm.

Saigon, Lammsgasse 8 (☎244 86 57), off Albrecht-Dürer-Str. The small bar swims in smoke and the croonings of Billie Holiday. You'd better know you're cool already—you wouldn't have come here otherwise. Espresso DM3, cocktails DM10.50-12, sushi service until midnight. Open Su-W 9pm-3am, Th-Sa 9pm-4am.

Cartoon, An der Sparkasse 6 (☎22 71 70), is a popular gay bar off Theatergasse, near Lorenzpl. Traditional Kneipe interior gets revamped by its patrons. Baguettes with ham, salad, or cheese DM7. Beer DM4.40 for 0.5L, many harder offerings at higher prices. Open M-Sa 11am-1am, Su 2pm-1am.

DANCE CLUBS

Sound Express, Kohlenhofstr. 1a, south of the Altstadt. From the train station, follow Frauentorgraben west, turn left onto Steinbühlerstr., then right onto Kohlenhofstr; the complex is recessed about 50m from the street on the left. This center of vice houses a pool hall, several bars and cafes (some with gogo dancing after midnight), and two discos (cover DM10) with well-known DJs. Open W, Th 10pm-4am, F-Sa 10pm-5am.

Mach 1, Kaiserstr. 1-9 (☎20 30 30), in the center of the Altstadt near Karlsbrücke. Grooving patrons change size, shape, and drapery depending on the day. Thursday attracts the mellow "Best of the 70s to 90s" crowd; Friday functions with "funk" and hip-hop; Saturday signifies house. Dress for the occasion, or you risk getting turned away at the door. Also, do your pre-gaming elsewhere; drinks are expensive (DM6 for 0.3L beer). Open Th-F 10pm-4am (cover DM8), Sa 10pm-5am (cover DM10-20).

Green Goose, Vordere Sterngasse 25 (☎20 84 48), in the south-east corner of the Altstadt. Having earned a reputation twenty years ago as a hangout for American servicemen, this dance club has since made an about-face. Today, a good mix of Americans and Germans shakes some booty on the tiny dance floor to everything from rock to techno. All drinks DM4 from 9pm-midnight. Open W, Th 9pm-4am, F-Sa 9pm-5am. Cover DM7 for men, which includes DM4 off the price of the first drink.

BAYREUTH ☎0921

Once you've turned off Tristanstr. onto Isoldenstr., walked past Walküregasse, and finally ducked into the *Parsifal* Pharmacy, there will be little doubt that you're in Bayreuth, the adopted home of Richard Wagner (see p. 25 and p. 29) and the site of the annual *Festspiele*—a pilgrimage of BMW-driving devotees coming to bask in his operatic masterpieces. Wagner retreated to Bayreuth in 1872 to escape his creditors and other folks he had burned. The remote town promised privacy, an 18th-century opera house, and an enchanting ego-fluffing concept—

BAVARIA

fans would now have to trek great lengths to experience a true Wagner performance. The grandiosity of it all has left Bayreuth a treasure trove of gorgeous buildings. The town bases nearly its entire existence around the man and the legend that is Richard Wagner; even for those who are not crazy Wagner-maniacs, the town is an interesting and attention-holding study in how a society can be built around a single obsession.

⁊ PRACTICAL INFORMATION

Bayreuth is pronounced "buy-royt," *not* "bay ruth"; you will be scorched by light-ning should you speak otherwise.

Trains: The train station lies 5min. north of the Altstadt; exit to the left and walk down Bahnhofstr. to reach the center. Trains zoom to **Nürnberg** (1hr., change at Lichtenfels, DM24.60); **Bamberg** (1½hr., DM24.60); and **Regensburg** (2hr., DM40).

Tourist Office: Luitpoldpl. 9 (☎885 88; fax 885 55), about four blocks to the left of the station in the building marked "Reisebüro Bayreuth." Offers maps, accommoda-tion lists, a monthly calendar of events, and city **walking tours.** (DM8, students DM5. Tours May-Oct. Tu-Sa 10am; Nov.-Apr. Sa only.) **Private rooms** are only available during the *Festspiele* (DM10 fee if the tourist office makes arrangements for you); at other times, the staff finds rooms in hotels and *Pensionen* for a DM5 fee. The office sells tickets to Bayreuth's theater, opera, and musical venues. Open M-F 9am-6pm, Sa 9:30am-1pm.

Currency Exchange: Citibank, Maximilianstr. 46. Open M, Tu, Th 9am-1pm and 2-6pm, W 9am-1pm, and F 9am-1pm and 2-5pm.

Internet Access: In the cyberbar on the second floor of the **Hertie** department store on the Markt by the streetcar stop. Open M-F 9am-8pm, Sa 9am-4pm. DM5 for the first half hr., DM3 for each half hr. after the first.

Post Office: Kanzleistr. 1, 95444 Bayreuth. Located off Maximilianstr. on the Markt. The **postal code** is 95444. Open M-F 8am-7pm, Sa 8am-1pm.

⌐ ACCOMMODATIONS

If you visit during the *Festspiele* and forgot to book a room ahead, expect to shell out the cash if you want to stay in Bayreuth. Almost any other time, prices are rea-sonable and beds are available.

Jugendherberge (HI), Universitätsstr. 28 (☎76 43 80; fax 51 28 05). Bayreuth's hostel lies outside the city center past the Hofgarten near the university. Take bus #4 (DM2.70) from the Marktpl. to "Mensa," walk out of the *Uni* onto Universität-str., and turn left. Or walk down Ludwigstr. from the city center, take a left onto Friedrichstr., then veer left onto Jean-Paul-Str., which merges with Universitätsstr. Friendly but runs like clockwork; check-in and check-out times strictly observed. Breakfast included. Sheets DM5.50. Reception 7am-noon and 5-9:30pm. Lockout 9:30-11am. Curfew 10pm; ask at the desk for a key. Open Mar. to mid-Dec. Dorm beds DM21.

Gasthof Hirsch, St. Georgen 26 (☎267 14 and 85 31 42). A 10min. walk behind the train station, on a corner with a rainbow of geraniums spilling out the windows. Exit the train station in the back, beyond track five and take a left onto Brandenburger Str., and left on St. Georgen. 18 clean beds. Singles DM35-40, doubles DM70-80.

Gasthof zum Brandenburger, St. Georgen 9 (☎78 90 60; fax 78 90 62 40). The rooms are nice and sunny, as is the beer garden, and spiffy ivy wallpaper adorns the third floor. Singles DM35, with shower DM60; doubles DM60, with shower DM130.

Gasthof Schindler, Bahnhofstr. 9 (☎262 49). Close to the station. Clean rooms and a basement restaurant. Singles DM50; double DM85-120. Reception M-Sa 8am-10pm, Su 9am-3pm.

FOOD

Bayreuth's abundance of traditional Bavarian fare will make your head (and stomach) spin. For cheaper eats, head to the **Norma** supermarket, Maximilianstr. 62 (open M-F 8:30am-7pm, Sa 8am-4pm), or check out the **market** in the Rotmainhal near Hindenburgstr. (open W 7am-12:30pm and Sa 7am-1pm).

Mensa (☎ 60 81). Fill 'er up at the university cafeteria for DM3-6; any student ID should do. Take bus #4 (DM2.70) from the Marktpl. to "Mensa," then walk past the buildings straight ahead. The enormous, low-roofed *Mensa* is to the right up the steps. Trade the cashier your ID and DM5 for a card, then put money on the card at the *Automaten* in the hall. After using the card to buy food, get your DM5, plus any balance left on the card, back from the cashier. The *Mensa* offers cheap meals including pizzas for DM4, also to be had "zum mitnehmen" (to go). Open Mar.-Apr. and Oct. 8am-6pm, May-July and Nov.-Feb. 8am-8:30pm.

Gaststätte Porsch, Maximilianstr. 63 (☎ 646 49). Enormous portions at great prices. *Schnitzel* and steak meals DM13-24. Open M-F 7am-8:30pm, Sa 7am-5pm.

Brauereischänke am Markt, Maximilianstr. 56 (☎ 649 19). The *bayerische Küche* comes up big with *Bratwurst* with potato salad or *Kraut* (DM8.80) and hearty steaks (DM17). Open M-Sa 9am-noon, Su 11:30am-6pm.

Hansl's Holzofen Pizzeria, Jean-Paul-Pl. (☎ 543 44). A cheaper alternative to the local cuisine. Pizza DM8-17. Open daily 10am-10:30pm.

Café Wundertüte, Richard-Wagner-Str. 33 (☎ 51 47 48), has a cup of coffee and a slice of raspberry *Torte* with your name on it (DM5.80), served in a wood-paneled atmosphere. Delightful selection of small salads, sausages, and cheeses (DM4-10). Open M-F 10am-6:30pm, Sa 10am-5pm.

SIGHTS

FESTSPIELHAUS. Wagner devotees visiting Bayreuth when the *Festspiele* are over console themselves with a tour of the **Festspielhaus.** From the train station, go right and up at the end of Siegfried-Wagner-Allee. To fund the 1872 construction, the composer hit up Ludwig II, who was in the midst of his own egocentric building spree. Ludwig responded with modest amounts of cash, resulting in a semi-spartan structure—Wagner fans must endure cushionless seats and limited leg room. (☎ 787 80. *Tours Sept.-Oct. and Dec.-May at 10, 10:45am, 2:15, and 3pm. DM2.50.*)

RICHARD-WAGNER-MUSEUM. Haus Wahnfried was once home to Bayreuth's famed composer. It houses an inexhaustible and kitschy—yet valuable—collection of scores, costumes, and stage sets. See Wagner stamps, coins, and playing cards, as well as his spoons, mirror, and little *Wotan* and *Sieglinde* dolls (the Wagnerian Ken and Barbie). Three death masks provide morbid pleasure: Wagner's, composer Carl Maria von Weber's, and that of Wagner's friend Ludwig II. Inch by inch the museum painstakingly covers Wagner's childhood, art, family, and the course of the Festspiel after his death. The thousands of exhibits are in German only—it might behoove you to pick up the melodramatic English guide-booklet (DM3). Those who fail to appreciate his *Gesamtkunstwerke* ("Total Works of Art," as he modestly referred to them) should recall Mark Twain's fiendishly accurate assessment of Wagner's music: "It's better than it sounds." Behind the house lie the graves of Wagner, his wife Cosima, and Russ, his big black dog. (*Richard-Wagner-Str. 48. ☎ 757 28 16. Open Apr.-Oct. M, W, and F 9am-5pm, Tu and Th 9am-8pm; Nov.-Mar. daily 10am-5pm. DM4, students DM2. 1-day passes for the Wagner Museum, the Jean-Paul-Museum, and Franz-Liszt-Museum available for DM6; 3-day passes to 6 museums for 1 adult and 2 children under 15 DM14.50. Wagner's compositions are played in the drawing room daily at 10am, noon, and 2pm; videos are shown at 11am and 3pm.*)

BAVARIA

FRANZ-LISZT-MUSEUM. Just to the left of the haughty Wagner Museum, the **Franz-Liszt-Museum** exhibits the composer's pianos and music sheets and displays the room in which he died (again, complete with death mask). In Bayreuth, Liszt is probably best known for fathering Wagner's wife—musical virtuosos also inbreed. For more on Liszt, see p. 29. *(Wahnfriedstr. 9.* ☎ *757 28 18. Open daily 10am-noon and 2-5pm; July & Aug. daily 10am-5pm. DM3, students and seniors DM1.)*

JEAN-PAUL-MUSEUM. This museum celebrates the life of Bayreuth's greatest poet with an endless collection of notebooks and chairs. *(Wahnfriedstr. 1.* ☎ *757 28 17. Open daily 10am-noon and 2-5pm. DM3, students and seniors DM1. Ring to get in.)*

DEUTSCHES FREIMAURERMUSEUM. Inside the **Hofgarten,** an English-style park, sits the **Deutsches Freimaurermuseum.** If you've wondered what's inside those windowless Freemason temples, this museum of the world's oldest secular fraternity is the place for you. The rituals of masonic brotherhood have transpired in Bayreuth for 225 years. *(Hofgarten 1.* ☎ *698 24. Open Tu-F 10am-noon and 2-4pm, Sa 10am-noon. DM2, students DM1. Ring to get in.)*

NEUES SCHLOß. The 18th-century Baroque castle is the former residence of Friedrich the Great's sister, **Margravine Wilhelmine.** Considered one of Europe's most brilliant and cultured women, she married the Margrave of Bayreuth and ended up stuck in what must have seemed a provincial cow town. After a mysterious castle fire, she redecorated and rococoed like mad King Ludwig, and when she finished gilding the home furnishings, she swept her eyes across Bayreuth and strove to cosmopolitanize it. *(*☎ *759 69 21. Castle open Apr.-Sept. Tu-Su 10am-5pm; Oct.-Mar. Tu-Su 10am-3pm. DM4, students DM3.)*

MARKGRÄFLICHES OPERNHAUS. The lavishly ornate 1748 opera house is the tangible fruit of Wilhelmine's labours. Wagner originally thought this theater's pomp appropriate for his production, but its 500 seats and stage proved much too small for his grandiose needs. *(Opernstr.* ☎ *759 69 22. Tours, including multimedia light show, every 45min. Open daily 9:15am-5:30pm. DM7; students DM5.)*

KREUZSTEINBAD. If you're sweating from Bayreuth's palatial magnificence, make a splash in Bayreuth's fabulous outdoor pool, whose opulence proves that grand Wagnerian style is not limited to 18th-century opera houses. Complete with waterslides and jungle gyms, it'll bring out the kid in everyone. *(Universitätsstr. 20.* ☎ *661 07. Open May-Sept. daily 7am-8pm. DM5, students DM2.50; "Abendtarif" (entrance after 5pm) DM2.50.)*

THE WAGNER FESTSPIELE

For Wagnerians, a devotional visit to Bayreuth is like a pious pilgrimage to Mecca. Every summer from July 25 to August 28, thousands of visitors pour in for the **Bayreuth Festspiele,** a vast and bombastic—in a word, Wagnerian—celebration of the composer's works. The music fills the **Festspielhaus** theater that Wagner built for his "music of the future." The world's operatic darlings, directors, and conductors have been taking on *The Flying Dutchman, Der Ring des Nibelungen,* and *The Meistersinger* here since 1876. Judging from the number of German Wagner societies and clubs, the spectacle will probably continue for as long as the Holy Grail is old. Tickets for the festival (DM80-300, obstructed view DM40-50) go on sale several years in advance and sell out quickly. Wagnerophiles write to Bayreuther Festspiele, 95402 Bayreuth well before September *every year* and hope for the best. You'll be notified some time after mid-November. Reserve a room in town when you get tickets.

BAMBERG
☎ 0951

Largely overlooked by non-European travelers, Bamberg boasts a history spanning a thousand years. Emperor Heinrich II liked the town so much that he made Bamberg the center of his empire and crowned it with a colossal cathedral. The magnificent building is but one shining example of the city's beauty—it is also blessed with an imperial palace, frescoes, and widely-varied architecture.

◨ GETTING THERE AND GETTING AROUND

Trains: The main station is on Ludwigstr. Trains to **Nürnberg** (1hr., 3 per hr., DM17); **Würzburg** (1¼hr., 2 per hr., DM27); **Munich** (2½-4hr., 1-2 per hr., DM80); and **Frankfurt** (3¼hr., 1 per hr., DM68).

Public Transportation: An excellent transportation net centers around the large, yellow **ZOB** (Zentralomnibusbahnhof) on Promenadestr. off Schönleinspl. Single ride within the inner zone DM1.80. 5-ride ticket DM7. The *Touristenticket,* valid for two days, offers unlimited travel within the inner and outer zones (DM10). For information, head to **i Punkt** (☎ 772 80). Open M-F 7am-7pm, Sa 9am-2pm. All tickets and maps can be purchased from machines.

Taxi: Bamberger Taxizentrale, ☎ 150 15 or 345 45.

Bike Rental: Fahrradhaus Griesmann, Kleberstr. 25 (☎ 229 67). Walk straight on Luitpoldstr. from the station, right on Heinrichsdamm after the bridge, left at the next bridge, and take the first right on Kleberstr. DM12 per day. ID required. Open M-F 9am-12:30pm and 2-5:45pm, Sa 9am-1pm.

✴◪ ORIENTATION AND PRACTICAL INFORMATION

The heart of Bamberg lies on an island between the **Rhein-Main-Danube** canal and the **Regnitz River** (named for its location at the confluence of the Regen and the Pegnitz Rivers). Across the Regnitz away from the train station and past the island lie the winding streets of the Altstadt. From the station, walk down Luitpoldstr., cross the canal, and walk straight on Willy-Lessing-Str. until it empties into Schönleinspl. Turn right onto Lange Str. and left up Obere Brückestr., which leads through the archway of the Rathaus and across the Regnitz (25-30min.). Or grab any city bus in front of the station to "ZOB" for a quick ride into town.

The **Bamberg Card,** valid for 48 hours, gets you free public transportation within the city, a walking tour of Bamberg, and admission to five different museums, as well as a complimentary copy of the *Fränkischer Tag,* Bamberg's answer to the *New York Times* (1 person DM13, 2 people DM24, 3 people DM35, 4 people DM46). It can be purchased at the tourist office or at the Deutsche Bahn Service Point in the train station.

Tourist Office: Fremdenverkehrsamt, Geyerswörthstr. 3 (☎ 87 11 61; fax 87 19 60; e-mail touristinfo@bamberg.de; www.bamberg.de), on an island in the Regnitz. Follow the directions to the Altstadt, above. Once through the Rathaus, take two lefts and re-cross the Regnitz on the wooden footbridge; the tourist office is on the right under the arches. Avoid paying DM0.50 for a map by picking up a free hotel list, which has a better map. The staff books **rooms** for a DM5 fee. Open Apr.-Oct. and Dec. M-F 9am-6pm, Sa 9am-3pm., Su 10am-2pm; Nov. and Jan.-Mar. closed Su.

Tours: 2hr. city tours meet in front of the tourist office Apr.-Oct. M-Sa 10:30am and 2pm, Su 11am; Nov.-Dec. M-Sa 2pm, Su 11am; Jan.-Mar. M-Sa 2pm. DM8, students DM5, children under 14 free with parent. Tours of the cathedral and the Neue Residenz meet at the Neue Residenz and leave when there are enough people. Apr.-Sept. daily 9am-noon and 1:30-5pm; Oct.-Mar. 9am-noon and 1:30-4pm. DM4, students DM3.

Currency Exchange: Citibank, on Schönleinspl. (☎ (0180) 332 21 11). Open M-W 8:30am-6:30pm, Th-F 9am-6:30pm.

Bookstore: Görres Bücher, Lange Str. 24 (☎98 08 40, www.sov.de), stocks a good selection of contemporary novels in English and French on the ground floor. Open M-F 9am-6:30pm, Sa 9am-4pm.

Laundromat: SB Waschsalon, (☎384 95) in the 2nd floor of the Atrium mall just east of the station. Wash DM8, dry DM1 per 8min. Open daily 7am-10pm.

Women's Resources: A woman's cafe pops up every Tuesday evening from 7:30-11pm in **cafe Jenseits,** Promenadestr. 5 (☎210 94), off Schönleinspl. The same building becomes a women's center M 9am-1pm.

Emergency: ☎110. **Police,** Schildstr. 81 (☎912 95 09). **Fire** and **Ambulance,** ☎112.

Rape Crisis Line: ☎582 80.

Pharmacy: Martin-Apotheke, Grüner Markt 21, has a list of 24hr. pharmacies in the window. Open M-F 8:30am-6pm, Th 8:30am-7pm, Sa 9am-2pm.

Hospital: Klinikum Bamberg, Buger Str. 80 (☎50 30). Bus #18 to "Klinikum."

Post Office: Ludwigstr. 25, 96052 Bamberg, across from the train station. Open M-F 7:30am-6pm, Sa 8am-12:30pm.

ACCOMMODATIONS AND CAMPING

Most inexpensive lodgings can be found near **Luitpoldstr.,** the street that runs from in front of the train station.

Jugendherberge Wolfsschlucht (HI), Oberer Leinritt 70 (☎560 02 or 563 44; fax 552 11). Bus #18 (direction: "Bug") to "Rodelbahn" (M-F every 20min., Sa-Su every hr.; DM1.80). Far from the city center, but rooms are tidy and the view of the Regnitz is pleasant. Breakfast included. Sheets DM5.50. Reception 7am-1pm, 5-10pm. Curfew 10pm, but you can get a house key. Because it's the only hostel in Bamberg, it fills up quickly; call very early for summer reservations. Closed mid-Dec. to mid-Jan. Four- or six-bed dorms DM21.

Bamberger Weissbierhaus, Obere Königstr. 38 (☎/fax 255 03), 10min. from the station. Turn left off Luitpoldstr. before the river. Spacious, clean rooms with balconies overlook a pleasant courtyard. Breakfast included. Delectable dinners from DM13. Reception 9am-midnight. Singles DM39; doubles DM70, with shower DM80.

Hotel Hospiz, Promenadestr. 3 (☎98 12 60; fax 981 26 66). Central location off Schönleinspl. Balconies, sparkling white sheets, telephones in every room, and a generous breakfast allow for a night of luxury. Reception 7am-9pm. Check-out 11am. Phone, fax, or mail reservations. Singles DM50, with bath DM70; doubles with shower DM80-85, with bath DM90-100; triples with shower DM114, with bath DM138.

Fässla, Obere Königstr. 19-21 (☎265 16; fax 20 19 89). 10min. from the station. Go right off Luitpoldstr., above one of the most popular beer halls in town. All rooms have TVs, phones, and baths. Breakfast buffet included. Closed Su after 1pm. Singles DM63; doubles DM98; triples DM130.

Camping: Campingpl. Insel, Am Campingpl. 1 (☎563 20). Bus #18 (direction: "Bug") to "Campingplatz." Prime riverside locale. Showers, toilets, washing machines. DM7.50 per adult, DM5.50 per child, DM6 per tent, DM6 per car.

FOOD

Bamberg boasts several breweries, but its most unusual specialty is **Rauchbier** (smoke beer). The daring can try its sharp, smoky taste at **Schlenkerla,** Dominikanerstr. 6 (☎560 60), *Rauchbier's* traditional home since 1678 (0.5L DM3.60, 0.5L bottles available for purchase, DM1.90). The smoke brewery lies at the foot of the steps leading up to Dompl. **Der Beck am Hauptwacheck,** Hauptwachstr. 16, offers scrumptious baked goods and pastries (open M-F 6:30am-6:30pm, Sa 6:30am-4pm). **Edeka,** Lange Str. 14, sells **groceries** (open M-F 8:30am-7pm, Sa 7:30am-4pm).

BAMBERGER RAUCHBIER Since 1678, the Schlenkerla tavern in Bamberg has been the world's fountain of *Rauchbier* (literally, "smoke beer"), an original and savory brew. *Rauchbier* is an aromatic, dark, bottom-fermented beer with an alcohol content slightly higher than 5%. Its smoky flavor is achieved by exposing the malt to burning beech-wood logs before the addition of hops and the subsequent maturation period. What results is a brew which is surprising—if not shocking—on first sip. Yet, as one beer melts into another, the taste becomes quite mellow and enjoyable. Incidentally, the name of the tavern and brewery is Franconian dialect for *Schlenkerer* (staggerer); drink too many of these strong brewskies and you might be schlenkering yourself around town the next day. More information on the *Rauchbier* can be found at www.smokebeer.com.

Mensa, Austr. 37, off Obstmarkt, serves the cheapest meals in town; under DM5. Menu changes daily. Any student ID will do. Open M-F 11:30am-2pm; **snack hall** until 7pm.

Weinstube Zeis, Obstmarkt 3 (☎208 24 66). Cheap cheesy *Käsespätzle* (DM10.80), *Schnitzel* with french fries (DM13.50), and *Bamberger Bratwurst* with *Fränkische Sauerkraut*, mustard, and bread (DM 9.80) on picnic tables that sprawl across a secluded pondside site. Open daily 9am-3am.

Ristorante Ferrari, Synagogenpl. 6. (☎282 77). In a garden that looks like the remains of Pompeii, only happier. Pricey but delicious Italian food. Spaghetti and salads DM15-17. Open W-M noon-2pm and 5:30pm-midnight.

Café Zeitlos, Am Heinrichsdamm 7 (☎208 03 33); enter on Willy-Lessing-Str. Coffee and cake on the 2nd floor of a building that survived the war. Step back into Germany's golden years. Various coffees DM6.90, salads DM8.50-13.50, house baguette DM7.20. Open M-F 10am-1am, Sa 6pm-1am, Su 2pm-1am.

 SIGHTS

DOM. Founded by Emperor Heinrich II, the cathedral was consecrated in 1012, burned down twice, and rebuilt in its present-day form in 1237. The most famous object within the Dom is the equestrian statue of the **Bamberger Reiter** (Bamberg Knight), which dates from the 13th century and depicts the chivalric ideal of the medieval warrior-king. Just beneath the rider is the tomb of Heinrich II and Queen Kunigunde, with their life-size figures on the top and their histories carved into the side. Heinrich sponsored the construction of the cathedral and was later canonized. On the left side of the Dom is the entry to the **Diözesanmuseum,** which includes the **Domschatz** and the perfectly preserved garments of 10th- to 12th-century saints, Popes, and Kaisers. *(Across the river and up the hill from the Rathaus. **Dom** ☎50 23 30; open Apr.-Oct. daily 8am-6pm; Nov.-Mar. daily 8am-5pm. **Museum** ☎50 23 25; open Tu-Su 10am-5pm; DM4, students and seniors DM2, children under 14 free. Organ concerts May-Oct. Sa noon. 1½hr. **tours** of Dom and Domschatz gather Tu-Sa 10:30am inside the main entrance of the cathedral. DM3, students DM1.50.)*

ALTES RATHAUS. The old town hall guards the middle of the Regnitz, the left arm of the Main, like an anchored ship. Built in the 15th century, the Rathaus was strategically placed to keep up the appearance of equal preference of the church and state powers on either side of the river. You can see one of the two bridges from its half-*Fachwerk*, half-Baroque facade with a Rococo tower in between. There are some strange visual effects in the frescoes—painted cherubs have three-dimensional dimpled legs and arms that jut from the wall where sculpted stone has been attached. The Rathaus also contains a Fayence and porcelain exhibit in its **Glanz des Barock** galleries. Don't break anything—you'll deprive someone else of an extremely boring afternoon. *(☎87 18 71. Gallery open Tu-Su 9:30am-4:30pm. DM6, students and children DM4.)*

BAVARIA

NEUE RESIDENZ. The largest building in Bamberg, the **Neue Residenz** was built from 1600 to 1703 and served as the residence of Bamberg's ecclesiastical and secular rulers, the prince-bishops. Only two hallways are open as a museum, holding art from the period of the palace's construction, but entry to the museum also includes a tour of the parade rooms of the palace. The highlight of the castle is the rose garden that lies beneath it. *(Dompl. 8. Opposite the Dom. ☎563 51. Open Apr.-Sept. Tu-Su 9am-6pm; Oct.-Mar. Tu-Su 10am-4pm; last entry 30min. before closing. DM6, students and seniors DM4. Tours meet one floor above the cashier's desk every 15min. Apr.-Oct. daily.)*

PFAHLPLÄTZCHEN. The streets between the Rathaus and the Dom are lined with 18th-century Baroque houses, many of which are not yet renovated. At Pfahlplätzchen, the pink house on the corner of Judenstr., behold the bay window from which Hegel peered while editing the proofs of *Phenomenology of Spirit.* At the time, unable to find a university teaching position, the philosopher was working as editor of the Bamberg newspaper.

E.T.A.-HOFFMANN-HAUS. The rickety house in which the author wrote his nightmarish *Der Sandmann* lies across the river. *(Schillerpl. 26. Open May-Oct. Tu-F 4-6pm, Sa-Su and holidays 10am-noon. DM2, students DM1.)*

🎵🎭 ENTERTAINMENT AND NIGHTLIFE

Nightlife centers around **Obere Sandstr.** in the Altstadt, a small alley which at least 10 bars and clubs call home.

Plapper Storch, Obere Sandstr. 11 (☎509 05 31). A very happening bar with a young clientele, Plapper serves up 17 different beers, among them various German beers (DM5 for 0.5L) and Guinness (DM6). Spins everything from rock and pop to techno on their 300-disc CD player. Open Su-F 7pm-1am, Sa 7pm-2am.

Live Club, Obere Sandstr. 7 (☎50 04 58), offers varied disco to a very young crowd. Scene changes with the day, mixing everything from R&B to hip-hop to hardcore. Open M and Th 9pm-1am, Sa 9pm-2am. Cover DM6-20 for live events. Monday night drinks are half-price with DM6 cover.

Soul Food, Obere Sandstr. 20 (☎550 25). A more mature crowd of music lovers congregates to hear classic rock, jazz, blues, and soul. Beer DM4; Mexican beers (including Corona) DM6. Open M-F 6pm-1am and Sa 6pm-2am.

ASCHAFFENBURG   ☎ 06021

The tourist office calls Aschaffenburg "a town waiting to be discovered," and yet for nearly 1000 years powerful people—including Napoleon and the Bavarian king Ludwig I—have stopped by to visit, some deciding to stay. The city that served as a second residence for the electors of Mainz still retains much of its past charm. i

🛈 **PRACTICAL INFORMATION.** King Ludwig I's "Bavarian Nice" lies near the low, forested Spessart mountains on a high bank at a bend in the Main. Aschaffenburg is easily accessible by **train** from **Frankfurt** (1hr., every 20 min., DM12.60) or **Würzburg** (1hr., 2 per hr., DM23.40). An extensive network of **buses** centered around the train station provides travel within the city and region (single ride within the city DM2, day card DM3.50); fare and route information can be found at the tourist office. To reach the castle and the **tourist office,** Schloßpl. 1, from the train station, cross Ludwigstr. in front of the station and turn left. Walk about 30m and turn right onto Frohsinnstr. Take the first right onto Erthalstr., which brings you into the heart of the **pedestrian zone.** After another 300m, take a left onto Strickergasse. Located on the ground floor of the town's ultra-modern library, the office books **rooms** (DM30-40, often in the suburbs) for free, gives out excellent maps of the Altstadt, and sells even better maps of the entire city for DM1. (☎39 58 00 or 39 58 01; fax 39 58 02; email tourist@info-aschaffenburg.de; www.info-aschaffenburg.de. Open M-F 9am-5pm, Sa 10am-1pm.) If the tourist office is closed, try the information desks across the square in the **Schloßmuseum,** the **Schlo-ßweinstuben,** or the **Galerie Jesuitenkirche** in the **Stadtgalerie. Tours** of the town in German meet in front of the tourist office from May-Oct. (1½hr. Su at 2pm. DM5, under 12 free.) A **laundromat, SB Waschsalon,** Beckerstr. 26, is on the corner of Kneippstr. close to the hostel. (Open M-Sa 9am-9pm. Wash DM5, dry DM6, soap DM1.) Rent a **bike** at **Radstation,** Ludwigstr. 2-4, on the west end of the train station (☎37 42 88, www.wiedia-bike.de. Open M-F 9am-6pm, Th until 8pm, Sa 9am-2pm. From DM10 per day.) The **post office,** 63739 Aschaffenburg, is to the left of the train station as you exit (open M-F 7:30am-6:30pm, Sa 8:30am-1pm.)

▟▞ ACCOMMODATIONS AND FOOD. Aschaffenburg's **Jugendherberge (HI)** is at Beckerstr. 47. From the train station, take bus #5 (direction: "Dörrmorsbach"), 40 (direction: "Dammbach"), 41 (direction: "Hösbach-Bahnhof"), or 63 (direction: "Dornau") to "Sälzer Weg" (DM2). Cross the street, walk a couple paces back towards the city, and turn right onto Gentilstr.; then turn left onto Beckerstr., and the hostel is on the right. A friendly place run by die-hard *Fußball* fans. Serene running and cycling paths through woods and meadows surround the hostel. (☎93 07 63; fax 97 06 94. Breakfast included. Sheets DM5.50. Closed Dec.-Jan. Reception 8-9am, noon-1pm, and 5-7pm. Curfew 11:30pm, though you can get a key at the desk. DM19; DM26.50 with breakfast and lunch; DM32.50 for all three meals.) Just outside the pedestrian zone and across from the Schöntal garden, the cheerful owner of **Hotel Garni Pape,** Würzburger Str. 16, provides a filling home-cooked breakfast with her rooms. From Schloßpl., follow Schloßgasse or Pfaffengasse and turn left onto Dalbergstr., which turns into Sandgasse and then into Würzburger Str. (☎226 73; fax 226 22. Singles DM50; doubles DM90.) **Hotel Syndikus,** Löherstr. 20 (☎235 88; fax 292 80; www.hotel-syndikus.com) offers a few singles with phone, TV, and hallway bathrooms and showers for DM48 per night.

For cheap **groceries,** try **Norma,** Friedrichstr. 25 (open M-F 8:30am-6:30pm, Sa 8am-2pm). Hidden just inside the city wall, **Zum Roten Kopf** has mastered hearty food—strong enough for Bavarians, but pH-balanced for tourists hungry for *Schnitzel* with salad (DM15) and liver soup (DM4.50). From Schloßpl., go down to the river by the castle parking lot, take a right onto Suicardusstr., and walk to the end of the street. (☎293 00. Open M and W-F 4pm-midnight, Sa-Su 10am-midnight.) Also convenient is **Stadtschänke,** Fohsinnstr. 29, a traditional Bavarian restaurant and bar across the street and a little to the left of the train station. Daily menu options (DM8-13) include spaghetti and salad and beer for DM4.30. (☎283 39. Open M-F 10am-10pm, Sa 10am-7pm, Su 11am-7pm.)

▩ SIGHTS. Schloß Johannisburg, the former domain of the Mainz bishops, is now an extensive museum of art filled with Dutch and German masters and an amusing display of cork models of classical buildings such as the Colosseum. (☎38 67 40. *Museum open Apr.-Sept. Tu-Su 9am-6pm; Nov.-Mar. Tu-Su 10am-4pm. Last entry 30min. before morning and afternoon closing. DM5, students DM4.)* A set of 48 chromatically-tuned bronze bells rings across the landscape daily at 9:05am, 12:05, and 5:05pm. The **Schloßgarten** possesses intricate pathways, ivy-canopied benches, and old town walls, forming a secluded haven for romance *(open Apr.-Sept. 6am-9pm, Oct.-Mar. 7am-5pm).* Sweetly tucked behind the Schloßgarten is the **Pompejanum,** a Pompeii-style house built for Ludwig I in the mid-19th century. *(☎21 80 12. Open Apr.-Sept. Tu-Su 9am-6pm. Last entry 30min. before closing. DM3, students DM2.)* Walking south on Schloß-gasse, turn left at Dalbergstr. to find the 10th-century **Stiftskirche St. Peter und Alexander,** whose style is a curious mix of Gothic, Romanesque, and Baroque. The repository of a millennium of cultural history, the **Stiftsmuseum** collection includes a 10th-century crucifix, Matthias Grünewald's painting *Beweinung Christi* (Mourning of Christ), and Vischer's *Magdalenenaltar.* *(☎33 04 63. Open M and W-Su 10am-1pm and 2-5pm. DM5, students DM2.)* Continuing down Dalbergstr. as it becomes Sandgasse, beautiful half-timbered houses pepper the path to the **Sandkirche,** a carefully-preserved 1756 Rococo church *(open daily 8am-9pm).*

Just past the tightly packed Altstadt lie the famous **Schönbusch gardens** and their principal building, **Schloß Schönbusch,** a country house built between 1778 and 1781 for the archbishop of Mainz. From the train station, take bus #4 (direction: "Stockstadt") to "Schönbusch" (DM2). The view from the **Chamber of Mirrors** (preserved from the original house and hence a bit distorted) reveals the city basking in the rich backdrop of the Spessart forests. The archbishop allowed no vegetation between his summer home and **Schloß Johannisburg** (3km away), and the two castles remain in that aristocratic see-you-see-me stance today. *(Castle ☎ 873 08; open Apr.-Sept. Tu-Su 9am-6pm. Admission and tour DM5, students and seniors DM4.)* The park was built by Elector Friedrich Karl Joseph in 1775 as an experiment in English-style landscape architecture, and was one of the earliest landscape gardens in German-speaking countries. Embellished with artificial ponds, islands, and bridges, as well as tiny buildings like the **Freundschaftstempel** (friendship temple) and the **Philosophenhaus,** the park reeks of fairy tale fantasy. The 1829 **Irrgarten,** close to the restaurant at the park's entrance, is a maze formed by trimmed bushes. To hedge the fate of the minotaur, climb the wooden tower to gain an overhead view before tackling the labyrinth. *(Open daily 9am-dusk. Free.)*

■ **ENTERTAINMENT.** For a trip to the disco the locals swear by, visit the **Colos-Saal,** Roßmarkt 19. (☎ 272 39. Open 9pm-late.) Revellers also congregate at Q-bar, Sandgasse 53, a lively Cuban-themed *Kneipe* with many original happy hour themes. Hit the Hemingway Hour (M-F 5-6pm), during which you get a complimentary cigar or cigarello for every cocktail or whiskey you buy. (☎ 36 22 52. Open M-F 5pm-1am, Sa-Su 10am-1am. Beer DM4, wraps DM10.50-14.50.) Pick up the monthly *Fritz* magazine (www.fritz-magazin.de) from the tourist office for a full listing of nightclubs in and around the city. Locals and tourists indulge in the city's home-brewed pride and joy, Heylands beer, as they party with fireworks and merry-go-rounds for 11 days straight during the **Volksfest** (June 15-25, 2001). In July, the **Kippenburg** and **Schloß wine festivals** attract wine aficionados to the city (first 3 weekends and last 3 weekends in July 2001, respectively). The annual **Carillion-Fest,** held the first weekend in August, brings renowned singers from around the globe and tourists who come to swim in the musical swell (August 4-5, 2001).

BADEN-WÜRTTEMBERG

Once upon a time, Baden, Württemberg-Hohenzollern, and Württemberg-Baden were three distinct states. When the Federal Republic was founded in 1951, the Allies masterminded a shotgun wedding, and the three became one: Baden-Württemburg. However, the Badeners and the Swabians (*never* "Württembergers") still proudly proclaim their distinct regional identities. Today, two powerful German stereotypes—the brooding romantic of the Brothers Grimm and the modern *homo economicus* exemplified by Mercedes-Benz—battle it out in Baden-Württemberg. Pretzels, cuckoo clocks, and cars were all invented here, and the region is as diverse as its homegrown products. Rural customs and traditions live on in the bucolic hinterlands of the Schwarzwald (Black Forest) and the Schwäbische Alb, while the modern capital city of Stuttgart celebrates the ascendancy of the German industrial machine. The province also hosts the ritzy millionaires' resort of Baden-Baden, the lovely vacation getaways of the exquisite Bodensee (Lake Constance), and the historic university towns of Freiburg, Tübingen, and Heidelberg.

HIGHLIGHTS OF BADEN-WÜRTTEMBERG

Heidelberg's (p. 337) cobblestone streets, literary past, historic buildings, and hopping nightlife draw droves of tourists. Ride the **cablecar** up to the crumbling Schloß or indulge in contemplative thought and stunning views in strolling the **Philosophenweg.**

A modern, corporate culture lies among lush greenery in **Stuttgart** (p. 354). The **Schloßgarten** beautifies the city with fountains and flower gardens, while **mineral baths** provide hours of indulgent relaxation.

Red-roofed **Tübingen** (p. 361) is known for its university and its **half-timbered houses.** The untouristed **Altstadt** showcases medieval German architecture at its finest.

Hikers live out their fantasies in the **Schwarzwald** (p. 376). Stretches of pine forest and serene lakes cover the slopes of towering mountains from **Freiburg** (p. 369) in the south to **Baden-Baden** (p. 367) in the north.

About as tropical as Germany gets, the **Bodensee** (p. 384) boasts beautiful beaches with turquoise waters. Gaze at the **Alps** from a boat or roam amid the animals made from flowers in the manicured gardens of **Mainau** (p. 387).

HEIDELBERG ☎ 06221

This sunlight-coated town by the Neckar and its crumbling Schloß have lured numerous writers and artists—Mark Twain, Wolfgang von Goethe, Friedrich Hölderlin, Victor Hugo, and Robert Schumann, to name a few. During summer, roughly 32,000 tourists *per day* also answer the call. Even in the off-season, legions of camera-toting fannypackers fill the length of Hauptstr., where postcards and T-shirts sell like hotcakes and every sign is in four languages. Yet the incessant buzz of mass tourism is worth enduring to experience Heidelberg's beautiful hillside setting, famous university, and lively nightlife.

▐ GETTING THERE AND GETTING AROUND

Trains: Frequent trains run from **Mannheim** (10min., 5 per hr., DM7.80); **Stuttgart** (40min., 1 per hr., DM31); and **Frankfurt** (40min., 2 per hr., DM23.40). Other trains run regularly to towns in the **Neckar Valley.**

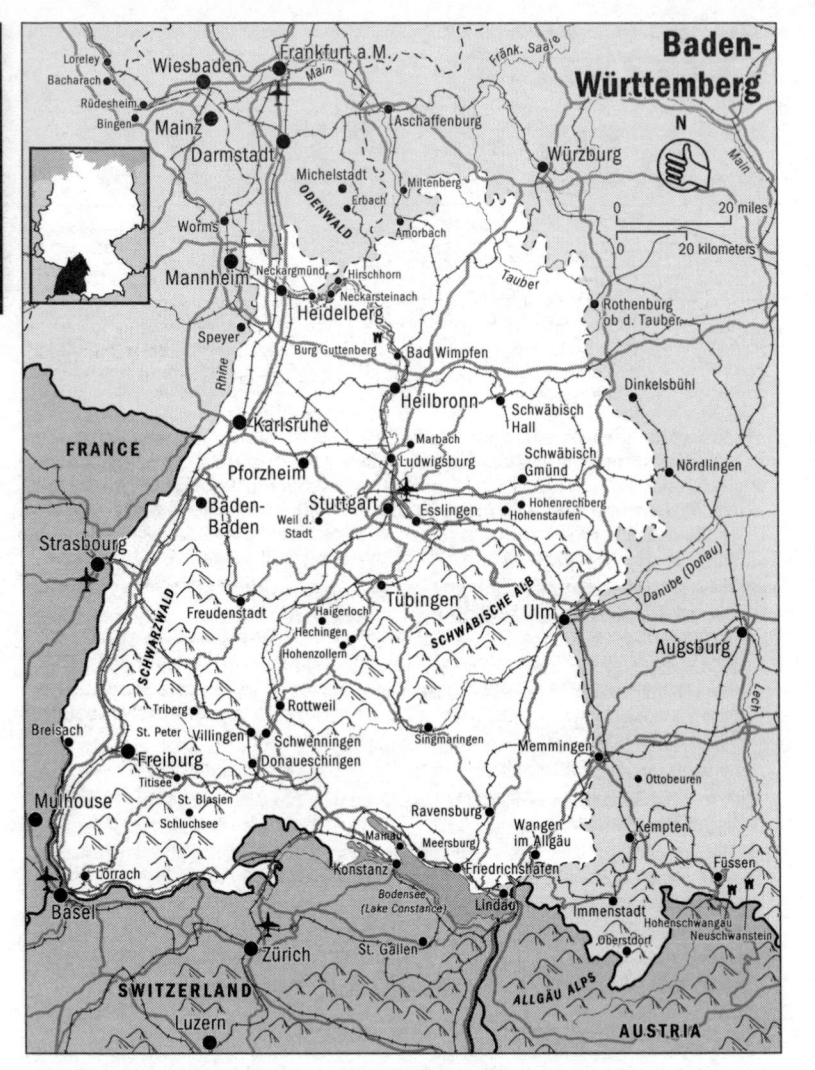

Public Transportation: Single ride tickets DM3.30. A day pass is valid for 24 hours from the time of purchase for up to 5 people on all streetcars and buses (DM10.50). Passes are available at the tourist office, ticket machines, and other tourist-friendly venues.

Ferries: Rhein-Neckar-Fahrgastschiffahrt (☎201 81), on the southern bank in front of the *Kongresshaus,* runs ferries to river ports all over Germany and provides round-trip Neckar cruises to Neckarsteinach (1½hr., runs Easter-Oct. 9:30am-3:30pm, DM12.50).

Taxi: ☎30 20 30.

Bike Rental: Per Bike, Bergheimer Str. 125 (☎16 11 48; fax 16 11 09). Half-day DM15, full day DM25, additional days DM20. Weekend special DM55. DM50 deposit or ID required. Open M-F 9am-6pm; Apr.-Oct. also open Sa 9am-1pm.

Boat Rental: Rent paddleboats and rowboats on the north shore of the Neckar by the Theodor-Heuss-Brücke at **Bootsverleih Simon.** 3-person boat DM15 per hr. 4-person boat DM20. Open daily 10am-sundown.

Mitfahrzentrale: Bergheimer Str. 125 (☎246 46; fax 14 59 59), matches riders and drivers. **Freiburg** DM24, **Köln** DM28, **Hamburg** DM54, **Paris** DM51. Open M-F 9am-5pm; Apr.-Oct. also Sa 9am-noon.

Hitchhiking: Let's Go does not recommend hitchhiking as a safe mode of transportation; hitchers recommend walking to the western end of Bergheimer Str. for all directions.

ORIENTATION AND PRACTICAL INFORMATION

About 20km east of the Neckar's confluence with the Rhein, Heidelberg stretches along the river's shores for several kilometers, with almost all of the city's attractions clustered in the eastern quadrant on the southern shore. To get to the Altstadt from the train station, take any bus or street car to "Bismarckpl.," where **Hauptstraße** leads into the city's heart. Known as the longest pedestrian street in Germany, Hauptstr. is the city's backbone. To save money, buy the **Heidelberg Card** (valid two days), which includes use of public transit and admission to the Schloß and most sights, available at the tourist office (DM19.80).

Tourist Office: Tourist Information (☎13 88 121; fax 13 88 111; www.cvb.heidelberg.de), in front of the station. Pick up a copy of the mags Meier (DM2) and Heidelberg Aktuell (DM1) to see what's up. The office offers tours (DM22) Th-Su, and **books rooms** with an 8% deposit for a DM5 fee. Be aware that the office often steers guests toward more expensive places; rooms start at approx. DM70. Open Mar.-Dec. M-Sa 9am-7pm, Su 10am-6pm; Jan.-Feb. closed Su. Additional tourist offices at the **Schloß** (☎211 44; open daily 9am-5pm; closed in winter) and at **Neckarmünzplatz** (open daily 9am-6:30pm; closed Sept. 30-May 31).

Currency Exchange: Change cash at the **Sparkassen** on Universitätspl. and Bismarckpl. Or try the exchange office in the train station. Open M-Sa 7am-8:30pm, Su 9am-1pm.

American Express: Brückenkopfstr. 1 (☎450 517; fax 45 55 84), at the north end of Theodor-Heuss-Brücke. Holds mail for members and owners of traveler's checks. Open M-F 10am-6pm, Sa 9am-1pm. 24-hr. refund hotline ☎0130 853 100.

Emergency: ☎110. **Police:** Römerstr. 2-4, ☎990. **Fire** and **Ambulance,** ☎112.

Women's Resources: Emergency hotline, ☎18 36 43. **Buchhandlung Himmelheber,** Theaterstr. 16 (☎222 01; fax 230 92), stocks books by, for, and about women, and also hosts readings. Open M-W and F 9am-6:30pm, Th 9am-8pm, Sa 9am-2pm.

Aids Hotline: ☎194 11.

Post Office: Sofienstr. 8-10 (☎91 24 10), 69155 Heidelburg, off Bismarkpl. Open daily 9am-6:30pm.

Internet Access: La Tapa, Steingasse 16 (☎18 35 11). Open M, Tu, Th-Sa 11am-8pm, Su 12-5pm. DM1.50 for 10 min.

ACCOMMODATIONS AND CAMPING

Finding a bed in Heidelberg can be extremely taxing. During the summer, save yourself a major headache by arriving early in the day or, better yet, calling ahead. Possible options for those with some ingenuity and a railpass are the countless little towns and villages scattered around Heidelberg. There are **youth hostels** in: **Neckargemünd** (10min. away, ☎(06223) 21 33; DM22, DM27 for over 26); **Eberbach** (25min., ☎(06271) 25 93; DM22,27); and **Zwingenberg** (35min., ☎(06251) 759 38; DM18,23). All these Neckar Valley towns lie along the Heidelberg-Heilbronn railroad; train service is reliable and regular between them. Better yet, the **Mannheim Jugendherberge** is only five minutes from Mannheim's train station, 15-20 minutes from Heidelberg (see p. 347).

Jugendherberge (HI), Tiergartenstr. 5 (☎41 20 66; fax 40 25 59). From Bismarckpl. or the station, bus #33 (direction: "Zoo-Sportzentrum") to "Jugendherberge." In peak season, call or fax your reservation at least a week ahead. Crowded and noisy, but its small **disco** can be fun (open nightly). As in any crowded hostel you should keep a close eye on your valuables. Sheets DM5.50. Reception until 11:30pm. Lockout 9am-1pm. Curfew 11:30pm; stragglers admitted at 1am. Partial wheelchair access. Members only. Dorms DM24, over 26 DM28.

Jeske Hotel, Mittelbadgasse 2 (☎237 33). From the station, bus #33 (direction: "Ziegelhausen") or 11 (direction: "Karlstor") to "Rathaus/Kornmark"; Mittelbadgasse is the second left off the square. English-speaking Euro-roamers fill this delightfully antiquated Altstadt facility, and for good reason—it's a great value with an unbeatable location. Reservations only accepted an hour ahead of time. Doubles DM52.

Schmidts, Blumenstr. 54 (☎27 29 6). From Bismarckkpl., follow Rohrbacher Str. away from the river and turn right on Blumenstr., one block after Bunsenstr. Schmidts' rooms are relatively cheap by Heidelberg standards. Singles DM70, with shower DM120.

Hotel-Pension Elite, Bunsenstr. 15 (☎257 33 or 257 34; fax 16 39 49). From Bismarktpl., follow Rohrbacher Str. away from the river and turn right on Bunsenstr.; the *Pension* is on the left. From the train station, take streetcar #1 to "Poststr."; the hotel is on the second street behind the Holiday Inn. Nice rooms with high ceilings, bath, and TV. Breakfast buffet included. Show your *Let's Go* guide to get these reduced rates. Singles DM75; doubles for one person DM85; for two persons DM100; DM20 per extra person. DM5 credit card surcharge.

Camping Haide (☎(06223) 21 11; email camping.haide@t-online.de), between Ziegelhausen and Neckargemünd. Bus #35 to "Orthopädisches Klinik," then cross the river and turn right; the campground is on the right 20min away. Open Apr.-Oct. Reception 8am-11:30am and 4:30-7:30pm. DM14.50-20 per person, DM2 per car. Cabins DM14.50-20. **Camping Heidelberg-Schlierbach** is located on the other bank (☎80 25 06). Bus #35 (direction: "Neckargemünd") to "Im Grund." Check-in 8am-12pm, 2pm-10pm. DM10 per person, DM4-12 per tent, DM2 per car.

⬛ FOOD

Eating out tends to be depressingly expensive in Heidelberg; most of the restaurants on and around Hauptstr. are exorbitantly priced. Just outside this central area, historic student pubs offer better values. Fill up a picnic basket at **Handelshof supermarket,** Kurfürsten-Anlage 60, 200m in front of the train station on the right (open M-F 7:30am-8pm, Sa 7:30am-4pm). W and S a **fruit market** is held on Marktpl.

Mensa, in the *Marstall* on Marstallstr. Bus #35 to "Marstallstr." Or, from the Alte Brücke, with your back to the old city, take a left along the river; it's the red fortress on the left. DM3-7, depending on your selections. Lunch M-F 11:30am-2pm. Dinner M-Sa 5pm-10pm. A popular **cafe** next door serves coffee, snacks, and beer (DM3). Open M-F 9am-12:30am, Sa 11am-1am.

Großer Wok, Bergheimer Str. 1a (☎60 25 28), near Bismarckkpl. Appetizing aromas whet your taste buds for Chinese specialties (DM4-13) served quickly to go or to eat atop bar stools. Open M-Th and Su 11am-11pm, F-Sa 11am-midnight.

Goldener Anker, Untere Neckar 52 (☎18 42 25), near the river and the Alte Brücke. Although most of the traditional German dishes are on the high end of the price scale, some are affordable (DM8-15). Open M-Sa 6pm-midnight.

Hemingway's Bar-Café-Meeting Point, Fahrtgasse 1 (☎16 50 53), at the corner of Neckarstaden. Open daily 9am-1am. Lunch menu DM7.90.

Thanner, Bergheimer Str. 71 (☎252 34), is a swank cafe with an eclectic international menu and the only *Biergarten* in Heidelberg allowed to play music (open until 11pm). Entrees DM7-29. Open M-Th and Su 9am-1am, F-Sa 9am-2am.

👁 SIGHTS

■ **HEIDELBERGER SCHLOß.** The jewel in the crown of an already striking city, the Schloß stands careful watch over the armies (of tourists) who dare approach Heidelberg. Its construction began early in the 14th century, and after

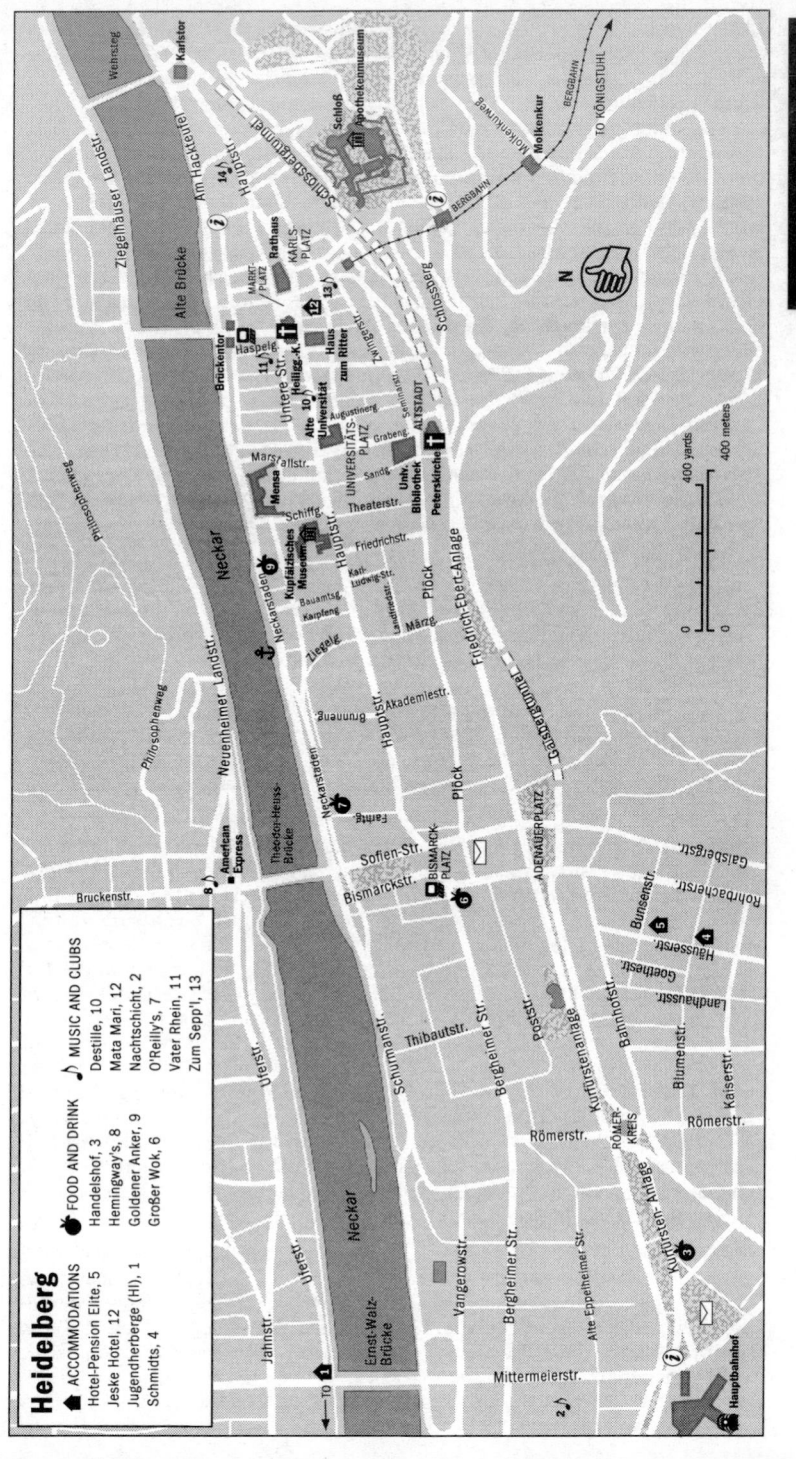

Heidelberg

▲ ACCOMMODATIONS
Hotel-Pension Elite, 5
Jeske Hotel, 12
Jugendherberge (HI), 1
Schmidts, 4

● FOOD AND DRINK
Handelshof, 3
Hemingway's, 8
Goldener Anker, 9
Großer Wok, 6

♪ MUSIC AND CLUBS
Destille, 10
Mata Mari, 12
Nachtschicht, 2
O'Reilly's, 7
Vater Rhein, 11
Zum Sepp'l, 13

1329 it housed the prince electors, whose statues decorate the facade in front of the entrance. Over a period of almost 400 years, the castle's dwellers commissioned their distinctive additions; the conglomeration of styles ranges from Gothic to High Renaissance. Thrice destroyed, twice by war (1622 and 1693) and once by nature (lightning in 1764), the castle's regal state of disrepair is best viewed from inside or from the **Philosophenweg** high above the northern bank of the Neckar; be prepared for an uphill hike. While walking around the castle grounds, visitors can cool off in the musty wine cellar. Its *Großer Faß* is the largest wine barrel ever made, holding 221,726 liters; the kleiner *Faß* holds a mere 45,000L. Local lore tells of a court jester and *Faß* guardian who drank nearly 18 bottles per day and finally perished after accidentally drinking a glass of water; a lesson is to be learned from this. The *Schloß* is accessible by an uphill path or the **Bergbahn,** the world's oldest cable car, which runs from the "Bergbahn/Rathaus" bus stop to the castle. *(Castle ☎ 53 84 14 or 538 40. Cable car round-trip DM4.70. Trams take off from the Kornmarkt parking lot next to the bus stop every 10 minutes from 9am to 7:45pm. Take bus #11 towards "Köpfel" or 33 towards "Karlstor." Obligatory English tours daily 15 min. past the hour from 11am-3pm. DM4, students DM2. Grounds open daily 8am-dusk. DM3, students DM1.50, charged from 8am-5:30pm only.)* The **Apothekenmuseum,** also in the castle, stopped dishing out the goods in 1693 but still features creepy displays on pharmaceuticals and alchemy. *(☎ 258 80. Open daily 10am-5:30pm. Free with entrance to castle grounds. Tour 2:30pm.)*

MARKTPLATZ. The Altstadt centers on the Marktplatz, a cobbled square where a contemplative Hercules directs water at **Hercules' Fountain,** and where, in the 15th century, accused witches and heretics were burned at the stake; now tourists recline on a legion of plastic chairs. The two oldest structures in Heidelberg border the square. During Louis XIV's invasion of the town, terrified inhabitants scurried to the 14th-century **Heiliggeistkirche.** A wall dividing the church into Catholic and Protestant sections was torn down in 1936; now the church is used for Protestant worship. *(Open M-Sa 11am-5pm; Su 1-5pm. Free. Church tower DM1, students DM0.50.)* Opposite the church's southern face, the ornate facade of the **Haus zum Ritter** dates from the 16th century. The stately **Rathaus** stands at the far end of the square.

UNIVERSITÄT. Heidelberg is home to Germany's oldest and perhaps most prestigious university, established in 1368. It was at Heidelberg that Clemens Brentano compiled *Des Knaben Wunderhorn,* a collection of folk poetry that led to the Brothers Grimm's own prose compilation. It was also here that sociology became a legitimate academic subject under the leadership of Max Weber. The oldest remaining buildings border the stone lion fountain of the Universitätsplatz. Other university buildings dot the western Altstadt. Before 1914, in the aristocratic tradition, students were exempt from prosecution by civil authorities; instead, the crimes of naughty youths were tried and punished by the university faculty. Guilty students were jailed (at their leisure) in the **Studentenkarzer.** The walls are covered with graffiti—nothing can snuff the creativity of a willingly incarcerated college student (see p. 583). *(Augustinergasse 2. ☎ 54 23 34. Open Apr.-Oct. M-F 10am-4pm., Nov.-Mar. Tu-F 10am-4pm. DM5; students DM4.)* After some time in jail, test your literacy skills on the **Bibliothek's** collection of precious medieval manuscripts. *(Plöck 107-109. ☎ 54 23 80. Open M-Sa 10am-7pm. Free.)*

KURPFÄLZISCHES MUSEUM. The museum is crammed with artifacts such as the jawbone of an unfortunate *homo Heidelbergensis,* a.k.a. "Heidelberg man," one of the oldest (deceased) humans discovered. Elsewhere in the museum stand well-preserved works of art by Dürer and a spectacular archaeology exhibit. *(Hauptstr. 97. ☎ 58 34 02 or 58 34 00. Open Tu and Th-Su 10am-5pm, W 10am-9pm. DM5, students DM3; Su DM3, students DM2.)*

KARL-THEODOR-BRÜCKE. No trip to Heidelberg would be complete without a visit to the northern bank of the Neckar. Walk across the modern Karl-Theodor-Brücke; on the south side of the bridge stands a plump statue of the bridge's namesake prince elector, which he commissioned as a symbol of his modesty.

PHILOSOPHENWEG. If train schedules haven't given you enough time to contemplate the Other, or if you just need a romantic place to kiss the Other, take a walk on the "philosopher's path." A high path opposite the Neckar from the Altstadt, the Philosophenweg offers the best views of the city. It traverses the **Heiligenberg,** with its ruins of the 9th-century **St. Michael Basilika,** the 13th-century **Stefanskloster,** and an **amphitheater** built under Hitler in 1934 on the site of an ancient Celtic gathering place. *(To the west of the Karl-Theodor-Brücke, in the direction of the Theodor-Huess-Bruecke. Take streetcar #1 or 3 to "Tiefburg," a castle in neighboring Handschuhsheim, to begin the hike upwards, or use the footpath 10m west of the Karl-Theodor-Bruecke.)*

🎵🖼 ENTERTAINMENT AND NIGHTLIFE

The first Saturday in June and September and the second Saturday in July, draws giant crowds to fireworks and pageants with the Schloß as a backdrop. The **Faschingsparade** (carnival) struts through the city on Shrove Tuesday. The **Hand-Schuhsheim Fest** lures revelers the third weekend in June, while the **Schloßfestspiele Heidelberg** features a series of concerts and plays at the castle in the month of August (☎583 52 for tickets). On September 30th, the **Heidelberger Herbst** brings a medieval market to the Altstadt, which later witnesses the **Weihnachtsmarkt** (Dec. 1-23). For more on Heidelberg events, try the InfoLife (☎60 45 20).

The **Marktplatz** is the hub of the city's action; most popular nightspots fan out from here. **Unter Straße,** on the Neckar side of the Heiliggeistkirche, boasts the most prolific—and often congested—conglomeration of bars in the city. During fair weather, drunken revelers fill the narrow way until 1 or 2am. **Hauptstraße** also harbors a fair number of venues, and a few dot the north side of the river as well.

Nachtschicht (☎16 98 32), in Landfried-Komplex. From Hauptbahnhof, take Mittermaierstr. past a metal dinosaur; take the first left onto Alte Eppenheimerstr., and enter the parking lot on the right. A variety of music plays in a basement resembling an abandoned warehouse. W-Sa 10am-4pm, closed Su-Tu. DM6; half-price W, F for students.

VaterRhein, Untere Neckarstr. 20-22 (☎213 71), close to the river near the *Stadthalle.* College students converge after midnight to chill here among the vintage 1950s ads that decorate the wood-paneled walls. Cheap food and drinks. Spaghetti DM2.50, pizza DM11.50, pilsner DM4.50. Open daily 8pm-3am.

O'Reilly's (☎410 140), on the corner of Brückenkopfstr. and Uferstr. Cross Theodor-Heuss-Brücke, turn right, and follow the noise to Guinness's "Best Irish Pub in Germany 1999," where a young crowd drinks Guinness (DM7.50) by the liter. Open M-F 5pm-1am, Sa-Su 1pm-3am.

Destille, Unterstr. 16 (☎228 08). A crowded bar where English is heard as often as German, and a gathering spot for local students and tourists alike. *Pils* DM5. Open daily from 12pm-1am.

Zum Sepp'l, Hauptstr. 213 (☎143 30). Hosts a loud crowd that's been partying since 1634. Meals DM19-29. Beer DM5.50, "the Boot" (2L of beer) DM7.20. Get kicked. Open daily 11:30pm-1am.

Mata Hari (☎18 18 08), on Zwingerstr. near Oberbadgasse. Cramped, subdued gay and lesbian bar. Tu men only. Beer DM5. Open daily 10pm-3am. Closed M.

Schwimmbad Musikclub, Tiergartenstr. 13 (☎47 02 01), across the river. Conveniently located up the street from the hostel, but a trek otherwise, it's the city's main catwalk for bands with names like "Fatal Function." W is independent alternative. Open W-Th 8pm-3am, F-Sa 8pm-4am.

NECKARTAL (NECKAR VALLEY)

The Neckartal—a stretch of the thickly forested **Odenwald** sliced by the Neckar River—reaches from Heilbronn to Heidelberg. Centuries ago, a series of enterprising royals decided to build castles with the lofty goal of protecting merchants from pirates as well as the not-so-lofty goal of charging tolls for their services. Today, their medieval castles dot the hilltops of the Neckartal and form part of the **Burgenstraße** (the Castle Road) that stretches from Mannheim to Prague. Largely unspoiled by tourism, the Neckartal is an excellent daytrip from Heidelberg.

Two train lines connect Heidelberg and Heilbronn, with stops in the small towns along both sides of the valley. One of the best ways to explore the valley is by biking along the well-maintained 85km route. In Hirschhorn, **Josef Riedel,** Hainbrunnerstr. 6 (☎(06272) 20 17), rents bikes for DM5 per half-day, DM10 per day. The **Rhein-Neckar Fahrgastschiffahrt** (p. 338) runs **boat tours** from Easter through late-October between Heidelberg, Neckargemünd, Neckarsteinach, Hirschhorn, and Eberbach. Round-trips cost DM4-19.50. For information and departure times, call ☎(06221) 201 81 or (06229) 526. Local buses also traverse the Neckar Valley; often these are faster than the infrequent trains. Schedules are posted at bus stops.

NECKARSTEINACH   ☎06229

At the north end of the valley, 14km upstream from Heidelberg, Neckarsteinach is renowned for its four medieval **castles** that peek proudly out of the pine trees and dominate the fishing village below. All within three kilometers of one another along the north bank of the Neckar River, the castles were built by the Steinachs, feudal tenants of the Bishop of Worms, during the 12th and 13th centuries. The two westernmost castles stand in ruins, while the two to the east tower in splendor; they are privately occupied, however, and visitors are not allowed inside. All can be reached by foot via the **Burgenweg.** From the train station, turn right on Bahnhofstr. and follow it until you reach Hauptstr. Turn left and follow the bend in the road; a cross marks the beginning of the *Schloßsteige*, a brick path leading upward and to the right which connects to the Burgenweg. At the end of the brick path, turn right to reach the first two private castles. Follow the Burgenweg to the left to reach the third, ruined, castle. To reach the fourth castle, follow the Burgenweg behind the third castle. Fifty meters beyond the shed, the trail intersects with another trail; this junction is partially hidden by a large tree. Take the trail that doubles back on higher ground, which will bring you around the mountain and to the last castle. You should see the Neckar within 10 minutes. (Open Mar.-Oct. M-Sa 9am-8pm.) Fireworks will light the sky above the town on the second Saturday after *Pfingsten* in June and on the last Saturday in July for the **Vierburgenbeleuchtung** (four-castle lighting).

Neckarsteinach's **tourist office,** Hauptstr. 7, inside the Rathaus, is one block down from Bahnhofstr. in the same direction as the *Schloß-steige*. The office has a list of private **rooms.** (☎920 00; fax 318. Open M-W 8am-noon and 1:30-3:30pm, Th 8am-noon and 1:30-5pm, F 8am-noon.) Or try the only hotel in town, **Vierburgeneck,** Unterhalb der Ruine. (☎542. TV, private bath, and breakfast included. DM65 per room.) For **camping,** head across the river to **Unterm Dilsberg.** Leave your campsite cleaner than you found it, since the owners are local sheriffs. (☎(06223) 725 85. Open Apr.-Sept. DM7 per site, DM6 per person.) The **postal code** is 69239.

HIRSCHHORN AM NECKAR   ☎06272

Just south of Neckarsteinach lounges Hirschhorn am Neckar, a town whose reconstructed medieval Altstadt appears to be floating on the river from a distance. The settlement was ruled for centuries by the Knights of Hirschhorn, who built their castle on Stockelberg mountain in 1200, displacing a herd of reindeer. History repeated itself hundreds of years later, when an enterprising young capitalist bought the knights out; the mountain is now a posh hotel/restaurant complex (☎(06272) 13 73. DM120 for basic room, DM250 for honeymoon suite). Nevertheless, the surrounding countryside is excellent for hiking, and **Schloß Hirschhorn** is worth a peek. By foot, follow the gray brick of Schloßstr. diagonally across from the *Bürgerhaus* intersection (15min.); unless you are in a car, do not follow the road signs. The castle's terraces offer a fine panorama, and an even better one can be had from the top of the tower (DM0.30). Stone stairs curl from the castle down to the Altstadt; along the way, they pass the 15th-century **Karmeliter Klosterkirche,** with its Gothic interior and graceful altar.

Maps of local hiking trails are available at the **tourist office,** Alleeweg 2, which also books **rooms** (from DM40) for free. From the station, turn left on Neckarsteinacher Str. and follow it to the intersection as it curves to the right. Turn right and walk downhill toward the river past the hotel. The office is in the rear of the yellow building on the right. (☎17 42 or 92 31 40. Open M-F 8am-noon and 2-5pm; Apr.-Oct. also Sa 9am-noon.) The building also houses the **Langbenmuseum,** an art and natural history museum with a collection of 17th- and 18th-century wooden statues, weaponry, and a diorama that crams more than 100 native fauna into a space the size of a king-size bed. (Open Tu and Th-F 2-4pm, Su 10am-noon and 2-4pm. DM1, children DM0.50.) The **post office,** Hauptstr. 27, 69434 Hirschhorn, is on the main drag (open M-F 8:30am-12:30pm and 2:30-6pm, Sa 8:30am-noon).

For overnight accommodations, check the hotels and *Pensionen* along Hauptstr. and the board outside the tourist office. **Haus La Belle,** Hauptstr. 38 (☎14 00), has cushy rooms with bath, TV, and breakfast included (from DM35 per person). Camp at **Odenwald Camping,** Langenthaler Str., one kilometer outside of town in the direction of the castle; follow the signs from the tourist office. (☎809; fax 36 58. Open Apr. to mid-Oct. DM 12 per site, DM8.50 per person.)

BURG GUTTENBERG

Thirty kilometers south of Hirschhorn towers **Burg Guttenberg,** which houses a **museum** detailing its 800-year history. (☎(06266) 91 020 Open Apr.-Oct. daily 10am-6pm.) Also within the castle walls is an **aviary** for birds of prey, maintained by prominent ornithologist Claus Fentzloff. Each day (Apr.-Nov. at 11am and 3pm; Mar. and Nov. 3pm only), Fentzloff or a well-trained assistant sends eagles and vultures flying inches above the heads of the crowds, plucking chickens out of the sky, while he launches into lengthy scientific diatribes. (Museum and castle DM5. Bird show DM12. All DM16.) To reach Burg Guttenberg by rail, get off at "Gundelsheim", cross the big bridge past the camping site, and walk 2km following the signs along the road, past tobacco fields and terraced hillsides (30min).

BAD WIMPFEN   ☎07063

Downstream from Heilbronn reposes the village of Bad Wimpfen, whose fairy-tale demeanor was once one of the best-kept secrets in southwest Germany. The immaculately preserved Altstadt is a 10-minute walk from the ornate train station. Follow Karl-Ulrich-Str. or take the steep hiking trail to the right of the station. Laid out along the northern side of the old castle walls, easily accessible points on the ancient battlements offer incredible views of the valley and the surrounding countryside. Next to the **Roter Turm** *(open Sa-Su 10am-noon and 2-5pm),* the **Pfalzkapelle** hosts the **Kirchenhistorisches Museum,** which exhibits ecclesiastical artifacts from the town's monastery and churches, including a Luther Bible. *(Open Apr.-Oct. Tu-Su 10am-noon and 2-4pm. DM1.50, students DM1.)* The **Blauer Turm,** Burgviertel 9, offers a stunning view to those willing to climb the 169 steps. At the top of the stairs lives the tower's watchwoman and her family, who'll give you your ticket to the top. *(☎89 68. Open Tu-Su 10am-6pm. DM2.)* Next door, the sandstone **Steinhaus** contains the **Historisches Museum,** a somewhat sparse collection of artifacts both ancient and medieval. *(Open Apr.-Oct. Tu-Su 10am-noon and 2-4:30pm. DM2, students DM1.)* The **Galerie der Stadt** features a small exhibit on contemporary artwork, while the **Reichstädtisches Museum** recounts the history of Bad Wimpfen. *(Both open Tu-Su 10am-noon and 2-5pm. Admission to the Galerie is free; to the museum DM3, students DM2.)* The world's only **Pig Museum,** Kronengäßchen 2, off Hauptstr. near the *Kulturamt,* details the history of swine (considered a good luck symbol in Germany) with collectors' items, lucky charms, and live pigs on the premises. (☎66 89. *Open daily 10am-5pm. DM5, students DM2.50.*) A **museum pass** is available to the Museum in Stienhaus, Museum in Alten Spital, Museum in der Pfalzkapelle, Blauer Turm, and Roter Turm for DM5, students DM3.

The friendly **tourist office** in the train station finds **rooms** from DM25-30 (☎972 00; fax 97 20 20. Open M-F 9am-1pm and 2-5pm, Sa-Su 10am-noon and 2-4pm.) **Tours** depart Sunday at 2pm from the tourist office (DM3). **Hotel Garni Neckarblick,** Erich-Salier-Str. 48, offers affordable luxury with a capital "L," incredibly hospitable management, and a stunning view of the valley. Call to be picked up from the train station, or take a right from the Hauptbahnhof and follow Hauptstr. to the street and hang a right. Proceed for 15 minutes along Erich-Salier-Str. as it curves around the hillside; the hotel is on the right. All rooms include TV, telephone, and bath. They also rent **bikes** (DM5 for guests, DM15 for non-guests) and offer to pick guests up at the end of a day of biking to bring them back to the hotel. (☎96 16 20; fax 85 48. Breakfast included. Call ahead or fax reservations. Singles DM80, doubles DM115-140, triples DM175.) Closer to the station, **Pension zur Traube,** Hauptstr. 1, offers less cushy but still comfortable rooms with showers. (☎95 05 21; fax 95 05 21. Breakfast included. Singles DM55; doubles DM105.) For traditional fare, try **Dobel's Maultaschen,** Hauptstr. 61, where *Maultaschen* (Swabian meat and spinach ravioli, DM9-16) and beer draw locals around the bar. The salad bar (DM7) is a rare source of edible green in the Neckar Valley. (☎82 12. Open M-Sa 10am-midnight, Su 10am-10pm.) The *"kleine portion"* at **Hirsch,** 88 Hauptstr., comes with a filling main dish, salad, and *Spaetzle* (Swabian noodles) for DM16 (M, W-F, 11am-2pm, 5:30-11pm, Sa-Su 11am-11pm). **Grocery** stores are located on the other side of the Altstadt along Rappenauerstr.

MANNHEIM   ☎0621

For nearly a thousand years, Mannheim existed merely as a simple fishing village. In 1720, however, history took a step forward, when Elector Karl Phillipp made the city the capital of Rheinland-Pfalz. Mannheim's heady days as a capital came to an end a mere 57 years later when the court packed up and marched off to Munich. *Auf Wiedersehen,* baby. The desertion appears to have had little effect on the city; today's Mannheim is one of the most urbanized locales in southwest Germany. The easily navigable streets and almost nonexistent tourist population make Mannheim a worthy destination for city-loving travelers.

ORIENTATION

Mannheim is centered on the peninsula created by the junction of the Rhein and Neckar rivers. The **Innenstadt** is bounded by a horseshoe (Parkring to the west, Luisenring to the northwest, Friedrichsring to the northeast, and Kaiserring to the east) whose southern ends are connected by Bismarkstr. The train station is just outside the southeast corner. **Kurpfalzstraße** bisects the horseshoe, which is divided into a grid of 144 blocks. Each block is designated by a letter and a number; blocks along Kurpfalzstr. are numbered 1, and the number increases moving away from the central axis. Blocks to the west of Kurpfalzstr. are designated south to north by the letters **A** through **K** starting with Bismarkstr., while streets to the east are similarly lettered **L** through **U**. East of Kaiserring, streets assume regular names; perhaps the Pfalz electors saw that they were running out of letters.

PRACTICAL INFORMATION

Trains run twice per hour to **Stuttgart** (40min., DM57) and **Frankfurt** (45min., DM40). Mannheim's **streetcars** cost DM1.20 per ride in the Innenstadt and DM3.20 for rides beyond that. The *Ticket 24 Plus,* valid 24hr., costs DM10. The **tourist office,** Willy-Brandt-Platz 3, a block from the station, distributes maps and information on accommodations. (☎10 10 11; fax 241 41; email info@tourist-mannheim.de; www.tourist-mannheim.de. Open M-F 9am-7pm, Sa 9am-noon.) The office also offers a **Mitfahrzentrale** ride-share service. A **laundromat, Schnell & Sauber,** awaits on block G7 on the Luisenring side. (Wash DM7. Dry DM1 per 15min. Open daily 6am-11pm, last entry 10pm.) A **pharmacy, Bahnhof-Apotheke,** is at block L15, across from the station and to the left. (☎ 12 01 80. Open M-F 7am-8pm, Sa 7:30am-4pm.) **Email** addictions can be fed at **Chat Corner,** M7, 2 blocks from the train station. (Open M-Sa 9am-3am, Su 10am-3am. DM1 per 10min.) The **post office,** 68161 Mannheim, is one block east of the station (open M-F 7am-7pm, Sa 7am-1pm).

ACCOMMODATIONS AND FOOD

Mannheim's **Jugendherberge (HI),** Rheinpromenade 21, provides somewhat cramped rooms, but its delectable breakfast and super-convenient location 10 minutes from the station more than make up for the aging facilities. Walk through the underground passage (toward track 10), exit at the back of the station, and take a right. Follow Joseph-Kellner-Str., cross the tracks, and take a left; with the park on your right, continue down for about a block, and enter at the first entrance by the yellow mailbox. Or take streetcar #7 (direction: "Neckarau") to "Lindenhofpl." (☎ 82 27 18; fax 82 40 73. Breakfast buffet included. Sheets DM6. Reception 8-9am, 4-5pm, and 6-8pm. Curfew 12:30am. Members only. Dorm beds DM23, over 26 DM28.) The next best value is the spotless and conveniently located **Pension Arabella,** block M2, #12, two blocks north of the Schloß. (☎ 230 50; fax 156 45 27. Breakfast DM7.50. Singles DM40-45; doubles DM70-80; triples DM100.) **Goldene Gans,** Tattersallstr. 19, two blocks northeast of the train station, has its entrance under ivy covering on Bismarkpl. during the day, but after midnight it's around the corner. Pleasant rooms are marred by noise on street-side suites. (☎ 10 52 77; fax 422 02 60. Breakfast included. Reception M-Sa 6am-midnight, Su 7am-8pm. Singles DM60-70, with shower DM75-85; doubles DM105-150.)

Butchers, bakers, and grocers gather at the **market** in the square at the intersection of Kurpfalzstr. and Kirchstr. at the center of the city grid (open Tu, Th, and Sa 7am-2:30pm). The cheapest meals in town are at the government-subsidized **Studentenwerk Mannheim Mensa** (open M-F 11:30am-2pm) and the adjacent, slightly more expensive **cafeteria** (open July-Aug. M-Th 8:30am-4pm; Sept.-June M-Th 8:30am-6pm). The *Mensa* is located behind the Residenzschloß in the southwest corner. DM3.90 buys a *Schnitzel* with fries or a big salad. Antiques fill **Harlekin,** Kaiserring 40, on the corner of Moltkestr. Sandwiches, pasta, and *Maultaschen* usually cost less than DM16. (☎ 10 33 54. Open M-F 9am-1am, Su 5pm-1am.) Folks of all ages congregate at **Stonehenge Irish Pub,** M4, #8-9, which offers live Irish music a few times a week in the winter and Irish breakfasts every Sunday for DM13.50. (☎ 122 39 49. Open M-Th and Su 12:30pm-1am, F-Sa until 3am.) *Imbiße* and ethnic restaurants abound in the Innenstadt. Blocks G2 through J6 have a particularly dense array. Blocks **G7** and **H7** teem with lots of busy bars.

SIGHTS

Mannheim's real attraction is its bustling commercial area, which centers around **Paradeplatz** at block O1 and extends for several teeming blocks in all directions, though most densely to the north and east. Restaurants, department stores, cafes, and movie theaters combine with the city's funky layout to form an urban space of an intensity rarely found in European roads. The city also has several substantial Old Europe offerings, beginning with its emblematic masterpiece, the **Wasserturm** and surrounding gardens on **Friedrichsplatz.** Finished in 1889 and restored to its original glory in 1956, the elegant sandstone tower topped by a statue of Amphitrite almost lives up to its billing as "the most beautiful water tower in the world." On the south side of the manicured foliage and crystalline fountains of Friedrichspl. crouches the **Kunsthalle**, Moltkestr. 9, a museum surveying art from the mid-19th century to modern times, including works by Manet, Monet, Cézanne, and Beckmann. *(From the station, walk north on Kaiserring. ☎ 293 64 30. Open Tu-W and F-Su 10am-5pm, Th noon-5pm. Hours extended for special exhibitions. DM4, students DM2.)*

The giant **Residenzschloß**, the largest palace of the Baroque period, it now houses the **Universität Mannheim**. In the oddly gaudy **Schloßkirche**, the sleek coffer of the crypt holds Karl Phillip's third wife, Violante von Thurn und Taxis. Even odder, a Masonic symbol and a post horn decorate the altar, suggesting a bizarre link between efficient mail and eventual Masonic world domination. *(☎ 292 28 90. Tours Apr.-Oct. Tu-Su 10am-1pm and 2-5pm; Nov.-Mar. Sa-Su 10am-1pm and 2-5pm. Entrance free. Entrance to Schloß DM5, students DM3.)* The extensive **Reißmuseum** consists of three buildings which contain exhibits on archaeology, ethnology, and natural science. In 2001, expect an exhibit on "Europe in 1000AD". *(Around block C5, northwest of the Schloß. ☎ 293 31 50. Open Tu-W and F-Su 10am-5pm, Th noon-5pm. DM4, students DM2, free on Thursday afternoons. Special exhibits DM14, students DM10.)* The **Jesuitenkirche** was built as a symbol of the Pfalz court's reconversion to Catholicism. The poet Friedrich Hölderlin called it "the most splendid building I have encountered during my travels." This is perhaps poetically licentious, but the church is fantastic. *(Between the museum and the Schloß at block A4. Open daily 8am-noon and 2-6:30pm.)*

On the other side of the Innenstadt, several blocks northeast of the Wasserturm, the 100-acre **Luisenpark** sprouts away. *(☎ 41 00 50. Open daily May-Aug. 9am-9pm; Sept.-Apr. 9am-dusk. DM5, students DM4.)* The greenhouses, flower gardens, aviary, zoo, water sports, mini-golf, frequent afternoon concerts, and eerily self-propelled boat rides offer something for everyone. South of Luisenpark, seven blocks due east of Friedrichspl. on the **Augustanlage**, lies the terrific **Landesmuseum der Technik und Arbeit**, Museumstr. 1, which displays the inner workings of big, creaky, rusty things through fun hands-on exhibits. Get a tetanus shot. In its six stories connected by tunnels and ramps, the museum covers "250 years of technical and social change and industrialization in southwest Germany." There's a working waterwheel, printing press, and BMWs galore. *(Take streetcar #6 (direction: "Neuostheim") to "Landesmuseum." ☎ 429 89. Open Tu, Th, and F 9am-5pm, W 9am-8pm, Sa 10am-5pm, Su 10am-6pm. DM5, students DM3, families DM7.)* Nearby, and behind the ADAC building, is a very early **planetarium**, still projecting spacey visions. *(☎ 41 56 92. Shows Tu 10am and 2:30pm, W and F 2:30 and 7:30pm, Th 2:30pm, Sa-Su 4:30 and 6pm. DM8, students DM6.50.)* The **Museumsschiff "Mannheim"** floats in the Neckar, just by the Kurpfalzbrücke. Once the steamer Mainz, which sank in 1956, it has been retrieved from the Rhein's murky depths and now houses a history of navigation. *(☎ 156 57 56. Open Tu-Su 10am-6pm. DM2, students DM1.)*

SCHWÄBISCHE ALB (SWABIAN JURA)

The limestone plateaus, sharp ridges, and pine-forested valleys that stretch from Tübingen in the north to the Bodensee in the south are collectively known as the Schwäbische Alb, a region often considered an ugly cousin of the adjacent Schwarzwald. Its rough-hewn landscape is scenic yet stubborn, with a harsh climate that often vents its wrath on travelers. The powerful medieval dynasties that held the area found the Swabian peaks perfect sites for fortification, and big-time families like the Hohenstaufens filled the region with castles and abbeys. Now some placid herds of sheep, lofty castle ruins, and the region's name—Staufenland—are all that remain of the their legacy. The **Schwäbische Albstraße** (Swabian Jura Road) bisects the plateau, intersecting with the Romantische Straße at Nördlingen (p. 315). A web of trails serves hikers; maps are available at regional tourist offices in most towns. Train service to many points is roundabout and often incomplete, but bus routes pick up the slack.

SCHWÄBISCH HALL   ☎0791

An urban oasis in the Swabian countryside, Schwäbisch Hall is a colorful gathering of red roofs, cathedral towers, and crumbling stone walls. Its steeply-sloping and many-staired Altstadt is one of the most expansive and well-preserved in Germany, relatively undamaged by the World Wars. Luckily, tourism is still in its infancy in Schwäbisch Hall, leaving the town almost entirely to its residents and the few travelers wandering its ancient streets.

❷ ORIENTATION AND PRACTICAL INFORMATION

From the Schwäbisch Hall train station, walk left with your back to the station and cross Steinbacherstr. via the footbridge, following the signs to the **Altstadt.** Head down the stone steps and footpath toward the river. Turn right on Mauerstr., cross the wooden covered footbridges that connect the islands in the Kocher, and follow the winding cobblestone streets to the **Marktplatz.** Schwäbisch Hall has two **train** stations. The **Hauptbahnhof** is close to town, but the more important station is in **Schwäbisch Hall-Hessental,** on the main rail line to **Stuttgart** (1¼hr., 1 per hr., DM20). Bus #1 and 4B connect the station to Schwäbisch Hall proper (2-3 per hr.; DM2, Sa-Su DM1). All **bus** lines at "Am Spitalbach" stop one block west and a few blocks down from the tourist office. On board, buy a *Tageskarte,* a day pass valid on all buses (DM6). Rent **bikes** at **2-Rad Zügel,** Johanniterstr. 55 (☎97 14 00), on the north side of the Friedensbrücke, or closer to the Hessental area, **Radsport Fiedler,** Kirchstr. 4 (☎93 02 40). Prices start at DM10 per day. For a **taxi** call ☎61 17. Schwäbisch Hall's **tourist office,** Am Markt 9, has maps and books **rooms** for free. (☎75 12 16; fax 75 13 97. Open May-Sept. M-F 9am-6pm, Sa-Su 10am-3pm; Oct.-Apr. M-F 9am-5pm.) The **post office** 74523 Schwäbisch Hall, sits behind the Rathaus (open M-F 8:30am-12:30pm and 2:30-5:30pm, Sa 8:30am-noon). The **postal code** is 74523.

▐▛♫ ACCOMMODATIONS AND FOOD

Schwäbisch Hall's **Jugendherberge (HI),** Langenfelder Weg 5, is beyond the Michaelskirche on the Galgenberg. Follow Crailsheimer Str. up 200m from the church and take a left onto Langenfelder Weg. The hostel is the orange building on the corner. (☎410 50; fax 479 98. Breakfast buffet included. Sheets DM5.50. Reception 4:30-7pm. Curfew 10pm. Members only. Dorm beds DM24, over 26 DM29.) **Gasthof Krone Semir,** Klosterstr. 1, offers basic, clean rooms. Follow the street to the right of Michaelskirche all the way up and around the corner on the right. (☎/fax 60 22. TV in every room. Breakfast included. Singles DM40; doubles DM80.) There is a **Campingplatz** at Steinbacher See. Take bus #4 to "Steinbach/Mitte," then backtrack and follow the signs. (☎29 84. DM7 per person, under 16 DM5. Campsite DM9.)

   You can find an **HLMarkt** three blocks down from the Marktplatz on Neue Str. Restaurants along **Gelbinger Gasse** offer a variety of ethnic specialties, including typically Swabian fare at **Sonne,** Gelbinger Gasse 2 (☎97 08 40), and Greek platters at **Alt Hall,** down the street from Sonne. Across the river, **Taverne bei Vangeli,** Bahnhofstr. 15, serves a bewildering array of Grecian specialities with a sizable vegetarian section. (Entrees DM9-15. ☎67 43. Open daily 11:30am-2pm and 5pm-midnight.) **Warsteiner Ilge,** Im Weiler 2 (☎716 84) is where twentysomethings go to drink delicious yogurt shakes (DM4-6) and beer (DM3-5).

▐♪ SIGHTS AND ENTERTAINMENT

On summer evenings from May to August, the **Freilichtspiele,** a series of plays running the gamut from Shakespeare to Brecht, are performed on the steps of the Michaelskirche and in the imitation **Globe** theater. Contact the tourist office for tickets (DM20-50, student discounts up to 30%, some tickets DM6-10). On the Saturday, Sunday, and Monday of Pentecost, Schwäbisch Hall celebrates the **Kuchen- und Brunnenfest,** during which locals don 16th-century costumes to dance traditional jigs. During the **Sommernachtsfest** (the last Sa in August), 30,000 little candles light patterns along the Ackeranlage.

ALTSTADT. Three times charred by flames, Hall's half-timbered center was built in the 18th century. *(Use the church tower as a beacon. From the Schwäbisch Hall-Hessental train station, take bus #1 to "Spitalbach Ost," the last stop (20min.). DM2.)* The convex **Baroque Rathaus** confronts the Romanesque tower and Gothic nave of the **Michaelskirche,** first built in 1156, which perches atop a steep set of stone stairs. The church is Lutheran due to the town's pride and joy, Johannes Brenz, the reformer who converted Hall to Protestantism in the 1520s. Organ music often echoes in the church, rattling the pile of human bones and skulls in the medieval ossuary, an underground room behind the altar. The Turmzimmer atop the church's tower provides an great view of the town. *(Open Mar. to mid-Nov. M 2-5pm, Tu-Sa 9am-noon and 2-5pm, Su 11am-noon and 2-5pm; mid-Nov. to Feb. Tu-Su 11am-noon and 2-3pm. Tower DM1.)*

A number of narrow, half-timbered alleys wind their way outwards from Marktpl. To the east, Obere Herrngasse leads to the eight-story Romanesque **Keckenturm,** on Keckenhof, which houses the **Hällisch-Fränkisches Museum.** Located in the medieval tower, the museum contains a smashing Baroque room and extensive exhibits on the history of Schwäbisch Hall, much of which is recounted through the museum's collection of 18th-century bullet-riddled practice targets. *(☎ 75 12 89. Open Tu-Su 10am-5pm, W 10am-8pm. Tours in German W 6:30pm and Su 11am. Free.)* The covered **Henkersbrücke,** near Mauer- and Bahnhofstr., delivers a view of Schwäbisch Hall's Kocher River. In the northern part of the Altstadt, the **Gelbinger Gasse** is the town's most beautiful section. For a relaxing walk along the river, the gardens of the **Ackeranlage** back the architectural vista with tall, shady trees.

KLOSTER GROßCOMBURG. Above town, Steinbach, the only suburb of Hall that remained Catholic during the Reformation, appropriately holds Kloster Großcomburg, a former castle and Benedictine monastery dating from the 11th century. The 460m wall provides peep holes for views of the valley, but you must take a tour (in German only) to see the museum and Midas-touched interior of the Baroque church, reconstructed in the 18th century. *(Take bus #4B to "Steinbach/Mitte," cross the street, and head uphill away from town and around the curve for 100m until you reach the parking lot and trailhead. ☎ 93 81 85. Tours Apr.-Oct. Tu-F at 10, 11am, 2, 3, and 4pm, Sa-Su at 2, 3, and 4pm; Nov.-Mar. call ahead. DM4, students DM2. Castle grounds free.)*

HOHENLOHER FREILANDMUSEUM. The Hohenloher Freilandmuseum in Museumsdorf Wackershofen reenacts the life of an old German agricultural village with 50 authentic low-ceilinged houses in the middle of scenic countryside. Let the fumes from the haystacks guide you to pigs, sheep, and cows. Watch Schnapps being made. *Prost! (Ride bus #7 to "Wackershofen" (direction: Gailenkirchen), head down the path slightly before the stop, and follow the signs. ☎ 97 10 10. Open July-Aug. daily 9am-6pm; May-June and Sept. Tu-Su 9am-6pm; Apr. and Oct. Tu-Su 10am-5:30pm. DM9, students DM5.)*

SCHWÄBISCH GMÜND   ☎ 07171

On the northern cusp of the range, Schwäbisch Gmünd provides a good base for excursions into the region. Billed as the oldest town in the Staufenland, it's been a center for gold and silversmithing since the 14th century. Beautifully wrought jewelry can be found in many shops in the town center, which bristles with Baroque plaster facades and half-timbered buildings from the 15th and 16th centuries.

To reach the cafe-filled Marktplatz from the train station, turn left onto Lorchenstr., using the pedestrian underpass to cross the first street, and cross the street in front of you which becomes Ledergasse and eventually leads to the square. Farther southwest, Münsterplatz hosts the 14th-century **Heiligkreuzmünster** (Holy Cross Cathedral), the oldest church with a Gothic nave in Southern Germany. The architect Peter Parler, born in Gmünd in 1330, designed one wing and later replicated it in his plan of Prague's principal cathedral. An engineer must have fallen asleep at the drafting table, however, because in the late 1400s, the towers of the church collapsed, and the boxy compromise renders the building decidedly non-ecclesiastic in appearance. Perhaps to compensate for this shortcoming, the powers-that-be have covered the exterior with frightening statues that protrude horizontally in every direction. The bizarre collection ranges from screaming, tortured human figures to fanged beasts. The **Silberwaren- und Bijouteriemuseum,** across from the tourist office, features silversmiths tooling silver in the traditional style each Sunday. The museum and its staff exhibit the cluttered detritus of silver-, gold-, and leathersmiths. (☎389 10. Open M-Sa 2-5pm, Su 11am-5pm. Tour 2pm in German. DM5, students DM2.) The 16th-century **Kornhaus,** an old grain storage building off Marktpl., two blocks behind the Rathaus, now houses the **tourist office.** The staff **books rooms** for free and offers many maps. (☎603 42 50; fax 603 42 99. Open M-F 9am-5:30pm, Sa 8am-noon.) The **post office,** 73525 Schwäbisch Gmünd, is opposite the train station (open M-F 8am-noon and 2:30-5:30pm, Sat 8am-noon).

Sadly, Schwäbisch Gmünd has no hostel, though there is one nearby in Hohenstaufen (see below). **Gasthof Weißer Ochsen,** Parlerstr. 47 (☎28 12), has decent singles (DM38) and one double (DM70). An **open-air market** fills Münsterpl. on Wednesday and Saturday (7am-noon), while **supermarkets** can be found a block north along Bocksgasse. **Gasthaus Zum Lamm,** Rinderbacher Gasse 19, has a daily menu of Swabian specialties for DM11-26. (☎26 61. Open M 4:30pm-midnight, Tu 10:30am-2pm and 6pm-midnight, W-F 10:30am-2pm and 4:30pm-midnight, Sa and Su 11am-2pm.) **Gasthaus zur Kanne,** Rinderbacher Gasse 17, serves filling portions of Italian dishes for DM8-30. (☎25 18. Open daily 11am-2pm, 5pm-midnight. Closed several times a month for holidays.)

THE KAISERBERGE

South of Schwäbisch Gmünd lie the three conical peaks, **Hohenstaufen, Hohenrechberg,** and **Stuifen,** which make up the **Dreikaiserberge.** Hohenstaufen was named after the castle that once graced its summit, built by the Hohenstaufen family. Only the castle's foundations remain, but the panoramic view of the entire valley, as far as the Schwarzwald or the range of Schwabian Alps, is spectacular, including a glimpse of tomorrow's weather in the distance. To reach Hohenstaufen from Schwäbisch Gmünd, take bus #11 or 12 to "Göppingen ZOB" from the bus station platform 4, then transfer to bus #13 and get off at "Hohenstaufen Jugendherberge" (1 per hr.; last bus leaves at 7pm). Bus #13 goes directly there on Sundays and holidays, but the second and final bus rolls away at noon. If you catch it, get off at "Juhe" and put yourself right in the middle of the hills around **Jugendherberge Hohenstaufen,** Schottengasse 45, which has six- and eight-bed rooms on a gently sloping plain. (☎(07165) 438; fax 14 18. Breakfast included. Sheets DM5.50. Curfew 10pm. Call ahead. Dorm beds DM23, over 26 DM28.) The Jugendherberge is up and to the right of the bus station. The footpath to the top begins to the left of the Jugendherberge; all diverging upward paths lead to the Hohenstaufen, though degrees of steepness vary. Hiking maps (DM2) are available from the tiny Hohenstaufer museum up the street from the Youth Hostel (9am-12pm and 2pm-5pm, daily from Mar. 15-Nov.15; museum free).

Another prime hiking trail winds around **Hohenrechberg** to the east, and boasts a mysterious **castle ruin** and a Baroque **Wallfahrtskirche** (pilgrimage church) at its summit. The **Burgruine** is halfway up; pay DM3 (DM1 for students) to catch a breathtaking glimpse of the Schwäbische Alb from inside the castle's walls. Hohenstaufen is best viewed from the Burgruine; Stuifen is visible from the church. To reach Hohenrechberg, take bus #4 (direction: "Wißgoblingen") to "Rechberg Gasthof Rad." Walk up Hohenstaufenstr.; the trail starts between the Volksbank and Jägerhof. The last bus to Schwäbisch Gmünd leaves around 6pm. The **tourist office** in Schwäbisch Gmünd (see p. 351) has a guide to the hiking trails. All buses to the Kaiserberge depart from Schwäbisch Gmünd's train station, and most also stop at Marktpl.

ULM ☎ 0731

When Napoleon designated the Danube as the border between Württemberg and Bavaria, Ulm was split into two distinct cities, Ulm and Neu-Ulm. Brochures claim that they are Siamese twins, but it's pretty clear from a tourist's perspective that Ulm got the good end of the deal. Residents of both cities may proudly whistle the "Blue Danube" as they promenade along the river, but only those in Ulm can brag about living in the city with the tallest church steeple in the world. The towering peak of the *Münster* looms over every corner of town and inspires a lively pedestrian district crowded with shoppers and beer-drinking people-watchers. Ulm also resonates with scientific history: both Einstein and Albrecht Berblinger, "tailor of Ulm." Berblinger, tailor by day, inventor by night, made one of the first serious attempts at human flight in 1811 when he tried to cross the Danube on his "kite-wings" and nearly drowned. Perhaps to discourage any other residents from such ventures, the city constructed many charming bridges over the Venetian-style canals leading from the river. These, the towering *Münster*, and the exuberance in the streets make Ulm a very pleasant excursion.

🔢 ORIENTATION AND PRACTICAL INFORMATION

Ulm is connected by **train** to all of southern Germany, with trains to **Munich** (1¼hr., 1 per hr., DM40) and **Stuttgart** (1hr., 2 per hr., DM26). Rent **bikes** from **Ralf Reich,** Frauenstr. 34. (☎211 79. DM15 per day, DM30 per weekend, DM80 per week; 15% discount with *BahnCard.*) The contrast between the strikingly modern white building that houses the **tourist office,** Münsterpl. 50, and the towering, ornate spire of the adjacent *Münster* epitomizes Ulm's strange unity of past and present. The helpful office sells maps of the Innenstadt (DM0.50), finds **rooms** for free (rooms start at DM40), and offers daily guided tours of Ulm. (☎161 28 30; fax 161 16 41; email info@tourismus.ulm.de; www.ulm.de. Open M-F 9am-6pm, Sa 9am-1pm.) The *Automat* outside sells a list of accommodations (DM1). Satisfy pharmaceutical fancies at the **Neue Apotheke,** Bahnhofstr. 13, or check the posted list to find out which **pharmacies** in town are open after hours. (☎600 74. Open M-F 8am-7pm, Sa 8am-4pm.) The **post office,** Bahnhofpl. 2, 89073 Ulm, is left of the station (open M-F 8am-6pm, Sa 8am-1pm).

🏠🍴 ACCOMMODATIONS AND FOOD

Ulm's **Jugendherberge Geschwister Scholl (HI),** Grimmelfinger Weg 45, looks like a high school, only with sparkling facilities, communal showers, and four- to eight-bed rooms. Take bus #1, 3, 8, or 10 from the bus platform at the train station in front of McDonald's to "Ehinger Tor," and change to bus #4 or 8 (direction: "Kuhberg"). Walk up the sidewalk and through the underpass just up the road, then follow the *Sport-Gaststätte* signs and go down a set of stairs on the right side of the building. Cut through the parking lot to the left of the basketball courts and follow the lone *Jugendherberge* sign. The hostel is named in memory of a brother and sister who were executed in 1943 for conspiring against Hitler. (☎38 44 55; fax 38 45 11. Breakfast included. Sheets DM5.50. Reception 5-9:45pm. Curfew 10pm. Dorm beds DM24, over 26 DM29.) **Münster-Hotel,** Münsterpl. 14, is located to the left of the *Münster*. Relish small, yet adequate rooms, but beware the early morning bells. (☎/fax 641 62. Breakfast included. Singles DM45, with shower DM65; doubles with shower DM90, with bath DM110.) Across the river in Neu-Ulm, **Gasthof Rose,** Kasernstr. 42a, has lovely rooms in a quiet district. (☎/fax 778 03. Breakfast included. Singles from DM40, doubles from DM80.)

A **farmer's market** springs up on Münsterpl. on Wednesday and Saturday mornings (8am-12pm). Ulm's restaurants reflect the culinary influences of

both Schwaben and Bayern, including the unusual *Schupfnudel*, a half-potato, half-wheat noodle. Cheap and greasy *Imbiß* fare lines the way to the *Münster* along **Bahnhofstr.** and **Hirschstr.** For the most variety and the densest collection of restaurants, the territory between **Neue Str.** and the river is prime grazing ground. **Restaurant zur Zill,** Schwörhausgasse 19, serves regional specialties in an inviting local-joint atmosphere. Meals run DM9-14. (☎ 659 77. Open M-F 11am-2pm and 5pm-midnight, Sa 11am-2pm and 5pm-1am.) Close to the *Münster*, **Zum Anker,** Rabengasse 2 (☎ 632 97), has a "daily recommendations" (*Tagesempfehlung*) menu that offers cheap and filling Bavarian and Schwabian specialties (DM8-10).

 SIGHTS

At 161m, the steeple topping the **Münster** is the tallest in the world. During the Middle Ages, members of guilds and other wealthy men decided to fund the building of a cathedral in their city, and so in 1377 the foundation stone was laid. Unfortunately, its conceivers and many successive generations passed away before the enormous steeple was completed 513 years later in 1890. When Ulm converted to Protestantism in 1530, many altars and ornate decorations were destroyed. Of those saved is *The Man of Sorrows*, a famous stone sculpture of Christ by 15th-century sculptor Hans Multscher, situated next to the front portal of the cathedral. Inside the looming Gothic walls, wooden choir stalls carved by Jörg Syrlin the Elder form a community of emotional busts. Climb the 768 dizzying corkscrew steps of the spire on a clear day to see the Alps. (☎ 15 11 39. *Church open daily Apr.-June and Sept. 8am-6:45pm; July-Aug. 8am-7:45pm; Oct. 8am-5:45pm; Nov.-Jan. 9am-4:45pm; Mar. 9am-5:45pm. Tower closes 1hr. earlier. DM4, children DM2.50. Free summer organ concerts M-Sa 11am, Su 11:30am.*)

Nearby, the white building that houses the tourist office is also home to the **Stadthaus.** Designed by New York architect Richard Meier, its postmodern style, in conspicuous contrast to the Gothic *Münster*, raised great controversy among Ulm's residents. The basement holds interesting archaeological and historical exhibits on the Münsterpl. and the painstakingly slow construction of the *Münster*. (*Open M-W and F-Sa 9am-6pm, Th 9am-8pm, Su 11am-6pm.*) Towards the river on Neue Str., the **Rathaus,** built in 1370, is decorated with brilliantly-colored murals and an elaborate astronomical clock, both dating from 1540. The old **Fischerviertel** (fishermen's quarter), down Kronengasse from the *Rathaus*, is full of classical half-timbered houses, narrow cobblestoned streets, and canal-spanning footbridges. Don't miss the **Schiefes Haus** (crooked house) at Schwörhausgasse 6. One of the oldest houses in Ulm, it now serves as a hotel.

On the other side of the Rathaus is the **Ulmer Museum,** Marktpl. 9, which features outstanding exhibits on both contemporary art and the archaeological past of the region. (☎ 161 43 00. *Open Tu-W and F-Su 11am-5pm, Th 11am-8pm. DM5, students DM3. Free on F. Special exhibits DM8, students and seniors DM5.*) The **Deutsches Brotmuseum,** Salzstadelgasse 10, documents 6,000 years of bread-making and waxes philosophical about "the *Leitmotiv* of Man and Bread." (☎ 699 55. *Open daily 11am-5pm, W 10am-8:30pm. Last entrance 1hr. before closing. DM5, students DM4.*) Well curated, it's a cultural history fan's dream come true. Don't miss "cake—the pride of the housewife" or "corn and bread in arts and crafts." One can easily overlook the tiny monument marking **Albert Einstein's birthplace,** donated to Ulm by India. It's on Bahnhofstr., up the street from the train station and across from the *McDonald's*. Einstein's home long ago gave way to a glass-and-chrome bank. Every year on the penultimate Monday in July, the mayor of Ulm takes the stand at the **Schwörhaus** (Oath House) to carry on a centuries-old tradition by swearing allegiance to the town's 1397 constitution, during much excessive drinking on the Danube.

STUTTGART   ☎0711

Leave your half-timbered houses and *lederhosen* at home; *Porsche, Daimler-Benz*, and a host of other corporate thoroughbreds keep Stuttgart speeding along in the fast lane. After almost complete destruction in WWII, Stuttgart was rebuilt in a thoroughly modern, functional, and uninspiring style. Thankfully, Stuttgart's verdant setting of forested hills, leafy parks, and lush vineyards provides a welcome tranquility to the busy capital of Baden-Württemberg.

▐ GETTING THERE AND GETTING AROUND

Flights: Flughafen Stuttgart (☎94 80). Take S-Bahn #2 or 3 to get to the city (30min.; one-way DM4.70).

Trains: The transportation hub of southwestern Germany, Stuttgart has direct rail links to most major German cities. Trains roll to **Frankfurt** (1½hr., 1 per hr., DM88), **Munich** (2½hr., 1 per hr., DM73), **Berlin** (5½hr., every 2hr., DM256), **Basel** (3hr., 1 per hr., DM85), and **Paris** (6hr., 3 direct trains per day, DM136). Call ☎(0180) 599 66 33 for 24hr. schedule information.

Ferries: Neckar-Personen-Schiffahrt (☎54 99 70 60; www.neckar-kaeptn.de). Boats leave from the Bad Cannstatt dock, by Wilhelma Zoo. Take U-Bahn #14 (direction "Remseck") to "Wilhelma." Ships cruise to towns along the Neckar (1-2 per day) from May to late Oct. Round-trip DM8-50. Watch out for older folks dancing the polka on board; bring your accordion or your earplugs. **Harbor tours** daily at 11am, 2, and 4:15pm (2hr., DM18, DM9 for students).

Public Transportation: Find the name of the stop you're going to in the alphabetical list of stations and punch the corresponding number to receive a ticket. Single ride DM3.20-9.60. A 4-ride Mehrfahrkarte (DM10.40-36.40) saves 10% off single-ride rates. A Kurzstrecke (DM2) covers distances of under 2km, a good value when traveling between two points in the city center. Or buy a Tageskarte, valid on all trains and buses for 24hr. (DM12). Nachtbus (night bus) stops are marked with purple and yellow signs. The best deal for visitors is a 3-day tourist pass, valid on the U-Bahn (DM13) or the entire transit system (DM20); purchase these at the tourist office. There is also an information desk (☎194 49) at the tourist office near the Hauptbahnhof; look for the desk under the VVS sign.

Car Rental: All have offices in the station near track 16. **Hertz** (☎226 29 21) open M-F 7:30am-9pm, Sa 8am-5pm, Su 11am-7pm. **Europcar** (☎224 46 30) open M-Sa 7:30am-9pm, Su 8:30am-9pm. **Sixt/Budget** (☎223 78 22 23) open M-F 8am-9pm, Sa 8am-5pm, Su 10am-6pm. **Avis** (☎223 72 58) open M-F 7am-9pm, Sa 8am-4pm.

Bike Rental: Rent a Bike, Kronenstr. 17 (☎209 90), in Hotel Unger. DM8 per hr., DM25 per day. Bikes are allowed on the U- and S-Bahn M-F 8:30am-4pm and 6:30pm until closing and Sa-Su all day; they're forbidden on buses and streetcars.

Mitfahrzentrale: 3 locations. **Stuttgart West,** Lerchenstr. 65 (☎636 80 36). Bus #42 (direction: "Schreiberstr.") to "Rosenberg/Johannesstr." **Hauptstätter Str. 154** (☎60 36 06). U-Bahn #14 (direction: "Heslach/Vogelrain") to "Marienplatz." **Zaeim-Bashi,** Calwerstr.38 (☎226 03 71). Open M-F 9am-6pm, Sa 9am-2pm, Su 11am-2pm.

✳▐ ORIENTATION AND PRACTICAL INFORMATION

Along the Neckar valley lies the heart of Stuttgart—an enormous pedestrian zone where shops and restaurants stretch as far as the eye can see. **Königstraße** and the smaller **Calwerstraße** are the main pedestrian thoroughfares; from the train station, both are accessible by the underground at **Arnulf-Klett-Passage.** To the left lies the tranquil **Schloßgarten,** to the right the thriving business sector, including **Rotebühlplatz** two blocks right from the end of Königstr. A number of discount packages and passes are available to tourists; among these is the **Stuttcard** (DM25), which offers three days of inner city transportation, admission to seven museums, and discounts for guided tours, theaters, the zoo, mineral baths, and other sights. Also

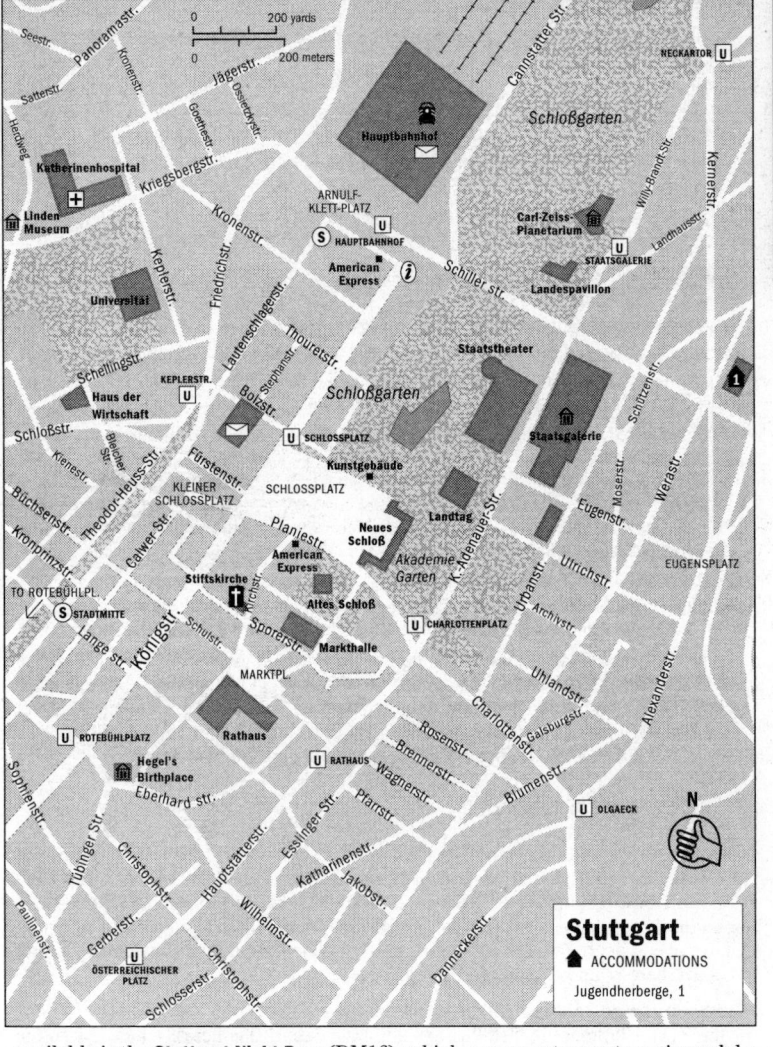

Stuttgart
🏠 ACCOMMODATIONS
Jugendherberge, 1

available is the **Stuttgart Night Pass** (DM16), which covers entrance to various clubs and free drinks at others. Call the tourist office for more information.

Tourist Offices: I-Punkt, Königstr. 1 (☎222 80; fax 222 82 53; email info@stuttgart.tourist.de; www.stuttgart-tourist.de), directly in front of the down escalator into the Klett-Passage. They may be busy, but they book **rooms** for free, sell excellent maps (DM1), and distribute bus and train schedules. The *Monatsspiegel* (DM3.50) lists museum hours, cultural events, and musical performances, and includes a guide to food and nightlife. Open May-Oct. M-F 9:30am-8:30pm, Sa 9:30am-6pm, Su and public holidays 11am-6pm; Nov.-Apr. same hours but Su and holidays 1-6pm. **tips 'n' trips,** Rotebühlpl. 26 (☎222 27 30; fax 222 27 33; email jugendinformation@tips-n-trips.de; www.tips-n-trips.de), in the underground U-Bahn passage at Theodor-Heuss-Str. and Fritz-Elsas-Str near the Rotebühlstr. exit. The knowledgeable, helpful staff hands out reams of youth-oriented pamphlets about travel and the Stuttgart scene. A great resource. Open M-F noon-7pm, Sa 10am-2pm. Sells ISICs.

Consulates: South Africa, Erich-Herion-Str. 27 (☎58 64 41). **UK,** Breite Str. 2 (☎16 26 90).

American Express: Schillerpl. 4 (☎162 49 33; fax 223 87 50), near Schloßplatz. Holds mail, cashes traveler's checks, and doubles as a travel agency for members. A **second branch,** Arnulf-Klett-Platz 1 (☎226 92 67; fax 223 95 44), holds mail and cashes checks. Open M-F 9:30am-1pm and 2-6pm, Sa 9:30am-12:30pm.

Bookstore: English Shop, Schellingstr. 11 (☎226 09 02). Specializes in all things British, sells classics and current best-sellers, and rents English videos. **Buchhaus Wittwer,** Königstr. 30 (☎250 70), sells books in English. Open M-F 9:30am-8pm, Sa 9am-4pm.

Gay and Lesbian Resources: Weißenburg, Weißenburgstr. 28a (☎640 44 92), is Stuttgart's gay and lesbian center. Office open M-F 7:30-9:30pm. Cafe open 3-10pm.

Erlkönig, Nesenbachstr. 52 (☎63 91 39), is a popular gay and lesbian bookstore. Open M-F 10am-1:30pm and 3-8pm, Sa 10am-4pm.

Women's Resources: Fraueninformationzentrum, Landhausstr. 62 (☎26 18 91).

AIDS Resources: Hölderlinpl. 5a (☎22 46 90). Open M-F 10am-noon and M-Th 2-5pm. Anonymous hotline (☎194 11) open M and Th-F 6:30-9:30pm.

Laundromat: SB Waschsalon, Kienbachstr. 16. S-Bahn #13 to "Kienbachstr." Wash DM8, dry DM2 per 10min. Open daily 8am-10pm.

Emergency: ☎110. **Police,** Hahnemannstr. 1, ☎899 01. **Fire,** ☎112.

Hospital: Bürgerhospital, Tunzhofer Str. 14-16 (☎253 00).

Pharmacy: Internationale, Königstr. 70 (☎22 47 80). Open M-W and F 8:30am-6:30pm, Th 8:30am-8:30pm, Sa 8:30am-2pm.

Post Office: At the **Hauptbahnhof,** 70001 Stuttgart. Open M-F 8am-7pm, Sa 8am-12pm. The post office at **Bolzstr. 3** does not hold mail. Open M-F 9am-8pm, Sa 9am-2pm. Another branch exists at **Blumenstr. 8.** Open M-F 9am-6:30pm, Sa 9am-1pm.

Internet Access: tips 'n' trips offers the best deal in town at DM5 per hr. for students (see **Tourist Offices,** above). If you don't want to stand in line for their lone computer, visit the top floor of the **Kaufhof** department store near the train station. DM3 per 30min. Open M-F 9:30am-9pm, Sa 9am-4pm. Or try the 3rd floor of the **Karstadt** store across the way. DM5 per 30min. Open M-F 9:30am-8pm, Sa 9am-4pm.

◤ ACCOMMODATIONS

Most of Stuttgart's budget beds are located on the two ridges surrounding the downtown area and are easily accessible by streetcar. Hotels around the pedestrian zone and train station cater to customers used to paying top Mark—call ahead for better deals. Contact **tips 'n' trips** (see **Tourist Offices,** above) for information on cheap accommodations in Stuttgart. Though a commute away, the hostel in **Ludwigsburg** is also a good alternative (see p. 361).

Jugendherberge Stuttgart (HI), Haußmannstr. 27 (☎24 15 83; fax 236 10 41). Take the "ZOB" exit from the Klett-Passage and walk through the Schloßgarten. Exit to the right of the statue of two men in an uncomfortable position and cross Willy-Brandt-Str. Continue up the path past the police station and climb the staircase on the other side of Schnützerstr. Or take streetcar #15 (direction: "Heumaden") to "Eugensplatz" and go down Kernerstr., the street starting at the *Apotheke;* the entrance is about 5min. down Kernerstr. A lively mix of nationalities shacks up in slightly crowded 6-bed rooms, most with spectacular city views. Often full; *always* call a week ahead. Breakfast included. Sheets DM5.50. Reception 7-9am and noon-11:30pm. Lockout 9am-noon. Strict curfew 11:30pm. Doors open briefly at 1am. Dorm beds DM24, over 26 DM29.

Jugendgästehaus Stuttgart, Richard-Wagner-Str. 2 (☎24 11 32 and 248 97 30). Streetcar #15 (direction: "Ruhbank") to "Bubenbad." Continue in the direction of the streetcar on the right side of the street and veer right immediately around the corner; the hostel is on the right, situated in a quiet residential neighborhood. Spotless rooms with a great view, though those in the basement are slightly less spectacular. Breakfast included. Dinner DM8. Key deposit DM20. Reception M-F 9am-8pm, Sa-Su 11am-8pm.

No curfew. Singles DM40, with bath DM45, with bath and shower DM50; DM35 per additional person, with bath and shower add DM10.

Hotel Espenlaub, Charlottenstr. 27 (☎21 09 10; fax 210 91 55). Take U-Bahn #5 or 6 or streetcar #15 or 16 to "Olgaeck." High on the price scale, but a great location and nice accommodations. Breakfast, TV, phone, and bath included. Singles start at DM60; doubles DM100.

Camping: Campingplatz Cannstatter Wasen, Mercedesstr. 40 (☎55 66 96; fax 55 74 54), on the river in Bad Cannstatt. S-Bahn #1, 2, or 3 to "Bad Cannstatt." Exit through the back of the station, and follow the signs for "Wasen." After the tunnel, head diagonally left across the never-ending parking lot. Reception 7am-noon and 2-10pm. DM9 per person; DM4 per child. Campsite DM6-8. Car DM4.

◘ FOOD

Due to a sizable contingent of guest workers, Stuttgart's culinary scene is heartily spiced up by Greek, Turkish, African, and Asian restaurants. But the cuisine of the Schwaben region is itself one of the most appealing varieties of German food. *Spätzle* (thick noodles) and *Maultaschen* (pasta pockets filled with meat and spinach) are especially popular. For basic fruits and veggies as well as staples like bread and cheese, head to the **Wochenmarkt** on Marktpl. and Schillerpl. (open Th and Sa 8am-3pm). For **groceries,** try the basement of **Kaufhof,** near the end of Königstr. on Eberhardstr. (open M-F 9am-8pm, Sa 9am-4pm).

Mensa, Holzgartenstr. 11. From the train station, take Kriegsbergstr. to Holzgartenstr. Turn left and go down the right side of the street over the underpass; the cafeteria is on the right. Or take bus #40, 42, or 43 to "Hegelplatz." A plain but functional establishment where quantity compensates for quality. Meals DM4-5. Open during the semester M-F 11:15am-2:00; the rest of the year M-F 11:15am-1:30pm.

Iden, Eberhardstr. 1 (☎23 59 89). U-Bahn to "Rathaus." Good vegetarian fare served cafeteria-style. Fifty kinds of salads (DM2.78 per 100g, which adds up quickly), various noodle and potato dishes, served in a bright atmosphere with lots of Nordic furniture. More desserts than you can imagine. Open M-F 11am-9pm, Sa 10:30am-5pm.

Weinhaus Stetter, Rosenstr. 32 (☎24 01 63). U-Bahn to "Charlottenplatz," walk down Esslinger Str., and take a left onto Rosenstr. This local favorite offers intriguing Swabian specialties (DM7-9) and an incredible wine selection (DM5-7). Open M-F 3-11pm, Sa 10am-3am. Kitchen open M-Sa 3-11pm.

Akademie der schönsten Künste, Charlottenstr. 5 (☎24 24 36). U-Bahn to "Charlottenplatz." High ceilings, art-covered walls, a garden, and fewer seats than necessary at such a paragon of European sophistication. Considered the perfect date restaurant among trendy Stuttgarters. Light fare isn't the cheapest (DM4-15), but the ambience makes up for it. Open M-F 9am-1am, Sa-Su 9am-6pm.

SIGHTS

▨ MINERALBÄDER. Stuttgart harbors amazing mineral baths, formed from the most productive mineral springs in Western Europe. The 22 million liters of spring water pumped out every day contain chemical combinations with curative powers. All baths offer a spectacular array of pools, saunas, and showers—the perfect remedy for budget traveler exhaustion. Most require a swim cap and swimsuit. Loll in the **Mineralbad Leuze,** an official health care facility. *(Am Leuzebad 2-6. U-Bahn to "Wilhelma." Cross the pedestrian footbridge and head toward the volcano-like fountains. ☎216 42 10. Open daily 6am-9pm. Day card DM25, students DM16; 3hr. soak DM15, students DM11; 1¼hr. DM9.50, students DM6. Massage DM36.)* **Mineralbad Berg** is a little less posh. *(Am Schwanenplatz 9. U-Bahn #1 or 14 or streetcar #2 to "Mineralbäder," then walk behind the U-Bahn station toward the river. ☎26 10 60. Open M-F 6am-7:30pm, Sa 6am-6:30pm, Su 6am-12:30pm. Day card DM10. Massage DM30.)*

SCHLOßGARTEN. Almost 20% of Stuttgart is under a land preservation order, resulting in something known as "the green U," much of which composes the **Schloßgarten,** Stuttgart's principal municipal park. Running from the station southward to the Neues Schloß and northeast to the Neckar, the Schloßgarten is crammed with fountains and beautifully tended flower gardens. An 8km-long pedestrian bridge beginning at the Schloßgarten weaves a path above the city without ever leaving the parks. The north end of the Schloßgarten contains the expansive **Rosensteinpark,** which also holds the **Wilhelma,** a large zoological and botanical garden that claims 9,000 species of animals and plants. *(Take U-Bahn #14 or Bus #52, 55, or 56 to "Wilhelma." ☎540 20. Open daily Mar.-Oct. 8:15am-5pm; Nov.-Feb. 8:15am-4pm. DM14, students DM7; after 4pm and from Nov.-Feb. DM9, students DM4.50.)*

SCHLOßPLATZ. The Schloßgarten runs to **Schloßplatz,** off Königstr., upon which reposes the elegant Baroque **Neues Schloß,** now home to stodgy bureaucrats and the 40 or so mythological statues on its roof. The 16th-century **Altes Schloß,** across the street on Schillerplatz, offers a graceful, colonnaded Renaissance courtyard.

CARL-ZEISS-PLANETARIUM. Stuttgart's stargazers get their fix at the Karl-Zeiss-Planetarium, enjoying shows with informative German voice-overs, cool visual effects (comets shooting, black holes sucking), and cliché background music. Karl Zeiss is perhaps the most famous telescope manufacturer in the galaxy. *(Willy-Brandt-Str. 25. U-Bahn #1, 9, or 14, or streetcar #2 or 4 to "Staatsgalerie," or walk from the south exit of the train station into the Schloßgarten for about 200m. ☎162 92 15. Shows Tu and Th 10am and 3pm; W and F 10am, 3, and 8pm; Sa-Su 2, 4, and 6pm. DM9, students DM5.)*

HEGEL'S BIRTHPLACE. To interface with the *Weltgeist* (world-spirit), head to Hegel's birthplace, which is a few doors down from a busy porn shop. The house provides a thorough exegesis of the philosopher's life through letters, manuscripts, and notes. *(Eberhardstr. 53, a couple blocks east from the end of Königstr. Take S-Bahn #1-6, U-Bahn #14, or streetcar #2 or 4 to "Rotebühlplatz (Stadtmitte)." ☎216 67 33. Open Tu and F 10am-5:30pm, Th 10am-6:30pm.)*

🏛 MUSEUMS

A plethora of outstanding and diverse museums compensates for Stuttgart's paucity of monumental history. In addition to the magnificent art galleries and archaeology exhibits, the city offers displays on some of the more hedonistic aspects of everyday life: beer, cars, and playing cards. The monthly *Monatsspiegel*, available at the tourist office, lists information on all museums.

■ **STAATSGALERIE STUTTGART.** An absolutely superb collection housed in two wings: the stately paintings in the **old wing** date from the Middle Ages to the 19th century, while the **new wing,** a colorful stroke of postmodern daring, contains an excellent collection of moderns including Picasso, Kadinsky, Beckmann, and Dalí. *(Konrad-Adenauer-Str. 30-32. ☎212 40 50. Open W and F-Su 10am-6pm, Tu and Th 10am-8pm. DM5, students DM3.)*

■ **MERCEDES-BENZ MUSEUM.** A must for car-lovers. The original workshop where Herr Daimler built the first generation of *Mercedes-Benzes* now houses an elaborately modern exhibit; visitors ooh and aah at a century's worth of gleaming models. Hold high-tech "soundsticks" to your ear and learn all about the little German engine that could (soundsticks in 4 languages). Tight security weeds out BMW spies; you even need to take a special bus from the parking lot to the entrance. *(Mercedesstr. 137, in Stuttgart-Untertürkheim. S-Bahn #1 to "Daimlerstadion"; walk left under the bridge and follow the signs. ☎172 25 78. Open Tu-Su 9am-5pm. Free.)*

LINDENMUSEUM STUTTGART. The museum features in-depth ethnological collections from America, the South Seas, Africa, and Asia. Western hegemonists can satisfy their curiosity about the exotic with films, lectures, and discussions.

(Hegelpl. 1. 10 min. west of the train station along Kriegsbergstr. Take bus #40, 42, or 43 to "Hegelplatz." ☎ *202 24 56. Open Tu, Th, and Sa-Su 10am-5pm, W 10am-8pm, F 10am-1pm. Free, except for special exhibits.)*

SCHWÄBISCHES BRAUEREIMUSEUM. Only in Germany could an entire museum be devoted to beer. Five millennia of the beverage's history culminate in a brew-it-yourself exhibit of current beer production. Everything's free but the samples. *(Robert-Koch-Str. 12, in Stuttgart-Vaihingen. U-Bahn #1, 3, or 6 or S-Bahn #1, 2, or 3 to "Vaihingen Bahnhof." Walk along Vollmoellerstr. and turn right onto Robert-Koch-Str.* ☎ *737 02 01. Open Th-Su 10:30am-5:30pm. DM3.50-4 per beer.)*

WÜRTTEMBERGISCHES LANDESMUSEUM. Located in the *Altes Schloß*, the museum details the Swabian region and people, with an emphasis on the abundant local archaeology. Excellent exhibits on Bronze Age Celtic metalwork, along with fascinating skulls, crown jewels, and Roman pillars. *(Schillerpl. 6.* ☎ *279 34 00. Open Tu 10am-1pm, W-Su 10am-5pm. Wheelchair accessible. DM5, students DM3.)*

KUNSTGEBÄUDE. Houses both the **Württembergischer Kunstverein** (☎ 22 33 70) and the **Galerie der Stadt** (☎ 216 21 88). Contemporary art in a variety of media. *(Schloßpl. 2, directly across from the Altes Schloß. Both museums open Tu and Th-Su 11am-6pm, W 11am-8pm. Free, but special exhibits usually DM8, students DM5.)*

PORSCHEMUSEUM. A glorified showroom, but Porsche fans will enjoy gawking at this large gathering of sexy curves. *(Porschestr. 42, in Stuttgart-Zuffauhausen. S-Bahn #6 (direction: "Weil der Stadt") to "Neuwirtshaus"; exit the station to the right (don't go under the tracks).* ☎ *827 56 85. Open M-F 9am-4pm, Sa-Su 9am-5pm. Free.)*

🎵🎭 ENTERTAINMENT AND NIGHTLIFE

The **Staatstheater,** across the plaza from the Neues Schloß, is Stuttgart's most famous theater, with operas, ballets, plays, and concerts by the dozen. (24hr. ticket information ☎ 197 03; reservations ☎ 20 20 90. Box office open M-F 10am-6pm, Sa 9am-1pm, and 1hr. before performance. DM16-90.) There are 25 other local theaters, and tickets for them are usually much cheaper (DM10-25, students DM5-15). The tourist office provides schedules and sells tickets, which can also be purchased at the **Kartenhäusle,** Geißstr. 4 at Hans-im-Glück-Brunnen. (☎ 210 40 12. Open M-F 9am-6pm, Sa 9am-2pm; order by phone 9am-noon and 2-5pm.) **Corso Kinoprogramm,** Hauptstr. 6 (☎ 73 49 16), shows films in their original language, with frequent special festivals and revivals. Take U-Bahn #1 to "Schillerpl." Schedules in English are available at the tourist office.

Stuttgart also offers a vibrant selection of annual festivals to please camera-toting tourists and liquored-up locals. The **Stuttgarter Weindorf** (wine village) is the largest wine festival in Germany. For 10 days starting in late August, wine lovers will descend upon Schillerpl. and Marktpl. to sample more than 350 kinds of wine as well as scrumptious Swabian specialties. Beer gets 16 days of its own adulation in the **Cannstatter Volksfest,** in late September and October.

From pleasant chats over fine Italian coffee to hypnotic, techno-fueled hysteria, Stuttgart offers a full spectrum of nightlife nastiness. Serious prowlers should pick up either *Prinz* (DM5) or *Stuttgart Lift* (DM4.50) at any city newsstand; both contain detailed information on what's happening. **Tips 'n' trips** (see tourist office above) also publishes up-to-date guides to the evening scene in German and English. Be assured, Dionysus never sleeps in this city. The area along Königstr. and Calwerstr. gets going in the early evenings with chatter and beer spilling from numerous cafes; later on, the nightlife clusters around Eberhardstr., Rotebühlplatz, and Kleines Schloßplatz. To appease sin-seeking tourists, there's the **Stuttgart Night Pass,** good for three nights' admission and free second drinks at various clubs, bars, and discos (DM16); ask at the tourist office for details.

Palast der Republik, Friedrichstr. 27 (☎ 226 48 87). This wooden bungalow emanates loud music as stylish after-hours aficionados congregate outside to down reasonably priced drinks (DM4-12). Open M-W 11am-2am, Th-Sa 11am-3am, Su 3pm-2am; in winter M-W and Su 11am-1am, Th-Sa 11am-2am.

Radio Bar, Rotebühlpl. 23 (☎ 62 87 09). Popular with a young preppy crowd, this place offers drinks (DM4-10), a lively dance floor, and pulsating house music 'til late. Open M-Th and Su 11:20am-2am, F-Sa 11:30am-4am. No cover.

Oblomow, Torstr. 20 (☎ 236 79 24). A cafe that throws open its doors late at night so passersby can hear its upbeat music. Fußball and pinball games. Vegetarians accommodated. Food DM4-8. Open daily 4pm-5am.

Zap, Hauptstätter Str. 40 (☎ 23 52 27), in the Josef-Hirn-Platz. This glitzy social mecca is a thriving cesspool of fun. Open Tu 9pm-3am, W-Su 10pm-4am. Cover DM8-15.

Lauras Club, Rotebühlpl. 4. Gay club blasts house and techno while S&M mannequins pose in cages. Open Th-Su 10pm-5am. No cover.

⚏ DAYTRIP FROM STUTTGART: MARBACH

Friedrich Schiller was born in Marbach, a fact that is difficult to ignore. From drug stores to hair salons, the name of the prominently-nosed poet is ubiquitous. The stately **Schiller-Nationalmuseum** offers a detailed account of Schiller's life and work, and also looks at his Swabian contemporaries. Follow the signs from the train station. *(Schillerhöhe 8-10. ☎(07144) 60 61. Open daily 9am-5pm. DM4, students DM2.)* Adjacent to the museum is the **German literature archive** *(☎(07144) 60 61)*, one of the largest of its kind in the country. Call ahead if you plan to visit. Die-hard Schiller devotees also visit the **Schiller-Geburtshaus,** where the author was born in 1759. Not an astounding amount to see here, except some Schiller artifacts and an animated video on the man. To get there, follow the signs through town. *(Niklastorstr. 31. ☎(07144) 175 67. Open daily 9am-5pm. DM3, students DM1.50.)* From the Schiller-Nationalmuseum, you'll pass through the half-timbered **Bürgerturm** and **Marktplatz.** The nearby **Rathaus** has information on walking tours, hotels, and restaurants. *(Marktstr. 23. Open M 9-11am and 4-6pm, Tu and Th-F 9-11am, W 2-4pm.)* To reach Marbach from Stuttgart, take S-Bahn #4 to the end.

⚏ DAYTRIP FROM STUTTGART: LUDWIGSBURG

Ludwigsburg popped out of the blue in the early 18th century, the narcissistic love child of Duke Eberhard of Ludwig. His modest idea: to erect a residential castle in the duchy's new capital bearing his own name. Unfortunately, Eberhard died before his playground was born, and although his successors finished decorating the castle, they preferred to live in Stuttgart. Even without the aristocratic element, Ludwigsburg became a lively Baroque city with a luxurious trio of palaces.

The opulent Baroque **Residenzschloß** is definitely worth seeing, even if you find yourself lost among German office fieldtrips. The 1¼-hr. guided journey is the only way to see Ludwig's 3m-long bed (he was larger than life: almost 7 ft. tall) and the rest of the lavish gold, marble, and velvet interior. *(Open mid-Mar. to Nov. daily 9am-noon and 1:30-5pm. Tours in English at 1:30pm; German tours Nov. to mid-Mar. M-F 10:30am and 3pm. DM8, students DM4. Combination ticket including Favoritschloß tours, DM10, students DM5.)* The "Swabian Versailles" is situated in an expansive 30-hectare garden that earned Ludwig's complex the tourist brochure epithet **Blühendes Barock,** or "blooming Baroque." *(Open mid-Mar. to early Dec. daily 7:30am-8:30pm. Main entrance on Schondorfer Str. open 9am-6pm.)* Inside, a perennial **Märchengarten** recreates scenes from major fairy tales in a large park of wild vegetation. *(Open 9am-6pm. Adults DM12, students DM5.)* Join 100 kids shouting *Rapunzel, Rapunzel, laß deinen Zopf herunter.* (Rapunzel, Rapunzel, let down your hair). The **Favoritschloß,** behind the *Residenzschloß* garden, is an excellent destination for a stroll or picnic. The small Baroque gem was built as a hunting lodge and party venue for Duke Carl Engler. *(☎(07141) 18 64 40. Open mid-Mar. to Oct. daily 9am-noon and 1:30-5pm; Nov. to mid-Mar.*

10am-noon and 1:30-4pm. Frequent guided tours mid-Mar. to Nov. daily 9am-noon and 1:30-5pm; Nov. to mid-Mar. Tu-Su 10am-noon and 1-4pm. DM4.) If you're not all *Schloβed*-out yet, continue for 30 minutes up the alley through the **Favoritenpark** *(open Apr.-Aug. 8am-7pm, Sept.-Oct. 9am-6pm, Nov.-Jan. 9am-4pm, Feb.-Mar. 9am-5pm)* and marvel at the third Ludwig palace—the Rococo **Monrepos** (☎*(07141)* 225 50). Unfortunately, the castle is now a luxury hotel and is closed to visitors, but you can chill out by renting a **boat** and rowing on the peaceful lake nearby.

All three palaces host the annual **Ludwigsburger Schloβfestspiele,** a series of open-air concerts and performances that runs from early June to late September. For information on tickets, call the Forum am Schloβpark. (☎*(07141)* 91 71 00. Open M-F 8:30am-6:30pm, Sa 9am-1pm.) Even without renowned musicians in the neighborhood, Ludwigsburg offers a sense of refined, classy tranquility. No bumpy medieval cobblestone to be found here: the **Marktplatz** is smooth and spacious, with cotton-candy churches contemplating one another across an aristocratic divide.To reach Ludwigsburg from Stuttgart, hop on S-Bahn #4 or 5 (direction: "Marbach" or "Bietigheim"; 20min.; DM4.30), or take the **boat** run by Neckar-Personen-Schiffahrt (see p. 354). The **tourist office,** across from the *Rathaus* at Wilhelmstr. 10, books **rooms** for free. (☎*(07141)* 910 22 74 or 910 22 52; email info@lust.ludwigsburg.de. Open M-F 9am-6pm, Sa 9am-2pm.) **Grocery stores** and bakeries run rampant along Myluisstr. and Arsenalstr. There are several restaurants on **Holzmarkt,** near Marktpl. **Corfu,** Holzmarktstr. 2, serves daily Greek specials, including a giant bean salad (DM6) and vegetarian entrees. (DM8.50-20. ☎92 08 24. Open daily 11:30am-2:30pm and 5pm-midnight.)

TÜBINGEN   ☎07071

With nearly half its residents affiliated with its 500-year-old university, Tübingen is academic and proud of it. The university has been a source of unrest from the Middle Ages to the student uprisings of the late 60s and beyond; students have boycotted classes to protest everything from the educational system to the Nazi pasts of politicians to Vietnam. The Altstadt, sheltering a lively student life, earned Tübingen the distinction of "highest quality of life" in a recent magazine poll.

▌ GETTING THERE AND GETTING AROUND

Thirty kilometers south of Stuttgart, Tübingen straddles the Neckar on the edge of the Schwarzwald. Easily reached by rail, it is one of the larger cities in the area, and it is connected by bus and train to many small towns in the Schwäbische Alb.

Trains: Chug daily to **Stuttgart** (1hr., 2 per hr., DM17).

Taxis: Taxizentrale, ☎243 01.

Bike Rental: RADlager, Lazarettgasse 19-21 (☎55 16 51; fax 55 17 51), in the Altstadt. DM18 per day. Open M-F 9am-6:30pm, Sa 9:30am-2:30pm.

Boat Rental: Bootsverleih Märkle (☎315 29), on the river by the tourist office. Rowboats DM12 per hr. Paddleboats DM16 per hr. Open Apr.-Sept. daily 11am-8pm.

Mitfahrzentrale: Provenceweg 2, in the French quarter (☎194 40). Matches riders and drivers. **Munich** DM24, **Frankfurt** DM24, **Köln** DM39, **Berlin** DM62. Open M-F 10am–7pm, Sa-Su 11am-2pm. Call 1-2 days in advance.

▌ PRACTICAL INFORMATION

Tourist Office: Verkehrsverein (☎913 60; fax 350 70; email mail@tuebingen-info.de; www.tuebingen-info.de), on the Neckarbrücke. From the front of the station, turn right and walk to Karlstr., turn left and walk to the river. The office books **rooms** (DM30-100) for free and sells maps (DM1-8). Open M-F 9am-7pm, Sa 9am-5pm, Su 2-5pm; Oct.-Easter closed Su.

Tours: In German. Leave from the tourist office Apr.-Oct. W 10am, Sa-Su 2:30pm. DM5.

Mitwohnzentrale: Wilhelmstr. 2-3 (☎ 194 45; fax 55 10 70). Arranges apartments for stays of 1 month or longer. Open M, Tu, Th 9am-noon and 2-5pm, W 2-5pm, F-Sa 10am-1pm.

Bookstores: The 400-year-old **Osiandersche Buchhandlung,** Wilhelmstr. 12 (☎ 920 10), carries a large selection of English and American literature. Open M-W 9am-7pm, Th-F 9am-8pm, Sa 9am-4pm. **Bücherkabinett Antiquariat,** Bachgasse 13 (☎ 55 12 23), has 20,000 used books, 5% in English. Open M-F 10am-6:30pm, Sa 10am-4pm.

Cultural Center: German-American Institute, Karlstr. 3 (☎ 340 71). Open M-F 9am-noon and 2-5pm.

Laundromat: City-Wash, on the corner of Rappstr. and Herrenberger Str., across from Marquardtei (see **Food,** below). DM8 wash. Open M-Sa 8am-9pm.

Women's Resources: Frauencafé, Karlstr. 13 (☎ 328 62), in the magenta house a block from the station, is a hopping, women-only night spot/safe zone. Open Sept.-June M-F 8pm-midnight. **Frauenbuchladen Thalestris,** Bursagasse 2 (☎ 265 90), is a women's bookstore. Open M-F 10am-7pm, Sa 10am-2pm.

Rape Crisis Hotline: Frauenhaus, ☎ 666 04.

Emergency: Police, ☎ 110. **Fire and Ambulance,** ☎ 112.

Post Office: Europapl. 2, 72072 Tübingen. 100m to the right of the station. Open M-F 7:30am-6:30pm, Sa 7:30am-12:30pm.

ACCOMMODATIONS AND CAMPING

Most of the lodgings in the city are not priced to please the budget traveler; ask about **private rooms** at the tourist office.

Jugendherberge (HI), Gartenstr. 22/2 (☎ 230 02; fax 250 61). Cross the bridge past the tourist office and make a right. Or take bus #12 to "Jugendherberge." The entrance is on Herman-Kurz-Str. Recently renovated; a terrace overlooks the Neckar. Breakfast included. Reception 5-8pm and 10-11pm. Curfew midnight. Lockers DM5 deposit. Wheelchair access. Members only. Dorm beds DM28, over 26 DM33.

Hotel am Schloß, Burgsteige 18 (☎ 929 40; fax 92 94 10), on the hill leading to the Schloß. 3-star lodgings in a picturesque location. All rooms have phone and TV. Breakfast included. Reserve by fax. Singles DM55, with shower DM72, with bath DM99-150; doubles with bath DM130-195.

Hotel Kürner, Weizsäckerstr. 1 (☎ 227 35; fax 279 20), 20min. from the Altstadt. Follow Wilhelmstr. past the university and go right on Weizsäckerstr. Or bus #1, 2, 6, 7, or 15 to "Lothar-Meyer-Bau." Friendly management, 70s decor, and restaurant. All rooms have phone and TV. Breakfast included. Singles DM58-68, doubles DM108.

Camping: Rappenberghalde (☎/fax 431 45). Go upstream from the Altstadt or left from the station; cross the river at the Alleenbrücke and turn left (25min.). Follow the blue signs. Or take bus #9 to "Rappenberg" and follow the river to your left. Bike rental DM15 per day. Laundry DM7.50. Reception daily 8am-12:30pm and 2:30-10pm. Open Mar. to mid-Oct. DM9.50 per person. Campsite DM7.

FOOD

With the smell of pungent herbs and fresh bread in the air, Tübingen's superb restaurants seduce students and tourists alike. Most inexpensive eating establishments cluster around **Metzergasse** and **Am Lutznauer Tor.** Buy **groceries** at **HL-Markt,** Europapl. 8, across from the post office (open M-F 7am-8pm, Sa 7am-4pm). The Altstadt bristles with bakeries and cafes.

Mensa, on Wilhelmstr. between Gmelinstr. and Keplerstr. Meals DM3.90 for Tübingen students, DM8.90 for guests. Salad bar DM1 per 100g. Open M-Th 11am-2pm and 6-8:15pm, F noon-2pm, Sa 11:45am-1:15pm. The **cafeteria** downstairs has cold food and dessert under DM5. Open M-Th 8am-8pm, F 8am-7pm. Mensa closed in Aug.

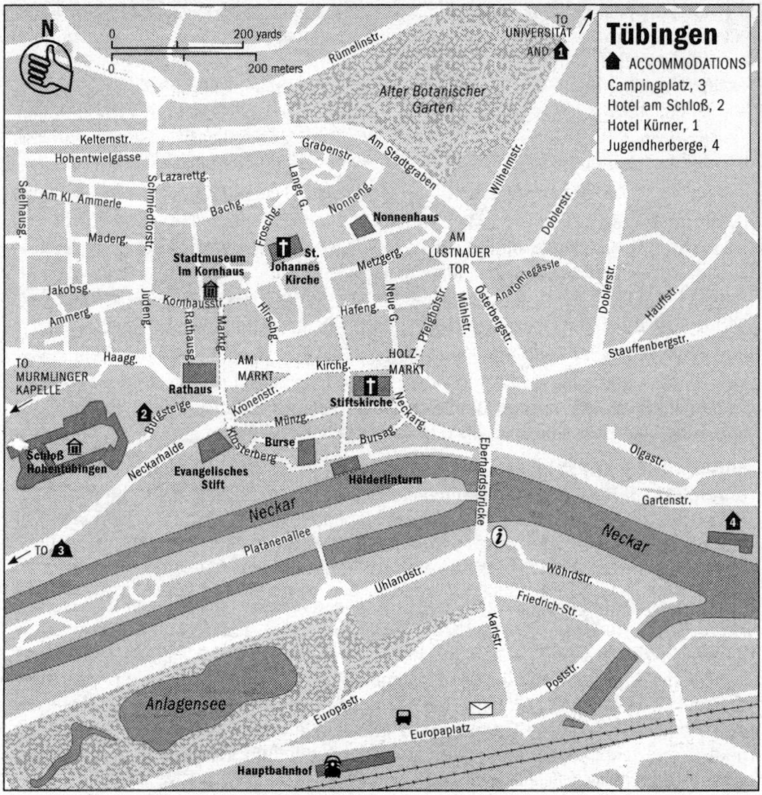

N

0   200 yards
0   200 meters

TO UNIVERSITÄT AND 🏠

Tübingen

🏠 ACCOMMODATIONS
Campingplatz, 3
Hotel am Schloß, 2
Hotel Kürner, 1
Jugendherberge, 4

Rümelinstr.
Alter Botanischer Garten
Keltemstr.
Hohentwielgasse
Lazarettg.
Am Kl. Ammerle
Seehaus
Maderg.
Jakobsg.
Ammerg.
Haagg.
TO MÜRMLINGER KAPELLE
Schloß Hohentübingen
Schmiedtorstr.
Bachg.
Froschg.
Lange G.
Grabenstr.
Nonneng.
Am Stadtgraben
Nonnenhaus
Metzerg.
Stadtmuseum im Kornhaus
St. Johannes Kirche
Kornhausstr.
Jüdeng.
Rathausg.
Markt.
Hirschg.
Hafeng.
Neue G.
Pfleghofstr.
AM LUSTNAUER TOR
Wilhelmstr.
Dobrestr.
Anatomiegässle
Osterbergstr.
Mühlstr.
Dobrestr.
Hauffstr.
Stauffenbergstr.
Rathaus
AM MARKT
Kronenstr.
Kirchg.
HOLZ-MARKT
Stiftskirche
Münzg.
Burse
Bursag.
Neckarg.
Olgastr.
Burgsteige
Neckarhalde
Kronenberg.
Hölderlinturm
Evangelisches Stift
TO 3
Neckar
Platanenallee
Uhlandstr.
Ebenhardsbrücke
Neckar
Gartenstr.
Wöhrdstr.
Friedrich-Str.
Karlstr.
Poststr.
Anlagensee
Europastr.
Europaplatz
Hauptbahnhof

Ratskeller, Haaggasse 4 (☎213 91). Entrance on Rathausgasse. Serves Swabian specialties and vegetarian platters (DM12-25) to loud locals and the occasional tourist (that's you). English menu available. Open M-Sa 6-11:30pm, Su 6-11pm.

Marquardtei, Herrenberger Str. 34 (☎433 86). Bus #8, 14, 16, or 30 to "Rappstr." Run by students, it serves *Schwäbisch* specialties (DM14-18), and vegetarian dishes (DM8-16). Open M-Sa 11:30am-2:30pm and 6pm-12:30am, Su 10am-12:30am.

Da Pino, Mühlstr 20 (☎55 10 86), is a small but eminently delicious eatery. Pizzas DM7-10. Take out available. Open daily 11:30am-2:30pm and 4:30pm-12:30am.

Wurstküche, Am Lustnauer Tor 8 (☎92 750), teaches you the Swabian dialect while you wait for a special (DM8-28). Open daily 11am-midnight, kitchen open 11:30am-11pm.

👁 SIGHTS

STIFTSKIRCHE. The 15th-century church serves as the focal point of the Altstadt's winding alleys. In the chancel lie the tombs of 14 members of the House of Württemberg. Life-size stone sculptures of the deceased top the tombs. The church tower offers a rewarding view for those who survive the climb. (☎420 46. *Open daily 9am-5pm. Chancel and tower open Apr.-July and Oct. F-Su 10:30am-5pm; Aug.-Sept. daily 10:30am-5pm. DM2, students DM1. Organ concerts July-Aug. Th at 6pm; Sept. Sa at 8pm.*)

SCHLOß HOHENTÜBINGEN. Atop the hill in the center of town stands the castle, dating from 1078. Check out the dark tunnel and the staircase on the far side of the courtyard; both lead through the castle wall to breathtaking views of the surrounding valleys. *(Accessible from above Am Markt. Castle grounds open daily 7am-8pm. Free.)* Occupied by various university institutes, the Schloß is also home to the excellent **Museum Schloß Hohentübingen,** the largest university museum in Germany, which features an extensive collection of ethnographic and archaeological artifacts. Don't miss what is purported to be the **oldest surviving example of handwork** (an ivory horse sculpture that's 35,000 years old) or the ethereal hall with plaster casts of classical sculptures. *(Burgsteig. ☎ 297 73 84. Open May-Sept. W-Su 10am-6pm; Oct.-Apr. W-Su 10am-5pm. Tours Su at 3pm. DM4, students DM2.)*

HÖLDERLINTURM. The great 18th- and 19th-century poet Friedrich Hölderlin lived out the final 36 years of his life in the nearby Hölderlinturm in a state of clinical insanity, spending his days writing neat quatrains on the four seasons. The tower now contains a museum dedicated to his life. *(Behind Bursagasse on the river. Open Tu-F 10am-noon and 3-5pm, Sa-Su 2-5pm. Tours Sa-Su 5pm. DM3, students DM2.)*

PLATANENALLEE. The buildings of the **Neckarfront** are best viewed from this tree-lined avenue that runs the length of the man-made island on the Neckar. Punting trips down the Neckar are available from university students; a good place to call or check is the Evangelisches Stift. *(☎ 56 10. DM7-12 per person.)*

WURMLINGER KAPELLE. The simple but beautiful chapel sits atop an idyllic pastoral hill, worlds away from Tübingen's crunchy academia. Follow the red-blaze signs from the Schloß to the Wurmlinger Kapelle trail (6km) for impressive views of several valleys, or take bus #18 (direction: "Oberndorf") to "Rössle", and follow the road up and to the left in the direction of Tübingen.

AROUND MARKTPLATZ. On the square is **Buchhandlung Heckenhauer Antiquariat,** where Hermann Hesse worked from 1895 until 1899. The store still offers rare books. *(Holzmarkt 5. ☎ 230 18. Open M 2-6:30pm, Tu-F 10am-6:30pm, Sa 10am-3pm.)* Nearby, the **Kornhaus** contains the **Stadtmuseum,** with exhibits on the city's history. *(Kornhausstr. 10. ☎ 20 41 711. Open Tu-F 3-6pm, Sa 11am-6pm.)* A block below Marktpl., on Kronenstr. dwells the **Evangelisches Stift.** Once a monastery, now a dorm for theology students, its alumni include such academic luminaries as Kepler, Hölderlin, and Hegel. *(Klosterberg 2. ☎ 56 10.)*

🎵🎭 ENTERTAINMENT AND NIGHTLIFE

Tübingen's nightlife is laid-back, mostly revolving around cafes in the Altstadt that begin brewing quiet cups of coffee at 10am and stay open into the night, serving beer to groups of students. Tübingen also has two major theaters: the progressive **Zimmertheater,** Bursagasse 16 (☎ 927 30; open M-F 10am-1pm and 3-6pm, Sa 2-7pm; tickets also available at the tourist office and Mensa), and the larger, more conservative **Landestheater,** Eberhardstr. 8 (☎ 931 31 49). Tickets (DM10-30) and schedules are available at the tourist office and at the box office at Eberhardstr. 6 (open Tu-F 2-7pm, Sa 10am-1pm). For **gay and lesbian nightlife,** head to **Südhaus** (below) on Wednesday nights for a mixed bar; gay afternoons are held on Sundays at **Luscht Café,** Herrenberger Str. 9.

Jazzkeller, Haaggasse 15/2 (☎ 55 09 06; fax 221 63), moves from jazz to funk to salsa and back again. There's also a disco downstairs. Open M 7pm-2am, Tu-Th and Su 7pm-1am, F and Sa 7pm-3am. Opens 1hr. later July and Aug.

Südhaus, Hechinger Str. 203 (☎ 746 96). Take bus #3 or 5 to "Fuchsstr.," or night bus N9 and go under the busy road. A "socio-cultural center" featuring wacky art films, dance parties, and live acts. Schedules are plastered all over town. Cover DM10-25.

Tangente-Night, Pfleghofstr. 10 (☎ 230 07), by the Lustnauer Tor corner. A premier student hangout for beer that buzzes at night, but is also good for a book and cappuccino in the morning (0.3L *Pils* DM3.50; coffee DM3). Most fun Sept.-Apr. Th-Su, when a DJ spins house, acid jazz, and techno. Open daily 10am-3am.

Neckarmüller, Gartenstr. 4 (☎278 48), is close to the youth hostel and next to the bridge. Young and old alike drink and schmooze at picnic tables under shady trees. The only way to get closer to the Neckar is to rent a boat. Try the house brew; light or dark DM3.90 for 0.3L. Food starts at DM5. Open daily 10am-1am.

O'Donovan's Irish Pub, Burgsteige 7 (☎55 29 77), near the Schloß. With occasional live music acts and bar quizzes, this bit o' Eire keeps students and travelers flushed and happy, especially in the winter. Su Irish brunch from 11am-5pm (DM14). Open M-F 5pm-1am, Sa 2pm-1am, Su 11am-1am.

Marktschenke, Am Markt 11 (☎220 35). With a few drinks, the cartoons on the walls are sure to amuse you. 0.5L *Hefeweizen* DM5.20. Open daily 9am-1am.

KARLSRUHE   ☎0721

By European standards, Karlsruhe was born yesterday. In 1715, Margrave Karl Wilhelm built a castle retreat for himself and his mistresses (hence the name, meaning "Karl's rest"). He then designed a city radiating out from the castle in the shape of a fan. Karlsruhe is home to Germany's two highest courts, the Federal Supreme Court and the Federal Constitutional Court. For travelers, the city offers a break from the burden of antiquity. For residents, Karlsruhe offers something even better—more than 1,700 hours of sun per year, earning it the title of "Sun City."

🛈 ORIENTATION AND PRACTICAL INFORMATION

From the station, the town center is a 25-minute walk along Ettlinger Str. and Karl-Friedrich-Str., or you can take any streetcar to "Marktpl." or "Europapl." The **S-Bahn** costs DM3.50 per ride within the city, DM8 for a 24-hour ticket. For a **taxi** call ☎94 41 44. The **tourist office,** Bahnhofpl. 6, across the street from the station, books **rooms** for free. The staff gives out the amazing (and free) ▨*Karlsruhe Extra,* an annually updated guide (in English) with great maps. (☎355 30; fax 35 53 43 99; email vv@karlsruhe.de; www.karlsruhe.de. Open M-F 9am-6pm, Sa 9am-1pm.) A **branch office,** Karl-Friedrich-Str. 22, provides the same services, but is closer to the Schloß. (☎35 53 43 76. Open M-F 9am-6pm, Sa 9am-12:30pm.) **Braunsche Universitätsbuchhandlung,** Kaiserstr. 120, has a small, popular selection of English-language books. (☎232 96; fax 291 16. Open M-F 9am-8pm, Sa 9am-4pm.) **Waschhaus** resides at the corner of Scheffelstr. and Sophienstr. (Open M-Sa 8am-11pm. Wash DM7, soap included; dry DM1 per 10min.) The **main post office,** 76133 Karlsruhe, sprawls near Europapl., but until renovations are done in late 2001, use the location on Kaiserstr. near Hirschstr. (open M-F 8:30am-6:30pm, Sa 8:30am-1pm).

🛏🍴 ACCOMMODATIONS AND FOOD

Karlsruhe's **Jugendherberge (HI),** Moltkestr. 24, is convenient to the Schloß and university, but far from the train station. Take the S-Bahn to "Europapl.," then follow Karlstr. until it ends. Turn left onto Seminarstr. and turn left again on Moltkestr.; it's on the right. (☎282 48; fax 276 47. Breakfast included. Sheets DM6. Reception briefly at 5, 7, and 9:30pm. Curfew 11:30pm. Lockout 9am-5pm. Call for reservations between 8 and 8:30am. Members only. Dorm beds DM25, over 26 DM33.) **Hotel Augustiner,** Sophienstr. 73, offers affordable rooms in the city near the sights. (☎84 55 80; fax 85 33 20. Breakfast included. Single DM50, with shower DM65; doubles DM100.) On the boundary of the city center, next to Mühlberger Tor, is the **Hotel Handelshof,** Rheinhold-Frank-Str. 46a (☎91 20 90; fax 91 20 988. Breakfast included. Singles DM50, with shower DM95; doubles DM130.) Camp at **Turmbergblick,** Tiengererstr. 40, in Durlach. Take S-Bahn #2 from the station to "Durlach Turmberg." (☎49 72 36; fax 49 72 37. Reception 8am-1pm and 3-9pm. Open Mar.-Sept. DM7-10 per person. Campsites DM7.)

A trade school's **Mensa** is located near the youth hostel. From the hostel's front door, walk straight ahead across the lawn between two buildings to the lowrise. (Meals DM4.50-9. Open M-Th 11:30am-2pm, F 11:30am-1:45pm.) **Krokodil,** Waldstr. 63, offers salads, *Schnitzel*, breakfasts, and pastas (DM5-17) served in a mirrored bar and beer garden. (☎273 31. Open daily 8am-1am.) For traditional German fare, try **Goldenes Kreuz,** Karlstr. 21a, around the corner from Ludwigspl., where entrees run DM12.30. (☎220 54. Open daily 11am-10pm.) *Imbisse* line Kaiserstr. to the west. Buy produce at the **market** on Marktpl. (open M-Sa 7:30am-12:30pm). Many cafes on Ludwigspl. stay open until 1am. **Harmonie,** Kaiserstr. 57, is a pub plastered with vintage posters and offering food (regional specialties DM7-12; beer DM3.60-6) and live music. (☎37 42 09. Open M-F 8am-1am, Sa 10am-1am, Su 9:30am-1am.)

🛈 SIGHTS

The most spectacular sight in Karlsruhe is the locus of the city—all roads lead to the classical yellow **Schloß.** The **Schloßgarten,** with its impeccably maintained swathes of green and inviting benches, stretches out behind the castle for nearly half a kilometer. *(Open until 10pm daily. Free.)* The Schloß houses the **Badisches Landesmuseum,** with elaborate special exhibits and a permanent collection of antiques including the flashy **Türkenbeute** (Turkish booty), a legacy of Turkish invaders. *(Take any train to "Marktpl." ☎926 65 14. Open Tu-Th 11am-5pm, F-Su 10am-6pm. DM5, students DM3.)* The **Museum beim Markt,** dedicated to design and illustration after 1900, has a particularly fascinating Art Deco collection. *(Karl-Friedrich-Str. 6. ☎926 65 78. Open Tu-Th 11am-5pm, F-Su 10am-6pm. DM3, students DM2. Free F after 2pm.)* Around the corner are the **Kunsthalle,** and **Kunsthalle Orangerie,** two top-notch art museums. European masterpieces from the 15th to the 19th centuries adorn the Kunsthalle—don't miss Grünewald's *Crucifixion*—while the Orangerie contains a smaller collection of modern art. *(Kunsthalle Hans-Thoma-Str. 2; ☎926 33 55. Orangerie Hans-Thoma-Str. 6. Take any train to "Europapl." Both open Tu-F 10am-5pm, Sa-Su 10am-6pm. DM5, students DM3.)* The **Kunstverein,** changes its modern art every six weeks. Though small, the gallery will pique your aesthetic curiosity. *(Waldstr. 3. Take any train except #2 to "Herrenstr." Open Tu-F 11am-7pm Sa-Su 11am-5pm. DM4, students DM2.)*

Occupying the upper floors of a former mansion, the recently renovated **Prinz-Max-Palais** has a local history display that includes the purported **first bicycle in the world.** *(Karlstr. 10. ☎133 42 34. Open Tu, W, F, Sa 10am-6pm, Th 10am-8pm, Su 2-6pm. Free.)* The quirkiest of Karlsruhe's museums is indisputably the **Museum für Literature,** in the same building and dedicated to poets such as von Scheffel and Hebel. *(☎84 38 18. Same hours as Prinz-Max-Palais museum. Free.)* A block in front of the Schloß and flanked on the west by the shopping district is the placid **Marktplatz.** To one side stands the rose-colored **Rathaus;** to the other, the imposing columns of the **Stadtkirche.** The red, sandstone pyramid in the center of the square is the symbol of the city and Karl's final resting place.

The unremarkable **Bundesverfassungsgericht** (Federal Constitutional Court) stands next to the Schloß. It may be ugly, but give it some respect: it houses Germany's strongest legal safeguard against totalitarian rule. Near Friedrichspl., the **Bundesgerichtshof** (Federal Supreme Court) is pumped with formidable security.

Perhaps to balance all this heavy-duty legal responsibility, Karlsruhe relaxes to the max with a number of huge cultural festivals. Every February, Karlsruhe hosts the **Händel-Festspiele,** a 10-day series of performances of Händel's works (Feb. 23-Mar. 4, 2001). The appetizing **Brigande-Feschd** takes place in late May, bringing a huge display of dishes from local restaurants. Local breweries play an essential role in the reveling **Unifest** in late July. The 10-day orgy of live music, food stands, and roaming students clutching mugs of beer takes place at the end of Günther-Klatz-Anlage and is the largest free open-air concert in Germany.

BADEN-BADEN   ☎ 07221

Anyone who ever wanted to lead the life of a pampered Old World aristocrat can have a ball in Baden-Baden. In its 19th-century heyday, Baden-Baden's guest list read like a *Who's Who* of European nobility. Although its status has declined, the spa town on the northern fringes of the Schwarzwald remains primarily a playground for the well-to-do; minor royalty, nouveaux riches, and the like gather here year-round to bathe in the mineral spas and drop fat sums of money in the elegant casino. The ritzy atmosphere is worth tolerating for the chance to experience the incredible (and surprisingly affordable) baths and to stroll down the luxurious tree-lined boulevards of the chic downtown area.

🛈 ORIENTATION AND PRACTICAL INFORMATION

Baden-Baden's **train station** is inconveniently located 7km from town. If you're not up for the 90 minute walk along the park path, take bus #204, 205, or 216 (direction: "Stadtmitte") or #201 (direction "Oberbeuren") from the station to "Leopoldspl." or "Augustapl." (DM3.50). For a **taxi** call ☎ 381 11 or 621 10. A **branch** of the **tourist office** is located at the city entrance at Schwarzwaldstr. 52, a few blocks from the train station toward town. The **main office** is at Trinkhalle on Kaiserallee, next to the casino. Take bus #201 to "Hindenburgpl." The staff offers free maps and a hotel list. (☎ 27 52 00; fax 27 52 02; email info@baden-baden.com; www.baden-baden.de. Open May-Oct. M-Sa 10am-6:30pm, Nov.-Apr. M-Sa 10am-5:30pm.) Dig up your Armani for a night on the town at the **Waschsalon**, Scheibenstr. 14. (☎ 248 19. Open M-Sa 7:30am-10pm.) The **main post office**, 76486 Baden-Baden, is located in the Wagener department store next to Hindenburgpl. below the Rathaus (open M-F 9am-7pm, Sa 9am-4pm). Check your **email** at **Café Contact**, Eichstr. 5, near Augustapl. (Open daily 11am-2pm. DM5 per 30min.)

⌂🍴 ACCOMMODATIONS AND FOOD

The cheapest bed in town is at the modern **Werner-Dietz-Jugendherberge (HI)**, Hardenbergstr. 34, between the station and the town center. Take bus #201, 205, or 216 to "Grosse-Dollen-Str." and follow the signs uphill. (☎ 522 23; fax 600 12. Sheets DM6. Reception 5-11pm. Curfew 11:30pm. Wheelchair accessible. Write in advance for reservations. Members only. Dorm beds DM25, over 26 DM30.) Rooms in the center of town are expensive with few exceptions. **Hotel am Markt**, Marktpl. 18, is next to the Friedrichsbad and the Stiftskirche. (☎ 270 40; fax 27 04 44; email hotel.am.markt.bad@t-online.de. Breakfast included. Dinner DM8-15. Reception 7am-10pm. Singles DM56, with shower DM80-90; doubles DM115, with shower DM140-150. *Kurtaxe* DM5.) The unassuming **Hotel Löhr**, Adlerstr. 2, inconveniently has its reception a block and a half away at **Café Löhr**, Lichtentaler Str. 19, across the street and back toward the station from the "Augustapl." bus stop. The rooms are clean but small. (☎ 262 04 or 313 70; fax 383 08. Singles DM45-70; doubles DM110.) Most restaurants in Baden-Baden aren't compatible with budget travel. For **groceries** head to **Pennymarkt**, at the "Grosse-Dollen-Str." bus stop near the hostel (open M-W 8:30am-6:30pm, Th-F 8:30am-7pm, Sa 8:30am-2pm). **Pizzeria Roma**, Gernsbacher Str. 14, offers affordable pasta (DM10-15) in a prime location below the Rathaus (closed on Tu).

◖ SPAS

Baden-Baden's history as a resort goes back nearly two millennia to the time when the Romans started soaking themselves in the area's **thermal baths.** The **Friedrichsbad**, Römerpl. 1, is a beautiful 19th-century bathing palace where visitors are parched, steamed, soaked, scrubbed, doused, and pummeled by trained professionals for three hours. There are 15 tubs of varying temperatures, as well as saunas, showers, and hot rooms that await the nude, and at the end everyone gets wrapped up like a mummy in pink blankets for a 30-minute nap. It's a marvelous experience, and not a stitch of clothing is permitted. (☎27 59 20. Open M-Sa 9am-10pm, Su noon-8pm. Last entry 3hr. before closing. Baths are co-ed Tu and F 4-10pm, and all day W and Sa-Su. Standard Roman bath DM36, with soap and brush massage DM48. DM6 discount with hotel or hostel coupon.) More modest or budget-minded cure-seekers should try next door at the astounding **Caracalla-Thermen,** Römerpl. 1, which is cheaper, more public, and allows bathing suits except in the saunas upstairs. Indoor and outdoor pools, whirlpools, and solaria of varying sizes and temperatures pamper the weary traveler at a very reasonable price. Whichever bath you choose, the experience will be unforgettable. (☎27 59 40. Open daily 8am-10pm. 2hr. DM19; 3hr. DM25; 4hr. DM29. Discount with hotel or hostel coupon.) The large, public **swimming pool** next to the hostel has a curvy slide and is the cheapest way to bathe in Baden-Baden. (Open 10am-8pm in good weather. Last entry 7pm. DM4.50, students DM3.)

SIGHTS AND HIKING

When they're not busy pruning themselves at the baths, Baden-Baden's affluent guests head to the oldest **casino** in Germany, which, according to Marlene Dietrich, is the "most beautiful casino in the world." Modeled after Versailles, it prompts oohs and aahs from even the most well-traveled aristocrat. In earlier days, no citizens of Baden-Baden were allowed inside. These rules no longer apply, but a slew of others still do: you must be 21+ in order to gamble here, and men must wear a coat and tie while women must have a dress or suit. The minimum bet is DM5, maximum bet DM20,000. (☎275 200. Open M-Th and Su 2pm-2am, F-Sa 2pm-3am. DM5. Tours Apr.-Sept. 9:30-11:45am. English language tours by special arrangement. DM6.) There is no dress code for the **slot machine wing,** located in the Alter Bahnhof on Lange Str. (Open M-Th and Su 2pm-midnight, F-Sa 2pm-1am. DM2.) Next to the casino is the massive Neoclassical **Trinkhalle,** which contains a gold-plated fountain, souvenir shop, and a gallery of murals immortalizing local folktales. The free *Heilwasser* (healing water) tastes like it's good for you: warm and saline. Bring it on. (Open daily 10am-6pm. Free.) A few blocks in the opposite direction, down the paths of the verdant Lichtentaler Allee, the **Kunsthalle** showcases modern art, rotating its exhibits every six weeks. (☎30 07 63. Open Tu and Th-Su 11am-6pm, W 11am-8pm. Admission usually DM10, students DM6.) For a stunning view of the surrounding valleys, head up the steep stairwell from Marktplatz to the **Neues Schloß.** Once the home of the Margraves of Baden, the castle now hosts the **Stadtgeschichtliche Sammlungen,** which houses exhibits on the wet and wild history of Baden-Baden. (Open Tu-Th 2-5pm, F-Su 11am-5pm. DM2, students and seniors DM1.) For an even more exquisite view extending all the way to the French frontier, head to the 12th-century **Altes Schloß.** Its majestic ruins, the **Ruine Hohenbaden,** are accessible from the trail starting from behind the Neues Schloß. From the trailhead, glance over at the visible Altes Schloß to orient yourself. Take the direct path to the forest, turn left, and at the information stand follow the trail that leads up and to the right; keep an eye out for poorly-marked signs for Altes Schloß on rocks and trees. The view is undeniably worth it. Or take bus #214 (direction: "Ebersteinburg") to the end of the line and follow the signs. Alternatively, bus #215 makes two loops on Sundays and holidays at 1:15pm and 4:15pm between Augustapl. and the Schloß. (☎269 48. Open Apr.-Oct. Tu-Su 10am-8pm, Nov.-Mar. Tu-Su 10am-7pm. Free.)

To rise above the decadence, escape to the nearby hills. The best place for immediate hiking is at the 668m **Merkur** peak east of town. Take bus #204 or 205 from Leopoldpl. to "Merkurwald," then ride the *Bergbahn* to the top, where a slew of trails plunge into the Schwarzwald. (Bergbahn runs daily 10am-10pm, every 15min. DM4 one-way, DM7 round-trip.) The *Bergbahn* station at the bottom is crossed by the **Panoramaweg.** Marked by white signs with a green circle, the Panoramaweg connects the best look-out points nearby. Pick up a map at the tourist office (DM2-10).

FREIBURG IM BREISGAU ☎ 0761

It's not difficult to see why German Luftwaffe pilots mistakenly bombed their own city of Freiburg in May 1940. Tucked in the far southwest corner of Germany, Freiburg enjoys a persistent French influence, which has helped its genial, humor-loving citizens to flout the dour German stereotype. Despite its status as the "metropolis" of the Schwarzwald, Freiburg has yet to succumb to the hectic rhythms of city life. The surrounding hills brim with greenery and fantastic hiking trails, paths link the medieval **Schwabentor** to the German trail network, and all traces of urbanity dissolve into serene countryside a few kilometers from the city.

▶ GETTING THERE AND GETTING AROUND

Trains: To **Karlsruhe** (1hr., 2 per hr., DM37); **Stuttgart** (1½hr., 1 per hr., DM61); **Straßbourg** (1¾hr., 1 per hr., DM27); and **Basel** (45min., 1-2 per hr., DM17).

Public Transportation: Single fare on Freiburg's many bus and streetcar lines DM3.40. Day pass DM8; for 2 people DM10. Get the scoop on regional travel at **PlusPunkt,** Salzstr. 3 (☎500), in the Altstadt, which serves your every transportation need. Open M-F 8am-7pm, Sa 9am-4pm. Most public transportation stops running around 12:30am, but a system of **night buses** (named after the planets) covers most major stops through the wee hours (DM7 per ride; DM4 with Day-Card). The streetcar platform in the train station is on the overpass at the end of the tracks.

Taxis: ☎444 44. Four you.

Mitfahrzentrale: City-Netz, Belfortstr. 55 (☎194 44), south of the station, just off Schnewlingstr. **Munich** DM38, **Paris** DM46, **Zurich** DM17. Open M-F 9am-7pm, Sa 9am-1pm, Su 10am-1pm.

Bike Rental: Mobile, Ventzinger 15 (☎319 65 05), behind the train station. DM15 for 6hrs., DM25 per day. Open daily 5am-1:30am. **Velo Doctor,** Klarastr. 63 (☎27 64 77). DM15 per day, DM45 per week. Open M-F 9am-7pm, Su 9am-2pm.

Hitchhiking: Let's Go does not recommend hitchhiking. Hitchers have been known to take public transit to departure points. For points north, take S-Bahn #5 (direction: "Zähringen") to "Reutebachgasse" and walk back 50m. West: S-Bahn #1 to "Padua-Allee," then bus #31 or 32 to "Hauptstr." East: S-Bahn #1 (direction: "Littenweiler") to "Lassbergstr.," then bus #18 (direction: "Langmatten") to "Strombad."

◢✱ ▮ ORIENTATION AND PRACTICAL INFORMATION

Most of the city's sights and restaurants lie within walking distance from one another in the Altstadt, a 15-minute walk from the main train station down tree-lined Eisenbahnstr. to Rathauspl.

Tourist Office: Rotteckring 14 (☎388 18 82; fax 388 18 87; email touristik@fwt-online.de; www.freiburg.de), 2 blocks down Eisenbahnstr. from the station. The staff finds **rooms** for DM5 and has free maps, but prefers to sell the comprehensive Freiburg Official Guide (in German or English) for DM6 or a smaller guide for DM1. 24hr. automated displays in front of the office and the train station can help you find accommodations if the staff is too busy. Open June-Sept. M-F 9:30am-8pm, Sa 9:30am-5pm, Su 10am-noon; Oct.-May M-F 9:30am-8pm, Sa 9:30am-2pm, Su 10am-noon.

Currency Exchange: The closest to the main train station is the **Volksbank** across the street and to the right. Open M-W, F 8am-4:30pm, Th 8am-6pm. **24hr. ATM.**

Bookstore: Walthari, Bertoldstr. 28 (☎38 77 70). A fairly large collection of English-language paperbacks and guides to the Schwarzwald region. Open M-W, F 9am-7pm, Th 9am-8pm, Sa 9am-4pm.

Laundromat: Waschsalon, Grünwälderstr. 19. Great location, wash and dry DM7, soap included. Open M-F 9am-7:30pm, Sa 9am-5pm.

Emergency: Police, ☎110. **Fire and Ambulance,** ☎112.

Rape Crisis Hotline: ☎ 333 39.

Gay Resources: Rosa Hilfe, ☎ 251 61.

Internet Access: in the **Galeria Kaufhof,** at the corner of Schusterstr. and Dreherstr. DM2 per 15min., DM3 per 30min. Open M-F 9:30am-8pm, Sa 9am-4pm. **Ping-Wing,** Niemenstr. 3, near Martinstor between Löwenstr. and Universitätstr. DM5 per 30min. Open M-F 11am-10pm, Sa 10am-11pm.

Post Office: Eisenbahnstr. 56-58, 79098 Freiburg. One block straight ahead of the train station. Open M-F 8:30am-6:30pm, Sa 8:30am-2pm.

▎ ACCOMMODATIONS AND CAMPING

Most of Freiburg's hotels and *Pensionen* are expensive and located outside the city center. The tourist office books cheaper rooms (singles DM25-45, doubles DM45-80) in private homes. These are usually the most affordable accommodations in Freiburg. Freiburg's youth hostel is large, nondescript, and far from the Altstadt. If your accommodation is far away, purchase the transportation daypass to save money (see **Public Transportation,** p. 369).

Jugendherberge (HI), Kartäuserstr. 151 (☎ 676 56; fax 603 67). S-Bahn #1 (direction: "Littenweiler") to "Römerhof," cross the tracks and backtrack 20m, then walk left down Fritz-Geiges-Str., cross the stream, and follow the footpath for about 10min. to the right. Rampant schoolchildren sleep in packed rooms amidst bright colors. In-house disco or movie nights. Sheets DM6. DM28, over 26 DM33. *Gästehaus* sheets included. Members only. Reception 7am-10pm. Curfew 11pm. Dorm beds DM38.

■ **Pension Gisela,** Am Vogelbach 27 (☎ 89 78 980; fax 897 898 20; www.hausgisela.de). Bus #10 (direction: "Padua-Allee") to "Hofackerstr.," then double back 1 block and turn left, walk 250m, and turn right on Hasenweg before the train tracks. Luxurious studio apartments pose as budget travel. Each room has kitchen, shower, and toilet. Breakfast included. Call ahead. Singles DM60-70; doubles from DM90.

Hotel Zum Löwen, Breisgau Str. 62 (☎ 809 72 20; fax 840 23), up the street from Gästehaus Hirschen (see below). A great deal. With the marble floors it sure doesn't feel like budget travel. Enter in the parking lot; the front door is also labeled "Löwen" but leads into a more expensive place. Breakfast and TV included. Singles DM50, with shower and toilet DM70; doubles DM90, with shower from DM130.

Hotel Schemmer, Eschholzstr. 63 (☎ 20 74 90; fax 20 74 950). From the train station, take the overpass at the end of track 1, go past the church and turn left. Friendly management and about the best location available. Some rooms with balcony. Breakfast included. Singles DM65, with bath DM75; doubles DM90, with bath DM105.

Haus Lydia Kalchtaler, Peterhof 11 (☎ 671 19). Streetcar #1 (direction: "Littenweiler") to "Lassbergstr.," then bus #17 (direction: "Kappel") to "Kleintalstr." Turn around and follow Peterhof up and to the left to the large wooden farmhouse with the water trough in front. Peace, quiet, and space all at an unbeatable price. A rustic, idyllic atmosphere and available kitchen counter with the inconvenience of a 45min. commute to the center. Sheets extra. DM25 per person.

Gästehaus Hirschen, Breisgauer Str. 47 (☎ 821 18; fax 879 94). Take streetcar #1 to "Padua-Allee," backtrack 30m along the tracks, and walk down Breisgauer Str. for 5min. Be careful: this *Gästehaus* is on the other side of town from the hotel of the same name; also, it isn't the same as Hirschengarten-Hotel, which is right next door. Old farmhouse in a quiet neighborhood with rooms as cozy as the exterior would lead you to believe. TV and breakfast included. Singles DM50, with shower DM80; doubles DM85, with shower DM110; triples DM120.

Camping: Hirzberg, Kartäuserstr. 99 (☎ 350 54; fax 28 92 12; email hirzberg@freiberg.de; www.freiburg-camping.de), has sparkling new camping facilities 20min. by foot from the Altstadt. Endlessly helpful multilingual staff. Streetcar #1 to "Stadthalle", then cross the street to the left via the underpass and walk straight (north) on Hirzbergstr. Cross the river at Max-Miller-Steg, keep going untill you reach the busy

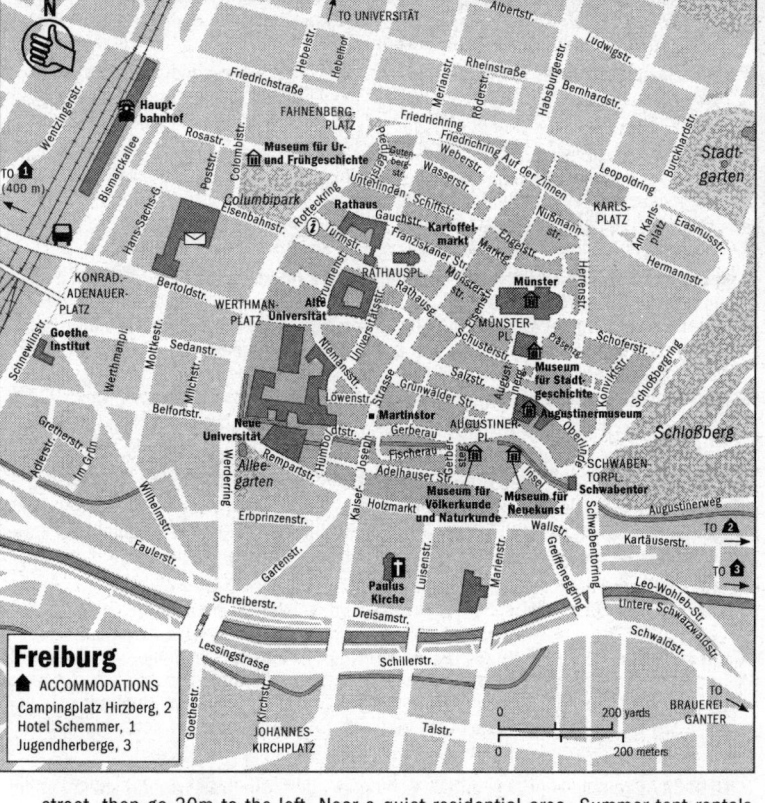

Freiburg

♠ ACCOMMODATIONS

Campingplatz Hirzberg, 2
Hotel Schemmer, 1
Jugendherberge, 3

street, then go 30m to the left. Near a quiet residential area. Summer tent rentals DM10-15 per day. Bikes DM15 per day. Laundry DM5. Reception 8am-10pm. DM9 per person; DM5 per child. DM6-8 per tent.

Camping: Mosle Park, Waldeseestr. 77 (☎729 38; fax 775 78). S-Bahn #1 to "Stadthalle." Head south on Möslestr., cross the tracks, and follow Waldseestr. (about 15 min.). Beautiful forested location, ideally situated for hiking. Wash and dry laundry DM13. Reception 8am-noon and 3-10pm. Open Apr.-Oct. DM8 per person; DM5 per child. DM4 per tent. DM9 per car.

🍴 FOOD

In the early 15th century, the humanist Dietrich von Nieheim noted admiringly that in Freiburg "the supply of victuals is good and readily available." With more than 23,000 university students to feed, Freiburg's budget eateries carry on the fine tradition. Many restaurants and cafes offer student menus and other deals. During the daytime, the **Freiburger Markthalle,** next to the Martinstor, is home to foodstands serving ethnic specialties for less than DM15. The main entrance is one block up on Grünwälderstr. (☎38 11 11. Open M-F 7am-7pm, Sa 7am-4pm.) The **open-air market** on Münsterpl. sells everything from fresh radishes to an offer to etch your name onto a grain of rice (M-Sa 7am-1pm). Get **groceries** at **Edeka,** Eisenbahnstr. 39, opposite the post office (open M-F 8am-8pm, Sa 8am-2pm).

Mensa: Two university *Mensen*—the blue-trimmed building on **Rempartstr.** in the Altstadt (lunch only) and on the main campus one block north of **Hebelstr.** (lunch and dinner).

Three kinds of meal tickets buy everything from a bowl of soup to a trayful of cheap eats. DM3.90-8.30, depending on size. Rempartstr. location open M-F 11:30am-2pm, Sa 11:30am-1:30pm. Hebelstr. location open M-F 11am-2pm and 5:30-7:30pm.

■ **Brennessel,** Eschholzstr. 17 (☎28 11 87). A plucky student tavern that fills the student gullet without emptying the student wallet. Funk and jazz abound. Don't miss the spaghetti *bolognese* (DM3.50) from 6-8pm, or *Pfannkuchen* (pancakes; DM5). Open M-Sa 6pm-1am, Su 5pm-1am. Kitchen open until 12:30am.

Greiffenegg-Schlößle, Schloßbergring 3 (☎327 28). Drink, eat, and look down over Freiburg from a terrace above the city. This mellow, chatty restaurant boasts a fabulous view. Seats 800 and fills up when the weather cooperates. Beer DM5-7. Half-price salad buffet 11am-2pm. Entrance across from the Schwabentor. Open year-round daily 11am-midnight.

Hausbrauerei Feierling, Gerberau 46 (☎266 78). 2 gleaming copper vats form the centerpiece of this airy Freiburg institution. Across the way, the *Biergarten* sports thick chestnut trees. Wheat beer (0.5L DM5.90) produced from ecologically-sound ingredients accompanies traditional German fare (DM10-26). The place is packed at night, keeping the student waitresses on their toes. Open Su-Th 11am-midnight, F-Sa 11am-1am. Kitchen open noon-2pm and 6-10pm. Biergarten open daily 11am-11pm.

Freiburger Salatstuben, Löwenstr. 1 (☎351 55), near Martinstor. A health-food haven with an array of imaginative vegetarian fare (100g DM2.30) that belies the absence of vegetarian pretension. Even the desserts (DM4-5) are smart. Open M-F 11am-8pm, Sa 11am-4pm, 1st Sa of the month 11am-6pm.

Milano, Schusterstr. 7 (☎337 35), 1 block from Münsterpl. With its salmon-leather interior and prime location, feels more high-brow than the prices might suggest. Authentic, delicious pizza (DM8-15) and pasta (DM7.50-15.50). Try the spaghetti marinara...mmm. Service with Italian flair. Open daily 11am-midnight.

◉ SIGHTS

What buildings the errant *Luftwaffe* bombers didn't hit, the Allies finished off one night in 1944, obliterating most of the old city. Since then, the citizens of Freiburg have painstakingly recreated the city's architecture and public spaces.

MÜNSTER. Freiburg's pride and joy is its majestic cathedral, which towers 116m above camera-wielding hordes of tourists. With sections constructed between the 13th and 16th centuries, this architectural melange immortalizes, in stained glass, the different medieval guilds that financed its construction. Stumble up more than 300 steps to ascend the tower, from which you can watch the **oldest bell in Germany** (her name's Hosanna) and 26 others swing into motion. Protect your eardrums when the hour strikes. (☎20 27 90. Open M-Sa 10am-6pm, Su 1-6pm. Tower open May-Oct. M-F 9:30am-5pm, Su 1-5pm; Nov.-Apr. Tu-Sa 9:30am-5pm, Su 1-5pm. DM2.50, students DM1.50. Summer organ concerts Tu at 8:15pm. Free.)

SCHLOßBERG. From the Schwabentor, take the pedestrian overpass across the heavily-trafficked Schloßbergring and climb the glorified Schloßberg for a superb view of the city. From there, a number of hiking trails explore the forested hills. Try the **Langbuckweg** or its alternate, the **Waldfahrtstr.-Hirzberg-St. Ottilien** trail.

ADELHAUSERMUSEUM NATUR- UND VÖLKERKUNDE. The museum of natural history rotates exhibits animal, vegetable, and mineral, including a staircase devoted entirely to beetles. The folk museum holds wonderfully obscure anthropological collections that change every four months. (Gerberau 32. ☎201 25 66. Open Tu-Su 10am-5pm. Free, but donations are requested.)

MUSEUM FÜR NEUE KUNST. Freiburg's Museum of Modern Art displays the works of 20th-century German artists such as Otto Dix in a clean-lined, modern building. Borrow the extremely helpful English language guide for an enlightening lesson on modern German art. (Marienstr. 10a. ☎201 25 81. Open Tu-Su 10am-5pm. Tours Sa 3pm and Su 11am. Free. Special exhibits DM5, students DM3.)

BRAUEREI GANTER. The brewery conducts tours tracking the production of their malt beverage. The grand finale of the one-hour tour consists of a portion of *Fleischkäse*, bread, potato salad, and lots of beer atop one of the factory buildings. Call ahead to get in on the group tours. *(Schwarzwaldstr. 43.* ☎ *218 51 81. S-Bahn #1 to "Brauerei Ganter." Tours Tu and Th at 1:30pm. Free.)*

AUGUSTINERMUSEUM. A good bet for those who dig lots of medieval art, the Augustiner impresses with its heart-warming depictions of Schwarzwald life. Included is admission to the **Wentzingerhaus Museum für Stadtgeschichte,** which displays paraphernalia related to Freiburg's colorful history. *(Augustiner at Salzstr. 32. Housed in a former monastery 2 blocks south of the Münster.* ☎ *201 25 31. Wentzingerhaus on Münsterpl.* ☎ *201 25 15. Both open Tu-Su 10am-5pm. DM4, students DM2; free 1st Su of every month. Special exhibits DM6, students DM3.)*

MUSEUM FÜR UR- UND FRÜHGESCHICHTE. An immaculate, early Victorian *Schloß* sits atop a hill of vineyards and wildflowers; inside is a museum of ancient history. Myriad crumbling odds and ends illuminate the fascinating prehistory of the South Baden region. *(*☎ *201 25 71. Along Eisenbahnstr. across from the tourist office. Open Tu-Su 10am-5pm. Free, but DM3.50 donation requested, students DM2.)*

SCHWABENTOR AND MARTINSTOR. On the south side of Münsterpl. wobbles the pink-tinted Kaufhaus, a merchants' hall dating from the 1500s. Two medieval gates—the Schwabentor and the Martinstor—stand within blocks of each other in the southeast corner of the Altstadt. The Martinstor, which served as a revolutionary barricade in the politically tumultuous year of 1848, has since been indelibly profaned by a set of golden arches. Now that's progress, Ronald.

OTHER SITES. Tucked away in the blocks between the *Münster* and the tourist office are the **Rathaus,** an amalgam of older buildings whose bells chime daily at noon, and the oddly named **Haus zum Walfisch** (House of the Whale), where Erasmus of Rotterdam lived in exile from Basel for two years following the Reformation. This gold-trimmed wonder is a recreation of the original, destroyed in WWII.

ENTERTAINMENT AND NIGHTLIFE

Freiburg claims to be a city of wine and music, and true to its word, it is awash with *Weinstuben* and *Kneipen*, though club offerings are less abundant. For the current events listings, pick up a free copy of *Freiburg Aktuell* from the tourist office or drop by the *Badische Zeitung* office at Martinstor, where you can buy tickets for upcoming shindigs. (☎ *49 64 67. Open M-Th 9am-5:30pm, F 9am-4:30pm, Sa 9am-1pm.)* The **Freiburger Weinfest** is a weekend-long festival held on Münsterpl. the first weekend in July. Stagger around and sample some 300 different vintages (DM3-6 per glass) while a swing band plays. The triennial three-day ◼**Street Party,** next in 2003, transforms the Altstadt. The annual two-week **Zeltmusikfestival** (the first week in July) brings big-name classical, rock, and jazz performers to two circus tents pitched at the city's edge. Tickets (DM15-40) sell surprisingly fast and can be bought by calling ☎ *50 40 30,* or at the *Badische Zeitung* office. Take S-Bahn #5 to "Bissierstr." and catch the free shuttle bus to the site. In addition, the **Narrenfest** (Fools' Festival) is held the weekend before Ash Wednesday, and the **Weihnachtsmarkt** (Christmas market) runs from Dec. 25-Jan. 6, 2001.

Freiburg's nightlife keeps pace with its students—afternoon cafes become pubs and discos by night. The streets around the university (**Niemensstr., Löwenstr., Humboldtstr.,** and the accompanying alleyways) form the hub of the city's scene.

◼ **Exit,** Kaiser-Josef-Str. 248 (☎ 365 36). Despite its inhospitable name, thousands pour in and stay. Open M and W-Th 10pm-3am, F-Sa 10pm-4am. No cover Th and Sa with student ID, ISICs not accepted. 18+. Cover DM6.

Jazzhaus, Schnewlingstr. 1 (☎ 349 73), across from the train station and to the right. Featuring live performances almost every night, this spacious underground grotto, founded 30 years ago by Miles Davis, has become a mainstay of the Freiburg cultural scene. Open M-Th and Su 10pm-3:30am, F-Sa 8pm-3am. Cover under DM10 for small acts, DM10-45 for better-known performers. Call for tickets or show up after 7pm.

Jos Fritz, Wilhelmstr. 15 (☎300 19). Just follow the noise to this indoor/outdoor enclave for trendy Freiburgers. Open Sa, M 10am-1am, Tu 10am-7pm, W 10am-8pm, Th 10am-1am, F 10am-8pm and 9pm-1am. F 9pm-1am alternates weekly between gay and lesbian night.

Dampfross, Löwenstr. 7 (☎259 39). The small *Kneipe* with big beer. Tiny student bar, with dark wood and American movie posters. *Pils* DM3.60 for 0.3L; salads and pasta DM7-13. The most popular dish is *Pommes mit Kräutercreme* (fries with herb cream; DM5.80). Out the back door is the cafe **Marias,** Löwenstr. 3-5, which plays stylish to Dampfross's traditional. More room, too. Beer DM4, drinks DM11 and up. Both open M-F 10am-2am, Sa from 11am, Su 5pm-1am. Food until 11pm, F and Sa until midnight.

Agar, Löwenstr. 8 (☎38 06 50), next to Martinstor. Lots of attitude. See or be seen. Th is 80s night; other nights range from house to hip-hop. Open Su, Tu, and Th 10pm-3am, F-Sa 11pm-4am. Tu free with student ID. Last entry 1hr. before closing. Cover DM6.

🄽 HIKING AND DAY HIKE

Freiburg's plentiful accommodations, easy access by train, and location make it a superior base for hikes in the Schwarzwald. Mountain biking trails also traverse the Schwarzwald; look for symbols with bicycles to guide you. Maps abound in all the bookstores and at the tourist office. All trails are marked with symbols such as diamonds and circles, and the marker will usually appear 50m after every trail junction if not at the junction itself. For safety precautions to observe while hiking, and the necessary equipment, see p. 57.

A good starting spot in Freiburg is **Schauinsland.** Take streetcar #4 to "Dorfstr.", then bus 21 to "Talstation." From the station, the red circle trail takes you to the top, or you can ride the spectacular 3.6km **Bergbahn.** (☎29 29 30. One-way DM13, students DM11. Runs 9am-5pm) and take the trail down (2hrs.).

Slightly longer, the yellow circle from the top of the mountain connects "Scheminsland Gipfel," "Rappeneck," and "Kappel," after which you can take a bus back to Freiburg (4hr.). A **Rundweg** also exists from the Bergstation that takes you in a panoramic circle around the top (2hrs.). Trails around Shauinsland are mostly forested and are loaded with vistas of Freiburg and the Schwarzwald.

Another good starting spot is **Feldberg.** From the Feldberg-Barental train station, the blue circle and trail 100m to your right leads to the Feldsee, a glacial lake impressively guarded by cliffs (3.5hrs. roundtrip). From the Feldsee, the Feldberg is a steep hike uphill (2hrs.); red diamonds and the bike symbols will guide you. The **Feldbergbahn** will carry you part of the way (DM9) if you want. On a clear day, the Swiss Alps are visible, along with the alarmingly unfenced drop into the Feldsee. Several paths extend from the top, including trails to Titisee.

For a **day-hike,** part of the red diamond **Westweg Pforzheim-Basel** connects Freiburg to Feldberg. The hike requires about 8 hours from **Schauinsland** to **Feldberg-Barental** and offers a glimpse of all aspects of the Schwarzwald—cow pastures, meadows, barns, logging, extreme panoramas, and soaring trees. Particularly noteworthy are the scenic meadows and thick forest between Feldberg and Notschrei. To reach the trail from Schauinsland Bergstation, take a right and head down the driveway to the parking lot. Follow the blue diamond trail to "Halden" and keep going; it meets the red diamond Westweg between "Halden" and "Notschrei" (3-4hrs.).

BREISACH AND THE KAISERSTUHL   ☎07667

Twenty-five kilometers west of Freiburg, Breisach is separated from French Alsace by the Rhein and a few meters of beach on either side. The town's exquisite location comes replete with a beautiful Altstadt surrounded by unending hills of vineyards. Near Breisach is the **Kaiserstuhl,** a clump of lush green hills that were volcanoes in their heyday. Now they attract hikers and bikers who come to see the flora and fauna, many of which are normally found only in warmer climates.

⫶ GETTING THERE. Trains arrive from **Freiburg** every 30min. (DM8). The Freiburg-Breisach train also stops at the towns of Ihringen and Wasenweiler, both located on the range's southern fringes. **Buses** handle the route straight into the hills; check the schedule at the Breisach Hauptbahnhof. Rent **bikes** at **Firma Schweizer,** Richard-Müller-Str. 22, behind the main pedestrian thoroughfare. (☎76 01. Open M-F 9am-12:30pm and 2-6:30pm. DM15 per day.) Jaunts along the Rhein in big white ships are available through **Breisacher Fahrgastschiffahrt,** Rheinuferstr. on the Rhein (☎94 20 10; fax 94 20 30). Two-hour joyrides run DM15; the company also runs ships to Strasbourg and Basel that can be used for one-way travel when not fully booked. Buy tickets at the dock or tourist office.

◪ PRACTICAL INFORMATION. For hiking and biking maps, visit the Breisach **tourist office,** Marktpl. 16. The staff books **rooms** for a DM1 fee. From the train station, turn left on Bahnhofstr., follow Neutorpl. from the rotary intersection, keep the fountain with the huge spinning globe on your right, and go down Rheinstr. into the Marktpl. (☎94 01 55; fax 94 01 58, email breisach-touristik@breisach.de; www.breisach.de. Open May-Oct. M-F 9am-6pm, Sa 10am-1pm, Su 1-4pm; Nov.-Apr. M-F 9am-12:30pm and 1:30-5pm.) The **post office** is one block from the train station (open M-F 8am-noon and 2:30-5:30pm, Sa 8:30am-noon).

⫶◘ ACCOMMODATIONS AND FOOD. Breisach's superb, modern **Jugendherberge,** Rheinuferstr. 12, boasts a stunning riverside location. From the train station, take a left and then go left again at the rotary intersection. After 20m, take the path leading under the main road. Head away from the underpass and cross the bridge, then turn right and walk along the river. Turn left at the hostel sign. (☎76 65; fax 18 47. Meals DM8.70. Sheets DM6. Reception 5-10pm. Curfew 11:30pm. Members only. Dorm beds DM27, over 26 DM32.) There is a **Mini-Mal grocery store** next door to the train station (open M-F 9am-8pm, Sa 9am-4pm).

◪ SIGHTS. Breisach's **Münster** dramatically crowns a steep riverfront promontory crowded with clapboard houses. Constructed between the 12th and 15th centuries, the church is plain compared to nearby cathedrals. Only the writhing, twisting wooden altar, the work of the 16th-century Master Haus Lou, and the 15th century silver arc holding relics of St. Gervasius and Protasius come close to flamboyance. Climb the statue of Zeus and Europa in the courtyard; the uninspired might mistake it for a triangle standing on a bull.

Continuing northward along Radbrunnenallee, a walled hilltop **fortress** boasting well-preserved medieval gates and excellent views of the countryside culminating in the garden atop the **Schloßberg.** The entrance to the garden is on Tullagasse, next to Kapuziner Hotel. In summer, the garden becomes a theater for the annual **Festspiele,** hosting several plays every weekend between mid-June and mid-September. (DM15-20. Call the tourist office for tickets.) Breisach also hosts the **Weinfest Kaiserstuhl und Tuniburg,** where local wines are sampled, sprayed, and supped on the banks of the Rhein during the last weekend in August. Close by in the 17th-century **Rheintor,** the **Museum für Stadtgeschichte,** Rheintorpl. 1, contains a large collection of city artifacts, including 3,000-year-old ceramics and chain-link undergarments from the 15th century—kinky stuff. (☎70 89. Open Tu-F 2-5pm, Sa 11:30am-5pm, Su 11:30am-6pm. Free.)

Wine connoisseurs can register for a tour of **Badischer Winzerkeller,** Zum Kaiserstuhl 16 (☎90 02 70; fax 90 02 32), one of the largest wine cellars in Europe; English speakers should call the tourist office in advance for a tour (3-7 samples DM5-9.50). The cellar is a 1km walk east of town. From the train station, go right on Bahnhofstr. and keep truckin' on Im Gelbstein; it's at the end. Closer by are two cellars specializing in sparkling wine that also offer wine sampling and tours: the **Geldarmann Privatsektkellerei,** Am Schloßberg 1 (☎83 42 58; fax 83 43 51), pours bubbly alcohol from Baden, as does its neighbor, **Gräflich von Kageneck'sche Wein & Sektkellerei,** Kupfertorstr. 35 (☎90 11 37; fax 90 11 99).

The most famous of the Kaiserstuhl's lush trails is the **Kaiserstuhl Nord-Südweg**, which braves the densely-vegetated hills and valleys, forging from Ihringen 16km northward to Endingen. From the Ihringen train station, walk down Eisenbahnstr. for 5 minutes; pass the church to turn right; the trail begins a block later at an alley on your left. The Nord-Südweg is marked by a blue diamond on a yellow field.

SCHWARZWALD (BLACK FOREST)

It might be a bit of an overstatement to say that Germans are obsessed with the dark, but from the earliest fairy tales to Franz Kafka's disturbing fiction, a sense of the uncanny and the sinister has long lurked in the German cultural consciousness. Nowhere is this collective mystique more at home than in the Schwarzwald, a tangled expanse of evergreen covering the southwest corner of Baden-Württemberg. While the Schwarzwald owes its foreboding name to the eerie darkness that prevails under its canopy of vegetation, it is also the source of inspiration for the most quintessential German fairy tales, including the adventures of Hänsel and Gretel as well as a slew of poetry and folk traditions. Many of these regional quirks are now exploited at the pervasive cuckoo-clock-*Lederhosen-Bratwurst*-keychain-and-ice-cream kiosks, which conspire, along with the devastating effects of acid rain, to erode the region's authenticity. Innumerable trails wind through the region, leading willing hikers into more secluded parts of the forest. Skiing is also available in the area; the longest slope is at Feldberg (near Titisee).

The main entry points to the Schwarzwald are Freiburg, in the center; Baden-Baden to the northwest; Stuttgart to the east; and Basel, Switzerland, to the southwest. Most visitors use a bike, as public transportation is sparse. Rail lines encircle the perimeter, with only one **train** penetrating the region. **Bus** service is more thorough, albeit slow and less frequent. The **Freiburg tourist office** (p. 369) is the best place to gather information about the Schwarzwald.

HOCHSCHWARZWALD (HIGH BLACK FOREST)

Arguably the most enthralling neck of the woods, the Hochschwarzwald is so named for its high, pine-carpeted mountains, towering dramatically above lonely lakes and remote villages. The best source of information for the area is the **Freiburg tourist office**, Rotteckring 14 (☎(0761) 368 90 90; fax 37 00 37).

At 1493m, **Feldberg** is the Schwarzwald's tallest mountain. The ski lift runs in summer and winter (round-trip DM10). Call the **tourist office,** Kirchgasse 1, for information about Feldberg and 16 other ski slopes in the area. (☎(07655) 80 19; fax 801 43; www.feldberg-schwarzwald.de. Open M-Tu and Th-F 10am-noon and 3-5pm, W 10am-noon.) To get to Feldberg from the Feldberg-Bärental train station, head right upon exiting and follow the signs to Feldsee or Feldberg (7km). Sporadic bus service also exists from the train station and regional towns such as Titisee to Feldbergerhof, right next to the ski lift. The tourist office is between the buses and ski lift, in the ground floor of the Feldberger Hof hotel. At 1234m above sea level, Feldberg's **Jugendherberge Hebelhof (HI),** Passhöhe 14, may be the highest in Germany. Take the Titisee-Schluchsee train to Feldberg-Bärental, then the bus to "Hebelhof." (☎(07676) 221; fax 12 32. Reception 8am-10pm. Curfew 10:45pm. Reservations for winter. Members only. Dorm beds DM26, over 26 DM31.) For a **ski and weather report,** call ☎(07676) 12 14.

TITISEE   ☎07651

The Titisee and Schluchsee are two of the most beautiful lakes in the region. The more touristed Titisee (pronounced: TEE-tee-zay) is mobbed by Germans on hot summer days, and its lakeside pedestrian zone is a cheesy strip of souvenir shops and *Imbiß* stands. The 45-minute train ride from Freiburg glides through the scenic **Höllental** (Hell's Valley). Between the Hintergarten

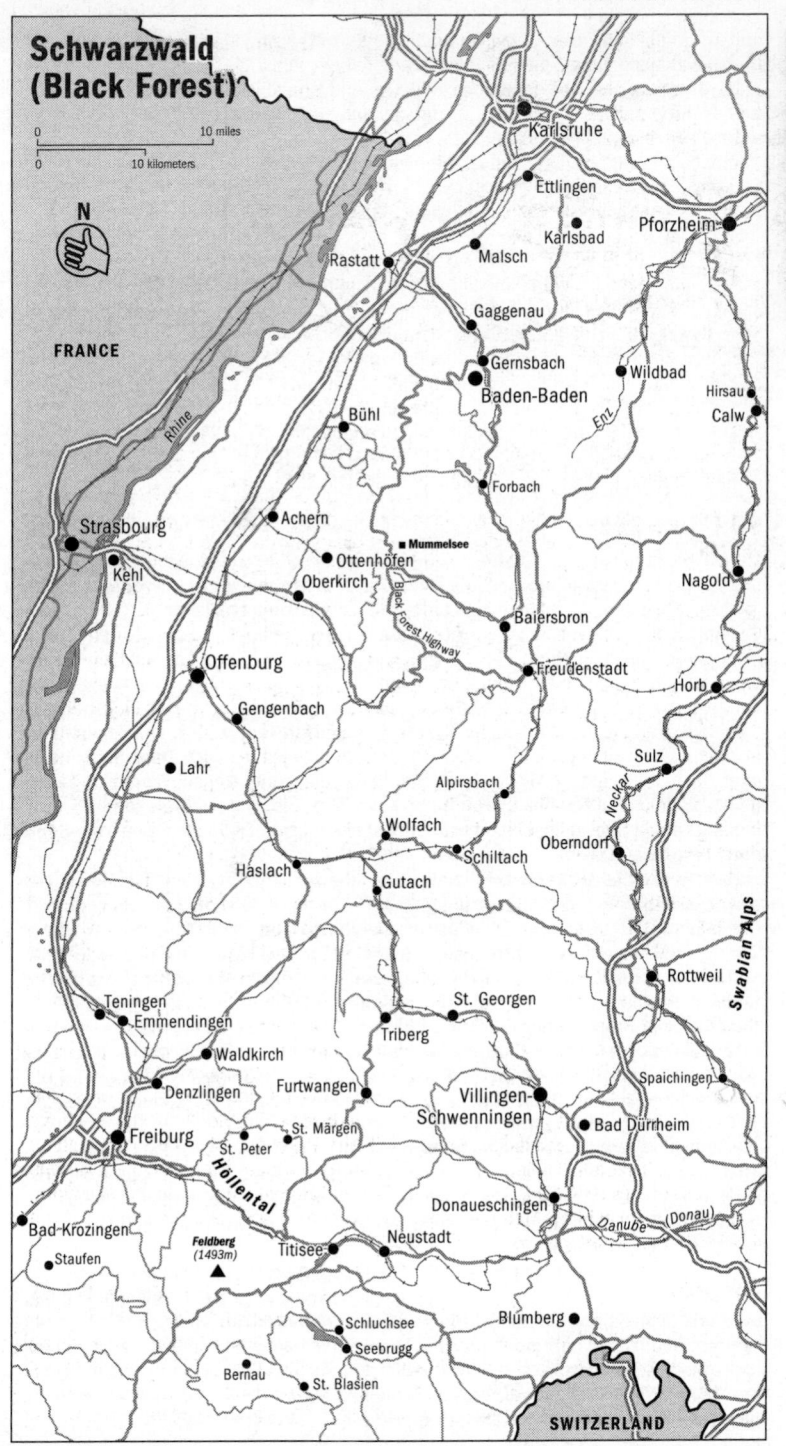

Schwarzwald (Black Forest)

0   10 miles
0   10 kilometers

N

FRANCE

Karlsruhe

Ettlingen

Pforzheim

Karlsbad

Malsch

Rastatt

Gaggenau

Gernsbach

Baden-Baden

Wildbad

Hirsau

Calw

Bühl

Forbach

Enz

Achern

■ Mummelsee

Strasbourg

Kehl

Ottenhöfen

Oberkirch

Nagold

Black Forest Highway

Baiersbron

Offenburg

Freudenstadt

Horb

Gengenbach

Sulz

Lahr

Alpirsbach

Wolfach

Oberndorf

Neckar

Schiltach

Haslach

Gutach

Rottweil

Swabian Alps

St. Georgen

Teningen

Emmendingen

Triberg

Waldkirch

Spaichingen

Denzlingen

Furtwangen

Villingen-Schwenningen

Bad Dürrheim

Freiburg

St. Peter

St. Märgen

Höllental

Donaueschingen

Bad Krozingen

Feldberg
(1493m)

Titisee

Neustadt

Danube (Donau)

Staufen

Blumberg

Schluchsee

Seebrugg

Bernau

St. Blasien

SWITZERLAND

Rhine

and Himmelreich train stops, in a gap of sky in the midst of tunnels, watch for the Hirschsprung, a regal statue of a stag that crowns the cliff in a harrowingly narrow part of the valley. According to legend, the statue was created because a deer once narrowly escaped a hunter's arrow by making the impossible leap across the chasm.

Titisee's **tourist office,** Strandbadstr. 4, books **rooms** for a DM4 fee and rents **bikes** for DM15 per day; they also dispense maps (DM1-15) of the 130km of nearby hiking trails. From the station, hang a left on Parkstr., take a left after Strandbadstr., and then follow Seestr. as it curves to the right. The office is behind a set of flags. (☎980 40; fax 98 04 40; www.titisee.de. Open July-Sept. M-F 8am-6pm, Sa 9am-noon and 3-5pm, Su 10am-noon; Oct.-June M-F 9am-noon and 1:30-5:30pm.) Hiking trails start in front of the office. Consider the placid **Seerundweg,** or keep going along Strandbadstr. and turn right on Alte Poststr. for more challenging trails. Rent **boats** from vendors along Seestr. (paddleboats and rowboats DM7 per 30min., DM11 per hr.). Guided **boat tours** depart from the same area, run by **Bootsverleih Winterhalder.** (☎82 14. 25min. DM6.) Titisee's **Jugendherberge HI, Veltishof am Titisee,** Bruderhalde 27, is 2km outside of town by a farm-like valley. (☎238; fax 756. Sheets DM6. Reception 5-10pm. Members only. Call ahead. Dorm beds DM27, over 26 DM32.)

SCHLUCHSEE   ☎07656

If the tourist density in Titisee is too great, head south to the Schluchsee, home to a slew of first-rate hiking trails. The simple **Seerundweg** circumvents the lake (18km, about 4hr.). More difficult and rewarding trails depart from the **Sportplatz** parking lot, a 15-minute walk up Dresselbacher Str. past the huge resort hotel. For an 18km, 6-hour trek, follow TK6, which leads past the **Vogel-haus,** which houses a folk museum (open daily 1-6pm). Then follow signs for Hingerhäuser, Fischbach, Bildstein, and Aha before returning to Schluchsee. Cruise around the lake on the **Gisele Seerundfahrten,** which runs **boat trips** between Schluchsee, Seebrugg, Aha, and Blasiwald. (☎449. June-Sept. daily every hr. 10am-5pm. DM4-7.) In Schluchsee, the boats depart from the beach near the **Aqua Fun Spaßbad,** which has several pools, water slides, and a sandy beach. Facing Schluchsee, it's to the left of the harbor. (☎77 32. Open May-Sept. daily 9am-7pm. DM6.)

Hourly double-decker **trains** make the 30-minute jaunt from Titisee to the towns of Schluchsee and Seebrugg (DM3.40). **Buses** #7255 and 7257 also connect the lakes (DM3.50). Rent **bikes** at the gas station on Freiburger Str. towards Titisee (DM12 per day). Schluchsee's **tourist office** is a block into the pedestrian zone in the *Kurhaus.* From the train station, turn right, walk through the underpass, and turn left up the brick sidewalk of Kirchsteige. The office sits at the corner of Fischbacher Str. and Lindenstr. The staff books **rooms** for free and offers a *Wanderwochen* deal, by which you can get a week's stay in a private room and hiking maps galore for DM280 and up. (☎77 32; fax 77 59; www.schluchsee.de. Open May-Sept. M-F 8am-6pm, Sa-Su 10am-noon; Oct.-Apr. M-F 8am-noon and 2-6pm.)

The **Jugendherberge Schluchsee-Wolfsgrund (HI),** Im Wolfsgrund 28, is ideally situated on the shore with a stunning lake view and comfortable facilities. From the station, cross the tracks and hop the fence, then follow the path right, over the bridge parallel to the tracks, and to the hostel's front door. (☎329; fax 92 37. Dinner DM8.70. Laundry DM6. Reception closed 2-5pm. Curfew 11pm. Dorm beds DM25, over 26 DM30. May-Oct. DM2-3 *Kurtaxe.*) **Haus Bergfrieden,** Dresselbacher Str. 23, is uphill from the village center. Its tidy rooms are a steal. (☎309. Breakfast included. DM25-28 per person.) Pitch a tent at **Campingplatz Wolfsgrund.** Walk left up Bahnhofstr. and continue onto Freiburger Str., take a left on Sägackerweg, follow it past Am Waldrain, and take another left. (☎573. DM9.50 per person. Campsite DM12.) Stock up on **groceries** at **Schmidt's Markt,** Im Rappennest 2. (☎15 54. Open M-F 7:30am-8pm, Sa 7:30am-4pm.)

NO BREAD CRUMBS THIS TIME
The Schwarzwald may be a hiker's paradise, but with its labyrinth of twisting trails it can easily become a tangled hell for novices. Even the trail markers are baffling: red diamonds, blue dots, green circles...purple horseshoes, anyone? Thankfully, the **Schwarzwaldverein** (Black Forest Association) has set up a system of markers for the major trails in the area. The trails are always marked by a diamond and are at least 10km of intense hiking each. These odysseys include the **Freiburg-Bodensee Querweg** (half-red, half-white diamond on a yellow field) and the 280km **Pforzheim-Basel Westweg** (always marked by a red diamond). Blue diamonds often mark trails with lots of uphill climbing and rewarding panoramas. **Terrain-Kurwege,** or TK, are well-marked trails that explore the local territory and are rarely longer than 10km. They are numbered in order of difficulty. A **Rundweg** is a connect-the-dots loop; a **Seerundweg,** which follows the shoreline of a lake, will be less taxing. A **Panoramaweg,** most popular with tourists, offers stunning views of the surrounding landscape. After trail junctions and intersections, look for a trail marker 50m down the path to confirm you're on the right track.

SEEBRUGG
☎ 07656

Three kilometers down the lake at the end of the train line, the town of Seebrugg consists of nothing but a train station, a beach, and the **Jugendherberge Schluchsee-Seebrugg (HI),** Seebrugg 9. Then again, what more could you want? The splendid, renovated building couched among pine trees is a five-minute walk along the paved path from the train station. (☎494; fax 18 89; email jh-schluchsee-seebrugg@t-online.de. Sheets DM6. Reception 12:30-1pm, 5-6pm, and 6:30-10pm. Curfew 10pm. Members only. Dorm beds DM25, over 26 DM30. May-Oct. *Kurtaxe* DM1.90.) Next to the hostel, a red diamond **hiking trail** darts into the forest, heading for the neighboring village of **Blasiwald** and its hillside cottages. This trail connects to the easier red dot **Seerundweg,** both crossing the admirable dam that spans a narrow neck of the lake. Debut your dental floss thong at the **Strandbad** beach to the left of the station. (☎13 65. Open daily May-Sept. from 10am. DM2.50.) **Boat rental** is also available here (DM6 per 30 min., DM10 per hr.).

ST. BLASIEN
☎ 07672

Were it not for its towering cathedral, St. Blasien would be an average town tucked into the southern mountains of the Black Forest. Third in size only to St. Peter's in Rome and Les Invalides in Paris, the **Dom**'s dome is constructed in a monumental classical style, rising above a charming Altstadt and immaculate white **Rathaus.** The origin of the cathedral stretches back to the 9th century, when the relics of St. Blasius were to be brought from Rome to Rheinau. On the way, the Benedectine monks chose to settle the well-protected Alb valley. Since then, the monastery has weathered a peasant's revolt and four fires, resulting in its late 18th-century neoclassical resurrection. (Open May-Sept. daily 8am-6:30pm, Oct.-Apr. 8:30am-5:30pm. Free concerts July-Aug. Tu and Sa 8:15pm.) In the same building as the tourist office sits the **Museum St. Blasien,** with exhibits on the Dom's past and town history. (Open Tu-Su 2:30-5pm. DM3, students DM1.) Every two years, St. Blasien hosts an international wood-carving contest for one week in late August. The next face-off will take place in 2002.

No trip to St. Blasien is complete without a hike up the northern hillside for an unparalleled glimpse of the Dom. Stick to Todtmooser Str. in the pedestrian zone, cross the river and head straight uphill. Cross Luisenstr., continue onto Dr.-Determan-Weg; after turning the corner, a set of stone stairs to the left leads to the forest. From there, a number of trails offer excellent views of the Dom. Particularly popular is Unterer Philosophenweg; turn left. Or turn right on Blasiwalder Weg for its famous vista and **Windberg** waterfall. On the other side of town, more trails scale the idyllic **Holzberg** (Wood Mountain). Or facing the right side of the Dom, take Tuskulumweg and follow it through the pedestrian tunnel, following signs for **TK1.** A plethora of trailheads await on the other side of the highway.

A sublime 20 minute **bus** ride (#7319) connects St. Blasien with **Seebrugg** and the train system (1 per hr., DM6.20). The **tourist office,** Am Kurgarten 1-3, has hiking maps and a catalog of **rooms.** From the main bus station, cross Umgehungsstr., enter the pedestrian zone, and bear right under the orange-trimmed gate. The tourist office is on the left. (☎414 30; fax 414 38; email tourist-information@st-blasien.de; www.st-blasien.de. Open M-F 10am-noon and 3-5pm and Sa 10am-noon; Oct.-May closed Sa.)

Most accommodations are in **Menzenschwand** (see **bus,** above). The **Jugendherberge Menzenschwand (HI),** Vorderdorfstr. 10, offers the cheapest lodgings in the area. (☎(07675) 326; fax 14 35. Sheets DM6. Breakfast included. Call ahead. Dorm beds DM25, over 26 DM30.) **Private rooms** in Menzenschwand run from DM22 per night, considerably cheaper than those in St. Blasien. Contact the Menzenschwand **tourist office,** Hinterdorfstr. 15, near the "Hirschen/Hintertor" bus stop. (☎(07675) 930 90; fax 17 09; email tourist-information@st-blasien-menzenschwand.de. Same hours as the St. Blasien tourist office.) If you miss the last bus to Menzenschwand, the cheapest night's stay in St. Blasien is **Hotel Garni Kurgarten,** Fürstabt-Gerbert-Str. 12, across the street from the tourist office. (☎527. Singles from DM28, doubles DM50.) **Edeka,** across from the Dom, has **groceries.**

ST. PETER AND ST. MÄRGEN

Sunk deep into a valley of cow-speckled hills 17km from Freiburg, St. Peter and St. Märgen exude an air of balmy tranquility. **Bus** #7216 runs from **Freiburg** to St. Märgen via St. Peter, but the more common route requires a **train** ride along the Freiburg-Neustadt line to "Kirchzarten" (3rd stop), where bus #7216 heads to St. Peter. Only half the buses continue on to St. Märgen; always check with the driver.

St. Peter, closer to Freiburg and surrounded by cherry orchards, juts high in the curative air, breaking through a crust of dark pine. Its **Klosterkirche** rises above the otherwise uneventful skyline, egging the rest of town on with a gaudy interior of turquoise and mauve. *(☎(07660) 910 10. Open 24hr. Tours Su 11:30am, Tu 11am, Th 2:30pm. DM5. Organ concerts July-Sept. Su 5pm. DM10, students DM7.)* The **tourist office** is in the Klosterhof. Get off the bus at "Zähringer Eck"; the office is right in front of the church under the *Kurverwaltung* sign. The staff has a list of affordable **rooms** starting at DM25. (☎(07660) 91 02 24; fax 91 02 44. Open M-F 8am-noon and 2-5pm; June-Oct. Sa 11am-1pm.) Many hiking paths—most of them well marked—begin at the tourist office and abbey. A relatively easy, but very scenic 8km path leads to **St. Märgen;** follow the blue diamonds of the **Panoramaweg.** From the abbey, make a sharp right alongside the Klosterkirche (do not cross the stream and main road), heading for the *Jägerhaus;* then cross the highway.

With links to all major Schwarzwald trails and a number of gorgeous day hikes, St. Märgen rightfully calls itself a *Wanderparadies.* One of the more challenging local trails leads to the **Zweibach waterfall;** follow signs with a black dot on a yellow field (16km, 4hr.). To reach the start of the trail from the town center, walk downhill along Feldbergstr., turn left onto Landfeldweg, and follow signs for *Rankmühle.* The **tourist office** sits in the Rathaus 100m from the "Post" bus stop. The staff provides good hiking and biking maps (DM5) and finds **rooms** for free. (☎(07669) 91 18 17; fax 91 18 40. Open M-F 8am-noon and 2-5pm; June-Aug. also Sa 10am-noon; Nov.-Dec. closed afternoons.)

CENTRAL BLACK FOREST

More than just hiking and biking, the thing that makes the central Black Forest tick is clocks. In 1667, the first wooden **Waaguhr** came into existence in Waldau. Since then, the Black Forest has become a breeding ground of ticking timepieces, with 12,000 clockmakers churning out 60 million clocks a year. The **Deutsche Uhrenstraße** (German clock route) winds its way through a number of towns, connecting glitzy clock museums and historic clock factories with tourist-hungry shops. Along the way, hikers haul past the Neckar and Danube rivers, and the famed **Schwarzwaldbahn** chugs through tunnels and over steep chasms.

DONAUESCHINGEN   ☎ 0771

A ten-year-old Mozart stopped in Donaueschingen on his way from Vienna to Paris and played three concerts in the castle. Since then, Donaueschingen has cultivated its status as a rest-stop for musical luminaries and the average traveler alike. Located on the Baar Plateau between the Schwarzwald and the Schwäbische Alb, it is an ideal starting place for forays into the **Schwarzwald**, the **Lake Konstanz** region, and the **Wutach Schlucht** (Wutach Gorge) 15km to the south.

▮ PRACTICAL INFORMATION. Trains connect Donaueschingen to **Freiburg** (1½hr., 1 per hr., DM20), **Triberg** (30min., 1 per hr., DM12), and **Rottweil** (30min., 1 per hr., DM12). Rent **bikes** at **Zweiradhaus Rothweiler,** Max-Egon-Str. 11 for DM10-20 per day, depending on the length of your cycling trip. (☎ 131 48; fax 127 95. Open Mar.-Sept. M-Tu and Th-F 9:30am-12:30pm and 2:30-6pm, W 9:30am-12:30pm.) The **tourist office**, Karlstr. 58, books **rooms** for free. Cross the bridge and veer right up the hill past the Schloß and turn left at Karlstr. (☎ 85 72 21; fax 85 72 28; email tourist.info@donaueschingen.de; www.donaueschigen.de. Open June-Aug. M-F 9am-6pm, Sa 10am-12:30pm; Sept.-May M-F 8am-noon and 2-5pm.) The office provides information about Donaueschingen's annual **Musiktage** in mid-October, a modern music festival. **Internet access** is available at **Internet-Café,** Raiffeisenstr. 13 in Freizeit Center. (Open M-F 10am-midnight, Sa 1-10pm, Su 10am-8pm. DM5 per ½ hr.) The **post office** is on the corner of Schulstr. and Kronenstr., near the tourist office (open M-F 8:30am-noon and 2-6pm, Sa 8:30am-noon). The **postal code** is 78166.

▮▮ ACCOMMODATIONS AND FOOD. Rest your weary feet at **Hotel Bären,** Josefstr. 7-9, on the street leading from the train station to town. (☎ 25 18. Basic breakfast buffet included. Large singles with same-floor shower DM45, doubles DM90.) Donaueschingen offers many pricey restaurants along Josefstr., although most have specials running DM10-14. Try **Fürstenberg Bräustübe,** Postpl. 1-4 (☎ 36 69), across the bridge in the corner of the pink house. **Pizzeria da Alfredo,** Villinger Str. 6, near the Rathaus, satisfies Italian cravings for DM8-30 (open daily 11am-2:30pm and 5:30pm-midnight).

▣ SIGHTS. Donaueschingen's spurious claim to fame is its status as the "source" of the 2840km Danube, the second-longest river in Europe and the only major one to flow west to east. Actually, the Danube begins where the Brigach and Brey Rivers converge, but the townsfolk decided to overlook this minor detail and build a monument to the river anyway. The **Donauquelle** (source of the Danube) is an unimpressive, shallow, rock-bottomed basin encased by mossy 19th-century stonework in the garden of **Schloß Fürstenberg,** located (by some inexplicable coincidence) right next to the Fürstenberg souvenir booth. The Schloß contains the oldest known medieval manuscript of the epic **Nibelungenlied,** spectacular tapestries, and a glorious bathroom—a shining marble cave with a massage-shower (no, you don't get to try it). The obligatory tour departs hourly. *(Open Easter-Sept. M and W-Su 9-11:30am and 2-4:30pm. DM5, students DM4. Garden always open.)* Across the street from the Schloß the **Fürstenberg Sammlungen,** Karlspl. 7, is a museum cluttered with former possessions of the princes of Fürstenberg. Diversity is the key with a room of clocks, an overgrown rock and mineral collection, and the thoroughly horrifying skeleton(s) of infant Siamese twins. *(☎ 865 63. Open Tu-Sa 10am-1pm and 2-5pm, Su 10am-5pm.)* The museum, the Schloß, and the adjacent puddle are all within a 10-minute walk of the train station. Take a right in front of the station and walk one block before turning left at Josefstr., then cross the bridge and turn right before the church.

If the Fürstenberg decor leaves you covetous, you can at least get royally smashed on free samples of the family beer at the **Fürstliche Fürstenberger Brauerei,** Postpl. 1-4, behind Haldenstr. *(☎ 862 06. 90 min. brewery tours held on weekdays. DM7. Call to arrange in advance.)* Bike fiends rejoice: Donaueschingen is a terminus of the Danube **bicycle trail,** which skirts the river all the way to Vienna. The tourist office sells a map (DM18.80). Take Josefstr. from the station and turn right on Prinz-Fritzi-Allee into the **Fürstenberg Park,** where bicycle trails abound. Hikers can also take heart: part of the Schwarzwald rings the western edge of town. Follow Karl-str. to the blue **Rathaus,** then take Villinger Str. away from town, making a left at the *Jägerhaus* sign. From there, a few trails venture into the forest.

TRIBERG   ☎07722

Tucked in a lofty valley 800m above sea level, the touristy whistle stop of Triberg has attitude about its altitude.

▐▌ PRACTICAL INFORMATION. Trains chug from Triberg to **Freiburg** (1¾hr., 1 per hr., DM32) and **Rottweil** (1½hr., 1 per hr., DM15). Triberg's **tourist office** hides on the ground floor of the local *Kurhaus.* From the train station, cross the bridge, go under it, and head up steep Féjusstr., which turns into Hauptstr. Pass the Markt-platz (10min.) and a little farther up at Hotel Pfaff take a left; the office is in the building behind the flags. Alternatively, look for signs just before the Marktplatz that lead to a shorter but more complicated route. Their staff gives out brochures, sells town maps (DM1), and dispenses a mammoth catalog of all hotels, *Pen-sionen,* and private rooms in the region. (☎95 32 30; fax 95 32 36; www.triberg.de. Open M-F 9am-5pm; May-Sept. also Sa 10am-noon.)

▐▛▌ ACCOMMODATIONS AND FOOD. The town's sparkling, modern **Jugendherberge (HI),** Rohrbacher Str. 35, straddles a mountain and offers spectacu-lar views of two valleys, though getting there requires a masochistic 30-minute climb up Friedrichstr. (which turns into Rohrbacher Str.) from the tourist office. The sleek, spacious facilities are quite luxurious. (☎41 10; fax 66 62. Sheets DM6. Reception 5-7pm and at 9:45pm. Call ahead. Dorm beds DM25, over 26 DM30.) For those apprehensive about the climb, the **Hotel Zum Bären,** Hauptstr. 10, offers worn-in rooms, most with showers, close to the town center and the waterfall entrance. (☎44 93. Breakfast included. Singles DM37, with shower and toilet DM45; doubles with sink DM66, with shower and toilet DM84.) Look for cuckoos at **Tick-Tack Stube,** Marktpl. 5, while you wait for traditional German fare (DM10-20. ☎68 19. Open daily 10am-2pm and 4-10pm.) Next to the waterfall entrance, **Lilie,** Wallfahrtsstr. 3, offers good deals despite its touristy location. (☎44 19. Open daily 10am-10pm. Daily specials DM9 and up.)

▣ SIGHTS. The inhabitants brag in superlatives about the **Gutacher Wasserfall**—the **highest waterfall in Germany**—a series of bright cascades tumbling over moss-covered rocks for 163 vertical meters. Swarming with more than 400,000 visitors every year, these falls are tame by Niagara standards; however, the idyllic hike through the lush, towering pine trees makes up for the unimpressive trickle. The somewhat steep climb dissuades the less-than-fit from ascending **Kaskadenweg** to the top of the waterfall. *(park admission DM2.50, students DM1.)* The signs within the park for the **Wallfahrtskirche** point along Kulturweg to the small **Pilgrim Church,** where pious ones have, according to legend, been miraculously cured since the 17th century. Keep going along Kroneckweg and follow the *Panoramaweg* signs for some hiking with an excellent view of the Schwarzwald valley. The **Schwarzwald Museum,** Wallfahrtsstr. 4, back in town, is directly across the street from the waterfalls. The museum is packed with Schwarzwald paraphernalia of every imaginable variety, from re-enactments of the daily life of the *Schwarzwald Volk* (complete with slimy wax people) to a Schwarzwald model railroad (DM1 to watch it go) that chugs away along a highly detailed cardboard landscape. (☎44 34. *Open daily 10am-5pm, closed on weekends in Nov. and Dec. DM6, students DM3.)* Beyond these attractions, the region's splendid natural surroundings promise some scrumptious hiking. Numerous trail signs on the outskirts of town point the way to a portion of the Pforzheim-Basel **Westweg**—look for red diamond trail markers. The tourist office sells hiking maps (DM5.50), and more detailed guides are avail-able at the town's bookstores and souvenir shops.

ROTTWEIL   ☎ 0741

High up on a plateau with a view of the Swabian Alps, Rottweil bears the distinction of being the oldest city in Baden-Württemberg. An independent city under the Holy Roman Empire, Rottweil's contributions to the world's well-being have included both flameless gunpowder and certain pernicious canines. It comes as no surprise that the city is a bustling, ferocious little village that knows how to party. Chief among its shindigs is Rottweil's famous **Fasnet** celebration, which draws gawkers from all over Germany to watch 4,000 *Narren* (fools) storm through town in wooden masks and expensive costumes in a festive attempt to expel winter; the next outbreak is February 26-27, 2001. The **Fronleichnam** (feast of Corpus Christi) ceremony (June 14, 2001) reignites old Protestant-Catholic feuds in an innocent re-enactment.

⚡🄷 ORIENTATION AND PRACTICAL INFORMATION. Lying on the Stuttgart-Zürich rail line, Rottweil is easily accessible by hourly **trains** to **Stuttgart** (1½hr., DM30). The train station lies in the valley below the town center, which translates into a 20-minute uphill climb. Turn right upon leaving the station and head upward. When you reach the bridge, take another right to cross it. Hauptstr., the second block on your left, is the center of the town's action. Or take one of the frequent buses from the train station to "Stadtmitte." Halfway up the street on the right-hand side is the **tourist office,** Hauptstr. 23. The office books **rooms** for free and offers maps, an English guide to the city, and *Freizeit Spiegel*—a free publication detailing artistic offerings. (☎ 49 42 80 or 49 42 81; fax 49 43 73; email tourist-information@rottweil.de; www.rottweil.de. Open Apr.-Sept. M-F 10am-6pm, Sa 9am-1pm; Oct.-Mar. M-F 10am-1pm and 2-5pm.) Free 90-minute **tours** depart from the tourist office every Saturday at 2:30pm. Rent **bikes** at **Alfred Kaiser,** Balingerstr. 9, at the end of the bridge leading out of town from Hauptstr. (☎ 89 19. DM30 per day, mountain bikes DM40. Open M-W 9am-12:30pm, 2-6:30pm, Th-F 9am-12:30pm, 2-7pm, Sa 9am-3pm.) **Internet access** is available at **GNet,** Bruderschaftgasse 2-4. (☎ 49 43 53. Open M, W 5-10pm, F 6-11pm.) The **post office,** 78628 Rottweil, is at Königstr. 12 (open M-F 8am-12:30pm and 2-6pm, Sa 8am-12:30pm).

🄵🄾 ACCOMMODATIONS AND FOOD. Inexpensive accommodations are difficult to find in the summer months; call early. To reach the small and homey **Jugendherberge (HI),** Lorenzgasse 8, turn right on Hauptstr. and left onto Lorenzgasse. Go right at the ivy-covered building, and take a quick left at the faded *Jugendherberge* sign. Many of the cramped six- to eight-bed rooms in this half-timbered house face out onto the terrifically steep plunge into the Neckar. The hostel is closed for renovations until late spring of 2001. (☎ 76 64. Breakfast included. Sheets DM6. Reception 5-10:30pm. DM23, over 26 DM28.) The *Pension* **Goldenes Rad,** Hauptstr. 38, is often booked solid several weeks in advance. (☎ 74 12. Reception M-Sa 11:30am-2pm and 5pm-midnight, Su 11:30am-2pm and 6pm-midnight. Singles DM38; doubles DM70.) For traditional regional cooking, head to **Zum goldenen Becher,** Hochbrücktorstr. 17. A family restaurant where meals run DM12-30. (☎ 76 85. Open Tu-Su 11am-midnight.) At **Rotuvilla,** Hauptstr. 63, feast on many incarnations of wood-oven pizza (DM9-16) in a half-timbered dining room. (☎ 416 95. Open M and W-Su 11:30am-2pm and 5pm-midnight.)

🄶 SIGHTS. Rottweil's fanatic adherence to old traditions is not limited to celebrations. The town is a living architecture museum, its buildings graced with historic murals and meticulously crafted windows. At the summit of the hill looms the 13th-century **Schwarzes Tor,** built in 1289 and enlarged in 1571 and 1650. Higher yet the **Hochturm** offers a stunning view of the Swabian Alps from its top. To scale all 54m, pick up the key to the tower from the tourist office for DM2 and an ID. On weekends, the key is available next door at Café Schädle. Across Hauptstr. from the tourist office and the Gothic **Altes Rathaus** stands the **Stadtmuseum,** Hauptstr. 20, which houses a 15th-century treaty between Rottweil and nine Swiss cantons—still valid to this day—and a collection of wooden masks from the *Fasnet* celebrations. (☎ 49 42 56. Open Tu-Sa 10am-noon and 2-5pm, Su 10am-noon. DM1.)

Behind the Altes Rathaus, the Gothic **Heilig-Kreuz-Münster** (Cathedral of the Holy Cross) houses an interesting array of gilded lanterns that are carried through town annually in the **Corpus Christi** procession. Subject to the winds of architectural fashion, this cathedral flip-flopped from 12th-century Romanesque to 15th-century Gothic to 17th-century Baroque and back to 19th-century Gothic revivalism. Behind the pink Rococo **Predigerkirche** stands the refreshingly modern **Dominikanermuseum**, on Kriegsdamm. The museum is home to a collection of medieval sculptures of saints and an excellent exhibit on Rottweil's Roman past, highlighted by a 570,000-tile 2nd-century mosaic. (☎ *78 62; fax 49 43 77. Open Tu-Su 10am-1pm and 2-5pm. DM3.*) For medieval stone sculptures, drop by the neighboring art collection in the **Lorenzkapelle,** Lorenzgasse 17. (☎ *49 42 98. Open Tu-Su 2-5pm. DM1.*)

BODENSEE (LAKE CONSTANCE)

Nearly land-locked Germany has long suffered from something of a Mediterranean complex. For this cold country, there are no white sand beaches of the Riviera, no sparkling waters of the Greek islands, none of the sun-bleached stucco of Italy—except for a strip of land on the **Bodensee.** In this stretch of southern Baden-Württemberg, potted palms line the streets, public beaches are filled with sunbathers tanning to a melanomic crisp, and daily business is conducted with a thoroughly un-German casualness. Looking out across the lake, it's easy to see how the deception works so smoothly, as the surprisingly warm waters glow an intense turquoise blue more typically found in the Caribbean than in European lakes. With the snow-capped Swiss and Austrian Alps soaring in the background, the Bodensee is one of Germany's most stunning destinations.

Getting to the region by **train** is easy; **Konstanz** and **Friedrichshafen** have direct connections to many cities in southern Germany. Rail transport within the region requires long rides and tricky connections due to the absence of a single route that fully encircles the lake. The bright white boats of the **BSB** (Bodensee-Schiffs-Betriebe) and other local and international ferry lines, known collectively as the **Weiße Flotte,** provide a more therapeutic and usually quicker alternative. Ships leave hourly from Konstanz and Friedrichshafen for all ports around the lake. Those who plan to spend at least a week here should invest in the 7-day **Bodensee-Pass,** which includes one day of free ship travel and a 50% discount on all rail, bus, and gondola-lift tickets (DM93). Three-day passes are also available at tourist offices. To contact the BSB, look for an office next to the dock, or call the office in Konstanz (☎ 28 13 98; fax 28 13 73).

KONSTANZ (CONSTANCE) ☎ 07531

Spanning the Rhein's exit from the Bodensee, the elegant university city of Konstanz has never been bombed. Part of the city extends into neighboring Switzerland, and the Allies were leery of accidentally striking neutral territory. The proximity of Switzerland and Austria gives the city an open, international flair. Its narrow streets wind around beautifully painted Baroque and Renaissance facades in the central part of town, while gabled and turreted 19th-century houses gleam with a confident gentility along the river promenades. The waters of the Bodensee lap the beaches and harbors, and a palpable jubilation fills the streets.

▮ ORIENTATION AND PRACTICAL INFORMATION

Tickets for the **BSB** ship line to **Meersburg, Mainau,** and beyond are on sale in the building behind the train station (open Mar. to mid-Oct. daily 7:40am-6:35pm). Follow the underground passage near the tourist office to the harbor or buy your tickets on the ship. **Giess Personenschiffahrt** (☎ (07533) 21 77; fax (07533) 986 66) runs private boats hourly from Dock 2 to **Freizeitbad Jakob** and **Freibad Horn** and leads tours of the Bodensee. (45min. June-Aug. daily 10:50am-5:50pm; May and Sept. Su only. DM9, children DM4.50.) **Buses** in Konstanz cost DM2.50 per ride, DM5 for a

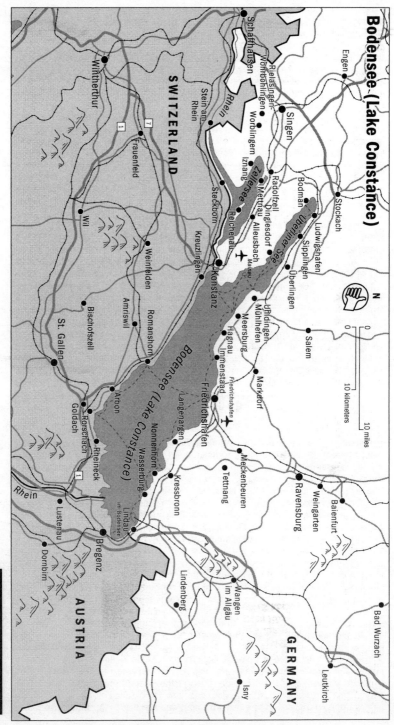

Bodensee (Lake Constance)

N

0 10 kilometers

0 10 miles

SWITZERLAND

Schaffhausen
Engen
Winterthur
Rielasingen-Worblingen
Wohlhausen
Worblingen
Stein am Rhein
Singen
Stockach
Frauenfeld
Iznang
Radolfzell
Bodman
Mettnau
Dingelsdorf
Allensbach
Reichenau
Überlinger See
Ludwigshafen
Sipplingen
Überlingen
Steckborn
Wil
Kreuzlingen
Konstanz
Mainau
Salem
Weinfelden
Überlingen
Mühlhofen
Amriswil
Romanshorn
Meersburg
Hagnau
Immenstaad
Markdorf
St. Gallen
Bischofszell
Bodensee (Lake Constance)
Friedrichshafen
Arbon
Langenargen
Meckenbeuren
Goldach
Nonnenhorn
Wasserburg
Kressbronn
Tettnang
Ravensburg
Weingarten
Rorschach
Rheineck
Lindau im Bodensee
Baienfurt
Lustenau
Bregenz
Wangen im Allgäu
Lindenberg
Dornbirn
Isny
Leutkirch
Bad Wurzach

AUSTRIA

GERMANY

Rhein

Tageskarte, and DM7 for a one-day ticket for two adults and three children. The **Gästekarte**, available at any place of accommodation in the city with a stay of two nights or more (including the youth hostel) costs DM1.50 per day and provides public transit within Konstanz, free or discounted admission to some sights, and one free dunk in the Jakobsbad. Rent **paddleboats and rowboats** at Am Gondelhafen, next to the Stadtgarten. (☎218 81. Open Apr.-Oct. daily 10am-dusk. Rowboats DM14 per hr., paddleboats DM16 per hr.) Rent **bikes** from **Kultur-Rädle**, Bahnhofpl. 29. (☎273 10. Open M-F 9am-12:30pm, 2:30-6pm; Sa 9am-12:30pm; Su 10am-12:30pm. DM17 per day.) For a **taxi**, call ☎222 22.

The friendly but busy **tourist office**, Bahnhofpl. 13, to the right of the train station, provides a helpful walking map (DM0.50) and lots of information about the area. The staff finds **rooms** in private homes for a DM5 fee (three-night minimum stay), or in hotels for shorter stays. (☎13 30 30; fax 13 30 60; email info@tourist information.stadt.konstanz.de. Open Apr.-Oct. M-F 9am-6:30pm, Sa 9am-1pm; Nov.-Mar. M-F 9am-noon and 2-5pm.) City **tours** (DM10) depart from the office as well (Apr.-Oct. M-Sa at 10:30am and Su at 2:30pm). Find the latest *Harry Potter* and other books in English at the **English Bookshop**, Münzgasse 10. (☎150 63. Open M-F 9am-6:30pm, Sa 9am-2pm.) Clean your clothes at **Waschsalon und Mehr**, Hofhalde 3. (Wash DM7, dry DM5 per 10min. Open M-F 10am-7pm, Sa 10am-4pm.) Some establishments list prices in Swiss Francs (SFr); see p. 42 for **exchange rates**. The **post office**, 78462 Konstanz, Markstatte 4, is near the train station (open M-F 8:30am-6pm, Sa 8:30am-noon). Check **email** at **Schulze & Schultze Internet Café**, Pfauengasse 2, near the Schnetztor in the southwest corner of the Altstadt. (☎152 74. Open until 1am. DM7.50 per ½hr.)

ACCOMMODATIONS AND FOOD

Finding lodging in popular Konstanz can induce some massive migraines. Call ahead to secure a place at the marvelous **Jugendherberge Kreuzlingen (HI)**, Promenadenstr. 7. South of the border in Kreuzlingen, Switzerland, but actually closer to downtown Konstanz than the Konstanz hostel, it commands the tip of a small lakefront hill and features cushy leather furniture and a multilingual staff practically breaking their necks to serve you. From May-June, however, the hostel is almost always booked by school groups on vacation. Lone travelers are occasionally given luxurious rooms in vacant student apartments nearby for the same price. The best way there is by foot (20min.). From the train station, turn left, cross the metal bridge over the tracks, turn right, and go through the parking lot to the checkpoint "Klein Venedig." Bear left and walk along Seestr. until the sharp right curve. Instead of following the street, continue straight ahead on the gravel path through the gate, past the billy goats (**goat feed** SFr1), right through the Seeburg castle parking lot, and right up the hill to the building with a flag on top. The hostel rents mountain bikes for SFr15 per day, kayaks for SFr12 per 2hr. (From Germany call ☎(00 41 71) 688 26 63, from Switzerland call ☎(071) 688 26 63; fax 688 47 61. Breakfast and sheets included. Reception 8-9:30am and 5-9pm. Curfew 11pm. Open Mar.-Nov. SFr23 or DM29—both currencies accepted.)

Jugendherberge "Otto-Moericke-Turm" (HI), Zur Allmannshöhe 18, is considerably less luxurious, with cramped rooms in a former water tower next to a graveyard. However, it has a terrific view and is being renovated and reconstructed, with the new additions expected to be finished early in 2001. Take bus #4 from the train station to "Jugendherberge" (7th stop); backtrack and head straight up the hill. (☎322 60; fax 311 63. Breakfast and dinner included. Sheets DM6. Reception Apr.-Oct. 3-10pm; Nov.-Mar. 5-10pm. Curfew 10pm. Lock-out 9:30am-noon. Call ahead. Members only. DM37, over 26 DM42.) **Jugendwohnheim Don Bosco**, Salesianerweg 5, offers cheap, rustic lodgings. From the station, take bus #1 to "Salzberg." Walk toward the intersection along Mainaustr. and keep on going. Or take bus #4, 9B, or 15 to the same stop, but cross Mainaustr. at the intersection and turn left. Walk 200m past the intersection, and follow the sign down the path to the right. Choose from 39 channels in the lively dayroom. (☎622 52; fax 606 88; email don.bosco@telda.net. Breakfast included. Sheets DM6.50. Curfew 10pm. DM29 per person.) Or fall asleep with the lapping waves at **Campingplatz Konstanz-Bruderhofer,** Fohrenbühlweg 50. Take bus #1 to "Staad." The campground is on the waterfront. Call ahead, as it fills up fast. (☎313 88 or 313 92. DM6 per person; DM6-8 per tent.)

Most restaurants in Konstanz are on the expensive side, but some budget-friendly options do exist. For **groceries,** head to **Edeka,** on Münzgasse near the Fischmarkt (open M-F 8am-8pm, Sa 8am-4pm). Stroll through the small streets surrounding the *Münster's* northern side: it is the oldest part of Konstanz, and now the center of its vibrant alternative scene, with health-food stores, left-wing graffiti, and student cafes. The University's **Mensa** on floor K6 dishes out Konstanz's cheapest food. Lunches, including dessert and a view of the lake, cost DM8-9, DM3-5 with any student ID. Buy tokens from the counters on K5 (open M-F 11:15am-1:30pm). The **cafeteria** immediately adjacent has *a la carte* fare and doesn't require ID. (DM2-5. Open M-Th 7:45am-6:30pm, F 7:45am-5pm; Aug. M-F 11am-2pm.) Take bus #9 from the train station to "Universität." The **Fachhochschule Mensa** overlooks the Rhein. An international student ID is required for a changecard; ask the attendant. The hassle is worth it—meals cost DM3.90-4.40 (open M-F 8:30am-4pm).

◆ SIGHTS

Konstanz's **Münster,** built over the course of 600 years, has a 76m soaring Gothic spire and a display of ancient religious objects. Unfortunately, the tower is undergoing renovations until 2003. *(Church open M-Sa 10am-6pm, Su noon-6:30pm. Candlelight tours 7pm on W during the summer. Free.)* The **Rathaus** tells the tale of Konstanz's history with its elaborate frescoes. Wander down **Seestraße,** near the yacht harbor on the lake, or down **Rheinsteig** along the Rhein, to two picturesque waterside promenades. The tree-filled **Stadtgarten,** next to Konstanz's main harbor, provides an unbroken view of the Bodensee and of the statue of the voluptuous *Imperia* who guards the harbor. Across the Rhein from the Altstadt, near the "Sternenplatz" bus stop, is the **Archäologisches Landesmuseum,** Benediktinerpl. 5, a three-floor assemblage of intriguing things from Baden-Württemberg—old town walls, re-assembled skeletons, and spearheads. *(☎980 40; fax 684 52. Open Tu-Su 10am-6pm. DM4, students DM3.)* Follow the aquatic life of the Rhein from its source to the North Sea at the **Sea-Life Museum,** Hafenstr. 9, near the docks. Coming early saves you from the crush of tourists in the afternoon. *(☎12 82 70; fax 128 27 27; www.sealife.de. Open July-Sept. daily 10am-7pm; Apr.-Jun. and Oct. daily 10am-6pm; Nov.-May F 10am-5pm, Sa-Su 10am-6pm. DM17, students DM14.)* Included in admission to the Sea-Life Museum is admission to the adjacent **Bodensee-Naturmuseum,** a large floor of minerals, fossils, and stuffed animals. *(☎12 87 39 00. Open May-Aug. daily 10am-8pm; Sept.-Apr. daily 10am-6pm. DM4, DM3 for students.)*

Konstanz boasts a number of **public beaches;** all are free and open May to September. **Strandbad Horn** *(☎635 50; take bus #5),* is the largest and most crowded; it sports a nude sunbathing section modestly enclosed by hedges. **Strandbad Konstanz-Lizelstetten** offers quieter surroundings *(☎99 88 13; bus #4 to "Wallhausen Hafen").* In inclement weather, head to **Freizeitbad Jakob,** Wilhelm-von-Scholz-Weg 2, near Strandbad Horn, a modern indoor-outdoor pool complex with thermal baths and sun lamps. *(Walk 30 minutes along the waterfront from the train station, or take bus #5 to "Bodensee Therme/ Freizeitbad Jacob." ☎611 63. Open daily 9am-9pm. DM8, students DM5.)*

▶ DAYTRIP FROM KONSTANZ: MAINAU

From the Konstanz train station, take bus #4 (direction: "Bettingen") to "Mainau" (15min., 2 per hr.). Boat trips leave from behind the train station. One-way DM5.40, round-trip DM9. ☎30 30; fax 30 32 48. Island open mid-Mar. to Oct. 7am-8pm; Nov. to mid-Mar. 9am-6pm. DM18.50, students DM9.50, seniors DM15.50, children DM6.50; after 6pm and Nov. to mid-Mar. DM10, students and children free.

The island of **Mainau** is a rich and magnificently manicured garden, the result of the horticultural prowess of generations of Baden princes and the Swedish royal family. A lush arboretum, exotic birds, and huge animals made of flowers surround the pink Baroque palace built by the Knights of the Teutonic Order, who lived here from the 13th to the 18th century. Now thousands of happy tourists scamper across the foot bridge from Konstanz to pose with the blooming peacock and take in the unparalleled view of the Bodensee amidst 30 different varieties of butterflies and a near-tropical setting. In summer, preserve your rapidly diminishing D-Marks by waiting until after 6pm, when students get in for free and the island is swathed by sunsets.

NEAR KONSTANZ: MEERSBURG ☎ 07532

Glaring over the Bodensee, the massive medieval fortress of **Burg Meersburg** is the centerpiece of the gorgeous town of Meersburg. Begun in the 7th century, Germany's **oldest inhabited castle** now houses deer antlers, rusting armor, and a very deep dungeon. (☎ 800 00. Open Mar.-Oct. daily 9am-6:30pm; Nov.-Feb. 10am-6pm. DM10, students DM8, children DM6.) In the 18th century, a prince bishop had declared the **Altes Schloß** unfit to house his regal self, so he commissioned the sherbet-pink Baroque **Neues Schloß**. Elaborately frescoed, it now houses the town's art collection, the **Schloßmuseum**, and the **Dorniermuseum**, with models of Dornier airplanes. (☎ 41 40 71. Open Apr.-Oct. daily 10am-1pm and 2-6pm. DM6, students DM5.) Meersburg's quirky, crowded **Zeppelinmuseum**, Schloßpl., between the two castles, presents anything remotely connected with zeppelins, including silverware from the *Hindenburg* and Zeppelin's own models of the flying cigars. (☎ 79 09. Open Mar.-Nov. daily 10am-6pm. DM5.) To catch a view of the Bodensee against an alpine backdrop, trek up past the Altstadt, cross the intersection at Stettenerstr., and turn left onto Droste-Hülshoff-Weg, before the orange house. Head up the hill or stroll the **Uferpromenade** along the harbor.

Meersburg is 30 minutes from Konstanz by **boat** (2 per hr., DM5.60). The town has no train station but the nearest accessible one is in **Überlingen,** 30 minutes away via bus #7395 (DM5, every 30min.) or in **Konstanz.** The **tourist office,** Kirschstr. 4, provides free city maps, useful for the tangled Altstadt, and a list of accommodations. Climb the stairs from the sea-level Unterstadtstr. past the stone wall and the half-timbered houses, and continue through the Marktplatz towards the church; it's on the right. (☎ 43 11 10; fax 43 11 20; email info@meersburg.de; www.meersburg.de. Open May-Sept. M-F 9am-6:30pm, Sa 10am-2pm; Oct.-Apr. M-F 9am-noon and 2-5pm.) In the summer, the office offers city **tours** Wednesday at 10:30am and Saturday at 2pm (DM5). Ask here for information about **wine-tasting tours** as well. To reserve **rooms,** consult the **Zimmervermittlung,** Untere Stadtstr. 13, half a block toward the castle from the dock. (☎ 804 40; fax 804 48. Open M-F 8:30am-12:30pm and 2-6pm, Sa 9am-noon. DM2 fee.) **Haus Mayer Bartsch,** Stettenerstr. 53, has rooms with flower-covered balconies. From Marktpl., go up Obertorstr. through the gate, then head straight and bear right onto Stettenerstr.; it's on the left past the gas station. (☎/fax 60 50. Singles DM38-45, with bath DM65; doubles DM85, with bath DM135.) For tasty pizza and spaghetti (DM9-20, slices DM3), **Da Nico,** Untere Stadtstr. 39, offers speedy pasta service. (☎ 64 48. Open daily 11am-11:30pm.)

FRIEDRICHSHAFEN ☎ 07541

A former construction base for Zeppelins, Friedrichshafen had trouble getting back up off the ground after Allied bombings in 1944. The current town was rebuilt with sweeping, wide promenades and tree-lined boulevards that open up onto breathtaking panoramas of the Alps across the water. The city's flagship attraction is the superb **Zeppelinmuseum,** which details the history of the flying dirigibles and their inventor. The fleet of 16 scale models is overshadowed by a 33m reconstruction of a section of the *Hindenburg*, which went up in flames in Lakehurst, New Jersey in 1937. Climb aboard for a peek at the recreated passenger cabins. (Seestr. 22. ☎ 380 10. Open May-Oct. Tu-Su 10am-6pm; Nov.-Apr. 10am-5pm. Last admission 1hr. before *closing. DM12, students DM6.)* The **Schulmuseum** documents school life in Germany as it has grown and flourished over the last 12 centuries; unfortunately, it also features hordes of schoolchildren from this century. Don't miss the "punishment" exhibit or the Third Reich room. *(Friedrichstr. 14. ☎ 326 22. Open Apr.-Oct. daily 10am-5pm; Nov.-Mar. Tu-Su 2-5pm. DM2.)* The 17th-century **Schloßkirche** almost burned to the ground in 1944. Today it stands in its rebuilt glory, despite a tacky marble high altar that only a mother could love. *(On Friedrichstr. to the right of the station. Open daily mid-Apr. to late-Sept. 9am-6pm; Oct. 9am-5pm. Closes W 2:30pm.)* The beach is at the **Strandbad.** *(Königsweg 11. Follow the hedged path to the right of the Schloßkirche entrance for 15min. ☎ 280 78. Open daily mid-May to mid-Sept. 9am-8pm. DM2.50.)*

Popular among avid cyclists, Friedrichshafen provides direct access to a number of **biking paths,** including the much-beloved **Bodensee-Radweg,** which whisks spandex the entire 260km around the Bodensee. The *Bodensee-Radweg* is marked by signs with a cyclist whose back tire is filled in blue (for the lake, get it?). The less hard-core can follow any of the other clearly marked routes, accessible from Friedrichstr.

There are two train stations in Friedrichshafen: the larger **Stadtbahnhof** and the easterly **Hafenbahnhof,** behind the Zeppelinmuseum and near the harbor and Buchhornpl. **Trains** connect the two stations (2-4 times per hr.). Trains run to **Munich** (3 hr., 1 per hr., DM84, youth DM67) and **Lindau** (30min., 1 per hr., DM7.80). Friedrichshafen is also connected by frequent **buses** and **boats** to Lindau and **Meersburg.** The boat to **Konstanz** (1½hr.) costs DM12.40. Buy boat tickets on board or at the ticket counter next to the Zeppelinmuseum (open M-F 8:10am-5:45pm, Sa-Su 9am-5:45pm). Rent your own boat (but don't attempt to get to Konstanz with it) at the **Gondelhafen** by Seestr. (☎ 217 46. Open May-Sept. daily 9am-8pm. Rowboats and paddleboats DM9-12 per 30min., motor boats DM30-32.) Rent **bikes** from the *Reisezentrum* counter of the Stadtbahnhof (DM15 per day). The **tourist office,** Bahnhofpl. 2, across the square to the left of the city train station, sells maps (DM0.50), details biking routes, and **reserves rooms** for a DM5 fee. (☎ 300 10; fax 725 88; tourist-infofriedrichshafen@t-online.de; www.friedrichshafen.de. Open Oct.-Mar. M-F 9am-noon and 2-5pm; May-Sept. M-F 9am-5pm, Sa 10am-2pm.) The **post office,** Friedrichshafen 88045, is next to the Stadtbahnhof (open M-F 8:30am-6pm and Sa 8:30am-1pm).

Friedrichshafen's quality **Jugendherberge Graf Zeppelin (HI),** Lindauer Str. 3, is clean, renovated, and 50m from the water's edge. Call ahead; this place fills up fast, especially in summer. From the Hafenbahnhof, walk 10min. down Eckenerstr. away from Buchhornplatz. From the Stadtbahnhof, walk left down Friedrichstr., and turn down Eckenerstr. (20min.) Or take bus #7 (direction: "Hafenbahnhof") to "Eberhardstr." (☎ 724 04; fax 749 86. Breakfast included. Sheets DM5.50. Laundry facilities. Reception 7-9am, 2-7:30pm, and 8-10pm. Curfew for guests under 18 10pm. Lockout 9am-noon. DM26, over 26 DM31.) For **groceries,** head to **Lebensmittel Fehl** on the corner of Seestr. and Salzgasse (open M-F 8am-6:30pm, Sa 8am-2pm). **Naturkost am Buchhornplatz,** Buchhornpl. 1 (☎ 243 35), serves home-cooked vegetarian food and offers take-out.

LINDAU IM BODENSEE   ☎ 08382

When geological forces crunched their way through southern Germany during the last Ice Age, Mother Nature decided that Lindau should be a resort. Connected to the lakeshore by a narrow causeway, the island sits cupped in aquamarine waters, enjoying a view of the Alps that's almost the same as the one you see on good chocolates. Tourists started floating in by steamship in 1835, and now close to a million come every year to soak in the balmy climate and wander among 14th-century gabled houses on **Maximilianstr.,** which forms the central part of town. Halfway along Maximilianstr., the **Altes Rathaus** is a fruity blend of frescoes. The **Cavazzen-Haus** in the Marktpl. houses the **Stadtmuseum,** which displays a collection of musical instruments and art ranging from fine French porcelain to 17th-century portraits of ugly German bluebloods. (☎ 94 40 73. Open Apr.-Oct. Tu-Su 10am-noon and 2-5pm. DM5, students DM3.) A walk down **In der Grub**—the less touristed equivalent of Maximilianstr.—leads to the ivy-covered **Diebsturm** (robbers' tower), which looks more like Rapunzel's tower than the prison it once was. For properly dressed adults, the **Spielbank** (casino) by the Seebrücke offers the regular spinning of roulette wheels and thinning of wallets. The bet ceiling is DM18,000, so don't worry about losing too much money. (☎5051. Open 3pm-3am. Admission DM5 and a passport—please daaarling, no jeans; tie required after 5pm. 21+.)

Lindau has four beaches. **Römerbad** is the smallest and most familial, located left of the harbor on the island. (☎68 30. Open M-F 10:00am-7:30pm and Sa-Su 10am-8pm. DM4, students DM3.) To reach the quieter **Lindenhofbad,** take bus #1 or 2 to "Anheggerstr." and then bus #4 to "Alwind." (☎66 37. Open daily 10am-8pm. DM4, students DM3.) In the same park complex as Lindenhofbad is **Strandbad Bad Schachen,** in the shadow of a posh hotel and serving much of its clientele. (Open 9am-7pm daily. Daypass DM19 on weekends, DM14 weekdays.) Lindau's biggest beach is **Eichwald,** a 30 min. walk to the East along Uferweg. Alternatively, take bus #1 or 2 to "Anheggerstr.," then bus #3 to "Karmelbuckel." (☎55 39. Open M-F 9:30am-7:30pm, Sa-Su 9am-8pm. DM5.)

Ferries link Lindau with **Konstanz,** stopping at **Meersburg, Mainau,** and **Friedrichshafen** along the way (3.5hr., 3-6 per day. DM18.80). The **train** to Konstanz takes two hours (DM28). Fun-lovers rent **boats** 50m to the left of the casino, next to the bridge, or next to the train causeway. (☎55 14. Open mid.-Mar. to mid.-Sept. daily 9am-9pm. Rowboats DM12-18, paddleboats DM14-18 per hr., motor boat DM45.) One-hour excursions leave from the dock behind the casino at 11:30am, 1, 2:30, and 6pm. (☎/fax 781 94. DM12, children DM6.) Rent **bikes** at the train station. (☎212 61. Open Mar. to late Dec. M-F 9am-1pm and 3:30-6pm, Sa 9:30am-1pm, Su 9am-noon. DM13 per day.) The **tourist office,** Ludwigstr. 68, across from the train station, finds **rooms** for a DM10 fee, but only if you send a letter. (☎26 00 30; fax 26 00 55; email tourist-information.lindau@t-online.de; www.lindau-tourismus.de. Open mid-June to early Sept. M-Sa 9am-1pm and 2-7pm; May to mid-June and Sept. M-F 9am-1pm and 2-6pm, Sa 9am-1pm; Apr. and Oct. M-F 9am-1pm and 2-5pm, Sa 9am-1pm; Nov.-Mar. M-F 9am-noon and 2-5pm.) **Tours** leave from the office at 10am (Tu and F in German, M in English. DM6, students and overnight guests DM4.) The **post office,** 88131 Lindau im Bodensee, is 50m to the right of the train station (open M-F 8am-6pm, Sa 8:30am-noon). Check **email** at **Bamboo's Internet Café,** Dammsteggasse 2. (☎94 27 67. DM10 per hr. Open Tu-Th, Su 5pm-1am, F-Sa 5pm-3am.)

The spectacular **Jugendherberge (HI),** Herbergsweg 11, lies across the Seebrücke off Bregenzer Str. Walk for 20min. or take bus #1 or 2 from the train station to "Anheggerstr.", then transfer to Bus #3 (direction: "Zech") to "Jugendherberge." (☎967 10; fax 496 71 50. Under 27 and families with small children only. Breakfast included. Reception 7am-midnight. Curfew midnight. Call ahead. DM29.) You could eat off the floor in the rooms at **Gästehaus Holdereggen,** Näherweg 4. Follow the railroad tracks across the causeway to the mainland; turn right onto Holdereggengasse and left onto Jungfernburgstr. Näherweg is on the left after 20min. (☎65 74. DM2 *Kurtaxe* per person for one-night stands. Showers DM2. Singles DM39; doubles DM74.) **Park-Camping Lindau Am See,** Frauenhofer Str. 20, is 3km east of the island on the mainland. It's within spitting distance of the Austrian border. *Let's Go* does not recommend spitting at foreign countries. Take bus #1 or 2 to "Anheggerstr.," then bus #3 (direction: "Zech") to the end. (☎722 36; fax 26 00 26. Showers included. DM9.50 per person. DM4 per tent. *Kurtaxe* DM1.50.) For **groceries** try **Plus,** in the basement of the department store at the intersection of In der Grub and Cramergasse (open M-F 8:30am-6:30pm, Sa 8am-1pm).

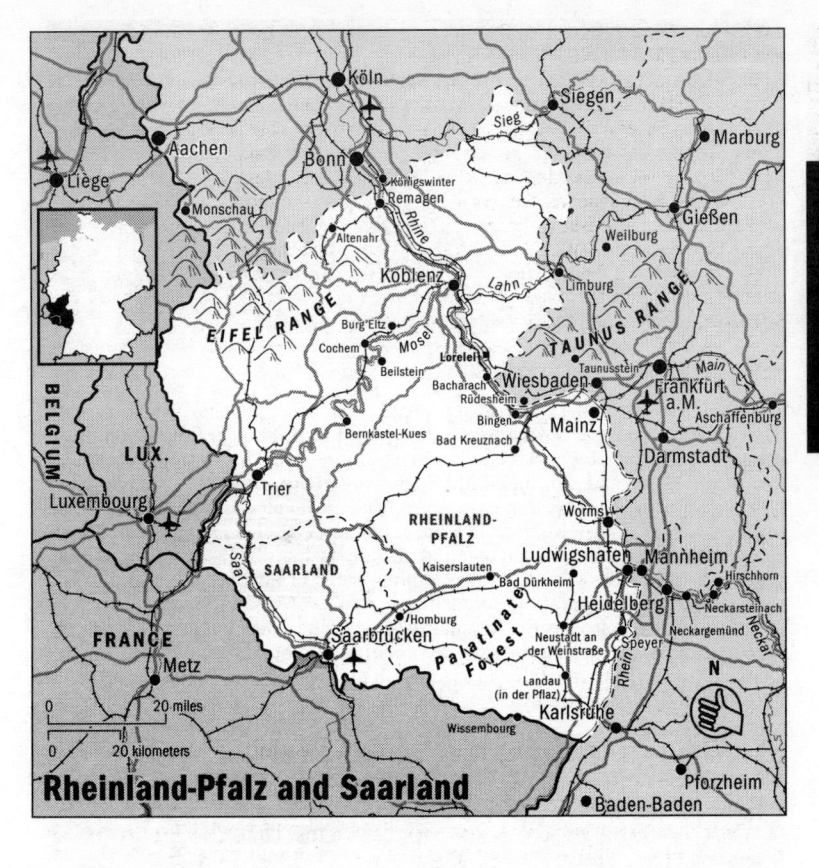

RHEINLAND-PFALZ
AND SAARLAND

The valleys, castles, and wine towns of Rheinland-Pfalz make the region a visual feast, as the Mosel River curls downstream to the soft, castle-backed shores of the Rhein Valley. Centuries of literature attest to its beauty as well, from the *Nibelungenlied* to the Lorelei revelry. The Rheinland also provides a literal feast: a rich agricultural tradition keeps produce in abundance, and the many vineyards in the Rhein and Mosel Valleys produce sweet, delicious wines. Trier is a millennia-old collage of Roman sights, while the medieval towns of Mainz, Worms, and Speyer bow down to glorious cathedrals. The Rheinland has been politically potent since the days when its electors were the king-makers of the Holy Roman Empire. Saarland, on the other hand, has long been the locus of political contention; the little *Land*'s mineral wealth has been making both Germany and France covetous for centuries.

391

HIGHLIGHTS OF RHEINLAND-PFALZ

The **Rheintal** is a poet's dream come true. From its mystical **Lorelei cliffs** to its majestic castles and famous wineries, the Valley cannot fail to impress (p. 396).

For *really* old sights, head to **Trier,** (p. 405) where 2,000-year-old Roman ruins make the typical German Schloß seem like a sandcastle.

Tiny hamlets with half-timbered houses abound in the **Moseltal** (p. 402). The many well-touristed towns in the region keep up the German tradition of gorgeous, ubiquitous castles and are surrounded by endless vineyards.

Mainz (p. 400) was once home to Johannes Gutenberg, inventor of the printing press. Copies of his famous Bibles are on display at the Gutenberg Museum, while the fantastic Dom draws the devout.

KOBLENZ   ☎0261

The etymology of "Koblenz," a corruption of Latin for "confluence," symbolizes the city's volatile history. Over the past 2,000 years, Rome, France, Prussia, and Germany have all fought for control of this lovely city, coveting its location at the junction of the Mosel and the Rhein. Although wars of conquest have died down in recent years, the frenetic activity has not. Unlike the plethora of sleepy tourist towns along the Rhine, Koblenz is a busy, modern city. Trains rattle along both sides of the river, and barges flanked by flirtatious speedboats plow through the water. The rivers draw in tourists as shining paths of history and legend, while serving a more practical function as the conduits of German industry. Before reunification, Koblenz was the Republic's largest munitions dump; today the only pyrotechnics that light up the city are decorative, not destructive. During the annual **Rhein in Flammen** (Rhine in Flames) in mid-August, the city is transformed into a fabulous flaming fiesta.

◨ GETTING THERE AND GETTING AROUND

Trains: Koblenz lies along the line that connects Frankfurt to Köln. Trains to **Köln** (1hr., 3-4 per hr., DM25); **Mainz** (1hr., 3 per hr., DM25); **Trier** (2hr., 1 per hr., DM30); and **Frankfurt** (2hr., 2 per hr., DM36).

Public Transportation: 10 main lines bus around the city and into the 'burbs for DM2.20-4.80 per ride. Day pass DM9. Tickets available from the driver. **Zentralplatz,** accessible by every bus line, offers the most convenient access to the Altstadt.

Taxi: Taxi Koblenz (☎330 55) or **Funk Taxi** (☎194 10).

Bike Rental: Biking the Rhein and Mosel is more satisfying than traveling by boat or train. See the pamphlet *Rund ums Rad,* sold in many bookstores, for detailed information. **Fahrradhaus Zangmeister,** Am Löhrrondell (☎323 63), offers bikes for DM10 per day. ID required. **Fahrrad Franz,** Hohenfelder Str. 7 (☎91 50 50), rents bikes for DM20 per day. Open M-F 9:30am-7pm, Sa 9:30am-4pm. **Vélo,** Konrad-Adenauer-Ufer 1 (☎151 02), will outfit you for DM15 per day. At peak season, reserve in advance.

◧◪ ORIENTATION AND PRACTICAL INFORMATION

Koblenz's sights cluster in the strip of Altstadt between the **Deutsches Eck** (a spit of land jutting into the confluence of the Mosel and the Rhein) and the **Markt.** The train station lies far inland from either of the rivers, but busy **Löhrstr.** runs from it to the Markt, lined with shops, groceries, hotels, and eateries.

Tourist Offices: The main office, Löhrstr. 141 (☎313 04; fax 100 43 ?8; email touristik@koblenz.de; www.koblenz.de), a sharp left as you exit the train station, hands out boat schedules and city maps with hotel, restaurant, and pub listings. They also find **rooms** (from DM60). Open M-F 9am-8pm, Sa-Su 10am-8pm. The **branch** located in the Rathaus (in the

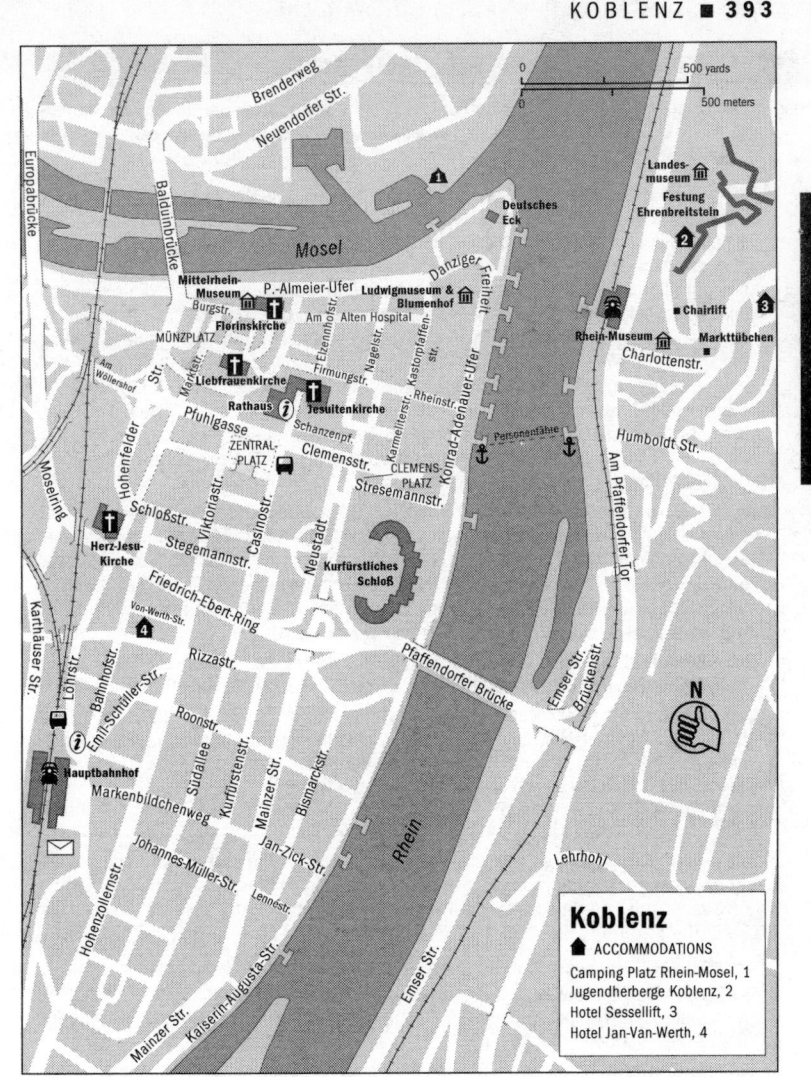

Koblenz

🏠 ACCOMMODATIONS

Camping Platz Rhein-Mosel, 1
Jugendherberge Koblenz, 2
Hotel Sessellift, 3
Hotel Jan-Van-Werth, 4

entrance to Jesuitenplatz) offers the same services. (☎ 13 09 20; fax 130 92 11. Open until Nov. M-F 9am-8pm, Sa-Su 10am-8pm, after Nov. M-F 9am-5pm, Sa 10am-5pm.)

Bookstore: Reuffel, Löhrstr. 90-92 (☎ 30 30 70), has lots of English paperbacks, and internet service upstairs (DM5 for 30min). Open M-F 9am-8pm, Sa 9am-4pm.

Laundromat: Wasch Center, on the corner of Rizzastr. and Löhrstr. Wash DM6, dry DM1 or DM2 per 15min, depending on the load. Soap included. Open M-Sa 6am-midnight, last wash 11pm.

Emergency: Police, ☎ 110. **Fire** and **Ambulance,** ☎ 112.

Pharmacy: Rosen-Apotheke, Löhrstr. 139 (☎ 361 35), to the left when leaving the train station and next door to the tourist office, posts a list in its front window of other pharmacies providing emergency services. Open M-F 8am-6:30pm, Sa 8:30am-1pm.

Post Office: Hauptpostamt, 65068 Koblenz, to the right of the train station exit. Open M-F 7am-7pm, Sa 7am-2pm.

RHEINLAND-PFALZ

ACCOMMODATIONS AND CAMPING

Since private rooms and most hotels in Koblenz are expensive, it may be worthwhile to trek across the river to the hostel. The difficult hike deters few, so call a day or two ahead.

■ **Jugendherberge Koblenz (HI)** (☎737 37; fax 702 707), in the Festung (see **Festung Ehrenbreitstein**, p. 395). For spectacular locations this hostel wins the prize; it sports a breathtaking view of Koblenz and the meeting of the Rhein and Mosel valleys. Since inaccessibility was the fortress's *raison d'être*, however, getting there is less than half the fun, and may be a deterrent for the travel-weary. Take bus #9 or 10 from the stop on Löhrstr. across the street from the tourist office to "Charlottenstr." If you intend to hike uphill, continue along the Rhein side of the mountain on the main road, following the DJH signs. Within minutes you'll come to a footpath leading to the Festung (20 min.). A chairlift is a block away in the same direction (operates daily Mar.-Sept. 9am-5:50pm. DM4; round-trip DM6, DM9 for non-hostel guests; includes Festung fee.) Fortunately, the hostel is friendly, clean, and worth the hike. Breakfast included. Dinner or lunch DM9.50, both DM14.50. Reception 7:30am-11:30pm. Curfew 11:30pm. DM25.90; doubles DM31.90 per person.

Hotel Jan. van Werth, Van-Werth-Str. 9 (☎365 00; fax 365 06). This classy family-run establishment is inexpensive living with a touch of elegance, and one of the best values in Koblenz. From the station, walk up Bahnhofstr. to the market district and take a right on Van-Werth-Str. The hotel is a green building. Gummi bears and a large breakfast buffet included. Reception 6:30am-10pm. Singles from DM40, with shower and toilet DM75; doubles DM85-100, with shower and toilet DM120.

Hotel Sessellift, Obertal 22 (☎752 56; fax 768 72), next to the "Obertal" bus stop. Friendly staff and functional rooms. Breakfast included. Singles DM45; doubles DM80; triples DM110.

Camping: Campingplatz Rhein-Mosel, Am Neuendorfer Eck (☎827 19), across the Mosel from the Deutsches Eck. A day ferry crosses the river (DM0.60). Reception 8am-noon and 2-8pm. Open Apr.-Oct. 15. DM6.50 per person. DM5 per tent.

FOOD AND NIGHTLIFE

Koblenz's multinational origins have found culinary expression, and the city is never at a loss for dining options. For **groceries,** head to **Plus,** Roonstr. 49-51 (open M-F 8:30am-7pm and Sa 8am-2pm). **Theater tickets** can be purchased from the box office in the Rathaus branch of the tourist office. (☎129 16 10. Open M-F 9am-8pm, Sa-Su 10am-8pm.)

■ **Marktstübchen,** Am Markt 220 (☎755 65), at the bottom of the hill from the hostel. Authenticity's last stand, it serves real German food for real budget prices. Most entrees DM10 or less. Open M-Tu, Th, and Sa-Su 11am-midnight, W 11am-2pm, F 4pm-1am.

Salatgarten (☎364 55), where Casinostr. becomes Gymnasialstr. near the Jesuiten-kirche. A salad-bar style restaurant that goes beyond your basic greens; arteries (and taste buds) cry out for the vegetarian wonders here. Self-service keeps prices low. Daily specials around DM9. Open M-F 9:30am-7pm, Sa 9:30am-4pm.

Altes Brauhaus, Braugasse 4 (☎15 001), in the shadow of the Liebfrauenkirche. Popular with locals and tourists, the pub dishes out German food (around DM15) and home brew. Open M-Sa 10am-1am.

Café Galleria Bistro & Pizzeria, Bahnhofpl. (☎337 58), near Hohenstaufenstr. Delicious pizzas and pastas from DM7. Open daily 10am-midnight.

Rizza Obst & Gemüse, Rizzastr. 49, has an assortment of drinks, fresh fruit, veggies, and other necessities. Open M-F 7:30am-7pm, Sa 7:30am-4pm.

Tatort, Münzplatz 15 (☎42 19). Grungy rock and roll bar that occasionally serves as a stage for local bands. Open Su-Th 7pm-1pm, F-Sa7pm-2am

Atelier Filmtheater, Löhrstr.78 (☎311 88), has English-language screenings approximately once a week. DM12-13, students DM9.

 **SIGHTS**

FESTUNG EHRENBREITSTEIN. If ground-level viewing has got you down, head to Festung Ehrenbreitstein, a fortress at the highest point in the city. The Prussians used it to accommodate French troops in past centuries; today, the German state uses it to accommodate you (see **Jugendherberge Koblenz,** p. 394). *(Non-hostel guests DM2; students DM1. Tours, DM6.)*

DEUTSCHES ECK. German nationalism and Germany's two greatest rivers, converge at the Deutsches Eck (German Corner). A peninsula at the confluence of the Rhein and Mosel, it purportedly witnessed the birth of the German nation in 1216 when the Teutonic Order of Knights settled here. Today, the **Mahnmal der Deutschen Einheit** (Monument to German Unity) stands on the right, commemorating a rather different sort of union. Erected in 1897, it stands in tribute to Kaiser Wilhelm I for forcibly reconciling the internal conflicts of the German Empire (though the Kaiser played second fiddle to Bismarck; see p. 10). The 14 meter tall equestrian statue of the Kaiser that once topped the monument was toppled in 1945; the statue was replaced by a duplicate in 1993.

CHURCHES. Attractions of a less fervent sort can be found in the many churches of Koblenz's Altstadt, within a few blocks of the Markt, many of which were restored after WWII. The 12th-century **Florinskirche** lost some of its luster in the 19th-century wars when Napoleon used it as a military encampment. *(Open daily 11am-5pm. Free.)* The oval Baroque towers of the **Liebfrauenkirche** rise nearby. The church's emerald and sapphire stained glass and intricate ceiling latticework are stunning; the choir windows document the role of women in the Passion and Resurrection of Christ. *(Open M-Sa 8am-6pm, Su 9am-12:30pm and 6-8pm, Sun. in summer 9am-8pm. Free.)* The masterful *Rheinisch* facade of the **Jesuitenkirche** on the Marktplatz conceals a startlingly modern interior. *(Open daily 7am-6pm.)* Koblenz's most mischievous monument lurks outside; the **Schängelbrunnen,** a statue of a boy that spits water on passersby, drives kids into frenzied glee.

BLUMENHOF. Behind the Mahnmal, in the beautiful, unassuming flower garden, lurks more national *braggadocio*, though this time not on the Germans' part. Napoleon erected the fountain to commemorate the "certain impending victory" in his Russian campaign. The Russians, after routing the French army, added the mocking inscription "seen and approved."

MUSEUMS

MUSEUM LUDWIG IM DEUTSCHHERRENHAUS. The hilarious bronze sculpture in the courtyard gives this collection a well-deserved thumbs up! Mostly contemporary French art, but expect anything and everything in their continuously changing special exhibits. *(Danziger Freiheit 1. Behind the Mahnmal. ☎ 30 40 40. Open Tu-Sa 10:30am-5pm, Su 11am-6pm. DM5, students DM3.)*

MITTELRHEINMUSEUM. Contains three floors of art, much of which focuses on religious sculpture and painterly landscapes of the Rhein Gorge. The second floor holds changing exhibits. *(Next door to the Florinskirche. Open Tu-Sa 10:30am-5pm, Su 11am-6pm. DM5, students DM3.)*

LANDESMUSEUM KOBLENZ. Exhibits include antique automobiles, cannons, wine, tobacco, and guns. A dangerous combination. Alas, no live ammo or tasty samples. *(Hohe Ostfront, in Festung Ehrenbreitstein. ☎ 970 30. Open mid-Mar. to mid-Nov. M-Sa 9am-5pm, Su 10am-5:30 pm. Last entrance 15min. before closing. DM3, students DM2.)*

RHEINMUSEUM. A private museum devoted to all things *Rheinisch*, four floors of maritime history including old boats, engines, and fish. *(Charlottenstr. 53a. Bus #9 or 10 to "Charlottenstr." ☎ 70 34 50. Open daily 10am-5pm. DM5, children DM3.)*

RHEINLAND-PFALZ

RHEINLAND-PFALZ

RHEINTAL (RHINE VALLEY)

At present, the sun and moon alone cast their light upon these old buildings famed
in story and gnawed by time, whose walls are falling stone by stone into the Rhein,
and whose history is fast fading into oblivion. O noble tower! O poor, paralyzed
giants! A steamboat packed with travelers now spews its smoke in your faces!
    —Victor Hugo

Though the Rhein River runs all the way from Switzerland to the North Sea, the
Rhein of the imagination exists only in the 80km of gorge stretching from Bonn to
just north of Mainz. Here the river rolls by treacherous whirlpools and craggy
shores surrounding the castles of aristocrats. This is the Rhein of sailors' night-
mares and poets' dreams. From the Lorelei cliffs, legendary sirens lured passing
sailors to their deaths on the rocks below. Heinrich Heine immortalized the spot
with his 1823 poem "Die Lorelei," but he can hardly claim sole credit for the literary resonance felt along the river. The renowned Rhein wines from the hillside
vineyards have inspired many a different illusion.

Two different train lines (one on each bank) traverse this fabled stretch; the line
on the west bank runs between Koblenz and Mainz and sticks closer to the water,
providing superior views. If you're willing to put up with lots of tourists, the best
way to see the sights is probably by boat. The **Köln-Düsseldorfer (KD) Line** (p. 444)
covers the Mainz-Koblenz stretch three times per day during the summer, while
more frequent excursions travel along shorter stretches of the river.

LORELEI CLIFFS AND CASTLES

The mythic Rhein explodes into rocky frenzy along the cliffs of the Lorelei. This
section of the river, with its switchbacks and boulders, was so difficult to navigate
that a sailors' song developed about it. The song, immortalized by the poet Heinrich Heine, told the story of the siren Lorelei, who seduced shipmen with her
intoxicating song and drew them onto the rocks. Protected by the plush interiors
and tinted windows of the ubiquitous Loreley Express tour buses, or watching
from cruise ships where the crew has learned to turn a deaf ear, most of today's
Rhein travelers avoid such grim fates. Near the cliffs and the beloved statue of the
maiden siren are the towns **St. Goarshausen** and **St. Goar,** on either side of the
Rhein. These two Loreley towns host the spectacular **Rhein in Flammen** firework-
filled celebration at the end of every summer (September 15, 2001). St. Goarshausen, on the east bank, provides access by foot to the Lorelei statue and the
infamous cliffs. Facing the Rhein, follow Rheinstr. left past the last houses and to
the peninsula on which the statue rests. To reach the cliffs, take the stairs across
the street from the beginning of the peninsula (45min.).

Directly above St. Goarshausen, the fierce **Burg Katz** (Cat Castle) eternally stalks
its prey, the smaller **Burg Maus** (Mouse Castle). Fortunately, the mouse escapes a
Kafka-esque fate by hiding away upstream in the Wellmich district of Goarshausen. *Burg Katz* is unfortunately not open to tourists, but *Burg Maus* offers
spectacular falconry demonstrations daily at 11am and 2:30pm (one extra demonstration Su 4:30pm) and 20min. tours (daily; DM12, students and children DM10).
Call 76 69 for information, or visit St. Goarshausen's **tourist office,** Bahnhofstr. 8.
(☎ (06771) 91 00; fax 910 15; email loreley-tourist-info@t-online.de. Open M-F 9am-
1pm and 2-5:30pm, Sa 9:30am-noon.) Two minutes from the Lorelei Cliffs, the hostel **Jugendheim Loreley** lures travelers with the friendly ditties of hip hostelers, only
to drown them in crashing waves of schoolchildren. From the cliffs, walk past the
red and white parking gate down the road a few hundred meters and take a left. (☎
(06771) 26 19; fax 81 89; email Loreley-Jugendherberge@t-online.de. Breakfast
included. Curfew 10pm. DM23.50.) Back in town, face the Rhein and go right on
Rheinstr. and then Rheinpromenade to get to **Campingplatz Loreleystadt** (☎25 92),
an eight-minute walk from the station. To be closer to the famed cliffs, try **Campingplatz Auf der Loreley** (☎ (06771) 430. DM8.50, tent DM5).

The **"Loreley V" ferry** crosses the river to and from St. Goar (6am-11pm, DM 1.50 round-trip DM2.50), which provides a pleasant base for Lorelei explorations. The view from the cliffs on the eastern side is spectacular, and **Burg Rheinfels** (☎ (06741) 383) is dazzling. Tour the sprawling, half-ruined castle and its underground passageways—it doesn't get more *romantisch* than this. (Open daily 9am-6pm; last entrance 5pm. DM6, students and children DM4. Bring a flashlight, or purchase a candle in the castle's museum for DM1.) St. Goar's **tourist office,** Heerstr. 6, is in the pedestrian zone (☎ (06741) 383; fax 72 09; email TalderLoreley@t-online.de; www.talderloreley.de. Open M-F 8am-12:30pm and 2-5pm, Sa 10am-noon). The office reserves **rooms** in town for no fee, except on Mondays. The **Jugendherberge (HI),** Bismarckweg 17, is conveniently-located 10 minutes from the station. With your back to the tracks, follow Oberstr. left and veer left on Schloßberg; Bismarckweg is the next right. (☎ 388; fax 28 69. Breakfast and sheets included. Reception 8-9am, 5-6pm, and 7-8pm. Curfew 10pm, but you can get a key. DM22.) ◪**Hotel Hauser,** Heerstr. 77, offers centrally-located, spotless, and relaxing rooms with balconies. (☎ (06741) 333; fax 14 64. Breakfast included. Singles DM46-95, doubles DM98-140.) St. Goar's **postal code** is 56329.

BACHARACH ☎ 06743

Bounded by a lush park on the river, a resilient town wall, and dramatically sloping vineyards, Bacharach maintains the kind of low profile coveted by glamour queens, B-movie has-beens, and royalty. All the sequestering has paid off: this hidden gem retains an irrepressible sense of identity in the face of increasing tourist traffic. The village's name is derived from the fact that it was once the home of an altar stone to Bacchus. Like any holy city, Bacharach fills with pilgrims who come from near and

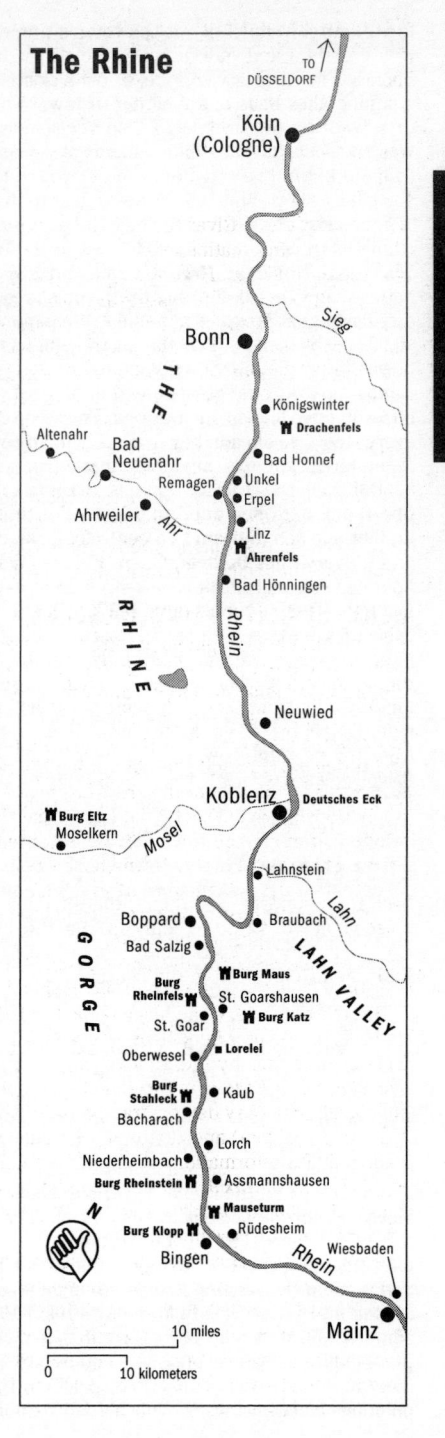

The Rhine

TO DÜSSELDORF

Köln (Cologne)

Bonn

Sieg

Königswinter
Drachenfels

Altenahr
Bad Neuenahr
Remagen
Bad Honnef
Unkel
Erpel

Ahrweiler
Ahr
Linz
Ahrenfels
Bad Hönningen

THE RHINE

Rhein

Neuwied

Koblenz   Deutsches Eck

Burg Eltz
Moselkern
Mosel
Lahnstein
Lahn

Boppard
Braubach
Bad Salzig
LAHN VALLEY

GORGE

Burg Maus
Burg Rheinfels
St. Goarshausen
St. Goar
Burg Katz

Oberwesel
Lorelei

Burg Stahleck
Kaub

Bacharach

Lorch
Niederheimbach
Assmannshausen
Burg Rheinstein

Mauseturm
Rüdesheim
Burg Klopp
Wiesbaden
Bingen
Rhein

N

Mainz

0   10 miles
0   10 kilometers

far to worship dutifully at the town's numerous *Weinkeller* and *Weinstuben* (wine cellars and pubs), scattered throughout well-preserved half-timbered houses. Find love, sweet love, at **Die Weinstube,** Oberstr. 63 (☎ 12 08), behind the stunning **Altes Haus** in the center of town. This family-owned business makes its own wine on the premises. Also accessible from Oberstr. is the 14th-century **Wernerkapelle,** the ghost-like remains of a red sandstone chapel that took 140 years to build but only a few hours to destroy in the Palatinate War of Succession in 1689. It's a short climb up the steps next to the late-Romanesque **Peterskirche.**

The **tourist office,** Oberstr. 45, and the *Rathaus* share an old building at one end of the town center. (☎ 91 93 03; fax 91 93 04. Open Apr.-Oct. M-F 9am-5pm, Sa 10am-4pm; Nov.-Mar. M-F 9am-1pm and 1:30-5pm, Sa 10am-1pm.) Hostels get no better than the unbelievable ◧**Jugendherberge Stahleck (HI),** a gorgeous 12th-century castle that provides an unbeatable panoramic view of the Rhein Valley for its 40,000 yearly visitors. Painstaking thought has gone into the minutest details of the hostel, from the individually named rooms (you might stay in *Falcon's Nest* or *Castle View*) to the great selection of local wines in the bar downstairs and the cheerful plaid sheets on your bed. The steep 20-minute hike to the hostel is worth every step. Call ahead; they're usually full by 6pm. From the station, turn left at the Peterskirche and take any of the marked paths leading up the hill. (☎ 12 66; fax 26 84. DM25.90, DM31.90 for doubles. Breakfast included. Dinner buffet DM9.70. Curfew 10pm, bar open until midnight.) For those weary of uphill treks, a dynamic mother and son duo run two centrally-located pensions. Frau Dettmar runs clean and flowery **Haus Dettmar,** Oberstr. 8 (☎/fax 26 61; DM 25-35), while son Jürgen operates **Pension Ferienwohnungen,** Oberstr. 64 (☎ 17 15; fax 29 79) in an even better location. (Double rooms only. DM70.) Or stay in the lap of luxury at the **Gästehaus Schloß Furstenberg,** Mainzer Str. 22 (☎ 91 90 00; fax 91 90 10) where the rooms are large and clean, the staff is friendly, and full apartments (bedroom, bath, and liv. room/kitchen) start at just DM75 a night. From the station turn left; the hotel is a 2 minute walk from the town center. (Singles w/bath from DM44, doubles w/bath from DM55; prices go down for stays over 4 days.) Turn right from the station (heading downhill towards the river), then walk south for 10 minutes to reach **Campingplatz Bacharach,** to camp directly on the Rhein. (☎ 17 52. DM8 per person. DM10 per plot. Tent DM5.) The price is right at the **Café Restaurant,** on Oberstr. 40, where three-course meals go for DM12-20, and smaller meals are DM5-12.50.

RÜDESHEIM ☎ 06722

Seen from opposite the Rhein, Rüdesheim is a romantic's dream come true. Terraced vineyards stretch steeply up from the tiny town framed by two stone castles. Up close, however, commercialism has found a home in the heart of town. Rüdesheim's location in the center of the Rheingau wine-producing region has made the town a tourist magnet. The picturesque 12th-century **Brömserburg,** Rheinstr. 2, like the rest of Rüdesheim, now succumbs to Bacchanalian indulgence—it's a wine museum bordered on both sides by a small vineyard. From the station or ferry docks, walk 5 minutes toward town along Rheinstr. (☎ 23 48. Open daily Mar.-Nov. 9am-6pm. Last admission 5:15pm. DM5, students and children DM3.) The fortress boasts an eclectic architecture from the Middle Ages through Art Deco. Servings of kitsch are available along nearby **Drosselgasse,** a tiny alley and the true tourist's dream, where merchants peddle fake cuckoo clocks, lots of wine, and plenty of "authenticity." Up Drosselgasse to the left are signs for **Siegfrieds Mechanisches Musikkabinett,** Oberstr. 29. This museum pays tribute to a rich history of mechanical musical instruments. One of the world's largest collections of music boxes and player pianos tinkle alongside carousel organs, organ grinders, and even musical chairs. And you thought your ballerina-in-a-box was cool! (☎ 492 17; fax 45 87. Open daily Mar.-Nov. 10am-10pm. 45min. mandatory tours every 15min. DM9, students DM5.) The **Mittelalterliches Foltermuseum,** Grabenstr. 13, displays medieval devices prisoners endured to "salvage" their souls. (☎ 475 10. Open daily Apr.-Nov. 10am-6pm. DM8, students DM4.) Eighty instruments as well as paintings and drawings provide a grisly exhibition.

The **Niederwalddenkmal,** a 38m monument crowned by the unnervingly nationalistic figure of Germania wielding a 1400kg sword, looms high above town. Erected to commemorate the establishment of the Second Reich in 1871, the central frieze features legions of 19th-century aristocrats pledging loyalty to the Kaiser flanked by winged emblems of war and peace. A **chairlift** *(Seilbahn)* runs to and from the statue (10min. each way) from the top of Christoffelstr.; take a left directly before the tourist office. (Open daily mid-Mar. to mid-Nov. 9:30am-7pm. DM6.50, round-trip DM10.) To reach the monument by foot (about 40min.), go towards the station on Oberstr. and turn onto Feldtor. Follow Feldtor as it winds through the vineyard towards the monument.

The **tourist office**, Rheinstr. 16, is perched along the river. The staff offers many brochures and tourist newspapers, internet access (10min. DM3, ½hour DM5) and books rooms (DM40-50) for free. (☎ 29 62 1 94 33; fax 34 85; www.ruedesheim.de. Open Apr. to mid-Sept. M-F 9am-6pm, Sa 1:30-5:30pm.) The **post office,** (Rheinstr. 4, towards Brömserburg) has an **ATM.** (Open M-F 8:30am-noon and 2:30-5pm, Sa 8:30-11:30am.)

The **Jugendherberge (HI),** Am Kreuzberg, is in the vineyards high above the town, but the 25 minute walk through flowers, vines, and silence is aesthetically rewarding. Call ahead—they're often booked solid. From the station, walk down Rheinstr. and take a left on any street that catches your fancy. At Oberstr., turn right. Bear left at the fork onto Germaniastr. and follow it to Kuhweg and the Jugendherberge signs. (☎ 27 11; fax 482 84. Sheets DM6. Breakfast included. Reception 8-9am, 1-2pm, and 5-9pm. Curfew 11:30pm. Members only. DM22, over 26 DM27.) **Campingplatz am Rhein** has prime riverside real estate for those with portable roofs. From the station, walk past town along the Rhein to the campsite. (☎ 25 28. Open May-Sept. Reception 8am-10pm. DM7.20 per person. Tent plots DM8.50.)

MAINZ   ☎ 06131

As the capital of Rheinland-Pfalz, much of Mainz has metamorphosed into a modern metropolis, but the monumental Dom and the maze of minuscule streets in the Altstadt remain the heart of the city and embody its character. Mainz seamlessly meshes its concrete and cobblestone. Since the 1450s, when native son **Johannes Gutenberg** invented the printing press, Mainz has been at the center of Germany's media industry. The Altstadt is full of history: Mainz was founded and ruled in its early years by the clergy, and there are many sights and local traditions reminiscent of this older age for the visitor to enjoy.

▛ GETTING THERE AND GETTING AROUND

Trains run from **Frankfurt** (½ hr., DM24); **Koblenz** (1 hr., DM33); and **Heidelberg** (1 hr., DM33).

Public Transportation. Mainz shares a transportation system with Wiesbaden, making daytrips easy. (To Wiesbaden, streetcar #8 runs 3 per hr. on weekdays, 2 per hr. on weekends.)

Ferries. The **Köln-Düsseldorf ferry** (☎ 23 28 00; fax 23 28 60) docks in Mainz and departs from the wharves on the other side of the Rathaus.

▟ ORIENTATION AND PRACTICAL INFORMATION

Streets running parallel to the Rhein sport blue nameplates, while streets perpendicular to the river bear red ones.

Tourist office doles out free maps and reserves **rooms** (from DM50) for a DM5 fee. ☎ 28 62 10; fax 286 21 55; www.info-mainz.de. Open M-F 9am-6pm, Sa 9am-1pm. **Tours** leave from the Markt near the Dom. 1½hr., daily 2pm, in German and English; Jul.-Aug. also at Sa 10am. DM10.

AIDS-Hilfe hotline, ☎ 22 22 75, has the scoop on gay and lesbian life in the city.

Post Office, 55001 Mainz, is a block down Bahnhofstr. from the station. Open M-F 8am-6pm, Sa 8:30am-12:30pm.

ACCOMMODATIONS AND FOOD

Jugendgästehaus (HI), Otto-Brunfels-Schneise 4 (☎ 853 32; fax 824 22), is in Weisenau in a corner of the Volkspark. Take bus #22, 62, 63, or 92 to "Jugendherberge/Viktorstift" (20 min.) and follow signs to the hostel. This model hostel has bright, clean rooms with a private bath in each! A little far but worth it once you get there. Wheelchair accessible. Breakfast included. Reception 7am-midnight. Doubles DM40; rooms with 4-6 beds, DM30 per person.

Altstadt Hotel Rebstock, Heiliggrabgasse 6 (☎ 23 03 17; fax 23 03 18), consists of eight clean, basic rooms over a small wine-house and boasts a friendly staff and a great location in the middle of the Altstadt. Take almost any bus from the Hauptbahnhof to "Höfchen." Breakfast included. Singles DM65, with shower DM85; doubles DM95, with shower DM104.

Hotel Stadt Koblenz, Rheinstr. 49 (☎ 22 76 02; fax 22 33 07), has inexpensive, finely furnished rooms across the street from the *Rathaus* on the outskirts of the *Altstadt*. Take your choice of several buses to "Rheingoldhalle." Breakfast included. Singles DM75, with shower and bathroom DM100; doubles DM95, with shower and bathroom DM130; triples DM150.

On Tuesdays, Fridays, and Saturdays in the warm months the **Domplatz** offers the quintessential German shopping and eating experience: an enormous outdoor **Markt** with fresh meats, fruits, vegetables, and even beer and sweets. If you're in a hurry or short on cash, stop on almost any street-corner in Mainz and pick up a fresh pretzel or cheese bread from one of the **Ditsch** stands (M-F 9am-9pm, Sa 9am-7pm, DM1-2.50). For groceries try **Supermarkt 2000,** Am Brand 41, under the *Sinn-Leffers* department store (open M-F 9:30am-8pm, Sa 9am-4pm).

Central Café, corner of Rheinstr. and Heugasse (☎ 22 56 66), near the *Dom,* has the decor of a city diner and delicious food; burgers and traditional German fare are less than DM15. Open M-Th and Su 10am-1am midnight, F-Sa 10am-1am.

News Cafe, Göttelmannstr. 40 (☎ 98 98 37), in the **Volkspark** adjacent to Mainz's Jugendgästehaus, provides an ideal backyard to the hostel with playgrounds, roller rinks, wading pools, ice cream stands, and a choo-choo train that goes around the whole park for the kiddies. Open 10am-1pm, all entrees less than DM20.

Taverne Academica (☎ 38 58 50) serves good, cheap food and drink to a student crowd. All entrees DM5-15. Take the bus to "Universität" and make a left. Open M-F 10am-4am, Sa noon-3pm and 7pm-4am.

▣ SIGHTS

MARTINSDOM. This colossal sandstone cathedral, the resting place of the archbishops of Mainz, lies at the heart of the city. Their extravagant tombstones line the walls and their faces appear in a stained-glass time line extending back to 975 AD (☎ 253 176/253 414. Open Apr.-Sept. M-F 9am-6:30pm, Sa 9am-4pm, Su 12:45-3pm and 4-6:30pm; Oct.-Mar. M-F 9am-5pm, Sa 9am-4pm, Su 12:45-3pm and 4-5pm. Free.)

CHURCHES. For some modern flavor in the Altstadt, visit **St. Johanneskirche,** an almost shocking hybrid of religion and contemporary art. (Across the street from the Dom). On a hill south of the Dom stands the Gothic **Stephanskirche,** most notable for its stunning stained-glass windows created by Russian artist-in-exile Marc Chagall. On sunny days, the windows bathe the church in eerie ocean-blue light. (From the Dom, take Ludwigstr. until it ends at Schillerpl. and follow Gaustr. up the hill to the church. ☎ 23 42 27. Open daily 10am-noon and 2-5pm.) **Pfarrkirche St. Christoph,** the reputed site of Gutenberg's baptism, was seriously damaged in WWII; today it

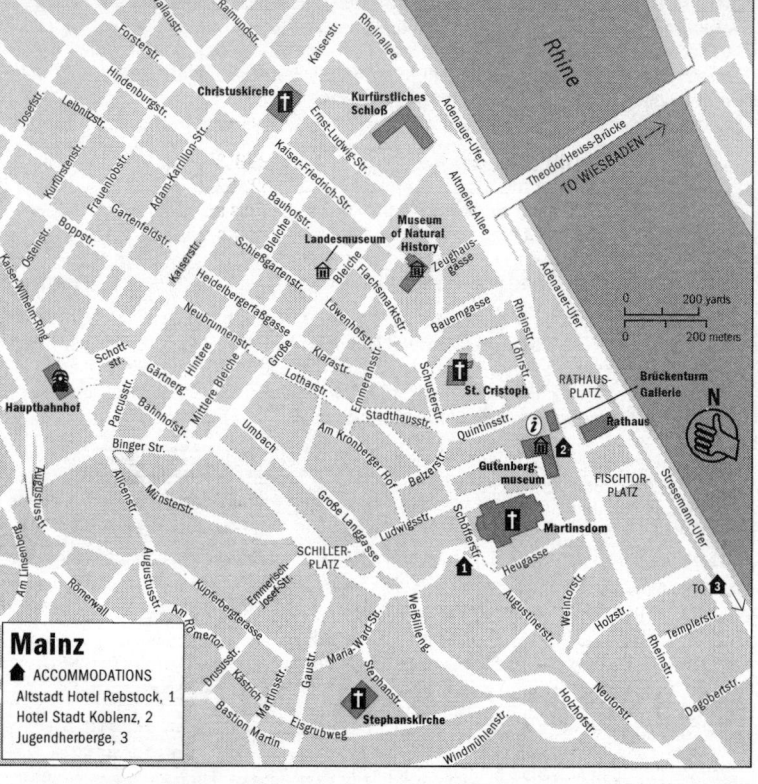

Mainz

⌂ ACCOMMODATIONS
Altstadt Hotel Rebstock, 1
Hotel Stadt Koblenz, 2
Jugendherberge, 3

stands as a poignant reminder of war to an otherwise gilded city. The tower is still used for services, but the main body lies in ruins. *(North of Marktpl. on Christophstr. Open M-F 8:30am-4:30pm.)*

🏛 MUSEUMS

The four main museums in Mainz (**Bischöfliches Dom** and **Diözesean-Museum**, **Gutenberg-Museum** and **Stadtarchiv**, the **Landesmuseum**, and the **Museum of Natural History**) have one informational telephone line (☎ 28 62 10), and offer reduced ticket rates (DM18, students DM9) if you plan to visit multiple museums in one day.

DIÖZESANMUSEUM. Adjacent to the *Martinsdom*, the **Diözesanmuseum** looks out on a beautiful courtyard, and houses changing exhibitions. *(Enter at the back of the Dom. ☎ 25 33 46/25 33 44; fax 25 33 49. Open Tu-Sa 9am-5pm, Su 11am-6pm. DM6, students DM3.)*

GUTENBERG-MUSEUM. Johannes Gutenberg, the father of movable type, is immortalized at the **Gutenberg-Museum.** The museum contains several Gutenberg Bibles, a replica of his original press (which really works!), an impressive collection of text art, early Asian calligraphy, and several other relics of the early printing industry. If you have time, there's even a marionette show about the famous printer. *(Across from the Dom, Liebfrauenpl. 5. ☎ 12 26 40. Open Tu-Su, 10am-5pm, DM6, students DM3. Show M-F 10:30am, Sa-Su 3pm.)* The **Druckladen,** an experimental print shop, lets visitors try their luck at Gutenberg's craft by setting and printing their own designs. *(Next to the Museum, Seiliggrasse 1. ☎ 12 26 86. Open M-F 10am-5pm, Sa 11am-2pm. Free.)*

GROSSE BLEICHE. Grosse Bleiche is home to many of Mainz's museums. The **Museum of Natural History** has exhibits on German and worldwide species. *(☎ 12 22 68. Open W, F-Su 10am-5pm, Tu, Th 10am-8pm. DM3, students DM2).* A comprehensive collection of art and archaeology, including a Judaica division and enormous Roman arches, awaits in the **Landesmuseum.** *(Up the street at Große Bleiche 49-51. Open Tu 10am-8pm, W-Su 10am-5pm. DM5, students DM3; Sa free.)* The **Romische-Germanische Zentralmuseum** is also on Grosse Bleiche, across from the Musuem of Natural History. Exhibits include ancient chariots, helmets, swords, sculpture, and jewelry. *(Open Tu-Su, 10am-6pm. Free.)*

NIGHTLIFE

Mainz sports a number of **Weinhäuser**; one wandering through the Altstadt is likely to find a selection of beer and wine cafes open until midnight or 1am. During the third weekend in June, Mainz celebrates **Johannisnacht,** three days of old-fashioned revelry dedicated to Gutenberg (June 22-25, 2001). Movable type and Bacchanalian revelry do not easily combine, but Mainz manages it in high style. For more active entertainment, visit one of the several clubs.

KUZ (Kulturzentrum), Dagobertstr. 20b (☎ 28 68 60), Mainz's standard, horribly hip disco and beer-garden. Take bus #60, 61, 71, 73, or 90 to "Holzturm/Fort-Malakoff-Park," face the shopping center across the street, and turn right. Walk just over one block and turn left on Dagobertstr. Open W 9pm-3am and F-Sa 10pm-4am. Cover DM8.

Jazzid, in the basement of Fort Malakoff Park (Dagobertstr. & Rheinstr.) is spicier and a little more posh than *KUZ* (which is directly across the street); the younger clientele here revels in a world of loud dance music and style that screams "glam disco," not "German brew house." Open Tu-Th, Su 9pm-3am, F-Sa 9pm-5am. Cover DM7.

MOSELTAL (MOSEL VALLEY)

Trying to avoid its inevitable surrender to the Rhein at Koblenz, the Mosel River slowly meanders past the sun-drenched hills, pretty towns, and ancient castles of the softly cut Moseltal. The headwaters of the Mosel flow from the Vosges Mountains of France, following a northeasterly course that winds over 200km of German territory from Trier to Koblenz. The slopes aren't quite as steep as the Rhein's narrow gorge, but the countless less-touristed vineyards on the gentle hillsides have been pressing quality wines since the Romans first cultivated the vines 2,000 years ago. The only local complaints heard about the region is that summers are too dry (the least of worries for a visitor) and the winters too wet. For a few days, the mellow Mosel goes berserk, flooding the valley.

The best way to view the valley's scenery is by boat, bus, or bicycle; the train line between Koblenz and Trier strays frequently from the course of the river, cutting through the unremarkable countryside. Although passenger boats no longer make the complete Koblenz-Trier run, several companies run daily trips along shorter stretches in summer.

COCHEM ☎02671

Like so many German wine-making villages, the hamlet of Cochem has become a repository of national nostalgia, its quintessential quaintness voraciously consumed by busloads of elderly German city-dwellers. Despite their presence, Cochem's impressive vineyard-covered hills and sparkling **Reichsburg** simply can't be cheapened into run-of-the-mill tourist attractions. High atop a hill adjacent to the village, the castle's elaborate turrets lend the town a pleasant, fairy-tale quality enhanced by the gnarled streets lined with clapboard houses.

GETTING THERE. Unlike much of the Mosel Valley, Cochem is easily accessible by **train** from **Koblenz** (1hr., 2-3 per hr., DM12), and **Trier** (1hr., 2 per hr., DM17).

Although Cochem is equidistant to the two cities, the route to Koblenz hugs the Mosel, making for some spectacular views; the trip to Trier traverses serene but not fantastic countryside. The **Moselbahn bus** service links DB trains to the rest of the Mosel Valley in Bullay, a town one stop away from Cochem (10min., 2 per hr., DM4.80).

◪ PRACTICAL INFORMATION. The **tourist office,** Endertplatz 1, next to the bus station, books **rooms** (from DM30) for free. From the train station, go to the river and turn right. (☎600 40 or 194 33; fax 60 04 44; email verkehrsamt.cochem@lcoc.de; www.cochem.de. Open Apr.-Oct. M-Th and Sa 9am-5pm, F 9am-6pm, Su 10am-noon. Nov.-Mar. M-F 9am-1pm and 2-5pm.) Along the way, you'll pass **Fahhrad-Shop Kreutz,** behind the Shell gas station along the river, which rents an array of **bikes.** (☎911 31. DM14 per day, DM70 per week. Kids' bikes DM7 per day. Open M-F 9am-6pm, Sa 9am-1pm. Passport required.) The **post office** is at the corner of Ravenestr. and Josefstr., one block from Endenplatz (open M-F 8am-5pm, Sa 8am-noon).

◪◪ ACCOMMODATIONS AND FOOD. Cochem's friendly, basic **Jugendherberge (HI),** Klottener Str. 9, is 15 minutes from the train station on the opposite shore. Cross the Nordbrücke to the left as you exit the station; the youth hostel is next to the bridge on the right. Beware the echoes that make schoolchildren seem much louder than usual. (☎86 33; fax 85 68. Breakfast and sheets included. Reception daily noon-1pm and 5-10pm. Curfew 10pm, but they'll give you a key with a DM10 deposit. Dorm beds DM22.90, with dinner 31.90.)For the best deals on hotel rooms, head in from the river. Family owned and operated **◪Hotel Holl,** Endertstr. 54, combines large, bright, and comfortable rooms with good food and friendly hospitality. (☎ 43 23; fax 8414; www.hotel-holl.de. Breakfast included. Single, doubles, and apartments, all with baths, for DM40-70 per person per night; less for extended stays.) Right down the street comfortable rooms await at **Gästehaus Onkel Willi,** Endertstr. 39, another welcoming family-operated guesthouse and restaurant combination. (☎ 735; fax 91 06 60. All doubles with baths, DM48-55 per person per night. Breakfast included.) If you've got your own portable party palace, walk down the path below the hostel to the **Campingplatz am Freizeitzentrum** on Stadionstr. (☎44 09. Wash and dry DM1.50. Bike rental DM14 per day. Reception 8am-10pm. Open Easter-Oct. DM6.50 per person, DM6-12 per tent.)

At the cheesy, good-hearted **Weinhexenkeller,** on Hafenstr. across and next to the Moselbrücke, indulge in food (DM8-15) and divine Mosel wine. Local legend says that guests who imbibe too much fall under a witch's spell. Modern science says they become drunk. Either way, you'll have a perfect excuse to go nuts when the live music and dancing kicks in Th-Sa at 7pm. (☎977 60. Open M-F 11am-1am, Sa 10am-2am.) On the Marktplatz next to the bridge, take a seat at the **Café-Restaurant Mosella** for a cup of coffee or a hearty meal (dishes DM4-20, open M-Sa, 10am-10pm). **La Baia Ristorante Pizzeria,** Liniusstr. 4 (☎80 40), on the train station side of the Mosel near the Moselbrücke, serves excellent pizza (from DM6.50) and pasta (from DM7.50) on a nice second-floor terrace.

◪◪ SIGHTS AND ENTERTAINMENT. The glorious interior of the **Reichsburg** hides its war-ravaged past. Originally built in the 11th century, the castle was destroyed in 1689 by French troops under Louis XIV; in 1868, a wealthy Berlin merchant rebuilt it as a luxurious villa in neo-Gothic style. The view from the castle grounds alone warrants the 15-minute climb along Schloßstr. from the Marktplatz. Unfortunately, a peek into its opulent interior can be taken today only as part of a guided tour. (☎ 255; fax 5691. Open daily mid-Mar. to Oct. 9am-5pm, Nov.-Dec. 11am-5pm. Frequent 40min. tours; written English translations available. DM7, students DM6, children DM3.) Take the tiny lane to the left as you walk down from the castle to the 15th-century **Peterskapelle,** enclosed by high walls and vine-covered trellises. The other popular hillside attraction in town is the **Sesselbahn** on Edenstr., a chair lift that runs to the **Wildpark, Märchenwald,** and the **Pinnerkreuz,** a lone cross standing on a high peak illuminated by 10,000-watt bulbs at night. (☎ 98 90 63; fax 98 90 64. Lift runs daily Apr. to mid-Nov. 10am-6pm. One-way DM6.90, round-trip DM9.50; children DM3.20 and DM4.50, respectively). For even more theme park style thrills 'n' spills, head across the river and follow the *Freizeitzentrum* signs to reach the gigantic **Moselbad,** a sprawling complex of pools, saunas, jacuzzis, and waterslides located five minutes north of the *Nordbrücke,* the bridge near the train station. (☎979 90; fax 97 99 22. Open daily May-June 10am-7pm, July-Aug. 10am-8pm. Day ticket DM19, students DM11, ages 6-11 DM7, under 6 free. Outdoor pool only DM5, students DM3.)

The **Weinwoche** begins a week and a half after **Pfingsten** (Pentecostal Monday) with some of the Mosel's best vintages (DM1-2 per 100ml taste). On the last weekend of August, the **Heimat-und-Weinfest** culminates in a dramatic fireworks display.

🄳 DAY TRIP: BURG ELTZ. Originally constructed in the 11th and 12th centuries, **Burg Eltz** is one of the only intact Medieval castles remaining in the Rheinland. The Burg rests on a small hill in a lush valley, belying its function as a fortress for the three branches of the Eltz family. Nature conspired in the defense: the Eltz brook flows on either side of the Burg's hill, providing a natural moat, while the sheltering woods were once favored hunting grounds. The Eltz party was crashed, however, in the 1330s by Baldwin, Elector of Trier. Two years and a lot of rock-slinging later, the Eltz family surrendered to Baldwin's terms: they retained possession of the castle as his minions...uh, vassals. But the arrangement was successful, because what now exists of the Burg was constructed mostly during the 15th century. Today the family Eltz still has rooms in the castle, but chooses to live outside Cochem, leaving more of the Burg open to tourists.

The castle's interior can only be seen with a tour. Two 15th-century Flemish tapestries, called verdures for their dominant greenish hues, give a fantastical artist's rendering of new animals described by explorers of the Americas and Africa. Sharing the room with these glorified rugs is Lucas Cranach the Elder's *Madonna with Grapes.* Various ornate and dazzling gold and silver pieces both functional and decorative are locked away in the **Schatzkammer** (treasure room), which is not part of the tour. (☎ (02672) 95 05 00; fax 950 50 50; www.burg-eltz.de. Open daily Apr.-Oct. 9:30am-5:30pm. Tours every 15min.; English tours given only upon sufficient demand, typically once an hour. DM9, students DM6, Schatzkammer DM4.)

The nearest town to Burg Eltz accessible by **train** is **Moselkern.** Trains from **Cochem** run hourly (20min, DM6). With your back to the train station, head right on Oberstr. through town until it passes under a bridge and becomes a slightly winding backwoods road along the Eltz brook. The road ends at **Ringelsteiner Mühle**—from here the path through the woods is well marked. The train station information center stores luggage (open M-F 5am-10pm, Sa-Su 5:40am-10pm).

BEILSTEIN ☎02673

A tiny hamlet of half-timbered houses, crooked cobblestone streets, and about 170 residents, Beilstein takes pride in being the smallest official town in Germany (it received town rights in 1319). Spared in WWII, Beilstein's untarnished beauty has made it the idyllic backdrop of several movies and political summits. Adenauer and DeGespari created the European Economic Community (now the European Union) here. By day, Beilstein's natural charm draws a tourist crowd that exponentially increases its population, but after 6pm, the spell breaks, and the peaceful town is yours. **Burg Metternich** is the resident castle; the French sacked it in 1689, but the view from the tower is still spectacular. (☎ 936 39; fax 936 388. Open daily Apr.-Oct. 9am-6pm. DM3, students DM2, children DM1.) Also worth a look is the Baroque **Karmelitenkirche,** with its intricately carved wooden altar and the famous **Schwarze Madonna von Beilstein,** a 16th-century Montserrat sculpture left behind by Spanish troops reintroducing Catholicism to the region (open daily 9am-8pm).

The town can be reached by **bus** #8060, which departs from both Endertplatz and the station in **Cochem** (15min; M-F 14 per day, Sa 7 per day, Su 3 per day; DM4.90). The boats of **Personnenschiffahrt Kolb** also float to Beilstein. (☎15 15; fax 15 10. 1hr.; May-Oct. 4 per day. One-way DM13, round-trip DM18.) Beilsteins's **tourist office** (☎/fax 90 01 91) makes its home in Café Klapperburg, a block uphill from the bus stop and on the left. Lay down your sleepy head at **Hotel Gute Quelle,** Marktplatz 34 where large, bright rooms fill a fairy-tale-perfect house. (☎14 37; fax 13 99. Breakfast included. Doubles, all with bath, DM45-60 per person.) Or try **Winzerschenke,** An der Klostertreppe 39, which has comfortable doubles in the shadow of the **Karmelitenkirche.** (☎/fax 13 54. Breakfast included. Doubles, all with bath, DM35-45 per person.) The **Klostercafé** outside the church offers outstanding traditional food (DM10-16), fantastic Mosel wine, and a view that beats them both. (☎16 74 and 16 53; fax 16 88. Open M-Sa 9am-7pm.)

TRIER ☎0651

The oldest town in Germany, Trier has weathered more than two millennia in the western end of the Mosel Valley. Founded by the Romans during the reign of Augustus, Trier reached the height of its prominence in the early 4th century as the capital of the Western Roman Empire, becoming an important center for Christianity in Europe. Today the town is a patchwork quilt of uncommon design and grace, having seen an eclectic range of architectural styles. The vitality of Trier's visitors and students blends harmoniously with the dignity and beauty of its incredible Roman ruins and well-preserved Altstadt.

▌ GETTING THERE AND GETTING AROUND

Trains: Depart to **Saarbrücken** (1½hr., 2 per hr., DM23); **Koblenz** (1¾hr., 2 per hr., DM30); **Köln** (2½ hours, 2 per hr.); and **Luxembourg** (45min., 1 per hr.; DM15).

Ferries: Personen-Schiffahrt (☎263 17) sails to **Bernkastel-Kues** from the Kaiser-Wilhelm-Brücke. May-Oct. daily at 9:15am. Round-trip DM45.

Taxi: Taxi-Funk (☎330 30).

Bike Rental: Tina Fahrradvermietung Trier (☎ 14 88 56), in the main building on track 11 at the train station. 3-speed bikes DM8 per day, 7-speed DM10, with a DM50 deposit. Open Apr.-Oct. daily 9am-7pm.

◆▌ ORIENTATION AND PRACTICAL INFORMATION

Trier lies less than 50km from the Luxembourg border on the Mosel. Most of the sights sit in the vicinity of the compact Altstadt. The gate to the Altstadt, **Porta Nigra** (Black Gate) is a 10-minute walk from the train station down Theodor-Heuss-Allee or Christophstr. Although most sights are within walking distance, the bus system can carry you anywhere for DM3. A **Trier Card,** available at the tourist office, offers admission to six museums, free bus fare, and discounts on the Roman ruins, tours, and theater performances over a 3-day period (DM21, family card for DM39).

Tourist Office: Tourist-Information (☎97 80 80; fax 447 59 or 70 00 48; email info@tit.de; www.trier.de), in the shadow of the Porta Nigra, offers daily **tours** in English at 1:30pm (DM10, DM3 for children). Open Jan.-Feb. M-F 10am-5pm, Sa 9am-1pm; Mar. M-Sa 9am-6pm, Su 9am-1pm; Apr.-Oct. M-Sa 9am-6:30pm, Su 9am-3:30pm; Nov.-Dec. M-Sa 9am-6pm, Su 9am-3:30pm. During these hours, the staff hands out free maps, sells the Trier Card (see above) and books rooms for free.

Bookstore: Akademische Buchhandlung, Fleischstr. 62 (☎97 99 01). Small selection of English paperbacks. Open M-F 9am-7pm, Sa 9am-4pm.

Wine Information: Vinothek, Margaritengässchen 2a (☎994 05 40), near the Porta Nigra. Staff advises on **wine tasting** in the Mosel region. Open daily 10am-7pm.

RHEINLAND-PFALZ

Laundry: Wasch Center, Brückenstr. 19-21, down the street from Karl Marx's old house. Wash DM8, dry DM3 per 25min. Open M-Sa 8am-10pm.

Internet Access: Net Café, Saarstr. 51-53 (☎970 99 18). Part of a bar, this cafe offers drinks and online time for DM1.50 per fifteen minutes.

Gay and Lesbian Resources: Rosatelefon (☎194 46).

Post Office: 54292 Trier, on Bahnhofpl. across from the Bahnhof. Open M-F 8am-7pm, Sa 8am-1pm.

▌ ACCOMMODATIONS AND CAMPING

Jugendgästehaus (HI), An der Jugendherberge 4 (☎14 66 20 or 29292; fax 146 62 30 or 24080). Bus #2 or 87 (direction: "Trierweilerweg" or "Pfalzel/Quint") to "Zur Laubener Ufer," and walk 10min. downstream along the river embankment. Or from the station follow Theodor-Heuss-Allee as it becomes Nordallee, forks right onto Lindenstr., and ends at the bank of the Mosel (30min.). Breakfast and sheets included. Reception open sporadically 7am-midnight. Singles DM54; doubles DM39.40; quads DM29.90 (all prices per person).

▨ **Jugendhotel/Jugendgästehaus Kolpinghaus,** Dietrichstr. 42 (☎97 52 50; fax 975 25 40), one block off the Hauptmarkt. Large, clean rooms and comfortable beds in an unbeatable location. Breakfast and sheets included. Reception 8am-11pm. Call as far ahead as possible. Dorm beds DM27; singles DM39; doubles DM80.

Hotel Haus Runne, Engelstr. 35 (☎289 22). Follow Theodor-Heuss-Allee from the station and turn right on Engelstr. after the Porta Nigra. Large 70s-style rooms with TV. Breakfast included. Singles DM45; doubles DM90; quads DM160.

Camping: Trier City Campingplatz, Luxemburger Str. 81 (☎869 21). From Hauptmarkt, follow Fleischstr. to Bruckenstr. to Karl-Marx-Str. to the Römerbrücke. Cross the bridge, head left on Luxemburger Str., and then left at the camping sign. Reception daily 8am-10pm. Open Apr.-Oct. DM8. Tent DM5.

◗ FOOD

For **groceries,** head to **Kaufmarkt,** at the corner of Brückenstr. and Stresemannstr. (open M-F 8am-8pm, Sa 8am-4pm), or check out **Plus** near the Hauptmarkt, Brotstr. 54 (open M-F 8:30am-7pm, Sa 8:30am-4pm).

▨ **Astarix,** Karl-Marx-Str. 11 (☎722 39), is squeezed in a passageway next to Miss Marple's. If you get to the sex shops, you've gone too far. Excellent food at unbelievable prices. Hip waitstaff without the attitude. Tortellini DM7.50, pizzas from DM9. Open M-Th 11:30am-1am, F-Sa 11:30am-2am, Su 6pm-1am. Kitchen open M-Th and Su noon-11:30pm, F-Sa noon-12:30am.

Italienisches Restaurant Fornelli, Jocobstr. 34 (☎433 85) serves up large scrumptious pizza (DM11-14) and pasta dishes for the lunch and dinner crowds. Open daily 11:30am-11:30pm.

Warsberger Hof, Dietrichstr. 42 (☎ 97 52 50), in the Kolpinghaus Hotel (see above). Walk from Porta Nigra to the Hauptmarkt and turn right. Lunch specials and vegetarian fare from DM10. Open daily 11am-midnight. Kitchen open 11:30am-11:30pm. **Cafeteria** in the back serves cheaper meals (DM6-9). Open daily 11:30am-2:15pm.

Woorscht & Kneissjen, on Fleischstr. off the Hauptmarkt. Combined bakery and butcher shop sells tasty sandwiches on one side (DM4-5) and different kinds of Wurst on the other (from DM2).

Bierakademie, Bahnhofstr. 28 (☎ 994 31 95), half a block from the station. Today's geography lesson: around the world in 100 beers! For those who foolishly insist that man cannot live on beer alone, simple baguettes, hot dogs, and chicken wings are priced under DM10. Open M-Sa 11am-1am, Su 3pm-1am.

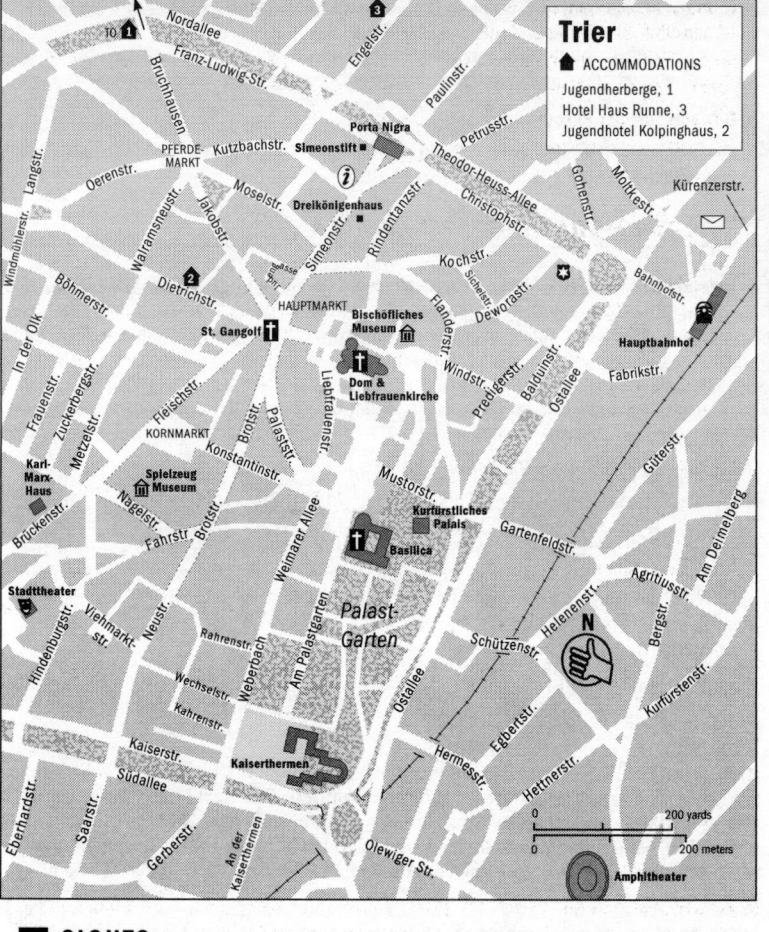

Trier

▲ ACCOMMODATIONS

Jugendherberge, 1
Hotel Haus Runne, 3
Jugendhotel Kolpinghaus, 2

SIGHTS

To save money, buy a one-day combination ticket valid at all Roman monuments. (Palm Sunday to Sept. DM9, students DM4.50; Oct.-Nov. and Jan. to Palm Sunday DM4.50; Dec. DM4.)

PORTA NIGRA. Trier has its belly full of its Roman past, the most impressive remnant of which is the Porta Nigra (Black Gate). Built in the 2nd century AD, the massive stone gate gained its name from the centuries of grime that metamorphosed its originally light-yellow sandstone face into uneven shades of gray. In the past, the gate served as the strongest line of defense against attacks on the city; now, throngs of tourists penetrate the barrier every day. Head to the top for a great view of Trier. *(Open daily Palm Sunday to Sept. 9am-6pm; Oct.-Nov. and Jan. to Palm Sunday 9am-5pm; Dec. 10am-4pm. DM4, students DM2. Last entry 30min. before closing.)*

DOM. With a delightfully impressive interior, the 11th-century cathedral's many nooks and crannies shelter the tombs of archbishops. What is reputedly the Tunica Christi (Holy Robe of Christ) is enshrined at the eastern end of the cathedral. Tradition holds that this relic was brought from Jerusalem to Trier around 300 by St. Helena, mother of Emperor Constantine. It was last shown to the public in 1996. Also in the Dom, the Schatzkammer touts a treasury of religious artifacts. Behind the Dom is the Bischöfliches Dom- und Diözesanmuseum, a surprisingly modern building showcasing holy art of all sorts. The museum also boasts large archaeological collections and beautifully restored frescoes. *(Dom open Apr.-Oct. daily 6:30am-6pm; Nov.-Mar. daily 6:30am-5:30pm. Free. Schatzkammer open Apr.-Oct. M-Sa 10am-5pm, Su 2-5pm; Nov.-Mar. F-Sa 11am-4pm, Su 1:30-4pm. DM2, students and children DM1.30. Diözesanmuseum, Windstr. 6-8. ☎ 710 52 55; fax 710 53 48; www.museum.bistum-trier.de. Open M-Sa 9am-5pm, Su 1-5pm. DM4, students DM2.)*

AMPHITHEATER. Leave the Altstadt for an imaginary concert at the remains of the 2nd-century Amphitheater. Had the Rolling Stones toured in 169 AD (and they probably did), this 20,000-seat venue, one of the largest in the Roman Empire, certainly would have been on the itinerary. Instead, it held a spectacle even more appalling than an aged Mick Jagger: the theater hosted demonstrations of the most spectacular and gruesome ways of inflicting pain (and death) on humans and animals. Explore the underground labyrinths for yourself. The amphitheater is now a stage for city productions; check with **Theater Trier** for a list of performances. *(A 5min. walk uphill from the Kaiserthermen along Olewiger Str. Admission and times same as the Porta Nigra above, but closed Dec.)*

HAUPTMARKT. Fruit stalls, florists, and ice cream vendors crowd the Hauptmarkt in central Trier. The colorful Gothic **Dreikönigenhaus,** on the left hand side of the Hauptmarkt as you walk away from the Porta Nigra, bears eloquent testimony to class antagonisms in old Europe. The front door of the merchant's home is located on the second story above street level, accessible only by a ladder, and was pulled inside when the angry *Lumpenproletariat* besieged the lavishly adorned house.

KAISERTHERMEN. The ruins of the Roman baths where Constantine once scrubbed himself still retain long, dark underground passages that make it easy to get lost. *(At the southeast corner of the walls. Same hours and admission as Porta Nigra above.)*

KARL-MARX-HAUS. Growing up in this neighborhood, it's no surprise that Marx was inspired to write his theory of class conflict. The Karl-Marx-Haus, where young Karl first walked, talked, and dreamed of labor alienation, still stands and is a must-see for indefatigable Marxists. Busts and copies of the *Manifesto* abound. *(Brückenstr. 10. ☎ 430 11. Open Apr.-Oct. M 1-6pm, Tu-Su 10am-6pm; Nov.-Mar. M 2-5pm, Tu-Su 10am-1pm and 2-5pm. DM3, students DM2.)*

LIEBFRAUENKIRCHE. Adjacent to the Dom is the magnificent Gothic Liebfrauenkirche. Unlike the stained glass in most churches, which remains a pretty but peripheral decoration, the angular and stylized red- and blue-patterned windows of this basilika dominate its interior. *(Liebfrauenstr. 2. ☎ 42 554; fax 40 313. Open daily 8am-noon and 2-6pm.)*

AROUND THE BASILIKA. The Basilika was originally the location of Emperor Constantine's throne room. *(Open M-Sa 9am-6pm, Su 11:30am-6pm. Free.)* Next door lies the bubble-gum pink **Kurfürstliches Palais,** a former residence of the archbishop-electors of Trier that today houses municipal government offices. It overlooks the well-kept **Palastgarten.** Along the eastern edge of the garden lies the **Landesmuseum,** an impressive collection of Roman stonework, sculpture, and mosaics, as well as a few other random relics, including a 2,700-year-old Egyptian mummy. The museum also hosts continually-changing exhibits. *(Ostallee 44. Open Tu-F 9:30am-5pm, Sa-Su 10:30am-5pm. DM10, children DM3.)*

SIMEONSTIFT. An 11th-century monastery enveloped by the Porta Nigra's courtyard, the Simeonstift holds the **Städtisches Museum,** which has special exhibitions and a permanent collection of oils and sculptures. *(☎ 718 14 50; fax 718 17 58. Open Apr.-Oct. daily 9am-5pm; Nov.-Mar. Tu-F 9am-5pm, Sa-Su 9am-3pm. DM6, students DM5.)*

SPIELZEUGMUSEUM. Placate your inner child at the **Spielzeugmuseum** with two centuries of dolls and teddy bears. *(Nagelstr. 4-5. ☎ 758 50; fax 994 38 75. Open Apr.-Oct. daily 11am-5pm; Nov.-Mar. Tu-Su noon-4pm. DM7.50, ages 10-18 DM4, under 10 DM3.)*

SCHWEBELBAHN. If you're simply not impressed with man-made wonders, ride the Schwebelbahn (gondola) across the Mosel to the Stadtwald and admire the primeval forest, the murmuring pines, and the hemlocks. *(☎ 14 72 30. Open M-F 9am-6pm, Sa-Su 9am-7pm. One way DM4.50, children DM3; round-trip DM8, children DM4.)*

🎵🎭 ENTERTAINMENT AND NIGHTLIFE

Several annual festivals spice up Trier's atmosphere. The **Altstadtfest** brings live music, wine, and beer to the streets during the fourth weekend in June. The second weekend in July welcomes the **Moselfest,** with Saturday night fireworks over the water. The first weekend in August brings on the **Weinfest** in the nearby town of Olewig, kicked off by Friday fireworks.

The **Theater Trier,** Am Augustinerhof, has three stages, and a wide variety of shows with tickets ranging from DM11-46. (☎718 18 18; www.theatertrier.de. Box office open Tu-F 9:30am-2pm, and 3:30-8pm, Sa 10am-12:30pm and 6:30-7:30pm, Su 11am-noon and 6:30-7:30pm.)

Pubs, clubs, and *Kneipen* of all flavors fan out from the Hauptmarkt, with dense collections on **Judengasse** and the **Pferdemarkt.** Check posters and the free weekly *Der kleine Dicke* for parties and concerts.

Palais Walderdorff, (☎410 62), across from the Dom. By day a mellow cafe, by night a multi-room bar and disco. Beautifully advertised themes. Cafe open daily 10am-10pm. Bar and disco open daily 10pm-3am, dancing kicks in around 12:30am. Cover DM7.

Blaues Blut, Pferdemarkt (☎412 57). Mellow blue lighting and tiles on the bar evoke the floor of a swimming pool. Instead of getting an eyeful of chlorine, enjoy this outdoor/indoor bar. Open M-Th 9:30am-1am, F-Sa 9:30am-2am, Su 9:30am-1am.

The Dive, Judengasse 21 (☎444 24). Descending into the first subterranean bar, you feel like you're on a surreal beach, replete with plastic bamboo and wooden parrots. Keep going—the disco downstairs caters to a happy crowd with high-intensity dance music. Open M and F-Sa 9pm-3am, Th 9am-2am. Cover DM5.

SAARBRÜCKEN   ☎0681

For centuries, Saarbrücken's proximity to the French border and rich natural resources have made it a center of one violent conflict after another, leaving virtually none of its Altstadt intact and clearing the way for rampant industrial development. Officially French until 1935, French influences linger everywhere. Road signs, cuisine, and an unmistakably cosmopolitan pulse point to Saarbrücken's cultural past, while postmodern architecture, countless factories and power plants, and a surprisingly dynamic downtown area point to its future. If you're looking for history, Saarbrücken isn't the place, but with its urban atmosphere and a plethora of punks and other young progressives, the city may be one of the least touristed centers of the modern European cultural scene.

🛈 PRACTICAL INFORMATION

Saarbrücken is connected twice hourly by **train** to Trier (1½hr., DM30) and **Mannheim** (1½hr., DM36). **Der Fahrradladen,** Nauwieser Str. 19, rents **bikes.** (☎370 98. Open M 2-7pm, Tu-F 10am-7pm, Sa 10am-2pm. DM10-20 per day.) The **tourist office,** Reichstr. 1, is across from the station near the McDonalds. The staff finds **rooms** for a DM3 fee. (☎938 09 39; email kontour@kontour-saar.de; www.saarbruecken.de. Open M-F 9am-8pm, Sa 9am-4pm.) The handy **Saarbrücken Card** (DM13 for 2 days) provides transportation, free entrance to several sights, and theater discounts. Do your **laundry** at **Waschhaus,** Nauwiesenstr. 22, two blocks from the Rathaus. (Wash DM6, dry DM1 per 10min. Soap DM0.50. Open daily 8am-10pm.) The **post office,** 66111 Saarbrücken, is to the right of the station (open M-F 7am-6:30pm, Sa 7am-2pm, Su 9am-3pm). Get **internet access** at the **inter@ctive café,** Ufergasse 2, to the right off Bahnhofstr. (☎320 80. DM4 per 30min. Half price on Th. Open M-Th and Su 2-10pm, F-Sa 2pm-midnight.)

 ACCOMMODATIONS AND FOOD

The **Jugendgästehaus Europa (HI),** Meerwiesertalweg 31, is a 25-minute walk from the station. Head downhill and to the left; at the intersection veer left on Ursulinenstr., turn right onto Mozartstr., left onto Dudweilerstr., and right onto Meerwiesertalweg. Or take bus #19 to "Prinzenweiher" and backtrack to the hostel. It's colorful and modern with a friendly staff. (☎330 40; fax 37 49 11; email jh-saarbruecken@djh-info.de. Breakfast and sheets included. Reception 7:30am-1am. Curfew 1am. Doubles DM39 per person; quads DM30 per person.) **Gästehaus Weller,** Neugrabenweg 8, offers larger rooms with shower, phone, TV, and amazing color coordination. Go down Ursulinenstr, right on Mozartstr., carry on to Schumannstr., left on Fichtestr., and cross the bridge to Neugrabenweg. (☎37 19 03; fax 37 55 65. Reception M-Sa 8am-11pm, Su 6-11pm. Call ahead. Singles DM69-79; doubles DM89-105.) **Hotel Schloßkrug,** Schmollerstr. 14, at the corner of Bruchwiesenstr., is 15 minutes from the station in a quiet, convenient location. Go left onto Ursulinenstr., right on Richard-Wagner-Str., and right on Schmollerstr. (☎354 48; fax 37 50 22. Singles DM50, with shower and bath DM68; doubles DM95, with shower DM110, with bath DM145; triples with bath DM170.) **Campingplatz Saarbrücken,** Am Spicherer Berg, is far from the station. Take bus #42 to "Spicherer Weg," then cross Untertürkheimstr. and head uphill on Spicherer Weg. (☎517 80. Reception 7am-1pm and 3-10pm. Open Mar.-Oct. DM6 per person. Tent DM8.)

   Hela, at the end of Ursulinenstr., gives you **groceries** in a massive store (open M-F 8am-8pm, Sa 8am-4pm). The streets around **St.-Johanner-Markt** brim with bistros, beer gardens, and ethnic restaurants. The buzzing **Schnokeloch,** Kappenstr. 6, serves pizza and pasta for DM9-12. (☎333 97. Open M-F noon-2:30pm and 6pm-1am, Sa noon-1am, Su 6pm-1am.) **Blue Moon,** on the corner of Schmollerstr. and Martin-Luther-Str., serves eclectic entrees (DM9-14) and boasts a funky ambience. (☎317 80. Open M-F 10am-3pm and 6pm-1am, Sa 6pm-1am, Su 10am-1am.) Come nightfall, students fill *Kneipen* in the **Chinesenviertel** a few blocks further, between Rotenbergstr., Richard-Wagner-Str., Dudweilerstr., and Großherzog-Friedrich-Str.

■♫ **SIGHTS AND ENTERTAINMENT**

While Saarbrücken is mainly remarkable for its super-modern commercial district, **St.-Johanner-Markt** does boast some pretty pieces of old Europe. The details on the bronze doors of the **Basilika St. Johann** have faded since its 1754 construction, and now it's difficult to tell whether the engraved figures are writhing in hell-fire or ecstatic with heavenly bliss. *(Take Kappenstr. from the market and then turn right at the intersection with Katherinen-Kirche-Str.; the church is on the left. Open daily 9am-5pm. Free.)* The massive mustard **Staatstheater** stands south of the market next to the Alte Brücke; it was presented to Hitler after the Saarland was re-integrated into Germany in 1935. A walk along Am Stadtgarten leads to the **Moderne Galerie.** The gallery features such superstar artists as Picasso, Rodin, and Beckmann. Part two, the **Alte Sammlung,** is across the street. Medieval Madonnas, French porcelain, and antique jewelry are all here. Attached is the **Landesgalerie,** introducing some of the more promising regional artists. *(Moderne Galerie Bismarckstr. 11-19. ☎996 40. Alte Sammlung Karlstr. 1. All museums open Tu and Th-Su 10am-6pm, W 10am-8pm. DM3, students and children DM1.50. Special exhibits DM8, students DM4.)*

The **Saarbrücker Schloß,** on the other side of the Saar river, has morphed many times since the 9th century and now has a sparkling glass facade. Currently it houses offices of local officials. *(☎ 50 62 47. Tours in German given W-Su at 4pm. Open M-F 8:30am-6pm, Sa-Su 10am-6pm. Free.)* The Schloßplatz is officially the **Platz des unsichtbaren Mahnmals** (Place of the Invisible Reminder) and home to one of the most interesting monuments you'll never see. In 1990, students at a nearby art school, under cover of darkness, dug up 2146 stones in the plaza and carved the names of former Jewish cemeteries on their undersides; this thoughtful memorial was the result. Three museums surround the plaza. To the south, adjacent to the Schloß, the **Historisches Museum** includes cars, chairs from the 70s, and a disturbing collection of war propaganda. Don't miss the prison cell once used by WWI secret police, with graffiti in Russian and German. *(☎ 50 65 49. Open Tu-W, F, and Su 10am-6pm, Th 10am-8pm, Sa noon-6pm. DM4, students DM2; Th after 5pm free.)* To the north, the **Museum für Vor- und Frühgeschichte,** Schloßpl. 16, has finds that include a Celtic countess's grave and jewelry from the 4th century BC. *(☎ 95 40 50. Open Tu-Sa 9am-5pm, Su 10am-6pm. Free.)* The 1498 **Rathaus** west of the Schloß hosts the wacky **Abenteuermuseum,** which crams a lot of anthropological loot into a few rooms, all of it collected by the original globe trotter Heinz Rox Schulz on his rampages through Asia, New Guinea, Africa, and South America. *(☎ 517 47. Open Tu-W 9am-1pm, Th-F 3-7pm. DM3, children DM2.)* The **Ludwigskirche** is an architectural gem five minutes down Schloßstr. and to the right. Its bright white interior is a respite from the usual Gothic gloom. *(Open Tu 3-5pm, W 10am-noon, Sa 4-6pm, Su 11am-noon. Also open W 4-5:30pm in summer.)*

WORMS ☎ 06241

Of course you've heard of Worms. It was in European history class, when an unfortunate student (maybe it was you) raised his hand and asked what the whole class was thinking: "What's a diet of worms?" The teacher chuckled for a little longer than necessary and replied with characteristic wit, "I don't know what a diet of worms is, but the DEE-ATE of VOHRMS *(the Diet of Worms)* was the imperial council that sent Martin Luther into exile for refusing to renounce his heretical doctrines." Remember how funny that was? No? No matter—a visit to Worms will certainly refresh your memory, especially since little else of comparable import has happened here in the centuries since the famous gathering. Today's Worms is a fairly modern conglomerate of businesses with several fantastic historic and architectural sites scattered throughout. Its tourist office proudly proclaims a trip through the city is "two thousand years, on foot"; travel through time and spend a day or two thousand years at the many churches, monuments, and museums.

7 PRACTICAL INFORMATION. Worms is 45 minutes from **Mainz** by **train** (1 per hr., DM13). The **tourist office,** Neumarkt 14, is in a shopping complex across the street from the Dom St. Peter. (☎ 250 45; fax 263 28; email touristinfo@worms.de; www.worms.de. Open M-F 9am-6pm, Sa 9am-noon; Nov.-Mar. closed Sa.) Walking **tours** in German meet at the south portal of the Dom (2hr., Apr.-Oct. Sa at 10am and Su at 3pm; DM5). **Exchange money** at the *Deutsche Bank* down Wilhelm-Leuschner-Str. from the station (open M-W 8:30am-12:30pm and 2-4pm, Th until 6pm, F until 3:30pm). The **post office,** Kämmerstr. 44, 67547 Worms, is at the northern end of the pedestrian zone (open M-F 8am-6pm, Sa 8:30am-12:30pm). Assuage the pangs of email withdrawal at **Internet-Cafe-Zwiebel,** on the corner of Kaemmerstr. and Friedrichstr. (DM4.50 per ½hr., DM3.50 for students).

🖥 ACCOMMODATIONS AND FOOD. To get to the **Jugendgästehaus (HI),** Dechaneigasse 1 (☎257 80; fax 273 94), follow Bahnhofstr. right from the station to Andreasstr., turn left and walk until the Dom is on your left; the hostel is on your right. Enjoy bright two- to six-bed rooms, each with private bath.

(Breakfast and sheets included. Reception 7am-11:30pm. Strict curfew 11:30pm. DM27.80.) A relaxed staff runs **Weinhaus Weis** (a *Pension*, not a drinking establishment), Färbergasse 19, supplying soft beds in spacious rooms. (☎ 235 00; call at least two weeks ahead; breakfast included; singles DM40, doubles DM70.)

The university **Mensa** is your ticket to cheap food—tastier than a diet of worms. Travelers technically need an ID for the hot food, but they often get by with language ability. Turn right as you exit the station, go right across the first bridge, walk down Friedrich-Ebert-Str., and turn left after eight blocks on Erenburger Str. It's a block and a half up on your right, past the US Army barracks (open M-F 9am-7pm; warm food served only during meal times). The sounds of intense haggling at the **farmer's market** echo across Marktpl. (M, Th, and Sa mornings).

■ ⛶ **SIGHTS AND ENTERTAINMENT.** The site of Luther's confrontation with the *Diet*, during which he shocked the membership by declaring, *"Hier stehe Ich. Ich kann kein anders"* ("Here I stand, I can do no other"), is memorialized at the **Lutherdenkmal**, a larger-than-life statue erected in 1868 three blocks southeast of the station along Wilhelm-Leuschner-Str. Across the walkway toward the Dom stands the **Kunsthaus Heylshof**, which showcases a small collection of late Gothic and Renaissance artifacts including Rubens' *Madonna with Child* and an impressive group of beer steins. (Open May-Sept. Tu-F 11am-5pm, Su 10am-5pm; Oct.-Dec. and Feb.-Apr. Tu-F 2-4pm, Su 10am-noon and 2-4pm. DM5, students DM2.) The inviting greenery and paths of the **Heylshofgarten** surround the museum.

Chief among Worms's architectural treasures is the **Dom St. Peter,** a magnificent Romanesque cathedral with posture-improving pews and a spooky crypt. Let your vampire fantasies run wild or stand and face the hounds of hell. According to the *Nibelungenlied*, Siegfried's wife Kriemhilde had a spat with her sister-in-law Brunhilde in the square in front of the Dom. (Open daily 9am-6pm in Summer, until 5 in Winter. Donation requested.) Nearby behind the Jugendherberge stands the **Museum der Stadt Worms**, with a bevy of artifacts dating from the Stone Age to the present. (☎ 946 39 11. Open Tu-Su 10am-5pm. DM4, students DM2.)

The 900-year-old **Heiliger Sand**, the oldest Jewish cemetery in Europe, is the resting ground for sundry rabbis, martyrs, and celebrities. Enter the cemetery through the gate on Willi-Brandt-Ring, just south of Andreasstr. and the main train station. On the opposite end of the Altstadt, the area around **Judengasse** stands witness to the thousand-year legacy of Worms's Jewish community (once known as "Little Jerusalem"), which prospered during the Middle Ages but was wiped out in the Holocaust. The **Synagogue,** just off Judengasse, was the center of Jewish learning north of the Alps until WWII. (Open daily 10am-12:30pm and 1:30-5pm. from Apr.-Oct., 10am-noon and 2-4pm daily Nov.-Mar. Required kappas available at the door.) Behind the synagogue is the **Jüdisches Museum** in the **Raschi-Haus**, which traces the history of Worms's Jews and houses commentary by the famous Talmudic interpreter Rabbi Shlomo Ben-Yitzhak, better known as Raschi. (☎ 85 33 45 and 85 33 70. Open Tu-Su 10am-12:30pm and 1:30-5pm. DM3, students DM1.50.)

In the basement of the building opposite the *Mensa* is the **Taberna**, a groovy *Studentenkneipe* with a weekly disco. (Open M-Th 3pm-1am. Disco open Th 9pm-late. Often closed July-Sept.) A swank young crowd swims in colorful tropical drinks at **Ohne Gleich**, Kriemhildenstr. 11, down Bahnhofstr. to the right of the station. You'll feel like you've stepped into a Magritte painting. (☎ 41 11 77. Open M-Th and Su 9am-1am, F-Sa 9am-2am.) The Worms open-air **jazz festival** takes place each summer (June 29-July 1, 2001), while the **Backfischfest** brings a wine-drenched party of 70,000 people to Worms for nine days beginning the last weekend in August (Aug. 25-Sept. 2 2001).

SPEYER ☎ 06232

Speyer's political star rose and fell early. During the reign of the mighty Salian emperors in the 11th century, the town served as a principal meeting place for the Imperial Diets. As the emperors' power waned, Speyer slipped in significance, until ultimately the entire city was burned to the ground during the Palatinate War of Succession. By the time the two World Wars rolled around, Speyer escaped destruction; its gracefully ramshackle **Altstadt** and several glorious churches, until recently well off the beaten path of mass tourism, were spared from the bombings.

🛈 PRACTICAL INFORMATION. Speyer is easily reached by **train** from **Mannheim** (30min. 1 per hr.) and **Ludwigshafen** (25 min., 2 per hr., DM20). **Bus** #7007 from **Heidelberg** (1½hr.) deposits passengers at the steps of the Kaiserdom. The **tourist office**, Maximilianstr. 11, two blocks before Dom, has maps and a list of accomodations. From the station, take the city shuttle to "Maximilianstr." (☎ 14 23 92; fax 14 23 32; email tourist@speyer.de; www.speyer.de. Open May-Oct. M-F 9am-5pm, Sa 10am-4pm, Su 11am-3pm; Nov.-Apr. closed Su.) **Tours** of the city depart from in front of the tourist office. (Apr.-Oct. Sa-Su 11am. DM5.) A **shuttle bus** runs the length of the city every 10 minutes (day ticket DM1). The **post office**, 67346 Speyer, is on Postpl., next to the Altpörtel (open M-F 8am-6pm, Sa 8am-12:30pm).

🍴🛏 ACCOMMODATIONS AND FOOD. Speyer is blessed with the incredible new **Jugendgästehaus Speyer (HI)**, Geibstr. 5, where fun is guaranteed by the nearby pool and sunbathers' park and the hostel's backyard ball pit. (☎ 615 97; fax 615 96. Reception daily 8am-9pm. Curfew 10pm. Members only. Dorm beds DM29.10; singles DM54.40; doubles DM39.80.) **Pension Grüne Au**, Grüner Winkel 28, has comfortable rooms with gleaming sinks. From Maximilianstr., go left on Salzgasse, continue to St. Georggasse. Walk in the direction the fish statue faces and take a right onto Salzturmgasse, which turns into Grüner Winkel; the hotel is on the right. (☎ 721 96, fax 29 28 99. Singles DM50-75, doubles DM75-90.)

Next to the Altpörtel is a **Tenglemann** for groceries (open M-F 8am-8pm and Sat 7:30-4:30). North of Maximilianstr., **Korngasse** and **Große Himmelsgasse** shelter excellent restaurants. The **Gaststätte Zum Goldenen Hirsch**, Maximilianstr. 90a, offers traditional fare three blocks from the Dom. (☎ 726 94. Open M-F and Su 11am-1am, Sa 11am-2am.)

The second weekend in July (July 13-15, 2001) hosts the **Bretzelfest** (pretzel festival); the festivities involve concerts and parades. The second weekend in August (Aug. 10-12, 2001), the **Kaisertafel Speyer** takes place—tables are set up along the streets and visitors are herded along and stuffed full of regional specialties.

📷 SIGHTS. Since its construction in the 12th century, the **Kaiserdom** has been the symbol of Speyer. The immense Romanesque cathedral is noted for its main portals, flanked by seven statues recounting the Crucifixion on each side. The crypt under the east end coddles the remains of eight Holy Roman Emperors and their wives (open Apr.-Oct. M-Sa 9am-7pm, Su 9am-5pm; Nov.-Mar. M-Sa 9am-5pm, Su 1:30-5pm). South of the Dom, the **Historisches Museum der Pfalz**, Dompl., offers a comprehensive presentation on Palatinate history including a wine museum and Roman museum and hosts highly-touted special exhibits on anything from pop art to Napoleon. Among the exhibits are the exquisite **Domschatzkammer** and the **oldest bottle of wine in the world**—a slimy leftover from some wild Roman blowout in the 3rd century. (☎ 132 50. Open Tu and Th-Su 10am-6pm, W 10am-7pm. DM8, students and children DM5; Tu after 4pm free. Free tours Su at 11am.) From the Dom, take Große Plaffengasse one block and turn right on Judengasse to reach the **Judenbad**, a Jewish *mikwe* (ritual bath-house) from the 12th century. (☎ 62 04 90. Open Apr.-Oct. M-F 10am-noon and 2-5pm, Sa-Su 10am-5pm. DM1.50).

Maximilianstr., Speyer's main thoroughfare, spreads westward from the Dom, culminating in the medieval **Altpörtel,** an exquisitely preserved five-story village gate. Climb it for a great view. (Tower open Apr.-Oct. M-F 10am-noon and 2-4pm, Sa-Su 10am-5pm. DM1.50.) From the Altpörtel, a southward jaunt on Gilgenstr. leads to the **Josefskirche** and, across the street, the **Gedächtniskirche** (both open May-Oct. daily 10am-6pm; Nov.-Apr. M-Sa 10am-noon and 2-5pm, Su 2-5pm). For something slightly more up-to-the-minute, the **Technikmuseum,** Geibstr. 2, fills a gigantic warehouse with 30,000 cubic meters of trains, planes, and automobiles, as well as an **IMAX theater** (☎ 67 08 50) and the "Adventure-simulator." (Take the city shuttle to "Technikmuseum," or walk through the Dom Garten until you see the IMAX sign. (☎ 670 80; fax 67 08 20. Museum open daily 9am-6pm. DM13, children DM9. IMAX DM13, children DM9. Combination ticket DM24, children DM16.)

THE GERMAN WINE ROAD

Stretching 85 km through Germany's most productive wine-growing region, the Wine Road (or *Weinstrasse*) offers a taste of countless vineyards, small villages, and some of the world's best *Wein*. The Palatinate vineyards produce more wine than any other region in Germany, the most famous of which is the mighty Riesling. Every town and village hosts festivals in tribute to this juice of life; in fact, a different festival occurs almost every weekend during the summer some-where along the Wine Road; check the tourist offices for details. If the drink alone doesn't make you relax, the scenery undoubtedly will. The Wine Road is flanked by the Haardt mountains and Palatinate forest, and castle ruins, orchards, and half-timbered houses dot the way.

NEUSTADT AN DER WEINSTRASSE   ☎ 06321

Bordering the Palatinate forest and the Haardt mountains, Neustadt and its surrounding villages are the midpoint of the German wine road, and also the most easily accessible, with trains to Mannheim every hour (DM8.10) and occasional trains to Saarbrücken (DM11.60).Neustadt's tourism industry is centered on the numerous, family-owned *Weinguts* in the area, where you can taste and buy wines. The surrounding villages, especially Haardt and Deidelsheim, regularly produce international award-winning wines, and are ten minutes away from Neustadt by bus. Though customers with the intention of buying wines can taste them at will, an official wine-tasting of all a Weingut has to offer, including 7-9 wines and something to eat will last 1-3 hours and cost from DM18 and up. Usually you need a group of 10 to schedule one; call the *Weingut* for details. The tourist office can provide you with a list of local wine cellars. In Haardt, **Weingut Probsthof**, Probstgasse 7, offers a wine-tasting for DM10, with *sekt*, the German equivalent of champagne, for DM12. (☎6315; fax 60215. Open M-F 9am-5pm, Sa 9am-2pm. Call ahead.). Take bus #512 to "Haardt, Winzer" and walk up the street, then turn right. In Diedesfeld, **Schönhof**, Wein-str. 600, provides the same services through its in-house restaurant. (☎861 98; fax 868 23. DM14 for 7 wines. Open F-Sa 5-11:30pm, Su 3-10pm. Call ahead.). Ride bus #501 to "Diedesfeld Winzergenossenschaft" and walk up the street. In town, the **Haus des Weines,** Rathausstr. 6 sells hundreds of wines and introduces you to the regional specialties (☎35 58 71. Open Tu-F 10am-1pm, 2:30-6:30pm, Sa 9:30am-3pm).

If all this wine leaves you dizzy, clear your head with a hike through the Palatinate forest to the Hambacher schloss, once a favorite retreat of the Speyer bishops. Dating to the beginning of the 11th century, the Hambach castle is perhaps more famous as a monument to German democracy, thanks to an 1832 "Hambach Festival" held by local vintners and attended by 20,000 people that called for political freedom and national unity. The trail starts from the end of Waldstr; make friends with the red dashes (90 min.). (Castle grounds free. Requisite museum DM9, students DM3. Falconry exhibitions DM5, students DM3.)

The **tourist office**, Hetzelpl. 1 (☎92 68 92; fax 92 68 91; email touristinfo@neustadt.pfalz.com; www.neustadt.pfalz.com), is across from the train station and offers free hotel lists, maps, and a **room** reservation service. Hiking maps of the Palatinate forest can be bought for DM10-18. Neustadt boasts a youth hostel, the **Jugendgästehaus Neustadt**, Hans-Geiger-Str. 27 which offers small but private rooms and a well-run cafe/bar. (☎22 89; fax 829 47; email jh-neustadt@djh-info.de; www.djh-info.de. Sheets and breakfast included. Reception open 8:30am-11pm. DM30, over 26 DM35.) Buy **groceries** at Borchers, 48 Hambacherstr. (open M-F 7:30am-12:30pm, 2:30-6:30pm). Check **email** at **Net-Cafe,** on Konrad-Adenauer-Str. 5 (DM5 per 30min. Open M-Sa 11am-10pm, Su 3pm-midnight.) The **post office** is on Bahnhofstr. 2, 67434 Neustadt and der Weinstraße, next to the train station.

BAD DÜRKHEIM   ☎06322

Thanks to the vibrant wine community and the natural baths, Dürkheim (only outsiders use the *Bad*) boasts a surprisingly diverse population, a dense collection of restaurants, and more convertibles than one would expect in such a small town. In front of the train station are **Römerpl.** and **Stadtpl.**,which are the center of the old city. Down the pedestrian zone from Römerpl. is the **Spielbank**, Schloßpl. 6-7 (☎942 40. Open daily from 2pm until you lose all your money.) Behind the Spielbank is the **Kurpark**, several acres of grass, flowers, and fountains with unnatural amounts of algae. The **Salinarium** (☎93 58 65) that put the "Bad" in Bad Dürkheim offers a swimming pool and sauna and lies outside the Kurpark (☎93 58 65), or the **Kurzentrum**, Kurbrunnenstr. 14 (☎96 40), next to the Spielbank offers water activities for convalescents and the older generations. What would Dürkheim be without wine? A block away from the Kurzentrum exit of the Kurpark is the **Große Faß**; the largest wine barrel in the world with capacity of 1,700,000L it eclipses the Faß in Heidelberg, though it's purely a tourist attraction and has never been used. Taste a few glasses at **Weingut Fitz-Ritter**, Weinstr. Nord 51, across the street from the Große Faß (☎53 89; fax 660 05. Open M-F 8am-noon and 1-6pm, and Sa 9am-1pm. Wine tasting free; official tour, wine tasting of 9 wines and 2 sekts and meal DM260, divided by the number of people in your group.) Dürkheim hosts the **Wurstmarkt**, the world's largest wine festival (Sept. 7-11, 14-17, 2001), which originated from pilgrims walking up to the nearby **Michaelskapelle** on St. Michael's Day.

Residents make use of the salt springs with the incredible ◪**Gradierbau salina**, near the salinarium. As brine springs to the surface, it's pumped up and across a 330meter long three-story high wall and trickles down what seem like giant fish gills. The surrounding air tastes like the ocean and is purported to be good for you. One kilometer from the city center is the **Pfalzmuseum für Naturkunde**, devoted to indigenous life. (DM3, students DM2. Open Tu, Th-Su 10am-5pm, W 10am-8pm.) The ruins of **Schloß Limburg**, 2 km west of Römerpl. (follow the blue stripes from the cemetery), date from 9th century Salic princes. Several people were buried on castle grounds, including the 11th century German Emperor Henry III's wife.

The **tourist office**, Mannheimerstr. 24 is one block to your right after you exit the train station. It books rooms for free and sells hiking maps for DM1-12. (☎93 51 56; fax 93 51 59; email verkehrsamt@bad-duerkheim.de; www.bad-duerkheim.de. Open M-W, Fr 8am-5pm, Th 8am-6pm, May-Oct. Sa 10am-noon.). Rent **bikes** at Agip Tankstelle, Weinstr. Nord 57 (☎660 12. DM 20 per day, DM10 per half day). The **post office** is across from the train station at Mannheimerstr. 11, 67098 Bad Dürkheim (open M-F 8am-6:30pm, Sa 8am-1pm). The **Jugendgästehaus St. Christopherus-Haus**, Schillerstr. 151 has cheap and clean singles and doubles; its multi-bed rooms are reserved for school groups. From the train station, turn left and follow Leningerstr. and continue along Schillerstr. (☎ 631 51; fax 624 42. Sheets and breakfast included. DM29 for single, DM39 with shower.) Find lodging with a cleanliness usually reserved for hospitals at the **Pension Am Amtspl.**, Weinstr. Süd 14. From the train station, turn left on Mannheimerstr. until it reaches Weinstr., a 10min. walk. (☎/fax 83 61. Singles DM35-60 doubles DM65-90.) Römerpl. and Stadtpl. hold the greatest number of restaurants; most are pricey, and cheaper restaurants are found on the blocks heading away from Römerpl. The cheapest food in the city center is undoubtedly the glorified *Imbiß* **Kochlöffel** on Römerpl.

HESSEN

Prior to the 20th century, Hessen was known for exporting mercenary soldiers to rulers such as King George III, who sent them off to put down an unruly gang of colonials on the other side of the Atlantic in 1776. Hessen ceased to exist as a political entity when it was absorbed by Bismarck's Prussia in 1866, until the Allies reinstated its *Land* status in 1945. Today, the region is the busiest commercial center in the country, led by the banking metropolis of Frankfurt. Overshadowed by this transit and commerce metropolis, the rest of Hessen attracts little attention from tourists, leaving the medieval delights of Marburg's *Uni*-culture and the fascination of Kassel blessedly off the beaten path.

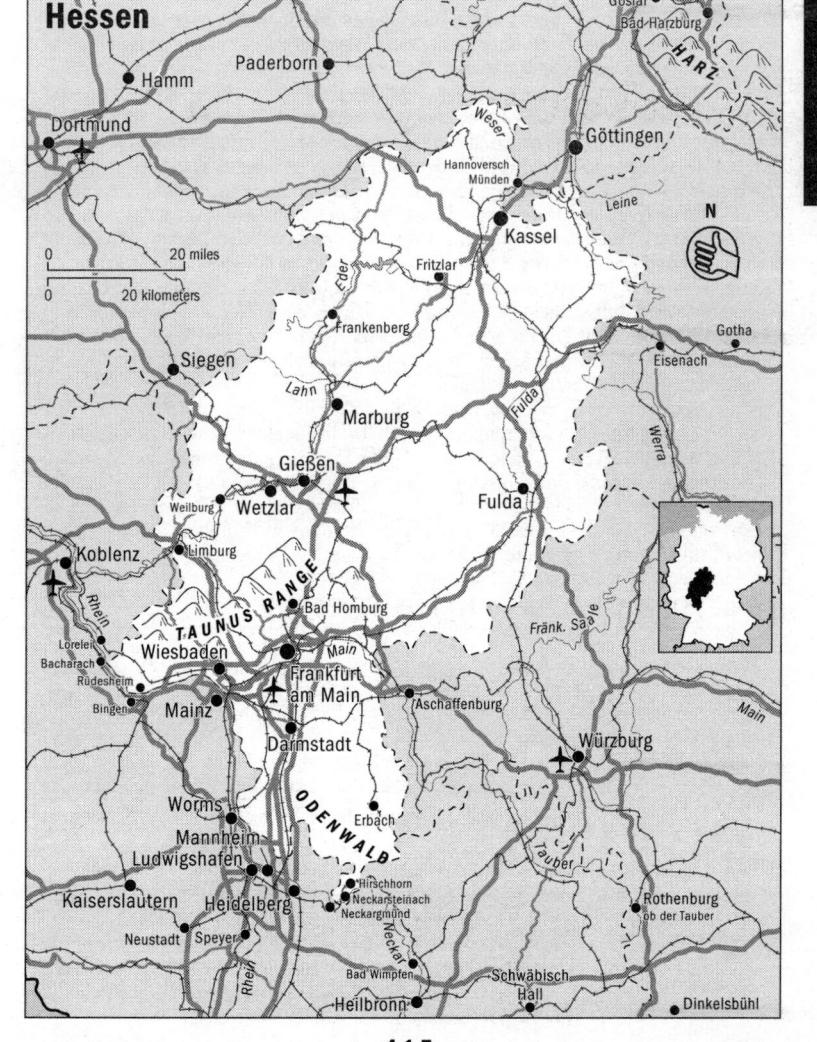

HIGHLIGHTS OF HESSEN

With its historical **Römerberg,** happening nightlife scene, and superb museums, **Frankfurt** (p. 418) is a fast-paced city, respectable for much more than its central high-traffic airport and train station.

The **Lahntal** (p. 431) is a treasure trove of outdoor fun, and **Weilburg's** 14th-century Schloß and **crystal caves** are not to be missed (p. 432).

The university town of **Marburg** (p. 432) influenced the writings of the **Brothers Grimm** and has spawned a hip youth culture.

The fairy-tale castles and waterfalls of **Wilhelmshöhe Park** and the cutting-edge **documenta** modern art exhibitions successfully merge in the curiously cosmopolitan city of **Kassel** (p. 436).

FRANKFURT AM MAIN   ☎069

Skyscrapers loom over crowded streets, investment bankers scurry to and fro—it's not hard to see how cell-phone-infested Frankfurt acquired the derisive nicknames "Bankfurt" and "Mainhattan." Many visitors view Frankfurt as the most Americanized city in Europe, a claim quickly verified by the flashy McDonald's on every street corner and the city's unusually high crime rate. While lacking the architectural beauty of more traditional German cities, Frankfurt's integral economic role as home to the central bank of the EU lends it a glitzy vitality.

Frankfurt made its first appearance when Charlemagne put the "Ford of the Franks" on the map in 794. In 1356, the **Golden Bull** of imperial law (see p. 8) made the trade center the site of emperors' elections and coronations until the Holy Roman Empire's dissolution. Since then, hordes of Frankfurters have gone on to influence western culture. **Goethe** and **Anne Frank** lived here, families such as the **Oppenheims** and **Rothschilds** influenced Frankfurt's economic development, and **Frankfurt School** members **Theodor Adorno, Max Horkheimer,** and **Walter Benjamin** elaborated their theories of art and society despite their temporary eviction to the United States during WWII (see p. 27).

After Allied bombers destroyed close to 100% of the city in 1944, Frankfurt received a complete concrete makeover paid for, ironically, by the same countries that had demolished it a decade earlier. Today the city government spends more on cultural attractions and tourism than any other German city, and an equally rich *Kulturszene* thrives under the city's patronage. If all this isn't enough to make you visit, the likelihood of arriving in Germany at Frankfurt's Rhein-Main Airport, the country's main hub, probably is.

▐ GETTING THERE AND GETTING AROUND

Flights: The ultra-modern Frankfurt airport, **Flughafen Rhein-Main** (☎69 00), welcomes hundreds of airplanes and thousands of businesspeople from all over the world daily. Each terminal is divided into lettered halls and has separate floors for arrivals and departures. From the airport, S-Bahns #14 and 15 travel to the Hauptbahnhof every 15min. Buy tickets (DM6.10) from the green *Automaten* marked *Fahrkarten* before boarding. Most public transportation departs from Terminal 1; a free streetcar runs between the terminals every 15min. Trains to Köln, Munich, and Hamburg also depart from Terminal 1 of the airport

Trains: Trains from all over Europe frequently roll in and out of Frankfurt's **Hauptbahnhof** to **Köln** (2½hr., 2 per hr., DM70, under 26 DM61); **Munich** (3½-4½hr., 2 per hr., DM212, under 26 DM118); **Berlin** (5-6hr., 2 per hr., DM207, under 26 DM166); **Hamburg** (6hr., 2 per hr., DM191, under 26 DM153); **Amsterdam** (5hr., every 2 hr., DM120, under 26 DM126.50); **Paris** (6-8hr., every 2 hr., DM140, under 26 DM115); **Rome** (15hr., 1 per hr., DM279, under 26 DM228). Call ☎(0180) 599 66 33 for schedules, reservations, and information.

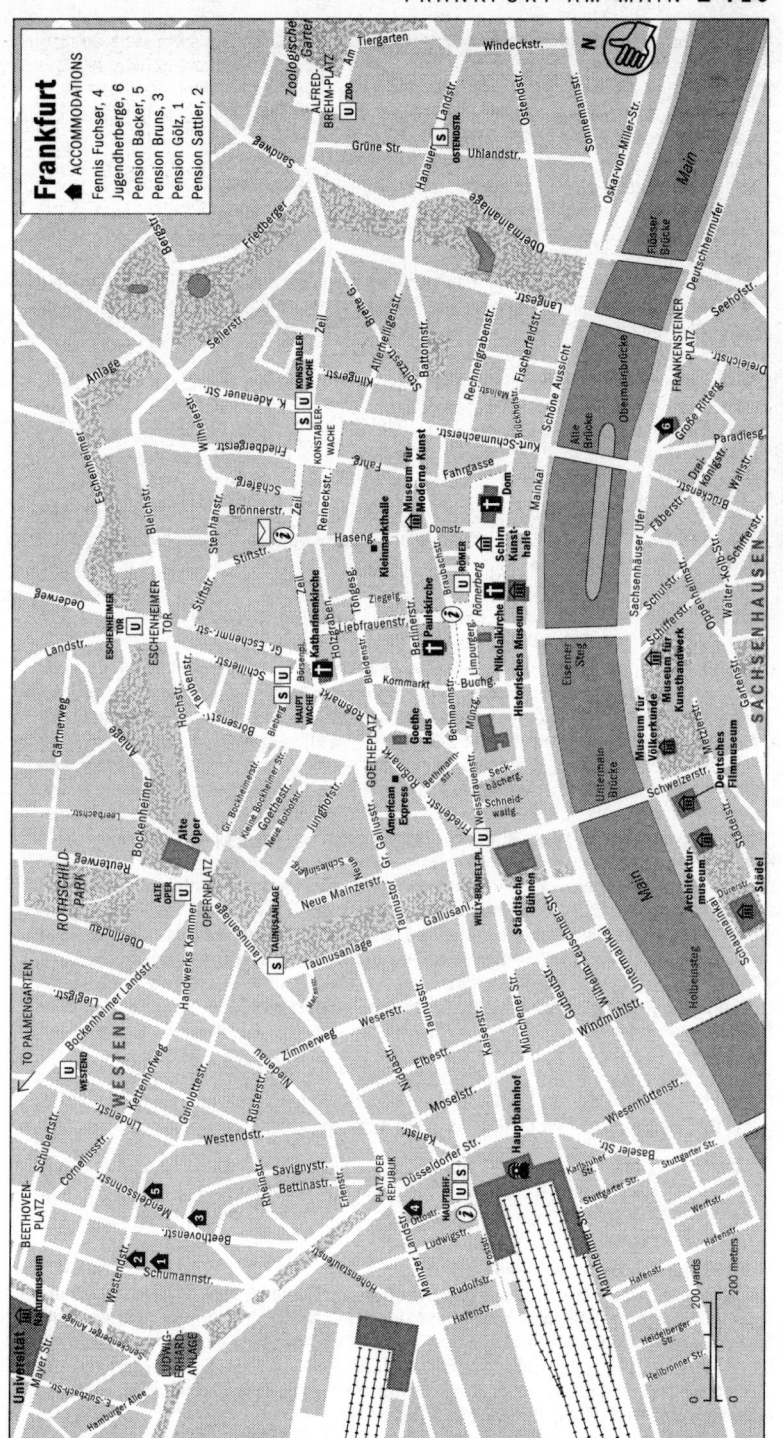

Frankfurt

▲ ACCOMMODATIONS
Fennis Fuchser, 4
Jugendherberge, 6
Pension Backer, 5
Pension Bruns, 3
Pension Gölz, 1
Pension Sattler, 2

HESSEN

Public Transportation: Refer to the subway map in the inside covers of this guide. Single-ride tickets are valid for 1hr. in one direction, transfers permitted (DM2.10, rush hour DM2.90). Eurail passes valid only on S-Bahn trains. For unlimited access to the S-Bahn, U-Bahn, streetcars, and buses, the *Tageskarte*, a pass valid until midnight of the day of purchase is available from machines in every station (DM8.50, children DM5). Some hotels offer a 2-day transportation pass (DM10) as well. Some machines take VISA/MC (Eurocard)/AmEX. **Passengers without tickets face a DM60 fine.** At the Hauptbahnhof, the S-Bahn departs from the level below the long distance trains. Escalators to the U-Bahn platforms are in the shopping passage. Streetcars #10, 11, 16, 19, and 21 pass by the island platform directly outside the main (northeast) entrance, while buses #35, 37, and 46 leave from just outside and to the right of the main entrance. This system is certainly intimidating if not outright confusing; luckily, the Hauptbahnhof has an information desk on the main level. The public transportation system shuts down around 1am every night.

Taxi: Call ☎23 00 01 or 25 00 01, find a taxi stand, or show some leg to flag one down. Taxis cost DM 2-3 per kilometer, depending on time of day.

Mitfahrzentrale: Baseler Str. 7 (☎23 64 44 or 23 64 45). Take a right on Baseler Str. at the side exit of the Hauptbahnhof (track 1), and walk 2 blocks. Connects riders with drivers for a fee. Arranges rides to Berlin (DM32), Athens (DM168), and everywhere in between. Open M-F 8am-6:30pm, Sa 8am-4pm, Su 10am-2pm.

Bike Rental: Most convenient is the **Handgepäckaufbewahrung** counter (☎26 53 48 31) in the Hauptbahnhof across from the tourist information desk and next to a flower shop. Passport required. Open daily 6am-midnight.

Boat Rides: Several companies offer tours on the Main, departing near the Römerberg (1¾hr., 2 per hr., DM13; DM 9,50 for 50 min).

Hitchhiking: *Let's Go* does not recommend hitchhiking as a safe mode of transport. Hitching on the highway itself is strictly forbidden. However, hitchers report that those heading south to Munich from Konstablerwache take buses #36 or 960 to the *Autobahn* interchange. To Köln or Düsseldorf, take S-Bahn #1 or 8 to "Wiesbaden Hauptbahnhof," then S-Bahn #21 (direction: "Niedernhausen") to "Auringen-Medenbach." Turn right, walk 800m, proceed under the *Autobahn,* and take the access road to the *Autobahn* rest stop.

■★■ ORIENTATION AND PRACTICAL INFORMATION

A sprawling conglomeration of steel, concrete, glass, and scaffolding, Germany's fifth-largest city bridges the **Main** (pronounced Mine) 35km east of its confluence with the Rhein. The station lies at the end of Frankfurt's red light district, which, in typical Frankfurt fashion, brings together international airline offices, sex bars, and banks. From the station, the town center is a 20-minute walk down Kaiserstr. or Münchener Str., which lead from the newer part of the city to the Altstadt. Located just north of the Main, the Altstadt contains the **Römerberg,** the well-touristed domain of old German kitsch. Take U-Bahn #4 (direction: "Seckbacher Landstr.") to "Römer" or walk down Liebfrauenstr. from the larger "Hauptwache," (S-Bahn #1-6, 8, or U-Bahn #1-3,6,7). A few blocks north of Römer lies the commercial heart of Frankfurt, an expanse of department stores and ice cream vendors that stretches along Zeil from **Hauptwache** (S-Bahn #1, 2, 3, 4, 5, 6, or 8, two stops from the Hauptbahnhof) to **Konstablerwache** (one stop farther) to **Opernplatz** (U-Bahn #6 or 7 to "Alte Oper"). Students, cafes, stores, and services cluster in **Bockenheim.** Take U-Bahn #6 or 7 to "Bockenheimer Warte." Across the Main, **Sachsenhausen** draws the *Ebbelwei*-lovers, the pub-crawlers, and the museum-goers. Take U-Bahn #1, 2, or 3 to "Schweizer Pl."

The **Frankfurt Card,** available at tourist offices and in most travel agencies, allows unlimited travel on all trains and buses including the airport line; it also gets you 50% off admission to 15 museums, the *Palmengarten*, the zoo, and that veritable carnival funhouse, the airport visitors' terrace (one day DM12, two days DM19). The **Museumsufer Card** gives you admission to the same museums, without any travel privileges (DM 15, students DM 7.50).

TOURIST AND FINANCIAL SERVICES

Tourist Office: (☎21 23 88 00; email info@tcf.frankfurt.de; www.frankfurt-tourismus.de). In the Hauptbahnhof, on the right side of the reception hall as you go through the main exit. Maps (DM1-2), brochures, souvenirs, tours, and lots more. Books rooms for a DM5 fee. Call or email ahead to reserve a room for free. Open M-F 8am-9pm; Sa-Su and holidays 9am-6pm. Another **branch** borders Römerplatz at Römerberg 27 (☎21 23 87 08), but the staff doesn't book rooms. Open M-F 9:30am-5:30pm, Sa-Su 10am-4pm. **City-Info,** Zeil 94a, is an information stand in the center of the commercial district. Open M-F 10am-6pm, Sa 10am-4pm.

Tours: Depart daily from the Römerberg tourist office and from the Hauptbahnhof tourist office 15min. later. 10am and 2pm; in winter only 2pm. DM44, students DM22. Eight different languages offered.

Consulates: Australia, Gutleutstr. 85 (☎273 90 90; fax 23 26 31). Open M-Th 8:30am-1pm and 2-5pm, F 8:30am-1pm and 2-4:15pm. **South Africa,** Ulmenstr. 37 (☎719 11 30). Open M-F 8am-noon. **UK,** Bockenheimer Landstr. 42 (☎170 00 20; fax 72 95 53). Open M-F 9am-noon and 2-4pm; phone hours M-Th 8:30am-1pm and 2-5pm, F 8:30am-1pm and 2-4:30pm. **US,** Siesmayerstr. 21 (☎753 50; fax 74 89 38). Open to the public M-F 8-11am; phone hours M-F 8am-4pm.

Currency Exchange: In various airport banks (open daily 7:30am-9pm) or the Hauptbahnhof (open daily 6:30am-10pm). Better rates are available at any bank.

American Express: Kaiserstr. 8 (☎21 93 88 60; fax 21 93 88 66; 24hr. hotline 9797-1000). Does not hold mail. Exchanges foreign currency, handles traveler's checks, and arranges hotel reservations and car rentals. Services are free for cardholders or traveler's check customers. Open M-F 9:30am-6pm, Sa 9:30am-12:30pm.

LOCAL SERVICES

Budget travel: STA Travel, Bockenheimer Landstr. 133 (☎70 30 35), near the university. Books flights and sells ISICs. V/MC. Open M-F 10am-6pm.

Bookstores: Süssman's Presse und Buch, Zeil 127 (☎131 07 51), by the Katharinenkirche. Mostly English titles for those who need their Shakespeare. Open M-W and F 9am-7pm, Th 9am-8pm, Sa 9am-4pm. **British Book Shop,** Börsenstr. 17 (☎28 04 92). Classics and popular novels in English. Open M-F 9:30am-7pm, Sa 9:30am-4pm.

Laundromat: Schnell & Sauber, Wallstr. 8, near the hostel in Sachsenhausen. Wash DM6, dry DM1 per 15min., soap included. Change machine. Open daily 6am-11pm. **Miele Washworld,** Moselstr. 17, is a 10 min. walk from the Hauptbahnhof. Wash DM7, dry DM3. Open daily 8am-11pm.

EMERGENCY AND COMMUNICATIONS

Emergency: ☎110. **Fire** and **Ambulance:** ☎112.

Gay and lesbian hotline: Rosa Hilfe Frankfurt (☎194 46). Open Su 6-9pm. In an emergency, call ☎(0171) 174 57 21.

AIDS hotline: ☎405 86 80.

Women's Helpline: ☎70 94 94.

Disabled travelers: Frankfurt Forum, Römerberg 32 (☎21 24 00 00), publishes a guide to handicapped-accessible locations in Frankfurt. Ask for Mr. Schmidt. Open M and W 10am-4:30pm, Tu 10am-6pm, and Th-F 10 am-2pm.

Pharmacy: (☎23 30 47; fax 24 27 19 16). In the Einkaufs passage of the train station. Open M-F 6:30am-9pm, Sa 8am-9pm, Su and holidays 9am-8pm. If pharmacies are closed, call ☎192 92 for emergency prescriptions.

Post Office: Main branch, Zeil 90, 60313 Frankfurt (☎13 81 26 21; fax 13 81 26 24), inside the *Hertie* department store. U- or S-Bahn to "Hauptwache." Take a right on Zeil with your back to the church until you see the *Hertie* building. Open M-F 9:30am-8pm, Sa 9am-4pm. **Branch office,** 60036 Frankfurt, on the upper level of the Hauptbahnhof. Open M-F 7am-9:30pm, Sa 8am-4pm.

Internet Access: Alpha, in the Hauptbahnhof's gambling salon, past track 24 on the north side of the station. DM1 per 4min. Get the hotel discount at **Telemark,** Elisabethen Str. 45-47. DM 6 per 30 min (DM5 with discount). Open 10am-10 pm. Satisfy further email withdrawal at **CyberRyder Internet Café,** Töngesgasse 31 (☎92 08 40 10). DM6 per 30min. Open M-Th 9am-11pm, F-Sa 9am-1am, Su 2pm-11pm.

▌ ACCOMMODATIONS

The hotel industry has no doubt decided to follow the city motto "show me the money." There are, however, a few cheap and charming options in the Westend/University area. Also, ask *pensionen* about cheaper, showerless rooms. Trade fairs occur often and make rooms scarce. If all else fails, there are three other hostels less than 45 minutes away: **Darmstadt** (S-Bahn #12; see p. 429), **Mainz** (S-Bahn #14; see p. 399), and **Wiesbaden** (S-Bahn #1 or 14; see p. 427).

Jugendherberge (HI), Deutschherrnufer 12 (☎610 01 50; fax 61 00 15 99; www.jugendherberge_frankfurt.de). Take Bus #46 from the main train station (DM2.40, rush hours DM2.90) to "Frankensteiner Pl." Turn left along the river; the hostel sits at the end of the block. After 7:30pm M-F, 5:45pm Sa, and 5pm Su, hop on S-Bahn #2, 3, 4, 5, or 6 to "Lokalbahnhof"; make sure to walk down Darmstädter Landstr. with your back to the train bridge above. Walk on the right side of the street and take a right before the *Commerzbank* onto Dreieichstr.; continue on until you reach the Main River and the intersection with Deutschhermufer. Take a left and the hostel will be on your left. Bordering the Sachsenhausen pub and museum district, the hostel tends to be lively and busy with student groups and youthful travelers. Breakfast with unlimited buffet—except orange juice and meat—included (7:30-9am); lunch and dinner also available (DM8.50). Vegetarian meals available. 24hr. reception. Check-in after 12pm. Check-out 9:30am. No lockout. Curfew 2am. Reservations by phone or fax. DM27, over 26 DM33. Singles (DM53) and doubles (DM43 per person) are *very rarely* available.

▨ **Pension Bruns,** Mendelssohnstr. 42 (☎74 88 96; fax 74 88 46). From the Hauptbahnhof, take a left onto Düsseldorfer Str. and walk north. After 2 blocks veer right on Beethovenstr. At the circle, go right on Mendelssohnstr. (10-15min.). Located in the wealthy Westend area near the university, Bruns houses 9 spacious Victorian rooms with high ceilings, hardwood floors, phones, and cable TV, and free breakfast in bed! Ring the bell; it's on the second floor. Call ahead. Showers DM2. Doubles DM79; triples DM105; quads DM140.

▨ **Pension Backer,** Mendelssohnstr. 92 (☎74 79 92). Two subway stops from the city center, Pension Backer offers the best deal in town. Take U-Bahn #6 (direction: "Heerstr.") or #7 (direction: "Hausen") to "Westend." The cheapest of these impeccable rooms are on the fifth floor. Breakfast included. Showers 7am-10pm (DM3). Reservations with deposit only. Singles DM25-50; doubles DM60; triples DM78.

Hotel an der Galluswarte, Hufnagelstr. 4 (☎73 39 93; fax 73 05 33). Run by the same folks as the Pension Bruns. Offers rooms at comparable prices available only to *Let's Go* readers: mention the guide and live in luxury on the cheap! Take S-Bahn #3 (direction: "Hohenmark"), 4 (direction: "Kronberg"), 5 (direction: "Friedrichsdorf"), or 6 (direction: "Galluswarte") to "Galluswarte." Exit under the sign marked "Mainzer Landstr.", take a right, walk a bit, and then take another right onto Hufnagelstr. Includes breakfast, TV, and phone. *Let's Go* prices: singles DM80; doubles DM100.

Hotel-Pension Gölz, Beethovenstr. 44 (☎74 67 35; fax 74 61 42; email hotel-goelz@aol.com). One street north of Pensions Backer and Bruns. U-Bahn #6 or 7 to "Westend." Quiet and beautiful rooms with tons of amenities: TV, phone, couch, and some with balconies. Big breakfast included. Reservations recommended. Singles DM69-85, with shower DM85-98; doubles with shower DM135-178; triples with shower DM165-188. Add $25 for a third person.

Fennis Fuchser, Mainzer Landstr. 95 (☎25 38 55). Located near the Hauptbahnhof, this hotel is a convenient place to crash. From the train station, take a left on Düsseldorfer Str., walk two blocks, and take a left onto Mainzer Landstr.; the hotel is one block down on the left. Enter through the restaurant downstairs. Special rates for stays longer than 1 night. Singles DM55; doubles DM85; triples DM120.

Pension Sattler, Beethovenstr. 46 (☎ 74 60 91; fax 74 84 66). Though its usual singles (DM120) and doubles (DM160) are pricey, the basement singles without showers are more reasonable at DM70. Some report that bargaining with the manager can lower the price to DM60.

🍴 FOOD

While cheap eats in Frankfurt are not nearly as rare as cheap beds, light eats may prove harder to come by, especially if you plan to stick with local culinary gems. Traditional German sausages and beer are popular in Frankfurt, but the region also treasures some dishes of its own: *Handkäse mit Musik* (cheese curd with raw onions), Goethe's favorite; *grüne Sosse* (a green sauce with various herbs, usually served over boiled eggs or potatoes); and *Ebbelwei.* Large mugs (0.3L) of this apple wine (or *Äpfelwein* up north) should never top DM3. Don't expect anything akin to the sharp sweetness of cider or the dryness of chardonnay; this isn't a wine to be sipped. Non-German foods abound: tasty crepes, T-bone steaks, samosas, lo mein, and those ubiquitous *Döner.*

For those on a tight budget, **supermarkets** are in plentiful supply. Just a few blocks from the youth hostel is a fully-stocked **HL Markt,** Dreieichstr. 56 (open M-F 8am-8pm, Sa 8am-4pm) while a **Tengelmann,** Münchener Str. 37, is close to the Hauptbahnhof (open M-F 8:30am-7:30pm, Su 8am-2pm). The most reasonably priced kitchens surround the university in Bockenheim and nearby parts of Westend (U-Bahn #6 or 7 to "Bockenheimer Warte"), and many of the pubs in Sachsenhausen serve food at a decent price. Take U-Bahn #1, 2, or 3 to "Schweizer Pl." Bockenheim, the Zeil, and Römerplatz attract carts and stands.

Mensa, U-Bahn #6 (direction: "Heerstr.") or 7 (direction: "Hausen") to "Bockenheimer Warte," then follow the "Mensa" signs to Building 133 of Goethe U. Your best bet for a filling, hot meal (DM5) with some collegiate attitude. Open M-F 11am-3pm.

🍴 **Adolf Wagner,** Schweizer Str. 71 (☎61 25 65). Sauce-soaked German dishes (DM5-27) and mugs of *Äpfelwein* (DM2.70 per 0.3L) keep the patrons of this famous corner of old-world Frankfurt jolly, rowdy, and coming back for years. Open daily 10am-1am.

Zum Gemalten Haus, Schweizer Str. 67 (☎61 45 59), four doors down from Adolf Wagner. The long wooden tables of this Sachsenhausen institution have seen generations of talkative locals treat their bellies to a quick *Wurst, Kraut,* and home-brewed wine (DM13). Celebrate meat with the hefty *Frankfurter Platte* and sit outdoors in the *Gartenlokal* (garden area). Open W-Su 10am-midnight.

Ban Thai Imbiß und Restaurant, Leipziger Str. 26 (☎77 26 75; 70 43 10 for takeout). Sizzling Thai dishes for those on the fly. Vegetarian options. Open daily 11:30am-10pm. Seating only after 7pm.

Pizzeria da Romeo, Mendelssohnstr. 83 (☎74 95 01). Typical Italian dishes (DM6-12). Open M-F 10:30am-3pm and 4-9:30pm.

Kleinmarkthalle, on Hasengasse between Berliner Str. and Töngesgasse, is a 3-story warehouse with several bakeries, butchers, fruit and vegetable stands, and more. Cutthroat competition between the many vendors pushes prices way down. Enough meat and sausages here to feed a small nation. Open M-F 7:30am-6pm, Sa 7:30am-4pm.

Römerbergstr. 13, in the corner of Romer next to the Alte Nikolaikirche, serves creatively fruity sundaes (DM6-16) and milkshakes (DM4) to rejuvenate tourists travelling between moo-seums. Hours vary, open daily.

👁 SIGHTS

Much of Frankfurt's historic splendor lives on only in memories and in reconstructed monuments nostalgic for the time before the bombing of 1944. Industrious Frankfurters, well aware that the same city could not be built twice, engineered its resurrection as a combined testament to pre- and post-modern times. A walk through the city center quickly reveals this architectural eclecticism.

RÖMERBERG. A pedestrian's voyage through Frankfurt should begin in the center of the Altstadt, among the half-timbered architecture and medieval fountains that grace most postcards of Frankfurt. To celebrate the 13 coronations of German emperors that were held in the city, the statue of Justice in the center of the square once sprouted wine; unfortunately for all she has since sobered up.

RÖMER. At the west end of the Römerberg, the gables of Römer have marked the site of Frankfurt's city hall since 1405; it's also where the merchants who began the city's trade tradition stopped on the Main to sell their goods. Only the building's upper floors are open to the public. These include the Kaisersaal, a former imperial banquet hall adorned with portraits of the 52 German emperors from Charlemagne to Franz II. *(Open daily 10am-1pm and 2-5pm. Obligatory hourly tour DM3, students DM1.)*

DOM. East of the reconstructed Römerberg stands the only building in the city that survived the bombings. The red sandstone Gothic cathedral contains several splendidly elaborate altarpieces. The seven electors of the Holy Roman Empire selected the emperors here, and the Dom served as the site of coronation ceremonies between 1562 and 1792. A viewing tower atop the Dom is currently undergoing reconstruction and is slated to reopen in 2002. *(Open daily 9am-noon and 2-6pm.)* The **Dom Museum** inside the main entrance contains architectural studies of the Dom, intricate chalices, and the venerated robes of the imperial electors. *(Open Tu-F 10am-5pm, Sa-Su 11am-5pm. DM3, students DM1.)*

ALTE NIKOLAIKIRCHE. South of the Römerberg, this church raises its considerably more modest spires. The minimalist interior is home to occasional fits of organ music. *(Open daily Apr.-Sept. 10am-8pm; Oct.-Mar. 10am-6pm. Free.)*

PAULSKIRCHE. St. Paul's Church stands directly across Braubachstr. from the Römerberg. Now used as a political memorial and conference venue, the unusual, round church was rebuilt in a more modern and simplistic style after WWII. Originally it served as the gathering place for Germany's first democratic National Assembly, which convened to draft a constitution for the fledgling German republic in the wake of the revolutionary tremors that swept through Europe in 1848-49 (see p. 10). Realizing that Germany could not unify without the assent of powerful Prussia, the assembly attempted to cajole Prussia's Friedrich Wilhelm IV into accepting the crown of a constitutional monarchy. The king replied that he ruled by the grace of God, and the whole episode ended with the bloody repression of the democratic movement. *(Open daily 10am-5pm. Free.)*

GOETHEHAUS. Of the half-dozen or so German cities that claim Goethe as their native son, Frankfurt legitimately possesses his early years. The master was born in Frankfurt in 1749, found his first love (a girl named Gretchen, said to be the inspiration for Marguerite in *Faust*), and penned some of his best-known works here, including *The Sorrows of Young Werther*. Unless you're a huge Goethe fan, the house is little more than a typical 18th-century showroom for a well-to-do family. It was one of the first buildings to be reconstructed after the war and refurnished with the family's original belongings, many of which the renowned author hated. *(Großer Hirschgraben 23-25, a few blocks northwest of the Römer. ☎ 13 88 00. Open*

Apr.-Sept. M-F 9am-6pm, Sa-Su 10am-4pm; Oct.-Mar. M-F 9am-4pm, Sa-Su 10am-4pm. Tours must be arranged in advance. DM7, students DM3.)

HISTORISCHER GARTEN. Between the Dom and the rest of the Römerberg lie the **Schirn Kunsthalle** (see **Museums,** p. 425) and the plantless "garden," dating back to the 2000-year-old Roman settlement.

PALMENGARTEN. Couples, tourists, families, and an extensive variety of native and exotic birds take refuge in the sprawling grounds of this garden in the northwest part of town. Rent a wooden boat and pretend you're rowing on the Main (DM4 per 30min.). The garden's greenhouses contain seven different "worlds," from the tropics to the plains. In summer, the grounds host a number of performances and exhibitions. *(Siesmayerstr. 61-63. U-Bahn #6 or 7 to "Bockenheimer Warte." ☎ 21 23 39 39. Open daily Mar.-Oct. 9am-6pm; Nov.-Jan. 9am-4pm; Feb. 9am-5pm. Admission DM10, students DM4.50.)*

ZOO. For animal lovers, over 650 species ranging from the commonplace to the exotic are represented east of the city center. The daily feeding times of the animals (around 11am) ups the entertainment value. *(Alfred-Brehm-Platz 16. ☎ 21 23 37 35. U-Bahn #6 or 7 to "Zoo." Open mid-Mar. to Sept. M-F 9am-7pm, Sa-Su 8am-7pm; Oct. to mid-Mar. daily 9am-5pm. DM11, students DM5; with U-Bahn ticket DM9, students DM4. Last Saturday of every month DM5.50, students DM2.50; with U-Bahn ticket DM4, students DM2.)*

🏛 MUSEUMS

Pick up a **Frankfurt Card** (see p. 420) for big savings on museum visits; or visit on Wednesdays, when most museums are free.

MUSEUMSUFER

The **Museumsufer** hosts an eclectic collection of museums. Located on the Schaumainkai along the south bank of the Main between the Eiserner Steg and the Friedensbrücke, the museums are housed in both opulent 19th-century mansions and in more contemporary buildings. The Museumsufer is also home to Frankfurt's weekly **flea market** (open Sa 9am-2pm during the warm months), and the **Museumsuferfest,** a huge cultural jamboree that draws more than a million visitors over three days in late August. Frankfurt also has nearly 50 spectacular commercial art galleries clustered around Braubachstr. and Saalgasse.

MUSEUM FÜR ÄNGEWANDTE KUNST. Arts and crafts imagined by human minds and made by human hands from Europe and the Near and Far East. *(Schaumainkai 17. ☎ 21 23 40 37 or 21 23 85 30. Open Tu and Th-Su 10am-5pm, W 10am-8pm. DM8, students DM4. Free on Wednesdays.)*

MUSEUM FÜR VÖLKERKUNDE. The Museum of Ethnology holds rare collections from the Pacific, Indonesia, Africa, and America. Call ahead for current exhibitions. *(Schaumainkai 29. ☎ 21 23 15 10. Open Tu-Su 10am-5pm, W 10am-8pm. DM6, students DM3. W free)*

GALERIE 37. A small gallery of rotating exhibitions of ethnically-oriented art. *(Schaumainkai 37. ☎ 212 57 55. Museum with gallery DM8, students DM4. Open Tu-Su 10am-1pm and 1:30pm-5pm, W until 10 pm.)*

DEUTSCHES FILMMUSEUM. Exhibits the development of filmmaking in an entertaining, interactive style. You can film yourself flying on a carpet above the Frankfurt skyline, or take in an old movie on the 3rd floor. *(Schaumainkai 41. ☎ 21 23 88 30. Museum and adjoining cafe open Tu, Th-F, and Su 10am-5pm, W 10am-8pm, Sa 2-8pm. Tours Su 3pm. DM5, students DM2.50. Free on Wednesday. Films DM9, students DM7.)*

ARCHITEKTURMUSEUM. Architecture buffs would enjoy this survey of the last 10 years in German architecture housed in a beautiful space. *(Schaumainkai 43. ☎ 21 23 88 44. Open Tu and Th-Su 10am-5pm, W 10am-8pm. Tours Su 3pm. DM8, students DM4.)*

DEUTSCHES MUSEUM FÜR KOMMUNIKATION. To remind you that Grandma didn't have email and that cell phones weren't ringing in restaurants 10 years ago, the museum exhibits the history of German communication and travel. The third floor houses a haunting retrospective on the role of media in the Nazi movement. Interactive video displays in German; English audio tours available. *(Schaumainkai 53. ☎ 606 00. Open Tu-Su 10am-5pm. Free.)*

STÄDEL. One of Germany's leading art museums, with an excellent collection of Old Masters, housed in a stately mansion. *(Schaumainkai 63, between Dürerstr. and Holbeinstr. ☎ 605 09 80. Open Tu and Th-Su 10am-5pm, W 10am-8pm. DM8, students DM4.)*

LIEBIEGHAUS. The castle-like building and gardens contain medieval, Renaissance, Baroque, Rococo, and Classical busts, statues, friezes, and other sculpted material. Hungry art lovers chill in the cafe on the patio. *(Schaumainkai 71. ☎ 21 21 86 17. Open Tu and Th-Su 10am-5pm, W 10am-8pm. Tours W 6:30pm and Su 11am. DM5, students DM2.50. Cafe open in the summer Tu-F 11am-10pm, Sa 11am-6:30pm, Su 10am-8pm.)*

ELSEWHERE IN FRANKFURT

■ **MUSEUM FÜR MODERNE KUNST.** Not to be missed. Just a few blocks up the street from the Dom, the triangular building's interior (the "slice of cake") is an ideal setting for the stunning modern art housed within, including impressive works by Claes Oldenburg, Roy Liechtenstein, and Jasper Johns. Art in every medium imaginable, guaranteed to push the borders of your mind. The basement shows films and slides. *(Domstr. 10. ☎ 21 23 04 47. Open Tu and Th-Su 10am-5pm, W 10am-8pm. DM10, students DM5; W free.)*

SCHIRN KUNSTHALLE. A postmodern art gallery hosting visiting exhibits in wide open spaces. *(Next to the Dom, entrance in a narrow alley. ☎ 299 88 20. Open Tu and F-Su 10am-7pm, W-Th 10am-10pm. DM12, students DM7.)*

HISTORISCHES MUSEUM. A series of exhibitions on the history of Frankfurt, including a permanent *Äpfelweinmuseum*, an exhibit of Frankfurt porcelain, and a comparative display of the city before and after the WWII bombings. *(Saalgasse 19. ☎ 21 23 55 99. Open Tu and Th-Su 10am-5pm, W 10am-8pm. DM8, students DM3.)*

NATURMUSEUM. Features several fully mounted dinosaur skeletons, impressive works of taxidermy, and some big whales thrown in for kicks. The largest natural history museum in Germany attracts the largest school groups in Frankfurt. *(Senckenberganlage 25. ☎ 754 20. U-Bahn #6 or 7 to "Bockenheimer Warte." Open M-Tu and Th-F 9am-5pm, W 9am-8pm, Sa-Su 9am-6pm. DM7, students DM3.)*

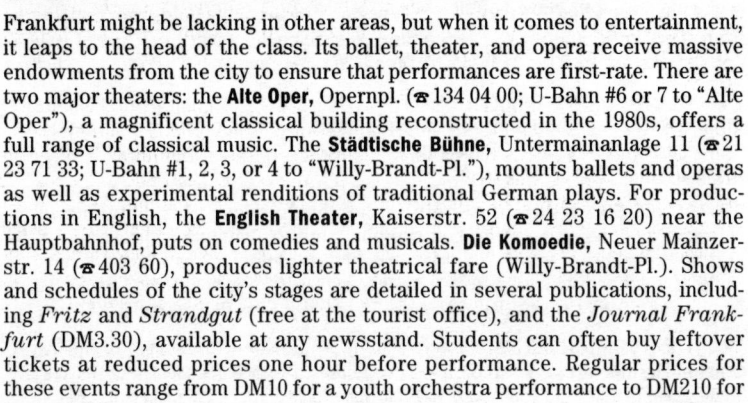 **ENTERTAINMENT AND NIGHTLIFE**

Frankfurt might be lacking in other areas, but when it comes to entertainment, it leaps to the head of the class. Its ballet, theater, and opera receive massive endowments from the city to ensure that performances are first-rate. There are two major theaters: the **Alte Oper,** Opernpl. (☎ 134 04 00; U-Bahn #6 or 7 to "Alte Oper"), a magnificent classical building reconstructed in the 1980s, offers a full range of classical music. The **Städtische Bühne,** Untermainanlage 11 (☎ 21 23 71 33; U-Bahn #1, 2, 3, or 4 to "Willy-Brandt-Pl."), mounts ballets and operas as well as experimental renditions of traditional German plays. For productions in English, the **English Theater,** Kaiserstr. 52 (☎ 24 23 16 20) near the Hauptbahnhof, puts on comedies and musicals. **Die Komoedie,** Neuer Mainzerstr. 14 (☎ 403 60), produces lighter theatrical fare (Willy-Brandt-Pl.). Shows and schedules of the city's stages are detailed in several publications, including *Fritz* and *Strandgut* (free at the tourist office), and the *Journal Frankfurt* (DM3.30), available at any newsstand. Students can often buy leftover tickets at reduced prices one hour before performance. Regular prices for these events range from DM10 for a youth orchestra performance to DM210 for a prime opera seat. For information on tickets at almost any venue, call **Frankfurt Ticket** (☎ 134 04 00).

For a night out drinking, head to the **Alt-Sachsenhausen** district between Brückenstr. and Dreieichstr., home to a huge number of rowdy pubs and taverns specializing in *Äpfelwein*. The complex of cobblestoned streets centering on **Grosse** and **Kleine Rittergasse** teems with cafes, bars, restaurants, and gregarious Irish pubs.

Frankfurt has a number of thriving discos and prominent techno DJs, mostly in the commercial district between Zeil and Bleichstr. In general, things don't really heat up until after midnight. Wear something dressier than jeans—unless they're *really* hip jeans—if you plan to get past the picky bouncers. Most clubs are for folks 18 or older; cover charges run DM10-20. For more on Frankfurt's club scene, visit www.technoclub.de.

U60311, Roßmarkt, on the corner of Goetheplatz. A popular addition to the house scene with the well-known DJ Sven Väth. Hopping hangout of the young and trendy; the lines start at 10pm F night. Open M-F 10pm-10am, Sa-Su 10pm-6am. Cover DM15-30.

Dorian Gray, (☎ 69 02 21 21) in Terminal 1 at the airport, right outside the U-Bahn exit (see p. 418). Don't plan on coming here until 1am. The far-out location explains the late hours of this expansive, sumptuous club. Young crowd, techno galore. Special guests on Saturdays and free breakfast at 5am on weekday mornings. Strict dress code. No trains run back to the Hauptbahnhof after 1am; plan on dancing 'till dawn or splurging on a cab. Open Th 10pm-4am, F-Sa 10pm-8am. Cover DM15.

The Cave, Brönnerstr. 11. Features hip-hop, house, and reggae every night in a catacomb-like locale. Open M-Th 10pm-4am. Sa-Su 10pm-6am. Cover DM5.

Der Jazzkeller, Kleine Bockenheimer Str. 18a (☎ 28 85 37). An appreciative crowd swings and swigs in this grotto-like mainstay of the Frankfurt jazz scene. Call for a schedule. Open Tu-Su 9pm-3am. Cover W and F DM20, varies other nights.

Blue Angel, Brönnerstr. 17 (☎ 28 27 72). A Frankfurt institution and one of the liveliest gay men's clubs around. Techno music, flashing lights, and police whistles dominate the interior. Ring the bell to be let in. Open daily 11pm-4am. Cover DM11.

Das Opium, Broennerstr. 7 (next to the lion). An enormous disco ball lights up a spacious, fleshy dance floor. House is the mainstay, but rotating DJ's add variety. Dance lessons occasionally offered. Open Th-Sa 10pm-4am. Cover DM12-20.

WIESBADEN ☎ 0611

While most German cities flaunt their castles and cathedrals, Wiesbaden's center of gravity is its ritzy casino. The city's designer boutiques and hip citizens still pay homage to the heady years of the 19th century when Europe's aristocracy came to frolic away its time and money. A bit of the old Wiesbaden is still here for the taking; you can shop on the cobblestone streets of the Marktplatz, take the hydraulic funicular to the top of the Neroberg, and, provided that you're formally attired, gamble away your life's savings at the casino.

PRACTICAL INFORMATION. Trains depart to Wiesbaden from **Frankfurt** (45 min., DM20); **Heidelberg** (1½ hr., DM40); **Koblenz** (1½ hr., DM34); and **Mainz** (15 min., DM7). Wiesbaden's **tourist office,** Marktstr. 6, down Bahnhofstr. from the train station, books **rooms** (from DM70) for a DM6 fee. (☎ 172 97 80/194 33; fax 172 97 98; www.tourist.wiesbaden.de. Open M-F 9am-6pm, Sa-Su 9am-3pm.) Wiesbaden is a convenient daytrip from Mainz (p. 399), as the two cities share a **public transportation** system. Ask about the day pass for buses. The **Mitfahrzentrale,** Bahnhofstr. 49-53, in a camper halfway between the pedestrian zone and the station, arranges ride shares. (☎ 33 35 55 or 194 40. Open M-F 9am-6pm, Sa 9am-noon.) The **post office,** Kaiser-Friedrich-Ring 81, is to the left as you come out of the station (open M-F 8am-6pm, Sa 8am-noon). For internet access, visit the **Surf Inn** at the **Galerie Kaufhof,** Kirchgasse 28 (☎ 175 30 4; email wiesbaden@surfinn.com. 15min. DM2, 30min. DM3).

█▛▐▌ ACCOMMODATIONS AND FOOD. Inexpensive accommodations are hard to come by in Wiesbaden. The **Jugendherberge (HI),** Blücherstr. 66, provides cheap beds, good facilities, and a friendly staff. Take bus #14 (direction: "Klarental") to "Gneisenaustr." The bus lets you off on Blücherstr. Turn left, cross Gneisenaustr. and continue to the end of the street. (☎486 57; fax 44 11 19. Breakfast included. Sheets DM6. Reception until midnight. Check-in after 2pm. Curfew midnight. DM24, over 26 DM29.) The **Ring-Hotel,** Bleichstr. 29, is a few minutes up the street towards the Marktplatz. This family-owned hotel used to house music's greatest (Jimi Hendrix, Tom Jones, to name a few). Now you can stay in their old stomping grounds, where the rooms are clean and the staff is friendly. (☎949 02 77. Breakfast included. Singles DM65, w/full bath & TV DM100, doubles w/shower DM120.) **Victuals** can be obtained at **HL Markt,** 46-48 Friedrichstr. (☎99 91 70. Open M-F 8am-8pm, Sa 8am-4pm.) The pedestrian zone is brimming with pubs and restaurants, and spice abounds in the ethnic joints around **Schwalbacher Str.** between Pl. der Deutschen Einheit and Einserstr. **Kebab House,** Schwalbacher Str. 61, dishes out gigantic servings of ready-made Turkish food for unbeatable prices. (☎30 63 45. DM5-11. Open daily 10am-1am.) Further into the city, the Marktplatz also has much to offer, with fruit stands, bakeries, and cafes. **The Irish Pub,** Michelsberg 15, rocks with live music every evening (starting around 9pm), offers enormous Irish breakfasts on Sundays (11am-3pm; DM14), and serves beer, wine, coffee, and specialty drinks until the wee hours. (☎30 08 49. Open M-Th 5pm-1am, F 5pm-2am, Sa 3pm-2am, Su 11am-1am.) A little further towards the Marktplatz, choose from a number of Italian restaurants on Goldgasse, open daily from around noon to 1am or 2am. For more traditional fare, sample a dish at **Setzkasten,** Wagemannstr. 33. The jolly staff serves up scrumptious Bavarian specials for under DM14. (☎30 64 75. Open daily 4pm-4am. Kitchen closes at 3am.)

▨▐▌ SIGHTS AND ENTERTAINMENT. The patrons of the **Spielbank** casino gambol about within a large, posh compound alternately used for business conferences, parades, and local art exhibitions. Compulsive gambler Fyodor Dostoevsky squandered the last 30 rubles that stood between him and destitution while visiting Wiesbaden, and so can you; a coat and tie are all you need. (☎53 61 00; fax 53 61 99; www.Spielbank-Wiesbaden.de. Open daily 3pm-3am. 21+.) Or flout the dress code and get down and dirty with the slots next door at **Kleines Spiel.** (Open daily 2pm-2am. DM2. 21+.) Situated off Wilhelmstr., the complex is bordered on two sides by the expansive **Kurpark,** where locals unwind under century-old willow trees. Take bus #1 or 8 to "Kurhaus/Theater." On the other side of the *Kurhaus* is the stately **Staatstheater,** inscribed with the ominous instruction *Der Menscheit Würde ist in Eure Hand gegeben, bewahret Sie.* ("The dignity of mankind is in your hands, preserve it.") The *Staatstheater* and neighboring **Kleines Haus** present traditional and modern ballets, operas, and plays; tickets occasionally sell for as little as DM9-15. Even if you don't have the time or funds for a show, catch a glimpse of the red-velvet theater and the gilded intermission ballroom; the house is open to the public until an hour before performance time. (☎13 23 25. Box office for Staatstheater and Kleines Haus open Tu-F 11am-6pm, Sa-Su 11am-1pm, and 1hr. before performance.) On Burgstr. west of the *Staatstheater* warbles the **world's biggest cuckoo clock,** topped by a giant moose head. The birds strut every half hour from 8am to 8pm. Toward the train station on Friedrich-Ebert-Allee, the **Museum Wiesbaden** houses temporary exhibits of modern German art. (☎335 21 70; fax 335 21 92. Open Tu 10am-8pm, W-F 10am-4pm, Sa-Su 10am-5pm. DM5, students and seniors DM2.50, children DM1.) The angular, red-brick **Marktkirche** is on the Markt near the tourist office. Catch a concert while you stroll through the square; every Saturday at 11:30am there is a ½-hour organ concert followed by a ½-hour carillon concert, courtesy of the Kirche's 21-ton, 49-bell instrument. (Open Tu and F-Sa 10:30am-12:30pm, W 10:30am-noon, Th 3:30-5:30pm.)

▨**Neroberg,** a low hill at the north end of town, provides an alternative to Wiesbaden's bustle. The hill is crowned by the **Nerobergturm.** Head a little bit down the hill and take a dip at the *Opelbad* or tan with the locals on the side of the hill. *(☎ 17 29 885. Open 7am-8pm, DM11, or DM7 after 5pm; students and "people under 1 meter tall" DM7.50.)* A few more feet down the mountain is the **Russisch-Griechische Kapelle,** the most impressive monument in the city. The painstakingly decorated Russian Orthodox chapel, modelled after the Cathedral of Christ the Redeemer in Moscow, was built in 1855 as a mausoleum for Princess Elizabeth of Nassau, the niece of a Russian Czar who was married to a local duke and died in childbirth at age 19. Her tomb dominates the chapel's inspiring interior. *(Open daily Apr.-Oct. 11am-5pm. DM1, students and children DM0.50.)* Take bus #1 to "Nerotal" and walk or take the **Nerobergbahn** hydraulic funicular to the summit of the 254m hill. *(☎ 780 22 22. Funicular open May-Aug. daily 9:30am-8pm; Apr. and Sept. W and Sa noon-7pm, Su 10am-7pm; Oct. W and Sa-Su noon-6pm. DM2; round-trip DM3.)*

DARMSTADT ☎ 06151

Despite the fact that German speakers may translate Darmstadt as "intestine city," the town is actually quite lovely. Home to the venerable German Academy of Language and Literature, which annually awards the most prestigious honor in German letters, one would expect Darmstadt to be staid and reserved. But its other great distinction—a collection of superb pieces of late 19th-century *Jugendstil* (art nouveau) architecture—graces the city with a lighthearted, colorful appearance. Darmstadt's cultural traditions are complemented by its lively, bazaar-like streets, making it a surprisingly diverse, largely untouristed destination just a short trip from Frankfurt.

▐ GETTING THERE AND GETTING AROUND

Darmstadt is accessible from Frankfurt by frequent **trains** (30min., 3 per hr.) or by S-Bahn #3 (both DM10.80). **S-Bahn** and **bus** tickets cost DM2.20, DM5.10 for 1 day, or DM30.60 for a 7-day ticket (students DM23). For a **taxi,** call **Funk** (☎ 194 10) any time of the day or night. Rent **bikes** at **Minigolf** in **Prinz-Emil-Garten,** next to the pond. Take S-Bahn #1 to "Prinz-Emil-Garten." (☎ 66 40 90. Open M-F 8am-8pm, Sa-Su 2-8pm. Bikes DM7 per day; mini golf DM3, students DM2.)

▐ PRACTICAL INFORMATION

The **tourist office** in front of the main train station provides city maps and hotel guides and finds rooms (☎ 13 27 82; email tourco@stadt.darmstadt.de; www.darmstadt.de; open M-F 9am-6pm, Sa 9am-noon). A **branch office,** at Luisenpl. 5, is located in a glass tower in the Luisencenter; they expect to move inside the Luisencenter in 2001 (☎ 13 27 81; open M-F 9am-6pm, Sa 10am-1pm). For English books, visit **Duckbill & Gooseberry's British Shop,** Alexanderstr. 26, on the corner of Mauerstr. (☎ 753 80. Open M-F 10am-7pm, Sa 10am-4pm.) **Louisetta,** (☎ 78 35 15) Mauerstr. 4, a **gay and lesbian cultural center,** shows movies (some M and each Tu at 8pm) and serves brunch (Su from 4pm). Take Bus F or K to "Alexanderstr./TU." Send an **email** to everyone back home from **Cantina y Bar Mexicano,** Luisenpl. 5, on the second floor (DM10 per hr.). The **post office,** 64283 Darmstadt, sends telegrams and faxes. There are two branches: **Postamt 1,** to your left as you exit the main train station (open M-F 7am-7pm, 8am-12:30pm), and **Postamt 11,** at Luisenpl. 3 (open M-F 9am-6pm, Sa 9am-2pm). **STA Travel,** Alexanderstr. 39 (☎ 225 22), books flights all over the world and handles other travel needs.

╭╮ ACCOMMODATIONS AND FOOD

The **Jugendherberge (HI),** Landgraf-Georg-Str. 119, offers spotless rooms and friendly service. Take Bus D (direction: "Ostbahnhof") to "Woog." (☎452 93; fax 42 25 35. Breakfast included. Check-in after 9:30am. Reception until 1am. Lockout 1-6am. Members only. DM24, over 26 DM29.) The hostel overlooks **Großer Woog,** an artificial lake and swimming hole. (☎13 23 93. Open daily mid-May to mid-Sept. Sa-M 9am-8pm, Tu-Fr 8am-8pm. DM3.50, students DM2. Boats DM6 per hr.) **Zentral Hotel,** Schuchardstr. 6, is a great bargain with a convenient location and well-appointed rooms. From Luisenplatz, walk along Luisenstr. with the Luisencenter mall on your right and turn left onto Schuchardstr. (☎264 11; fax 268 58. Breakfast included. Singles DM60, with shower DM90; doubles DM120, with shower DM150.)

Eating in Darmstadt can be pricey. Try **Plus,** the **grocery** store across from the Schloß on Marktpl (open M-F 8:30am-7pm, Sa 8am-4pm). Every morning but Sunday fresh fruits and cold cuts crowd the Marktplatz for the outdoor **Markt.** Most of the city's inexpensive dining can be found in **Martinsviertel,** a student area northeast of the city center. The university **Mensa** dishes out cheap meals. With your back to the northern side of the Schloß, cross Alexanderstr., then take a right and walk past the yellow *Staatsarchiv* on your left. Once past this, turn left down the stairs, then right and head upstairs into the University's *Otto-Bernd-Halle.* A decent selection of generous sandwiches is available for DM1, and light fare runs DM3-6 (meals served M-Th 8am-4pm, Fr 8am-3pm). **Efendi's,** Landgraf-Georg-Str. 13, has generous, spicy portions of Mediterranean dishes, including vegetarian options and large salads (DM3-9). Take a right when facing the southern side of the Schloß and walk straight. Cross the intersection and Efendi's will be one block up on the right. (☎29 38 09. Open Su-Tu 11am-1am, W-Sa 11am-midnight.)

◉ SIGHTS

MATHILDENHÖHE. The mecca of Darmstadt's Jugendstil architecture (see p. 23), this artists' colony on a hill west of the city center was founded by Grand Duke Ernst Ludwig in 1899. The Duke fell in love with *Jugendstil* and invited seven artists to build a "living and working world" of art, funding them to transform the urban landscape with a nature-friendly predecessor to Art Deco. The result was this startling architectural complex, heavy on flowered trellises and somber fountains. *(Walk east from the Luisenplatz along Erich-Ollenhauer-Promenade, or take bus F to "Lucasweg/Mathild." then take a right on Lucasweg.)*

HOCHZEITSTURM. This "wedding tower" in the Mathildenhöhe was the city's wedding present to Grand Duke Ernst Ludwig in 1908. Rising like a monstrous jukebox against the German sky, the 48m tower offers a scenic view of Darmstadt. *(Open Mar.-Oct. Tu-Su 10am-6pm. DM3, students DM1.)*

MUSEUM DER KÜNSTLERKOLONIE. This collection, also in the Mathildenhöhe, houses Art Nouveau furniture and exhibits of modern art. *(Alexandra Weg 26. ☎13 27 78. Open Tu-Su 10am-5pm. Tours 11am on the first Su of each month. DM5, students DM3.)*

RUSSISCHE KAPELLE. The "Russian Chapel," a gilded, three-domed Russian Orthodox Church, also rests on the Mathildenhöhe. The chapel was imported stone by stone from Russia at the behest of Czar Nicholas II upon his marriage to Darmstadt's Princess Alexandra. *(Nikolaiweg 18. ☎42 42 35. Open Apr.-Sept. 9am-6pm, Oct.-Mar. 9:30am-5pm. DM1.50, students DM1.)*

BRAUN MUSEUM. The home of the Braun design collection, which showcases the evolution of the company's renowned electrical appliances since 1955—everything from Aunt Sally's prized blender to Uncle Jörg's cutting-edge electric razor. *(Eugen-Bracht-Weg 6. Right off of Alexandraweg near Mathildenhöhe. ☎480 08. Open Tu-Sa 10am-6pm, Su 10am-1pm. Free.)*

ROSENHÖHE. This brooding park houses a rose garden and a mausoleum of the city's deceased dukes. The garden was planted in 1810 at the request of Grand Duchess Wilhelmine, who wanted a garden that breathed "the free, noble Spirit of Nature." With its overgrown lawns, hulking evergreens, and cemetery-like serenity, it seems to fulfill Wilhelmine's wish. *(Corner of Seitersweg and Wolfskehlstr.)*

SCHLOß. The gigantic coral and white palace is smack-dab in the middle of the city. Built between 1716 and 1727, it was modeled after Versailles by a wistful Frenchman. Since WWII, the Schloß has served as a public university library and police station. A small museum tucked in the eastern wing holds 17th- to 19th-century ducal clothing and furniture. *(☎ 642 83. Open M-Th 10am-1pm and 2-5pm, Sa-Su 10am-1pm. DM5, students DM3.)* What's a *Schloß* without a *Garten?* **Herrngarten,** a lush expanse of well-maintained greenery north of the Schloß, provides space for loafing students, gamboling dogs, and ducks (which you aren't allowed to feed). Even more exquisite is the **Prinz-Georg-Garten,** arranged in Rococo style and maintained by a brigade of six gardeners. *(Open Apr.-Sept. 7am-7:30pm; Oct.-Mar. 8am-dark.)* Next to it, the recently renovated **Porzellanschlößchen** (little porcelain castle) flaunts an extensive collection of porcelain. *(Schloßgartenstr. 7. ☎ 78 85 47. Open M-Th 10am-1pm and 2-5pm, Sa-Su 10am-1pm. DM8, students DM5.)*

LANDESMUSEUM. An establishment catering to those with a geological, paleontological, or zoological bent. Its doors are framed by two lions. *(Friedenspl. 1. ☎ 16 57 03. At the southern end of the Herrngarten across from the Schloß. Open Tu-Sa 10am-5pm, also W 7-9pm, Su 11am-5pm. DM5, students DM2.)*

 NIGHTLIFE

Locals recommend **Nachrichten-Treff,** Elisabethenstr. 20, where beers (DM4) are served and karaoke resounds in the winter. *(☎ 238 23. Open 9am-1am.)* From Luisenpl. take Luisenstr. and the first right onto Elisabethenstr. Pool action can be found at **Kuckucksnest,** a happening after-hours establishment two blocks from the Schloß. The music is loud and beer runs DM3-7. *(Cover DM5. Open daily 8pm-3am.)* For late-night *Kneipe*-hopping, the Martinsviertel, always full of college students, is best. *Journal Frankfurt* (DM3.30) reports on nightlife in Darmstadt as well. Darmstadt parties annually during **Heinerfest** with beer, music, fireworks, and rides in the city's center (June 28-July 2, 2001).

LAHNTAL (LAHN VALLEY)

The peaceful Lahn River flows through verdant valleys, bounteous vineyards, and delightful *Dörfer*. The valley is an understandably popular destination for German families wishing to enjoy the great outdoors. Every spring and summer, campgrounds and hostels fill with people who have come to take advantage of the hiking, biking, and kayaking available along the Lahn. Rail service runs regularly between Koblenz in the West and Gießen at the eastern end of the valley, as well as between Frankfurt and Limburg.

LIMBURG AN DER LAHN   ☎ 06431

Limburg an der Lahn flourished during the Middle Ages as a bridge for merchants traveling from Köln to Frankfurt. Today, it serves much the same function. As the most important train station between Koblenz and Gießen, Limburg is an excellent base for exploring the Upper Lahn Valley. Largely unscathed by WWII, Limburg prides itself on its well-preserved medieval town houses scattered throughout the Altstadt. Often confused with a notoriously cheesy Dutch city of the same name, Limburg an der Lahn is known for **St. Georg-Dom,** a majestic cathedral that rests on the peak of the Altstadt. This architectural hybrid of Romanesque and Gothic styles shelters a series of galleries and carefully restored frescoes which take on an unearthly glow as the sun shines through the windows. From the train station, follow Bahnhofstr. until it ends in the Altstadt and take a left on Salzgasse. Take a sharp right onto the Fischmarkt and from there follow Domstr. all the way up to the Dom. Next to the cathedral the **Diözesanmuseum und Domschatz,** Domstr. 12, display a small but impressive collection of medieval religious artifacts dating back to the 12th century. The serene statues, jewel-encrusted crucifixes, and elaborate robes are quite a sight to behold. (☎ 29 52 33. Open mid-Mar. to mid-Nov. Tu-Sa 10am-1pm and 2-5pm, Su 11am-5pm. DM3, students DM1.)

The **tourist office,** Hospitalstr. 2, books **rooms** (from DM35) for free if you stop by (DM1 to book by phone). Turn left on the street in front of the station and make a quick right on Hospitalstr. The office also provides details about the local **Oktoberfest,** which begins the third week of October. (☎ 61 66; fax 32 93. Open Apr.-Oct. M-F 8am-12:30pm and 2-5pm, Sa 10am-noon; Nov.-Mar. M-Th 8am-12:30pm and 2-5pm, F 8am-1pm.) The **Jugendherberge (HI),** Auf dem Guckucksberg, in Eduard-Horn-Park, has fuzzy green beds and sparkling facilities. From the station, go right through the underpass and take the left exit toward Frankfurter Str. Follow Im Schlenkert right until it empties onto a larger road, and take this right until it branches with Frankfurter Str. on the left; the hostel is on the right along Frankfurter Str. Or take bus #603 from Hospitalstr. (direction: "Am Hammerberg"; every hour on the hour from 8am-6pm) to "Jugendherberge." (☎ 414 93; fax 438 73. Breakfast DM8. Sheets DM6. Reception 5-10pm. Curfew 11:30pm. DM20.50, over 26 DM25.50.) There's a **Campingplatz** in a riverside location on the far side of the Lahn. Follow directions to the Dom until the Fischmarkt, then bear left (instead of right on Domstr.) downhill to Brückengasse and the Lahnbrücke. On the other side of the Lahn, turn right onto Schleusenweg and walk 10 minutes along the Lahn to the campground. (☎ 226 10. Reception 8am-1pm and 3-10pm. Open May to mid-Oct. DM7.50 per person. DM4.50 per tent.) **Café Bassin,** Bahnhofstr. 8a, has excellent small meals from DM5-9 and daily specials from DM5-12. The large variety of cakes is definitely worth gawking over. (☎ 66 70. Open M-Sa 7am-7pm, Su 10am-7pm.) **Felix Imbiss**, located in the Bahnhof, offers a surprisingly comfortable place to relax for a moment and gobble down french fries (DM1.70) or Bratwurst (DM2), and wash it all down with a beer.

MARBURG   ☎ 06421

In 1527, Landgrave Philip founded the world's first Protestant university in **Marburg,** then an isolated location on the banks of the Lahn River. Since then, the university has produced an illustrious list of alumni, including Martin Heidegger, T.S. Eliot, Richard Bunsen (the burner man), and, of course, the Brothers Grimm. With its rich history and towering Schloß, Marburg now attracts crowds of tourists who mingle among the older buildings, occasionally rubbing elbows with the active Uni population of 15,000 students. A range of watersports, outdoor cafes, historical monuments, and nightclubs give residents of all ages plenty to choose from.

■✦🛈 ORIENTATION AND PRACTICAL INFORMATION

Marburg is served by frequent trains from Frankfurt and Kassel. Rudolphsplatz lies at the foot of the elevated Oberstadt, which is the heart of the city. From the train station, take buses #1, 2, 3, 5 or 6 or follow Bahnhofstr. over the Lahn until the road ends. Take a left on Elizabethstr., which becomes Pilgrimstein and eventually merges with Biegenstr., shortly thereafter bringing you to Rudolphspl. (25min.). Pilgrimstein's narrow staircases and steep alleys lead to the Oberstadt, as does the Oberstadt-Aufzug elevator. (Operates daily 6am-2am. Free.)

Trains: Trains go to **Frankfurt** (1hr., 1 per hr., DM20.30); **Hamburg** (3½hr., 6 per day, DM46); **Kassel** (1½hr., 1 per hr., DM27); and **Köln** (3¼hr., 1 per hr., DM55).

Public Transportation: A single ticket gets you anywhere in the city (DM2.20).

Taxi: Funkzentrale, ☎477 77 or **Minicar,** ☎144 44.

Bike Rental: Velociped, Alte Kasseler Str. 43 (☎245 11). DM15 per day. Open M-F 10am-4pm.

Tourist Office: Pilgrimstein 26 (☎991 20; fax 99 12 12), 150m from Rudolphspl. Bus #1, 2, 3, 5 or 6 to "Rudolphspl.," and exit to the north along Pilgrimstein; the office is on the left. Sells maps (DM0.50) and books **rooms** (from DM35) for free. Open M-F 9am-6pm, Sa 10am-2pm.

Bookstore: N.G. Elwert, Pilgrimstein 30 (☎17 09 34), 1 block from Rudolphspl., has a selection of English books. There is an annex of the store at Reitgasse 7. Open M-F 9:30am-7pm, Sa 9:30am-4pm.

Laundromat: Wasch Center, at the corner of Gutenbergstr. and Jägerstr. Sip a beer (DM3-5.50) in the adjacent **Bistro Waschbrett** during rinse cycle. Wash DM6, dry DM1 per 15min. Open M-F 8am-10pm, Sa 8am-9pm, Su 2-9pm.

Women's Resources: Autonomes Frauenhaus, Alter Kirchainer Weg 5 (☎16 15 16). Open M and W 10am-1pm, Th 4-7pm.

Emergency: Police, ☎110. **Fire,** ☎112. **Ambulance,** ☎192 92.

Post Office: Bahnhofstr. 6, 35037 Marburg, a 5min. walk from the train station on the right. Open M-F 9am-6pm, Sa 9am-noon.

Internet Access: On Pilgrimstein, right across from the tourist office. Sip espresso (DM2.50) or choose from a variety of hot and cold drinks (DM2.30-4), while checking your email or surfing the web (DM4 per ½ hour).

▌ACCOMMODATIONS AND CAMPING

Although small, Marburg boasts more than 30 hotels and Pensionen; unfortunately, competition hasn't done too much to keep prices down. Plan ahead if you intend to spend less than DM60.

Jugendherberge (HI), Jahnstr. 1 (☎234 61; fax 121 91). From the train station walk down Bahnhofstr. and make a left on Elizabethstr., which becomes Pilgrimstein after the church. This leads to Rudolphspl.; cross the bridge and turn right onto the riverside path. Continue to the small wooden bridge.; the hostel is on the other side. The hostel's prime location provides a scenic and welcoming resting place on the banks of the Lahn, but remains close to the action of the town center. Clean, spacious rooms; some with bath. Call ahead; the hostel quickly fills with school groups. Breakfast included. Sheets DM6. Reception 9am-noon and 1:30-11:30pm, but house keys are available with ID or DM50 deposit. DM24.50, over 26 DM29.50.

Tusculum-Art-Hotel, Gutenbergstr. 25 (☎227 78; fax 153 04). Follow Universitätsstr. from Rudolphspl. and take the first left on Gutenbergstr. The modern-art themed decor and bright, airy rooms complete with cable TV make Tusculum a pleasant stay. Kitchen open 24hr. Reception 10am-6pm. Singles DM60-70, with shower DM80-90; doubles DM100-120, with shower DM125-140.

Camping: Camping Lahnaue, Trojedamm 47 (☎213 31), on the Lahn River. Follow directions to the hostel and continue down-river for another 5min. Tent DM5. DM10 deposit for use of electricity and toilets. DM7 per person. The **Terrassencafe** offers moderately priced food and drink on location. Open Apr.-Oct. Call ahead.

◘ FOOD

Marburg's cuisine caters to its large student population; most establishments offer Würste or several kinds of pizza, along with the omnipresent Marburger beer. The streets surrounding the Markt are full of standing-room only cafes serving sandwiches for around DM5. **Aldi,** Gutenbergstr. 19, caters to your grocery needs. (open M-F 9am-6:30pm, Sa 8am-2pm). Vegans and health food junkies will enjoy **Bio Eck,** Gutenbergstr. 11, a natural foods grocery store with a large cosmetic section. (☎06421; M-F 9am-7pm, Sat 9am-5pm. From Rudophplatz, walk down Univerisitystr. and turn left on Gutenbergstr. Bio Eck is on your left.)

Mensa, Erlenring 5. Cross the bridge at Rudolphspl., make the 2nd left on Erlenring and follow the signs. Satisfy your hearty appetite with the university crowd. 3-course meals DM3-6. Open during the semester M-F 8:15am-8pm, Sa noon-2pm; during semester breaks M-F 8:15am-7:30pm, Sa noon-2pm.

■ **Bistro-Café Phönix,** Am Grün 1 (☎16 49 69). Tucked in a short alley between Rudolphspl. and Universitätsstr., the bistro serves traditional dishes as well as lighter fare. Sip 1 of a variety of cocktails, like the ice-cold piña coladas (DM9), while soaking in the warmth of the desert-colored walls. Open M-Th 10am-2am, F 10am-3am, Sa 6pm-3am, Sun 6pm-2am.

Café Barfuß, Barfüßerstr. 33 (☎253 49), is packed with locals. Big breakfast menu (DM5.50-12.50) served until 3pm. In the summer enjoy your Pils outside on one of the hefty brown picnic tables. The menu has amusing cartoons made even funnier by any of the 5 beers on tap (DM2.80-6.50). Open daily 10am-1am.

Café Vetter, Reitgasse 4 (☎258 88), is a traditional cafe proud of its terrace on the edge of the Oberstadt. Cake and coffee runs DM8. Open M and W-Sa 8:30am-6:30pm, Tu 11am-6:30pm, Su 9:30am-6:30pm.

◉ SIGHTS

■ **UNIVERSITÄTSMUSEUM FÜR BILDENDE KUNST.** The university's impressive collection of 19th- and 20th-century painting and sculpture is housed in a modest-looking building surrounded by a city that doesn't seem to notice. The variety of paintings includes masterpieces by Cranach and Kandinsky, as well as cutting-edge collections of contemporary work. The section on Expressive Realism depicts the lost generation of artists who matured during the Nazi period. *(Biegenstr. 11. ☎28 23 55. Open Tu-Su 11am-1pm and 2-5pm. Free.)*

LANDGRAFENSCHLOß. The exterior of this Schloß almost looks as it did in 1500 as the haunt of the infamous Teutonic knights. Later, Count Philip brought rival Protestant reformers Martin Luther and Ulrich Zwingli to his court in 1529 to convince them to kiss and make up. He was on the verge of success when an epidemic made everyone grumpy and uncooperative. Inside, the Schloß has been completely renovated to house the Museum für Kulturgeschichte, which exhibits Hessian history and art, including medieval shields, ornate crosses, and recently-unearthed 9th-century wall remnants. The Landesherrschaft floor is a war buff's dream come true. *(From Rudolphspl. or Markt take bus #16 (direction: "Schloß") to the end, or hike up the 250 steps from the Markt. Open Apr.-Oct. Tu-Su 10am-6pm; Nov.-Mar. Tu-Su 11am-5pm. Last entry 30min. before closing. DM3, students DM2.)*

ELISABETHKIRCHE. Save some ecclesiastic awe for the oldest Gothic church in Germany, modeled on the French cathedral at Rheims. The name of the church honors the town patroness, a widowed child-bride (engaged at four, married at 14) who took refuge in Marburg, founded a hospital, and snagged sainthood four years after death. The reliquary for her bones is so overdone, it's glorious. The somber brown interior is illuminated by glowing stained-glass windows. *(Elisabethstr. 3.*

☎655 73. *With your back to the train station, walk down Bahnhofstr. 5min. and turn left on Elisa-bethstr. Open daily Apr.-Sept. 9am-6pm; Oct. 9am-5pm; Nov.-Mar. M-Sa 10am-4pm, Su after 11am. Church free; reliquary DM3, students DM2.)*

RUDOLPHSPLATZ. The modern university building was erected in 1871, but the original Alte Universität on Rudolphspl. was built on the rubble of a monastery conveniently vacated when Reformation-minded Marburgers ejected the resident monks. As the central point on campus, the **Aula**, or main hall, bears frescos illuminating Marburg's history. The nearby houses with technicolor flags are former fraternities.

MARKT. In front of the 16th-century Gothic Rathaus lies a plaza surrounded by open-air cafes and local shops. For a glance at some really modern art, check out the **Kunstverein.** The gallery displays special exhibits by contemporary artists and an annual show featuring pieces by local talent. *(Markt 16.* ☎*258 82; www.marburg.de/kunstverein. Open Tu-Th and Sa 10am-1pm and 2-5pm, F 10am-1pm and 2-8pm, Su 11am-1pm. Free.)*

OTHER SIGHTS. The 13th-century **Lutherische Pfarrkirche St. Marien** features amber-colored stained glass and an elaborate organ. The view overlooking the old city rivals that of the Schloß. *(Lutherische Kirchhof 1.* ☎*252 43. Open daily 9am-5pm. Free organ concerts Oct.-July Sa at 6:30pm.)* Down Kugelgasse, the 15th-century **Kugelkirche** (sphere church) owes its peculiar name not to its shape but to the *cuculla* (hats) worn by the religious order that founded it.

🎵🎵 ENTERTAINMENT AND NIGHTLIFE

Bars and pubs in Marburg breed faster than rabbits; in the Oberstadt alone there are more than 60 fine establishments. Live music, concert, theater, and movie options are listed in the weekly *Marburger Express,* available at many bars and pubs. Posters plastered all over the main streets announce touring bands, DJs, and larger events. Things get hopping on the first Sunday in July, when costumed citizens parade onto the Markt for the rowdy **Frühschoppenfest.** Drinking officially kicks off at 11am when the brass rooster on top of the 1851 Rathaus flaps its wings. Unofficially, however, the barrels of Alt Marburger Pils are tapped at 10am when the ribald old Marburger Trinklieder (drinking ballads) commence.

■ **Barfly/Café News/Hollywood Stars/Down Under Dance Club,** Reitgasse 5 (☎212 05/ 26). All your nightlife needs in one convenient location. **Barfly** is a bistro and terrace cafe, claiming the highest platform of its kind. Open daily 11am-1am. **Café News** is a trendy spot occupying the main floor of the complex. Open daily 9am-1am. **Hollywood Stars,** down the spiral staircase, serves special drinks and American fare. Happy "hour" daily 6-7:30pm. Open daily 6pm-1am. **Down Under** raves on weekends—a dance mecca. Open F-Sa 9pm-1am.

Discothek Kult, Temmlerstr. 7 (☎941 83). Bus #A1 (direction: "Pommernweg") or A2 (direction: "Cappeler Gleiche") to the first stop after the Südbahnof. This warehouse-like building is the place to shake your groove thang, along with Marburg's massive teenage population. Take your pick from 1 of 3 dance floors, with music ranging from bass-throbbing techno to hip-hop to oldies. If you prefer, join the older set at 1 of 4 bars. Open Tu-W 9pm-3am, F-Sa 9pm-4am. Cover DM3-5.

Bolschoi Café, Ketzerbach (☎622 24). From Rudolfspl. walk up Pilgrimstein until you reach the Elizabethkirche and turn left on Ketzerbach; it's at the end of the block. The Communist kitsch here will warm the cockles of any Cold Warrior's heart—red candles, red walls, red foil ceiling, and 20 brands of domestic and imported vodka (DM3-6). But it's the decor, not the clientele, that is red. Those in search of "Komrads" might be disappointed—only native Marburgers here. Open M-W and Su 8pm-1am, F-Sa 8pm-2am.

Hinkelstein, Markt 18 (☎242 10). This cavernous underground bar provides a hangout for dart-playing locals listening to Hendrix and Jackson Brown. A welcome respite from the techno scene. Open daily 7pm-1am.

KASSEL ☎0561

After Napoleon III and his soldiers were captured in the Battle of Sedan in 1870, the Aacheners jeered *"Ab nach Kassel"* ("off to Kassel") at the crestfallen monarch as he crossed the border to Schloß Wilhelmshöhe. Today, hordes of travelers answer the call, coming to see Kassel's many treasures. The steeped traditions of Wilhelmshöhe and the grand hillside parks that inspired the Brothers Grimm to record their famous fairy tales contrast with the cutting-edge thinking of the documenta contemporary art exhibitions. Complemented by an active *Uni* setting and the head-throbbing nightlife to match, Kassel is one of Hessen's hottest locales.

▐ GETTING THERE AND GETTING AROUND

Trains: To Frankfurt (2½hr., 2 per hr., DM54); Hamburg (2½hr., 2 per hr., DM99); Düsseldorf (3½hr., 1 per hr., DM145); and Munich (5hr., 1 per hr., DM172).

Ferries: Personenschiffahrt Söllner, Die Schlagd/Rondell (☎77 46 70; fax 77 77 76), at the Fuldabrücke near the Altmarkt, offers Fulda Valley tours (3hr.) mid-June to Aug. daily 2pm, May to mid-June and Sept. W and Sa-Su 2pm. One-way DM10, round-trip DM16, children half-price.

Public Transportation: Kassel's sophisticated system of buses and streetcars is integrated into the **NVV** (Nordhessischer Verkehrsverbund). Tickets priced by distance; single tickets range from DM2.50 (up to 4 stops) to DM43.70 (anywhere in the area). The **Multiticket** (DM8.50) is valid for 2 adults and 3 kids for a weekday or weekend. Ask questions at the **NVV-Center,** Königsplatz 366 (☎70 75 80).

Taxi: ☎881 11.

Car Rental: City-Rent Autofairmietung, Kurt-Schumacher-Str. 25 (☎77 08 21).

Bike Rental: FahrradHof, Wilhelmshöher Allee 253 (☎31 30 83), in the Wilhelmshöhe train station. Bikes from DM20 per day, DM80 per week. Open M-F 9am-1pm and 2-5:30pm, Sa 9am-3pm.

✦ ☐ ORIENTATION AND PRACTICAL INFORMATION

Kassel is a diffuse city, the product of a frantic building boom that followed the postwar housing shortage. Get a free map of the city at the tourist office or at the hostel to navigate the more remote parts of the city. Deutsche Bahn chose Kassel to be an InterCity Express connection and rebuilt **Bahnhof Wilhelmshöhe-Kassel** to streamlined contemporary specs. The Wilhelmshöhe station is the point of entry to Kassel's ancient castles and immense parks on the west side; the older **Hauptbahnhof** is the gateway to the tightly packed and entirely modernized Altstadt. Now a model of extravagant hipness, the Hauptbahnhof's recent remodeling saturated it with postmodern adornments, including the Gleis 1 nightclub, and one of the documenta exhibitions, the **caricatura.** IC, ICE, and most IR trains only stop at Wilhelmshöhe. Frequent trains, city buses, and streetcars shuttle between the stations; catch most other bus and streetcar lines at either the "Rathaus" or "Am Stern" stops. From the Hauptbahnhof, take streetcar #7 or 9 to "Rathaus," and streetcar #4, 7, or 9 to "Am Stern"; from Wilhelmshöhe, take streetcar #1, 4, or 6 to "Rathaus" or "Am Stern." The underground walkway in front of the Hauptbahnhof is often full of shady-looking types; don't walk there alone after dark. **Treppenstraße,** Kassel's original pedestrian zone (the first in all of Germany), and **Königsstraße,** the current pedestrian zone, are areas well worth exploring.

Tourist Office: Tourist-Information (☎340 54; fax 31 52 16), in Kassel-Wilhelmshöhe train station, sells maps (DM1.50), and books **rooms** for a DM5 fee. Ask about the **Kassel Service Card,** which provides access to public transportation and other discounts. 24hr. card DM12, 3-day card DM19. Open M-F 9am-1pm and 2-6pm, Sa 9am-1pm.

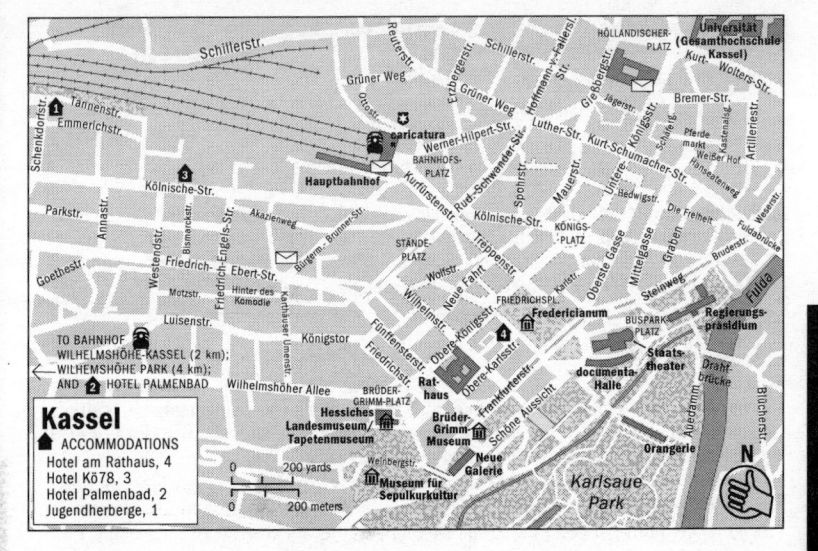

Kassel

🏠 ACCOMMODATIONS

Hotel am Rathaus, 4
Hotel Kö78, 3
Hotel Palmenbad, 2
Jugendherberge, 1

Bookstore: Buchladung Vaternahm, Obere Königsstr. 7 (☎78 98 40). Broad selection of paperbacks in English. Open M-F 9:30am-8pm, Su 9am-4pm.

Laundromat: Schnell & Sauber, Friedrich-Ebert-Str. 83, near the hostel. Wash DM6. Dry DM1 per 11min. Soap included. Open M-Sa 5am-midnight.

Women's Resources: Frauenhaus Kassel, Frankfurter Str. 65 (☎89 88 89). **Beratungsstelle Schwarzer Winkel,** Goethestr. 44 (☎10 70 25).

AIDS Hotline: Frankfurter Str. 65 (☎28 39 07). Open daily 10am-1pm.

Emergency: Police, ☎110. **Fire** and **Ambulance,** ☎112.

Hospital: Städtische Klinik, Mönchebergstr. 41-43 (☎98 00).

Post Office: Hauptpostamt, Untere Königsstr. 95, 34117 Kassel, between Königsplatz and the university. Open M-F 8am-6pm, Sa 8am-noon.

Internet Access: InterDock Mediencafé, Untere Karlsstr. 4 (☎316 12 05), in Dock 4 cultural center, behind Museum Friedricianum. DM8 per hr. Open Th-Sa 2-9pm.

▚ ACCOMMODATIONS AND CAMPING

Hotels in Kassel actively seek conventioneers and business crowds, but the large accommodations industry generally has a surplus of moderately priced rooms.

Jugendherberge am Tannenwäldchen (HI), Schenkendorfstr. 18 (☎77 64 55; fax 77 68 32). Streetcar #4 or 6 from the Rathaus or Bahnhof Wilhelmshöhe (direction: "Ottostr." or "Lindenberg") to "Annastr." Continue walking up Friedrich-Ebert-Str., and make a right on Schenkendorfstr. Or walk from the Hauptbahnhof: leave from the *Südausgang*, turn right on Kölnische Str., and turn right again onto Schenkendorfstr. A spacious cafeteria, clean rooms, and a location just a short walk from the city center make this hostel one of the more desirable gems of the DJH system. The hostel is popular with school groups; call ahead. HI members only. Breakfast included. Sheets DM6. Reception 9am-11:30pm. Curfew 12:30am. DM24.50, over 26 DM29.50.

▨ **Hotel Kö78,** Kölnische Str. 78 (☎716 14; fax 179 82). From the Hauptbahnhof, exit through the *Südausgang*, walk up the stairs, and follow Kölnische Str. uphill and to the right. From Bahnhof Wilhelmshöhe, follow the directions to the Jugendherberge, and from the train stop walk up Annastr. Turn right onto Kölnische Str. The hotel's handsome exterior shelters positively luxurious rooms at reasonable prices. Breakfast included. All rooms have cable TV. Reception M-F 6am-10pm, Sa-Su 8am-10pm. Singles from DM59, with shower from DM69; doubles from DM98, with shower from DM119.

Hotel-Restaurant Palmenbad, Kurhausstr. 27 (☎/fax 326 91). Streetcar #3 (direction: "Ihringshäuser Str.") to "Wigandstr.," then 5min. uphill on An den Eichen. Or walk from Bahnhof Wilhelmshöhe up Wilhelmshöher Allee (towards Herkules), left on Baunsberg-str., and right on Kurhausstr. Cozy quarters, friendly staff. Reception M-F 5:30-11pm, Sa 10am-11pm, Su 10am-3pm. Singles DM49; doubles DM90, with shower DM95.

Camping: Kurhessen-Kassel, Giesenallee 7 (☎224 33). Bus #16 (direction: "Auesta-dion") or bus #25 (direction: "Bebelplatz") to "Damaschkebrücke." The campground boasts a stunning spot on the Fulda close to Karlsaue park. Reception 8am-1pm and 3-10pm. Open Mar.-Oct. DM5 per adult, DM2 per child. Tents DM10-20.

◖ FOOD

Many of Kassel's culinary offerings take a bite out of the budget. **Friedrich-Ebert-Str.,** the upper part of **Wilhelmshöher Allee,** and the area around **Königsplatz** have super-markets and cafes sprinkled among department stores and fashion boutiques. **E Activ** sells groceries on Friedrich-Ebert-Str. near Bismark St. (open M-F 7am-7pm; Sa 7-4pm). Or pick through goodies at the **Markt** on Königsplatz. Inexpensive meals await in the university complex. From Bahnhof Wilhelmshöhe, take street-car #1 to "Holländischer Pl.," cross through the underground passage, and con-tinue in the same direction. Walk along the left side of the university to the back and hang a right onto Arnold-Bode-Str. As in most large German cities, Kassel's Altstadt has food stands, bakeries, and *Imbiße*.

Mensa (☎804 25 87), on Arnold-Bode-Str. in the back left corner of the University, 100m across a gorge from the big red brick tower. Look for the *Mensa* sign—it's the only way to tell this brick building from the 50-odd others. Students with ID DM3-5, others tack on DM2. Lunch M-F 11:45am-2:15pm. The **Moritz-Restaurant** in the same building serves a more elaborate lunch with much shorter lines. Students DM5, others DM7. Open M-F 11am-2:30pm. Just around the corner, the **Studentwerke-Pavillon,** Diagonale 13, slaps together meals later in the day for the same prices. Open M-F 5-9pm. The café downstairs sells the cheapest ice cream around (DM0.80 per scoop).

▨ Lohmann Biergarten, Königstor 8 (☎122 90). From the Rathaus, walk up Fünffensterstr. and make a left on Königstor. The only outdoor *Biergarten* in Kassel open late. One of Kassel's oldest and largest beer gardens, it serves tasty food at great prices. Spaghetti bolognese DM8, huge baguettes DM7, Greek salad DM8. Wash your meal down with beer (DM5 for 0.5L) or *Äpfelwein* (DM3). Open daily noon-2am.

Bistro & Restaurant Eckstein, Obere Königstr. 4 (☎71 33 00), at the corner of Fünffen-sterstr. The selection is as large as the portions. Pizza DM6-13, veggie meals from DM9. Lunch M-F noon-5pm, DM9. Open M-Th and Su 11am-1am, F-Sa 11am-2am.

Da Zhang, Kurfürstenstr. 8 (☎739 88 53), between the Hauptbahnhof and Treppenstr. Chinese specialties served in a classical Chinese-restaurant interior with a fountain and a goldfish pond. Though main courses cost DM10-20, the *Schnellmenü* offers entrees for DM7.80 M-F 11am-2:30pm. Open daily 11am-2:30pm and 5:30-11pm.

▧ SIGHTS

Kassel's sights are geographically centered around two main areas: the Rathaus, and the far end of Wilhelmshöhe Allee. The Rathaus area is home to many muse-ums, a large portion of which are devoted to Kassel's fervent passion, **Documenta.** The area surrounding the Schloß Wilhelmshöhe offers an adventurous jaunt into Germanic history. Most of the museums—Schloß Wilhelmshöhe, Ballhaus, Hessi-sches Landesmuseum, Neue Galerie, and Orangerie—belong to **Staatliche Museen Kassel** and are covered by a package deal: the **Verbundkarte** offers admission to and is for sale at all of these museums (DM15, students DM10).

DOCUMENTA

Hordes of art-lovers, dilettantes, and camera-toting curiosity-seekers descended upon Kassel in the summer of 1997 to take part in the world's preeminent exhibition of contemporary art, **Documenta X.** During the past fifty years, Documenta has pushed the boundaries defining the role of contemporary art within the larger culture; indeed, Documenta's lasting influence has challenged the old-guard traditions which in the past controlled the very definition of 'art'. The contributors emphasized the soul-searching and democratic potential of new media that subverts traditional notions of artistic form. Amid collections of giant Chia Pets and ironic images of "ideal" cityscapes, the show included a bevy of internet pieces which were broadcast worldwide in real-time (www.documenta.de). With memories of the recent exhibition still fresh, Kassel is preparing to launch Documenta into the new millennium. **Documenta XI** will take place in Kassel from June 8 to September 15, 2002.

DOCUMENTA AND RATHAUS AREA

In 1997, the Kassel hosted Documenta for the 10th time since 1955. Several of the past Documentas have become permanent exhibitions: visit Claes Oldenburg's *Pick-axe* on the banks of the Fulda near the Orangerie and Joseph Beuys' *7,000 oak trees*, both from Documenta VII in 1982.

■ MUSEUM FÜR SEPULKRALKULTUR. An ultramodern structure houses this extensive collection of death-ritual-related paraphernalia. The museum's intent is to "arrest the taboo process which surrounds the subject of 'death and dying' in today's world, and open it to public discussion." Painted skulls, black mourning garb, frequently changing art exhibits, and elaborate metal crucifixes and stone monuments that seem to reflect style over sadness are sure to satisfy your morbid fascinations. *(Weinbergstr. 25-27. From the Rathaus, cross Funffenster to Wilhelmshöhe, and go left on Weinberg; follow curves to the museum.* ☎91 89 30. *Open Tu-Su 10am-5pm, Wed 10am-8pm. Adults DM6, students DM4.)*

MUSEUM FRIEDRICIANUM. This enormous building is the oldest museum building on the Continent and houses the lion's share of Documenta-related exhibitions. *(Friedrichspl. 18,* ☎707 27 70. *Open W and F-Su 10am-6pm, Th 10am-8pm. Single exhibition DM8, students DM5; entire museum DM12, students DM8.)*

DOCUMENTA-HALLE. Located between Museum Friedricianum and the Orangerie, the newest edition to the world of Documenta houses changing exhibitions of modern art. *(Du-Ry-Str.* ☎70 72 70. *Open Tu-Su 10am-5pm. DM5, students DM3.)*

CARICATURA. Even the Hauptbahnhof has gotten in on the Documenta action. Renamed **KulturBahnhof,** it houses the self-proclaimed "gallery for bizarre art." Changing exhibitions try relentlessly to convince skeptics that Germans *do* have a sense of humor. *(Bahnhofspl. 1.* ☎77 64 99. *Open Tu-F 2-8pm, Sa-Su noon-8pm.)*

DOCUMENTA-ARCHIVES. In Dock 4 cultural center, behind Museum Friedricianum. For those who can never get enough of Documenta. *(Untere Karlsstr. 4.* ☎787 40 22. *Open M-F 10am-2pm.)*

NEUE GALLERIE. This museum includes not only ultra-contemporary work from the most recent Documenta exhibitions, but a well-rounded collection including paintings dating back to the 1700s and important works from the *Neue Sahlichkeit* movement. Wander through the halls of serene rosy-cheeked beauties, or examine the bug-like creatures crafted from camping equipment in the installation. *(Schöne Aussicht. Walk toward the Fulda from Friedrichspl., cross via the underpass, and turn right on Schöne Aussicht. Open Tu-F 10am-5pm. DM5, students DM3.)*

KARLSAUE. The English Garden of Karlsaue sprawls along the Fulda. At its southern tip is the **Insel Siebenbergen**—Karlsaue's unique "Island of Flowers." From Königsplatz, hop on bus #16 (direction: "Auestadion") to "Siebenbergen." The **Orangerie,** Karlsaue 20c (☎715 43), located at the north end of the park in a bright yellow manor house, is home to the **astronomy and technology museum.** Inside, you'll find mechanical and optical marvels as well as a planetarium. *(Open Tu-Sa 10am-5pm. DM5, students DM3. Free on F. Planetarium shows Tu and Sa 2pm, W and F 3pm, Th 2pm and 8pm, Su 3pm. DM7, students DM5.)*

BRÜDER-GRIMM-MUSEUM. Exhibits the Brothers' handwritten copy of *Kinder- und Hausmärchen*, their fabled collection of fairy tales, and translations into dozens of languages. Don't miss the artistic interpretations of the tales on the second floor. *(Schöne Aussicht 2. ☎ 787 20 33, in Palais Bellevue near the Orangerie. Walk toward the Fulda from Friedrichspl. and turn right on Schöne Aussicht. Open daily 10am-5pm. DM3, students DM2.)*

HESSISCHES LANDESMUSEUM. Features the only **wallpaper museum** in the world: this place is floor-to-ceiling fun! Surprises include 16th-century embossed leather-and-gold Spanish hangings, a rare depiction of the battle of Austerlitz, a six-color wallpaper printer, and a letter from Goethe to Schiller mentioning an order of wallpaper. The museum also houses several other collections, including a floor of prehistoric artifacts. *(Brüder-Grimm-Pl. 5. ☎ 784 60. In the yellow Landesmuseum near the Rathaus. Open Tu-Su 10am-5pm. DM5, students DM3; free on F.)*

WILHELMSHÖHE

The Wilhelmshöhe area is a hillside park with one giant Greek hero, two castles, three museums, and five waterfalls, all punctuated by rock gardens, mountain streams, and innumerable hiking trails. The whole park experience—a cross between the halls of Montezuma and a Baroque theme park—takes up half a day; approach it with humor, cynicism, or a good pair of hiking boots. From Bahnhof Wilhelmshöhe, take streetcar #1 to Wilhelmshöhe, at the southern end of the park.

SCHLOß WILHELMSHÖHE. The building is the mammoth former home of the rulers of Kassel. Napoleon III was imprisoned here after being captured in the Battle of Sedan. The **Schloßmuseum** records the extravagant royal lifestyle. *(☎ 937 77. From the streetcar stop, walk under the overpass, and take the path straight or right. Open Mar.-Oct. Tu-Su 10am-5pm; Nov.-Feb. Tu-Su 10am-4pm. Tours of private suites leave when there are enough people. Last tour one hour before closing. DM7, students DM5.)*

SCHLOß LÖWENBURG. Perched atop a misty peak above Schloß Wilhelmshöhe, the castle is an amazing piece of architectural fantasy. It was built by Wilhelm in the 18th century with stones deliberately missing to achieve the effect of a crumbling medieval castle. To accentuate further the ancient look, the material used was a rapidly deteriorating basalt. For some reason, this Teutonic Don Quixote was obsessed with the year 1495 and fancied himself a time-displaced knight. In order to supplement the credibility of this pretense, he even built a Catholic chapel on the Schloß to date it before the Reformation, even though he himself was Protestant. Despite his claims of chivalry, the castle was built as a bedroom for his favorite concubine, who bore him 15 children—13 more than his wife. *(☎ 935 72 00. Facing up the hill at Schloß Wilhelmshöhe, take the path on the left of the pond; follow it as it bends left after the small waterfall, and then go left again at the road. Open Mar.-Oct. Tu-Su 10am-5pm; Nov.-Feb. Tu-Su 10am-4pm. Entry only with a tour. Tours every hour; last tour one hour before closing. DM7, children DM5.)*

CASCADES. Be warned: when there isn't enough water, the cascades aren't quite "cascading." If you arrive at the top of Herkules on a Sunday or Wednesday, check out the **fountain displays** at 2:30pm; they're timed so that a walk down the clearly designated path lands you at the next waterfall as the show begins (Easter-Sept. only). The grand finale comes at 3:45pm when the displays end in a grand 52m-high gush. Stake out a vantage point early. *(Follow the road uphill from Schloß Löwenburg to the base of the fountain.)*

HERKULES. Kassel's emblem, the mighty Greek stands atop a massive pedestal, jeering at his conquered foe, the giant Encelades, whose head pokes out of the rocks at the top of the cascades. An English author traveling in the 18th century described it as "one of the most splendid structures in all of Europe, not excluding those in Versailles, Frascati, or Tivoli." Visitors can climb up onto Herkules's pedestal and, if they're brave enough, into his club. *(Access to the base of the statue free. Pedestal and club open mid-Mar. to mid-Nov. Tu-Su 10am-6pm. DM3, students DM2.)*

 ENTERTAINMENT AND NIGHTLIFE

Dozens of music bars, pubs, cafes, and discos spice up Kassel's Altstadt. The stretch along Friedrich-Ebertstr. and Goethestr. between Bebelplatz and Königsplatz and extending south along Rathenauallee toward the Rathaus packs in the party *Geist.* The free magazines *Fritz* and *Xcentric*, available at the tourist office, list an indispensable schedule of parties at the city's clubs. Kassel also fosters a lively **film** culture. Theaters cluster around the Altstadt; **Bali** (☎70 15 50) in the Hauptbahnhof shows movies in their original language. Kassel hosts an **outdoor film festival** every summer behind the Museum Friedricianum at the theater **Dock 4** (☎787 20 67). Take Streetcar #1 or 3 to "Friedrichspl." Shows (DM10) range from the artsy pretense of Godard to the authentic power of *Star Wars*. The **Staatstheater** (☎109 42 22) on Friedrichspl. hosts plays, concerts, operas, and ballet performances from mid-September to early July.

- **Musiktheater,** Angersbachstr. 10 (☎840 44). Bus #27 to "Angersbachstr." A disco-party mecca. 3 humongous dance floors occupying 2 city blocks host techno, house, and pop. The walk is dimly-lit and sparsely traveled; use caution or take public transportation. Open F-Sa after 8:30pm, sometimes also Th. Cover DM5.

- **Mr. Jones,** Goethestr. 31 (☎71 08 18). Walking distance from the hostel at the corner of Querallee. Excellent food of the Tex-Mex variety DM8-12. Open M-Th and Su 10am-1am, F-Sa 10am-midnight.

- **Café-Bar Suspekt,** Fünffensterstr. 14 (☎10 45 22). Popular gay and lesbian pub belies its name with a laid-back and friendly ambience. During the day a pleasant cafe (Tu-Su 1-8pm), at night a bar (M-Th and Su 8pm-1am, F-Sa 8pm-2am).

- **SPOT,** Oelmuelenweg 10-14 (☎56 209). Turn up the bass and get ready to move. Techno, drum 'n bass, gay/lesbian night, and 3 floors of "Projekt Nachsicht" on Tuesdays. Most nights start at 10pm. Call or check listings in *Fritz* or *Xcentric* (www.kassel-szene.ed/spot).

- **Music Club Blaque,** Burgermeister-Brunner-Str. 19 (☎739 57 48). Hip Hop and R&B mixed up on "Blaque Friday" and Saturday.

NEAR KASSEL: FRITZLAR   ☎05622

The birth of the town of Fritzlar as *Frideslar* (Place of Peace) dates to a not-so-peaceful act of St. Boniface, who, in 723, chopped down the huge **Donar's Oak,** the pagan religious symbol of the tribal Chats. The "Apostle of Germany" used the timber to build his own wooden church, which today is the beautiful Petersdom. It was also here that Heinrich I was proclaimed king in 915, inaugurating the medieval incarnation of the Holy Roman Empire. Since then, this diminutive medieval town has become isolated from the main routes of buzzing commerce and affluence. Nevertheless, having survived both WWII and the zeal of the post-war building projects unscathed, Fritzlar is content with its role as a postcard-perfect town of half-timbered houses on the **Märchenstraße,** the German fairy tale road.

The gem of Fritzlar is the 12th-century **Petersdom,** with its elaborate altar and sizeable treasury, which includes the diamond and pearl-covered **Heinrichkreuz** as well as numerous precious robes and relics. (Open May-Oct. M-Sa 10am-noon and 2-5pm, Su 2-5pm; Nov.-Apr. Su-M 2-4pm, Tu-Sa 10am-noon & 2-4pm, Su 2-4pm. DM5, students DM2. Tours DM5, children DM2.) On the western extremity of the still-standing medieval city wall, the 39m **Grauer Turm** is the tallest defense tower in Germany. Though it no longer serves its original purpose, the view remains one of the best in the area (key available at the tourist office). The **Hochzeitshaus,** on Burggrabenstr., has hosted weddings and festivals since the 16th century. It also houses the **Regionalmuseum,** which does its best to reflect all aspects and stages of Fritzlar's bumpy history. (☎98 86 28. Open Mar.-Nov. M-F and Su 10am-noon and 3-5pm; Dec.-Feb. M-F 10am-noon and 3-5pm. DM3, children DM1.) Little towns spawn big festivals, and Fritzlar's *Wunderkinder* are no exception: the **Pferde-markt** (July 13-15, 2000) and the **Altstadtfest** (Aug. 18-19, 2000) draw out *Lederho-sen*, traditional music, and beer goggles.

Fritzlar is an ideal afternoon jaunt from Kassel. It can be reached from either of the main stations in Kassel by train (40min., twice daily, DM12.50) or bus (40min.). The **tourist office,** Zwischen den Krämen 5, sits next to Fritzlar's Rathaus, the old-est official building in Germany, built in 1109. Make a left out of the train station and a quick right onto Gießener Str. After the bridge, make a left onto Fraumün-sterstr., and then a right onto Georgengasse. At the top of the hill you'll find Gießener Str. (again). Hang a left, walk through the Marktplatz, and make a left onto Zwischen den Krämen. The office provides maps, makes room reservations (from DM50), and has a very friendly staff. (☎98 86 43; fax 98 86 26; www.frit-zlar.de, stadt@fritzlar.de. Open M 10am-6pm, Tu-Th 10am-5pm, F 10am-4pm, Sa-Su 10am-noon.) **Tours** leave from the Rathaus, but only if there is a minimum of five people. (1½hr. May-Sept. Tu-Sa 10:30am, Su 11am. DM5.) The **post office,** 34560 Fritzlar, is at the corner of Nikolausstr. and Gießener Str., near the Markt (open M-F 9am-noon and 2:30-6pm, Sa 9am-noon).

Nordrhein-Westfalen

NORDRHEIN-WESTFALEN
(NORTH RHINE-WESTPHALIA)

In 1946, the victorious Allies attempted to speed Germany's recovery by merging the traditionally distinct regions of Westphalia, Lippe, and the Rhineland to unify the economic and industrial nucleus of post-war Germany. The resulting *Land*, Nordrhein-Westfalen, meets no typical German stereotype. The region's dense concentration of highways and rail lines form the infrastructure of the most heavily populated (17 million inhabitants) and economically powerful area in Germany. The industrial boom of the late 19th century sparked social democracy, trade unionism, and revolutionary communism—the popular moniker "Red Ruhr" didn't refer to the color of the water. Despite downturns in heavy industry and persistently high unemployment, the great industrial wealth of the region continues to support a multitude of cultural offerings for the citizens and visitors of its lively towns and beautiful river valleys. While the region's industrial squalor may have inspired the philosophy of Karl Marx and Friedrich Engels, the natural beauty of the Teutoburg and Eifel mountains and the intellectual energy of Köln, Aachen, and Düsseldorf have spurred the muses of writers from Goethe to Heine to Böll.

443

HIGHLIGHTS OF NORDRHEIN-WESTFALEN

The crowning glory of German piety, **Köln's Dom** is the largest example of High Gothic architecture in the world. **Köln** (p. 444) shines beyond its cathedral with a collection of world-class museums, great nightlife—including a burgeoning gay scene—and a fountain that gushes forth perfume.

Düsseldorf (p. 466) is a wealthy, wealthy city, with a glitzy strip of designer boutiques (the "Kö") and a palpably cosmopolitan air. Budget travelers enjoy the **Kunstsammlung Nordrhein-Westfalen** and the shrine to hometown writer-hero **Heinrich Heine.**

Bordering Belgium and the Netherlands, beautiful **Aachen** (p. 461) exudes internationalism in a sophisticated university town atmosphere.

See Germany's erstwhile capital, **Bonn** (p. 454), in its new, bureaucrat-free incarnation.

KÖLN (COLOGNE) ☎0221

Founded as a Roman colony (*colonia*, hence Köln) in AD 48, Köln was Petrarch's "city of dreams" when the rest of Germany was just wilderness. The city's location at the intersection of several international trade routes ushered in a Golden Age during the Middle Ages and the Renaissance, bolstering Köln's present status as Germany's commercial, technical, and communications center *par excellence*. Today, nearly a million citizens call the city home.

Köln's major attraction is the majestic and legendary Dom. Designed to exceed all other churches in splendor, the Gothic structure took an amazing 632 years to build. During WWII, at least 14 bombs struck the cathedral, which somehow survived and has since become a powerful symbol of Köln's miraculous recovery from the Allied raids, which left 90% of the city center in ruins. Today, Köln is the largest city in Nordrhein-Westfalen and its most important cultural center, with a full plate of world-class museums and theatrical offerings. It is a prosperous, modern city with a penchant for bibulous celebrations.

Modern Köln is also the city of Nobel Prize-winning novelist Heinrich Böll, who set *The Lost Honor of Katharina Blum* and the scandalous *Clown* here. The novels explore the venom of press slander and the violation of civil liberties—topics appropriate to a city steeped in literary and journalistic tradition. Köln is the base for many national media networks, just as it was during the days of Karl Marx, who began his revolutionary career here as a local newspaper editor. Although Köln's citizens conduct their own communications in the impenetrable *Kölsch* dialect, the locally brewed *Kölsch* beer offers a savory experience that brings to the taste buds the kind of euphoria that the heavenly Dom delivers to the eyes.

▐ GETTING THERE AND GETTING AROUND

Flights: Flights depart from **Köln-Bonn Flughafen;** a shuttle to **Berlin** leaves 24 times per day. Call ☎(01803) 80 38 03 for flight information. Bus #170 leaves stop #3 at the train station daily at 5:30, 6, and 6:30am, and then every 15min. 7am-8pm, and every 30min. 8-11pm; it stops at Köln-Deutz 5min. before proceeding to the airport (20min., DM8.70, children DM4.50).

Trains: Direct train lines to **Düsseldorf** (45min., 5 per hr., DM12.60, DM10 for students); **Frankfurt** (2 hrs., 3 per hr., DM61, DM49 for students); **Hamburg** (5hrs., 3 per hr., DM123, students DM98); **Berlin** (6½hrs., 2 per hr., DM172, students DM138); **Munich** (6hrs., 4 per hr., DM173, students DM138). Trains also run every 2hr. to **Brussels** (2½hr., DM54); **Amsterdam** (4hr., DM79); and **Paris** (4hr., DM128).

Ferries: Köln-Düsseldorfer (☎08 83 18; fax 208 345; www.k-d.com), begins its ever-popular Rhein cruises here, where Salzgasse meets the Rhein. Sail upstream to **Koblenz** (DM59.80, round trip DM66.40) or the fairy-tale castle-land in the **Rhein Gorge** (to the Loreley towns DM99, round trip DM112). Or take the Rhein-Jet instead of a train to **Bonn** (DM11.20, round trip DM17.80.) Students and children ages 4-12 half-

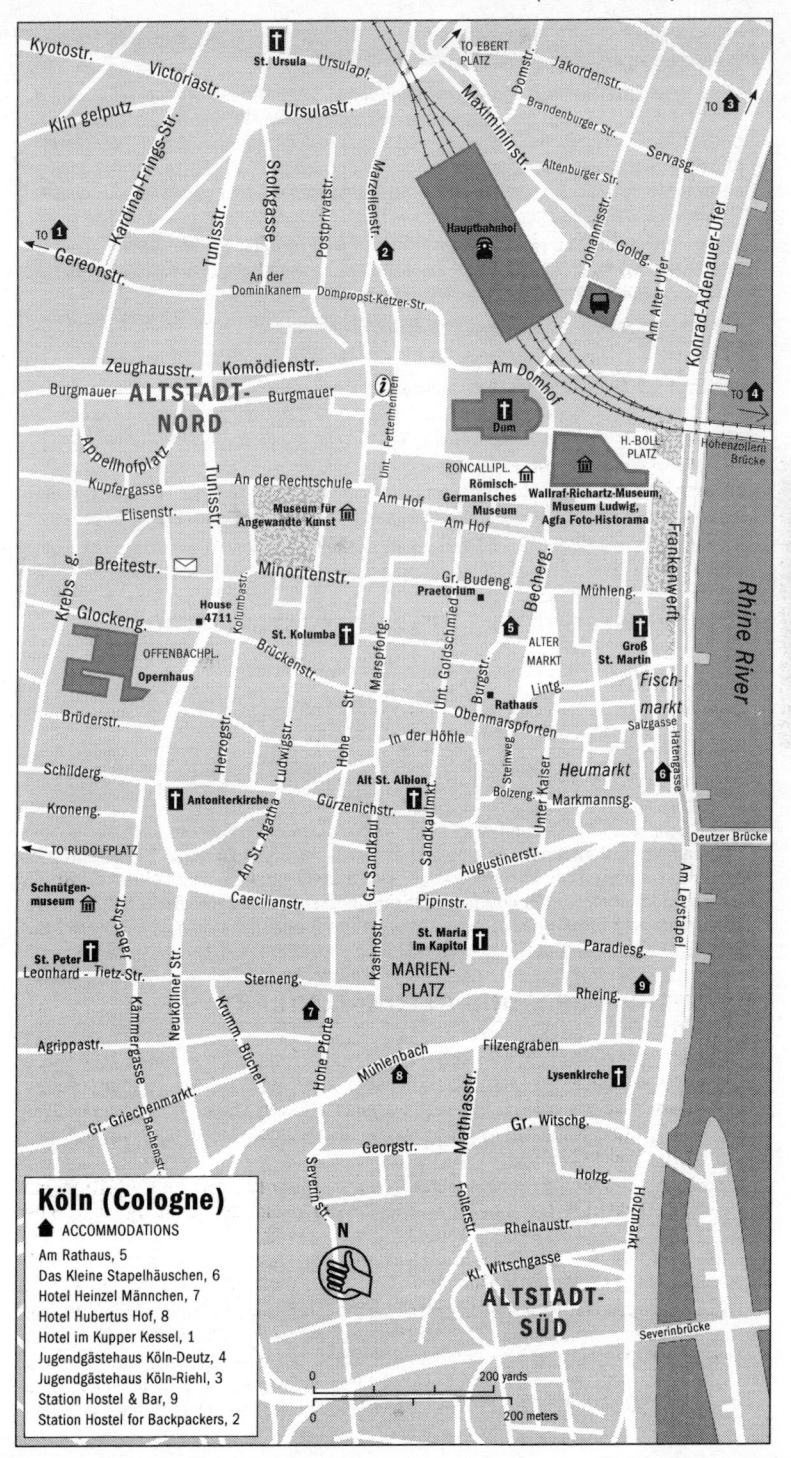

NORDRHEIN-WESTFALEN

Köln (Cologne)

⌂ ACCOMMODATIONS

Am Rathaus, 5
Das Kleine Stapelhäuschen, 6
Hotel Heinzel Männchen, 7
Hotel Hubertus Hof, 8
Hotel im Kupper Kessel, 1
Jugendgästehaus Köln-Deutz, 4
Jugendgästehaus Köln-Riehl, 3
Station Hostel & Bar, 9
Station Hostel for Backpackers, 2

0   200 yards
0   200 meters

price, seniors half-price on M and F (on all trip excluding Rhein-Jet). Most trips (excluding hydrofoils) covered by Eurail and German railpasses.

Public Transportation: VRS (*Verkehrsverbund Rhein-Sieg*) offices have free maps of the S- and U-Bahn, bus, and streetcar lines; one office is downstairs in the *Hauptbahnhof*, at the U-Bahn station. Major convergence points include the train station, **Neumarkt, Appellhofplatz,** and **Barbarossaplatz.** Single ride tickets DM2.20-14.50, depending on distance traveled. Day pass DM9.50. The *Minigruppen-Ticket* allows up to 5 people to ride all day after 9am for DM13-36.

Gondola: Rheinseilbahn (☎547 41 84), U-Bahn #16 (direction: "Ebertplatz/Mülheim") to "Zoo/Flora." Float over the Rhein from the *Zoo* to the *Rheinpark*. DM6.50, children DM3.50; round-trip DM10, children DM5. Open daily 10am-5:45pm.

Taxi: Funkzentrale, ☎28 82. Cold medinas not available.

Car Rental: Avis, Clemensstr. 29 (☎23 43 33); **Hertz,** Bismarckstr. 19 (☎51 50 84).

Bike Rental: Kölner Fahrradverleihservice, Markmannsgasse (☎0171 629 87 96), in the Altstadt on the Rhein. DM4 per hr., DM20 per day, or DM95 per week. Discounts if you take a K-D ferry. Open daily 9am-6pm. Daily 3hr. city **tour** Apr.-Oct. in German and English at 1:30pm, DM29.

Mitfahrzentrale: Citynetz Mitfahrzentrale, Maximinstr. 2 (☎194 40), to the left of the train station, matches riders and drivers. Open daily 9am-7pm.

Hitchhiking: *Let's Go* does not recommend hitchhiking. For all destinations, hitchers take a choice of many buses to the *Hauptbahnhof* or bus #170 to the airport.

✴🛈 ORIENTATION AND PRACTICAL INFORMATION

Eight bridges unite Köln across the Rhein, but nearly all sights can be found on the western side. The train station is in the northern part of the *Innenstadt*. The *Altstadt* is split into two districts; *Altstadt-Nord* is near the station, and *Altstadt-Süd* is just south of the *Severinsbrücke*. Many high-end hotels in the *Innenstadt* sell the unbeatable **Köln Tourismus Card,** a packet of vouchers entitling the bearer to a city tour, discounts on Rhein cruises, a three-day pass to all city museums, and use of the public transportation system (DM30).

Tourist Office: Verkehrsamt, Unter Fettenhennen 19 (☎22 12 33 45 or 194 33; fax 22 12 33 20; email koelntourismus@koeln.org; www.koeln.de), across from the main entrance to the *Dom,* provides a free city map and books rooms for a DM6 fee, DM5 for last minute reservations. Pick up the *Monatsvorschau* (DM2), a booklet with essential information and a complete monthly schedule of events, or a booklet with maps and overviews of all the sights for DM3. Open May-Oct. M-Sa 8am-10:30pm, Su 9am-10:30pm; Nov.-Apr. M-Sa 8am-9pm, Su 9:30am-7pm.

Budget Travel: STA Travel, Zülpicher Str. 178 (☎44 20 11). Open M and Th 10am-8pm, Tu-W and F 10am-6pm.

Currency Exchange: An office at the train station is open daily 7am-9pm, but the service charges are lower at the post office (see below).

American Express: Burgmauerstr. 14 (☎925 90 10), near the Dom. **24hr. ATM.** Members' mail held 4 weeks. Open M-F 9am-5:30pm, Sa 10am-1pm.

▨ **Bookstore: Mayersche Buchhandlung,** Neumarkt 2 (☎20 30 70; www.mayersche.de), has a fabulous paperback selection including a separate room of books in English. Open M-F 9am-8pm, Sa 9am-4pm.

Cultural Centers: Amerika Haus, Apostelnkloster 13-15 (☎20 90 10; fax 25 55 43; email ahk@usconsulate.de; www.usembassy.de/cologne), is also known as the US Consulate General's Public Affairs section. They offer English cultural activities. English language **library** open Tu-F 2-5pm, by appointment only. The **British Council,** Hahnenstr. 6 (☎20 64 40), right around the corner on *Neumarkt,* offers the same services with a better *Monty Python* collection. Open Tu 2-7pm, W-F 1-5pm. Closed July 20-Aug.20.

Gay and Lesbian Resources: Schulz Schwulen-und Lesbenzentrum, Kartäuserwall 18 (☎93 18 80 80), near Chlodwigplatz. Information, advice, movies, youth activities, library, and popular cafe. The tourist office also offers a "Gay City Map" with listings and locations of gay-friendly hotels, bars, and clubs.

Women's Resources: Frauenamt, Markmansgasse 7 (☎22 12 64 82), fields questions on cultural services. Open M-Th 8:30am-1pm and 2-4pm, F 8:30am-12:30pm, but it's best to make an appointment. **Women's crisis hotline,** ☎420 16 20.

Laundry: Eco-Express, at the corner of Richard-Wagner-Str. and Händelstr. Wash DM6, dry DM1 per 10min. Soap included. Open M-Sa 6am-11pm.

Emergency: Police, ☎110. **Fire and Ambulance,** ☎112.

Pharmacy: Dom-Apotheke, Komödienstr. 5 (☎257 67 54), near the station, posts a list of after-hours pharmacies. English spoken. Open M-F 8am-6:30pm, Sa 9am-1pm.

Post Office: Hauptpostamt, 50667 Köln, at the corner of Breite Str. and Tunisstr. From the Dom, head down Hohe Str. and take a right on Minoritenstr. The **post office** is on the right in the *WDR-Arkaden* shopping gallery, but you can't miss the yellow marquee. Open M-F 8am-8pm, Sa 8am-4pm.

Internet Access: In FuturePoint (see **Food,** p. 449), and in the **Station Hostel** (see **Accommodations,** p. 447).

⌐ ACCOMMODATIONS AND CAMPING

The brisk convention and tour business in Köln produces a wealth of rooms; the trick is pinning one down. Hotels fill up (and prices set sail) in the spring and fall when trade winds blow conventioneers into town. Summer is high season for Köln's two hostels, both of which brim to the beams from June to September. The main hotel haven centers around **Brandenburger Str.,** on the less interesting side of the train station. The **Mitwohnzentrale,** An der Bottmühle 16, finds apartments for longer stays. (☎194 45. Open M-F 9am-1pm and 2-4pm.) Scrounging for a last minute room during Karneval is futile—most people book a year in advance for the festivities.

Jugendherberge Köln-Deutz (HI), Siegesstr. 5a (☎81 47 11; fax 88 44 25), just over the *Hohenzollernbrücke.* Take S-Bahn #6, 11, or 12 to "Köln-Deutz." From the main exit of the S-Bahn station, walk down Neuhöfferstr. and take the first right; the hostel is in a tree-lined courtyard. Small but clean rooms in a good location, with two pinball machines and free access to washing machines (soap DM1). Breakfast and sheets included. Lunch or dinner DM7. Reception 11am-1am. Curfew 1am. Call ahead. Dorm beds DM33, over 26 DM37.

Jugendgästehaus Köln-Riehl (HI), An der Schanz 14 (☎76 70 81; fax 76 15 55), on the Rhein north of the zoo. U-Bahn #16 (direction: "Ebertplatz/Mülheim") to "Boltenstern-str." Or walk along the Rhein on Konrad-Adenauer-Ufer until it becomes Niederländer Ufer and finally An der Schanz (40min.). Big common areas and lockers big enough to hide in. Breakfast and sheets included. Reception 24hr. No curfew. Call ahead. 4- to 6-bed rooms DM38.50; singles DM63.50.

⊠ Station Hostel and Bar, Rheingasse 34-36 (☎23 02 47; email station@t-online.de; home.t-online/home/station), is the new addition to the *Station* hostel family, where the friendly staff provides larger and cleaner rooms for just a few marks more than the old location. Right across the street from the Rhein and the **Chocolate Museum,** this hostel's location may not be so central, but it is certainly scenic. And for nightlife at your fingertips, the bar downstairs is always jumping with hostelers and regulars; they show all the big games here. Reception at all hours except 1-5pm, reserved rooms are held until 6pm. Singles DM50; doubles DM80; triples DM108; quads DM132.

Station Hostel for Backpackers, Marzellenstr. 44-48 (☎912 53 01; fax 912 53 03; email station@t-online.de; www.hostel-cologne.de). From the station walk 1 block along Dompropst-Ketzer-Str. and take the first right on Marzellenstr. The independent hostel has brightly colored, functional rooms, a chill atmosphere, and friendly staff. It's everybody-friendly and the location could only be more central if it were in the Dom. Sheets DM3. Wash DM3, dry DM3, soap is one big ol' scoop for DM1.50. Internet access DM1, and then 10 pfennigs per minute. 24hr. reception. No curfew. Check-in is 2pm, checkout is noon; call by 3pm on the day of arrival to confirm reservations. 6-bed dorms DM27; singles DM40; doubles DM70; tripes DM96; quads DM120.

Jansen Pension, Richard-Wagner-Str. 18 (☎ 25 18 75). U-Bahn #1, 6, 7, 15, 17, or 19, to "Rudolfplatz" and follow Richard-Wagner-Str. nearly 2 blocks. The *Pension* is just before the intersection with Brüsseler Str. Beautifully decorated, bright rooms with sky-high ceilings in a Victorian house. Walk in and be happy. Breakfast included. Singles DM55 or 70, depending on size, drops to DM50 or DM65 for stays over one night; doubles DM110, two nights or more DM100.

Hotel Im Kupferkessel, Probsteigasse 6 (☎ 13 53 38; fax 12 51 21). From the *Dom,* follow Dompropst-Ketzer-Str. as it becomes An der Dominikan, Unter Sachsenhausen, Gereonstr., and finally Christophstr.; Probsteigasse is on the right. Well decorated, clean rooms, and young, friendly owners. Singles DM55-DM88, doubles from DM120. Breakfast included. Call ahead.

Hotel Heinzelmännchen, Hohe Pforte 5-7 (☎ 21 12 17; fax 21 57 12). Bus #132 (direction: "Frankenstr.") to "Waidmarkt," or walk down the Hohe Str. shopping zone until it becomes Hohe Pforte. Bright, elegantly decorated rooms with balconies and firm mattresses. Less for stays over 2 days. Breakfast included. Reception 6am-11pm; call if you're arriving later. Singles DM65-72; doubles DM115; triples from DM125.

Hotel Hubertus Hof, Mühlenbach 30 (☎ 21 73 86; fax 21 89 55). Follow the directions above to Hohe Pforte and turn left on Mühlenbach. This gay-friendly hotel has fuzzy carpets and monster-sized rooms. Showers and toilets off the hall. Breakfast included. Reception 7am-9pm. Singles DM60, doubles DM80-85.

Am Rathaus, Burgerstr. 6 (☎ 257 76 24; 258 28 29). Standing on the front porch of the *Rathaus,* Am Rathaus is immediately on your right. This place is all about location. Breakfast included. Singles DM50-65, doubles DM90-140.

Das Kleine Stapelhäuschen, Fischmarkt 1-3 (☎ 257 78 62; fax 257 42 32). Cross the *Altenmarkt* from the back of the *Rathaus* and take Lintgasse to the *Fischmarkt.* Everything is perfectly elegant in this *Rheinisch* inn replete with oak furnishings and a stunning circular staircase. A friendly staff and a lovely view of the Rhein complete the image, making this hotel an enjoyable splurge. Breakfast included. Singles DM75-87, with shower and TV DM98-125, with full bath and TV DM125-135; doubles DM125-135, with shower and DM170-185, with full bath and TV DM195-235.

Hotel Berg, Brandenburger Str. 6 (☎ 12 11 24; fax 139 00 11; email hotel@hotelberg.com; www.hotel-berg.com). Bear left on Johannisstr. from the back exit of the train station and take the third left on Brandenburger Str. Well-kept rooms and a homey breakfast area. Breakfast included. 24hr. reception. Singles from DM50; doubles from DM80, with shower from DM100.

Camping: Campingplatz Poll, Weidenweg (☎ 83 19 66), on the Rhein, southeast of the *Altstadt.* U-Bahn #16 to "Marienburg" and cross the *Rodenkirchener Brücke.* Reception 8am-noon and 5-8pm. Open Apr.-Oct. DM8 per person. DM4 per tent. DM4 per car.

◖ FOOD

Small cafes packed with students and cheap restaurants line Zülpicher Straße. Take U-Bahn #7 or 9 to "Zülpicher Platz." Mid-priced restaurants with a fine selection of ethnic cuisine are concentrated around the perimeter of the *Altstadt,* particularly from Hohenzollernring to Hohenstaufenring. For glitzy cafes, the city's wealthy head to *Neumarkt.* Köln offers hungry visitors scrumptious *Rievekoochen* (potato pancakes), slabs of fried potato dunked in *Apfelmus* (apple sauce). Don't pass through Köln without sampling the city's smooth *Kölsch* beer. Local brews of the delightful stuff include *Sion, Küppers, Früh,* and the devout *Dom.* An open-air **market** on **Wilhelmsplatz** takes over the northern **Nippes** neighborhood to offer farm-fresh joys (open M-Sa 7am-noon). A number of authentic German eateries surround the *Domplatz*. The city's best inexpensive eats are found in the Turkish district on Weidengasse. **HL**, Hohenzollernring 20, sells **groceries.** (☎257 29 66. Open M-F 9am-8pm, Sa-Su 8:30am-4pm.) There's a big selection at **Mini-Mal**, Hohenstaufenring 30. (☎923 36 57. Open M-F 8am-8pm, Sa 8am-4pm.)

■ **Brauhaus Früh am Dom,** Am Hof 12-14 (☎258 03 97). Offers the best *Kölsch* in town. Patrons enjoy a number of Kölner and German specialties while basking in the warm glow of the lit *Dom* and lit Germans in the outdoor *Biergarten*. Meals DM9-30. Open daily 8am-midnight, menu until 11:45pm.

Päffgen-Brauerei, Friesenstr. 64-66 (☎13 54 61; fax 13 92 005). A local favorite since 1883. Legendary *Kölsch* is brewed on the premises and consumed in cavernous halls or in the *Biergarten*; there is room to seat 600 in this Mecca of breweries. Oh, and if you've come for more than to quench your thirst, sample a hearty meal for DM3-DM30. Open daily 10am-midnight. Kitchen open 11am-11pm.

Café Magnus, Zülpicherstr. 48 (☎24 16 14 69). Funky indoor/outdoor cafe with beautifully presented meals at low prices, and a perfect location for watching the attractive university crowd. Pizzas and salads from DM6, pasta from DM10. Open daily 9am-3am.

Sushi Nara, Friesenstr. 70 (☎12 01 70). Good sushi at unbeatable prices. Meals from DM10. Open M-F noon-3:30pm, and 5:30pm-midnight; Sa noon-midnight, Su 6-11pm.

Sasmus Island, Heinsberg 11a (☎23 34 98), at the corner of Heinsberg and Zülpicherstr. Serves Spanish, Creole, Cajun, and South American dishes, and equally exotic drinks to match, in a bright decor. Meals from DM10. Open daily 8am-1am, with breakfast M-Sa served until 1pm, Su until 3pm.

FuturePoint, Richmodstr. 13 (☎206 72 06), gives its sleek clientele just what it wants: a huge drink menu, esoteric snacks, and cheap internet access (DM2 per 15min.) in a chic cafe straight out of *The Jetsons*. Open daily 9am-1am.

Joe Champs, Hohenzollernring 1-3 (☎257 28 54). A 2-story bar serving huge burgers, both veggie and meat, and motley cocktails. Shows major US sporting events on the biggest bar screen in town. Happy hour 5-7pm. Open M-Th and Su noon-1am, F-Sa noon-3am.

Ganesha, on the corner of Händelstr. and Richard-Wagner-Str.(☎21 31 65) Dinner prices at this Indian restaurant are good (DM12-19), but the lunch menu is a steal at DM8.50-10. Open M-Su 6pm-midnight, Tu-Su also 12:30-3pm.

SIGHTS

■ DOM

☎52 19 77. Directly across from the train station. ***Open*** daily 6am-7pm. Free. ***Tours in German*** M-Sa 11am and 12:30, 2 and 3:30pm, Su 2 and 3:30pm; DM6, students and children DM3. ***Tours in English*** M-Sa 10:30am and 2:30pm, Su 2:30pm; DM7, children DM4. ***Organ concerts*** mid-June to Aug. Tu 8pm; free. ***Tower*** open Nov.-Feb. 9am-4pm, May-Sept. 9am-6pm, Mar., Apr., and Oct 9am-5pm; DM3, students DM1.50. ***Domschatzkammer*** open Apr.-Oct. M-Sa 9am-5pm, Su 1-4pm; Nov.-Mar. M-Sa 9am-4pm, Su 1-4pm; DM3, students DM1.50. ***Diözesanmuseum*** open M-W and F-Su 10am-5pm; free.

When sight-seeing in Köln, it's impossible to save the best for last. Most train stations offer only drunks, beggars, and transients, but visitors exiting Köln's station are immediately treated to the beauty, power, and sorrow that emanate from the colossal Dom, Germany's greatest cathedral. Visually overwhelming in intricacy and scale, the Dom is a pure example of High Gothic style, the largest of its kind in the world. Over six centuries passed from this edifice's start to its completion in 1880. For 500 years, the giant wooden crane, now kept inside, was as much Köln's trademark as the two massive towers. The stunning stained glass windows—enough to cover the floor twice—cast a harlequin display of colored light over the interior. Moving toward the front, the section to the right of the center altar bears the **Dombild triptych,** a masterful 15th-century painting and gilded altarpiece. The enormous sculpture shining brilliantly behind the altar is the **Shrine of**

the Magi, a reliquary of the Three Kings in blinding gold, brought to the city in 1164. The Magi are the town's holy patrons; they stand behind the altar in a magnificent 1531 woodcut of the town by Anton Woensam, and their three crowns grace Köln's heraldic shield. Tapestries of Rubens' *Triumph of the Eucharist* line the central nave. Look for the 976 **Gero crucifix** in the fenced off area to the left of the center altar, behind the floor mosaics; it is the oldest intact sculpture of **Christus patiens** (a crucified Christ with eyes shut), as well as Ruben's *Crucifixion of St. Peter.*

Five hundred and nine steps and 15 minutes are all it takes to scale the **Südturm** and peer down at the river below. Catch your breath at the *Glockenstube* (about halfway up), a chamber for the tower's nine bells. But eardrums beware of being there when the clock strikes on the hour! Four of the bells date from the Middle Ages, but the 19th-century upstart known affectionately as **Der große Peter** (at 24 tons, the world's heaviest swinging bell) rings loudest. Hailed as "Germany's Bell on the Rhein," it bears an engraved call for national unity. The **Domschatzkammer,** in a corner of the cathedral, holds the requisite clerical artwork and reliquaries: thorn, cross, and nail bits, as well as pieces of 18 saints. Find more ecclesiastic treasures in the **Diözesanmuseum,** just outside the south portal in the red building.

The allure of the cathedral illuminated from dusk to midnight is irresistible, drawing natives and tourists to the expansive **Domvorplatz** for a daily carnival of relaxation, art, and activism. Since time and acid rain have corroded much of the Dom's original detail, every piece is gradually being reproduced and replaced with new, treated stone. To expedite this task, play the "Dom lottery" at posts around the plaza and save a statue's fingernail. *(DM1-2.)*

INNENSTADT

In the shadow of the cathedral, the **Hohenzollernbrücke** crosses the Rhein. The majestic bridge empties out onto a promenade guarded by equestrian statues of the imperial family. A monumental flight of stairs leads to **Heinrich-Böll-Platz** and its cultural center (see **Museums,** p. 452), a complex of modern architecture that complements the Dom. Farther on, the squares and crooked streets of the **Altstadt** and old **Fischmarkt** district open onto paths along the Rhein; the cafe patios give way to an expanse of grass along the river, perfect for a picnic serenaded by musicians.

HOUSE #4711. In the 18th-century, Goethe noted "How grateful the women are for the fragrance of Eau de Cologne." This magic water, once prescribed as a drinkable curative, made the town (via the oft-mimicked export) a household name. If you're after the authentic article, be sure your bottle says *Echt kölnisch Wasser* (real Köln water); or look for the world-renowned "4711" label. Its name comes from the Mühlens family house, labeled House #4711 by the Napoleonic system that abolished street names. It has been converted into a boutique, with a small fountain continually dispensing the famous scented water. Visit the upstairs museum gallery for a full history of the famous fragrance; come on the hour to hear the *Glockenspiel,* which plays a pre-programmed selection every hour from 9am-8pm. *(Glockengasse, at the intersection with Tunisstr. From Hohe Str., turn right on Brückenstr., which becomes Glockengasse. Open M-F 9:30am-8pm, Sa 9:30am-4pm.)*

RÖMISCHES PRAETORIUM UND KANAL. Classical historians and *Ben Hur* fans will be impressed by the excavated ruins of the former Roman military headquarters. Looking like an abandoned set from a gladiator movie, the underground museum displays remains of Roman gods and a befuddling array of rocks left by early inhabitants. *(From the Rathaus, take a right towards the swarm of hotels and then a left onto Kleine Budengasse. Open Tu-F 10am-4pm, Sa-Su 11am-4pm. DM3, students DM1.50.)*

RATHAUS. Bombed in WWII, Köln's city hall has been reconstructed in its original mongrel style. The Gothic tower stands guard over Baroque cherubs flying around an ornate 1570 Renaissance arcade called the *loggia,* the only section to survive the war. The tower is adorned with a diverse array of historical and cultural figures; Marx and Rubens loom above rows of popes and emperors. A Glockenspiel offers a titillatingly tintinnabulary experience daily at noon and 5pm. *(Open M-Th 7:30am-5pm, F 7:30am-2pm. Tours W at 3pm. Free.)*

MIKWE JUDENBAD. The glass pyramid to the left as you exit the *Rathaus* shelters the 12th-century Jewish ritual bath that burrows 15m down to groundwater. Medieval bathers generally went in naked, but you'll need at least a passport (ooohh…sexy moneybelt, stud) to obtain a key from the *Praetorium* on Kleine Budengasse. *(Open M-Th 8am-4:45pm, F 8am-12:30pm, Sa-Su 11am-4pm. Free.)*

OTHER SIGHTS. Köln-Riehl's Zoo, aquarium, and botanical garden offer respectable, though rarely unique, exhibition where you can have your animal, fish and plant fixes. *(Take a gondola (see Rheinseilbahn, p. 446) to "Zoo," or U-Bahn #16 to "Zoo/Flora."* ☎778 51 22. *Zoo open daily Apr.-Oct. 9am-6pm; Nov.-Mar. 9am-5pm, last entrance is ½hr. before closing. Aquarium open daily 9am-6pm. Garden open daily 9am-9pm. Combined admission too zoo and aquarium DM17, students DM9.50, children DM7.50. Garden Free).*

CHURCHES

Köln's success in building awe-inspiring churches began hundreds of years before the idea for the Dom was conceived. The Romanesque period from the 10th to mid-13th century saw the construction of 12 churches roughly in the shape of a semi-circle around the Altstadt, using the holy bones of the saints to protect the city. The churches attest to the sacred glory and tremendous wealth of what was, at the time, the most important city north of the Alps. The city's piety received poetic embodiment in a Samuel Taylor Coleridge poem: "In Köln, a town of monks and bones/And pavements fanged with murderous stones/And rags, and hags, and hideous wenches/I counted two-and-seventy stenches…." Probably the perfume.

GROSS ST. MARTIN. Along with the Dom, **Groß St. Martin** defines the Rhein panorama of Köln. Near the Rathaus in the Altstadt, the church was reopened in 1985 after near destruction in WWII. Crypts downstairs house an esoteric collection of stones and diagrams. *(An Groß St. Martin 9.* ☎257 79 24. *Open M-F 10:15am-6pm, Sa 10am-12:30pm, and 1:30-6pm, Su 2-4pm. Church free. Crypt DM1, children DM0.50.)*

ST. GEREON. One of the first medieval structures to use the unique decagon layout, **St. Gereon** houses a floor mosaic of David hacking off Goliath's head. *(Gereonsdriesch 2-4.* ☎13 49 22. *Open M-Sa 9am-12:30pm and 1:30-6pm, Su 1:30-6pm.)*

ST. CÄCILIEN. The founding of this church dates back to the ninth century; centuries and post-WWII restorations later, the church is no longer used for services. **St. Cäcilien** is now home to a collection of religious artifacts and artwork as the **Schnütgen Museum.** On the portal behind the church stands "Death"—the masterpiece of a professional sprayer, not drunken vandals. *(Cäcilienstr. 29. Accessible only through Schnütgenmuseum, p. 452.* ☎221 23 10. *Open Tu-F 10am-5pm, first W of every month 10am-8pm. Sa-Su 11am-5pm.)*

ST. MARIA IM KAPITOL. Visitors are treated to amazingly ornate carved wooden panels detailing the life of Christ. *(Marienpl. 19. Entrance around the corner on Kasinostr.* ☎21 46 15. *Open daily 8am-6pm.)*

ST. URSULA. North of the Dom, the church commemorates Ursula's attempts to maintain celibacy despite her betrothal. She and 11 virgins under her tutelage were mistaken for Roman legionnaires and burned at sea. More than 700 skulls and innumerable reliquaries line the walls of the **Goldene Kammer.** *(Ursulapl. 24.* ☎13 34 00. *Open M-F 9:45am-1pm and 2-5:15pm. Sa 9am-1pm, and 2-4pm, Su after the mass. Church free. Kammer DM2, children DM1.)*

ALT ST. ALBAN. Behind the *Rathaus*, inside the overgrown ruins of the bombed church, parents mourn the children lost in war in a statue created by Käthe Kollwitz. *(On Unter Golschmied.)*

🏛 MUSEUMS

Köln's cultural, religious and economic significance in Europe stocks its museums with a vast and impressive array of holdings. The main museums are free with the **Köln Tourismus Card** (see p. 446).

NEAR THE DOM

▨ **HEINRICH-BÖLL-PLATZ.** Designed to maximize natural light, the unusual building houses three complementary collections. The **Wallraf-Richartz Museum** features crackly masterpieces from the 13th to the 19th century, from the Italian Renaissance through the French Impressionists. The **Museum Ludwig** spans Impressionism through Dalí, Lichtenstein, Warhol, and to art where the glue and paint have yet to dry. It also has one of the world's largest Picasso collections. The **Agfa Foto-Historama** chronicles chemical art of the last 150 years, including a rotating display of Man Ray's works. *(Bischofsgartenstr. 1. Behind the Römisch-Germanisches Museum. ☎ 22 12 23 82. Open Tu 10am-8pm, W-F 10am-6pm, Sa-Su 11am-6pm. Tours Tu 6pm, W 4:30pm, Sa 11:30am, and Su 11:30am. DM10, students DM5.)*

RÖMISCH-GERMANISCHES MUSEUM. Built on the ruins of a Roman villa, the displays include the world-famous Dionysus mosaic, the tomb of Publicus, an intimidating six-breasted sphinx, and some naughty candle-holders. *(Roncallipl. 4., between the Dom and Diözeansmuseum. ☎ 22 12 44 28. Open Tu-Su 10am-5pm, W 10am-7pm. DM10, students and children DM5.)*

MUSEUM FÜR ANGEWANDTE KUNST. A giant arts-and-crafts fair spanning seven centuries with a fabulous 20th-century design display and helpful English captions. *(An der Rechtschule. West of the Dom across Wallrafpl. ☎ 22 12 67 14. Open daily 11am-5pm, W 11am-8pm. Tours W 6pm, Sa-Su 2:30pm. DM5, students and children DM2.50.)*

ELSEWHERE IN KÖLN

▨ **SCHOKOLADENMUSEUM.** Better than Willy Wonka's Chocolate Factory (well, maybe that's not possible, but it's at least more real). Salivate at every step of chocolate production from the rainforests to the gold fountain that spurts streams of silky, heavenly, creamy…there's even a chocolate factory! Resist the urge to drool and wait for the free samples from the chocolate fountain...*Mmmmm*. *(Rheinauhafen 1a. Near the Severinsbrücke. From the train station, head for the river, and walk along the Rhein heading right. Proceed under the Deutzer Brücke and take the first footbridge across to the small bit of land jutting into the Rhein. ☎ 931 88 80; fax 931 88 814. Open M-F 10am-6pm, Sa-Su 11am-7pm. Last entry 1hr. before closing. DM10, students, seniors, and children DM5. Tours Sa at 2 and 4pm, Su at 11:30am, 2, and 4pm. DM3.)*

NS-DOKUMENTATIONS-ZENTRUM. Once Köln's Gestapo headquarters, the museum now portrays Köln as it was during the Nazi regime, including a display of the 1,200 wall inscriptions made by political prisoners who were kept in the building. See the actual prison cells in the basement. All informational plaques and film clips in German. *(Am Appellhofpl. 23-25. At the corner of Elisenstr., on the far side from the Dom. ☎ 22 12 63 31. Open Tu-F 10am-4pm, Sa-Su 11am-4pm. Tours first Sa of the month at 2pm. DM5, students DM2.)*

KÄTHE-KOLLWITZ-MUSEUM. The world's largest collection of sketches, sculptures, and prints by the brilliant artist and activist (see p. 23). Her images are dark and deeply moving, chronicling early 20th-century Berlin in stark black-and-white. There are also changing exhibits by other modern artists. *(Neumarkt 18-24. On the top floor in the Neumarkt-Passage. Take U-Bahn #12, 14, 16, or 18 to "Neumarkt." ☎ 227 23 63. Open Tu-F 10am-6pm, Sa-Su 11am-6pm. Tours Su at 3pm. DM5, students DM2.)*

SCHNÜTGENMUSEUM. The collection showcases ecclesiastical art from the Middle Ages to the Baroque, including tapestries and priestly fashions. *(Cäcilienstr. 29. ☎ 22 12 23 10; fax 22 12 84 89; email schnuetgen@netcologne.de. In St. Cäcilien, p. 451. Open*

Tu-F 10am-5pm, Sa-Su 11am-5pm. First W of the month 10am-8pm. Tours Su at 11am, W at 2:30pm. DM5, students DM2.50.)

♪ ENTERTAINMENT

Köln explodes in celebration during **Karneval,** a week-long pre-Lenten festival. Celebrated in the hedonistic spirit of the city's Roman past, Karneval is made up of 50 neighborhood processions in the weeks before Ash Wednesday. **Weiberfastnacht,** Feb. 21, 2001, is the first major to-do; the mayor mounts the platform at Alter Markt and abdicates leadership of the city to the city's *Weiber* (an archaic and not-too-politically-correct term for women). They then traditionally go and find their husbands at work and chop their ties off. In the afternoon, the first of the big parades begins at Severinstor. The weekend builds up to the out-of-control parade on **Rosenmontag,** the last Monday before Lent (Feb. 26, 2001). Everyone's in costume and gets and gives a couple dozen *Bützchen* (Kölsch dialect for a kiss on a stranger's cheek). Arrive early, get a map of the route, and don't stand anywhere near the station or cathedral—you'll be pulverized by the crowds. While most revelers nurse their hangovers on Shrove Tuesday, pubs and restaurants set fire to the straw scarecrows hanging out their windows. For more information on the festival and tickets to events, inquire at the **Festkomitee des Kölner Karnevals,** Antwerpener Str. 55 (☎57 40 00), or pick up the Karneval booklet at the tourist office.

Köln's traditional entertainment is a site of fierce competition with more than 30 theaters, including the **Oper der Stadt Köln** and **Kölner Schauspielhaus** near Schildergasse on Offenbachpl. The **box office** for the Schauspielhaus sells tickets for both. (☎84 00. Open M-Sa 9am-2pm.) **KölnTicket,** a ticket agent located in the same building as the Römisch-Germanisches Museum (see p. 452), sells tickets for the opera and everything else too—Köln's world-class **Philharmonie,** open-air rock concerts, and everything in between. (☎28 01. Open M-W and F 9am-6:30pm, Th 9am-8pm, and Sa 9am-4pm.) For more on Köln's theaters, check the *Monatsvorschau,* available at the tourist office. For information on special summertime productions, check out the KölnTicket's website: www.koelnersommerfestival.de. The **Cinemathek** (☎257 59 21) entrance is on the ground floor of the three-museum building in Heinrich-Böll-Pl.; current movies are screened almost daily, with most films in the original language. **Metropolis** (☎72 24 36), on Ebertpl., shows mostly English language movies. From Apr. to Oct, catch the **craft market** the last weekend of every month in the *Altstadt,* around Groß St. Martin church (see p. 451).

♦ NIGHTLIFE

Celebrating with lavish festivities has long been a tradition in Köln. Roman mosaics dating back to AD 3 record the wild excesses of the city's early residents. But instead of grape-feeding and fig-wearing, modern life in Köln now focuses on house music and a more sophisticated bump-and-grind. The closer to the Rhein or Dom you venture, the more quickly your wallet gets emptied. Students congregate in the **Bermuda-Dreieck** (triangle). The area is bounded by Zülpicherstr., Zülpicherplatz, Roonstr., and Luxemburgstr. The center of gay nightlife runs up Matthiasstr. to Mühlenbach, Hohe Pforte, Marienpl., and up to the Heumarkt area by *Deutzer Brücke.* Radiating westward from Friesenpl., the **Belgisches Viertel** is spiced with slightly more expensive bars and cafes.

Worshippers of Bacchus boozed themselves into stupors here, and the tradition of getting plastered is still highly practiced in Köln. At the various *Brauhäuser,* where the original *Kölsch* is brewed, waiters will greet you with a friendly "Kölsch?" and then proceed to bring one glass after another until you fall under the table unless you place your coaster over your glass. Make sure that the lines on your coaster correspond to the number of beers you actually drank—it's said they might count on the fact that you won't be able to count.

Café Waschsalon, Ehrenstr. 77 (☎13 33 78). Filled with decorative washing machines; turn on the spin cycle in your head with their drinks. Breakfast served until 4pm. Lunch from DM8. Open M-Th 8am-1am, F 8am-3am, Sa 10am-3am, Su 10am-1am.

Das Ding, Hohenstaufenring 30-32 (☎24 63 48). Smoky, and very *noir*. Techno and other flavors. A popular bar and disco for students. Open M and W 9pm-2am, Tu and Th-Su 9pm-3am. Cover DM8.

Papa Joe's Jazzlokal, Buttermarkt 37 (☎257 79 31), defines Köln's jazz scene with traditional, high-caliber live jazz and oodles of New Orleans atmosphere. Live music nightly. For diehards, "Non-Stop Jazz" M-Sa after 8pm, Su after 3:30pm. Open M-Sa 7pm-2am, Su 3:30-11pm. No cover.

MTC, Zülpicherstr. 10 (☎240 41 88). A veritable smörgåsbord of olfactory and ol' factory fun. Schizophrenic musical offerings, alternating between punk/grunge, rock 'n' roll, live concerts, and recorded bar tunes. Open M, W, and Su 9pm-2am, Tu and Th-Sa 9pm-3am. Cover DM6, including one drink.

Taco Loco, Zülpicherstr. 4a (☎240 15 16). With a daily happy "hour" from 6-8pm and tasty margaritas, it's not just the tacos that get crazy here. Generous nacho dishes satisfy late-night hunger. Livin' la...ah, shyat up. Ricky not included. Open M-Th and Su 10am-2am, F-Sa 10am-3am.

Broadway, Ehrenstr. 11 (☎25 52 14). Appropriately located in a gutted theater box-office, the funky cafe with movie-marquee decor is haunted by Köln's hippest artists and intellectuals. Open M-Sa 10am-12:30am, Su 3pm-12:30am.

Café Stövchen, Ursulakloster 4-6 (☎13 17 12; www.stoevchen.de), in the shadow of the *Ursulakirche*. A laid back coffee shop by day, a slightly swankier beer bar by night. Sink into a couch, beer in hand, and lay down some smack at *Jenga* or *Othello*. Local flavor, in the scene as well as the small menu. Open M-F 11am-1am, Su 10am-1am.

The Corkonian, Alter Markt 51 (☎257 69 31). A change of pace. Not a *Biergarten*, a *Bierstube*, or *Kneipe*, the Corkonian is pure *pub*. Throw in your lager for a dark beer topped with a clover. Open M-Th noon-1am, F-Sa noon-3am, and Su 11am-1am. After 8pm 20+.

GAY AND LESBIAN VENUES

Vampire, Rathenaupl. 5 (☎240 12 11). The gay and lesbian bar has such a chill atmosphere and dark, soothing interior that anyone should come to enjoy a delicious holy water, and another... Happy hour 8-9pm. Disco F and Sa. Open Tu-Th and Su 8pm-1am, F-Sa 8pm-3am. No garlic.

Gloria, Apostelnstr. 11 (☎258 36 56). Crowded, popular, and plastered with cellophane wall-coverings, the cafe and occasional club is at the nexus of Köln's trendy gay and lesbian scene. Open M-Th 9am-1am, Su 10am-1am. Cover around DM15.

TIMP, Heumarkt 25 (☎258 14 09; www.timp.de), right across from the bus stop. This outrageous gay-friendly club attracts crowds by hosting nightly cabaret shows for no cover. Shows daily from 1am-4am.

Star-Treff, Alte Wallgasse (☎25 50 63), at the corner of Ehrenstr. This schmaltzy gay-friendly cabaret shines with lavish drag shows in an ocean of cigarette smoke and red velvet. Showtimes W-Th and Su 8pm, F-Sa 7pm and 10:10pm.

BONN   ☎0228

No longer Germany's capital, Bonn can finally go back to just being Bonn instead of being pointedly not Berlin. Known derisively for the past 50 years as the *Hauptdorf* (capital village), Bonn was basically a non-entity before falling into the limelight by chance. Konrad Adenauer, the Federal Republic's first chancellor, resided in the suburbs, and the ever-considerate occupying powers made Bonn the "provisional capital" of the Western Occupation Zone before they baptized it as the capital of the fledgling Republic. The summer of 1991 brought headlines of "Chaos in Bonn" as Berlin fought for the right to reclaim the seat of government in a political catfight that cleaved every party from the CDU to the

Greens. By the narrowest of margins, Berlin won. In 1999, the *Bundestag* packed up and moved on. Bonners have taken the loss well. Although Berliners joke that Bonn is "half the size of a Chicago cemetery and twice as dead," the sparkling streets of the *Altstadt* bustle with notable energy and eclecticism. The well-respected university and excellent museums bolster a thriving cultural scene. Bonn is fast becoming a center for Germany's computer-technology industry, and is nursing a hip cyber-culture.

GETTING THERE AND GETTING AROUND

The **Regio Bonncard,** available in the tourist office for DM24 per day, covers transportation costs after 9am (all day Sa-Su) and admission to more than 20 museums in Bonn and the surrounding area. For DM46 get the *Regio Bonncard* for a three-day period instead.

Flights: Köln-Bonn Flughafen (☎(02203) 40 40 01 02). Bus #670 runs from the train station. Every 20min. 5am-10pm. DM12.60, children DM6.30.

Trains: Trains depart for **Köln** (30min., 6 per hr., DM10), **Koblenz** (1hr., 3 per hr., DM14.80), and **Frankfurt** (1½hr., 1 per hr., DM59).

Public Transportation: Bonn is linked to Köln and other riverside cities by the massive **VRS** *(Verkehrsverbund Rhein-Sieg)* S-Bahn and U-Bahn network. Areas are divided into **Tarifzonen;** the farther you go, the more you pay. Single tickets (DM2.20-14.20), 4-ride tickets (DM8-12.80), and day tickets (DM9.50-35) are available at *Automaten* and designated vending stations. With the *Minigruppenkarte* (DM13-36 per day) 5 people can ride M-F after 9am and all day on weekends. Stop by the **Reisezentrum** under the train station to pick up a network map. Open M-Sa 5:30am-10pm, Su 6:30am-10pm.

Taxi: Funkzentrale, ☎55 55 55. The funk never grows old.

Car Rental: Hertz, Avis, InterRent Europcar, and **Alamo** have airport offices. **Kurscheid** (see **Bike Rental,** below) also rents cars.

Mitfahrzentrale: Herwarthstr. 11 (☎69 30 30), behind the train station, matches riders and drivers. Open M-F 10am-6pm, Sa 10am-2pm, Su for phone calls only 11am-2pm.

Bike Rental: Kurscheid, Römerstr. 4 (☎63 14 33), charges DM15 per day and offers a DM20 weekend special. Also rents cars. ID required for both. Open M-Sa 7am-7pm, Su 9am-1pm and 3-7pm.

Internet Cafe: Surf Inn, on the second floor of the SportArena. Remgiusstr. 6-8, (☎516 513). 15min for DM2, 30min for DM3.

PRACTICAL INFORMATION

Tourist Office: Windeckstr. 2 (☎1 94 33 or 77 50 00; fax 77 50 77; email bonninformation@bonn.de; www.bonn-region.de), am Münsterpl., near the big cathedral. The staff doles out free maps or fantastic maps (DM1), offers tours (daily Apr.-Oct., pick from eleven different tours) and **books rooms** for a DM3-5 fee (☎910 41 60). Open M-F 9am-6:30pm, Sa 9am-4pm, Su 10am-2pm.

Budget Travel: STA Travel, Kaiserstr. 22 (☎22 14 71) Open M-F 9am-6pm, Sa 10am-noon.

Bookstore: The mammoth **Bouvier,** Am Hof 28 (☎729 01 64), has a wide range of foreign books on the top floor. Open M-F 9:30am-8pm, Sa 9:30am-4pm.

Gay and Lesbian Resources: Schwulen- und Lesbenzentrum, Am Frankenbad 5 (☎63 00 39; fax 65 00 50; www.zentrumbonn.de, www.lesbenbonn.de), is located in a *Mobil Autoöl* parking lot. From Münsterpl., follow Windeckstr., which becomes Sternstr., to Berliner Pl. Cross Berliner Pl. to Bornheimer Str. and after about 3 blocks take a right on Adolfstr.; Am Frankenbad is 2 blocks down the street and to the left (about 15min.). For **counseling** call 194 46; **gay assault hotline** 192 28. Open M-Tu and Th 8pm-midnight, W 7pm-midnight.

Women's Resources: Frauenberatungstelle, Kölnstr. 69 (☎65 95 00). Open M and Th 5-7:30pm, W and F 10am-noon.

Laundromat: Eco-Express Waschsalon, Bornheimer Str. 56 (☎24 02 333). Wash DM5, with soap DM6, dry DM1 per 10min. Open 6am-11pm. Last wash at 10:15pm.

Emergency: Police, ☎110. **Fire** and **Ambulance,** ☎112.

Pharmacy: Bahnhof-Apotheke Poststr. 19. A list of night pharmacies is posted on the door. Open M-W and F 8:30am-7pm, Th 8:30am-7pm, Sa 9am-4pm.

Post Office: Münsterpl. 17, 53111 Bonn. Walk down Poststr. from the station. Open M-F 8am-8pm, Sa 8am-4pm.

ACCOMMODATIONS AND CAMPING

Most hotels in Bonn are tailored to wealthy tax-subsidized politicians, a vestige of its capital days. With one *Jugendgästehaus* but no *Jugendherberge*, even hosteling gets expensive in Bonn.

Jugendgästehaus Bonn-Venusberg (HI), Haager Weg 42 (☎28 99 70; fax 289 97 14; email jgh-bonn@t-online.de), is far from the center of town. Take bus #621 (direction: "Ippendorf Altenheim") to "Jugendgästehaus," or bus #620 (direction "Venusberg/Klinikum") to "Sertürnerstr.," turn left on Haager Weg and walk for 10min. A sparkling, super-modern place in the suburbs; it even has glass doors that slide open automatically and a nightly bar. Wheelchair accessible. Breakfast and sheets included. Laundry DM10. Reception 9am-1am. Curfew 1am. Dorm beds DM39.

Hotel Mozart, Mozartstr. 1 (☎65 90 71 74; fax 65 90 75). From the south exit of the station turn right onto Herwarthstr., left on Bachstr., then right on Mozartstr. From the piano in the front foyer to the large, trim rooms, this hotel delivers just the kind of Viennese elegance you'd expect in such a conveniently located, classical neighborhood. Breakfast included. Singles DM75-88, with bath DM135-150; doubles DM105-115, with bath DM165-185.

Hotel Bergmann, Kasernenstr. 13 (☎63 38 91; fax 63 50 57). From the station follow Poststr., turn left at Münsterpl. on Vivatsgasse, then right on Kasernenstr.; after 10min., the hotel is on the left. Cozy, elegant rooms. *Very* pink bathrooms in the hall. Reception hours sporadic—call ahead. Singles DM60, doubles DM95.

Hotel Virneburg, Sandkaule 3a (☎63 63 66). Walk up Poststr. and bear right on Acherstr. at the north end of Münsterpl. Turn left on Rathausgasse and left again on Belderberg, which runs into Sandkaule. Or take U-Bahn #62, 66, or 67 to "Bertha-von-Suttner-Platz." Functional rooms, unbeatable price and location. Breakfast included. Singles DM35-45, with shower DM55-65; doubles DM65-70, with shower DM90-95.

Hotel Hofgarten, Fritz-Tillman-Str. 7 (☎22 34 82 or 22 34 72; fax 21 39 02). From the station turn right onto Maximilianstr., continue on Kaiserstr., and then turn left on Fritz-Tillman-Str. Live like an ambassador in this stately hotel. A fabulous splurge. Breakfast included. Call ahead. Singles DM60-140; doubles DM125-185.

Camping: Campingplatz Genienaue, Im Frankenkeller 49 (☎34 49 49). U-Bahn #16 or 63 to "Rheinallee," then bus #613 (direction: "Giselherstr.") to "Guntherstr." Turn left on Guntherstr. and right on Frankenkeller. Rhein-side camping in the suburb of Mehlem. Reception 9am-noon and 3-10pm. DM8 per person. Tent DM5-8.

FOOD

The **market** on **Münsterplatz** teems with haggling vendors and determined customers trying to get the best meat, fruit, and vegetables at the lowest prices. At the end of the day voices rise and prices plummet (open M-Sa 9am-6pm). There is also a **supermarket** located in the basement of the *Kaufhof* department store on Münsterpl. (open M-F 9:30am-8pm, Sa 9am-4pm).

Mensa, Nassestr. 11, a 15min. walk from the station along Kaiserstr. In Bonn's glory days it swung with cosmopolitan flair. Reagan would sip *Dom Perignon* out of Maggie

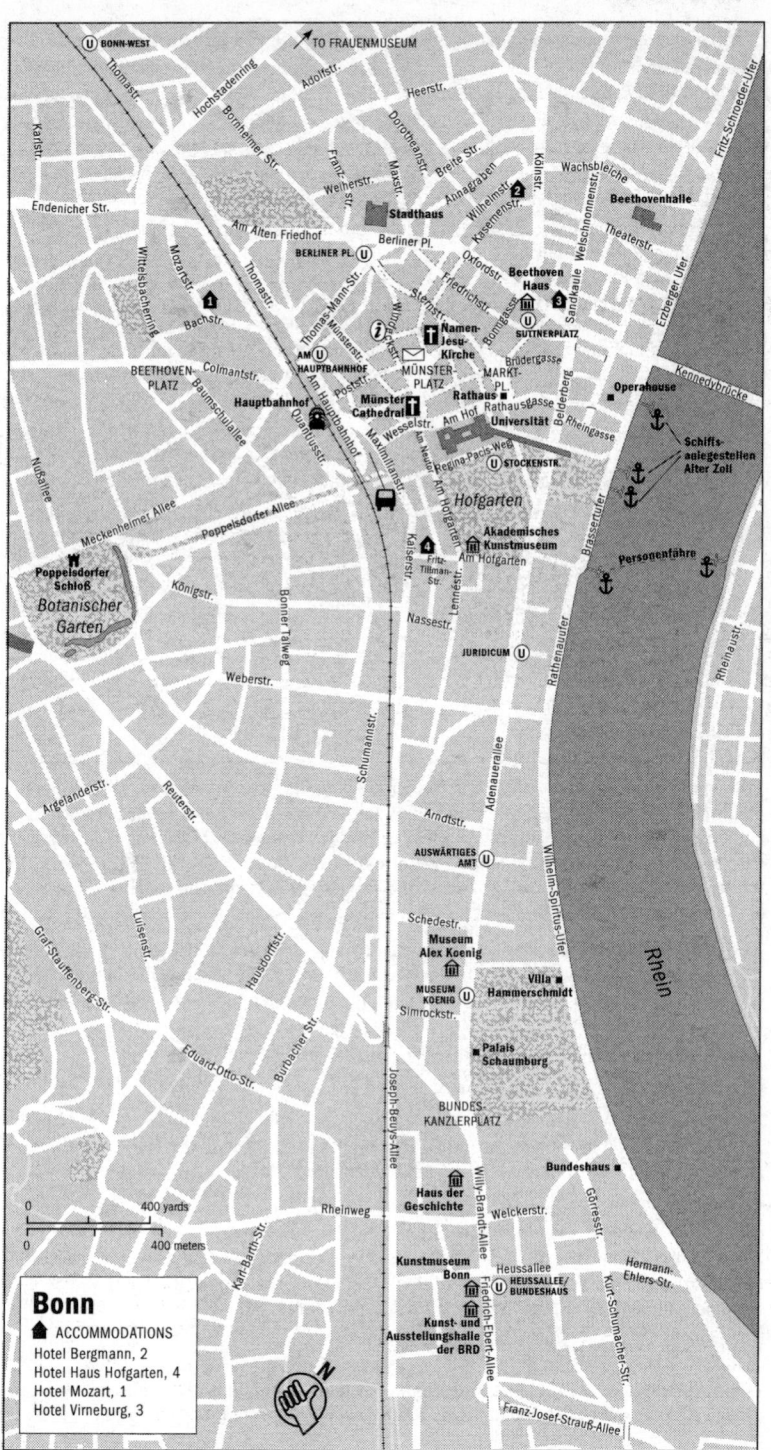

Bonn

ACCOMMODATIONS
Hotel Bergmann, 2
Hotel Haus Hofgarten, 4
Hotel Mozart, 1
Hotel Virneburg, 3

Thatcher's stilleto heels, and Helmut Kohl would lead the crowd in a round of bawdy German drinking songs. Now, it's just another *Mensa*. Pick up a monthly menu. Cheap meals DM2-5.50. DM1 extra for non-students. Lunch M-Th 11:30am-2:15pm, F 11:30am-2pm, Sa noon-1:45pm. Dinner M-F 5:30-7:30pm.

■ **Cafe-Bistro Bonngoût,** Remigiuspl. 2-4 (☎65 89 88) serves well-presented, generous meals in an attractive setting. Wash it down with a selection of alcoholic drinks, coffees, and refreshing milkshakes. Sit outside or enjoy the same kind of view through the floor-to-ceiling windows. Huge breakfasts (DM8-18) served M-F until noon, Sa until 1pm, Su until 3pm. M-Sa 9am-1am, Su 10am-1am.

Carl's Mensa-Bistro, Nassestr. 15, has restaurant-quality meals served cafeteria-style at a price only slightly more expensive than the Mensa. Chili and burritos DM6-7, burgers DM6-8, steaks DM6-11, salad DM1.20 per 100g. Open M-Th 10:30am-10pm, F 10:30am-3pm. Hot food served from 11:30am-½hour before closing.

Cassius-Garten, Maximilianstr. 28d, at the edge of the Altstadt facing the station. A scrumptious veggie bar where zealous disciples of health consume 50 kinds of salads (or create their own), noodles, and whole-grain baked goods in a sunny cafe off an atrium. DM2.70 per 100g. Careful on your first time through: the weight really adds up. Bistro open M-F 9am-8pm, Sa 9am-4pm, restaurant open M-Sa from 11:30am.

Café Blau, Franziskanerstr. 5 (☎65 07 17), across from the university. Serves light meals (breakfast DM2.50-6, salads DM5-11, crepes DM7-8), and fills up with loud crowds of students in the evening. Open daily 9am-1am.

Brauhaus Bönnsch, Sterntorbrücke 4 (☎65 06 10), pours its own highly civilized *Bönnsch*, the smooth-as-butter illegitimate son of Köln's *Kölsch* (DM2.50 for 0.2L). The delicious *Bönnsche Flammkuchen,* made from a 250-year-old Alsatian recipe, comes in many vegetarian (and non-vegetarian) varieties (DM13-17). Open M-Th and Su 11am-1am, F-Sa 11am-3am.

🔎 SIGHTS

The postwar architectural mandate to turn this small city into a world-class capital produced goofy results. While most of Bonn's bureaucracy has been packed up and shipped out, the hulls remain; most of the governmental buildings now serve as ministries, easing the transition from capital to government-lite. These erst-while seats of power have a historical and novelty factor, but the castles, palaces, and museums that lend Bonn its cultural wealth lie just outside the city center.

BEETHOVENHAUS. Attracting music aficionados of all sorts, this museum, located in the house where Beethoven was born, hosts a fantastic collection of the composer's personal effects—from his primitive hearing aids to his first violin. Check out the face casts upstairs to get a picture of the man behind the music. The symphonic ghost haunts Bonn annually during the **Beethoven Festival.** The first fête, in 1845, was a riot, with Franz Liszt brawling with French nationalist Berlioz while King Ludwig's mistress Lola Montez table-danced. Call the tourist office or the Beethoven festival information hotline (☎20 10 345) for information. *(Bonngasse 18-20. ☎981 75 25. Open Apr.-Sept. M-Sa 10am-6pm, Su 11am-4pm; Oct.-Mar. M-Sa 10am-5pm, Su 11am-4pm. Last entry one hour before closing. DM8, students DM6.)*

RATHAUS. This Baroque building is pink, white, and gold, and in many ways rem-iniscent of a voluptuous birthday cake. The town hall presides over the Markt-platz; in the similarly colorful 60s, de Gaulle, Kennedy, and Elizabeth II visited together for a photo-op. The Marktplatz pavilion and the scenic *Rathaus* as back-drop provide a performance space for town presentations.

MÜNSTER. The cathedral holds three stories of arches within arches that finally yield a gorgeous gold-leaf mosaic; a 12th-century cloister laced with crossways and latticed passages branches off under the doorway labeled "Kreuzgang." Keep an eye out for the incongruous blue-red Expressionist windows. *(Münsterpl., or Ger-*

hard-von-Are-Str. 5. ☎ 98 588 10; fax 98 588 33; email pfarrbuero@bonner-muenster.de. Cloister open M-Sa 9am-5:30pm, Su 1:30-6pm.)

BUNDESTAG. In its governmental heyday, the vaguely *Bauhaus* structure earned the title of "least prepossessing parliament building" in the world. *(Take U-Bahn #16, 63, or 66 to "Heussallee/Bundeshaus" or bus #610 to "Bundeshaus.")*

PALAIS SCHAUMBURG. Come see the former home of the German president! The less majestic **Denkmal** on the street outside the Palais was erected in honor of Konrad Adenauer, one of Germany and Bonn's most prominent personas. Nicknamed *der Alte* (the old guy), the postwar chancellor was Bonn's guiding light, but the 3m hollow-cheeked bust looks like a skull lifted from a pirate flag. Engraved into his cranium are allegorical figures—various animals, a pair of bound hands, and two French cathedrals. *(Adenauerallee 135-141.)*

OTHER SIGHTS. Forty thousand students study within the **Kurfürstliches Schloß**, the huge 18th-century palace now serving as the center of Bonn's **Friedrich-Wilhelms-Universität**. The *Schloß* is the gateway to the refreshing **Hofgarten** and **Stadtgarten**, forever filled with students and punks. To uncover Bonn's "other" palace, stroll down Poppelsdorfer Allee to the 18th-century **Poppelsdorfer Schloß**. The palace touts a French facade and an Italian courtyard, as well as beautifully manicured **botanical gardens**. *(Gardens open Apr.-Sept. M-F 9am-6pm, Su 9am-1pm; Oct.-Mar. M-F 9am-4pm. Su 9am-1pm. Free M-F, DM1 Su. Greenhouses open year round M-F 10:30am-noon and 2-4pm, Apr.-Sept. Su 9am-1pm also. Free.)*

🏛 MUSEUMS

Bonn's museums are superb. The city enjoyed nearly 50 years of generous federal funding, and much of this wealth has been channeled into more than 20 museums in Bonn and the surrounding region. The **"Museum Mile"** begins at the **Museum Alexander König**. Take U-Bahn #16, 63, or 66 to "Heussallee" or "Museum König." The **Bonncard** provides free admission to most museums.

▧ HAUS DER GESCHICHTE. A futuristic museum dedicated to critical and "interactive" German history. Thoughtful exhibits are highlighted by some antique VWs and a black enclosure with the scrolling names of Holocaust victims. *(Adenauerallee 250/Willy-Brandt 4. ☎916 50. 1 block from the Kunstmuseum. Open Tu-Su 9am-7pm. Free.)*

KUNSTMUSEUM BONN. A stunning contemporary building houses a superb selection of Expressionist and modern German art. *(Friedrich-Ebert-Allee 2. ☎77 62 60. Open Tu and Th-Su 10am-6pm, W 10am-7pm. DM5, students DM3.)*

KUNST-UND AUSSTELLUNGSHALLE DER BRD. The art here is so new you can smell the paint; check out the ultra-modern media-art room. The 16 columns flanking the *Ausstellungshalle* represent the 16 federal states of united Germany. *(Friedrich-Ebert-Allee 4. ☎917 12 00. Open Tu-W 10am-9pm, Th-Su 10am-7pm. DM10, students DM5.)*

MUSEUM ALEXANDER KOENIG. If taxidermy has a *Louvre*, this is it. Realistic and not at all creepy, the specimens in the exhibit are intriguing for anyone interested in animals. *(Adenauerallee 160. ☎912 22 15 or 912 22 19. Open Tu-F 9am-5pm, Sa 9am-12:30pm, Su 9:30am-5pm. DM4, students DM2.)*

FRAUENMUSEUM. The vast galleries glitter with interactive, modern art pieces by women. The second floor covers medieval art. Peculiar pieces on the roof and a Yoko Ono room provide more thought-provoking works. *(☎69 13 44. U-Bahn #61 to "Rosental/Herrstr." Open Tu-Sa 2-5pm, Su 11am-5pm. DM8, students DM5.)*

AKADEMISCHES KUNSTMUSEUM. Lazy sculpture fans can forget about going abroad to see the masterpieces because they're all here, in the largest collection of plaster casts in Germany. Exhibits include Venus de Milo, the Colossus of Samos, and Laocöon. *(On the far side of the Hofgarten, facing the Kufürstliches Schloß. ☎73 77 38. Open M-W, F, and Su 10am-1pm, Th 10am-1pm and 4-6pm. DM1, students free.)*

NORDRHEIN-WESTFALEN

NIGHTLIFE

Bonn's bombastic and versatile nightlife forcefully debunks myths suggesting that the city is boring. Of Bonn's monthly glossies, *Schnüss* is unbeatable; it's more complete than the free *Szene Bonn*. Bonn's theater world is also very extensive; tickets for all performances can be bought at the tourist office through **BonnTicket.**

The Jazz Galerie, Oxfordstr. 24 (☎ 65 06 62). A hub for jazz and rock concerts, or a jumping bar and disco. Open daily M-Th and Su 9pm-3am, F-Sa 9pm-4am. On concert nights opens at 8pm, but shows begin around 9:15pm. Cover for concerts DM10-20, for discos DM13, with 2 free drinks.

Pantheon, Bundeskanzlerplatz (☎21 25 21), in the shadow of an enormous *Mercedes* logo. Follow Adenauer-Allee out of the city until you reach Bundeskanzlerpl. The popular disco caters to eclectic tastes; it hosts concerts, stand-up comedy, and art exhibits. Open M-Sa 8pm-3am. Cover DM10.

Café Gottlich (☎65 99 69), on tiny Fürstenstr. behind the *Rathaus* and near the university. Serves drinks into the wee hours of the morning. Open M-Sa 9am-4am, Su noon-2am. Restaurant open M-Sa noon-3:30pm and 6pm-midnight, Su 6pm-midnight.

Schicht N8, Bornheimer Str. 20-22 (☎963 83 08). Quirkiest club in Bonn. Themed evenings range from Britpop parties to Gothic-industrial "funerals." Open daily 10pm-5am. Cover Sa-Su DM5.

Sharlies, Theaterstr. 2 (☎69 07 61; email sharliebn@aol.com; home.t-online.de/home/sharlie.bonn), at the corner of Theaterstr. and Kölner Str. Hopping gay and lesbian bar. Open M-Th 9pm-3am, F-Sa 9pm-5am, Su 9pm-1am.

Café Z, in the **Schwulen- und Lesbenzentrum** (see p. 455). This upstairs bar with colorful wall art hosts gay night Tu, youth-group (ages 16-27) W, and mixed gay-lesbian Th. Lesbian party 2nd Sa in the month. Open M-Tu and Th 8pm-midnight, W 9pm-midnight.

DAYTRIP: KÖNIGSWINTER AND DRACHENFELS

"The castled crag of Drachenfels frowns o'er the wide and winding Rhein," wrote Lord Byron in *Childe Harold's Pilgrimage*. According to the *Nibelungenlied* and to local lore, epic hero Siegfried slew a dragon who once haunted the crag. Siegfried then bathed in the dragon's blood and would have been invincible if not for the bare spot left by a leaf on his back. The ruins and the incredible view of the **Drachenfels** can be reached from Bonn and **Königswinter,** the town in the valley below the ruins. From Bonn, take U-Bahn #66 (direction: "Königswinter/Bad Honnef") to "Königswinter Fähre" (30min., every 20min., DM5.30). Or take the **Bonner Personen Schiffahrt** ferry (DM13.50 round trip; leaves 4 times a day, up to 8 times a day in later summer). From Königswinter, follow Drachenfelsstr. (about 45min.). The less energetic take the **Drachenfelsbahn,** Drachenfelsstr. 53, a railway leading to the top. (☎(02223) 920 90. DM11 up, DM9 down, DM14 round-trip.) Or ride a donkey. But they poop a lot. The **Nibelungshalle,** where the dragon once munched on tasty young virgins, is now a **reptile zoo** and **museum** with more than 150 live reptiles. (☎(02223) 241 50. Open mid-Mar. to mid-Nov. daily 10am-6pm; mid-Nov. to mid-Mar. Sa-Su 11am-4pm. DM6, students DM5.) The *Drachenfels'* little brother **Schloß Drachenburg** (☎90 19 70), an impressive nineteenth-century castle, raises its ornate turrets halfway between the museum and ruin. Tours through the castle's fine interior depart hourly. (Open Apr.-Oct. Tu-Su 11am-6pm. Tours of the castle DM4, students and children DM3, or just DM1 to stroll through the grounds.)

AACHEN ☎ 0241

Aachen jives day and night in four different languages, exuding a youthful internationalism in spite of its age. The town lies at Germany's borders with the Netherlands and Belgium, which accounts for noticeable French influences. Charlemagne and made Aachen the capital of his Frankish empire in the 8th century; his palace and an impressive cathedral are Aachen's big attractions. Though it has been tossed back and forth among empires for centuries, Aachen has held onto its historical treasures, ranging from Roman ruins to medieval architecture to the remains of great kings. Though Charlemagne (and all his pieces) have given the city its place on the map, Aachen has drawn flocks of pilgrims since Roman times for its magnificent thermal baths. In the midst of all this history Aachen is also renowned as a thriving forum for modern, up-and-coming European artists. The sights and tastes of Aachen make it a beautiful daytrip from nearby Köln or a relaxing and fulfilling longer stay, with Tivoli and the Netherlands just a few blocks from your door.

GETTING THERE AND GETTING AROUND

Trains: Chug from Aachen to **Köln** (1hr., 2-3 per hr., DM20); **Brussels** (2hr., 1 per hr., DM51); and **Amsterdam** (4hr., 1-2 per hr., DM102). A **shuttle** (Airport Aixpress) goes to and from the Düsseldorf and the Köln/Bonn Airports. (☎18 20 00; fax 18 20 027; www.taeter.de).

Public Transportation: The main **bus** station is on the corner of Peterskirchhof and Peterstr. Tickets are priced by distance, with one-way trips running DM2.30-9.30. *24-Stunden* tickets provide a full day of unlimited travel within Aachen for DM8. For those under 21, a weekend pass for all buses can be purchased on Saturdays for DM5. Some hotels also offer a DM7 *Hotelgastkarte* good for 2 days of unlimited travel.

Mitfahrzentrale: Roermonder Str. 4 (☎194 40). Matches riders and drivers. Open M-Sa 10am-6pm; phone lines open 9am-9pm.

Bike Rental: Bike Shop, Pontstr. 141-149 (☎401 33 60). DM12 per day.

ORIENTATION AND PRACTICAL INFORMATION

Aachen is at the crossroads of Germany, Belgium, and the Netherlands. Many travelers cross the Dutch border to stock up on cheese.

Tourist Office: ☎180 29 60; fax 180 29 31. In the Atrium Elisenbrunnen on Friedrich-Wilhelm-Pl., an ivory colored pillared building. The office dispenses literature, runs **tours,** and finds **rooms** from DM35 for free. From the train station, cross the street and head up Bahnhofstr., turn left onto Theaterstr., which becomes Theaterpl., then right onto Kapuzinergraben, which becomes Friedrich-Wilhelm-Pl.; the atrium is to the left. Open M-F 9am-6pm, Sa 9am-2pm.

Currency Exchange: At the post office in the train station. Open M-F 9am-6pm, Sa 9am-1pm, Su 10am-noon. Also at the **Hauptpostamt** near the tourist office.

Gay and Lesbian Resources: Schwulenreferat, Kasinostr. 37 (☎346 32). Hosts a weekly cafe Tu after 8pm. Office open Tu 8-9pm, Th noon-2pm.

Laundromat: SB Waschsalon, Jülicher Str. 3. Wash DM5, DM4 on Wednesday. Dry DM1 per 10min. Open M-Sa 8:30am-10pm.

Emergency: Police, ☎110. **Fire** and **Ambulance,** ☎112.

Internet Access: Öffentliche Bibliothek, Couverstr. 15. City library open Tu-W and F 11am-5:45pm, Th 1:15-8pm, Sa 10am-1pm. DM6 per hr., but available from DM1. **The Web,** Kleinmarschierstr. 6. Open M-F 10am-11pm, Sa 10am-midnight, Su noon-8pm. DM8 per hr.

Post Office: **Hauptpostamt,** Kapuzinergraben, 52064 Aachen, to the left of the train station. Walk down Lagerhausstr., right down Franzstr., and then right on Kapuzinergraben. Open M-F 9am-6pm, Sa 9am-1pm.

■ ACCOMMODATIONS AND CAMPING

Aachen has too much history for a town of its size, and the oodles of visitors push the lodging prices up. The **Mitwohnzentrale,** Süsterfeldstr. 24 (☎87 53 46), sets up lodging for longer stays. Take bus #7 (direction: "Siedlung Schönau") or #33 (direction: "Vaals") to "Westbahnhof" (open M-F 9am-1pm and 3-6pm).

Euroregionales Jugendgästehaus, Maria-Theresia-Allee 260 (☎71 10 10; fax 71 19 120). Two buses go to the hostel leaving from the "Finanzamt" bus stop. To get to this departure point from the station, walk left on Lagerhausstr. until it intersects Karmeliterstr. and Mozartstr.; the bus stop will be on the other side of the street. Bus #2 (direction: "Preusswald") to "Ronheide" or #12 (direction: "Diepenbenden") to "Colynshof." Super-clean and bright, with interior decorating that would please Armani, and completely renovated facilities (including a bar with projection TV), this feels more like an expensive convention center than a youth hostel. The hostel's bistro is open from 4:30pm to 12:30am, providing a late night respite from the kiddie tour groups. Large breakfast buffet and sheets included. Laundry is DM3, including soap. Computer facilities also available. Curfew 1am. Dorm beds DM38.50.

Hotel Marx, Hubertusstr. 33-35 (☎375 41; fax 267 05). From the station, take a left on Lagerhausstr. which becomes Boxgraben. Turn right on Stephanstr., and then left on Hubertusstr. Friendly hotel with a great location 2 blocks from the Altstadt. Breakfast included. Singles with bath DM85; doubles DM110, with bath DM140.

Hotel Cortis, Krefelder Str. 52 (☎15 60 11; fax 15 60 12). From the central bus station, take bus #51 to "Tivoli." Backtrack down Krefelder Str. about 300m. Located outside Aachen proper, this hotel offers bright, comfortable rooms above a small bar. Breakfast included. 24hr. reception. Singles DM50-65; doubles DM75-120.

Hotel Am Tivoli, Krefelder Str. 86 (☎/fax 91 95 20 or 91 95 21). Bus #51 to "Tivoli"; backtrack 100m on Krefelder Str. and the hotel will be on your left. A small inn with local flavor. Breakfast included. Singles with bath DM65; doubles with bath DM100.

ETAP-Hotel, Strangenhäuschen 15 (☎91 19 29; fax 15 53 04). From the bus station, take bus #5 to "Strangenhäuschen." A chain, clean budget hotel far from the city center with rooms following a cookie-cutter pattern. Breakfast DM8.90. Reception 6:30-10am and 5-11pm. Checkout noon. Singles DM64; doubles DM76. F-Su all rooms DM64.

◗ FOOD

Much of **Pontstraße** seems to be an exercise in creating the perfect 90s cafe—Euro-simplistic furniture and signs cut from sheet metal and lit by fluorescent light are separated by more traditional *Imbiße* and cheap Italian pizza places. But beware—this region is also the prowling ground of the *Bahkauv*, a fearsome mythical blend of dog, puma, and dragon, which pounces on drunken revelers, inducing head-splitting hangovers. While in Aachen, be sure to try the native *Printen*, a tremendously appetizing (and addictive!) spicy gingerbread biscuit refined from an old Belgian recipe. It's now a world-famous snack with an annual production of 4,500 tons. For the budget traveler, **Plus,** Marienbongard 27, off Pontstr. and inside a small gallery, has an erratic selection of very cheap **groceries** (open M-F 8am-8pm, Sa 8am-4pm).

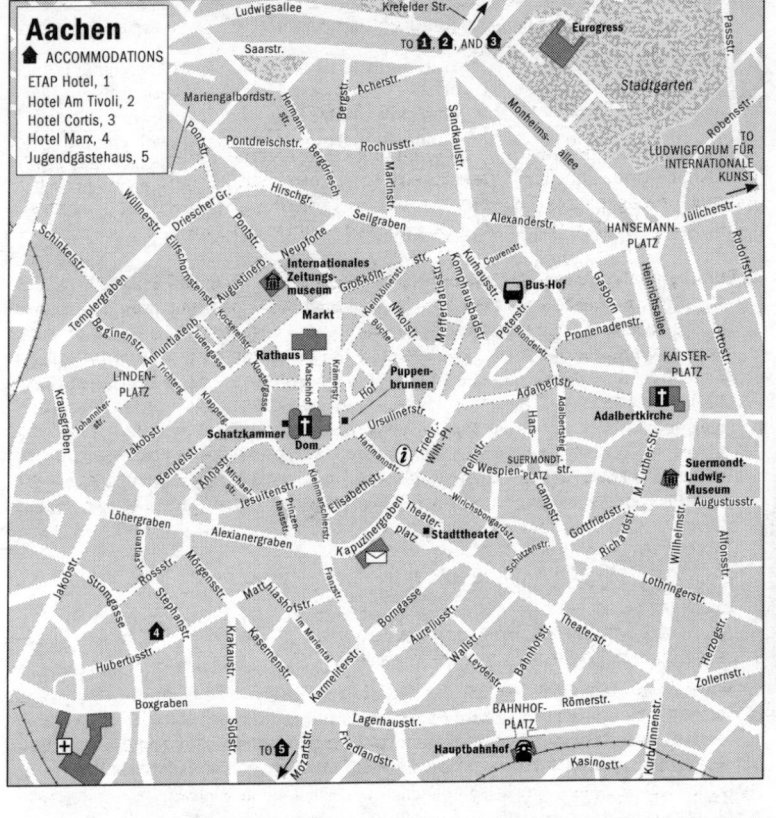

Aachen

🏠 ACCOMMODATIONS

ETAP Hotel, 1
Hotel Am Tivoli, 2
Hotel Cortis, 3
Hotel Marx, 4
Jugendgästehaus, 5

Mensa (☎ 80 37 92), in the green-trimmed building on Pontwall, near the Ponttor. Meals DM3-7.50. Open M-F 11:30am-2pm.

🖼 **Pera,** Marienbongard 2 (☎ 40 93 780), on the corner of Pontstr. Is it a Swedish furniture exhibition or a cafe? Minimalism reaches new heights here, but not on the drink list, which is as long as the bar stools are high. Dine on all sorts of generous Mediterranean dishes as you enjoy the classy atmosphere. Open daily 11am-1am.

Katakomben Studentenzentrum, Pontstr. 74-76 (☎ 470 01 41), encloses **Café Chico Mendes,** a vegetarian co-op cafe of the Catholic College. Entrees DM8-12. Half-off a very long list of drinks during the rare happy hour (Su 8:30-9:30pm). Open M-F 4:30pm-1am, Sa-Su 6pm-1am.

Van den Daele, Büchel 18-20 (☎ 357 24), just off the Markt. The finest selection of baked goods in Aachen's oldest house. Built in 1655, this *Printen* factory was made famous by artist/baker Leo van den Daele. The atmosphere is pure 18th-century, and the house speciality is *Reisfladden* (rice pudding)—DM4 buys you one huge slice. Open M-F 9am-7pm, Sa 9am-9pm, Su 11am-7pm.

🔆 SIGHTS

In 765, the Frankish King Pepin the Short took a dip in the hot springs north of Aachen's present city center. When his son **Charlemagne** (Karl der Große) assumed power, he made the family's former vacation spot the capital of the rapidly expanding kingdom, and later of the Holy Roman Empire. Many of Aachen's sights are heavily influenced by its early political importance.

■ DOM. The emperor's presence still dominates the city, in part through a local legend that claims that in WWII, a bomb aimed at the cathedral was deflected by a statue of Charlemagne. The 8th-century dome at its center tops three tiers of marble arches that separate the gilded roof from the mosaic floor. The careful golden mosaic tilework is awe-inspiring in its elegance. What you see there now is a reconstruction of the original ceilings; samples of the old mosaic tiles are kept in the Rathaus museum. The neo-Byzantine structure demonstrates Charlemagne's attempt to transplant the grandeur of Constantinople to his own capital. His throne on the second level is a simple chair of marble slabs. For a while, scientists and scholars weren't sure if the throne were actually Charlemagne's, or Otto III's. Careful carbon dating has shown it to be the seat of the infamous "big" king, who now is laid to rest (well, partially) in the large gold and jewelled reliquary casket behind the altar. Stained glass rings the 15th-century Gothic choir, a "new" addition to the church which was once the coronation place of kings and queens. (☎47 09 127; fax 477 09 150; www.aachendom.de. Open daily 7am-7pm; visiting hours, outside of service hours, 11am-7pm, Su 12:30-7pm. Tours M 11am and noon; Tu-F 11am, noon, 1, 2:30, and 3:30pm plus 4:30 and 5:30 on demand; Sa-Su 12:30, 1:30, 2:30, and 3:30pm. DM3 to get in above the first floor. A 3-in-1 ticket is available for DM15, DM9 for students, and is good for the Dom, Schatzkammer, and Rathaus, all within a few blocks of each other in the Altstadt.)

SCHATZKAMMER. Old Karl cuts even more of a figure in the Schatzkammer. The most famous likeness of the emperor, a gold-plated silver bust, was made in Aachen in 1349, donated by Charlemagne's successor Charles IV. Inside is Charlemagne's skull. The bust was carried to the city gates each time a new king was crowned so Charlemagne could "welcome" his successors. The crown jewels also shine brightly in this rich treasury, just around the corner from a gigantic golden arm statue that holds his radius and ulna bones. Other reliquaries hold bits and pieces of famous Jerusalemites—look for the remains of the Cross, nails, Christ's scourging robe, and John the Baptist's hair and ribs. (Klosterpl. 2. Around the corner to the right from the Dom, tucked into the Klostergasse. ☎477 09 127; fax 477 09 150. Open M 10am-1pm, Tu-W and F-Su 10am-6pm, Th 10am-9pm. Last entrance 30min. before closing. Tours must be arranged by phone. DM5, students, seniors, and children DM3.)

MARKTPLATZ. The 14th-century stone **Rathaus,** built on the ruins of Charlemagne's palace, looms over the wide Marktplatz beside the cathedral. Seventeenth-century citizens with a decorative obsession added Baroque flourishes to the facade. On the northern face stand 50 statues of former German sovereigns, 31 of whom were crowned in Aachen (not to mention the 12 queens who were also coronated here but didn't make the Rathaus cut). (☎432 73 10. Open daily 10am-6pm, Th until 9pm, last entrance 40min. before closing. DM3, students and children DM1.50.) A copy of the famed Charlemagne statue draws a picnicking crowd that sits in the square talking on cell phones and playing cards. The **Puppenbrunnen,** a fountain whose lovable characters represent Aachen's clever townspeople, spews forth at the intersection of Krämerstr. and Hofstr.

 MUSEUMS

Although the range of museums in Aachen is limited, the Altstadt shelters numerous little galleries worth browsing.

■ LUDWIGFORUM FÜR INTERNATIONALE KUNST. It's the building with the large clown in drag in front. The Forum follows a contemporary trend of scorning the title "museum," and its collection is cutting-edge. In the converted

Bauhaus umbrella factory, works of the current greats (Jeff Koons' gigantic sex dolls) are exhibited next to the soon-to-be-greats (a three-foot Marge Simpson stone fertility doll). For you traditional types, there's Renaissance art here too...on Band-Aids. **The Space,** underneath the museum, is a forum for dance, music, and theatre. *(Jülicher Str. 97-109. ☎ 180 71 04; fax 180 71 03; email ludwigforum@aachen.heimat.de; www.CONTINENTALSHIFT.org. Open Tu and Th 10am-5pm, W and F 10am-8pm, Sa-Su 11am-5pm. Tours Su 11:30am and 3pm. Last entrance 30min. before closing. DM6, students DM3.)*

INTERNATIONALES ZEITUNGSMUSEUM. "What's black and white and re(a)d all over?" This classy museum houses more than 120,000 different international newspapers, including press from the revolutions of 1848, the World Wars, the day Hitler died, and reunification. *(Pontstr. 13. Just up the street from the Markt. ☎ 432 45 08; fax 409 06 56. Open Tu-F 9:30am-1pm and 2:30-5pm, Sa 9:30am-1pm. Free.)*

SUERMONDT-LUDWIG-MUSEUM. The 14th-century statues placed in the distinctly contemporary interior are slightly disconcerting, but this recently expanded museum holds 44 galleries of sculptures, paintings, engravings, and crafts, starting with the modern and ending with the medieval. *(Wilhelmstr. 18. ☎ 47 98 00 or 47 98 020. Open Tu and Th-F 11am-7pm, W 11am-9pm, Sa-Su 11am-5pm. Last entry 30min. before closing. DM6, students and children DM3.)*

🎵🎭 ENTERTAINMENT AND NIGHTLIFE

Aachen has a lively theater scene, beginning with the **Stadttheater,** on Theaterplatz in the central city. (☎ 478 41; www.theater-aachen.de. Box office open M-Sa 9am-1pm, 5-7pm, and 30min. before performance.) Tickets range from DM16-51, with operas being the most expensive. Student rates, which are significantly cheaper, are available on tickets bought at the door. A small strip of newer, unconventional theaters lines **Gasborn,** spearheaded by the **Aachener Kultur-und Theaterinitiative,** Gasborn 9-11 (☎ 274 58). At night, the streets come alive as swarms of students hit the cafes and pubs for a study break with the *Bahkauv* (see **Food,** p. 462). *Klenkes Magazin* (DM4), available at most newsstands, offers readers movies and music listings galore. *Stonewall TAC,* available in most cafes near the university and at some newsstands, has a thorough listing of gay and lesbian events.

Atlantis, Pontstr. 141 (☎ 242 41), fills all entertainment needs with a multi-screen cinema, a mellow terrace cafe, a space-age underground *Kneipe,* and a grab-and-go bar outside the cinema for the requisite pre-movie beer run. Cafe and *Kneipe* open 9:30am-3am daily. Movie times vary—check out their weekly schedule.

Café Kittel, Pontstr. 39 (☎ 365 60). Posters smother the door with announcements for live music, parties, and special events in this cafe that is ever-so-slightly grittier than its neighbors; but this fact is made up for by an ever-so-friendly staff. Enjoy beer or coffee in the outdoor *Biergarten* or in the greenhouse. Drinks from DM2, pizza from DM8. Open M-Th 10am-2am, F-Sa 10am-3am, Su 11am-2am

Zum Eulenspiegel, Pontstr. 114 (☎ 373 97). Named after the mischievous German elf, this bar is proud of its laminated Ted Nugent album adorning the wall. On Thursday nights locals and tourists alike revel in *Kölsch* (DM2), *Hefeweizen* (DM3), Guinness (DM3), and a *really* inexpensive drink menu. Open daily 6pm-3am (or later).

B9, Blondelstr. 9. A fairly run-of-the-mill disco that fills nightly with students and Gen-Xers getting down to a diverse selection of music. Check any of the multi-colored party posters all over town. Open daily M-Th 10pm-3am, F-Sa 10pm-5am, drinks DM3.60-6.

NORDRHEIN-WESTFALEN

DÜSSELDORF
☎0211

As Germany's modish fashion hub and multinational corporation base, as well as the capital of densely-populated Nordrhein-Westfalen, the rich city of Düsseldorf crawls with German patricians and wanna-be aristocrats. Founded in the 13th century, the city has endured a series of terrific pummellings. Düsseldorf rebounded after suffering calamitous destruction during the Thirty Years War, the War of Spanish Succession, and WWII, each time with an indefatigable independence that translates into fierce pride among the city's residents. Set on the majestic Rhein, Germany's "Hautstadt" (a pun on *Hauptstadt* (capital) and the French *haute*, as in *haute culture*) is a stately, modern metropolis, with an Altstadt that sponsors the best nightlife along the Rhein in authentic German style. Some residents claim that Düsseldorf is not on the Rhein but on the Königsallee (also known as the Kö), a kilometer-long catwalk that sweeps down both sides of the old town moat. At night, propriety (and sobriety) are cast aside as thousands of Düsseldorfers flock to the 500 pubs in the Altstadt, trading their monocles and Rolexes for beer goggles and a very good time.

GETTING THERE AND GETTING AROUND

Flights: Frequent S-Bahn train #7, bus #727, and a Lufthansa shuttle travel from the main train station to **Flughafen Düsseldorf.** Call ☎421 22 23 for flight information. Open 5am-12:30am.

Trains: Düsseldorf is connected by train to **Frankfurt** (3hr., 3per hr., DM79, student DM65); **Hamburg** (3½hr., 2 per hr., DM116, student DM93); **Berlin** (4½hr., 1 or 2 per hr., DM170, student DM137); **Munich** (6hr., 2 or 3 per hr., DM184, student DM147); **Amsterdam** (3hr., 1 per hr., DM55); **Brussels** (3¼hr., 1 per hr., DM59); and **Paris** (4½hr., 7 per day, DM140). It's a little slower but cheaper to take the S-Bahn to **Aachen, Dortmund, and Köln.**

Public Transportation: The **Rheinbahn** includes subways, streetcars, buses, and the S-Bahn. Single tickets, DM2.10-12, depending on distance traveled. The Tagesticket (DM11-32, depending on distance traveled) is the best value—up to 5 people can travel for 24hr. on any line. Tickets are sold by vending machine; pick up the Fahrausweis brochure at the tourist office for instructions. Düsseldorf's S-Bahn is integrated into the mammoth regional **VRR** (*Verkehrsverbund Rhein-Ruhr*) system, which connects most surrounding cities. For schedule information, call ☎582 28.

Taxi: ☎33 333, or 99 999. Rhein-Taxi service ☎21 21 21.

Car Rental: Hertz, Immermannstr. 65 (☎35 70 25). Open M-F 7am-5pm, Sa 8am-noon. Rates start at DM400 per week.

Mitfahrzentrale: Konrad-Adenauer-Pl. 13 (☎37 60 81), to the left as you exit the train station, and upstairs over a tiny travel office. Arranges ride shares. Open daily 9am-6pm. **City-Netz Mitfahrzentrale,** Kruppstr. 102 (☎194 44), is a chain with slightly higher prices. Open M-F 9am-7pm, Sa 9am-2pm.

Bike Rental: Zweirad Egert, Ackerstr. 143 (☎66 21 34). S-Bahn #6 (direction "Essen") to "Wehrbahn," turn right from the exit on Birkenstr., then right onto Ackerstr. and walk 10min. Call ahead to check availability. Bikes DM23.30 per day, DM100 per week. DM50 deposit and ID required. Open M-F 9:30am-6:30pm, Sa 10am-2pm.

C'MON RIDE THE TRAIN. Riding the Düsseldorf subway is half practicality and half entertainment. Brand-new, huge high-definition television screens line the walls of the stations, displaying everything from weather forecasts to remarkably accurate horoscopes. Even cartoon shorts grace the screens, proving that the German travel authorities do indeed have a sense of humor—who knew? Nearby, Aachen's Hauptbahnhof subway station, lit entirely with fluorescent blue lights, is similarly entertaining, projecting cheery yellow streetcars that move back and forth while you wait for the real one to come along. If you're truly enjoying yourself in the station, gather your friends and stay all night—Deutsche Bahn's "Party Bahn" option allows devoted customers to rent a train car filled with drinks and music for an evening (☎ 194 40; conductors not included).

⁊ PRACTICAL INFORMATION

Tourist Office: Konrad-Adenauer-Pl. (☎ 17 20 20; fax 35 04 04; www.duesseldorf.de). Walk up and to the right from the train station and look for the Immermanhof building. This shiny office with friendly staff is a bastion of information, and its free monthly *Düsseldorfer Monatsprogramm* details all goings-on about town. Open for concert and theater ticket sales (12% fee...not a bad idea; at the door there is a 20% surcharge) and general services M-F 8:30am-6pm, Sa 9am-12:30pm. Books **rooms** (DM55 and up) for a DM5 fee M-Sa 8am-8pm, Su 2-8pm. The **branch office,** Heinrich-Heine-Allee 24 (☎ 899 23 46), specializes in cultural listings. Open M-F 9am-5pm.

Consulates: Canada and **UK,** Yorckstr. 19 (☎ 944 80). Open M-F 8:30am-noon. **US,** Kennedydamm 15-17 (☎ 47 06 10).

Currency Exchange: Deutsche Verkehrsbank, in the train station and the airport. Open M-Sa 7am-9pm, Su 8am-9pm.

American Express: Benzenbergstr. 39-47 (☎ 90 13 50). Mail held up to 4 weeks for card members. Open M-F 9am-6pm, Sa 10am-6pm, Su 9am-1pm.

Bookstore: Stern-Verlag, Friedrichstr. 24-28 (☎ 388 10). A good selection of paperbacks in many languages. Open M-F 9:30am-8pm, Sa 9:30am-4pm.

Women's Resources: Frauenbüro, Mühlenstr. 29 (☎ 899 36 03), 2nd floor, entrance next door to Mahn-und Gedenstätte. Walk-ins M-Th 8am-4pm, F 8am-2pm.

Gay and Lesbian Resources: Oberbilker Allee 310 (☎ 77 09 50). S-Bahn #6 to "Oberbilk" or U-Bahn #74 or 77 to "S-Bhf. Oberbilk." The **Aids-Hilfe Zentrum** is open M-Th 10am-1pm, and 2-6pm, F 10am-1pm, 2-4pm.

Laundromat: Wasch Center, Friedrichstr. 92, down the street from the Kirchpl. S-Bahn stop. Wash DM6. Dry DM1 per 15min. Soap included. Open M-Sa 6am-11pm.

Emergency: Police, ☎ 110. **Ambulance** and **Fire,** ☎ 112.

Pharmacy: Apotheke im Hauptbahnhof, open M-F 7am-8pm, Sa 8am-4pm. Staff speaks English. Closed pharmacies post lists of nearby open ones. **Emergency pharmacy,** ☎ 0115 00. **Emergency doctor,** ☎ 192 92.

Post Office: Hauptpostamt, Konrad-Adenauer-Pl., 40210 Dusseldorf, a stone's throw to the right of the tourist office. Open M-F 8am-6pm, Sa 9am-2pm. Limited service M-F 6-8pm. **Branch office** in Hauptbahnhof open M-F 8am-6pm, Sa-Su 2pm-midnight.

Internet Access: Convenient to the train station is **Telenet-Center,** Fritz-Vomfelde-Str. 34 (☎ 53 88 32 11; fax 53 88 32 13). Open daily 9am-11pm. DM3 per ½hour. Otherwise, Düsseldorfers do internet in the true cafe style; with plenty of food and drink to accompany those surfing hours. See **g@rden** (p. 473) or **Ratin Gate** (p. 470).

ACCOMMODATIONS AND CAMPING

Düsseldorf is a hugely popular international convention city where corporate crowds make rooms scarce and costly; it's not unusual for hotels to double their prices during a convention. Call at least a month ahead if possible. For a budget hotel stay, call the tourist office for trade fair dates and show up during a lull. Most rooms go for at least DM50 per person even in the off season. Fairly cheap hotels populate the seedy train station neighborhood.

Jugendgästehaus Düsseldorf (HI), Düsseldorfer Str. 1 (☎55 73 10; fax 57 25 13, email jgh-duesseldorf@t-online.de), is conveniently located just over the Rheinkniebrücke from the Altstadt. U-Bahn #70, 74, 75, 76, or 77 to "Luegplatz," then walk 500m down the BMW-lined Kaiser-Wilhelm-Ring. The hostel fills with whirlwind-tour-of-Europe groups making a pit stop in Düsseldorf. An unbeatable location makes up for moderately clean facilities and moderately high prices. Reception 7am-1am. Curfew 1am, but doors open every hour on the hour 2-6am. DM38, over 26 DM42.

Hotel Schaum, 63 Gustav-Poengsen Str. (☎31 16 510; fax 31 32 28). From the main train station, exit going left on Graf-Adolf-Str. Take your first left and follow it along the tracks to Gustav-Poengsen-Str. Or take the S-Bahn one stop to "Düsseldorf-Friedrichstadt," and exit onto Hüttenstr. You can see the large "Hotel" sign from there. Huge rooms and a friendly, family staff make this new hotel a great deal. TV, phone, and breakfast buffet included. Singles DM60, with bath DM80; doubles DM100-120.

Hotel Bristol, Aderstr. 8 (☎37 07 50; fax 37 37 54), 1 block south of Graf-Adolf-Str. at the bottom tip of Königsallee. The well-appointed and newly-renovated hotel offers large rooms and elegance in profusion—even by the Kö's standards. TV, phone, and breakfast included. Singles DM75-95; doubles DM120-140.

Hotel Manhattan, Graf-Adolf-Str. 39 (☎37 02 44; fax 37 02 47), 2 blocks from the station. The ghost of mid-1980s consumer America—the mirror-plated reception hallway reflects neon and Coca-Cola posters into infinity. The rooms are less glitzy, but no less chintzy; every room takes on some American character, and incorporates a Coke poster, of course. A young, lively hotel with seven floors of rooms. TV, phone, and breakfast buffet included. 24hr. reception. Singles DM68-105; doubles DM100-150.

Bahn-Hotel, Karlstr. 74 (☎36 04 713; fax 36 49 43). Coming out from the station on Konrad-Adenauer-Pl., turn right on Karlstr. A big orange sign welcomes you. Breakfast included. Singles DM80, with half-bath DM95, full bath DM130. Doubles are similarly DM110, DM120, and DM160. Triples DM190.

Hotel Diana, Jahnstr. 31 (☎37 50 71; fax 36 49 43), 5 blocks from the station. Head left down Graf-Adolf-Str., left on Hüttenstr., and then make a quick jog to the right on Jahnstr. Worn carpet, ugly tile, and really bad tapestry art, but it's all clean. Breakfast included. 24hr. reception. Singles DM65, with bath DM80-90; doubles DM90, with bath DM100-135.

Jugendherberge Duisburg-Wedau, Kalkweg 148e (☎(0203) 72 41 64; fax 72 08 34; www.jh-duisburg@dmx.net). S-Bahn #1 or 21 to "Duisburg Hauptbahnhof," then bus #934 to "Jugendherberge." Quite far from the city, the neighboring town of Duisburg is accessible by frequent streetcars (40min.), but public transportation closes by 1am and the hostel is too far for a taxi. Wash and dry DM2.50 each. Breakfast included. Reception 8am-10pm. Closed mid-Dec. to mid-Jan. DM27, over 26 DM32.

Hotel Amsterdam, Stresemannstr. 20 (☎840 58; fax 840 50), between Oststr. and Berliner Allee. From the station, start up Graf-Adolf-Str. and turn right at Stresemannstr. Recently renovated; now each room has a different color scheme. No-frills singles DM70, with TV and breakfast DM80-95; doubles DM140. Reception 7am-midnight.

Camping: Kleiner Torfbruch (☎899 20 38). S-Bahn to "Düsseldorf Geresheim," then bus #735 (direction: "Stamesberg") to "Seeweg." Pitch your palace and live like a king. DM7.50 per person, children DM4.50. DM10 per tent.

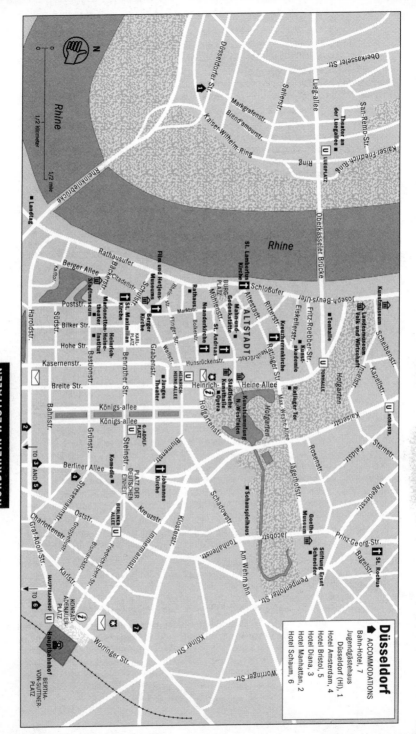

Düsseldorf

ACCOMMODATIONS
- Bahn-Hotel, 7
- Jugendgästehaus Düsseldorf (HI), 1
- Hotel Amsterdam, 4
- Hotel Bristol, 5
- Hotel Diana, 3
- Hotel Manhattan, 2
- Hotel Schaum, 6

FOOD

For a cheap meal, the endless eateries in the Altstadt can't be beat. Rows of pizzerias, *Döner* stands, and Chinese diners reach from Heinrich-Heine-Allee to the banks of the Rhein, supplying standing meals by day and standing beers by night. The **Markt** on Karlsplatz offers shoppers plenty of foreign fruits and a local favorite, *Sauerbraten* (pickled beef). To watch well-dressed people pay high prices for mediocre food, enjoy a cup of espresso on the **Kö**. Otto Mess, a popular **grocery** chain, should satisfy all your DIY needs. The most convenient location is at the eastern corner of Karlsplatz in the Altstadt (open M-F 8am-8pm, Sa 8am-4pm). Another supermarket is in the basement of the **Galeria Kaufhof**, on Bahnhofstr. between Oststr. and Berlinerstr. (open M-F 9:30am-8pm, Sa 9am-4pm).

La Copa, Bergerstr. 4 (☎323 88 58). Sammy, Deano, and Barry Manilow have left the building, but not without bequeathing their beloved Copa 50 tasty tapas dishes (DM8-15). Wash it down with sangría. Open daily noon-midnight.

Marché, Königsallee 60 (☎32 06 81), in the Kö-Galerie mall. If you must dine on the Kö, Marché, a classy cafeteria-style restaurant safely hidden in a corner far from Armani's gaze, is one of the few places you can eat without blowing a week's budget. Entrees from DM7. Open M-Th and Su 9am-9pm, F-Sa 9am-10pm.

Galerie Burghof, Burgallee 1-3 (☎40 14 23), in Kaiserwerth next to Friedrich's Rhein ruins. U-Bahn #79 to "Klemensplatz." Walk down Kaiserwerther Markt and turn left on the Rhein promenade. Somewhat touristy, but delicious pancakes, a marvelous view of the Rhein and the Kaiserwerth ruins, as well as a 1932 Rolls Royce filled with stuffed chickens and a wedding-gowned mannequin covered with butterflies make eating here an oddly visual experience. Open daily 11am-1am. Pancakes served M-F 6-10:45pm, Sa 2-10:45pm, Su 2-11pm.

Zum Uerige, Bergerstr. 1 (☎86 69 90). Some pheromone in the air inexplicably draws cool Germans to this seemingly average, heavy-wood, heavy-food restaurant. Try house specialties of *Blutwurst* (blood sausages; DM4) and Mainz cheese (DM4). When (if) you finish eating, settle down with a *Schlösser Alt* beer and soak up the crisp *Rheinisch* zephyrs. Open daily 10am-midnight. Kitchen open M-F 6-9pm, Sa 11am-4pm.

Zum Csikos, Andreasstr. 9 (☎32 97 71). This colorful little *Kneipe* is bursting with character and Hungarian food and drink. Try the *Gulyassuppe* (DM9) and watch out for famous *Düsseldorfers.* Open Tu-Su 6pm-3am.

Schnabelewojski, Bolkerstr. 53 (☎13 32 00), housed in Heinrich Heine's birthplace, has a smattering of cafe food and inexpensive wine, but its real draw is the "poetry cafe" at 8pm, the first Tuesday of each month, when customers read original or published poetry in many languages (snap your fingers, everyone...). Open M 4-11pm, Tu-F 3pm-midnight, Sa noon-1am, Su 11am-11pm.

Ratin Gate, Ratinger Str. 8 (☎32 20 40), is an internet cafe of the genuine variety; where food and drink accompany web-surfing. During happy "hour" (11pm-1am), it's not only the drinks, but also the web that's half-price. Internet access DM9 per hr., or DM5 for students. Open M-Th and Su 1pm-1am, F-Sa 1pm-3am.

SIGHTS

 **KÖNIGSALLEE.** The glitzy Kö, located just outside the Altstadt, embodies the vitality and glamour of wealthy Düsseldorf. While it doesn't have the fashion-center status of Milan or New York, it's just as glittery and twice as pretentious. If you don't get run over by models, you too can window-shop at Armani or ogle at the Beemer parked outside. *(Head 10min. down Graf-Adolf-Str. from the train station.)*

Properly called the Königsallee, the *belle époque* expanse was laid out over a century ago. Stone bridges span the little river that runs down the middle to trickle at the toes of a decadent statue of the sea god Triton. Midway up is the awesome **Kö-Galerie,** a gaudy marble-and-copper highbrow shopping mall of one haughty store after another. Items *start* at DM200, and even the mannequins have attitude.

SCHLOß BENRATH. The castle sits in the suburbs of Düsseldorf, a monument to the inadequacy complexes of the aristocracy. The castle was originally built 200 years ago as a pleasure palace and hunting grounds for Elector Karl Theodor. The architect used strategically placed mirrors and false exterior windows to make the squat, pink castle appear larger than it is, but the enormous, neurotically geometrical garden tempers the effect. *(S-Bahn #6 (direction: "Köln") to "Benrath." Castle open Tu-Su 10am-5pm. Tours every 30min. DM7, students and children DM3.50.)*

HEINRICH-HEINE-INSTITUT. Beloved poet **Heinrich Heine** is Düsseldorf's melancholic son. His birthplace and homestead are marked by plaques, and every third restaurant and fast-food stand bears his name. The institute is the official shrine, with a collection of manuscripts and an unsettling death mask. *(Bilker Str. 12-14. ☎899 55 71. Open Tu-Su 11am-5pm, Sa 1-5pm. DM4, students DM2.)*

KAISERWERTH. North on the Rhein but still within Düsseldorf dwell the **ruins** of Emperor Friedrich's palace in the tiny town of Kaiserwerth. Built in 1184, the palace was destroyed in 1702 in the War of Spanish Succession, but the gloomy frame remains. In case you're curious, the seemingly out-of-place **tower,** with the blinking lights visible from the Rhein at night, is actually a clock called the **Rheinturm.** From bottom to top, the dots represent one second, 10 seconds, one minute, 10 minutes, one hour, and 10 hours. *(Take U-Bahn #79 to "Klemenspl.," then follow Kaiserwerther Markt to the Rhein, and walk left another 150m.)*

HOFGARTEN. At the upper end of the Kö, the Hofgarten park is an oasis of green inside urban Düsseldorf and is the oldest public park in Germany. Stroll through to the eastern end of the garden, where the 18th-century **Schloß Jägerhof** houses the **Goethemuseum** (see **Museums,** see p. 472) behind its pink facade and white iron gates. The Hofgarten meets the Rhein at the Ehrendorf, museum plaza. The Neoclassical **Ratinger Tor** gatehouse leads into the garden from Heinrich-Heine-Allee. Twilight walks along the east bank of the Rhein are breathtaking.

BURGPLATZ. Farther up the Altstadt on the Rhein, Burgplatz used to be the site of a glorious castle, but tired citizens have saved only a single tower. The castle was built in 1324, burnt in 1490, rebuilt in 1559, razed in 1794, rebuilt in 1851, and flattened in 1872, at which point the townsfolk gave up—only the tower was reconstructed in 1900, and *that* was bombed to rubble in WWII. The pessimistic citizens waited until 1984 to rebuild the tower. The Burgplatz opens onto the scenic **Rheinuferpromenade,** a 2km walk that is second only to the Kö. The glittering river looks its best glamorously and romantically lit up at night; sit along the wall or in one of the many cafes along the promenade and admire.

EKO-HOUSE. Düsseldorf has the largest Japanese population of any European city. The EKO-House, across the Rhein from the Altstadt, is a beautiful garden and cultural center with frequent tea ceremonies and readings from Buddhist texts. *(Brüggener Weg 6. Take U-Bahn #70 or 74-77 to "Belsenpl." Follow Quirinstr. to Comeniuspl. and turn left again on Niederkasseler Str. ☎57 40 71. Open Tu-Su 1-5pm. DM5, students DM3.)*

🏛 MUSEUMS

Düsseldorf's museums are numerous, large, and good—not only are the Top 40 of the art world well represented, but so is anybody who ever influenced them. Art clusters around **Ehrenhof** above the Altstadt and **Grabbeplatz** near the city center. The **ArtTicket** (DM20) includes entrance to all museums, and can be purchased at the tourist office or any museum.

ALTSTADT

KUNSTSAMMLUNG NORDRHEIN-WESTFALEN. The art museum is the black glass edifice west of the Hofgarten. Skylights lavish sunshine on Matisse, Picasso, Surrealists, and Expressionists. The collection of works by hometown boy Paul Klee is one of the most extensive in the world. The museum hosts many changing exhibits of modern art and film as well. *(Grabbepl. 5. U-Bahn #70, 75, 76, 78, or 79 to "Heinrich-Heine-Allee." Walk north 2 blocks, or take bus #725 to "Grabbepl." ☎ 838 10; fax 838 12 02; email info@kunstsammlung.de; www.kunstsammlung.de. Open Tu-Th and Sa-Su 10am-6pm, F 10am-8pm. Tours Su 11am, W 3:30pm, and F 6pm. DM5, students DM3. Special exhibits DM12, students DM8. Tours are free.)*

KUNSTHALLE. Across the square from the Kunstsammlung Nordrhein-Westfalen, it's not a museum, mind you, but a forum for modern exhibits of every shape and size. Open your mind and step inside. The stove-pipe on the museum is an art piece by Joseph Beuys intended to symbolize the link between art and the real world. Breathe deeply as you pass. *(Grabbeplatz. 4. ☎ 32 70 23; fax 32 90 70; www.kunstverein-duesseldorf.de. Admission depends on the exhibit; usually DM10, students and children DM7. Open Tu-Su 11am-6pm.)*

KUNSTMUSEUM DÜSSELDORF. A strong collection of Baroque and Romantic art in one wing balances an early 20th-century and contemporary collection in the other. On the ground floor, glassware, tapestries, dishes, and some astonishingly intricate locks memorialize 11 centuries of aristocratic decor. The **Kunstpalast** is an extension of the Kunstmuseum devoted to rotating contemporary exhibits. *(Ehrenhof 5. ☎ 899 62 40; fax 899 24 60. Open Tu-Su 11am-6pm. Tours Su 11am. DM5, students and children DM2.50.)*

GOETHEMUSEUM. The museum makes up for its lack of hometown advantage with a massive collection—30,000 souvenirs memorialize the poet and his friends. Everything in the mini-palace is furnished as Goethe would have wished it—to evoke his character. *(Jakobistr. 2. In Schloß Jägerhof, at the east end of the garden. Streetcar #707 or bus #752 to "Schloß Jägerhof." ☎ 899 62 62. Open Tu-F and Su 11am-5pm, Sa 1-5pm. Library open Tu-F 10am-noon and 2-4pm. DM4, students and children DM2.)*

ELSEWHERE IN DÜSSELDORF

FILMMUSEUM AND HETJENSMUSEUM. The film museum displays everything from shadow plays and hand-puppets to German-dubbed clips from the master directors. The connected **Hetjens** museum fills four floors with 8,000 years of pottery and ceramics. The **Black Box** theater, a cinema specializing in art-house flicks, is in the same complex. See **Entertainment,** p. 473. *(Schulstr. 4. South of the Schloßturm on Rheinuferstr. ☎ 899 42 10; fax 899 37 68. Both open Tu and Th-Su 11am-5pm, W 11am-9pm. Admission to each DM6, students DM3.)*

NEANDERTHALMUSEUM. A museum where low-brows, thick-skulls, and knuckle-draggers can feel comfortable. The first remains of a being identified as Neanderthal Man were found here; the museum introduces you to his 60,000-year-old relatives. *(Thekhauser Quall, in the suburb of Erkrath. S-Bahn #8 to "Hochdahl," then bus #741 to "Neanderthal."* ☎*(02104) 311 49. Open Tu-Su 10am-6pm. DM2, students DM1.)*

STADTMUSEUM. The building clashes with its 18th-century neighbors, but its exhibits aptly summarize the city's consumer history. *(Berger Allee 2. By the Rheinkniebrücke.* ☎*899 61 70. Open Tu and Th-Su 11am-5pm, W 11am-9pm. DM6, students DM3.)*

MAHN- UND GEDENKSTÄTTE. A small museum and document collection commemorates victims of the Third Reich and displays artwork by children returning from concentration camps. *(Mühlenstr. 29.* ☎*899 62 06, or 899 61 92 for tours; fax 892 91 37. Open Tu-F and Su 11am-5pm, Sa 1-5pm. Free.)*

🎵🎭 ENTERTAINMENT AND NIGHTLIFE

Folklore holds that Düsseldorf's 500 pubs make up *die längste Theke der Welt* (the longest bar in the world). Pubs in the Altstadt are standing-room-only by 6pm, and foot traffic is shoulder-to-shoulder by nightfall, when it is nearly impossible to see where one pub ends and the next begins. **Bolkerstr.** is jam-packed nightly with street performers of the musical and beer-olympic varieties. *Prinz* (DM5) is Düsseldorf's fashion cop and scene detective; it's often given out free at the youth hostel. *Facolte* (DM4), a gay and lesbian nightlife magazine, is available at most newsstands. The free cultural guides *Coolibri* and *Biograph* are less complete but still sufficient.

Das Kommödchen is a tiny, extraordinarily popular theater behind the Kunsthalle at Grabbepl. (☎32 94 43. Box office open M-Sa 1-8pm, Su 3-8pm. Tickets usually DM38, students and children DM28.) Ballet and opera tickets are best bought (without service charge) at the **Opernhaus,** Heinrich-Heine-Allee 16a. (☎890 82 11. Box office open M-F 11am-6:30pm, Sa 11am-1pm, and 1hr. before each performance.) **Black Box,** Schulstr. 4 (☎899 24 90), off Rathausufer along the Rhein, serves the art-film aficionado with unadulterated foreign flicks (DM8, students DM6). Other theaters include the **Capitol Theate** (Erkrather Str. 30, ☎73 440) which houses Broadway shows in German and touring companies, and children's theater spaces like the **Puppentheater** (Helmholtzstr. 38, ☎37 24 01). Tickets for all events are available over the phone, at the box office, or from the tourist office.

🎭 **Pam-Pam,** Bolkerstr 34. (☎854 93 93). This basement disco is filled to overflowing by midnight, and yet the crowds keep coming. Dance the night away to house, rock, pop, and plenty of American music. Open F-Sa 10pm-dawn. No cover.

La Rocca, Grünstr. 8 (☎88 00 441). Just off the Kö, this posh club serves as a showcase for purchases made during the day. But they do know how to throw a party. A mostly 20-something crowd dances the night away to house. Open Th-Sa from 10pm-5am (often later). Cover DM8.

Zum Uel, Ratinger Str. 16 (☎32 53 69). The quintessential German Kneipe. The locals know what's up too; the crowd in front of Zum Uel renders the street impassable. Stop at the hugely popular pub for a glass of *Schlösser Alt,* (DM2.80 for 0.2l). Open M-Tu, Th, and Su 10am-1am, W and F 10am-3am.

Unique, Bolkerstr. 30 (☎323 09 90). Lives up to its name, at least in the context of Düsseldorf's Altstadt. Surrounded by an endless beerfest, the red-walled club draws a younger, trendier crowd. Open daily 10pm-late. Cover DM10.

g@rden, Rathausufer 8 (☎86 61 60). In addition to internet access and a great view of the Rhein, the futuristic cafe hosts DJs who spin everything from funk to R&B to techno. Cafe open 11am-1am, club after 9pm.

Stahlwerk, Ronsdorfer Str. 134 (☎ 73 03 86 81). U-Bahn #75 to "Ronsdorfer Str." This classic factory-turned-disco in one of Düsseldorf's grittier areas packs in 1,500 of the city's most divine. Open F-Sa and the last Su of every month after 10pm. Cover DM10.

Café Rosa, Oberbilker Allee 310 (☎ 77 52 42). The socio-cultural mecca of Düsseldorf's gay community, this do-it-all Kulturzentrum offers self-defense classes and throws killer parties. Tu men only; F lesbians only. Open Tu-Sa 8pm-1am, later on weekends.

NEAR DÜSSELDORF: MÖNCHENGLADBACH   ☎02161

Mönchengladbach, known to all as MG (em-gay), has always stayed way ahead of the times. Pre-Neanderthals set up one of the largest communities in the region here over 300,000 years ago. In 974, Archbishop Gero founded a prominent Benedictine monastery and intellectual center, **Abteiberg,** a structure that still dominates the skyline. About 800 years later, the French kicked the monks out, and since then the deserted monastery has served as the **Rathaus.** Next door towers the 11th-century **Münster,** a church whose ecclesiastical treasures include a portable altar and a bust of the Saxon St. Vitus, the city's guardian. (Church open M-F 7:15am-8pm, Sa 7:15am-6:45pm, Su 8am-6:45pm. Museum open Tu-Sa 2-6pm, Su noon-6pm.) Around the corner, the mirrored **Städtisches Museum Abteiberg,** Abteistr. 27, just beyond the Rathaus, houses a collection of 20th-century art including pieces by Andy Warhol, Roy Lichtenstein, and George Segal. (☎25 26 37. Open Tu-Su 10am-6pm. DM8, students and children DM4.) Also at the top of the Abteiberg is the **Alter Markt,** an old cobblestone square now studded by small diners and craft shops. To reach the Alter Markt, turn left out of the train station and head up Hindenburgstr. past the shopping district, or take bus #13 or 23 up the hill.

After your walk, treat yourself to some delicious eats at **Spaghetti-Haus,** Sandradstr. 15, right off the Alter Markt. The portions are huge, and the mouth-watering pizzas start at DM10. (☎/fax 20 65 13. Open daily 11:30am-3pm, and 5:30pm-midnight.) Gaze down at the residential district, a dense blanket of pastel decorated houses with flowers spilling out of windows. Five parks—**Geropark, Bundespark, Kaiserpark, Hardtor Wald,** and **Volksgarten**—lie within MG proper, but most affecting is the **Bunter Garten** (Garden of Colors), in the center of town, accessible from Alter Markt by following Sandvadstr. for ten minutes. The park includes a botanical garden within its maze of forested paths.

Just outside of town stands the majestic **Schloß Rheydt.** From the station, take bus #6 to "Bonnenbroich" and then bus #16 to "Schloß Rheydt" (30min., but worth it). This pristine Renaissance palace is upstaged only by its own beautiful grounds, prize peacocks, and a tranquil, Monet-esque moat. The museum inside houses rotating art and historical exhibits. (☎66 92 89 00. Open Apr.-Sept. Tu-Su 11am-7pm, Oct.-Mar. Tu-Sa 11am-4pm, Su 11am-6pm. DM5, kids DM2.50.)

Mönchengladbach is best seen as a day trip from Düsseldorf, about 30 minutes away by train. Nevertheless, the **tourist office,** Bismarckstr. 23-27, located in the *First Reisebüro* (travel agency) one block to the left of the train station, finds rooms (from DM45) for free. (☎220 01; fax 27 42 22. Open M-F 9:30am-8:30pm, Sa 9:30am-1pm.) The **Jugendherberge Hardter Wald,** Brahmstr. 156, lies at the boundary of a wheat field and a forest. From the station, take bus #13 or 23 to "Hardtmarkt" (20min.), walk straight and make a left at the *Jugendherberge* sign onto Brahmstr. (1.2km). The facilities are excellent but the hostel's bucolic location far from Mönchengladbach and really, really far from Düsseldorf rules out debaucherous nightlife action. (☎56 09 00. Breakfast included. Sheets DM6. Reception 8am-10pm; last check-in 6pm. Dorm beds DM26, over 26 DM31.)

RUHRGEBIET (RUHR REGION)

Both Germany's modern wealth and working class were forged from the coal and steel of the Ruhr Valley. After 1850, the Ruhr provided for the railroad expansion and the immense manufacturing demands of a newly unified (and bellicose) Germany, quickly becoming the foremost industrial region in Europe. Not everything ran smoothly in this era, however; the growing exploitation of the workers led to numerous strikes and strong socialist leanings. Nevertheless, Ruhr residents remained loyal to the government, and the Ruhr was torn apart not by Marxist revolution but by Allied bombers in WWII. The reconstruction program in the following years yielded numerous parks to brighten the region's smoggy visage, and travelers weary of the bleak landscape can get their aesthetic fix at many excellent museums and cultural centers. The Ruhr's sprawling conglomeration of streetcar, bus, and U-Bahn systems still offers the densest concentration of rail lines in the world, providing a snapshot of its industrial past.

ESSEN
☎0201

For a millennium, Essen was just another German cathedral town. By the eve of WWI, however, Essen had advanced to become the industrial capital of Germany, thanks to seemingly limitless deposits of coal and iron. After its destruction in WWII, the city reformed its image as a soot-belching monstrosity by emphasizing its religious and cultural faces. As a result, the city is alive with concerts and museums, but huge department stores and office buildings dominate the atmosphere and Essen's high-tech factories remain the industrial cornerstone of the Ruhr.

NORDRHEIN-WESTFALEN

🛈 **PRACTICAL INFORMATION.** Trains run from Essen to **Düsseldorf** (½hr., 5 per hr., DM18) and **Dortmund** (20min., 4 per hr., DM18). Essen's U-Bahn and streetcar lines cost DM3.20 per ride. The spiffy new **tourist office,** Am Hauptbahnhof 2, across from the station, books **rooms.** (☎194 33; fax 887 20 44; email touristikzentrale@essen.de; www.essen.de. Open M-F 9am-5:30pm, Sa 10am-1pm.)

🛏🍴 **ACCOMMODATIONS AND FOOD.** The **Jugendherberge (HI),** Pastoratsberg 2, sits in the middle of a quiet forest in Werden, a suburb notable for its 8th-century Abteikirche and Luciuskirche, the oldest parish north of the Alps. Take S-Bahn #6 to "Werden" (25min.) and bus #190 to "Jugendherberge." Rooms are standard but far from the city. (☎49 11 63; fax 49 25 05. Breakfast included. Sheets DM6. Reception 7am-11:30pm. Curfew 11:30pm. Dorm beds DM27, over 26 DM32.) The basic, comfortable **Hotel Kessing,** Hachestr. 30, is close to the train station. (☎23 99 88; fax 23 02 89. Breakfast included. Singles DM59, with bath DM85; doubles DM118, with bath DM138. Prices go up when conferences are in town.) Camp at **Stadt-Camping Essen-Werden,** Im Löwental 67, on the west bank of the Ruhr. Take the S-Bahn to "Essen-Werden" and continue south along the river. (☎49 29 78. Reception 7am-1pm and 3-9pm. DM7.50 per person. Tent DM15.)

The maze of stairs and escalators at **Porscheplatz,** near the Rathaus, crawls with vendors of cheap mall food. Take the U-Bahn to "Porschepl." The **Mensa** is in the yellow-trimmed cafeteria building at the university. Take the U-Bahn to "Universität" and follow the signs to the building. (☎18 31. Open M-F 7:30am-4pm, Sa 7:30am-3:30pm.) Just across the street, **Beaulongerie,** on Segerothstr., offers delicious baguettes (DM4.50) with a variety of fillings and sauces. (☎32 62 12. Open M-F 10am-11pm, Sa 11am-11pm.) The **Drospa** in the train station meets basic **grocery** needs (open M-Sa 6:30am-9:30pm, Su 9am-9:30pm). The **post office,** 44137 Essen, is on Hachestr. 4 (open M-F 8am-7pm, Sa 8:30am-3:30pm).

🔲 **SIGHTS.** The **Museumszentrum** at Goethestr. 41 houses three museums. Take streetcar #101, 107, or 127 or U-Bahn #11 to "Rüttenscheider Stern." Follow signs to the Museumzentrum and continue (north) on Rüttenscheiderstr., then turn left on Kuhrstr., and right onto Goethestr. The internationally-renowned **Museum Folkwang** (☎884 53 00, www.museum-folkwang.de) drops all the big names in modern art from Courbet to Pollack and hosts superstar special exhibits. The Folkwang's **Fotographische Sammlung,** takes on camera work from the early days, and the **Ruhrlandmuseum** (☎884 010) hosts exhibits on the Ruhr in its industrial heyday. Experience the miner's life in the Weimar Republic without dirtying your hands. *(All three open Tu-Th and Sa-Su 10am-6pm, F 10am-midnight. The photography collection is closed during summer holidays. Combined admission DM5, students and children DM3.)*

Nineteenth-century arms and railroad mogul **Alfred Krupp** perfected steel-casting in industrial Essen. **Villa Hügel,** the Krupp family home (read: palace) for decades, was given to the city in the 1950s in order to brighten the company's image, which was tarnished by its Nazi affiliation. Even the gargantuan mahogany staircases and intricate carvings pale in comparison to the **Korea exhibit,** which fills the main building with all things bright and beautiful from the East. *(☎48 37. Take S-Bahn #6 to "Essen-Hügel." Open Tu-Su 10am-7pm. DM12, children and seniors DM8.50.)*

Essen's **Münsterkirche,** close to the city center on Burgplatz, is an ancient, cloistered string of flowering courtyards and hexagonal crypts founded in 852. The 1,000-year-old, doll-like *Goldene Madonna* stands beside the nave. *(☎22 04 206. Open daily 7:30am-6:30pm. Schatzkammer open Tu-Sa 10am-5pm, Su 12:30-5pm.)* Although Nazis gutted Essen's **Alte Synagoge,** Steeler Str. 29, in 1938, it stands today as the largest synagogue north of the Alps. Take the U-Bahn to "Porscheplatz" and follow the signs to the Schützenbahn; as you head south on the Schützenbahn, the synagogue is on your left. Inside, slides and pictures from the Third Reich era make up the *Dokumentationsforum,* a monument to the Jews of Essen. *(☎84 52 18/23; fax 88 45 225. Open Tu-Su 10am-6pm. Free.)* The **Deutsches Plakatmuseum** sits on the third floor of the shopping mall at the intersection of Rathenaustr. and Am Glockenspiel. The poster museum has everything from the unusual (elephants in elephant-suits) to the bizarre (two pig heads eating a human heart), as well as a Gutenberg press. From the station, walk through Will-Brandt-Pl., and up Kettwiger Str. Turn left on Am Glockenspiel. *(Open Tu-Su noon-8pm. Free.)* Across the street is the **Theaterplatz.** Performances happen here, at the Grillo theater, and in the Rathaus theater. *(Box office in the Rathaus open M-Sa 10am-1pm and M-F 3-5pm. Or call ☎81 22 200.)*

DETMOLD   ☎05231

Worlds away from the industry of the Ruhrgebiet crouches Detmold, the premier city of the Teutoburger Wald. Until 1918 the royal seat of the Lippe-Detmold principality, Detmold has since been raking in the tourists.

🔲 **PRACTICAL INFORMATION.** Detmold's location makes it an ideal base for exploring the Teutoburger Wald. **Trains** run from Detmold to **Osnabrück** (1¼hr., 1 per hr., DM23); **Hannover** (2hr., 2 per hr., DM35); and **Köln** (3½hr., 3 per hr., DM80). Though infrequently open, **Fahrradbüro Detmold,** Richtenhofstr. 14 (☎97 74 01; fax 30 02 01) rents out old **bikes.** (Open Apr.-Oct. Tu and Th 5-7pm, Sa 10am--1pm. DM6 per day, DM30 per week. Passport or ID and DM50 deposit required.) The **tourist office,** Rathaus am Markt, is stocked with everything you need. From the station, head left on Bahnhofstr., turn right on Paulinenstr., then left on Bruchstr. into the pedestrian zone, and walk another five minutes to the Rathaus. The tourist office is on the right side of the building. The city brochure is excellent, with a map detailed enough for hikes to the *Denkmal* and the surrounding area (DM1). The staff books **rooms** (from DM35) for free and posts an accommodations list outside the building. (☎97 73 28; fax 97 74 47; email info@detmold.de; www.touristikdetmold.de. Open M-Th 10am-8pm, F 10am-4pm, Sa 10am-1pm.) Tours of the Altstadt take off from the main entrance of the Residenzschloß. (Apr.-Oct. Sa at 10am, Su at 11am. DM4, students DM2.)

ACCOMMODATIONS AND FOOD. In addition to the regular pack of wild school children, the **Jugendherberge Schanze (HI)**, Schirrmannstr. 49, features its own mule. From Bussteig 3 at the train station, take bus #704 (direction: "Hiddesen") to "Auf den Klippen," and walk 10 minutes down the trail. It's approximately a 45min. walk from the station. Make a right on Paulinenstr., and a right on Freiligrathstr. (which becomes Bandelstr.), then a left on Bülowstr., followed by a right onto Schützenberg. (☎247 39; fax 289 27. Breakfast included. Lunch DM8.30, Dinner DM7.10. Sheets DM6.50. Reception until 8pm. Curfew 10pm, but guests are provided with keys. Dorm beds DM24.50, over 26 DM29.50.) Enjoy delicious crepes (DM3-6), baked potatoes (DM2-7), and salads (DM5) at **Knollchen,** Lange Str. 21. (☎283 99. Open M-F 11am-7pm, Sa 10am-4pm.) **Kaiser's,** Bruchstr. 18-20, provides **groceries** (open M-F 8am-7pm, Sa 8am-2pm).

SIGHTS. Towering over the dense forest, the striking **Hermannsdenkmal** commemorates the Teutonic chief Hermann, proclaiming him liberator of the German people. Over-eager nationalists erected Hermann's monolithic likeness on an old encampment in 1875, and Kaiser Wilhelm I came to cut the ribbon. Complete with winged helmet, the statue wields a 7m sword with the disconcerting inscription, "German unity is my power, my power is Germany's might." Research continually relocates the battle to other hills; the only consensus reached is that the colossus does *not* mark the spot of the battle. *(Open Mar.-Oct. daily 9am-6:30pm; Nov.-Feb. 9:30am-4pm. DM2.50, children DM1.)* The hike is beautiful but rather steep for the inexperienced (or lazy) hiker and like most of Detmold's attractions, it lies far from the city. Bus #792, which leaves from the train station, makes the ascent easier. *(Apr.-Oct. M-F 8:10, 9:10am, and 3:10pm; Sa 9:10am and 3:10pm; Su and holidays 10am and 1:10pm.)* No less impressive and far more exhilarating is the **Adlerwarte,** featuring more than 80 birds of prey. Time your arrival with bus #701 from Detmold (direction: "Weidmüller") to "Adlerwarte" to catch a free flight exhibition. The falcons buzz the crowd, passing inches above startled faces and raising shrieks from children and adults alike. *(☎471 71. Open daily mid-Mar. to Oct. 9:30am-5:30pm; Nov. to mid-Mar. 10am-4pm. Displays mid-Mar. to Oct. 11am, 3, and 4:30pm; Nov. to mid-Mar. 11am and 2:30pm. DM7, children DM3.50.)* Save money with the tourist office's **combination ticket,** *der Fliegende Hermann.* *(DM11, children DM4.50.)* The ticket is valid at the Hermannsdenkmal, Adlerwarte, and the **Vogel- und Blumenpark** (bird and flower park). *(☎474 39. Open Apr.-Nov. daily 9am-6pm. DM7, students DM5, children DM3.50.)* On weekends, the ticket also lets you ride the shuttle connecting the three sights for free. Detmold's **Westfälisches Freilichtmuseum,** is less touristy, more original, and just plain cooler than most of Detmold's sights. Spread over 80 hectares, this outdoor museum consists of more than 100 restored and rebuilt 17th- to 19th-century German farm buildings as well as a village where blacksmiths still smith and milk-churners still churn. A horse-drawn carriage takes you from the entrance to the far end of the museum, where the central village is located. *(DM3, children DM2.)* Take bus #701 (direction: "Weidmüller") to "Freilichtmuseum." *(☎706 105. Open Apr.-Oct. Tu-Su 9am-6pm. DM7, children DM3.)* In the Altstadt, cannons still arm the courtyard of the **Fürstliches Residenzschloß,** a Renaissance castle in the town's central park. *(☎700 20. Can only be seen with tours, which leave daily Apr.-Oct. on the hour, noon-5pm; Nov.-Mar. no 5pm tour. DM6, children DM3.)*

MÜNSTER ☎0251

Perhaps even more than other tranquil, medium-sized German cities, Münster maintains a level of repose and dignity that reflects its history as a place of peaceful reconciliation. As the capital of the Kingdom of Westphalia, Münster presided over the 1648 peace that brought the Thirty Years War to an end, defining the borders of scores of German mini-states for centuries. But the Münster of today offers much more than historic sights: the 45,000 reveling students of the Wilhelmsuniversität know how to punctuate the peace.

▐ GETTING THERE AND GETTING AROUND

Flights: Flughafen Münster-Osnabrück, located to the northeast of the city, has flights to major European cities. Bus #S50 shuttles between the train station and the airport. **Flight Information:** ☎(02571) 940.

Trains: To **Düsseldorf** (1½hr., 3 per hr., DM35); **Köln** (2hr., 3 per hr., DM50); and **Bremen** (1¼hr., 1 per hr., DM54).

Car Rental: Hertz, Hammerstr. 186 (☎773 78). Open M-F 7:30am-6pm, Sa 7:30am-1pm, Su 9:30-11:30am.

Bike Rental: Münster's train station has an impressive bike rental service (☎484 01 70; fax 484 01 77), with hundreds of bikes and amazingly long hours. Just look for the big glass triangle outside of the main entrance to the train station. Open M-F 5:30am-11pm, Sa-Su 7am-11pm. DM11 per day, DM9.50 for Deutsche Bahn customers who've traveled over 100km. DM45 per week.

Mitfahrzentrale: AStA, Schloßpl. 1 (☎405 05). Open M-F 8:30am-4pm.

✷ ❼ ORIENTATION AND PRACTICAL INFORMATION

Münster is located at the confluence of the lower channels of the Ems River, in the midst of the Münsterland plain. The magnificent Promenade surrounds the Altstadt, which lies west of the train station.

Tourist Office: Klemensstr. 10 (☎492 27 10; fax 492 77 43; email amt80@stadt-muenster.de; www.muenster.de). Just off the Marktplatz. From the station, cross Bahnhofstr. and head into the walking zone that is Windthorstr. Follow this street, veering right as it becomes Stubengasse; the office is on your left as Stubengasse crosses Klemenstr. and becomes H.-Bruning-Str. Staff books **rooms** (from DM50) for free and offers **tours** and theater tickets. Open M-F 9am-6pm, Sa 9am-1pm.

Laundromat: Wasch Center, Moltkestr. 5-7. Wash DM7, soap included. Dry DM1 per 15 min. Open M-F 6am-11pm.

Budget Travel: STA Travel, Frauenstr. 24-26 (☎41 43 90). Open M-F 10am-6pm, Sa 10am-2pm.

Bookstore: Phönix Bücher, Prinzipalmarkt 24. (☎41 86 00). Has a good selection of English paperbacks and classics. Open M-F 9am-8pm, Sa 9am-2pm.

Post Office: Berliner Pl. 37, 48143 Münster. Located directly to the left of the train station. Open M-F 8am-7pm, Sa 8am-1pm.

Internet Access: Surf Inn, in the Galeria Kaufhof across from the tourist office, on the corner of Klemensstr. and Ludgeristr. 15min. DM2, ½hr. DM3. Open M-F 9:30am-8pm, Sa 9am-4pm. **Universitäts Bibliothek,** Krummer Timpen 3-5. From the entrance, turn right into the computer catalog room. Free. Open M-F 8am-9pm, Sa 9am-5pm.

▐ ACCOMMODATIONS AND CAMPING

Münster's accommodations are less than adequate for budget travel. The shiny *Jugendgästehaus* is not cheap, and hotels fill up quickly, so be sure to call several days ahead. In a pinch, there's a hostel in **Nottuln,** a 50-minute bus ride

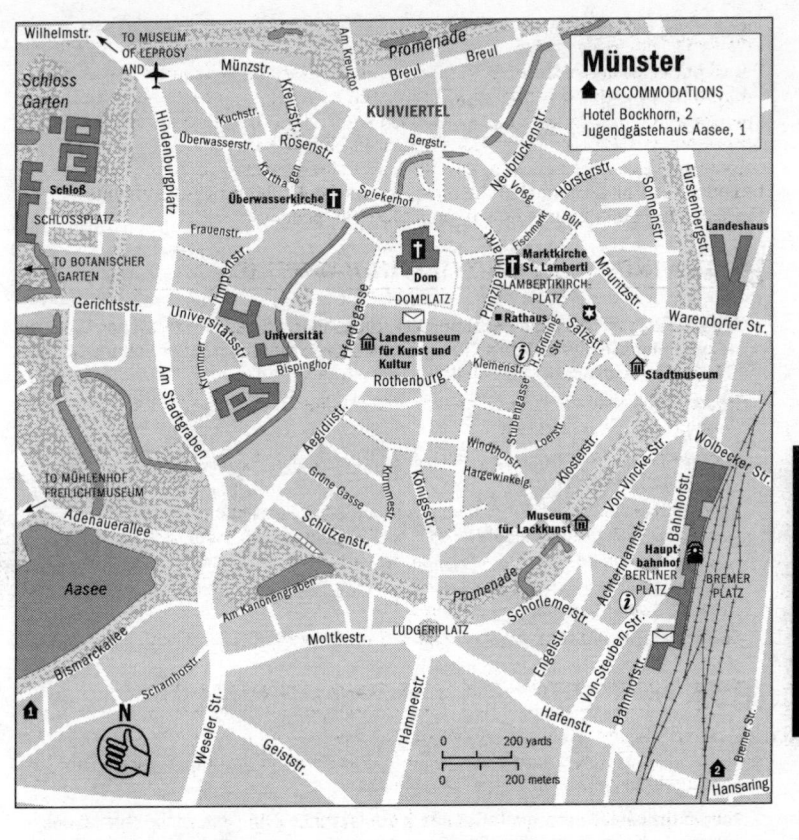

Münster

🏠 ACCOMMODATIONS

Hotel Bockhorn, 2
Jugendgästehaus Aasee, 1

away. Take bus #560 or 561 to "Rodeplatz," then follow the signs. (☎(02502) 78 78; fax 96 19. Breakfast included. Sheets DM6. Reception 8am-10pm. DM24, over 26 DM29.)

Jugendgästehaus Aasee, Bismarckallee 31 (☎53 24 70/53 24 77; fax 52 12 71; email Jugendgaestehaus-Muenster-DJH@t-online.de). Bus #10 (direction: "Roxel") or 34 (direction: "Zentralklinikum") to "Hoppendamm." A huge, luxurious brick hostel overlooking the peaceful river, newly and beautifully renovated. Bike rental DM10 per day. Toilet and bath in each room. Breakfast buffet and sheets included. Reception 7am-1am. Lockout 1am. Doubles DM50.50 per person; quads DM40.50.

Hotel Bockhorn, Bremer Str. 24 (☎655 10), a 5min. walk from the station. From the rear exit of the train station, walk right on Bremer Str. for 400m. Tidy, no-frills rooms are convenient to the Altstadt and to the train. The breakfast room is decorated with a piece of 17th-century furniture somehow obtained from the Schloß. Breakfast included. 24hr. reception. Singles from DM60; doubles DM120.

Haus vom Guten Hirten, Lindenweg 61 (☎378 70; fax 37 45 44). Bus #14 to "Mauritz Friedhof." Or take a long (40min.) walk from the rear entrance of the train station, turn left on Bremer Str., right on Wolbecker Str., left on Hohenzollernring, right on Manfred-von-Richthofen-Str., and finally left on Lindenweg. Managed by the Church, this hotel offers huge suites that debunk the myth that monks and nuns mustn't indulge. Breakfast included. Reception 6am-9pm. Singles DM58; doubles DM98; triples DM138.

Hotel An'n Schlagbaum, Weseler Str. 269 (☎/fax 79 21 80). Bus #7, 15, or 16 to "Inselbogen." 11 affordable rooms above a faded restaurant. Breakfast included. Singles DM55; doubles DM90.

Camping: Campingplatz Münster, Auf der Laer 7 (☎31 19 82). Bus #320 to "Wersewinkel." Reception 8am-midnight. DM7 per person. DM4 per tent.

FOOD AND NIGHTLIFE

A **farmer's market** takes over the plaza in front of the Dom, offering fresh fruit, fresh meat, and second-hand clothes (W and Sa 7am-2pm). Fridays at 1pm bring the **biomarkt,** the politically correct, organically grown version of the regular market. The student district, **Kuhviertel** (literally, "cow quarter"—gives you an idea of how much Münster loves its students), is dotted with fairly inexpensive eateries and cafes. Bars line the streets across from the Schloß in the student quarter, and discos abound father southwest between the train station and the harbor. Free in university buildings, *Gig* provides monthly print coverage of nightlife and art openings in Münster and the surrounding area. Münster also has a large performance scene; tickets for all concerts can be bought through the tourist office or directly from the box office. (☎41 46 71 00; fax 59 09 205. Open Tu-F 9am-1:30pm, and 3:30-7pm, Sa 9am-1pm.)

C.u.b.a., Achtermannstr. 10-12 (☎582 17). A hotspot for Münster's alternative crowd. This cultural center, disco, and *Kneipe* throws a massive Cuba-fête every 1st, 3rd, and 4th Saturday of the month (9pm-3am). Open daily 5pm-1am, but the cool kids don't come out to play until 11pm.

Cavete Akademische Bieranstalt, Kreuzstr. 38 (☎457 00). Founded by students for students in 1959, the first student pub in Westfalen serves homemade spinach noodles in thick sauces (DM10) in a dark, carnivalesque atmosphere. Open daily 7pm-1am. Kitchen closes M-Th and Su 11:30pm, F-Sa 12:30am.

Diesel, Windthorstr. 65 (☎57 96), in the Altstadt, at the intersection of Windthorststr., Stubengasse, and Loerstr. Fuel pumps, Keith Haring artwork, a red neon shrine filled with plastic flowers, and funky bossa nova music surround the pool table that takes up most of the cafe. A big screen TV graces those that choose to drink on the terrace. Daily specials DM6-12. Open daily 10am-1am.

Brauerei Pinkus Müller, Kreuzstr. 7 (☎451 51). Directly across the street from the Cavete. This beer hall, which takes up half the block, is about as hip as an elbow and filled with tourists, but one of Germany's most intense joys is drinking beer in the house where it's brewed. Open M-Sa 11:30am-midnight.

Le Différent, Hörsterstr. 10 (☎51 12 39), at the fork in the road, is the center of Münster's gay nightlife. Techno and charts on 2 dance floors. 18+. Open F-Sa 11pm-5am.

SIGHTS

DOM. The heartbeat of Münster's religious life echoes through the huge St. Paulus-Dom on Domplatz in the center of the Altstadt. The church was founded under the direction of Charlemagne in 792. The cathedral that stands today, however, is a construction dating back to the thirteenth century. Though bombed in WWII, this cathedral has been beautifully restored. The Bishop's peaceful inner courtyard is open to the public. A stone from the similarly bombed Cathedral of Coventry stands in the entrance-way, carrying a wish for mutual forgiveness between Britain and Germany. From his pulpit in the cathedral, Bishop Clemens von Galen delivered a courageous sermon against the Nazi program of euthanasia for so-called "incurables." After wide distribution of the sermon, pressure from the church prompted a rare partial retreat by Hitler. Also inside the church, a statue of St. Christopher points its massive toes to the 16th-century astronomical clock, which recreates the movements of the planets and plays a merry Glockenspiel tune. *(M-Sa noon, Su 12:30pm. Church open Tu-Sa 10am-noon and 2-6pm, Su 2-6pm. DM2.)* The remnants of past diocesan fashions are on display in the basement; the splendid robes could make Armani jealous. *(Dom open M-Sa 6am-6pm, Su 6:30am-7:30pm. Courtyard open Tu-Sa 10am-noon and 2-6pm, Su 2-6pm. Domkammer open daily 11am-4pm.)*

MARKTKIRCHE ST LAMBERTI. Münster's piety takes a turn towards the macabre at the Marktkirche St. Lamberti, where three cages hang above the clock face. The cages were used in the 16th century to display the dead bodies of rebel anabaptists who refused to submit to King Jan van Leiden's order to relinquish all property and be rebaptized as polygamists. The grim cages still hang as a "reminder." Suspended inside is Germany's only free-hanging organ. *(Kirchhermgasse 3, off the Prinzipalmarkt. ☎448 93. Free concerts are given the first Saturday of every month at noon.)*

PROMENADE. When Goethe's carriage turned onto the huge linden tree-lined Promenade encircling the Münster Altstadt, he would slow it and smell the flowers. The Promenade is idyllic all the way around with bicyclers in the middle and couples licking ice cream and strolling in droves on either side. In the west, the Promenade meets the Schloßgarten, where 19th-century trees are still growing, moss-covered and majestic. The Schloß itself, built from 1702-1787, now is part of the university. *(Open Apr.-Sept. 7am-10pm, Oct.-Mar. 7am-8pm.)* The botanical gardens, on the campus of the Wilhelmsuniversität, are especially beautiful. *(☎83 23 810; fax 83 23 823. Open mid-Mar.-mid-Oct. daily 8am-7pm; mid-Oct. to mid-Mar. 8am-4pm.)*

FRIEDENSSAAL. Across from the church, the Friedenssaal (Hall of Peace), which kept one unknown woodcarver very busy for a very long time, commemorates the end of the Thirty Years War. The infamous "Peace of Westphalia" treaty was signed in these hallowed halls in 1648. During WWII, all the important (and breakable) artifacts were stored away for safe-keeping, so after a little post-bombing reconstruction, it was possible to restore the hall to its actual original state. Inside, a centuries-old human hand is on display, guarded by a nearby golden cockerel. Nobody knows who it's from or what it's for, so don't ask. *(Open M-F 9am-5pm, Sa 9am-4pm, Su 10am-1pm. DM1.50, children and students DM0.80.)*

🏛 MUSEUMS

Münster treasures its historical and cultural artifacts in a well-maintained **Landesmuseum,** but its real gems are the small collections that celebrate the random. Ask the tourist office for information about all of the city's offerings, including its **Railway Museum, Carnival Museum,** and **Museum of Organs** (unrelated to the **Leprosy Museum**), all located in the suburbs.

LANDESMUSEUM FÜR KUNST UND KULTUR. Contains modern sculptures and ancient paintings, arranged on 3 floors around a central atrium. *(Domplatz 10. ☎59 07 01. Open Tu-Su 10am-6pm. DM5, students and children DM2, family pass DM10. F free.)*

STADTMUSEUM. This large museum used to be a department store, but now it's a historical odyssey through Münster from its small beginnings early in the 8th century. *(Salzstr. 28. Open Tu-Su 10am-6pm. Tours Su 11am. Free.)*

MUSEUM OF LEPROSY. A little far away, but you should definitely drop by. The exhibits, including playful little leper-puppets, are strictly hands-off. *(Kinderhauser Str. 15. To the northwest of the Altstadt; take bus #6, 9, or 17 to "Kristiansandstr." ☎285 10; fax 285 11 29. Open Su 3-5pm. Free. Call for an appointment on other days.)*

MÜHLENHOF-FREILICHTMUSEUM. The museum is a reconstructed 18th-century farm town. Have a picnic lunch on a millstone from 1868, pick up a loaf of indestructible *Schwarzbrot* (DM2) or some authentic wooden clogs (DM20, DM24 for big feet). *(Theo-Breider-Weg, near the Aasee and Torminbrücke. ☎ 981 200; fax 981 20 40. Open mid-Mar. to Oct. daily 10am-6pm, Nov. to mid-Mar. Tu-Sa 1-4:30pm and Su 11am-4:30pm. DM5, students and seniors DM3, children DM2.)*

MUSEUM FÜR LACKKUNST. The world's only exhibition of all things lacquered. Highlights from shiny empires of the past fill perfectly polished cases, while videos tell you how to make your living room the shiniest on the block. Visiting modern exhibits glisten in the basement. *(Windthorststr. 26, just off the Promenade. ☎ 41 85 10; fax 41 85 120. Open Tu noon-8pm, W-Su noon-6pm. DM3, students DM1.50. Free on Tu.)*

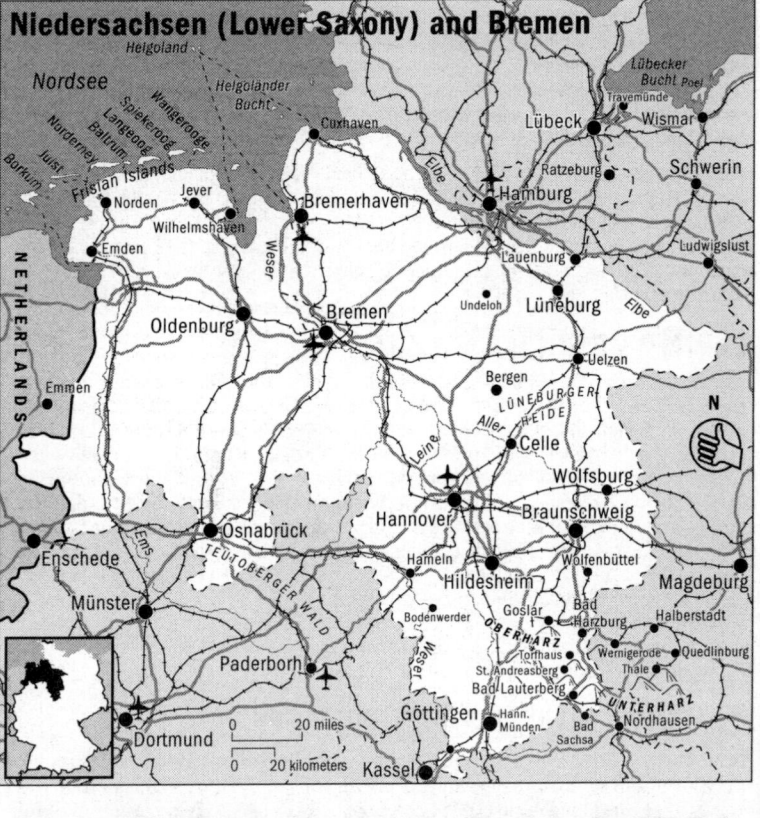

Niedersachsen (Lower Saxony) and Bremen

NIEDERSACHSEN
(LOWER SAXONY)
AND BREMEN

Niedersachsen extends from the Ems River to the Harz Mountains and from the North Sea to the hills of central Germany. Within its relatively small cities, residents strive for economic success and contact with contemporary international culture—everything has a web address, and cultural and arts events are over-advertised in public transportation, phone booths, and the door of the scummiest rest room. Most towns, as well as the spectacular East Frisian islands, resist this trend as they cling to traditional professions and ways of life. Topographically, Niedersachsen has two distinct flavors: old hills in the east and flatlands in the west. The mainland is used almost exclusively for agricultural purposes; a train ride through the region often becomes a blur of green corn, barley, windmills, and bovine rumps. Since the Middle Ages, Niedersachsen has been the seat of intense regionalism, and it still treasures its autonomy, harkening back to the Hanseatic traders who made the coast's fortune. A pocket of the region belongs to Bremen and Bremerhaven, two seafaring cities united in a unique case of state federalism to form Germany's smallest *Land*.

HIGHLIGHTS OF NIEDERSACHSEN AND BREMEN

Hannover (p. 484) is Niedersachsen's metropolis, boasting an explosive cultural scene, a great modern art collection in the **Sprengel Museum**, and rollicking nightlife.

Surrounded by rolling hills and filled with young folks, **Göttingen** (p. 491) is the quint-essential university town.

It's no surprise that the city of **Bremen** (p. 515) is an independent *Land* within Niedersachsen—the residents are feisty, the political climate especially liberal, and the nightlife in the student-dominated **Viertel** can't be contained.

A respite from the German city circuit can be found along the North seacoast, where the **East Frisian islands** (p. 528) offer barren beauty and a string of **superb beaches**.

HANNOVER (HANOVER) ☎0511

Despite its relatively small size, Hannover puts on a show of culture and cosmopolitan charm to rival cities twice as large. As the most important railway center in northwestern Germany, the city's myriad attractions lure travelers out of the Berlin-Hamburg-Köln triangle. But Hannover has seen darker times. Because of an unusual marriage that bound the Hanoverian royalty to the United Kingdom, the city found itself repeatedly attacked by foreign powers striking at the British throne. When the city later came under Prussian control, it benefited from the empire's prosperity, but WWII put a stop to the good run, flattening 60% of the city. Yet resilient Hannover, accustomed to severe poundings, emerged like a Phoenix, leaping joyfully from the ashes. Today, with great economic vigor, a wealth of museums, a supreme opera hall, and a tradition of outdoor festivals, Hannover reigns as Niedersachsen's cultural and political capital.

⌐ GETTING THERE AND GETTING AROUND

Available at youth hostels and **ÜSTRA** offices, the **Hannover Card** provides public transportation within the city and to the airport, as well as admission or discounts at several museums (DM14 for 1 day, DM23 for 3 days; group ticket for up to 5 people DM30 for one day, DM50 for 3 days). Plan ahead: the card is only valid from 7pm on the day of purchase, so you must buy your ticket one day ahead of time.

Flights: Hannover's airport is 20-30min. from the Altstadt. *Schnellbuslinie* (express bus) #60 runs from the Hauptbahnhof to the airport (M-F 5am-7pm, every 20min.; 7-10:30pm, every 30 min.; Sa-Su 5:30am-10:30pm, every 30min.; DM9). Flights depart to many European cities. For flight information, call 977 12 23; fax 977 18 98.

Trains: Hannover is well connected to cities in Northern Europe, especially within Germany. Trains leave at least one every hour for **Hamburg** (1½hr., DM50); **Berlin** (2½hr., DM78.60); **Köln** (2hr., DM93); **Frankfurt** (3hr., DM157); **Munich** (9hr., DM241); and **Amsterdam** (4½-5hr., DM80).

Public Transportation: ÜSTRA, Hannover's mass-transit system, is extremely thorough and fast. From the station, walk to the aluminium grey stand in front of King August or at the "Raschpl." bus stop behind the station, and pick up the free map of the U-Bahn and bus lines (open M-W and F 8am-6pm, Th until 7pm, Sa 9am-2pm). Tickets can be bought at machines or from drivers. Hannover has 3 zones, so prices vary. *Kurzstrecke* (3 stops) DM2; single ride DM3-5, children 6-11 DM 1.60; day ticket DM6-10; group ticket for up to 5 people DM12-18. The Mitte and Altstadt are both in Zone 1; check list for other streets. *Remember to punch your ticket at the blue machines, or risk a DM60 fine.* A **Schüler-Wochenkarte** opens up the magical world of public transportation to students for 1 week; you'll need a student ID and a passport-sized photo to hand over (DM17.50). For more info and maps, call the **ÜSTRA customer service office** (☎ 16 68

22 38) in the Kröpcke station. Open M-W and F 8am-6pm, Th 8am-7pm, Sa 9am-2pm. The **Hannover Card** provides more comprehensive savings (see above).

Bike Rental: Radgeber Linden, Kötnerholzweg 43 (☎210 97 60). U-Bahn #10 to "Leinaustr." DM15 per day. Open M-Tu, Th-F 10am-1pm and 3-6pm.

Taxi: Taxi Ruf, ☎38 11.

✦7 ORIENTATION AND PRACTICAL INFORMATION

The old Saxon *"Hon overe"* means "high bank," referring to the city's position on the river **Leine**. In the heart of Hannover (the Mitte) lies the Hauptbahnhof, where a statue of Ernst August, first king of Hannover, beams from the saddle of his horse, surveying the city he founded. Bahnhofstr. extends from the horse's hooves, leading to the landmark **Kröpcke Café** and, farther, into the Altstadt. Below the statue's feet sprawls the underground **Passerelle,** a bizarre conglomeration of cheap diners and souvenir shops. Behind the station is **Raschplatz,** home to a disco and club scene. A pedestrian zone connects most of the center, including the shopping districts along **Georgstraße** and the Altstadt. The most interesting area for budget travelers is the student quarter surrounding the university.

Tourist Office: Hannover Information, Ernst-August-Pl. 2 (☎116 849 710). Outside the main entrance of the train station, facing the large rear of the king's splendid steed, turn right. In the same building as the post office. The superb staff finds **rooms** for any budget for a steep DM10 fee (**reservation line** ☎01805 65 10 00; fax 01805 65 11 11), provides maps and information on cultural events, sells tickets to concerts and exhibits (☎168 497 20), and runs a full travel agency. Free hotel list available. Open M-F 9am-7pm, Sa 9:30am-2pm.

Tours: The **tourist office** offers 24 theme tours—"Hannover's Cemeteries" or "Artistic Hannover," for example (☎16 84 97). DM12-25, students DM7-10. To experience Hannover fully, follow the **Red Thread,** a 4km walking tour guided by a painted red line connecting all the major—and minor—sites. The accompanying Red Thread Guide (DM3), available from the tourist office, details the tour in English.

Student Travel Office: RDS, Fortunastr. 28 (☎44 60 37), off Limmerstr. The basics for the budget traveler. Flights and train packages. Open M-F 9am-6pm. Or **STA,** Callinstr. 23 (☎13 18 531; www.sta.de), in the same building as the Mensa.

Consulate: UK, Karl-Weichert-Allee 50 (☎388 38 08). U-Bahn #4 (direction: "Roderbruch") to "Medizinische Hochschule." At the end of the parking lot, go right onto Carl-Neuberg-Str., which runs into Karl-Weichert-Allee. Open M 11am-7pm, Tu-Th 9am-3pm.

Currency Exchange: ReiseBank, to the left inside the main exit of the train station, is the most convenient location, with the longest hours and decent commissions. Open M-Sa 7am-10pm, Su 9am-10pm.

American Express: Georgstr. 54 (☎368 10 03; 24hr. refund assistance 0130 85 31 00), across from the opera house. Travel agency and full cardmember services. Mail held for a maximum of 4 weeks for card members, traveler's check clients, and travel agency customers. Open M-F 9am-12pm and 1pm-6pm, Sa 10am-1pm.

Bookstores: Schmorl und von Seefeld, Bahnhofstr. 14 (☎367 50; fax 367 52 41), has English-language novels downstairs. Open M-F 9:30am-8pm, Sa 9:30am-4pm.

Laundromat: Wasch Center, at the corner of Hildesheimer Str. and Siemensstr. Take U-Bahn #1 (direction: "Sarstedt"), to "Altenbekener Damm," or #10 (direction: "Ahlem") to "Leinaustr." Wash DM6, dry DM1 per 15min. Open daily 6am-11pm.

Information: ☎11 88 33, English ☎11 88 37, Turkish ☎11 88 36.

Emergency: Police, ☎110 or 10 90. **Fire,** ☎112. **Ambulance,** ☎192 22.

Medical Assistance: EMS, ☎31 40 44. **Medical Information,** ☎31 40 44.

Gay and Lesbian Resources: ☎194 46.

Women's Resources: Rape Crisis Line, ☎33 21 12. **Shelter,** ☎66 44 77.

Pharmacy: Europa-Apotheke, Georgstr. 16 (☎32 66 18; fax 363 24 63), near the train station. English spoken. Open M-F 8am-8pm, Sa 8am-4pm. Posts emergency information after hours.

Post Office: 30159 Hannover, in the same building as the tourist office. Open M-F 9am-8pm, Sa 9am-4pm. Mail held above on first floor.

Internet Access: In **Daily Planet** (see **Nightlife,** p. 491).

ACCOMMODATIONS

Finding budget accommodations in Hannover is difficult but not impossible. The youth hostel and two *Naturfreundehäuser* (similar to hostels, but not part of HI) provide affordable respites, as do private accommodations through the tourist office. Call the **reservation hotline** (☎811 35 00; fax 811 35 41). Should all else fail, traveling to the hostels in nearby Braunschweig or Celle may be cheaper than bedding down in one of Hannover's royally priced hotels.

> **!** **Safety Warning:** Hannover's hostel and *Naturfreundehäuser* are situated in parks and woods on the outskirts of town. Walkways in these areas are deserted and poorly lit at night; anyone planning to stay out past curfew should use caution.

Jugendherberge Hannover (HI), Ferdinand-Wilhelm-Fricke-Weg 1 (☎131 76 74; fax 185 55). U-Bahn #3 or 7 (direction: "Wettbergen") to "Fischerhof/Fachhochschule." From the station, cross the tracks and walk on the path through the school's parking lot; follow the path as it curves, and cross the street. Go over the enormous red footbridge and turn right. The hostel is 50m down on the right, within walking distance of the Maschsee and Schützenfestplatz. Some may find the 6- to 12-bed rooms in the old building a bit crowded. Major renovations and additions produced a new building with more spacious accommodations. Sheets included. Reception 7:30-11:30pm. After 11:30pm, doors open every hour, on the hour. DM27-29, over 26 add DM5.

Naturfreundehaus Stadtheim, Hermann-Bahlsen-Allee 8 (☎69 14 93; fax 69 06 52; nfh-elienriede@t-online.de; www.nfh-elienriede.de). U-Bahn #3 (direction: "Lahe") or 7 (direction: "Fasanenkrug") to "Spannhagengarten." Walk 15m back to the intersection and follow Hermann-Bahlsen-Allee to the left for about 5min.; follow the sign to your right down the paved road 200m to the hostel on the left. Tiny rooms, with a superior breakfast included. Reception 8am-noon and 3-10pm. No curfew. DM49.

Naturfreundehaus Misburg, Am Fahrhorstfelde 50 (☎and fax 58 05 37). Take U-Bahn #3 (direction: "Lahe") to the end. Then hop aboard bus #124 to "Misburg Garten"; once there, switch to bus #631 to "Waldfriedhof." Stroll up Am Fahrhorstfelde to the very end, go 10m straight ahead on the trail, and follow the sign. At least an hour's travel from the Hauptbahnhof. On a beautiful lake brimming with ducks. 4- to 6-bed rooms decked out in homey brown. Sheets DM7.50. Breakfast included. Reception Tu-F after noon. No curfew. The 30 beds fill quickly—reservations are necessary. DM39.50.

Hotel am Thielenplatz, Thielenpl. 2 (☎32 76 91 93; fax 32 51 88). From the station, take a left onto Joachimstr. and go one block to Thielenpl. Luxurious furnishings in a miniature lobby filled with all types and 150 beds in well-maintained rooms, all with TV. Rooms on the top floor (#279 and higher) have panoramic views of the city. Breakfast buffet included. Check-out 11:30am. Singles with shower DM78-190; doubles with shower DM180-300; cheaper on weekdays.

FOOD

Kröpcke, the once-renowned food court-cafe at the center of the pedestrian zone, now owned by Mövenpick, a touristy restaurant chain, can hook you up with small snacks (from DM2.50) or nice sit-down meals (from DM13.50). The **Mövenpick Café** has reasonably-priced lunch specials and an all-you-can-eat salad bar (weekdays, 11:30am-11pm), sandwiches (DM4-8), and delicious ice cream treats (DM3-10.80). The **Lister Meile** area behind and inside the train station also offers cafes with pleasant seating

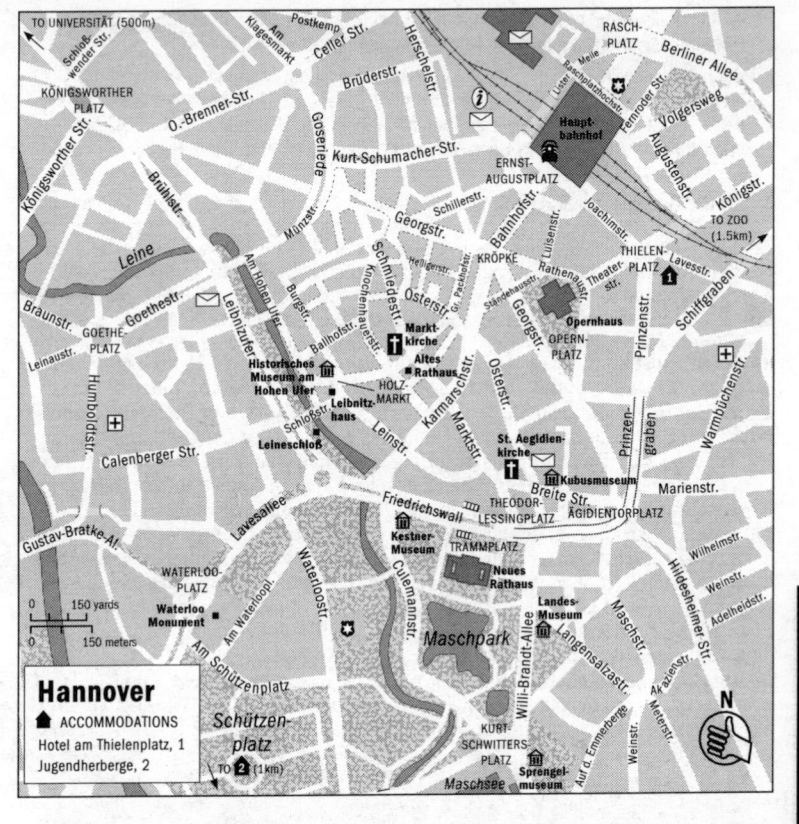

Hannover

▲ ACCOMMODATIONS

Hotel am Thielenplatz, 1
Jugendherberge, 2

options, and more fast-food stands than you can count, but not much going on in the way of interesting food (pizza or, um, pizza). **Spar supermarkets** sit by the Lister Meile and Kröpcke U-Bahn stops (open M-F 7am-7pm, Sa 8am-2pm). An **Edeka,** at the corner of Pfarrlandstr. and Limmerstr. (U-Bahn #10 to "Leinaustr."), gets in on the **grocery** action (open M-F 7am-8pm, Sa 8am-4pm). For a more international flavor, ride on down from the *Hauptbahnhof* to the **Markt-halle,** where a variety of snacks, meals, and booze awaits (open M-W 7am-6pm, Th-F 7am-8pm, Sa 7am-4pm).

Mensa, Callinstr. 23 (☎ 768 80 35). U-Bahn #4 or 5 to "Schneiderberg." Take a right up Schneiderbergstr., just past the small bridge in the green-trimmed building. DM3 gets you the card on which you can deposit however much you want to spend. Meals DM2.20-3.70, DM6-8.50 for guests. If you miss the tight lunch hours, turn right off Schneiderbergstr. onto Callinstr., where several inexpensive cafes wait, most with outdoor seating. Open M-F 11:40am-2:30pm.

Uwe's Hannenfaß Hannover, Knochenhauerstr. 36 (☎32 16 16). Located in the center of the Altstadt, in the timber-framed house where the master brewer of Hannover once lived. The steaming *Niedersachsenschmaus* (DM8.90), a potato casserole, steadies the stomach while a *Bowle* of the house-brewed *Hannen Alt* lightens the head (DM5.40). The traditional German fare of Jägerschnitzel (DM12) and Bremsklotz (DM6) overshadows the healthier prepared salads (DM8.90). Daily specials served noon-3:30pm. Open M-Sa noon-2am, Su 3pm-2am.

Jalda, Limmerstr. 97 (☎212 32 61), serves a delightful combination of Italian, Greek, and Arabic dishes. Lunch specials M-F noon-4pm (DM10-13). Pizzas, veggie fare, and Arabic *Pfanne* DM 6-12, meaty chow DM15-19. Take out or eat in with candlelight and funk in the background. Diverse crowd—students at one table, grandma and grandpa in the corner booth. Open M-Th and Su 11:30-midnight, F-Sa noon-1am.

Peach Pit, Lister Meile 5 (☎ 34 34 32). A late night/early morning haven for the drunk, tired, and hungry. Although you won't run into Brenda or Brandon, you will likely see happy inebriates looking for a sandwich (DM2.80-7), milkshake (DM3.50), or more beer. Open W 8pm-2am, Th 6am-2am, and F 6am until Su at 2pm—that's 56 continuous hours of 90210 antics!

Ahrberg, Bahnhofstr. 3, right outside the station. For a quick snack, have a traditional bratwurst (DM3), or, to satisfy a deeper hunger, an entire chicken (DM11). Open M-F 7am-8pm, Sa 7am-4pm.

SIGHTS

HERRENHAUSEN. In 1714, George I, the son of Electoral Princess Sophie, ascended the throne of the United Kingdom. His descendants continued as the rulers of Hannover and the United Kingdom until 1837, when the Hanoverians refused to accept an English queen—Sophie's great-great-great-great-granddaughter, Victoria. The city owes much to Princess Sophie, who furnished the three paradisiacal **Herrenhausen gardens.** The centerpiece is the Baroque **Großer Garten.** Its **Herrenhausen palace,** built in the 18th century and bombed to ruins in 1943, opens onto a garden roofed by topiary trees and populated by copies of Renaissance sculptures of mythical heroes and heroines. During the "illuminations," geyser-like fountains shoot from the ground to glow in the warm backlighting—gushing in their midst is Europe's highest garden fountain, the **Große Fontäne.** Originally 32m high, it has been gradually built up to 80m. Concerts and the performing arts enliven the garden from June to August. Call for schedule (☎ 16 84 12 22). Not as large as the **Großer Garten,** the **Georgengarten** is a maze of open fields and tree-lined avenues, while the **Berggarten** showcases an indoor rain forest (DM8.50). The fireworks contests held in summer provide dazzling displays. *(Take U-Bahn #4 (direction: "Garbsen") or 5 (direction: Stöcken") to "Herrenhäuser Gärten." Georgengarten open 24hr. Free. Großer Garten and Berggarten open Apr.-Oct. M-Tu 8am-8pm, W-Su 8am-10pm; daily Nov.-Mar. 8am-dusk. DM3. Light show W 5-7:30pm. DM5. Fountains M-F 11am-noon and 3-5pm, Sa-Su 11am-noon and 2-5pm. DM3.)*

ALTSTADT. Many sights stand in Hannover's otherwise-modern **Altstadt,** a 15-minute walk from the train station. Walk down Bahnhofstr. and continue along as it becomes Karmarschstr.; take a right on Knochenhauer Str.—an old 14th-century church, the **Marktkirche,** will be on your left. *(In the center of Hans-Lilje-Pl. Open daily 10am-4pm; check for concerts.)* Used for official purposes until 1913, Hannover's former **Rathaus** has become, in a final burst of glory…a shopping area and cafe. Best to gawk at the lovely exterior; most everything inside is pricey.

LEIBNIZHAUS. A beautifully restored Baroque mansion, the house was home to brilliant mathematician, philosopher, man of letters, and royal advisor Gottfried Wilhelm Leibniz until his death in 1716. Tread carefully—this site cost DM22 million to restore. *(Holzmarkt 5. ☎ 62 44 50. Open Su 10am-1pm and 1:30-6pm.)*

HANN("FESTIVALS ARE NEVER")OVER: If a world expo were to be held in Germany, it could only be at Hannover. No stranger to festivals, it was the choice for World Expo 2000. Swing by the 160-hectare fair grounds (in the southeastern suburbs, near Laatzen) to check out the aftermath or entertain yourself with some live action. Festivals, city-wide events, and special performances are held all year-round. Drive away the winter blues at the annual concert of the Niedersachsen State Orchestra **(Operhaus),** or heat up the summer with the firework competition **(Herrenhausen).** There is something for everyone, anytime, anywhere…as long as it is in Hannover. Check www.hannover.de for the entire year's schedule.

ST. ÄGIDIENKIRCHE. A jog down Leinstr. brings you past the magnificent **Leineschloß,** seat of the Diet of Niedersachsen, to the ivy-covered shell of the **St. Ägidienkirche.** The massive damage suffered by the church during WWII was intentionally left untouched and memorial plaques were put up as reminders of the folly of war.

NEUES RATHAUS. On the outskirts of the Altstadt, among the museums, stands the more spectacularly modern **Neues Rathaus.** Hanoverians painstakingly recreated this palatial turn-of-the-century complex after WWII. Step inside to see models of the city in 1689, 1939, 1945, and today. Take the slanted elevator up the tower to behold the real thing (DM3, students DM2). From up high, you can scout out Hannover's many parks, including the **Maschsee,** a 2km long lake just south of the Rathaus that's covered with sailboats and rowboats during the summer and ice skaters in winter. *(Rathaus Open Apr.-Oct. M-F 9:30am-5:30pm, Sa-Su 10am-5pm.)*

ZOO. Lions, tigers, and bears, oh my! Hannover's large and classy zoo, offers a reptile house and an African "jumbo" safari. Or just be entertained with the guinea-pig city by the entrance (free!). *(From the Altstadt, follow Schiffstr., which becomes Fritz-Behrens Allee, for 40min. Or take U-Bahn #4 (direction: "Roderbruch") to "Clausewitzstr." and switch onto #11 (direction: "Zoo") until the end of the line. Open M-Sa 9am-7pm. Adults DM24.50, children DM19.50, dogs DM10.)*

 **MUSEUMS**

■ **SPRENGEL MUSEUM.** A 20th-century art lover's dream with works by James Turrell, Henry Moore, Dalí, Picasso, Magritte, and Horst Antes. Learn to appreciate a wide range of modern art, including 5 inch lego sculptures and giant inflatable lily pads. Good bistro with beautiful view of the Maschsee (snacks DM8-20). *(Kurt-Schwitters-Pl. At the corner of the Maschsee and Maschpark, near the Neues Rathaus. ☎ 16 84 38 75. Open Tu 10am-8pm, W-Su 10am-6pm. Permanent collection DM7, students DM3.50; excellent special exhibits DM12, students DM8.)*

■ **KESTNER-MUSEUM.** Decorative arts of Medieval and Renaissance Europe, ancient Egypt, Greece, and Rome arranged creatively on three floors. Eat at the cafeteria on the second floor surrounded by 18th-century porcelain and 20th-century furniture. *(Trammpl. 3. Next to the Neues Rathaus. ☎ 16 84 21 20. Open Tu and Th-Su 11am-6pm, W 11am-8pm. DM5, students DM3; free on F.)*

WILHELM-BUSCH-MUSEUM. Just reopened after architectural improvements, this cartoon museum dazzles with wit, sarcasm, and vivid colors. Take a break from the laughing on the shores of the neighboring pond. *(Georgengarten 1. U-Bahn #4, direction: "Gorbsen," or #5, direction: "Stöcken," to "Schneiderberg." ☎ 71 40 76.)*

KUBUSMUSEUM. This Hanoverian artists' co-op shows contemporary art in a single room space on the second floor. *(Theodor-Lessing-Pl. 2, near the Ägidienkirche. ☎ 16 84 57 90. Open Tu-F 11am-6pm, Sa-Su 11am-4pm. Free.)*

LANDESMUSEUM. A child-friendly cultural museum with an outdoor bistro (DM7-20) that hosts concerts. The tame ground floor has an aquarium, a non-European "cultural" exhibit (read: jumble of African masks and Inuit huts), and Neanderthal skulls. A few wonderful paintings on the top floor, including Rubens and the appetizing "Stilleben beim Wildhändler" by Frans Snyders. *(Willy-Brandt-Allee 5. ☎ 980 75. Open Tu-Sa 10am-5pm, Th 10am-7pm. DM6, students DM3.)*

HISTORISCHES MUSEUM AM HOHEN UFER. Sits in a 1960s "replica" of a 10th-century fortress. A very thorough exposition of Hannover's history and its cultural links with Britain. Also houses a huge collection of dioramas depicting scenes from battlefields. *(On Burgstr. next to the Leibnizhaus. ☎ 16 84 30 52. Open Tu 10am-8pm, W-F 10am-4pm, Sa-Su 10am-6pm. DM5, students and children DM3. F free.)*

NIEDERSACHSEN

ENTERTAINMENT AND NIGHTLIFE

More than 20 theaters make their homes in Hannover, supplying ballet, opera, drama, and Broadway musicals. The four largest are the **Opernhaus,** Opernpl. 1, the **Ballhof,** Ballhofstr. 5, the **Schauspielhaus,** on Theaterpl., and the **Theater am Aegi,** on Ägidientorpl. Tickets for most of the theaters (from DM12) are sold at the tourist office; call their ticket line at 30 14 30. Advance tickets for the opera and the *Schauspielhaus* are also sold at the Opernhaus M-F 10am-7:30pm, Sa 10am-2pm, or by calling ☎99 99 11 11 one hour after the box office opens. Most theaters offer student tickets 60 minutes before each show at a 25% discount. For the line on theater dates, festival dates, and other items of interest, pick up the monthly *Hannover Vorschau* (DM 3) from the tourist office or the free *Hannover Live.* The Opernhaus provides its own free, thick guide to opera and ballet. The **UFA-Arthouse Thielenplatz,** Lavesstr. 2 (☎32 18 79; open M-F 4:45pm, Sa-Su 1:45pm), shows movies in English. The enormous **Cinemaxx,** Nikolaistr. 8 (☎130 93; tickets 126 32 00; Open 11am-11pm), and the **Palast Filmtheater,** Bahnhofstr. 5 (☎32 28 73), show dubbed American blockbusters.

If you're within a 100km radius of Hannover the first week in July, detour to its **Schützenfest** (marksmanship festival), the largest such *fête* in the world. Every summer since 1539, Hanoverians have congregated—weapons in hand—to test their marksmanship and retreat to the beer gardens to get *Schützen*-faced. The 10-day festival comes complete with parade, fireworks, chintzy stuffed animals, and rickety amusement park rides, but its main attraction is the *Lüttje Lage,* a feisty traditional drink. Without spilling, you must down the contents of two shot glasses simultaneously, holding them side by side in one hand; one glass contains *Weiß-bier,* the other *Schnapps.* For more information, contact the **Hannoversches Schützenfest** (☎161 18 54; fax 161 18 55). And if this isn't enough fun for you, Hannover delivers a nifty one-two punch. After giving the liver a brief respite, the **Maschseefest** (late July-early Aug.) hits you with another wild combination of concerts, masked balls, and street performances. For anyone left standing, the knock-out blow falls with the **Altstadtfest** in the first or second weekend in August. All the big *Kneipen* and cafes convene for one last hurrah until next year. And for those folks who feel they must drop some cash in the streets every weekend, the **Floh-markt** (flea market) on the **Leibnizufer** hits town every Saturday from 7am to 2pm.

When the sun goes down, Hannover lets 'em rip with an impressive array of packed cafes and pumping discos. The happening university crowds swarm the area of Linden-Nord, between Goetheplatz and Leinaustr., filling the cafes and *Kneipen.* For parties, snoop around the Mensa for signs (see **Food,** p. 487), or check either *Prinz* (DM2) or *Schädelspalter* (DM5), outstanding guides to nightlife in the city. The free *MagaScene* lists dance clubs and concerts. For live music, check out **The Capitol** (see below) or **Altro Mondo,** Bahnhofstr. 8 (☎32 33 27), in the City-Passage. Tickets are available by phone at ☎41 99 99 40.

■ **The Loft,** Georgstr. 50b (☎363 13 76). Right near Kröpcke, this hip joint is packed with students and smoke on the weekends. Open M-Th 9pm-2am, F-Sa 9pm-5am, Su 9pm-2am. Go through the back door to enter the alternative bistro-bar **Masa.** Enjoy falafel (DM6.50) and milkshakes (DM5.50) by candlelight. Both offer half-price drinks during the happy hours of 12pm-4pm and 12am-closing. Masa open F-Sa noon-5am, Su-Th noon-2am.

The Capitol, Schwarzer Bär 2 (☎44 40 66), sets the floor thumping with dance hits. Loosen up in a sea of bumping bodies. Next to the bar, a smaller floor for hard rock gets heads banging. The Capitol offers live music, while its neighbor **The Capitol Rockdisco,** has a dance floor. Open F-Sa 10pm. Cover around DM8.

Osho Disco, Raschpl. 7L (☎34 22 17). A lounge area surrounding the dance floor is a great place to meet (pick up) folks. Every Wednesday is "over 30-night"—no cover for anyone over 30. Open W-Su at 10pm. Cover W-and Su DM5, Th-Sa DM8.

Daily Planet, Ägidientorpl. 1 (☎32 30 02). Jump out of your phone booth and stop the friggin' presses. A cool news bar with **internet access** (30min DM3), burgers, beers, and a wealth of hard liquor. Open M-Sa 11:30am-11pm.

Finnegan's Wake, Theaterstr. 6 (☎32 97 11). A place to chill with real Dubliners, where everybody knows *Ulysses's* name. Heats up early (9pm) even on weeknights; a good place to practice speaking English. Daily happy hour (4-6pm) and live Irish music (F-Su 9pm) liven the scene. Open M-F 4pm-2am, Sa-Su noon-2am.

Schwule Sau, Schaufeldstr. 30 (☎700 05 25). U-Bahn #6 or 11: "Kopernikusstr." This extremely popular gay and lesbian bar is located in the university district. On good nights, the 3-person sofa in the corner seats 15. Tu ladies only. W men only. Sunday afternoons are tea. Next door, the radical left meets techno beat at **KNHO,** Schaufeldstr. 33. Open Tu, W, and F 8pm-3am, Sa 9pm-7am, Su 3pm-2am. Cover DM6.

GÖTTINGEN ☎0551

Home to Europe's first free university, Göttingen remains a college town to the core. The Georg-August-Universität boasts Otto von Bismarck as an alumnus and the Brothers Grimm as former faculty members, but its real fame comes from its spectacular track record in hard science. Forty-two Nobel laureates have been students or faculty members, including Max Planck (the father of quantum mechanics) and Werner Heisenberg (author of the famous Uncertainty Principle). Heisenberg was the head of the German A-Bomb project, but a fundamental, and perhaps intentional, mistake in calculations lead his research teams down fruitless paths and kept the Bomb out of Hitler's hands. The university has historically taken radical positions jumping all over the political spectrum—left in 1734 after its founding, reactionary right in the 1920s, and in the fifties back again, earning a reputation as a *rote Uni* (red university). Today, the political climate is less urgent, and yet the leftist roots are evident in the independent stylings of the student body. Those in search of *Animal House* will be disappointed—the cast of characters here looks more like *Run Lola Run.*

NIEDERSACHSEN

▐ GETTING THERE AND GETTING AROUND

Trains: Frequent trains to **Berlin** (2½hr., 1 per hr., DM100); **Frankfurt** (2hr., 1 per hr., DM66); **Hannover** (1hr., 2 per hr., DM30); and **Hamburg** (2hr., 2 per hr., DM80).

Public Transportation: Almost all city buses depart from the "Markt" and "Kornmarkt" stops. Single ride DM2.70, one transfer permitted.

Taxis: Hallo Taxi, "Göttingen's friendly taxis." Call 340 34 and say hallo.

Car Rental: Sixt, Groner Landstr. 33b (☎54 75 70). Open M-F 8am-6pm, Sa 8am-1pm.

Mitfahrzentrale: Mitfahrbüro Cheltenham House, Friedrichstr. 1 (☎48 59 88), hooks up riders and drivers. To Frankfurt DM25, Berlin DM30, Munich DM44. Open M-F 10am-6pm, Sa 10am-1:30pm.

Bike Rental: Fahrrad-Parkhaus (☎599 94), to the right of the station's main exit. Bikes from DM15 per day. Open M-Sa 5:30am-10pm, Su 8am-11pm.

▐ ORIENTATION AND PRACTICAL INFORMATION

The Altstadt lies within the confines of a horseshoe-shaped ring road. At its center lie the **Altes Rathaus** and **Wilhelmsplatz,** site of the original university building.

Tourist Office: Tourist-Information, Markt 9 (☎540 00; fax 400 29 98; tourismus@goettingen.de), in the Altes Rathaus. From the station, cross Berliner Str. to perpendicular Goetheallee. Follow it several blocks as it becomes Prinzenstr. and turn right onto Weender Str., which runs into the Markt. The staff books rooms (from DM30) for free. Open Apr.-Oct. M-F 9:30am-5pm, Sa-Su 10am-4pm; Nov.-Mar. M-F 9:30am-

1pm and 2-6pm, Sa 10am-1pm. A smaller Tourist-Center, Bahnhofspl. 5 (☎560 00; fax 531 29 28), is at the train station. Open M-F 9am-6pm, Sa 9am-2pm.

Tours: Depart from the main hall of the Rathaus daily at 11:30am if 5 or more people attend. DM7. Tours in English available for large groups only.

Currency Exchange: Commerzbank, Prinzenstr. 2 (☎40 80), has the best rates in town. Open M-W 8:30am-4pm, Th 8:30am-6pm, F 8:30am-3:30pm.

American Express: Goetheallee 4a (☎52 20 70). Open M-F 9am-6pm, Sa 9:30am-12:30pm.

Bookstore: Deuerlich, Weender Str. 33 (☎49 50 00). Smaller branches at Weender Landstr. 6 and Theaterstr. 25. Open M-W and F 9am-7pm, Th 9am-8pm, Sa 9am-4pm.

Laundromat: Wasch-Salon, Ritterplan 4, opposite the Städtisches Museum. Wash DM4, soap DM1. Dry DM1 per 12min. Open M-Sa 7am-10pm.

Pharmacy: Goethe-Apotheke, Goetheallee 17-18 (☎563 64). Open M-F 8am-6:15pm, W 8am-4pm, and Sa 9am-1pm.

Emergency: ☎110. **Police,** Am Steingraben 19 (☎49 11). **Fire,** ☎112. **Ambulance,** ☎192 22.

Women's Resources: Frauenhaus (☎483 20). Open 24hr. Some English spoken.

AIDS Hotline: AIDS-Beratung, ☎400 48 31.

Post Office: Heinrich-von-Stephan-Str. 1, 37073 Göttingen, to the left of the train station. Open M-F 7am-6:30pm, Sa 8am-1pm.

ACCOMMODATIONS

The abundance of students and visitors in Göttingen makes the housing market tight but not unreasonable. Fortunately, the hostel is reasonably priced and generally has room available, while those wishing to stay a few days or even a few months can check the **Mitwohnzentrale,** Rasenweg 8a, which matches up potential roommates. (☎194 30. Open M-F 10am-6pm, Sa 10am-2pm.)

Jugendherberge (HI), Habichtsweg 2 (☎576 22; fax 438 87). From the station, turn left onto Berliner Str., which becomes Nikolausberger Weg; bear right at the Nonnensteig fork, and then follow the signs to the hostel (45min.). Or take bus #8, 10, 11, 15, or 18 to "Kornmarkt," then bus #6 (direction: "Klausberg") to "Jugendherberge." A helpful staff and many facilities make the hostel a first choice for many. Lots of singles available (for an extra DM5). Breakfast and sheets included. Room keys require DM20 deposit. Reception 6:30am-11:30pm. Curfew midnight, or get a key with a DM30 deposit. HI members only. DM27, over 26 DM 32.

Hotel-Gaststätte Berliner Hof, Weender Landstr. 43 (☎38 33 20; fax 383 32 32; email BerlinerHof.Göttingen@T-Online.de; www.berlinerhof.de). Take bus #20 or #24 to "Kreuzbergring." Or walk left out of the station up Berliner Str. and turn left on Weender. At the edge of the university, Berliner Hof offers cheery rooms and a friendly staff. All rooms with TV. Reception 3-11pm. Large 3 bedroom suites (DM150) are ideal for families or groups. Singles DM60, with shower DM70; doubles with the works DM100.

Hotel Garni Gräfin Holtzendorff, Ernst-Ruhstrat-Str. 4 (☎639 87; fax 63 29 85). Remotely located in an industrial area, but a worthwhile option if everything else is booked. From the station, take bus #13 (direction: "Harrenacher") to "Florenz-Sautorius-Str." Continue walking in the direction of the bus and take the second left. Comfortable singles DM49, with shower DM70; doubles DM85, with shower DM95.

FOOD

Göttingen is blessed with a high-quality **Mensa** and vegetable **Markt.** Perhaps the most appetizing produce comes from the **fruit market** adjacent to the Deutsches Junges Theater (Tu, Th, and Sa 7am-1pm) and in the square in front of the Rathaus (Th 2-8pm). The most central supermarket is **Plus,** Prinzenstr. 13, across from the

Göttingen

🏠 ACCOMMODATIONS
Hotel Gräfin Holtzendorff, 1
Hotel-Gaststätte Berliner Hof, 2
Jugendherberge, 3

library. (Open M-F 8am-7:30pm, Sa 8am-4pm.) **Vollkorn Naturkostmarkt,** on 73 Lange Geismarstr., hawks natural foods (M-F 9am-5:30pm, Sa 9am-2:30pm.) **Goetheallee,** running from the station to the city center, has late-night Greek, Italian, and Turkish restaurants. Bakeries and other places good for a quick snack line **Weender Str.** and **Jüdenstr.** The streets surrounding Wilhelmsplatz have a variety of pizza joints and other restaurants that cater to the student population.

Zentral-Mensa, Pl. der Göttinger Sieben 4 (☎39 51 51). Follow Weender Landstr. onto Pl. der Göttinger Sieben, turn right into the university complex, and walk through the central plain to the cavernous *Studentenwerk* building on the left. Swarming with people and plastered with events listings, the cafeteria serves meals for DM5-6. Tickets sold downstairs—buy one or you can't eat. Open M-F 11:30am-2:15pm, Sa 11:30am-2pm. The **Central Café** sells baguettes and snacks. Open M-Th 9am-8pm, F 9am-7pm.

🦜 **Shucan,** Weender Str. 11 (☎48 62 44). Soak up some sun under the colorful bird and do a little people watching outside in the Marktplatz. Baguettes (DM5-8) are a slice above most. Open M-Th and Su 9am-2am, F-Sa 10am-3am.

Nudelhaus, Rotestr. 13 (☎442 63). Oodles of noodles (27 different varieties), most DM8-15, served up in generous portions in a Mediterranean meets German atmosphere. A beer garden in back facilitates merry slurping. English menu available. Open Su-Th 10am-midnight, F-Sa 10am-1am (kitchen closes at midnight).

Pizzeria Sorrento, Jüdenstr. 13a (☎550 20). With Göttingen's plethora of gyro-joints, how does one choose? Here's the local pick, just far enough off the main pedestrian routes to avoid total discovery. Gyros DM6-10, pizzas DM7-13. They deliver. Open M-Th and Su 11am-2am, F-Sa 11am-3am.

Mr. Jones, Goethealle 8 (☎531 45 00). Tex mex food and lots of funny colored liquids to wash it down are the order of the day at this hip cafe/bar featuring a *Biergarten* and a substantial drink menu. Open daily from 11:30am.

🍴 SIGHTS

ALTES RATHAUS. The courtyard of the Altes Rathaus serves as the meeting place for the whole town; however, the savviest onlookers tend to pull up chairs in one of the numerous cafes lining its perimeter. The meter-tall Gänse-liesel (goose-girl) on the fountain in front of the Rathaus is Göttingen's symbol, edging out Madonna as "the most-kissed girl in the world"; graduating students, particularly budding doctors, line up to plant one on this deceptively innocent little nymphet. The repressed city council imposed a "kissing ban" in 1926, prompting one incensed (or perhaps just, uh, frustrated) student to sue. He lost, but town officials now turn a blind eye to extracurricular fountain activities. The bronze lion-head doorknob on the south portal of the **Rathaus** was crafted in 1300, making it the oldest town hall door knob in Germany. Not quite the pyramids, but good trivia nonetheless. Inside, elaborate murals depict 19th-century life in Göttingen.

GEORG-AUGUST-UNIVERSITÄT. The renowned university's campus fills an area bounded by Weender Landstr., Humboldtallee, and Nikolausberger Weg. Free-form fashioned students of all persuasions rush in and out, many via bicycle.

BISMARCK SIGHTS. The **Bismarckhäuschen,** outside the city wall, is a tiny stone cottage built in 1459 where 17-year-old law student Otto von Bismarck took up res-idence after authorities expelled him from the inner city for boozing it up. *(☎48 62 47. Open Tu 10am-1pm, Th and Sa 3-5pm. Free.)* The **Bismarckturm** commemorates the larger-scale trouble-making of his later career (see Bismarck and the Second Reich, p. 10). From the top of the old stone tower, there's a Göttingen-wide view. These sights are a bit distant and forgotten, but remain a significant part of the area's history. *(Im Hainberg. ☎561 28. Take bus A to "Bismarckstr./Reitsaal." Open Sa-Su 11am-6pm. Free.)*

MEDIEVAL CHURCHES. Göttingen hosts a number of notable churches. The **Jakobikirche's** 72m tower rises up next to the stone lambda structure called Der Tanz. Inside, it's fun to play with the miniature model of the impressive 1402 altar triptych. *(☎575 96. At the corner of Prinzenstr. and Weender Str. Open daily 10am-5pm. Tower open Sa from 11am. Free organ concerts F at 6pm.)* Down Weender Str. behind the Altes Rathaus stands the fortress-like **Kirche St. Johannis.** The interior is unexceptional, but the tower in which students have lived since 1921 is more interesting. *(☎48 62 41. Open daily 10:30am-12:30pm. Tower open Sa 2-4pm.)*

STÄDTISCHES MUSEUM. The municipal museum gives a detailed examination of the city over the last several millennia or so. Jewelry from the bronze age, altarpieces and robes from times long forgotten, and 50s furniture fill out the more benign elements of city history. The real chills come from an era when Theaterplatz was renamed Adolf-Hitler-Platz: gas masks, Hitler youth paraphernalia, and explanations of the SS, ISK, SPD, KPD, and BDM. The Jewish tapestries on the third floor provide a solemn contrast. The upper floor houses an exhibit dedicated to the university's tradition of resistance. *(Ritterplan 7. One block north from the Jakobikirche on Jüdenstr. ☎400 28 43. Open Tu-Su 10am-5pm. Permanent exhibit DM3, students DM1; temporary exhibits DM3, students DM2.)*

SYNAGOGUE MEMORIAL. On Untere Maschstr., the steel sculpture stands over a space with plaques listing the names of those killed when a Göttingen synagogue was razed in 1938. Viewed from above, the structure spirals into a monumental Star of David.

🎵🎭 ENTERTAINMENT AND NIGHTLIFE

Göttingen's entertainment industry covers the entirety of the theatrical spectrum with many world-class performances and locales.

🎭 Deutsches Theater, Theaterpl. 11 (☎ 49 69 11), puts on the classics with tickets as low as DM11. Check out the slick *DT* catalogue for the schedule, available at the box office. Open M-F 10am-1:30pm and 5-7pm, Sa 10am-noon, and 1hr. before performance.

Junges Theater, Hospitalstr. 6 (☎ 49 50 15), a more edgy alternative that presents a new outlook on both the classic and the innovative. (Tickets DM19, students DM12.) The Junges Theater also houses the **KAZ-Keller** (☎ 471 45), a pleasant *Kneipe* that draws the local artsy crowd, hosting concerts and dances. Open daily 8pm-2am.

Cinema: Film buffs can indulge in the perverse pleasure of ruthlessly dubbed blockbusters and German-language flicks at **Capitol 3 Cinema,** Prinzenstr. 13 (☎ 48 48 84), or at the nine screens of the gigantic **Cinemaxx** (☎ 521 22 00) complex behind the train station. The artsy **Lumière,** Geismarer Landstr. 19 (☎ 48 45 23), is more cosmopolitan (DM9, students DM8).

Although Göttingen's disco and pub scene centers on the Altstadt, a few popular clubs perch on the outskirts of the university.

Outpost, Königsallee 243 (☎ 662 51). This aptly named club mixes up the best dance music in town, with "Kamikaze Club" on Tuesday. Open Tu and F-Sa from 10pm.

Blue Note, Wilhelmspl. 3 (☎ 469 07), under the Alte Mensa, Wilhelmsplatz 3. The chillest venue for music and hanging out in the Altstadt. There's a different musical theme each day of the week, and live bands at least once a week. Jazz, reggae, and African pop are well represented. Open daily from 8pm. Cover for concerts DM8-30.

Nörgelbuff Musik-Kneipe, Groner Str. 23 (☎ 438 85), located next to the "Kornmarkt" bus stop, has that old-school, cheap-beer, rock-n-roll feel, and hosts a fairly broad range of musical events a couple times per week, some of which rock harder than others. Open M 10pm-2am, F-Sa 7pm-3am, Su 9pm-2am.

Irish Pub, Mühlenstr. 4 (☎ 456 64), is one of the most popular student watering holes, with a seemingly infinite supply of Guinness and a ton of Gaelic *Gemütlichkeit*. Open daily 6pm-2am.

GOSLAR ☎ 05321

Goslar's immaculately-preserved Altstadt, tucked snugly into the rolling hills of the Harz mountains, is bound to leave most visitors positively enchanted. During WWII, Goslar's citizens proclaimed it neutral and free of soldiers, painting red crosses atop their homes. Under the Geneva convention, this act rendered the town a non-target for bombing, saving it from destruction. The charm of the tightly-packed half-timbered houses is enhanced by exciting museums and provocative sculptures, designed and crafted by artists such as Henry Moore and Botera, scattered throughout the village. As the hub of an extensive bus network, Goslar can spin you into any part of the region. Goslar's postcard perfection and its perch at the edge of the peaceful and popular Harz mountains has, however, turned it into something of a tourist trap. Those in search of the authentic German experience might be disappointed; in its quest to become a tourist mecca, Goslar's local character seems somewhat strained.

🛈 ORIENTATION AND PRACTICAL INFORMATION

Trains roll hourly to **Hannover** (1½hr., 1 per hr., DM23) and **Göttingen** (1¼hr., 1 per hr., DM23). Goslar is a good base for a bus or hiking tour of the Harz Mountains. **Harz Bike,** Bornhardtstr. 3-5, rents **bikes** for DM50 per day. (☎ 820 11. Open M-F 10am-5pm, Sa 10am-4pm.) The **tourist office,** Markt 7, across from the Rathaus, books **rooms** (from DM30) for free and offers maps of the Harz. (☎ 780 60; fax 230

05; email goslarinfo@t-online.de; www.goslarinfo.de. Open May-Oct. M-F 9:15am-6pm, Sa 9:30am-4pm, Su 9:30am-2pm; Nov.-Apr. M-F 9:15am-5pm, Sa 9:30am-2pm.) **Tours** (DM5.50-9) depart regularly from the Marktplatz. **Harzer Verkehrsverband,** Marktstr. 45, inside the Industrie- und Handelskammer building, handles regional tourism and provides information on the Harz. (☎340 30; fax 34 94 66. Open M-F 8am-4pm.) The **Frauenzentrum Goslar,** Breite Str. 15a, provides counseling for women. The entrance is on Bolzenstr. (☎422 55. Open M 9am-noon and 3-5pm, W 9am-noon, and F 9-11am.) The **post office** is at Klubgartenstr. 10, 38640 Goslar (open M-F 8am-5:30pm, Sa 9am-noon).

While the Oberharz Mountains loom over Niedersachsen and Thüringen, information about the entire Harz region can be found in Sachsen-Anhalt (see Harz Mountains, (p. 201).

 ACCOMMODATIONS AND FOOD

The half-timbered Goslar **Jugendherberge (HI),** Rammelsberger Str. 25, wins the prize for being the most confusingly-located hostel in the book. From Marktpl., take twisty Bergstr. southwest until it ends at Clausthaler Str. Directly across the street, between the trees, a stairway marked with a *Wanderweg* sign awaits. Take this pleasant path through the pines and head right at the fork at the path's midpoint to end up in the hostel's backyard (20min.). Or, take bus C from the train station (direction: "Bergbaumuseum") to "Theresienwall"; continue along in the same direction as the bus, and take a sharp left up the hill at the big white *Jugendherberge* sign (10 min.). The path is poorly lit at night. The hostel features smallish two- and six-bed rooms with new furniture. (☎222 40; fax 413 76. Members only. Breakfast included. Linen DM6. Reception 8:30am-2:30pm and 3-10pm. Curfew midnight. Dorm beds DM22, over 26 DM27.) **Gästehaus Elisabeth Möller,** Schiefer Weg 6, offers a dollhouse-like ambience with its lacy, pastel decor, puffy beds, and delightful garden. From the station, take a right on Klubgartenstr., which becomes Am Heiligen Grabe; cross Von-Garssen-Str., and turn right on Schiefer Weg. (☎230 98. Singles DM40, with shower DM50, with full bath DM60; doubles DM80-110.) **Campingplatz Sennhütte,** Clausthaler Str. 28, is 3km from town along the B241. (☎224 98 or 225 02. DM5.50 per person. Tent DM4. Car DM3.)

The town's mountain **Markt** yodels every Tuesday and Friday (open 8am-1pm). The beautiful market square is ringed with restaurants, but most of them are priced and geared toward the tourist crowd. **Markt Treff,** Fleiseharren 6, (☎306 761) serves German favorites, like curry bratwurst with french fries (DM7.50), at prices that put the other outdoor cafes surrounding the square to shame. Cheaper bistros and cafes can be found along Hokenstr., where *Imbiß* stands provide meals for DM4-8. **Mac Döner,** Marktstr. 36, serves fast Turkish food, but no *Happy Meals.* (☎12 30. Open M-Th 11am-11pm, F-Sa 11am-1pm.) Music, beer, and the local crowd converge at **Kö Musik-Kneipe,** Marktstr. 30. (☎268 10. Open M-Th and Su 4pm-2am, F-Sa 4pm-3am.)

SIGHTS

Guarded by a pair of bronze Braunschweig lions, the austere **Kaiserpfalz,** Kaiserbleek 6, is a massive Romanesque palace that served as the ruling seat for 11th- and 12th-century emperors. The palace fell into sad decay by the 19th century but was extensively restored by Prussian aristocrats. The interior of the **Reichssaal** is plastered with murals; the huge paintings display carefully selected historical incidents in a uniquely mythic, pompous manner. In the palace's **Ulrichskapelle,** Heinrich III's heart lies tucked away inside a massive sarcophagus. *(Kaiserpfalz. ☎70 43 58. Museum and tomb open Jan.-Oct. daily 9am-5pm; Nov.-Dec. 10am-4pm. Last entry 30min. before closing. DM8, youth DM4.)* Below the palace is the **Domvorhalle,** a restoration of a 12th-century imperial cathedral destroyed 170 years ago. *(Kaiserbleek 10. ☎75 780.)*

The central **Marktplatz** is an adorable hodgepodge of ornate woodwork and trellises. The **Hotel Kaiserworth,** a former guild house, was for many years an eccentric but striking addition to the square, with superb gable spires and wooden statues of emperors gracing the facade. However, the stately nature of this landmark was recently altered by a garish red paint job, complete with the addition of green "vines." The statues were also painted; the lack of plastic packaging is all that differentiates these colorful beings from action figures. Each day in the market square, small **Glocken- und Figurenspiel,** figures of court nobles and the miners whose work made the region prosperous, dance to the chime on the treasury roof *(9am, noon, and 6pm).* The Rathaus's **Huldigungssaal,** Markt 1, is coated with early 16th-century depictions of prophecies concerning Christ's return. *(☎ 757 80. Open Apr.-Oct. 9am-5pm, Nov.-Mar. 10am-4pm.)* The twin towers of the reconstructed 12th-century **Marktkirche** loom behind the Rathaus. The church hosts the stained-glass saga of St. Cosmas and St. Damian, third-century twin doctors and martyrs. In a classic instance of the Roman empire's overkill, the saints were disciplined and punished by drowning, burning at the stake, stoning, and crucifixion. *(☎ 229 22. Open Apr.-Sept. Tu-W 10:30-3:30pm, Th-Sa 10:30am-6pm, Sun. noon-6pm; Oct.-Mar. Th. 3pm-6:30pm, F-Sa 10:30am-4pm, Sun. 11:30am-4pm.)*

The **Mönchehaus** exhibits a grand modern art collection, including Anselm Kiefer, Calder, Miró, and Joseph Beuys. *(Mönchestr. 3. ☎ 29 570; fax 42 199. Open Tu-Sa 10am-1pm and 3-5pm, Su 10am-1pm. DM5, Students DM 2.50.)* On the way back from the Kaiserpfalz, the fantastic **Musikinstrumente- und Puppenmuseum** is not to be missed. The owner has spent more than 40 years assembling the largest private instrument collection in Germany, including one of the world's first accordions, a snakeskin mandolin, and a digerido. Visit the museum which sits on a shelf inside, billed as the "smallest musical instrument museum in the world" with a Guiness article to prove it. *(Hoher Weg 5. ☎ 269 45. Open daily 11am-5pm. DM6, children DM3.)* Goslar gets funky at the end of August with its **Altstadtfest**—a G-rated *Oktoberfest.*

HAMELN (HAMELIN)   ☎ 05151

In the 700 years since the Pied Piper first strolled out of town, some might say that Hameln has transformed itself from a rat trap to a tourist trap. The original story was sordid enough: after Hameln failed to pay the piper his rat-removal fee, on June 26, 1284, he walked off with 130 children in thrall. But today the legend of the *Rattenfänger,* as he is known in German, draws tourists as mysteriously as his flute drew rodents seven centuries ago. Making your way through the souvenir-choked streets of the tiny Altstadt, you can almost hear the mayor consoling grieving parents, "You haven't lost a child, you've gained a lucrative tourist industry." With so much rat and piper paraphernalia crowding those *Straßen,* it's easy to forget the town's residents. Most do their best to avoid the legend altogether, and beyond the Altstadt lies a completely normal town.

☑ ORIENTATION AND PRACTICAL INFORMATION

Hameln bridges the Weser Rivera and lies 45 minutes from Hannover by **train** (2 per hr., DM15). For a **taxi,** call 74 77. **Oberweser-Dampfschiffahrt,** Inselstr. 3, runs **ferries** up and down the Weser to Bodenwerder, Holzminden, and Hannoversch Münden, and offers a complete package of tours. *(☎ 93 99 99; fax 93 99 933.* 1hr. expedition DM8, kids DM 5; 2hr. DM16, children DM5. Call for a schedule. Operates Mar.-Oct.) Rent **bikes** from **Fahrradverleih Troche,** Kreuzstr. 7. *(☎ 136 70.* Open M-F 9:30am-1pm and 2:30-6pm, Sa 9:30am-12:30pm. DM20 per day.) The hostel (see **Accommodations,** below) also has a few old bikes to rent to guests (DM8 per day). The **tourist office,** Deisterallee 1, on the Bürgergarten, tracks down **rooms** (from DM25) for free. They also give out a very comprehensive list of hotels and *Pensionen.* The just-finished, *über*-modern building, along Piper-free Diesterallee, is the town's small step away from Grimm's antique fairy tale. From the station, cross Bahnhofplatz, make a right onto Bahnhofstr., and turn left onto Deisterstr., which becomes Deisterallee.

NIEDERSACHSEN

(☎95 78 23; fax 95 78 40; email tourist-info@hameln.de; www.hameln.de. Open May-Sept. M-F 9am-1pm and 2-6pm, Sa 9:30am-12:30pm and 2-4pm, Su 9:30am-12:30pm; Oct.-Apr. M-F 9am-1pm and 2-5pm.) **Buchhandlung Matthias,** Bäckerstr. 56, has a limited selection of English paperbacks (☎947 00; open M-F 9-6:30pm, Sa 9am-4pm; May-Sept. also open Su 12:30-4pm). The **post office** is at Am Posthof 1, 31785 Hameln (open M-F 8am-6pm, Sa 8am-1pm).

ACCOMMODATIONS AND FOOD

The beautifully-located, Piper-festooned **Jugendherberge (HI),** Fischbeckerstr. 33, sits on a dreamy bend in the Weser. From the station, take bus #2 to "Wehler Weg," and turn right onto Fischbeckerstr. On foot, cross Bahnhofplatz, make a right onto Bahnhofstr., turn left on Deisterallee, and then go right around 164-er Ring (along the Hamel rivulet) to Erichstr. as it bends into Fischbeckerstr (about 30min.). German school kids *love* dreamy bends in rivers, so call a couple of weeks in advance if possible. (☎34 25; fax 423 16. Breakfast included. Sheets DM6. Reception 12:30-1:30pm and 5-10pm. Curfew 10pm, but key available with DM30 deposit. DM22, over 26 DM27.)

Hameln's tourist boom has resulted in a large number of *Pensionen*. The **Gästehaus Alte Post,** Hummenstr. 23, is located in the Altstadt. Colorful rooms complete with Picasso prints, television, telephone, and clock radio. A coffee maker and refrigerator are available for use. (☎434 44; fax 414 89. Breakfast included. Checkout 11am. DM50-85.) Southeast of the city center, on the gracious shores of Tönebon lake, lies **Campground Jugendzeltplatz,** Tönebonweg 8, equipped with warm showers. Take bus #51 to "Südbad." (☎262 23. Reception Su-Th until 10pm, F-Sa until 11pm. Open May-Sept. DM5 per person.)

Hamelners flock for fruit, vegetables, and other treats to the open-air **market** on the Bürgergarten (W and Sa 8am-1pm). **Batman Market,** Deisterallee 18d, awaits outside the Altstadt to rescue you from unfresh-vegetable villains (open M-Sa 7am-7pm). The streets of the Altstadt around Osterstr. and Pferdemarkt are lined with restaurants and cafes, but the chances of finding a bargain are slim. A few good deals loom along Bäckerstr. near the *Münster*. Duck into **Julia's Restaurant,** Bäckerstr. 57, a dimly lit cafeteria which serves spaghetti (DM 6.90) various sorts of *Schnitzel* and *Wurst,* and crispy salads for DM3.50-8. (☎444 32. Open M-F 10am-8pm, Sa 10am-4pm; May-Sept. also Su 11:30am-5pm.) **Mexcal,** Osterstr. 15, serves excellent *Deutsch*-Mexican meals, and the lunch specials are a good deal (burritos DM9.90). Daily happy "hour" (all day except 6-9pm) gets you cheap drinks (DM8.90—they're BIG. ☎428 06. Open daily noon-midnight.) Need to email your friends to share the Piper-love? Check out the **Witte Internet Cafe,** Kopmanshof 69, which specializes in computers, not cuisine. Fortunately, the food is as inexpensive as the internet. Be prepared to negotiate around local teens, as Witte is the only internet connection around. (☎94 440. 30min. DM5, student DM2.50.) Hameln boasts an impressive array of edible rodents (if you swallow them whole, the fur will tickle your throat…mmm!). To catch these rats, pay to the tune of DM0.35 for tiny marzipan critters and up to DM6 for a jumbo pastry rat. Little crusty breadrats cost DM3 at the excellent bakery in the **Schnelz Reformhaus,** Osterstr. 18, in the Altstadt. It also sells all-natural foodstuffs of every sort, a delight for the vegetarian. (Open M-F 8:30am-6pm, Sa 8:30am-2pm.)

SIGHTS

If you cringe at the thought of small rodents or little flute players in motley capes, Hameln is probably not the best vacation spot; the Piper motif can seem inescapable. One of the few buildings unadorned by rodentia is the gray, modern **Rathaus** (did we say RAT Haus?). In the courtyard out front, however, several elfin children with bowl cuts hang suspended in mid-air as they follow a 1975 piper statue by Karl-Ulrich Nuss to the **Rattenfängerbrunnen** (the "Piper fountain"). The **Bürgergarten,** across Rathausplatz, lends small but soothing relief to the tourist rat race. *(Open daily 7am-10pm; fountains run daily Apr.-Oct. 11am-noon, 3-4pm, and 7:30-8:30pm.)* Also at Rathausplatz is the **Theater Hameln,** where a musical about the piper plays—along with some genuine theater, opera, and dance. *(For information ☎ 91 62 22, for tickets ☎ 91 62 20. Box office open Tu-F 10am-7pm and Sa 10am-1pm.)* Down Osterwall, the **Rattenfängerhaus,** built in 1603, is decked out with startled-looking figureheads and a sad inscription recalling the sudden surge in the average age of townsfolk. Trek 100m into the Fussgängerzone to the **Leiesthaus,** Osterstr. 8-9, where the Museum Hameln exhibits the Piper in 20 poses and 20,000 books. *(☎ 20 22 15. Open Tu-Su 10am-4:30pm. DM3, students and children DM1.)* The grim *Rattenfänger* tale is re-enacted each Sunday at noon in a **Freilichtspiel** (open-air show) at the 1610 Hochzeithaus. Small children dressed as rats chase a man with a large wooden instrument in his mouth wearing a multicolored suit and tight pants; it's simply saucy. (May-Sept., weather permitting. Free.) At 9:35am, the **Glockenspiel** on the Hochzeithaus plays the *Rattenfängerlied* (Pied Piper song); at 11:45am you're serenaded by the *Weserlied;* and at 1:05, 3:35, and 5:35pm, a tiny stage emerges from the Hochzeithaus, and "rats" circle around a wooden flautist. After a fill of *Ratfänger* time, head to the **Glashütten Hameln,** Pulverturm 1, where you can watch people who don't care about rats or multi-colored tights fill their cheeks with air and blow molten glass into shape. *(☎ 272 39; fax 272 40. Open M-F 9:30am-1pm and 2pm-6pm, Sa 9:30am-2pm, Su 10am-5pm. DM2, children DM1.50, under 6 free.)*

HANNOVERSCH MÜNDEN   ☎ 05541

Hannoversch Münden lies between the forested hills where the Fulda and the Werra combine—with the newborn Weser River popping out as a result of the consummation. Alexander von Humboldt called it "one of the seven most beautifully located cities in the world." With more than 700 preserved *Fachwerkhäuser*, this is one of the most attractive of Germany's six zillion half-timbered towns. The impeccable Altstadt remains refreshingly free of tourists despite its picture-book setting at the foot of the *Deutsche Märchenstraße* (German fairy tale route). To taste the flavor of the town, strolling aimlessly through the Altstadt might offer a richer palate than dragging yourself between sights. Either way, Münden offers a tiny world of architectural beauty and authenticity.

🛈 PRACTICAL INFORMATION. Münden is easily accessible by **train** from Göttingen (40min., 1 per hr., DM10) and Kassel (30min., 1 per hr., DM8). **Ferries** navigate the Fulda and Weser rivers with **water tours** of the town (DM10-12). Ask for information at the tourist office (see below), or walk to **Weserstein** at the tip of the island *"Unterer Tanzwerder"* and hop on a ferry. The **tourist office** in the Rathaus **books rooms** (from DM25) for free. (☎ 753 13; fax 754 04; www.hann.muenden.de. Open June-Sept. M-F 9am-6pm, Sa 10am-noon, 1-4pm, Su 11am-4pm; Oct.-May Su-F 9am-4pm.) Help is also on hand from the information counter in the same building after the office closes. (☎ 750. Open daily May-Sept. until 9pm; Oct.-Apr. until 8pm.) **Tours** of the Altstadt leave from the tourist office (June-Sept. M-Su 2pm. DM4, children DM2). Rent **bikes** and **boats** at **Busch Freizeit,** located at **Campingplatz Münden.** (See below. ☎ 66 07 77; fax 660 778. Open 8am-6pm. Bikes DM13, boats DM25 per day.)

🛏🍴 ACCOMMODATIONS AND FOOD. The **Jugendherberge (HI),** Prof.-Oelkers-Str. 10, sits just outside the town limits on the banks of the Weser. From the station, walk down Beethovenstr., turn left at Wallstr., cross the Pionierbrücke, and turn right along Veckerhäger Str. When the road makes a left turn, turn with it (40min.). Or take bus #135 from the train station (direction: "Veckerhäger-/Kasseler Str.") to "Jugendherberge." This hostel has spacious 2-6 person rooms, good facilities, and a cheery location on the river. (☎ 88 53; fax 734 39. Breakfast included. Sheets DM5.70. Reception 5-7pm and 9:45-10pm. Curfew 10pm, but a key to the front door is available. Call ahead. Closed 2 random weekends per month June-Sept. DM22, over 26 DM26.) Pitch your tent in view of the city walls at **Campingplatz Münden,** Oberer Tanzwerder, 10 minutes from the train station on an island in the Fulda River off Pionierbrücke. Follow Kasseler Schlagd along the city walls and turn left on Tanzwerder. A bridge leads over to the island. (☎ 122 57; fax 66 07 78. From DM5.50 per tent. Reception 7am-10pm. DM7.50 per person, DM5 per child.)

The cheapest eats can be found at bakeries along **Lange Str.** or at the **Markt** behind the Rathaus (W and Sa 7am-1pm). **Plus,** Marktplatz 5, stocks **groceries** (open M-F 8am-6:30pm, Sa 8am-2pm).Restaurants of all sorts abound in the area around the **Altmarkt,** but they tend to be pricey. For something affordable, try **Zeus,** at the corner of Loh-Str. and Mühlenstr. near the Rathaus, which sells Greek food (DM5-14) in a classy *Imbiß* setting. (☎26 08. Open daily, 1:30-3:30pm, 5:30-11:30pm.) **Pizza Eck,** Rosenstr. 14, serves hefty pizza and pasta plates. (☎20 94. DM6-9. Open M-Sa 11am-11pm, Su 5-11pm.)

🏛 **SIGHTS.** The town centers around the ornate **Rathaus,** a prime example of the Weser Renaissance style that originated in the area around 1550. Centuries-old markings of Weser flood heights mark the Rathaus' corners, and coloring book scenes from the city's past line the walls inside. Figurines appear in the upper windows of the Rathaus and dance, juggle, and hit each other with heavy hammers to the ringing of the bells daily at noon, 3, and 5pm. *(From the station, cross the street and walk down Beethovenstr.; make a right onto Burgstr. and a left on Marktstr.; the Rathaus will be on the left immediately after Lange Str.)* Outside of the Rathaus sits the wagon of Münden's former resident and favorite tourist gimmick, **Doctor Eisenbart,** an 18th-century traveling physician whose ability to treat many illnesses was overshadowed by his reputation as a quack and a swindler. The story of his life is played out on the stage in front of the Rathaus *(Late June-Aug., 11:15am. DM4, children DM2).*

The **Blasiuskirche,** opposite the Rathaus, is decked out in periwinkle and emerald, with ornate Solomonic columns surrounding the altar and 15th-century crucifix. *(Open May-Oct. 1-6pm daily. Free.)* On the banks of the Werra, the austere **Welfenschloß** proves that not all Weser Renaissance buildings look like over-iced birthday cakes. The gray parts of the building are remnants of the original Gothic structure that burned down in 1560, but the bulk of the structure is a more recently-constructed peach building. The interior can only be admired on a guided tour *(DM4. May-Sept. Su 2:30pm; meet in front of the Rathaus),* but it's not worth the price. The Schloß also houses the **Städtisches Museum,** which exhibits a sizable antique collection and several of Gustav Eberlein's neo-Baroque sculptures as well as local archaeological relics dating back to the 12th century. *(From the Rathaus, follow Markstr. to the Museum. Open M-F 10am-noon and 2:30-5pm, Sa 10am-noon and 2:30-4pm, Su 10am-12:30pm.)*

Weave through the angled side streets to admire the 14th-century *Fachwerkhäuser;* some of the oldest and most impressive are tucked away on **Ziegelstr.** and **Hinter der Stadtmauer.** Note the memorial plaque on **Hinter der Stadtmauer 23,** a Jewish school since 1796, which was gutted in 1938. On the edges of the city, seven of the original defense towers still stand, as well as the **Alte Werrabrücke,** built in 1329, and the 12th-century **Ägidienkirche.**

Münden's three islands—**Doktorwerder, Unterer Tanzwerder,** and **Oberer Tanzwerder**—are all easily accessible by small bridges on the outskirts of the Altstadt. The islands are an excellent place for a stroll, especially the park on Doktorwerder, which comes complete with sculptures. Unterer Tanzwerder has several small parks, and a biergarten and ice cream stand which cater to the tourist crowd. The camp grounds lie on Oberer Tanzwerder. To see the valley from above, cross the Pionierbrücke and hang a left. Follow the sign to the path. The climb includes rugged paths and steep hills which will challenge even the most athletic traveler. The best view of the valley is from across the Fulda atop the **Tillyschanze** tower (☎18 90), built in 1882 to commemorate May 30, 1626. On this day during the Thirty Years War, General Tilly stormed through Münden, slaughtering more than 2,000 citizens. *(Open M 9am-1pm, Tu-Sun 9am-8pm. DM2, children DM1.)*

HILDESHEIM ☎05121

The *tausendjähriger Rosenstock* (Thousand-Year-Old Rose Bush) symbolizes the prosperity of the town of Hildesheim. According to legend, Emperor Ludwig der Fromme (the Pious) lost his way after a hunt and fastened his relic of the Virgin Mary to the branch of a conspicuous rose bush. He managed to find his way home, and the next day, remembering his relic, returned to find it frozen to the branch. Since it was the middle of summer, he interpreted this as a divine sign and erected a chapel on the site, around which grew the majestic Dom and the town of Hildesheim. As long as the bush flourishes, so will Hildesheim. On March 22, 1945, Allied bombers flattened the town, yet the remarkable bush survived. The collapsed ruins of the Dom sheltered the roots from the flames. Eight weeks later, 25 buds were growing strong.

■ PRACTICAL INFORMATION. Hildesheim is 45km southeast of Hannover, with hourly **trains** to **Hannover** (30min., DM10) and **Göttingen** (30min., DM32). **Bus** tickets within the city cost DM2.20 and are valid for one hour; a *Tagesticket* (DM6.50) is valid all day. Rent **bikes** at Räder-Emmel, Dingworthstr. 20-22; it's on your way down the mountain from the hostel (☎438 22; open M-F 9am-1pm and 3-6pm, Sa 9am-1pm; DM8.50 per day). The **tourist office,** Am Ratsbauhof 1c, two blocks from the Rathaus, offers brochures and passes out maps and city guides. From the Hauptbahnhof, walk straight up Bernwardstr., which becomes Almsstr., which in turn becomes Hoher Weg; turn left onto Rathausstr., and turn right down Ratsbauhof. (☎179 80; fax 17 98 88; email tourist-info@hildesheim.com; www.hildesheim.com. Open M-F 9am-6pm, Sa 9am-1pm.) The tourist office also offers two-hour city **tours** (Apr.-Oct. M-F 2pm, Sa 10am and 2pm, Su 2pm; DM7). **Die Gerstenbergsche,** Hoher Weg 10 and Rathausstr. 20, offers a limited selection of English-language novels and chairs to lounge in (☎10 66; open M-F 9am-7pm, Sa 9am-4pm). **Internet access** awaits in @ Il Giornale, Judenstr. 3. (Open M-Sa 9:30am-9:30pm. 40min. connection DM5.) The post office, Bahnhofplatz 3-4, is diagonal from the train station (open M-F 8am-6pm, Sa 8am-1pm).

⌐⌐ ACCOMMODATIONS AND FOOD. Hildesheim's pastoral **Jugendherberge (HI),** Schirrmanweg 4, perches on the edge of a bucolic farm with a gorgeous view of the city. There's a backyard disco for the *Schulkinder*, and fruit candies will be placed on your blue and white bedding. Take bus #1 (direction: "Himmelsthür") to "Dammtor." There, switch to bus #4 (direction: "Bockfeld") to "Triftstr." Cross the street and climb 10 minutes uphill to the hostel. (☎427 17; fax 478 47. Sheets DM6. Breakfast included. Reception M-Sa 8-9:30am, 5-7pm, and 9:45-10pm, Su 6-7pm and 9:45-10pm. Check-out 10am. Curfew 10pm, but key available with an ID. DM24, over 26 DM29.) Along the *Fussgängerzone* off Küsthardstr. rests **Pension Kurth,** Küsthardstr. 4. From the Marktplatz take Judenstr. to a left turn onto Schustr. After the intersection with Zingel Str., take a right onto Küsthardstr, which is across the Hindenburgplatz. Cable TV and plush sofas will have you feeling like a million Marks, but you'll only spend DM50 (☎36 272. Breakfast included.)

Hildesheim has a diverse culinary scene, with plenty of variety and reasonable prices. To the far right of Bahnhofsplatz, savvy shoppers enjoy **Plus Supermarkt,** Hannoversche Str. 28. (Open M-F 8am-7pm, Sa 8am-2pm.) Cultural shoppers will prefer the open-air **market** on Sundays and Wednesdays. The **Amsthausstuben,** Markt 7, serves German dishes from DM14. (☎323 23. Open daily from 10am, kitchen 11:30am-10pm.) For fresh vegetarian and vegan fare, check out **Scheidemann's Salad & Toast Bar,** Osterstr. 18, a stand-up cafe with over 20 salads to choose from, DM5-16.50. Sandwiches and pizzas cost DM5-8. Meat dishes are available, too. (☎390 04. Open M-Th 9am-8pm, F 9am-6pm, Sa 10am-2pm.) **Paulaner im Kneip,** Marktstr. 4, offers a piece of Munich in Hildesheim. Lunch dishes start at DM5, but the real draw is the beer—sweet *Münchener* Paulaner (0.5L DM5.80; *Maß* DM10.50). After happy hour (M-F 5-7pm; 0.3L beer DM2.50), some may want to take a quick swim in the nearby Rathaus fountain. *Some.* (☎360 13. M-Sa 10am-midnight, Su 8am-midnight.)

⊙ SIGHTS. Hildesheim is a city of many churches, and the best way to see all of them is to follow the Rosenroute (rose path), a do-it-yourself tour of spray-painted white blossoms that wends around town. The tourist office has an English guide (DM2). Ludwig's favorite chapel, the Annenkapelle, and the famous *Tausendjäh-riger Rosenstock* bush are featured in the **Dom's** courtyard. *(Open M-Sa 9:30am-5pm, Su* *noon-5pm. Courtyard DM0.50, children and students DM0.30.)* The Dom-Museum and Dom-schatz, around to your left as you exit the Dom, showcase the Marian relic of old Ludwig—it's #8 on the *Schlacht bei Dinklar* exhibit—and other ecclesiastical goodies. *(☎17 91 63; open Tu-Sa 10am-5pm, Su noon-5pm; DM4, students DM1.50.)* The Marktplatz is a plaza of reconstructed half-timbered buildings and archways featuring the majestic ▨Knochenhaueramtshaus (butcher's guild house), reputed to be the most beautiful wooden structure in the world. The facade is lavishly decorated with colorful paintings and German proverbs (e.g., *Arm oder reich, der Tod macht alles gleich*— "poor or rich, death treats all the same"). South of the city center at the intersection of Gelber Stern (Yellow Star) and Lappenberg lie the remains of Hildesheim's synagogue. The temple was torched on *Kristallnacht* in 1938, and a memorial has been placed on the site. Further to the left, drop into the **Römer- und Pelizaeus-Museum,** Am Steine 1, featuring a colorful collection of Egyptian art and artifacts as well as frequent and extensive special exhibits related to ancient cultures. *(☎93 69 31; www.roemer-pelizaeus-museum.de. Open everyday 9am-6pm. DM12, students DM8.)*

🎭 **ENTERTAINMENT.** Opened in 1999, the Theaterhaus Hildesheim, Ostertor 11, hosts visiting theater and dance companies, plays artsy flicks, and stages concerts. *(☎542 76.)* The students in the area get down at Vier Linden, Alfelder Str. 55b, a hip dance-mecca with a popular bar. The first Saturday of every month is "Independence Night": they won't play anything you can hear on the radio. What *do* they play? Cool man. It's cool. *(☎252 55. Open M and Th 10pm-3am; bar open W-Su 6pm-1am.)* The Irish *Kneipe* Limerick, Klaperhagen 6, has lunch specials (11am-4pm; DM9-13), omelettes (DM8-13) and British draughts. *(☎13 38 76; open M-Th and Su 11am-1am, F-Sa until 2am).* For more information on nightlife, check out the free magazine *Public.*

BODENWERDER   ☎05533

In the land of Baron von Münchhausen, the legendary King of Liars, you might not be sure what to believe. It is said that the baron first related his fabulous tales of flying to the moon and navigating an ocean of milk to a cheese isle here, on the banks of the Weser. And it would seem likely that the baron himself is an elaborate fabrication of Bodenwerder's tourist industry, an attempt to out-fable Hameln, except that the little town's church ledgers have birth and death listings for Baron Hieronymus Carolus Fredericus von Münchhausen. The Baron is long gone, but Bodenwerder remains nestled in the hills of the German countryside.

🛈 **PRACTICAL INFORMATION.** Bodenwerder is best reached by bus from Stadtoldendorf, a town on the Altenbeken-Braunschweig train line. Take bus #523 (direction: "Kemnade") to "Weserbrücke, Bodenwerder." from the main bus stop, which is down the hill in front of the station and to the right. Caution—plan your trip ahead and coordinate bus schedules with the train—the bus runs rather infrequently, and only goes straight from Stadtoldendorf to Bodenwerder every few hours. A series of transfers is possible, but the buses in this area tend to run a few minutes late, complicating the problem. From Hameln, take bus #520 (direction: "Stadtoldendorf"). Rent **bikes** from **Karl-Heinz Greef,** Danziger Str. 20. *(☎33 34. Open Mar.-Oct. daily 8:30am-6pm. DM10 per day.)* The **tourist office,** Weserstr. 3 *(☎405 41; fax 61 52; email Touristinformation@bodenwerder.de; www.bodenwerder.de)* hands out free *Weg und Fähre,* which lists events, and has various bits of other information (Open M-F 9am-12:30pm and 2:30-6pm, Sa 9am-1pm; closed Sa Nov.-Mar.) **Tours** meet in front of the office (May-Sept. W at 3pm. DM3). The **post office** is located across the street from the Rathaus, 37619 Bodenwerder. (open M-F 8:30am-noon and 2:30-5pm, Sa 8:30-11:30am).

🏠 **ACCOMMODATIONS AND FOOD.** The tourist office prints a list of hotels and **private rooms** available for rent (from DM25). Bodenwerder's **Jugendherberge (HI),** Richard-Schirmann-Weg *(☎26 85; fax 62 03),* is a 15-minute walk from the pedestrian zone, but the last 100m is steep, steep, steep. Walk across the Weser and turn left, then right on Siemensstr., and follow the signs up Unter dem Berge. While the hike up might be difficult, the view of the town through the cafeteria windows. The institutional exterior conceals a fun-filled interior brimming with *Fußball* and ping-pong. (Breakfast included. Lunch DM8.70, dinner DM6.80. Sheets DM5.70. Reception 4-7pm and 9:30-10pm. Curfew 10pm, but you can get a key to the side door. Members only. 6-bed dorms DM24, over 26 DM29.) The **Campingplatz und Gasthaus Rühler Schweiz,** Großes Tal, are located on the Weser, south of the Altstadt on the opposite side of the river. Cross the Weserbrücke and make a right on the path by the river. All rooms have showers and bathrooms. (☎28 27 or 28 23. Reception daily 2-6pm. Open Mar.-Oct.)

Bodenwerder's culinary offerings are nothing shocking: pizza, baked goods, ice cream. Grill **Akropolis,** Große Str. 44 (☎35 44) cooks up tasty, budget-friendly Greek food, with pitas starting at DM6, and heaping grill plates from DM12. For **groceries** check out **Niedrig Preis,** just across the Weserbrücke from the post office (open M-F 8am-8pm, Sa 8am-4pm).

◉🎵 **SIGHTS AND ENTERTAINMENT.** On Münchhauspl., the mansion-turned-**Rathaus,** the Baron's birthplace, holds the **Münchhausenzimmer und Heimatmuseum.** Inside, you'll find color illustrations of his exploits along with the legendary pistol with which he shot his horse off a steeple. (☎405 41. Open after Apr., 10am-noon and 2-5pm. DM2, children DM1.20.) The streets lining the pedestrian zone are riddled with 114 half-timbered houses; the oldest dot Königstr., Homburgstr., and Große Str. Farther up the pedestrian zone is a beautiful fountain depicting three of the baron's most outrageous adventures. Once a month, a **play** in the spa gardens reenacts Münchhausen's exploits (May-Oct. First Su of the month at 3pm. Free). On the second Saturday of August, Bodenwerder sets the Weser ablaze with its pyrotechnic **festival of lights.**

BRAUNSCHWEIG   ☎ 0531

Now that Braunschweig's Cold War border town duties are over, this middleweight city is pumping up its cultural attractions. The history of Braunschweig (sometimes called **"Brunswick"** in English) began in 1166, when Heinrich der Löwe (Henry the Lion) settled here. After hanging up his hat, Heinrich set about building a kingdom: he erected the famous Braunschweig lion statue—now the city's emblem—built Burg Dankwarderode, the castle around it, and inaugurated Braunschweig's growth into a thriving religious and commercial center. The town is saturated with cathedrals and other monuments that once marked the free city's economic importance to the Holy Roman Empire. Today, the monuments are almost overwhelmed by the fast-paced shopping centers, and the laid-back ambience of the nightlife has a distinctly cosmopolitan feel. A former member of the Hanseatic League, Braunschweig now boasts a robust economy, which, combined with its brash bids for tourism, make it one of Niedersachsen's most vital cities.

■ **GETTING THERE AND GETTING AROUND**

Trains: Braunschweig lies on the main line between Hannover and Berlin. Trains roll frequently to **Hannover** (45min., 2 per hr., DM16.40); **Magdeburg** (45min., 2 per hr., DM29); and **Berlin** (1¼hr., 1 per hr., DM84).

Public Transportation: A thorough system of **streetcars** and **buses** laces Braunschweig and its environs, which comprise 3 zones. Braunschweig proper is zone 1, Wolfenbüttel (see p. 509) and suburbs make up zone 2, and even farther out, true suburbia comprises zone 3. For info on routes, call ☎ 194 49; for times and ticket prices, call ☎ 383 27 10. A 90 min. ticket, valid for any number of transfers, costs DM2.80, or buy two for DM5. A daypass costs DM7, and a family day ticket (valid for up to 2 adults and 3 kids) costs DM9. Pick up a free, credit card-sized **map** at the booth in front of the train station or at the tourist offices. Most buses make their final run around 10:30pm, but a system of 15 **night buses** (NachtExpress), centered at the Rathaus stop, will get you where you need to go (2 per hr., M-Th 10:30pm-12:30am, F until 1:30am, Sa-Su until 2:30 am).

Bike Rental: Glockmann + Sohn, Ölschlägern 29-30 (☎469 23), in the Magniviertel, off of Am Magnitor. Open M-F 9am-6:30pm, Sa 9am-1pm.

Car Rental: Europcar, Berliner Pl. 3 (☎24 49 80; fax 244 98 66), across from the train station, under the pink *Hotel Mercure* sign on the left. Open M-F 7:30am-6pm, Sa 8am-noon, Su 9-11am.

Mitfahrbüro, Wollmarkt 3 (☎194 40), matches riders and drivers. Walk to the northern tip of the pedestrian zone and up Alte Waage, which turns into Wollmarkt. Open M-F 10am-6pm, Sa 10am-2pm.

Taxis: ☎555 55, 666 66, 59 91, or 621 21. Call 444 44 for **Frauennacht-Taxi** (women's taxi).

🔅🛈 ORIENTATION AND PRACTICAL INFORMATION

Braunschweig hunkers like a dozing lion between the Lüneburger Heide and the Harz Mountains. The Hauptbahnhof sits southeast of the city center, which is essentially an island ringed by the **Oker** river. Walking straight from the train station brings you across Berliner Platz to **Kurt-Schumacher-Str.,** with a major S-Bahn line and a low fence cutting down its center. This street curves to the left to meet **John-F.-Kennedy-Platz,** a major crossroad at the southeast corner of the central city. Following Auguststr. northwest from JFK-Platz leads to **Ägidienmarkt,** which brings you to **Bohlweg,** the wide street that is the eastern boundary of the main pedestrian zone. Turn left at Langer Hof to get to the Rathaus. Braunschweig's downtown attractions are mostly within this great circle, formed by the branching Oker. The multiple streets going forth from the several markets are sometimes confusing. Streetcars and buses criss-cross the city; most lines pass through either the "Rathaus/Bohlweg" stops (downtown) or "JFK-Platz/K.-Schumacher-Str." stops (a 10min. walk from the train station). Streetcars #1 and 2 from the station head to all these stops.

Tourist Office: There are 2 tourist offices in town; one is inside the train station (open M-F 8:30am-5pm, Sa 9am-noon), and the other sits a block from the Neues Rathaus, on Bohlweg (☎273 55 30 or 273 55 31; fax 273 55 19; www.braunschweig.de). Open M-F 9:30am-6pm, Sa 9:30am-2pm, Su 9:30am-12:30pm. Both offices find **rooms** in hotels and *Pensionen* for free (DM39 and up), but you can also just get a free copy of the hotel list from them. A few brochures are available in English, but all of the **tours** (DM4-27), which depart from the Bohlweg branch, are *auf Deutsch*.

Mitwohnbüro: Wollmarkt 3 (☎130 00; fax 152 52), in the same office as the Mitfahrbüro (see above). Finds apartments and sublets. Open M-F 10am-6pm, Sa 10am-2pm.

Currency Exchange: Dresdner Bank, at the corner of Neue Str. and Gördelingerstr., near the Altstadtmarkt. **24 hr. ATM.** Open M and F 8:30am-4pm, Tu and Th 8:30am-6pm, W 8:30am-1pm.

Bookstore: Pressezentrum Salzman, in the Burgpassage near the stairs, sells paperback pulp novels, as well as a limited selection of English and American magazines and newspapers. Open M-F 9:30am-8pm, Sa 9am-4pm. Also in the Burgpassage, near the escalators, **Karl Pfannkuch,** Kleine Burg 10, has novels in English, as well as an excellent collection of German classics. Open M-F 9:30am-8pm, Sa 9:30am-4pm.

Library: Öffentliche Bücherei, Hintern Brüdern 23 (☎470 68 38), right off Lange Str. Main building open M-Tu and Th-F 10am-7pm, Sa 10am-2pm, but the **foreign language library** is only open Tu noon-6pm and F 11am-4pm.

Emergency: Police, ☎110. **Ambulance,** ☎192 22. **Fire,** ☎112.

Pharmacy: Apotheke am Kennedy-Platz, Auguststr. 19 (☎439 55). Open M-F 8:30am-6:30pm, Sa 9am-1pm. **Emergency service** information posted on the door (☎440 33).

Post Office: The main office, 38106 Braunschweig, is in the 16-story building to the right of the train station. Open M-F 8am-6pm, Sa 8am-1pm.

Internet Access: In **Hound Dog** (see **Entertainment and Nightlife,** p.450).

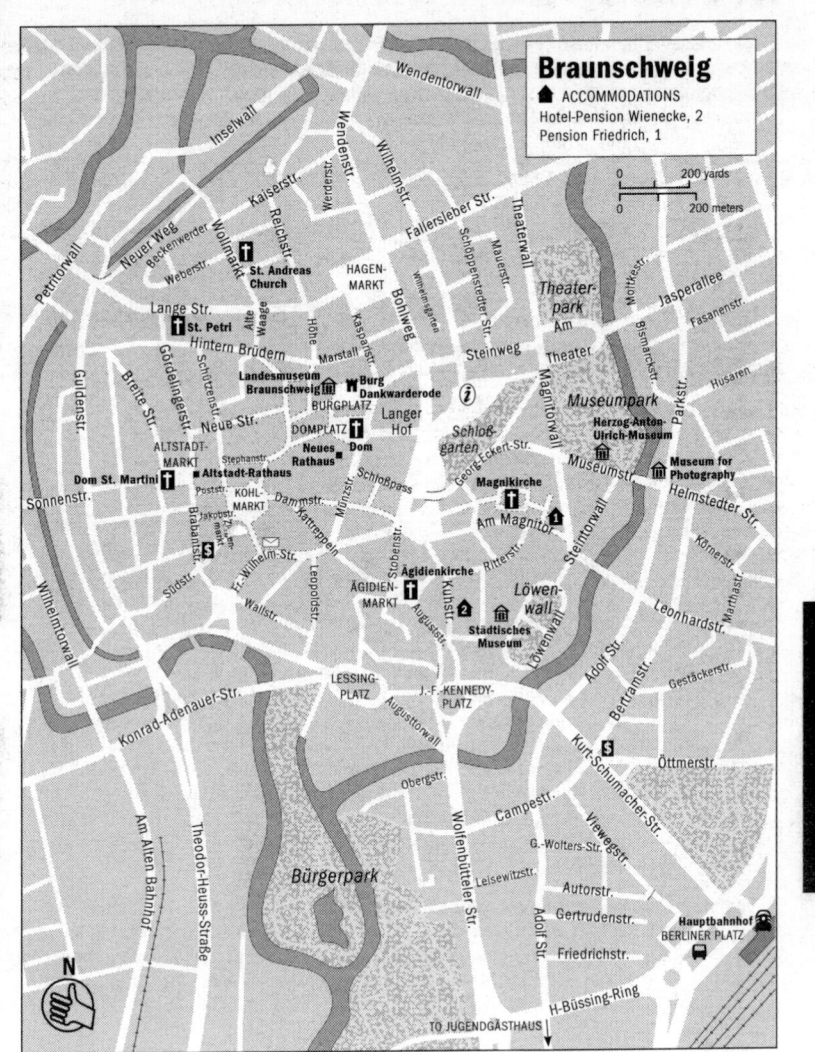

ACCOMMODATIONS

Considering the city's size, Braunschweig's inexpensive housing pickings are pretty slim. But the good news is that the cheap *Pensionen* are only about 10 minutes outside of the action in the city center, and if you've got the money, the rooms are pretty swank. Pick up a free copy of *Hotels und Gaststätten* at the tourist office; it includes a listing of accommodations and cafes with prices, phone numbers, and city maps.

Jugendgästehaus (HI), Salzdahlumerstr. 170 (☎26 43 20; fax 264 32 70). From the station, take bus #11 (direction: "Mascherode"), or bus #19 (direction "Stöckheim") to "Klinikum Salzdahlumerstr." The hostel is across from the train station, on the left. By foot, walk left from the station on Berliner Pl. to H.-Büssing-Ring, turn left on Salzdahlumerstr. and go under the overpasses. (Some find the overpass area a bit sketchy after dark—use your best judgement, or spend a few extra dollars for a cab.) Keep walking straight, but it's going to take awhile. The antiseptic buildings contain bright, spacious rooms, a huge backyard with little white pavilions, and kitchen facilities. Breakfast DM7. Sheets included. Key deposit DM30. Reception 7-10am and 4-10pm in the separate building on the left, through the little green metal gate. Members only. DM18.50-37, depending on the number of bunks and bathroom facilities; over 26 DM22.50.

Hotel-Pension Wienecke, Kuhstr. 14 (☎464 76; fax 464 64). From the station, walk up Kurt-Schumacher-Str. to JFK-Platz, bear right onto Auguststr. and then Kuhstr. (15min.). Quiet, comfortable rooms on a pedestrian street near the city center with big windows, private bathrooms, and TVs. Breakfast buffet included. Singles DM79-86, with bath DM89-99; doubles with bath DM125-145; apartments for 1-4 people DM95-220.

Pension Friedrich, Am Magnitor 5 (☎417 28). In the Magniviertel, right by the Städtisches Museum. Feel like you're part of the city as the friendly chatter from the cafes below drifts in through the windows of this cozy little *Pension*. Spacious, airy singles; top floor doubles with sofas and large bathrooms are to die for. TV and stereo in all rooms. DM60-80.

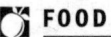 FOOD

A plethora of bars and *Imbiße* along **Bohlweg** proffer pizzas, salads, soups, and small sandwiches at reasonable prices. There's a produce market in the Altstadt every W and Sa 8am-1:30pm. The Kohlmarkt area, southeast of the Altstadtmarkt in the city center, is a bustling, open space with many pleasant (though not terribly cheap) cafes and restaurants. The Magniviertel's winding streets, boutiques, and half-timbered houses provide a great setting for a meal or drink. Several malls—the **Burgpassage Galerie, Weltenhof,** and **City Point**—also have excellent food stands. Two supermarkets are at the ready on Porschestr. near the Ägidienmarkt: the run of the mill **Aldi,** Porschestr. 10 (open M-F 9am-6:30pm and Sa 8am-1pm); and next door, the more exotic **A. Chau,** an Asian specialty market that also has the basics. (Open M-F 9:30am-7pm, Sa 9am-4pm.) For the late-night cavorters, Friedrich-Wilhelm-Str. has a wealth of excellent Turkish delis and fast food, located conveniently close to the clubs and bars in and around the pedestrian zone.

☒ Vegetarisches Vollwert-Restaurant Brodocz, Stephanstr. 1 (☎422 36), across from the Karstadt perfume department, This garden-themed restaurant serves up heaping portions of artfully prepared, primarily vegetarian, cuisine. A touch of candle-lit ambience makes it the perfect place to have a glass of wine with that special someone. Daily special with salad and soup DM16.50. Open M-Sa 11am-11pm, Su 3-10pm.

Tolle Knolle, Stobenstr. 15-16 (☎437 33), near the "Bohlweg/Damm" stop. Potato soups (DM3.50-5.50), potato omelettes (DM8-10.50), potato salads (DM4-8), baked potatoes (DM4-14), and even "Potatoes of the World" from DM10.50. Mr. Potato Head gives his blessing from the bar, while some suspiciously similar characters stand smiling on the center of the menu. Open M-F and Su 11:30am-3pm and 5:30-10pm.

Delicato, Münzstr. 9 (☎40 07 16), 3 blocks from Burgpl., protruding from the corner of Münzstr. and Kattreppeln. This gourmet Turkish deli packs up salads and spicy, freshly cooked meats that stand a step above the typical Turkish fast food, at prices that won't break the bank. Everything sold by weight; a plateful costs around DM10. Open M-F 9am-8pm, Sa 9am-4pm.

Café MM, Kuhstr. 6 (☎422 44), near Hotel-Pension Wienecke. Offers omelettes (DM6.80-10.50), salads (DM6-11.50), and exciting pastas (DM6.80-10.50). The ritzy sidewalk bistro has Manet's cafe scenes re-created in a kind of meta-mural inside. Open M-Th and Su 9am-midnight, F-Sa 9am-1am.

TOUCHDOWN ON THE TENTH MERIDIAN

Braunschweig was the site of the first-ever European soccer match in 1874, and since then it's been an extremely vigorous and athletic town. Within the last decade, Braunschweig's seemingly endless sporting energy has been channeled into an American favorite: football. Yes, American football. In 1997, the Braunschweig *Lions* (name courtesy of Heinrich der Löwe) dominated the German bowl, bringing the coveted trophy home to their stadium north of the city. Encouraged by victory, they've been clashing shoulder pads even more fiercely ever since.

👁 SIGHTS

All of Braunschweig was once crowded on a small island surrounded by offshoots of the Oker; the streams now form a slim moat around the Altstadt. Braunschweig's medieval sights ring the cobbled **Burgplatz**, at the center of which the city's (and Heinrich's) emblem, a **bronze lion**, stands guard. Heinrich's leonine symbol of regional dominance was first cast in 1166, as Braunschweig was positioning itself as a commercial center.

DOM ST. BLASI. One of Heinrich's architectural projects, the Dom looms at the southwest corner of the city center. In 1173, Heinrich oversaw the destruction of a tiny wooden church on the spot and the beginning of the Dom's construction, a project that would take another 22 years. The finished basilica shows only one telltale sign of its inheritance: a wooden crucifix above the Nave. Fast-fading frescoes color the ceiling and archways of the interior, illustrating the lives of Christ, Mary, John the Baptist, and Thomas of Canterbury. Below in the gloomy granite **crypt** rest the sarcophagi of Heinrich and his consort Mathilde. *(Dom open daily 10am-5pm. Crypt DM2.)*

NEUES RATHAUS. For the aspiring architects, here is neo-Gothic style in perfect form. This structure houses the present city offices and also hosts various exhibitions in the front foyer. *(Take streetcar #1 or 2 to "Rathaus" from the train station; or walk (15min.) along Kurt-Schumacher-Str., bear right at JFK-Pl. through Ägidienmarkt onto Bohlweg.)*

ALTSTADT-RATHAUS. The Burg and Dom lie at the eastern border of the pedestrian zone; at the western edge of the Altstadtmarkt stands this stately grey building, its medieval trim preserved in good character. The Rathaus is flanked by an open plaza, which at times seems a bit empty, as most of the pedestrian action has moved closer to Kohlmarkt.

DOM ST. MARTINI. Built concurrently with the Dom St. Blasi, the cathedral's magnificently ornamented interior includes an altar decorated with sculptures of the Wise and Foolish Virgins, who look like they carry larger than life Martini glasses. Wise were the Virgins who had enough lamp oil as they waited for their grooms, fools were those who got left alone in the dark. *(Next door to the Altstadt-Rathaus. Open Tu-F 10am-1pm and 3-5pm, Sa 10am-5pm, Su 10am-noon and 3-5pm. Free.)*

ST. ÄGIDIENKIRCHE. If your ecclesiastical hunger is not yet satiated, check out the spectacular St. Ägidien church and neighboring monastery, just up Auguststr. from JFK-Platz at the highest geographic spot in the Altstadt. St. Ägidienkirche earns its historical brownie points as the only Gothic cathedral in the city. However, what separates it from the rest are the slightly overgrown heroic statues which gaze at you out of the corners of their moss covered eyes. You'll find yourself looking over your shoulder as you walk past them into the monastery, which now houses the Jüdisches Museum (see **Museums,** below).

LÖWENWALL. Looking for the place to lie down in the grass and talk about Fussball without actually playing any? Löwenwall is the place, a circular park backing up the Städtisches Museum. The obelisk, flanked by lions and two splashing fountains, is a monument to the city nobles who died in the Napoleonic Wars. *(Walk up Kurt-Schumacher-Str. from the train station; the Löwenwall will be on your right just before you reach JFK-Platz.)*

NIEDERSACHSEN

MAGNIVIERTEL. Braunschweig's friendliest social center is lined with pale cobblestoned streets and cafes centered around the **Magnikirche.** The laid-back ambiance of the evening makes Am Magnitor one of the most desirable places to sit down with a beer and converse with the locals. The quarter features the only half-timbered houses in Braunschweig, which escaped destruction in WWII and have been well-preserved since.

MUSEUMS

If you're planning to do a run of Braunschweig's museums in one day, you may want to purchase a *Braunschweiger Museumsverbund Tageskarte* (DM10), a day pass valid at all museums, available at all museum desks and tourist offices.

■**LANDESMUSEUM BRAUNSCHWEIG.** This museum has several branches in town, and one in neighboring Wolfenbüttel. The main collection is here in the **Vieweg-Haus.** One of the larger museums in Braunschweig, the displays range from equine armor to dainty Victorian dollhouses; a collection of dolls books with Hitler on the cover and other WWII-related playthings are also featured. *(Burgpl. 1. To the left of the Dom.* ☎ *484 26 02. Open Tu-W and F-Su 10am-5pm, Th 10am-8pm. DM5, students DM2.50.)*

■**MUSEUM FOR PHOTOGRAPHY.** This constantly evolving museum hosts a different artist's work every couple months. The building is small, but the spaces are light. *(Helmstedter Str. 1. Just down Museumstr. from the Ulrich museum, or take bus #13 or 43 to "Steintor".* ☎ *750 00. Open Tu-F 1-6pm, Sa-Su 2-6pm. DM5, students DM3.)*

JÜDISCHES MUSEUM. A branch of the Landesmuseum, the Jewish museum's reconstruction of the main room of the old synagogue is a disturbing complement to memorials to victims of the Holocaust. The synagogue's furniture and altar are authentic, rescued from the deteriorating building, including the small dome and chandelier which hang in eerie silence. Complemented by menorahs, pamphlets from the Concentration Camp Theater, and other relics of German Jewish culture, this museum paints a broader picture of a people. *(Hinter Ägidien.* ☎ *484 25 59. Open Tu-W and F-Su 10am-5pm, Th 10am-8pm. DM5, students DM3.50; free entry with ticket from main museum, and vice versa.)*

HERZOG-ANTON-ULRICH MUSEUM. This was the first European museum to open its doors to the general public. It houses a collection of the tried-and-true greats of Western art, highlighted by the Dutch Masters, including works by Van Dyck, Vermeer, Rubens, and Rembrandt. *(Museumstr. 1.* ☎ *484 24 00. From the pedestrian zone, walk across Bohlweg and down Georg-Eckert-Str., which turns into Museumstr.; or ride streetcar #5 to "Museumstr." Open Tu and Th-Su 10am-5pm, W 1-8pm. DM5, students DM3.)*

BURG DANKWARDERODE. This 19th-century reconstruction of Henry the Lion's castle today shows off of his precious medieval collectables in gray gloom. The newly renovated **Rittersaal** (knights' hall) dazzles with its golden technicolor paintings, and the original Braunschweig lion stands at a level suitable for a face-off. *(Burgpl.* ☎ *484 24 00. Museum open Tu and Th-Su 11am-5pm, W 1-2:30pm and 4-8pm. Rittersaal open Tu and Th-Su 10-11am, W 2:30-4pm. DM5, students DM2.50.)*

STÄDTISCHES MUSEUM. This specialized "domestic museum" includes historical originals of furniture, appliances, living room bric-a-brac, and the world's first motorcycle. From time to time, this museum also houses special exhibitions; check with the tourist office or call for more information. *(Löwenwall 16.* ☎ *470 45 05. Open Tu-Su 10am-5pm., Th 10am-8pm.)*

 **ENTERTAINMENT AND NIGHTLIFE**

The high-water marks of Braunschweig's theatrical scene were stained in 1772 with the first performance of Lessing's *Emilia Galotti*, and in 1829 with the premiere of Goethe's *Faust*. The monumental **Staatstheater** (☎ 123 40) built in the Florentine Renaissance style, was erected in 1861 to replace the old theater hall. The

Großes Haus, Am Theater (☎484 28 00) is only one of three stages run by the state theater; the other two are the **Kleines Haus,** Magnitorwall 18 (☎484 28 00), and the **Theaterspielplatz,** Hinter der Magnikirche 6a (☎484 27 97). The Großes Haus plays big-name operas, ballets, and musicals (DM8-51) and orchestral concerts (DM19-45); the Kleines Haus and Theaterspielplatz have everything from Goethe to Mamet to modern dance, priced at DM6-35. (☎500 01 41 for information. Tickets to the Großes Haus available M-F 10am-6:30pm, Sa 10am-1pm.) The **LOT Theater,** Kaffeetwete 4a (☎173 03), is the home of the local avant-garde theater company. Walk up Gördelingerstr. from the Altstadtmarkt. (Box office open M-F 11am-2pm. Tickets DM13-20.) The **Stadthalle,** Leonhardpl. (☎707 07), is home to the **Braunschweiger Staatsorchester,** the city orchestra. Many movie theaters crowd Braunschweig; **Lupe,** Gördelingerstr. 7 (☎493 11), and **Broadway,** Kalenwall 3 (☎455 42), show artsy films. Pick up a copy of the free magazine *Filmtips* for a schedule.

Braunschweig has several free monthly magazines offering the details on local events: *Subway, Da Capo,* and *Cocktail.* It's telling that these magazines sometimes direct readers to cities as far away as Hamburg. Still, the Braunschweig scene heats up to a steady simmer on weekends. The most lively area is the square formed by the intersection of Sack, Vor der Burg, and Schuhstr., as well as Neue Str. nearby. The Magniviertel brims with cafes, bars, and Braunschweig charm.

Movie, Neue Str. 2 (☎437 26), is a bar with a pop music theme. Lots of beer on tap, cheap food (2 *Wieners* DM4.50), and rock and blues constitute the "feature presentation." Open daily 9am-2am.

Pupasch-Kneipe, Neue Str. 10-12 (☎445 61), just down the street from Movie. They're *die total verrückte Kneipe* ("the totally crazy bar"). Maybe the loudest and largest bar on Neue Str, this is a place where the pints flow frequently and chatter grows in proportion. Open M-Th and Su noon-midnight, F-Sa noon-4am.

The Jolly Joker, Broitzemerstr. 220 (☎281 46 60). Bus #5, #6, or #19 to "Broitzemerstr." This titanic joint has it all, including 3 dance floors: one spinning chart-toppers mixed up to dancing beats, another two with a more alternative edge, a *Biergarten,* more bars than you care to count, fast food, and movies. The club's biggest fans are the under-21 crowd, but the floor is open to anyone who can match their fast-paced dance moves. W and Sa disco nights. Open M 9:30pm-2am, Tu and Th 9:30pm-2:30am, F-Sa 9pm-4am. Cover DM3; movies free.

Hound Dog, Breite Str. 23 (☎416 61), just off the Altstadt Markt, has a peachy pink interior decorated with the glories of the freeway, electronic gambling, a friendly owner, and of course, a hound- err, sheep-dog. But what brings homesick backpackers to this neck of the woods? The holy grail: one computer, set back behind the bar, with internet access (DM10 per hr.). Open daily from 1pm.

WOLFENBÜTTEL ☎05311

Just a few kilometers from Braunschweig lies Wolfenbüttel, its pretty little sister city. Hop on bus #21 from Braunschweig's Hauptbahnhof, or take a 10min. train ride (DM10, 2 per hr.). For the most part, Wolfenbüttel's Baroque-era architecture remains intact; the key historical treasures are oozing with recently-painted color, while many of the half-timbered houses are correspondingly well-maintained, carrying a healthy dose of distinctly German flavor. The friendly streets of the town rustle with pedestrian chatter, while the shady parks and quiet river insulate the clamor. Though a savvy tourist industry has made Wolfenbüttel extremely accessible to visitors, its child-like bliss is thankfully not lost.

🛈 PRACTICAL INFORMATION. The Wolfenbüttel **tourist office** is located at Stadtmarkt 7, in the heart of the city market. From the station, exit right, then hang a left on Bahnhofstr., and another left on Schulwall. Turn right onto Löwenstr., and follow the curves as it becomes Krambuden. When the space to your right opens up, turn right and walk down the right side of the market to the tourist's office. The office has a list of hotels, pension, and a few private rooms, as well as some information about the city available in English, including maps. They also lead **tours** from the Schloß. (☎ 862 80; fax 867 77 08; email stadt@wolfenbuettel.de; www.wolfenbuettel.de. Office open M-F 9am-12:30pm and 2-4pm, Apr.-Oct. also Sa 9am-1pm. Tours in German Apr.-Dec. Sa 2:30pm and Su 11am; Oct.-Mar. Su 11am. DM5, under 14 free.) Wolfenbüttel's **postal code** is 38300.

🏠🍴 ACCOMMODATIONS AND FOOD. Wolfenbüttel has a very affordable **Jugendgästehaus,** Jägerstr. 17. From the train station, go right and then head left on Bahnhofstr. and take a left at Schulwall. Continue on the same street when you reach Schloßplatz; you'll cross a little river and end up on Dr.-Heinrich-Jasper-Str. Make a left at Jägerstr (10 min.). Concealed by a peeling exterior, the rooms are spacious and bright (☎ 271 89; fax 90 24 45. Breakfast included. Sheets DM3. Bikes DM5 per day or DM10 per week. Free canoe rental. DM24, over 25 DM30. Full pension DM33, over 25 DM44.) **Krambuden** and **Lange Herzogstr.,** just off the center of the Stadtmarkt, have many fruit stands and bakeries. Löwenstr.'s curves hold a great variety of inexpensive Italian, Chinese, and Turkish cuisine, such as mini pizzas (DM3.50), Asian specials (DM8), and the ubiquitous *Döner* (DM4). Down the street, a **Plus supermarket** sells inexpensive foodstuffs. (Open M-W 8:30am-7pm, Th-F 8:30am-8pm, Sa 8am-4pm.) While in Wolfenbüttel, don't miss the delicious coconut macaroons (DM1.20) served in bakeries around town. Resist the temptation to chew on the houses, though.

🏛 SIGHTS. The phrase "paint the town red" (or mauve, or crimson) might as well have been coined in Wolfenbüttel, where many of the historic sights have been slathered in candy-colored hues bright enough to fulfil the wildest coloring-book pipe-dreams of any kindergartner. The pink **Trinitiaskirche** in the Holzmarkt looks more like a palace than a church; only a viewing of the elaborate interior with three levels of balconies and a glorious altar reveals its true purpose. (Open Tu 11am-1pm, W 11am-1pm and 2-4pm, Th 3-5pm, Sa 11am-4pm.) The crimson **Kanzlei,** Kanzleistr. 3, could pass for a medieval comedy club, or perhaps just some jester's bad joke, with its absurd silver sculpture that appears to have forks for hands. In fact, it serves a much more serious purpose: houses the pre-history collection of the **Landesmuseum Braunschweig**—rocks, fossils, primitive tools, and the like. (☎ 270 71. Open Tu-F and Su 10am-5pm. DM5, students DM2.50.)

In recent years, even the **Schloß** has jumped in on the radical red action with a new paint job. The castle has the foundation of a 13th-century fortress of the Guelphs, but its current appearance is pure Baroque with a beautifully proportioned 17th-century clock tower. A tour through the front rooms of the **Schloßmuseum,** Schloßplatz 13, is like walking through a giant dollhouse; it's a real taste of royal life, right down to the banquet, which is regretfully inedible. (☎ 924 60. Museum and castle interior open Tu-Su 10am-5pm. Museum DM5, students DM3.) Open-air performances take place in the Schloß's enclosed courtyard nearly every day from mid-June to mid-July; musicals, choral performances, chamber music concerts, jazz shows, and ballets are all on offer. Tickets are available at the *Braunschweiger Zeitung* office in Wolfenbüttel, Löwenstr. 6 (☎ 800 10).

Across the street from the Schloß is the yellow **Lessinghaus,** a compact mansion that was the local duke's gift to big-time *litterateur* **Gotthold Ephraim Lessing,** the court librarian of the nearby August-Bibliothek. The **museum** inside recalls Lessing's life and work through manuscripts, letters, and paintings, but beautiful moldings are what make it worthwhile. Those lacking the German skills to do a bit of intense translating might appreciate the building best from the exterior. (☎ 80 80. Open Tu-Su 10am-5pm.) Behind the Lessinghaus, the stately **Herzog-August-Bibliothek** guards a priceless collection of medieval and Renaissance books. Under the loving care of bookworm Duke August, the library became the largest in Europe. Today, the library is designed for a steady stream of visitors, with many of the most precious calligraphic scripts displayed in glass cases. A series of medieval manuscripts culminates with a facsimile of the famous **Braunschweiger Evangelier,** a kaleidoscopically illuminated gospel drawn up in the late 12th century at the request of Henry the Lion; the state of Niedersachsen shelled out millions for the manuscript in 1983. The original is locked safely away. Also worth checking out are miniature oil portraits of Martin Luther and his wife, Katharin von Bora. (☎80 82 14. Open Tu-Su 10am-5pm.) Across from the castle is the 17th-century **Zeughaus**, whose magenta high-gabled facade belies its former role as an armory. It now serves as a library annex holding the other half of the Herzog-August collection. (Open M-F 8am-8pm, Sa 9am-1pm.) The two libraries and the Lessinghaus sell **combination tickets** valid at all three sights. (DM6, students DM4, under 19 DM2, family DM12.) Had enough bright colors for one day? The city's other major sight, the **Hauptkirche Beate Mariae Virgins**, stretches its hulking, neutral spires across town in the Heinrichstadt section. A jutting four-faced clock tower and life-sized statues of saints grace the church's exterior. (Open Tu-Sa 10am-noon and 2-4pm. Suggested donation DM1.)

LÜNEBURGER HEIDE (LÜNEBURG HEATH)

The shrub-covered Lüneburger Heide stretches between the Elbe and Aller rivers. Many German literary greats have appreciated the symbolic power of the heath: the delicate *Heideröslein* ("heath rose") found a role in one of Goethe's *Lieder*, while Heine charmingly compared one lady's bosom to the "flat and bleakly desolate" landscape of the *Heide*. The undulating countryside moves quickly back and forth from farm to forest; green gives way to purple from July to September, when the bushes flower. If you want to see the grassy *Heide* during the flowering season, but would prefer not to sleep on it, put down the book and make reservations now. All of Germany comes here to bike, hike, motor, and otherwise frolic in the late summer. The most important regional towns are **Lüneburg** and **Celle**. In Lüneburg, the **Fremdenverkehrsverband Lüneburger Heide**, Barckhausenstr. 35 (☎ (04131) 737 30; fax 426 06), finds rooms in remote hamlets barely on the map. The staff also provides information on the Heide's *Heu-Hotels* ("hay hotels"), functioning barns with rooms that farmers rent out to travelers for around DM20. They're called hay hotels because that's where you sleep (bring a sleeping bag). But all have showers and toilets, and many are surprisingly luxurious.

To see the greater Heide, a bike is your best bet. The tourist offices in both Lüneburg and Celle offer information on self-guided and group tours. Extensive and detailed maps outline the *Heide's* major bike tours. The most popular is an 80km tour leaving from Lüneburg; this tour takes you along main roads and through the endless woods and pastures of the suburbs and countryside of Lüneburg and neighboring Harburg. But grab a map; the tour is marked only with tiny 4x6 white signs with green bicycles. The 350km Heide-Rundtour, is the most comprehensive, passing through both Celle and Lüneburg. The tourist offices are not so helpful in directing hopeful hikers; your best bet for hiking information is the bookstore, where there are a number of hiking and biking guides for the area.

LÜNEBURG ☎04131

Perhaps because there is no salt-god, or perhaps because the name Salzburg was already taken, Lüneburg derives its name from the moon-goddess Luna. Regardless, this is a city built literally and figuratively on salt. The city made a 13th-century fortune with its stores of "white gold." The citizens' salt monopoly held Northern Europe in an iron grip until plague and war struck the town in the 1620s. Although "salt shocks" no longer pose a threat to the world economy, and Lüneburg's wealth and power have faded, neither the salt nor the town are obsolete. The salt is channeled into the city's famed rejuvenating baths, and the town, with its Gothic brick Altstadt and elegant half-timbered houses, retains its ancient grace. Lüneburg native Heinrich Heine penned one of Germany's greatest and most melancholic Romantic poems, the *Lorelei*, in this enjoyable town.

NIEDERSACHSEN

■ ORIENTATION AND PRACTICAL INFORMATION

Lüneburg serves as the transportation center of the Heide. By train, the city lies between **Hamburg** (40min., 4 per hr., DM12.60) and **Hannover** (1hr., 1 per hr., DM35, students DM28). Rent **bikes** at **Radspeicher am Bahnhof**, next to the train station. (☎557 77. Open daily 6am-10pm. DM15 per day. They also have a great weekend deal: F-Su for DM30. DM200 deposit and ID required.) The **tourist office**, Am Markt, in the Rathaus, books **rooms**. From the train station, head downhill away from the bus station and post office, take a left on Lünertorstr., and turn left on Bardowicker Str. at the end. If the inconsistent "Lüne-" streets are confusing, just head towards the big brick tower on the skyline: that's St. Nikolai, and Bardowicker Str. is on the other side of it. (☎30 95 93 or 322 00; fax 30 95 98; hotline ☎207 66 44; www.luneburg.de. Open July-Aug. M-F 9am-7pm, Sa-Su 9am-4pm; May-June M-F 9am-6pm, Sa-Su 9am-4pm; Oct.-Apr. M-F 9am-5pm, Sa-Su 9am-4pm.) Daily **tours** of the Altstadt leave daily at 11am and 2pm (DM6, children DM4). **Internet access** is available at Lünestr. 6-7 for DM10 per hr. (open M-F 10am-7pm, Sa 10am-1pm). The **post office**, 21332 Lüneburg, is on the corner of Soltauer Str. and Saltztorstr (open M-F 8am-6pm, Sa 8am-noon).

■ ACCOMMODATIONS AND FOOD

Hotels fill up rather quickly when the Heide blooms in July through September. At **Jugendherberge Lüneburg (HI)**, Soltauer Str. 133, cheap and charming walk hand in hand. Small rooms have new furnishings and clean floors. Until 7pm during the week and Sunday after 1pm, bus #11 (direction "Rettmer/Hecklingen") runs from the train station to the hostel; get off at "Scharnhorststr./DJH." During off hours, take bus #7 from "Auf dem Klosterhof" behind the Rathaus to "Ginsterweg," and walk 200m farther along Soltauer Str. Or brace yourself for a long haul from the station (30min.): turn left on Bahnhofstr., right at the bottom onto Altenbrückentorstr., then left onto the very long Berliner Str. Follow the street as it turns into Uelzener Str., make a right at Scharnhorststr., and continue until you meet Soltauer Str. (☎418 64; fax 457 47. Breakfast included. Sheets DM5.70. Laundry DM5. Reception until 10pm. Curfew 10pm, but pocket a house key with a DM20 deposit. Call ahead. DM22, over 26 DM27.) **Hotel Stadt Hamburg**, Am Sande 25, is right on one of the town's main squares in the Altstadt, and will put a grin on your face, unlike the dour visages of famous Lüneburgers whose portraits line the staircase. (☎444 38; fax 40 41 98. Breakfast included. 24hr. reception. Call ahead. Singles DM50, with shower DM55; doubles DM100-130.) There are a number of official **camping** places along the Elbe river and in the woods of the small suburbs; call the tourist office for further information.

The overabundance of salt makes Lüneburgers thirsty—at one time the tiny city was padded with 80 breweries. For cheap food, try the **Mensa** on the university campus next to the hostel, which serves hot breakfasts and dinners (open 8:45-10:45am and 11:15am-2:15pm). The adjacent cafe, **Building 26**, features live music (open M-Th 10am-7pm, F 10am-7pm and from 8pm, Sa only if there's a party, Su 11am-3pm). Many cafes and nicer restaurants line Schröderstr. Imbibe Lüneburg's own *Pilsner* (DM3.80) in a late 15th-century beer hall at **Kronen-Brauerei**, Heiligengeiststr. 39-41. (☎71 32 00. Open daily 11:30am-10pm.)

■ SIGHTS AND ENTERTAINMENT

Legend has it that Lüneburg's salt stores were discovered when a wild boar fell into a pit and, clawing his way out, shook salt loose from his bristles. The **Deutsches Salzmuseum**, Sülfmeisterstr. 1, presents much, *much* more than you ever wanted to know about salt. Did you get the necessary 19 grams today? From the Rathaus, take Neue Sülze to Salzstr.; at Lambertipl., take the path behind the supermarket. Dine among salt-caked rafters in the attached **salt café**. *(☎450 65; fax*

Hmm, call home or eat lunch?
With **YOU**™
you can do both.

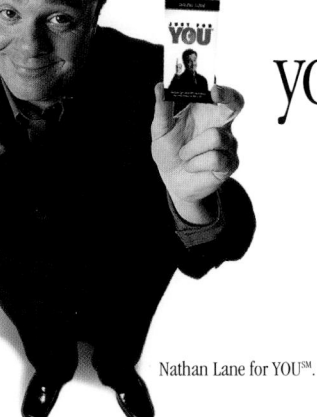

Nathan Lane for YOU℠.

No doubt, traveling on a budget is tough. So tear out this wallet guide and keep it with you during your travels. With YOU, calling home from overseas is affordable and easy.

If the wallet guide is missing, call collect 913-624-5336 or visit www.youcallhome.com for YOU country numbers.

Pack the Wallet Guide

and save 25% or more* on calls home to the U.S.

It's lightweight and carries heavy savings of 25% or more* over AT&T USA Direct and MCI WorldPhone rates. So take this YOU wallet guide and carry it wherever you go.

To save with YOU:
- Dial the access number of the country you're in (see reverse)
- Dial 04 or follow the English voice prompts
- Enter your credit card info for easy billing

Service provided by Sprint

450 69. Open Apr.-Oct. M-F 9am-5pm, Sa-Su 10am-5pm; Nov.-Mar. daily 10am-5pm. DM7, students DM5, children DM4.50. Tours M-F at 11am, 12:30, and 3pm; Sa-Su at 11:30am and 3pm. DM1.50, students DM1.) Lüneburg's other offbeat museums should be taken with a grain of... nevermind. The **Brauereimuseum,** Heiligengeiststr. 39-41, was a working brewery for 500 years until its copper vats became museum pieces in 1985. The museum explains exactly how hops, malt barley, and water make the magic potion that keeps Germany going, going, and gone. *(☎ 410 21. Open Tu-Su 1-4:30pm. Free.)*

The **Kloster Lüne,** on Domänehof, just over the Lünertor bridge, proudly displays its 15th-century face. *(☎ 523 18. Open Apr.-Oct. M-Sa 10am-12:30pm and 2:30-5pm, Su 11:30am-12:30pm and 2-5pm. DM5.)* Lüneburg boasts three big brick churches. At Bardowicker and Lünerstr., **St. Nikolai,** whose gigantic steeple is visible from the train station, sits in tall and impressive splendor on the edge of the Rathausplatz. *(Open daily 9am-5pm. Open market concerts Sa at 11am during the summer.)* Side streets with old, ivy-covered houses and boutiques lead to the Gothic **Michaeliskirche,** on Johann-Sebastian-Bach-Platz in the Altstadt. The imposing brick, wood, and ceramic church was built in 1418 on a foundation of salt; the massive pillars have warped somewhat since then. Bach was a regular visitor to the church between 1700 and 1702. *(☎ 314 00. Open M-Sa 10am-5pm.)* The spire of the **Johanniskirche,** Am Sande, soars over the gables of the streets. Late 13th-century walls shelter a Gothic altar and Baroque organ. *(☎ 445 42. Open M-Th 10am-5pm, F 10am-5:30pm, Sa 10am-6pm, Su 9am-5pm.)*

During the week, nightlife piles up around the Lünertor bridge, while locals pack the cafes along Am Stintmarkt. Strike it up at **Garage,** Auf der Hude 72. Frequent live acts, raves, and theme parties complement the regular dance scene. *(☎ 358 79. Open W and F-Sa after 10pm. Cover W DM2; F DM2 before 11pm, DM6 thereafter; Sa DM2 before 11pm, DM8 after.)*

CELLE ☎ 05141

The powerful prince electors of Lüneburg moved to Celle (pronounced "TSEL-luh") in 1398 after the Lüneburg War of Succession and remained here until 1705 when the last duke died. During those 307 years, the royalty lavished funds on their residence, building a massive castle and promoting the city's growth. The well-maintained half-timbered houses that line the streets used to be taxed by the number of crossed diagonal beams on their houses; the beams quickly became coveted status symbols—a precursor of the Mercedes-Benz logo.

NIEDERSACHSEN

⊿ ORIENTATION AND PRACTICAL INFORMATION. Celle is connected by frequent **trains** to **Hannover** (½hr., 3 per hr., DM12.60) and **Braunschweig** (1½hr., 2 per hr., DM20.20). Rent a **bike** from **Fahrrad Werner,** Kanzielstr. 14, near the tourist office. *(☎ 211 79. Open M-F 9am-1pm and 3-6pm, Sa 9am-1pm. DM10 per day, ID required.)* The **tourist office,** Markt 6 in the Altes Rathaus, reserves **rooms** for free and distributes a list of concerts and musical productions. The office also serves as a ticket office for numerous productions around Celle, the Lüneburger Heide, and greater North Germany. From the train station, walk up Bahnhofstr. as it becomes Westcellertorstr., turn left onto Poststr., which becomes Markt. Or take bus #2 or 3 to "Schloßpl." and follow the signs. *(☎ 12 12; fax 124 59; email touristinfo@celle.de; www.celle.de. Open June-Oct. daily 9am-10pm; Apr.-May M-F 9am-7pm, Sa 10am-4pm, Su 11am-2pm; Nov.-Mar. M-F 9am-5pm, Sa 10am-1pm.)* **Tours** start from the bridge in front of the Schloß. *(1½hrs. Apr. and Nov. Sa 2:30pm and Su 11am; May-Oct. and Dec. M-Sa 2:30pm, Su 11am. DM5.)* **Bike tours** of the countryside leave Saturdays at 10:30am, call the tourist office for reservations. *(June-Sept. DM5.)* **Internet access** is available for DM5 per 30min. at **Spiel-Treff,** Am Heiligen Kreuz 7 (open M-Sa 8am-11pm, Su 11am-11pm). The **post office,** 03100 Celle, is on Schloßplatz (open M-F 8am-6pm, Sa 8am-1pm).

⌂⌂ ACCOMMODATIONS AND FOOD. The **Jugendherberge (HI),** Weghausstr., covered with sky-blue siding and conveniently located near an aromatic cow pasture, reaches new levels in barn-chic. From the train station, take bus #3 (direction: "Boye") to "Jugendherberge." Or from the train station, walk up the pedestrian path as it becomes Biermannstr., turn left on Bremer Weg, and turn up the first right onto Petersburgstr. (☎532 08; fax 530 05. Breakfast included, lunch DM8.50. Sheets DM5.70. Reception until 10pm, but best time for check-in is 5-7pm. Curfew 10pm, but house keys are available with a DM50 deposit. Dorm beds DM22, over 26 DM27.) Across the street at **Pension Luhmannshof,** Dorfstr. 8, a little chocolate on each bed adds a touch of elegance to spacious rooms, while rusty farm equipment gives the yard a country image. From Petersburgstr., it's the first building on the right after Weghausstr. (☎530 94. Breakfast included. All rooms with full bath. Reception until 9pm. Reservations recommended. Singles DM60; doubles DM110.) **Hotel Blühende Schiffahrt,** Fritzenwiese 39, is considerably closer to the Altstadt. (☎227 61. Breakfast included. Call ahead. DM60 per person.) **Campingplatz Silbersee** lies 7km northeast of the town. Take bus #6 (direction: "Vorwerk") to "Silbersee." (☎312 23. DM5.50 per person.)

Café Fricke, Neue Str. 14, at the intersection with Brandplatz, cooks up crepes from DM5. (☎21 49 18. Open daily 10:30am-6pm.) **Alex's Antikcafé,** Schuhstr. 6 makes its home in a secluded patio off the street, offering cheap, simple food (soup and sandwich combo DM10), and a spectrum of alcohol and coffee. (☎21 75 40. Open M-Su 9am-6pm.) Nearby **Scallawags,** Schuhstr. 11, offers delicious, inexpensive entrees. (Menu items DM5-15. Open Su-Th 9am-1am, F-Sa 9am-2am.)

🆔 **SIGHTS.** Some of the city's finest half-timbered houses are tucked away on side streets; to find them, wander down any of the smaller streets radiating from Schloßplatz or Großer Platz in the Altstadt. The **oldest house** in the area is at Am Heiligen Kreuz 26, and was built in 1526. The **Stadtkirche** stands just outside the massive pedestrian zone that dominates the Altstadt. The church hosts concerts and art exhibitions, as well as regular services, and the tower provides a view of red- and brown-shingled roofs fading into the countryside. (☎77 35. Church open Tu-Su 10am-6pm. Tower open Apr.-Oct. Tu-Su 10am-noon and 2-4pm. DM2, children DM1.) In the Altstadt, the **Rathaus** is richly wrought in the Weser Renaissance style. Directly across the road, fine figures out of Celle's colorful history mark the hour on the **Glockenspiel** (daily at 10, 11am, noon, 3, 4, and 5pm).

The **Herzogschloß,** Schloßpl. 13, just west of the Altstadt, flaunts foundations that date back to 1292, and beautiful grounds with a peaceful pond. One of the most renowned residents of the castle was Caroline-Mathilde; she was granted asylum here in 1772 after her marriage to the King of Denmark collapsed when her affair with the King's minister was exposed. (☎123 73. Open Tu-Su 10am-5pm. Tours Tu-Su Apr.Oct. 10am-4pm on the hour; Nov.-Mar. 11am and 3pm. DM4, students DM2.) Caroline-Mathilde's weeping likeness is found in the **Französischer Garten,** south of the Altstadt. Directly across from the Schloß is the 🏛**Bomann-Museum Celle,** Schloßplatz 7. This museum's got everything from rooms modeled after early Cellean houses, to a history of the town and the *Heide* (including an exhibit on Celle's famous Zweiback) to modern art. Amazing and extensive special exhibits on the top and bottom floors. (☎123 72; fax 125 35; email bomann-museum@t-online.de. Open Tu-Su 10am-5pm. DM4, students DM2.) The 1740 Baroque **Synagoge,** Im Kriese 24, is one of the oldest standing places of Jewish worship in Germany and a memorial to Celle's once-thriving Jewish community. (☎55 07 14. Open Tu-Th 3-5pm, F 9-11am, Su 11am-1pm. Free.)

NEAR CELLE: BERGEN-BELSEN ☎05051

The Bergen-Belsen **concentration camp** was founded in 1940 as a "labor camp" for prisoners of war. For five years, about 20,000 Soviet prisoners were held there, performing futile, torturous "labor," like rolling heavy stones up and down hills, or digging ditches only to refill them. In January 1945, the POW camp was dissolved and the SS took over, bringing in thousands of Jews, homosexuals, and political dissidents who were evacuated from Auschwitz and other concentration camps. For four unimaginable months, tens of thousands of people lived in cramped conditions and suffered the mindless torture of the Nazis. Over 35,000 died of hunger and typhoid fever, including **Anne Frank,** whose symbolic gravestone is near the Jewish memorial. In total, Bergen-Belsen claimed more than 100,000 lives. In the documents building, a permanent exhibit displays the history of the camp and a film taken by British liberation forces. The grounds of the camp contain no original buildings; these were burned after liberation to prevent the spread of disease. Instead, a cemetery of mass graves stands on the site. A stone obelisk commemorates the 30,000 Jewish victims and a wall is inscribed with memorial phrases in the languages of the victims. The memorial (☎60 11) is open daily from 9am to 6pm. Take bus #911 from the Celle train station to "Belsen-Gedenkstätte." (1hr., M-Sa at 11:55pm and inconsistently at 1:40pm, return at 4:54pm. DM8.90.)

BREMEN ☎0421

Much like Hamburg, its Hanseatic sister city to the north, Bremen has given over its once famed medieval ambience to a thriving cosmopolitan swirl in which churches compete with video art for tourists' attention. The donkey, dog, cat, and rooster of the Brothers Grimm's fairy tale *Die Bremer Stadtmusikanten* (The Musicians of Bremen) were en route to Bremen when they terrified a band of robbers with their singing. The transients singing for attention at the city's train station maintain the tradition, and the tourist office pushes the theme whenever it can, much to the chagrin of those who would turn Bremen into a center for contemporary German art. Bremen's other famous symbol is a key, which you will undoubtedly see on such things as manhole covers and homemade Beck's beer bottles. The city's most enduring trait, however, is a strong desire for independence: despite continuing struggles, Bremen and its daughter city Bremerhaven remain their own tiny, autonomous *Land* surrounded by Lower Saxony. This feisty streak has helped foster a liberal political climate that erupted into violent battles between police and demonstrators in 1980.

◼ GETTING THERE AND GETTING AROUND

Flights: Bremen's international **airport** (☎559 50) is 3.5km from the city center; take S-Bahn #5 (10min.). Frequent flights to major German cities, the East Frisian Islands, and international destinations.

Trains: Roll to **Hannover** (1¼hr., 2 per hr., DM34); **Hamburg** (1½hr., 2 per hr., DM33); **Bremerhaven** (45min., 2 per hr., DM17); and **Osnabrück** (1¼hr., 2-3 per hr., DM33).

Public Transportation: An integrated system of streetcars and buses centered on the train station covers the city and suburbs. The best deal by far is the **Bremer Kärtchen,** with unlimited rides for 2 adults for 1 calendar day, *not* 24hr. from time of purchase; DM8. Single rides DM3.20, children under 16 DM1.60. 4-ride ticket DM9.60. Across from the Hauptbahnhof is a **VBN** information center with tickets and transportation maps (DM1). Open daily 6am-9pm.

Ferries: Schreiber Reederei (☎32 12 29) shuttles to the suburbs and towns along the Weser and ends up at Bremerhaven. 3½ hr.; May 16-Nov. 16 W-Th and Sa at 8:30am. One-way to Bremerhaven DM21, round-trip DM34. **Reederei Warrings** ferries also begin at Bremen on their daily path to and from Helgoland and Wangerooge, stopping at all port towns in between.

Taxi: Pick up a taxi waiting at the front or back exits of the Hauptbahnhof or call ☎140 14. **Frauen Nachtaxi** (☎133 34) operates a women's taxi service daily 7pm-4am.

Car Rental: Avis, Kirchbachstr. 200 (☎21 10 77). Open M-F 7am-6pm, Sa 8am-1pm.

Bike Rental: Leave a DM50 security deposit and a photo ID, and pedal away from the **Fahrrad Station** (☎30 21 14), a red stand on the right of the train station's exit. DM15 per day, children DM9; DM60 per week, children DM45. Open Mar.-May and Oct.-Dec. M-F 10am-5pm; June-Sept. M and W-F 10am-5pm, Sa-Su 10am-noon and 5-5:30pm.

◆🛈 ORIENTATION AND PRACTICAL INFORMATION

Bremen lies south of the mouth of the Weser River on the North Sea, making the city perfect for meandering, but take care on the blocks surrounding Ostertorsteinweg and Am Dobben late at night; as you move out of the Altstadt, the city's anthropomorphic patrons won't follow. Bremen has four distinct neighborhoods: the tourist-filled **Altstadt,** where most of the sights and the oldest architecture are; the **Alte Neustadt,** a residential neighborhood south of the Weser river; the **Schnoor,** an old neighborhood turned shopping village; and the **Viertel,** a student quarter filled with hip kids, clubs, and cheap food.

A **Tourist Card Bremen,** available at the tourist office, provides free travel on city transportation, 20% discounts to theater shows and city tours, and 50% off admission to many of Bremen's museums. (2-day card for 1 adult and 1 child DM19.50, 3-day card DM26; 2-day group card for up to 5 people DM35, 3-day DM46.)

Tourist Office: The souvenir-jammed central office (☎308 00 51; fax 308 00 30), sits in its own little building in the center of the plaza in front of the Hauptbahnhof, and offers **room** listings. It also provides guides to museum exhibits and theater schedules, and sells tickets for concerts and festivals. A smaller **kiosk,** next to the Rathaus, performs the same tasks during the same hours. Open June-Oct. daily 9:30am-10pm; Nov.-May M-W 9:30am-6:30pm, Th-F 9:30am-8pm, Sa-Su 9:30am-4pm.

Consulate: UK, Herrlichkeit 6 (☎590 90). Open M-Th 8:30am-12:30pm and 2:30-3:30pm, F 8:30am-12:30pm.

Bookstores: Thalia, Sögerstr 36-38 (☎302 920) in the walking district, has an excellent selection of English paperbacks and classics, but you have to look a little in the "international" section as well. Open M-F 9:30am-8pm, Sa 9:30am-4pm.

Gay Resources: ☎70 41 70. Provides information about gay events and services. Open M-W and F 10am-1pm, Th 4-5pm.

Women's Resources: Am Hulsberg 11 (streetcar: "Am Hulsberg"). Info pertinent to travelers is available in the lobby. **Frauenbuchladen Hagazussa,** Friesenstr. 12 (☎741 40), stocks over 3000 books of particular interest to women. Only women are admitted. Open M 10am-2pm, Tu-F 10am-6pm, Sa 10am-2pm.

Laundromat: Wasch Center, Vor dem Steintor 75. Follow Ostertorsteinweg to the bitter end. DM3 per kilo for wash, soap, and spin dry; another DM1 per 10min. to dry. Open daily 7am-10pm. Or try **Schnell & Sauber,** a few doors down at Vor dem Steintor 107. DM6, soap included, dry DM1 per 15 minutes. Open 6am-11pm.

Internet Access: Internet Center Bremen, Bahnhofsplatz 22-28 (☎277 66 00), in the DGB building to the left of the main entrance. DM2.50 for 30min. Open M-W, F 11am-8pm, Sa 11am-4pm.

Pharmacy: Päs Apotheke, Bahnhofspl. 5-7 (☎144 15) across the *Platz* from but not facing the station. Stated hours M-F 8am-6:30pm, Sa 8am-2pm, though there may be someone around later, or on Sunday, to help if you call or pass by.

Emergency: Police, ☎110. **Fire and Ambulance,** ☎112.

Post Office: Main office at Domsheide 15, 28195 Bremen (☎367 33 66), near the Markt. Open M-F. Another office is on Bahnhofspl. 21, by the train station. Both open M-F 9am-8pm, Sa 9am-2pm.

⛰ ACCOMMODATIONS AND CAMPING

The key phrase is "call ahead." Inexpensive hotels exist, but they fill fast. The tourist office's free *Hotel-Liste* lists a few rooms in the DM20-40 range, but prices quickly rocket up to DM100.

Jugendgästehaus Bremen (HI), Kalkstr. 6 (☎17 13 69; fax 17 11 02). From the train station, take Bahnhofstr. to Herdentorsteinweg, go right at Am Wall, then turn left onto

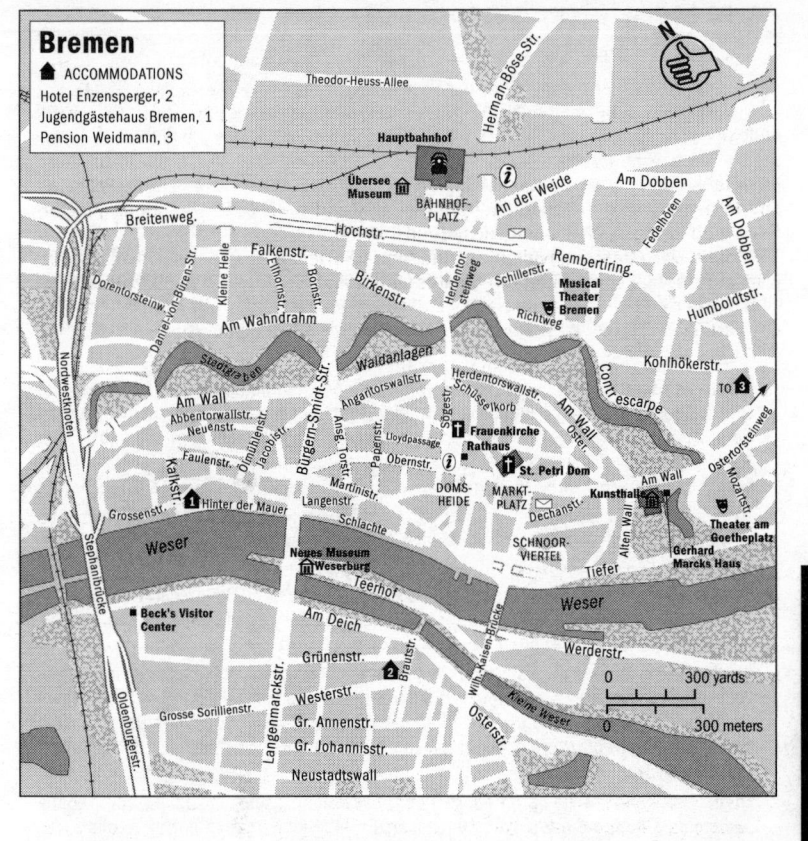

Bremen

⬆ ACCOMMODATIONS
Hotel Enzensperger, 2
Jugendgästehaus Bremen, 1
Pension Weidmann, 3

Bürgermeister-Smidt-Str. and right along the water to the hostel. The glowing Beck's Brewery sign across the Weser lulls you to sleep with visions of malt dancing in your head. Breakfast and sheets included. 24hr. reception. Check-in 2pm. Check-out 10am. No curfew. Dorm beds DM29.90, over 27 DM34.90.

Hotel-Pension Garni Weidmann, Am Schwarzen Meer 35 (☎498 44 55). Ostertorsteinweg eventually becomes Am Schwarzen Meer; follow it. The plush comforters and cavernous rooms—complete with coffee-makers—are fit for royalty. Pampering at bargain prices. Reservations recommended. Singles from DM40; doubles from DM80.

Hotel Enzensperger, Brautstr. 9 (☎50 32 24). From the Markt, cross the Wilhelm-Kaiser Brücke over the Weser, turn right on Osterstr., and right on Brautstr. Clean, no-frills accommodations. Rooms have TV, phones, and sometimes views. Restaurant and bar downstairs. Breakfast included. Call a few days ahead. Singles DM48; doubles DM90.

Hotel Weltevreden, Am Dobben 62 (☎780 15; fax 70 40 91), just off Ostertorsteinweg. Comfortable rooms, good prices, close to Bremen nightlife. Breakfast included. Reception open M-Sa 7am-10pm, Su 7:30am-1pm and 5-10pm. Call a few days ahead. Singles DM60; doubles DM100, with shower DM120.

Camping: Campingplatz Bremen, Am Stadtwaldsee 1 (☎21 20 02; fax 21 98 57). S-Bahn #5 or #8 to "Külen Campf," then Bus #28 to the door. Open all year. Washers and dryers DM4 each. 2-person tent DM7.50, 3-person tent DM9.50, 4 or more DM11. DM4.50 per child. Free showers and electrical hookup.

🍴 FOOD

A cheap way to eat well is in the open-air **market** (daily 8am-2pm).In the Rathaus, Bremen's renowned **Ratskeller** is worth a visit. Dating back to 1405, it's one of the oldest wine bars in Germany. Settle in a cozy leather-and-wood booth or among huge barrels to enjoy one of 600 German wines; most are moderately priced (DM7-8 per 0.2L glass), but the meals run around DM40. (☎32 16 76. Open daily 11am-midnight; kitchen open noon-2:30pm and 6-11pm.) In the Marktplatz, bronze pigs herd pedestrians into take-out cafes on **Sögerstr.**, where shops sell everything from chocolate truffles to fish sandwiches. The restaurants of the **Schnoorviertel** are sweetly styled as old-fashioned German inns—this means they're overpriced. Student pubs proliferate farther east in the **Viertel**, and on and around **Ostertorsteinweg** (see **Nightlife**, p. 520). **Comet**, at the corner of Vor dem Steintor and Friesenstr., brings grocery shopping to the heart of the hip Viertel. Posters for parties and concerts line the walls.

> **Mensa Academia,** Dechanatstr. 13-15 (☎364 91 67), downstairs at the Hochschule für Künste, just behind the post office. Eat, drink, and "be" a student (necessary, but how is up to you) under ivy trellises in a stone courtyard while listening to the opera ingenues. Open M-F 10am-very late, Sa noon-very late.

> **Moto,** Schlachte 22 (☎30 21 13), is a cheap but classy pan-Asian place beside the Weser in a row of expensive cafes, all with good views of water and people. Try the soup or noodle dishes (DM5.50-17.50). Many veggie options. Open daily noon-midnight.

> **Basilikum,** Langemarckstr. 129 (☎59 25 57). From the Altstadt the Bürgermeister-Smidt-Br. becomes Langemarckstr. Fresh banana, orange, tomato, and apple juice alongside soups (DM5), immense gyros (DM9.50-12.50), pizza (DM8-15), and salads (DM3-10) fill students and old men in a candlelit atmosphere.

> **Café Harlekin Bookshop,** Lahnstr. 65b (☎50 19 11). From Langemarckstr. walk away from Beck's Brewery along Lahnstr. Bremen's best breakfast selection (served all day) is flanked by an alternative bookstore. The generous *Türkisches Frühstück* ("Turkish Breakfast," *Fladenbrot*, feta, olives, and cucumbers, DM7.50) makes a filling lunch. Open daily 10am-6:30pm.

> **Engel,** Ostertorsteinweg 31-33 (☎766 15). Enjoy simple, elegant dining and people-watching in both the art-nouveau interior and on the leafy terrace outside. Lunch specials (DM10.50) include dessert. Other artful entrees DM10-19. Concerts on the terrace on summer weekends. Open daily from 9am.

📷 SIGHTS

ST. PETRI-DOM. A survivor of WWII, the **St. Petri-Dom** next to the Rathaus has a mosaic exterior depicting the crucifixion. Below are stone saints; at their feet, lions and griffons gnaw on squirming victims. It's a pretty building—really. Inside the Dom are frescoed ceilings. The foundation dates to 798, when Charlemagne had the first stone placed here. Once you've seen the inside, climb the tower to gaze down upon the hubbub of the market square below. (*Sandstr. 10-12.* ☎36 50 40. *Cathedral open M-F 10am-5pm, Sa 10am-1:45pm, Su 2-5pm. Free. Tower open May-Oct. M-F 10am-4:30pm, Sa 10am-1:45pm, Su 2-5pm. DM1.*) In a corner of the cathedral is the **Dom Museum,** housed in part of the original foundation with frescoes dating back 500 years. (*☎365 04 11. Open Apr. 15-Nov. M-F 10am-5pm, Sa 10am-noon, Su 2-5pm; Dec.-Apr. 15 M-F 11am-4pm, Sa 10am-noon, Su 2-5pm. DM3, students and children DM2.*) Walk around the church and into the **Bibelgarten** behind the church; the courtyard features glorified plants, and also serves as a colorful walkway to another Dom attraction. Your museum ticket is good for a DM1 discount on an entrance to the macabre **Bleikeller,** in the basement of the Dom. The mummified corpses of workers who fell from the roof of the cathedral were discovered here in 1695 and have been on exhibit (with other random mummies, just for good measure), for three centuries._(Open May-Oct. M-F 10am-5pm, Sa 10am-2pm, Su noon-5pm; Nov.-Apr. daily 1-5pm. DM2, children DM1. Admission ticket likewise good for DM1 discount at the Dom museum above.)

RATHAUS. Bremen's Altstadt centers around the **Rathaus** and its 15th-century base decorated by an ornate Renaissance facade. Surprisingly, it and the surrounding market square are the original structures. The survival of the buildings here is thanks to the generosity of the English WWII bomber assigned to bomb the area; he deliberately missed the target. (Adults DM5, children DM2.50.) Just left of the entrance to the town hall is Gerhard Marcks's famous 1951 sculpture *Die Musikanten*, which shows the Grimms' donkey, dog, cat, and rooster in their robber-foiling stance. (Open for guided tours M-Sa 11am, noon, 3pm, and 4pm; Su 11am and noon. DM6, students and children DM3.)

OTHER SIGHTS. Just past the *Domshof*, turn left on Domsheide for the **Schnoorviertel**, a district of red-roofed gingerbread houses, dainty shops, and dog salons. Between the Marktplatz and the Weser lies the narrow cobblestone **Böttcherstr.** Once a crowded artisans' quarter, the street offers gilded archways, stained-glass windows, boutiques, and craft shops. It's worth standing with all the tourists at noon, 3, or 6pm for the magic of the Böttcherstraße **Glockenspiel.** Bells ring and part of the building swings open to deliver a performance by mechanical figurines, re-enacting wild sea and air exploits from the building's early memory. Come early—the prime gawking spots fill up quickly. The smell of the brew lures the helpless across the Weser to **Beck's Brewery.** They will happily treat you to an hour long tour, followed by taste-tests and samples of Germany's best-selling beer...2L of free beer! Unlike its exported counterparts, homegrown Beck's offers the famous full bouquet expected in a German beer; try the special brews while you're here, because they're not available anywhere in the world but North Germany. The history is almost as rich as the brew here; although Beck's is shipped all over the world, horse-drawn carriages still deliver the hometown beer to all stores and restaurants in Bremen. (Am Deich 18/19. ☎50 94 55 55. Hourly tours Tu-Sa 10am-5pm, Su 10am-3pm. English tours at noon. DM5, children free.)

🏛 **MUSEUMS**

The persistence of the four traveling animals theme throughout the Altstadt might lead you to believe otherwise, but Bremen is a city of high culture. The city's sophistication and intelligence are most notably on display in Bremen's museums.

▧ **NEUES MUSEUM WESERBURG BREMEN.** The museum crouches on the island between the Klein Weser and the Weser in four red brick buildings that once served as warehouses. Inside is a new universe: white rooms on five floors filled with strange, beautiful installations of modern works by international artists. (Teerhof 20. Off the Bürgermeister-Schmidt Brücke. ☎59 83 90; fax 50 52 47. Open Tu-F 10am-6pm, Sa-Su 11am-6pm. DM8, students and children DM5. Tours daily in German; DM11, students and children DM8. Free CD listening tour.)

KUNSTHALLE. Bremen's main collection includes Impressionist, Expressionist, and contemporary works. (Am Wall 207. ☎32 90 80. Open Tu 10am-9pm, W-Su 10am-5pm. DM8, students DM4. Tours Su 11:30am, Tu 6pm.)

ÜBERSEE MUSEUM. Promises a *"Weltreise im Minutentakt"* (a trip around the world in a matter of minutes). With animals stuffed into tasteful poses in life-like "habitats" and displays of cultural artifacts in still life, it does just that...sort of. Exhibits ranging from a Shinto garden to a South Sea fishing village attempt to show the world outside Germany's borders. An exhibit on Bremen's history is on the third floor. The special exhibits are *much* more fun than the museum's basic selection. (Bahnhofspl. 13, next to the train station on the right. ☎361 91 76; fax 361 92 91. Open Tu-Su 10am-6pm. DM10, students DM5, children DM5.)

GERHARD-MARCKS-HAUS. An indoor and outdoor sculpture garden of works by the sculptor of *Die Musikanten*. Changing exhibitions of modern sculpture and graphic art. *(Am Wall 208. Next to the Kunsthalle. ☎32 72 00. Open Tu-Su 10am-6pm. Tours Th at 5pm. DM6, students and children DM4.)*

🎭 🎵 ENTERTAINMENT AND NIGHTLIFE

There's opera in the **Theater am Goetheplatz**, Am Goethepl. 1-3 (☎365 33 33; fax 365 33 32), new drama in the **Schauspielhaus**, Ostertorsteinweg 57a (☎365 33 33), and auldies but goodies in the **Bremer Shakespeare Company**, Theater am Leibnizplatz (☎50 03 33; fax 50 33 72). The **Theater im Schnoor**, Wüste Stätte 11 (☎32 60 54; fax 32 75 96), does cabarets and revues, from postmodern Shakespeare (nothing is sacred) to parodies of the *Wehrmacht*. International blockbusters appear at **Musical Theater Bremen**, near the train station on Richtweg 7-13 (☎554 43 21). For the slightly more bizarre, check out the show at **Madame Lothar's Variete Theater**, Kolpingstr. 9 (☎337 91 91) which puts on a cabaret "travestie" comedy nightly W-Sa at 9:30pm.

Summertime brings performances to parks around the city; a children's production of the famous Bremen fairy tale happens right on the main *Platz* every Su at noon and 1:30pm from May-Oct. Discount tickets for all events are usually held for students. Check the tourist office, the theaters, or the publication *Bremer Umschau* (DM3) for schedules and prices, as well as information on free performances. *Foyer*, free at many museums, lists theater, music, film, and art events. The tourist office also has a booklet with these listings and an excellent map of the city. *Belladonna* lists cultural events of special interest to women. *Prinz* has comprehensive nightlife listings and the full scoop on the Bremen *Szene* (DM4.50 at the tourist office and newsstands). *Partysan*, a magazine based in Hamburg, also lists big parties in Bremen (free at Engel and other cafes).

During the last two weeks of October, Bremen drinks beer and eats tubs of lard cakes in honor of its trading heritage and freedom as a *Land* with the colorful **Freimarkt** fair, an annual event since 1095. And Bremen rocks—big concerts are often held in the **Weserstadion** (☎43 45 00) behind the train station. Tickets and information for small- and large-scale events are available at the tourist office. **Modernes Complex**, Neustadtswall 28 (☎50 55 53; fax 50 66 90; take trams #1 or 8, or bus #26/27 to "Bremen Universität"), hosts films, plays, concerts, and dancing. Times and cover charges vary. Bremen offers a well-developed and raucous pub culture, and the *Viertel* is the place to be. Find the true pulse of the nightlife on the densely populated **Ostertorsteinweg**. A lively gay and lesbian scene is scattered around the city, with centers at the edge of the *Viertel* on Am Dobben and Humboldtstr.

🏅 **Moments,** Vor dem Steintor 65 (☎780 07). A wildly popular disco with well-advertised and well-attended parties. The music invariably improves during happy hour (10-11pm) with half-price drinks. Open daily 10pm-late.

Litfass, Ostertorsteinweg 22 (☎70 32 92). An all-day, all-night bastion of alternative chic that poses as a bar. As the eyes of the supermodel on the wall cast flirting glances toward you, coolly take down one of their piping hot coffees (from DM2.90). The extensive outdoor terrace and open facade make it the place to see and be seen. Open M-Th and Su 10am-2am, F-Sa 10am-4am.

Confession, Humboldtstr. 156 (☎738 22). A swingin' gay and lesbian club featuring live blues, jazz, and alternative bands. Sit outside at the red picnic tables and stare at the yellow nipples on the front of the building. Is this fun or what? Open M-Th and Su 7pm-2am, F-Sa 9pm-late. Saturday women only.

TheaLit, Im Krummen Arm 1 (☎70 16 32). An evening club and center for women's and lesbian events. Bar, buffet dinners (DM38), salads (DM16), and "fingerfood" (DM3.50 a piece). Women only. Office open Tu-F 10am-12pm. Bar open Tu-Sa 7pm-12:30am.

BREMERHAVEN
☎ 0471

Bremerhaven holds extra significance for Americans: since the 18th century, it has been the main emigration port for Germany. The sea calls Bremerhaven—Bremen's younger, saltier sister city—but these days, no one is home. The city's residents would rather pack the **Columbus Center mall** than crowd the decks of any of the town's numerous antique (and land-locked) vessels. The beautiful **Große Kirche** (Great Church) sits across the street from the Columbus Center. To get here from the train station take bus #501, 502, 505, 506, 508, 509, or 511 to "Columbus Center". The street there is the crowded, commercial **Bürgersmidt Str.**; avoid it unless you need an ATM or a McDonald's. The **Alter Hafen** (Old Harbor) is a place of many delights and many, many German grandparents with their grandchildren. It's a block behind the Columbus Center, or take bus #526 from the Hauptbahnhof to "Alter Hafen." **Ferries** sail daily for **Helgoland,** Germany's own Fantasy Island, at 9:45am. The ◼**Deutsches Schiffahrts-Museum,** Hans-Scharoun Pl. 1, has scurvy, cabin-fever, and whatever other boat-related psychoses you can think of. It's crazy for ships, with models and relics inside the building and real full-scale museum ships outside. After you've explored the floors and floors of navy exhibits, head to the basement to play captain of your own ship, or race a friend. (Open Apr.-Oct. daily 10am-6pm; Nov.-Mar. Tu-Su 10am-6pm. Admission DM8, students, seniors, and children DM4.) Docked across the bridge, you can crawl around the inside of the **Technikmuseum U-Boot Wilhelm Bauer,** one of the only German submarines from WWII that was neither sunk nor scrapped. (Open Apr.-Oct. daily 10am-6pm. DM4, under 18 DM3.) The other boats on display are more expensive, and the view from the shore is probably enough. At the **Zoo am Meer,** farther up the harbor, German schoolchildren scream and careen through the garden, while animals on the other side of the bars (polar bears, sea lions, monkeys, etc.) sit calmly and watch. If the babes jangle your nerves, there is a soothing aquarium downstairs. (Open May-Aug. daily 8am-7pm; Apr. and Sept. 8am-6:30pm; Oct.-Mar. 8am-5pm. DM4, students and children DM2. Free tours available with reservation, call ☎ 420 71.)

Bremerhaven is 45 minutes from **Bremen** by **trains** that leave and arrive at least hourly; a **ferry** leaves Bremen daily at 8:30am (see Bremen, p. 515). Ferries also depart from Bremerhaven to **Helgoland** daily at 9:45am. The **tourist office,** on the second floor of the Columbus Center, finds rooms from DM30 for free. (☎ 430 00. Open M-W 9:30am-6pm, Th-F 9:30am-8pm, Sa 9:30am-4pm.) The **Verkehrsamt,** Van-Ronzelenstr. 2, provides the same services. (☎ 94 64 60; fax 460 65. Open M-F 8am-4pm.) **Internet access** is available at **Interface,** Grazerstr. 68, behind the Columbus Center. (☎ 41 91 209. Open daily 1pm-midnight.) You can rent **bikes** from **Fahrrad-Verleih** on Bürgermeister-Schmidt-Str. 138 (☎ 941 38 30; fax 941 30 31. DM14 per day, DM38 for 3 days, DM65 per week. Open M-F 9:30am-1pm and 2-6:30pm, Sa 9am-12:30pm.) The **post office,** 27570 Bremerhaven, directly to the left as you leave the Hauptbahnhof, offers **currency exchange** and cashes traveler's checks for a DM6 fee (open M-F 8am-6pm, Sa 8am-1pm). Bremerhaven's number one combo platter, the ◼**Jugendgästehaus-Jugendherberge (HI),** Gaußstr. 54-56, offers a dazzling array of conveniences. Take bus #502, #509, or #511 to "Gesundheitsamt." Work out in the mini-gym or visit their Volkswagen-sized sauna. The rooms are clean and all of them in the *Gästehaus* are private. (☎ 856 52 or 98 20 80; fax 874 26. Breakfast and sheets included. Special handicapped-access rooms also available. Reception 7am-6am. Make reservations a week in advance. Hostel DM28, over 26 DM31.50. *Jugendgästehaus* DM29.90.)

HELGOLAND
☎ 04725

Seduced by duty-free prices, German tourists endure a two- to four-hour ferry ride, jump into tiny skiffs to row ashore, and then run all over the island, snatching up as many cartons of cigarettes, meter-tall bottles of liquor, and rounds of cheese as they can legally carry before the ship departs at 4pm. A different kind of mayhem reigned at the conclusion of WWII, when the British navy evacuated the strategically valuable island and attempted to obliterate it with thousands of tons of dynamite. The island bears battle scars, including concrete docks that extend into the ocean, but the glitz and glam of consumerism give it a flashy veneer.

Helgoland isn't a great day trip on rainy days: a ferry ride on the high seas will not put you in a cheese-eating mood, and the best way to enjoy the island is to go for a walk under a clear sky. The three hours the ferry allows is plenty of time to buy a lunch at one of the carry-out places near the dock and climb or take the **elevator** to the top of the dunes, where fields of Queen Anne's lace, red paths, red cliffs, and a view out to sea await. (Daily until 11pm; one-way DM1, round-trip DM1.50.) There's also the beach to comb, and ferries leaving every half-hour for **Dünne,** Helgoland's little sister island, which is one big beach. (Ferries run 8am-8pm. Buy a *Fahrkarte* from machines on the dock.) Helgoland's **museum, aquarium, swimming pool, mini-golf,** and **tennis courts** aren't as exciting as its cliffs, but if you plan to stay more than one day, they might be of interest. Hours and prices vary; check the notices in the glass cases on the dock. Helgoland's claim to fame however, is at its northwest tip: the **Lange Anna** is a free standing rock tower, and the island's most famous landmark. Time is not an obstacle—it only takes a half hour walk—but in a storm watch out for high winds!

The cheapest and most reliable way to get to Helgoland is through Norddeich, Bremerhaven, or Cuxhaven. The **MS Frisia III,** operating from **Norddeich,** offers a lower fare but a longer ride (4hr.) and a skimpier schedule. (Departs May-June Tu 8am; July-Aug. Tu and F 8am. Daytrips DM43, under 13 DM27.) **Reederei Warrings** (☎ (04464) 949 50; fax (04464) 94 95 30; email info@reederei-warrings.de; www.reederei-warrings.de) sends the **MS Helgoland** and the **MS Speedy** from **Bremerhaven.** (3hr. Daily at 9:45am, return trip at 4pm. Daytrip DM58, ages 11-18 DM38, 4-11 DM30; open-ended return DM70, ages 11-18 DM40, 4-11 DM29.) **Reederei Warrings** also sends Helgoland ships from **Wilhelmshaven** (daily at 9am, 3hrs. Daytrip DM58, open-ended return DM70.) and **Bremen.** (Daily at 7am, 5hrs. Daytrip DM62, ages 12-18 DM32, ages 4-11 DM42.) The **MS Wappen von Hamburg,** which sails via **Cuxhaven,** is quickest. (☎ (04721) 55 48 95. 2hrs. May-Sept. daily 10:30am. Daytrips DM55, ages 12-18 DM36; open-ended return DM68, ages 12-18 DM40.)

With thousands of visitors each year, Helgoland's **tourist office** greets travelers as they step off the skiff. Their free brochure offers a wealth of information, including a list of accommodations. (☎813 711; fax 81 37 25. Open M-F 9am-5pm, Sa-Su 11:30am-3pm.) Helgoland's **Jugendherberge (HI),** Postfach 580, sits right on the beach, a 10-minute walk from the ferry dock. Follow the maps and signs. (☎341; fax 74 67; email Haus-des-Jugend-Helgoland@t-online.de. Sheets DM10. Reception Apr.-Oct. 10am-2pm and 5-7pm. Curfew 10pm. Call or fax 4-6 weeks ahead. DM25, with 3 meals DM41, over 4 nights with 3 meals DM38 per night; kids and families DM24 per person.)

OSNABRÜCK ☎0541

Around 1300, the inhabitants of Osnabrück built a wall around two villages that had been developing for centuries, and called the unified town Osnabrück. It quickly developed into a commercial center, and when the warring parties sat down in 1648 to end the Thirty Years War, it was in Osnabrück. On October 25 of that year, the peace was announced to the town's citizens. They stood incredulous for a few minutes, then broke out in song. The townspeople eventually finished their song and went home, but a spirit of peacefulness remained. Three hundred and fifty years after the Peace of Westphalia, Osnabrück is as tranquil as ever.

◪ PRACTICAL INFORMATION. Trains run from Osnabrück to **Hannover** (1½hr., 1 per hr., DM36), **Münster** (½hr., 2 per hr., DM20), and **Düsseldorf** (2hr., 1 per hr., DM60). **Buses** travel around the city center (DM1.30) and to the outer zones (DM2.20), but the best deal is a *Tageskarte* (DM4.50), good for a day of unlimited travel after 9am. Rent **bikes** at the **Fahrradverleih** in the train station. (☎25 91 31. Open M-F 6am-8pm, Sa 7am-2pm. DM8 per day, DM35 per week. ID and DM20 deposit required.) For a **taxi,** call ☎320 11. The **tourist office,** Krahnstr. 58, is just off the Rathaus. From the station, walk up Möserstr. as it turns into Herrenteich Str., follow the curve around, and turn onto Krahnstr. The staff books **rooms** (from DM30 per person) for free. (☎323 22 02; fax 323 27 09; email tour-info@osnabrueck.de. Open M-F 9:30am-6pm, Sa 9:30am-1pm. City tours Sa 11am, W 3pm, DM7, children DM3.) Internet access is available at the **Stadtbibliothek** above the tourist office (open Tu-F 10am-6pm, Sa 10am-1pm). Launder your duds at **Wasch Center,** on the corner of Kommenderiestr. and Johanisstorwall. (Open daily 6am-11pm. Wash DM7, including soap, dry DM1 per 15 min.)

▐▐▐ ACCOMMODATIONS AND FOOD. South of the city center is the newly outfitted ▓**Jugendgästehaus Osnabrück,** Iburger Str. 183a. From the station, take bus #62 (direction: "Zoo") to "Kinderhospital." The rooms are clean and large, and the light-up map in the lobby is as good as any tourist office. (☎542 84; fax 542 94. Breakfast included. Sheets DM6. Reception 3-6pm and 8-10pm. Wheelchair accessible. Call ahead. Dorm beds DM24.70, over 26 DM30.) Clean rooms fill the **Hotel Jägerheim,** Johannistorwall 19a. From the station, turn left on Konrad-Adenauer-Ring, which becomes Petersburgerwall and then Johannistorwall. (☎216 35. Reception until 9pm. Singles DM40-45, with bath DM64; doubles DM80, with bath DM104.) For **camping,** try **Freizeitpark Attersee,** Zum Attersee 50. From the station, take bus #22 to "Attersee." (☎12 41 47. DM6.50 per person.)

A number of discount **supermarkets** line Johannisstr. The new **Pub'lic,** Markt 25, takes trendiness to new levels. Recline in the shadow of the Marienkirche and indulge in the creative drink menu, or any of the soups, baguettes, pastas, and salads for DM5-15. (☎205 18 18. Open Su-Th 11am-2am, F-Sa 11am-3am.) Next door is the ▓**Creperie,** Markt 24, which serves huge salads and amazing crepes with an endless complimentary bread basket. (☎227 15. Open 11:30am-midnight.) **Lagerhalle,** Rolandsmauer 26, is the town's one-stop nightlife center, with a popular *Kneipe,* a restaurant with international and vegetarian specials from DM5, an art-house film theater, and frequent rock concerts, cabarets, and dance parties; Lagerhalle boasts over 500 events a year. (☎33 87 40. Open Tu-Th 6pm-1am, F 6pm-2am, Sa 7pm-2am, Su 6:30-11pm.) **Theater Osnabrück** is next door to the Dom. (Box office open Tu-F 10am-5:30pm, Sa 10am-1pm, and 1hr. before all performances.)

▣ SIGHTS. Osnabrück's stunning **Friedenssaal** (Hall of Peace) hides inside the perfectly preserved **Rathaus.** *(Open M-F 8am-6pm, Sa 9am-4pm, Su 10am-4pm. Tours Su 10:30am. Free.)* Next to the Rathaus stands the **Marienkirche,** completely destroyed during the war, and fully rebuilt thereafter. Tread lightly; the floor of the choir is an impressive sea of stones marking the graves of the clergymen buried below. *(Open Apr.-Sept. M-Sa 10am-noon and 3-5pm; Oct.-Mar. M-Sa 10:30am-noon and 2:30-4pm. Tours of the tower Su from 11:30am-1pm; DM2, children DM1.)* The immense **Dom,** Kleine Domsfreiheit 24, has been collecting priceless religious relics since the 14th century. The courtyard is worth a stroll. *(☎31 84 81; fax 31 84 82. Open Tu-F 10am-1pm and 3-5pm, Sa-Su 11am-2pm. Tours Su at noon, or after the service. Domschatzkammer DM1.50.)*

The warm afterglow of Westphalia quickly fades amidst the permanent **Felix Nussbaum** exhibit at the **Kulturgeschichtliche Museum;** Nussbaum was deported to a camp in 1940. He escaped, but painted the images he saw there for the rest of his life. While in hiding in 1943 he could no longer use oil paints for fear of being sniffed out, but continued to paint until he was deported to Auschwitz in 1944. Nussbaum's paintings symbolically depict the tragedy of the Holocaust, and are displayed in cold, concrete hallways to complete the atmosphere. *(Open Tu-F 11am-6pm, Sa-Su 10am-6pm. DM8, students DM4.)* Osnabrück's most famous son is Erich Maria Remarque, the acclaimed author of *Im Westen nichts Neues (All Quiet on the Western Front).* Though Allied bombing completely destroyed his house on Hafenstr., literary travelers can tour the **Erich-Maria-Zentrum,** Am Markt 6, which documents his life and work. *(☎969 45 11. Open Jan.-Nov. Tu-F 10am-1pm and 3-5pm, Sa 10am-1pm, first Su of the month 11am-5pm.)* The **Osnabrück Zoo,** Am Waldzoo 2-3, is fantastic. Take bus #62 to "Zoo" to watch the tigers and bears frolic. *(☎95 10 50. Open daily Apr.-Oct. 8am-6:30pm; Nov.-Mar. 9am-dark. Last entrance 1hr. before closing. DM15, students DM10, children DM8, including the aquarium.)* Next door is the **Museum am Schölerberg,** Am Schölerberg 8, which has a planetarium. *(☎56 00 30; fax 56 00 337. Open Tu 9am-8pm, W-F 9am-6pm, Sa 2-6pm, Su 10am-6pm. DM6, children DM3.)*

OLDENBURG ☎ 0441

Founded in 1108, the city of Oldenburg was spared the destruction of the Thirty Years War largely because its count at the time, Anton Günther, raised the most beautiful horses in Germany. Today's Oldenburg is much more than a one-trick pony—the unique Frisian culture runs deep in this city, and all its residents are actively involved in its preservation. Most tourists will miss the beautiful residential neighborhood west of Alexanderstr., the cemetery, and the green, green *Schloßgarten*, which doesn't bother *Oldenburgers*, who are friendly, but not about to divulge all their secrets.

⚡ GETTING THERE AND PRACTICAL INFORMATION

Oldenburg is easily accessible by **train** from **Bremen** (½hour, 2-3 per hr., DM15.60); **Osnabrück** (1¾hr., 1-2 per hr., DM31); and **Jever** (1hr., every 2 hrs., DM15.40). The old, moated city lies along an offshoot of the Weser river, and serves as a take-off point for excursions to East Frisia. The **tourist office,** Wallstr. 14, finds **rooms** (from DM30; call ahead) and piles visitors with numerous North Sea brochures. (☎ 157 44; fax 248 92 02; email info@oldenburg.de; www.oldenburg-tourist.de. Open M-F 10am-5pm, Sa 10am-1pm.) The tourist office also serves as a ticket office for shows in Oldenburg and as far away as Bremen. **Rent bikes** at the **Fahrradstation,** Neuesstr. 5, across the street from the tourist office. (☎ 163 45. Open M-Th 7am-11pm, Sa 8am-11pm. DM15 per day for the first two days, after that DM5 per day.) **Oldenburgische AIDS-Hilfe,** Bahnhofstr. 23, offers information on AIDS and gay resources, and has English-speaking counselors. (Hotline ☎ 194 11. Open M 9am-noon and 2-4pm, W 9am-noon and 2-6pm, Tu and Th-F 9am-noon.) For internet access, head to **FutureWorld,** Staustr.18. (☎ 998 76 88. Open M-Sa 10am-10pm, Su 1-10pm. ½hour for DM4.) The **post office,** 26123 Oldenburg, is directly to the right as you exit the train station (open M-F 7:30am-7:30pm, Sa 7:30am-1pm).

🏠🍴 ACCOMMODATIONS AND FOOD

The city's modern **Jugendherberge (HI),** Alexanderstr. 65, is 1.5km from the station. From the train station, turn right on Molestr. At the post office, look to your right: take the walkway over the station, and turn left onto Karlstr. Follow it as it becomes Milchstr. and go left on Lindenstr. Alexanderstr. is to the left of the cemetery; walk 3min. to your new home. Or take bus #7, 9, or 12 to "Lappen"; then, across the street, catch bus #2 or 3 to "Von Finckstr." (☎ 871 35. Breakfast included. Reception 5-11pm. Curfew 10pm, but you can get a key. The hostel fills quickly, so call several days ahead. Dorm beds DM22, over 26 DM28.20.) The **Hotel Hegeler,** Donnerschweerstr. 27, has bright, clean, large rooms and a bowling alley—really! From the station, cross the walkway over the tracks and follow the road to the left to Donnerschweerstr., then turn left and walk 150m. (☎ 875 61; fax 885 03 59. Call ahead. Singles DM45-50, with bath DM80; doubles DM60-100, with shower DM140. In a pinch, doubles as singles are DM60, or DM100 with bath.)

Picknick, Markt 6, serves up regional specialties like potato pancakes with apple sauce (DM9) and baguettes from DM7. (☎ 273 76. Open M-Sa 10am-late.) **Marvin's Biergarten,** Rosenstr. 8, is as laid-back as it gets. Interesting art, inside and out. You'll know you've found the right place when you see the eyes painted between the second floor windows. "Beer on tab" DM2.20-5.80. "Food & Good" DM4-8. From the train station, head up Bahnhofstr. and go left on Rosenstr. (open M-Th and Su 7pm-2am, F-Sa 8pm-3am). **Tandoor,** Staustr. 18, serves gyros (DM11), pasta (DM9-14), and lunch specials (DM10). The *bunter Salatteller* ("colorful salad plate") will restore your faith in mankind. Scribble your order on the scraps of paper provided at the tables, then hand it to the man behind the counter; he knows what to do. (☎ 170 75. Open Su-Th noon-1am, F-Sa noon-3am.) Wallstr. has a good selection of cheap late-night pizza and pasta places; try **New York, New York,** Wallstr. 24 where the dining is ever-so-slightly classier than most. (☎ 157 11. Open M, Tu, Th 11am-2am, W 11am-3am, F-Sa 11am-5am, Su 4pm-2am.)

📷🗼 SIGHTS AND ENTERTAINMENT. Every morning, the city's residents jockey for position with hundreds of tourists as a **daily market** bustles on the main square surrounding the 1887 **Rathaus.** The adjacent 13th-century **Lambertikirche** has endured Baroque and Neoclassical additions to its Gothic structure, which have rendered its interior shockingly…nondescript. *(Open Tu-F 11am-12:30pm and 2:30-5pm, Sa 11am-12:30pm. Free.)* A well-organized meetingplace for the 15th and 20th centuries, the **Landesmuseum,** Schloßpl. 26, in the lemon-yellow castle with white and copper trim, houses Oldenburg's best collections. The city's history is told through decorative and religious art displayed in rooms with individual soundtracks and videos. *(Open Tu 9am-8pm, W-F 9am-5pm, Sa-Su 10am-5pm. DM4, students, seniors, and children DM2.)* The **Augusteum,** Elisabethstr. 1, is an extension of the *Landesmuseum.* The lower floor showcases special exhibitions, while upstairs is home to Kirchner's Expressionist street scenes (see p. 23) and groggy Surrealist dreamscapes. *(☎220 26 00. Open Tu-F 9am-5pm, Sa-Su 10am-5pm. Call for tours. DM4, students, children, and seniors DM2.)* For slightly less esoteric action, walk another 300m to the **Naturkunde und Vorgeschichte Museum** (natural and prehistory museum), Damm 38-44. Displays of Jewish life in the early 20th century are informative—except for the strange omission of the Holocaust. Also check out the spearheads and mastodons upstairs. *(☎924 43 00; fax 924 43 99; www.logiplan.de/museum. Open Tu-Th 9am-5pm, F 9am-3pm, Sa-Su 10am-5pm. DM3, students and children DM1.50.)* Down Lappen and across the street, the **Stadtmuseum,** Am Stadtmuseum 4-8, holds printing presses, stamps, and postcards from the city's history. *(Open Tu-F 9am-5pm, Sa 9am-noon, Su 10am-5pm. Free.)* Where Alexanderstr. and Nadorstr. diverge, the **Getrudenfriedhof,** Oldenburg's ancient cemetery, stretches its mausoleum- and headstone-covered lawn.

Oldenburg's nightlife centers around a curious man named "Popeye" who runs the club **JFK's** at Wallstr. 3. Despite the campy and strangely morbid motif, Popeye injects some pulse into Oldenburg after hours, organizing numerous raves, dance parties, and beach parties. Just ask him what's going on. Oldenburg also offers **Pulverfass,** Kaiserstr. 24, a popular men-only gay disco. *(☎126 01. Open F-Sa 11pm-5am. Cover DM5.)* **Der Schwann,** Stau 44 across from Kaiserstr., is a beer garden with live music on weekends. Watch the pretty boats sail across the harbor while downing cheap beer. *(☎261 89. Open daily 9am-2am. Breakfast served until 2pm.)*

OSTFRIESLAND (EAST FRISIA)

Germany's North Sea shoreline and the seven sandy islands that hug the coast appear to belong to an entirely different country. The flat landscape, dotted with windmills, dramatic cloud scenes, and foreboding seascapes, seems to bear no relationship to the rest of the country's cheerful river valleys and bustling cities. Caught up in such dramatic scenery, it's easy to forget that people actually live here, but Frisian culture is still quite prominent. The seafaring Frisians treasure their delicious **tea,** which is often served with sugar candies called *Kluntje* in elaborate porcelain sets. To complement the tea, try some *Ostfriesische Rosinenstütten,* a sweet loaf chock-full of juicy raisins; it's on display in every bakery. The Frisian dialect is actually the closest linguistic relative to English.

Twice a day, around 8am and 8pm, the tide goes out on the Frisian coast, exposing the ocean floor—called the **Watt**—between the mainland and the islands. Guides, called *Wattführer,* are numerous and well advertised; check at the tourist office or on posters everywhere for a schedule of *Watt* tours.

> **!** Never venture onto the *Watt* without a guide—quicksand pits abound, and the tide's rapid return is extremely dangerous.

Although the region has a number of HI youth hostels, don't expect to stay there unless you have a reservation; Ostfriesland is as popular with school groups as it is with tourists. Hostels on the mainland are well-kept and surprisingly cheap, but on the more touristed islands, prices rise higher than the choppy *Nordsee* waves. The best bet for the budget traveler is a **private room,** *(Privatzimmer)* booked through a tourist office, which start at DM25-30. If you plan on staying longer than a few days, and especially if you're traveling in a group, renting a **vacation apartment** *(Ferienwohnung)* is the best option. These apartments usually include a kitchen and start at about DM60 per night. Consult a tourist office. If you plan to be on the move, having or renting a car will allow you to see more of the towns. Buses and trains are often inconvenient and infrequent. Miles of breathtaking beaches, green fields, and rolling dunes more than compensate for all the planning required.

JEVER ☎ 04461

Four hundred and fifty years ago, Jever received city rights from its patroness, Lady Mary, who promoted its culture by commissioning art and building fortifications and a school. Now the local brewery, famous throughout Germany, does the same. Located on Elisathufer north of the Altstadt, the **Fresisches Brauhaus** (☎ 137 11; fax 137 04; www.jever.de) offers a **tour** of the futuristic glass brewing complex that puts Jever on the map—and on tap—all over northern Germany. (2hrs., every 30min. Apr.-Oct. M-F 9:30am-12:30pm and 1:30-6pm, Sa 9am-1pm. DM10, including a souvenir mug, pretzel, and two glasses of beer. Call ahead.)

Jever's other industry is tourism. The main marketplace conveniently holds most of the worthy sights. Most Jeverians dismiss their famed barley fetish, claiming that their finest offering is the castle located across from the tourist office at Alter Markt 18. The salmon-colored, 15th-century **Schloß,** along with the statue outside (the town's greatest memorial to their patron lady), houses an engaging museum filled with art and trinkets dating back 500 years. (☎21 06; fax 91 22 14; email schlossmuseum-jever@ewetel.net; www.schlossmuseum.de. Open Mar. to mid-Jan. Tu-Su 10am-6pm; July-Aug. also open M 10am-6pm. DM4, students DM2, children DM1.50.) The Renaissance **Rathaus** in the main square sits behind a mask of scaffolding. On Kirchplatz, the **Stadtkirche** is Jever's monument to persistence; after being burned down, it was reconstructed and modernized. Adjacent to the church and across from the tourist office at the Hof von Oldenurg is a **Glockenspiel,** which goes off at 11am, noon, 3, 4, 5, and 6pm, releasing figurines from Jever's history through its trap doors. The little people extend their hands to you in welcome, and as the tourist office will tell you, you're meant to take it personally. For a more restful atmosphere, take the bus to **Hooksiel** (every 2 hours), a small coastal town northwest of Jever, with quiet **beaches** and cozy campgrounds.

Getting to Jever can be tricky; let Deutsche Bahn do the work for you at one of their information desks. They'll give you a ticket that works for both **trains** and **buses** in the Jever region. Trains arrive in Jever about once an hour; bus schedules are available from the train station or the tourist office. The **tourist office,** Alter Markt 18, across from the Schloß, books **rooms** for free and directs brew-seeking visitors to their Shangri-La. (☎ 710 10; fax 93 92 99. Open May-Sept. M-F 10am-6pm, Sa 10am-2pm; Oct.-Apr. M-Th 9am-5pm, F 9am-1pm.) For a **taxi** call ☎ 30 30.

The **Jugendherberge Jever (HI),** Mooshütterweg 12, idles on a small street behind the Schloß. Unlike most hostels in the region, rooms are generally available. (☎ 35 90; fax 35 65. Breakfast included. Sheets DM5. Ring at the front desk to be let in. Curfew 10pm. Open Apr.-Oct. Dorm beds DM19, over 26 DM24.)

PORT TOWNS

Only two mainland ports are accessible by train: **Emden,** the ferry port for Borkum, and **Norddeich,** the ferry port for Norderney and Juist. The departure points for all other islands lie in a string of tiny ports on the coast—all connected by the overpriced **Bäderbus,** which runs from **Norden.** The ferry companies servicing **Baltrum** run a separate bus from the train area which is conveniently timed with the ship.

Beware: *the Bäderbus is not scheduled to connect with departing ferries,* and its driver is not concerned with getting you to your port on time. Pick up a bus schedule from the train station in Norden and plan at least a day ahead, or you may get stuck waiting for hours with no bus *or* ferry. Watch for new ferry services and specials; companies often run inter-island trips or excursions to the duty-free haven of Helgoland (see p. 521). **Trains** run from **Bremen** to **Norden** (2-2½hr., 1 per hr., DM42) and **Norddeich** (2½hr., 1 per hr., DM47). They also head from **Oldenburg** to **Norden** (1½-2hr., 1 per hr., DM30) and **Norddeich** (1½-2hr., 1 per hr., DM32).

NORDEN AND NORDDEICH ☎ 04931

Norden is the transportation polestar for any excursion around Ostfriesland. By **train,** it connects to **Emden** and **Norddeich** (1 per hr., DM3-5), and as the anchor of the **Bäderbus,** it provides easy access to every other port town. Pick up a bus schedule ahead of time; this service is not always convenient to trains and ferries. Call or visit the **tourist office,** next to the **Rathaus,** for specific transportation information or to book **rooms** (from DM25) for free. (☎ 98 62 01; fax 98 62 90. Open M-F 9am-1pm and 2-5pm, Sa 9am-4pm.)

The main marketplace and walking district centers around Osterstr. and Neuerweg. From the Rathaus, it's impossible to miss the gigantic tower on the other side of the market green belonging to the 15th-century **Ludgerkirche** (open Apr.-Sept. M 10am-12:30pm, Tu-Sa 10am-12:30pm and 3-5pm). Experience the church's **Glockenspiel** at 9am, noon, 3, or 6pm: two minutes before each hour the bells tinkle out a line from a German song about our hearts and our friends. If you are so moved, stay the whole day and sing along—the words are printed on the church bulletin board. If you're any good, the swells drinking in the square may throw you a beer. The great East Frisian fascination with tea is explained at the **East Frisian Tea Museum,** Wesserstr. 1, in the old Rathaus on the west side of the Marktplatz. For DM1 on Wednesdays (May-Aug. only), participate in an East Frisian **tea ceremony.** Be careful: if you raise your pinky when you drink, someone may cut it off—play it cool, Anglophiles. The ceremony takes place at tea time (2 and 3pm), of course. (☎ 121 00. Open Mar.-Oct. Tu-Sa 10am-4pm. DM4, children DM1.50, family card DM12.) The **Heimatmuseum** in the same building explains the early culture of Ostfriesland, including dike construction and shoemaking (same admission and hours as tea museum). For some actual treasures of the sea, try the **Mushel-&Schnecken-Museum,** a collection of shells inside an old windmill. (☎ 126 15. Open Apr.-Oct. Tu-F 2:30-6pm. DM2.50, children DM1.)

Often passed through only en route to Norderney or Juist, the suburban port **Norddeich** actually offers spectacular land- and seascapes well worth an extra look. The town's **Jugendherberge (HI),** Strandstr. 1, is an excellent base for exploring the region; it's convenient (in the middle of Norddeich, the main port for island ferries), clean, and inexpensive. From the Norddeich-Mole station (the end of the line), walk away from the boats along the big green *Deich,* a grass hump between surf and turf. Descend and turn left on the little white street just past the Hotel Regina Maris; the hostel will be on the next corner on the left. The main hostel compound is almost always filled with schoolchildren, but the newly built pine cabins *(Blockhütten)* in the backyard allow you to escape the shrill *Schulkinder* and the 10pm curfew. (☎ 80 64; fax 818 28. Breakfast DM6.60, sheets included. Reception 5-8pm. Dorm beds DM14.90, over 26 DM19.90. DM9 to pitch your own tent in the backyard.) **Nordsee-Camp,** Deichstr. 21, is 20 minutes farther down Badestr., which turns into Deichstr. It has impressive views, but dike-side camping gets chilly. (☎ 80 73; fax 80 74. Open mid-Mar. to Oct. DM5 per day, DM8.25 per person. *Kurtaxe* DM3.)

Ferries leave Norddeich daily for Norderney and Juist. Pick up schedules in the ferry ticket offices right outside of the Norddeich-Mole train station. The Norddeich **tourist office,** Dörper Weg 22, is at the very end of the street which opens off of Badestr. The staff finds **rooms** in *Pensionen* (DM23-35) for free, doles out ferry schedules, and arranges **Watt tours.** (☎ 986 02; fax 98 62 90. Open M-F 9am-6pm, Sa 9am-4pm, Su 10am-noon.) Numerous **bike** rental shops line Dörper Weg; many will also rent you a go-cart (single or family-size) from DM6 per hr. Take advantage of the bike trails criss-crossing the fields around Norden and Norddeich. (Bikes about DM10 per day, DM40 per week. Passport required.) For a **taxi,** call ☎ 800. The **postal code** is 26506.

NIEDERSACHSEN

OSTFRIESISCHE INSELN (EAST FRISIAN ISLANDS)

The East Frisian islands are seven in number and float in the southernmost part of the North Sea. They begin to warm up in early June, and every summer thousands of Germans vacation here, shrieking and shouting as they jump into the frigid waters. Six or seven ferry companies have set up shop on the mainland, making for dependable transportation to all the islands, but no main transit hub exists. Unless you want to take a tiny, vibrating plane for upwards of DM100, you can't travel between islands—you always have to return to the mainland. Fortunately, the **Bäderbus** runs from **Norden** to all the ferry ports, meaning that a 9am departure from the bus stop should have you on your island by noon. However, don't count on the buses leaving more than once every 2-3 hours or getting you there in time for the ferry. DeutscheBahn offers Bäderbus schedules for free. To comprehend all the ins and outs of your chosen island, buy its brochure at a tourist office in the region. These pamphlets contain extensive accommodation listings and everything you ever wanted to know about each particular piece of sand.

BORKUM   ☎ 04922

Lodged in an inlet halfway between Germany and the Netherlands, Borkum is where the industrious Germans go to do nothing. The island is festive and laidback. A tiny painted train carts vacationers through a serene, flower-filled landscape to the shiny happy town at the far end of the island. The town centers on a 19th-century **lighthouse,** a lovely structure that provides a great view from the top.

AG-EMS (☎ (04921) 89 07 22; fax (04921) 89 07 42; office in the Emden train station open M-F 8:30am-5pm) runs a ferry from Emden's *Außenhaven* (see p. 527) out to the island four times a day, returning three times to the mainland. (2hr. Same-day round-trip DM25, children DM12.50. Ticket window opens 1hr. before departure.) For more money, you can get to the island in half the time on the **catamaran** (DM39.50, children DM24.50). On Borkum, rent **bikes** at the **Fahrradverleih** at the train station. (DM3 per hr., DM8 per day. Open M-F 7am-6pm; Sa 7-8am, 9amnoon, 1-2pm, and 3-5pm; Su 7-8am, 9am-noon, 1-2pm, and 4-6pm.) Borkum's **tourist office,** Am-Georg-Schütte-Pl. 5, at the train station in town, books **rooms** for free and sells the island's brochure (DM1) and maps. (☎ 93 30; fax 93 31 22; email kurverwaltung@borkum.de. Open M-F 10am-2:30pm, 4-5:30pm, Sa 10am-noon.)

NIEDERSACHSEN

Ostfriesische Inseln (East Frisian Islands)

Borkum's **Jugendherberge (HI),** Reedestr. 231, a five-minute walk from the dock, fills up quickly. A written request one month in advance is necessary in order to secure a room. (☎579; fax 71 24; email jh-borkum@djh-unterweser-ems.de. Three meals included. Curfew 10:30pm, but house keys are available. Dorm beds DM40, over 26 DM45.) **Insel-Camping,** Hindenburgstr. 114, is 15 minutes from the train station by foot. (☎10 88. Open Mar.-Oct. DM23.50 per person, tent included.)

NORDERNEY
☎04932

More "civilized" than the mainland, the island of Norderney is Germany's oldest North Sea spa. Once visited by the likes of Bismarck and Heinrich Heine, the island now houses numerous white turn-of-the-century hotels and lots of postcard and beach-bucket shops. One spot of peace is the town's tiny **church,** built in 1578, and its equally tiny **graveyard.** The church is covered with roses and ivy; inside, model ships hang from the ceiling, and the local priest plays the organ all day long. (Open M-Th 8am-5pm, Su after the service-5pm. Free.) Away from town, the dunes and beaches of the eastern two-thirds of the island are part of the **Wattenmeer national park.** Some parts of the endless beach are known as **FKK** (nude beach). To get to the spa, tides, or surrounding nature wonderland, you have two options: a walk through the Watt or a ferry. For *Watt-wanderungs* call local expert seaman Kurt Knittel ((04931)30 96); his tour is 3hrs. to the island, complete with a bus tour to Nessmersiel, an explanation of sea creatures, and most importantly, a ferry ticket back. (DM36.50; pick up a schedule at the ferry office or call, tours leave around 8am). Or, employ the services of **Ferry Company Frisia,** which runs a ferry from Norddeich. (☎in Norden (04931) 98 71 24; fax 98 71 31; in Norderney ☎913 13; fax 913 10. Leaves 9-13 times a day; call or check with the tourist office for schedules. 1hr. day-trip DM27, open-ended return DM38.) On Norderney, two **bike** rental shops are conveniently located just beyond the harbor. **Dicki Verleih** is on Gorch-Fock-Weg. (☎33 78. Open daily 9am-6:30pm. DM3 per hr., DM12 per day.) Or try the **Fahrradverleih am Hafen,** 300m down Hafenstr. as you step off the ferry. (☎13 26. Open daily 9am-6pm. Same prices as Dicki.) For **groceries,** head to **Comet,** across the street from Dicki on Gorch-Fock-Weg (open M-F 8am-1pm and 3-6pm, Sa 8am-1pm). For a **taxi,** call 33 45 or 33 33. To spend the night, check in with the friendly folks at the **tourist office,** Bülowallee 5, at the end of Hafenstr. The staff finds **rooms** in *Pensionen* or private homes from DM26 for a DM7.50 fee. (☎918 50; fax 824 94. Open M-F 9am-6pm, Sa 10am-12:30pm and 2-4pm, Su 11am-2pm.)

NIEDERSACHSEN

Norderney has two **youth hostels,** both of which are full of German school children and very expensive; guests must pay for three meals a day for the duration of their stay. However, the owner of the hostel at **Südstr.** takes pains to provide a haven for stranded travelers. Follow Zum Fähranleger to Deichstr., then turn onto Südstr. (☎24 51; fax 836 00. Full board included. Sheets DM5. Reception 8:30-9am, 5:15-6pm, and 9:45-10pm. HI members only. Open Mar.-Oct. Dorm beds DM37.50, including *Kurtaxe*.) Somewhat less inviting due to its inconvenient location in the middle of the island (5km away from the city) is the hostel **In den Dünen 46.** If you miss the hourly bus to "Leuchtturm," you'll have to rent a **bike** in town or suffer the 1½- to 2-hour walk. Follow Deichstr. to its end, and head left on Karl-Reger-Weg, where signs point you to the hostel. (☎25 74; fax 832 66. Full board included. Reception 8:30-10am. Open Mar.-Oct. Dorm beds DM37.50, over 26 DM42.50.) **Camping** is available in summer for HI members only. (☎16 14. DM11 per person with breakfast.) **Haus Westend,** Friedrichstr. 40, offers elegant rooms across the street from the beach for surprisingly low prices. Those on the top floor have ocean views. (☎26 85; fax 832 61. Singles DM68, with bath DM70-80, doubles DM110-140. 10-20% off during low season.) Another slightly less classy option is the nearby **Hotel Adriatic,** Friedrichstr. 8. (☎26 62; fax 841 54. Singles DM65-68; doubles DM130-136.) The main camp site on the island is **Camping Booken,** Waldweg 2, the next best thing to the hostels. Call ahead. (☎448 or 23 96; fax 478. Wash DM6, dry DM5. Reception 10am-noon. Open year-round. DM12 per person, DM12 per tent. Warm showers included.)

BALTRUM   ☎04939

The smallest of the Frisian Islands, with a population of 500, **Baltrum** is the ideal escape from civilization. The island prides itself on its silence (due to an absolute ban on motor vehicles) and its wilderness. Horses graze everywhere, and only a small (but well-provisioned) town interrupts the pristine landscape. **Watt tours** are available here; call the local *Wattführer*, Hans-Jürgen Broul, at ☎918 20. (1½hr. tours DM4, children DM2. 2½hr. tour DM5, children DM3.)

To reach Baltrum, take the bus from the Norden train station (one short stop from Norddeich; DM4, children DM2) to **Neßmersiel** to catch the ferry. (Open-ended return DM36, children DM18. Daytrip DM24, children DM11.) Trains, buses, and boats (30min.) are all timed for a convenient rendezvous. (June-Nov. 2-3 per day. Last ferry to the island does not have a corresponding ferry back.) Note that daytripping visitors must pay a DM2 *Kurtaxe*. Transportation on Baltrum is provided by a **horse-drawn "taxi"** (☎316). You can't bring a bike over, nor can you rent one on arrival, but the island is small enough to traverse on foot. For more information, call the ferry company, **Reederei Baltrum Linie** (☎913 00; fax 91 30 40) or visit the **tourist office,** on the left as you leave the harbor. The office also offers hotel information and books private **rooms** for free. (☎91 40 03; fax 91 40 05; www.baltrum.de. Open M-F 8:30am-12:30pm and 1:30-5pm.) Sorry HI fans, **no hostel** here; the tourist office's list of *Privatzimmer* is your best bet.

HAMBURG

The largest port city in Germany, Hamburg radiates an inimitable recklessness. Calling its atmosphere "liberal" or "alternative" does not do the city justice. With a fiercely activist population of squatters and a thriving sex industry comparable only to Amsterdam's, the city is a crazy coupling of the progressive and the perverse. As a busy port, Hamburg gracefully grew over the centuries into an industrial center of nearly two million inhabitants. Straddling several rivers, it was an early hub for overland trade from the Baltic Sea, and the first German stock exchange convened here in 1558. In 1618, Hamburg gained the status of Free Imperial City, a proud tradition of autonomy that endures to this day, as it wields considerable political power as one of Germany's sixteen *Länder*.

Poised on the crest of Germany's breakneck industrialization and naval construction drive, Hamburg became one of Europe's wealthiest cities by the beginning of WWI. The *Hamburg-Amerika Linie* ruled the oceans of industry as the largest shipping firm in the world. At the onset of WWII, the city suffered a severe pummeling as the first stop on Royal Air Force bombing raids. The port was a primary target for the Allies; a single air raid killed 50,000 civilians, many of whom lived in crowded tenements along the waterfront. The conflagration in the streets reached temperatures of 1,000°C, leaving nearly half of the city's buildings in ruins. Fortunately, Germany's richest city could afford the reconstruction of much of its copper-roofed architecture. Since the late 60s, an active conservation movement has steadily and successfully lobbied for the restoration of historic buildings, including museums, hotels, and houses. In the early 80s, however, violent riots erupted when police attempted to evacuate warehouses occupied by anarchists and left-wing intellectuals who were protesting property speculators' acquisition of the real estate. Today, Hamburg expresses its restlessness less violently, by exuding the energy of a city that has become a center of contemporary artists and intellectuals as well as reveling party-goers who live it up in Germany's self-declared "capital of lust."

HIGHLIGHTS OF HAMBURG

Befitting the second-largest city in Germany, Hamburg's **museums** (p. 541) are world-class: the **Hamburger Kunsthalle** displays a huge collection of art from medieval times to the present, while the **Deichtorhallen** hosts contemporary creations, and the **Museum für Kunst und Gewerbe** specializes in decorative arts.

Hamburg is also damn sexy, with its **Reeperbahn red-light district** (p. 534), second only to Amsterdam's, and its **Erotic Art Museum** (p. 541).

A staggering **nightlife** scene will make you dance, fool, dance (p. 543).

◩ GETTING THERE AND AWAY

Flights: Lufthansa (☎35 92 55) and **Air France** (☎50 75 24 59) are the two heavy hitters that fly to Hamburg's **Fuhlsbüttel Airport** (☎507 50). **Jasper** buses (☎227 10 60) make the 25min. trip from the Kirchenallee exit of the Hauptbahnhof to the airport daily every 20min. 5am-9:20pm. DM8.50, under 13 DM4. Or take U-Bahn #1 or S-Bahn #1 to "Ohlsdorf," then take an **express bus** to the airport, which runs every 10min. (daily 5:30am-11pm). DM3.90.

Trains: The **Hauptbahnhof** handles most traffic with hourly connections to **Berlin** (2¾hr., DM93); **Frankfurt** (3¾hr., DM191); and **Munich** (6hr., DM260). Further trips to **Hannover** (1½hr., 3 per hr., DM70); **Copenhagen** (6hr., 3 per day, DM102); and **Amsterdam** (5½hr., 3 per day, DM105). The efficient staff at the **DB Reisezentrum** sells tickets and books vacation packages. Open daily 5:30am-11pm. **Dammtor** station is near the university, and **Altona** station is in the west of the city. Most trains to and from Schleswig-Holstein stop only at Altona. Frequent trains and the S-Bahn connect the 3 stations. **Lockers** are available 24hr. for DM2-4 per day.

Hamburg

ACCOMMODATIONS
Hotel Alt-Nürnberg, 23
Hotel Annerhof, 21
Hotel Terminus Garni, 22
Hotel Florida, 15
Instant Sleep, 5
Jugendherberge, 19
Schanzenstern Übernachtungs-
    und Gasthaus, 7

NIGHTLIFE
Absolut, 14
Cave, 16
Cotton Club, 20
Frauenkneipe, 10
Große Freiheit 36/ Kaiser
    Keller, 12
Indra, 11
La Cage, 13
Logo, 2
Mojo Club, 18
Molotow, 17
Rote Flora, 8

FOOD
Asia Imbiß Bok, 6
Falafel König, 4
Geo Pizza, 1
Machwitz, 3
Noodles, 9

HOHELUFTBRÜCKE

HARVESTEHUDE

Hallerstr.

Laundromat

Grindelhof

Grindelallee

Schlüterstr.

Hohe Weide

G.-Falke-Str.

Beim Schlump

Bundesstr.

Rentzelstr.

Grindelallee

Universität

CHRISTUS-
KIRCHE

Schäferkampsallee

SCHLUMP

Schröderstiftstr.

Moorweidenstr.

An der Verbindungsbahn

E.-Siemers-

Tiergartenstr.

Altonaer Str.

Sternschanzenpark

STERNSCHANZE   Sternschanze

TV
Turm

Planten un
Blomen

Lagerstr.

Karolinenstr.

St. Petersburger Str.

Marseiller Str.

Botanischer
Garten

Max-Brauer-Allee

Schulterblatt

Bartel-Str.

Susannenstr.

Bahrenfeldstr.

Schanzenstr.

Sternstr.

Grabenstr.

MESSEHALLEN

Bei den Kirchhöfen

Jungiusstr.

Gorch-

Stresemannstr.

Holsten-Glacis

Kleine Wallanlagen

Gorch-Fock-Wall

Dammtorwall

Wohlers Allee

Bernstorffstr.

Lerchenstr.

Neuer Kamp

Marktstr.

Glashüttenstr.

SIEVEKING-
PLATZ

Musikhalle

Drehbah

GÄNSE-
MARKT

Caffamacherreihe

Valentins
kamp

Thadenstr.

FELDSTR.   Feldstr.

JOHANS-
BRAHMS-PLATZ

Backerbreitergasse

Otzenstr.

PAULINEN
PLATZ

Heiligengeistfeld

Speckstr.

Kaiser-Wilhelm-Str.

Kohlhöfen

Fuhlentwiete

ABC
Str

Gilbertstr.

Willistrasse

ST. PAULI

Glacischaussee

Große Wallanlagen

Holstenwall

ENCKE
PLATZ

Pilatuspool

Poolstr.

Neustädter-
str.

Thielbek

Kurzestr.

Komödogr.

NEUSTADT

Rademachergang

Stadthausbrücke

TO ALTONA
(1.2 km)

Kl.
Freiheit

Große
Freiheit

Paul-Roosen-Str.

Detlev-Bremer-Str.

Budapester Str.

Simon-von-Utrecht-Str.

Peterstr.

Neander-str.

Markus-
str.

Wexstr.

GROßE
NEUMARKT

Alter Steinweg

Düsternstr.

Nobistor

Erotic
Art
Museum

Königstr.

ST. PAULI

Neuer Steinweg

Hütten

Helgoländer

STADTHAUS-
BRÜCKE

REEPERBAHN

Reeperbahn

Spielbudenplatz

ALBERS-
PLATZ

MILLERNTOR-
PLATZ

Reeperbahn

Ludwig-Erhard-Str.

Michaelskirche

Ost-West-Str.

Rödings-Markt

Herrengraben

Pepermölenbek

HEIN-
KÖLLISCH-
PLATZ

Davidstr.

Elbpark

Gerstäckerstr.

Rothesoodstr.

Böhmkenstr.

Kravenkamp

Teilfeld

Martin-Luther-Str.

Admiralität Str.

Steinhöft

Rödings-Markt

Holstenstr.

Bernhard-Nocht-Str.

St.-Pauli-Hafenstr.

Zirkusweg

Seewartenstr.

Helgoländer Allee

Stintfang

Venusberg

SCHAAR-
MARKT

Schaar-
steinweg

Neustädter
Neuerweg

Vorsetzen

Stubbenhuk

Baumwall

Fischmarkt

St.-Pauli-Fischmarkt

Landungsbrücke

LANDUNGS-
BRÜCKEN

Karpfangerstr.

Johannisbollwerk

Baumwall

BAUMWALL

Nordereibe

Old
Elbe
Tunnel

Windjammer
Rickmer
Rickmers

Binnenhafe

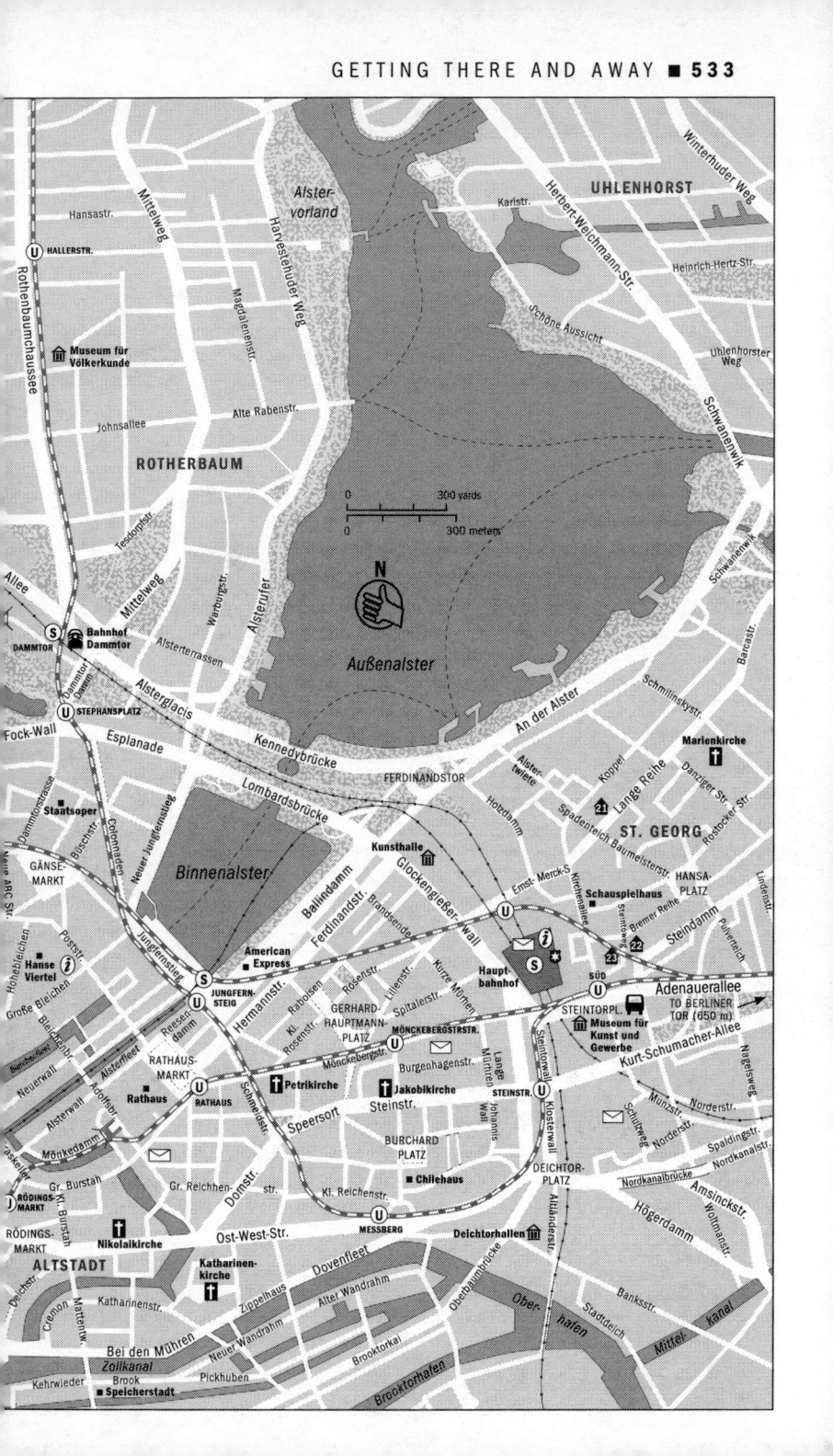

PHONE CODE. Hamburg's phone code is 040.

Buses: The **ZOB** is located across Steintorpl. from the Hauptbahnhof. To **Berlin** (2½hr., 8 per day, DM41), **Paris** (15hr., daily, DM115), and **Copenhagen** (6hr., 2 per day, DM63). **Polenreisen** has good deals to Poland. Open M-F 9am-8pm, Sa 9:30am-1:30pm and 4-8pm, Su 4-8pm. **Lockers** are located in the main hall but cannot be accessed between 9pm and 5:30am (DM2).

Ferries: DFDS Seaways, Van-der-Smissen-Str. 4 (☎389 03 71; fax 38 90 31 41), about 1km west of the Fischmarkt (S-Bahn #1 or 3 to "Königstr."), sets sail to England and Ireland. Overnight ferries run to Harwich, England (20hr.), every other day. The cheapest tickets cost DM208 (DM106 in the winter); students receive a 25% discount. Other destinations include Copenhagen, Oslo, and Amsterdam. Open M-F 10am-4:30pm; phone reservations M-F 9am-6pm, Sa 9am-2pm.

Hitchhiking: *Let's Go* does not recommend hitchhiking as a safe mode of transportation. Those headed to Berlin, Copenhagen, or Lübeck take U-Bahn #3 to "Rauhes Haus" then walk up Mettlerkampsweg and turn right on Sievekingsallee to Hamburg Horn (a treacherous traffic rotary at the base of the *Autobahn*). Hitchers aiming for points south take S-Bahn #3 to "Wilhelmsburg" and wait at Raststätte Stillhorn.

⌐ GETTING AROUND

Public Transportation: HVV operates an efficient U-Bahn, S-Bahn, and bus network. Single tickets within the downtown area cost DM1.80. There are also 1- and 3-day tickets (DM9.50 and 23.30); consider buying a **Hamburg Card** instead (see below). All tickets can be bought at orange *Automaten*.

Taxis: Taxiruf, ☎194 10.

Car Rental: Hertz has an office in the Hauptbahnhof's ReiseBank (see **Currency Exchange,** below; ☎33 54 70; fax 24 53 78). Rates start at DM400 per week.

Mitfahrzentrale: City Netz Mitfahrzentrale, Ernst-Merk-Str. 8 (☎194 40). Ride-sharing deals. Berlin DM31, Köln DM44, Amsterdam DM60, Paris DM95. Open daily 8am-9pm.

Boat Rental: Rent sailboats, paddleboats, and rowboats on the Außenalster from **Segelschule Kpt. Pieper,** An der Alster (☎24 75 78), directly across from the Hotel Atlantic at the foot of the Kennedybrücke. Sailboats DM32 per hr. for 1-2 people (additional skippers DM3 per person), paddleboats and rowboats DM20 per hr. Sailing license required to rent sailboats. Open daily 10am-9pm.

⊞ ORIENTATION

Hamburg's fame as a North Sea port relies upon its huge harbor 100kilometers inland, on the north bank of the **Elbe.** The city center sits between the river and the two city lakes, **Außenalster** and **Binnenalster,** formed by the confluence of the Alster and Bille with the Elbe. Most major sights lie between the **St. Pauli Landungsbrücken** port area in the west and the Hauptbahnhof in the east. Both the **Nordbahnhof** and **Südbahnhof** U-Bahn stations exit onto the Hauptbahnhof.

The **Hanseviertel** is a quarter thick with banks, shops, art galleries, and auction houses. The area's glamour turns window-shopping into an aesthetic pleasure, while the nearby shipping canals manage to give the quarter a pseudo-Venetian charm. North of the downtown, the **university** dominates the **Dammtor** area and sustains a vibrant community of students and intellectuals. To the west of the university, the **Sternschanze** neighborhood is a politically active community home to artists, squatters, and a sizeable Turkish population. The **Altona** district, with its own major train station, was once an independent city ruled by Denmark; as Hamburg grew, the Danes were ousted. At the south end of town, an entirely different atmosphere reigns in **St. Pauli,** whose raucous **Fischmarkt** (fish market) is juxtaposed by the equally wild (and no less smelly) **Reeperbahn,** home to Hamburg's infamous sex trade.

🛈 PRACTICAL INFORMATION

TOURIST AND FINANCIAL SERVICES

Tourist Offices: Hamburg's two main tourist offices supply free maps and pamphlets. The **Hauptbahnhof office**, near the Kirchenallee exit (☎30 05 12 00; fax 30 05 13 33; email info@hamburg-tourism.de; www.hamburg-tourism.de), **books rooms** for a DM6 fee. Open M-F 6am-10pm, Sa and Su 7am-10pm. The less-crowded **St. Pauli Landungsbrücken office** is located between piers 4 and 5 (☎30 05 12 00). Open daily 10am-7pm. A third office is in the **Hanseviertel** mall. Open daily 9am-6pm. For advanced reservations and information, call the **Hamburg Hotline** (☎30 05 13 00; open daily 8am-8pm). The offices all sell the **Hamburg Card,** a great means of exploring the city. For a fairly low price, it provides unlimited access to public transportation, admission to most museums, and discounts on bus and boat tours. 1 day DM12.50; 3 days DM26, without transportation DM10. An even better deal is the **Group Card,** which provides the same deals for up to five people. One day DM24; 3 days DM42, without transportation DM21.

Tours: Top-Tour-Hamburg (☎227 10 60) operates summertime sight-seeing tours leaving every 15 minutes from 9:30am to 4:45pm from the Kirchenallee exit of the Hauptbahnhof and the St. Pauli Landungsbrücken. Adults DM22, children DM11; with Hamburg Card DM4 and DM2. **Hamburg Vision** (☎31 79 01 27) offers a similar tour with additional stops at the Rathaus and Michaeliskirche. DM25, students DM19, under 12 free. Tours last between 1¼hr. and 2hr. **O'Neil Bikes,** Beethovenstr. 37 (☎22 12 16), offers German-language bike tours of the city and environs. Prices from DM49 for a 3-4hr. tour. **Alster-Touristik** (☎347 42 40), across from Hotel Atlantic on the Außenalster (two blocks north of the Hauptbahnhof), leads 1hr. jaunts around the lakes. Daily 10am-5pm on the quarter hour. DM13, seniors DM9, children DM6.50.

Consulates: Canada, (☎35 55 62 90). **Ireland,** Feldbrunnenstr. 43 (☎44 18 62 13). U-Bahn #1 to "Hallerstr." Open M-F 9am-1pm. **New Zealand,** Heimhuder Str. 56 (☎442 55 50). Open M-Th 9am-5:30pm, F 9am-4:30pm. **UK,** Harvestehuder Weg 8a (☎/fax 448 03 20). U-Bahn #1 to "Hallerstr." Open M-F 9am-noon and 2-4pm. **US,** Alsterufer 27 (☎41 17 10), on the Außenalster's west side. Open M-F 9am-noon.

Currency Exchange: ReiseBank, on the second floor of the Hauptbahnhof near the Kirchenallee exit, arranges money transfers for Western Union, cashes traveler's checks, and exchanges money for a DM5 fee. Open daily 7:30am-10pm. Otherwise, try one of the dozens of banks downtown. Generally open M-W and F 9am-1pm and 2:30-4pm, Th 9am-1pm and 2:30-6pm. There's also a **ReiseBank branch** in the Altona train station and at Ballindamm 16.

American Express: Ballindamm 39, 20095 Hamburg (☎30 39 38 11 12; fax 30 39 38 12). Mail held for cardmembers up to 4 weeks; all banking services. Open M-F 9am-6pm, Sa 10am-1pm.

LOCAL SERVICES

Bookstores: Heine Buch, Grindelallee 24-28 (☎441 13 30), in the university district, has a superb selection of German literature. It also has an impressively comprehensive English-language section. Open M-F 9:30am-7pm, Sa 10am-4pm.

Library: Staats- und Universitätsbibliothek, Von-Melle-Park 3 (☎428 38 22 33). Hamburg's university library includes a fine English-language collection. Open M-F 9am-9pm, Sa 10am-1pm; Aug. only M-F 9am-7:30pm, Sa 10am-1pm.

Gay and Lesbian Resources: Hein und Fiete (☎24 03 33), Pulverteich 21, in the rainbow-striped building. Open M-F 4-9pm, Sa 4-7pm. **Magnus-Hirschfeld-Centrum,** Borgweg 8 (☎279 00 69). U-Bahn #3 or bus #108 to "Borgweg." Daily films and counseling sessions. Evening cafe open daily 5pm-midnight. Center open M and F 2-6pm, Tu-W 7-10pm. Private meetings available at the **Leben- und Schwulenberatung** (call ☎33 58 45, Tuesdays 6-8pm to make an appointment).

Women's Resources: See **Frauenbuchladen und Café**, p. 538.

Laundromat: **Schnell und Sauber**, Grindelallee 158, in the university district. S-Bahn #21 or 31 to "Dammtor." Wash 6kg DM6, soap included. Dry DM1 for 15min. Open daily 7am-10pm. There are also several laundromats on Simon-von-Utrecht-Str., heading towards the Altona station from St. Pauli.

EMERGENCY AND COMMUNICATIONS

Emergency: Police, ☎110. From the Kirchenallee exit of the Hauptbahnhof, turn left and follow the signs for "BGS/Bahnpolizei." There's also a police statioℂ on the **Reeperbahn** at the corner of Davidstr. and Spielbudenplatz. **Fire** and **Ambulance**, ☎112.

Rape Crisis Line: ☎25 55 66. Open M and Th 10am-1pm and 3-7pm, Tu 9:30am-1pm and 3-4pm, W 3-4pm, F 10am-1pm. English speaking staff members available.

Pharmacy: Exit the Hauptbahnhof on Kirchenallee and turn right. The staff of the **Senator-Apotheke** speaks English. Open M-F 7am-8pm, Sa 8am-6pm.

Post Office: Branch at the Kirchenallee exit of the Hauptbahnhof, 20097 Hamburg. Open M-F 8am-8pm, Sa 9am-6pm, Su 10am-4pm. **Poste Restante**, 20099 Hamburg, in the main branch on Grosser Burstah 3. Open M-F 8am-6pm, Sa 8am-noon.

Internet Access: **Cyberb@r** is located on the 3rd floor of the gigantic **Karstadt** department store on Mönckebergstr. DM5 per 30min.

▐ ACCOMMODATIONS

Hamburg's single rooms, from DM60, reflect the price of the city's accommodations. Many establishments are tawdry with few comforts. A slew of small, relatively cheap *Pensionen* line **Steindamm, Steintorweg, Bremer Weg**, and **Bremer Reihe**, around the Hauptbahnhof. While the area is filled with drug addicts and wannabe-*mafiosi*, the hotels are for the most part safe. The tourist office's free *Hotelführer* aids in navigating past the filth. For stays longer than four weeks, try the **Mitwohnzentrale, Homecompany**, at Schulterblatt 112. (☎194 45; www.homecompany.de; Open M-F 9am-1pm and 2-6pm, Sa 9am-1pm.) Take S-Bahn #21 or 31 or U-Bahn #3 to "Sternschanze." A passport is required, as well as a deposit of the 1st, 2nd, or 3rd month's rent.

HOSTELS AND CAMPING

Jugendherberge auf dem Stintfang (HI), Alfred-Wegener-Weg 5 (☎31 34 88; fax 31 54 07; email jh-stintfang@t-online.de; www.schoelzel.com/jh-hamburg/index.shtml). S-Bahn #1, 2, or 3, or U-Bahn #3 to "Landungsbrücke." A great location near the Reeperbahn and the subway and a beautiful view of the harbor compensate for the regimental house rules. Very clean rooms, showers, and kitchen. All halls same-sex. The hostel also features an email, internet, fax, phone, and word-processing facility. Sheets and breakfast included. Lunch and dinner DM8.50. Reception 12:30pm-1am. Lockout 9:30-11:30am. Curfew 1am. Call ahead. Private rooms available for couples and families. DM29.50, over 26 DM34.50. Non-members pay a DM6 surcharge.

Jugendgästehaus und Gästehaus Horner-Rennbahn (HI), Rennbahnstr. 100 (☎651 16 71; fax 655 65 16; email jgh-hamburg@t-online.de), U-Bahn #3 to "Horner-Rennbahn" or bus #160 from Berliner Tor. From the main exit of the station, turn right—the hostel is about 10min. by foot at the corner of Tribünenweg. Inconveniently far from the center, located next to a horse-racing track, but extremely clean and secure. Members only. Family rooms available. Reception 7-9:30am and noon-1am. Curfew 1am, stragglers admitted at 2am. DM38, over 26 DM38; slightly less for longer stays.

▧ **Schanzenstern Übernachtungs-und Gasthaus**, Bartelsstr. 12 (☎439 84 41; fax 439 34 13; email info@schanzerstern.de; www.schanzerstern.de). S-Bahn #21 and #3 or U-Bahn #3 to "Sternschanze." Left onto Schanzenstr., right on Susannenstr., and left to Bartelsstr. Located in the middle of an electrifying neighborhood of students, working-class Turks, and left-wing dissenters, the Schanzenstern is managed by a politically and ecologically progressive cooperative. Situated on the upper floors of a renovated fountain pen factory, the hotel's 50 rooms are clean, quiet, bright, and tastefully decorated with Swedish wood furniture, plants, and cheerfully painted walls. Breakfast buffet DM11. Reception 6:30-2am, no curfew. Wheelchair accessible. Reservations are a must in the summer and at New Year's. Dorm beds DM33; singles DM60; doubles DM90; triples DM115; quads DM140; quints DM140.

■ **Instant Sleep,** Max-Brauer-Allee 277 (☎43 18 23 10; fax 43 18 23 11; email backpack-erhostel@instantsleep.de; www.instantsleep.de). S-Bahn #3, 21, or 31 or U-Bahn #3 to "Sternschanze." From the station go straight on Schanzenstr., turn left on Altonaer Str., and follow it until it becomes Max-Brauer-Allee. This spic-and-span hostel overlooks the progressive Sternschanze neighborhood. Guests lounge and make evening plans in the lobby. Each room is painted with a different brightly-colored design. Sheets DM5. Internet access available (15min. DM2.50), as well as a communal kitchen and laundry room. Reception 9am-2pm. No curfew. Call ahead. Prices per person: dorm beds DM27; singles DM49; doubles DM40; triples DM35.

Camping: Campingplatz Rosemarie Buchholz, Kieler Str. 374 (☎540 45 32). From Altona train station, take bus #182 or #183 to "Basselweg" (10 min.), then walk 100m in the same direction as traffic. Leafy setting near a very busy road. Showers DM1.50. Reception 8am-noon and 2-10pm. Quiet hours 10pm-7am. Check-out noon. Call ahead. DM7 per person, tents DM12.50 per night.

HOTELS

Hotel Alt-Nürnberg, Steintorweg 15 (☎24 60 24; fax 280 46 34). From the station, go right on Kirchenallee and left onto Steintorweg. Heidi-themed decor in the heart of Hamburg's somewhat sketchy Hauptbahnhof neighborhood. Very convenient to trains. Each clean, safe, and smallish room features a telephone, some with TV. Call ahead. Singles DM60, with shower DM90; doubles DM90, with shower DM130.

Hotel Florida, Spielbudenpl. 22 (☎31 43 94). U-Bahn #3 to "St.Pauli," or S-Bahn #1 or 3 to "Reeperbahn." Located in the heart of Hamburg's thriving nightlife and sex industry, Hotel Florida offers small but clean rooms adjacent to Hamburg's biggest clubs. Breakfast included. Singles DM60; doubles DM95; triples DM135.

Hotel Terminus Garni, Steindamm 5 (☎280 31 44; fax 24 15 18). From the Hauptbahnhof's Kirchenallee exit, turn right. Breakfast included. 24hr. reception. Doubles DM90, with shower DM120; triples with bath DM165.

Hotel Annerhof, Lange Reihe 23 (☎24 34 26; fax 24 55 69). From the train station's Kirchenallee exit take the 2nd left. Hall showers. Breakfast DM8. Call ahead. Singles DM50, doubles DM82.

◘ FOOD

The most interesting part of town from a culinary standpoint is **Sternschanze,** where Turkish fruit stands, Asian *Imbiße*, and avant-garde cafes entice the hungry passersby with good food and, equally important, atmosphere. **Schulterblatt, Susannenstr.** and **Schanzenstr.** host a slew of funky cafes and restaurants. Slightly cheaper establishments abound in the **university** area, especially along **Rentzelstr., Grindelhof,** and **Grindelallee.** In **Altona,** the pedestrian zone leading up to the train station is packed with ethnic food stands and produ e shops. Check out the market inside Altona's massive **Mercado** mall, which includes everything from sushi bars to Portuguese fast-food. There's even a **Safeway** (open M-F 10am-8pm, Sa 9am-4pm). In a pinch, the shopping arcade at the **Hauptbahnhof** has about a dozen fast food joints (open daily 6am-11pm).

STERNSCHANZE

Take S-Bahn #21 or 31 or U-Bahn #3 to "Sternschanze."

■ **Noodles,** Schanzenstr. 2-4 (☎439 28 40). Along with innovative pasta creations, Noodles serves up veggie entrees alongside a full bar. Trippy ambient music provides an appropriate acoustic background for the alternative community of Sternschanze. Try the broccoli with cheese and ham (DM12) or one of their generous salads. Breakfast from DM7.50. Beer DM5. Open M-Th and Su 10am-1am, F-Sa 10am-3am.

HAMBURG

Machwitz, Schanzenstr. 121 (☎ 43 81 77). Join the hip student crowd in the funky angular interior or people-watch outside. The CD collection is even better stocked than the bar. Creamy soups DM6, entrees DM12-17. Occasional concerts from local bands. Open Su-Th 10am-4am, F-Sa 10am-8am. Kitchen closes at midnight during the week and 2am on the weekends.

Asia Imbiß Bok, Bartelstr. 29. *Imbiß* is a misnomer here—this joint serves real restaurant food. Try the spicy Thai noodles or some of the other savory Korean and Chinese options (DM10-17). Open daily 11:30am-11:30pm.

Falafel-König, Schanzenstr. 113. An excellent option for vegetarians, this tiny Lebanese *Imbiß* is indeed the seat of the "Falafel-King." Basic falafel DM5, with one of half a dozen toppings DM6. Open M-Th and Su 11:30am-midnight, F-Sa 11:30am-3am.

UNIVERSITY

Mensa, Schlüterstr. 7. S-Bahn #21 or 31 to "Dammtor," then head left on Rothenbaumchaussee, left on Moorweidenstr., then right onto Schlüterstr. Check bulletin boards for special events. Meals DM2-7 with student ID, more for non-students. Open daily 10am-7:30pm; serves warm meals M-F 11:15am-6:30pm.

Geo Pizza aus dem Holzbackofen, Beim Schlump 27 (☎ 45 79 29). U-Bahn #2 or 3 to "Schlump." Delectable pizzas (DM9-16) and a large vegetarian selection. The Inferno Pizza (DM11.80-13.80), topped with an incendiary blend of jalapeños, red peppers, beef, onions, salsa, and corn, transforms humans into fire-belching beasts. Open M-F 5pm-1am, Sa-Su11am-1am.

ALTONA

Duschbar, on A.-Wartenburg-Pl. Attracts a lively 20-something crowd with its ultra-modern decor and drink menu. Happy "hour" 6-9pm. Open daily 11am-late.

Indian Tandoori, Ottenser Hauptstr. 20, in the pedestrian zone near Altona train station. Whether you eat inside or outdoors in the *Fußgängerzone*, Indian Tandoori's food is sure to jump-start your Teutonically-impaired taste buds. If you're in a hurry, grab an order of samosas (DM6); otherwise, feast on their namesake tandoori chicken (DM12) or chicken tikka masala (DM10). There are also a number of vegetarian options; try the palak paneer (DM13.50). Open daily noon-11pm.

ELSEWHERE IN HAMBURG

Frauenbuchladen und Café, Bismarckstr. 98 (☎ 420 47 48). U-Bahn #3 to "Hoheluftbrücke." A primarily lesbian, women-only establishment. Pick up the *Hamburger Frauenzeitung* (DM6) if you read German. Open M-F 10am-7pm, Sa 10am-3pm.

◨ SIGHTS

ALTSTADT

GROßE MICHAELSKIRCHE. The gargantuan 18th-century Michaelskirche is the grand-daddy of all Hamburg churches. It is affectionately and somewhat fearfully referred to as *"der Michael."* While the exterior is a bit imposing—the statue of St. Michael above the doorway mischievously grins at the passing tourists—the interior's scalloped walls are reminiscent of a concert hall. *Der Michael's* bulbous Baroque tower is the official emblem of Hamburg; it's also the only one of the city's six spires that can be ascended, by foot or by elevator. On weekends, the tower is used to project a multimedia presentation about Hamburg's millennial existence onto a five-meter-high screen. (☎ 37 67 81 00. Open Apr.-Sept. M-Sa 9am-6pm, Su 11:30am-5:30pm; Oct.-Mar. M-Sa 10am-4:30pm, Su 11:30am-4:30pm. DM1. Screenings Th-Su hourly 12:30-3:30pm. DM5, students, children, and Hamburg Card holders DM2.50. Organ music Apr.-Aug. daily at noon and 5pm. Tower DM5, students and children DM2.50. Crypt DM2.50 for the living.)

RATHAUS. The copper spires of the town hall, a richly-ornamented, neo-Renaissance monstrosity that serves as the political center of Hamburg, rise above the city center. The Rathausmarkt in front of it is the place for constant festivities, ranging from political demonstrations to medieval fairs. *(☎428 31 20 64. Tours of the Rathaus in German every 30min. M-Th 10am-3pm, F-Su 10am-1pm. Tours in English and French every hour M-Th 10:15am-3:15pm, F-Su 10:15am-1:15pm. Free.)*

NIKOLAIKIRCHE. In the city center rest the somber ruins of the old Nikolaikirche, a reminder of Hamburg's time as an Allied bombing target. A 1943 air raid flattened this example of early neo-Gothic architecture. City officials have left the ruins unrestored as a memorial to the horrors of war. In front of its bombed-out hull lies the **Hopfenmarkt,** home to a motley melange of *Imbiße*, book, and clothing stands. Behind the church ruins is a zig-zagging maze of canals and bridges centered on the **Alte Börse** (old stock market). The buildings along nearby **Trostbrücke** sport huge copper models of clipper ships on their spires—a reminder of sea-trade's role in Hamburg's wealth. *(Just south of the Rathaus, off Ost-West-Str.)*

SPEICHERSTADT. East of the docks near the copper dome of the **St. Katherinenkirche** *(open daily 9am-5pm; free organ concerts W at 12:30pm)* lies the historic warehouse district of Speicherstadt. These elegant, late 19th-century brick storehouses are filled with cargo, spices, and swarms of stevedores.

KONTORHAUSVIERTEL. At the corner of Burchardstr. and Pumpen, the **Chilehaus** showcases architecture of a different generation. Designed to look like the sails of a ship when viewed from the plaza to the east, this 1922 *trompe l'oeil* office building is the work of Expressionist architect Fritz Höger, who also designed the **Sprinkenhof** building across the street. The Great Fire of 1842 unfortunately consumed many of the quarter's 17th- to 19th-century office buildings, some of which are carefully restored. On summer afternoons, locals gather in the sidewalk cafes.

MÖNKEBERGSTRASSE. The pedestrian shopping zone, which stretches from the Rathaus to the Hauptbahnhof along Mönckebergstr., is punctuated by two spires. The first belongs to the **St. Petrikirche,** site of the oldest church in Hamburg. *(Free concerts W 5:15pm. Open M-Tu and F 10am-6:30pm, W-Th 10am-7pm, Sa 10am-5pm, Su 9am-6pm.)* The second church in the area is the **St. Jakobikirche,** known for its 14th-century Arp-Schnittger organ. *(☎32 77 49. Open F-Sa 10am-5pm.)*

ELSEWHERE IN CENTRAL HAMBURG

ST. PAULI LANDUNGSBRÜCKEN. Hamburg's harbor, the largest port in Germany, lights up at night with ships from all over the world. More than 100,000 dockers and sailors work the ports, and their presence permeates Hamburg. Numerous companies offer harbor cruises: **Kapitän Prüsse** departs every 30 min. from Pier 3. *(☎31 31 30. DM15, children DM7.50.)* **HADAG** offers more elaborate cruises of outlying areas from Pier 2. *(☎311 70 70. Every 30min. 9:30am-6pm. DM15, children DM7.50.)* After sailing the East Indies, the 19th-century **Windjammer Rickmer Rickmers** was docked at Pier 1 and restored as a museum ship. Old navigation equipment, all brass and polish, is juxtaposed with modern nautical technology. *(☎35 69 31 19. Open daily 10am-6pm. DM6, students DM5, children under 12 DM4.)* The elevator to the **old Elbe tunnel,** built in 1907 and running 1200meters under the Elbe, protrudes through the floor of the building behind Pier 6. With all of its machinery exposed, the building looks like a nautilus machine built for the gods.

PLANTEN UN BLOMEN. To the west of the Alster near the university area, the park features dozens of obsessively planned and trimmed flower beds surrounding two lakes and a handful of outdoor cafes *(open 7am-11pm)*. From May to September, daily performances ranging from Irish step-dancing to Hamburg's police orchestra shake the outdoor **Musikpavillon;** there are also nightly **Wasserlichtkonzerte,** lighted fountain arrangements put to music. *(May-Aug. 10pm, Sept. 9pm.)*

ALSTER LAKES. To the north of the city center, the two Alster lakes, bordered by tree-lined paths and parks, provide refuge from crowded Hamburg. Elegant promenades and commercial facades surround **Binnenalster,** while windsurfers, sailboats, and paddleboats dominate the larger **Außenalster.** Ferries, more personal than the bigger Hamburg boats, depart here (see **Tours,** p. 535).

FISHMARKT. Veritable anarchy reigns as charismatic vendors haul in and hawk huge amounts of fish, produce, and other goods. The market fascinates in the morning, as early risers mix with flashy revelers trying to rally and keep the night going. Listen for cries of *"Ohne Geld!"* ("No Money!") and keep your head up—to grab attention, the fruit vendors toss free pineapples into the crowd. *(U- or S-Bahn to "Landungsbrücken" or S-Bahn to "Königstr." Open Su 6-10am, off-season 7-10am.)*

BEYOND THE CENTER

GEDENKSTÄTTE JANUSZ-KORCZAK-SCHULE. In the midst of warehouses, the school serves as a memorial to 20 Jewish children brought here from Auschwitz for "testing" and murdered by the S.S. only hours before Allied troops arrived. Visitors are invited to plant a rose for the children in the flower garden behind the school, where plaques with the children's photographs line the fence. *(Bullenhuser Damm 92. S-Bahn #21 to "Rothenburgsort." Follow the signs to Bullenhuser Damm along Ausschlaeger Bildeich and across a bridge; the school is 200m down. ☎ 428 96 03. Open Su 10am-7pm and Th 2-8pm. Free.)*

ERNST-THÄLMANN-GEDENKSTÄTTE. In 1923, Communist leader Ernst Thälmann led a march on the police headquarters, setting off a riot that resulted in the death of 61 protestors and 17 police officers. Thälmann was later murdered by the Nazis at Buchenwald and subsequently became the first martyr of the GDR. His life and times are chronicled in this small museum. *(Ernst-Thälmann-Platz. ☎ 47 41 84. Open Tu-F 10am-5pm, Sa-Su 10am-1pm. Donation requested.)*

ALTONAER BALKON. Ships from the four corners of the world pass under the Altonaer Balkon. The top of the bluffs upstream from Hamburg's harbor have been converted into a popular flower-covered park and scenic overlook. To the south, along the Elbe, are the fields of cranes unloading cargo and to the east is the Hamburg skyline. A perfect place to let Altona's ethnic food settle in the stomach. *(S-Bahn #3, 31, or 1 to "Altona". Walk south along Max-Brauer-Allee until you hit the overlook.)*

KZ NEUENGAMME. An idyllic agricultural village east of Hamburg provided the backdrop for the Neuengamme concentration camp. Here the Nazis killed 55,000 prisoners through slave ¹abor. In 1948, Hamburg prison authorities took over the camp and demolished all of the buildings to construct a German prison on the site; the mayor at that time believed that the facility would cleanse Neuengamme's sullied reputation. In 1989, the Hamburg senate moved the prison in order to build a more appropriate memorial on the site. Banners inscribed with the names and death-dates of the victims, along with four 500-page books listing their names, hang in the **Haus des Gedenkens.** *(Jean-Doldier-Weg. Take S-Bahn #21 to "Bergedorf," then bus #227, which runs hourly on the :40. About 1hr. from Hamburg to "Jean-Doldier-Weg." ☎ 723 10 31. Open May-Oct. Tu-Su 10am-6pm, Sept.-Apr. 10am-5pm.)*

🏛 MUSEUMS

Hamburg's many museums are filled with everything from African war masks to 18th-century pornography. The one- or three-day **Hamburg Card** (see p. 535) provides access to most of these museums, with the exception of the Deichtorhallen and the Erotic Art Museum. Hamburg also has a thriving and exciting contemporary art scene; pick up a list of the city's galleries and their current exhibits at either tourist office. At noon on Wednesdays, most museums offer a short presentation or lecture on topics ranging from Cézanne to Korean shamanism; the free newspaper *Die Museen* lists topics and current exhibits.

HERZLICHEN GLÜCKWUNSCH! Need a place to celebrate your birthday while on vacation? For DM75-100, the **Museum für Kunst und Gewerbe** will lead you and your friends around its hallowed halls on appropriately themed tours. Topics include *amor vincit omnia* (depictions of love) or the indubitably more popular *in vino veritas*, which traces the importance of wine and is, of course, followed by ample samplings of the "devil's elixir." *Prost!*

HAMBURGER KUNSTHALLE. This sprawling first-rate art museum is three-pronged: the first part of the collection contains superb German and Dutch art from the medieval era through the 19th century. The next assortment contains works by 19th-century French painters such as Millet, Courbet, Manet, and Monet. The newly built **Galerie der Gegenwart** displays Warhols, Picassos, and a pair of Levi's nailed to the wall. (*Glockengießerwall 1. Turn left from the "City" exit of the Hauptbahnhof and cross the street. ☎ 428 54 26 12. Open Tu-W and F-Su 10am-6pm, Th 10am-9pm. DM15, students DM10, family pass DM21.*)

DEICHTORHALLEN HAMBURG. Hamburg's contemporary art scene resides here in two buildings that were former fruit market halls. New exhibits each season showcase up-and-coming artists. Outstanding, but expensive. (*Deichtorstr. 1-2. U-Bahn #1 to "Steinstr." Follow signs from the subway station; look for two entwined iron circles. ☎ 32 10 30. Open Tu-Su 11am-6pm, Sa-Su 10am-6pm. Each building DM10, students DM8.*)

MUSEUM FÜR KUNST UND GEWERBE. A rich collection of handicrafts, china, and furnishings ranging from ancient Egyptian and Roman to Asian and *Jugendstil*. Sure to inspire you to new heights of interior decoration. The museum also has an extensive photography collection. Check for special exhibitions. (*Steintorpl. 1. One block south of the Hauptbahnhof. ☎ 428 54 27 19. Open Tu-Su 10am-6pm. DM14, students and seniors DM7, under 15 DM5.*)

EROTIC ART MUSEUM. Follow the silver sperm painted on the floor as they lead you through four floors of tactful iniquity. The first two floors examine postcard-sized sketches of assorted aristocrats and their voluptuous maids, while the top two levels focus on the art of bondage. The Reeperbahn location is home to the permanent collection, while the building at Bernhard-Nocht-Str. entertains exhibits that are just passing through. The museum is in surprisingly good taste, as evidenced by the Haring originals on the fourth floor and the sonorous classical music. The Reeperbahn peep-show crowd tends to head elsewhere. (*Nobistor 12, and Bernhard-Nocht-Str. 69. S-Bahn #1 or 3 to "Reeperbahn." ☎ 31 78 41 26. Open Tu-Su 10am-midnight. DM15, groups DM10.*)

HAMBURGISCHES MUSEUM FÜR VÖLKERKUNDE. With two floors of glass cases brimming with weapons, clothing, and cooking utensils, the exhibits are treasure troves of imperial plunder from Indonesia to the Caribbean, and everywhere in between. (*Rothenbaumchaussee 64. U-Bahn #1 to "Hallerstr." ☎ 428 48 25 24. Open Tu-W and F-Su 10am-6pm, Th 10am-9pm. DM7, Hamburg card DM4, students and seniors DM3.50, under 16 DM2. Half-price F.*)

⬛ ENTERTAINMENT

As the cultural capital of the North, Hamburg patronizes the arts with money and attention. Federal and municipal subsidies of high culture lower ticket prices significantly, and most box offices offer generous student discounts.

MUSIC

The **Staatsoper,** Dammtorstr. 28, houses one of the best opera companies in Germany, tending toward the modern, but also playing a steady stream of Bizet and Puccini. The associated **ballet company** is the acknowledged dance powerhouse of the nation. Tickets start at DM7. (☎ 35 17 21. Take U-Bahn #1 to "Stephansplatz."

HAMBURG

Open M-F 10am-6:30pm, Sa 10am-2pm.) **Orchestras** abound—the Philharmonie, the Norddeutscher Rundfunk Symphony, and Hamburg Symphonia, the big three, all perform at the **Musikhalle** on Johannes-Brahms-Platz. (☎34 69 20. Take U-Bahn #2 to "Gänsemarkt" or "Messehallen.") The Musikhalle also hosts **chamber music** concerts on a regular basis, as well as the odd jazz performance. Call ☎41 80 68 for tickets. Hamburg's many churches (see **Sights,** above) offer a wide variety of classical concerts that are usually free.

Live music prospers in Hamburg, satisfying all tastes. Superb traditional jazz swings at the **Cotton Club** and **Indra** (see **Nightlife,** below). On Sunday mornings, good and bad alike play at the **Fischmarkt** (see **p. 540**). Rock groups jam at **Große Freiheit,** Große Freiheit 36 (☎31 42 63), and at **Docks,** Spielbudenpl. 19 (☎31 78 83 11). The renowned **Fabrik,** Barnerstr. 36 (☎39 10 70), in Altona, features everything from funk to punk. Cover runs about DM12. For more information, the magazine *Szene* (DM5) has an exhaustive listing of events. The **West Port** jazz festival, Germany's largest, runs in mid-July. Call ☎44 64 21 for tickets. The most anticipated festival, however, is the "Love Parade of the North." The **G-Move** grooves into town early in June, but unlike its techno brother in Berlin, it only draws crowds in the high thousands. Check www.g-move.com for the dates and performers.

The **Hafengeburtstag,** or "harbor birthday," is the city's biggest bash. Hamburg owes its prosperity to May 7, 1189, when Friedrich Barbarossa granted the town the right to open a port. The city still celebrates the anniversary for a weekend in early May, featuring music and other events. During April, August, and November, the **Heiligengeistfeld** north of the Reeperbahn metamorphoses into the **"Dom,"** a titanic amusement park with fun-booths, kiosks, and merry-go-rounds. The festival's beer and wild parties have eclipsed its historical connection to the church.

THEATER AND FILM

Most theaters sell half-price tickets to students at the regular box office as well as at the evening box office, which generally opens one hour before performances. In July and August, many theaters close down, but only to make way for the **Hamburger Sommer** arts festival; pick up a schedule at any kiosk.

The **Deutsches Schauspielhaus,** Kirchenallee 39, is located across from the Hauptbahnhof. The theater presents a full venue: Ibsen, Brecht, Fassbinder, and *Rent*. (☎24 87 13. Box office open 10am-showtime. Student tickets as low as DM10.) The **English Theater,** Lerchenfeld 14, entertains both natives and tourists with its English-language productions. (☎227 70 89. U-Bahn #2 to "Mundsgurg." Performances M-Sa at 7:30pm; matinees Tu and F at 11am.) **Thalia,** Alstertor 1, sets up adventurous avant-garde musicals, plays, and staged readings. (☎32 26 66. S-Bahn #1 or 3 or U-Bahn #1 or 2 to "Jungfernstieg.") Regular performances are also held in the **Hamburger Kunsthalle** (see **Museums,** p. 541).

The German **cabaret** tradition is still alive and kicking at a number of venues, including **Das Schiff,** on Holzbrückestr. (☎36 47 65. U-Bahn #3 to "Rödingsmarkt") and the drag theater **Pulverfass,** Pulverteich 12, off of Steindamm, near the Hauptbahnhof. (☎24 97 91. Shows daily at 8:30 and 11:30pm, Friday and Saturday also at 2:30am. DM20 minimum.)

The movie scene in Hamburg is dauntingly diverse, ranging from the latest American blockbusters to independent film projects by university students. The **Kommunales Kino Metropolis,** Dammtorstr. 30a (☎34 23 53), a non-profit cinema, features new independent films and revivals from all corners of the globe, focusing on pieces from the US, France, Germany, and Italy. **Kino 3001,** Schanzenstr. 75 (☎43 76 79), shows artsy alternative flicks. The **City** theater, a block east of the Hauptbahnhof at Steindamm 9 (☎24 44 63), screens American blockbusters in their original English F-M.

☑ NIGHTLIFE

The Sternschanze and St. Pauli areas monopolize Hamburg's crazy nightlife scene. The infamous **Reeperbahn,** a long boulevard which makes Las Vegas look like church on a Sunday, is the spinal cord of St. Pauli; sex shops, strip joints, peep shows, and other establishments seeking to satisfy every libidinal desire compete for space along the sidewalks. Crowds meander up and down the Reeperbahn like ants, occasionally crossing the street to peek into a shop window or dodge one of the many greaseballs who beckon passersby to enter the "erotic" interiors of their strip clubs. Though the Reeperbahn is reasonably safe for both men and women, it is not recommended for women to venture to the adjacent streets. Herbertstr., Hamburg's only remaining legalized prostitution strip, runs parallel to the Reeperbahn, and is open only to men over 18. The prostitutes flaunting their flesh on Herbertstr. are licensed professionals required to undergo health inspections, while the streetwalkers are venereal roulette wheels. Men (mostly) and women flock to this district to revel all night long in an atmosphere simmering with sultry energy. The sleaze peddlers have failed to stifle the vital spark of the many clubs that cater to those not seeking sex for sale. Backgrounded by sex shops and prostitutes, many of Hamburg's best bars and clubs fill with a young crowd that leaves the smut outside.

Students trying to avoid the hypersexed Reeperbahn head north to the spiffy streets of **Sternschanze.** Unlike St. Pauli, these areas are centered around cafes and weekend extravaganzas of an alternative flavor. Filled with spectacular graffiti that crosses the boundary into "public art" and posters that could easily be the products of high-end design schools, the neighborhood hums with creative energy and creatively-dressed people. Much of Hamburg's **gay scene** is located in the **St. Georg** area of the city, near Berliner Tor. Gay and straight bars in this area are more welcoming and classier than those in the Reeperbahn. In general, clubs open late and close late, with some techno and trance clubs remaining open until noon the following day. *Szene*, available at newsstands (DM5), lists events and parties, while *Hinnerk* lists gay and lesbian events.

STERNSCHANZE

▨ **Rote Flora,** Schulterblatt 71 (☎ 439 54 13). Held together both figuratively and literally by the spray paint and posters that cover all its vertical surfaces, this graffiti-covered mansion serves as the nucleus of the Sternschanze scene. The Flora lights up on weekends, with huge dub and drum 'n' bass parties inside the spooky and decrepit ruin. A little more mellow during the week, this squatter's community center and cafe does it all, from vegan cooking parties to screening of political films to motorbike repair. Cafe open M-F 6-10pm. Opening times vary. Weekend cover DM8 or more.

Logo, Grindelallee 5 (☎ 410 56 58). If you can play it live (and loud), you can play it at Logo. Nightly live music at this friendly club near the university gives locals a chance to be rock stars. Open nightly from 9:30pm. Cover varies.

Frauenkneipe, Stresemannstr. 60 (☎ 43 63 77), S-Bahn #21 or 3 to "Holstenstr." A bar and meeting place for women. Visitors who are disconcerted by the Reeperbahn and drunken-sailor scene will find another option here. For women only, gay or straight. Open M-F from 8pm, Sa from 9pm, Su from 6pm.

ST. PAULI

▨ **Mojo Club,** Reeperbahn 1 (☎ 43 52 32), has more attitude than it knows what to do with and a dance floor filled with all kinds of smoke. The attached **Jazz Café** attracts the trendy and features acid jazz. Usually open 11pm-4am. DM12 cover on weekends.

La Cage, Reeperbahn 136. If you're rich and pretty, make an appearance at the prettiest club in Hamburg, where glitz drips from cascades of hanging beads and two big silver cages dominate the dance floor. The club sends out special invitations to modeling agencies in order to fill the floor with faces whose perfection adds to the decor. Open F-Sa after 11pm. Cover DM15-25.

Absolute, Hans-Albers-Pl. 15 (☎317 34 00), hosts the gay scene Sa nights as it spins intense house to a younger crowd that grooves (and cruises) until well after the sun is up. Open after 11pm. Cover DM10.

Cave, Reeperbahn 48. Hamburg's house for "house". Descend into the smoky neon Cave, where nothing but wild, raving techno at 100bpm spins with enough bass to turn your eardrums inside out. The pounding might not always be the music: Thursdays, women can drink DM50 worth for free, and every drink is DM1 on Sunday. More than a great club, Cave is also one of Hamburg's best accommodation deals. In exchange for a DM15 cover charge, you can stay from opening time at 1am until the close at noon without having to worry about any curfew. Breakfast not included.

Indra, Große Freiheit 64 (☎31 79 63 08), is a haven of calm live jazz just off the adren-aline-powered Reeperbahn. Cool cats talk quietly in low light over a million cigarettes. Open W-Su from 9pm; music starts around 11pm. Cover DM5-10.

Molotow, Spielbudenpl. 5 (☎31 08 45), parallel to the Reeperbahn. This basement lives at the fringes of Hamburg's club scene. The DJ spins an eclectic mix of indepen-dent rock and underground soul. Open Th-Sa from 10pm onwards. Cover DM10.

Große Freiheit 36/Kaiser Keller, Große Freiheit 36 (☎31 77 780). The Beatles played on the small stage downstairs during their early years. Today, everyone from Ziggy Mar-ley to Matchbox Twenty stomps about on the big stage upstairs. The basement dance floor opens at 10pm; students admitted to the downstairs only for free on Tuesdays. Call for show times and ticket prices (DM5-30) for the upstairs stage. Open daily.

Cotton Club, Alter Steinweg 10 (☎34 38 78; fax 348 01 23); U-Bahn #3 to "Rödings-markt." Gives a different jazz, swing, or skittle band a chance every night. Smoky atmo-sphere, mostly older crowd, great jazz. Open M-Sa 8pm-midnight. Shows start at 8:30pm. Cover around DM12.

SCHLESWIG-HOLSTEIN

The only *Land* to border two seas, Schleswig-Holstein's past and present livelihood is based on the trade generated at its port towns. In between the coasts, verdant plains, populated mainly by sheep and plump bales of hay, produce much of northern Germany's agricultural goods. Although Schleswig-Holstein became a Prussian province in 1867 following Bismarck's defeat of Denmark, the region retains close cultural and commercial ties with Scandinavia. Linguistically, Schleswig-Holstein is also isolated from its southern neighbors by its various dialects of *Plattdeutsch* and, to a lesser extent, the Frisian spoken within its borders. The most noticeable difference is the local greeting *Moin*, a *Plattdeutsch* salutation used throughout the day.

LÜBECK   ☎ 0451

Lübeck wears its skyline of neo-classical townhouses and copper 13th-century spires so well, you would never guess that the greater part of the city was razed in WWII. The town's present appearance is thanks to a painstaking reconstruction undertaken in the 1950s. In its heyday, Lübeck was the capital of the Hanseatic League, carrying a big stick on account of its control of trade across Northern Europe. Though no longer a center of political and commercial influence, Lübeck was home to literary giants Heinrich and Thomas Mann and retains the pulse and energy of a bustling city, beyond the glitz of marzipan and the sheen of tour buses.

█ GETTING THERE AND GETTING AROUND

Trains: Frequent departures for **Hamburg** (45min., 2 per hr., DM17); **Kiel** (1¼hr., 1 per hr., DM24); **Schwerin** (1¼hr., 1 per hr., DM21); **Rostock** (1¾hr., 1 per hr., DM37); and **Berlin** (3¼hr., 1 per hr., DM97).

Public Transportation: Although the Altstadt is easily seen on foot, Lübeck has an excellent bus network. The **ZOB** (central bus station) is across from the train station. Single ride DM3.50, children DM1.90. **Mehrfahrtkarten** (books of 6 tickets) DM17. The best value is the **Lübeck Card**—it's valid on all local buses, including those going to Travemünde, allows the bearer to take 2 children along for free on weekends and holidays, and offers significant discounts at most museums (1 day DM10). Direct questions to **Service Center am ZOB**, ☎ 888 28 28. Open M-F 6am-8pm, Sa 9am-1pm.

Ferries: Quandt-Linie, An der Obertrave (☎ 777 99), has cruises around the Altstadt and harbor every 30min. 10am to 6pm daily from the bridge in front of the *Holstentor*. DM12, students DM9.

Car Rental: Hertz, Willy-Brandt-Allee 1 (☎ 018 05 33 35 35), by the train station, next to the Mövenpick. Open M-F 7am-6pm, Sa 7am-1pm, Su 9-10am.

Bike Rental: Konrad Renta-Bike, in a white trailer on Adenauerstr. near the station; left from main entrance. DM1 per hr., DM8 per day. Open M-F 10am-7pm, Sa 10am-4pm, Su noon-4pm.

Mitfahrzentrale: Hinter der Burg 1a (☎ 707 14 70), arranges ride shares.

█ █ ORIENTATION AND PRACTICAL INFORMATION

Because *Wasser* surrounds Lübeck, the key to navigation is remembering that water seeks the lowest ground. Moving around the city can be a very Kafka-esque experience, particularly at night, when everything looks the same and you're never sure where you are or whether you've been there before. When confused, a good rule of thumb is to head uphill, towards **Königstr.** and **Breite Str.**, the two main streets which crest the ridge on which Lübeck stands.

Tourist Office: Avoid the tourist office in the train station (☎86 40 75; fax 86 30 24; open M-Sa 1pm-6pm); they charge DM4 for maps and rob you blind for **booking a room** (DM5 *plus* 10% of your hotel bill). Instead, head for the helpful office in the Altstadt at Breite Str. 62 (☎ 122 54 13 or 122 54 14; fax 122 54 19). They don't book rooms, but staff can point you in the right direction and give you a free map. Open M-F 9:30am-7pm, Sa-Su 10am-3pm.

Currency Exchange: In the station near the exit. Open M-Sa 9:30am-6:30pm, Su 9:30am-1pm.

Laundromat: McWash, (☎ 702 03 57) on the corner of An der Mauer and Hüxterdamm. Wash 7kg DM7 (includes soap). Dry 10kg DM1.20 per 15min. Open M-Sa 6am-10pm.

Emergency: Police, ☎ 110. **Fire,** ☎ 112. **Ambulance,** ☎ 192 22.

Rape Crisis Center: Marlegrube 9 (☎ 70 46 40). Open daily 5-7pm.

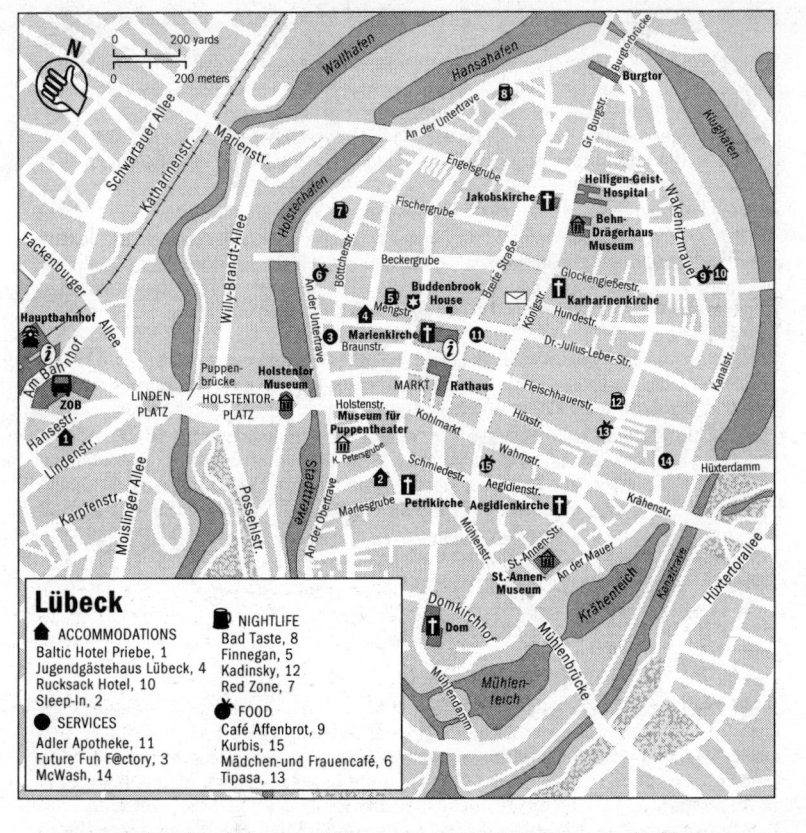

Lübeck

♠ ACCOMMODATIONS
Baltic Hotel Priebe, 1
Jugendgästehaus Lübeck, 4
Rucksack Hotel, 10
Sleep-In, 2

● SERVICES
Adler Apotheke, 11
Future Fun F@ctory, 3
McWash, 14

◗ NIGHTLIFE
Bad Taste, 8
Finnegan, 5
Kadinsky, 12
Red Zone, 7

◗ FOOD
Café Affenbrot, 9
Kurbis, 15
Mädchen-und Frauencafé, 6
Tipasa, 13

Women's Resources: Anarat, Steinrader Weg 1 (☎ 408 28 50). A center for women to share information about art, culture, etc. Open W 4-6pm, Th 5-7pm. **Mixed Pickles,** Kanalstr. 70 (☎ 702 16 40), is a center for girls and women, especially those who are disabled. Pick up a copy of *Zimtzicke,* a women's events calendar containing other important numbers and addresses, at the tourist office.

Pharmacies: Adler-Apotheke, Breite Str. 71 (☎ 798 85 15), across from the Marien-kirche. Open M-F 8am-7pm, Sa 8:30am-4pm.

Post Office: Königstr. 44-46, across the street from the Katharinenkirche. **24hr. ATM.** Open M-W and F 8am-6:30pm, Th 8am-7pm, Sa 8am-1pm. The **postal code** is 23552.

Internet Access: Cyberb@r, on the 4th floor of the **Karstadt** department store, across the street from the tourist office. **Future Fun F@actory,** An der Untertrave 103. DM3 per 15min., DM5 per 30min. (open M-Sa 11am-11pm).

SCHLESWIG-HOLSTEIN

⚑ ACCOMMODATIONS AND CAMPING

Jugendgästehaus Lübeck (HI), Mengstr. 33 (☎ 702 03 99; fax 770 12). From the station head for the Holstentor, cross the river, make a left on An der Untertrave and turn right on Mengstr. The hostel is in a historic building, conveniently close to Lübeck's sights. Breakfast and sheets included. Lockout midnight, but guests over 18 can get a key. Reception 7:30am-noon, 1:15-6pm, and 7:15pm-midnight. Members only. Call ahead. Triples and quads 1st night DM31, over 26 DM39.50; additional nights DM28.50, over 26 DM37. Doubles DM33, over 26 DM42.

■ **Rucksack Hotel,** Kanalstr. 70 (☎ 70 68 92 or 261 87 92; fax 707 34 26), on the north side of the Altstadt by the canal. From the station, walk past the Holstentor, left on An der Untertrave, right on Beckergrube, which becomes Pfaffstr. and then Glockengießer-str; the hostel is on the corner of Kanalstr. (20min.). Or take bus #1, 11, 13, 21, or 31 from the station to "Pfaffenstr.," and turn right at the church on Glockengießerstr. Bright, cheery rooms in a former-factory filled mostly with backpackers. Breakfast DM8, sheets DM6. Reception 9am-1pm and 4-10pm. Wheelchair accessible. Key to front door given. Self-serve kitchen. 6-bed dorms DM26; 10-bed dorms DM24. Double with bath DM80; quads DM112, with bath DM136.

Sleep-In (CVJM), Große Petersgrube 11 (☎ 719 20; fax 789 97), near the Petrikirche in the Altstadt, 10min. from the station. Walk past the Holstentor, turn right on An der Obertrave, left on Große Petersgrube, and look to the right for the sign. "Lively" does not quite capture the scene in the pub downstairs during the weekends. Raucous. These are good accommodations for travelers who prefer not to get up until late afternoon. Break-fast DM7. Sheets DM8. Reception M-F 8am-10pm, Sa-Su 8am-noon and 5-7:30pm. No locked rooms or lockers. Key with DM20 deposit. 4- to 8-bed dorms DM17, doubles DM20-40. Apartments DM30-40 per person.

Baltic Hotel, Hansestr. 11 (☎855 75; fax 838 31; www.baltic-hostel.de), across the street from the *ZOB*. Small but clean rooms 2min. from the station and 5min. from the Altstadt. Telephone and TV in every room. Filling breakfast buffet included. Reception 8am-10pm. Singles DM60-90; doubles DM110-130; triples from DM150.

Camping: Campingplatz Lübeck-Schönbocken, Steinraderdamm 12 (☎89 30 90 or 89 22 87), on a distant site northwest of the city. Showers, washing machines, and cook-ing facilities available. From the *ZOB,* bus #8 (direction: "Bauernweg") to the end, then walk 300m along Steinraderdamm toward the city. DM8 per person. Tent DM6.

⦿ FOOD

While the rest of Germany swims in beer, Lübeck drowns in coffee, with no point more than a saucer's throw away from a caffeine fix. Of course this is still Ger-many, so Lübeck's cafes function as the nightlife venue of choice by staying open until the wee hours to serve beer. Hipper, more popular cafes lie along **Mühlenstr.** in the eastern part of the city. A local specialty is *Lübecker Marzipan,* a delecta-ble candy made with sugar and almonds. The confectionery **I.G. Niederegger,** Breite Str. 89, across from the Rathaus, is the place to purchase marzipan pigs, jellyfish, and even the town gate. (☎530 11 26. Open M-F 9am-7pm, Sa 9am-6pm, Su 10am-4pm.) A **Co-op supermarket** is at the corner of Sandstr. and Schmiedstr (open M-F 8:30am-7pm, Sa 9am-4pm).

■ **Tipasa,** Schlumacherstr. 12-14 (☎706 04 51). The hip waitstaff leisurely weaves through the candle-lit interior, carrying pizza, pasta, and vegetarian dishes to hungry students. Even with all the coffee, diners lounge in their chairs listening to the constant flow of *U2* from the speakers. Try the *Tipasa-Topf,* a spicy stew of tomatoes, beef, mush-rooms, and peppers (DM12.50), or the pizza (DM7-11). *Biergarten* in back. Open M-Th and Su noon-1am, F-Sa noon-2am. Kitchen closes 30min. earlier.

Kurbis, Mühlenstr. 9 (☎70 70 126). A laid-back atmosphere permeates the outside tables, main floor, and inside balcony. Try one of the vast selection of *Pfanne,* a wide range of ingredients cooked in a pan with melted cheese on top (DM9-11), or the more conventional pasta, all while sitting under exposed oak rafters and above hardwood floors. Open Su-Th 11am-1am, F-Sa 11am-2am.

Café Affenbrot, Kanalstr. 70 (☎721 93), on the corner of Glockengießerstr. A vegetar-ian cafe. Dine on monkey-bread burgers (pineapples, berries, salad, and cheese on whole wheat DM8) at tables made from old-fashioned sewing machines. Meals DM8-11. Open daily 9am-midnight. Kitchen closes at 11:30pm.

Mädchen- und Frauencafé, An der Untertrave 97 (☎122 57 46), on the 2nd floor of the women's center. A friendly women-only cafe serving coffee, tea, and cake. Live music on F, 8pm-1am. Open Su 3-8pm. Breakfast W-Th 10am-1pm.

SIGHTS

To see Lübeck from above, hop on the double-decker **LVG Open-Air-Stadtrundfahrt.** The red bus stops at all municipal bus stops in town and runs frequently every day. Prices are the same as regular public transportation.

RATHAUS. On the eve of Palm Sunday, 1942, Allied bombers flattened most of Lübeck. After the war, the city used Marshall Plan funds to begin the daunting task of renovating the leveled Altstadt. At its center lies the Rathaus, comprising three very distinct parts. Begun with a striking 13th-century structure of glazed black and red bricks, new, major wings were added in the 14th and 15th centuries. *(Open M-F 9:30am-6pm, Sa-Su 10am-2pm. Tours M-F at 11am and noon. DM4, students DM2.)*

MARIENKIRCHE. The brick twin towers (standing at a precarious angle) of the Marienkirche dominate the Lübeck skyline. Begun in the Romanesque style around 1200 but finished as a Gothic cathedral in 1350. The picture-perfect interior was once graced by the equally beautiful music of Bach. The church's music comes from the **largest mechanical organ in the world.** The saints literally come marching in at noon on the church's newly restored **astronomical clock.** The famous medieval **Totentanzbild** used to encircle the chapel opposite the astronomical clock, but it was destroyed in 1942; all that remains is a reproduction, including the *Kaiser* holding hands with two wooden skeletons representing the plague. *(Open daily in summer 10am-6pm; in winter 10am-4pm. Tours W and Sa 3:15pm. Organ concerts daily at noon, Tu at 6:30pm, Th at 8pm, and Sa at 6:30pm. DM9, students DM6.)*

BUDDENBROOKHAUS. Literary giants **Heinrich** and **Thomas Mann** lived here as children. The house is now a museum dedicated to the life and works of both brothers. Thomas's works expressed his fierce opposition to Nazism and a profound ambivalence about German culture. While Thomas received the Nobel Prize for literature in 1929, his brother also wrote a number of important works, including *Professor Unrat,* on which the famous Marlene Dietrich film *Der Blaue Engel (The Blue Angel)* is based. The house holds special summer events, including a "literary walk" through Lübeck on weekends from June to September. *(Mengstr. 4. Opposite the Marienkirche. ☎ 122 41 92. Open daily 10am-5pm. DM8, students DM5. Walks DM12, students DM10.)*

MUSEUM BEHN- UND DRÄGERHAUS. Modern art clashes beautifully with the neo-classical architecture of an 18th-century townhouse. The first floor features works by contemporary Lübeck artists, while the second houses a small collection with paintings by Edvard Munch, Max Liebermann, and Max Beckmann. The artists' cooperative in the **sculpture garden** outside showcases local artists. *(Königstr. 11. ☎ 122 41 48. Open Tu-Su Apr.-Sept. 10am-5pm; Oct.-Mar. 10am-4pm. DM5, students DM3. Free first F of every month. Sculpture garden free.)*

KATHARINENKIRCHE. With a floor made completely of tombs, this unusually ornate church, formerly part of a 14th-century Franciscan monastery, hosts more dead people than living in its congregation on any given Sunday. *(Königstr. 7. ☎ 122 41 80. Open Tu-Su 10am-1pm and 2-5pm. Free.)*

JAKOBIKIRCHE. Traditionally a place of worship for seafarers, the whitewashed, high-ceilinged church contains a beautifully ornamented organ. *(North of the Rathaus on Breite Str., near Koberg. Open daily 10am-6pm. Organ concerts F 8pm. Free.)*

PETRIKIRCHE. An elevator climbs to the top of the 13th-century steeple for a sweeping view of the Altstadt and Lübeck's many spires. The nave exhibits local modern art. *(East of the Rathaus on Schmiederstr. Church open daily 11am-4pm. Tower open Apr.-Oct. 9am-7pm. Admission DM3.50, students DM2.)*

HEILIGEN-GEIST-HOSPITAL. The long barn with rows of tiny cabins inside was built as a hospital in 1820 and now attracts tourists who cannot believe that it also served as a home for aged people from 1851 to 1970. The **cloister** in front contains several medieval murals. *(Am Koberg 9. Open May-Sept. Tu-Su 10am-5pm; Oct.-Apr. Tu-Su 10am-4pm. Free.)*

HOLSTENTOR. Between the Altstadt and the station is the massive Holstentor, one of Lübeck's four 15th-century gates and the symbol of the city. Inside, the **Museum Holstentor** displays exhibits on ship construction, trade, and quaint local implements of torture. *(☎ 122 41 29. Open Apr.-Sept. Tu-Su 10am-5pm; Oct.-Mar. 10am-4pm. DM5, students DM3, under 19 DM1.)*

DOM. Founded by Henry the Lion in 1173, as evidenced by his trademark lion statue, the rather unremarkable cathedral features a late Gothic crucifix. *(Domkirchhof. At the southernmost end of the inner island. ☎ 747 04. Open Apr.-Sept. 10am-6pm; Mar. and Oct. 10am-5pm; Nov. 10am-4pm; Dec.-Feb. 10am-3pm. Free.)*

ST.-ANNEN-MUSEUM. Displays 16th century crosses, tablets, altars, and other paraphernalia of the opiate of the masses from Lübeck's own churches, as well as an exhibit upstairs recounting the city's cultural history. *(St.-Annen-Str. 15. Off Mühlenstr. ☎ 122 41 37. Open Apr.-Sept. Tu-Su 10am-5pm; Oct.-Mar. Tu-Su 10am-4pm. DM5, students DM3. Free first F of every month.)*

MUSEUM FÜR PUPPENTHEATER. The largest private puppet collection in the world. Thirteen rooms are filled with more than 700 laughing, dancing puppets made of wood, from all corners of the globe. Call for info on shows. *(Kolk 16. Just below the Petrikirche. ☎ 786 26. Open daily 10am-6pm. DM6, students DM5, children DM3.)*

🎵🎭 ENTERTAINMENT AND NIGHTLIFE

Lübeck is world-famous for its **organ concerts.** The **Jakobikirche** and **Dom** offer a joint program of concerts every Friday at 8pm (DM10, students DM6). The smaller **Propsteikirche Herz Jesu,** Parade 4, near the Dom, has free concerts Wednesdays at 8pm; call ☎ 328 58 for details. For entertainment listings, pick up *Piste, Szene, Zentrum,* or (for women) *Zimtzicke* from the tourist office. Lübeck's two major theaters offer generous student discounts. The huge **Theater Lübeck,** Beckergrube 10-14, puts on operas, symphonies, and mainstream German and American plays. (☎ 745 52 or 767 72. Box office open Tu-Sa 10am-1pm, Th-F 4-6:30pm, and 30min. before performance. Tickets DM25-50.) The smaller **Theater Combinale,** Hüxstr. 115, gets down with avant-garde works (☎ 788 17; tickets DM15-20).

Kandinsky, Fleischhauerstr. 89. More than 30 tables in the street, a mile-long drink list, and live jazz in the evenings. Open M-Tu and Su 1pm-1am, F-Sa 1pm-2am.

Finnegan, Mengstr. 42 (☎ 711 10). The Irish pub serves *Guinness* and other dark, yeasty beers (DM4-6) guaranteed to make you go *Bragh* the next morning. Very popular with locals. Open M-F 4pm-1am, Sa-Su 4pm until late.

Bad Taste, An der Untertrave 3a. Draws healthy crowds to watch local bands rock out under camouflage netting and disco balls. There's something enjoyably obnoxious every night, with weekends reserved for theme parties, from "Dark Wave" to reggae. Times and cover vary; check posters around town.

Red Zone, An der Untertrave 81-83. Red Zone successfully juggles the usually-opposing forces of hip-hop and techno/house; they're just not played on the same weekend night. Older crowd. One of the few discos in Lübeck. Times and cover vary.

NEAR LÜBECK: RATZEBURG ☎ 04541

The island town of Ratzeburg, founded in the 11th century by Henry the Lion, swims in the Ratzeburger See, 24km south of Lübeck. The natural beauty of the town's environs makes bikers and hikers rush to the lakeside, along with the German Olympic crew team, which trains daily on the huge *See.* Other than the scenery, Ratzeburg's main means of seduction is its art—two small but significant museums offer unique collections by 20th-century artists A. Paul Weber and Ernst Barlach, who lived in the town, as well as Günter Grass, who resided nearby.

Weber's astounding satirical lithographs and watercolors are on display, along with the artist's workshop and printing press, at the ■A.-Paul-Weber-Haus. *(Domhof 5. From the Markt, turn left (coming from Lüneburger Damm) onto Domhof, the second street exiting the square. ☎86 07 20. Open Tu-Su 10am-1pm and 2-5pm. DM3, students DM1.)* Ratzeburg's **Dom,** down the street from the Weberhaus, was built by Henry the Lion soon after he colonized Schleswig-Holstein and houses galleries of religious works *(open Apr.-Sept. daily 10am-noon and 2-6pm; Oct.-Mar. Tu-Su 10am-noon and 2-4pm).* Between the Weberhaus and the Dom lies the **Kreismuseum** in the **Herrenhaus,** the summer residence of Duke Adolf Friedrich IV. The museum is filled with a random mishmash of Biedermeier furniture, art by Weber, Grass, and Barlach, and the obligatory pointy Prussian helmet display. *(☎123 25. Open Tu-Su 10am-1pm and 2-5pm. DM2, students DM1.)* A larger collection of Barlach's work sits on the opposite side of Marktpl. from the Dom in the **Ernst-Barlach-Gedenkstätte.** Haunting, meditative bronzes and manuscripts from the early 20th century are on display. *(Barlachpl. 3. ☎37 89. Open Mar.-Nov. Tu-Su 10am-1pm and 2-5pm. DM5, students DM3.)*

The **train station** is a 30-minute walk from Marktpl. With your back to the station, turn right and follow Bahnhofsallee as it becomes Lüneburger Damm, Unter den Linden, and finally Herrenstr. Or take bus #2 to "Marktpl." Hourly **trains** connect Ratzeburg with **Lübeck** (15min., DM7.60) and **Lüneburg** (40min., DM15). The **tourist office,** Schloßwiese 7, is between the train station and the Marktpl. From the station, head down Bahnhofsallee until it becomes Lüneburger Damm (15min.) or take bus #2 to "Alter Zoll"; it's behind a small parking lot on the left. The staff books **rooms** (DM30-40) for free (☎85 86 65; fax 53 27. Open M-Th and F 9am-5pm, Sa-Su 10am-4pm). Join the hordes of nature-lovers and rent a **bike** from **Fahrradverleih Schloßwiese** on the lake, just past the tourist office. (☎44 66. Open daily 10am-6pm. DM18 per day.) The **post office,** 23909 Ratzeburg, is at Herrenstr. 12 (open M-F 8am-noon and 2-6pm, Sa 8am-noon).

To reach Ratzeburg's **Jugendherberge (HI),** Fischerstr. 20, take any bus from the train station to Marktpl. or follow the directions to the square above. Continuing straight through the Markt down Langenbrückenstr., turn right onto Schrongenstr. and follow it until it becomes Fischerstr.; it's at the end of the street. (☎37 07; fax 847 80. Sheets DM6. Laundry DM6. Reception 7am-10pm. Curfew 10pm, but you can ring the bell until 11:30pm, or get a key. DM22, over 26 DM27.) **Groceries** await at **Edeka** on the corner of Herrenstr. and Barlachstr. (open M-F 8am-8pm, Sa 7:30am-4pm). **Pinocchio,** Herrenstr. 14, is just about the cheapest option in *Imbiß*-free Ratzeburg. The menu features pizza (DM8-20) and pasta (DM11-16) in lots of exciting Italian varieties (open daily noon-10:30pm).

LAUENBURG AN DER ELBE   ☎04153

Lauenburg an der Elbe takes quintessential European quaintness to new levels. The cobblestones are perfectly aligned, the streets are perfectly narrow, and the houses are perfectly medieval, or at least look like it after restoration. Was that Mother Goose around the corner? Easy transport to Lauenburg is one of many remnants of its successful past; the town earned its bread as a stop on the great medieval canals connecting the mines of the Lüneburger Heide to the salt-starved towns of the Baltic coast.

The Lauenburg Altstadt consists of two halves—the **Unterstadt** down by the river, and the **Oberstadt** up above, joined by pathways of narrow steps. Most of the sights are located in the Unterstadt, an uninterrupted half-timbered strip built over the **Sperrmauer,** a stone embankment. The **Uferpromenade** is a narrow cobblestoned path (quaint, of course) between the houses which runs along the river's edge, and is ideal for walking or biking. Lauenburg's houses, many of which date back to the 16th century, are distinctive for their elaborately painted wood-and-brick framework. The **Mensingschehaus,** Elbstr. 49, off Kirchpl., is one of very few survivors of a catastrophic 1616 fire that claimed the Duke, his young wife, and most of the posher houses in town. The former **Rathaus,** Elbstr. 59, now houses the **Elbschiffahrtsmuseum,** which documents the town's shipping industry. (☎512 51. Open

SCHLESWIG-HOLSTEIN

Mar.-Oct. daily 10am-1pm and 2-5pm; Nov.-Feb. W and F-Su 10am-1pm and 2-5pm. DM2.) The house at **Elbstr. 97** (☎522 20) takes this cuteness thing a little bit too far. At about six feet wide, it is one of the smallest in Germany. You can even rent it if you really want to live out your Grimms' fairy tale fantasies. In the center of the Altstadt, the **Maria-Magdalena-Kirche,** Kirchpl. 1, stands tall and solid over the city; the church tower was a signal to returning sailors that they were home at long last (open M-Sa 10am-5pm, Su 9am-5pm). To the left of the church is a pretty 17th-century square, filled with sagging half-timbered houses whose beams are inscribed with religious messages. Above the church in the Oberstadt's Amtsplatz is the **Schloßturm,** built between 1457 and 1477. After the town burned down in 1616, the tower served as a state-of-the-art vantage point from which vigilant watchdogs observed the town burn down six more times. Now the tower can be climbed for a view of Lauenburg that is only moderately better than the one from the hill. (Open M, Tu, F 8:30am-12:30pm and 1:30-4:30pm, W 8:30am-12:30pm and 1-3pm, Th 8:30am-12:30pm and 1:30-7pm. Free.) Nothing remains of the **Schloß** except one wing, now used to house municipal offices.

Frequent trains run to **Lüneburg** (15min., 1 per hr., DM6) and **Lübeck** (1hr., 1 per hr., DM20). From Hamburg, **bus** #31 makes the 40-minute trip to Lüneburg from the "Bergedorf" S-Bahn stop (DM9.10). To reach the town from the train station, cross the bridge and turn left; the Altstadt will appear about 20m after you pass the giant **Hitzler** (don't forget the z!) **wharfs. The tourist office,** Elbstr. 91, is in the only modern-looking building on Elbstr. (☎520 267; email deopenhoor@t-online.de; www.lauenburg-elbe.de. Open Tu-Su 9am-5pm, closed M.) The **Jugendherberge Lauenburg (HI),** Am Sportpl. 7, is a pleasant 20 minute hike from the Altstadt. At the fork in the road at Elbstr. 20, follow the Radweg zur Jugendherberge sign left to the Uferpromenade. Go right onto Elburferweg; after about 10 minutes the paved promenade ends. Make a right here onto Kuhgrund (unmarked). Turn left at the *Jugendherberge* sign and take the dirt path through the woods (5min.). The hostel is the big brick building at the top of the hill. The hill has a view of the Elbe and the woods to one side, and the *Sportplatz* on the other. The brightly colored hostel, packed with school groups, offers game rooms with ping pong and a TV. (☎25 98. Breakfast included. Sheets DM7. Closed Dec. 15-Jan. 15. Call ahead. Dorm beds DM22, over 26 DM27.) *Pensionen* abound in the Altstadt, mostly closer to the train station; look for *Zimmer frei* signs. Private rooms run DM 30-60 per person.

The outdoor cafes on the waterfront tend to cater to the wealthier tourists who frequent the river cruises (fish dishes DM16-30). Cheaper eats can be had along the main drag of Hamburger Str. and in the Oberstadt's pedestrian zone. There is also an **Aldi** supermarket, Alte Wasche 15 (open M-F 8am-6pm, Sa 8am-1pm).

HOLSTEINISCHE SCHWEIZ (HOLSTEIN SWITZERLAND)

Spanning the countryside between Lübeck and Kiel, the Holsteinische Schweiz is the province's vacation playground. Placid lakes, lush forests, and moderately relaxed vacationing Germans populate this idyllic expanse with the fish and fowl.

PLÖN   ☎ 04522

The small town of Plön balances on a narrow strip of land that runs between two gigantic lakes, the **Kleiner Plöner See** and the **Großer Plöner See.** Even as this natural "bridge" threatens to buckle under the weight of German and Scandinavian tourists and school groups, the town continues to hold weekly festivals during the summer and maintain a surprisingly large number of monuments. Plön is a resort town dominated by its baroque **Schloß.** These days, most *Deutsch* tourists bypass the town for the surrounding lakes and tree-sheltered trails whose shady seduction once attracted the royal family.

⊉ PRACTICAL INFORMATION. Plön lies on the main rail line between Lübeck and Kiel. **Trains** travel hourly to **Kiel** (30min., DM12), **Lübeck** (40min., DM12), and **Eutin** (15min, DM5). For a **taxi**, call ☎66 66 or 35 35. Rent **bikes** at **Wittich**, Lange Str. 34. (☎27 48. Open M-Sa 9am-6pm. DM12 per day.) Rent **boats** at the **Kanucenter**, Ascheberger Str. 76, near the camp ground. (☎41 43. Kayaks DM8-12 per hr., DM25-45 per day; canoes DM10-40 per hr., DM40-120 per day.) **Großer Plöner Seerundfahrt** chugs around the lake from the dock on Strandweg. (10 min. past the hr. daily 10am-5pm. DM14, students under 20 DM8.) The **tourist office**, Am Lübschen Tor 1, lies between the station and the Markt. Follow the signs to the left from the station. The staff sells a good map (DM4) and books **rooms** for free. (☎50 950; fax 50 95 20; email touristinfo@ploen.de; www.ploen.de. Open M-F 9am-6pm, Sa-Su 10am-1pm.) The **post office**, 24306 Plön, is next to the station (open M-F 8:30am-noon and 3-6pm, Sa 8:30am-noon).

▟▚ ACCOMMODATIONS AND FOOD. If you're staying for a week or longer, your best bet is a vacation home; otherwise, private rooms (DM21-52) are a good deal. Plön's **Jugendherberge (HI)**, Ascheberger Str. 67, is—brace yourself—brimming with Britney Spears-adoring *Schulkinder*. Walk left from the station along Bahnhofstr. as it becomes Lübecker Str. and then Lange Str. through the center of town. Keep going as Lange Str. becomes Hamburger Str., Ascheberger Chaussee, and finally Ascheberger Str; the hostel is on the left (30min.). Two- to six-bed rooms let you get to know your roommates *well*, though some have large windows. (☎25 76; fax 21 66. Breakfast included. Sheets DM6. Front door locked 10pm-7am, but you can get a key. Checkout 9am. Members only. Dorm beds DM22, over 26 DM27.) **Hotel Zum Hirschen**, Bahnhofstr. 9, across from the station, has small, clean rooms and a convenient location. (☎24 23. Singles DM55-70, doubles DM100.) **Campingplatz Spitzenart**, Ascheberger 75-76, is next to the hotel (☎27 69. DM8 per person. Tents DM6-10. Open Apr.-Oct.) Plön's restaurants are unexciting and expensive. The pedestrian zone around the **Markt** supports a healthy, if not particularly hip, cafe culture. **Sky**, Lübecker Str. 32, has the lowest prices and the longest hours of any **grocery store** (open M-F 8am-8pm, Sa 8am-4pm). **Kochlöffel**, across from the Nikolaikirche on the Markt, sells delicious chicken dishes, all under DM5 (open M-Sa 9am-10:30pm, Su 11am-10:30pm). **Antalya-Grill**, Lange Str. 36, offers grill platters (DM3-16) and spicy pizzas. (☎39 82. DM8-14. Open daily 11am-midnight.)

◪ SIGHTS. Plön's main attraction is the late Renaissance **Schloß**. On top of the Schloßberg, the palace affords a spectacular view out over the surrounding lake. Further away from town is the lush **Lustgarten** and the modest **Prinzenhaus**. The brick 18th-century beauty was the private *Lusthaus* (heh, heh) of the last duke, who enjoyed participating in boyish sports. Down the eastern slope of the Schloß-berg is Plön's small 19th-century **Rathaus**. From there, Schloßbergstr. dips down into the Markt, the current commercial center of Plön and the site of its many festivals, which often involve small carnival rides and *always* involve beer. The Markt is also Plön's religious center, hosting the heavenly **Nikolaikirche**. Some of its original 12th-century splendor was dumbed down in 1542 in response to the anti-pomp fashions of the Reformation; the church was later torn down and rebuilt because it was falling apart from old age. It then burnt to a crisp in June of 1864, necessitating yet another reconstruction *(open daily 10am-4pm)*.

The town's other archaic attraction is the **Museum des Krieses**, Johannisstr. 1. The museum is housed in a former apothecary and displays 17th-century glassware, porcelain, and other goodies swiped from the Schloß. *(☎74 32 69. Open mid-May to Sept. Tu-Sa 10am-noon and Tu-Su 3-6pm; Nov. to mid-May Tu-Sa 10am-noon. DM3, students DM1.)* Next door to the museum is the **Johanniskirche**, on Johannisstr. The church was built in 1685 for the ducal couple, Johann Adolph and Dorothea Sophie, and has a small graveyard alongside it. *(Open 10am-4pm. Free.)* Far east of the town center on the ridge that runs between the two lakes, the **Parnaßturm,** a former lookout tower, provides an amazing view well worth the 20-minute climb up Rodomstorstr. from the Gänsemarkt, just west of the station. *(Open Easter-Oct. 9am-7pm. Free.)* West of the center, the **Prinzeninsel** stretches out from the mainland into the Großer Plöner See. A tiny canal spanned by a footbridge divides it from the shore. The island shelters a sandy beach complete with snack bar. The lake has quite a pungent odor, making a swim an experience. Perhaps walking the trails to get here is a nicer one.

EUTIN ☎ 04521

Plön may pack more of an historical punch, but as the region's main shopping center, Eutin has the power of cash. The daily town market is more like a fair, with jewelry, sailor suits, and housewares mixed in with the usual fruit, vegetables, meat, and cheese. Like Plön, Eutin sits between two lakes: the **Großer Eutiner See** to the east and the **Kleiner Eutiner See** to the west. A series of dukes made the city more culturally attuned during the 17th century, and in the 18th century, composer Carl Maria von Weber provided it with a tourist industry to last for years to come (he wrote some music, too).

⚑ PRACTICAL INFORMATION. Eutin lies on the rail line between Lübeck and Kiel. Hourly **trains** run to **Lübeck** (20min., DM9); **Kiel** (1hr., DM15); and **Plön** (15min., DM5). Rent **bikes** at the stand at the tourist office. (DM12 per day. Open daily 9am-7pm.) The **tourist office,** Bleekergang 6, also provides an overwhelming array of brochures and books **rooms** for free. (☎ 709 70; fax 70 97 20. Open May-Sept. M-F 9am-6pm, Sa-Su 10am-1pm; Oct.-Apr. M-Su 9am-5pm.) From the station, turn left on Bahnhofstr. and right on Plöner Str. Follow the street to Voßpl. and head straight on tiny Rosengartenweg to the Strandpromenade. Turn left at the lake; the office will be on your left. The **post office,** 23701 Eutin, Peterstr. 18-22, in the mall off Marktpl., **exchanges money** (open M-W 7am-6pm, Th-F 7am-7pm, Sa 7am-2pm).

⚏⚐ ACCOMMODATIONS AND FOOD. The **Jugendherberge (HI),** Jahnhöhe 6, often has space. Follow the directions to the tourist office (above) to Voßpl. Turn left on Riemannstr. and left again on Jahnhöhe; the hostel is on the right. The local swimming pool is only two minutes away. (☎ 21 09; fax 746 02. Breakfast included. Sheets DM7. Curfew 11pm, but you can get a key. Dorm beds DM22, over 26 DM27.) The **Markt** offers a number of cafes as well as more hum-drum fast food joints. For **groceries,** try **Sky Market,** Königstr. 10, at the Markt (open M-F 8am-7pm, Sa 8am-4pm).

⚏⚐ SIGHTS AND ENTERTAINMENT. Two stone monkeys squat on the bridge leading across the moat to Eutin's central monument, the **Eutiner Schloß,** Schloßpl. The austerity of the complex's sparse rooms and plain marble floors somehow inspire more vivid images of 16th-century nobility. (☎ 709 50. *Obligatory tours daily on the hour 10am-4pm, except 1pm. DM7, students DM5, children DM3, family card DM15.)* The landscaped **Eutiner Schloßgarten** has a few buildings hidden amidst its lush lawns. The **Seepavillon** pokes out of the Großer Eutiner See. The **Küchengarten,** south of the castle, has an **Orangerie** and other horticultural goodies. Farther from the Schloß, the **Tempelgarten** contains a "Chinese" bridge and the **Monopteros,** a faux ancient Greek temple. *(Open 24hr. Free.)* Next door to the Schloß, the **Ostholstein-Museum,** Schloßpl. 1, makes a valiant effort at filling its two floors with portraits of the town's dukes and Carl Maria von Weber. (☎ 701 80. *Open Apr.-Sept. Tu-Su 10am-1pm and 2pm-5pm; Oct.-Jan. and Mar. Tu-Su 3-5pm. DM3, students DM2.)* Climb aboard a **lake cruise** with **Eutiner Seerundfahrten,** which leave the Strandpromenade daily at 12:15pm, 1:30pm, and 2:45pm *(1hr., DM8),* or expand your Romantic fantasies on the **Nachtwächterrundgang** ("the night watchman's rounds"), a role-playing tour of Eutin that meets at the Schloß gates. *(Daily at 7:30pm. DM6.)*

KIEL
☎ 0431

Site of the 1936 and 1972 Olympic sailing events, the waters around Kiel swim ceaselessly with brightly colored sails. These multiply in the last full week of June, when the annual **Kieler Woche** (☎901 24 16) takes place. The largest in the world, this internationally renowned regatta enlivens the harbor and floods the town with music, food, and beer. During the rest of the year Kiel offers little to visitors besides ferry connections to Scandinavia and access to the world's busiest artificial waterway, the Nord-Ostsee-Kanal, unless they have a fetish for nautical machinery. Allied bombings here were typically ruthless, destroying 80% of the city. Unfortunately, Kiel has retained little of its historic beauty.

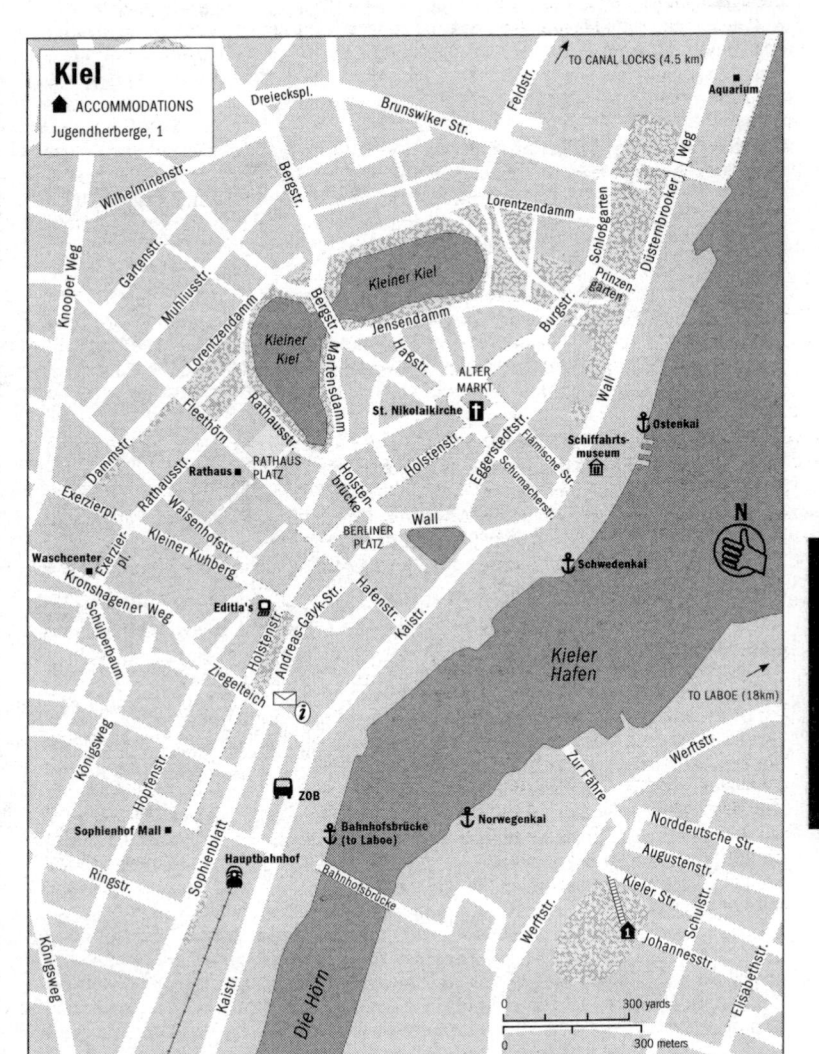

Kiel

ACCOMMODATIONS
Jugendherberge, 1

SCHLESWIG-HOLSTEIN

📠 GETTING THERE AND GETTING AROUND

Hourly **trains** run daily from Kiel to **Hamburg** (1½hr.); **Lübeck** (1½hr.); and **Flensburg** (1hr.). The **Mitfahrzentrale,** Sophienblatt 52a, two blocks south of the train station, matches riders and drivers for DM0.10 per km. (☎194 40; fax 67 67 42. Open M-W and F 9am-6pm, Th 9am-7pm, Sa 10am-3pm, Su noon-3pm.) At DM3.10 per ride, Kiel's extensive **public transportation** system will quickly result in a massive cash hemorrhage. Avoid the fiscal bloodletting with the **Kieler Karte,** which also offers discounts at many sights (1 day DM12, 3 days DM17). Most of Kiel's buses pass through the rows of stops outside the train station; the ones on the train station side of the street *generally* head north, while the ones on the Sophienhof side go south. All **ferries** except those bound for Norway and the Baltics leave from the piers on the west side of the harbor. **Baltic Line,** on the west side near the station at **Schwedenkai** (☎20 97 60), will take you to Sweden. **Color Line** at **Norwegenkai,** on the opposite side of the harbor, sails to **Oslo.** (☎730 03 00; fax 730 04 00. Single cabin DM134-174, double DM150-202.) **Langeland-Kiel,** on the west side of **Ostenkai,** ships out to Bagenkop, Denmark (☎97 41 50; fax 945 15. 2½hr. DM7, in July DM9). Boats bound for **Kaliningrad** and the **Baltics** leave from **Ostuferkai.**

🛈 PRACTICAL INFORMATION

Kiel's **tourist office,** Andreas-Gayk-Str. 1, is located in the post office building, two blocks north of the train station. It finds rooms for free and books them for a DM5 fee. (☎679 100; fax 679 10 99. Open M-F 9am-7pm, Sa 9am-4pm, Su 9am-1pm.) Call 750 00 for a **taxi.** Rent **bikes** at Radsport Center Kiel, Kranshagener Weg 38 (☎170 10; fax 52 91 64). Do laundry at **Waschcenter,** Exerzierpl. on Ziegelteich (open M-Sa 6am-midnight). **Exchange money** at the adjacent **Postbank** (same hours as the post office; closes at 1pm on Saturdays). Internet connection at **Editla's,** Alter Markt 13 (open M 6pm-1am, Tu-Sa 11am-1am, Su 4pm-1am). The **post office,** 24044 Kiel, Stresemannpl. 1-3, is on the other side of the bus station from the train station (open M-F 8am-7pm, Sa 8:30am-2pm).

🏠🍴 ACCOMMODATIONS AND FOOD

Kiel's boss hostel, **Jugendherberge Kiel (HI),** Johannesstr. 1, has uncrowded quads, each sharing a shower and bathroom with the neighboring room. Take bus #4 from the train station on the Sophienhof side to "Kieler Str.," and backtrack one block, then turn right on Johannesstr.; or take the "Cinemaxx" exit from the train station and walk toward the harbor. Take the bridge across and walk in the same direction through the construction site to the overpass. Turn left, following the small, white signs through the garden to the hostel, a 15 min. journey (☎73 14 88; fax 73 57 23. Breakfast and sheets included. Reception 7am-1am. Checkout 7am-9am. Curfew 1am. Members only. Dorm beds DM28, over 26 DM33.) **Campingplatz Falckenstein,** Palisadenweg 171, is a distant 13km from the center. Take bus #44 (direction: "Strand") to "Seekamp." Backtrack to Scheidekoppel and hike 20 min. through wheat fields until Palisadenweg, then turn left down toward the beach. (☎39 20 78; fax 39 20 78. Open Apr.-Oct. DM8 per person. Tent DM6-12.)

Get groceries at **Edeka** on the ground floor of the Sophienhof Mall (open M-F 9am-8pm, Sa 8:30am-4pm). **Günther's Cafe,** located portside, serves everything from lasagna to chili (DM7-11) to a serenade of seagulls and ships' horns. From the main entrance of the train station, take a right to the pedestrian bridge (open M-F 8am-9pm, Sa-Su 9am-9pm). On dry land, the *Fussgängerzone* offers **Sandwich,** Holstenstr. 92, which counts on tourists' thirst for expensive Coca-Cola; fight the power by bringing your own drink and enjoy the yummy little sandwiches. (DM2.50-5. Open M-F 6:30am-6pm, Sa 7am-2pm.) The **Kieler Brauerei,** Alter Markt 6, has dark suds (DM3-6) and expensive breadbaskets (DM12-15), but at least this barley center is somewhat authentic. (☎90 62 90. Open M-Th and Su 11am-1am and F-Sa 11am-2am.)

"EIN BITT, BITTE!" Two things become clear during a road trip from Munich north to Flensburg: the land becomes flatter and the beer become more bitter. Northern Germans like beer to pack a punch to keep things lively during those long winter months, so their beer harbors a much more bitter taste than its southern cousins of Bavaria. The odd-man-out is *Alsterwasser* (literally "water from the Alster", one of Hamburg's lakes), which is a mix of lemonade and beer. Sticking to the classic recipes are *Astor* and *Holsten* from Hamburg, which are bearable to untested taste buds. Farther north, *Flensburger Pilsner* (Felnsburg) and *Asgaard* (Schleswig) dominate the menus. *Budweiser* (the original), from the Czech Republic, squeezes its way in. But dominating it all is *Jever*, the undisputed champion of bitterness.

◎ SIGHTS

The sights and sounds of the harbor, the city's focal point, are omnipresent in stolid, modern Kiel. The highlight is the largest team of **canal locks** in the world. The view of the canal and the harbor is amazing. *(Take bus #4 to "Kanal," then the ferry that runs every 15 min. (free). Walk right 10 minutes along Kanalstr. from the ferry dock to the Schleuseninsel. Alternatively, landlubbers can take bus #1 or 41 to "Schleuse." (30min. Obligatory tours daily 9am-3pm, every 2hr. DM3, students DM1.)* Hugging the west coast of Kiel's harbor, the **Schiffahrtsmuseum** displays a collection of model ships as diverse as the real ships that have graced Kiel's harbor throughout its history. *(Wall 65. ☎ 34 28. Open mid-Apr. to mid-Oct. daily 10am-6pm; mid-Oct. to mid-Apr. Tu-Su 10am-5pm. Free.)* At the end of the Holstenstr. shopping district stands the 13th-century **Nikolaikirche,** Altermarkt. The church is frequently the site of free concerts. *(☎ 929 37. Open M-F 10am-1pm and 2-6pm, Sa 10am-1pm.)*

SCHLESWIG ☎ 04621

At the southernmost point of the Schlei inlet, Schleswig bills itself as the "friendly city of culture," a title earned by its picture-perfect fishing settlements, 16th-century castle, and extensive museum collections. Originally settled by Vikings, Schleswig became an important fishing and trade center in the Middle Ages. The city was subsequently the seat of the Gottorfer dukes, small-time nobles who set themselves up in a showy castle on the banks of the Schlei. Today Schleswig's laid-back pace, beautiful surroundings, and millennium-long history provide visitors with a relaxing tour of an interesting cross-section of European history.

SCHLESWIG-HOLSTEIN

Gehege Tiergarten · Suadicanistr. · Spielkoppel · Lutherstr. · Kartöffels · Schnell & Sauber · Stadtweg · Königstr. · Wiesenstr. · ZOB · Lange Str. · St. Petridom · Rathaus · Holmer Noor · Waldmühle · Schloßallee · Flensburger Str. · Loliuß · Schleistr. · Kreuzstall · Landesmuseen · Nydamhalle · Schloß Gottorf · Norderdomstr. · Süderdomstr. · Töpferstr. · Hafengang · Rathausmarkt · Süderholmstr. · Am Hafen · HOLM · Adliges Johanniskloster · Stadthafen · Gottorfdamm · LOLLFUSS · Callisenstr. · Viking Tower · N · Schlei Inlet · Friedrichstr. · Bahnstr. · Städtisches Museum · B76 · Hauptbahnhof · Manstenstr. · Haddebyer Chaussee · Strandweg · Landstr. · Haddebyer Damm · TO VIKING MUSEUM HAITHABU (300m)

0   300 yards
0   300 meters

Schleswig

⌂ ACCOMMODATIONS
Campingplatz, 3
Jugendherberge (HI), 1
Pension Schleiblick, 2

☷ ORIENTATION AND PRACTICAL INFORMATION

Unlike most German towns, Schleswig centers around its **bus terminal** *(ZOB)* rather than its train station. The town center, part shopping mall, part conscientiously preserved Altstadt, sits on the north bank of the **Schlei**, while the train station lies 20 minutes south of town. **Stadtweg** is a major commercial and *Fussgänger* zone; Schleswig's sights are south of it. To get to the train station, take bus #1, 2, 4, or 5 from the stop outside the *ZOB*, which is close to the Altstadt. **Trains** head hourly to **Kiel, Flensburg,** and **Hamburg** (via Neumünster). Single rides on Schleswig's **bus** network cost DM1.90. To avoid being stripped of cash and dignity, purchase a **Schleswig Card** (DM13), valid for three days of public transit and admission to most sights. Rent **bikes** at **Peters Fahrradverleih,** Bahnhofstr. 14a. (☎376 88. DM10 per day.) The **tourist office,** Plessenstr. 7, is up the street from the harbor; from the *ZOB*, walk down Plessenstr. toward the water. The staff books **rooms** for DM25-60. (☎98 16 16; room reservations ☎98 16 17; fax 98 16 19. Open May-Sept. M-F 9am-12:30pm and 1:30-5pm, Sa 9am-noon; Oct.-Apr. M-Th 9am-12:30pm and 1:30-5pm, F 9am-12:30pm.) **Schnell und Sauber,** Stadtweg 70, washes 6kg of **laundry** for DM6 (open M-Sa 6am-10pm). The **post office,** 24837 Schleswig, is on Stadtweg 53-55 (open M-F 9am-6pm, Sa 9am-1pm).

☷☐ ACCOMMODATIONS AND FOOD

The **Jugendherberge (HI),** Spielkoppel 1, is close to the center of town. Take bus #2 (direction: "Hühnhauser Schwimmhalle") from either the train station or the *ZOB* to "Schwimmhalle"; the hostel is across the street. For those shunning the bus, walk (with your back to the *ZOB*) right along Königstr. and turn right onto Poststr. Keep going in this direction as it changes to Moltkestr. and then turn left onto Bellmannstr. Follow this street to Spielkoppel, which will be on your left; the hostel is on the right across from the school. Great location and a view of the Schlei inlet. (☎238 93. Breakfast included. Sheets DM7. Reception 7am-1pm and 5-11pm. Curfew 11pm. Dorm beds DM21, over 26 DM26.) For a night in a former *Fischerhaus* overlooking the water (or for the TV in every room), try **Pension Schleiblick,** Hafengang 4. Follow Plessenstr. toward the harbor. Continue as it turns into Am Hafen, then bear left onto Hafengang. (☎234 68; fax 234 68. Reception daily until 11pm. Breakfast included. Singles DM65, doubles DM110-130.) The **Wikinger Campingplatz,** Am Haithabu, is across the inlet from the Altstadt (☎324 50; fax 331 22. DM6 per person). **Da Paolo,** Stadtweg 65, serves traditional pizza and pasta (DM9-16) on red-checkered tablecloths. (☎298 97. Open daily noon-3pm and 5:30pm-midnight.) Also try the seafood—fresh and cheap—at the *Imbiße* down by the **Stadthafen.** Schleswig's own **Asgaard-Brauerei,** Königstr. 27, keeps the Viking tradition, looting and pillaging (at least metaphorically) with golden ale, though you must supply the hornèd headwear. Sandwiches are expensive (DM7.50-11.50), but—praise Odin— the beer's not: DM3-6! (☎292 06. Open M-Th 5pm-midnight, F-Sa 11am-2am, Su 11am-midnight.)

☷ SIGHTS

Schleswig's Altstadt, located a few blocks up from the harbor, is stuffed to the gills with meandering cobblestoned streets leading along the town's unusually hilly terrain. **Stadtweg,** the main pedestrian zone, is lined with smart shops and a department store. Towering over it all is the copper steeple of the 12th-century **St. Petri-Dom,** renowned for its successful combination of Romanesque and high Gothic architecture, as well as for its intricately carved 16th-century **Bordesholmer Altar** by Brüggemann. Untouched by the war, the cathedral still displays original frescos and glazed brick. Climb the 112-meter tower. In the summer the church offers a choral and organ concert series. *(Open May-Sept. M-Th and Sa 9am-5pm, F 9am-3pm, Su 1-5pm; Oct.-Apr. M-Th and Sa 10am-4pm, F 10am-3pm, Su 1-4pm. Tower DM2, children DM1.*

SCHLESWIG-HOLSTEIN

Concerts W evenings; DM10-15, students DM5-8.) Two blocks beyond the Dom, the narrow alleys unfold onto the **Rathausmarkt,** a quiet square adjacent to the 15th-century **Rathaus.** Beyond Knud-Laward-Str. begins the **Holm,** a small fishing village with a tiny church in the main square, which doubles as Holm's cemetery.

A 20-minute walk along the harbor from the Altstadt, 18th-century **Schloß Gottorf** and its surrounding buildings house the **Landesmuseen,** a treasure trove of artwork and artifacts in six museums. The castle is home to most of the exhibits; the first floor consists of 16th- and 17th-century Dutch and Danish artwork, alongside tapestries, suits of armor, and the Gottorfs' apartments. Upstairs the path leads to the incredibly ornate **Kapelle** (chapel), built in 1591. The grand finale is the appropriately named **Hirschsaal,** whose deer-endowed walls feature real antlers. The second floor is also home to the excellent **Jugendstilmuseum,** a collection of art deco paintings and furniture. Wipe your shoes before going in—even the carpets are part of the exhibit. One floor up are the main exhibits of the **Archäologisches Landesmuseum.** Along with telling the prehistoric story of Schleswig-Holstein, the Middle Ages are seen through the eyes of different classes, from pauper to emperor. The rest of the museum is in the **Nydamhalle** adjacent to the castle, including a 4th-century fishing boat and an exhibit on the Saxon migration to England. On the other side of the castle, the **Kreuzstall** and the adjacent buildings house the **Museum des 20. Jahrhunderts,** an extensive collection devoted to the artists of the Brücke school, including Emil Nolde, Max Pechstein, and Ernst Ludwig Kirchner, as well as a well-rounded presentation of adherents to the *Neue Sachlichkeit.* Finally, the park surrounding the castle holds an **outdoor sculpture museum** featuring contemporary German sculptors. *(☎81 32 22. All museums open daily Mar.-Oct. 9am-5pm; Nov.-Feb. 9:30am-4pm. DM9, students DM5.)*

If you find yourself longing to see the remains of a civilization of tall, attractive people who seem to have made a lot of combs and beautiful boats, ferries *(DM2.50 one-way)* travel from the Stadthafen near the Dom to the **Wikinger Museum Haithabu.** The museum, next to a former **Viking settlement,** covers all aspects of Viking life in three huts. Despite the throngs of tourists, it's not a hokey place: the area around the museum has walking paths that lead to a strikingly landscaped cemetery and a stone church straight out of the dark ages. *(Open daily Apr.-Oct. 9am-5pm; Nov.-Mar. Tu-Su 9am-4pm. DM5, students DM3, families DM12.)* About five minutes up the road heading to the station, the **Städtisches Museum,** Friedrichstr. 9-11, houses documents and *objets trouvés* from Schleswig's history. *(☎814 280. Open Tu-Su 10am-5pm.)*

FLENSBURG   ☎0461

With the Danish border only a hop, skip, and a stumble away, Flensburg is Germany's northernmost city. You can't go anywhere in northern Germany without encountering the quality *Flensburger Pilsner* on tap, and the town itself is swimming in it. Although Lady Luck seemed to wink propitiously during WWII, when few Allied bombs fell on the town. Flensburg's good condition attracted the fleeing Nazi government, which named the town Germany's provisional capital and then surrendered it almost immediately afterwards on May 7, 1945. Now, however, the untouched Altstadt and peaceful beaches attract a different kind of German. Bypassing the Baltic Sea's other coastal towns, young, wealthy Germans and Danes flock to this cosmopolitan outpost during the summer months. Along with daylight, tourists, locals, and students flood the pedestrian area and harbor-side well into the wee hours of the morning. Fueling the merry feasting is the recent boom in ethnic restaurants. Once a safe haven for Nazis, Flensburg is transforming into a home for anyone wanting a more relaxed pace of life with an ocean view.

█ PRACTICAL INFORMATION

Trains link the city to **Schleswig** (1hr.); **Kiel** (1hr.); and **Hamburg** (1½hr.) every hour, while others head north to **Copenhagen** (5hr., twice daily) and many other Danish cities. **Buses** also cross the border to the Danish towns of **Sønderborg**

SCHLESWIG-HOLSTEIN

(1¼hr.) and **Aabenrå** (50min.) from gate B4. Flensburg's **public transportation** system saves a lot of uphill walking in town; most buses circulate through the *ZOB* two blocks from Holm below the harbor (single ride DM1.90). From the west bank of the harbor, **Hansalinie**, Eckernförder Landstr. 2, runs five **ferries** a day between Flensburg and **Glücksburg** in Germany and **Gravenstein** and **Kollund** in Denmark (☎980 01; fax 989 01. DM6, children 7-14 DM4). The **tourist office**, Speicherlinie 40, lies off Große Str.; follow the signs through the courtyard. The staff books **rooms** (DM20-35) for free and arranges summer tours of the brewery for DM5 every Tuesday. (☎909 09 20; fax 909 09 36. Open M-F 9am-6pm, Sa 10am-1pm.) The **post office** is near the train station at Bahnhofstr. 40, 24939 Flensburg (open M-F 8am-6pm, Sa 8am-1pm). The **postal code** is 24939. **Internet connections** at **Netg@te**, 63 Ferienschanze. (60min DM10. Open M-F 10am-8pm, Sa 10-6pm, Su 3-6pm.)

ACCOMMODATIONS AND FOOD

Flensburg's **Jugendherberge (HI)**, Fichtestr. 16, offers no escape from exercise, whether it be running laps on the nearby track or making the long walk into town. From the train station, take bus #1 (direction: "Lachsbach") or 4 (direction: "Klueshof") to "ZOB" and change to #3 or 7 (direction: "Twedter Plack") to "Stadion," then follow the signs. (☎377 42; fax 31 29 52. Sheets DM6. Reception 8-8:45am, 5-6pm, and 9:30-10pm. Dorm beds DM22, over 26 DM27.) Among the overpriced hotels on Süderhofenden there is ☒**ETAP Hotel**, Süderhofenden 14, right at the bus station. With a credit card, check in any time at the front door. (☎48 08 920. Breakfast DM8.90. Reception M-Sa 7am-10am, 5-10pm. Beds DM59.) With trendy shops and equally trendy cafes lining the pedestrian zone, cheaper eats will be found in the bakeries or along Schiffbrucke Str. The **Nordermarkt** simmers with a slew of cafes and bars. For those itching to see what a metric hangover feels like, **Hansen's Brauerei**, Schiffbrucke 16, serves home-brewed beer by the meter for DM26 (12 drinks for the price of 10!) and German food in equally absurd quantities. Their whopping Sunday special bloats you with 1kg of ribs for DM14. (☎222 10. Open M-Th and Su 11am-midnight, F-Sa, 11am-2am.)

SIGHTS

Flensburg surrounds the natural harbor formed by the inland banks of the **Flensburger Förde**; streets run up from the water's edge into the hills. The **Deutsches Haus**, on Neumarktstr., is a Bauhaus-style concert hall donated to Flensburg in recognition of the city's loyalty in the 1920 referendum. In the **Südermarkt**, the beautiful 14th-century **Nikolaikirche** boasts a gargantuan organ, the *Organ Maximus.* *(Open Tu-F 9am-5pm, Sa 10am-1pm. Free.)* Down Große Str., beyond the **Nordermarkt**, stands the **Marienkirche** with its bizarre 1950s-era stained-glass windows. *(Open M-Sa 10am-5pm. Free.)* The **Marientreppe**, Norderstr. 50, offers a glimpse of Denmark atop its 146 stairs. The **Schiffahrtsmuseum**, documents Flensburg's nautical history and role in Denmark's once-thriving Caribbean trade. *(Schiffbrücke 39. ☎85 29 70. Open Tu-Sa 10am-5pm, Su 10am-1pm. DM5, students DM2.50.)* The last weekend in May hosts the **Rum Regatta**.

SYLT
☎04651

The sandy, windswept island of Sylt stretches far into the North Sea, culminating in Germany's northernmost point. The 10km long **Hindenburgdamm** connects Sylt—traditionally a favorite spot for government luminaries and other wealthy vacationers, but now a more democratic affair—to the mainland. The beauty of Sylt's undulating dunes and pine forests attracts large crowds, especially to **Westerland.** The mother of all *Kurtowns* and the largest town on the island, Westerland is abuzz with bourgeois types traipsing down the boardwalk. Parts of the island are heinously overdeveloped; others are deserted.

SCHLESWIG-HOLSTEIN

◪ PRACTICAL INFORMATION. Trains from Hamburg's **Altona** station travel to Westerland via **Husum** (2½hr., 1 per hr.). **Public transportation** on the island is quite expensive but very thorough (DM6.40 to reach either hostel from Westerland, day card DM20). Buses leave from the *ZOB* terminal to the left of the train station. Rent a **bike** from **Fahrrad am Bahnhof** at the station, across from track 1. (DM9 per day, DM49 per week. Open daily 9am-1pm and 2-6:30pm.) Sylt levies a *Kurtaxe* on any easy riders hoping to hit the beaches. (June-Sept. DM6, May and Oct. DM5.50 per day, Nov.-Apr. DM3; under 18 free.) **Ferries** run seven to 11 times a day from List harbor to **Havneby** on the Danish island of **Rømø**. (50min. One-way DM65, round-trip DM99, same-day return DM90.) Call **Rømø-Sylt Linie** (☎310 30 30) in **List** for reservations and information. **Adler-Schiffe**, Boysenstr. 13 (☎987 00), in Hörnum, runs daytrips to **Amrum**. The **tourist office** in the train station books **rooms** (DM35 and up) for a minimum DM10 fee or 8% of your bill. (☎99 88; fax 99 81 00. Open daily in summer M-Sa 9am-6pm, Su 11am-4pm.) For **rooms** in List, call ☎952 00; in Hörnum, ☎96 26 26; in Kampen, ☎46 98 33. The **post office,** 25992 Sylt, is on Kjeirstr. 17, near the exit of the train station (open M-F 8am-6pm, Sa 8am-noon).

◤ ACCOMMODATIONS. Sylt offers two youth hostels. Those neither wayward nor lucky enough to earn a spot in Hörnum's reform school will have to settle for the adjacent **Jugendherberge Hörnum (HI),** Friesenpl. 2. The hostel offers a convenient location next to a bus stop with a **SPAR grocery store** 1km down the road (☎88 02 94; fax 88 13 92. Open M-Sa 7:30am-6:30pm, Su 10am-noon). From the *ZOB*, take bus #2 (direction: "Hörnum Hafen") to "Hörnum-Nord" and continue along Rantumer Str., turning left at the *Jugendherberge* sign. Across the street from the hostel, a secluded beach stretches for miles. (Sheets DM7. Reception noon-1pm and 5-10pm. Curfew 11pm. Reservations recommended. Dorm beds DM25, over 26 DM29.) List's **Jugendherberge Mövenberg** offers much more room, but gives new meaning to "in the middle of nowhere." Catch bus #1 (direction: "List Hafen") from the Westerland *ZOB* and take it to the end of the line (DM6.20). If you're lucky you can change for the infrequent bus #5 to "Mövenberg"; otherwise, return to the second intersection before the bus stop, turn right and follow the *Jugendherberge* sign for 35min., past the sheep and dunes. Be aware that school groups covet the hostel's proximity to the youth beach. (☎87 03 97; fax 87 10 39. Breakfast included. Reception 8-9am, noon-2pm, and 3-8pm. Curfew 11pm. Reservations strongly advised. Open mid-Mar. to Oct. Dorm beds DM25, over 26 DM29.)

◧◪ SIGHTS AND HIKING. From Westerland, the best way to explore the 39km-long island is by bicycle. The main bike path follows the highway, making it good for inter-town travel, while the smaller dirt and gravel paths meander through the dunes, affording stunning views of the ocean. Outside the recreational chaos of the main town, where shopping is everyone's favorite summer sport, Sylt offers sparsely populated beaches, including the (in)famous **Bühne 16,** whose nude bathers reveal that water wings do not a swimsuit make. Sylt's beaches also provide the only locales in Germany where windsurfing is possible. While they're no Waikiki, the beaches at **Wellingstedt, Hörnum,** and **Strandhalle** all produce rideable surf. While Westerland is a convenient starting-point for an island adventure, its rows of designer shops and overpriced restaurants can become claustrophobic in the high season. To avoid (most of) the crowds, head north. Beyond Westerland's city limits, unpopulated dune trails and small vacation villages await; both ends of the island are nature reserves. North of **Kampen** (one town north of Westerland), the main road leads through rolling grass-covered dunes and fields sparsely inhabited by cows and horses. **List,** Sylt's northernmost town, is an excellent base for hikers and bikers wishing to explore the trails leading into the remote dunes of **Ellenbogen,** 8km north of town, the northernmost point in Germany.

AMRUM
☎ 04682

The closest island to Sylt, **Amrum** draws (mostly wealthy) visitors with its cliff-sized dunes, fragrant pine forests, and miles of sandy beaches. Nine square kilometers of Amrum are sand; the other 20 square kilometers support five towns: **Wittdün,** the main town; **Steenodde; Süddorf; Nebel,** winner of the highest-percentage-roofs-thatched prize; and **Norddorf. Wittdün** has a pleasant main street **(Hauptstr.),** as well as a souvenir- and *Imbiß*-free **Strandpromenade.** But the island's main attraction is the **Kniepsand**—kilometers of the whitest sand bordering the North Sea. Between the *Kniepsand* and the towns lies a narrow strip of grassy dunes interspersed with lakes and hiking trails, crowned by the **Amrumer Leuchtturm,** the tallest lighthouse on Germany's North Sea coast (open Apr.-Oct. M-F 8:30am-noon). Use the lighthouse as a lookout point, or climb to one of the **Aussichtsdünen** that dot the walkways through the dunes. Amrum has two museums, both of which are worth a once-over, even if only from the outside. Both are located in **Nebel.** The **Mühlenmuseum,** in a shaggy windmill, has exhibits on the history and prehistory of Amrum, the lighthouse, and some model boats. (☎ 38 89. Open M-W 10am-noon, Th-Su 3-6pm.) To learn more about Frisian culture, step inside the **Ömrang Hüüs** Waaswai 1, an 18th-century captain's home. (☎ 41 53. Open M-F 10am-1pm and Saturday afternoons in summer.) **St. Clemens,** Nebel's church, is also worth a visit.

Getting to Amrum provides its own excitement for folks who **run** to the island across the **Wattenmeer** from Sylt at low tide. The path connecting the two islands contains a few **quicksand** pits, making it advisable to take a guided tour (☎ 21 75; DM6). For the less adventurous, **Adler-Schiffe** (☎ (04651) 987 00; fax 264) runs boats to Wittdün from **Hörnum** on Sylt. (50min. 10:05, 11:55am and 5:05pm. Round-trip DM35, children DM17.50.) Amrum has two **bus lines.** Bus #1 services Norddorf, Nebel, Süddorf, and Wittdün, while bus #2 services Wittdün, Süddorf, Steenodde, and Nebel. (Single ride DM2-2.50. Day-card DM9). **Bikes** are available for rent *everywhere* on the island, but prices go up the closer you are to Wittdün and the ferry. (A good price is around DM6 per half-day, DM10 per day.) Amrum's transportation authorities would prefer that cyclists keep off the main road, so two main paths running along either side of the island have been paved. The **green trail** goes through pine forests to the west, while the **yellow trail** rolls through the pastures and villages in the east. The **tourist office** (☎ 940 30; fax 94 03 20), near the ferry, **books rooms** for DM15 per person.

Although Amrum has nearly 1,000 guest beds available, they are almost all full in summer. Adventurers may have some luck in the mornings at the tourist office. The **Jugendherberge Wittdün,** Mittelstr. 1, has large, clean rooms, some with beach views. From the ferry, walk straight away from the boat and turn right onto Mittelstr. Note that *Pensionen* of equivalent price and greater tranquility can be found. If you really want to stay here anyway, you'll need a reservation, unless there's a miracle. (☎ 20 10. Sheets DM7. Reception 7-9am, noon-1pm and 3-10pm. Members only. Open Apr.-Nov. Dorm beds DM24, over 26 DM29, plus *Kurtaxe*.) Restaurants in Wittdün tend to be fairly expensive, but fortunately there are two **SPAR supermarkets** on Hauptstr. (open M-F 9am-6pm, Sa 9am-1pm). The **post office** is on Hauptstr. 30 (open M-F 9am-noon and 2:30-5pm, Sa 9am-noon).

MECKLENBURG-VORPOMMERN

More than 1,700 lakes, the marshy coast of the Baltic Sea, and labyrinthine medieval towns make up the lonely landscape of Mecklenburg-Vorpommern. Once a favored vacation spot for East Germans, this sparsely populated northernmost province of the former GDR retains the sturdy, raw-boned natural beauty of the *Bundesboonies*. Cyclists and hikers flock to Mecklenburg's lakes and Rügen, which offer some of Germany's most spectacular scenery. And as restoration work in the region's main cities continues, dramatic Hanseatic architecture emerges from the rubble. Tourists are again beginning to fill seaside resorts that were the playground of the early 20th-century glitterati, and the area is gradually getting back on its feet. With an unemployment rate hovering around 20%, however, Mecklenburg-Vorpommern's cities remain economically and politically troubled, and the presence of neo-Nazis is, unfortunately, palpable.

Mecklenburg-Vorpommern

HIGHLIGHTS OF MECKLENBURG-VORPOMMERN

Rostock (p. 569), perched on an inlet of the Baltic, is a dynamic and complicated city filled with beautiful architecture and a left-leaning student population.

Swarms of Germans descend upon the island of **Rügen** (p. 576) every summer—and for good reason. The spectacular cliffs and great beaches, some protected by a national park, make for a fantastic getaway.

Unlike many decayed eastern cities, **Schwerin** (p. 564) shines with a fantastic Altstadt and a slew of lush gardens.

SCHWERIN   ☎0385

First recognized in 1018, Schwerin is the grandfather of Mecklenburg-Vorpommern's cities, and with the *Wende*, the city regained its status as capital of the *Land*. Surrounded almost entirely by lakes and largely free of Communist "architectural innovations," Schwerin's Altstadt brims with well-preserved townhouses and remnants of its past life as an elegant spa town. Fueled by the state government and tourists, both German and foreign, seeking refuge from the west's Americanization, every crumbling building is a neighbor to one in the midst of repair. It will only be a few years before visitors will no longer be able to see the old East Germany, as *Der Mauer im Kopf* ("the wall in the head"), a metaphorical description of the East/West divide in mentality, also steadily disappears. A number of galleries and performance spaces house dozens of art festivals and concerts throughout the year, but high culture isn't all the city has to offer. On weekends, the streets fill with chic club-hoppers, making it possible to take in an opera and a rave in the same night (and morning).

🛈 ORIENTATION AND PRACTICAL INFORMATION

Schwerin lies on the Magdeburg-Rostock rail line and is easily accessible from all major cities on the Baltic coast. **Trains** connect Schwerin to **Rostock** (1¼hr., 1 per hr., DM22) and **Lübeck** (1½hr., 1 per hr., DM20). The **tourist office**, Am Markt 1, **books rooms** (DM30-50) for free and has calendars of concerts and openings. From the train station, go right on Grundthalplatz and continue as it turns into Wismarsche Str.; take a left on Arsenal, a right on Mecklenburgstr., and another left on Schmiedestr. (☎592 52 12; fax 55 50 94. Open M-F 10am-6pm, Sa-Su 10am-2pm.) The **Apotheke am Markt,** Puschkinstr. 61, just off Marktpl., has an emergency bell. (☎59 23. Open M-F 8am-6pm, Sa 9am-1pm.) **Schnell & Sauber,** on Pl. der Freiheit, keeps you clean. (Wash 6kg for DM4, soap included. Dry DM0.50 for 12 minutes. Open M-Sa 6am-11pm.) The main **post office** resides at Mecklenburgstr. 6, 19053 Schwerin. From the Markt, go down Schmiedestr. and turn right (open M-F 8am-7pm, Sa 9am-4pm).

🏠 ACCOMMODATIONS AND FOOD

The **Jugendherberge (HI),** Waldschulweg 3, is located south of town in the woods by the lake. From the station, take a right down Wismarschestr. to Marienpl. Take bus #14 to "Jugendherberge," get off at the last stop, and walk to the right, toward the zoo; the hostel is on the left. With Schwerin's increasing popularity, the friendly hostel frequently fills, so phone ahead. (☎/fax 326 00 06. Breakfast included. Sheets DM6. Reception 4-10pm. Curfew 10pm. Dorm beds DM25, over 26 DM30.) The cheapest place to catch a bite to eat is at the **Edeka supermarket,** just off the Markt on Schmiedestr. (open M-F 8am-8pm, Sa 8am-4pm) or at a string of fast food joints in the **Wurm,** a mall on Marienpl. (open M-F 9:30am-8pm, Sa 9:30am-4pm, Su 11am-4pm). The mephistophilean ambiance at **Café Faust,** at (of course) Goethestr. 101, may draw you in; pull up a barstool in the *Gestalt* of a pile of books and drink in the draughts of hell (open daily from 11am). For a less jarring experience, wile away the night at the mustard-yellow **Bernstein Café,** Voßstr. 46, a 10-minute walk

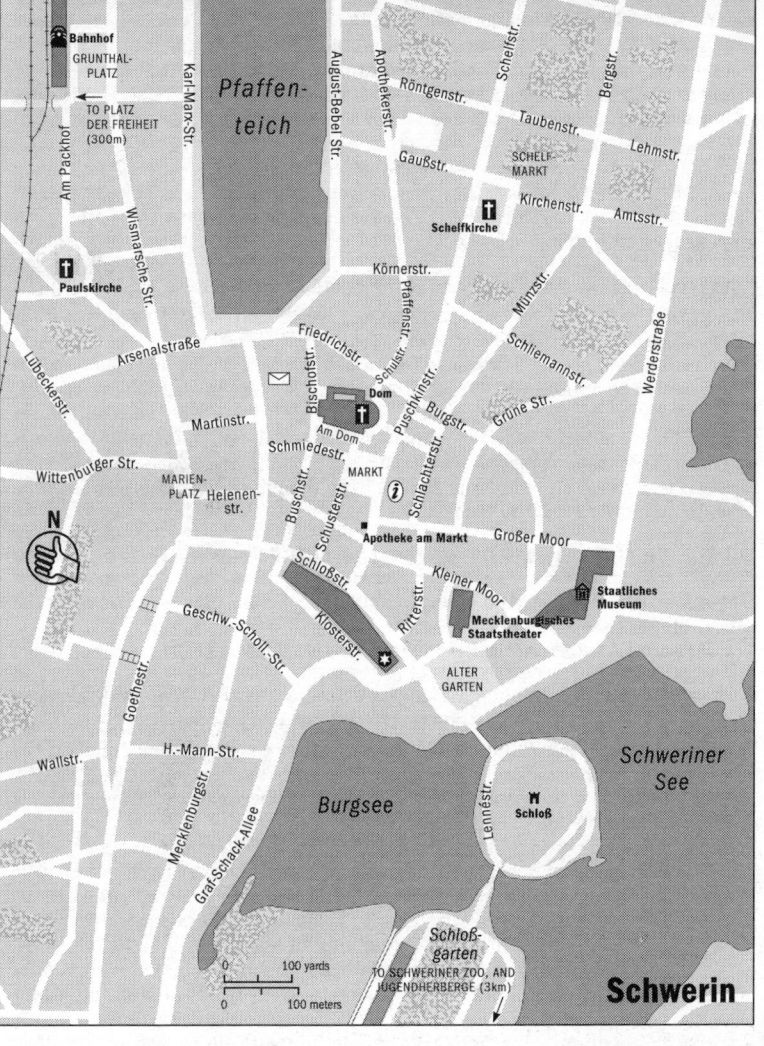

off the beaten path down Wallstr., which serves marvelous coffee and inexpensive but good breakfast. (DM4.50-8.50. Open daily from 9am.) Tucked among Schwerin's medieval back streets hides **Domhof,** Domstr. 6, just of the Markt. Enjoy the traditional side of German dining surrounded by half-timbered houses and a modern art gallery. Entrees DM7-16 (open daily from 11am).

SIGHTS

Schwerin's **Schloß,** located on an island just south of the city center, is everything a castle should be; the building's ridiculous amalgamation of architectural styles is both majestic and gaudy. Begun in the 1500s, additions were made into the 19th century when the castle served as the seat of the dukes of Mecklenburg, who ruled the area until the 1918 upheaval chased the monarch from power. The castle's gilded Baroque cupolas runneth over with luxury—the red

M.-VORPOMMERN

silk wallpaper and mahogany floors pale in comparison to the sumptuous throne room with its gilt and marble columns. (☎ *56 57 58. Open Tu-Su 10am-6pm. DM8, students DM5.)* Across from the Schloß, the **Alter Garten** was the site of mass demonstrations preceding the downfall of the GDR in 1989. Atop a cascade of stairs on the right sits the **Staatliches Museum,** which houses a good collection of 15th- to 19th-century Dutch and German art, including a few works by Rembrandt, Cranach the Elder, and Rubens. *(Open Tu 10am-8pm, W-Su 10am-6pm. DM7, students DM4.)* Looking uphill, the nearest spire belongs to the 13th-century Gothic **Dom.** *(Open M-Sa 10am-5pm, Su noon-5pm. For DM2, sweat your way up the 110m tower. Organ music M at 2:30pm. Free.)* The **Schleswig-Holstein-Haus** generally hosts high-quality art exhibitions. *(Puschkinstr. 12.* ☎ *55 55 27. DM6, students DM4.)* Schwerin's former **synagogue** reposes silently at Schlachterstr. 3, off Marktpl.; the temple was destroyed in a pogrom in 1938. The building formerly housed the region's memorial to its Jewish community, but closed several years ago after an interior looting by local skinheads.

Animals cavort at the **Schweriner Zoo,** which borders the hostel adjoining the **Fauler See.** (☎ *39 55 10; fax 395 51 30. Open Apr.-Sept. M-F 9am-5pm, Sa-Su 9am-6pm; Oct.-Mar. daily 10am-4pm. DM9, students and children DM5.)* The zoo specializes in water fowl, but it has its share of ferocious mammals. Another option for nature lovers is the reserve on **Kaninchenwerder** island set in the Schweriner See. In summer, **ferries** leave at least once an hour from the docks to the left of the Schloß to visit the island's rabbits *(one-way DM9, children DM2.50).*

🎵📺 ENTERTAINMENT AND NIGHTLIFE

The striking cream-pillared building next door to the museum (see above) is the **Mecklenburgisches Staatstheater Schwerin,** currently in the midst of a dramatic revival (☎ 53 00 01 23. call for ticket service). **Kultursommer '01,** available from the tourist office for free, has lists of both public sculptures and theatrical performances. Tickets for most shows can be bought through **Ticketservice Behnke,** in the tourist office. (☎ 56 05 00. Open M-F 10am-6pm, Sa 10am-noon.) Schwerin's best sights often double as performance spaces; each summer, the steps of the museum are converted into an opera stage, and in the nearby Schloß, the throne room is a grand venue for monthly concerts (DM50, students DM35). The **Schelfstadt** neighborhood houses a number of galleries and performance spaces; everything from literary readings to folk music concerts takes place in **Der Speicher,** Röntgenstr. 22, entrance on Schelfstr. (☎ 56 05 00). The **Kammerkino,** Röntgenstr. 12 (☎ 55 50 78), around the corner, shows international independent films. Loud crowds flock to **Louis,** Wittenburger Str. 50, where frequent live bands keep the party going into the early morning. (☎ 758 84 84. Open Th-Sa from 9pm.) For those who get tired, respite can be found next door at **Pub-Pela;** the music is only a few decibels quieter, but chairs and tables replace sweaty dancing bodies. Discotheques are starting to bloom along Arsenalstr., beginning by the Markt and ending with **Unity,** Arsenalstr. 35, a brand-new student club (open daily at 6pm).

MECKLENBURGISCHE SEENPLATTE (MECKLENBURG LAKE PLAIN)

When things got hectic in Berlin, Bismarck often found refuge among the reserved but sincere folk of the Mecklenburgische Seenplatte. The reminders of the GDR are not as obvious here as in other regions of Eastern Germany, perhaps because the Socialist-era architects were wise enough to leave the forests and hills alone. A popular vacation area for the last century, the Seenplatte attracts plenty of summer crowds; consider advance reservations.

M.-VORPOMMERN

WAREN
☎ 03991

Conveniently located within an hour of Rostock and two hours of Berlin, Waren is the gateway to the ■ **Müritz National Park.** The park, located on the northeastern shore of the Müritz, Germany's largest freshwater lake, offers a unique combination of deep dark forest and marshland inhabited by rare birds. Visitors can best appreciate the park by taking a small-group tour, arranged at the tourist office, by purchasing the **Müritz-Nationalpark-Ticket,** which is good for a day of travel on a combination of bus, rail, and ferry connections (DM10-30, students DM5-18), or by bike following Eichhofstr. east.

☐ GETTING THERE. Waren is easily reached from **Rostock** (1hr., every 2hr., DM22); **Berlin** (1¾hr., every 2hr., DM51); and **Güstrow** (30min., 1 per hr., DM15). **Warener Schiffahrtsgesellschaft,** Am Stadthafen (☎ 12 56 24; fax 12 56 93), and **Müritzwind Personenschiffahrt,** Strandstr. (☎ 66 66 64; fax 66 58 79), both offer **boat tours** of the Müritz lake that vary in length from one to four hours (DM7-22, children half-price). Rent **bikes** around the corner from the train station at **Bureau Mobil,** Lloydstr. 2b. (☎ 73 25 50. Open M-F 9am-6pm, Sa 9am-noon. DM10 per day.)

☑ PRACTICAL INFORMATION. **Waren Information,** Neuer Markt am Stadthafen, in the town square, has maps of the park and brochures and finds **rooms** (DM30) for a DM5 fee. The office runs both park and town **tours** in German. (M, W, and F 10am; Sa-Su 11am. DM5, students DM3.) From the train station, turn right onto the footpath and follow it across the footbridge over Schweriner Damm; go left on Friedenstr. and left again on Lange Str. (☎ 66 61 83; fax 66 43 30. Open Apr.-Oct. daily 9am-8pm; Nov.-Mar. M-F 10am-4pm.) A **pharmacy, Fontane-Apotheke,** Lange Str. 55, keeps you fit. (☎ 642 70. Open M-F 8am-6pm, Sa 8am-12:15pm.) The **post office,** Neuen Markt 19, 17192 Waren, is also in the central market (open M-F 9am-5:30pm, Sa 9am-noon).

▐▞ ACCOMMODATIONS AND FOOD. The **Jugendherberge (HI),** Auf dem Nesselberg 2, is in the woods south of town. From the station's Schweriner Damm exit, go left on Schweriner Damm, bear right at the fork in the road, and then walk along the harbor down the successive streets Zur Steinmole, Strandstr., Müritzstr., and Am Seeufer. When you reach the wooded hill on the left, head up the stairs and to the right (25min.). Or walk 100m to the left as you leave the train station and take bus #3 (direction: "Ecktannen") to "Wasserwerk." The 60 beds book quickly, but the hostel boasts a lovely location, and the friendly management will set up tents outside if they're full. (☎/fax 66 76 06. Breakfast DM7. Sheets DM7. Reception 4-6pm and 8pm, or ring the bell. Members only. Dorm beds DM17, over 26 DM22.) There is camping at **Azur,** on Fontanestr. Follow the directions to the youth hostel (above), but keep going on Am Seeufer until you reach Fontanestr. 10min. past the hostel. Or take bus #3 or 5 (direction: "Ecktannen") to the last stop. (☎ 26 07. DM6 per person, DM3 per tent.) The **City Ristorante,** Friedenstr. 8, offers everything from pizzas (DM5-12) to *schnitzel* (DM9). (☎ 66 87 03. Open daily 10am-11pm.) A **Spar supermarket** is at Neuer Markt 23 (open M-F 8am-8pm, Sa 8am-2pm).

▣ SIGHTS. Since Waren's primary attractions are nature-related, it's not surprising that restoration of the Altstadt is not a top priority. Sitting on the quiet **Alter Markt,** the weather-beaten 14th-century **Altes Rathaus,** the 290-year-old **Altes Schulhaus** (old schoolhouse) and the **Alte Feuerwasche** (old fire station), have all seen better days. The Alte Feuerwasche, however, now holds an **internet cafe** and youth center *(open M-F 2-9pm).* Next door, the **Georgenkirche** lost its roof to fire in 1699 and received only a modest, flat replacement. The **Müritz Museum,** on Friedensstr., holds a modest **aquarium** and **aviary.** *(Open Mar.-Sept. Tu-F 9am-6pm, Sa-Su 9am-5pm; Oct.-Apr. Tu-F 10am-4pm, Sa-Su 10am-noon and 2-5pm. DM5, students DM3.)*

M.–VORPOMMERN

GÜSTROW
☎ 03843

Were it not home to a huge collection of works by the prolific 20th-century artist Ernst Barlach, Güstrow would be like most of Mecklenburg-Vorpommern's towns: a mass of crumbling buildings with satellite dishes and *Imbiße* poking out of the brickwork. A model city for Germany's EXPO 2000 urban renewal project, Güstrow has begun pulling itself out of its decrepit state. In addition to filling the city with pacifist sculptures, Barlach fiercely opposed German nationalism and fascism, causing the Nazis to condemn his work as *Entartete Kunst* (degenerate art). Güstrow is also the hometown of Uwe Johnson, a GDR author subjected to constant surveillance and forced into exile in 1959 for "subversive" writings that criticized the divisions between East and West—at this time the town's only monument to the author is a street that bears his name.

◪ **PRACTICAL INFORMATION.** Central Güstrow lies south of the train station. To get there, follow Eisenbahnstr. until it becomes Lindenstr., then go about 45m farther on Lindenstr. before turning left onto Pferdemarkt. Güstrow is connected to **Rostock** (45min., 1 per hr., DM12) and **Waren** (30min., 1 per hr., DM15). **Fahrrad Dräger**, Langestr. 49, rents **bikes** for DM10 per day. (☎ 68 40 10. Open M-F 9am-noon and 1-6pm, Sa 9am-noon.) **Güstrow Information,** Domstr. 9, finds **rooms** (DM30 and up) for a DM5 fee. (☎ 68 10 23; fax 68 20 79. Open Mar.-Sept. M-F 9am-6pm, Sa-Su 9:30am-1pm; Oct.-Apr. closed Su.) The office offers city **tours** that leave from Franz-Parr-Pl. daily at 11am. (May-Oct. DM4, students DM2.) Do laundry at **SB Waschsalon,** Pferdemarkt 35. (Wash DM6, dry DM2. Open 7am-10pm.) The **post office** is at Pferdemarkt 52 (open M-F 8am-6pm, Sa 9am-noon). The **postal code** is 18271. **Internet** access is available at **Lenny's Computer,** Greviner Str. 23, 30min for DM4. Open M-F 10am-1pm and 2-6pm, Sa 9:30am-1pm.

▛▛ **ACCOMMODATIONS AND FOOD.** Güstrow's cute but distant **Jugendherberge (HI),** Heidberg 33, is 4km from town, and serviced by bus #224, which runs only 5 times a day. Take the same route as to the Barlach Atelierhaus (see **Sights,** below); stay on the path until it hits Heidberg and bear left. (☎ 84 00 44. Breakfast included. Curfew 10pm. DM28, over 26 DM34) Also consider using the room-finding service at the tourist office (☎ 84 00 44). **Café Küpper,** on Domstr., serves sweets, pizza (DM7) and an extensive breakfast for DM5 (open M-F 8am-6:30pm, Sa and Su 1-6pm).

◩ **SIGHTS.** The Barlach tour of Güstrow begins on the southwest side of town with the **Dom,** which houses Barlach's most famous work, *Der Schwebende Engel* (The Hovering Angel). Created as a testament to the horrors of war, the angel was originally designed to hang above the pews of the Dom but is now tucked away in a corner. The statue was originally cast in 1926, but was then publicly melted down and made into bullets by the Nazis in 1941. After WWII, a plaster cast of the statue was found buried in West Germany, and, in 1952, the angel was restored and rededicated to the war's victims. *(Open M-Sa 10am-5pm, Su 2-4pm.)*

Walking back to Domstr., the recently renovated **Schloß** towers ahead. A grand example of Renaissance architecture, it is complete with a cute **Schloßgarten** surrounded by an ingenious shrub wall, gates and windows included. The **Schloßmuseum** is proud of its works by Barlach. (☎ 75 20. Open Apr.-Oct. Tu-Su 9am-5pm; Nov.-Mar. Tu-Su 10am-5pm. DM6, students DM2.) On the west side of town, the **Gertrudenkapelle** houses a collection of Barlachs in an octagonal white chapel and peaceful garden. *(Gertrudenpl. 1.* ☎ 68 30 01. Open Mar.-Oct. Tu-Su 10am-5pm; Nov.-Feb. Tu-Su 11am-4pm. DM3, students DM2.) The only church in town neglecting Barlach is the **Pfarrkirche St. Marien.** Although sitting in the shadow of the Dom, the church outshines its neighbor with an imposing organ, a recently restored altarpiece from 1522, and over 180 sculpted figures by Brussels artist Jan Borman. Organ music echoes in the church on Wednesdays at 12:15pm. *(Open M-F 10am-5pm, Sa 10am-4pm.)*

Barlach's **Atelierhaus** (studio) hosts the largest collection of his works, in the house in which they were created. Though its setting is beautiful, Barlach was never happy working here, and the studio was functional for only a few years. *(Heidberg 15. It's a one-hour walk from the Altstadt, and bus #4a comes here only every three to four hours. Renting a bike is the best way to visit. Head down Greviner Str. from the Marktpl. and follow it as it turns into Plauer Str. until you see the "Barlachweg" signs. Follow this path around the lake past the grassy beach; continue 100m through the woods and the museum will be on the left. ☎ 822 99. Open Tu-Su 10am-5pm.)*

ROSTOCK   ☎ 0381

Construction workers are carefully removing the scaffolding that had enveloped Rostock, revealing a fresh face. The new look of the city's center signals a rebirth; Rostock is now poised to regain much of the prosperity that it formerly held as the GDR's largest port. The familiar energy in the deep water docks, a growing university and beaches a streetcar ride away are responsible for the massive amount of reconstruction and the droves of people crowding the pedestrian shopping zone. This modern picture of Rostock shows how much the scars of 1992 have healed. On August 24 of that year, a hostel for foreigners seeking political asylum in Germany was attacked and set ablaze by neo-nazi youths. Today, however, the neo-nazi presence is almost invisible, except in parts of the suburbs—it is the left-leaning student population that takes center stage. Tourists on the way to the beach—or Scandinavia—pause in Rostock for the 12th-century buildings, lively nightlife, and cosmopolitan feel.

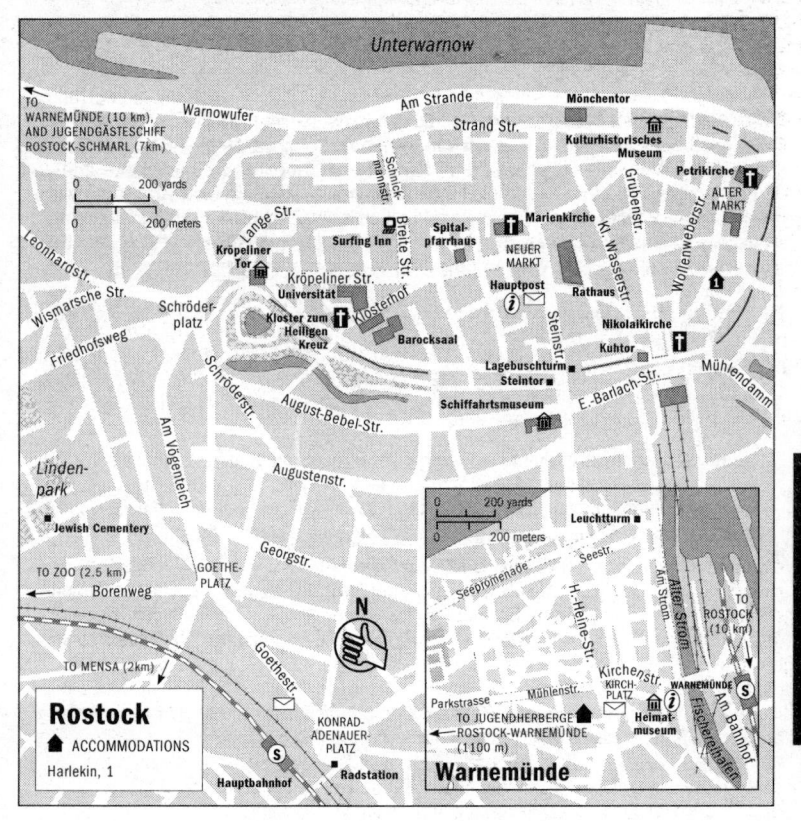

▌ GETTING THERE AND GETTING AROUND

Trains: Call ☎ 493 44 54 for information. Hourly connections to **Schwerin** (1hr., DM22.20); **Stralsund** (1½hr., DM19.40); and **Wismar** (1¼hr., DM22.20). Numerous daily connections to **Berlin** (2½hr., DM65); **Hamburg** (3hr., DM76.20); and **Dresden** (7hr., DM118).

Public Transportation: Streetcars #11 and 12 shuttle from the main station to the Altstadt. A single ticket is DM2.20, but the *Tageskarte*, a one-day ticket for streetcar, bus, and S-Bahn, is worth it at DM4.50, for traveling around the city center. The S-Bahn leaves from the main station for Warnemünde and the suburbs every 15min. To get to the **bus station** for lines to smaller towns, leave the train station through the Südstadt exit. Bus service thins out at night, leaving only the *Fledermaus* (bat) buses connecting a few central stops. Late night buses bear blue circles with pictures of bats on them.

Ferries: Boats for **Scandinavia** leave from the **Überseehafen** docks. **TT-Linie,** Hansakai (☎ 67 07 90; fax 670 79 80) runs to **Trelleborg, Sweden** (5hr., 6 per day; one-way DM50, students and children DM25). **Scandlines Europa GT Links** (☎ 34 34 35; fax 670 66 71) sails to **Gedser, Denmark** (2hr., 8 per day. One-way DM8 Th-Su, DM5 M-Th, children DM2.50).

Bike Rental: Radstation (☎ 240 11 53), on your right by the train station. DM12 per day, DM8 per day for 5+ days. ID required. Open M-F 10am-6pm, Sa 10am-1pm.

▌ ORIENTATION AND PRACTICAL INFORMATION

The majority of Rostock's sights lie in the downtown area, with the exception of **Warnemünde,** a peaceful fishing village and resort town to the northwest. The city's suburbs consist of huge brick-and-concrete apartment blocks linked by long, wide roads. These areas are not well lit, and local thugs have been known to be hostile toward foreigners. **Single travelers, particularly women, should avoid these areas at night.** Rostock is served by an extensive network of S-Bahn trains, buses, and trams; they run less frequently during the late hours and at night, so check schedules before you set out.

Tourist Office: Neuer Markt 3 (☎ 194 33; fax 38 12 601). From the train station, take streetcar #11 or 12 to "Steintor.," in the same building as the post office. *Zimmervermittlung* finds **rooms** (DM30-40) for free. Staff leads 1½hr. **tours** in German through the town (May-June and Sept. W and F-Su at 2pm. DM7, children under 12 free). Open M-F 10am- 7pm, Sa-Su 10am-4pm. Oct.-Apr. closed two hours earlier on weekdays.

Currency Exchange: Citibank, on Kröpeliner Str. near Universitätspl., charges DM5 for exchanging cash. **24hr. ATM.** Open M-F 9am-1pm and M, Tu, Th 2-6pm, F 2-5pm. **Deutsche Bank,** Kröpeliner Str. 84, exchanges cash without a fee and travelers checks for a DM5 fee. Open M, T, Th 9am-6pm, W 9am-1pm, F 9am-3pm.

Emergency: Police, ☎ 110. **Ambulance and Fire,** ☎ 112.

Gay and Lesbian Resources: rat + tat, Leonhardstr. 20 (☎ 45 31 56). Open M 10am-1pm and 3-5pm, Tu and Th 2-6pm.

Pharmacy: Rats-Apotheke, Neuer Markt 13 (☎ 493 47 47). Open M-F 8am-7pm, Sa 8am-1pm.

Post Office: Hauptpostamt, Neuer Markt, 18055 Rostock. Open M-F 8am-6pm, Sa 8am-1pm.

Internet: Surfing 'inn, on the third floor of the **Galleria Kaufhof** on Lange Str. 30min for DM3. Open M-F 9am-8pm, Sa 9am-6pm.

ACCOMMODATIONS

Because both of Rostock's hostels are quite far from town and in somewhat dangerous neighborhoods, your best bet is the tourist office.

Jugendherberge Rostock-Warnemünde (HI), Parkstr. 46 (☎54 81 70; email JH.Warne@t-online.de). Provides spacious, clean rooms and ping pong. Take the S-Bahn (direction: "Warnemünde") to the end, cross the bridge, and head straight on Kirchenstr. as it becomes Mühlenstr. and then Parkstr., a 20-25min. journey. Or ride the S-Bahn to "Warnemünde Werft" and then bus #36 (direction: "Warnemünde-Strand") to "Parkstr." Breakfast included. Sheets DM7, dinner DM8. Reception 8-9am, 2:30-5pm, and 7-10pm. Curfew 10pm, but you can ring the bell until 11pm. Doubles DM25.50, over 26 DM30.50.

Jugendgästeschiff Rostock-Schmarl (☎71 62 24; fax 71 40 14). Past travelers have complained of harassment by aggressive hooligans while walking to the hostel, but once inside, the kind staff will guide you around their hostel-boat-museum-bar. Take the S-Bahn (direction: "Warnemünde") to "Lütten Klein," then bus #35 (direction: "Schmarl Fähre") to the end. Follow the buoy-lined street to the *Traditionsschiff;* reception is on the 2nd fl. Unfortunately, the last #35 bus through the dangerous harbor area imposes an 8pm curfew. Breakfast and sheets included. Dorm beds DM27.50, over 26 DM34.

Harlekin, Lohgerberstr. 37 (☎454 99 11; fax. 454 99 12). Some of the cheapest rooms to be found in the Altstadt. This modern pension also houses a **gay bar** and restaurant. From the station, take streetcar #4 to "Gerberbruch", then walk up the hill to Lohgerberstr. Breakfast included. Restaurant open 11am-2pm and 6-11pm, bar from 8pm until the party ends. Rooms DM60-100.

FOOD

While no one will ever accuse Rostock of being a gastronome's heaven, eating here doesn't necessarily mean chowing on *ein Whopper* and *Pommes Frites*. **Neue Markt,** on Seinstr. across from the Rathaus, sprouts into a small market of fruits and vegetables and various roasted meats (open M-F 8am-5pm, Sa 8am-1pm), while the bakeries on Kröpeliner Str. offer an array of cheap sandwiches and pastries. In **Warnemünde,** several restaurants along the beach fish up the bounties of the sea.

Mensa, on the corner of Südring and Albert-Einstein-Str. From the train station or the Altstadt, streetcar #11 (direction: "Neuer Friedhof") to the end and bus #89 or 39 (direction: "Stadthalle/ZOB") to "Mensa" (one stop). Or take bus #26 from the train station (direction: "Mensa") to the end. In the new building, students load their trays; a full meal will run about DM8. Open M-F 8am-2:30pm. Opposite the Mensa entrance, a bulletin board advertises all major parties and club shows, while on weekends the *Mensa* holds what students claim is the best **disco** in Rostock. Open Th-Su after 10pm. Call ☎459 12 48 for the program. Cover DM5 and up.

Gorki Park, Margaretenpl., by the Lindenpark (☎203 68 95). Gorki Park succeeds where the communist experiment failed: great food and drawings of nudes on the walls. A *soviet* for students and professors alike. Entrees DM7-14; try the micro-brewed Rote Oktober DM5. Open daily noon-3am.

Café 28, Mühlenstr. 28 (☎524 67), in Warnemünde on the way to the hostel, is a shiny, happy hangout. Soups, salads, and small but tasty dishes run DM6-16. Open May-Oct. M-F noon-late, Sa-Su 10am-late.

🔍 SIGHTS

MARIENKIRCHE. This 13th-century beast of a brick basilica is near the main square at the Steintor end of Kröpeliner Str. In the final days of the 1989 turmoil, the services here overflowed with political protesters who came to hear the inspiring sermons of Pastor Joachim Gauck. In one of his more heroic gestures, Pastor Gauck began to publicly chastise the secret police by calling out the names of those *Stasi* members he could identify from the pulpit. After reunification, Gauck was entrusted with the difficult job of overseeing the fate of the *Stasi* archives. The confusing 12m **astronomical clock** dates from 1472. At noon and midnight, mechanical apostles strut in a circular procession, but only 11 make it inside before the door closes. *(Open M-Sa 10am-5pm, Su 11am-noon. DM2 donation requested.)*

KRÖPELINER STRAßE. Relics of Rostock's past as a center of Hanseatic trade still stand. Although half of the city was destroyed in WWII, many of the half-timbered and glazed-brick houses have been restored. Kröpeliner Str. (or simply "Kröpe"), the main pedestrian mall, runs east to the sturdy 12th century Kröpeliner Tor, the former town gate. The main buildings of the Universität Rostock, one of the oldest universities in North Central Europe, are near the middle of Kröpeliner Str. Next to the university, along the remains of the city wall, sits the **Kloster zum heiligen Kreuz,** a restored cloister which was originally built by the Danish Queen Margaret in 1270. The museum contains medieval art, sculptures by the omnipresent Ernst Barlach, and special exhibits. *(Open Tu-Su 10am-5pm. DM6, students DM2.)*

RATHAUS. A strawberry-pink wedding cake of a building, now in the midst of restoration, the town hall on the Neuer Markt was originally composed of three separate *Bürger* houses united by a Gothic wall with seven towers; elaborate detailing can still be seen above some of the portals. The Steintor, Kuhtor, and Lagesbuschturm sit in close proximity to Steinstr., connected by remnants of the recently renovated town wall.

ALTER MARKT. Rostock's pre-war commercial center is now almost completely restored, as is the 13th century church. Strike a Quasimodo pose as you ascend the reconstructed tower of the **Petrikirche,** from which you can see all of Rostock, including the ominous cooling towers of its nuclear power plant. *(Open M-F 9am-noon and 2-5pm, Sa-Su 11am-5pm. Tower DM3.50.)*

ZOO. Rostock's stunning zoo housed some of its animals in public offices during the war; the apes were guests of the police station. Now the extensive collection of animals lives on its own land. *(Take streetcar #11 (direction: "Neuer Friedhof") to "Zoo." Open Apr.-Oct. daily 9am-7pm, Nov.-Mar. 9am-5pm. DM12, students and children DM6.)*

SCHIFFAHRTMUSEUM DER HANSESTADT. Displays tell tales of wild seafaring along the rocky Baltic coast. Amused guards look on as visitors try to copy ship knots at a hands-on exhibit. *(August-Bebel-Str. 1. Take streetcar #11 to "Steintor." ☎ 492 26 97. Open Tu-Su 10am-6pm. DM6, students DM2.)*

JEWISH ROSTOCK. Rostock was once home to a substantial Jewish population; little remains, however, of Rostock's Jewish community. The SA razed the synagogue on Augustenstr., and the SS began the deportations soon after. Only partially destroyed in the war, the **Jewish cemetery** still stands. In the 1970s, the government decided to embed the gravestones face-down in the earth to create the city's **Lindenpark.** Pressure from the international Jewish community forced the city to right most of the stones and add a memorial in 1988. *(Take streetcar #1, 3, or 11 to "Saarpl.," then go south through the park.)*

WARNEMÜNDE. To the north of Rostock and accessible by S-Bahn lies the beach town **Warnemünde.** The **Alter Strom** (old harbor), across the bridge from the train station, rings with the sounds of fishing boats, fish hawkers, and the shattering of teeth on rock candy. Warnemünde's sunny beach stretches far into the distance; walk long enough, and you can bare all (look for *FKK* signs at beach entrances). Near the Alter Strom toward the sea stands a **lighthouse** whose 30m tower can be scaled (DM3). For a comprehensive survey of those tiny, colorful *Pfister* houses, visit Warnemünde's **Heimatmuseum,** Alexandrinerstr. 31, just off the Kirchenpl. *(Open W-F 10am-6pm, Sa-Su 10am-8pm. DM6, students DM2.)* The first full week in July is the city festival of **Warnemünde Woche.**

 **NIGHTLIFE**

At night, Rostock's student population of about 10,000 comes out to play, congregating along Kröpeliner Str. and around Wismarische Str. and Barnstorfer Weg. Check out *Rostock Szene,* which lists local clubs and performances, and *Nordost Eventguide,* a chic little booklet that covers clubs in all of Mecklenburg-Vorpommern. Both are available at the tourist office for free.

Studentenkeller (☎ 45 59 28), through the big yellow building on Universitätspl. *The* night-time destination of Rostock's students. Four rooms and an outdoor patio packed with Euro fashion, cell phones, and fluorescent hair. Open M-Sa 10pm-late.

Spiecher, Am Strande 3A (☎ 492 30 31), has it all: a cool venue and a rip-roaring good time. In an old warehouse on the shore, one of the few discotheques near the Altstadt. Times vary, check the graffiti-painted announcement by the door.

La Lupina, Leonhardstr. 20 (☎ 459 14 07), is a sleek bar with an alternative clientele and drink menu. Wear black. Open daily 7pm-2am.

Central, Leonhardstr. 22 (☎ 490 46 48), next door, hops with a twenty-something crowd that spills out into the street. Open M-Sa 2:30pm-2am, Su 10am-2am.

Mephisto, Seestr. 16 in Warnemünde, is where vacationing students satisfy their need for drink and music; stick around long enough and you might get breakfast (DM6). Open W-Su 7pm-late.

Harlekin, see "Accommodations," above.

STRALSUND ☎ 03831

Albrecht von Wallenstein, commander of the Catholic army during the Thirty Years War, lusted after Stralsund. "Even if it were chained to heaven, I'd want to have it," he panted; yet Stralsund resisted his advances. After years of neglect, the city is gradually regaining its former beauty. The GDR years spent little money on Stralsund, causing priceless 13th-century buildings to fall into decay, but also preserving its skyline almost exactly as it appeared in 1293, when it helped to found the **Hanseatic League** (see p. 8) and asserted itself as a trading and shipbuilding center. Today the key to Stralsund's charm is its unique geography; the hill of the Altstadt is bordered to the south and west by two natural ponds and slopes gently north toward the **Strelasund,** the strait that separates **Rügen** from the mainland.

✦ ❷ ORIENTATION AND PRACTICAL INFORMATION

Stralsund's major sights and attractions are concentrated in the **Altstadt,** where the distinctive spires of the city's three churches make excellent navigational beacons. **Ossenreyerstr.,** which runs north-south, is the main pedestrian zone. Two of the city's gates, the **Kutertor** and the **Kniepertor,** sit to the west and north, respectively. The train station is across the bridge, down the street from the Kutertor.

Trains: Stralsund is connected to **Rostock** (1hr., 1 per hr., DM 20.20), and hourly to **Binz** and **Saßnitz** on Rügen (both about 1hr, DM15.40); several trains also leave daily for **Berlin** (3½hr., DM68) and **Hamburg** (4hr., DM73.20).

Buses: Intercity buses depart from **Frankenwall,** south of the train station.

Public Transportation: Bus lines #1-6 circle the Altstadt, serving the outskirts of town. Single ride DM2.50; day pass DM5.

Ferries: Reederei Hiddensee (☎(0180) 321 21 50) runs 3 times per day to the ports of Kloster, Vitte, and Neuendorf on Hiddensee (round-trip DM24-26, children DM13-15, bikes DM10) and to Schaprode on Rügen's west coast (DM7, children DM3.50).

Bike Rental: ☎28 01 55. At the service desk in the train station. DM10 per day. Open M-F 6am-9pm, Sa 7am-2:30pm, Su 9am-4:30pm.

Tourist Office: Stralsund Information, Alter Markt 9 (☎246 90; fax 24 69 49; e-mail INFO-HST@t-online.de). From the station, head straight on Jungfernstieg, turn right onto the path at the intersection about 300m from the train station to trans-verse Knieper Teich; continue straight through the Kütertor, and turn left on Ossen-reyerstr. Or take bus #4 or 5 to "Kütertor." The office distributes free maps, finds **private rooms** (DM25-100) for a DM5 fee, and sells tickets for **tours** through the Altstadt (DM7). They also offer a **tourist coupon** (DM1) that reduces admission prices for most of the city's sights and museums. Open June-Sept. M-F 9am-7pm, Sa 9am-2pm, Su 10am-2pm; Oct.-May M-F 10am-6pm, Sa 10am-2pm.

Women's Resources: Frauen in Not (☎29 51 12). 24hr. hotline.

Pharmacy: Bahnhofsapotheke, Tribseer Damm 6 (☎29 23 28), by the train station. Open M-F 8am-6pm, Sa 8am-noon.

Emergency: Police, ☎110. **Fire** and **Ambulance,** ☎112.

Post Office: Neuer Markt, 18439 Stralsund, in the red-brick building opposite the Marienkirche. Open M-F 9am-6pm, Sa noon.

Internet Access: Future, Langenstr. 64. 15min DM3. Open daily 1pm-midnight.

▐ ACCOMMODATIONS

Jugendherberge Stralsund (HI), Am Kütertor 1 (☎29 21 60; fax 29 76 76). The hostel is a gorgeous 15min. walk from the train station. Follow the directions to the tourist office, but stop at Kütertor; the hostel shares a wall with the *Tor.* Located in a 17th-cen-tury town hall with a courtyard, the hostel is convenient, but watch those low ceilings. Many school groups in summer. Breakfast buffet included. Sheets DM7. Reception 7-9am and 3-10pm. Lockout 9am-3pm. Curfew 10pm, but you can ring the bell until 1am. Dorm beds DM25, over 26 DM30.

Jugendherberge Stralsund-Devin (HI), Strandstr. 21 (☎49 02 89). From the station, take bus #3 to "Devin" (25min., DM2.50), then walk straight into the woods. Take the trail on the left side of the dreary-looking *Kurhaus-Devin,* and turn left when you hit Strandstr. (5min.). Located in the nearby village of Devin, this hostel is bigger than the one in Stralsund, but much harder to reach. The 20 buildings are close to the beach. Breakfast included. Sheets DM7. Bike rentals to guests DM10 per day. Reception 7:30am-10:30pm. Curfew 10:30pm. Open Mar.-Oct. Dorm beds DM28, over 26 DM33.

FOOD

Large portions and decent prices rarely keep company in Stralsund these days; even supermarket bills are pretty steep. Stock up on **groceries** at **Lebensmittel-Feinkost,** Ossenreyerstr. 49, in the Ost-West Passage (open M-F 8am-7pm, Sa 8am-6pm). Or indulge in cake and coffee at **Stadtbäckerei und Café,** Ossenreyerstr. 43. (☎29 40 82. Open M-F 8am-6pm, Sa 8am-5pm.)

Al Porto, Seestr. 14 (☎28 06 20). Stralsund's beautiful people get their noodle fix at this mildly pretentious harbor restaurant and cafe. While much of the food is on the more expensive side, the pizza is decently priced (DM10-15). Open daily 11am-11pm.

Galerie Café, Badenstr. 44 (☎29 07 65), serves artistic food as well as a new vegetarian dish every day (DM5-10). The selection of international magazines is even greater than the selection of coffees. Open M-F 10am-7pm, Sa 2-7pm.

Hansekeller, Mönchstr. 48 (☎ 70 38 40), occupies a Renaissance basement where customers down *Wurst* and guzzle *Bier* (DM7-25). Come hungry. Open 11am-midnight.

Essbar, Kleinschmeidstr. 22 (☎29 81 76), has a small Italian-French menu, and is a hangout for artists after the theater. Entrees around DM16. Open 5:30pm-midnight.

Speicher-Café, Katherinenburg 34 (☎29 70 93), is the local teen hangout by day, and a club by night. Special dance parties a couple times each month. Open 11am-late.

SIGHTS

■**DEUTSCHES MUSEUM FÜR MEERESKUNDE UND FISCHEREI.** Between the Alter and Neuer Markt, Stralsund's two major museums have replaced the monks in the *Kirche* and adjoining buildings of the **St. Katharinen** monastery. A good way to use the tourist coupon is to visit the most popular museum in northern Germany, which contains a shark tank, the mandatory diagrams of Baltic fishing, and footage of a live "fossil fish." Bring a camera, as the gift shop doesn't sell any postcards of the five-foot-long whale penis on display. *(On the corner of Monchstr. and Bielkenhagen. ☎265 00. Open May-June daily 10am-5pm; July-Aug. daily 9am-6pm; Nov.-Apr. Tu-Su 10am-5pm. DM7, students DM3.50.)*

ALTER MARKT. Stralsund's compact Altstadt island is free of GDR-era architecture. The Alter Markt, to the north, is surrounded by several of the town's oldest buildings. The remarkably well-preserved 14th-century red-brick facade of the Gothic **Rathaus** displays the coats-of-arms of the other major players in the Hanseatic League, as well as Stralsund's trademark green and gold 12-point stars. From the early 15th century, **St. Nikolaikirche,** behind the Rathaus, is the oldest church in town. Its twin towers are reminiscent of Lübeck's Marienkirche, even though one is missing a capping spire. *(Open M-Sa 10am-5pm, Su 2-4pm.)*

NEUER MARKT. After the wealthier half of Stralsund built their church, merchants from the other side of the tracks responded by erecting the Gothic **Marienkirche** on Neuer Markt. The church houses a rare mid-17th-century Stellwagen organ as well as a rather phallic Soviet memorial in the front yard. Climb the church tower for the best view of Stralsund. Getting to the top is an adventure; after climbing the narrow, winding staircase, you have to ascend the last 150 feet on a ladder. *(Open daily 10am-5pm. Tower DM3.)*

M.-VORPOMMERN

ST. JAKOBI. The third of Stralsund's monumental churches, on Böttcherstr., was heavily damaged in 1944 and further harmed during GDR days. Its organ's pipes were removed and used as rain gutters; the church is currently being restored.

JOHANNISKLOSTER. An alternate route from the Alter Markt follows Külpstr. to Schillstr., ending at the Johanniskloster, a Franciscan monastery built in 1254—45 years after St. Francis of Assisi founded the order. The monastery is down by the harbor and is a glory of Gothic hallways, 14th-century mosaics, murals (rescued from 30 layers of peeling paint), roses, and red-brick walls. Next to the monastery is the former **Johanniskirche;** ruined in 1944, it now hosts occasional open-air concerts and theater. *(Monastery open W-Su 10am-6pm. DM4, students DM3, including a tour; free last Wednesday of every month.)* The quiet court-yard contains a dramatic Ernst Barlach *pietà*, as well as a **memorial** to Stral-sund's lost Jewish community. The memorial used to sit on the Apollonienmarkt, near the former site of the synagogue, but was placed in the cloister after it was vandalized by neo-Nazis in 1992; graffiti marks still remain *(courtyard free.)*

OTHER SIGHTS. A stroll along the **Sundpromenade** at sunset reveals the rolling green hills of Rügen across the bay. Another beautiful walk runs along **Knieperwall,** the **Knieperteich** (pond), and the remains of the **town wall.** The **Knieper Tor** and **Küter Tor** date back to the 13th century.

RÜGEN

Bathing in the Baltic Sea northeast of Stralsund, Germany's largest island offers a varied landscape of white beaches, rugged chalk cliffs, farmland, beech forests, heaths, and swamps. Stone Age ruins and megalithic graves (easily identified piles of stones) are scattered about like enormous paperweights. Teutonic tribes were pushed out by Slavs during migrations in the 5th century; 500 years later, the rule of the pagan inhabitants was broken by invading Danes, who in turn converted the not-so-eager Slavs to Christianity. In the 19th century, it was the nobility who invaded the island, transforming Rügen into a resort stacked with ritzy Neoclassical villas that are today slowly being renovated after decades of neglect.

Today, the tourist industry in Rügen is treading water. Once the prime getaway for east Germans, tourism has decreased somewhat as former GDR residents explore western Germany's vacation spots. Still, summer months are busy. *Let's Go* strongly recommends booking a room in advance by phoning or writing ahead. For groups of three or more, a *Ferienwohnung* (vacation apartment) can be a surprisingly affordable option at DM20-40 per person. There are only two hostels, one in **Prora** and the other in **Binz,** and the latter is almost constantly booked.

Rügen is so close to Stralsund's coast that you could almost swim there; however, since **trains** leave hourly for **Binz** and **Saßnitz** (DM15-20), you can probably leave your water wings at home. It's only an hour from Stralsund to Saßnitz, which makes daytrips an option, especially if the hostels on Rügen are booked. **Buses** connect Stralsund with Rügen's largest towns, and a **ferry** runs to Schaprode, near Hiddensee, on Rügen's west coast.

Once on the island, public transportation is reliable but expensive and infre-quent—most visitors come with cars. Trains connect Stralsund with Binz, Prora, and Saßnitz via **Bergen,** an unattractive town in the center of the island. To get to **Kap Arkona** in the north or **Göhren** in the south, however, you'll have to take an **RPNV** bus (which runs every hour); check schedules carefully, and make sure you know when the last bus leaves, lest you get stuck. The **Rasender Roland,** a narrow-gauge rail line, runs every two hours from Putbus to Göhren (DM12) with stops in

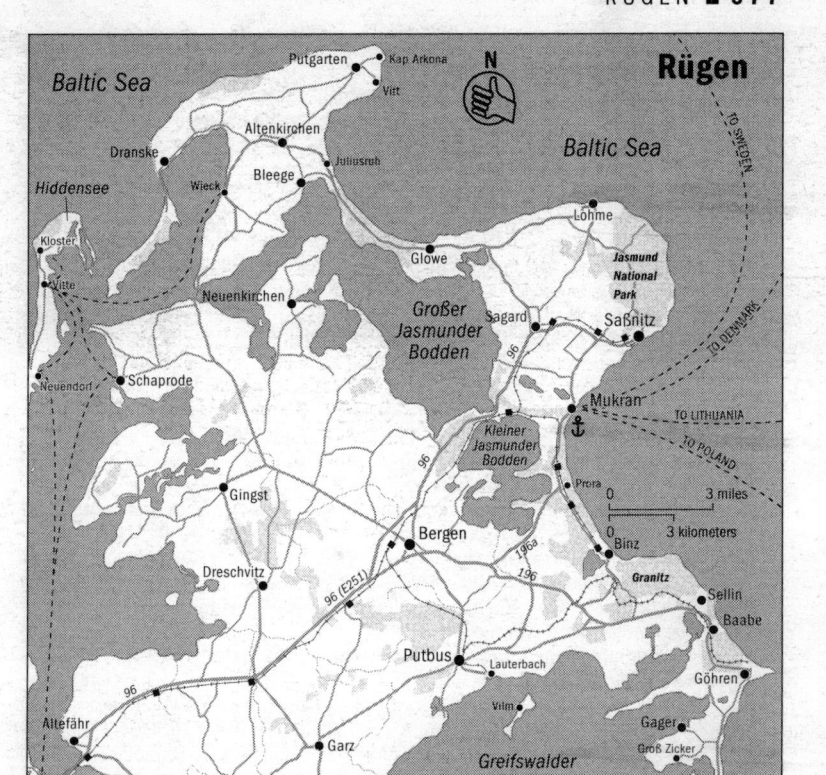

many spa towns; unfortunately, the railway is more of a tourist attraction than a means of practical transportation. Although the island is large, the major points of interest lie no more than 20km from one another. The best way to get around is by combining the train and buses with walking, hiking, and biking. Well-marked **trails** cover the entire island.

🏔 DAY BIKE: TOUR DE RÜGEN
Estimated time: 6hrs.; estimated distance 60km.

A combination of Rügen Island's trails offers not-quite-off-road-biking; the best ride is from **Sassnitz** to **Kap Arkona** (3hrs one way). This worthwhile excursion includes four stages. For safety precautions to observe while hiking, and the necessary equipment, see p. 57.

Stage 1: The woods around the remains of the GDR. From Sassnitz station take Birkenweg to a right on Merkelstr. At the Lanken station, take a right onto **Am Kreidebuch Str,** then an immediate right on **Klementelvitzer Weg;** continue straight as this dwindles into a footpath. At the first factory, go right, then immediately left and choose the low road. At the second factory, again choose the low road after a left. Once at Sagard station, take a right through **Sagard.**

Stage 2: Lakeside Farmland. At the other side of town, take a right onto the cobblestone highway. Take a left at the sign for **Polchow.** Follow this road almost until the end, and take a right at the sign for **Glowe.**

Stage 3: The coastal pine forest. Once at **Glowe,** take a right and follow the paved bike path until **Juliusruth.**
Stage 4: The windswept cape. Right after Juliusruth, follow the signs for **Arkona** and the camping grounds to the right. After reaching the camp grounds, follow the back road on the cape's edge to the **lighthouses.**

BINZ   ☎ 038393

"They paved paradise and put up a parking lot." Joni Mitchell's words ring painfully true in Binz, the main beach town on Rügen. The beat on the street here is the sound of jackhammers working furiously to resurrect Binz as Germany's "other Sylt." Recently restored seaside mansions, many of which are rapidly reopening as spiffed-up luxury hotels, hearken back to Binz's former incarnation as a fashionable, aristocratic resort. While there isn't much to see in Binz, there is plenty to do, with miles of sandy beach perfect for swimming, sunbathing, windsurfing, or playing badminton with accountants from Düsseldorf. There are also two **nude beaches** tastefully situated at the far ends of the town beach, suitable for just hanging out. Where Hauptstr. meets the beach, take in the family entertainment at the outdoor stage; crooners and oompah bands produce tunes that may leave you in tears. Luckily, Binz leaves a better taste in the mouth than in the ears, as it teems with restaurants, bars, and ice cream stands. The **Strandcafé Binz/Pizza Ristorante da Barbara,** Strandpromenade 29, serves pasta and herring specialties. Try the *gnocchi alla gorgonzola* (DM 12.50), or one of a dozen pizzas. (DM9-15. Open daily 11am-late.) More restaurants and a **crazy billiards** game (miniature golf with pool cues, DM3 for 18 holes) are in the **Vitarium,** a greenhouse-type building at the north end of the beach, for occupation on rainy days.

Accommodations in Binz fill up quickly and are DM10-15 more expensive than on other parts of the island. The main **tourist office,** Hauptstr. 1, **books rooms** (DM40-70) for free. From the station, take a left on Dollahner Str., which becomes Jasmuder Str., and follow until Haupstr. (☎ 134 60; fax 134 615. Open Su-Th 9:30am-7pm, F-Sa 9:30am-8pm.) The **post office** is at Zeppelinstr. 3 (open M-F 9am-6pm, Sa 9am-noon). The **postal code** is 18609.

The scarcity of rooms carries over to the better of Rügen's two youth hostels, **Jugendherberge Binz (HI),** Strandpromenade 35, which underwent a DM7.8 million renovation in 1997. (☎ 325 97; fax 325 96; email Jugendherberge_Binz@t-online.de. Breakfast included. Sheets DM7. Reception 8:15-9am and 6-9:30pm. Curfew 10:30pm, but you can get an access code. Dorm beds DM34; over 26 DM41.50.) Less likely to fill but exponentially less attractive accommodations await in the **Jugendherberge Prora (HI),** a "family hostel" which only rents out rooms. To get there, take either the Bergen-Binz train or the Binz-Saßnitz bus to "Prora-Ost" (not "Prora"), cross the tracks and follow the signs. (☎ 328 44; fax 328 45. Reception 7-9am and 4-10pm. Curfew 11pm. Call ahead or show up by 4pm. All rooms DM40.) The **Edeka supermarket,** at the corner of Schillerstr. and Zeppeliastr., boasts long hours and long lines (open M-F 8am-8pm, Sa 8am-6pm, Su 2-6pm).

SAßNITZ   ☎ 038392

Saßnitz has fallen hard since Prussian author Theodor Fontane penned in *Effi Briest:* "To travel to Rügen means to travel to Saßnitz." Today, the town consists of crumbling masses of apartment blocks interspersed with recently refurbished seaside villas. While Saßnitz is little more than an enclave of GDR nostalgia, its proximity to the stark chalk cliffs and bucolic forests of **Jasmund National Park** (see below) make it an attractive base for hikers and other nature-lovers. Below the town is the *Hafen,* which can be reached by following Hafenstr. down the hill. Tourists stroll along the seawall and among the warehouses; the promenade ends at the **Museum für Unterwasserarchaeologie,** displaying remnants of a 10th-century fishing boat and hands-on exhibits. (DM5, students DM3. Open 10am-6pm.)

Saßnitz also serves as Rügen's ferry station. **Ferries** leave for **Sweden, Denmark, Russia,** and **Lithuania** (DM50-100 with car, DM10-30 just for cabin) from the *Fährhafen* in **Mukran.** Take bus #414b from the train station to "Saßnitz Fährhafen" (15min.). Other companies send boats on **water tours** around the national park and to **Kap Arkona** from the *Stadthafen* below the town. (Daily 9am-5pm. DM15-25.) Shorter hauls to the Danish island of **Bornholm** and to **Świnoujście, Poland** also depart from the *Stadthafen* (DM50 with car). Rent a **bike** at Hafenstr. 19b, off of Hauptstr. (☎350 75. DM10-15 per day. Open M-F 9:30am-1pm and 2-5:30pm, Sa 10am-noon.) Saßnitz's **tourist office,** Seestr. 1, is in the 11-story Rügen Hostel. From the train station, walk down Bahnhofstr. and take a left on Hauptstr. The staff **books rooms** (DM30-40) for a DM8 fee. (☎51 60; fax 516 16. Open Apr.-Oct. M-Sa 9am-5pm.) Billiards and the **internet** await at **Cafe Blue,** Mukraner Str. 1, on the second floor of the strip mall. (30min DM3.50. Open daily 4pm-until late.) The **post office** is at Ruegengalerie 12, 18546 Saßnitz, to the left of the train station (open M-F 9am-6pm, Sa 10am-1pm).

The closest campground is **Campground Nipmerow,** under ancient beech trees next to the national park, near the *Königstuhl.* Catch bus #408 (direction: "Stubbenkammer") from the train station and get off at "Nipmerow". (☎(038302) 92 44. Wash DM5; no dryers. Reception 8am-10pm. DM8 per person. DM4-6 per tent.) Pick up groceries for your hike at **Plus,** Bahnhofstr. 1 (open M-F 8am-6:30pm, Sa 8am-1pm).

■ JASMUND NATIONAL PARK

The spectacular chalk cliffs rising just north of Saßnitz and culminating in the famous **Großer Stubbenkammer** were forged by massive glaciers 12,000 years ago; despite some erosion, they'll still give you the chills. There are a couple of options for approaching the cliffs. The most direct (but also the least fun) is to take bus #408 to "Stubbenkammer" from the stop outside the Saßnitz train station (DM2.50); it runs every half hour during the summer and lets you off about 10m away from the **Königstuhl** (king's chair), the most famous of the cliffs. To avoid the air-conditioned bus route, take the bike trail next to the church at the end of Hauptstr. in Saßnitz. A good vantage point can be found by following signs to "Waldhalle," then hiking about a kilometer south to the bike trail's end; steps will take you down to a chalky beach. The path to the *Königstuhl* is also clearly marked. For the best views, take the ◪**Hochuferweg** (high coastal trail) all the way from Saßnitz to the *Stubbenkammer.* Despite the intimidating name, the 8.5km trail (a 3hr. hike) is fairly easy and runs from one incredible scenic lookout to the next. To pick up the trail, follow the "Stubbenkammer" signs through Saßnitz up the hill until you reach the parking lot, where there's a detailed map of the park showing all the trails and their blazes—follow the ones for "Hochuferweg."

The trail leads first to the **Wissower Klinken** (3km), which you might recognize from Caspar David Friedrich's paintings—these were his favorite chalk cliffs. Even though they've lost about 3m to erosion since he painted them, their beauty still seems almost supernatural. Continuing for another 5km, you'll reach the **Victoriasicht** lookout, and then the famous *Königstuhl.* If you follow the mob to the lookout area, you'll have to pay for the view, which isn't much better than what you've already seen for free (DM2, students DM1).

Look up to the left, and you'll see a small guard post once used by GDR authorities to make sure no one escaped by boat to Sweden. For a bit of solitude, walk down the steep and windy paths to the flint-covered beach. Another trail leads from the *Königstuhl* to the lovely **Herthasee,** a lake named after the German harvest goddess Hertha. According to myth, Hertha drowned her mortal servants in this lake, and their spirits supposedly still gather on the banks each night, although we didn't stick around to find out. Nearby, the **Herthaburg,** a U-shaped earth wall built by the Slavs in the 7th century, recalls the less peaceful periods of this violently beautiful landscape.

M.-VORPOMMERN

GRANITZ AND GÖHREN   ☎038308

The **Jagdschloß Granitz** is an odd-looking, castle-like hunting lodge designed and built in 1836 by Prussian architect Friedrich Schinkel, whose unmistakable creations can be seen all over the island. Built atop the Tempelberg hill, its 38m tower offers a breathtaking panorama of the island. Faint of heart, beware: Bambi's family tree is mounted on the walls of the **Jagdmuseum** (hunting museum) inside the "castle." (Open Tu-Su 9am-6pm. DM5, students DM4.) The *Roland* stops at the Jagdschloß, as does the **Jagdschloßexpress,** which makes round-trips from the *Kurhaus* in Binz (DM10, children DM6). From the "Jagdschloß" *Roland* stop, head uphill on the trail off to the right to reach the castle. To walk or bike the 5km from Binz, take the trail near the "Binz Roland" station. Heading south from the *Roland* "Jagdschloß" stop to the village of Lancken-Granitz, you'll pass a bunch of huge prehistoric graves; one dates back to 2300 BC.

The *Roland's* final stop is **Göhren,** on the easternmost tip of the forested **Mönchgut peninsula,** which was settled in the 13th century by monks who believed in total self-sufficiency. The slower pace of life here reflects the smaller number of tourists and obligatory tourist attractions. The city sits on a hill, and from the church off Strandstr. one can look across the sea at Greifswald. Göhren, like every other town worth its salt on Rügen, has a nice beach; it's also the base of numerous **hiking and biking trails** leading through peaceful beaches, forests, and the rolling hills of the **Zickersche Alpen.** Göhren's main attraction is the **Mönchguter Museum,** composed of four tiny museums in the town's center, which display local history in a schoolhouse, a 17th-century cottage, a thatched-roof barn, and a ship. (All museums open May-June and Sept.-Oct. Tu-Su 10am-5pm; July-Aug. daily 10am-6pm. Each museum DM4, students DM3; with *Kurkarte* DM3, students DM2. Day card for all 4 museums DM14, students DM10; with *Kurkarte* DM10, students DM6.)

Navigating in Göhren requires little effort, as almost everything lies either on **Strandstr.** or just off it. To get to the center of town from the train station, follow Strandstr. up the hill. Frequent **buses** connect Göhren to **Binz, Bergen,** and **Saßnitz** to the north and **Klein Zicker** to the south (DM5-10). The **Fahrradverleih,** Kastanienalle 8, rents touring bikes for DM8 and mountain bikes for DM10. (☎254 06. Open daily 9-11am and 4-6pm.) The **tourist office,** Poststr. 9, provides information and **books rooms** for a 10% fee. From the train station, follow Strandstr. up the hill and to the right; after a couple blocks it turn into Poststr. (☎21 50 or 259 10; fax 259 11; www.goehren.de. Open M-Th 8am-6pm, F 8am-1pm and 4-6pm, Sa-Su 4-6pm.) The **post office,** 18586 Gohren, is inside the **Edeka grocery store** on Strandstr. (open M-F 8am-6pm, Sa-Su 4-6pm).

The **campground** is near the train station and the beach. From the station, turn right and follow the signs. The staff **rents bikes** and runs a restaurant, cinema, and **laundromat.** (☎901 20; fax 21 23. Reception M-F 7am-1pm and 3-7pm, Sa-Su 9am-1pm and 3-6pm. DM6 per person; DM4.50-8 per tent.) **Ostseeresidenz Göhren** (☎912 55), on the beach down the hill from Strandstr., has expensive fish and vegetarian entrees served in a ballroom overlooking the sea. Try the *Rotbarschfilet* (DM19).

KAP ARKONA AND VITT   ☎038391

At the northern tip of Rügen, Kap Arkona—Germany's only cape, flanked on either side by the villages of Putgarten and Vitt—stretches into the Baltic. The main attractions of the area, two lighthouses and Vitt itself, are beautiful but unfortunately infested with souvenir shops and busloads of tourists. **Buses** run hourly from **Saßnitz** (#419, 40min., DM7.40) and **Bergen** (#110, 50min., DM9) to **Altenkirchen,** where you can transfer to bus #403 to **Putgarten** (20min., DM2). The horribly slow *Arkonabahn,* a humiliating motorized train, connects to Putgarten, Vitt, and the lighthouses for a modest cost. (30min., every 30min.

DM3 each stop or DM8 round-trip; students DM2 per stop, DM5 round-trip.) **Horse-drawn carts** offer even less efficient transportation between **Putgarten** and the lighthouses for the same prices as the slightly faster *Arkonabahn*. Before reunification, the two lighthouses on Kap Arkona resided in a restricted area belonging to the GDR's National People's Army; the **Leuchtfener Arkona**, designed by Schinkel, has been open to the public since 1993. Built in 1826, it guarded the GDR's sea borders. Nearby, the **Marinepeilturm** was built in 1927 and rigged with a fancy electronic system that could eavesdrop on British radio communications. Now it houses archaeological finds from the **Tempel-burg Arkana**, a Slavic fortification built in the 8th century and destroyed by the Danes in 1168. (Lighthouses open daily 11am-5pm. Each lighthouse DM4, students DM3. Combination ticket DM10, students DM8.) By the Marinepeilturm is the underground **Bunker Arkona**, with paintings and sculptures of local artists (DM1 donation requested. Open daily 11am-5pm.) Thatched-roofed **cafes** in Vitt offer crepes and coffee.

The combination souvenir shop and **tourist office,** in the parking lot by Kap Arkona, 300m down the road from Putgarten's bus stop, **books rooms.** (☎41 90; fax 419 17. Open Jan.-Mar. daily 10am-4pm; Mar.-May 10am-5pm; June-Oct. 10am-7pm.) Pick up a free guide or rent a **bike** to wheel around (DM3 per hr., DM10 per day). The **Wittower Campground** is east of Altenkirchen. (☎133 20. DM9 per person, DM9 per tent. Reception 8am-10pm. Open Apr.-Oct.)

⊡ DAYTRIP FROM RÜGEN: HIDDENSEE. West of Rügen lies the slender island of Hiddensee, known in the *Plattdeutsch* dialect as *dat söte Länneken* (the sweet island). Free of youth hostels, campgrounds, motor vehicles, and other sources of pollution, Hiddensee remains the same sliver of unadulterated natural beauty that drew Sigmund Freud, Albert Einstein, and Käthe Kollwitz to its shores. Ferries serve Hiddensee's three towns: Neuendorf, Vitte, and Kloster. Of the three, **Neuendorf** is the least spectacular; like the heath surrounding it, the town rests silently except in winter, when local plants are picked for *Sanddorn*, a rust-colored, honey-like drink, served hot or cold in most of the island's restaurants. (DM5 per bottle, DM15-25 for the alcoholic variant.) North of Neuendorf lies **Vitte,** the island's main town and the home of Hiddensee's sandiest beach. As Hiddensee has neither a hostel nor a campground, visit the **tourist office,** Norderende 162, reached by following signs to the Rathaus. (☎(038300) 642 26; fax 642 25; email inselinformation.hiddensee@t-online.de. Open M-F 9am-5pm, Sa 10am-noon.) By the Rathaus is **Edeka**, offering fresh food for a picnic lunch (open M-F 8am-7pm, Sa 8am-6pm, and Su 1-6pm). The island's beauty and action climax in **Kloster,** the northernmost town. The great naturalist author and social dramatist **Gerhardt Hauptmann** summered in Kloster from 1930 to 1943 and is buried here; there is a memorial to him and his work. The huge wine cellar, Kirchweg 13, reveals that Hauptmann loved the bottle nearly as much as the pen. (☎(038300) 397. Open May-Oct. 10am-5pm; Nov.-Apr. 11am-4pm. DM3, students DM1.50.)

Kloster's museums and sandy beaches are mere appetizers for the hills above the town which make up the **Dornbusch,** an area so pristine that not even bikes are allowed. Though ferries dump loads of tourists who crawl the mountains, the plethora of trails let you pretend you're alone. Follow the trails which run along the grassy hillsides carpeted with wildflowers to reach the **Leuchtturm,** which affords a view of the entire island. (DM4, DM2.50 with *Kurkarte*. Open daily 10:30am-6pm.) At the northern end, lonely trails fall and rise with the cliffs overlooking the Baltic Sea. Fully enjoying Hiddensee requires renting a **bike,** preferably a burly one with plenty of gears and nice fat tires, as the majority of the island's roads are either muddy country trails or sandy beach paths. Bike rentals *(Fahrradverleih)* are everywhere on the island; the standard rate is DM10 for a three-speed. For those seeking real solitude, spend a night on the island; the only ferry arrives in **Vitte** at 11:30am and leaves at 4:30pm.

M.–VORPOMMERN

Ferry connections are available to Hiddensee from **Stralsund** on the mainland and **Schaprode** on Rügen's west coast. Ferries leave **Schaprode** approximately four times per day. (45min. DM11, children DM7; round-trip DM21, children DM13.)

GREIFSWALD ☎ 03834

Endowed with one of the oldest universities in Germany and an array of youth-oriented shops, Greifswald clearly belongs to its students who zoom through the city on bikes. Their 543 years of professors are commemorated by scores of plaques around the city. The city's young blood has allowed gigantic leaps to be made in the Altstadt's restoration, but, like most former GDR cities, outer neighborhoods still crumble. The talented hands of Caspar David Friedrich (see p. 23) painted the skyline and the nearby cloister ruins into art-world fame in the late 19th century. Greifswald has managed to hold on to a few of his works, which are at least partially responsible for the German Romantics' obsession with humanity's insignificance; unfortunately, most of the paintings have been snatched up by bigger museums in Berlin and Düsseldorf.

⚡ PRACTICAL INFORMATION

Greifswald is the easternmost city on Germany's Baltic coast, lying 30km southeast of and 60km west of the Polish frontier.

Trains: Chug to **Stralsund** (20min., 1 per hr., DM10.40); **Rostock** (2½hr., 8 per day, DM28); **Schwerin** (3½hr., 5 per day, DM52); and **Berlin** (3hr., 1 per hr., DM60).

Buses: Cover the inner city and suburbs from the ZOB across from the station (single ticket DM2.30, day card DM5).

Taxi: Stands are outside the train station and the Rathaus.

Tourist Office: Schuhagenstr. 22, offers free maps and guided tours in German (☎and fax 19 433. Open M, W, and F at 2pm; DM10). They also **book rooms** (DM30-50) for free (open M-F 9am-6pm, Sa 9:30am-12:30pm).

Exchange Money: at the **Deutsche Bank** on the Markt. Open M, Tu, Th 8:30am-6pm, W and F 8:30am-2pm. **24hr. ATM** available.

Gay and Lesbian Resources: Rosa Greif, Lange Str. 49 (☎89 70 34; email rosagreif@gmx.de). Open Tu 3-5pm, Th 5-9pm.

Women's Resources: at the **Frauenausbildungs- und Beratungszentrum Baltic,** Spiegeldorfer Wende 2.

Pharmacy: The **Rats-Apotheke,** Am Markt 2 (☎82 03 43), fills all your pharmaceutical needs. Open M-F 7:30am-6:30pm, Sa 9am-noon.

Internet Access: Check your e-mail at **Billiard Café,** Wollweberstr. 22. Open Tu-F 5:30-11pm, Sa-Su 2:30-11pm.

Post Office: Am Markt 15-19, 17489 Greifswald (open M-F 9am-6pm, Sa 9am-noon).

🏠🍴 ACCOMMODATIONS, FOOD, AND NIGHTLIFE

In May of 2001, Greifswald's **Jugendherberge (HI),** Pestalozzistr. 11, will celebrate its first birthday. This highly touted hostel is part of the new wave of youth hostels hitting Germany. From the station, take a right on Bahnhofstr., another right on Guetzkower Str., then a left on Pestalozzistr. (☎51 69 0; fax 51 69 10. Breakfast included. Sheets DM7. 24hr. reception. Call way ahead. Dorm beds DM29, over 26 DM34.) The **Spar** supermarket is located inside the Altstadt's monstrous Dompassage shopping center (open M-F 8am-8pm, Sa 8am-4pm). While Greifswald's culinary options are scant, its night life is not. The **Mensa,** Am Schiesswall (☎86 17 11), opens for breakfast at 8am and remains open for lunch through 3:30pm; buy a magnetic card outside the cafeteria (DM2-4). Most nights it reopens as *Mensaclub*, though hours and programs vary; check out the posters on the first floor to see what's going down. The cheapest eats can be had at **Cafe mal Anders,** inside the *Soziokulturelles Zentrum*, Lange Str. 49. Not-too-big entrees cost DM4-6 (open Tu-Th 11:30am-5pm, F 11:30am-4pm). In contrast to the usual *Biergarten* that line Lange Str., (non-alcoholic) drinks are hidden at **Cafe Lichtblick,** Domstr 13. (open M-F 9am-5pm). In the mornings, locals gather at **Klex,** Lange Str. 14, a youth center that doubles as a breakfast cafe, and irregularly as a dance club. (☎89 83 30. Open M-F 9am-noon.) At the end of Lange Str., in a building combining Neoclassicism and a eight-year-old color scheme, is **Cafe Quark,** Karl-Marx-Pl. 19 (☎50 22 35), a popular hangout. The most happening dance club, **Fly-In**, Grauss Str. 12 (☎876 20) is a 35min. ride from the Altstadt. Take bus #30 to "Max-Plank-Str."

◎ SIGHTS

Stretching high above the Greifswald skyline is the tower of the **St. Nikolaikirche.** A small viewing platform has been built around the tower of the 14th- century basilica; climb through a maze of wooden beams to the rickety heights of the building and survey Greifswald in all its glory (DM3, students DM1.50). The city has still not removed the cannonballs that were lodged in the east wall of the 13th- century **St. Marienkirche** by an angry elector of Brandenburg in 1678, but the early Gothic interior is worth a look (open M-F 10am-noon and 2-4pm, Sa-Su 10am-noon).

The unkindness of the university's professors has been memorialized in the **Karzer,** a prison where naughty students would endure several days of solitary confinement—bringing a whole new dimension to the repercussions of missed deadlines. Greifswald's Karzer is notable because students locked up there maliciously painted beautiful coats-of-arms on the walls and carved their names in impeccable script on the doors. The crown jewel **Pommersches Landesmuseum** is still under construction, but the art wing is open to the public. The **Gemäldgalerie,** on Muehlenstr., displays a precious few of Friedrich's works (open Tu-Su 10am-6pm). Near the train station, the university's **botanical gardens,** Münterstr. 11, has a greenhouse that will take you from Saharan Africa to the jungles of Indochina in 3 seconds flat. (☎86 11 30. Open M-F 9am-3:45pm, Sa-Su 1-3pm.) Running around the city is a tree-lined pedestrian boulevard; when the town wall was razed in the late 1700s, these kilometers of greenery replaced it. At 700 years old, the **house** at Markt 13 is the oldest (if not the prettiest) in Greifswald.

A few kilometers east of Greifswald, the coastal villages of **Wieck** and **Eldena** keep the city supplied with fresh fish. Make a trip to the carefully preserved **Klosterruine** in Eldena, across from Wolgaster Str. This 12th-century Cistercian monastery once housed Danish monks, but was, in great part, destroyed by Swedish soldiers plundering for raw materials. Friedrich immortalized the ruins in a series of Romantic images; stop by and contemplate your insignificance. In June, the cloisters become a venue for open-air Bach recitals. Take bus #60 (direction: "Wieck Brücke") to the end of the line.

LOCK 'IM UP, JOHNNY Turn-of-the-century professors would never have been accused of softness of heart by their students, as a number of *Karzer* scattered throughout Germany's many university towns testify. These small prison cells—hence, in*karzer*ation—were used to punish students for various offences, including chasing "strange women" and drinking too much. The rowdiest academics served sentences of up to 10 days, although by the early 20th century it was common practice to let student prisoners out of the *Karzer* for a couple of hours each day to eat and socialize. Even locking them up didn't cure their mischievous tendencies, however; some of the best parties were purportedly held in *Karzer* cells, as students would climb walls to be let in the windows.

M.–VORPOMMERN

USEDOM

Usedom is probably more interesting for what it was than what it is. The late 19th century drew crowds of wealthy Berliners to this island. Their millions of Reichmarks built the beaches into an elitist playground, nicknamed "Berlin's bathtub." Depression and war sent them scattering, but their beach toys—enormously gaudy houses and long piers—remain, albeit in various states of decay. Today the island is the bathtub of the *petit bourgeoisie*; a less glittering crowd of middle-class families fills the beaches and rents rooms in a few of the restored palaces. An astonishing amount of the island has been neither restored nor destroyed, and the quiet, cavernous buildings lend the area a haunting atmosphere.

■ **ORIENTATION AND GETTING AROUND.** Usedom is the northeastern most point in Germany; the eastern part of the island is part of Poland. The island still fills up in July and August, when the beaches become crowded with *Strandkörbe* (people-baskets that block the sun), so it's a good idea to reserve accommodations in advance. Usedom is connected to the national rail system at **Zuessow**, via **Wolgast.** From the station at Zuessow, take the **Usedom Baederbahn (UBB)** to get onto the island (DM7 to Zinnowitz); the UBB also connects all Usedom's towns (DM2-10, daypass DM15). Alternatively, **Adler-Schiffe** (☎03 83 78 or 325 83) runs **ferries** from the Usedom resorts to **Saßnitz** (see p. 578) on the island of **Rügen** (4hr., 1 per day, DM43.50). A *Kurkarte* is a good investment (DM4, students DM2); your hotel should provide you with one; these cards offer access to all beaches as well as discounts at many of Usedom's tourist spots.

ZINNOWITZ   ☎038377

Larger and less naturally striking than the other resorts on the island, Zinnowitz nonetheless benefits from a minimum of tourists and a plentiful supply of cheap accommodations. The sparkly new **Kurverwaltung** (spa administration), at the corner of Neue Strandstr. and Dünenstr., provides free maps of the island and books rooms (DM30-60) for free. (☎49 20; fax 422 29. Open M-F 9am-7pm, Sa-Su 10am-3pm.) This tourist office also offers **bike tours** (M and W-Th at 10am; DM5, DM3 with *Kurkarte*). Rent **bikes** at the **Fahrradverleih,** Dr.-Wachsmann-Str. 5. (☎428 69. DM6-10. Open daily 8am-noon and 1-7pm.) There is a **pharmacy** at Neue Strandstr. 39. (☎20 24 62. Open M-F 8am-6pm, Sa 8:30am-noon.) The **post office** is at Neue Strandstr. 38, 17454 Zinnowitz (open M-F 9am-6pm, Sa 9am-1pm).

If the *Zimmervermittlung* at the tourist office leaves you looking for cheaper accommodations, check out the **Sportschule,** Dr.-Wachsmann-Str. 30, which in addition to rooms also offers a large track, soccer field, handball court, and ping-pong tables. (☎22 68; fax 22 80. DM35 per person; sheets DM5.) Just down the street, **Campingplatz Pommernland,** Dr.-Wachsmann-Str. 40, has several expensive but very new bungalows and rents camping places. (☎403 48; fax 403 49. Doubles DM140; quads DM180. Camping DM8.50, tents DM7-10. Reception open daily 8am-noon and 2-9pm.) Next to the post office there is an **Edeka** supermarket (open M-F 9am-6pm, Sa 9am-1pm), and across the street is **Mamma Mia,** offering pizza (DM8-14) and the standard Italian menu (open daily 11am-late).

KOSEROW   ☎038375

Probably the best way to imagine Koserow is to play forest-and-beach relaxation tapes at full blast with your eyes closed. At the narrowest and highest part of Usedom (58m), Koserow's remarkable forests of moss-covered trees fall sharply onto a surreally perfect sandy beach in what is, refreshingly, the least touristy of Usedom's resort towns. The **tourist office,** Hauptstr. 34 offers free maps and hiking tips (☎204 15. Open M-F 9am-6pm, Sa-Su 9am-noon.) You'll have to go to the **Zimmervermittlung,** in the same building as the tourist office, to get yourself a room. (☎210 62. Reservation service free, but call early in the year for the summer months. DM30-60.) Most services line Koserow's Hauptstr., which leads conveniently to the train station. Buy your (legal) drugs at the **Vineta-Apotheke** at the corner of Schulstr. and Hauptstr. (☎202 35. Open M-F 8am-6:30pm, Sa 8am-noon.) **Internet access** can be found at **Hotel Nautic,** Hauptstr. 46e. (DM8 per hr. Open daily 10am-9pm.) The **post office** is near the train station at Hauptstr. 49a., 17459 Koserow (open M-F 8:30am-12:30pm and 2:30-5:30pm, Sa 9-11am).

While nearly every house in the small town advertises rooms for rent, they are usually booked well in advance. **Wald und Meer,** perched in the woods on the west end of town at the end of Forster-Schrödter-Str., offers fairly spartan bungalow accommodations in 2-6 bed rooms. (☎26 20; fax 262 40. Breakfast included. DM35 per person.) Pitch your tent at **Campingplatz Am Sandfeld** to enjoy the cheapest accommodations and best views on the island. By the station end of Haupstr. take a right onto Siemenstr. and follow the signs. (☎207 59; fax 214 05. DM8 per person. Wash DM4. Beach access DM1. Like its neighboring towns, the best places to eat in Koserow are the bakeries and fish huts. Several places along Hauptstr. churn out fresh bread, and fish is for sale north of the pier. For **groceries,** stop by **Netto** on Hauptstr., by the train station (open M-F 7am-8pm, Sa 7am-6pm, Su 11am-5pm).

HERINGSDORF ☎038378

Heringsdorf was once the most elite of the three resort towns; check out the now privately owned abode of Kaiser Wilhelm II, Delbrückstr. 6, for a taste of the village's imperial past. The tourist industry is once again on the rise here; the shiny combination of the new pier, shopping center, and the glassy **Platz des Friedens** at the center of town are the result of many vacation *Marks*. To get to the Platz, turn left on Bülowstr. from the station, right on Friedenstr., and follow it to the end. The beach is obviously Heringsdorf's main attraction; the salty sea climes and clean air have survived a century of political struggle unharmed. They haven't gone unnoticed, however, and the beaches can get claustrophobically crowded in season. The **Villa Irmgard,** Maxim-Gorki-Str. 13, traces the rise and fall of 19th century Usedom resort life. This former home of Russian writer **Maxim Gorki** has been converted into a museum and now houses an exhibit of Gorki's personal possessions (probably interesting only to Gorki fanatics), as well as a more interesting collection of intricate swimsuits and everything else that the rich and famous needed at the beach. (Open Tu-Su 10am-6pm. DM6, with *Kurkarte* DM5, students a couple marks cheaper.)

Heringsdorf's **tourist office** is at Kulmstr. 33, next to the Rathaus. (☎24 51; fax 24 54. Open M-F 9am-6pm, Sa-Su 10am-3pm.) Most other services cluster around the Platz. The **Sparkasse** exchanges money for DM3 or a 1% fee and has **24hr. ATMs** (☎23 60. Open M, Tu, F 8:30am-noon and 1:30-4pm, W 8:30am-noon, Th 8:30am-noon and 1:30-6pm). The **Apotheke** at Seestr. 40 lists the phone numbers of local doctors in the window. (☎25 90. Open M-F 8am-6:30pm, Sa 8am-12:30pm.) For a **taxi,** call ☎225 26. During the high season (July and Aug.), it is virtually impossible to find accommodations in Heringsdorf; most vacationers reserve early in the year for the summer months. The **Jugendherberge Heringsdorf (HI),** Puschkinstr. 7-9, has taken over a beach house between Heringsdorf and Ahlbeck. From the train station, turn right on Liehrstr. and follow the signs.

M.-VORPOMMERN

(☎223 25; fax 323 01; www.jh-heringsdorf.de. Breakfast included. Sheets DM7. Reservations required. Reception open 8-9am, noon-1pm, and 6-10pm. Curfew 10pm. DM29, over 26 DM36. Beach tax May-Sept. DM3.80, Oct.-Apr. DM1.90.) If the hostel is full, call the *Zimmervermittlung* in Ahlbeck (see below). Food in Heringsdorf is unremarkable. **Schwenn's,** a couple doors down from the tourist office, offers a small array of **groceries** (open M-F 7am-8pm, Sa 7am-7pm, Su 8am-7pm).

APPENDIX

CARDINAL NUMBERS										
0	1	2	3	4	5	6	7	8	9	10
null	eins	zwei	drei	vier	fünf	sechs	sieben	acht	neun	zehn
11	12	20	30	40	50	60	70	80	90	100
elf	zwölf	zwanzig	dreizig	vierzig	fünfzig	sechzig	siebzig	achtzig	neunzig	hundert

ORDINAL NUMBERS					
1st	2nd	3rd	4th	10th	20th
erste	zweite	dritte	vierte	zehnte	zwanzigste

CLIMATE

Germany's climate is varied but for the most part unexceptional; the southern parts of the country are not substantially warmer than the northern regions. Rain is common year-round, though it is especially prevalent in the summer, when the weather can change with surprising disjointedness from one hour to the next. Temperatures typically range between -1 to 2 °C (30-36 °F) in deep winter to 12 to 25 °C (55-77 °F) in July and August.

SEASONAL	JANUARY			APRIL			JULY			OCTOBER		
TEMP. (HI-LO), precipitation	°C	°F	mm	°C	°F	mm	°C	°F	mm	°C	°F	mm
Berlin	-3-1	26-35	48	2-12	37-54	41	13-22	56-73	75	5-13	42-56	51
Frankfurt	-1-3	30-38	45	3-13	39-56	58	13-23	57-75	60	6-13	43-57	55
Hamburg	-1-3	30-38	60	2-11	37-52	45	12-21	55-70	81	6-12	43-55	60
Munich	-4-2	24-36	48	2-11	36-53	71	12-22	54-72	127	4-12	40-55	60

TEMPERATURE CONVERSIONS							
°Celsius	-5	5	15	20	25	30	35
°Farenheit	23	41	59	68	77	86	95

To convert from °C to °F, multiply by 1.8 and add 32. To convert from °F to °C, subtract 32 and multiply by 0.55.

TIME ZONES

Germany uses West European time (abbreviated MEZ in German). Add six hours to Eastern Standard Time and one hour to Greenwich Mean Time. Subtract nine hours from Eastern Australia Time and 11 hours from New Zealand Time. Germany, like the rest of Western Europe, observes Daylight Savings Time, and so the time differential remains constant.

TELEPHONE CODES

In Germany, dial 00 to get an international line, then dial the code:

Australia	61	Ireland	353
Austria	43	Netherlands	31
Belgium	32	New Zealand	64
Czech Republic	420	Poland	48
Denmark	45	South Africa	27
France	33	Switzerland	41
Hungary	36	United Kingdom	44
Italy	39	US and Canada	1

CITY CODES

When calling Germany from abroad, before entering the regional number, drop the first zero and then enter the following codes for the relevant city:

Aachen	0241	Kassel	0561
Bayreuth	0921	Kiel	0431
Berlin	030	Köln	0221
Bonn	0228	Leipzig	0341
Braunschweig	0531	Lübeck	0451
Bremen	0421	München	089
Dessau	0340	Münster	0251
Dresden	0351	Nürnberg	0911
Düsseldorf	0211	Passau	0851
Erfurt	0361	Regensburg	0941
Frankfurt	069	Rostock	0381
Freiburg	0761	Stuttgart	0711
Göttingen	0551	Trier	0651
Hamburg	040	Tübingen	07071
Hannover	0511	Weimar	03643
Heidelberg	06221	Würzburg	0931

MEASUREMENTS

Like the rest of the rational world, Germany uses the metric system. Keep this in mind whenever you see a road sign or any other distance indicator—those are kilometers, not miles, so whatever distance is being described is not as far away as Americans and Brits might think. Also, all German recipe books use metric measurements. And, unfortunately, gasoline isn't as cheap as it looks to those used to gallons: prices are *per liter*.

MEASUREMENT CONVERSIONS

1 inch (in.) = 2.54cm	1 centimeter (cm) = 0.39 in.
1 foot (ft.) = 0.30m	1 meter (m) = 3.28 ft.
1 yard (yd.) = 0.914m	1 meter (m) = 1.09 yd.
1 mile = 1.61km	1 kilometer (km) = 0.62 mi.
1 ounce (oz.) = 28.35g	1 gram (g) = 0.035 oz.
1 pound (lb.) = 0.454kg	1 kilogram (kg) = 2.202 lb.
1 fluid ounce (fl. oz.) = 29.57ml	1 milliliter (ml) = 0.034 fl. oz.
1 gallon (gal.) = 3.785L	1 liter (L) = 0.264 gal.
1 acre (ac.) = 0.405ha	1 hectare (ha) = 2.47 ac.
1 square mile (sq. mi.) = 2.59km^2	1 square kilometer (km^2) = 0.386 sq. mi.

LANGUAGE

Life is too short to learn German.
—Thomas Love Peacock

Although the majority of Germans speak at least elementary English, you'll have many real face-to-face encounters with people who don't, especially when traveling in Eastern Germany. Mastering the grammar of German is quite an accomplishment. However, a rudimentary knowledge can be attained rather quickly with a good book. Before asking someone a question in English, always preface your query with a polite *Sprechen Sie Englisch?* (do you speak English?).

PRONUNCIATION

Although you cannot hope to speak correct German without studying it, you can make yourself understood by learning only a little German. The first step is to master the pronunciation system. Unlike English, German pronunciation is for the most part consistent with spelling; there are no silent letters.

Consonants are pronounced as in English with the following exceptions: **J:** always pronounced as a Y. **K:** always pronounced, even before an N. **QU:** pronounced KV. **S:** pronounced as Z. **V:** pronounced as F. **W:** pronounced as V. **Z:** pronounced as TS. The hissing, aspirant **CH** sound, appearing in such basic words as *Ich* (I), *nicht* (not), and *sprechen* (to speak), is quite tricky for untrained English-speaking vocal cords. After A, O, U, or AU, it is pronounced as in the Scottish, "loch"; otherwise it sounds like a soft CH, as in "chivalry." If you can't hack it, use an SH sound instead. The diphthong **SCH,** found at the beginning of many German words, is pronounced SH, as in the word "shut," while **ST** and **SP** are pronounced "SHT" and "SHP," respectively.

German has one consonant that does not exist in English, **the "ß,"** which is alternately referred to as the *scharfes S* (sharp S) or the *Ess-tsett.* It is a shorthand symbol for a **double-S,** and is pronounced just like an English "ss." The letter appears only in lower case and shows up in two of the most important German words for travelers: *Straße*, "street," which is pronounced "SHTRAH-sseh" and abbreviated "Str."; and *Schloß*, "castle," pronounced "SHLOSS." Note that the use of the "ß" is being phased out in an effort to standardize spelling (see **The Woeful Decline of the ß,** p. 32).

German vowels and diphthongs also differ from their English counterparts: **A:** as in "father." **O:** as in "oh." **U:** as in "fondue." **AU:** as in "wow." **IE:** as in "thief." **EI:** like the I in "wine." **EU:** like the OI in "boil." An **umlaut** over a letter (e.g., ü) changes the pronunciation. An umlaut is sometimes replaced by an E following the vowel, so that "schön" becomes "schoen." An **Ä** sounds a lot like the short "e" in "effort," while an **Ö** is pronounced like the "e" in "perm." To make the **Ü** sound, round your lips to say "ooh," keep them in this position, and then try to say "ee" instead. Germans are very forgiving toward foreigners who butcher their mother tongue. There is, however, one important exception—place names. If you learn nothing else in German, learn to pronounce the names of cities properly. Berlin is "bare-LEEN," Hamburg is "HAHM-boorg," Munich (München) is "MEUWN-shen," and Bayreuth is "BUY-royt."

NUMBERS, DATES, AND TIMES

A space or period rather than a comma is used to indicate thousands, so 10,000 is written 10 000 or 10.000. Instead of a decimal point, Germans use a comma, e.g., 3.1415 is written 3,1415. Months and days are written in the reverse of the American manner, e.g., 10.11.92 is November 10. The numeral 7 is written with a slash through the vertical line, and the numeral 1 is written with an upswing, resembling an inverted "V." Note that the number in the ones place is pronounced before the number in the tens place; thus "fünfundsiebzig" (FUHNF-oont-ZEEB-tsish; literally "five and seventy") is 75, *not* 57. This can be hard to keep in mind.

The months in German are *Januar, Februar, März, April, Mai, Juni, Juli, August, September, Oktober, November, Dezember.* The days of the week are *Montag, Dienstag, Mittwoch, Donnerstag, Freitag, Samstag/Sonnabend,* and *Sonntag.* Germany uses the 24-hour clock for all official purposes: 20.00 equals 8pm. Thus, *fünfzehn Uhr* (15.00) is 3pm, etc. When Germans say "half eight" (*halb acht*), they mean 7:30; "three quarters eight" (*dreiviertel acht*) means 7:45 and "quarter eight" (*viertel acht*) means 7:15.

GLOSSARY

Abendessen: dinner
ab/fahren: to depart
Abfahrt: departure
Abteil: train compartment
Achtung: beware
Altstadt: old town, historic center
Amt: bureau
an/kommen: to arrive
Ankunft: arrival
Apotheke: pharmacy
Arbeit: work
auf/steigen: get off
Ausgang: exit
Auskunft: information
Ausstellung: exhibit
Ausweis: ID
Auto: car
Autobahn: highway
Autobus: bus
Bad: bath, spa
Bahn: railway
Bahnhof: train station
Bahnsteig: train platform
Berg: mountain, hill
Bett: bed
Bibliothek: library
Bundesrepublik Deutschland (BRD): Federal Republic of Germany (FRG)
Brot: bread
Brücke: bridge
Brunnen: fountain
Bundestag: parliament
Burg: fortress
Busbahnhof: bus station
Damen: ladies
Dennkmal: memorial
Dusche: shower
Dom: cathedral

Dorf: village
echt: real
ekelig: disgusting
Ehefrau: wife
Ehemann: husband
Einbahnstraße: one-way street
Eingang: entrance
ein/steigen: board
Eintritt: admission
Essen: food
Fähre: ferry
Fahrplan: timetable
Fahrrad: bicycle
Fahrschein: train ticket
Feiertag: holiday
Fernseher: TV set
Festung: fortress
Flohmarkt: flea market
Flughafen: airport
Flugzeug: airplane
Fluß: river
Fremdenverkehrsamt: tourist office
Frühstück: breakfast
Fußgängerzone: pedestrian zone
Gasthaus: guest house
Gaststätte: local bar with restaurant
Gedenkstätte: memorial
geil: cool OR horny
Gleis: track
Hafen: harbor
Hauptbahnhof: main train station
Hauptpostamt: main post office
Herren: Gentlemen
Hof: court, courtyard
Innenstadt: city center
Imbiß: fast-food stand

Insel: island
Jugendgästehaus: youth hotel
Jugendherberge: youth hostel
Karte: ticket
Kino: cinema
Kiosk: newsstand
Kirche: church
Kneipe: bar
Kreuz: cross, crucifix
Kunst: art
Kurort: spa town
Kurtaxe: overnight resort tax
Kurverwaltung: *Kurort* tourist office
Land: German state/province
Lesbe: lesbian (n.)
Markt: market
Marktplatz: market square
Mauer: wall
Meer: sea
Mensa: university cafeteria
Mitfahrzentrale: ride-share service office
Mitwohnzentrale: long-term accommodation service
Münster: cathedral
Museum: museum
Notausgang: emergency exit
Notfall: emergency
Notruf: emergency hotline
Paß: passport
Pension: cheap hotel
Platz: square
Polizei: police
Postamt: post office

Privatzimmer: room in a private home
Quittung: receipt
Rathaus: town hall
Rechnung: bill, cheque
Reisebüro: travel agency
Reisezentrum: travel office in train stations
S-Bahn: commuter rail
Sammlung: collection
Schatzkammer: treasury
Schiff: ship
Schloß: castle
Schule: school
schwul: gay (adj.)
See: lake
Speisekarte: menu
Stadt: city
Strand: beach
Straße: street
Straßenbahn: streetcar
Tankstelle: gas/petrol station
Teich: pond
Tor: gate
Turm: tower
U-Bahn: subway
umsteigen: to make a transit connection
Universität: university
Veganer/in: vegan
Vegetarier/in: vegetarian
Viertel: quarter, district
Vorsicht: caution
Wald: forest
wandern: to hike
Wanderweg: hiking trail
Weg: road, way
Wurst: sausage
Zeitung: newspaper
Zimmer: room
Zug: train

GERMAN PHRASEBOOK

The following phrasebook is meant to provide only the very rudimentary phrases you will need in your travels. Nothing can replace a full-fledged phrasebook or a pocket-sized English-German dictionary. The German numbering system is especially confusing; look in the **Language** section above for further explanation. German features both an informal and formal form of address (see p. 35); in the tables below, the polite form follows the familiar form in parentheses.

ENGLISH	GERMAN	ENGLISH	GERMAN
GREETINGS			
Hello.	Hallo.	Good-bye.	Tschüß! (informal); Auf Wiedersehen! (formal)
Excuse me/sorry	Entschuldigung/ Verzeihung.	My name is...	Ich heiße...

ENGLISH	GERMAN	ENGLISH	GERMAN
Could you please help me?	Können Sie mir bitte helfen?	What is your name?	Wie heißt Du (heißen Sie)?
How old are you?	Wie alt bist Du (sind Sie)?	Where are you from?	Wo kommst Du (kommen Sie) her?
Good morning.	Guten Morgen.	How are you?	Wie geht's (geht es Ihnen)?
Good afternoon.	Guten Tag.	I'm fine.	Es geht mir gut.
Good evening.	Guten Abend.	Do you speak English?	Sprichst Du (sprechen Sie) Englisch?
Good night.	Gute Nacht.	I don't speak German.	Ich kann kein Deutsch.

USEFUL PHRASES

Thank you (very much).	Danke (schön).	Please.	Bitte.
What?	Was?	I am a student (male/female).	Ich bin Student (m)/ Studentin (f).
When (what time)?	Wann?	Are there student discounts?	Gibt es Studentenermäßigungen?
Why?	Warum?	No problem.	Kein Problem.
Where is...?	Wo ist?	I don't understand.	Ich verstehe nicht.
I'm from...	Ich komme aus...	Please speak slowly.	Sprechen Sie bitte langsam.
America/USA	Amerika/den USA	Please repeat.	Bitte wiederholen Sie.
Australia	Australien	Pardon? What was that?	Wie bitte?
Canada	Kanada	Yes/No	Ja/nein
Great Britain	Großbritannien	Maybe	Vielleicht
Ireland	Irland	I would like...	Ich möchte...
New Zealand	Neuseeland	I'm looking for...	Ich suche...
South Africa	Südafrika	I need...	Ich brauche...
I'm not feeling well.	Mir ist schlecht.	How much does that cost?	Wieviel kostet das?
I have a headache.	Ich habe Kopfweh.	Where is the phone?	Wo ist das Telefon?
I need a doctor.	Ich brauche einen Arzt.	I don't know.	Ich weiß nicht.
Leave me alone.	Laß mich in Ruhe.	Where is the toilet?	Wo ist die Toilette?
I'll call the police.	Ich rufe die Polizei.	I have potato salad in my Lederhosen.	Ich habe Kartoffelsalat in meine Lederhosen.
Help!	Hilfe!	What does that mean?	Was bedeutet das?
No thanks.	Nein, danke.	Are there any vacancies?	Gibt es ein Zimmer frei?
Do you have anything cheaper?	Haben Sie etwas billigeres?	How do you say that in German?	Wie sagt man das auf Deutsch?

DIRECTIONS & TRANSPORTATION

(to the) right	rechts	(to the) left	links
straight ahead	geradeaus	Where is...?	Wo ist...?
next to	neben	opposite	gegenüber
How do I find...?	Wie finde ich ...?	It's nearby.	Es ist in der Nähe.
How do I get to...?	Wie komme ich nach...?	Is that far from here?	Ist es weit weg?
Where is this train going?	Wohin fährt der Zug?	When does the train leave?	Wann fährt der Zug ab?

TIME & HOURS

open	geöffnet	closed	geschlossen
morning	Morgen	opening hours	Öffnungszeiten
afternoon	Nachmittag	today	heute
night	Nacht	yesterday	gestern
evening	Abend	tomorrow	morgen
What time is it?	Wie spät ist es?	break time, rest day	Ruhepause, Ruhetag

ENGLISH	GERMAN	ENGLISH	GERMAN

FOOD & RESTAURANT TERMS

English	German	English	German
bread	Brot	rice	Reis
meat	Fleisch	water	Wasser
vegetables	Gemüse	tap water	Leitungswasser
cheese	Käse	roll	Brötchen
wine	Wein	beer	Bier
sausage	Wurst	pork	Schweinefleisch
chicken	Huhn	beef	Rindfleisch
potatoes	Kartoffeln	french fries	Pommes frites
sauce	Soße	coffee	Kaffee
tea	Tee	jelly	Marmelade
It tastes good.	Es schmeckt gut.	It tastes awful.	Es schmeckt widerlich.
Check, please.	Rechnung, bitte.	I would like to order...	Ich hätte gern...
I'm a vegan.	Ich bin Veganer (m)/ Ich bin Veganerin (f).	I'm a vegetarian.	Ich bin Vegetarier/Vegetarierin.
Give me chocolate.	Gib (Geben Sie) mir Schokolade.	Give me a nutella sandwich.	Gib (Geben Sie) mir ein Nutellabrötchen.

OPPOSITES ATTRACT

English	German	English	German
together	zusammen	alone	allein/e
good	gut	bad	schlecht
happy	glücklich	sad	traurig
big	groß	small	klein
young	jung	old	alt
full	voll	empty	leer
hot	heiß	cold	kalt
safe	sicher, ungefährlich	dangerous	gefährlich
alive	lebendig	dead	tod
besonders	special	einfach	simple
mehr	more	weniger	less
vor	before	nach	after
pretty	schön	ugly	häßlich

NEVER, NEVER GONNA GET IT

English	German	English	German
You're cute	Du bist hübsch.	I'm...	Ich bin...
You're friend is cute.	Dein Freund/Deine Freundin ist hübsch.	drunk	betrunken
I have...	Ich habe...	bisexual	bi
a boyfriend/girlfriend	einen Freund/ eine Freundin	gay	schwul
a venereal disease	eine Geschlechtskrankheit	lesbian	Lesbe
no inhibitions	keine Hemmungen	straight	hetero
no money	kein Geld	not sure	mir nicht sicher
handcuffs	Handschellen	That'll be fifty Marks.	Das macht fünfzig Mark.
You're da bomb.	Du bist die Bombe.	Get lost.	Hau ab.
The hostel is close.	Die Jugendherberge ist in der Nähe.	Oops. The hostel just closed.	Huch. Die Jugendherberge hat gerade zugemacht.
What's your sign?	Was ist dein Sternzeichen?	Really? I'm a Cancer. Do you want to dance?	Wirklich? Ich bin Krebs. Willst Du tanzen?
Can I buy you a drink?	Kann ich Dir einen Drink kaufen?	My boyfriend would like to meet you.	Mein Freund möchte Dich kennenlernen.

DISTANCES (KM) AND TRAVEL TIMES BY TRAIN

	Aachen	Berlin	Bonn	Bremen	Dresden	D-Dorf	Frankfurt	Freiburg	Hamburg	Hannover	Kassel	Köln	Leipzig	München	Nürnberg	Rostock	Stuttgart
Aachen		642	90	387	649	80	263	541	484	351	307	68	576	650	503	638	450
Berlin	5½hr.		608	390	214	565	564	827	285	285	388	583	192	587	431	219	652
Bonn	1½hr.	5hr.		349	570	78	181	422	450	317	273	26	497	588	399	604	357
Bremen	4hr.	4hr.	3½hr.		488	298	467	700	119	133	281	324	370	745	573	297	657
Dresden.	9hr.	3hr.	8hr.	6hr.		568	471	724	485	371	337	578	124	494	346	474	572
Düsseldorf	1½hr.	4hr.	45min.	3hr.	7hr.		231	492	423	272	228	41	493	618	449	577	414
Frankfurt	3½hr.	4hr.	2hr.	4hr.	6hr.	3hr.		272	497	362	194	192	398	399	223	651	216
Freiburg	5hr.	6½hr.	4hr.	6hr.	9hr.	4½hr.	2hr.		755	613	454	443	661	340	369	994	179
Hamburg	5hr.	2½hr.	4½hr.	1hr.	5hr.	3hr.	3½hr.	6hr.		163	311	425	377	775	607	184	679
Hannover	4hr.	2hr.	3hr.	1hr.	4½hr.	3hr.	2½hr.	5hr.	1½hr.		176	292	263	640	478	338	565
Kassel	5hr.	3hr.	4hr.	2½hr.	5½hr.	4hr.	2hr.	4hr.	2½hr.	1hr.		248	276	479	304	465	397
Köln	1hr.	4½hr.	30min.	3hr.	7½hr.	30min.	2½hr.	4hr.	4hr.	3hr.	4hr.		505	579	432	579	379
Leipzig	7hr.	2hr.	6hr.	4hr.	1½hr.	6hr.	3¾hr.	7hr.	4½hr.	3hr.	3½hr.	6hr.		422	274	366	499
München	7½hr.	7hr.	5hr.	6hr.	7hr.	6hr.	3½hr.	4½hr.	6hr.	4½hr.	4hr.	5½hr.	6hr.		162	761	221
Nürnberg	6hr.	5hr.	4hr.	4hr.	5hr.	5hr.	2hr.	4½hr.	4½hr.	3hr.	2½hr.	4½hr.	4hr.	2hr.		618	247
Rostock	8hr.	3hr.	8hr.	4hr.	6hr.	7hr.	6hr.	9hr.	2hr.	4hr.	5hr.	7hr.	5½hr.	9hr.	7½hr.		833
Stuttgart	4½hr.	5½hr.	3hr.	5hr.	7hr.	4hr.	1½hr.	2hr.	5½hr.	4hr.	3hr.	3hr.	6hr.	2hr.	2½hr.	8hr.	

Liberty, Justice,
....
and Globe-trotting
....
for all.
....

Sip espresso in Paris. Cheer the bulls in Barcelona. Learn the waltz in Saltzburg. 85 years after the Wright brothers discovered flying was easier than walking, wings are available to all. When you Name Your Own Price^{SM} on airline tickets at priceline.com, the world becomes your playground, the skies your road-less-traveled. You can save up to 40% or more, and you'll fly on top-quality, time-trusted airlines to the destinations of your dreams. You no longer need a trust fund to travel the globe, just a passion for adventure! So next time you need an escape, log onto priceline.com for your passport to the skies.

priceline.com^{SM}
Name Your Own Price^{SM}

INDEX

www.lowealpine.com

If I had my life
to live over again,

I would relax. I would limber up. I would take more chances.

I would take more trips.

I would climb more mountains, swim more rivers, and watch more sunsets.

I would go places and do things and travel lighter than I have.

I would ride more
merry-go-rounds.

Excerpt from Nadine Stair, 85 years old / photo> John Norris

Lowe
alpine

technical packs & apparel

Will you have enough stories to tell your grandchildren?

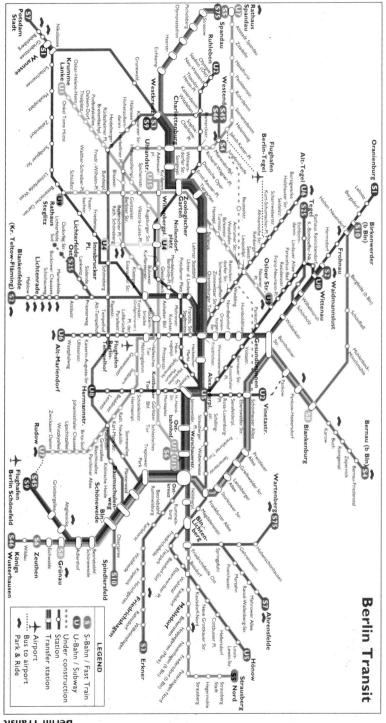

Berlin Transit

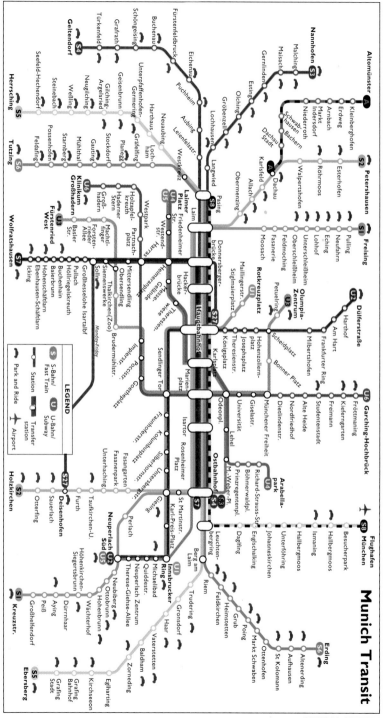

Munich Transit

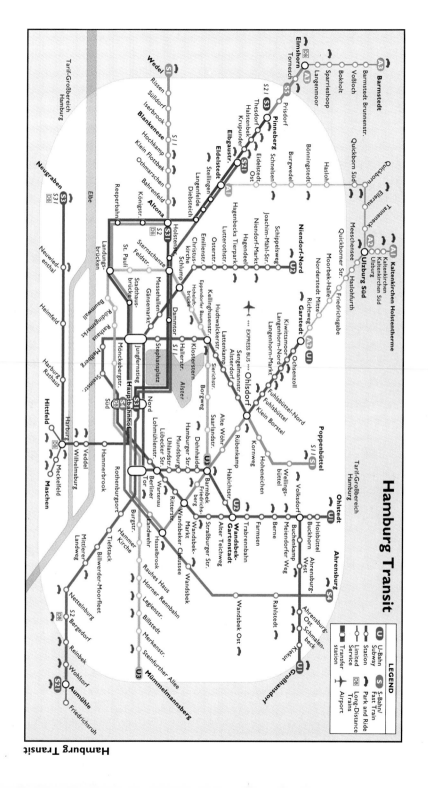

Hamburg Transit

Frankfurt Transit

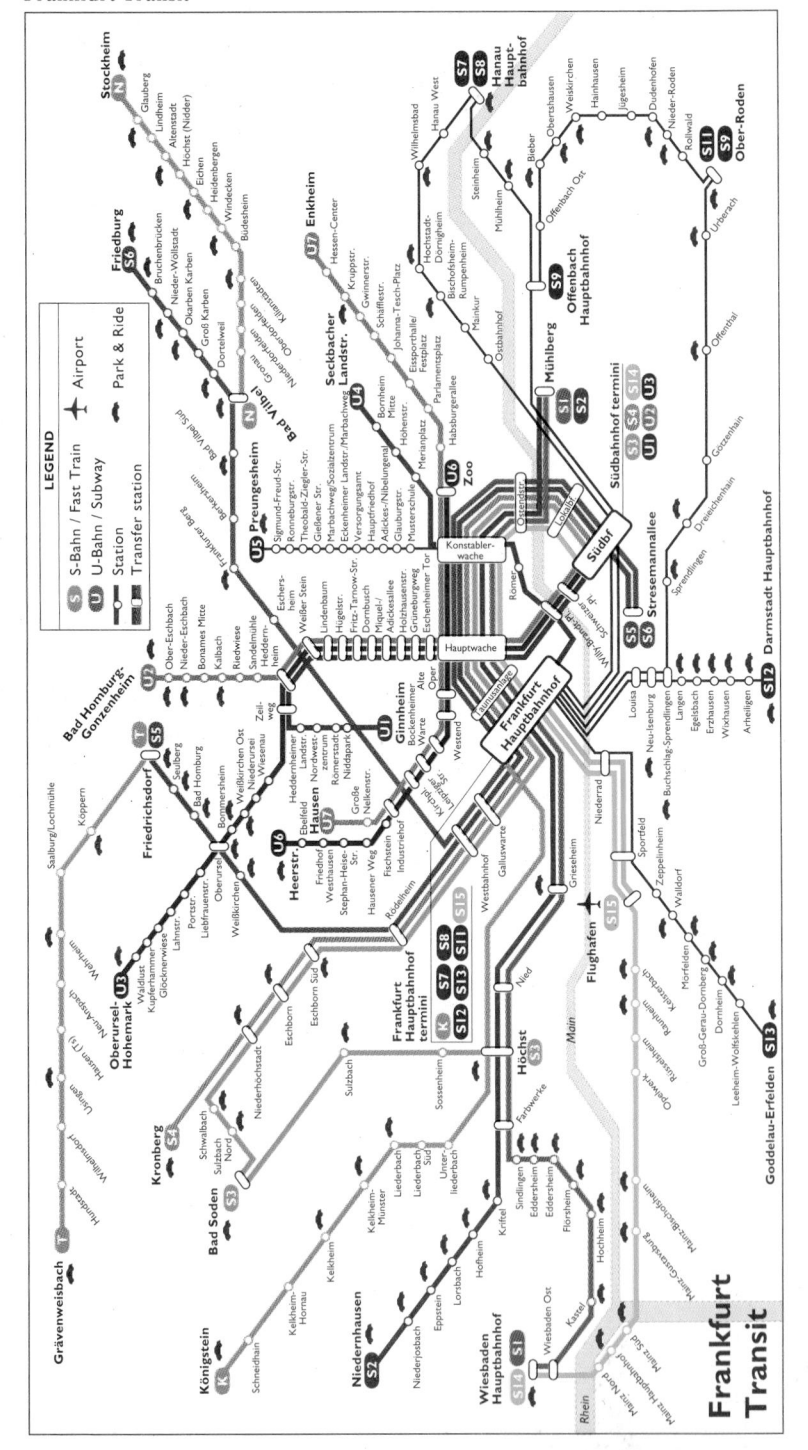